# CADE'S

## CAMPIN
## TOURING AND
## MOTOR CARAVAN
### *SITE GUIDE*

## 2 0 0 6

*Compiled and Edited by*
Reg Cade and Barry Gallafent

---

*Published by*
Marwain Publishing Limited,
Marwain House, Clarke Road, Mount Farm, Milton Keynes MK1 1LG
Tel: 01908 643022
Email: enquiries@cades.co.uk
Website: www.cades.co.uk

*Design and Administration*
Vicky Jones

*Advertisement Manager*
Derek Inall

---

*Printed by*
Rotographik, Barcelona, Spain

---

*Distribution (Booktrade)*
Kuperard
59 Hutton Grove, London, N12 8DS

*(Camping and Caravan Trade)*
Marwain Publishing Limited

ISBN 0 - 905377 - 97 - 4

# Come Touring with us!

## caravan +camping

## Excellent on site amenities and touring facilities

Choose from **21** of the finest Beachside, Seaside & Woodland Locations in the UK

### Wales & Scotland

1. Kiln Park, South Wales
2. Penally Court, South Wales
3. Greenacres, North Wales
4. Presthaven Sands, North Wales
5. Craig Tara, Scotland
6. Seton Sands, Scotland

### Yorkshire & The North

7. Haggerston Castle, Northumberland
8. Blue Dolphin, Yorkshire
9. Primrose Valley, Yorkshire
10. Reighton Sands, Yorkshire
11. Lakeland, Cumbria
12. Marton Mere, Blackpool

### East of England

13. Thorpe Park, Cleethorpes
14. Golden Sands, Lincolnshire
15. Wild Duck, Norfolk

### Dorset Coast

16. Rockley Park, Dorset
17. Seaview, Dorset
18. Littlesea, Dorset

### Devon, Cornwall & Somerset

19. Devon Cliffs, Devon
20. Perran Sands, Cornwall
21. Burnham-on-Sea, Somerset

Quote: TO_CADES

**Call now or book online**

## 08705 033 03

www.touringholidays.co

Welcome to the 2006 edition of 'Cade's Camping, Touring & Motor Caravan Site Guide'.

In this publication you will find details on approximately 1,800 Touring Parks throughout England, Scotland and Wales. The information we feature has been provided to us by the owners or operators of each park and has been updated, as always, for this edition. We believe Cade's is probably the most up to date Touring Park Guide available.

We are not agents for the parks, nor they of us and we publish only such information as is supplied to us by them, in good faith. The Trade Descriptions Act binds Park owners and operators to accurately describe their facilities, however you should always check directly with the park that any particular facility, which is important to you during your stay, would be available at that time. Certain things such as entertainment, site shops, swimming pools etc. are often only available during peak season and obviously our publication cannot allow for every eventuality. Most parks produce a brochure or leaflet of their own describing them in greater detail, and they are happy to send them out on request.

Discount Vouchers to the value of £20 can be found at the back of this guide, which will entitle you to a fifty-pence per night reduction on pitch fees at certain parks throughout the guide. Look out for the voucher symbol 🅴 on the facilities line in the park descriptions. Use of the vouchers can save you almost three times the cover price of this guide.

For 2006 we are pleased to introduce an index to parks open all year, along with our fishing index and the adults only index. These can be found towards the back of the guide.

All that remains now is for me to thank you for choosing Cade's and to wish you all the very best for your touring holidays in 2006.

*Barry M Gallafent*

Barry M Gallafent
**Managing Director**
**Marwain Publishing Limited**

# INDEX

# Whatever, wherever, whenever...

## ...there's a superb Caravan Club Site that's perfect for you!

With around 200 top class Sites to choose from in fabulous locations throughout the British Isles, finding your perfect holiday location has never been easier.

You don't have to be a member to stay on many Club Sites but members save up to £7 per night on pitch fees

Morvich

Lleithyr Meadow

Sandringham

Plymouth Sound

N
E
S

Whatever holiday experience you're looking for there's a Club Site to suit you, including over 30 Sites open all-year-round.

Whichever Site you choose, you can be assured of excellent facilities, a friendly welcome from our Resident Wardens, and consistently high standards.

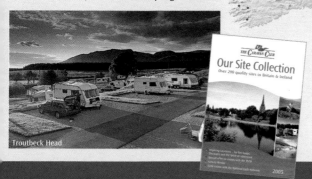

Troutbeck Head

**Our Site Collection**
Over 200 quality sites in Britain & Ireland

2005

## THE CARAVAN CLUB

The Caravan Club, East Grinstead House, East Grinstead, West Sussex RH19 1UA

## SYMBOLS

- ⋏ Tents
- ⊟ Motor Caravans
- ⊡ Touring Caravans
- ⇌ Nearest Station
- ♿ Facilities for Disabled
- ⚡ No Motorcycles
- ⨍ Electricity Hook-ups
- ⊟ Fully Serviced Pitches
- ⊡ Hard Standings
- ⊞ Flush Toilets
- ⚲ Water
- ⌐ Showers
- ☺ Shaver Points
- ⊿ Washing Facilities
- ◢ Ironing Facilities
- ▣ Launderette
- ♜ Chem. Toilet Disposal
- S♒ Site Shop
- M♒ Mobile Shop
- l♒ Local Shop
- ☐ Gas
- ☎ Public Telephone
- ✕ Café Restaurant
- ♈ Licensed Club
- ⊞ T.V.
- ♠ Games Room
- ⋒ Childs Play Area
- ⤳ Outdoor Pool
- ⤳ Indoor Pool
- ✿ Sports Area
- ⇥ Pets Welcome
- ▣ Parking by Unit
- ⊞ Credit Cards Accepted
- ▣ Money-Off Vouchers Accepted
- A Adults Only Park
- ⚶ Seasonal Pitches
- ℘ Secure Storage

Nearby Facilities
- ⌐ Golf
- ✐ Fishing
- ⚓ Sailing
- ⤳ Boating
- ∪ Riding
- ⇗ Water Ski-ing
- ℘ Tennis
- ⤳ Climbing

## SYMBOLES FRANÇAIS

- ⋏ Tentes
- ⊟ Auto-Caravanes
- ⊡ Caravanes
- ⇌ Gare Locale
- ♿ Handicapés
- ⨍ Branchments Electrique Pour Caravanes
- ⊟ Emplacement Service Complet
- ⊡ Emplacement Surface Dure
- ⚡ Motorcyclettes Non-Admises
- ⊞ Toilettes
- ⚲ Eau
- ⌐ Douches
- ☺ Prises Electrique pour Rasoirs
- ⊿ Bains
- ◢ Repassage
- ▣ Laverie Automatique
- ♜ Décharge pour W.C. Chemique
- S♒ Magasin du Terrain
- M♒ Magasin Mobile
- l♒ Magasin du Quartier
- ☐ Gaz
- ☎ Cabines Téléphoniques
- ✕ Café
- ♈ Club/Bar Patenté
- ⊞ Salle de Télévision
- ♠ Salle de Jeux
- ⋒ Terrain de Jeux Enfants
- ⤳ Piscine du Terrain
- ⤳ Piscine a l'interieur
- ✿ Terrain de Sports et de Jeux
- ▣ Stationment à côté de la caravane permis
- ⊞ Carte Credit Accepter
- ▣ Bon Remise 'Cades' Accepter
- A Camping Seulment Adulte
- ⚶ Emplacements pour La Saison
- ℘ Gardiennage

Nearby Facilities
- ⌐ Golf
- ✐ Pêche
- ⚓ Voile
- ⤳ Canotage
- ∪ Equitation
- ⇗ Ski Nautique
- ℘ Tennis
- ⤳ Ascension

## Accessories for Caravan & Motorhome Owners

### CARALEVEL

Fully automatic **Caravan Levelling System**. At the turn of a key the caravan will level itself in just 2½ minutes, making life so much easier! The advanced electronic system activates motors on the four corner steadies. Ideal for the disabled and back sufferers. Get it fitted at our Fitting Centre, by your local dealer, or one of our mobile engineers will fit it at your home. DIY Kit is available from £725 for home fitting in about 6 hours. Weight 10kg. 12 Months Warranty.

### CARAMOVER

British made quality **Caravan Mover** from the makers of Caralevel. Advanced features make this the best mover of its kind, driving the road wheels. ✓ Remote Control Handset with cable back-up. ✓ Full control when going up or down hill. ✓ Better ground clearance. ✓ Soft start up. ✓ Overload protection. ✓ Wider fixings mean less stress on the caravan. Avaialble Fully Fitted or as a DIY Kit. Price on application. Full Warranty for peace of mind.

### CARALIFT

Makes the Hitching & Un-Hitching of your caravan easy, at just the touch of a button! **1.** Simply plug in the remote control and turn the Caralevel key to LEVEL. **2.** With the touch of the remote control button you can lower or lift your caravan gently on or off the tow bar. **3.** Raise the legs with the key switch ready to depart, or to level the caravan on arrival at your site, after first removing the remote control.
A useful optional extra to the Levelling System at a price of £90.

### POWER STEADIES for MOTORHOMES

On arrival at your site, simply turn the key on the dashboard and the caravans legs turn themselves down until they reach the ground. Sensors detect ground level for each leg. To retract the legs just turn the key to the up position. ✓ Convenient for roadside stops. ✓ No need to leave the drivers seat, ideal for bad weather. ✓ Effortless. Ideal for the disabled and back sufferers. ✓ Warning device when in operation. Whole system is lightweight, weighing less than 6kg. Avaialble Fully Fitted or as a DIY Kit. Price from £498.

*For More Information Contact the Suppliers:*

Springhill Farm • Great Horwood Road
Little Horwood • Milton Keynes • MK17 0NZ
Tel/Fax: **01296 713 476**

# Presenting the 2006 Collection of Caravan Awnings and Porches

## HARRISON
### THE BIG NAME IN AWNINGS

Harrison's are believed to be the longest established manufacturer of quality awnings, porches and motor annexes in Europe with over 44 years' experience. We have a solid reputation that has been earned by producing top quality products at competitive prices, with the ultimate aim of delivering maximum customer satisfaction and enjoyment.

We recognise that families and couples who enjoy caravanning and camping require a very high standard of product that delivers security, excitement and long lasting durability all at competitive prices. With this year's collection there's an awning, porch or motor annexe to suit your needs.

This year sees many changes throughout our entire range, all of which can be viewed in our catalogue. With some new materials, colours and design features, you can be sure that by choosing Harrison's you will be buying a robust, well designed product that will give years of pleasure.

If you want that extra bit of space, or the children want to bring some friends along, why not extend your awning by adding one of our Tall or Standard Optional Annexes – you may even decide to add both – giving you more space and privacy.

Visit our website at www.harrisonawnings.co.uk

The new Harrison catalogue is available now. Call for your free copy.

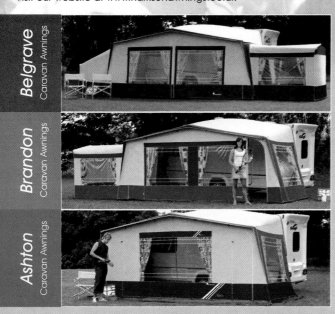

**Belgrave** Caravan Awnings

**Brandon** Caravan Awnings

**Ashton** Caravan Awnings

Unique Harrison Twister Poles supplied with each full awning

Fixon Pad

Mosquito Net Side Wall

S T Harrison (Bristol) Limited, 28 Lyppiatt Road, St George, Bristol, BS5 9HR, U.K.
Tel: 0117 955 8423 • Fax: 0117 935 0415 • Email: mail@harrisonawnings.co.uk

# ENGLAND

## BERKSHIRE

### DORNEY REACH

**Amerden Caravan Site,** Off Old Marsh Lane, Dorney Reach, Nr Maidenhead, Berkshire, SL6 0EE
**Tel:** 01628 627461
**Pitches For** ▲ � ♦
**Facilities** 📶 ⚡ 🆚 🚿 ⌒ ☉ 🍴 🛒 🅿 🚽
🏪 🔥 🛁 💈 🍴 🅿
**Nearby Facilities** ⌒ ✧ ⚓ U
**Acreage** 3 **Open** April **to** October
**Access** Good **Site** Level
Near River Thames.
**Nearest Town/Resort** Maidenhead
**Directions** Leave M4 junc 7, Slough West, then A4 towards Maidenhead. Third turn left signposted Dorney Reach and caravan site, then first turn right.
⚐ Taplow

### HURLEY

**Hurley Riverside Park,** Shepherds Lane, Hurley, Nr Maidenhead, Berkshire, SL6 5NE
**Tel:** 01628 823501/824493 **Fax:** 01628 825533
**Email:** info@hurleyriversidepark.co.uk
**www.** hurleyriversidepark.co.uk
**Pitches For** ▲ ⌣ ♦ **Total** 200
**Facilities** 👤 📶 🅿 🆚 ⚡ ⌒ ☉ 🍴 🛒 🅿 🚽
🏪 🍴 🚿 🔥 💈 🍴 🅿 🚽
**Nearby Facilities** ⌒ ✧ ✦ ⚓
**Acreage** 15 **Open** March **to** October
**Access** Good **Site** Level
On picturesque River Thames. Ideal touring centre for Henley, Windsor (Legoland), Oxford and London. Slipway. Walks along riverside and into nearby forest. Disabled toilet facilities. David Bellamy Gold Award.
**Nearest Town/Resort** Maidenhead/Henley-on-Thames.
**Directions** Maidenhead, A4130 west towards Henley. After 3¼ miles turn right, ¾ mile past Hurley Village, into Shepherds Lane. Entrance 200 yards on left.
⚐ Maidenhead/Henley-on-Thames

### NEWBURY

**Oakley Farm Caravan Park,** Oakley Farm House, Penwood Road, Wash Water, Newbury Berkshire, RG20 0LP
**Tel:** 01635 36581
**www.** oakleyfarm.co.uk
**Pitches For** ▲ ⌣ ♦ **Total** 30
**Facilities** 📶 🅿 🆚 ⚡ ⌒ ☉ 🛒 🅿 🚽
🏪 🍴 🚿 🔥 💈 🍴 🅿
**Nearby Facilities** ⌒ ✦
**Acreage** 3 **Open** March **to** October
**Access** Good **Site** Gentle Slope

Not suitable for caravans over 22 foot long.
**Nearest Town/Resort** Newbury.
**Directions** From the A34 south of Newbury take the exit marked Highclere and Wash Common. Turn left onto the A343 towards Newbury, turn right after ¼ mile (by car sales garage) into Penwood Road. Site is then 400 metres on your left.
⚐ Newbury

### WOKINGHAM

**California Chalet & Touring Park,** Nine Mile Ride, Finchampstead, Wokingham, Berkshire, RG40 4HU
**Tel:** 0118 973 3928 **Fax:** 0118 932 8720
**Email:** california.dodd@virgin.net
**www.** californiapark.co.uk
**Pitches For** ▲ ⌣ ♦
**Facilities** 👤 📶 🅿 🆚 ⚡ ⌒ ☉ 🍴 🛒 🅿 🚽
🏪 🏪 🔥 💈 🅿
**Nearby Facilities** ⌒ U ✦
**Open** 1 March **to** 31 Dec
**Access** Good **Site** Level
Lakeside park. Ideal for visiting Windsor, Legoland, Ascot Races, Thorpe Park and Chessington Zoo.
**Nearest Town/Resort** Wokingham
**Directions** From Wokingham take the A321 towards Sandhurst, turn right onto the B3016. At the junction with the B3430 turn right, site is ½ a mile.
⚐ Wokingham

# BRISTOL (County of)

## BRISTOL

**Baltic Wharf Caravan Club Site,** Cumberland Road, Bristol, BS1 6XG
**Tel:** 0117 926 8030
**www.** caravanclub.co.uk
**Pitches For** ⌣ ♦ **Total** 58
**Facilities** 👤 📶 🅿 🆚 ⚡ ⌒ 🅿 🚽
🏪 🍴 🔥 💈 🅿
**Nearby Facilities** ⌒ ⚓ ✦
**Acreage** 2½ **Open** All Year
**Access** Good **Site** Level
Quiet waterside site ½ mile from the town centre. River ferry service to the city centre in Summer. Near to Bristol Zoo, SS Great Britain and museums. Non members welcome. Booking essential.
**Nearest Town/Resort** Bristol
**Directions** Leave the M5 at junction 18 and take the A4. After Clifton Suspension Bridge keep in left lane and follow signs to harbour. At lights stay in right lane through Hotwells, go over the crossing and move to left lane, go over bridge following signs for SS Great Britain. Site is 500 yards on the left.
⚐ Bristol Temple Meads

## BRISTOL

**Brook Lodge Touring Caravan & Camping Park,** Cowslip Green, Bristol, BS40 5RD
**Tel:** 01934 862311 **Fax:** 01934 862311
**Email:** brooklodgefarm@aol.com
**www.** brooklodgefarm.com
**Pitches For** ▲ ⌣ ♦ **Total** 29
**Facilities** 📶 🅿 🆚 ⚡ ⌒ ☉ 🍴 🛒 🅿 🚽
🏪 🍴 🔥 🔥 💈 🅿 🔥
**Nearby Facilities** ⌒ ✦ U ✧ ✦
**Acreage** 4½ **Open** 18 March **to** 1 Nov
**Access** Good **Site** Mostly Level
Beautiful grounds with mature trees, lawns and garden. Cowslip Green is nestled in view of the nearby Mendip Hills. Trout fishing at Blagdon Lake 2 miles. Bird life and walks. Swimming pool open in warm weather. ETB Graded 3 Stars, AA 3 Pennants, ANWB Approved, Green Tourism Award, Welcome to Excellence ETB Award.
**Nearest Town/Resort** Bristol/Bath
**Directions** From Bristol take A38 south west for 9 miles, Park is signposted on the left. Or from the M5 junc 18 take A4 then A370, turn left to Barrow Gurney on B3130 to A38. After Bristol Airport Park is 3 miles. 1 mile from the Darlington Arms to the bottom of the hill, opposite the Holiday Inn.

# BUCKINGHAMSHIRE

## BEACONSFIELD

**Highclere Farm Country Touring Park,** Newbarn Lane, Seer Green, Nr Beaconsfield, Buckinghamshire, HP9 2QZ
**Tel:** 01494 874505 **Fax:** 01494 875238
**Email:** highclerepark@aol.com
**www.** highclerefarmpark.co.uk
**Pitches For** ▲ ⌣ ♦ **Total** 60
**Facilities** 📶 🅿 🆚 ⚡ ⌒ ☉ 🍴 🛒 🅿 🚽
🏪 🍴 🔥 🔥 💈 🅿
**Nearby Facilities** ⌒ U ✦
**Acreage** 6 **Open** 18 March **to** January
**Access** Good **Site** Level
Near to Legoland, Chiltern Air Museum, Miltons Cottage, Odds Farm (Rare Breeds), Bekonscot, Amersham and London.
**Nearest Town/Resort** Beaconsfield
**Directions** Leave the M40 at junction 2, go into Beaconsfield and take the A355 towards Amersham. After 1 mile turn right to Seer Green and follow tourist signs.
⚐ Seer Green

## NEWPORT PAGNELL

**Lovat Meadow Caravan Park,** London Road, Newport Pagnell, Buckinghamshire, MK16 9BQ
**Tel:** 01908 610858
**Email:** newportptc@aol.com

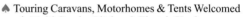

www. members.aol.com/newportptc/
**Pitches For** ♿ ♨ **Total** 40
**Facilities** ♪ ⓑ♒✠ ♒
**Nearby Facilities** ✦
**Open** March **to** January
**Access** Good **Site** Lev/Slope
Riverside location, ideal for fishing.
Adjacent to our own indoor heated
swimming pool. Pets are welcome if kept
on leads.
**Nearest Town/Resort** Newport Pagnell
**Directions** 1½ miles from the M1 junction
14. Follow signs to Newport Pagnell along
the A509, cross the roundabout onto the
B526, park is 500 yards on the left.
➧ Milton Keynes

## OLNEY
**Emberton Country Park**, Emberton, Nr
Olney, Buckinghamshire, MK46 5DB
**Tel:** 01234 711575 **Fax:** 01234 711575
**Email:** embertonpark@milton-
keynes.gov.uk
**www.** mkweb.co.uk/embertonpark
**Pitches For** ⚊ ♿ ♨ **Total** 58
**Facilities** ⚒ ♪ ⓦⓔ ♒ ♒ ⊙ ♒ ♒
⚡ ⓑ✕♒✠♒
**Nearby Facilities** ✦ ✦ ∪ ♒
**Acreage** 5 **Open** April **to** Oct
**Access** Good **Site** Level
Set in a 200 acre Country Park with 5 lakes
and 1 mile of the River Great Ouse. Three
rally fields.
**Nearest Town/Resort** Olney
**Directions** 1 mile south of Olney on the
A509.
➧ Milton Keynes Central

# CAMBRIDGESHIRE
## BURWELL
**Stanford Park**, Barron Cove, Weirs Drove,
Burwell, Cambridgeshire, CB5 0BP
**Tel:** 01638 741547
**Email:**
enquiries@stanfordcaravanpark.co.uk
**www.** stanfordcaravanpark.co.uk
**Pitches For** ⚊ ♿ ♨ **Total** 90
**Facilities** ⚒ ♪ ⓦⓔ ♒ ♒ ⊙ ♒ ♒
⓵ⓑ⚐♒✠♒
**Nearby Facilities** ✦ ✦ ∪ ♒
**Acreage** 20 **Open** All Year
**Access** Good
Near to Ely Cathedral, Newmarket Race
Course, Cambridge Universities and
National Trust properties. Ideal for touring.
**Nearest Town/Resort** Newmarket
**Directions** From the B1102 in Burwell follow
international camping signs. 4½ miles north
west of Newmarket.
➧ Newmarket

## CAMBRIDGE
**Appleacre Park**, London Road, Fowlmere,
Royston, Hertfordshire, SG8 7RU
**Tel:** 01763 208354
**Email:** appleacrepark@aol.com
**www.** appleacrepark.co.uk
**Pitches For** ⚊ ♿ ♨ **Total** 20
**Facilities** ♪ ⓦⓔ ♒ ♒ ⊙ ♒ ♒ ♒
⚡ⓑ♒
**Nearby Facilities** ✦ ✦
**Acreage** 3 **Open** All Year
**Access** Good **Site** Level
A small pleasant park at the southern end
of a village with trees and shrubs. Within
easy reach of Duxford Imperial War
Museum.
**Nearest Town/Resort** Cambridge
**Directions** 9 miles south of Cambridge on
the B1368 through Fowlmere Village.
➧ Shepreth

## CAMBRIDGE
**Cherry Hinton Caravan Club Site**, Lime
Kiln Road, Cherry Hinton, Cambridgeshire,
CB1 8NQ
**Tel:** 01223 244088
**www.** caravanclub.co.uk
**Pitches For** ⚊ ♿ ♨ **Total** 60
**Facilities** ⚒ ♪ ⓗ ⓦⓔ ♒ ♒ ⊙ ♒ ♒ ♒
⓵ⓑ♒✠ⓔ♒
**Nearby Facilities** ✦ ✦
**Acreage** 5.5 **Open** All Year
**Access** Good **Site** Level
Set in old quarry works with imaginative
landscaping. Only ½ a mile from
Cambridge town centre. Close to the
American War Cemetary, Duxford Imperial
War Museum, Wicken Fen Nature
Reserve, Wimpole Hall and Audley End
House & Gardens. Non members
welcome. Booking essential.
**Nearest Town/Resort** Cambridge
**Directions** From the south west on the A10,
pass over the M11 junction 11 and continue
onto the A1309 signposted Cambridge. At the
fifth set of traffic lights turn right into Long
Road (A1134). After 1½ miles at the
roundabout continue to Queen Ediths Way,
after 1 mile turn right into Lime Kiln Road.
PLEASE NOTE - Traffic calming and mini
roundabouts the length of Cherry Hinton High
Street have made towing through the village
inadvisable.
➧ Cambridge

## CAMBRIDGE
**Highfield Farm Touring Park**, Highfield
Farm, Long Road, Comberton,
CambridgeCambridge, CB3 7DG
**Tel:** 01223 262308 **Fax:** 01223 262308
**Email:**
enquiries@highfieldfarmtouringpark.co.uk
**www.** highfieldfarmtouringpark.co.uk
**Pitches For** ⚊ ♿ ♨ **Total** 120
**Facilities** ♪ ⓗ ⓦⓔ ♒ ♒ ⊙ ♒ ♒ ♒
⓵ⓗ ⓑ⚛ⓐⓜⓗ ♒ ♒
**Nearby Facilities** ✦ ✦ ∪
**Acreage** 8 **Open** April **to** October
**Access** Good **Site** Level
Well maintained, long established family
run Touring Park. Close to the historic
University City of Cambridge, and the
Imperial War Museum, Duxford. Calor
Caravan Park Awards 2002, Best Park in
England (Finalist).
**Nearest Town/Resort** Cambridge
**Directions** From Cambridge - Leave A1303/
A428 (Bedford) after 3 miles, follow camping
signs to Comberton. From M11 - Leave
junction 12, take A603 (Sandy) for ½ mile
then B1046 to Comberton (2 miles).
➧ Cambridge

## CAMBRIDGE
**Roseberry Tourist Park**, Earith Road,
Willingham, Cambridgeshire, CB4 5LT
**Tel:** 01954 260346 **Fax:** 01954 260346
**Pitches For** ⚊ ♿ ♨ **Total** 80
**Facilities** ♪ ⓗ ⓦⓔ ♒ ♒ ⊙ ♒ ♒ ♒
ⓑ ♒✠ⓔ♒
**Nearby Facilities** ✦ ✦ ✠
**Acreage** 10 **Open** All Year
**Access** Good **Site** Level
Ideal for touring.
**Nearest Town/Resort** Cambridge
➧ Cambridge

## EARITH
**Westview Marina**, High Street, Earith,
Huntingdon, Cambridgeshire, PE28 3PN
**Tel:** 01487 841627
**Pitches For** ⚊ ♿ ♨ **Total** 28
**Facilities** ♪ ⓦⓔ ♒ ♒ ⊙ ♒ ♒
**Nearby Facilities** ✦ ✦ ✠ ✠

**Acreage** 2 **Open** March **to** October
**Access** Good **Site** Level
River frontage. Ideal touring.
**Nearest Town/Resort** St. Ives (Cambs)
**Directions** 5 miles from St. Ives and 12 miles
from Cambridge.
➧ Huntingdon

## ELY
**Riverside Caravan & Camping Park**, 21
New River Bank, Littleport, Ely,
Cambridgeshire, CB7 4TA
**Tel:** 01353 860255
**Email:** riversideccp@btopenworld.com
**www.** riversideccp.co.uk
**Pitches For** ⚊ ♿ ♨ **Total** 49
**Facilities** ♪ ⓗ ⓦⓔ ♒ ♒ ⊙ ♒ ♒ ♒
**Nearby Facilities** ✦ ✦ ⚐ ✠
**Acreage** 4 **Open** All Year
**Access** Good **Site** Level
Under new ownership. Alongside the Great
Ouse River, fishing adjacent. Ideal for
touring Cambridgeshire and Norfolk.
**Nearest Town/Resort** Ely
**Directions** Site is signposted off the A10
(Ely/Littleport By-Pass) on the right once
across the River Ouse. Please telephone for
further details.
➧ Littleport

## GRAFHAM
**Old Manor Caravan Park**, Church Road,
Grafham, Huntingdon, Cambridgeshire,
PE28 0BB
**Tel:** 01480 810264 **Fax:** 01480 819099
**Email:** camping@old-manor.co.uk
**www.** old-manor.co.uk
**Pitches For** ⚊ ♿ ♨ **Total** 80
**Facilities** ⚒ ♪ ⓗ ⓦⓔ ♒ ♒ ⊙ ♒ ♒ ♒
⓵⚡ⓑⓐⓜ♒✠ⓔ♒
**Nearby Facilities** ✦ ✦ ⚐ ✠ ∪ ✠
**Acreage** 6½ **Open** Mid Jan **to** Mid Dec
**Access** Good **Site** Level
Near to Grafham Water. Refurbished
amenity block. David Bellamy Gold Award
for Conservation 2004.
**Nearest Town/Resort** Huntingdon
**Directions** From the A1 at Buckden
roundabout follow caravan park signs. From
the A14 leave at Ellington and follow caravan
park signs from the village.
➧ Huntingdon

## GREAT SHELFORD
**Cambridge Camping & Caravanning
Club Site**, 19 Cabbage Moor, Great
Shelford, Cambridgeshire, CB2 5NB
**Tel:** 01223 841185
**www.** campingandcaravanningclub.co.uk
**Pitches For** ⚊ ♿ ♨ **Total** 120
**Facilities** ⚒ ♪ ⓗ ⓦⓔ ♒ ♒ ⊙ ♒ ♒ ♒
⓵ⓑⓐⓜ♒✠ⓔ ♪ ♒
**Nearby Facilities** ✦ ✦ ∪
**Open** March **to** October **Site** Level
On the outskirts of the city of Cambridge. 6
miles from Duxford Imperial War Museum
and the American Cemetery. Boat
launching. BTB 4 Star Graded and AA 3
Pennants. Non members welcome.
**Directions** Leave the M11 at junction 11 onto
the B1309 signposted Cambridge. At the first
set of traffic lights turn right, after ½ mile you
will see the site sign on the left hand side
pointing down the lane.
➧ Great Shelford

## HUNTINGDON
**Houghton Mill Caravan Club Site**, Mill
Street, Houghton, Huntingdon,
Cambridgeshire, PE28 2AZ
**Tel:** 01480 466716
**www.** caravanclub.co.uk
**Pitches For** ⚊ ♿ ♨ **Total** 65

# CAMBRIDGESHIRE

**Facilities** ⚿ ⌁ 🏚 🚿 ⌂ 🚻 🛝 🅿 🍴⌆🔌
**Nearby Facilities** ⌁ ⚓ ♨ ♣
**Acreage** 8½ **Open** March **to** Oct
**Access** Good **Site** Level
On the banks of the River Great Ouse. Adjacent to Houghton Mill working watermill. Ideal for walkers, bird watchers and wildlife enthusiasts. Non members welcome. Booking essential.
**Nearest Town/Resort** Huntingdon
**Directions** From the A1(M)/A1 turn onto the A14 signposted Huntingdon, then take the A141. At Texaco roundabout turn onto the A1123 signposted Houghton, after 1¼ miles turn right signposted Houghton, continue into Mill Street, pass the church and site is on the left.
⚑ Huntingdon

## HUNTINGDON

**Huntingdon Boathaven & Caravan Park,** The Avenue, Godmanchester, Huntingdon, Cambridgeshire, PE18 8AF
**Tel:** 01480 411977
**Email:** boathaven.hunts@virgin.net
**Pitches For** ⚿ ⌂ 🚐 **Total** 23
**Facilities** ⚿ ⌁ 🚿 🏚 ⚿ 🍴 ⌂ ⌆ 🔌 🍴
⌆ 🛝 ⌂🔌🅿 ✂
**Nearby Facilities** ⌁ ⚓ ♨ ♣
**Acreage** 2 **Open** March **to** October
**Access** Good **Site** Level
Marina and caravan park situated on the Great River Ouse. Near to many tourist attractions. Limited fishing on site.
**Nearest Town/Resort** Cambridge
**Directions** From the A14 turn off to Godmanchester and travel towards Huntingdon. Turn left before the fly-over to Huntingdon Boathaven.
⚑ Huntingdon

## HUNTINGDON

**Quiet Waters Caravan Park,** Hemingford Abbots, Huntingdon, Cambridgeshire, PE28 9AJ
**Tel:** 01480 463405
**Email:** quietwaters.park@btopenworld.com
**www.** quietwaterscaravanpark.co.uk
**Pitches For** ⚿ ⌂ 🚐 **Total** 20
**Facilities** ⚿ ⌁ 🚿 🏚 🍴 ⌂ ⌆ 🔌 🍴 ⌂ 🍴
⌆ ⌂ 🚿🅿🔌 ✂
**Nearby Facilities** ⌁ ⚓ ♨ ∪
**Acreage** ½ **Open** April **to** October
**Access** Good **Site** Level
In the centre of a riverside village, good for fishing and boating.
**Nearest Town/Resort** St Ives/Huntingdon
**Directions** Junction 25 off the A14. West of Cambridge on the A14, after 12 miles look for Hemingford Abbots, we are 1 mile into the village. 3 miles east of Huntingdon on the A14.
⚑ Huntingdon

## HUNTINGDON

**Stroud Hill Park,** Fen Road, Pidley, Huntingdon, Cambridgeshire, PE28 3DE
**Tel:** 01487 741333
**Email:** stroudhillpark@btconnect.com
**www.** stroudhillpark.co.uk
**Pitches For** ⚿ ⌂🔲 **Total** 54
**Facilities** ⚿ ⌁ 🚿 🏚 🍴 🏚 ⌂ ⌆ 🔌 🍴
🕌 ⌂ ⌁🚿🅿🔲⌂🅰
---

**Nearby Facilities** ⌁ ⚓
**Acreage** 6 **Open** All Year
**Access** Good **Site** Lev/Slope
Quiet, attractive, rural, ADULTS ONLY site. Set in ancient bluebell woodland on a 150 acre family farm. Tennis on site. 18 hole golf course next door. Non members welcome. Booking essential.
**Nearest Town/Resort** St. Ives
**Directions** From the A141 turn onto the B1040 signposted Pidley. In 2¾ miles turn left past the church into Fen Road, site is ¾ miles on the right.
⚑ St. Ives

## HUNTINGDON

**The Willows Caravan Park,** Bromholme Lane, Brampton, Huntingdon, Cambridgeshire, PE18 8NE
**Tel:** 01480 437566
**Email:** willows@willows33.freeserve.co.uk
**www.** willowscaravanpark.com
**Pitches For** ⚿ ⌂ 🚐 **Total** 70
**Facilities** ⚿ ⌁ 🚿 🏚 🍴 ⌂ 🍴 ⌂ ⌆ 🔲 ⌂ 🍴
🕌 ✗ ⌂🚿🅿🔌 ✂
**Nearby Facilities** ⌁ ⚓ ♨ ♣ ⚲
**Acreage** 4 **Open** All Year
**Access** Good **Site** Level
Situated on Ouse Valley Way, attractive walks. Launching area for boats and canoes. Fishing and boating available. Separate tent field. Heated toilet block. Resident wardens on site. Country park, Grafham Water and sports facilities nearby. Site is Caravan Club, Camping & Caravanning Club and AA Listed.
**Nearest Town/Resort** Huntingdon
**Directions** Brampton is situated between the A1 and the A14 (formerly A604). Follow the B1514 through Brampton towards Huntingdon, taking right hand signposted turning into Bromholme Lane.
⚑ Huntingdon

## HUNTINGDON

**Wyton Lakes Holiday Park,** Banks End, Wyton, Huntingdon, Cambridgeshire, PE28 2AA
**Tel:** 01480 412715
**Email:** loupeter@supanet.com
**www.** wytonlakes.com
**Pitches For** ⚿ ⌂ 🚐 **Total** 40
**Facilities** ⚿ ⌁ 🚿 🏚 🍴 ⌂ 🍴 ⌂ ⌆ 🍴
🕌 ⌂🚿🅿🔲🅰✂
**Nearby Facilities** ⌁ ⚓
**Acreage** 12½ **Open** March **to** Oct
**Access** Good **Site** Level
ADULTS ONLY site situated alongside a river with four fishing lakes on site.
**Nearest Town/Resort** Huntingdon
**Directions** Leave the A14 at junction 23 and follow signs for the A141 March. On the 4th roundabout take the A1123 for St. Ives, park is approx. 1 mile on the right.
⚑ Huntingdon

## MARCH

**Floods Ferry Marina Park,** Staffurths Bridge, March, Cambridgeshire, PE15 0YP
**Tel:** 01354 677302
**Pitches For** ⚿ ⌂ 🚐 **Total** 40
**Facilities** ⚿ ⌁ 🚿 🏚 🍴 🏚 ⌂ 🍴 ⌂ ⌆ 🍴
⌂ 🚿 ⚲ ⌂🚿🅿 ✂
**Nearby Facilities** ⌁ ⚓ ♣
---

**Acreage** 7 **Open** All Year
**Access** Good **Site** Level
Relaxed, remote location adjacent to the Old Nene River. Marina, slipway for boat launch and a ramp for disabled access. Long/short term moorings. Occasional live music in the clubhouse. Ideal for walking and bird watching. Cycle route. Facilities for assited disabled. Disabled fishing access. Views across Fenland. Holiday lodges for sale. Barrier controlled. Bar snacks available in the Bar.
**Nearest Town/Resort** March
**Directions** 4 miles from March. Take the A141 from March towards Chatteris, look for Floods Ferry and golf course sign and take this turn, continue for 3 miles and look for park sign on the right, single lane road to the park.
⚑ March

## PETERBOROUGH

**Ferry Meadows Caravan Club Site,** Ham Lane, Peterborough, Cambridgeshire, PE2 5UU
**Tel:** 01733 233526
**www.** caravanclub.co.uk
**Pitches For** ⚿ ⌂ 🚐 **Total** 254
**Facilities** ⚿ ⌁ 🚿 🏚 🍴 🏚 ⌂ 🍴
🕌 ⌂ 🚿🅰⌂🔌
**Nearby Facilities** ⌁ ⚓ ♨ ♣ ⚲
**Acreage** 30 **Open** All Year
**Access** Good **Site** Level
Set in a country park with plenty of activities available nearby, and a 6 acre shopping complex. Near to Nene Valley Steam Railway. Non members welcome. Booking essential.
**Nearest Town/Resort** Peterborough
**Directions** From South on the A1, do not turn onto the A1139, instead turn left at next junction just past the service station signposted Showground. At the T-junction turn left, continue and turn left signposted Nene Park, continue and site is on the left.
⚑ Peterborough

## ST. NEOTS

**Camping & Caravanning Club Site,** Hardwick Road, Eynesbury, St. Neots, Cambridgeshire, PE19 2PR
**Tel:** 01480 474404
**www.** campingandcaravanningclub.co.uk
**Pitches For** ⚿ ⌂ 🚐 **Total** 180
**Facilities** ⚿ ⌁ 🚿 🏚 🍴 ⌂ 🍴 ⌂ ⌆ 🍴 ⌂ 🍴
🕌 ⌂ 🚿🅰⌂🅿🔲 ✂
**Nearby Facilities** ⌁ ⚓ ♨ ♣ ⚲
**Acreage** 11 **Open** March **to** Nov
**Access** Good **Site** Level
On the banks of the River Ouse for boating, fishing and walking. Plenty of sports facilities in the area. Non members welcome.
**Nearest Town/Resort** Cambridge
**Directions** From the A1 take the A428 to Cambridge, at the second roundabout turn left to Tesco's, go past the sports centre and follow the international signs to the site.
⚑ Cambridge

## WISBECH

**Virginia Lake & Caravan Park,** Smeeth Road, St John's Fen End, Wisbech, Cambridgeshire, PE14 8JF
**Tel:** 01945 430585 **Fax:** 01945 430585
**Email:** mickandmarion@supanet.com

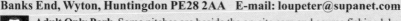

www. virginialake.co.uk
**Pitches For** ⚠ ⬜ ⬛ **Total** 82
**Facilities** ⚹ ♨ ⬜ ⬛ ♠ ⊙ ⌟ ⬛ ⬛ ⬛
⬛ ⬛ ⬛ ⬛ ✕ ♀ ⬛ ♠ ⬛ ⬛ ⬛ ⬛
**Nearby Facilities** ⌐ ✓ ⤢ U ♪
**Acreage** 5 **Open** All Year
**Access** Good **Site** Level
2 acre course fishing lake on site. Full
C.C.T.V. in operation and site is secured at
night. Motorhome waste disposal point. 30
mins from Sandringham and 45 mins from
the coast. ETB 4 Star Graded and AA 3
Pennants.
**Nearest Town/Resort** Wisbech/Kings Lynn
**Directions** On the A47 7 miles from Wisbech
and 7 miles from Kings Lynn. Follow tourist
board signs from the A47.
⬛ Kings Lynn

# CHANNEL ISLES

## GUERNSEY

**Fauxquets Valley Farm Camping Site,**
Fauxquets de Bas, Catel, Guernsey,
Channel Islands, GY5 7QA
**Tel:** 01481 255460 **Fax:** 01481 251797
**Email:** info@fauxquets.co.uk
www. fauxquets.co.uk
**Pitches For** ⚠ **Total** 90
**Facilities** ⚹ ♨ ⬜ ♠ ⌐ ⊙ ⌟ ⬛
⬛ ⬛ ⬛ ⬛ ✕ ⬛ ♠ ⬛ ♠ ⬛ ⬛ ⬛
**Nearby Facilities** ⌐ ✓ ⤢ U ♪ ♪
**Acreage** 3 **Open** May to 10 Sept
**Site** Level
1½ miles from sea, beautiful countryside,
quiet site. Fully equipped tents available
for hire. Licensed bar.
**Nearest Town/Resort** St. Peter Port
**Directions** Follow sign for Catel, turn left
onto Queens Road. Turn right at the sign for
the German Underground Hospital

## GUERNSEY

**La Bailloterie Camping,** Bailloterie Lane,
Vale, Guernsey, Channel Islands, GY3 5HA
**Tel:** 01481 243636 **Fax:** 01481 243225
**Email:** info@campinguernsey.com
www. campinguernsey.com
**Pitches For** ⚠ **Total** 150
**Facilities** ⚹ ⬜ ♠ ⌐ ⊙ ⌟ ⬛ ⬛ ⬛
⬛ ⬛ ⬛ ✕ ⬛ ♠ ⬛ ♠ ⬛ ⬛ ⬛
**Nearby Facilities** ⌐ ✓ ⤢ U ♪ ♪ ✕
**Acreage** 12 **Open** 15 May to 15 Sept
**Site** Sloping
Rural setting near a Blue Flag beach.
Close to services. Fully equipped 2, 4 and
6 berth tents available for hire plus private
camping.
**Nearest Town/Resort** St. Peter Port
**Directions** From St. Peter Port leave for norh
of the island. At the seafront leave a second
filter, turn right at the second set of traffic
lights, then turn first left.

## JERSEY

**Beuvelande Camp Site,** Beuvelande, St
Martin, Jersey, Channel Islands, JE3 6EZ
**Tel:** 01534 853575 **Fax:** 01534 857788
**Email:** info@campingjersey.com
www. campingjersey.com
**Pitches For** ⚠ **Total** 150
**Facilities** ⚹ ♨ ⬜ ✕ ♠ ♠ ⌐ ⊙ ⌟ ⬛
⬛ ⬛ ⬛ ✕ ⬛ ♠ ♠ ⬛ ⬛ ⬛
**Nearby Facilities**
**Acreage** 6 **Open** 1 April to 30 Sept
**Site** Level
Caravans are now allowed on the Channel
Islands by permit from Jersey Tourism. AA
5 Pennant Premier Park and listed under
Best Parks in Britain.
**Nearest Town/Resort** St. Martin
**Directions** From the harbour take the A6 to
St. Martin Church then follow signs to camp
site.

## JERSEY

**Rozel Camping Park,** Rozel, St Martin,
Jersey, Channel Islands, JE3 6AX
**Tel:** 01534 855200 **Fax:** 01534 856127
**Email:** rozelcampingpark@jerseymail.co.uk
www. jerseyhols.com/rozel
**Pitches For** ⚠ ⬜ ⬛ **Total** 160
**Facilities** ⚹ ♨ ⬜ ♠ ⌐ ⊙ ⌟ ⬛ ⬛ ⬛
⬛ ⬛ ⬛ ♠ ⬛ ⬛ ⬛ ⬛
**Nearby Facilities** ⌐ ✓ ⤢ ✕ U ♪
**Acreage** 3 **Open** May to Mid Sept
**Site** Level
Views of France. Nearby a picturesque
beach and harbour aswell as Gerald Durrell's
Zoo. Hire tents available, own tents, caravans
and motor homes welcome.
**Nearest Town/Resort** St. Helier
**Directions** 5 miles from St. Helier. A6 to
Martin's Church then B38 to Rozel.

# CHESHIRE

## CHESTER

**Chester Fairoaks Caravan Club Site,**
Rake Lane, Little Stanney, Chester,
Cheshire, CH2 4HS
**Tel:** 0151 355 1600
www. caravanclub.co.uk
**Pitches For** ⚠ ⬜ ⬛ **Total** 100
**Facilities** ⚹ ♨ ⬜ ⬜ ♠ ⌐ ⬛ ⬛
⬛ ⬛ ⬛ ⬛ ⬛
**Nearby Facilities** ⌐ ✓
**Acreage** 8 **Open** All Year
**Access** Good **Site** Level
Pleasant site with oak tree boundaries.
Close to Chester Cathedral and Zoo. Non
members welcome. Booking essential.
**Nearest Town/Resort** Chester
**Directions** Leave the M53 at junction 10 and
take the A5117 signposted Queensferry. After
¼ mile in Little Stanney turn left signposted
Chorlton. Site is ¼ mile on the left.

## CHESTER

**Chester Southerly Touring Park,**
Balderton Lane, Chester, Cheshire, CH4
9LF
**Tel:** 01244 671308
www. chestersoutherlytouringpark.co.uk
**Pitches For** ⚠ ⬜ ⬛ **Total** 70
**Facilities** ⚹ ♨ ⬜ ♠ ⌐ ⊙ ⌟ ⬛ ⬛
⬛ ⬛ ⬛ ⬛
**Nearby Facilities** ⌐ ✓ ⤢ ✕ U ♪
**Acreage** 8 **Open** Easter to End Oct
**Access** Good **Site** Level
Ideally positioned for Chester and North
Wales. Please note that cycles,
skateboards and all ball games are not
permitted.
**Nearest Town/Resort** Chester
**Directions** Well signposted from the A55/
A483. Just off the A483 south of Chester (2½
miles).
⬛ Chester

## CHESTER

**Manor Wood Country Caravan Park,**
Manor Wood, Coddington, Chester,
Cheshire, CH3 9EN
**Tel:** 01829 782990 **Fax:** 01829 782990
**Email:** info@manorwoodcaravans.co.uk
www. cheshire-caravan-sites.co.uk
**Pitches For** ⚠ ⬜ ⬛ **Total** 25
**Facilities** ⚹ ♨ ⬜ ⬜ ⬜ ♠ ⌐ ⊙ ⌟ ⬛ ⬛
⬛ ⬛ ⬛ ♠ ⬛ ✿ ⬛ ♪ ⬛ ⬛
**Nearby Facilities** ⌐ ✓ U ♪
**Acreage** 8 **Open** All Year
**Access** Good **Site** Level
Only 15 minutes from Chester. Local
attractions within 10 minutes radius. Good
cycleways and walking.
**Nearest Town/Resort** Chester

**Directions** From the A41 Whitchurch to
Chester road, at the roundabout take the A534
towards Wrexham. At the Cock O Bourton Pub
turn right and enter the village, go straight on
and the Park is 500 yards on the left.
⬛ Chester

## CHESTER

**Netherwood Touring Site,** Netherwood
House, Whitchurch Road, Nr Chester,
Cheshire, CH3 6AF
**Tel:** 01244 335583
**Email:** netherwood.chester@btinternet.com
www. netherwoodtouringsite.co.uk
**Pitches For** ⬜ ⬛ **Total** 15
**Facilities** ♨ ⬜ ♠ ⌐ ⊙ ⌟ ⬛ ⬛ ⬛ A
**Nearby Facilities** ⌐ ✓ ⤢ ✕
**Acreage** 1½ **Open** March to October
**Access** Good **Site** Level
Adults only site on Shropshire Union
Canal. 5 miles from Zoo.
**Nearest Town/Resort** Chester
**Directions** On A41, approx. 1 mile from
Chester bypass.
⬛ Chester

## CHESTER

**Northwood Hall Country Touring Park,**
Northwood Hall, Dog Lane, Kelsall,
ChesterCheshire, CW6 0RP
**Tel:** 01829 752569 **Fax:** 01829 751157
**Email:** enquiries@northwood-hall.co.uk
www. northwood-hall.co.uk
**Pitches For** ⚠ ⬜ ⬛ **Total** 30
**Facilities** ♨ ⬜ ⬜ ♠ ⌐ ⊙ ⌟ ⬛ ⬛
⬛ ⬛ ♠ ⬛ ⬛ ⬛
**Nearby Facilities** ⌐ ✓ ⤢ ✕ U ♪
**Acreage** 8 **Open** 31 March to 30 Oct
**Access** Good **Site** Gently Sloping
Rural site near Delamere Forest and the
walled city of Chester.
**Nearest Town/Resort** Chester
**Directions** 7 miles east of Chester off A556.
⬛ Chester

## MACCLESFIELD

**Capesthorne Hall Caravan Park,**
Siddington, Macclesfield, Cheshire, SK11
9JY
**Tel:** 01625 861221 **Fax:** 01625 861619
**Email:** info@capesthorne.com
www. capesthorne.com
**Pitches For** ⬜ ⬛ **Total** 30
**Facilities** ♨ ⚹ ♨ ⬜ ♠ ⌐ ⊙ ⌟ ⬛ ⬛ ⬛
⬛ ✕ ⬛
**Nearby Facilities** ⌐ U ♪
**Open** April to Oct
**Access** Good **Site** Level
Peaceful site in the grounds of
Capesthorne Hall stately home. Free
access to the gardens and lakes until 7pm.
**Nearest Town/Resort** Macclesfield
**Directions** Situated on the A34. From
Macclesfield take the A537 and turn left onto
the A34, site is 1 mile on the right.
⬛ Macclesfield

## MACCLESFIELD

**Strawberry Wood Caravan Park,** Home
Farm, Farm Lane, Lower Withington,
MacclesfieldCheshire, SK11 9DU
**Tel:** 01477 571407
**Email:**
strawberrywoodcaravanpark@yahoo.co.uk
www. http://uk.geocities.com/
strawberrywoodcaravanpark
**Pitches For** ⬜ ⬛ **Total** 25
**Facilities** ♨ ⬜ ⬜ ♠ ⌐ ⊙ ⬛ ⬛ ✕ ♪
**Nearby Facilities** ⌐ ✓
**Acreage** 5 **Open** March to October
**Access** Good **Site** Level
Large coarse fishing pond adjacent to the
site. ETB Graded 3 Stars.

**Nearest Town/Resort** Macclesfield
**Directions** Leave the M6 at junction 18 and take the A54 to Holmes Chapel. Then take the A535 to Macclesfield, after 4 miles turn right onto the B5392 (Farm Lane). The site entrance is 700 yards on the right hand side.
⇌ Goostrey

## WARRINGTON

**Holly Bank Caravan Park,** Warburton Bridge Road, Rixton, Warrington, Cheshire, WA3 6HU
**Tel:** 0161 775 2842
**Pitches For** ▲ ⌺ ⇌ **Total** 75
**Facilities** ᕦ ⚥ ⨍ 𝓤ᴱ ⚓ Ր ☉ ⌣ ◢ ◻ ☎
⚘ 𝄞 𝄆 ⏚ ♨ ⊞ ⌸ ◨
**Nearby Facilities** Ր ⚑ ⚓ ∪
**Open** All Year
**Access** Good **Site** Level
Dunham Park, Tatton Park, and ideal touring North Cheshire.
**Nearest Town/Resort** Warrington
**Directions** 2 miles from M6 junction 21 on A57 (Irlam) turn right at lights into Warburton Bridge Road entry on left, Warrington 5 miles.
⇌ Irlam

## WINSFORD

**Lamb Cottage Caravan Park,** Dalefords Lane, Whitegate, Northwich, Cheshire, CW8 2BN
**Tel:** 01606 882302 **Fax:** 01606 888491
**Email:** lynn@lccp.fsworld.co.uk
**www.** lambcottage.co.uk
**Pitches For** ⌺ ⇌
**Facilities** ᕦ ⨍ ⊟ 𝓗 𝓤ᴱ ⚓ Ր ☉ ⌣ ◢ ◻ ☎
⊞ 𝄐 ⏚ ⊞ ⧉ ♨
**Nearby Facilities** Ր ⚑ ∪
**Open** March to October
**Access** Good **Site** Level
Peaceful retreat for Adults only. Ideal for touring the heart of Cheshire.
**Nearest Town/Resort** Winsford
**Directions** 1 mile from the A556.
⇌ Cuddington


# CORNWALL

## BODMIN

**Camping & Caravanning Club Site,** Old Callywith Road, Bodmin, Cornwall, PL31 2DZ
**Tel:** 01208 73834
**www.** campingandcaravanningclub.co.uk
**Pitches For** ▲ ⌺ ⇌ **Total** 130
**Facilities** ⨍ 𝓤ᴱ ⚓ Ր ☉ ⌣ ◢ ◻ ☎
⚘ 𝄞 ⏚ ⧉ ⊬ ⊟ ⌸ ♨ ℘
**Nearby Facilities**
**Acreage** 11 **Open** March to Nov
**Site** Lev/Slope
On the edge of Bodmin Moor. Within easy reach of the coast and close to many places of interest. BTB 4 Star Graded and AA 3 Pennants. Non members welcome.
**Directions** From the north stay on the A30 until signpost 'Bodmin', turn right crossing over the dual carriageway in front of industrial estate, then turn immediately left at international sign. Site is on the left down Old Callywith Road.
⇌ Bodmin Parkway

## BODMIN

**Lanarth Hotel & Caravan Park,** St Kew Highway, Bodmin, Cornwall, PL30 3EE
**Tel:** 01208 841215
**Pitches For** ▲ ⌺ ⇌ **Total** 86
**Facilities** ⨍ 𝓤ᴱ ⚓ Ր ☉ ⌣ ◢ ⊟ ☎
⚘ 𝄐 ⏚ ⚥ 𝄞 ⏚ ⇥ ⧉ 𝄐 ♨ ℘
**Nearby Facilities** Ր ⚑ ⚓ ⚓ ∪ ⚓
**Acreage** 10 **Open** April to October
Beautiful rural setting, conveniently situated for beaches and moor. Ideal for touring Cornwall and Devon.
**Nearest Town/Resort** Wadebridge
**Directions** On the A39 at St. Kew Highway, approx 4 miles east of Wadebridge and 8 miles west of Camelford.
⇌ Bodmin

## BODMIN

**Ruthern Valley Holidays,** Ruthernbridge, Nr Bodmin, Cornwall, PL30 5LU
**Tel:** 01208 831395
**Email:** ruthern.valley@btconnect.com
**www.** self-catering-ruthern.co.uk
**Pitches For** ▲ ⌺ ⇌ **Total** 30
**Facilities** ⨍ 𝓤ᴱ ⚓ Ր ☉ ⌣ ◢ ◻ ☎
𝄐 ⏚ ⧉ ⌸
**Nearby Facilities** Ր ⚑ ⚓ ∪ ℘
**Acreage** 2 **Open** April to October
**Access** Good **Site** Level
Quiet peaceful wooded location centrally based for touring. ETC 4 Star Holiday Park, AA 3 Pennants and Bellamy Gold Award 2002.
**Nearest Town/Resort** Bodmin
**Directions** Through Bodmin on A389 towards St. Austell, on outskirts of Bodmin Ruthernbridge signposted right. Follow signs for Ruthern or Ruthernbridge.
⇌ Bodmin Parkway

## BODMIN

**South Penquite Farm,** South Penquite, Blisland, Bodmin, Cornwall, PL30 4LH
**Tel:** 01208 850491
**Email:** thefarm@bodminmoor.co.uk
**www.** southpenquite.co.uk
**Pitches For** ▲ ⇌ **Total** 25
**Facilities** 𝓤ᴱ Ր ⌣ ⚥ ⏚
**Nearby Facilities** Ր ⚑ ⚓ ⚓ ∪
**Acreage** 5 **Open** May to September
**Access** Good **Site** Level
South Penquite is a 200 acre organic sheep farm set high on Bodmin Moor. Interesting farm walk.
**Directions** Enter Cornwall on the A30 and drive for approx. 18 miles, take right turn signposted St. Breward, farm lane will be on the right after 3 miles.
⇌ Bodmin Parkway

## BOSCASTLE

**Lower Pennycrocker Farm,** St Juliot, Boscastle, Cornwall, PL35 0BY
**Tel:** 01840 250257
**www.** pennycrockerinternet.co.uk
**Pitches For** ▲ ⌺ ⇌ **Total** 40
**Facilities** ⨍ 𝓤ᴱ ⚓ Ր ☉ ⌣ 𝄐 𝄞 ⏚ ⇥ ⊟ ♨ ℘
**Nearby Facilities** ⚑ ⚓ ⚓ ∪
**Acreage** 4 **Open** Easter to September
**Access** Good **Site** Level
Scenic views, ideal touring.

**Nearest Town/Resort** Boscastle
**Directions** 2½ miles north of Boscastle on B3263, turn left signposted Pennycrocker.
⇌ Bodmin

## BOSCASTLE

**St. Tinney Farm Holidays,** Otterham, North Cornwall, PL32 9TA
**Tel:** 01840 261274 **Fax:** 01840 261575
**Email:** info@st-tinney.co.uk
**www.** st-tinney.co.uk
**Pitches For** ▲ ⌺ ⇌ **Total** 20
**Facilities** ⨍ 𝓤ᴱ ⚓ Ր ☉ ⌣ ◢ ◻ ☎
⚘ 𝄐 ⏚ ⚥ 𝄞 ⏚ ⧉ ⊞ ⌸
**Nearby Facilities** Ր ⚑ ∪
**Acreage** 34 **Open** Easter to 1 Nov
Own country pub and children's pony rides. David Bellamy Gold Award for Conservation.
**Nearest Town/Resort** Boscastle
**Directions** Bypass Launceston on the A30 then take the A395 for 8 miles to Hallworthy. Turn second right onto the B3262 to the junction with the A39, turn right for Bude, after 1 mile turn right for Otterham.
⇌ Bodmin

## BUDE

**Budemeadows Touring Holiday Park,** Poundstock, Bude, Cornwall, EX23 0NA
**Tel:** 01288 361646 **Fax:** 01288 361646
**Email:** holiday@budemeadows.com
**www.** budemeadows.com
**Pitches For** ▲ ⌺ ⇌ **Total** 140
**Facilities** ⨍ 𝓗 𝓤ᴱ ⚓ Ր ☉ ⌣ ◢ ◻ ☎
⚘ 𝄞 ⏚ ⧉ ⚥ ♨ ⊞ ⇥ ⊞ ⌸ ℘
**Nearby Facilities** Ր ⚑ ⚓ ⚓ ∪ ℘
**Acreage** 9 **Open** All Year
**Access** Good **Site** Level
1 mile from sandy beaches, cliff walks and rolling surf of Widmouth Bay. Spectacular coastal scenery. Licenced Bar.
**Nearest Town/Resort** Bude
**Directions** From Bude take A39 south for 3 miles.
⇌ Exeter

## BUDE

**Camping & Caravanning Club Site,** Gillards Moor, St Gennys, Bude, Cornwall, EX23 0BG
**Tel:** 01840 230650
**www.** campingandcaravanningclub.co.uk
**Pitches For** ▲ ⌺ ⇌ **Total** 100
**Facilities** ᕦ ⨍ 𝓗 𝓤ᴱ ⚓ Ր ☉ ⌣ ◢ ◻ ☎
⚘ 𝄞 ⏚ ⧉ ⊬ ⊟ ⌸ ♨ ℘
**Nearby Facilities**
**Acreage** 6 **Open** April to Oct
**Site** Lev/Slope
Near the coastal paths in the heart of King Arthur's Country. Table tennis on site. BTB 4 Star Graded and AA 3 Pennants. Non members welcome.
**Directions** Going south on the A39 the site is on the right in lay-by 9 miles from Bude. Going north on the A39 the site is on the left in lay-by 9 miles from Camelford, approx. 3 miles from the B3262 junction. Brown camping signs ½ mile either side of the site, also on both ends of the lay-by.
⇌ Bodmin

**BUDE**

**Cornish Coasts Caravan & Camping Park,** Middle Penlean, Poundstock, Bude, Cornwall, EX23 0EE
**Tel:** 01288 361380
**Email:** reception2@cornishcoasts.co.uk
**www.** cornishcoasts.co.uk
**Pitches For** Å ♠ 🚗 **Total** 45
**Facilities** ∮ ⊟ ⅏ ⅏ ♨ ⌂ ☉ ⊶ ≙ ◲ 🍴
🏤 ⊙ �Ⓜ 🏕 ⌹ ✈ ℓ
**Nearby Facilities** ⌐ ✐ ∪ ⚲
**Acreage** 3½ **Open** April **to** October
**Access** Good **Site** Level
Peaceful site with fantastic views. 2 miles from the beach. Ideal for touring.
**Nearest Town/Resort** Bude
**Directions** Take the A39 south for 5 miles, we are in a layby on the right hand side of the road.
🚆 Bodmin

**BUDE**

**Coxford Meadow,** Crackington Haven, Bude, Cornwall, EX23 0NS
**Tel:** 01840 230707
**Pitches For** Å ♠ 🚗 **Total** 20
**Facilities** ⅏ ♨ ⌂ ☉ 🏤 ✕ 🏕 ⌹ ≋
**Nearby Facilities**
**Acreage** 1 **Open** Easter **to** Sept
**Access** Poor **Site** Level
Set in farmland with views to the sea. A mile from the surfing beach at Crackington Haven.
**Directions** Take the A39 south from Bude and turn right at Wainhouse Corner, take the third turning on the right.
🚆 Bodmin

**BUDE**

**Ivyleaf Camping Site,** Ivyleaf Hill, Bush, Nr Bude, Cornwall, EX23 9LD
**Tel:** 01288 321442 **Fax:** 01288 321442
**www.** ivyleafcamping.co.uk

**Pitches For** Å ♠ 🚗
**Facilities** ∮ ⊟ ⅏ ⅏ ♨ ⌂ ☉ ⊶ ≙ ◲ 🍴
**Nearby Facilities** ⌐ ✐ ∪ ⚲ ℓ ⚲
**Acreage** 5 **Open** All Year
**Access** Good **Site** Level
Easy access to the North Cornwall coast for surfing etc..
**Nearest Town/Resort** Bude
**Directions** From Bideford take the A39 south, go past Kilkhampton and in approx. 2 miles, at sharp right hand bend, continue into lane, site is on the left below the summit of the hill.
🚆 Exeter

**BUDE**

**Penstowe Caravan & Camping Park,** Stibb Road, Kilkhampton, Bude, Cornwall, EX23 9QY
**Tel:** 01288 321601 **Fax:** 01288 321601
**Email:** camping@penstowecaravans.wanadoo.co.uk
**www.** penstoweholidays.co.uk
**Pitches For** Å ♠ 🚗 **Total** 120
**Facilities** ⌂ ∮ ⊟ ⅏ ⅏ ♨ ⌂ ☉ ⌂ 🍴
🏤 ⊙ ⅏ ✕ ℓ Ⓜ ℨ ⚲ 🏕 ≙ ⊟ 🔲 ≋ ℓ
**Nearby Facilities** ⌐ ✐ ✕ ∪ ℓ ⚲
**Acreage** 6 **Open** All Year
**Access** Good **Site** Level
Quiet site with lovely views. Touring caravan site attached to an established, highly rated holiday village with excellent facilities. Highly recommended.
**Nearest Town/Resort** Bude
**Directions** 4 miles north of Bude on the A39 at Kilkhampton.
🚆 Barnstaple/Exeter

**BUDE**

**Red Post Holiday Park,** Launcells, Bude, Cornwall, EX23 9NW
**Tel:** 01288 381305
**Email:** gsharp@redpostinn1.wanadoo.co.uk
**Pitches For** Å ♠ 🚗

**Facilities** ∮ ⊟ ⅏ ⅏ ♨ ⌂ ☉ ⊶ ≙ ◲ 🍴
Ⓡ 🔒 ✕ ⅏ 🏕 ✈ ≋
**Nearby Facilities** ⌐ ✐ ⚲ ∪ ℓ ⚲ ⚲
**Open** All Year
**Access** Good **Site** Level
Quiet, family run park near the beach. Secluded bays and good nightlife. Centrally located for exploring the coast and towns.
**Nearest Town/Resort** Bude
**Directions** 4 miles from Bude, 5 miles from Holsworthy and 3 miles from Widemouth Bay.
🚆 Bude

**BUDE**

**Upper Lynstone Camping & Caravan Park,** Upper Lynstone Farm, Bude, Cornwall, EX23 0LP
**Tel:** 01288 352017 **Fax:** 01288 359034
**Email:** reception@upperlynstone.co.uk
**www.** upperlynstone.co.uk
**Pitches For** Å ♠ 🚗 **Total** 65
**Facilities** ⌂ ∮ ⅏ ♨ ⌂ ☉ ≙ ◲ 🍴
🏤 ⊙ ⅏ Ⓜ ⊟ ⌹
**Nearby Facilities** ⌐ ✐ ✕ ∪ ℓ
**Acreage** 5 **Open** Easter **to** October
**Access** Good **Site** Lev/Slope
Within easy reach of good surfing beaches. Access to cliff walks. Families and couples only, no groups.
**Nearest Town/Resort** Bude
**Directions** ½ mile south of Bude on Widemouth Bay road.
🚆 Exeter

**BUDE**

**Widemouth Bay Caravan Park,** John Fowler Holidays, Widemouth Bay, Bude, Cornwall, EX23 0DF
**Tel:** 01271 866766 **Fax:** 01271 866791
**Email:** bookings@johnfowlerholidays.com
**www.** johnfowlerholidays.com
**Pitches For** Å ♠ 🚗 **Total** 200
**Facilities** ⌂ ∮ ⅏ ⅏ ♨ ⌂ ☉ ⊶ ≙ ◲ 🍴
🏤 ℓ ⊙ ⅏ ✕ ℨ Ⓜ 🔒 🏕 ℓ ℓ ≋ ⊟ ⊟ ≋ ≋

**CHOICE OF 3 LOVELY HOLIDAY PARKS**

NORTH DEVON & CORNWALL

*JOHN FOWLER HOLIDAY PARKS*

**TENT & TOURING PITCHES AT BARGAIN PRICES**

☆ *Close to Sandy Beaches*
☆ *No Silly Extras*

FREE Hot Showers  FREE Awning Space
FREE Entertainment  FREE Licensed Club

WRITE TO: DEPT. CC,
JOHN FOWLER HOLIDAYS, MARLBOROUGH ROAD,
ILFRACOMBE, N. DEVON EX34 8PF

**www.johnfowlerholidays.com**

☆ **Nightly Entertainment** ☆ **Club**
☆ **Heated Pools** ☆ **Children's Club**
☆ **Safe Playground** ☆ **Electric Hook-ups**
☆ **Shop & Take-Away**

**BOOKING HOT-LINE 01271 866766**

## The Setting

Sandymouth sits in twenty four acres of meadowland in an area with beautiful beaches, bustling coastal resorts and fishing villages. Whether you want to explore the countryside, wander into Devon or seek out Tintagel where King Arthur is reputed to have lived, Sandymouth gives you access to lots of different settings and places of interest. Inland, the rolling countryside is a fascinating contrast to the rugged coast near Sandymouth.

E-MAIL: reception@sandymouthbay.co.uk
WEB: www.dolphinholidays.co.uk
Online Booking Available
Sandymouth Bay, Bude, Cornwall EX23 9HW

## Facilities

Indoor Heated Swimming Pool  Solarium and Sauna  Toilet facilities for tourers  Clubhouse (FREE membership)  Restaurant and Takeaway  Entertainment and Cabaret  Mini-supermarket  Children's adventure playground  Games room  Public telephones  Breakfast available  Bingo/Quizzes  Kid's games  Face paint competitions  Discos  Karaoke  Speciality evenings & much more  Well stocked coarse fishing lake adjacent to park (moderate extra charge)

**TELEPHONE: 01288 352563**
**FAX: 01288 354 822**

---

**Nearby Facilities** ┌ ✓ ⚓ ⚲ ∪ ℛ
**Acreage** 50 **Open** March **to** October
**Access** Good **Site** Level
Close to one of Cornwall's finest surfing beaches. Perfect location for touring both Devon and Cornwall.
**Nearest Town/Resort** Bude
**Directions** From the M5 take the A361 then the A39 to Bude. Widemouth Bay is 4 miles west of Bude, clearly signposted.
⇌ Exeter

## BUDE

**Willow Valley Holiday Park,** Dye House, Bush, Bude, Cornwall, EX23 9LB
**Tel:** 01288 353104 **Fax:** 01288 353104
**Email:** willowvalley@talk21.com
**www.** willowvalley.co.uk
**Pitches For** ▲ ⊞ ➤
**Facilities** ╱ 🅼 ♨ ┌ ⊙ ᴒ ⬛ ◲ ➤
🆂 🅾 ⌂ ┩ ⊟ ⊡ ➤
**Nearby Facilities** ┌ ✓ ⚲ ∪ ℛ
**Acreage** 3 **Open** March **to** Dec
**Access** Good **Site** Level
River runs through the site. 2 miles from the nearest beach.
**Nearest Town/Resort** Bude
**Directions** On the A39 between Bude and Kilkhampton.
⇌ Exeter

## BUDE

**Wooda Farm Park,** Poughill, Bude, Cornwall, EX23 9HJ
**Tel:** 01288 352069 **Fax:** 01288 355258
**Email:** enquiries@wooda.co.uk
**www.** wooda.co.uk
**Pitches For** ▲ ⊞ ➤ **Total** 200
**Facilities** ⚿ ╱ 🄵 ⊞ 🅼 ♨ ┌ ⊙ ᴒ ⬛ ◲ ➤
🆂 🅸 🅾 ⊗ ✕ 🅃 ♠ ⋀ ⚒ ┩ ⊟ ⊡ ℛ ✗
**Nearby Facilities** ┌ ✓ ⚓ ⚲ ∪ ℛ ✗
**Acreage** 12 **Open** April **to** October
**Access** Good **Site** Lev/Slope

Overlooks sea and coastline, woodland walks, coarse fishing, large childrens play area, dog exercise field, short golf course. Sandy beaches 1½ miles. Licensed farm restaurant and take-away. Off License on site. Contact Mrs Q. Colwill.
**Nearest Town/Resort** Bude
**Directions** Take road to Poughill 1¼ miles, go through village. At crossroads turn left. Site 200yds along road on right hand side.
⇌ Exeter

## CAMELFORD

**Juliot's Well Holiday Park,** Camelford, Cornwall, PL32 9RF
**Tel:** 01840 213302 **Fax:** 01840 212700
**Email:** juliotswell@holidaysincornwall.net
**www.** holidaysincornwall.net
**Pitches For** ▲ ⊞ ➤
**Facilities** ╱ 🄵 🄷 🅼 ♨ ┌ ⊙ ᴒ ⬛ ◲ ➤
🆂 🄰 ✕ ⚲ ♠ ⋀ ⤳ ┩ ⊟ ⊡ ⚒ 🄿
**Nearby Facilities** ┌ ✓ ⚲
**Open** March **to** Oct
**Access** Good **Site** Lev/Slope
**Nearest Town/Resort** Camelford
**Directions** Turn off the A39 at Valley Truckle, signposted from there.
⇌ Bodmin

## CAMELFORD

**Lakefield Caravan Park,** Lower Pendavey Farm, Camelford, Cornwall, PL32 9TX
**Tel:** 01840 213279 **Fax:** 01840 213279
**Email:** lakefield@pendavey.fsnet.co.uk
**www.** lakefieldcaravanpark.co.uk
**Pitches For** ▲ ⊞ ➤ **Total** 40
**Facilities** ╱ 🅼 ♨ ┌ ⊙ ᴒ ⬛ ◲ ➤
🆂 🅾 ⌂ ⋀ ✿ ┩ ⊟ 🄿
**Nearby Facilities** ┌ ✓
**Acreage** 5 **Open** Easter **to** October
**Access** Good **Site** Level
Scenic views, own lake. Ideal for touring Cornwall. Full equestrian facilities

providing lessons, site rides and hacks for all the family. British Horse Society Qualified Instruction. Pets Corner and Tea Shop on site.
**Nearest Town/Resort** Camelford/Tintagel
**Directions** 1¼ miles north of Camelford on the B3266 Boscastle road.
⇌ Bodmin

## CARLYON BAY

**Carlyon Bay Camping Park,** Cypress Avenue, Carlyon Bay, St Austell, Cornwall, PL25 3RE
**Tel:** 01726 812735
**Email:** holidays@carlyonbay.net
**www.** carlyonbay.net
**Pitches For** ▲ ⊞ ➤ **Total** 180
**Facilities** ╱ 🄵 🄷 🄼 ♨ ┌ ⊙ ᴒ ⬛ ◲ ➤
🆂 🅾 ⊗ ✕ 🅃 ♠ ⋀ ⚒ ┩ ⊟ ⊡ 🄰
**Nearby Facilities** ┌ ✓ ⚲
**Acreage** 18 **Open** Easter **to** Oct
**Access** Good **Site** Level
Just a 5 minute walk to the beach.
**Nearest Town/Resort** St. Austell
**Directions** From St Austell head east on the A390, signposted.
⇌ Par

## COVERACK

**Little Trevothan Caravan Park,** Coverack, Helston, Cornwall, TR12 6SD
**Tel:** 01326 280260 **Fax:** 01326 280260
**Email:** mmita@btopenworld.com
**www.** littletrevothan.com
**Pitches For** ▲ ⊞ ➤ **Total** 60
**Facilities** ╱ 🄼 ♨ ┌ ⊙ ᴒ ⬛ ◲ ➤
🆂 🅸 🅾 ⊗ 🅃 ♠ ⋀ ┩ ⊟ ⊡
**Nearby Facilities** ┌ ✓ ⚓ ⚲ ∪
**Open** May to September
**Access** Good **Site** Level
Beach nearby, flat meadows, off road.
**Nearest Town/Resort** Helston
**Directions** A39 to Helston, follow B3083 to

Culdrose, turn left B3293 signposted to Coverack. Go past BT Goonhilly, turn right before Zoar Garage, third turning on left, 300yds on the right.
➥ Redruth

## COVERACK

**Penmarth Farm Camp Site,** Coverack, Helston, Cornwall,
**Tel:** 01326 280389
**Pitches For** ▲ ⚍ �btotal 28
**Facilities** ⚒ 🚽 ⚓ ⌯ ☉ ⊐ ☦ ⚘ ⊣
**Nearby Facilities** ⌯ ✈ ⚓ ↝ ∪
**Acreage** 2 **Open** March **to** October
**Access** Good **Site** Level
¼ mile woodland walk to the sea and beach.
**Nearest Town/Resort** Helston
**Directions** From Helston take the B3293 for approx. 10 miles.
➥ Cambourne

## CRACKINGTON HAVEN

**Hentervene Caravan & Camping Park,** Crackington Haven, Nr Bude, Cornwall, EX23 0LF
**Tel:** 01840 230365
**Email:** contact@hentervene.co.uk
www. hentervene.co.uk
**Pitches For** ▲ ⚍ ♛ **Total** 43
**Facilities** ⌯ 🚽 🚽 ⚓ ⌯ ☉ ⊐ ☦ ⚘ ☦
⌯ ⚘ ⚓ 🍴 ⚒ 🄰 ⊣ 🄿 🄲 ☀
**Nearby Facilities** ⌯ ✈ ⚓ ↝ ∪ ⟿ ♞ ⚂
**Acreage** 8¼ **Open** Easter **to** End Oct
**Access** Good **Site** Level
2 miles from the beach for sands, swimming and surfing. Ideal touring centre. Caravans for sale. Closed for camping only end of October to 1st April. Statics available all year.
**Nearest Town/Resort** Bude
**Directions** 10 miles southwest of Bude, turn off A39 at Otterham, signed Crackington

Haven. After 2½ miles turn left onto Crackington Road at Hentervene sign, park is ½ mile on right - 2 miles from beach.
➥ Bodmin

## CRANTOCK

**Treago Farm Caravan & Camping Park,** Treago Farm, Crantock, Newquay, Cornwall, TR8 5QS
**Tel:** 01637 830277 **Fax:** 01637 830277
**Email:** treagofarm@aol.com
www. treagofarm.co.uk
**Pitches For** ▲ ⚍ ♛ **Total** 100
**Facilities** ⌯ 🚽 🚽 ⚓ ⌯ ☉ ⊐ ☦ ⚘ ☦
⌯ 🄲 ⚘ 🍴 🄰 ⚒ 🄰 ⊣ 🄿 🄲 ☀
**Nearby Facilities** ⌯ ✈ ⚓ ↝ ∪ ♞
**Acreage** 5 **Open** Easter **to** 1 Nov
**Access** Good **Site** Lev/Slope
Footpath to two sandy beaches. Surrounded by National Trust land.
**Nearest Town/Resort** Newquay
**Directions** 2½ miles south west of Newquay, turn right off the A3075 signposted Crantock and Treago Campsite.
➥ Newquay

## DELABOLE

**Planet Park,** Westdown Road, Delabole, Cornwall, PL33 9BQ
**Tel:** 01840 213361
**Pitches For** ▲ ⚍ ♛ **Total** 30
**Facilities** ⌯ 🚽 ⚓ ⌯ ☉ ⊐ ☦ ⚘ ☦
⌯ 🄲 ⚘ 🍴 🄰 ⚒ 🄰 ⊣
**Nearby Facilities** ⌯ ✈ ↝ ∪ ⟿
**Acreage** 2 **Open** All Year
**Access** Good **Site** Level
Wonderful views, close to all the village facilities. Ideal for touring.
**Nearest Town/Resort** Tintagel
**Directions** On the B3314 coast road at the western end of village.
➥ Bodmin

## FALMOUTH

**Retanna Holiday Park,** Edgcumbe, Helston, Cornwall, TR13 0EJ
**Tel:** 01326 340643
**Email:** retannaholpark@lineone.net
www. retanna.co.uk
**Pitches For** ▲ ⚍ ♛ **Total** 24
**Facilities** ⚒ ⌯ 🚽 🚽 ⚓ ⌯ ☉ ⊐ ☦ ⚘ 🄰 ☦
⚘ ⌯ 🄲 ⚘ 🍴 ⚒ 🄰 🄿 🄲
**Nearby Facilities** ⌯ ✈ ⚓ ↝ ∪ ⟿ ♞
**Acreage** 8 **Open** April **to** October
**Access** Good **Site** Lev/Slope
Helford River area, close to a number of tourist attractions.
**Nearest Town/Resort** Falmouth/Helston
**Directions** Situated midway between Falmouth and Helston on the A394, on the right hand side immediately after Edgcumbe.
➥ Falmouth

## FALMOUTH

**Tregedna Farm Touring Park,** Tregedna Farm, Maenporth, Falmouth, Cornwall, TR11 5HL
**Tel:** 01326 250529
**Pitches For** ▲ ⚍ ♛ **Total** 40
**Facilities** ⌯ 🚽 ⚓ ⌯ ☉ ⊐ ☦ ⚘ 🄰 ☦
⚘ ⌯ 🄲 ⚘ 🍴 ⊣ 🄿 ☀
**Nearby Facilities** ⌯ ✈ ⚓ ↝ ∪ ♞
**Acreage** 10 **Open** May **to** September
**Access** Good **Site** Sloping
½ mile to Maenporth beach. Close to all well known NT Gardens. Ideal for touring South and West Cornwall.
**Nearest Town/Resort** Falmouth
**Directions** Take the A39 from Truro to Falmouth, turn off right at Hillhead roundabout and continue straight for 2½ miles.
➥ Penmere

# CORNWALL

## FOWEY
**Penhale Caravan & Camping Park,**
Fowey, Cornwall, PL23 1JU
**Tel:** 01726 833425 **Fax:** 01726 833425
**Email:** info@penhale-fowey.co.uk
www. penhale-fowey.co.uk
**Pitches For** ▲ ⊕ ⊟ **Total** 56
**Facilities** ⌁ ▥ ♨ ⌐ ⊙ ↵ ⌧
▣ ⓡ ◉ ☺ ⌁ ⊞
**Nearby Facilities** ⌐ ✓ ⚓ ⚒ ∪ ⊿ ♪
**Acreage** 5 **Open** April to October
**Access** Good **Site** Lev/Slope
Splendid views, close to sandy beaches with
many lovely walks nearby. Central for touring.
**Nearest Town/Resort** Fowey
**Directions** 1 mile west of Lostwithiel on the
A390, turn left onto the B3269. After 3 miles
turn right at the roundabout onto the A3082.
Penhale is 500yds on the left.
⇌ Par

## FOWEY
**Penmarlam Caravan & Camping Park,**
Bodinnick-by-Fowey, Fowey, Cornwall,
PL23 1LZ
**Tel:** 01726 870088 **Fax:** 01726 870088
**Email:** info@penmarlampark.co.uk
www. penmarlampark.co.uk
**Pitches For** ▲ ⊕ ⊟ **Total** 65
**Facilities** ⚹ ⌁ ▥ ♨ ⌐ ⊙ ↵ ⌧ ⊞
▣ ⊙ ⊬ ⊡ ⊡ ⊠ ♨
**Nearby Facilities** ⌐ ✓ ⚓ ⚒ ∪
**Acreage** 4 **Open** Easter to Oct
**Access** Good **Site** Lev/Slope
Quiet site two areas, one sheltered
and one with stunning views. Near the
Eden Project.
**Nearest Town/Resort** Fowey
**Directions** From the A38 eastbound, pass
Liskeard and turn left onto the A390 sp St.
Austell. In East Taphouse turn left onto the
B3359 sp Polperro & Looe. After 5 miles turn
right sp Bodinnick. Site is on the right in 5 miles.
⇌ Liskeard/Par/Looe

## FOWEY
**Polruan Holidays - Camping &**
**Caravanning,** Polruan-by-Fowey,
Cornwall, PL23 1QH
**Tel:** 01726 870263 **Fax:** 01726 870263
**Email:** polholiday@aol.com
**Pitches For** ▲ ⊕ ⊟ **Total** 47
**Facilities** ⚹ ⊟ ▥ ▥ ♨ ⌐ ⊙ ↵ ⌧ ⊞
▣ ⓡ ◉ ☺ ⊡ ⊬
**Nearby Facilities** ✓ ⚓ ⚒ ∪
**Acreage** 2 **Open** Easter to Sept
**Access** Good **Site** Lev/Slope
Coastal park surrounded by sea, river and
National Trust farmland.
**Nearest Town/Resort** Fowey
**Directions** From Plymouth A38 to Dobwalls,
left onto A390 to East Taphouse, then left
onto B3359. After 4¼ miles turn right
signposted Polruan.

## GOONHAVERN
**Roseville Holiday Park,** Goonhavern, Nr
Truro, Cornwall, TR4 9LA
**Tel:** 01872 572448 **Fax:** 01872 572448
www. rosevilleholidaypark.co.uk
**Pitches For** ▲ ⊕ ⊟ **Total** 90
**Facilities** ⚹ ⌁ ▥ ♨ ⌐ ⊙ ↵ ⌧ ⊞
▣ ⓡ ◉ ♠ ⊞ ⊬ ♨ ♪
**Nearby Facilities** ⌐ ✓ ⚓ ⚒ ∪ ⊿ ♪
**Acreage** 7 **Open** April to Sept
**Access** Good
Ideal for North Cornwall. Quiet, private site.
Families and mature persons only.
**Nearest Town/Resort** Newquay
**Directions** 6 miles from Newquay on the
A3075.
⇌ Truro

## HAYLE
**Atlantic Coast Park,** 53 Upton Towans,
Gwithian, Hayle, Cornwall, TR27 5BL
**Tel:** 01736 752071
**Email:** enquiries@atlanticcoast-
caravanpark.co.uk
www. coastdale.co.uk/atlanticcoast
**Pitches For** ▲ ⊕ ⊟ **Total** 15
**Facilities** ⚹ ▥ ♨ ⌐ ⊙ ↵ ⌧ ⊞
▣ ⊙ ☺ ⊬ ⊡ ⊡ ⊠ ♨
**Nearby Facilities** ⌐ ✓ ⚓ ⚒ ∪ ⊿ ♪ ✗
**Acreage** 4½ **Open** April to October
**Access** Good **Site** Level
Situated in sand dunes close to a bathing
and surfing beach, excellent walks.
**Nearest Town/Resort** Hayle
**Directions** When entering Hayle from
Camborne by-pass (A30), turn right at the
double roundabout onto the B3301, Atlantic
Coast Park is approx. 1 mile on the left.
⇌ Hayle

## HAYLE
**Beachside Holiday Park,** Hayle, Cornwall,
TR27 5AW
**Tel:** 01736 753080 **Fax:** 01736 757252
**Email:** reception@beachside.demon.co.uk
www. beachside.co.uk
**Pitches For** ▲ ⊕ ⊟ **Total** 90
**Facilities** ⚹ ▥ ♨ ⌐ ⊙ ↵ ⌧ ⊞
▣ ◉ ♡ ♠ ⋏ ⊬ ⊡ ♨
**Nearby Facilities** ⌐ ✓ ⚓ ⚒ ∪ ♪ ✗
**Acreage** 20 **Open** Easter to 30 Sept
**Access** Good **Site** Lev/Slope
Right beside a golden sandy beach. Sea
fishing from site.
**Nearest Town/Resort** Hayle
**Directions** Leave the A30 at Hayle and
follow brown tourist signs to 'Beachside'.
⇌ Hayle

## HAYLE
**Gwithian Farm Campsite,** Gwithian,
Hayle, Cornwall, TR27 5BX
**Tel:** 01736 753127
**Email:** holidays@gwithianfarm.co.uk
www. gwithianfarm.co.uk
**Pitches For** ▲ ⊕⊟ **Total** 120
**Facilities** ⚹ ⌁ ▥ ♨ ⌐ ⊙ ↵ ⌧ ⊞
▣ ⊙ ⊓ ☺ ⊬ ⊞ ♨
**Nearby Facilities** ⌐ ✓ ⚓ ⚒ ∪ ⊿ ♪
**Acreage** 7½ **Open** 3 April to 3 Oct
**Access** Good **Site** Level
Just a 10 minute walk from a stunning 3
mile long beach. Friendly, family run site in
a village, opposite a good pub. New
facilities built in 2005. 8 miles from St Ives.
**Nearest Town/Resort** St. Ives
**Directions** Leave the A30 at Hayle
roundabout and turn right onto the B3301
signposted Portreath. After 2 miles in
Gwithian, the site is on the left opposite the
Red River Inn.
⇌ Camborne/Hayle

## HAYLE
**Higher Trevaskis Caravan & Camping
Park,** Gwinear Road, Connor Downs,
Hayle, Cornwall, TR27 5JQ
**Tel:** 01209 831736
**Pitches For** ▲ ⊕ ⊟ **Total** 75
**Facilities** ⚹ ⊟ ▥ ♨ ⌐ ⊙ ↵ ⌧ ⊞
▣ ⓡ ◉ ☺ ⊬ ⊞ ♨
**Nearby Facilities** ⌐ ✓ ⚓ ⚒ ∪ ♪ ✗
**Acreage** 5¼ **Open** April to October
**Access** Good **Site** Level
Friendly, secluded, family run, countryside
park. Spacious, level pitches in small
enclosures. Designated play areas and our
renowned spotlessly clean facilities.
**Nearest Town/Resort** Hayle/St Ives
**Directions** At Hayle roundabout (Little Chef)
on A30 take the first exit (signposted Connor
Downs). After 1 mile turn right to Carnhell
Green. Park is on the right in ¾ of mile.
⇌ Hayle

## HAYLE
**Parbola Holiday Park,** Wall, Gwinear,
Cornwall, TR27 5LE
**Tel:** 01209 831503
**Email:** bookings@parbola.co.uk
www. parbola.co.uk
**Pitches For** ▲ ⊕ ⊟ **Total** 110
**Facilities** ⚹ ⌁ ▥ ♨ ⌐ ⊙ ↵ ⌧ ⊞
▣ ⓡ ◉ ☺ ⊓ ♠ ⋏ ⊬ ⊞ ♨
**Nearby Facilities** ⌐ ✓ ⚓ ⚒ ∪ ⊿ ♪
**Acreage** 14 **Open** April to September
**Access** Good **Site** Level
No dogs allowed during July and August.
**Nearest Town/Resort** Hayle
**Directions** Travel on A30 to Hayle, at
roundabout leave first exit to Connor Downs.
At end of village turn right to Carnhell Green,
right at T-Junction, Parbola is 1 mile on the left.

## HELSTON
**Boscrege Caravan Park,** Ashton, Helston,
Cornwall, TR13 9TG
**Tel:** 01736 762231 **Fax:** 01736 762231
www. caravanparkcornwall.com
**Pitches For** ▲ ⊕ ⊟ **Total** 50
**Facilities** ⚹ ⌁ ▥ ♨ ⌐ ↵ ⌧ ⊞
▣ ◉ ⊓ ♠ ⋏ ⊕ ☺ ⊬ ⊡ ⊡ ⊠ ♨ ∪ ♪ ✗
**Nearby Facilities** ⌐ ✓ ⚓ ⚒ ∪ ♪ ✗
**Acreage** 7 **Open** Easter/1 April to Oct
**Access** Good **Site** Level
Quiet family park in garden setting. No
club. Near sandy beaches. Ideal for
exploring West Cornwall. Microwave for
campers.
**Nearest Town/Resort** Praa Sands
**Directions** From Helston follow Penzance
road (A394) to Ashton, turn right by post
office along road signposted to Godolphin
and continue about 1½ miles to Boscrege
Park.
⇌ Penzance

## HELSTON
**Lower Polladras Touring Park,** Carleen,
Helston, Cornwall, TR13 9NX
**Tel:** 01736 762220 **Fax:** 01736 762220
**Email:** lowerpolladras@btinternet.com
www. lower-polladras.co.uk
**Pitches For** ▲ ⊕ ⊟ **Total** 60
**Facilities** ⚹ ▥ ♨ ⌐ ⊙ ↵ ⌧ ⊞
▣ ⓡ ◉ ☺ ♨ ⊬ ♪

**Tel: 01736 762220** *Lower Polladras Touring Park*
*Carleen, Nr. Helston, Cornwall TR13 9NX*
An attractive, peaceful and friendly, family run park. Just 10 minutes from
the nearest beach. Spotless facilities, free showers. Dog exercising field and
wildlife walk. All year caravan storage. **Low season special deals.**
*www.lower-polladras.co.uk*  E-mail: *lowerpolladras@btinternet.com*

**Nearby Facilities** ⌂ ✈ ⚓ ⚡ ⛳ ♨ ♿ ⚑ ⚘
**Acreage** 4 **Open** Easter/1 April **to** End Oct
**Access** Good **Site** Level
A family run park in an area of outstanding
natural beauty, overlooking classic Cornish
countryside. Centrally located for exploring
Cornwall and The Lizard. 10 minutes away
from safe, sandy, lifeguarded beaches.
Low season special deals.
**Nearest Town/Resort** Helston/Praa Sands
**Directions** From Helston take the A394 to
Penzance and turn right at the Hilltop Garage
onto the B3302. After ½ a mile turn left to
Carleen Village and follow signs to the park.
From the A30 take the exit to Camborne
West, turn left at the first roundabout then
right at the next three mini roundabouts, take
the B3303 for 6 miles, turn left at the junction
with the B3302, turn first right and follow
signs to Carleen.
✈ Penzance/Camborne

## HELSTON

**Poldown Caravan & Camping Site,**
Carleen, Breage, Helston, Cornwall, TR13
9NN
**Tel:** 01326 574560 **Fax:** 01326 574560
**Email:** poldown@poldown.co.uk
**www.** poldown.co.uk
**Pitches For** ⚐ ⚐ **Total** 13
**Facilities** ♒ ♿ ⚓ ⌂ ⊙ ⚡ ◻ ⚑ ↝ ⊡ ▣
**Nearby Facilities** ⌂ ✈ ⚓ ⚡ ♨ ⚑
**Acreage** 1¼ **Open** May **to** Sept
**Access** Good **Site** Level
Small, secluded, pretty site. Ideal for
touring West Cornwall. ETB 4 Star Graded.
**Nearest Town/Resort** Helston
**Directions** Take A394 (signed Penzance)
from Helston. At top of the hill on outskirts of
Helston take the B3303 signed Hayle/St Ives.
Take the second left on this road and we are
¼ mile along.
✈ Penzance

## ISLES OF SCILLY

**Garrison Holidays,** Tower Cottage, The
Garrison, St Mary's, Isles of ScillyCornwall,
TR21 0LS
**Tel:** 01720 422670 **Fax:** 01720 422625
**Email:** tedmoulson@aol.com
**www.** garrisonholidays.com
**Pitches For** ⚐ **Total** 120
**Facilities** ⚒ ♿ ⚓ ⌂ ⊙ ⚡ ◻ ⚑ ⚏ ⚐ ⚑
**Nearby Facilities** ⌂ ✈ ⚓ ⚡ ♨ ⚑ ⚘
**Acreage** 9½ **Open** Easter **to** Oct
**Site** Level
Small, family orientated campsite. No
formal marked out pitches. Small fields,
mostly sheltered. No vehicles on site.
Transport for luggage is available from the
ferry to the site for a small charge.
**Nearest Town/Resort** St Mary's

**Directions** From Penzance take a boat,
skybus or helicopter to Isles of Scilly. Park is
10 minutes walk from Hugh Town, St Mary's.
✈ Penzance

## ISLES OF SCILLY

**St. Martin's Campsite,** Middle Town, St
Martin's, Isles of Scilly, Cornwall, TR25 0QN
**Tel:** 01720 422888 **Fax:** 01720 422888
**Email:** info@stmartinscampsite.co.uk
**www.** stmartinscampsite.co.uk
**Pitches For** ⚐ **Total** 50
**Facilities** ⚒ ♿ ⚓ ⊙ ⚡ ◻ ⚏ ♿ ⚑
**Nearby Facilities** ✈ ⚓ ♨ ⚑
**Acreage** 2½ **Open** Easter **to** End Oct
**Site** Level
Adjacent to a south facing white sandy
beach on a peaceful, idyllic island.
**Directions** Take a ferry, plane or helicopter
from Penzance to St. Mary's. Launch from
St. Mary's to St. Martin's.
✈ Penzance

## KILKHAMPTON

**East Thorne Touring Park,** Kilkhampton,
Bude, Cornwall, EX23 9RY
**Tel:** 01288 321654
**Pitches For** ⚐ ⚐ ⚐ **Total** 29
**Facilities** ♒ ♿ ⚓ ⌂ ⊙ ⚡ ◻ ⚑ ⚏ ↝ ⊡
**Nearby Facilities** ⌂ ✈ ⚓
**Acreage** 2 **Open** Easter/April **to** Oct
**Access** Good **Site** Level
Set in farmland on the outskirts of
Kilkhampton Village. 3 miles from the beach.
**Nearest Town/Resort** Bude
**Directions** 5 miles north of Bude on the A39,
½ mile on the B3254.
✈ Bude

## LANDS END

**Cardinney Caravan & Caravan Park,**
Main A30, Lands End Road, Crows-an-
Wra, Lands EndCornwall, TR19 6HJ
**Tel:** 01736 810880 **Fax:** 01736 810998
**Email:** cardinney@btinternet.com
**www.** cardinney-camping-park.co.uk
**Pitches For** ⚐ ⚐ ⚐ **Total** 105
**Facilities** ♒ ⊞ ♿ ⚓ ⌂ ⊙ ⚡ ◻ ⚑ ⚐ ⚑
♿ ⚏ ⚒ ⚏ ⚑ ↝ ⊡ ▣
**Nearby Facilities** ⌂ ✈ ⚓ ♨ ⚑ ⚘
**Acreage** 5 **Open** 1 Feb **to** End Nov
**Access** Good **Site** Level
Sennen Cove Blue Flag, scenic coastal
walks, ancient monuments, scenic flights,
Minack Ampitheatre, trips to the Isles of
Scilly. Ideal for touring Lands End Peninsula.
BH & HPA Member and CTB 3 Star Graded.
**Nearest Town/Resort** Sennen Cove
**Directions** From Penzance follow Main A30
to Lands End, approx 5¼ miles. Entrance on
right hand side on Main A30, large name
board at entrance.
✈ Penzance

## LANDS END

**Lower Treave Caravan & Camping Park,**
Crows-an-Wra, St Buryan, Penzance,
Cornwall, TR19 6HZ
**Tel:** 01736 810559 **Fax:** 08700 553647
**Email:** camping@lowertreave.co.uk
**www.** lowertreave.co.uk
**Pitches For** ⚐ ⚐ ⚐ **Total** 80
**Facilities** ♒ ♿ ⚓ ⌂ ⊙ ⚡ ◻ ♿ ⚏ ↝ ⊡ ▣
**Nearby Facilities** ⌂ ✈ ⚓ ⚡ ♨ ⚑ ⚘
**Acreage** 5 **Open** Easter **to** Oct
**Access** Good **Site** Level
Quiet family site in the heart of Lands End
peninsula with panoramic rural views to
the sea. Sheltered, level grass terraces.
Blue Flag beach 2½ miles. All 3 Pennants,
Camping & Caravan Club Listed and
Caravan Club Listed.
**Nearest Town/Resort** Penzance
**Directions** On A30 Penzance to Lands End
road, site is signposted ½ a mile beyond the
village of Crows-an-Wra.
✈ Penzance

## LISKEARD

**Great Trethew Manor Camp Site,**
Horningtops, Liskeard, Cornwall, PL14 3PY
**Tel:** 01503 240663 **Fax:** 01503 240695
**Email:** great_trethew_manor@yahoo.com
**www.** great-trethew-manor.co.uk
**Pitches For** ⚐ ⚐ ⚐ **Total** 55
**Facilities** ♒ ♿ ⚓ ⌂ ⚡ ◻ ⚒ ⚏ ⚑ ↝ ⊡ ▣ ⚘
**Nearby Facilities** ⌂ ✈ ⚓ ⚡ ♨ ⚑ ⚘
**Acreage** 30 **Open** March **to** September
**Access** Good **Site** Level
On site features include fishing, tennis,
woodland walks, beautiful gardens and
hotel facilities. Near to beaches, moorland,
sea sports and many historic buildings.
**Nearest Town/Resort** Looe
**Directions** From Liskeard follow the A38 for
approx. 3 miles, turn right onto the B3251.
After ¼ mile turn left into drive entrance.
✈ Menheniot

## LISKEARD

**Pine Green Caravan Park,** Double Bois,
Liskeard, East Cornwall, PL14 6LE
**Tel:** 01579 320183
**Email:** maryruhleman@btinternet.com
**www.** pinegreenpark.co.uk
**Pitches For** ⚐ ⚐ ⚐ **Total** 50
**Facilities** ♒ ⊞ ♿ ⚓ ⌂ ⊙ ⚡ ◻ ⚏ ↝ ⊡ ❄
**Nearby Facilities** ⌂ ✈ ⚓ ⚡ ♨ ⚑ ⚘
**Acreage** 3 **Open** All Year
**Access** Good **Site** Level
Overlooking beautiful wooded valley and
open countryside.
**Nearest Town/Resort** Liskeard
**Directions** 3 miles from Liskeard towards
Bodmin. Just off the main A38 at Double
Bois.
✈ Liskeard

**BOSCREGE**
**CARAVAN & CAMPING PARK**
★ Special out of season offers
★ Award winning quiet family park close to local
   beaches and attractions with no bar or clubs
★ Free showers ★ Microwave facilities
★ Games room ★ Child's play area
★ Laundry ★ Pets welcome
For Brochure Telephone: **01736 762231**
Ashton, Nr Helston, Cornwall TR13 9TG
www.caravanparkcornwall.com
enquiries@caravanparkcornwall.com

# CAMPING CARADON TOURING PARK AA ▶

## Trelawne, Looe, Cornwall PL13 2NA Tel: 01503 272388

New owners Stephen & Lene Cox welcome return guests & new faces to **Camping Caradon**. Enjoy the peaceful, rural location midway between Looe & Polperro, 1½ miles from Talland Bay. 85 flat pitches, 60 electric hook-ups. Club House (with Non-Smoking Bar), Shop, Games Room & usual facilities. **www.campingcaradon.co.uk**

## LISKEARD

**Trenant Chapel House,** Trenant Caravan Park, St Neot, Liskeard, Cornwall, PL14 6RZ
**Tel:** 01579 320896
**Pitches For** ▲ ⊕ ⇔ **Total** 8
**Facilities** ⫟ ⊞ ⚲ Ր ⊙ ⇌ ⚄ ☎ ⌷✕⊟▣
**Nearby Facilities** ✓ ⚐ ⚲ ∪
**Acreage** 1 **Open** April **to** October
**Site** Level
Siblyback and Colliford Reservoirs close, fishing, boardsailing and bird watching. Site in sheltered corner upper Fowey valley bounded by tributary of Fowey river, close Bodmin moor, ideal walking, touring.
**Nearest Town/Resort** Liskeard
**Directions** Take St Cleer road off A38 at Dobwalls, 1 mile left signposted St. Neot, 1 mile right SP Trenant, ½ mile right signposted Trenant.
⇞ Liskeard

## LIZARD

**Gwendreath Farm Caravan Park,** Kennack Sands, Helston, Cornwall, TR12 7LZ
**Tel:** 01326 290666
**Email:** tom.gibson@virgin.net
**www.** tomandlinda.co.uk
**Pitches For** ▲ ⊕ ⇔ **Total** 30
**Facilities** ⫟ ⊞ ⚲ Ր ⊙ ⇌ ⚄ ▣ ☎
⚿ ⌷ ⊗ ⚑ ⟡✕⊟▣
**Nearby Facilities** Ր ✓ ⚐ ⚲ ∪
**Acreage** 3 **Open** Easter
**Access** Good **Site** Level
Attractive, peaceful family site overlooking the sea in an area of outstanding natural beauty. Short woodland walk to safe sandy beaches.
**Nearest Town/Resort** The Lizard
**Directions** A3083 from Helston, left on B3293 after R.N.A.S. Culdrose. After Goonhilly Earth Station, take the first right then first left. At end of lane go through Seaview Caravan Site to second reception.
⇞ Redruth

## LIZARD

**Henry's Campsite,** Caerthillian Farm, The Lizard, Helston, Cornwall, TR12 7NX
**Tel:** 01326 290596
**Pitches For** ▲ ⊕ ⇔ **Total** 30
**Facilities** ⫟ ⊞ ⚲ Ր ⊙ ⇌ ▣⌷ ⊗ ⚑⟡⊟
**Nearby Facilities** Ր ✓ ⚐ ⚲ ∪ ⟡ ✗

**Acreage** 1½ **Open** All Year
**Access** Good **Site** Lev/Slope
Outstanding views. Close to secluded or popular beaches and near coastal footpaths.
**Nearest Town/Resort** Helston
**Directions** Take the main A3083 Helston to Lizard road, enter the village and take the first turn right across the village green, then turn second right.
⇞ Redruth

## LIZARD

**Silver Sands Holiday Park,** Kennack Sands, Gwendreath, Ruan Minor, HelstonCornwall, TR12 7LZ
**Tel:** 01326 290631 **Fax:** 01326 290631
**Email:**
enquiries@silversandsholidaypark.co.uk
**www.** silversandsholidaypark.co.uk
**Pitches For** ▲ ⊕ ⇔ **Total** 34
**Facilities** ⫟ ⊞ ⚲ Ր ⊙ ⇌ ⚄ ⊗ ⚑ ⚿ ❀
⟡⊟▣
**Nearby Facilities** Ր ✓ ⚐ ⚲ ∪
**Acreage** 9 **Open** Easter **to** Mid Sept
**Access** Good **Site** Lev/Slope
800mts to safe sandy beach, ideal touring and walking. Quiet, family site in area of outstanding natural beauty.
**Nearest Town/Resort** Helston
**Directions** On entering Helston take the A3083 Lizard road, pass R.N.A.S. Culdrose then turn left at roundabout onto the B3293 signposted St Keverne. In 4 miles, immediately past Goonhilly Satellite Station, turn right to Kennack. After 1 mile turn left.
⇞ Redruth

## LOOE

**Camping Caradon Touring Park,** Trelawne, Looe, Cornwall, PL13 2NA
**Tel:** 01503 272388
**Email:** stephen.cox2@virgin.net
**www.** campingcaradon.co.uk
**Pitches For** ▲ ⊕ ⇔ **Total** 85
**Facilities** ⫟ ⊞ ⚲ Ր ⊙ ⇌ ⚄ ▣ ☎
⚿ ⊗ ✕ ⚑ ⟡⊟▣
**Nearby Facilities** Ր ✓ ⚐ ⚲ ∪ ⟡ ⚁ ♫
**Acreage** 3½ **Open** Easter **to** End Oct
**Access** Good **Site** Level
Rural countryside site, on the local bus route. 20 miles from the Eden Project (fast track tickets sold). Ideal base for touring.
**Nearest Town/Resort** Looe

**Directions** From Looe t\ake the A387 towards Polperro. After 2 miles turn right onto the B3359. Take the next turning right, and Camping Caradon is clearly signposted.
⇞ Looe

## LOOE

**Killigarth Manor Holiday Park,** John Fowler Holidays, Killigarth Manor, Polperro, Cornwall, PL13 2JQ
**Tel:** 01271 866766 **Fax:** 01271 866791
**Email:** bookings@johnfowlerholidays.com
**www.** johnfowlerholidays.com
**Pitches For** ▲ ⊕ ⇔ **Total** 125
**Facilities** ⚿ ⫟ ⊞ ⊞ ⚲ Ր ⊙ ⇌ ⚄ ▣ ☎
⚿ ⌷ ⊗ ⚑ ✕ ⚑ ⚑ ❄ ⟡⊟▣
**Nearby Facilities** Ր ✓ ⚐ ⚲ ∪ ♫
**Open** March **to** October
**Access** Good **Site** Level
Perfect location for touring Cornwall's picturesque villages, and visiting The Eden Project.
**Nearest Town/Resort** Looe/Polperro
**Directions** From Plymouth take the A38 then the A387 to Looe. Turn for Polperro and the Park is at the entrance to Polperro.
⇞ Looe

## LOOE

**Polborder House Caravan & Camping Park,** Bucklawren Road, St Martin, Looe, Cornwall, PL13 1NZ
**Tel:** 01503 240265
**Email:** rlf.polborder@virgin.net
**www.** peaceful-polborder.co.uk
**Pitches For** ▲ ⊕ ⇔ **Total** 36
**Facilities** ⚿ ⫟ ⊞ ⊞ ⚲ Ր ⊙ ⇌ ⚄ ▣ ☎
⚿ ⊗ ⚑ ⟡⊟▣ ⊗ ⚢
**Nearby Facilities** Ր ✓ ⚐ ⚲ ∪ ♫
**Acreage** 3 **Open** March **to** Oct
**Access** Good **Site** Level
Small, select, award winning park set in beautiful countryside, 1¼ miles from the sea.
**Nearest Town/Resort** Looe
**Directions** 2¼ miles east of Looe off B3253, follow signs for Polborder and Monkey Sanctuary.
⇞ Looe

## LOOE

**Tencreek Holiday Park,** Polperro Road, Looe, Cornwall, PL13 2JR
**Tel:** 01503 262447 **Fax:** 01503 262760
**Email:** reception@tencreek.co.uk
**www.** dolphinholidays.co.uk
**Pitches For** ⚠ ⊕ ⊜
**Facilities** ⚐ ⨍ ⊟ ⊞ ☎ ⌐ ⊙ ⊒ ⚑ ⊡ ☎
☒ ⊙ ⊜ ✕ ♀ ⊞ ♣ ⚘ ☂ ↘ ⊞ ⊡ ☯ ☇
**Nearby Facilities** ⌐ ✔ ⚓ ⤴ ∪ ♫
**Acreage** 20 **Open** All Year
**Access** Good **Site** Lev/Slope
Excellent coastal and countryside views. Good park facilities including indoor pool and a large modern club house with entertainment.
**Nearest Town/Resort** Looe
**Directions** 1¼ miles west of Looe on the A387 Looe to Polperro road.
⚒ Looe

## LOOE

**Trelay Farmpark,** Pelynt, Looe, Cornwall, PL13 2JX
**Tel:** 01503 220900 **Fax:** 01503 220900
**Email:** stay@trelay.co.uk
**www.** trelay.co.uk
**Pitches For** ⚠ ⊕ ⊜ **Total** 55
**Facilities** ⚐ ⨍ ⊞ ☎ ⌐ ⊙ ⊒ ⚑ ⊡ ☎
⚑ ⊙ ⊜ ☇ ⊞ ⊡
**Nearby Facilities** ⌐ ✔ ⚓ ⤴ ∪ ♫ ♫
**Acreage** 3 **Open** 1 April **to** 31 Oct
**Access** Good **Site** Level
A quiet, uncommercialised park surrounded by farmland. Wide views over open countryside. Large pitches on a gentle south facing slope. Immaculate facilities.
**Nearest Town/Resort** Looe/Polperro
**Directions** From Looe take the A387 towards Polperro. After 2 miles turn right onto the B3359. Trelay Farmpark is clearly signed ¾ mile on the right.
⚒ Looe

## LOSTWITHIEL

**Downend Camp Site,** Lostwithiel, Cornwall, PL22 0RB
**Tel:** 01208 872363
**Pitches For** ⚠ ⊕ ⊜
**Facilities** ⨍ ⊞ ☎ ⌐ ⊙ ☎ ☒ ⊙ ⊜ ☇ ⊡
**Nearby Facilities** ⌐ ✔ ∪
**Open** March to End Oct
**Access** Good **Site** Level
5 miles from the Eden Project.
**Nearest Town/Resort** Lostwithiel
**Directions** On the A390 approx. 1 mile east of Lostwithiel.
⚒ Lostwithiel

## LOSTWITHIEL

**Powderham Castle Tourist Park,** Lanlivery, Nr Bodmin, Cornwall, PL30 5BU
**Tel:** 01208 872277
**Email:** powderhamcastletp@tiscali.co.uk
**www.** powderhamcastletouristpark.co.uk
**Pitches For** ⚠ ⊕ ⊜ **Total** 75
**Facilities** ⨍ ⊞ ☎ ⌐ ⊙ ⊒ ⚑ ⊡ ☎
☒ ⊙ ⊜ ⊞ ♣ ♣ ☂ ⊞ ⊡
**Nearby Facilities** ⌐ ✔ ⚓ ⤴ ∪ ♫ ♫ ♫
**Acreage** 10 **Open** April/Easter **to** Oct
**Access** Good **Site** Level
Quiet spacious site, uncommercialised. Ideal for touring all of Cornwall and near the Eden Project. Battery charging, freezer pack service. Dish washing and vegetable preparation facilities. Putting green and a multiactivity games area.
**Nearest Town/Resort** Bodmin/St. Austell
**Directions** 1½ miles southwest Lostwithiel on A390, turn right at signpost, up road 400 yards.
⚒ Lostwithiel

## MARAZION

**Trevair Touring Site,** South Treveneague Farm, St Hilary, Penzance, Cornwall, TR20 9BY
**Tel:** 01736 740647

**Email:** philandval@trevair.freeserve.co.uk
**www.** trevairtouringpark.co.uk
**Pitches For** ⚠ ⊕ ⊜ **Total** 35
**Facilities** ⨍ ⊞ ☎ ⌐ ⊙ ⊒ ⚑ ⊡ ☎ ☒ ⊞ ⊡
**Nearby Facilities** ⌐ ✔ ⚓ ∪
**Acreage** 3½ **Open** End March **to** October
**Access** Good **Site** Level
Everyone is welcome at our clean and friendly site. Set in the peace and quiet of the countryside, yet within 2/3 miles of beaches, shops and pubs.
**Nearest Town/Resort** Marazion
**Directions** 3 miles from Marazion, B3280 through Goldsithney signposted South Treveneague.
⚒ St. Erth

## MARAZION

**Wheal Rodney Holiday Park,** Gwallon Lane, Marazion, Cornwall, TR17 0HL
**Tel:** 01736 710605
**Email:** reception@whealrodney.co.uk
**www.** whealrodney.co.uk
**Pitches For** ⚠ ⊕ ⊜ **Total** 30
**Facilities** ⨍ ⊞ ☎ ⌐ ⊙ ⊒ ⊙ ⊡ ⊜ ☂ ⊞ ⊡ ⊡
**Nearby Facilities** ⌐ ✔ ⚓ ⤴ ∪ ♫
**Acreage** 2½ **Open** March **to** October
**Access** Good **Site** Level
The nearest touring park to St. Michael's Mount.
**Nearest Town/Resort** Marazion
**Directions** On the A30 towards Penzance, at Crowlas turn left signposted Rospeath, 1½ miles on the right. Or from Marazion on the A30 turn opposite the Fire Engine Inn, site is 500 metres on the left.
⚒ Penzance

## MAWGAN PORTH

**Magic Cove Touring Park,** Mawgan Porth, Newquay, Cornwall, TR8 4BZ
**Tel:** 01637 860263
**Email:** magic@redcove.co.uk
**www.** redcove.co.uk

**Pitches For** **Total** 26
**Facilities**
**Nearby Facilities**
**Acreage** 1 **Open** Easter **to** Oct
**Access** Good **Site** Level
300yds from a sandy beach. Ideal centre for North Cornwall coast. Water adjacent to each pitch and TV points.
**Nearest Town/Resort** Newquay
**Directions** Take the A30 to Bodmin, 4 miles from the end of the dual carriageway, iron bridge ½ mile turn right onto the A3059. At the roundabout take the second left to Newquay, ¾ mile turn right to the airport, T-Junction turn right to Mawgan Porth.
≠ Newquay

## MAWGAN PORTH
**Marver Touring Park,** Marver Chalets, Mawgan Porth, Nr Newquay, Cornwall, TR8 4BB
**Tel:** 01637 860493 **Fax:** 01637 860493
**Email:** familyholidays@aol.com
**www.** marverholidaypark.co.uk
**Pitches For** **Total** 17
**Facilities**
**Nearby Facilities**
**Acreage** 2½ **Open** All Year
**Access** Good **Site** Level
Peaceful location in a valley with superb views. 300 yards to the beach, excellent coastal walks. Ideal base for touring Cornwall.
**Nearest Town/Resort** Newquay
**Directions** From Newquay take the B3276 coast road to Padstow. After 6 miles, on entering Mawgan Porth, turn right at the Mawgan Porth Stores, park is 300 yards on the left.
≠ Newquay

## MAWGAN PORTH
**Sun Haven Valley Holiday Park,** Mawgan Porth, Nr Newquay, Cornwall, TR8 4BQ
**Tel:** 01637 860373 **Fax:** 01637 860373
**Email:** traceyhealey@hotmail.com
**www.** sunhavenvalley.co.uk
**Pitches For** **Total** 118
**Facilities**
**Nearby Facilities**
**Acreage** 7 **Open** April **to** October
**Access** Good **Site** Level
¾ miles from Mawgan Porth beach, surrounded by countryside. Family bathrooms available.
**Nearest Town/Resort** Newquay/Padstow
**Directions** From the A30 4 miles after Bodmin turn right signposted Newquay and Airport. Continue to follow signs for the Airport and after 1½ miles turn right to St. Mawgan. Turn right at Mawgan Porth Garage.
≠ Newquay

## MEVAGISSEY
**Seaview International,** Boswinger, Gorran, St Austell, Cornwall, PL26 6LL
**Tel:** 01726 843425 **Fax:** 01726 843358
**Email:** holidays@seaviewinternational.com
**www.** seaviewinternational.com
**Pitches For** **Total** 189
**Facilities**
**Nearby Facilities**
**Acreage** 15 **Open** March **to** Oct
**Access** Good **Site** Level
England's TOP PARK. Beautiful level park overlooking the sea, surrounded by sandy beaches, nearest ½ mile. Free sports and pastimes on site. All facilities are centrally heated. Holiday caravans also for hire, all have Rose Award. AA Best Campsite of the Year 1995/6 and AA 5 Pennant Premier Park.
**Nearest Town/Resort** Mevagissey/St. Austell
**Directions** From St. Austell take B3273 to Mevagissey, prior to village turn right. Then follow signs to Gorran.
≠ St Austell

## MEVAGISSEY
**Tregarton Park,** Gorran, Nr Mevagissey, St Austell, Cornwall, PL26 6NF
**Tel:** 01726. 843666 **Fax:** 01726 844481
**Email:** enquiries@tregartonpark.co.uk
**www.** tregartonpark.co.uk
**Pitches For** **Total** 130
**Facilities**
**Nearby Facilities**
**Acreage** 12 **Open** April **to** October
**Access** Good **Site** Lev/Terraced
Beautiful sheltered park with glimpses of the sea through the valley. Nearest beach is 1½ miles. Lost Garden of Heligan only a 2 minute drive away and Eden Project 20 minutes.
**Nearest Town/Resort** Mevagissey
**Directions** From St Austell take the B3273 signposted Mevagissey. At the top of Pentewan Hill turn right signposted Gorran. Park is 3 miles on the right (signposted).
≠ St. Austell

## MULLION
**Franchis,** Cury Cross Lanes, Mullion, Helston, Cornwall, TR12 7AZ
**Tel:** 01326 240301
**Email:** enquiries@franchis.co.uk
**www.** franchis.co.uk
**Pitches For** **Total** 70
**Facilities**
**Nearby Facilities**
**Acreage** 4 **Open** Easter **to** Oct
**Access** Good **Site** Lev/Slope
Set in 17 acres of woodland and fields. Near to beaches and Helford River.
**Nearest Town/Resort** Mullion
**Directions** On the A3083, 5 miles south of Helston and 2 miles north of Mullion.
≠ Redruth

## MULLION
**Mullion Holiday Park,** Mullion, Nr Helston, Cornwall, TR12 7LJ
**Tel:** 0870 444 5344 **Fax:** 01326 241141
**Email:** touring@weststarholidays.co.uk
**www.** weststarholidays.co.uk
**Pitches For** **Total** 150
**Facilities**
**Nearby Facilities**
**Acreage** 49 **Open** May **to** September
**Access** Good **Site** Level
The ideal base for exploring Cornwall and its magical Lizard Peninsula. Spacious, level, serviced or super serviced pitches. Free modern showers and toilets. Free live entertainment.
**Nearest Town/Resort** Helston
**Directions** From the A30 take the A39 to Truro and continue on the Falmouth road. Take the A394 to Helston then the A3083 for The Lizard. After 7 miles we are on the left.
≠ Redruth

## MULLION
**Teneriffe Farm Caravan Site,** A B Thomas, Teneriffe Farm, Mullion, HelstonCornwall, TR12 7EZ
**Tel:** 01326 240293 **Fax:** 01326 240293
**Pitches For** **Total** 20
**Facilities**
**Nearby Facilities**
**Acreage** 3 **Open** Easter **to** October
**Access** Good **Site** Lev/Slope
Views of sea. Tumble drying facility. S.A.E. required for brochure.
**Nearest Town/Resort** Helston
**Directions** 10 miles Helston to The Lizard, turn right for Mullion. Take Mullion Cove road, turn left Predannack.
≠ Redruth

## NEWQUAY
**Camping & Caravanning Club Site,** Tregurrian, Nr Newquay, Cornwall, TR8 4AE
**Tel:** 01637 860448
**www.** campingandcaravanningclub.co.uk
**Pitches For** **Total** 90
**Facilities**
**Nearby Facilities**
**Acreage** 4½ **Open** April **to** Oct
**Access** Good **Site** Level
The glorious sandy beach of Watergate Bay is just ¾ miles away. There is a pretty coastal walk from the site to the beach. BTB 4 Star Graded, AA 3 Pennants and Loo of the Year Award. Non members welcome.

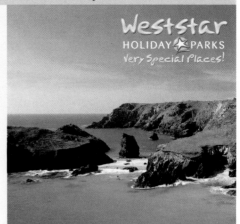

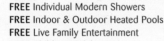

# CORNWALL

**Nearest Town/Resort** Newquay
**Directions** Leave the A30 after a prominent railway bridge by turning right signposted Newquay Airport, St Columb Major at roundabout on the A39. Join the A3059 to Newquay, after 1½ miles turn right signposted Newquay Airport and follow signs to Watergate Bay.
⇻ Newquay

## NEWQUAY
**Cottage Farm Touring Park,** Treworgans, Cubert, Newquay, Cornwall, TR8 5HH
**Tel:** 01637 831083
**Pitches For** ▲ ⊕ ⊞ **Total** 45
**Facilities** ⏸ 🏕 🔀 ᚛ ୮ ⊙ ⊋ 🍴 🛢 🔲 📮
**Nearby Facilities** ୮ ⊅ ⚓ ⚲ ∪ ♉
**Acreage** 2 **Open** April **to** October
**Access** Good **Site** Level
Within easy reach of three National Trust beaches. Small, family site, peaceful and in a rural location.
**Nearest Town/Resort** Newquay
**Directions** Newqauy to Redruth road A3075, turn right onto High Lanes. Follow signs to Cubert, before Cubert Village turn right signposted Crantock-Wesley road. Down the lane for ¼ mile then turn left signposted Tresean and Treworgans.
⇻ Newquay

## NEWQUAY
**Crantock Plains Touring Park,** Crantock, Newquay, Cornwall, TR8 5PH
**Tel:** 01637 830955
**www.** crantock-plains.co.uk
**Pitches For** ▲ ⊕ ⊞
**Facilities** ⏸ 🏕 🔀 ᚛ ୮ ⊙ ⊋ 🍴 🛢 🔲 🛟
🔀 ᚙ ⏻ 🛢 🉑 ⋔ ⊞ 📮 🔀 ᚛
**Nearby Facilities** ୮ ⊅ ⚓ ⚲ ∪ ♉
**Access** Good **Site** Level
Small site shop with limited stock.
**Nearest Town/Resort** Newquay
**Directions** Turn off the A30 onto the A392

and go over the roundabout. At Quintrell Downs pass Morrisons and turn left onto the A3075, take the second turn right to Crantock.
⇻ Newquay

## NEWQUAY
**Hendra Holiday Park,** Newquay, Cornwall, TR8 4NY
**Tel:** 01637 875778 **Fax:** 01637 879017
**Email:** enquiries@hendra-holidays.com
**www.** hendra-holidays.com
**Pitches For** ▲ ⊕ ⊞ **Total** 600
**Facilities** ᚛ ⏸ 🏕 🔀 🛢 ᚙ ୮ ⊙ ⊋ 🛢 ⊋ 🔲
🔀 ᚙ 🉑 ᚙ 🛢 ⋔ ⏻ 🉑 🛟 ⋔ 🛢 📮 📮 🔀 ᚛
**Nearby Facilities** ୮ ⊅ ⚓ ⚲ ∪ ♉
**Open** April **to** October
**Access** Good **Site** Level
Country views. Only 1½ miles from beaches. Indoor and outdoor Oasis Fun Pools.
**Nearest Town/Resort** Newquay
**Directions** 1½ miles from Newquay on the A392.
⇻ Newquay

## NEWQUAY
**Holywell Bay Holiday Park,** Holywell Bay, Cornwall, TR8 5PR
**Tel:** 01637 871111 **Fax:** 01637 850818
**Email:** enquiries@parkdeanholidays.com
**www.** parkdeanholidays.co.uk
**Pitches For** ▲ ⊕ ⊞ **Total** 56
**Facilities** ᚛ 🏕 🔀 ᚛ ୮ 🔲 ᚙ 🛢 🔀 ⚲
⏻ 🛢 🉑 ⋔ ✿ 📮 📮
**Nearby Facilities** ୮ ⊅ ♉
**Acreage** 40 **Open** March **to** Oct
**Access** Good **Site** Level
Beach is situated right off the park, with Newquay town centre only 2 miles away.
**Nearest Town/Resort** Newquay
**Directions** Follow the M4 to Exeter and take the A30 to Okehampton. Turn off at the first slip road to Newquay (A39), continue over

the roundabout to the A3075 towards Redruth, the park is 2 miles.
⇻ Newquay

## NEWQUAY
**Monkey Tree Holiday Park,** Scotland Rd, Rejerrah, Newquay, Cornwall, TR8 5QR
**Tel:** 01872 572032 **Fax:** 01872 573577
**Email:** enquiries@monkeytreeholidaypark.co.uk
**www.** monkeytreeholidaypark.co.uk
**Pitches For** ▲ ⊕ ⊞ **Total** 450
**Facilities** ᚛ ⏸ 🏕 🔀 ᚛ ୮ ⊙ ⊋ 🛢 🔲 🛟
🔀 ᚙ 🉑 🛢 🔀 ⚲ ⏻ 🉑 🔀 ⋔ ✿ 📮 📮 🔀 ᚛
♉
**Nearby Facilities** ୮ ⊅ ⚓ ⚲ ∪ ♉ ♉
**Access** Good **Site** Level
4 miles from Newquay and 8 miles from Truro. Easily accessible to all parts of Cornwall with its location adjacent to the A30.
**Nearest Town/Resort** Newquay
**Directions** From the A30 take the turning onto the B3285 to Perranporth. Take the second turning on the right signposted Monkey Tree Holiday Park. The park can be found 1 mile on the left hand side.
⇻ Newquay

## NEWQUAY
**Newperran Holiday Park,** Rejerrah, Newquay, Cornwall, TR8 5QJ
**Tel:** 01872 572407
**Email:** holidays@newperran.co.uk
**www.** newperran.co.uk
**Pitches For** ▲ ⊕ ⊞ **Total** 400
**Facilities** ᚛ ⏸ 🏕 🔀 ᚛ ୮ ⊙ ⊋ 🛢 🔲 🛟
🔀 ᚙ 🉑 🛢 🔀 ⚲ ⏻ 🉑 🔀 ⋔ ✿ 📮 📮 🔀 ᚛
♉
**Nearby Facilities** ୮ ⊅ ⚓ ⚲ ∪ ♉ ♉
**Acreage** 25 **Open** Easter **to** October
**Access** Good **Site** Level
Concessionary green fees, scenic views and central to nine golden beaches. AA 4 Pennants and BH&HPA.

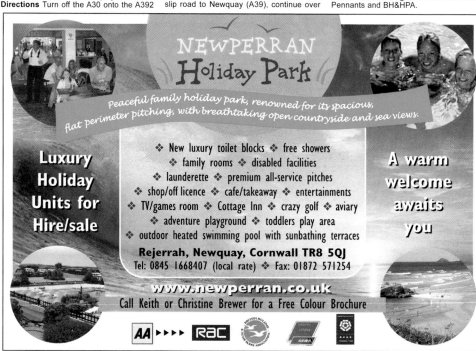

**Nearest Town/Resort** Newquay
**Directions** Take the A30 towards Redruth, turn right onto the B3285 signposted Perranporth and Goodhavern. At the junction at Goodhavern turn right onto the A3075 and turn left at the Newperran sign.
⇌ Newquay

## NEWQUAY
**Newquay Holiday Park,** Newquay, Cornwall, TR8 4HS
**Tel:** 01637 871111 **Fax:** 01637 850818
**Email:** enquiries@parkdeanholidays.com
**www.** parkdeanholidays.co.uk
**Pitches For** ⋏ � ⊞ **Total** 233
**Facilities** ⨍ ⊞ ⅃ ⌐ ⊙ ⌐ ⍁ Ⓠ ⊞
⛢ ⊠ ✗ ♀ ⊞ ♠ ⚿ ✣ ⌿ ⊞ ⌐ ⁂
**Nearby Facilities** ⌐ ✓ ♣
**Acreage** 60 **Open** March **to** Oct
**Access** Good **Site** Sloping
Set in rolling Cornish countryside, only 2 miles from eleven different beaches.
**Nearest Town/Resort** Newquay
**Directions** Follow the M4 to Exeter and take the A30 to Okehampton. Continue until you see the turn off for St. Mawgan, go along the road and take the A3059 to Newquay.

## NEWQUAY
**Porth Beach Tourist Park,** Porth, Nr Newquay, Cornwall, TR7 3NH
**Tel:** 01637 876531 **Fax:** 01637 871227
**Email:** info@porthbeach.co.uk
**www.** porthbeach.co.uk
**Pitches For** ⋏ ⊞ ⊞ **Total** 201
**Facilities** ⅃ ⅁ ⊞ ⊞ ⅃ ⌐ ⊙ ⌐ ⍁ Ⓠ ⎙
⚸ ⊙ ⍁ ⚿ ⌐ ⊞
**Nearby Facilities** ⌐ ✓ ⚘ ⋎ ∪ ⥿ ♣
**Acreage** 6 **Open** April **to** October
**Access** Good **Site** Level
200 yards from the beach and 1½ miles from Newquay. Ideal touring.

**Nearest Town/Resort** Newquay
**Directions** From the A30 turn west at Indian Queens onto the A392 to Newquay. 1 mile before Newquay turn right onto the B3276, Park is ½ a mile on the right.
⇌ Newquay

## NEWQUAY
**Riverside Holiday Park,** Gwills, Lane, Newquay, Cornwall, TR8 4PE
**Tel:** 01637 873617 **Fax:** 01637 877051
**Email:** info@riversideholidaypark.co.uk
**www.** riversideholidaypark.co.uk
**Pitches For** ⋏ ⊞ ⊞ **Total** 120
**Facilities** ⅃ ⊞ ⅃ ⌐ ⊙ ⌐ ⍁ Ⓠ ⎙
⛢ ⊙ ⊠ ✗ ♀ ⊞ ♠ ⚿ ✣ ⌐ ⁂
**Nearby Facilities** ⌐ ✓ ∪ ♣
**Acreage** 7 **Open** Easter **to** October
**Access** Good **Site** Level
In a peaceful position, beside the River Gannel. Only 2½ miles from the spectacular coastline and sandy beaches.
**Nearest Town/Resort** Newquay
**Directions** Approx. 2½ miles from Newquay town centre, situated 1 mile off the A392 Newquay road.
⇌ Newquay

## NEWQUAY
**Rosecliston Park,** Trevemper, Newquay, Cornwall, TR8 5JT
**Tel:** 01637 830326
**Email:** info@rosecliston.co.uk
**www.** rosecliston.co.uk
**Pitches For** ⋏ ⊞ ⊞ **Total** 150
**Facilities** ⅃ ⊞ ⅃ ⊞ ⅃ ⌐ ⊙ ⌐ ⍁
Ⓠ ⛢ ⊙ ⍁ ♀ ⊞ ♠ ✣ ⌐ ⊞ A
**Nearby Facilities** ⌐ ✓ ⥿ ∪ ♣
**Acreage** 10 **Open** May **to** Sept
**Access** Good **Site** Lev/Slope
ADULTS ONLY PARK. Close to Newquay with its nightlife, shopping and excellent

surfing beaches.
**Nearest Town/Resort** Newquay
**Directions** On the A3075 Newquay to Redruth road, 1 mile from Newquay Boating Lake.
⇌ Newquay

## NEWQUAY
**Sunnyside Holiday Village,** Quintrell Downs, Newquay, Cornwall, TR8 4PD
**Tel:** 01637 873338 **Fax:** 01637 851403
**Email:** info@sunnyside.co.uk
**www.** sunnyside.co.uk
**Pitches For** ⋏ ⊞ ⊞ **Total** 50
**Facilities** ⊞ ⅃ ⌐ ⊙ ⌐ ⍁ ⌐
Ⓠ ⛢ ⊙ ⊠ ✗ ♀ ⊞ ♠ ✣ ✣ ⊞ A ⁂ ⌿
**Nearby Facilities** ⌐ ✓ ∪ ♣
**Acreage** 16 **Open** 1 March **to** 2 Jan
**Site** Sloping
18-30's Holiday Centre catering solely for couples and groups (no children or families).
**Nearest Town/Resort** Newquay
**Directions** 3 miles inland from Newquay on the A392.
⇌ Newquay

## NEWQUAY
**The Meadow,** Holywell Bay, Newquay, Cornwall, TR8 5PP
**Tel:** 01872 572752
**www.** holywellbeachholidays.com
**Pitches For** ⊞ ⊞ **Total** 6
**Facilities** ⅃ ⊞ ⅃ ⌐ ⊙ ⌐ ⍁ ⌐ ⊞ ⌑ ⊞ ⊞
**Nearby Facilities** ⌐ ♣
**Acreage** 1½ **Open** Easter **to** October
**Access** Good **Site** Level
Sheltered site by the beach and a stream, in a small village.
**Nearest Town/Resort** Newquay
**Directions** From Newquay take the A3075, after 3 miles turn right heading towards Redruth.
⇌ Newquay

# CHOOSE YOUR BEST HOLIDAY EVER FROM ONE OF NEWQUAY'S FINEST PARKS...

# Trevella Park

## CARAVAN & CAMPING PARK

## NEWQUAY

**Trebarber Farm,** St Columb Minor, Newquay, Cornwall, TR8 4JT
**Tel:** 01637 873007 **Fax:** 01637 873007
**Pitches For** ▲ ♦ ⌂
**Facilities** ⊞ ♨ ⌂ ⊙ ⊣ ⊿ ▣ ☎ ✦ ⊡
**Nearby Facilities** ⌐ ✔ ⚓ ⚓ ∪ ⇗
**Acreage** 5 **Open** May **to** October
**Access** Good **Site** Level
Quiet, ideal family centre for touring and beaches. Within walking distance of Porth Reservoir (coarse fishing) and a golf course.
**Nearest Town/Resort** Newquay
**Directions** 3 miles from Newquay on A3059, Newquay to St. Columb Major road.
⇥ Newquay

## NEWQUAY

**Trekenning Tourist Park,** Trekenning, Newquay, Cornwall, TR8 4JF
**Tel:** 01637 880462 **Fax:** 01637 880500
**Email:** trekenning@aol.com
**www.** trekenning.co.uk
**Pitches For** ▲ ♦ ⌂ **Total** 75
**Facilities** ∮ ⊞ ⊞ ♨ ⌂ ⊙ ⊣ ⊿ ▣ ☎
⊗ ⅊ ⊙ ⊕ ✕ ▽ ⊡ ♠ ♫ ⤳ ✦ ⊡ ⊡
**Nearby Facilities** ⌐ ✔ ⚓ ⚓ ∪ ⇗ ⇗
**Acreage** 6½ **Open** All Year
**Access** Good **Site** Sloping
Family site, family run.
**Nearest Town/Resort** Newquay
**Directions** From Newquay take the A3059 to the Trekenning roundabout, site entrance is 20 yards on the right before the roundabout.
⇥ Newquay

## NEWQUAY

**Treloy Tourist Park,** Newquay, Cornwall, TR8 4JN
**Tel:** 01637 872063/876279 **Fax:** 01637 872063/876279
**www.** treloy.co.uk
**Pitches For** ▲ ♦ ⌂ **Total** 141

**Facilities** ♿ ∮ ⊞ ⊞ ⊞ ♨ ⌂ ⊙ ⊣ ⊿ ▣ ☎
⊗ ⅊ ⊙ ⊕ ✕ ▽ ⊡ ♠ ♫ ⤳ ✦ ⊡ ⊡ ☼
**Nearby Facilities** ⌐ ✔ ⚓ ⚓ ∪ ⇗
**Acreage** 20 **Open** April **to** September
**Access** Good **Site** Level
Ideal site for touring the whole of Cornwall. Coarse fishing nearby. Own golf course ½ mile, concessionary Green Fees. Free entertainment.
**Nearest Town/Resort** Newquay
**Directions** 5 minutes from Newquay off the A3059 Newquay to St Columb Major Road.
⇥ Newquay

## NEWQUAY

**Trenance Holiday Park,** Edgcumbe Avenue, Newquay, Cornwall, TR7 2JY
**Tel:** 01637 873447 **Fax:** 01637 852677
**Email:** enquiries@trenanceholidaypark.co.uk
**www.** trenanceholidaypark.co.uk
**Pitches For** ▲ ♦ ⌂
**Facilities** ∮ ⊞ ♨ ⌂ ⊙ ⊣ ⊿ ▣ ☎
⊗ ⅊ ⊙ ⊕ ✕ ♠ ⊓ ▣ ⊡
**Nearby Facilities** ⌐ ✔ ⚓ ⚓ ∪ ⇗ ⇗
**Open** Easter **to** 31 Oct
**Access** Good **Site** Sloping
1 mile from Newquay town centre and next door to Newquay Zoo and a council owned leisure centre.
**Nearest Town/Resort** Newquay
**Directions** On the main A3075 Newquay to Truro road.
⇥ Newquay

## NEWQUAY

**Trencreek Holiday Park,** Trencreek, Newquay, Cornwall, TR8 4NS
**Tel:** 01637 874210
**Email:** trencreek@btconnect.com
**www.** trencreekholidaypark.co.uk
**Pitches For** ▲ ♦ ⌂ **Total** 150
**Facilities** ∮ ⊞ ⊞ ⊞ ♨ ⌂ ⊙ ⊣ ⊿ ▣ ☎
⊗ ⅊ ⊙ ⊕ ✕ ▽ ⊡ ♠ ♫ ⤳ ⊡
**Nearby Facilities** ⌐ ✔ ⚓ ⚓ ∪ ⇗ ⇗ ✗

**Acreage** 10 **Open** April **to** September
**Access** Good **Site** Level
Coarse fishing on site, 15 minutes footpath walk to Newquay, 1 mile by road.
**Nearest Town/Resort** Newquay
**Directions** A392 to Quintrell Downs, turn right Newquay East/Porth, at Porth crossroads, ¾ mile outside Newquay, turn left to Trencreek.
⇥ Newquay

## NEWQUAY

**Trethiggey Touring Park,** Quintrell Downs, Newquay, Cornwall, TR8 4QR
**Tel:** 01637 877672 **Fax:** 01637 879706
**Email:** enquiries@trethiggey.co.uk
**www.** trethiggey.co.uk
**Pitches For** ▲ ♦ ⌂
**Facilities** ♿ ∮ ⊞ ⊞ ⊞ ♨ ⌂ ⊙ ⊣ ⊿ ▣ ☎
⊗ ⅊ ⊙ ⊕ ✕ ▽ ⊡ ♠ ♫ ⤳ ▣ ⊡ ☼ ☼ ⅊
**Nearby Facilities** ⌐ ✔ ⚓ ⚓ ∪ ⇗ ⇗
**Open** 2 March **to** 2 Jan
**Access** Good **Site** Level
2 miles from Newquay, ½ a mile from Dairyland and 12 miles from the Eden Project.
**Nearest Town/Resort** Newquay
**Directions** 2 miles south of Newquay on the A3058.
⇥ Newquay

## NEWQUAY

**Trevarrian Holiday Park,** Trevarrian, Mawgan Porth, Newquay, Cornwall, TR8 4AQ
**Tel:** 01637 860381 **Fax:** 01637 860993
**Email:** holiday@trevarrian.co.uk
**www.** trevarrian.co.uk
**Pitches For** ▲ ♦ ⌂ **Total** 180
**Facilities** ∮ ⊞ ⊞ ⊞ ♨ ⌂ ⊙ ⊣ ⊿ ▣ ☎
⊗ ⅊ ⊙ ⊕ ✕ ▽ ⊡ ♠ ♫ ⤳ ✦ ⊡
**Nearby Facilities** ⌐ ✔ ⚓ ⚓ ∪ ⇗ ⇗ ⅊ ✗
**Acreage** 8 **Open** Easter **to** 1 Oct
**Access** Good **Site** Level
Near the beach. Ideal for families and

couples. First class facilities. Always a friendly welcome.
**Nearest Town/Resort** Newquay
**Directions** Follow the A30 to Bodmin, continue until you go under a railway bridge then turn right sp St Mawgan. At the next roundabout take the Newquay road, turn right just after the garage so Mawgan Porth. Continue to the T-Junction and turn right, Park is ½ a mile on the left.
⚑ Newquay

## NEWQUAY

**Trevella Park,** Crantock, Newquay, Cornwall, TR8 5EW
**Tel:** 01637 830308
**www.** trevella.co.uk
**Pitches For** ⋏ ⌂ ⛟ **Total** 270
**Facilities** ⚒ ∮ 🏠 🍴 🎮 ⚓ ↻ ⌂ ⚐ ⚑ 🔥 ⚵ 🖥 ☎ ⚙ ✗ ♥ 🛢 ♠ ⛅ ⚘ ✣ 🅿 🍽 🔥
**Nearby Facilities** ⚐ ✒ ⚓ ⚘ ∪ 🌙 🎣
**Acreage** 15 **Open** Easter **to** October
**Access** Good **Site** Level
½ mile from the beach, concessionary green fees, own fishing lake. AA 4 Pennants.
**Nearest Town/Resort** Newquay
**Directions** 2 miles south of Newquay on the A3075, turn right signposted Crantock.
⚑ Newquay

## NEWQUAY

**Trevornick Holiday Park,** Holywell Bay, Newquay, Cornwall, TR8 5PW
**Tel:** 01637 830531 **Fax:** 01637 831000
**Email:** bookings@trevornick.co.uk
**www.** trevornick.co.uk
**Pitches For** ⋏ ⌂ ⛟ **Total** 500
**Facilities** ⚒ ∮ 🏠 🍴 🎮 ⚓ ↻ ⌂ ⚐ ⚑ 🔥 ⚵ 🖥 ☎ ⚙ ✗ ♥ 🛢 ♠ ⛅ ⚘ ✣ 🅿 🍽 🔥
**Nearby Facilities** ⚐ ✒ ⚓ ⚘ ∪
**Acreage** 30 **Open** Easter **to** September
**Access** Good **Site** Level
Next to the beach, stunning sea views. Tourers and static tents. Golf on site.
**Nearest Town/Resort** Newquay
**Directions** Take Newquay to Perranporth A3075 road. Take turning for Cubert/Holywell.
⚑ Newquay

## NEWQUAY

**Watergate Bay Holiday Park,** Watergate Bay, Newquay, Cornwall, TR8 4AD
**Tel:** 01637 860387 **Fax:** 01637 860387
email@watergatebaytouringpark.co.uk
**www.** watergatebaytouringpark.co.uk
**Pitches For** ⋏ ⌂ ⛟ **Total** 171
**Facilities** ⚒ ∮ 🏠 🍴 🎮 ⚓ ↻ ⌂ ⚐ ⚑ 🔥 ⚵ 🖥 ☎ ⚙ ✗ ♥ 🛢 ♠ ⛅ ⚘ ✣ 🅿 🍽 🔥 🅿
**Nearby Facilities** ⚐ ✒ ⚓ ∪ 🅿 ⚘
**Acreage** 30 **Open** March **to** November
**Access** Good **Site** Level
½ mile from Watergate Bay in a rural location

in an area of outstanding natural beauty.
**Nearest Town/Resort** Newquay
**Directions** 4 miles north of Newquay on the B3276 Coast Road to Padstow. Follow directions shown from Watergate Bay.
⚑ Newquay

## NEWQUAY

**White Acres Country Park,** Whitecross, Newquay, Cornwall, TR8 4LW
**Tel:** 0845 458 0065 **Fax:** 01726 860877
**Email:** enquiries@parkdeanholidays.com
**www.** parkdeanholidays.co.uk
**Pitches For** ⋏ ⌂ ⛟ **Total** 40
**Facilities** ⚒ ∮ 🏠 🍴 🎮 ⚓ ↻ ⌂ ⚐ ⚑ 🔥 ⚵ 🖥 ☎ ⚙ ✗ ♥ 🛢 ♠ ⛅ ⚘ ✣ 🅿 🍽 🔥
**Nearby Facilities** ⚐ ✒ ⚓ ⚘ ∪ 🅿 🎣
**Acreage** 167 **Open** 22 March **to** 1 Nov
**Access** Good **Site** Level
5 Star Park with fifteen coarse fishing lakes. Six beaches within 6 miles. 10 miles from the Eden Project.
**Nearest Town/Resort** Newquay
**Directions** Turn off the A30 onto the A392 in the direction of Newquay. Park is 6 miles outside Newquay at Whitecross Junction.

## PADSTOW

**Carnevas Farm Holiday Park,** Carnevas Farm, St Merryn, Padstow, Cornwall, PL28 8PN
**Tel:** 01841. 520230 **Fax:** 01841 520230
**Pitches For** ⋏ ⌂ ⛟ **Total** 198

# CORNWALL

**Facilities**   ♿ ⚡ 📶 ⬛ 🚻 😊 🍴 ⛽ 📷 ☎
⬛ ⓘ 🔥 ❄ 🅿 ✕ 🔥 🔥 🏪 🔥 ✂ 🔥
**Nearby Facilities** ⌐ ✈ ⚓ ⬥ ⚲ ∅ ♫
**Acreage** 8 **Open** April **to** October
**Access** Good **Site** Lev/Slope
Near numerous sandy beaches in lovely rural position, ideal touring, well run family park. AA 3 Pennants and ETB 4 Star Park.
**Nearest Town/Resort** Padstow
**Directions** Take Newquay coast road from Padstow, turn right at Tredrea Inn just before getting to Porthcothan Bay. Site ¼ mile up road on right.
🚉 Newquay

## PADSTOW

**Dennis Cove Camping Ltd.,** Dennis Cove, Padstow, Cornwall, PL28 8DR
**Tel:** 01841 532349
**Email:** denniscove@freeuk.com
**www.** denniscove.co.uk
**Pitches For** ⚡ 🚐 **Total** 42
**Facilities** 🔥 ♿ 🔥 📶 😊 🍴 ⛽ 📷 ⓘ 🔥 🏪
**Nearby Facilities** ⌐ ✈ ⚓ ⬥ ⚲ ∅ ♫
**Acreage** 5 **Open** April **to** September
**Access** Fair **Site** Lev/Slope
Scenic views. Site adjoins Camel Trail cycle track. 10 minute walk to Padstow centre. 5 Touring caravan pitches with electric hook-ups. Groups by permission only. Reservation essential.
**Nearest Town/Resort** Padstow
**Directions** Signposted off A389 on outskirts of Padstow Town.
🚉 Bodmin Parkway

## PADSTOW

**Dennis Farm,** Padstow, Cornwall, PL28 8DR
**Tel:** 01841 533513
**Pitches For** ⚡ **Total** 24
**Facilities** ♿ ⚡ 📶 📷 😊 🍴 ⛽ 📷 ☎
⬛ ⓘ 🔥 ❄ 🅿
**Nearby Facilities** ⌐ ✈ ⚓ ⬥ ⚲ ∅ ♫

**Acreage** 1 **Open** July **to** Sept
**Site** Lev/Slope
Tent only site by the River Camel, ten minutes walk to Padstow. Own slipway and moorings. ALSO OPEN Spring Bank Holiday week.
**Nearest Town/Resort** Padstow
**Directions** Take the A389 to Padstow. Take first turning on the right by Tesco, then turn second right into Dennis Lane, continue to the end of the lane.
🚉 Bodmin Parkway

## PADSTOW

**Higher Harlyn Park,** St Merryn, Padstow, Cornwall, PL28 8SG
**Tel:** 01841 520022
**Email:** pbharlyn@aol.com
**www.** cornwall-online.co.uk
**Pitches For** ⚡ 🚐 ⛺
**Facilities** & 🔥 ♿ ⚡ 🔥 📶 😊 🍴 ⛽ 📷 📷 ☎
⬛ ⓘ 🔥 📷 ✕ ♿ ❄ 🅿 🔥 ✂ ♫
**Nearby Facilities** ⌐ ✈ ⚓ ⬥ ⚲
**Open** Easter **to** Early Oct
**Access** Good **Site** Level
Less than ½ a mile from the beach. Outdoor heated swimming pool from June to Sept.
**Nearest Town/Resort** Padstow
🚉 Bodmin Parkway

## PADSTOW

**Maribou Holiday Park,** St Merryn, Padstow, Cornwall, PL28 8QA
**Tel:** 01841 520520 **Fax:** 01841 521154
**Pitches For** ⚡ 🚐 **Total** 100
**Facilities** 🔥 ♿ 🔥 📶 📷 😊 📷 ⛽ 📷 ☎
⬛ ⓘ 🔥 ❄ 🅿
**Nearby Facilities** ⌐ ✈ ∅ ⚲
**Open** Easter **to** Oct
**Access** Good **Site** Level
Near to seven beaches.
**Nearest Town/Resort** Padstow
**Directions** From the A30 take the B3274,

after the roundabout take the second turning left to St. Merryn.
🚉 Bodmin

## PADSTOW

**Music Water Touring Park,** Rumford, Wadebridge, Cornwall, PL27 7SJ
**Tel:** 01841 540257 **Fax:** 01841 540257
**www.** campingsites.co.uk
**Pitches For** ⚡ 🚐 **Total** 140
**Facilities** 🔥 ♿ 🔥 📶 😊 🍴 ⛽ 📷 📷 ☎
⬛ ⓘ 🔥 🏪 🔥 ❄ 🅿
**Nearby Facilities** ⌐ ✈ ⚓ ⬥ ⚲ ∅ ♫
**Acreage** 8 **Open** April **to** Oct
**Access** Good **Site** Lev/Slope
5 miles from beaches. Ideal touring base.
**Nearest Town/Resort** Padstow
**Directions** From Wadebridge take the A39 to Winnards Perch roundabout, then take the B3274. Turn first left and site is on the right.
🚉 Bodmin

## PADSTOW

**Old MacDonald's Farm,** Porthcothan Bay, Padstow, Cornwall, PL28 8LW
**Tel:** 01841 540829
**Email:** karen@old-macdonalds-farm.co.uk
**www.** old-macdonalds-farm.co.uk
**Pitches For** ⚡ 🚐 **Total** 40
**Facilities** & 🔥 ♿ 🔥 📶 🔥 📷 😊 ⚡ ✕ 🔥 🏪 🔥
**Nearby Facilities** ⌐ ✈ ∅
**Acreage** 3½ **Open** All Year
**Access** Good **Site** Level
½ mile to the beach. Campers have free access to old MacDonald's Farm Park and can help feed the animals. Pony rides, crazy golf and a miniature railway on site. Dutch speaking owners.
**Nearest Town/Resort** Padstow/Newquay
**Directions** Just off the B3276 coast road. 5 miles south of Padstow and 9 miles north of Newquay.

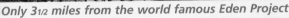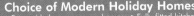

## PADSTOW

**Padstow Holiday Park,** Cliffdowne, Padstow, Cornwall, PL28 8LB
**Tel:** 01841 532289
**Email:** mail@padstowholidaypark.co.uk
www. padstowholidaypark.co.uk
**Pitches For** ⚊ 🚐 ⛺ **Total** 50
**Facilities** ⌇ 🔟 🔟 ♨ ⌇ ⊙ ⌣ ⚌ ⬚ 🛟 ⛱
🔟 🌀 🏕 🅿 🎆 ⚡ ♒
**Nearby Facilities** ⌇ ✈ ⚓ ↘ ∪ ⚲
**Acreage** 3 **Open** All Year
**Access** Good **Site** Level
Quiet location with no club or bar. 1 mile from a sandy cove. Footpath to Padstow (1 mile). 1 mile from a Tesco store.
**Nearest Town/Resort** Padstow
**Directions** From Wadebridge take the A389 to Padstow, site is on the right 1 mile before Padstow.
⚒ Bodmin

## PADSTOW

**Padstow Touring Park,** Trerethern, Padstow, Cornwall, PL28 8LE
**Tel:** 01841 532061 **Fax:** 01841 532289
**Email:** mail@padstowtouringpark.co.uk
www. padstowtouringpark.co.uk
**Pitches For** ⚊ 🚐 ⛺ **Total** 100
**Facilities** ⚊ ⌇ 🔟 🔟 ♨ ⌇ ⊙ ⌣ ⚌ ⬚ 🛟 ⛱
🌀 🔟 🌀 🏕 ♨ ⊞ 🅿 🌀 ♒
**Nearby Facilities** ⌇ ✈ ⚓ ↘ ∪ ⚲ ♒
**Acreage** 13¼ **Open** All Year
**Access** Good **Site** Level
Panoramic views, several sandy beaches within 3 miles. Extra large pitches, footpath to padstow. En-suite pitches. No statics. Separate dog exercise area. Free brochure.
**Nearest Town/Resort** Padstow
**Directions** On A389 1 mile south south west of Padstow.

## PADSTOW

**Seagull Tourist Park,** St Merryn, Padstow, Cornwall, PL28 8PT
**Tel:** 01841 520117
**Pitches For** ⚊ 🚐 ⛺ **Total** 100
**Facilities** ⌇ 🔟 ♨ ⌇ ⊙ ⌣ ⚌ ⬚ ⛱
🔟 🌀 🏕 🔟 🅿 🌀 ⤳ ♒
**Nearby Facilities** ⌇ ✈ ⚓ ↘ ∪ ⚲ ♒
**Acreage** 8 **Open** Easter/1 April to End Oct
**Access** Good **Site** Level
Seven golden sandy beaches within 10 minutes drive. Small family park, quiet farmland. Coastal walks, golf, fishing, boating, surf and cycle hire.
**Nearest Town/Resort** Padstow
⚒ Bodmin Parkway

## PAR

**Par Sands Holiday Park,** Par Beach, St Austell Bay, Cornwall, PL24 2AS
**Tel:** 01726. 812868 **Fax:** 01726 817899
**Email:** holidays@parsands.co.uk
www. parsands.co.uk
**Pitches For** ⚊ 🚐 ⛺ **Total** 200
**Facilities** ⚊ ⌇ 🔟 🌀 ♨ ⌇ ⊙ ⌣ ⚌ ⬚ 🛟 ⛱
🔟 🌀 🏕 🌀 ♨ 🏕 ♒ ⊞ 🅿 🌀 ♒
**Nearby Facilities** ⌇ ✈ ⚓ ↘ ∪ ♒
**Acreage** 12 **Open** April to October
**Access** Good **Site** Level
Alongside safe sandy beach and freshwater wildlife lake. Indoor heated swimming pool with aquaslide. Luxury extra wide caravan for hire. Rose Award. 3½ miles from the Eden Project. Heated toilet and shower block. Please see our colour advertisement.
**Nearest Town/Resort** St. Austell/Fowey
**Directions** 4 miles east of St Austell on road to Fowey A3082.
⚒ Par

## PENRYN

**Menallack Farm,** Treverva, Penryn, Cornwall, TR10 9BP
**Tel:** 01326 340333 **Fax:** 01326 340333
**Email:** menallack@fsbdial.co.uk
**Pitches For** ⚊ 🚐 ⛺ **Total** 30
**Facilities** ⌇ 🔟 ♨ ⌇ ⊙ ⌣ ⛱ 🛟 ⊞ 🌀 🔟
♒
**Nearby Facilities** ⌇ ✈ ⚓ ↘ ∪ ⚲
**Acreage** 1½ **Open** Easter to Oct
**Access** Good **Site** Lev/Slope
Secluded site with lovely views.
**Nearest Town/Resort** Falmouth
**Directions** From take the A39 "Asda" roundabout turn right up the hill to Mabe Burnthouse. At the crossroads turn left and follow the road, at crossroads turn right to Gweek, site is signposted 1½ miles.
⚒ Penryn

## PENTEWAN

**Pentewan Sands Limited,** Pentewan, Cornwall, PL26 6BT
**Tel:** 01726 843485 **Fax:** 01726 844142
**Email:** info@pentewan.co.uk
www. pentewan.co.uk
**Pitches For** ⚊ 🚐 ⛺ **Total** 482
**Facilities** ⌇ 🔟 🌀 ♨ ⌇ ⊙ ⌣ ⚌ ⬚ 🛟 ⛱
🛟 🔟 🌀 🏕 🗙 ♒ 🔟 ♨ 🌀 ⤳ ⊞ 🅿 🌀 ♒
**Nearby Facilities** ⌇ ✈ ⚓ ↘ ∪ ⚲ ♒ ♒
**Acreage** 32 **Open** April to Oct
**Access** Good **Site** Level
Pentewan Sands is located on its own private beach. Ideal for a family holiday with entertainment, bars, shop and heated swimming pool.
**Nearest Town/Resort** Mevagissey
**Directions** From St. Austell follow the B3273 towards Mevagissey. Site is 4 miles from St Austell on the left.
⚒ St. Austell

## PENZANCE

**Boleigh Farm Site,** Boleigh Farm, Lamorna, St Buryan, PenzanceCornwall, TR19 6BN
**Tel:** 01736 810305
**Pitches For** ▲ ⊕ ⊞ **Total** 30
**Facilities** ♪ 🛁 ♨ ⌂ ☺ ☎ ♈ ♊ ☷ ♒ ⊞ ☼
**Nearby Facilities**
**Open** April to October
**Access** Good **Site** Sloping
**Nearest Town/Resort** Penzance
**Directions** On the B3315 5 miles from Penzance, first farm house after Lamorna Cove turning.
⚆ Penzance

## PENZANCE

**Bone Valley Caravan & Camping Park,** Heamoor, Penzance, Cornwall, TR20 8UJ
**Tel:** 01736 360313
**Email:**
margaret@bonevalleycandcpark.co.uk
**www.** cornwalltouristboard.co.uk/bonevalley
**Pitches For** ▲ ⊕ ⊞ **Total** 17
**Facilities** ♪ 🛁 🛁 ♨ ⌂ ☺ ♊ ♒ ⊞ ☎
♒ ☷ ☺ ☷ ♈ ☷ ⊟ ☷
**Nearby Facilities** ✓ ∪ ♪
**Acreage** 1 **Open** All Year
**Access** Good **Site** Level
1 mile from Penzance, 3 miles from St Michaels Mount and 10 miles from Lands End. Coastal footpaths.
**Nearest Town/Resort** Penzance
**Directions** Follow the A30 (Penzance Bypass) to roundabout and turn right signposted Heamoor. Follow road through the village to camping/caravan sign and turn right, continue to next camping/caravan sign, signposted Bone Valley.
⚆ Penzance

## PENZANCE

**Garris Farm,** Gulval, Penzance, Cornwall, TR20 8XD
**Tel:** 01736 365806 **Fax:** 01736 365806
**Pitches For** ▲ ⊕ ♨
**Facilities** 🛁 ♨ ☎ ♈ ♊
**Nearby Facilities** ⚓ ✈ ∪
**Acreage** 8 **Open** May to October
**Access** Good **Site** Sloping
**Nearest Town/Resort** Penzance
**Directions** Leave A30 turning right at Growlas on road to Luogvan B3309 to Castlegate. Follow road to Chysauster ancient village.
⚆ Penzance

## PENZANCE

**Kenneggy Cove Holiday Park,** Higher Kenneggy, Rosudgeon, Penzance, Cornwall, TR20 9AU
**Tel:** 01736 763453
**Email:** enquiries@kenneggycove.co.uk
**www.** kenneggycove.co.uk
**Pitches For** ▲ ⊕ ♨ **Total** 60
**Facilities** ♪ 🛁 ♨ ⌂ ☺ ♊ ☷ ☷ ⊞ ☎
♒ ☷ ☺ ♊ ♒ ♈ ⊞
**Nearby Facilities** ✓ ∪ ⚓ ♈ ∪ ♪
**Acreage** 8 **Open** April to Nov
**Access** Good **Site** Level
A quiet site which operates a policy of no noise after 10pm. 12 minutes walk to the stunning beach and S.W. Coastal Path. Quality take-away food service from May to Sept.
**Nearest Town/Resort** Penzance
**Directions** Midway between Penzance and Helston on the A394. Take turn into lane signposted Higher Kenneggy towards the sea.
⚆ Penzance

## PENZANCE

**River Valley Country Park,** Relubbus, Penzance, Cornwall, TR20 9ER
**Tel:** 0845 601 2516 **Fax:** 01736 763398
**Email:** rivervalley@surfbay.dircon.co.uk
**www.** rivervalley.co.uk
**Pitches For** ▲ ⊕ ♨ **Total** 150
**Facilities** ♪ 🛁 🛁 ♨ ⌂ ☺ ☷ ☷ ♊ ⊞ ☎
♒ ☷ ☺ ♈ ⊞ ☷ ☼
**Nearby Facilities** ✓ ✈ ∪
**Acreage** 18 **Open** March to October
**Access** Good **Site** Level
Partly wooded park, situated in one of the most picturesque valleys in Cornwall. Alongside a small trout stream. Beaches nearby. Ideal touring base.
**Nearest Town/Resort** Penzance
**Directions** From the A30 at St. Michaels Mount roundabout, take the A394 towards Helston. Turn left at the next roundabout onto the B3280 to Relubbus, after approx. 3 miles turn left after the small bridge to River Valley.
⚆ Penzance

## PENZANCE

**Sennen Cove Camping & Caravanning Club Site,** Higher Tregiffian Farm, St Buryan, Penzance, Cornwall, TR19 6JB
**Tel:** 01736 871588
**www.** campingandcaravanningclub.co.uk
**Pitches For** ▲ ⊕ ♨ **Total** 75
**Facilities** ♨ ♪ 🛁 🛁 ♨ ⌂ ☺ ☷
♒ ☷ ☺ ♈ ♒ ☷ ⊞ ⊟ ☷
**Nearby Facilities** ✓ ♪ ✈
**Acreage** 4 **Open** April to Oct
**Access** Good **Site** Level
Situated on a farm in peaceful countryside. 2½ miles from the beach at Sennen Cove which has won numerous awards. BTB 4 Star Graded and AA 3 Pennants. Non members welcome.

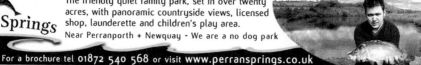

**Nearest Town/Resort** Penzance
**Directions** Follow the A30 towards Lands End, turn right onto the A3306 St. Just to Pendeen road, site is 50 yards on the left.
≠ Penzance

## PENZANCE

**Wayfarers Caravan & Camping Park,** St Hilary, Penzance, Cornwall, TR20 9EF
**Tel:** 01736 Penzance 763326
**Email:** wayfarers@eurobell.co.uk
**www.** wayfarerspark.co.uk
**Pitches For** ▲ ⊕ ⊜ **Total** 60
**Facilities** ⌁ ⊡ ⓌⓌ ⚓ Ր ⊙ ⊒
⊠ ⌕ ⊘ ⊜ ⊬ ⊡ ⊜ Ⓐ
**Nearby Facilities** Ր ✔ ⚓ ⌕ ∪ ⋡ Ɽ ⌇
**Acreage** 4 **Open** March to January
**Access** Good **Site** Level
ADULTS ONLY PARK. Tranquil, landscaped surroundings. Graded Excellent by the English Tourist Board. Pitches with 16amp hook-ups and awnings from £55 per week. Four luxury holiday homes for hire.
**Nearest Town/Resort** Marazion
**Directions** 2 miles east of Marazion on B3280.
≠ Penzance

## PERRANPORTH

**Penrose Farm Touring Park,** Goonhavern, Truro, Cornwall, TR4 9QF
**Tel:** 01872 573185
**www.** penrosefarm.co.uk
**Pitches For** ▲ ⊕ ⊜ **Total** 100
**Facilities** ⌁ ⌁ ⓌⓌ ⚓ Ր ⊙ ⊒ ⊒ ⊒ ⊠ ⓦ
⊠ ⌕ ⊘ ⊜ ⊬ ⊡ ⊜ ⊬
**Nearby Facilities** Ր ✔ ⚓ ⌕ ∪ ⋡ Ɽ
**Acreage** 9 **Open** April to October
**Access** Good **Site** Level
Quiet, clean and sheltered park with animal centre and adventure play area. Good spacing. Close to Perranporth beach. Award winning private 'Superloos'.
**Nearest Town/Resort** Perranporth
**Directions** Leave A30 onto the B3285 signed Perranporth, site 1½ miles on the left.
≠ Newquay/Truro

## PERRANPORTH

**Perran Sands Holiday Park,** Perranporth, Cornwall, TR6 0AQ
**Tel:** 01872 573742
**www.** touringholidays.co.uk

**Pitches For** ▲ ⊕ ⊜
**Facilities** ⌁ ⌁ ⌁ ⊡ ⚓ Ր ⊙ ⊒ ⊠ ⓦ
⊠ ⌕ ⊘ ⊘ ✘ Ր ⊡ ⚓ ⋔ ⌇ ⊬ ⊬⊡ ⊜ ⊬
**Nearby Facilities** Ր ✔ ⚓ ⌕ ∪ ⋡ Ɽ ⋡
**Open** April to Sept
**Access** Good **Site** Level
Just a 5-10 minute walk from the sandy beach.
**Nearest Town/Resort** Perranporth/Newquay
**Directions** From Exeter take the A30 through Devon and Cornwall. 1 mile beyond the Wind Farm roundabout turn right onto the B3285 towards Perranporth. Perran Sands is on the right hand side.
≠ Truro

## PERRANPORTH

**Perran Springs Holiday Park,** Goonhavern, Truro, Cornwall, TR4 9QG
**Tel:** 01872 540568 **Fax:** 01872 540568
**Email:** info@perransprings.co.uk
**www.** perransprings.co.uk
**Pitches For** ▲ ⊕ ⊜
**Facilities** ⌁ ⌁ ⓌⓌ ⊡ ⓣ ⓦ ✘ ⊡ ⊘ ⊘
⊠ ⌕ ⊘ ⊜ ⓥ ⚓ ⊛ ⊡ ⊘
**Nearby Facilities** Ր ✔ ⚓ ∪ Ɽ
**Acreage** 21 **Open** Easter to October
**Access** Good **Site** Level
Award winning, friendly, quiet family park offering: Coarse Fishing Lakes, Spacious Level Pitches, Electric Hook-ups, Caravan Holiday Homes, Eurotents, Licensed Shop, Launderette, Children's Play Area and Panoramic Countryside Views.
**Nearest Town/Resort** Perranporth
**Directions** Leave the A30 and turn right onto the B3285 signposted Perranporth. Follow the brown tourism signs marked 'Perran Springs' for 1½ miles. Entrance and flags will then be clearly seen.
≠ Truro

## PERRANPORTH

**Tollgate Farm Caravan & Camping Park,** Budnick Hill, Perranporth, Cornwall, TR6 0AD
**Tel:** 0845 166 2126
**Email:** tollgatefarm@aol.com
**www.** tollgatefarm.co.uk
**Pitches For** ▲ ⊕ ⊜ **Total** 120
**Facilities** ⌁ ⌁ ⓌⓌ ⚓ Ր ⊙ ⊒ ⊒ ⊠ ⓦ
⊠ ⌕ ⊘ ⊜ ⊬ ⊡ ⊜ ⊬
**Nearby Facilities** Ր ✔ ⚓ ∪ Ɽ
**Acreage** 10 **Open** Easter to Oct

**Access** Good **Site** Lev/Slope
Fantastic views from this quiet, friendly, family run site, less than 1 mile from the beach. Help feed the animals. Great for walking. Brand new facilities. Take-away food bar (peak season). Off-peak discounts available. Ideal base for touring.
**Nearest Town/Resort** Perranporth
**Directions** From the A30 take the B3285 signposted Perranporth, go through Goonhavern and site is 1½ miles on the right.
≠ Newquay

## POLPERRO

**Killigarth Manor Holiday Park,** John Fowler Holidays, Killigarth Manor, Polperro, Cornwall, PL13 2JQ
**Tel:** 01271 866766 **Fax:** 01271 866791
**Email:** bookings@johnfowlerholidays.com
**www.** johnfowlerholidays.com
**Pitches For** ▲ ⊕ ⊜ **Total** 125
**Facilities** ⌁ ⌁ ⊡ ⓌⓌ ⚓ Ր ⊙ ⊒ ⊒ ⊒ ⊠ ⓦ
⊠ ⌕ ⊘ ⊜ ✘ ⊡ ⚓ ⋔ ⋡ ⊘ ⊒
**Nearby Facilities** Ր ✔ ⚓ ⌕ ∪ Ɽ
**Open** March to October
**Access** Good **Site** Level
Perfect location for touring North Cornwall's picturesque villlages, and visiting The Eden Project.
**Nearest Town/Resort** Looe/Polperro
**Directions** From Plymouth take the A38 then the A387 to Looe, turn for Polperro, the Park is at the entrance to Polperro.
≠ Looe

## POLZEATH

**South Winds Camping & Caravan Park,** Old Polzeath Road, Polzeath, Nr Wadebridge, Cornwall, PL27 6QU
**Tel:** 01208 863267 **Fax:** 01208 862080
**Email:** paul@tristramcampsite.fsnet.co.uk
**www.** rockinfo.co.uk
**Pitches For** ▲ ⊕ ⊜ **Total** 100
**Facilities** ⌁ ⌁ ⓌⓌ ⚓ Ր ⊙ ⊒ ⊒ ⊠ ⓦ
⋔ ⊘ ⊘ ⊬ ⊡ ⊜
**Nearby Facilities** Ր ✔ ⚓ ∪ Ɽ ⋡ ⋡
**Acreage** 7 **Open** Easter to October
**Access** Good **Site** Level
Outstanding views of countryside and sea. ½ a mile from Polzeath Beach.
**Nearest Town/Resort** Polzeath
≠ Bodmin Road

STUNNING LOCATIONS CORNWALL
POLZEATH
EXCELLENT FACILITIES

One of the most spectacular, safest and best surfing beaches in Cornwall. Visitors return each year to enjoy the beauty and safety of its golden sands and clear blue sea.

We have two prime sites at Polzeath. Tristram above right and shown on the aerial picture is on the gently sloping cliff overlooking the beach with direct access to the beach. The site is private and safe for children. It also has its own shop, restaurant and take away on site. South Winds above left is different, families like the peace and quiet with beautiful sea and panoramic rural views yet only half a mile from the beach. Both sites have modern toilets, showers and laundry facilities.

01208 862215 (Tristram)
01208 863267 (South Winds)
www.rockinfo.co.uk

E-mail: paul@tristramcampsite.fsnet.co.uk    Fax: 01208 862080
South Winds, Polzeath, Cornwall PL27 6QU

## POLZEATH

**Tristram Camping & Caravan Park,** Polzeath, Nr Wadebridge, Cornwall, PL27 6TD
**Tel:** 01208 862215 **Fax:** 01208 862080
**www.** rockinfo.co.uk
**Pitches For** ▲ � ⌺ **Total** 150
**Facilities** & ⨍ ▥ ⌺ ℾ ☉ ⌁ ◪ ⌺ ❤
♀☎ ⌺ ⊖ ⊛ ✕ ⊬⊟ ▣
**Nearby Facilities** ┏ ✔ ⚓ ❈ ∪ ♬ ⚲
**Acreage** 10 **Open** March to Nov
**Access** Good **Site** Level
Set on a cliff top overlooking Polzeath beach. Private access onto the beach.
**Nearest Town/Resort** Polzeath
**Directions** From Wadebridge take the B3314 and follow signs to Polzeath.

## PORTHTOWAN

**Porthtowan Tourist Park,** Mile Hill, Porthtowan, Truro, Cornwall, TR4 8TY
**Tel:** 01209 890256 **Fax:** 01209 890256
**Email:** admin@porthtowantouristpark.co.uk
**www.** porthtowantouristpark.co.uk
**Pitches For** ▲ �0 ⌺ **Total** 50
**Facilities** & ⨍ ▥ ▣ ⌺ ℾ ☉ ⌁ ◪ ⌺ ❤
♀☎ ⊖ ⊛ ♠ ⊓ ⊬⊟
**Nearby Facilities** ┏ ✔ ⚓ ❈ ∪ ❈
**Acreage** 5½ **Open** Easter to October
**Access** Good **Site** Level
A level site with spacious pitches in an area of outstanding natural beauty. Close to a sandy surfing beach, cycle trail and coastal park. Superb new toilet/laundry facilities with free showers and family rooms. Ideal touring base.
**Nearest Town/Resort** Porthtowan/Truro
**Directions** Take signpost off A30 Redruth/Porthtowan. Cross the A30, through north country to T-Junction, right up the hill, park is ½ a mile on the left.

## PORTHTOWAN

**Rose Hill Touring Park,** Porthtowan, Truro, Cornwall, TR4 8AR
**Tel:** 01209 890802
**Email:** reception@rosehillcamping.co.uk
**www.** rosehillcamping.co.uk
**Pitches For** ▲ �0 ⌺ **Total** 50
**Facilities** & ⨍ ▥ ▣ ⌺ ℾ ☉ ⌁ ◪ ⌺ ❤
♀☎ ⌺ ⊖ ⊛ ⊓ ⊬⊟
**Nearby Facilities** ┏ ✔ ⚓ ❈ ∪ ❈
**Acreage** 3 **Open** April to October
**Access** Good **Site** Level
Friendly family run site, sheltered and situated in the coastal village of Porthtowan. Just 4 minutes level walk to the beach, pubs, restaurants and coastal path. 5 Star immaculate toilet block. Fresh crusty bread and croissants baked daily. No clubhouse or games room, just a bit of paradise surrounded by trees and bird

song. Close to a sandy beach.
**Nearest Town/Resort** St. Agnes
**Directions** From the A30 take the B3277 signposted St. Agnes and Porthtowan, after 1 mile turn left signed Porthtowan. Site is 100 yards past beach road.

## PORTREATH

**Cambrose Touring Park,** Portreath Road, Redruth, Cornwall, TR16 4HT
**Tel:** 01209 890747 **Fax:** 01209 891665
**Email:** cambrosetouringpark@supanet.com
**www.** cambrosetouringpark.co.uk
**Pitches For** ▲ �0 ⌺ **Total** 60
**Facilities** & ⨍ ▥ ⌺ ℾ ☉ ⌁ ◪ ⌺ ❤
♀☎ ⊖ ⊛ ✕ ⊓ ▥ ⌺ ⊬ ⊛ ⊬⊟ ✲
**Nearby Facilities** ┏ ✔ ∪ ❈
**Acreage** 7 **Open** April to Oct
**Access** Good **Site** Level
1½ miles from the beach. Near to tramway. Ideal for walks and touring.
**Nearest Town/Resort** Portreath
**Directions** From Redruth take the B3300 to Portreath, pass the Gold Centre on the left and after ¼ mile turn right signposted Porthtowan, Cambrose is 100 yards on the right.
⊭ Redruth

## PORTSCATHO

**Treloan Coastal Farm Holidays,** Treloan Lane, Portscatho, The Roseland, TruroCornwall, TR2 5EF
**Tel:** 01872 580899 **Fax:** 01872 580989
**Email:** holidays@treloan.freeserve.co.uk
**www.** coastalfarmholidays.co.uk
**Pitches For** ▲ ⌀ ⌺ **Total** 57
**Facilities** & ⨍ ▥ ▣ ▥ ⌺ ℾ ☉ ◪ ⌺
▥ ⌺ ⊖ ⊛ ⊬⊟ ✲ ⌀
**Nearby Facilities** ✔ ⚓ ❈ ∪
**Acreage** 35 **Open** All Year
**Access** Good **Site** Level
A working traditional and organic farm on the coastal path offering self catering, touring and camping in beautiful surroundings. Jersey cows, pigs and chickens. Access to three secluded beaches. Close to shops, pubs, etc.. Squash courts nearby. Shire horses. Sailing facilities on site.
**Nearest Town/Resort** Portscatho/Truro
**Directions** From Truro take the A390 through Tresillian and onto the by-pass, take second right turn onto the A3078 signposted Tregony and St. Mawes. At Trewithian turn left signposted Portscatho and follow signs.
⊭ Truro/St. Austell

## PRAA SANDS

**Lower Pentreath,** Lower Pentreath Farm, Praa Sands, Penzance, Cornwall, TR20 9TL
**Tel:** 01736 763221
**Email:** andrew.wearne@tinyworld.co.uk

**Pitches For** ▲ ⌀ ⌺ **Total** 15
**Facilities** ▥ ⌺ ℾ ☉ ⌁ ❤ ⌺
**Nearby Facilities** ┏ ✔ ⚓ ∪ ❈
**Acreage** 1 **Open** April to October
**Access** Good **Site** Lev/Slope
Small friendly site, 400 yards from the beach.
**Nearest Town/Resort** Penzance
**Directions** From Penzance take the A394 towards Helston. Go through Rosudgeon, take Pentreath Lane immediately before the garage on the right hand side, we are at the bottom of the hill.
⊭ Penzance

## REDRUTH

**Chiverton Park,** East Hill, Blackwater, Truro, Cornwall, TR4 8HS
**Tel:** 01872 560667 **Fax:** 01872 560667
**Email:** chivertonpark@btopenworld.com
**www.** chivertonpark.co.uk
**Pitches For** ▲ ⌀ ⌺ **Total** 12
**Facilities** ⨍ ▣ ▥ ▣ ⌺ ℾ ☉ ⌁ ◪ ⌺
♀☎ ⊛ ♠ ⊓ ⊬⊟
**Nearby Facilities** ┏ ✔ ⚓ ∪ ♬
**Acreage** 4 **Open** 7 Feb to 7 Jan
**Access** Good **Site** Level
Quiet park, close to beaches. Easy access to the north and south coast.
**Nearest Town/Resort** St Agnes
**Directions** Travel along the A30 to Chiverton Cross roundabout 4 miles north of Redruth. Take the B3277 St. Agnes road, after 500 yards turn left and the park is 200 yards down on the left.
⊭ Truro

## REDRUTH

**Globe Vale Holiday Park,** Radnor, Redruth, Cornwall, TR16 4BH
**Tel:** 01209 891183 **Fax:** 01209 890590
**Email:** info@globevale.co.uk
**www.** globevale.co.uk
**Pitches For** ▲ ⌀ ⌺ **Total** 40
**Facilities** ⨍ ▥ ▣ ⌺ ℾ ☉ ⌁ ◪ ⌺ ❤
♀☎ ⊓ ⊬⊟ ⊛ ✲ ⌀
**Nearby Facilities** ┏ ∪
**Acreage** 4 **Open** Easter to Oct
**Access** Good **Site** Level
Just a 10 minute drive from Portreath and Porthtowan beaches. Good access from the A30, ideal for visiting St. Ives, Penzance and Truro.
**Nearest Town/Resort** Redruth
**Directions** From Redruth follow signs to Portreath and Porthtowan from the A30 roundabout. At the double roundabout take the third exit to North Country. At the crossroads turn right signposted Radnor and follow signs. Approx. 4 miles from Redruth.
⊭ Redruth

# Pensagillas Farm Campsite

**01872 530808**

*Mevagissey • St Austell • Cornwall • TR2 4SR*  **Open All Year**

Friendly, family run campsite, just a few minutes drive from many sandy beaches. 5 minutes drive from The Lost Gardens of Heligan, and 10 minutes from the Eden Project. Toilets and hot showers. Food and drink served in our small Club House. Course fishing in our 2½ acre lake. *www.pensagillas-park.co.uk*

## REDRUTH
**Lanyon Holiday Park,** Loscombe Lane, Four Lanes, Nr Redruth, Cornwall, TR16 6LP
**Tel:** 01209 313474 **Fax:** 01209 313422
**Email:** jamierielly@btconnect.com
**www.** lanyonholidaypark.co.uk
**Pitches For ▲ ⊕ ⊟ Total** 50
**Facilities** ⚏ ⊟ ⊡ ⊞ ♨ ♪ ⊙ ⊣ ⊡ ☎
ℳ ⊠ ⚘ ♥ ⊡ ⚑ ⊕ ⊠ ⊡ ⊡ ⊠ ⊡ ☀ ⌂
**Nearby Facilities** ↑ ✈ ⚓ ⊀ ∪ ⊿ ♪ ⊁
**Acreage** 14 **Open** March to Oct
**Access** Good **Site** Level
Surrounded by open countryside. Heated indoor swimming pool. Three modern toilet/ shower blocks. Site shop during high season. Ideal touring base. 6 miles to the nearest beach.
**Nearest Town/Resort** Redruth
**Directions** From Redruth take the B3297 towards Helston for approx. 2 miles, as you enter the small village of Four Lanes park is 400 yards.

## REDRUTH
**Wheal Rose Caravan & Camping Park,** Wheal Rose, Scorrier, Redruth, Cornwall, TR16 5DD
**Tel:** 01209 891496
**Email:** les@whealrosecaravanpark.co.uk
**www.** whealrosecaravanpark.co.uk
**Pitches For ▲ ⊕ ⊟ Total** 50
**Facilities** ⚏ ♪ ⊟ ⊡ ♨ ♪ ⊙ ⊣ ⊟ ⊡ ☎
ℳ ⊠ ⊕ ⚘ ⊡ ♥ ⊡ ♨ ⊡ ⊡ ⊡ ℘
**Nearby Facilities** ↑ ✈ ⚓ ⊀ ∪ ⊿ ♪
**Acreage** 6½ **Open** March to Dec
**Access** Good **Site** Level
Adjacent to a mineral tramway. Cenral for all of West Cornwall's attractions.
**Nearest Town/Resort** Porthtowan
**Directions** From the A30 take the Scorrier slip road and turn right at the Plume of Feathers, follow signs to park.
⚘ Redruth

## RUAN MINOR
**The Friendly Camp,** Tregullas Farm, Penhale, Ruan Minor, HelstonCornwall, TR12 7LJ
**Tel:** 01326 240387
**Pitches For ▲ ⊕ ⊟ Total** 18
**Facilities** ⊞ ♨ ♪ ⊙ ⊣ ⊟ ⊠ ⊡ ⊕ ⊞ ⊡
**Nearby Facilities** ↑ ✈ ⊀ ∪
**Acreage** 1¼ **Open** April to November
**Access** Good **Site** Level

Lovely views and moorland walks. Ideal touring.
**Nearest Town/Resort** Mullion
**Directions** 7 miles south of Helston on left hand side of A3083, just before junction of B3296 to Mullion which is 1 mile.
⚘ Redruth

## SALTASH
**Dolbeare Caravan & Camping Park,** Landrake, Saltash, Cornwall, PL12 5AF
**Tel:** 01752 851332
**Email:** dolbeare@btopenworld.com
**www.** dolbeare.co.uk
**Pitches For ▲ ⊕ ⊟ Total** 60
**Facilities** ♪ ⊟ ⊡ ⊞ ♨ ♪ ⊙ ⊣ ⊟ ⊡ ☎
ℳ ⊕ ⊠ ⊡ ♥ ⊡ ⊡ ⊡ ⊡ ☀ ℘
**Nearby Facilities** ↑ ✈ ⚓ ⊀ ∪ ⊿ ♪
**Acreage** 9 **Open** All Year
**Access** Good **Site** Lev/Slope
Quality touring park in magnificent countryside. Free, plentiful hot water. Level hard standings and large grass areas. 30 minutes from the Eden Project. Only 6 miles from Europes first premier diving venue 'Seylla' at Whitsand Bay. Also close to the ferry port of Plymouth. Please telephone for a brochure.
**Nearest Town/Resort** Saltash
**Directions** 4 miles west of Saltash, turn off A38 at Landrake immediately after footbridge into Pound Hill, signposted.

## SALTASH
**Notter Bridge Caravan & Camping Park,** Notter Bridge, Saltash, Cornwall, PL12 4RW
**Tel:** 01752 842318
**Email:** holidays@notterbridge.co.uk
**www.** notterbridge.co.uk
**Pitches For ▲ ⊕ ⊟ Total** 29
**Facilities** ⚏ ♪ ⊟ ⊡ ⊞ ♨ ♪ ⊙ ⊣
⊡ ⊠ ⊕ ⊞ ⊡ ☀
**Nearby Facilities** ↑ ✈ ⚓ ⊀
**Acreage** 6¼ **Open** April/Easter to September
**Access** Good **Site** Level
Sheltered, level site in a picturesque wooded valley with river frontage. Fishing, pub food opposite. Indoor swimming pool nearby. Ideal centre for Plymouth, Cornwall and Devon.
**Nearest Town/Resort** Plymouth
**Directions** A38, 3½ miles west of Tamar Bridge, Plymouth, signposted Notter Bridge.
⚘ Plymouth

## SENNEN
**Seaview Holiday Park,** Sennen, Lands End, Cornwall, TR19 7AD
**Tel:** 01736 871266 **Fax:** 01736 871190
**Pitches For ▲ ⊕ ⊟ Total** 160
**Facilities** ⚏ ♪ ⊟ ⊡ ⊞ ♨ ♪ ⊙ ⊣ ⊟ ⊡ ☎
ℳ ⊠ ⊕ ⊠ ✗ ⊡ ⊡ ⊿ ⊕ ⊡ ⊡
**Nearby Facilities** ↑ ✈ ⚓ ⊀ ∪ ♪ ⊁
**Acreage** 11 **Open** All Year
**Access** Good **Site** Level
½ mile to Whitesands Bay Blue Flag beach with surfing. Sennen Cove, Lands End and coastal walks.
**Nearest Town/Resort** Penzance
**Directions** From Penzance take the A30 signposted Lands End. Stay on the A30 and Sennen Village is just before Lands End.
⚘ Penzance

## ST. AGNES
**Beacon Cottage Farm Touring Park,** Beacon Drive, St Agnes, Cornwall, TR5 0NU
**Tel:** 01872 552347/553381
**Email:** beaconcottagefarm@lineone.net
**www.** beaconcottagefarmholidays.co.uk
**Pitches For ▲ ⊕ ⊟ Total** 60
**Facilities** ⚏ ♪ ⊞ ♨ ♪ ⊙ ⊣ ⊟ ⊡ ☎
ℳ ⊕ ⊠ ⊡ ♥ ⊡ ⊡ ⊡ ☀
**Nearby Facilities** ↑ ✈ ⚓ ⊀ ∪ ♪ ⊁
**Acreage** 4 **Open** April to September
**Access** Good **Site** Level
On working farm, surrounded by National Trust land. Sandy beach 1 mile, beautiful sea views.
**Nearest Town/Resort** St. Agnes
**Directions** From A30, take B3277 to St. Agnes, take road to the Beacon. Follow signs to site.
⚘ Truro

## ST. AGNES
**Presingoll Farm Caravan & Camping Park,** St Agnes, Cornwall, TR5 0PB
**Tel:** 01872 552333
**Email:** pam@presingollfarm.fsbusiness.co.uk
**www.** presingollfarm.fsbusiness.co.uk
**Pitches For ▲ ⊕ ⊟ Total** 90
**Facilities** ⚏ ♪ ⊟ ⊡ ⊞ ♨ ♪ ⊙ ⊣ ⊟ ⊡ ☎
ℳ ⊠ ⊡ ⊞ ⊡
**Nearby Facilities** ↑ ✈ ∪ ♪ ⊁
**Acreage** 3½ **Open** Easter to End October
**Access** Good **Site** Level
Working farm overlooking the North

Cornwall coastline. Near the Cornish Coastal Path and surf beaches within 2 miles. Ideal for walking. Dogs must be kept on a lead.
**Nearest Town/Resort** St. Agnes
**Directions** Leave the A30 at Chiverton Cross roundabout and take the B3277 for St. Agnes. Site is 3 miles on the right.
⇌ Truro

## ST. AUSTELL
**Croft Farm Holiday Park,** Luxulyan, Bodmin, Cornwall, PL30 5EQ
**Tel:** 01726 850228 **Fax:** 01726 850498
**Email:** lynpick@ukonline.co.uk
**www.** croftfarm.co.uk
**Pitches For** ▲ ➡ **Total** 52
**Facilities** ⏚ 🏠 Ⅶ🄑 ♨ ☂ ⊙ ⏛ 🔌 🅿 🔲 ☎
♨ 🄑 ⚑ 🎱 🕮 🕂🄿 🄑 🄑 🔌 ☙ ∪
**Nearby Facilities** ⌐ ✔ ⌿ ☂ ↘
**Acreage** 4 **Open** 21 March **to** 21 Jan
**Access** Good **Site** Level
David Bellamy Gold Conservation Award winners.
**Nearest Town/Resort** St. Austell
**Directions** From A390 (Liskeard to St Austell) turn right past the level crossing in St Blazey (signposted Luxulyan). In 1¼ miles turn right at T-Junction, continue to next T-Juntion and turn right. The park is on the left within ½ mile. N.B. DO NOT take any other routes signposted Luxulyan/Lux Valley.
⇌ Luxulyan

## ST. AUSTELL
**Pensagillas Park,** Grampound, Truro, Cornwall, TR2 4SR
**Tel:** 01872 530808
**Email:** sales@pensagillas-park.co.uk
**www.** pensagillas-park.co.uk
**Pitches For** ▲ ➡☖ **Total** 65
**Facilities** ⏚ 🄕 Ⅶ🄑 ♨ ☂ ⊙ ⏛ 🔌 🅿 🔲 ☎
♨ 🄑 🎱 🕮 🕂🄿 🄑 🄑 🔌
**Nearby Facilities** ⌐ ✔ ⌿ ☂ ↘ ∪ ♪ ⚘ ✗
**Acreage** 10 **Open** March **to** Oct
**Access** Good **Site** Level
2½ acre course fishing lake, tennis court and small bar on site. Nature trail. Just a 10 minute drive to the beach and Mevagissey.
**Nearest Town/Resort** Mevagissey
**Directions** Take the A390 towards Truro, turn onto the B3287 signposted Tregony and St Mawes. Follow for 1½ miles, at the T-Junction turn left, Park is 1 mile on the right.

## ST. AUSTELL
**River Valley Holiday Park,** London Apprentice, St Austell, Cornwall, PL26 7AP
**Tel:** 01726 73533 **Fax:** 01726 73533
**Email:** river.valley@tesco.net
**www.** cornwall-holidays.co.uk
**Pitches For** ▲ ➡ **Total** 40
**Facilities** ⏚ 🄕 Ⅶ🄑 ♨ ☂ ⊙ ⏛ 🔌 🅿 🔲 ☎
♨ 🄑 ⚑ 🕮 🕂🄿 🄑 🄑 🔌 ⚘ ✗

**Nearby Facilities** ⌐ ✔ ⌿ ☂ ↘ ✗ ♪ ✗
**Acreage** 9 **Open** 15 March **to** 5 Oct
**Access** Good **Site** Level
Alongside a river with woodland walk and cycle trail to the beach.
**Nearest Town/Resort** St Austell
**Directions** Take the B3273 from St Austell to Mevagissey, 1 mile to London Apprentice, site is on the left hand side.
⇌ St Austell

## ST. AUSTELL
**Sun Valley Holiday Park,** Pentewan Road, St Austell, Cornwall, PL26 6DJ
**Tel:** 01726 843266
**Email:** reception@sunvalleyholidays.co.uk
**www.** sunvalleyholidays.co.uk
**Pitches For** ▲ ➡ **Total** 22
**Facilities** ⏚ 🄕 🄓 Ⅶ🄑 ♨ ☂ ⊙ ⏛ 🔌 🅿 🔲 ☎
♨ 🄑 ⚑ 🎱 🕮 🕂🄿 🄑♨ 🄑 🔌
**Nearby Facilities** ⌐ ✔ ⌿ ☂ ↘ ∪ ♪
**Acreage** 20 **Open** April **to** October
**Access** Good **Site** Level
Site situated in woodland and pasture surrounding. 1 mile from sea. Ideal touring centre. Tennis on site. Close to Eden Project.
**Nearest Town/Resort** Mevagissey
**Directions** Take B3273 from St. Austell, site 1 mile past 'London Apprentice', on right.
⇌ St. Austell

## ST. AUSTELL
**Trencreek Farm Country Holiday Park,** Hewas Water, St Austell, Cornwall, PL26 7JG
**Tel:** 01726 882540 **Fax:** 01726 883254
**Email:** reception@trencreek.co.uk
**www.** trencreek.co.uk
**Pitches For** ▲ ➡ **Total** 198
**Facilities** ⏚ ⏚ 🄕 Ⅶ🄑 ♨ ☂ ⊙ ⏛ 🔌 🅿 🔲 ☎
♨ 🄑 🄑 ⚑ 🕮 ♨ 🕂🄿 🄑♨ 🄑 🔌
**Nearby Facilities** ⌐ ✔ ⌿ ☂ ↘ ∪ ♪
**Acreage** 56 **Open** Easter **to** End October
**Access** Good **Site** Level
Kids Club in main season and 4 fishing lakes on site.
**Nearest Town/Resort** St. Austell
⇌ St. Austell

## ST. AUSTELL
**Treveor Farm Caravan & Camping Site,** Gorran, St Austell, Cornwall, PL26 6LW
**Tel:** 01726 842387 **Fax:** 01726 842387
**Email:** info@treveorfarm.co.uk
**www.** treveorfarm.co.uk
**Pitches For** ▲ ➡ **Total** 50
**Facilities** ⏚ Ⅶ🄑 ♨ ☂ ⊙ ⏛ 🔌 🅿 🔲 ☎
**Nearby Facilities** ⌐ ✔ ⌿ ☂ ↘
**Acreage** 4 **Open** April **to** Oct
**Access** Good **Site** Level
1 mile to the beach and coastal path. 3 miles from the Lost Gardens of Heligan and only 15 minutes from the Eden Project.
**Nearest Town** St Austell/Gorran Haven

**Directions** Take the B3273 from St Austell towards Mevagissey. After Pentewan at top of the hill turn right to Gorran. After approx 4 miles turn right into the park at the signboard.
⇌ St Austell

## ST. AUSTELL
**Trewhiddle Holiday Estate,** Pentewan Road, St Austell, Cornwall, PL26 7AD
**Tel:** 01726 879420 **Fax:** 01726 879421
**Email:** dmcclelland@btconnect.com
**www.** trewhiddle.co.uk
**Pitches For** ▲ ➡ **Total** 105
**Facilities** ⏚ Ⅶ🄑 ♨ ☂ ⊙ ⏛ 🔌 🅿 🔲 ☎
♨ 🄑 🄑 ⚑ 🎱 🕮 ♨ 🕂🄿 🄑 🄑 🔌 🔲
**Nearby Facilities** ⌐ ✔ ⌿ ☂ ↘
**Acreage** 16½ **Open** All Year
**Access** Good **Site** Lev/Slope
Only 15 minutes from Eden Project and Heligan Gardens. Three beaches within four miles.
**Nearest Town/Resort** St. Austell
**Directions** From St Austell take the B3273 towards Mevagissey. Trewhiddle is ¾ miles from the roundabout on the right.
⇌ St. Austell

## ST. BURYAN
**Tower Park Caravans & Camping,** St Buryan, Penzance, Cornwall, TR19 6BZ
**Tel:** 01736 810286
**Email:** enquiries@towerparkcamping.co.uk
**www.** towerparkcamping.co.uk
**Pitches For** ▲ ➡ **Total** 102
**Facilities** ⏚ ⏚ 🄕 Ⅶ🄑 ♨ ☂ ⊙ ⏛ 🔌 🅿 🔲 ☎
♨ 🄑 🄑 ⚑ 🕮 ♨ 🕂🄿 🄑 🔌
**Nearby Facilities** ⌐ ✔ ⌿ ☂ ↘ ∪ ♪ ✗
**Acreage** 12 **Open** March **to** January
**Access** Good **Site** Level
Quiet, rural park located midway between Penzance and Lands End. Ideal touring and walking in West Cornwall.
**Nearest Town/Resort** Penzance
**Directions** From the A30 Lands End road turn left onto the B3283 towards St. Buryan. In the village turn right again and the park is 300 yards on the right.
⇌ Penzance

## ST. BURYAN
**Treverven Touring Caravan & Camping Park,** Treverven Farm, St Buryan, Penzance, Cornwall, TR19 6DL
**Tel:** 01736 810200
**www.** chycor.co.uk/camping/treverven
**Pitches For** ▲ ➡ **Total** 115
**Facilities** ⏚ ⏚ 🄕 🄕 Ⅶ🄑 ♨ ☂ ⊙ ⏛ 🔌 🅿 🔲 ☎
♨ 🄑 🄑 ⚑ 🕂🄿 🄑 🄑 🔌
**Nearby Facilities** ⌐ ✔ ⌿ ☂ ↘ ∪ ♪ ✗ ✗
**Acreage** 7 **Open** Easter **to** End Oct
**Access** Good **Site** Level
In an area of outstanding natural beauty with wonderful scenery. Direct access onto the South West Coastal Path. Four

beaches within 3 miles.
**Nearest Town/Resort** Penzance
**Directions** From Penzance By-Pass take the A30 to Catchall, after approx. 3 miles turn left onto the B3283 and drive into St. Buryan Village. Go straight through the village and after 2 miles turn left onto the B3315.
♒ Penzance

## ST. IVES
**Ayr Holiday Park,** Ayr, St Ives, Cornwall, TR26 1EJ
**Tel:** 01736 795855 **Fax:** 01736 798797
**Email:** recept@ayrholidaypark.co.uk
**www.** ayrholidaypark.co.uk
**Pitches For** ⚊ ⊞ ⊞ **Total** 35
**Facilities** ⚭ ⎰ ▣ ▣ ▣ ♨ ⚑ ☉ ◡ ▱ ◻ ⊡
▥ ▯ ⊙ ⊟ ☜ ⚑ ⊞ ▱ ⊡ ◻
**Nearby Facilities** ⌐ ✔ ⚓ ⚲ ∪ ⇵ ♗ ⚞
**Acreage** 4 **Open** All Year
**Access** Good **Site** Sloping
Just a 10 minute walk to the town centre, harbour and beaches. Beautiful coastal views.
**Nearest Town/Resort** St. Ives
**Directions** To avoid the town centre, follow holiday route to St. Ives. From the B3306, ½ mile from the town centre turn left into Carnellis Road, follow road to the park entrance on the left.
♒ St. Ives

## ST. IVES
**Balnoon Camping Site,** Balnoon, Nr Halsetown, St Ives, Cornwall, TR26 3JA
**Tel:** 01736 795431
**Email:** nat@balnoon.fsnet.co.uk
**Pitches For** ⚊ ⊞ ⊞ **Total** 23
**Facilities** ⎰ ▣ ⌐ ☉ ☜ ⚑ ▱ ⊙⇥⊡
**Nearby Facilities** ⌐ ✔ ∪ ◿
**Acreage** 1 **Open** Easter **to** October
**Access** Good **Site** Level
Situated in the countryside with views of

adjacent rolling hills. Equidistant from the beautiful beaches of Carbis Bay and St. Ives, approx. 2 miles.
**Nearest Town/Resort** St. Ives
**Directions** From the A30 take the A3074 for St. Ives, at the second mini-roundabout turn first left signposted St. Ives Day Visitors (B3311), turn second right signposted Balnoon. Approx. 3 miles from the A30.
♒ St. Ives

## ST. IVES
**Higher Chellew,** Higher Trenowin, Nancledra, Penzance, Cornwall, TR20 8BD
**Tel:** 01736 364532 **Fax:** 01736 332380
**Email:** higherchellew@btinternet.com
**www.** higherchellewcamping.co.uk
**Pitches For** ⚊ ⊞ ⊞ **Total** 30
**Facilities** ⎰ ▣ ⚑ ⌐ ☉ ☜ ⚑ ▱ ◻ ⊙⇥⊡
**Nearby Facilities** ⌐ ✔ ⚓ ⚲ ∪ ⇵ ♗
**Acreage** 1¼ **Open** 1st Friday before Easter **to** End Oct
**Access** Good **Site** Level
Peaceful and private small site with spectacular walks in the area. Near St Michaels Mount.
**Nearest Town/Resort** St Ives/Penzance
**Directions** On the B3311 in between Penzance and St Ives.
♒ St Ives/Penzance

## ST. IVES
**Little Trevarrack Tourist Park,** Laity Lane, Carbis Bay, St Ives, Cornwall, TR26 3HW
**Tel:** 01736 797580
**Email:** littletrevarrack@hotmail.com
**www.** littletrevarrack.com
**Pitches For** ⚊ ⊞ ⊞ **Total** 232
**Facilities** ⚭ ⎰ ▣ ⚑ ⌐ ☉ ☜ ⚑ ▱ ◻ ⊡
▯ ⊙ ⚑ ⌂ ▱ ✿⇥▱ ◻ ⊡ ⚬
**Nearby Facilities** ⌐ ✔ ⚓ ⚲ ∪ ⇵ ♗
**Acreage** 20 **Open** Easter **to** Oct
**Access** Good **Site** Lev/Slope

Near the beach. Bus service to St. Ives in high season only. Ideal for touring West Cornwall. 2 dogs allowed per pitch.
**Nearest Town/Resort** St. Ives
**Directions** Turn off the A30 onto the A3074 towards St. Ives. At Carbis Bay the site is signposted left opposite the junction to the beach, turn left and follow for 150 yards to the crossroads, go straight across and the site is 150m on the right.
♒ Carbis Bay

## ST. IVES
**Penderleath Caravan & Camping Park,** Towednack, St Ives, Cornwall, TR26 3AF
**Tel:** 01736 798403 **Fax:** 01736 798403
**Email:** penderleath@aol.com
**www.** penderleath.co.uk
**Pitches For** ⚊ ⊞ ⊞ **Total** 75
**Facilities** ⚭ ⎰ ▣ ⚑ ⌐ ☉ ☜ ⚑ ▱ ◻ ⊡
▥ ▯ ⊙ ⊟ ☓ ⚑ ⌂ ⚑ ✿⇥▱ ◻ ⊡
**Nearby Facilities** ⌐ ✔ ⚓ ⚲ ∪ ⇵ ♗ ⚞
**Acreage** 10 **Open** Easter **to** Oct
**Access** Good **Site** Lev/Slope
Set in a classified area of outstanding natural beauty, with fabulous views over countryside to the sea. Very peaceful and tranquil. Outside the main season we offer an Adults Only Camping Area.
**Nearest Town/Resort** St. Ives
**Directions** From the A30 take the A3074 signposted St. Ives. At the second mini roundabout turn left, at the end of the road turn left then immediately right, turn left at next fork.

## ST. IVES
**Polmanter Tourist Park,** Halsetown, St Ives, Cornwall, TR26 3LX
**Tel:** 01736 795640 **Fax:** 01736 795640
**Email:** reception@polmanter.com
**www.** polmanter.com

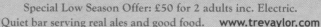
**Pitches For** ♦ ⚑ ⚑ **Total** 240
**Facilities** ⚎ ⏚ ⎕ ⎗ ⌂ ⏛ ⍾ ⎗ ☐ ❦
⚏ ⊙ ⊗ ✗ ⟟ ⚑ ↺ ✿ ⊞ ⊟ ⊡
**Nearby Facilities** ⌙ ✓ ⚓ ↺ ∪ ⚲ ♪ ⚡
**Acreage** 20 **Open** April **to** October
**Access** Good **Site** Level
Just 1½ miles from St. Ives and beaches.
Central for touring the whole of West
Cornwall. Tennis on park. Dump station for
motorised caravans.
**Nearest Town/Resort** St. Ives
**Directions** Take the A3074 to St. Ives from
the A30. First left at the mini-roundabout
taking Holiday Route to St. Ives (Halsetown).
Turn right at the Halsetown Inn, then first left.
⇌ St. Ives

## ST. IVES
**St. Ives Bay Holiday Park,** Upton Towans,
Hayle, Cornwall, TR27 5BH
**Tel:** 01736 Hayle 752274 **Fax:** 01736 754523
**Email:** stivesbay@btconnect.com
**www.** stivesbay.co.uk
**Pitches For** ♦ ⚑ ⚑ **Total** 200
**Facilities** ⎕ ⌂ ⊙ ⌣ ⎕ ⚏ ⊙ ⊗ ✗ ⏉
⟟ ⚑ ⎅ ⊟ ⎕
**Nearby Facilities** ⌙ ✓ ⚓ ↺ ∪ ⚲
**Acreage** 12 **Open** May **to** September
**Access** Good **Site** Lev/Slope
Park adjoining own sandy beach, onto St.
Ives Bay. Children very welcome. Sea
views. Dogs no longer accepted. Dial-a-
Brochure 24 hours, Mr R. White. (See our
display advertisement).

**Nearest Town/Resort** Hayle
**Directions** A30 from Camborne to Hayle, at
roundabout take Hayle turn-off and then turn
right onto B3301, 600yds on left enter park.
⇌ Hayle

## ST. IVES
**Trevalgan Touring Park,** Trevalgan, St.
Ives, Cornwall, TR26 3BJ
**Tel:** 01736 796433 **Fax:** 01736 796433
**Email:** recept@trevalgantouringpark.co.uk
**www.** trevalgantouringpark.co.uk
**Pitches For** ♦ ⚑ ⚑ **Total** 120
**Facilities** ⚎ ⌂ ⏚ ⎕ ⏛ ⌂ ⊙ ⌣ ⊟ ⎕ ⎗
⚏ ⎔ ⊙ ⊗ ✗ ⟟ ⚑ ⎅ ↺ ✿ ⊞ ⊟ ⎕
**Nearby Facilities** ⌙ ✓ ⚓ ↺ ∪ ⚲ ♪ ⚡
**Acreage** 8 **Open** May **to** Sept
**Access** Good **Site** Level
In delightful countryside with many walks.
Near the coastal footpath.
**Nearest Town/Resort** St. Ives
**Directions** Follow the B3306 St Ives to
Lands End road for 1½ miles, follow brown
Trevalgan sign.
⇌ St. Ives

## ST. JUST
**Roselands Caravan Park,** Dowran, St
Just, Penzance, Cornwall, TR19 7RS
**Tel:** 01736 788571
**Email:**
camping@roseland84.freeserve.co.uk
**www.** roselands.co.uk
**Pitches For** ♦ ⚑ ⚑ **Total** 30

**Facilities** ⏛ ⎕ ⚑ ⌂ ⊙ ⌣ ⊟ ☐ ⎗
⚏ ⊙ ⊗ ✗ ⚲ ⌣ ⟟ ⚑ ⊟ ⎕
**Nearby Facilities** ⌙ ✓ ⚓ ↺ ∪ ⚲ ♪ ⚡
**Acreage** 3 **Open** January **to** October
**Access** Good **Site** Level
Close to the sea. Ideal for walking and bird
watching. All attractions nearby. 5 miles
from Lands End. Cycle hire on site.
**Nearest Town/Resort** Penzance
**Directions** From the A30 Penzance by-pass
take the A3071 to St. Just for 5 miles, turn
left at sign and park is 800 yards.
⇌ Penzance

## ST. JUST
**Secret Garden Caravan Park,** Bosavern
House, St Just, Penzance, Cornwall, TR19
7RD
**Tel:** 01736 788301 **Fax:** 01736 788301
**Email:** mail@bosavern.com
**www.** secretbosavern.com
**Pitches For** ♦ ⚑ ⚑ **Total** 12
**Facilities** ⎕ ⏛ ⌂ ⊙ ⌣ ⊟ ☐ ⎗
⊗ ✗ ⟟ ⎕ ⊟ ⎕
**Nearby Facilities** ⌙ ✓ ⚓ ↺ ∪ ⚲ ♪ ⚡
**Acreage** 1 **Open** March **to** October
**Access** Good **Site** Level
Walled garden site surrounded by trees
and flowers. Excellent walking country,
good beaches nearby. Local authorities
licensed site.
**Nearest Town/Resort** St. Just/Penzance
**Directions** Take the A3071 from Penzance
towards St. Just. Approximately 550yds

**'Say Hello to a New Experience'**

**www.trethem.com**

**01875 580504**

ST. JUST-IN-ROSELAND,
TRURO, CORNWALL TR2 5JF

before St. Just turn left onto the B3306 signposted Lands End and airport. Bosavern Garden Caravan Park is 500yds from the turn off, behind Bosavern House.
⇥ Penzance

## ST. JUST

**Trevaylor Caravan & Camping Park,** Botallack, St Just, Cornwall, TR19 7PU
**Tel:** 01736 787016
**Email:** bookings@trevaylor.com
**www.** trevaylor.com
**Pitches For** ▲ ⚲ 🚐 **Total** 85
Facilities �🏂 🔟 ⚡ ♠ 𝄞 ⊙ ┙ 🝙 ◻ 🍺
♒ 🜨 🌢 ✕ ♫ 🅿️ ⊞ 🍴 🔲 ⅏
**Nearby Facilities** ┌ 🏌 ⚓ 🎣 ∪ ⅃ ⚞
**Acreage** 5 **Open** Mid March **to** October
**Access** Good **Site** Level
Easy access to the golden sands, rugged cliffs and white surf of the Atlantic Ocean. 500 metres from the coastal path and Crown Mines. Bar serving real ale and good food on site.
**Nearest Town/Resort** Sennen Cove/St. Just
**Directions** Situated on the B3306 Lands End to St Ives road, approx 1 mile to the north of St Just.
⇥ Penzance

## ST. MAWES

**Trethem Mill Touring Park,** St Just-in-Roseland, Truro, Cornwall, TR2 5JF
**Tel:** 01872 580504 **Fax:** 01872 580968
**Email:** reception@trethem.com
**www.** trethem.com
**Pitches For** ▲ ⚲ 🚐 **Total** 84
Facilities ⅃ ⏛ 🔟 ⚡ ♠ 𝄞 ⊙ ┙ 🝙 ◻ 🍺
♒ 🜨 🌢 🅿️ ⊞ 🔲 ⅏
**Nearby Facilities** ┌ 🏌 ⚓ 🎣 ∪ ⅃ ⅃
**Acreage** 4 **Open** April **to** Mid Oct
**Access** Good **Site** Lev/Slope
Discover the unexplored Roseland, staying on the only 5 Star Park on the Peninsula. Family owned and run, we offer a relaxing and tranquil setting. Ideally located for for walking, sailing, beaches and gardens. 'Caravan Park of the Year' Cornwall Tourist Board Awards 2002.
**Nearest Town/Resort** St. Mawes
**Directions** From Tregony follow the A3078 to St. Mawes. Approx. 2 miles after passing through Trewithian look out for caravan and camping sign.
⇥ Truro

## ST. MERRYN

**Tregavone Farm Touring Park,** St Merryn, Padstow, Cornwall, PL28 8JZ
**Tel:** 01841 520148
**Pitches For** ▲ ⚲ 🚐 **Total** 40
Facilities ⚡ ⅃ 🔟 ♠ 𝄞 ⊙ ┙ 🝙 🍺 🅿️⊞ 🔲
**Nearby Facilities** ┌ 🏌 ⚓ 🎣 ∪ ⅃ ⚞ ⅃
**Acreage** 4 **Open** March **to** October
**Access** Good **Site** Level
Quiet family run site situated near sandy surfing beaches, country views, well maintained and grassy. AA 2 Pennants.
**Nearest Town/Resort** Padstow
**Directions** Turn right off the A39 (Wadebridge-St. Columb) onto A389 (Padstow) come to a T-junction and turn right, in 1 mile turn left, entrance on left after 1 mile.
⇥ Newquay

## ST. MERRYN

**Trethias Farm Caravan Park,** St Merryn, Padstow, Cornwall, PL28 8PL
**Tel:** 01841 520323
**Email:** trethias@freeuk.com
**Pitches For** ▲ ⚲ 🚐 **Total** 62
Facilities ⅃ 🔟 ♠ 𝄞 ⊙ ┙ 🝙 🅿️ 🝙 ⊞ 🔲
**Nearby Facilities** ┌ 🏌 ⚓ ∪ ⅃
**Acreage** 12 **Open** April **to** September
**Access** Good **Site** Level
Near beach, scenic views. Couples and family groups only. ETB 3 Star Graded 2004 and David Bellamy Gold Award for Conservation 2004.
**Nearest Town/Resort** Padstow
**Directions** From Wadebridge follow signs to St. Merryn, go past Farmers Arms, third turning right (our signs from here).

## ST. MERRYN

**Trevean Farm Caravan & Camping Park,** St Merryn, Padstow, Cornwall, PL28 8PR
**Tel:** 01841 520772 **Fax:** 01841 520772
**www.** bhhpa.org.uk/treveanfarmc+cpark
**Pitches For** ▲ ⚲ 🚐 **Total** 36
Facilities ⅃ 🔟 ♠ 𝄞 ⊙ ┙ 🝙 ◻ 🍺
♒ 🅿️ 🜨 ♫ ⊞ 🔲 🍴 ⅏
**Nearby Facilities** ┌ 🏌 ⚓ 🎣 ∪ ⅃ ⅃
**Acreage** 2 **Open** April **to** October
**Access** Good **Site** Level
Situated near seaweed sandy, surfing beaches. ETC 3 Star Grading.
**Nearest Town/Resort** Padstow
**Directions** From St. Merryn village take the B3276 Newquay road for 1 mile. Turn left for Rumford, site ¼ mile on the right.
⇥ Newquay

## ST. MERRYN

**Treyarnon Bay Caravan & Camping Park,** Treyarnon Bay, Padstow, Cornwall, PL28 8JP
**Tel:** 01841 520681 **Fax:** 01841 520681
**www.** treyarnonbay.co.uk
**Pitches For** ▲ ⚲ 🚐 **Total** 60
Facilities ⅃ 🔟 ♠ 𝄞 ⊙ ┙ 🝙 ◻ ♒ 🍺 🜨 🔲
**Nearby Facilities** ┌ 🏌 ∪
**Acreage** 4 **Open** April **to** Sept
**Access** Good **Site** Level
200 yards from the beach, overlooking Treyarnon Bay. Ideal family park.
**Nearest Town/Resort** Padstow
**Directions** From Wadebridge take the A389 west and follow signs to St. Merryn and Treyarnon Bay. 3½ miles from Padstow.
⇥ Bodmin/Newquay

## ST. MINVER

**St. Minver Holiday Village,** St Minver, Wadebridge, Cornwall, PL27 6RR
**Tel:** 01208 862305 **Fax:** 01208 862265
**Email:** enquiries@parkdeanholidays.com
**www.** parkdeanholidays.co.uk
**Pitches For** ▲ ⚲ 🚐 **Total** 33
Facilities ⅃ 🔟 ♠ 𝄞 ⊙ ♒ 🝙 🜨 ✕ ♇ 🄿 ♣
🜨 ✈ 🌢 🅿️ 🔲 ⅏
**Nearby Facilities** ┌ ⅃ ⅃
**Acreage** 44 **Open** March **to** Oct
**Access** Good **Site** Level
Set in stunning Cornish countryside, only 2 miles from Rock and Polzeath beaches.
**Nearest Town/Resort** Wadebridge
**Directions** Follow the M4 to Exeter and take

the A30 signposted Okehampton to Bodmin. Then take the A389 to Wadebridge, head towards Port Isaac and Rock.
⇥ Wadebridge

## TINTAGEL

**Bossiney Farm Caravan Site,** Tintagel, Cornwall, PL34 0AY
**Tel:** 01840 770481
**www.** bossineyfarm.co.uk
**Pitches For** ▲ ⚲ 🚐 **Total** 54
Facilities ⅃ 🔟 ♠ 𝄞 ⊙ ┙
🔲 ♒ 🜨 🅿️ 🔲
**Nearby Facilities** ┌ 🏌 ⚓ ∪ ⅃
**Acreage** 2 **Open** April **to** October
**Access** Good **Site** Lev/Slope
Ideal touring centre, near beach, inland views.
**Nearest Town/Resort** Tintagel
**Directions** ¾ miles from centre of Tintagel on main Boscastle road.
⇥ Bodmin Parkway

## TINTAGEL

**The Headland Caravan & Camping Park,** Atlantic Road, Tintagel, Cornwall, PL34 0DE
**Tel:** 01840 770239 **Fax:** 01840 770925
**Email:** headland.caravan@btconnect.com
**www.** headlandcaravanpark.co.uk
**Pitches For** ▲ ⚲ 🚐 **Total** 60
Facilities ⅃ 🔟 ♠ 𝄞 ⊙ ┙ 🝙 🔲 🍺
♒ 🜨 🜨 ⊞ 🔲
**Nearby Facilities** ┌ 🏌 ⚓ ∪ ⅃
**Acreage** 4 **Open** Easter **to** October
**Access** Good **Site** Lev/Slope
Three beaches within walking distance. Scenic views. Ideal touring centre. Facilities for the disabled planned for the 2006 season.
**Nearest Town/Resort** Tintagel
**Directions** Follow camping/caravan signs from B3263 through village to Headland.
⇥ Bodmin Parkway

## TINTAGEL

**Trewethett Farm Caravan Club Site,** Trethevy, Tintagel, Cornwall, PL34 0BQ
**Tel:** 01840 770222
**www.** caravanclub.co.uk
**Pitches For** ▲ ⚲ 🚐 **Total** 124
Facilities ⅃ 🔟 ♠ 𝄞 ⊙ 🔲 🜨 🜨 ⊞ 🔲
**Nearby Facilities** ┌ 🏌
**Acreage** 15 **Open** March **to** Oct
**Access** Good **Site** Level
Breathtaking views overlooking Bossiney Cove. ½ mile from a sandy beach. Spectacular clifftop walks. Near Tintagel Castle, picturesque ports and harbours. Non members welcome. Booking essential.
**Nearest Town/Resort** Tintagel
**Directions** From NE on the A30, turn onto the A395 via slip road. After 11 miles at the T-junction turn right onto the A39, after 1 mile just before the transmitter turn left, at junction turn right onto the B3266. After 2½ miles at the junction on the bend turn left onto the B3263, site is on the right.

## TRURO

**Carnon Downs Caravan & Camping Park,** Carnon Downs, Truro, Cornwall, TR3 6JJ
**Tel:** 01872 862283

Email: info@carnon-downs-caravanpark.co.uk
www. carnon-downs-caravanpark.co.uk
Pitches For ⅄ ⬡ ⬢ Total 110
Facilities
Nearby Facilities
Acreage 20 Open All Year
Access Good Site Level
Quiet, family run park with good quality facilities. Ideally central for touring. Excellent location for sailing and water sports. David Bellamy Gold Award for Conservation and ETB 5 Star 'Exceptional' Graded.
Nearest Town/Resort Truro
Directions On the A39 Falmouth road, 3 miles West of Truro.
⚊ Truro

### TRURO

Chacewater Camping & Caravan Park, Coxhill, Chacewater, Truro, Cornwall, TR4 8LY
Tel: 01209 820762
Email: chacewaterpark@aol.com
www. chacewaterpark.co.uk
Pitches For ⅄ ⬡ ⬢ Total 100
Facilities
Nearby Facilities
Acreage 6 Open May to End September
Access Good Site Level
Exclusively for Adults. The ideal holiday base for the Over 30's.
Nearest Town/Resort Truro
Directions From A30 take the A3047 to Scorrier. Turn left at Crossroads Hotel onto the B3298. 1½ miles left to Chacewater ½ mile sign directs you to the park.
⚊ Truro

### TRURO

Cosawes Park, Cosawes Park Homes, Perranarworthal, Truro, Cornwall, TR3 7QS
Tel: 01872 863724 Fax: 01872 870268
Email: info@cosawes.com
www. cosawes.com
Pitches For ⅄ ⬡ ⬢ Total 50
Facilities
Nearby Facilities
Acreage 4 Open All Year
Access Good Site Lev/Slope
Situated in a 100 acre wooded valley, an area of outstanding natural beauty. New pitches for 2006. Near to local beaches, Flambards and the city of Truro.
Nearest Town/Resort Truro/Falmouth
Directions From Truro take the A39, as you exit the village of Perranarworthal take signposted turning on the right.

### TRURO

Summer Valley Touring Park, Shortlanesend, Truro, Cornwall, TR4 9DW
Tel: 01872 277878
Email: chris@summervalley.co.uk
www. summervalley.co.uk
Pitches For ⅄ ⬡ ⬢ Total 50
Facilities
Nearby Facilities
Acreage 3 Open April to October
Access Good Site Sloping
Ideal touring centre for all of Cornwall.
Nearest Town/Resort Truro
Directions 2½ miles north of Truro on the B3284 Perranporth road.

### TRURO

Veryan Camping & Caravanning Club Site, Tretheake Manor, Veryan, Truro, Cornwall, TR2 5PP
Tel: 01872 501658

www. campingandcaravanningclub.co.uk
Pitches For ⅄ ⬡ ⬢ Total 150
Facilities
Acreage 9 Open 25 March to 1 Nov
Access Good Site Sloping
Ideal for exploring the beaches and coves of the Cornish Coast. BTB 4 Star Graded and AA 3 Pennants. Non members welcome.
Nearest Town/Resort Veryan
Directions Take the A390 from St. Austell, leave at the A3078 sign on the left, turn left at the filling station and follow international signs.
⚊ Truro

### WADEBRIDGE

Gunvenna Caravan & Camping Park, St Minver, Wadebridge, Cornwall, PL27 6QN
Tel: 01208 862405 Fax: 01208 862405
Pitches For ⅄ ⬡ ⬢ Total 75
Facilities
Nearby Facilities
Acreage 10 Open Easter to October
Access Good Site Lev/Slope
Polzeath and rock beaches. Good sandy beaches.
Nearest Town/Resort Wadebridge
Directions Take the A30 to Bodmin then the A389 to Wadebridge. Take the A39 to Polzeath then the B3314, remain on this road and Gunvenna Caravan Park is on the right hand side.
⚊ Bodmin

### WADEBRIDGE

Little Bodieve Holiday Park, Bodieve Road, Wadebridge, Cornwall, PL27 6EG
Tel: 01208 812323
Email:
berry@littlebodieveholidaypark.fsnet.co.uk
www. littlebodieve.co.uk

Pitches For ▲ ⬤ ⬤ Total 195
Facilities ⬤ ! ⬛ ⬛ ⬛ ⬛ ⬛ ⬛ ⬛ ⬛ ⬛ ⬛ ⬛ ⬛ ⬛ ⬛ ⬛ ⬛
Nearby Facilities ⬛ ⬛ ⬛ ⬛ ⬛ ⬛
Acreage 22 Open Late March to October
Access Good Site Level
Friendly family park. Near to the Camel
Trail, close to superb beaches and golf
courses. Ideal touring centre, Eden Project
and many attractions within 25 minutes.
Free hot showers, heated outdoor pool,
crazy golf, pets corner, meals & take-away
and entertainment in main season. Luxury
caravans for hire and sale. Short breaks
available. Brochure on request.
Nearest Town/Resort Wadebridge
Directions 1 mile north of Wadebridge Town
centre off the A39 trunk road. 1/3rd mile on
the B3314 road to Rock and Port Isaac.
⇌ Bodmin Parkway

## WADEBRIDGE
**Ponderosa Caravan Park,** St Issey,
Wadebridge, Cornwall, PL27 7QA
**Tel:** 01841 540359
Pitches For ▲ ⬤ ⬤
Facilities ! ⬛ ⬛ ⬛ ⬛ ⬛ ⬛ ⬛ ⬛ ⬛ ⬛
Nearby Facilities ⬛ ⬛ ⬛ ⬛ ⬛ ⬛
Acreage 4 Open 1 April to Oct
Access Good Site Lev/Slope
Close to the Camel Trail, Creely Leisure
Park and the Eden Project.
Nearest Town/Resort Padstow
Directions On the main road between
Wadebridge and Padstow. 3½ miles from
Wadebridge.
⇌ Bodmin Parkway

## WIDEMOUTH BAY
**Widemouth Bay Caravan Park,** John
Fowler Holidays, Widemouth Bay, Bude,
Cornwall, EX23 0DF
**Tel:** 01271 866766 **Fax:** 01271 866791
**Email:** bookings@johnfowlerholidays.com
**www.** johnfowlerholidays.com
Pitches For ▲ ⬤ ⬤ Total 200
Facilities ⬤ ! ⬛ ⬛ ⬛ ⬛ ⬛ ⬛ ⬛ ⬛ ⬛
⬛ ⬛ ⬛ ⬛ ⬛ ⬛ ⬛ ⬛ ⬛ ⬛ ⬛ ⬛ ⬛
Nearby Facilities ⬛ ⬛ ⬛ ⬛ ⬛ ⬛
Acreage 50 Open March to October
Access Good Site Level
Close to one of Cornwall's finest surfing
beaches. Perfect location for touring both
Devon and Cornwall.
Nearest Town/Resort Bude
Directions From the M5 take the A361 then
the A39 to Bude. Widemouth Bay is 4 miles
west of Bude, clearly signposted.
⇌ Exeter

# CUMBRIA

## ALLONBY
**Manor House Caravan Park,** Edderside
Road, Allonby, Nr Maryport, Cumbria,
CA15 6RA
**Tel:** 01900. 881236 **Fax:** 01900 881160
**Email:** holidays@manorhousepark.co.uk
www.manorhousepark.co.uk
Pitches For ▲ ⬤ ⬤ Total 30
Facilities ! ⬛ ⬛ ⬛ ⬛ ⬛ ⬛ ⬛ ⬛
⬛ ⬛ ⬛ ⬛ ⬛ ⬛ ⬛ ⬛
Nearby Facilities ⬛ ⬛ ⬛ ⬛ ⬛
Acreage 2 Open March to 15th Nov
Access Good Site Level
1 mile from beach, quiet park. Ideal for
touring North Lakes.
Nearest Town/Resort Allonby
Directions B5300 from Maryport, through
Allonby, 1 mile turn right, park 1 mile on right.
Signposted on main road.
⇌ Maryport

## AMBLESIDE
**Great Langdale National Trust
Campsite,** Great Langdale, Near
Ambleside, Cumbria, LA22 9JU
**Tel:** 01539 437668 **Fax:** 01539 437668
**Email:** langdale.camp@nationaltrust.org.uk
www.langdalecampsite.org.uk
Pitches For ▲ ⬤ Total 300
Facilities ⬤ ⬛ ⬛ ⬛ ⬛ ⬛ ⬛ ⬛ ⬛ ⬛ ⬛
Nearby Facilities ⬛ ⬛
Open All Year Site Level
Spectacular mountain location at the head
of Great Langdale Valley.
Nearest Town/Resort Ambleside
Directions From Ambleside take the A593,
turn right at Skelwith Bridge and the campsite
is 6 miles on the left, just before The Old
Dungeon Ghyll Hotel.
⇌ Windermere

## AMBLESIDE
**Low Wray Campsite,** The National Trust
Campsite, Low Wray, Ambleside, Cumbria,
LA22 0JA
**Tel:** 015394 32810 **Fax:** 015394 32810
**Email:**
lowwraycampsite@nationaltrust.org.uk
www.lowwraycampsite.org.uk
Pitches For ▲ ⬤ Total 200
Facilities ⬤ ⬛ ⬛ ⬛ ⬛ ⬛ ⬛ ⬛ ⬛ ⬛ ⬛
Nearby Facilities ⬛ ⬛ ⬛
Acreage 10 Open Easter to End Oct
Site Lev/Slope
Beautiful lake shore location with
spectacular views.
Nearest Town/Resort Ambleside
Directions From Ambleside take the B5286
towards Hawkshead, signposted off to the
left, approx. 3 miles from Ambleside.
⇌ Windermere

## AMBLESIDE
**Skelwith Fold Caravan Park,** Skelwith
Fold, Ambleside, Cumbria, LA22 0HX
**Tel:** 015394 32277 **Fax:** 015394 34344
**Email:** info@skelwith.com
www.skelwith.com
Pitches For ⬤ ⬤ Total 150
Facilities ⬤ ! ⬛ ⬛ ⬛ ⬛ ⬛ ⬛ ⬛ ⬛ ⬛
⬛ ⬛ ⬛ ⬛ ⬛ ⬛ ⬛ ⬛ ⬛ ⬛ ⬛
Nearby Facilities ⬛ ⬛ ⬛ ⬛ ⬛ ⬛ ⬛
Acreage 130 Open 1 March to 15 Nov
Access Good Site Level
Ideal for walking or exploring the Lake
District.
Nearest Town/Resort Ambleside
Directions 1½ miles from Ambleside on the
B5286 heading for Hawkshead.
⇌ Windermere

## APPLEBY
**Hawkrigg Farm,** Colby, Appleby-in-
Westmorland, Cumbria, CA16 6BB
**Tel:** 017683 51046
Pitches For ▲ ⬤ ⬤ Total 15
Facilities ! ⬛ ⬛ ⬛ ⬛ ⬛ ⬛ ⬛
Nearby Facilities ⬛ ⬛ ⬛
Open All Year
Access Good Site Level
Good views of the Pennines. Ideal for
touring and walking. Near to the Lake
District. Swimming pool nearby. Two hard
standings available.
Nearest Town/Resort Appleby
Directions From Appleby take the B6260
turn west onto the Colby road. In Colby turn
left onto Kings Meaburn Road, take the first
turning right.
⇌ Appleby

## ·APPLEBY
**Silverband Park,** Silverband, Knock, Nr
Appleby, Cumbria, CA16 6DL
**Tel:** 01768 361218
Pitches For ⬤ ⬤ Total 12
Facilities ! ⬛ ⬛ ⬛ ⬛ ⬛ ⬛ ⬛
⬛ ⬛ ⬛ ⬛ ⬛ ⬛
Nearby Facilities ⬛ ⬛ ⬛ ⬛ ⬛
Acreage ½ Open All Year
Access Good Site Sloping
Ideal for touring the Lakes and Fells. Only
two fully serviced pitches available.
Nearest Town/Resort Appleby/Penrith
Directions Turn left off the A66 Penrith to
Scotch Corner road at Kirkby Thore. After 2
miles at T-Junction turn left, after 100 yards
take the first turn right, site is 1 mile on the
right.
⇌ Appleby/Penrith

**APPLEBY**

**Wild Rose Park,** Ormside, Appleby, Cumbria, CA16 6EJ
**Tel:** 017683 51077 **Fax:** 017683 52551
**Email:** reception@wildrose.co.uk
www.wildrose.co.uk
**Pitches For** ⚠ ⊕ ⊕ **Total** 230
**Facilities** ⬡ ⌁ 🔔 🏠 🚽 ⚡ 🌂 ⊙ 🍴 🔲 ☎
🔇 🚿 🐶 ✕ 🚿 🔫 ↷ ✦ ⤴ 🅿 🔲 🔋 ☇
**Nearby Facilities** ↑ ✎
**Acreage** 40 **Open** All Year
**Access** Good **Site** Lev/Slope
Quiet park in unspoilt Eden Valley, superb views. Midway between Lakes and Yorkshire Dales. Secure Storage from Nov to March.
**Nearest Town/Resort** Appleby
**Directions** Centre Appleby take B6260 Kendal for 1½ miles. Left Ormside and Soulby 1½ miles left, ½ mile turn right.
⚑ Appleby

**ARNSIDE/SILVERDALE**

**Fell End Caravan Park,** Slackhead Road, Hale, Nr Milnthorpe, Cumbria, LA7 7BS
**Tel:** 0870 774 4024 **Fax:** 01524 63810
**Email:** enquiries@southlakeland-caravans.co.uk
www.southlakeland-caravans.co.uk
**Pitches For** ⚠ ⊕ ⊕ **Total** 94
**Facilities** ⬡ 🚿 ⌁ 🔔 🏠 🚽 ⚡ ⊙ 🍴
🔲 ☎ 🔇 🚿 🐶 ✕ 🚿 🔫 ↷ ✦ 🅿 🔲 ☇ 🏊
**Nearby Facilities** ↑ ✎ ⤢ ✦ ∪ ⚡
**Acreage** 12 **Open** All Year
**Access** Good **Site** Lev/Slope
In an area of outstanding natural beauty, Fell End is a meticulously kept site with mature gardens and a country inn. Close to Lakes and Dales. Open all year to tourers. Please telephone for special offers.
**Nearest Town/Resort** Arnside/Silverdale
**Directions** Leave the M6 at junction 35, take the A6 north and turn left at Wildlife Oasis

after driving past Esso Fuel Station and follow caravan tourism signs.
⚑ Arnside

**ARNSIDE/SILVERDALE**

**Hall More Caravan Park,** Field House, Hall More, Hale, Nr MilnthorpeCumbria, LA7 7BP
**Tel:** 0870 774 4024 **Fax:** 01524 732034
**Email:** enquiries@southlakeland-caravans.co.uk
www. southlakeland-caravans.co.uk
**Pitches For** ⚠ ⊕ ⊕ **Total** 60
**Facilities** ⌁ 🏠 🚽 ⚡ ⊙ 🍴 🔲 ☎
🔇 🚿 ⤴ 🔲 ☇ 🏊
**Nearby Facilities** ↑ ✎ ∪ ⚡
**Acreage** 5 **Open** March **to** October
**Access** Good **Site** Level
Rural location, excellent for walking, rambling, etc.. Next to a Trout Fishery. Easy access to the Lake District.

# CUMBRIA

**Nearest Town/Resort** Arnside/Milnthorpe
**Directions** Leave the M6 at junction 35, take the A6 north and turn left at Wildlife Oasis (after passing Esso fuel station). Follow signs to Fell End Caravan Park and Hall More is signposted from there.
⚡ Arnside

## ARNSIDE/SILVERDALE
**Holgate's Caravan Parks Ltd.,** Cove Road, Silverdale, Nr Carnforth, Lancashire, LA5 0SH
**Tel:** 01524 701508 **Fax:** 01524 701580
**Email:** caravan@holgates.co.uk
www.holgates.co.uk
**Pitches For** ▲ ☲ ☷ **Total** 70
**Facilities** ᚼ ☕ ╱ ⎕ ⊞ ☷ ♠ ſ ⊙ ▱ ⎕ ☂
ՇҼ ◗ ☒ ✗ ♀ ♠ ⅄ ☼ ♦ ⊬ ⊟ ⊡
**Nearby Facilities** ſ ✔ ∪ ⋔ ♪
**Acreage** 10 **Open** 22 Dec **to** 7 Nov
**Access** Good **Site** Lev/Slope
On Morecambe Bay. In area of outstanding natural beauty. Spa bath, sauna and steam room. Restaurant and bar. Restricted facilities during Winter months. Silver Winner of Excellence in England Award 2002, AA Campsite of the Year Award 1995/96 and Regional Winner for Northern England.
**Nearest Town/Resort** Morecambe
**Directions** 5 miles northwest of Carnforth, between Silverdale and Arnside.
⚡ Silverdale

## BASSENTHWAITE
**Herdwick Croft Caravan Park,** Herdwick Croft, Ousebridge, Bassenthwaite, KeswickCumbria, CA12 4RD
**Tel:** 017687 76605
**Pitches For** ☲ ☷ **Total** 12
**Facilities** ſ ⊞ ⊞ ♠ ſ ⊙ ⌐ ⎕ ☷ ⊡
**Nearby Facilities** ſ ✔ ∪ ⋔ ♪ ⋔
**Open** 1 April **to** 1 Nov
**Access** Good **Site** Level
Easy access to Bassenthwaite for coarse & salmon fishing and sailing.
**Nearest Town/Resort** Keswick
**Directions** From the A66 take the B5291 at Dubwath and follow signs for Castle Inn. Site is on the left hand side after crossing the bridge.
⚡ Penrith

## BASSENTHWAITE
**North Lakes Caravan Park,** Bewaldeth, Bassenthwaite Lake, Nr Keswick, Cumbria, CA13 9SY
**Tel:** 017687 76510 **Fax:** 017687 76112
**Pitches For** ▲ ☲ ☷ **Total** 145
**Facilities** ſ ⊞ ⊞ ♠ ſ ⊙ ⌐ ⎕ ☷
◗ ⊟ ◗ ♀ ⅄ ♠ ⋔ ☷ ⊟ ☷ ⊬
**Nearby Facilities**
**Acreage** 30 **Open** Easter **to** Nov
**Access** Good **Site** Lev/Slope
Quiet, peaceful park. Approx. 2 miles to an Osprey viewpoint at Dodd Wood.
**Directions** Leave the M6 at junction 40 and take the A66 towards Keswick. Stay on the bypass to Crosthwaite roundabout then take the A591 towards Carlisle. Follow road for approx. 8 miles to the park.
⚡ Penrith

## BRAMPTON
**Irthing Vale Caravan Park,** Old Church Lane, Brampton, Cumbria, CA8 2AA
**Tel:** 016977 3600
**Email:** glennwndrby@aol.com
www.ukparks.co.uk/irthingvale
**Pitches For** ▲ ☲ ☷
**Facilities** ſ ⊞ ♠ ſ ⊙ ⌐ ⊟ ▱ ☂ ՇҼ ◗
**Nearby Facilities** ſ ✔ ∪ ⋔ ∪
**Open** March **to** Oct
**Access** Good

Ideal for Hadrian's Wall, touring and walking.
**Nearest Town/Resort** Brampton
**Directions** From the M6 junction 43 take the A69 to Brampton, then the A6071 signposted Longtown for ½ mile. Turn into Old Church Lane, site is on the left in 400yds (signposted).
⚡ Brampton

## BROUGHTON IN FURNESS
**Birchbank Farm,** Birchbank, Blawith, Ulverston, Cumbria, LA12 8EW
**Tel:** 01229 885277
**Email:** birchbank@btinternet.com
**Pitches For** ▲ ☲ ☷ **Total** 8
**Facilities** ſ ⊞ ⊞ ♠ ſ ⊙ ⌐ ☂ ⋔ ⊟
**Nearby Facilities** ⋏ ∪
**Acreage** ½ **Open** Mid May **to** October
**Access** Good **Site** Level
Small farm site. Next to open Fell, good walking area.
**Nearest Town/Resort** Coniston Water
**Directions** A5092 ¼ mile west of Gawthwaite turn for Woodland. Site is 2 miles on the right along an unfenced road.
⚡ Kirkby in Furness

## CARLISLE
**Dalston Hall Caravan Park,** Dalston, Carlisle, Cumbria, CA5 7JX
**Tel:** 01228 710165
**Email:** nigel@etmanco.fsnet.co.uk
www.dalstonhall.co.uk
**Pitches For** ▲ ☲ ☷ **Total** 55
**Facilities** ſ ⊞ ⊞ ♠ ſ ⊙ ⌐ ⎕ ▱ ☂
ՇҼ ℉ ◗ ✗ ♀ ♠ ⊞ ⎕ ⊟ ☷ ⊬ ♪
**Nearby Facilities** ſ ✔ ⚥ ∪ ♪
**Acreage** 3½ **Open** March **to** Oct
**Access** Good **Site** Level
Adjacent to a golf course (same ownership). Fishing rights on the adjacent river.
**Nearest Town/Resort** Carlisle
**Directions** Leave the M6 at junction 42 and take the road to Dalston. At Dalston take the B5299 towards Carlisle, site is on the right after 1 mile.
⚡ Dalston

## CARLISLE
**Dandy Dinmont Caravan & Camping Site,** Blackford, Carlisle, Cumbria, CA6 4EA
**Tel:** 01228 674611
**Email:** dandydinmont@btopenworld.com
www.caravan-camping-carlisle.itgo.com
**Pitches For** ▲ ☲ ☷ **Total** 47
**Facilities** ſ ⊞ ∪ ♠ ſ ⊙ ⌐ ☂
◗ ♠ ⋔ ⊟ ⊡
**Nearby Facilities** ✔ ♪
**Acreage** 4 **Open** March **to** October
**Access** Good **Site** Level
Historic Carlisle-Castle, Cathedral, Roman Wall, Border Country only 45 minutes to Lake District.
**Nearest Town/Resort** Carlisle
**Directions** On A7 at Blackford, 4¼ miles north of Carlisle. Leave M6 at junction 44, take the A7 Galashiels road (site approx 1½ miles on the right). After Blackford sign, follow road directional signs to site.
⚡ Carlisle

## CARLISLE
**Englethwaite Hall Caravan Club Site,** Armathwaite, Carlisle, Cumbria, CA4 9SY
**Tel:** 01228 560202
www.caravanclub.co.uk
**Pitches For** ☲ ☷ **Total** 63
**Facilities** ſ ⊞ ⊟ ℉ ◗ ☷ ♠ ⊟ ♪
**Nearby Facilities**
**Acreage** 5 **Open** March **to** Nov
**Access** Good **Site** Lev/Slope
Tranquil 15 acre estate in the Eden Valley with lovely views and Inglewood Forest as

a backdrop. Riverside walks. Near the Lake District, Yorkshire Dales and Hadrians Wall. Own sanitation required. Non members welcome. Booking essential.
**Nearest Town/Resort** Carlisle
**Directions** Leave the M6 or A6 at junction 42 and take the B6263 signposted Wetheral after 1¾ miles turn right signposted Armathwaite. Site is approx. 2¾ miles on the right. Warning! - Bumpy road, recommended max speed 35mph.
⚡ Carlisle

## CARLISLE
**Green Acres Caravan Park,** High Knells, Houghton, Carlisle, Cumbria, CA6 4JW
**Tel:** 01228 675418
www.caravanpark-cumbria.com
**Pitches For** ▲ ☲ ☷ **Total** 30
**Facilities** ſ ⊞ ⊞ ♠ ſ ⊙ ⎕ ☷ ⋔ ⊟ ⊡ ⊬
♪
**Nearby Facilities** ſ ✔ ♪
**Acreage** 3 **Open** Easter **to** October
**Access** Good **Site** Level
Ideal touring base for Hadrians Wall, Carlisle City, Lake District and Scottish Borders. AA 3 Pennant Graded.
**Nearest Town/Resort** Carlisle
**Directions** Leave the M6 at junction 44 (North Carlisle). Take the A689 for 1 mile, turn left signposted Scaleby. Site is 1 mile on the left.
⚡ Carlisle

## COCKERMOUTH
**Wheatsheaf Inn Caravan Park,** Low Lorton, Cockermouth, Cumbria, CA13 9UW
**Tel:** 01900 85268
**Email:** thewheatsheaf@tiscali.co.uk
www.wheatsheafinnlorton.co.uk
**Pitches For** ▲ ☲ ☷ **Total** 10
**Facilities** ſ ⊞ ♠ ſ ⊙ ⊟ ℉ ◗ ☒ ♀
⊞ ⋔ ⊟ ⊡ ⊬
**Nearby Facilities** ſ ✔ ⚥ ∪ ♪ ⋔
**Open** March **to** 1 Nov
**Access** Good **Site** Level
**Nearest Town/Resort** Cockermouth
**Directions** 4 miles from Cockermouth on the Buttermere and Loweswater road.
⚡ Penrith

## COCKERMOUTH
**Whinfell Camping,** Lorton, Nr Cockermouth, Cumbria, CA13 0RQ
**Tel:** 01900 85260/85057
**Pitches For** ▲ ☲ ☷ **Total** 40
**Facilities** ſ ⊞ ♠ ſ ⊙ ⊟ ℉ ◗ ⋔ ⊟
**Nearby Facilities** ſ ✔ ⚥ ∪ ♪ ⋔
**Acreage** 5 **Open** 15 March **to** 15 Nov
**Access** Good **Site** Level
Ideal touring and walking. Near to many attractions including Whinlatter Visitor Centre, Sellafield Visitor Centre, Ravenglass Miniature Steam Railway, Muncaster Castle & Gardens and an Owl centre.
**Nearest Town/Resort** Cockermouth
**Directions** Take the A66 then the B5292 at Braithwaite into Low Lorton, follow caravan and camping signs. Or take the 5289 from Cockermouth.
⚡ Workington

## COCKERMOUTH
**Wyndham Holiday Park,** Old Keswick Road, Cockermouth, Cumbria, CA13 9SF
**Tel:** 01900 822571/825238
**Pitches For** ▲ ☲ ☷ **Total** 30
**Facilities** ſ ⊞ ⊞ ♠ ſ ⊙ ⌐ ▱ ⎕ ☂
ՇҼ ◗ ☒ ✗ ♀ ⊞ ♠ ⋔ ⊟ ⊡
**Nearby Facilities** ſ ✔ ⚥ ∪ ♪ ⋔ ♪
**Acreage** 12 **Open** March **to** November
**Access** Good **Site** Lev/Slope
Cockermouth is the birthplace of

# CUMBRIA

Wordsworth also Fletcher Christian of Mutiny on the Bounty. Indoor swimming pool nearby.
**Nearest Town/Resort** Cockermouth
**Directions** ¼ of an hours drive from Keswick on the A66 or 3 minutes from Cockermouth town centre.
⚐ Workington

## CONISTON
**Coniston Hall Camping Site,** Coniston, Cumbria, LA21 8AS
**Tel:** 015394 41223
**Pitches For** ⚐ ⛺
**Facilities** 🆎 🚿 📶 ⊙⊿ ☕ 🏪 🔌 ⚡ ⊡ ⊞ ⊞
**Nearby Facilities** ✓ ⚓ ↖ ∪ ♣ ✈
**Acreage** 200 **Open** March to October
**Site** Level
Lake access. Dogs to be kept on leads.
**Nearest Town/Resort** Coniston
**Directions** 1 mile south of Coniston.
⚐ Windermere

## CONISTON
**Hoathwaite Farm Caravan & Camping Site,** Hoathwaite Farm, Torver, Coniston, Cumbria, LA21 8AX
**Tel:** 01539 441349 **Fax:** 01539 441349
**Pitches For** ⚐ ⛺
**Facilities** ☕🍴🔌⊡ ⊞
**Nearby Facilities** ✓ ⚓ ↖ ∪ ✈
**Acreage** 20 **Open** All Year
**Access** Good **Site** Lev/Slope
Lake access for canoeing, sailing and fishing. Ideal for walking, climbing and orienteering.
**Nearest Town/Resort** Coniston
⚐ Ulverston

## CONISTON
**Park Coppice Caravan Club Site,** Coniston, Cumbria, LA21 8LA
**Tel:** 01539 441555
**www.** caravanclub.co.uk
**Pitches For** ⚐ ⛺ **Total** 280
**Facilities** ⚓ 🍴 📶 🆎 🚿 ⊙ ☕
⚡ ⊞ ⊞ ⊟ ⊡ ⊞
**Nearby Facilities** ✓ ⚓ ↖
**Acreage** 20 **Open** March to Nov
**Access** Good **Site** Level
Situated between Coniston Water and mountains in 63 acres of National Trust woodland. Ideal for walking and bird watching, especially in Grizedale Forest. Post Office, junior orienteering course and Red Squirrel Nature Trail on site. Non members welcome. Booking essential.
**Nearest Town/Resort** Coniston
**Directions** On the A593, 1½ miles south of Coniston Village, just past the A5084 junction in Torver. NB: Approach is narrow in places.
⚐ Ulverston

## CONISTON
**Pier Cottage Caravan Park,** Pier Cottage, Coniston, Cumbria, LA21 8AJ
**Tel:** 01539 441497/441252
**Pitches For** ⚐ ⛺ **Total** 10
**Facilities** 🆎 🚿 📶 ⊙⊿ ☕ ⊟ ⊡ ⊞
**Nearby Facilities** ✓ ⚓ ↖ ∪ ♣ ✈
**Acreage** 1 **Open** March to October
**Access** Good **Site** Level
Lakeside site with boating, fishing and fellwalking.
**Nearest Town/Resort** Coniston
**Directions** 1 mile east of Coniston off the B5285 Hawkshead road.
⚐ Windermere

## CUMWHITTON
**Cairndale Caravan Park,** Cumwhitton, Headsnook, Brampton, Nr CarlisleCumbria, CA8 9BZ
**Tel:** 01768 896280
**Pitches For** ⚐ ⛺ **Total** 5
**Facilities** 🍴 📶 🆎 🚿 ⊙ ☕ 🔌⊡ ⊞

**Nearby Facilities** 🎣 ⚓ ↖
**Acreage** 2 **Open** March to October
**Access** Good **Site** Level
Scenic views, ideal touring, quiet site, water and electricity to individual touring sites. Windsurfing nearby.
**Nearest Town/Resort** Carlisle
**Directions** Follow A69 to Warwick Bridge and then follow unclassified road through Great Corby to Cumwhitton, approx. 9 miles.
⚐ Carlisle

## DENT
**Conder Farm,** Deepdale Road, Dent, Sedbergh, Cumbria, LA10 5QT
**Tel:** 015396 25277
**Email:** conderfarm@aol.com
**Pitches For** ⚐ ⛺ **Total** 47
**Facilities** 📶 🆎 🚿 ⊙ ☕ ⊞ ⊞ ⊿
**Nearby Facilities** 🎣 ∪ ✈
**Open** All Year
**Access** Good **Site** Lev/Slope
Ideal for touring and hill walking.
**Nearest Town/Resort** Sedbergh
**Directions** Leave the M6 at junction 37 and take the road for Sedbergh, Dent is 10 miles. At the George & Dragon take the right hand fork to Dent.
⚐ Dent

## DENT
**Ewegales Farm,** Dent, Sedbergh, Cumbria, LA10 5RH
**Tel:** 01539 625440
**Pitches For** ⚐ ⛺ **Total** 60
**Facilities** ⚓🍴📶 ⊙ ☕ ⊞ ⊞
**Nearby Facilities** ✓ ⚓
**Acreage** 5½ **Open** All Year
**Access** Good **Site** Level
Alongside a river.
**Nearest Town/Resort** Dent
**Directions** Leave the M6 at junction 37 and head towards Sedbergh then Dent, park is 3½ miles east of Dent Village.
⚐ Dent

## DENT
**High Laning Caravan & Camping Park,** High Laning, Dent, Nr Sedbergh, Cumbria, LA10 5QJ
**Tel:** 01539 625239 **Fax:** 01539 625239
**Email:** info@highlaning.co.uk
**www.** highlaning.co.uk
**Pitches For** ⚐ ⛺ **Total** 80
**Facilities** 🆎 🍴 📶 🆎 🚿 📶 ⊙⊿ ☕ ⊟ ⊡ ⊞
🏪 ⊞ 🔌⊞ ⊞
**Nearby Facilities** 🎣 ✓
**Acreage** 4½ **Open** All Year
**Access** Good **Site** Level
Dent is quaint and peaceful with lovely walks and beautiful scenery. Ideal for birdwatching. Historical attractions, cobbled village and The Three Peaks.
**Nearest Town/Resort** Dent
**Directions** Leave the M6 at junction 37 and take the A684 to Sedbergh, Dent is 5 miles from Sedbergh. Take the A1 then exit onto the A684 to Leyburn, Bainbridge and Hawes, Dent is 15 miles from Hawes.
⚐ Dent

## EGREMONT
**Home Farm Caravan Park,** The Nest, Home Farm, Rothersyke, EgremontCumbria, CA22 2US
**Tel:** 01946 824023
**Pitches For** ⚐ ⛺ **Total** 18
**Facilities** ⚓🍴📶 🆎 🚿 ⊙⊿ ☕ ⊡ ⊞
🏪 ⊞🔌⊞ ⊿ ✎
**Nearby Facilities** 🎣 ✓ ∪
**Open** March to October
**Access** Good **Site** Level
Beaches within 3 miles, river fishing ½ a mile. Ideal for touring.

**Nearest Town/Resort** Egremont
**Directions** From the south on the A595 to Calderbridge, take the first left after Blackbeck roundabout and follow St Bees signs on the B5345. 3 miles from St. Bees and 2 miles from Egremont.
⚐ St. Bees

## EGREMONT
**Tarnside Caravan Park,** Braystones, Nr Beckermet, Cumbria, CA21 2YL
**Tel:** 01946 841308
**www.** ukparks.co.uk/tarnside
**Pitches For** ⛺ ⚐ **Total** 20
**Facilities** 🆎 🍴 ⊞ 📶 🆎 🚿 ⊙⊿ 🔌⊟ ⊡ ⊞
🏪 🏪✈ ⊞ 🔌⊞ ⊞
**Nearby Facilities** 🎣 ✓ ∪
**Acreage** 10 **Open** All Year
**Access** Narrow Roads **Site** Level
Overlooking the sea and West Lake District Fells. Ideal base for touring the Lake District.
**Nearest Town/Resort** Egremont
**Directions** 2 miles south of Egremont, follow brown tourist signs on the B5345.
⚐ Braystones (On Site)

## GRANGE-OVER-SANDS
**Cartmel Caravan & Camping Park,** Wells House Farm, Cartmel, Grange-Over-Sands, Cumbria, LA11 6PN
**Tel:** 015395 36270 **Fax:** 015395 36270
**Email:** info@cartmelcamping.co.uk
**www.** ukparks.co.uk/cartmel
**Pitches For** ⚐ **Total** 59
**Facilities** 🆎 🍴 📶 🆎 🚿 ⊙⊿ 🔌⊟ ⊡ ☕
🏪 ⊞ 🏪⚓⊞🔌⊞
**Nearby Facilities** 🎣 ✓ ∪
**Acreage** 5 **Open** March to October
**Site** Level
Tranquil park set in picturesque surroundings, yet only 2 minutes from the village square. Cartmel, one of South Lakelands oldest and prettiest villages, has grown up around its famous 12th Century Priory.
**Nearest Town/Resort** Grange-over-Sands
**Directions** Enter Cartmel from the A590, turn right at the Pig & Whistle, turn next left and the entrance is shortly on the right hand side.
⚐ Grange-over-Sands

## GRANGE-OVER-SANDS
**Greaves Farm Caravan Park,** c/o Prospect House, Barber Green, Grange-over-Sands, Cumbria, LA11 6HU
**Tel:** 015395 36329/36587
**www.** ukparks.co.uk/greaves
**Pitches For** ⚐ ⛺ **Total** 10
**Facilities** 🆎🍴 📶 🆎 ⊙⊿ ☕ ⊟ ⊡ ⊞🔌⊞
**Nearby Facilities** 🎣 ✓ ⚓ ↖ ∪ ✈
**Acreage** 3 **Open** March to October
**Access** Good **Site** Level
Quiet, select, family run park. Ideal base for exploring the Lake District.
**Nearest Town/Resort** Grange-over-Sands
**Directions** Come off the A590 approx 1 mile south of Newby Bridge at the sign "Cartmel 4 miles". Proceed 1½ miles to sign for caravan park.
⚐ Grange-over-Sands

## GRANGE-OVER-SANDS
**Lakeland Leisure Park,** Moor Lane, Flookburgh, Nr Grange-ver-Sands, Cumbria, LA11 7LT
**Tel:** 01539 558556 **Fax:** 01539 558559
**www.** touringholidays.co.uk
**Pitches For** ⚐ ⛺ **Total** 125
**Facilities** 🆎 🍴 📶 🆎 🚿 ⊙⊿ 🔌⊟ ⊡ ☕
🏪 📶⊞⚓🏪✕ ▽ 🏪 ▲ 🏪 ✈🔌⊞ ⊞
**Nearby Facilities** 🎣 ✓ ⚓ ↖ ∪ ♣ ♣ ✈
**Open** March to October
**Access** Good **Site** Level

CADE'S CAMPING, TOURING & MOTOR CARAVAN SITE GUIDE 2006

Less than 15 miles from Lake Windermere. Ideal for touring and exploring.
**Nearest Town/Resort** Grange-over-Sands
**Directions** Leave the M6 at junction 36 onto the A590, turn left onto the A6/A590 for Barrow-in-Furness. Then take the B5277 through Grange-over-Sands, then Allithwaite and into Flookburgh. Turn left at the village square and travel 1 mile down this road to the Park.
⇻ Cark-in-Cartmel

## GRANGE-OVER-SANDS
**Meathop Fell Caravan Club Site,** Grange-over-Sands, Cumbria, LA11 6RB
**Tel:** 01539 532912
**www.** caravanclub.co.uk
**Pitches For** ⊕ ⇔ **Total** 130
**Facilities** ⬚ ∮ 🅗 🆖 ⚓ ⌐ ⊙ 🖾
🖾 🖾 🄰 ⊣🖪 🖰
**Nearby Facilities** ⌐ ⚓ ⚓ ⚓
**Acreage** 10 **Open** All Year
**Access** Good **Site** Lev/Slope
Peaceful site. Ideal base to explore North Lancashire and Southern Lake District. Close to Brockhole National Park Visitor Centre. Non members welcome. Booking essential.
**Nearest Town/Resort** Grange-over-Sands
**Directions** Leave the M6 at junction 36 and take the A590 signposted South Lakes. After 3¼ miles turn left via slip road signposted Barrow, at roundabout turn left onto the B5277 and immediately turn left signposted Meathop. Within ¾ miles turn right up incline and keep right at the top, in 200 yards fork left at green notice board, site is on the left in 150 yards. NB: Steep approach.

## GRANGE-OVER-SANDS
**Oak Head Caravan Park,** Ayside, Grange-over-Sands, Cumbria, LA11 6JA
**Tel:** 015395 Newby Bridge 31475
**Pitches For** ▲ ⊕ ⇔ **Total** 90
**Facilities** ∮ 🆖 ⚓ ⌐ ⊙ ⊣ 🖾 🖾 🖾
🖾 🖾 ⊕🖪 🖰 🗻
**Nearby Facilities** ⌐ ∕ ⚓ ⚓ U ⚓ ⚓ ⚓
**Acreage** 2½ **Open** March to October
**Access** Good **Site** Lev/slope
Scenic views, ideal touring. Within easy reach of all lakes.
**Nearest Town/Resort** Grange-over-Sands
**Directions** M6 junction 36 follow signs for Newby Bridge, site is signposted on left hand side of A590, 2 miles from Newby Bridge, 13 miles from M6.
⇻ Grange-over-Sands

## HAWKSHEAD
**Hawkshead Hall Farm,** Nr Ambleside, Cumbria, LA22 0NN
**Tel:** 015394 36221
**Pitches For** ▲ ⊕ ⇔ **Total** 50
**Facilities** 🅗 🆖 🖾 🖰
**Acreage** 5 **Open** March to October
**Access** Good **Site** Lev/Slope
**Nearest Town/Resort** Hawkshead
**Directions** 5 miles south of Ambleside on the B5286.
⇻ Windermere

## HAWKSHEAD
**The Croft Caravan & Camp Site,** North Lonsdale Road, Hawkshead, Nr Ambleside, Cumbria, LA22 0NX
**Tel:** 015394 36374 **Fax:** 015394 36544
**Email:** enquiries@hawkshead-croft.com
**www.** hawkshead-croft.com
**Pitches For** ▲ ⊕ ⇔ **Total** 100
**Facilities** ∮ 🅗 🆖 ⚓ ⌐ ⊙ ⊣ 🖾 🖾
🖾 🖾 ⊕🖪 🗻
**Nearby Facilities** ∕ U
**Acreage** 5 **Open** March to November
**Access** Good **Site** Level
ETB 4 Star Graded and Rose Award 2005.

**Nearest Town/Resort** Hawkshead
**Directions** From Ambleside 5 miles on the B5286 at village of Hawkshead.
⇻ Windermere

## KENDAL
**Ashes Exclusively Adult Caravan Park,** The Ashes, New Hutton, Kendal, Cumbria, LA8 0AS
**Tel:** 01539 731833
**Email:** info@ashescaravanpark.co.uk
**www.** ashescaravanpark.co.uk
**Pitches For** ⊕ □ **Total** 24
**Facilities** ⬚ ✗ ∮ 🅗 🆖 ⚓ ⌐ ⊙ 🖾
🖾 🖪 🄲 🄰
**Nearby Facilities** ⌐ ∕ ⚓ ⚓ U ⚓ ⚓
**Acreage** 1½ **Open** 1 March to 15 Nov
**Access** Good **Site** Lev/Slope
ADULTS ONLY SITE in a countryside setting with views of the Cumbrian Fells. Popular with walkers and ideal for visiting many local attractions. Close to the Lakes and the Yorkshire Dales.
**Nearest Town/Resort** Kendal
**Directions** Leave the M6 at junction 37 and take the A684 towards Kendal. In 2 miles at the crossroads turn left signposted New Hutton, site is in ¾ miles on the right.
⇻ Oxenholme

## KENDAL
**Camping & Caravanning Club Site,** Millcrest, Shap Road, Kendal, Cumbria, LA9 6NY
**Tel:** 01539 741363
**www.** campingandcaravanningclub.co.uk
**Pitches For** ▲ ⊕ ⇔ **Total** 50
**Facilities** ∮ 🅗 🆖 ⚓ ⌐ ⊙ ⊣ 🖾 🖾
🖾 ⊕ 🄰 ⊕🖪 🗻
**Nearby Facilities** ⌐ ∕ U ⚓
**Acreage** 3 **Open** March to Nov
**Site** Lev/Slope
Right in the middle of the Lake District. Tumble drier and spin drier on site. BTB 4 Star Graded and AA 3 Pennants. Non members welcome.
**Directions** On the A6, 1½ miles north of Kendal, site entrance is 100 yards north of the nameplate 'Skelsmergh'.
⇻ Kendal

## KENDAL
**Lambhowe Caravan Park,** Crosthwaite, Nr Kendal, Cumbria, LA8 8JE
**Tel:** 015395 68483
**Pitches For** ⊕ ⇔ **Total** 14
**Facilities** ∮ 🅗 🆖 ⚓ ⌐ ⊙ 🖾
🖾 ⊕ ⚲ ⊕🖪 🗻
**Nearby Facilities** ⌐ ⚓
**Acreage** 20 **Open** 1 March to 16 Nov
**Access** Good **Site** Level
Set in the delightful Lyth Valley. Just a 15 minute drive to Lake Windermere.
**Nearest Town/** Bowness on Windermere
**Directions** Leave the M6 at junction 36 and take the A590, then take the A5074 towards Bowness. Lambhowe is opposite the Damson Dene Hotel.
⇻ Windermere

## KENDAL
**Low Park Wood Caravan Club Site,** Sedgwick, Kendal, Cumbria, LA8 0JZ
**Tel:** 01539 560186
**www.** caravanclub.co.uk
**Pitches For** ⊕ ⇔ **Total** 161
**Facilities** ⬚ ∮ 🅗 🆖 ⚓ ⌐ ⊙ 🖾
🖾 ⊣🖪 🖰
**Nearby Facilities** ⌐ ∕
**Acreage** 20 **Open** March to Nov
Peaceful site with varied bird life and wild flowers. River fishing. Non members welcome. Booking essential.
**Nearest Town/Resort** Kendal

**Directions** Leave the M6 at junction 36 and take the A590 signposted South Lakes, after 3¼ miles leave via slip road signposted Barrow. At roundabout follow brown signs and turn into road signposted Sedgwick, After 150 yards turn left onto road running parallel with the River Kent. Fork right at the junction, site is on the left after ½ mile.
⇻ Kendal

## KENDAL
**Sampool Caravan Park,** Levens, Kendal, Cumbria, LA8 8EQ
**Tel:** 015395 52265
**Pitches For** ▲ ⊕ ⇔ **Total** 15
**Facilities** ⬚ ∮ 🅗 🆖 ⚓ ⌐ ⊙ ⊣ 🖾 🖾
🖾 🖾 ⊕ 🄰 ⊕🖪 🗻
**Nearby Facilities** ⌐ ∕ ⚓ ⚓ U ⚓ ⚓
**Acreage** 2½ **Open** 15 March to 31 October
**Access** Good **Site** Level
Alongside the River Kent and near the south lakes. Easy access from the M6 motorway (5 minutes).
**Nearest Town/Resort** Kendal
**Directions** 6 miles south of Kendal on the A6, at Levens Bridge turn right onto the A590, Park is 500 metres on the left.
⇻ Oxenholme

## KESWICK
**Bridge End Camp & Caravan Site,** Bridge End Farm, Thirlmere, Keswick, Cumbria, CA12 4TG
**Tel:** 01768 772166
**Pitches For** ▲ ⊕ ⇔ **Total** 20
**Facilities** ∮ 🆖 ⚓ ⌐ ⊙ ⊣ 🖾 🖾 🖪
**Nearby Facilities** ⌐ ∕ ⚓ ⚓ U ⚓ ⚓ ⚓
**Open** March to Nov
**Access** Good **Site** Lev/Slope
Central for the Lake District and all its attractions. Fishing on Thirlmere Lake 200 yards away.
**Nearest Town/Resort** Keswick
**Directions** 4 miles from Keswick on the A591 or 16 miles from Penrith on the A66.
⇻ Penrith

## KESWICK
**Burns Farm Caravan Site,** St Johns-in-the-Vale, Keswick, Cumbria, CA12 4RR
**Tel:** 017687 79225
**Email:** linda@burns-farm.co.uk
**www.** burns-farm.co.uk
**Pitches For** ▲ ⊕ ⇔ **Total** 40
**Facilities** ⬚ ∮ 🆖 ⚓ ⌐ ⊙ ⊣ 🖾 🖾 ⊕🖪 🖰
**Nearby Facilities** ⌐ ∕ ⚓ U ⚓ ⚓
**Acreage** 1¼ **Open** Easter to October
**Access** Good **Site** Level
Ideal touring, walking and climbing. Beautiful views, quiet family site. AA Graded.
**Nearest Town/Resort** Keswick
**Directions** Turn left off the A66 (Penrith to Keswick road) ½ mile past B5322 junction signposted Castlerigg Stone Circle. Site is on the right, farm is on the left. 2¼ miles from Keswick.
⇻ Penrith

## KESWICK
**Camping & Caravanning Club Site,** Derwentwater Caravan Park, Crow Park Road, Keswick, Cumbria, CA12 5EN
**Tel:** 01768 772579
**www.** campingandcaravanningclub.co.uk
**Pitches For** ⊕ ⇔ **Total** 44
**Facilities** ⬚ ∮ 🅗 🆖 ⚓ ⌐ ⊙ 🖾 🖾 🄰 🗻
**Nearby Facilities**
**Acreage** 16 **Open** 1 March to 14 Nov
**Access** Good **Site** Level
Within the heart of the Lake District National Park. BTB 4 Star Graded, David Bellamy Gold Award and AA 3 Pennants. Non members welcome.
**Nearest Town/Resort** Keswick

# CUMBRIA

**Directions** Leave the M6 at junction 40 and take the A66 signposted Keswick and Workington for 13 miles. Do not take the A591, stay on the A66. At the roundabout turn left signposted Keswick Town Centre, follow signs for caravan park to Derwentwater.
✈ Penrith

## KESWICK
**Camping & Caravanning Club Site,** Crow Park Road, Keswick, Cumbria, CA12 5EP
**Tel:** 01768 772392
**www.** campingandcaravanningclub.co.uk
**Pitches For** ⋏ ⌂ ⊟ **Total** 250
**Facilities** ⅄ ♿ 🏳 🏕 🐄 ♨ 🅿 ⊙ ⊐ 🚿 ◻ 🍴
♒ ⊙ 🏊 🚲 ⊩⊟ ⬓ ≋
**Nearby Facilities** ✔ ⚓ ⛵ 🎣 ⚔
**Acreage** 14 **Open** Feb **to** Nov
**Access** Good **Site** Level
Situated on the banks of Derwentwater, ideal for fishing and water sports. Boat launching for small boats. Good hillwalking area. Close to the centre of Keswick. BTB 4 Star Graded, David Bellamy Gold Award and AA 3 Pennants. Non members welcome.
**Nearest Town/Resort** Keswick
**Directions** From Penrith take the A5271, turn left into Main Street (Keswick), turn right to pass Lakes Bus Station, pass the rugby club and turn right, site is on the right.
✈ Penrith

## KESWICK
**Low Manesty Caravan Club Site,** Manesty, Keswick, Cumbria, CA12 5UG
**Tel:** 01768 777275
**www.**caravanclub.co.uk
**Pitches For** ⌂ ⊟ **Total** 60
**Facilities** ⅄ 🏳 🏕 🐄 ♨ ⊩⊟ ◻
**Nearby Facilities** ✔ ⚓ ⛵
**Acreage** 12 **Open** March **to** Nov
**Access** Good **Site** Level
Set in National Trust woodland, close to Derwentwater. Numerous walks from the site. Many visitor attractions within easy reach. Own sanitation required. Non members welcome. Booking essential.
**Nearest Town/Resort** Keswick
**Directions** Leave the M6 at junction 40 and take the A66, on the outskirts of Keswick keep right onto bypass. At roundabout within 1½ miles turn left signposted A5271 Keswick, follow signs onto the B5289. After 4¼ miles turn right over the bridge (care required), site is on the right in 1 mile.
✈ Keswick

## KESWICK
**Scotgate Holiday Park,** Braithwaite, Keswick, Cumbria, CA12 5TF
**Tel:** 017687 78343 **Fax:** 017687 78099
**Email:** info@scotgateholidaypark.co.uk
**www.** scotgateholidaypark.co.uk
**Pitches For** ⋏ ⌂ ⊟ **Total** 40
**Facilities** ⅄ 🏕 🐄 ♨ ⊙ ⊐ 🚿 ◻ 🍴
♒ 🏳 ⊙ 🏊 ✗ ♨ ⊩⊟ ◻
**Nearby Facilities** ✔ ✓ ⚔ ⚔
**Open** All Year
**Access** Good **Site** Level
Quiet site, central for good walks. River nearby.
**Nearest Town/Resort** Keswick
**Directions** Just off the A66, 2¼ miles from Keswick.
✈ Penrith

## KIRKBY LONSDALE
**New House Caravan Park,** Kirkby Lonsdale, Cumbria, LA6 2HR
**Tel:** 015242 71590
**Email:** colinpreece9@aol.com
**Pitches For** ⌂ ⊟ **Total** 50
**Facilities** ⅄ ⅃ 🏳 🏕 🐄 ♨ ⊙ ⊐ 🚿 ◻ 🍴
🅿 ⊙ 🏊 ⊩⊟

---

**Nearby Facilities** ⏃ ✓ ∪
**Acreage** 3½ **Open** March **to** End Oct
**Access** Good **Site** Lev/Slope
Situated near to the historic town of Kirkby Lonsdale and Devils Bridge. An ideal location to visit lakes and Yorkshire Dales.
**Nearest Town** Kirkby Lonsdale/Kendal
**Directions** From Kirkby Lonsdale take the A65 towards Settle, after approx. 1½ miles site is on the right 300 yards past Whoop Hall Inn.
✈ Carnforth

## KIRKBY LONSDALE
**Woodclose Caravan Park,** High Casterton, Kirkby Lonsdale, Cumbria, LA6 2SE
**Tel:** 015242 71597 **Fax:** 015242 72301
**Email:** info@woodclosepark.com
**www.** woodclosepark.com
**Pitches For** ⋏ ⌂ ⊟ **Total** 17
**Facilities** ⅄ 🏳 🏕 🐄 ♨ 🅿 ⊙ ⊐ 🚿 ◻ 🍴
♒ 🏳 ⊙ 🏊 ⊩⊟ ≋
**Nearby Facilities** ⏃ ✓ ⏃ ⚓ ∪ ♨ 🎣 ⚔
**Acreage** 9 **Open** March **to** Oct
**Access** Good **Site** Lev/Slope
Quiet, rural site within easy driving distance of the Lake District and the Yorkshire Dales.
**Nearest Town/Resort** Kirkby Lonsdale
**Directions** Leave the M6 at junction 36 and take the A65 for approx. 6 miles. Woodclose entrance is past Devil's Bridge on the left hand side.

## KIRKBY STEPHEN
**Bowberhead Caravan Site,** Bowberhead Farm, Ravenstonedale, Kirkby Stephen, Cumbria, CA17 4NL
**Tel:** 015396 23254 **Fax:** 015396 23254
**Email:** hols@cumbriaclassiccoaches.co.uk
**www.** cumbriaclassiccoaches.co.uk
**Pitches For** ⋏ ⌂ ⊟ **Total** 7
**Facilities** ⅄ 🏕 🐄 ♨ 🅿 ⊙ ⊐ ◻ 🍴 🅿 🏊 ♨ ⊩⊟
**Nearby Facilities** ✔ ✓ ∪ 🎣
**Acreage** 1¼ **Open** All Year
**Access** Good **Site** Lev/Slope
Settle to Carlisle Line, beautiful views, best fell walking. TV hook-up. Vintage coach excursions from the site.
**Nearest Town/Resort** Kirkby Stephen
**Directions** 4½ miles south of Kirkby Stephen off the A683 road to Sedbergh.
✈ Kirkby Stephen

## KIRKBY STEPHEN
**Pennine View Caravan Park,** Station Road, Kirkby Stephen, Cumbria, CA17 4SZ
**Tel:** 01768 371717
**Pitches For** ⋏ ⌂ ⊟ **Total** 43
**Facilities** ⅄ 🏳 🏕 🐄 ♨ 🅿 ⊙ ⊐ 🚿 ◻ 🍴
♒ 🏊 ⊩⊟ ≋
**Nearby Facilities** ✔ ✓ ∪ 🎣
**Acreage** 2½ **Open** Early March **to** End Oct
**Access** Good **Site** Level
On the edge of the River Eden and on the outskirts of the small market town of Kirkby Stephen. Ideal for walking and touring the Yorkshire Dales and the Lake District.
**Nearest Town/Resort** Kendal
**Directions** On the A685 approx. 1 mile from Kirkby Stephen town centre.
✈ Kirkby Stephen

## KIRKBY THORE
**Low Moor,** Kirkby Thore, Penrith, Cumbria, CA10 1XG
**Tel:** 017683 61231
**www.** lowmoorpark.co.uk
**Pitches For** ⋏ ⌂ ⊟ **Total** 12
**Facilities** ⅄ 🏕 🐄 ♨ 🅿 ⊙ 🍴 🅿
🏳 ⊙ 🏊 ⊩⊟ ≋
**Nearby Facilities** ✔
**Acreage** 1½ **Open** April **to** October
**Access** Good **Site** Level
Open country.

---

**Nearest Town/Resort** Appleby
**Directions** On the A66 7 miles south east of Penrith, between Temple Sowerby and Kirkby Thore villages.
✈ Penrith

## LAMPLUGH
**Dockray Meadow Caravan Club Site,** Lamplugh, Cumbria, CA14 4SH
**Tel:** 01946 861357
**www.** caravanclub.co.uk
**Pitches For** ⌂ ⊟ **Total** 53
**Facilities** ⅄ 🏳 🏕 🐄 ♨ 🅿 ⊩⊟ ◻
**Nearby Facilities** ✓
**Acreage** 4½ **Open** March **to** Nov
**Access** Good **Site** Lev/Slope
Sheltered site alongside a stream with fell scenery. Ideal for walkers. Own sanitation required. Non members welcome. Booking essential.
**Nearest Town/Resort** Lamplugh
**Directions** From the A66 Cockermouth bypass turn onto the A5086 signposted Egremont. After 6½ miles (300yds past Lamplugh Tip Pub) turn left at signpost for Loweswater. Within ¾ miles turn right signposted Croasdale, site is 50 yards on the left.

## LAMPLUGH
**Inglenook Caravan Park,** Fitzbridge, Lamplugh, Workington, Cumbria, CA14 4SH
**Tel:** 01946 861240 **Fax:** 01946 861240
**Email:** mesicp@fsbdial.co.uk
**www.** inglenookcaravanpark.co.uk
**Pitches For** ⋏ ⌂ ⊟ **Total** 53
**Facilities** ⅄ ⅃ 🏳 🏕 🐄 ♨ 🅿 ⊙ ⊐ ◻ 🍴
♒ ⅃ ⊙ 🏊 ♨ ⊩⊟ ≋ ∅
**Nearby Facilities** ✔ ✓ ∪ ⚔
**Acreage** 4 **Open** All Year
**Access** Good **Site** Level
2 miles from lakes and from the beach.
**Nearest Town/Resort** Maryport
✈ Workington

## LONGTOWN
**Camelot Caravan Park,** Sandysike, Longtown, Cumbria, CA6 5SZ
**Tel:** 01228 791248
**Pitches For** ⋏ ⌂ ⊟ **Total** 20
**Facilities** ⅄ 🏳 🐄 🅿 ⊙ ⊐ 🍴 ♒ ⊙ ⊩⊟
**Nearby Facilities** ⏃ ✓ ∪
**Acreage** 1¼ **Open** March **to** October
**Access** Good **Site** Level
Ideal for Solway coast, Carlisle Settle railway, romantic Gretna Green, base for Hadrians Wall and border towns, Carlisle Castle. AA 3 Pennants. Waiting List for Secure Storage.
**Nearest Town/Resort** Longtown
**Directions** On left 1¼ miles south of Longtown on A7, northbound leave M6 at exit 44, take A7 (Longtown) site on right in 4 miles.
✈ Carlisle

## LONGTOWN
**High Gaitle Caravan Park,** Longtown, Cumbria, CA6 5LU
**Tel:** 01228 791819 **Fax:** 01228 791819
**Pitches For** ⋏ ⌂ ⊟ **Total** 30
**Facilities** ⅄ ⅃ 🏳 🐄 ♨ 🅿 ⊙ ⊐ 🍴 🐕 ∅
**Nearby Facilities** ✔ ✓
**Acreage** 6 **Open** All Year
**Access** Good **Site** Level
Ideal touring location for the Lake District, Borders region, Gretna Green and Hadrians Wall.
**Nearest Town/Resort** Carlisle
**Directions** From Carlisle travel north on the A7 to Longtown, then take the A6071 north towards Gretna. Approx. 10 miles from Carlisle.
✈ Carlisle

---

# Flusco Wood

Quiet woodland setting with generous serviced pitches. Centrally heated shower building with free hot water, laundry, drying room and dishwash. 4 miles from Penrith and the M6 junction 40. Only 3½ miles from Ullswater, numerous visitor attractions nearby. *Luxury pine holiday lodges for sale.*

**FLUSCO, PENRITH, CUMBRIA CA11 0JB**
**TEL: 017684 80020   e-mail: admin@fluscowood.co.uk   www.fluscowood.co.uk**

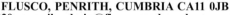

## MARYPORT

**Spring Lea Caravan Park,** Allonby, Maryport, Cumbria, CA15 6QF
**Tel:** 01900 881331 **Fax:** 01900 881209
**Email:** mail@springlea.co.uk
**www.** springlea.co.uk
**Pitches For** ▲ ⚑ ⚐ **Total** 35
**Facilities** ⌁ 🅷 🆄🅴 ♿ 🄿 ⊙ ⌿ ▄ ◨ ☂
🔟 🅿 🏪 ✕ 🐾 ⚑ ▥ ϟ✦🄿🄴 ☼
**Nearby Facilities** ⌿ ✦ ⚓ ↖ ∪
**Acreage** 5 **Open** March **to** October
**Access** Good **Site** Level
300 yards from the beach with views of Lakeland and Scottish hills. Leisure centre for sauna etc.. Bar/restaurant on site.
**Nearest Town/Resort** Maryport
**Directions** 5 miles north of Maryport on the B5300 coast road.
⇌ Maryport

## MEALSGATE

**The Larches Caravan Park,** Mealsgate, Wigton, Cumbria, CA7 1LQ
**Tel:** 016973 71379/71803 **Fax:** 71782
**Email:** melarches@btinternet.com
**www.** thelarchescaravanpark.co.uk
**Pitches For** ▲ ⚑ ⚐ **Total** 73
**Facilities** ⌁ ⌁ 🄵 🅷 🆄🅴 ♿ 🄿 ⊙ ⌿ ▄
🔟 🆂🅴 🄾 🏪 🝖 ▥ ϟ🅷🄴🄰
**Nearby Facilities** ⌿ ✦ ⚓ ↖ 🄿
**Acreage** 19 **Open** March **to** October
**Access** Good **Site** Lev/slope
ADULTS ONLY SITE. Ideal for couples, peace and quiet in the countryside with beautiful views. Excellent toilets.
**Nearest Town/Resort** Wigton
**Directions** From the north take the A57/A74/A7/A69 to Carlisle, follow the A595 to Mealsgate. From the south leave the M6 at junction 41, take the B5305 Wigton road as far as the A595. Turn left and follow the A595 to Mealsgate.
⇌ Wigton

## MELMERBY

**Melmerby Caravan Park,** Melmerby, Penrith, Cumbria, CA10 1HE
**Tel:** 01768 881311
**Email:** eric.carson@ntlworld.com
**www.** melmerbycaravanpark.co.uk
**Pitches For** ⚑ ⚐ **Total** 5
**Facilities** ⌁ ⌁ 🄵 🅷 🆄🅴 ♿ 🄿 ⊙ ⌿ ▄ ◨ ☂
🔟 🄾🝖🄴 ☼
**Nearby Facilities** ⌿ ✦ ⚓ ↖ ∪ 🄿 🄿
**Open** Mid-March **to** November
**Access** Good **Site** Level
Excellent walking country, ideal base for touring North Pennines, Eden Valley and Lake District.
**Nearest Town/Resort** Penrith
**Directions** Situated in Melmerby Village on the A686, 10 miles north east of Penrith.

## MILNTHORPE

**Waters Edge Caravan Park,** Crooklands, Nr Kendal, Cumbria, LA7 7NN
**Tel:** 015395 67708
**www.** watersedgecaravanpark.co.uk
**Pitches For** ▲ ⚑ ⚐ **Total** 32
**Facilities** ⌁ ⌁ 🅷 🆄🅴 ♿ 🄿 ⊙ ⌿ ▄ ◨ ☂
🆂🅴 🔟 🄾 🏪 🍴 🝖 🐾🝖🄿🄴 🄴 ☼
**Nearby Facilities** ⌿ ∪ 🄿
**Acreage** 3 **Open** March **to** November

**Access** Good **Site** Level
Set in quiet and pleasant countryside. Lakes, Yorkshire Dales and Morecambe Bay within easy reach.
**Nearest Town/Resort** Kendal
**Directions** A65 Crooklands, ¾ mile from M6 motorway junction 36.
⇌ Oxenholme

## NEWBY BRIDGE

**Hill of Oaks Caravan Estate,** Windermere, Cumbria, LA12 8NR
**Tel:** 015395 31578 **Fax:** 015395 30431
**Email:** enquiries@hillofoaks.co.uk
**www.** hillofoaks.co.uk
**Pitches For** ⚑ ⚐ **Total** 43
**Facilities** ⌁ ⌁ 🄵 🅷 🆄🅴 ♿ 🄿 ⊙ ⌿ ▄
🔟 🆂🅴 🄾 🝖🄿
**Nearby Facilities** ⌿ ✦ ⚓ ↖ ∪ 🄿 ✦
**Acreage** 31 **Open** 1 March **to** 14 Nov
**Access** Good **Site** Lev/Slope
One of the most beautifully secluded lakeside caravan estates, offering exclusive lake frontage for 1km onto Windermere. Boating on site.
**Nearest Town/Resort** Windermere
⇌ Windermere

## PENRITH

**Beckses Caravan Site,** Penruddock, Penrith, Cumbria, CA11 0RX
**Tel:** 017684 83224
**Pitches For** ▲ ⚑ ⚐ **Total** 23
**Facilities** ⌁ 🅷 🆄🅴 ♿ 🄿 ⊙ ⌿ ▄ ◨ ☂ 🄾
**Open** Easter **to** Oct
**Access** Good **Site** Lev/Slope
**Nearest Town/Resort** Penrith
**Directions** Take the A66 Penrith to Keswick road then the B5288, site is 400 metres on the right.
⇌ Penrith

## PENRITH

**Cross Dormont Camp Site,** Dunroamin, Cross Dormont, Howtown, PenrithCumbria, CA10 2NA
**Tel:** 017684 86537
**Email:** enquiries@crossdormont.co.uk
**Pitches For** ▲ ⚑ ⚐
**Facilities** 🆄🅴 ♿ 🄿 ⊙ ⌿ 🄸🝖🄷
**Nearby Facilities** ⌿ ✦ ⚓ ↖ ∪ 🄿
**Acreage** 5 **Open** March **to** November
**Access** Good **Site** Level
Quiet family run site, overlooking a lake with lake access. Near to a yacht club.
**Nearest Town/Resort** Penrith
**Directions** From Penrith follow the main road for approx. 5 miles then turn left into Howtown road. We are approx. 1½ miles along on the left hand side.
⇌ Penrith

## PENRITH

**Flusco Wood Caravan Park,** Flusco, Penrith, Cumbria, CA11 0JB
**Tel:** 01768 480020
**Email:** admin@fluscowood.co.uk
**www.** fluscowood.co.uk
**Pitches For** ⚑ ⚐ **Total** 50
**Facilities** ⌁ ⌁ 🄵 🅷 🆄🅴 ♿ 🄿 ⊙ ⌿ ▄ ◨ ☂
🆂🅴 🄾 🝖🄴🄷
**Nearby Facilities** ⌿ ✦ ⚓ ↖ ∪ ✦
**Acreage** 14 **Open** Easter **to** November

**Access** Good **Site** Sloping
Grassed and hard, serviced pitches set in woodland clearings. 1 mile from the Lake District. ETB 5 Star Graded and Bellamy Gold Award for Conservation.
**Nearest Town/Resort** Penrith
**Directions** Leave the M6 at junction 40 and travel west on the A66 for 4 miles.
⇌ Penrith

## PENRITH

**Gillside Caravan & Camping Site,** Glenridding, Penrith, Cumbria, CA11 0QQ
**Tel:** 017684 82346
**Email:** gillside@btconnect.com
**www.** gillsidecaravanandcampingsite.co.uk
**Pitches For** ▲ ⚑ ⚐ **Total** 65
**Facilities** ⌁ 🅷 🆄🅴 ♿ 🄿 ⊙ ⌿ ▄ 🔟 🄾 🝖🄿
**Nearby Facilities** ⌿ ✦ ⚓ ↖ ∪ 🄿
**Acreage** 8 **Open** March **to** Mid Nov
**Access** Good **Site** Level
Foot of Helvellyn, 5 minutes walk from Lake Ullswater.
**Nearest Town/Resort** Penrith
**Directions** A592 signposted Ullswater, 14 miles from Penrith. In Glenridding turn right, follow sign for Gillside.
⇌ Penrith

## PENRITH

**Hillcroft Park,** Roe Head Lane, Pooley Bridge, Penrith, Cumbria, CA10 2LT
**Tel:** 017684 86363 **Fax:** 017684 86010
**Pitches For** ▲ ⚑ ⚐
**Facilities** ⌁ ⌁ 🄵 🅷 🆄🅴 ♿ 🄿 ⊙ ⌿ ▄ ◨ ☂
🆂🅴 🄾 🏪 🝖🄿🄴
**Nearby Facilities** ⌿ ⚓ ↖ ∪
**Acreage** 7 **Open** 6 March **to** 14 Nov
**Access** Good **Site** Lev/Slope
Close to Lake Ullswater. Good fellwalking area and a convenient base to tour the Lake District.
**Nearest Town/Resort** Penrith
**Directions** Leave the M6 at junction 40 and take the A66, then the A592 to Ullswater. Go through Pooley Bridge, bear right at the church and go straight across the crossroads.
⇌ Penrith

## PENRITH

**Oaklands Country Park.** Great Strickland, Penrith, Cumbria, CA10 3DH
**Tel:** 01931 712371
**Facilities** ♿ 🝖
**Nearby Facilities**
**Acreage** 5 **Open** 1 March **to** 10 Jan
**Access** Good **Site** Level
Near to Lowther Park and a golf course.
**Nearest Town/Resort** Penrith
**Directions** From Penrith take the A6 towards Shap, Park is on the left after approx. 4 miles.
⇌ Penrith

## PENRITH

**Park Foot Caravan & Camping Park,** Howtown Road, Pooley Bridge, Penrith, Cumbria, CA10 2NA
**Tel:** 017684 86309 **Fax:** 017684 86041
**Email:** holidays@parkfootullswater.co.uk
**www.** parkfootullswater.co.uk
**Pitches For** ▲ ⚑ ⚐ **Total** 332
**Facilities** ⌁ ⌁ 🄵 🅷 🆄🅴 ♿ 🄿 ⊙ ⌿ ▄ ◨ ☂
🆂🅴 🄾 🏪 ✕ 🍴 🝖 🐾 🏍 🝖🄿🄴 🄱 ☼

# CUMBRIA

**Nearby Facilities** ⌐ ✔ ⚓ ⚲ ∪ ♪ ✗
**Acreage** 40 **Open** March to October
**Access** Good **Site** Lev/Slope
Family run park beside Lake Ullswater with boat and car launching access. Licensed bar, restaurant and takeaway. Pony trekking, mountain bike hire, tennis and table tennis on site.
**Nearest Town/Resort** Pooley Bridge
**Directions** 5 miles southwest of Penrith. Leave M6 at junction 40, then take A66 for Ullswater, next roundabout take A592 then road for Pooley Bridge and 1 mile on Howtown Road to site.
⇌ Penrith

## PENRITH
**Side Farm Campsite,** Side Farm, Patterdale, Penrith, Cumbria, CA11 0NP
**Tel:** 017684 82337
**Email:** sidefarm.fsnet.co.uk
**Pitches For** ▲ ⌂ **Total** 60
**Facilities** ⓌⒸ ⚡ ⌐ ⊙ ⌁ ▣ ⌯✚⌂
**Nearby Facilities** ✔ ⚓ ⚲ ∪ ♪ ✗
**Open** Easter to Oct **Site** Sloping
Near the lakeside with a bank down from the site to the lake. Ideal for boating, sailing, fishing, mountain biking, walking, or simply relaxing. Sorry, no single sex groups.
**Nearest Town/Resort** Ullswater
**Directions** On the A592 Penrith to Windermere road. Farm is signposted in Patterdale between the church and the school.
⇌ Penrith/Windermere

## PENRITH
**Stonefold,** Newbiggin, Stainton, Penrith, Cumbria, CA11 0HP
**Tel:** 01768 866383
**Email:** gill@stonefold.co.uk
**www.stonefold.co.uk**
**Pitches For** ⌂ ⌀ **Total** 15
**Facilities** ⨍ Ⓦ ⌐ ⊙ ⌁ ⛿✚⌂⊠ ☼
**Nearby Facilities** ⌐ ✔ ⚓ ⚲ ∪ ♪ ♪ ✗
**Acreage** 2 **Open** Easter to Oct
**Access** Good **Site** Level
Family run site with a panoramic position overlooking Eden Valley. An ideal base for exploring and enjoying the lakes. 5 miles from Ullswater. BH & HPA Member.
**Nearest Town/Resort** Penrith
**Directions** Leave M6 at junction 40 and take the A66 Keswick road. Turn right at the sign for Newbiggin and Stonefold is one minutes drive on the left.
⇌ Penrith

## PENRITH
**Thacka Lea Caravan Site,** Thacka Lea, Penrith, Cumbria, CA11 9HX
**Tel:** 01768. 863319
**Pitches For** ⌀ ⌂ **Total** 25
**Facilities** ⨍ ⌐ ⊙ ⌁ ⛿ ⊙ ✚⊠
**Nearby Facilities** ⌐
**Acreage** 1 **Open** March to October
**Access** Good **Site** Lev/Slope
Just a 10 minute walk from the town centre. Good touring.
**Nearest Town/Resort** Penrith
**Directions** From south, turn left off the A6, go past the Esso Station at the north end of town. From north, turn right at The Grey Bull.
⇌ Penrith

## PENRITH
**Troutbeck Head Caravan Club Site,** Troutbeck, Penrith, Cumbria, CA11 0SS
**Tel:** 01768 483521
**www.caravanclub.co.uk**
**Pitches For** ⌀ ⌂ **Total** 141
**Facilities** ⚓ ⨍ ⌾ Ⓦ ⌐ ⚡ ▣ ⌂
⊙⚡♠⛰✚⌁⊠
**Nearby Facilities** ⌐ ✔ ⚓ ⚲ ∪

**Acreage** 25 **Open** March to Jan
**Access** Good **Site** Level
Set in countryside, alongside a brook with fabulous views. Only 4 miles from Ullswater. Ideal for walkers and nature lovers. Rookin House Farm Centre adjacent offering go-karting, quad bikes, archery, horse riding and much more. Non members welcome. Booking essential.
**Nearest Town/Resort** Penrith
**Directions** Leave the M6 at junction 40 and take the A66 signposted Keswick. Go straight on at the roundabout and after approx. 7 miles turn left onto the A5091. Site is 1¼ miles on the right. NB: No arrivals before 12 noon.
⇌ Penrith

## PENRITH
**Waterfoot Caravan Park,** Pooley Bridge, Penrith, Cumbria, CA11 0JF
**Tel:** 017684 86302 **Fax:** 017684 86728
**Email:** enquiries@waterfootpark.co.uk
**www.waterfootpark.co.uk**
**Pitches For** ⌀◨ **Total** 38
**Facilities** ⚓ ⨍ ⌾ Ⓦ ⚡ ⌐ ⊙ ⌁ ⚡ ⊠ ⌂
⛿ ⊙ ♠ ♣ ⛰ ✚⌂
**Nearby Facilities** ⌐ ✔ ⚓ ⚲ ∪ ♪
**Acreage** 22 **Open** 1 March to 14 Nov
**Access** Good **Site** Lev/Slope
Parkland site in the grounds of a Georgian Mansion. A mix of hardstanding and lawn areas for awnings. Licensed Bar on site.
**Nearest Town/Resort** Penrith
**Directions** Leave the M6 at junction 40 and take the A66 for approx. 1 mile. Then take the A592 and Waterfoot can be found on the right hand side.
⇌ Penrith

## PENRITH
**Waterside Farm Campsite,** Waterside Farm, Howtown Road, Pooley Bridge, PenrithCumbria, CA10 2NA
**Tel:** 017684 86332 **Fax:** 017684 86332
enquire@waterside-farm-campsite.co.uk
**www.waterside-farm-campsite.co.uk**
**Pitches For** ▲ ⌂
**Facilities** ⚓ Ⓦ ⚡ ⌐ ⊙ ⌁ ⚡ ⊠ ⌂
⛿ ⊙ ♠ ⛰ ✚⌂
**Nearby Facilities** ⌐ ✔ ⚓ ⚲ ∪ ✗
**Open** March to October **Site** Lev/Slope
Genuine lakeside location with beautiful views of a lake and fells. Boat, canoe and mountain bike hire available. ETB 4 Star Graded and AA 3 Pennants.
**Nearest Town/Resort** Ullswater
**Directions** Leave the M6 at junction 40 and take the A66 for 1 mile, turn left onto the A592 for Ullswater and after 4 miles turn left to Pooley Bridge. Go through the village and turn right at the church then right again, we are 1 mile on the right past the other sites.
⇌ Penrith

## RAVENGLASS
**Ravenglass Camping & Caravanning Club Site,** Ravenglass, Cumbria, CA18 1SR
**Tel:** 01229 717250
**www.campingandcaravanningclub.co.uk**
**Pitches For** ▲ ⌀ ⌂ **Total** 60
**Facilities** ⨍ ⌾ Ⓦ ⚡ ⌐ ⊙ ⌁ ⚡ ⊠ ⌂
⛿ ⊙ ♠ ✚⌂⊠ ☼ ⌁
**Nearby Facilities** ✔ ✗
**Acreage** 5 **Open** March to Nov
**Access** Good **Site** Lev/Slope
Set in 5 acres of mature woodland, this is a walkers paradise on Cumbria's Western Coast, where the Lake District National Park meets the sea. Non members welcome.
**Nearest Town/Resort** Broughton
**Directions** From the A595 turn west for Ravenglass, before village turn left to site.
⇌ Ravenglass

## SEDBERGH
**Cross Hall Farm Caravan Park,** Cross Hall Farm, Cautley, Sedbergh, Cumbria, LA10 5LY
**Tel:** 015396 20668 **Fax:** 015396 21504
**Email:** crosshall@btopenworld.com
**www.dalescaravanpark.co.uk**
**Pitches For** ▲ ⌂ ⌀ **Total** 15
**Facilities** ⨍ Ⓦ Ⓤ ⚡ ⌐ ⊙ ⌾ ⌂✚⊠
**Nearby Facilities** ⌐ ✔ ∪ ✗
**Acreage** 1½ **Open** April to Oct
**Access** Good **Site** Level
Ideal for touring the Lake District and the Yorkshire Dales, also for climbing the Howgill Fells and Cautley Spout.
**Nearest Town/Resort** Kendal
**Directions** Leave the M6 at junction 37 and travel to Sedbergh. Then take the A683 towards Kirkby Stephen for 2½ miles, signposted.
⇌ Oxenholme

## SEDBERGH
**Yore House Farm Caravan Park,** Yore House Farm, Lunds, Sedbergh, Cumbria, LA10 5PX
**Tel:** 01969 667358
**Pitches For** ▲ ⌂ ⌀ **Total** 7
**Facilities** Ⓤ ⌑✚⌂
**Nearby Facilities**
**Open** Easter to End Sept
**Access** Good **Site** Level
Quiet, farm site beside the River Ure. In sight of the famous Settle to Carlisle railway.
**Nearest Town/Resort** Hawes
**Directions** On the A684 10 miles from Sedbergh and 6 miles from Hawes, near the Moorcock Pub. On the North Yorkshire and Cumbria border.
⇌ Garsdale

## SILLOTH
**Hylton Caravan Park,** Eden Street, Silloth, Cumbria, CA7 4AY
**Tel:** 016973 31707
**Email:** enquiries@stanwix.com
**www.stanwix.com**
**Pitches For** ▲ ⌀ ⌂ **Total** 92
**Facilities** ⚓ ⨍ ⌾ Ⓦ ⚡ ⌐ ⊙ ⌁ ⚡ ⊠ ⌂
⛿ ⊙ ♠ ⛰✚⌂⊠ ⊙ ☼
**Nearby Facilities** ⌐ ✔ ⚓ ∪ ♪ ♪
**Acreage** 18 **Open** 1 March to 15 Nov
**Access** Good **Site** Level
Quiet site convenient for the town centre. 213 holiday home pitches and 92 camping/touring pitches with mains service hook-ups. New luxury amenity block with toilets, bathrooms, launderette and disabled facilities. Sister park to Stanwix Park Holiday Centre with lots of super facilities which are free to Hylton residents.
**Nearest Town/Resort** Silloth
**Directions** This park is off Eden Street. Entering Silloth on the B5302 follow signs for ½ a mile.
⇌ Carlisle

## SILLOTH
**Moordale Park,** Blitterlees, Silloth, Cumbria, CA7 4JZ
**Tel:** 016973 31375
**Email:** manda@moordalepark.com
**www.moordalepark.com**
**Pitches For** ▲ ⌀ ⌂ **Total** 12
**Facilities** ⨍ Ⓦ Ⓤ ⚡ ⌐ ⊙ ⌁ ⚡ ⊠ ⌂
⛿ ⊙ ⛰✚⌂
**Nearby Facilities** ⌐ ✔ ⚓ ∪ ♪ ♪
**Acreage** 7 **Open** March to October
**Access** Good **Site** Level
A quiet and spacious site adjacent to the beach and a golf course. Convenient for the Lake District and Scotland.

## SILLOTH

**Nearest Town/Resort** Silloth
**Directions** From Silloth take the B5300 Silloth to Maryport road. Moordale is about 2 miles on the right hand side.
⚐ Wigton

## SILLOTH

**Rowanbank Caravan Park,** Beckfoot, Silloth-on-Solway, Cumbria, CA7 4LA
**Tel:** 01697 331653 **Fax:** 01697 331653
**Email:** phandjmorris@aol.com
www.rowanbankcaravanpark.co.uk
**Pitches For** ▲ ⬍ ⬍ **Total** 20
Facilities ≠ 🏠 🖽 🖵 ⌂ ♨ ◻ 🌣
🔥 🍴 🛒 🚻 🅿 🖭 ※
**Nearby Facilities** ⌂ ✔ ⚓ ⛵ ∪ ⋺ ♪
**Acreage** 3 **Open** 1 March to 14 Nov
**Access** Good **Site** Level
Across the road from the beach, overlooking the Scottish Hills. Ideal base to visit the Lakes and Scottish Borders.
**Nearest Town/Resort** Silloth
**Directions** 2 miles south of Silloth on the B5300.
⚐ Maryport

## SILLOTH

**Seacote Caravan Park,** Skinburness Road, Silloth, Carlisle, Cumbria, CA5 4QJ
**Tel:** 016973 33121/31031 **Fax:** 31031
**Pitches For** ⬍ ⬍ **Total** 20
Facilities ≠ 🏠 🖽 🖽 ⌂ ⌂ ♨ ◻ 🌣
🏮 ◻ 🛒 🚻 🅿 ※
**Nearby Facilities** ⌂ ✔ ∪ ♪
**Acreage** 5½ **Open** 1 March to 15 Nov
**Access** Good **Site** Level
Peace and tranquility, adjacent to Solway. Central to the Lake District and Scottish Borders.
**Nearest Town/Resort** Carlisle
**Directions** From Carlisle take the A595, then the A596 and finally the B5302 to Silloth.
⚐ Carlisle

## SILLOTH

**Solway Holiday Village,** Skinburness Drive, Silloth, Wigton, Cumbria, CA7 4QQ
**Tel:** 016973 31236 **Fax:** 016973 32553
www.hagansleisure.co.uk
**Pitches For** ▲ ⬍ ⬍
Facilities ≠ 🏠 🖽 🖽 ⌂ ⌂ 🌣 ♨ ◻ 🌣
♒ 🍴 🛒 🚻 ♀ 🍴 🏮 ⚒ 🌣 ◄🅿 🖭 ※
**Nearby Facilities** ⌂ ✔ ⚓ ∪ ♪ ⋺
**Open** March to October
**Access** Good **Site** Level
Near the beach. Golf course on site.
**Nearest Town/Resort** Silloth
**Directions** Drive into Silloth, turn right at the Raffa Club and follow road for ½ mile. Turn right at signpost for holiday village.
⚐ Wigton

## SILLOTH

**Stanwix Park Holiday Centre,** Silloth (West), Cumbria, CA7 4HH
**Tel:** 016973 32666 **Fax:** 016973 32555
**Email:** enquiries@stanwix.com
www.stanwix.com
**Pitches For** ▲ ⬍ ⬍ **Total** 121
Facilities ♿ ≠ 🏠 🖽 🖽 ⌂ ⌂ ♨ ◻ 🌣
♒ 🍴 🛒 🚻 ♀ 🍴 🏮 ⚒ 🌣 ◄🅿 🖭 ※
**Nearby Facilities** ⌂ ✔ ⚓ ⋺ ♪
**Acreage** 18 **Open** All Year
**Access** Good **Site** Level
Large holiday centre with full range of facilities for all the family, indoor and outdoor. Sunbeds, water shoot. Indoor leisure complex. See our display advertisment.
**Nearest Town/Resort** Silloth
**Directions** Enter Silloth on B5302, turn left at sea front, 1 mile to West Silloth on B5300. Site on right.
⚐ Carlisle

## SILLOTH

**Tanglewood Caravan Park,** Causewayhead, Silloth, Cumbria, CA7 4PE
**Tel:** 016973 31253
tanglewoodcaravanpark@hotmail.com
www.tanglewoodcaravanpark.co.uk
**Pitches For** ▲ ⬍ ⬍ **Total** 31
Facilities ≠ 🏠 🖽 🖽 ⌂ ⌂ ♨ ◻ 🌣
🔥 ♨ 🍴 🏮 🚻 🅿 🖭 ※
**Nearby Facilities** ⌂ ✔ ∪ ♪
**Acreage** 2 **Open** March to January
**Access** Good **Site** Level
Tree sheltered site, ideal for touring lakes and borders. Pets free of charge.
**Nearest Town/Resort** Silloth
**Directions** Take B5302, 1 mile inland from town on Wigton road.
⚐ Wigton

## TEBAY

**Westmorland Caravan Site Tebay,** Tebay Westmorland Services, M6 Northbound, Cumbria, CA10 3SB
**Tel:** 015396 24511 **Fax:** 015396 24511
**Email:** caravans@westmorland.com
www.wms.com
**Pitches For** ⬍ ⬍ **Total** 70
Facilities ♿ ≠ 🖽 🖽 ⌂ ⌂ ♨ ◻ 🌣
♒ 🍴 🛒 🚻 🅿 🖭 ※
**Nearby Facilities** ✔
**Acreage** 3½ **Open** Mid-March to October
**Access** Good **Site** Level
Ideal base for the Lake District and the Yorkshire Dales.
**Nearest Town/Resort** Penrith/Kendal
**Directions** M6 Motorway 1 mile north of junction 38, take the Westmorland Tebay Services exit and follow signs for Tebay Caravan Site. Access also from Tebay East Services M6 south, follow signs.
⚐ Penrith/Oxenholme

## TROUTBECK
**Gill Head Farm,** Troutbeck, Penrith, Cumbria, CA11 0ST
**Tel:** 017687 79652
**Email:** enquiries@gillheadfarm.co.uk
www.gillheadfarm.co.uk
**Pitches For ▲ ♠ ➡ Total** 80
**Facilities** ∮ 🏠 🛁 ♣ ↿ ⊙ ↵ ⟂ 🔲 ☎
🏠 🔘 🗢 🏕 ⍉ ⊁ ➡ 🎵 ⟂ ↳ ⟍ ∪ ♫ ↯
**Nearby Facilities** ↿ ✔ ⟂ ↳ ⟍ ∪ ♫ ↯
**Open** Easter **to** Nov **Access** Good **Site** Level
On a working hill farm in a lovely rural location with panoramic views of the Fells.
**Nearest Town/Resort** Keswick
**Directions** Take the A66 to Keswick then the A5091 towards Ullswater. After 100 yards turn right, after 1½ miles turn right again.
🚉 Penrith

## TROUTBECK
**Hutton Moor End Caravan & Camping Site,** Moor End, Troutbeck, Penrith, Cumbria, CA11 0SX
**Tel:** 01768 779615
**Email:** info@huttonmoorend.co.uk
www.huttonmoorend.co.uk
**Pitches For ▲ ♠ ➡ Total** 50
**Facilities** ♿ ∮ 🏠 🛁 ♣ ↿ ⊙ ↵ ⟂ 🔲 ☎
🏠 🔘 🗢 🏕 🏕 ➡ 🎵
**Nearby Facilities** ↿ ∪
**Acreage** 2½ **Open** Easter/1st Apr **to** Nov
**Access** Good **Site** Sloping
**Nearest Town/Resort** Keswick
**Directions** On A66 9 miles west of junc 40 M6. Turn left for Wallthwaite.
🚉 Penrith

## ULLSWATER
**The Quiet Caravan & Camping Site,** Ullswater, Nr Penrith, Cumbria, CA11 0LS
**Tel:** 0176 84 86337
**Email:** info@thequietsite.co.uk
www.thequietsite.co.uk
**Pitches For ▲ ♠ ➡ Total** 83
**Facilities** ♿ ∮ 🏠 🛁 ♣ ↿ ⊙ ↵ ⟂ 🔲 ☎
🏠 🔘 🗢 🏕 ♣ 🏕 ♣ ➡ 🎵 ⍉
**Nearby Facilities** ↿ ✔ ⟂ ↳ ⟍ ∪ ♫ ↯
**Acreage** 6 **Open** March **to** November
**Access** Good **Site** Lev/Slope
Idyllic setting amongst the fells, voted Best Campsite in Britain by Camping Magazine, AA Northern Campsite of the Year. Large

adventure playground and Olde Worlde Bar (probably the best campsite bar in Britain!). Family bathroom and shower rooms. Campers kitchen. ETB 'Exceptional' Graded.
**Nearest Town/Resort** Pooley Bridge
**Directions** Take A592 from Penrith, turn right at lake and right again at Brackenrigg Hotel follow road for 1½ miles, site on right hand side of road.
🚉 Penrith

## ULLSWATER
**Ullswater Caravan Camping & Marine Park,** Watermillock, Penrith, Cumbria, CA11 0LR
**Tel:** 0176 84 86666 **Fax:** 0176 84 86095
**Email:** info@uccmp.co.uk
www.uccmp.co.uk
**Pitches For ▲ ♠ ➡ Total** 155
**Facilities** ♿ ∮ 🏠 🛁 ♣ ↿ ⊙ ↵ ⟂ 🔲 ☎
🏠 🔘 🗢 🖥 ♣ 🏕 ➡ 🔲 ☎
**Nearby Facilities** ↿ ✔ ⟂ ↳ ⟍ ∪ ♫
**Acreage** 7 **Open** March **to** 14 November
**Access** Good **Site** Lev/Slope
Lake District National Park. Scenic views. Boat launching and moorings 1 mile.
**Nearest Town/Resort** Penrith
**Directions** A592 from Penrith, turn right at lake and right again at telephone kiosk, signposted Watermillock Church.
🚉 Penrith

## ULVERSTON
**Bardsea Leisure,** Priory Road, Ulverston, Cumbria, LA12 9QE
**Tel:** 01229 584712 **Fax:** 01229 580413
**Email:** reception@bardsealeisure.co.uk
www.bardsealeisure.co.uk
**Pitches For ▲ ♠ ➡ Total** 83
**Facilities** ∮ 🖥 🏠 🛁 ♣ ↿ ⊙ ↵ 🔲 ☎
🔘 🗢 ✗ 🏕 ➡ 🎵 ⍉
**Nearby Facilities** ↿ ✔ ♫
**Acreage** 10 **Open** All Year
**Access** Good **Site** Lev/Slope
Ideal for touring.
**Nearest Town/Resort** Ulverston
**Directions** Leave the M6 at junction 36 and take the A590 then the A5087.
🚉 Ulverston

## ULVERSTON
**Bigland Hall Caravan Park,** Haverthwaite, Nr Ulverston, Cumbria, LA12 8PJ
**Tel:** 015395 31702 **Fax:** 015395 31702
**Pitches For ♠ ➡ Total** 50
**Facilities** ∮ 🏠 🛁 ♣ ↿ ⊙ ↵ 🔲 ☎
🏠 🔘 🗢 🏕 ➡ ⍉
**Nearby Facilities** ✔ ⟂
**Acreage** 30 **Open** 1 March **to** 16 Nov
**Access** Good **Site** Level
Ideal central base for exploring lakeland. 10 minutes from Lake Windermere.
**Nearest Town/Resort** Ulverston
**Directions** Take the A590 towards Barrow-in-Furness, turn left opposite Steam Railway, at the T-junction turn left onto the B5278, Park is 1½ miles on the left.
🚉 Grange-over-Sands

## ULVERSTON
**Black Beck Caravan Park,** Bouth, Nr Ulverston, Cumbria, LA12 8JN
**Tel:** 01229 861274 **Fax:** 01229 861041
**Email:** reception@blackbeck.com
**Pitches For ♠ ➡ Total** 60
**Facilities** ♣ ∮ 🏠 🛁 ♣ ↿ ⊙ ↵ ⟂ 🔲 ☎
🏠 🔘 🗢 🖥 🗢 ⍉
**Nearby Facilities** ↿ ✔ ⟂ ↳ ⟍ ∪ ♫ ↯
**Open** 1 March **to** 15 Nov
**Access** Good **Site** Level
Beck through the centre of the park. Lake Windermere is easily accessible.
**Nearest Town/Resort** Ulverston
**Directions** On the A590 5 miles from Ulverston.
🚉 Ulverston

## ULVERSTON
**Crake Valley Holiday Park,** Water Yeat, Blawith, Via Ulverston, Cumbria, LA12 8DL
**Tel:** 01229 885203 **Fax:** 01229 885203
**Email:** crakevalley@coniston1.fslife.co.uk
www.crakevalley.co.uk
**Pitches For ▲ ♠ Total** 4
**Facilities** 🖥 ♣ ↿ ⊙ ⟂ 🔲 ☎ ➡ 🎵
**Nearby Facilities** ↿ ✔ ⟂ ↳ ⟍ ∪ ♫
**Open** May **to** Sept **Site** Level
Opposite Coniston Water. Ideal base for touring the Lakes.
**Nearest Town/Resort** Coniston
**Directions** Take the A590, turn right onto the A5092, after 2 miles turn right onto the A5084

**PARK CLIFFE** windermere

HOLGATES

Right in the **heart** of the
ke District National Park.

A tempting year-round
holiday in Silverdale.
Irresistible

for Coniston. The Park entrance is 3 miles on the left hand side, opposite Coniston Water.
⇌ Ulverston

## WALNEY ISLAND
**South End Caravan Park,** Walney, Barrow in Furness, Cumbria, LA14 3YQ
Tel: 01229 472823
Email: kathmulgrew@aol.com
www.walney-island-caravan-park.co.uk
Pitches For ▲ ⊞ ⊟ Total 60
Facilities ⚡ ∮ ⊡ ⊞ ⚓ ↑ ⊙ ↵ ⚰ ◻ ☎
⚑ ◙ ⊟ ▽ ⬚ ⋀ ⊁ ✻ ✦ ⊞ ⊟ ◻ ☀
Nearby Facilities ⌐ ✔ ∪
Acreage 7 Open Mar to Oct Site Sloping
Close to beach, good views.
**Nearest Town/Resort** Barrow in Furness
**Directions** A590 to Barrow, then follow Walney signs. Turn left after crossing bridge to Walney, 4 miles south from there.
⇌ Barrow

## WASDALE
**Church Stile Holiday Park,** Church Stile Farm, Wasdale, Cumbria, CA20 1ET
Tel: 019467 26252 Fax: 019467 26028
Email: churchstile@campfarm.fsnet.co.uk
www.churchstile.com
Pitches For ▲ ⊟ Total 70
Facilities ⚡ ∮ ⊡ ⊞ ⚓ ⌐ ⊙ ↵
◻ ⚰ ⊟
Nearby Facilities ⌐ ✔ ✗
Acreage 4 Open 21 Mar to 31 Oct Site Level
River, lake and beach. Fell walking and climbing.
**Nearest Town/Resort** Seascale/ Whitehaven
**Directions** From Gosforth take the A595 and follow signs for Nether Wasdale (approx. 4 miles). We are the only farm in the village.
⇌ Seascale

## WASDALE
**Wasdale National Trust Campsite,** Wasdale Head, Cumbria, CA20 1EX
Tel: 01946 726220
wasdale.campsite@nationaltrust.org.uk
www.wasdalecampsite.org.uk
Pitches For ▲ ⊟ Total 120
Facilities ⚡ ⊞ ⚓ ⌐ ⊙ ↵ ◻ ⚑ ◙ ⊟ ↑ ⊟
Nearby Facilities ✔ ✗
Open All Year Site Level
Spectacular mountain location, remote and peaceful. 100m from the head of beautiful Washwater.
**Nearest Town/Resort** Egremont
**Directions** Wasdale Head is reached via the A595. From the south turn right at Holmrook for Santon Bridge, then follow signs to Wasdale Head. From the north turn left at Gosforth.
⇌ Ravenglass

## WINDERMERE
**Braithwaite Fold Caravan Club Site,** Glebe Road, Bowness-on-Windermere, Windermere, Cumbria, LA23 3GZ
Tel: 01539 442177
www.caravanclub.co.uk
Pitches For ⊞ ⊟ Total 66
Facilities ∮ ⊡ ⊞ ⚓ ◙ ◻ ⊟ ↑ ⊟
Nearby Facilities ⌐ ✔ ⚓ ✗
Acreage 4 Open March to Nov
Access Good Site Level
Close to the shores of Lake Windermere (with sailing centre) and within walking distance of the town. Not suitable for very large awnings. Non members welcome. Booking essential.
**Nearest Town/Resort** Windermere
**Directions** Leave the M6 at junction 36 and the A590. After 3¼ miles continue onto A591 to Windermere. In Windermere DO NOT turn

first or second left into town, continue to the roundabout and turn left onto A592. Follow signs for Bowness Bay, immediately past the pier turn right into Glebe Road, site is on the right.
⇌ Windermere

## WINDERMERE
**Camping & Caravanning Club Site,** Ashes Lane, Staveley, Kendal, Cumbria, LA8 9JS
Tel: 01539 821119
www.campingandcaravanningclub.co.uk
Pitches For ▲ ⊞ ⊟ Total 250
Facilities ⚓ ∮ ⊡ ⊞ ⚓ ⌐ ⊙ ↵ ◻ ☎
⚑ ◙ ▽ ⊁ ⋀ ✦ ⊞ ⊟ ◻ ☀ ◿
Nearby Facilities ⌐ ✔ ∪
Acreage 24 Open 14 March to 14 Jan
Access Good Site Level
Ideal for touring the Lake District. Non members welcome.
**Nearest Town/Resort** Staveley
**Directions** From Kendal take the A591 towards Windermere for 1½ miles, follow signposts.
⇌ Kendal

## WINDERMERE
**Fallbarrow Park,** Rayrigg Road, Windermere, Cumbria, LA23 3DL
Tel: 0870 774 4024 Fax: 01524 732034
enquiries@southlakeland-caravans.co.uk
www.southlakeland-caravans.co.uk
Pitches For ⊞ ⊟ Total 38
Facilities ⚡ ∮ ⊡ ⊞ ⚓ ⌐ ⊙ ↵ ⚰ ◻ ☎
⚑ ◙ ⊟ ✗ ▽ ⬚ ⋀ ⊟ ⊟
Nearby Facilities ⌐ ✔ ∪
Acreage 32 Open March to Nov
Access Good Site Level
Set amidst wooded parkland on the shore of Lake Windermere. Extensive lake shore with boat launching facilities. 5 minutes walk to Bowness. Luxury holiday caravans for hire.
**Nearest Town/Resort** Windermere
**Directions** Leave the M6 at junction 36 and follow the A591 to Windermere until you reach the town centre. Turn left following signs for Bowness then turn right at the mini roundabout signposted Keswick & Steamboat Museum, Park is 300 yards on the left.
⇌ Windermere

## WINDERMERE
**Limefitt Park,** Patterdale Road, Windermere, Cumbria, LA23 1PA
Tel: 0870 774 4024 Fax: 01524 732034
enquiries@southlakeland-caravans.co.uk
www.southlakeland-caravans.co.uk
Pitches For ▲ ⊞ ⊟ Total 154
Facilities ⚡ ∮ ⊡ ⊞ ⚓ ⌐ ⊙ ↵ ⚰ ◻ ☎
⚑ ◙ ⊟ ✗ ▽ ⬚ ⋀ ⊁ ✦ ⊞ ⊟ ☀
Nearby Facilities ⌐ ✔ ⚓ ✦ ∪ ✗
Acreage 113 Open March to Nov
Access Good Site Lev/Slope
Spectacular lakeland valley location. Ten minutes drive from Lake Windermere. Luxury holiday caravans for hire.
**Nearest Town/Resort** Windermere
**Directions** Leave the M6 at junction 36 and follow the A591 to Windermere until you reach the town centre. About ½ mile north of Windermere turn right at the mini roundabout take the A592 Patterdale Road signposted Ullswater. Limefitt is 2½ miles on the right.
⇌ Windermere

## WINDERMERE
**Park Cliffe Camping & Caravan Estate,** Birks Road, Tower Wood, Windermere, Cumbria, LA23 3PG
Tel: 015395 31344 Fax: 015395 31971
Email: info@parkcliffe.co.uk
www.parkcliffe.co.uk

Pitches For ▲ ⊞ ⊟ Total 250
Facilities ⚡ ∮ ⊡ ⊞ ⚓ ⌐ ⊙ ↵ ⚰ ◻ ☎
⚑ ⚑ ◙ ⊟ ✗ ▽ ⚓ ⋀ ✦ ⊞ ⊟ ☀
Nearby Facilities ⌐ ✔ ⚓ ✦ ∪ ⊁ ✗
Acreage 25 Open 1 March to Mid Nov
Access Good Site Lev/Slope
Near to Lake Windermere with outstanding views of lakes and mountains, ideal touring. AA 4 Pennants and RAC.
**Nearest Town/Resort** Windermere
**Directions** M6 junction 36, A590 to Newby Bridge. Turn right onto A592, in 4 miles turn right into Birks Road. Park is roughly ½ mile on the right.
⇌ Windermere

## WINDERMERE
**White Cross Bay Leisure Park & Marina,** Ambleside Road, Windermere, Cumbria, LA23 1LF
Tel: 0870 774 4024 Fax: 01524 732034
enquiries@southlakeland-caravans.co.uk
www.southlakeland-caravans.co.uk
Pitches For ⊞ ⊟ Total 25
Facilities ⚡ ∮ ⊡ ⊞ ⚓ ⌐ ⊙ ↵
◻ ⚑ ◙ ⊟ ✗ ▽ ⚓ ⋀ ✦ ⊞ ⊟ ☀ ◿
Nearby Facilities ⌐ ✔ ⚓ ✦ ∪ ⊁ ✗
Acreage 60 Open March to Nov
Access Good Site Level
Natural woodland setting right on the shore of Lake Windermere. Restaurant, mini market, bar, sailing school, lake access and marina. Excellent base to explore.
**Nearest Town** Windermere/Ambleside
**Directions** Leave the M6 at junction 36 and follow direction signs to Windermere on the A591. Following signs for Ambleside, park is on the left hand side after approx. 2 miles.
⇌ Windermere

# DERBYSHIRE

## AMBERGATE
**The Firs Farm Caravan & Camping Park** Crich Lane, Nether Heage, Ambergate, BelperDerbyshire, DE56 2JH
Tel: 01773 852913
Email: thefirsfarmcaravanpark@btinternet.com
www.thefirsfarmcaravanpark.co.uk
Pitches For ▲ ⊞ ⊟ Total 60
Facilities ∮ ⊡ ⊞ ⚓ ⌐ ⊙ ↵ ☎
⚑ ⊞ ⊟ ⚑ ▽ ◿
Nearby Facilities ⌐ ✔ ⚓ ∪
Acreage 3½ Open All Year
Access Good Site Level
ADULTS ONLY SITE.
**Nearest Town/Resort** Ambergate
**Directions** 1½ miles south of Ambergate turn left off the A6 at sign for Firs Farm, follow signs for 1 mile.
⇌ Ambergate

## ASHBOURNE
**Bank Top Caravan & Camping,** Bank Top Farm, Fenny Bentley, Ashbourne, Derbyshire, DE6 1LF
Tel: 01335 350250
Pitches For ▲ ⊞ ⊟ Total 51
Facilities ∮ ⊞ ⚓ ⌐ ⊙ ↵ ⚰ ◻ ☎
⚑ ⊞ ⊟ ☀
Nearby Facilities ⌐ ✔ ⚓ ∪ ⊁ ⊁ ✗
Acreage 3 Open April to 1 Oct
Access Good Site Lev/Slope
Working farm with scenic views from the site. Ideal for touring Dovedale and other Dales, also pretty little villages.
**Nearest Town/Resort** Ashbourne
**Directions** From Ashbourne take the A515 north, then take the B5056 and the site is 200 yards on the right.
⇌ Derby

## Rivendale — Peak District
### Tel (01335) 310311

Surrounded by fabulous Peak District scenery with footpaths and trails from site, convenient for Chatsworth, Alton Towers, Dove Dale and Carsington Water.

* Licensed Cafe & Bar
* Open Xmas & New Year
* 10 acre amenity field
* Disabled Facilities.
* Hard-standing pitches
* Central-heated buildings
* Only Closed 10 Jan - 3 Feb
* Holiday Homes for sale

E-mail: cades@Rivendalecaravanpark.co.uk
www.RivendaleCaravanPark.co.uk

---

## ASHBOURNE
**Blackwall Plantation Caravan Club Site,** Kirk Ireton, Ashbourne, Derbyshire, DE6 3JL
Tel: 01335 370903
www.caravanclub.co.uk
Pitches For 🏠 🚐 Total 128
Facilities ⚅ ⅃ 🚽 🚿 🎣 ☐ 🛒 🍴 🅿 🛖 ⚿ 🅿
Nearby Facilities ✈ ⚓
Acreage 25 Open March to Oct
Access Good Site Level
Set in a beautifully landscaped pine plantation. Adjacent to Carsington Reservoir for fishing and sailing. BBQ's allowed with wardens permission. Non members welcome. Booking essential.
Nearest Town/Resort Ashbourne
Directions Take the A517 from Ashbourne, turn left after 4½ at signpost Carsington Water, after ¾ miles at crossroads turn right, site is 1 mile on the right.
✈ Ashbourne

## ASHBOURNE
**Callow Top Holiday Park,** Buxton Road, Ashbourne, Derbyshire, DE6 2AQ
Tel: 01335 344020 Fax: 01335 343726
Email: enquiries@callowtop.co.uk
www.callowtop.co.uk
Pitches For ⚑ 🏠 🚐
Facilities ⚅ ⅃ 🚽 🚿 🎣 🍴 ☐ 🅿 🛒 ☐ 🍴
🛒 🛖 ⚿ ✖ 🍴 🛒 ⚿ 🍴 ❧ ✦ 🅿 ☐
Nearby Facilities ✦ ✈ ⚓ ✦ ∪ ⚿ 🅿
Acreage 15 Open Easter to November
Access Good Site Level
Alton Towers only 20 minutes away, Tissington Trail cycle path is adjacent, Carsington Reservoir 5 miles. Many footpaths. Secure Storage for Winter.
Nearest Town/Resort Ashbourne
Directions The access to Callow Top is only ¼ mile from Ashbourne on the A515 Buxton road. The entrance is directly opposite

Sandybrook Garage, follow the private road for ½ mile to the end.
✈ Derby

## ASHBOURNE
**Highfields Farm Caravan Park,** Fenny Bentley, Ashbourne, Derbyshire, DE6 1LE
Tel: 0870 741 8000 Fax: 0870 741 2000
www.highfieldsfarmcaravanpark.co.uk
Pitches For ⚑ 🏠 🚐 Total 105
Facilities ⅃ 🚽 🚿 🎣 🍴 🅿 ❧ 🛒 ☐ 🍴
🛒 ☐ 🍴 🚽 🍴 ☐ ⚿
Nearby Facilities ✦ ✈ ⚓ ✦ ∪ 🅿 ✦
Acreage 30 Open March to October
Access Good Site Level
Next to the Tissington Trail. Ideal touring.
Nearest Town/Resort Ashbourne
Directions 3 miles north of Ashbourne on the A515 towards Buxton.

## ASHBOURNE
**Lees Hall Farm,** Boylestone, Ashbourne, Derbyshire, DE6 5AA
Tel: 01335 330259 Fax: 01335 330259
Pitches For ⚑ 🏠 🚐 Total 20
Facilities ⅃ 🚽 🅿 🍴 ☐ ✦
Nearby Facilities ✦
Acreage 2 Open March to Oct
Access Good Site Level
Near to Alton Towers.
Nearest Town/Resort Ashbourne
Directions From Ashbourne take the A515 Lichfield road for 6 miles, turn left for Boylestone then second right for Foston, turn first left for Sapperton then first right across Farm Drive.
✈ Uttoxeter

## ASHBOURNE
**Newton Grange Caravan Site,** Newton Grange, Ashbourne, Derbyshire, DE6 1NJ
Tel: 01335 310214
Pitches For ⚑ 🏠 🚐 Total 15
Facilities ⚿ ⅃ 🍴 ☐

Nearby Facilities ✦ ⚓ ∪
Acreage 1 Open Mid Mar to End Oct
Access Good Site Level
Close to Buxton, Matlock and Alton Towers. Tissington Trail adjacent for cycling and walking. Ideal touring.
Nearest Town/Resort Ashbourne
Directions On the A515 4½ miles north of Ashbourne.
✈ Derby

## ASHBOURNE
**Rivendale Caravan & Leisure Park,** Buxton Road, Alsop-en-le-Dale, Ashbourne, Derbyshire, DE6 1QU
Tel: 01335 310311 Fax: 01332 842311
enquiries@rivendalecaravanpark.co.uk
www.rivendalecaravanpark.co.uk
Pitches For ⚑ 🏠 🚐 Total 80
Facilities ⚅ ⅃ 🚽 🚿 🎣 🍴 🅿 ❧ 🛒 ☐ 🍴
🛒 ☐ 🍴 ✖ 🍴 🛒 🍴 🚽 🍴 ☐ 🍴 ⚿
Nearby Facilities ✦ ✈ ⚓ ✦ ∪ 🅿 ✦
Acreage 35 Open Feb to Jan
Access Good Site Level
Surrounded by scenic countryside, ideal for walking, cycling and outdoor hobbies. Convenient for Chatsworth, Alton Towers and many other attractions.
Nearest Town/Resort Hartington
Directions 6½ miles north of Ashbourne, directly accessed from the A515 (Buxton road).
✈ Buxton

## BAKEWELL
**Camping & Caravanning Club Site,** c/o Hopping Farm, Youlgreave, Bakewell, Derbyshire, DE45 1NA
Tel: 01629 636555
www.campingandcaravanningclub.co.uk
Pitches For ⚑ 🏠 🚐 Total 100
Facilities ⅃ 🍴 🚽 ☐ 🛒 ☐ 🍴 ⚿ 🅿
Nearby Facilities ✦ ✈ ∪ 🅿
Acreage 14 Open Marc to Nov Site Sloping
Ideally situated for the Peak District. Near

---

## Callow Top Holiday Park
### Buxton Road, Ashbourne, Derbyshire, DE6 2AQ
### Tel: 01335 344020 (brochure on request)
### www.callowtop.co.uk    enquiries@callowtop.co.uk

A select holiday park overlooking the Derbyshire Dales. Only 8 miles from Alton Towers. The quaint market town of Ashbourne is only 1 mile away. 10 minutes from Carsington Water for water sports & Trout fishing.

**Park facilities include:** Traditional Pub Serving Real Ale & Good Food, Heated Swimming Pool & Paddling Pool, Playground, Games Room, TWO Toilet & Shower Blocks, Disabled Toilet & Shower, Laundry and Pot Washing Room. Craft Brewery. On Site Fishing, Cycle Hire and Several Lovely Country Walks. Hard Standings, Winter Storage & Self Catering Accommodation available.

---

# DERBYSHIRE

to Haddon Hall and Chatsworth House. BTB 3 Star Graded and AA 1 Pennant. Non members welcome.
**Directions** Take the A6 Bakewell to Matlock road, turn onto the B5056 Ashbourne road. After ½ mile take the right hand branch to Youlgreave, turn sharp left after the church into Bradford Lane opposite The George Hotel. Continue ½ mile to club sign then turn right into Farmers Lane for ¼ mile.
✈ Matlock

## BAKEWELL
**Chatsworth Park Caravan Club Site,** Chatsworth, Bakewell, Derbyshire, DE45 1PN
**Tel:** 01246 582226
www.caravanclub.co.uk
**Pitches For** ▲ ⊞ ➡ **Total** 120
**Facilities** ⅃ ♒ 🝙 ⅊ 🖅 ⎍ 🔲 🕭 ➡ ⊡
**Acreage** 6½ **Open** March to Jan
**Access** Good **Site** Level
Situated in the old walled garden on the Chatsworth Estate with beautiful countryside views. Visit Chatsworth House, 1000 acre park and farm. Non members welcome. Booking essential.
**Nearest Town/Resort** Bakewell
**Directions** From Bakewell take the A619, after 3¾ miles (on the outskirts of Baslow) at the mini roundabout turn right signposted Sheffield. Site is 150 yards on the right.
✈ Bakewell

## BAKEWELL
**Greenhills Holiday Park,** Crowhill Lane, Bakewell, Derbyshire, DE45 1PX
**Tel:** 01629 813052 **Fax:** 01629 815760
**Email:** info@greenhillsleisure.com
www.greenhillsleisure.com
**Pitches For** ▲ ⊞ ➡ **Total** 233
**Facilities** ⅃ 🝙 ⅊ 🖅 ⎍ 🔲 🕭 ⊡
🝙 ⅊ 🖅 🕭 ⎐ ⊡ ➡ ⊡ ⚘
**Nearby Facilities** ⌐ ✓ ∪ ♀ ⚡
**Acreage** 8 **Open** March to Oct
**Access** Good **Site** Lev/Slope
In the heart of the Peak District. Close to Chatsworth House and Haddon Hall.
**Directions** 1 mile north west of Bakewell turn left into Crow Hill Lane, turn first right over the cattle grid.
✈ Matlock

## BAKEWELL
**Haddon Grove Caravan & Camping Site,** Haddon Grove Farm, Bakewell, Derbyshire, DE45 1JF
**Tel:** 01629 812343
**Pitches For** ▲ ⊞ ➡
**Facilities** ⅃ 🖅 🕭 ⅊ ⎐ ⎍ 🔲 🕭 ⊡
**Open** March to Oct
**Access** Good **Site** Level
**Directions** From Bakewell take the B5055 towards Monyash. Travel for 3½ miles then turn left at Haddon Grove sign.
✈ Chesterfield

## BAKEWELL
**Stocking Farm Caravan & Camp Site,** Stocking Farm, Calver Bridge, Calver, Hope ValleyDerbyshire, S32 3XA
Hope Valley 630516
**Pitches For** ▲ ⊞ ➡ **Total** 10
**Facilities** 🝙 🖅 🕭 ⅊ ⎐ 🕭 🕭
**Nearby Facilities** ∪ ⚡
**Acreage** 1½ **Open** April to October
**Access** Good **Site** Level
Scenic views, idea touring. Married couples and families only. Dogs must be kept on a lead.
**Directions** Out of Bakewell on the A619 fork left onto the B6001 to traffic lights. Turn right then first left, after Derbyshire Craft Centre first left again.
✈ Grindleford

## BRADWELL
**Eden Tree Caravan Park,** Eccles Lane, Bradwell, Hope Valley, Derbyshire, S33 9JT
**Tel:** 01433 623444
**Pitches For** ▲ ⊞ ➡ **Total** 20
**Facilities** ⅃ 🝙 🖅 🕭 ⅊ ⎐ 🕭 🔲 🔲 ⚘
**Nearby Facilities** ⌐ ✓ ⚓ ∪ ⚡
**Open** March to October
**Access** Good **Site** Sloping
In the heart of the Peak District National Park. Close to Chatsworth House, Castleton, Buxton and many other attractions.
**Nearest Town/Resort** Bakewell
**Directions** On the outskirts of the village of Bradwell, 10 miles from Bakewell.
✈ Hope

## BUXTON
**Cottage Farm Caravan Park,** Blackwell in the Peak, Derbyshire, SK17 9TQ
**Tel:** 01298 85330
**Email:** mail@cottagefarmsite.co.uk
www.cottagefarmsite.co.uk
**Pitches For** ▲ ⊞ ➡ **Total** 30
**Facilities** ⚒ ⅃ 🝙 🖅 🕭 ⅊ ⎐ 🕭 🔲 ⊡
**Nearby Facilities**
**Acreage** 3 **Open** March to October
**Access** Good **Site** Level
Centre of a National Park, ideal for walking and touring by car. Hotel and restaurant in 1 mile.
**Nearest Town/Resort** Buxton
**Directions** Turn off the A6 midway between Buxton and Bakewell, signposted.
✈ Buxton

## BUXTON
**Endon Cottage,** Hulme End, Buxton, Derbyshire, SK17 0HG
**Tel:** 01298 84617
**Pitches For** ▲ ⊞ ➡ **Total** 30
**Facilities** 🝙 🖅 🕭 ⎍
**Nearby Facilities** ✓
**Acreage** 2 **Open** 1 April to 15 Oct
**Access** Good **Site** Sloping
Ideal for walking and touring.
**Nearest Town/Resort** Leek/Buxton
**Directions** From the main A roads take the B5054 into Hulme End and follow Beresford Lane signs. 10 miles from Leek, Buxton and Ashbourne.
✈ Buxton

## BUXTON
**Grin Low Caravan Club Site,** Grin Low Road, Ladmanlow, Buxton, Derbyshire, SK17 6UJ
**Tel:** 01298 77735
www.caravanclub.co.uk
**Pitches For** ▲ ⊞ ➡ **Total** 117
**Facilities** ⅃ 🝙 🖅 🕭 ⅊ ⎐ 🔲 🕭
🝙 ⅊ 🖅 🕭 ⎍ ⊡
**Nearby Facilities** ⌐
**Acreage** 11 **Open** March to Oct
**Access** Good **Site** Level
Situated in the Peak District National Park. Ideal for walking and cycling. Near to many historic houses. No late night arrivals. Non members welcome. Booking essential.
**Nearest Town/Resort** Buxton
**Directions** From Buxton take the A53 Leek road, after 1½ miles turn left signposted Grin Low. After 300 yards turn left into site road, entrance is ¼ mile.
✈ Buxton

## BUXTON
**Lime Tree Park,** Dukes Drive, Buxton, Derbyshire, SK17 9RP
**Tel:** 01298 22988 **Fax:** 01298 22988
www.ukparks.co.uk/limetree
**Pitches For** ▲ ⊞ ➡ **Total** 100
**Facilities** ⅃ 🝙 🖅 🕭 ⅊ ⎐ 🖅 🕭 🔲 ⊡
🝙 ⅊ 🖅 🕭 ⎍ ⊡ ➡ ⊡ ⚘

**Nearby Facilities** ⌐ ✓ ⚓ ⎍ ∪ ♀ ⚡
**Open** March to October inc.
**Access** Good **Site** Lev/Slope
Ideal location for touring the Peak District. TV room.
**Nearest Town/Resort** Buxton
**Directions** From Buxton proceed south on the A515 for ½ mile, sharp left after Buxton Hospital, ½ mile along on the right.
✈ Buxton

## BUXTON
**Newhaven Caravan & Camping Park,** Newhaven, Nr Buxton, Derbyshire, SK17 0DT
**Tel:** 01298 84300
www.newhavencaravanpark.co.uk
**Pitches For** ▲ ⊞ ➡ **Total** 125
**Facilities** ⅃ 🝙 🖅 🕭 ⅊ ⎐ 🕭 ⎍ 🔲 ⊡
🝙 ⅊ 🖅 🕭 ⎐ ⎍ ➡ 🔲 ⊡ ⚘
**Nearby Facilities** ⌐ ✓ ⚓ ∪ ⚡
**Acreage** 27 **Open** March to October
**Access** Good **Site** Lev/Slope
Ideal centre for touring Peak District, National Park and Derbyshire Dales. Café/restaurant opposite site.
**Nearest Town/Resort** Buxton
**Directions** Midway between Ashbourne and Buxton on A515. At the junction with A5012.
✈ Buxton

## BUXTON
**Pomeroy Caravan & Camping Park,** Street House Farm, Pomeroy, Nr Flagg, BuxtonDerbyshire, SK17 9QG
**Tel:** 01298 83259
**Pitches For** ▲ ⊞ ➡ **Total** 40
**Facilities** ⚒ ⅃ 🖅 🕭 ⅊ ⎐ 🔲 🕭 ➡ 🔲 ⊡
**Nearby Facilities** ⌐ ∪ ⚡
**Acreage** 2 **Open** Easter/1 Apr to 31 Oct
**Access** Good **Site** Level
Site adjoins the northern end of Cromford High Peak Trail. Cycle hire centre 3 miles. Ideal walking and cycling.
**Nearest Town/Resort** Buxton
**Directions** From Buxton take the A515 towards Ashbourne, site is 5 miles on the right, go over the cattle grid, 200 yard tarmac drive to the site.
✈ Buxton

## BUXTON
**Waterloo Inn,** Main Street, Biggin by Hartington, Nr. Buxton, Derbyshire, SK17 0DH
**Tel:** 01298 84284
**Pitches For** ▲ ⊞ ➡ **Total** 20
**Facilities** ⅃ 🖅 🕭 ⅊ ⎐ ⎍ 🕭
🕭 ✕ ⚲ 🝙 ⚓ ➡ 🔲 ⊡
**Nearby Facilities** ⌐ ⎍ ⚓ ⚓ ∪ ⚡
**Acreage** 2 **Open** April to Oct
**Access** Good **Site** Lev/Slope
Ideal for walking and cycling, near the Derbyshire Dales (Dove Dale etc.) and the Tissington Trail.
**Nearest Town/Resort** Buxton/Ashbourne
**Directions** From Buxton take the A515 towards Ashbourne for approx. 10 miles, turn right signposted Biggin, site is through the village on the right.
✈ Buxton

## CASTLETON
**Losehill Caravan Club Site,** Castleton, Hope Valley, Derbyshire, S33 8WB
**Tel:** 01433 620636
www.caravanclub.co.uk
**Pitches For** ▲ ⊞ ➡ **Total** 78
**Facilities** ⅃ 🝙 🖅 🕭 ⅊ ⎐ 🔲 ⊡
🝙 ⅊ 🖅 🕭 ➡ 🔲 ⊡
**Nearby Facilities** ⌐ ✓ ∪ ⚡
**Acreage** 6½ **Open** All Year
**Access** Good **Site** Level
Set in the heart of the Peak National Park

with panoramic views. Ideal for outdoor activities such as walking, cycling, pothating, etc.. ½ mile from Peveril Castle. Non members welcome. Booking essential. **Directions** From South on the M1, leave at Junction 29 and take the A617. In Chesterfield turn onto the A619, after 8¾ miles in Baslow turn right at mini roundabout onto the A623. In Calver turn right onto the B6001, in Grindleford turn left at signpost Hathersage still on the B6001). After 2½ miles turn left onto the A6187, site is 5 miles on the right.

## CASTLETON
**Rowter Farm,** Castleton, Hope Valley, Derbyshire, S33 8WA
**Tel:** 01433 620271
www.lets.stay.uk/peakdistrictcampsites
**Pitches For** ▲ ⊕ ⊟ **Total** 30
**Facilities** ⬛ 🚻 ⟍ 🏪🚻⊟
**Nearby Facilities** ∪ ⅄
**Acreage** 4 **Open** End March to End Oct
**Access** Good **Site** Level
One static caravan available for hire.
**Nearest Town/Resort** Castleton
**Directions** From Castleton take the B6061 Winnats Pass road, go to the top and continue for 200 yards, turn left through the gate.
⚞ Hope

## DERBY
**Beechwood Park,** Main Road, Elvaston, Thulston, DerbyDerbyshire, DE72 3EQ
**Tel:** 01332 751938 **Fax:** 01332 751938
**Email:** colinbeech@btconnect.com
www.beechwoodparkleisure.co.uk
**Pitches For** ▲ ⊕ ⊟ **Total** 45
**Facilities** ⬡ ⨍ 🛁 ⬛ ⟍ 🏪⊙ 🍴 ⊡ 🖥 ⊟
😊 ⊙🚻⊟ ⊡
**Nearby Facilities** ⌐ ✑ ⚲ ⅄ ⊿
**Acreage** 5 **Open** All Year
**Access** Good **Site** Level
Superb level touring pitches. Three fishing lakes. Lovely country pub in the village.
**Nearest Town/Resort** Derby
⚞ Derby

## DERBY
**Shardlow Marina Caravan Park,** London Road, Shardlow, Derby, Derbyshire, DE72 2GL
**Tel:** 01332 792832 **Fax:** 01332 792832
**Pitches For** ▲ ⊕ ⊟ **Total** 40
**Facilities** ⨍ 🛁 🗑 ⬛ 🚿 ⟍ 🏪⊙ ⊿ 🖥 ⊟
😊 🗑⊙🛒❌🍴 ╌⅄ ℘
**Nearby Facilities** ⌐ ✑
**Open** March to Jan
**Access** Good **Site** Level
Near a river and canal.
**Nearest Town/Resort** Derby
**Directions** Junction 1 of A6/A50 Derby southern bypass. 5 miles from Derby.
⚞ Derby

## DOVERIDGE
**Cavendish Cottage Camping & Caravan Site,** Doveridge, Ashbourne, Derbyshire, DE6 5JR
**Tel:** 01889 562092
**Pitches For** ▲ ⊕ ⊟ **Total** 15
**Facilities** ⨍ ⬛⊙🍴 ⬛ 🗒 🛒❌
**Nearby Facilities**
**Acreage** 2 **Open** All Year
**Access** Good **Site** Level
Alton Towers, Dovedale, Sudbury Hall and many pleasant walks. Owner Mr G Wood.
**Nearest Town/Resort** Uttoxeter
**Directions** On the main road in Doveridge take the sign posts for (Doveridge)
⚞ Uttoxeter

## EDALE
**Fieldhead Campsite,** Edale, Hope Valley, Derbyshire, S33 7ZA
**Tel:** 01433 670386
**Email:** booking@fieldhead-campsite.co.uk
www.fieldhead-campsite.co.uk
**Pitches For** ▲ **Total** 45
**Facilities** ⬡ ⬛ 🚿 ⟍ 🏪⊙ ⊿ 🖥 🍴
**Nearby Facilities** ⌐ ✑ ⚲ ⚲ ∪ ⊿ ⌿ ⅄
**Acreage** 3 **Open** All Year **Site** Level
Alongside a river, next to Peak District Visitor Centre. 6 fields, 2 of which are by the river. All superb views of Mamtor Ridge and Kinder Scout. At the start of Pennine Way.
**Nearest Town/Resort** Castleton
**Directions** 4½ miles from Castleton.
⚞ Edale

## EDALE
**Highfield Farm,** Upper Booth, Edale, Hope Valley, Derbyshire, S33 7ZJ
**Tel:** 01433 670245
**Pitches For** ▲ ⊕ ⊟
**Facilities** ⬛ 🚿 ⬡ 🛒 ⊟
**Nearby Facilities** ∪ ⅄
**Acreage** 30 **Open** Easter to October
**Access** Good **Site** Lev/Slope
Good walking country, ideal for climbing and caves nearby. Sorry No Dogs allowed.
**Nearest Town/Resort** Buxton/Castleton
**Directions** Turn right off the A625 opposite Hope Church, take minor road to Edale. Follow the road up the valley, pass the turning for Edale Village, at bottom of the hill turn right, go past the viaduct and pass picnic area, round the corner and the house is up ahead.
⚞ Edale

## EDALE
**Waterside Camp Site,** Waterside, Barber Booth Road, Edale, Hope ValleyDerbyshire, S33 7ZL
**Tel:** 01433 670215 **Fax:** 01433 670293
**Email:** jenn.cooper@cw.com
**Pitches For** ▲ ⊕ ⊟ **Total** 50
**Facilities** ⨍ ⬛ ⬛ ⟍ 🏪⊙ ⊿ ⊟
**Nearby Facilities** ⌐ ✑ ∪ ⅄
**Open** Easter to End Sept
**Access** Good **Site** Level
Near to the Pennine Way, Blue John Caverns, Chatsworth House (18 miles) and Bakewell. Café ½ mile.
**Nearest Town/Resort** Buxton
⚞ Edale

## ELVASTON
**Elvaston Castle Caravan Club Site,** Borrowash Road, Elvaston, Derbyshire, DE72 3EP
**Tel:** 01332 573735
www.caravanclub.co.uk
**Pitches For** ▲ ⊕ ⊟ **Total** 44
**Facilities** ⨍ ⬛ ⟍ 🏪⊙ ⊿ 🛒❌⊟
**Nearby Facilities** ⌐ ✑ ∪
**Acreage** 3 **Open** March to Oct
**Access** Good **Site** Level
Set in a 280 acre country park which has a castle with museum and provides play facilities, horse riding and lovely walks. Within easy reach of Nottingham. No arrivals after 8pm as park gates are locked. Non members welcome. Booking essential.
**Nearest Town/Resort** Derby
**Directions** From north on the M1 leave at junction 24A onto the A50, at junction 2 leave via slip road signposted Alvaston. At roundabout turn right onto the B5010, continue left on the B5010 then, at 1 mile turn left into Elvaston Castle Country Park, site is on the left before the car park kiosk.
⚞ Derby

## GLOSSOP
**Crowden Camping & Caravanning Club Site,** Crowden, Glossop, Derbyshire, SK13 1HZ
**Tel:** 01457 866057
www.campingandcaravanningclub.co.uk
**Pitches For** ▲ **Total** 45
**Facilities** ⬛ ⬛ ⟍ 🏪⊙⊿ 🖥 🛒❌🖥 ⊟
**Nearby Facilities** ⅄
**Acreage** 2½ **Open** April to Oct
**Site** Sloping
In the heart of the Peak District National Park, close to the Pennine Way. BTB 3 Star Graded and AA 2 Pennants. Non members welcome.
**Directions** On the A628 Manchester to Barnsley road, in Crowden follow signs for car park, Youth Hostel and camp site. Camp site is approx. 300 yards from the main road.
⚞ Hadfield/Glossop

## HARTINGTON
**Barracks Farm Caravan & Camping Site,** Beresford Dale, Hartington, Buxton, Derbyshire, SK17 0HQ
**Tel:** 01298 84261
**Pitches For** ▲ ⊕ ⊟ **Total** 40
**Facilities** ⬛ ⬛ ⟍ 🏪⊙ 🍴 ⊙🛒❌🖥
**Nearby Facilities**
**Acreage** 5 **Open** Easter to End Oct
**Access** Good **Site** Level
Alongside river, scenic views and ideal touring.
**Nearest Town/Resort** Buxton
**Directions** Buxton A515 approx 10 miles. After leaving Buxton go on for 7 miles, turn right for Hartington B5054. Go through village for 1½ miles, turn left for Beresford Dale, continue for ¼ mile then turn left again signposted Beresford Dale. The site is second on the left.
⚞ Buxton

## HAYFIELD
**Camping & Caravanning Club Site,** Kinder Road, Hayfield, High Peak, Derbyshire, SK22 2LE
**Tel:** 01663 745394
www.campingandcaravanningclub.co.uk
**Pitches For** ▲ ⊕ ⊟ **Total** 90
**Facilities** ⬛ ⬛ ⟍ 🏪⊙ ⊿ 🖥 🛒❌🖥 ⊟
**Nearby Facilities** ∪
**Acreage** 6 **Open** March to Nov
**Access** Difficult **Site** Level
On the banks of the River Sett. Ideal for fell and moorland walkers. 6 miles from a Victorian style swimming pool. 12 miles from Granada Studios. BTB 3 Star Graded and AA 2 Pennants. Non members welcome (no caravans).
**Directions** On the A624 Glossop to Chapel-en-le-Frith road, the Hayfield by-pass. Well signed to the village, follow wooden carved signs to the site.
⚞ New Mills

## HOPE
**Hardhurst Farm,** Parsons Lane, Hope, Hope Valley, Derbyshire, S33 6RB
**Tel:** 01433 620001
**Pitches For** ▲ ⊕ ⊟ **Total** 37
**Facilities** ⨍ 🗑 ⬛ ⬛ ⟍ 🏪⊙ ⊿ 🖥 ⊟
🖥 🛒❌🍴 ⊟
**Nearby Facilities** ⌿ ∪ ⅄
**Acreage** 3 **Open** All Year
**Access** Good **Site** Level
Ideal touring base for the Peak District.
**Nearest Town/Resort** Castleton
**Directions** 10 miles west of Sheffield on the A625.
⚞ Hope

## HOPE

**Laneside Caravan Park,** Hope, Hope Valley, Derbyshire, S33 6RR
**Tel:** 01433 620215 **Fax:** 01433 620214
**Email:** laneside@lineone.net
www.lanesidecaravanpark.co.uk
**Pitches For** ▲ ⊕ ☻
**Facilities** ⚲ ╱ 🖪 🄷 🖽 ⚡ ⌐ ☉ ☐ ⚞ ◧ 🄰 ☎
🏧 🅻 🖸 🅰 🄷🄼🄿🄳 ⚡
**Nearby Facilities** ┌ ╱ ∪ ⅄
**Open** April **to** October
**Access** Good **Site** Level
Alongside the River Noe. Just a few minutes walk to the village shops, pubs and restaurant.
**Nearest Town/Resort** Hope
**Directions** Camp site borders river/bridge on the Hope Village boundary.
⚯ Hope

## MATLOCK

**Birchwood Farm Caravan Park,**
Wirksworth Road, Whatstandwell, Matlock, Derbyshire, DE4 5HS
**Tel:** 01629 822280 **Fax:** 01629 822280
**Pitches For** ▲ ⊕ ☻ **Total** 70
**Facilities** ⚲ ╱ 🖪 🄷 🖽 ⚡ ⌐ ☉ ⊿ 🄰 ◧ ☎
🏧 🖸 🄰🄼🄿🄳 ⚡
**Nearby Facilities** ┌ ╱ ⚓ ⅄ ⅃
**Acreage** 4 **Open** April **to** October
**Access** Good **Site** Lev/Slope
Near High Peak Trail, ideal touring area. Carsington Water 20 minutes. Table Tennis on site.
**Nearest Town/Resort** Matlock Bath
**Directions** Leave to A6 at Whatstandwell, take the B5035 towards Wirksworth, about 1 mile.
⚯ Whatstandwell

## MATLOCK

**Lickpenny Caravan Park,** Lickpenny Lane, Tansley, Matlock, Derbyshire, DE4 5GF
**Tel:** 01629 583040 **Fax:** 01629 583040
**Email:** lickpenny@btinternet.com
www.lickpennycaravanpark.co.uk
**Pitches For** ⊕ ☻ **Total** 90
**Facilities** ⚲ ╱ 🖪 🄷 🖽 ⚡ ⌐ ☉ ⊿ 🄰 ◧ ☎
🄰 ◧ 🄰🄼🄿🄳 ⚡
**Nearby Facilities** ┌ ╱ ⅄ ∪ ⅃ ⅄
**Acreage** 16 **Open** All Year
**Access** Good **Site** Level/Terraced
Ideal touring. Large individual hardstanding plots, some fully serviced pitches.
**Nearest Town/Resort** Matlock
**Directions** From Matlock Town centre take the A615 towards the M1 for 2½ miles.
⚯ Matlock

## MATLOCK

**Packhorse Farm Bungalow,** Packhorse Farm, Tansley, Matlock, Derbyshire, DE4 5LF
**Tel:** 01629 582781
**Pitches For** ▲ ⊕ ☻ **Total** 20
**Facilities** ╱ 🖪 ⚡ ⌐ ☉ ⚞ 🄷🄼🄿🄳 ⚡
**Nearby Facilities** ┌ ╱ ⚓ ∪ ⅃
**Acreage** 3 **Open** All Year
**Access** Good **Site** Level
Ideal for touring the countryside.
**Nearest Town/Resort** Matlock
**Directions** Take the A615 to Tansley Village, 1½ miles to the site. 4½ miles from Matlock.
⚯ Matlock

## WHALEY BRIDGE

**Ringstones Caravan Park,** Yeardsley Lane, Furness Vale, Whaley Bridge, Derbyshire, SK23 7EB
**Tel:** 01663 732152/747042
**Pitches For** ▲ ⊕ ☻

**Facilities** 🖽 ⚲ ⌐ ☉ ☎ ◧🄷◧🄳 ⚡ ╱ ☐
**Nearby Facilities** ┌ ╱ ⅄ ⚡ ⅃
**Acreage** 3 **Open** March **to** October
**Access** Good **Site** Lev/Slope
Near a restaurant and licenced club.
**Nearest Town/Resort** Whaley Bridge
**Directions** From Whaley Bridge take A6 towards Stockport, in Furness Vale turn left at Pelican crossing (Cantonese resturant on corner).
⚯ Furness Vale

## DEVON

### ASHBURTON

**Parkers Farm Holiday Park,** Higher Mead Farm, Ashburton, Devon, TQ13 7LJ
**Tel:** 01364 652598 **Fax:** 01364 654004
**Email:** parkersfarm@btconnect.com
www. parkersfarm.co.uk
**Pitches For** ▲ ⊕ ☻ **Total** 60
**Facilities** ⚲ ╱ 🖪 🄷 🖽 ⚡ ⌐ ☉ ⊿ 🄰 ◧ ☎
🏧 🅻 🖸 🄰☻✗ ⅄ ⚡ 🄰🄷🄼🄳 ⚡ ⅄
**Nearby Facilities** ┌ ╱ ⚓ ⅄ ∪ ⅃ ⚡ ⅃
**Acreage** 10 **Open** April **to** October
**Access** Good **Site** Level Terrace
A real working farm enviroment with goats, sheep, pigs, cows, ducks and rabbits set amidst beautiful countryside.
**Nearest Town/Resort** Ashburton
**Directions** Take the A38 to Plymouth, when you see the sign 26 miles Plymouth take second left at Alston Cross marked Woodland - Denbury. The site is behind the bungalow.
⚯ Newton Abbot

**SHBURTON**

**iver Dart Adventures,** Holne Park, shburton, Devon, TQ13 7NP
**el:** 01364 652511 **Fax:** 01364 652020
**mail:** enquiries@riverdart.co.uk
**ww.** riverdart.co.uk
**itches For** ⚠ ⛺ ♿ **Total** 170
**acilities** ⚙ 🚿 🔌 ⚡ 🛒 ⛱ ⛴ 🍴 ⚑
🕜 ⚙ 🚻 ⛽ 🎣 🛒 ⤳ 🚮 🅿 ☐ 🚽
**earby Facilities** 🏇 🚣 ⚓ 🎣 🏌 🏊
**.creage** 90 **Open** Easter/1 April **to** Sept
**.ccess** Good **Site** Level
**.agnificent** site alongside the River Dart.
.eal touring site for Dartmoor and the outh Devon coast.
**earest Town/Resort** Ashburton
**irections** A38 Devon expressway at xeter/Plymouth. From the A38 follow brown 'gns for River Dart Country Park.
⇌ Newton Abbot

**AXMINSTER**

**Andrewshayes Caravan Park,** Dalwood, Axminster, Devon, EX13 7DY
**Tel:** 01404 831225 **Fax:** 01404 831893
**Email:** info@andrewshayes.co.uk
**www.** andrewshayes.co.uk
**Pitches For** ⚠ ⛺ ♿ **Total** 150
**Facilities** ⚙ ⛽ ⛴ 🍴 🛒 ⚡ 🍴 🛒 ☐ ⚑
🕜 🕱 🚿 🚻 ⛴ ⚙ ⤳ 🚮 🅿 ☐ 🚽 ※
**Nearby Facilities** 🏇 🚣 ⚓ 🎣
**Acreage** 10 **Open** March **to** Dec
**Access** Good **Site** Sloping
Peaceful, clean park in beautiful countryside. Ideal for family holiday. Easy reach of resorts. Friendly bar and restaurant. Clean toilets with family and disabled rooms.
**Directions** Just off the A35 3 miles from Axminster and 6 miles from Honiton. Turn north at Taunton Cross and the site entrance is 100 yards.
⇌ Axminster

**AXMINSTER**

**Hunters Moon Country Estate,** Off B3165, Hawkchurch, Near Lyme Regis, East Devon, EX13 5UL
**Tel:** 01297 678402 **Fax:** 01297 678720
**Pitches For** ⚠ ⛺ ♿ **Total** 183
**Facilities** ⛴ ⛽ 🚿 ⚡ 🍴 🛒 ⛴ ⚡ ☐ ⚑
🕱 ⚙ 🚿 🚻 ⛴ ⚙ 🚮 🅿 ☐ 🚽 ※ ♿
**Nearby Facilities** 🏇 🚣 ⚓ 🎣 ⛵
**Acreage** 21 **Open** 15 March **to** 15 Nov
**Access** Good **Site** Level
Occupying a privileged location, protected by mature woodlands yet with commanding views over the Axe Valley. This tranquil park is remarkable. Only a few minutes drive from the spectacular Jurassic coastline of Lyme Regis.
**Directions** From Axminster take A35 towards Dorchester for 3 miles. At main crossroads take left B3165 towards Crewkerne. Follow for 2¼ miles turn left to Hunters Moon.
⇌ Axminster

**Brightlycott Caravan & Camping Site,**
Brightlycott Barton, Barnstaple, Devon,
EX31 4JJ
**Tel:** 01271 850330
**Email:** friend.brightlycott@virgin.net
**Pitches For** Å ⊕ ⊟ **Total** 20
**Facilities** ⌇ 🚿 ♨ ⌂ ☉ ⊐ 🛒 ☎
🏠 ♣ 🅰 🕪 🔁 ☒ ⋇ 🔎
**Nearby Facilities** ⌇ ⌇ ∪ ♬
**Acreage** 4 **Open** 15 March **to** 15 Nov
**Access** Good **Site** Lev/Slope
Extremely peaceful, small, friendly, family
run site situated on a former dairy farm
with panoramic views.
**Nearest Town/Resort** Barnstaple
**Directions** Leave Barnstaple on the A39
towards Lynton, turn right 1½ miles after the
hospital signposted Brightlycott and
Roborough.
�± 🚂 Barnstaple

## BARNSTAPLE
**Greenacres Farm Touring Caravan Park,**
Bratton Fleming, Barnstaple, North Devon,
EX31 4SG
**Tel:** 01598 763334
**Pitches For** ⊕ ⊟ **Total** 30
**Facilities** ⅃ ⌇ 🚿 ♨ ⌂ ☉ ⊐ 🛒 ☎
🏠 ☒ 🅰 ♣ 🕪 🔁 ☒
**Nearby Facilities** ⌇ ∪
**Acreage** 4 **Open** April **to** October
**Access** Good **Site** Level
Moors and coast 5 miles, towns 10 miles.
Peaceful, secluded park with scenic views.
Ideal for touring, walking and cycling.
**Nearest Town/Resort** Barnstaple
**Directions** From North Devon link road
(A361), turn right at Northaller roundabout
(by Little Chef). Take the A399 to Blackmoor
Gate, approx 10 miles. Park signed (300yds
from the A399).
➱ Barnstaple

## BARNSTAPLE
**Kentisbury Grange Country Park,**
Kentisbury, Barnstaple, Devon, EX31 4NL
**Tel:** 01271 883454 **Fax:** 01271 882040
**Email:** info@kentisburygrange.co.uk
**www.** www.kentisburygrange.co.uk
**Pitches For** Å ⊕ ⊟ **Total** 20
**Facilities** ⅃ ⌇ ⊟ 🚿 ♨ ⌂ ☉ ⊐ 🛒 ☎

♌ ⌇ 🚿 🕪 🔁 ☒ ⋇ 🔎
**Nearby Facilities** ⌇ ⌇ ⚓ ⚶ ∪ ♬ ♬ ⚡
**Acreage** 7 **Open** Easter **to** Sept
**Access** Good **Site** Lev/Slope
On the fringe of Exmoor, 5 miles from the
beach. Fishing nearby for trout (2 miles)
and carp (5 miles).
**Nearest Town/Resort** Combe Martin
**Directions** On the A39 midway between
Barnstaple and Lynton.
➱ Barnstaple

## BARNSTAPLE
**Tarka Holiday Park,** Braunton Road,
Barnstaple, North Devon, EX31 4AU
**Tel:** 01271 343691 **Fax:** 01271 326355
**Email:** info@tarkaholidaypark.co.uk
**www.** tarkaholidaypark.co.uk
**Pitches For** Å ⊕ ⊟ **Total** 95
**Facilities** ⅃ ⌇ ⊟ 🚿 ♨ ⌂ ☉ ⊐ 🛒 ☒ 🖩 ☎
♌ ⌇ ⊕ 🖉 🅰 🕪 🔁 ☒ ⋇
**Nearby Facilities** ⌇ ⌇ ⚓ ∪
**Open** March **to** October
**Access** Good **Site** Level
Close to the famous Tarka Trail for walking
and cycling. Discover the beautiful rugged
coastline of North Devon. Great shopping
in Barnstaple.
**Nearest Town/Resort** Barnstaple
**Directions** Take the A361 from Barnstaple
towards Ilfracombe, site is approx. 2 miles.
➱ Barnstaple

## BIDEFORD
**Steart Farm Touring Park,** Horns Cross,
Bideford, Devon, EX39 5DW
**Tel:** 01237 431836
**Email:** steart@tiscali.co.uk
**Pitches For** Å ⊕ ⊟ **Total** 70
**Facilities** ⅃ ⌇ ⊟ 🚿 ♨ ⌂ ☉ ⊐ 🛒 🖩 ☎
♌ ⌇ 🚿 🅰 🕪 🔁 ☒ ⋇
**Nearby Facilities** ⌇ ⌇ ∪ ⚡
**Acreage** 10¼ **Open** Easter **to** Sept
**Access** Good **Site** Lev/Slope
Set in 17 acres overlooking Bideford Bay, 1
mile from the sea. 2¼ acre dog exercise
area. 2 acre childrens play area.
**Nearest Town/Resort** Bideford
**Directions** From Bideford follow the A39
west (signed Bude). Pass through Fairy
Cross and Horns Cross, 2 miles after Horns

Cross site will be on the right. 8 miles from
Bideford.
➱ Barnstaple

## BRAUNTON
**Chivenor Caravan Park,** Chivenor Cross,
Braunton, Barnstaple, North Devon, EX31
4BN
**Tel:** 01271 812217
**Email:** chivenorcp@lineone.net
**www.** chivenorcaravanpark.co.uk
**Pitches For** Å ⊕ ⊟ **Total** 30
**Facilities** ⅃ ⌇ ⊟ 🚿 ♨ ⌂ ☉ 🖩 ☎
♌ ⌇ 🚿 🅰 🔁 ☒ ⋇
**Nearby Facilities** ⌇ ⌇ ⚓ ⚶ ∪ ♬ ♬ ⚡
**Acreage** 3 **Open** March **to** January
**Access** Good **Site** Level
100 yards from the Tarka Trail. Saunton
Sands 3 miles. Central for touring North
Devon.
**Nearest Town/Resort** Braunton
**Directions** On the A361 Barnstaple to
Braunton road, on the only roundabout
between the two.
➱ Barnstaple

## BRAUNTON
**Lobb Fields Caravan & Camping Park,**
Saunton Road, Braunton, Devon, EX33 1EB
**Tel:** 01271 812090 **Fax:** 01271 812090
**Email:** info@lobbfields.com
**www.** lobbfields.com
**Pitches For** Å ⊕ ⊟ **Total** 180
**Facilities** ⅃ ⌇ ⊟ 🚿 ♨ ⌂ ☉ ⊐ 🛒 🖩 ☎
♌ ⌇ 🚿 🕪 🔁 ☒
**Nearby Facilities** ⌇ ⌇ ⚓ ⚶ ∪ ♬ ⚡
**Acreage** 14 **Open** 24 March **to** 29 Oct
**Access** Good **Site** Gentle Slope
1½ miles from the beach. 1 mile from the
Tarka Trail. Disabled toilet and shower.
**Nearest Town/Resort** Braunton
**Directions** Take the A361 to Braunton, then
take the B3231. The park entrance is 1 mile
from Braunton centre on the right.
➱ Barnstaple

## BRIXHAM
**Centry Touring Caravans & Tents,**
Mudberry House, Centry Road, Brixham,
Devon, TQ5 9EY
**Tel:** 01803 853215 **Fax:** 01803 853261

## Upton Manor Farm Camping  BRIXHAM•TORBAY  01803 882384

Quiet and sheltered, friendly, family run site, on the outskirts of Brixham in lovely countryside near the beach. High standard of cleanliness in the toilet/shower blocks, Free hot water in showers and wash basins. Modern laundry facilities. Out of season Special Offers (per week) for couples. *E-mail: uptoncamp@aol.com*

**St. Mary's Road • BRIXHAM • Devon • TQ5 9QH** *www.uptonmanorfarm.co.uk*

**Email:** jlacentry.touring@talk21.com
**www.**ukparks.co.uk/centry
**Pitches For** ▲ ⊞ ➡ **Total** 30
**Facilities** ↯ ⅏ ⚓ ⌂ ⊙⊣ ❄ ⅋ ⊘↦⊟
**Nearby Facilities** ⌐ ✓ ⚓ ❅ ∪ ⅃ ♪ ⚡
**Acreage** 2 **Open** April **to** October
**Access** Good **Site** Level
Next to the coastal footpath and adjacent to Berry Head Country Park.
**Nearest Town/Resort** Brixham
**Directions** Entering Brixham on the A3022, bear right at the first set of traffic lights and follow signs to Berry Head.
⇥ Paignton

## BRIXHAM
**Galmpton Touring Park,** Greenway Road, Galmpton, Brixham, Devon, TQ5 0EP
**Tel:** 01803 842066
**Email:** galmptontouringpark@hotmail.com
**www.**galmptontouringpark.co.uk
**Pitches For** ▲ ⊞ ➡ **Total** 120
**Facilities** ⅙ ↯ ⅏ ⚓ ⌂ ⊙⊣ ⊿ ⊟ ⊘ ❄
₷ ⅃ ⊘ ⊗ Å ↦ ⊟ ⊟ ⊟
**Nearby Facilities** ⌐ ✓ ⚓ ❅ ⅃
**Acreage** 10 **Open** Easter **to** September
**Access** Good **Site** Lev/Slope
Terraced site with stunning River Dart views, in a central Torbay location. Pets are welcome but not in peak season (mid July to August).
**Nearest Town/Resort** Brixham
**Directions** Signposted right off the A379 Brixham road ¼ mile past the end of the A380 Torbay ring road.
⇥ Paignton

## BRIXHAM
**Hillhead Holiday Park,** Hillhead, Brixham, Devon, TQ5 0HH
**Tel:** 01803 853204
**www.**caravanclub.co.uk
**Pitches For** ▲ ⊞ ➡ **Total** 193
**Facilities** ⅙ ↯ ⅏ ⚓ ⌂ ⊙ ⊿ ⊟ ⊟
₷ ⅃ ⊘ ⊗ ❌ ▽ ⊞ Å ↻ ↦ ⊟ ⊟
**Nearby Facilities** ⌐ ✓ ⚓ ❅ ⅃
**Acreage** 20 **Open** March **to** Oct
**Access** Good **Site** Lev/Slope
In a great location with many pitches affording stunning views of the sea, South Devon and parts of Dorset. Ideal site for families. Kingswear-Paignton Steam Railway and Paignton Zoo nearby. Non members welcome. Booking essential.
**Nearest Town/Resort** Brixham
**Directions** From the A380 3 miles south of Newton Abbot turn right onto the ring road signposted Brixham. After 7 miles at traffic lights turn right onto the A3022, just past Churston Golf Course turn right onto the A379. At mini roundabout turn right and immediately fork left onto the B3205. Site is ¼ of a mile on the left.
⇥ Paignton

## BRIXHAM
**Upton Manor Farm Camping Site,** Upton Manor Farm, St Mary's Road, Brixham, Devon, TQ5 9QH
**Tel:** 01803 882384
**Email:** uptoncamp@aol.com
**www.**uptonmanorfarm.co.uk
**Pitches For** ▲ ⊞ ➡ **Total** 175

**Facilities** ↯ ⅏ ⚓ ⌂ ⊙⊣ ⊙ ⅃ ⊘ ❄ ⊟ ⊟ ⊟
**Nearby Facilities** ⌐ ✓ ⚓ ❅ ⅃
**Acreage** 7½ **Open** Spring B/H **to** Mid Sept
**Access** Good **Site** Level
Pets welcome if kept on leads.
**Nearest Town/Resort** Brixham
**Directions** In Brixham town centre turn right into Bolton Street, at the traffic lights go straight on, then turn left into Castor Road which leads to St. Mary's Road.
⇥ Paignton

## BUCKFAST
**Churchill Farm,** Buckfastleigh, Devon, TQ11 0EZ
**Tel:** 01364 642844
**Email:** a.pedrick@farmersweekly.net
**Pitches For** ▲ ⊞ ➡ **Total** 25
**Facilities** ↯ ⅏ ⚓ ⌂ ⊙⊣ ⊟ ⊟ ⊟
**Nearby Facilities** ⌐ ✓ ⚓ ❅ ∪ ♪ ⅃ ♪ ⚡
**Acreage** 2 **Open** April **to** October
**Access** Good **Site** Lev/Slope
Stunning views of Dartmoor and Buckfast Abbey, the latter being within easy walking distance as are the Steam Railway, Butterfly Farm, Otter Sanctuary and local inns. Seaside resort 10 miles.
**Nearest Town** Buckfastleigh/Buckfast
**Directions** Exit A38 at Dartbridge, follow signs for Buckfast Abbey, proceed up hill to crossroads. Turn left into no-through road towards church. Farm entrance is opposite the church 1½ miles from the A38.
⇥ Totnes

## BUCKFASTLEIGH
**Beara Farm Camping Site,** Colston Road, Buckfastleigh, Devon, TQ11 0LW
**Tel:** 01364 642234
**Pitches For** ▲ ⊞ ➡ **Total** 30
**Facilities** ⅙ ⅏ ⅏ ⚓ ⌂ ⊙⊣ ⊟ ❄ ↦ ⊟
**Nearby Facilities** ⌐ ∪ ⅃
**Acreage** 3¼ **Open** All Year
**Access** Good **Site** Level
Quiet, select, sheltered site adjoining River Dart. Within easy reach of sea and moors and 1½ miles southeast of Buckfastleigh.
**Nearest Town/Resort** Buckfastleigh
**Directions** Coming from Exeter take first left after passing South Devon Railway and Butterfly Centre at Buckfastleigh, signpost marked Beara, fork right at next turning then 1 mile to site, signposted on roadside and junctions.
⇥ Totnes

## CHAGFORD
**Woodland Springs Adult Touring Park,** Venton, Drewsteignton, Devon, EX6 6PG
**Tel:** 01647 231695
**Email:** enquiries@woodlandsprings.co.uk
**www.**woodlandsprings.co.uk
**Pitches For** ▲ ⊞ ➡ **Total** 85
**Facilities** ↯ ⅏ ⅏ ⚓ ⌂ ⊙⊣ ❄ ↦ ⊟ ⊟ Å ⅃ ❄
**Nearby Facilities** ⌐ ✓ ∪
**Acreage** 4 **Open** All Year
**Access** Good **Site** Level
ADULTS ONLY. Quiet, secluded site within the Dartmoor National Park, surrounded by wood and farmland. Good access for the larger units and large all-weather pitches. Off season breaks.

**Nearest Town/Resort** Okehampton
**Directions** From Exeter take the A30, after 17 miles turn left at Merrymeet roundabout onto the A382 towards Moretonhampstead, after ½ a mile turn left at the roundabout, site is 1 mile on the left signpost Venton.
⇥ Exeter

## CHUDLEIGH
**Holmans Wood Holiday Park,** Harcombe, Cross, Chudleigh, Devon, TQ13 0DZ
**Tel:** 01626 853785 **Fax:** 01626 853792
**Email:** enquiries@holmanswood.co.uk
**www.**holmanswood.co.uk
**Pitches For** ▲ ⊞ ➡ **Total** 100
**Facilities** ⅙ ↯ ⅏ ⅏ ⚓ ⌂ ⊙⊣ ⊿ ⊟ ⊟ ⊟
⅃ ⊘ ⊗ Å ⊟ ⊟ ❄ ⅃
**Nearby Facilities** ⌐ ✓ ⚓ ❅ ∪ ♪ ⚡ ⚡
**Acreage** 11 **Open** March **to** End October
**Access** Good **Site** Level
Picturesque setting. Ideal touring for Dartmoor, Haldon Forest, Exeter and Torbay. Holiday homes for sale.
**Nearest Town/Resort** Chudleigh
**Directions** From Exeter take the A38 Towards Plymouth. Go past the racecourse and after 1 mile take the B3344 for Chudleigh. We are on the left at the end of the sliproad.
⇥ Newton Abbot

## CLOVELLY
**Dyke Green Farm,** Nr Clovelly, Bideford, Devon, EX39 5RU
**Tel:** 01237 431279
**Pitches For** ▲ ⊞ ➡ **Total** 40
**Facilities** ↯ ⅏ ⚓ ⌂ ⊙ ❄ ₷ ⅃ ⊘ ↦ ⊟
**Nearby Facilities** ⌐ ✓ ⚓ ❅ ∪ ♪ ⚡
**Acreage** 3 **Open** Easter **to** Oct
**Access** Good **Site** Level
**Nearest Town/Resort** Clovelly
⇥ Barnstaple

## COMBE MARTIN
**Newberry Farm,** Woodlands, Combe Martin, North Devon, EX34 0AT
**Tel:** 01271 882334
**Email:** enq@newberrycampsite.co.uk
**www.**newberrycampsite.co.uk
**Pitches For** ▲ ⊞ ➡ **Total** 110
**Facilities** ⅙ ↯ ⅏ ⅏ ⚓ ⌂ ⊙ ⊿ ⊟ ❄
⅃ ⊘ Å ⊟ ⊟ ❄ ⅃
**Nearby Facilities** ⌐ ✓ ⚓ ❅ ∪
**Acreage** 20 **Open** Easter **to** October
**Access** Good **Site** Level
Beautiful countryside valley site. Combe Martin beach and village within 5 minutes walk. Course fishing lake. Woodland walks. Exmoor National Park nearby. 4 Star Graded. Sorry, no dogs.
**Nearest Town** Combe Martin/Ilfracombe
**Directions** Leave the M5 at junction 27 and take the A361 to Aller Cross Roundabout. A399 to Combe Martin.
⇥ Barnstaple

## COMBE MARTIN
**Sandaway Beach Holiday Park,** John Fowler Holidays, Sandaway, Nr Combe Martin, North Devon, EX34 9ST
**Tel:** 01271 866766 **Fax:** 01271 866791
**Email:** bookings@johnfowlerholidays.com

# DEVON

www.johnfowlerholidays.com
**Pitches For** ⚠ ⊕ **Total** 20
**Facilities** ⚒ ✦ 🔲 🆖 🔱 ✦ ⌐ ☉ ☐ 🔲 ☎
🕿 📶 🖲 🏊 ✕ 🍴 🛝 🔥 ⚓ ⌂ 🔲 🔲
**Nearby Facilities** 🏇 🖊 ⚓ ⤻ ∪ 🎣
**Open** March **to** October
**Access** Good **Site** Level
Own private beach. Fantastic walks and
scenery. Close to all major holiday
attractions.
**Nearest Town/Resort** Ilfracombe/Combe
Martin
**Directions** From the M5 take the A361
towards Barnstaple, then take the A399 to
Combe Martin. Sandaway is on the right at
the far end of the village. 5 miles from
Ilfracombe.
  ⚏ Barnstaple

## COMBE MARTIN
**Stowford Farm Meadows,** Combe Martin,
Devon, EX34 0PW
**Tel:** 01271 882476 **Fax:** 01271 883053
**Email:** enquiries@stowford.co.uk
www.stowford.co.uk
**Pitches For** ⚠ ⊕ ⊕ **Total** 700
**Facilities** ⚒ ✦ 🆖 🔱 ✦ ⌐ ☉ ☐ 🔲 ☎
🕿 🖲 🏊 ✕ 🍴 🛝 🔥 ⚓ 🛒 🔲 🔲 ✂ 🅿
**Nearby Facilities** 🏇 🖊 ⚓ ∪
**Acreage** 140 **Open** Easter **to** October
**Access** Good **Site** Lev/Slope
Set in 450 acres of beautiful countryside.
Ideal touring site at the heart of North
Devon. Renowned for our extensive range
of facilities at excellent value. Caravan
repair workshop, caravan accessories
shop and caravan sales.
**Nearest Town/Resort** Combe Martin
**Directions** Situated on the A3123 Combe
Martin/Woollacombe Road at Berry Down.
  ⚏ Barnstaple

## CREDITON
**Yeatheridge Farm Caravan & Camping
Park,** East Worlington, Crediton, Devon,
EX17 4TN
**Tel:** 01884 860330
**Email:** yeatheridge@talk21.com
www.yeatheridge.co.uk
**Pitches For** ⚠ ⊕ ⊕ **Total** 85
**Facilities** ⚒ ✦ 🆖 🔱 ✦ ⌐ ☉ 🛒 ☐ 🔲 ☎
🕿 🖲 🏊 ✕ 🍴 🛝 🔥 ⚓ ⌂ 🔲 🔲
**Nearby Facilities** 🏇
**Open** 1 April **to** 1 Oct
**Access** Good **Site** Lev/Slope
2½ mile woodland walk. Horse riding on
site.
**Directions** From Tiverton take the B3137 to
Witheridge, turn left onto the B3042 and
Yeatheridge is 3½ miles on the left.
  ⚏ Eggesford

## CROYDE BAY
**Bay View Farm Holidays,** Bay View Farm,
Croyde, Devon, EX33 1PN
**Tel:** 01271 890501
www.bayviewfarm.co.uk
**Pitches For** ⚠ ⊕ ⊕
**Facilities** ⚒ ✦ 🔲 🆖 ✦ ⌐ ☉ 🔲 ☎
📶 🖲 🏊 ✕ 🛝 🔥 🔲
**Nearby Facilities** 🏇 🖊 ⚓ ⤻ ∪ 🎣 🔱 🎣
**Acreage** 10 **Open** Easter **to** September
**Site** Level
Near beach, 5 mins walking, Scenic views,
ideal touring, booking advisable peak
season. Pets by advance booking only.
S.A.E. for information.
**Nearest Town/Resort** Croyde
**Directions** At Braunton on A361 turn west
on main road B3231 towards Croyde Village
  ⚏ Barnstaple

## CROYDE BAY
**Ruda Holiday Park,** Croyde Bay, North
Devon, EX33 1NY
**Tel:** 01271 890477 **Fax:** 01271 890656
**Email:** enquiries@parkdeanholidays.com
www.parkdeanholidays.co.uk
**Pitches For** ⚠ ⊕ ⊕ **Total** 372
**Facilities** ⚒ ✦ 🔲 🆖 🔱 ✦ ⌐ ☉ 🛒 ☐ 🔲 ☎
🕿 🖲 🏊 ✕ 🍴 🛝 🔥 ⚓ 🛒 🔲 🔲
**Nearby Facilities** 🏇 🖊 ⚓ ⤻ ∪ 🎣 🔱
**Acreage** 320 **Open** March **to** Oct
**Access** Good **Site** Level
Our own beach, Croyde Bay is immediately
adjacent to camping and touring pitches.
Excellent surfing and walking.
**Nearest Town/Resort** Barnstaple
**Directions** From Barnstaple take the A361
to Braunton. In the centre of Braunton at the
traffic lights turn left onto the B3231 and
follow signs to Croyde.
  ⚏ Barnstaple

## CULLOMPTON
**Forest Glade Holiday Park,** Cullompton,
Devon, EX15 2DT
**Tel:** 01404 841381 **Fax:** 01404 841593
**Email:** enquiries@forest-glade.co.uk
www.forest-glade.co.uk
**Pitches For** ⚠ ⊕ ⊕ **Total** 80
**Facilities** ⚒ ✦ 🔲 🆖 🔱 ✦ ⌐ ☉ 🛒 ☐ 🔲 ☎
🕿 🖲 🏊 ✕ 🔥 🛝 🔥 ⚓ 🔲 🔲 🔲 ✂ 🅿
**Acreage** 10 **Open** Mid March **to** End Oct
**Access** See Directions **Site** Level
Central for southwest twixt coast and
moors. Large flat sheltered camping
pitches. Caravans for hire. Free heated
indoor swimming pool and Paddling pool.
Riding and gliding nearby. Tennis on site.
**Directions** A373 Cullompton/Honiton, turn
for Sheldon at Keepers Cottage Inn, 2½ miles
east of Cullompton. Touring caravans via
Dunkeswell Road only.
  ⚏ Honiton/Tiverton Parkway

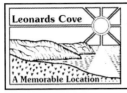

**Overlooking the sea on a cliff top:** Caravanning and camping in peaceful setting designated an area of outstanding natural beauty. Centered in coastal village with shop, restaurant and country pub. Walking distance famous Blackpool sands. Three miles Historic Port of Dartmouth. Ideal for rural and coastal walks, relaxing in peace and quiet. Regret no pets. Laundry available.

**Leonards Cove, Stoke Fleming, Dartmouth, Devon, TQ6 0NR
Tel: 01803 770206  Fax: 01803 770845
Or visit our Website: www.leonardscovecamping.co.uk**

See our advertisement on the back cover
www.coftonholidays.co.uk

---

Fleming, Dartmouth, Devon, TQ6 0NR
**Tel:** 01803 770206 **Fax:** 01803 770845
**Email:** enquiry@leonardscove.com
www.leonardscove.com
**Pitches For** ▲ ⬛ **Total** 40
**Facilities** ⌇ 🆚 ♨ ♥ ☉ ⬦ ⬛ ◻ ☕
🝙 🛢 🛒 ✕ 🄿
**Nearby Facilities** ☔ ✈ ⚓ ✗ ∪ ♨ ♠ ⚘
**Acreage** 12 **Open** Mid March **to** End Oct
**Access** Good **Site** Lev/Slope
Within walking distance of Blackpool
Sands beach. Sea views and woodlands.
**Nearest Town/Resort** Dartmouth
**Directions** From Dartmouth take the A379
towards Kingsbridge, we are in the village of
Stoke Fleming.
⚏ Totnes/Paignton

## DARTMOUTH
**Little Cotton Caravan Park,** Dartmouth,
South Devon, TQ6 0LB
**Tel:** 01803 832558 **Fax:** 01803 834887
**Email:** enquiries@littlecotton.co.uk
www.littlecotton.co.uk
**Pitches For** ▲ ⬛ **Total** 95
**Facilities** & ⌇ 🆚 ♨ ♥ ☉ ⬦ ⬛ ◻ ☕
🝙 🛢 🛒 ✕ 🄿 ⬛ ◻ ☕
**Nearby Facilities** ☔ ✈ ⚓ ✗ ⚘
**Acreage** 7½ **Open** 15 March **to** October
**Access** Good **Site** Lev/Slope
Scenic views, ideal touring. Park and ride
service in the next field. Luxurious new
toilet and shower facilities.
**Nearest Town/Resort** Dartmouth
**Directions** Leave the A38 ta Buckfastleigh,
A384 to Totnes, from Totnes to Halwell on
the A381. At Halwell take the A3122
Dartmouth road, park is on the right at
entrance to town.
⚏ Totnes

## DARTMOUTH
**Start Bay Caravan Park,** Strete, Nr
Dartmouth, South Devon, TQ6 0RU
**Tel:** 01803 770535 **Fax:** 01803 770773
**Pitches For** ▲ ⬛ **Total** 6
**Facilities** ⌇ 🆚 ♨ ♥ ☉ ⬦ ⬛ ◻ ☕
🝙 ✱ ⬛ ◻ ☕ ❄
**Nearby Facilities** ☔ ✈ ⚓ ✗ ∪ ♨ ♠
**Acreage** 1¼ **Open** Apr (Easter) **to** End Oct
**Access** Good **Site** Level
In the countryside, near the sea. Black
Pool Sands and Slapton Ley.
**Nearest Town/Resort** Dartmouth
**Directions** 5 miles from Dartmouth on the
coast road to Kingsbridge, turn right at Strete
Post Office for Halwell.
⚏ Totnes

## DARTMOUTH
**Woodlands Leisure Park,** Blackawton,
Totnes, Devon, TQ9 7DQ
**Tel:** 01803 712598 **Fax:** 01803 712680
**Email:** enquiries@woodlandspark.com
www.woodlandspark.com
**Pitches For** & ⌇ 🆚 ♨ ♥ ☉ ⬦ ⬛ ◻ ☕
🝙 🛢 🛒 ✕ ♠ ⬛ ◻ ☕ 🄿
**Nearby Facilities** ☔ ✈ ⚓ ✗ ∪
**Acreage** 16 **Open** Easter **to** Nov
**Access** Good **Site** Mostly Level
Alan Rogers 'Best Family Campsite in
Europe' Award and AA Campsite of the
Year for England 2004. Combining 5 Star
facilities with personal supervision.
Spacious pitches in beautiful countryside, 4
miles from Dartmouth coast. Excellent
bathrooms, laundry and Free hot showers.
Two nights stay gives FREE entrance to
our 60 acre Leisure Park. 3 watercoasters,
500m Toboggan Run and Arctic Gliders.
Master Blaster, Trauma Tower. Live

entertainment days, excellent indoor
Falconry Centre with flying displays. An
ocean of undercover play. Guaranteed fun
whatever the weather!
**Nearest Town/Resort** Dartmouth
**Directions** 4 miles from Dartmouth on main
road A3122 (formally B3207).
⚏ Totnes

## DAWLISH
**Cofton Country Holidays,** Starcross, Nr
Dawlish, Devon, EX6 8RP
**Tel:** 01626 890111 **Fax:** 01626 891572
**Email:** info@coftonholidays.co.uk
www.coftonholidays.co.uk
**Pitches For** ▲ ⬛ **Total** 450
**Facilities** & ⌇ 🆚 ♨ ♥ ☉ ⬦ ⬛ ◻ ☕
🝙 🛢 🛒 ✕ ♥ 🆚 ♠ 🗌 ♨ ✦ ✱ ⬛ ◻ ☕
**Nearby Facilities** ☔ ✈ ⚓ ✗ ∪ ♨ ♠
**Acreage** 16 **Open** Easter **to** October
**Access** Good **Site** Level
In beautiful rural countryside near to sandy
Dawlish Warren beach. Clean and tidy family
run park. Superb complex and swimming
pool. Swan Pub with family lounge and
meals. See our advert on the back cover.
**Nearest Town/Resort** Dawlish Warren
**Directions** On the A379 Exeter to Dawlish
road, ½ mile after the fishing village at
Cockwood.
⚏ Dawlish

## DAWLISH
**Golden Sands Holiday Park,** Week Lane,
Dawlish, South Devon, EX7 0LZ
**Tel:** 01626 863099 **Fax:** 01626 867149
**Email:** info@goldensands.co.uk
www.goldensands.co.uk
**Pitches For** ▲ ⬛ **Total** 60
**Facilities** & ⌇ 🆚 ♨ ♥ ☉ ⬦ ⬛ ◻ ☕
🝙 🛢 🛒 ✕ ♥ 🆚 ♠ 🗌 ✦ ✱ ⬛ ◻ ☕

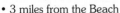

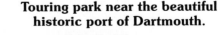

# Woodlands

## Caravan Park
### DARTMOUTH • DEVON

**SIT BACK & RELAX OR GET-UP & GO...**
enjoy the perfect balance between our
touring **CARAVAN PARK** and the **FUN PARK!**

Best in Europe Award

Alan Rogers

Best Family Campsite

Woodlands Leisure Park, Blackawton, Totnes, South Devon TQ9 7DQ
**Tel: 01803 712598 • Web: www.woodlandspark.com**
Woodlands Leisure reserve the right to close the park or any attractions without prior notice.

# Family Camping on the Coast

 **www.dawlishwarren.com**

**Nearby Facilities** ⌂ ✦ ⚓ ❄ ∪ ♪ ♫
**Acreage** 2¼ **Open** Easter **to** October
**Access** Good **Site** Level
Family run for family fun! Small touring park, 2/3rds of a mile from Dawlish Warren beach. Free nightly, family entertainment in the licensed club and our unique indoor/outdoor swimming pool (in season).
**Nearest Town/Resort** Dawlish
**Directions** From M5 junction 30 take the A379 Dawlish, through Starcross. After 2 miles Week Lane is the second left opposite the filling station, on the right.
≠ Dawlish

## DAWLISH

**Lady's Mile Holiday Park,** Exeter Road, Dawlish, Devon, EX7 0LX
**Tel:** 01626 863411 **Fax:** 01626 888689
**Email:** info@ladysmile.co.uk
www.ladysmile.co.uk
**Pitches For** ▲ ⌂ 🚐 **Total** 486
**Facilities** ⚿ ♿ 🚻 ♨ ♪ ⊙ ⅃ 🔥 ▣ ◙ ☎
⛟ 🅿 🅾 🛒 ✕ ♀ ⊞ ⚑ ⋔ ⚡ ❀⛽⇥▣ 🄲 ☀
♪
**Nearby Facilities** ⌂ ✦ ♫
**Acreage** 16 **Open** Mid March **to** End Oct
**Access** Good **Site** Lev/Slope
9 hole golf course on site. Very close to a Blue Flag beach and near to Dartmoor National Park. Ideal base for exploring Devon.

**Nearest Town/Resort** Dawlish
**Directions** On A379 road 1 mile north of Dawlish and 10 miles south of Exeter.
≠ Dawlish

## DAWLISH

**Leadstone Camping,** Warren Road, Dawlish, Devon, EX7 0NG
**Tel:** 01626 864411 **Fax:** 01626 873833
**Email:** post@leadstonecamping.co.uk
www.leadstonecamping.co.uk
**Pitches For** ▲ ⌂ 🚐 **Total** 137
**Facilities** ♪ ♿ ♨ ♪ ⊙ ⅃ 🔥 ▣ ◙ ☎
⛟ 🅿 🅾 🛒 ♀ ⚑ ⇥▣ 🄲 ☀
**Nearby Facilities** ⌂ ✦ ⚓ ❄ ∪ ♪ ♫
**Acreage** 7 **Open** 16 June **to** 3 Sept
**Access** Good **Site** Lev/Slope
Rolling grassland in a natural secluded bowl within ½ mile of sandy 2 mile Dawlish Warren Beach and nature reserve. Ideally situated for discovering Devon.
**Nearest Town/Resort** Dawlish
**Directions** Leave the M5 at junction 30 and take signposted road A379 to Dawlish. As you approach Dawlish, turn left on brow of hill, signposted Dawlish Warren. Our site is ½ mile on the RIGHT.
≠ Dawlish Warren

## DAWLISH

**Seaway Touring Park,** Warren Road, Dawlish Warren, Devon, EX7
**Tel:** 01626 866986 **Fax:** 01626 888659
**Email:** info@seawayholidays.co.uk
www.seawayholidays.co.uk
**Pitches For** ▲ ⌂ **Total** 450
**Facilities** ⚿ ♪ ♿ ♨ ♪ ⊙ ⅃ 🔥
🅿 🅾 🛒 🅾 ⚑ ⋔❄⇥ ☀
**Nearby Facilities** ⌂ ✦ ⚓ ❄ ∪ ♪ ♫
**Acreage** 18 **Open** Easter **to** Sept
**Access** Good **Site** Lev/Slope
Near the beach and the town. Ideal for short get aways.
**Nearest Town/Resort** Dawlish Warren
**Directions** From the A379 in Dawlish Warren, turn into Warren Road.
≠ Dawlish

## DAWLISH WARREN

**Peppermint Park,** Warren Road, Dawlish Warren, Devon, EX7 0PQ
**Tel:** 01626 863436 **Fax:** 01626 866482
**Email:** info@peppermintpark.co.uk
www.peppermintpark.co.uk
**Pitches For** ▲ ⌂ 🚐 **Total** 300
**Facilities** ⚿ ♪ ♿ ♨ ♪ ⊙ ⅃ 🔥 ▣ ◙ ☎
⛟ 🅿 🅾 🛒 ♀ ⊞ ⚑ ⋔ ❄⇥▣ 🄲
**Nearby Facilities** ⌂ ✦ ⚓ ❄ ♫
**Acreage** 16 **Open** Easter **to** September
**Access** Good **Site** Lev/Slope
Closest touring park to Dawlish Warren

# Lady's Mile
## Holiday Park

### Family run for over 48 years

- **TWO** Swimming Pools ● **TWO** Waterslides ● "The Mile" family bar
- **TWO** Launderettes ● Free hot water & showers ● Electric Hook-ups
- Licensed Shop ● Adventure Fort & Play Area ● Multi Sports
- Poolside Bar ● Families & Rallies welcome ● Takeaway
- Games room ● AJ's Family Disco
- Luxury Holiday Homes & Apartments

Phone for a FREE colour brochure 01626 863411 or visit www.ladysmile.co.uk
Mrs C Jeffrey, Ladysmile Holiday Park, Dawlish, South Devon EX7 9YZ

## Telephone 01626 863411  Fax 01626 888689
### www.ladysmile.co.uk

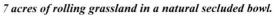

# Leadstone Camping ...a great little site!

## 7 acres of rolling grassland in a natural secluded bowl.

- ▶ Owned and managed by the same local family for 34 years.
- ▶ Friendly, quiet and uncommercialised.
- ▶ Half a mile from Dawlish Warren's Golden Sands
- ▶ One night stop-overs welcome.
- ▶ Ideal base for day-touring Devon.

*Electric hook-ups : Toilets : Showers : Launderette*
*Children's Adventure Playground*

*Write or phone for a full colour brochure.* Warren Road, Dawlish, S. Devon EX7 0NG
Tel: 01626 864411   Fax: 01626 873833   www.leadstonecamping.co.uk

beach (680 metres). The only 4 Star Graded touring park at Dawlish Warren. Grassland park sheltered by mature trees. Coarse fishing. Free nightly entertainment. David Bellamy Gold Award and AA Holiday Centre.
**Nearest Town/Resort** Dawlish
**Directions** Leave M5 at junction 30 and take the A379 Dawlish road. Approx. 2½ miles after Starcross take sharp left for Dawlish Warren. Park is approx. 1¼ miles down the hill on the left.
≉ Dawlish Warren

## EXETER
**Barley Meadow Caravan & Camping Park,** Crockernwell, Exeter, Devon, EX6 6NR
**Tel:** 01647 281629
**Email:** angela.waldron1@btopenworld.com
www.barleymeadow.co.uk
**Pitches For** ▲ ⊕ ⊖ **Total** 40
**Facilities** & ∮ ⊞ ⊞ ⊕ ⓡ ⊙ ⌿ ⊟ ⚋ ⊡ ⊜
ⓢ ⓘ ⊙ ⓢ �ⓣ ⚋ Ⅲ ⚋ ⊞ ⫰
**Nearby Facilities** ⌐ ⌿ ∪
**Acreage** 4½ **Open** March **to** November
**Access** Good **Site** Level
Very clean facilities on this quiet site on the edge of Dartmoor with superb views. 150 yards from Two Moors Way walk. Heated shower blocks. Small charge for dogs. Excellent access for touring Dartmoor.
**Nearest Town/Resort** Okehampton/Exeter
**Directions** 10 miles from Exeter on the A30 to Okehampton, turn left signposted Crockernwell, 3 miles site is on the left. From Okehampton travel for 7 miles towards Exeter, at large roundabout turn left, 3 miles site is on the right.

## EXETER
**Exeter Racecourse Caravan Club Site,** Kennford, Exeter, Devon, EX6 7XS
**Tel:** 01392 832107
www.caravanclub.co.uk
**Pitches For** ▲ ⊕ ⊖ **Total** 100
**Facilities** ∮ ⊞ ⚋ ⓡ ⊙ ⊜ ⓘ ⊙ ⊜ ⫰ ⊟
**Nearby Facilities** ⌐ ⌿
**Acreage** 10 **Open** March **to** Oct
**Access** Good **Site** Level
Free access to racing and a 9 hole practice

golf course. Large late night arrivals area. Near to Exeter Cathedral, Dartmoor National Park and Trago Mills Shopping Complex. Non members welcome. Booking essential.
**Nearest Town/Resort** Exeter
**Directions** From the M5 take the A38, just past Kennford keep to right hand lanes and continue on the A38 at A380 junction. After ½ mile move to nearside lane and at the top of steep Haldon Hill turn left signposted Exeter Racecourse then immediately right, follow signs to the site.
≉ Exeter

## EXETER
**Kennford International Caravan Park,** Kennford, Exeter, Devon, EX6 7YN
**Tel:** 01392 833046 **Fax:** 01392 833046
**Email:** ian@kennfordint.fsbusiness.co.uk
www.kennfordint.co.uk
**Pitches For** ▲ ⊕ ⊖ **Total** 137
**Facilities** & ∮ ⊞ ⊞ ⚋ ⓡ ⊙ ⌿ ⚋ ⊡ ⊜
ⅼ ⊙ ⊜ ⓧ ⓨ ⚋ Ⅲ ⚋ ⊞ ⊟ ⊜ ⫰
**Nearby Facilities** ⌐ ⌿ ∪
**Acreage** 15 **Open** All Year
**Access** Good **Site** Level
Kennford International is a family run park close to beaches and the city of Exeter. Fishing and the villages of Kenn and Kennford nearby. 10% discount for the over 50's (not available July & August). Special 7 night stay, £55 between 3 Sept and 1 Nov.
**Nearest Town/Resort** Exeter
**Directions** From the M5 join the A38 towards Plymouth and Torquay. Exit at Kennford Services, pass the garage, go over the bridge and we are on the left. Approx. 10 minutes from Exeter.
≉ Exeter

## EXMOUTH
**Castle Brake,** Castle Lane, Woodbury, Nr Exeter, Devon, EX5 1HA
**Tel:** 01395 232431
**Email:** reception@castlebrake.co.uk
www.castlebrake.co.uk
**Pitches For** ▲ ⊕ ⊖ **Total** 42
**Facilities** & ∮ ⊞ ⚋ ⓡ ⊙ ⌿ ⚋ ⊡ ⊜
ⅼ ⊙ ⊜ ⓧ ⓨ ⚋ Ⅲ ⚋ ⊞ ⊜ ⫰ ⌿
**Nearby Facilities** ⌐ ⌿ ⚋ ⚋ ∪ ⌿

**Acreage** 10 **Open** March **to** October
**Access** Good **Site** Level
Beautiful views of the River Exe. Exmouth beach 6 miles. Good touring centre for East Devon and beyond.
**Nearest Town/Resort** Exmouth
**Directions** M5 junction 30 take the A3052 to Halfway Inn. Turn right onto the B3180, after 2 miles turn right to Woodbury at the golf and caravan site sign, the park is 500yds on the right.
≉ Exmouth

## EXMOUTH
**Devon Cliffs Holiday Park,** Sandy Bay, Exmouth, Devon, EX8 5BT
**Tel:** 01395 226226 **Fax:** 01395 223111
www.touringholidays.co.uk
**Pitches For** ▲ ⊕ ⊖ **Total** 145
**Facilities** & ∮ ⊟ ⊞ ⚋ ⓡ ⊙ ⚋ ⊡ ⊜
ⓢ ⅼ ⊙ ⊜ ⓧ ⓨ Ⅲ ⚋ ⚋ ⊞ ⫰ ⊞ ⊡ ⊜
**Nearby Facilities** ⌐ ⌿ ⚋ ⚋ ∪ ⌿ ⚋
**Open** March **to** October
**Access** Good **Site** Sloping
Spectacular hillside setting, on top of the cliffs, overlooking the beautiful Sandy Bay, with access to our very own sandy beach. Dogs welcome if kept on leads. Motorcycles welcome but must not be ridden on the park.
**Nearest Town/Resort** Exmouth
**Directions** Turn off the M5 at exit 30 and take the A376 for Exmouth. Clear directions from Exmouth to Devon Cliffs, follow brown tourism signs.
≉ Exmouth

## EXMOUTH
**St. John's Caravan & Camping Park,** St John's Road, Exmouth, Devon, EX8 5EG
**Tel:** 01395 263170
**Email:** st.johns.farm@amserve.net
**Pitches For** ▲ ⊕ ⊖ **Total** 45
**Facilities** & ∮ ⊞ ⚋ ⓡ ⊙ ⓢ ⊙ ⊞ ⫰ ⊟
**Nearby Facilities** ⌐ ⌿ ⚋ ⚋ ∪ ⌿ ⌿
**Acreage** 6 **Open** March **to** Dec
**Access** Good **Site** Sloping
Family site situated in pleasant pasture land with rural views, yet only minutes away from 2 miles of sandy beaches or unspoilt heathland.
**Nearest Town/Resort** Exmouth
**Directions** From Exmouth town centre follow

Family run 4 Pennant Park with top quality facilities. We are conveniently situated 1 mile from the end of the M5, alongside the A38 and are an ideal centre for visits to Torquay, Dartmoor and the beaches of South Devon.   **Open All Year.**
**Please telephone for our brochure illustrating the local attractions and park facilities.**
**Kennford International Caravan Park,** Exeter, Devon EX6 7YN
**Tel/Fax: 01392 833046    Mr & Mrs Ian Hopkins, Mobile 07768240780**
**Website: www.kennfordint.co.uk    E-mail: ian@kennfordint.fsbusiness.co.uk**

signs for Budleigh Salterton B3178. Go past Tesco and take the next turn left, St John's Road is the fifth on the right.
✈ Exmouth

## GREAT TORRINGTON
**Greenways Valley,** Caddywell Lane, Great Torrington, Devon, EX38 7EW
**Tel:** 01805 622153
**Email:** cades@greenwaysvalley.co.uk
www.greenwaysvalley.co.uk
**Pitches For** ▲ ♠ ⊞ **Total** 4
**Facilities** ∮ 🅗 ♨ ⌐ ⊙ ⊣
⎕ ⊘ ⊛ ♣ ⋒ ⊃ ⊟
**Nearby Facilities** ⌐ ✔ ⚓ ⚘ ∪ ♪
**Acreage** 8 **Open** Mid March **to** October
**Access** Good **Site** Level
Peaceful well tended site with a southerly aspect overlooking a beautiful wooded valley. Tennis and heated pool on park. Holiday lodges for sale.
**Nearest Town** Torrington/Westward Ho!
**Directions** Site is just one mile from Torrington town centre. Take B3227 (to South Molton) turn left into Borough Road then 3rd left to site entrance.
✈ Barnstaple

## GREAT TORRINGTON
**Smytham Manor,** Little Torrington, Devon, EX38 8PU
**Tel:** 01805 622110 **Fax:** 01805 625451
**Email:** info@smytham.co.uk
www.smytham.co.uk
**Pitches For** ▲ ♠ ⊞ **Total** 45
**Facilities** & ∮ 🅗 🆖 ♨ ⌐ ⊙ ⊣ ⊿ ⊟ ♥
⊠ ⊜ ♀ ♣ ⋒ ⊃ ⊞ ⊟ ☼
**Nearby Facilities** ⌐ ✔ ♪
**Acreage** 25 **Open** March **to** Oct
**Access** Good **Site** Lev/Slope
Direct access to the Tarka Trail.
**Nearest Town/Resort** Great Torrington
**Directions** 2 miles south of Great Torrington on the A386.
✈ Barnstaple

## HARTLAND
**Hartland Caravan & Camping Park,** South Lane, Hartland, Bideford, North Devon, EX39 6DG
**Tel:** 01237 441876/441242 **Fax:** 441034

**Pitches For** ▲ ♠ ⊞ **Total** 60
**Facilities** & ∮ 🅗 🆖 ♨ ⌐ ⊙ ⊣ ⊡ ♥
🅘 ⋒ ⊞ ⊟ ⊠ ⊘ ₽
**Nearby Facilities** ⌐ ✔ ⚓ ⚘ ∪ ♪ ♪ ⚡
**Acreage** 6 **Open** All Year
**Access** Good **Site** Lev/Slope
Overlooking Hartland Village, woodlands and the Atlantic coast. Well kept, family run site boasting a new toilet/shower block with baby changing room, disabled and family room. Small fishing lake and BBQ area. 2 miles from beaches. Some hardstandings. Dishwashing facilities and washing machine. Just a 3 minute walk to shops and public houses. Close to Hartland Abbey and many other tourist attractions.
**Nearest Town/Resort** Bideford
**Directions** From the A39 take the B3248 to Hartland. On entering the village site is on the left.
✈ Barnstaple

## HOLSWORTHY
**Hedley Wood Caravan & Camping Park,** Bridgerule, Holsworthy, Devon, EX22 7ED
**Tel:** 01288 381404 **Fax:** 01288 382011
**Email:** alan@hedleywood.co.uk
www.hedleywood.co.uk
**Pitches For** ▲ ♠ ⊞ **Total** 120
**Facilities** & ∮ 🅗 🆖 ♨ ⌐ ⊙ ⊣ ⊿ ⊠ ⊟ ♥
⊠ ⊘ ⊜ ⊁ ♀ 🅘 ♣ ⋒ ⊞ ⊟ ₽
**Nearby Facilities** ⌐ ✔ ⚘ ∪ ♪
**Acreage** 16½ **Open** All Year
**Access** Good **Site** Lev/Slope
Open and sheltered camping areas with a 'laid back' atmosphere. Dog kennelling facility and a dog walk/nature trail.
**Nearest Town/Resort** Bude/Holsworthy
**Directions** From Holsworthy take the A3072 towards Bude, at Red Post crossroads turn south onto the B3254 to Launceston. After 2¼ miles turn right to Titson, site entrance is 500 yards on the right.
✈ Exeter

## HOLSWORTHY
**Newbuildings,** Brandis Corner, Holsworthy, Devon, EX22 7YQ
**Tel:** 01409 221305
**Pitches For** ▲ ♠ ⊞ **Total** 10
**Facilities** ∮ 🅗 ♨ ⌐ ♥ 🅘 ⚘
**Nearby Facilities** ⌐ ✔ ⚓ ∪ ♪ ♪

**Acreage** 4 **Open** March **to** Oct
**Access** Good **Site** Level
Central rural position, excellent for walking. 12 miles from beaches and the Moors. Licensed pub within ¼ mile.
**Nearest Town/Resort** Bude/Bideford/ Dartmoor
**Directions** Take the A30 to Okehampton then the A3079 through Halwill Junction to Dunsland Cross. Go straight across the A3072, and Newbuildings is on the left 200 yards down Farm Lane.
✈ Exeter

## HOLSWORTHY
**Noteworthy,** Bude Road, Holsworthy, Devon, EX22 7JB
**Tel:** 01409 253731 **Fax:** 01409 253731
**Email:** jmsb.0603@virgin.net
**Pitches For** ▲ ♠ ⊞ **Total** 12
**Facilities** ∮ 🅗 🆖 ♨ ⌐ ⊙ ⊣ ♥ ⊁ ⊟
**Nearby Facilities** ⌐ ✔ ♪
**Acreage** 5 **Open** All Year
**Access** Good **Site** Level
Quiet site with limited numbers of people. 7 miles from Cornish coast and beaches. Easy journeys to the moors.
**Nearest Town/Resort** Bude
**Directions** From Holsworthy travel west on the A3072 towards Bude. The site is 2.7 miles on the right.

## ILFRACOMBE
**Big Meadow Touring Caravan & Camping Park,** Watermouth, Ilfracombe, Devon, EX34 9SJ
**Tel:** 01271 862282
**Email:** bigmeadow@hotmail.co.uk
www.bigmeadow.co.uk
**Pitches For** ▲ ♠ ⊞ **Total** 125
**Facilities** ∮ 🅗 🆖 ♨ ⌐ ⊙ ⊣ ⊿ ⊠ ⊟ ♥
⊠ 🅘 ⊘ ⊜ ⊁ 🅘 ♣ ⋒ ⊞ ♨ ⊟
**Nearby Facilities** ⌐ ✔ ⚓ ⚘ ∪ ♪ ⚡
**Acreage** 9 **Open** Easter **to** Mid Sept
**Access** Good **Site** Level
Sheltered family site with stream running through. Near Watermouth Harbour and two beaches within walking distance.
**Nearest Town/Resort** Ilfracombe
**Directions** Situated on the A399 coastal road approximately 2 miles from Ilfracombe,

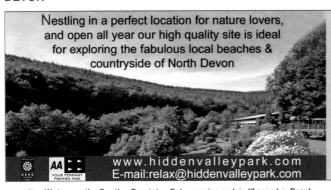

opposite Watermouth Castle Tourist Attraction.
⚏ Barnstaple

## ILFRACOMBE
**Brook Lea Caravan Club Site,** West Down, Ilfracombe, Devon, EX34 8NE
Tel: 01271 862848
www.caravanclub.co.uk
Pitches For ⚑ ⚑ Total 77
Facilities ƒ 🚿 ⓘⓔ 🅾 ⚑ ✿🕂🄳
Nearby Facilities ⌐ ✔ ⚓ ⚒
Acreage 6 Open April to Sept
Access Good Site Level
Elevated position with superb views and a woodland walkway. 5 miles from a sandy beach and near to Exmoor National Park and Tarka Trail Cycle Track. Own sanitation required. Non members welcome. Booking essential.
**Nearest Town/Resort** Ilfracombe
**Directions** From Barnstaple take the A361, at Mullacott Cross roundabout turn right onto the A3123. Turn right at caravan sign signposted West Down, site is 1 mile on the left.
⚏ Ilfracombe

## ILFRACOMBE
**Hele Valley Holiday Park,** Hele Bay, Ilfracombe, North Devon, EX34 9RD
Tel: 01271 862460 Fax: 01271 867926
Email: holidays@helevalley.co.uk
www.helevalley.co.uk
Pitches For ▲ ⚑ Total 50
Facilities ♿ ƒ ⓊⒷ 🅰 ⌐ ⊙ ⌂ 🛒 🄰 🅲 🍴
🅿️ 🅾 🅰🕂🄳🄳 🄴
Nearby Facilities ⌐ ✔ ⚓ ⚒ ∪ ℛ
Acreage 4 Open May to Sept
Access Good Site Level

Only camping park in Ilfracombe. Beach only a few minutes walk. Tranquil secluded valley, alongside a stream with scenic views.
**Nearest Town/Resort** Ilfracombe
**Directions** Take A399 to Ilfracombe turn at signpost Hele village, to bottom of lane, take righthand turning into Holiday Park.
⚏ Barnstaple

## ILFRACOMBE
**Hidden Valley Touring & Camping Park,** West Down, Nr Ilfracombe, North Devon, EX34 8NU
Tel: 01271 813837 Fax: 01271 814041
Email: relax@hiddenvalleypark.com
www.hiddenvalleypark.com
Pitches For ▲ ⚑ ⚑ Total 120
Facilities ♿ ƒ ⒻⓊⒷ 🅰 ⌐ ⊙ ⌂ 🛒 🄲
🅂🅀 🅾 🅰🅇 ♀ 🄼🕂🄳 🄲
Nearby Facilities ⌐ ✔ ⚓ ⚒ ∪ 🎣 ℛ 🏇
Acreage 25 Open All Year
Access Good Site Level
This beautiful owner-run touring park offers first class amenities - sheltered, level pitches, glorious tranquil surroundings, an excellent site shop, coffee shop and bar. Ideally located for exploring the North Devon coast and countryside.
**Nearest Town/Resort** Ilfracombe
⚏ Barnstaple

## ILFRACOMBE
**Napps Caravan Site,** Napps, Old Coast Road, Berrynarbor, IlfracombeNorth Devon, EX34 9SW
Tel: 01271 882557 Fax: 01271 882557
Email: bookings@napps.fsnet.co.uk
www.napps.co.uk
Pitches For ▲ ⚑ ⚑ Total 250

Facilities ƒ 🄷 ⒰ 🅰 ⌐ ⊙ ⌂ 🛒 🄰 🅾 🍴
🅂🅀 🅾 🄶🅇 ♀ 🄼🅰 ⚒🕂🄳 🄴 🗲 🄿
Nearby Facilities ⌐ ✔ ⚓ ⚒ ∪
Acreage 11 Open March to November
Access Good Site Level
Probably the most beautiful coastal setting you will see. Beach 200yds. Popular family site with woodland and coastal walks. Five-a-Side football pitch and tennis on site.
**Nearest Town/Resort** Ilfracombe
**Directions** On A399, 1¼ miles west of Combe Martin, turn right onto Old Coast Road (signposted). Site 400yds along Old Coast Road.
⚏ Barnstaple

## ILFRACOMBE
**Sandaway Beach Holiday Park,** John Fowler Holidays, Sandaway, Nr Combe Martin, North Devon, EX34 9ST
Tel: 01271 866766 Fax: 01271 866791
Email: bookings@johnfowlerholidays.com
www.johnfowlerholidays.com
Pitches For ▲ ⚑ ⚑ Total 20
Facilities ♿ ƒ ⒻⓊⒷ 🅰 ⌐ ⊙ ⌂ 🛒 🄲
🅂🅀 🄸🄴 🅾 🅰🅇 ♀ 🄼🅰 🄼🕂🄳 🄲 🄴
Nearby Facilities ⌐ ✔ ⚓ ⚒ ∪ ℛ
Open March to October
Access Good Site Level
Own private beach. Fantastic walks and scenery. Close to all major holiday attractions.
**Nearest Town/Resort** Ilfracombe/Combe Martin
**Directions** From the M5 take the A361 towards Barnstaple, then take the A399 to Combe Martin. Sandaway is on the right at the far end of the village. 5 miles from Ilfracombe.
⚏ Barnstaple

## IVYBRIDGE

**Cheston Caravan & Camping Park,** Folly Cross, Wrangaton Road, South Brent, Devon, TQ10 9HF
**Tel:** 01364 72586 **Fax:** 01364 72586
www.chestoncaravanpark.co.uk
**Pitches For** ▲ ⚏ ⚐ **Total** 24
**Facilities** ⚒ ✦ 🆚 🏛 ♨ ┌ ☉ ⌣ 🍽
🔥 ⓖ ✖ 🄿
**Nearby Facilities** ┌ ✓ ⚲ ⌖ ∪ ⚑ ♫
**Acreage** 1¾ **Open** March **to** Oct
**Access** Good **Site** Level
Set in beautiful Dartmoor. Perfect for touring, walking and bird watching. Nearest beach 9 miles. Pets welcome. Easy access from A38.
**Nearest Town/Resort** Ivybridge
**Directions** From Exeter, after by-passing South Brent, turn left at Wrangaton Cross slip road then right A38. From Plymouth take South Brent (Woodpecker) turn, at end of slip road turn right, go under A38 and rejoin A38 and follow directions from Exeter.

## KINGSBRIDGE

**Island Lodge,** Stumpy Post Cross, Kingsbridge, Devon, TQ7 4BL
**Tel:** 01548 852956
**Pitches For** ▲ ⚏ ⚐ **Total** 30
**Facilities** ⚒ ✦ 🆚 ♨ ┌ ☉ ⌣ 🍽 🄿 ⚏
🔥 ⓖ ⚏ ✖ 🄿
**Nearby Facilities** ┌ ✓ ⚲ ⌖ ∪ ⚑ ♫ ✗
**Acreage** 2 **Open** All Year
**Access** Good **Site** Level
Quiet site with sea views. Ideal for touring all attractions (cities, towns, moors and beaches). Licensed boat storage available. You can also telephone us on Mobile 07968 222007.
**Nearest Town/Resort** Kingsbridge
**Directions** 1 mile north of Kingsbridge on the A381. At Stumpy Post Cross continue on the A381 and take the first turn left.
⚐ Totnes

## KINGSBRIDGE

**Karrageen Caravan & Camping Site,** Bolberry, Malborough, Kingsbridge, Devon, TQ7 3EN
**Tel:** 01548 561230 **Fax:** 01548 560192
**Email:** phil@karrageen.co.uk
www.karrageen.co.uk
**Pitches For** ▲ ⚏ ⚐ **Total** 70
**Facilities** ⚒ ✦ 🆚 ♨ ┌ ☉ ⌣ 🍽 🄿 ⚏
**Nearby Facilities** ┌ ✓ ⚲ ⌖ ∪ ⚑ ♫
**Acreage** 7½ **Open** 15 March **to** 30 Sept
**Access** Good **Site** Lev/slope
Nearest and best park to Hope Cove, beaches 1 mile away. Situated in beautiful, scenic countryside and surrounded by superb National Trust coastline. Terraced,

level, tree lined pitches. Parents and baby room and family shower room. Hot take-away food. Superb cliff top walking. A site with a view. Caravans for hire. See our advertisement under Salcombe.
**Nearest Town/Resort** Salcombe
**Directions** Take the A381 Kingsbridge to Salcombe road, turn sharp right into Malborough Village. In 0.6 miles turn right (signposted Bolberry), after 0.9 miles the site is on the right and reception is at the house on the left.
⚐ Totnes/Plymouth

## KINGSBRIDGE

**Mounts Farm Touring Park,** The Mounts, Nr East Allington, Kingsbridge, South Devon, TQ9 7QJ
**Tel:** 01548 521591
**Email:** mounts.farm@lineone.net
www.mountsfarm.co.uk
**Pitches For** ▲ ⚏ ⚐ **Total** 50
**Facilities** ✦ 🆚 ♨ ┌ ☉ ⌣ 🍽 🄿 ⚏
🅱 🔥 ⓖ ⚏ ✖ 🄿 🍽 🄿
**Nearby Facilities** ┌ ✓ ⚲ ⌖ ∪ ⚑
**Acreage** 6 **Open** April **to** October
**Access** Good **Site** Level
In an area of outstanding natural beauty. Ideal for touring all South Devon.
**Nearest Town/Resort** Kingsbridge
**Directions** On the A381 Totnes/Kingsbridge. 3 miles north of Kingsbridge. Entrance from A381 - DO NOT go to East Allington Village.
⚐ Totnes

## KINGSBRIDGE

**Parkland,** Sorley Green Cross, Kingsbridge, Devon, TQ7 4AF
**Tel:** 01548 852723
**Email:** enquiries@parklandsite.co.uk
www.parklandsite.co.uk
**Pitches For** ▲ ⚏ ⚐
**Facilities** ⚒ ✦ 🅵 🆚 🏛 ♨ ┌ ☉ ⌣ 🍽 🄿 ⚏
🔥 ⓖ ⚏ ⚑ 🏛 ⚏ 🄿 ✖ 🄿
**Nearby Facilities** ┌ ✓ ⚲ ⌖ ∪ ⚑ ♫ ✗
**Acreage** 3 **Open** All Year
**Access** Good **Site** Level
PARKLAND is a high quality traditional site set in 3 acres of level grounds, located 1 mile north of Kingsbridge. Just a short distance from Bantham Beach and panoramic views of Salcombe and Dartmoor. FREE electric hook-ups. Full modern heated facilities, family and disabled suites. Large children's playground. Family adventure centre ¼ mile, course fishing ½ mile and leisure centre 1 mile. Special breaks available. All enquiries welcome.
**Nearest Town** Kingsbridge/Salcombe
**Directions** From Totnes follow the A381, main Kingsbridge road, to Sorley Green Cross. Go straight ahead and the site is 100 yards on the left.

## KINGSBRIDGE

**Slapton Sands Camping & Caravanning Club Site,** Middle Grounds, Slapton, Kingsbridge, Devon, TQ7 1QW
**Tel:** 01548 580538
www.campingandcaravanningclub.co.uk
**Pitches For** ▲ ⚐ **Total** 115
**Facilities** ⚒ ✦ 🆚 ♨ ┌ ☉ ⌣ 🍽 🔲 🄿
ⓖ ⚏ 🏛 ✖ 🄿 🄿 ✖
**Nearby Facilities** ┌ ✓ ∪
**Acreage** 5½ **Open** March **to** Nov
**Access** Good **Site** Lev/Slope
Overlooking Start Bay, just a few minutes from the beach. BTB 4 Star Graded and AA 3 Pennants. Club Member Caravans Only.
**Nearest Town/Resort** Dartmouth
**Directions** From Kingsbridge take the A379, site entrance is ¼ mile from the A379, beyond the brow of the hill approaching Slapton Village.
⚐ Totnes

## LYDFORD

**Camping & Caravanning Club Site,** Lydford, Nr Okehampton, Devon, EX20 4BE
**Tel:** 01822 820275
www.campingandcaravanningclub.co.uk
**Pitches For** ▲ ⚏ ⚐ **Total** 70
**Facilities** ⚒ ✦ 🆚 ♨ ┌ ☉ ⌣ 🍽 🔲 🄿
ⓖ ⚏ 🏛 ✖ 🄿 🄿
**Nearby Facilities** ✓ ⚲ ⌖ ∪ ⚑ ✗
**Acreage** 7½ **Open** March **to** Nov
**Access** Good **Site** Lev/Slope
Situated in a quiet rural setting, overlooking a river. On the edge of Dartmoor, close to the moors, Lydford Gorge and castle. BTB 4 Star Graded and AA 3 Pennants. Non members welcome.
**Nearest Town/Resort** Okehampton
**Directions** A30 take the A386 signposted Tavistock and Lydford Gorge. Pass the Fox Hounds Public House on the left, turn right signposted Lydford. At the war memorial turn right, right fork, site is on the left.
⚐ Lydford

## LYNTON

**Camping & Caravanning Club Site,** Caffyn's Cross, Lynton, Devon, EX35 6JS
**Tel:** 01598 752379
www.campingandcaravanningclub.co.uk
**Pitches For** ▲ ⚏ ⚐ **Total** 105
**Facilities** ✦ 🆚 🏛 ♨ ┌ ☉ ⌣ 🍽 🔲 🄿
ⓖ ⚏ 🏛 ✖ 🄿 🄿 ✖ 🄿
**Nearby Facilities** ✗ ∪ 🄿
**Acreage** 5½ **Open** March **to** Oct
**Access** Good **Site** Lev/Slope
Overlooking the Bristol Channel. 2 miles from Lynton and Lynmouth. BTB 3 Star Graded and AA 3 Pennants. Non members welcome.

**Nearest Town/Resort** Lynton
**Directions** Leave the M5 and take the A361 to Barnstaple. At South Molton turn right to Blackmoor Gate signposted Lynmouth and Lynton. After 5 miles turn left at the bus shelter, turn first left then first right to camp site.
⇌ Barnstaple

## LYNTON

**Channel View Caravan & Camping Park,** Manor Farm, Barbrook, Lynton, North Devon, EX35 6LD
**Tel:** 01598 753349 **Fax:** 01598 752777
**Email:** channelview@bushinternet.com
www.channel-view.co.uk
**Pitches For** ⋏ ⌑ ⊖ **Total** 110
**Facilities** ⓓ ⨍ 🚿 🎔 ⓤ ⚓ ⌐ ☉ 🍴 ⬛ ◻ ☕
🏧 ◉ ⬛ 🏧 ⊷ ⬜ ◻
**Nearby Facilities** ⌐ ✓ ⩍ ⟲ ∪ ♪ ♗ ⚑
**Acreage** 6 **Open** 15 March **to** 15 Nov
**Access** Good **Site** Level
Panoramic views, on the edge of Exmoor overlooking Lynton/Lynmouth. ETB 4 Star Graded.
**Nearest Town/Resort** Lynton/Lynmouth
**Directions** 2 miles south east of Lynton on the A39.
⇌ Barnstaple

## MODBURY

**Broad Park Caravan Club Site,** Higher East Leigh, Modbury, Ivybridge, Devon, PL21 0SH
**Tel:** 01548 830714
www.caravanclub.co.uk
**Pitches For** ⌑
**Facilities** ⓓ ⨍ 🎔 ⓤ ⚓ ⌐ ☉ 🍴 ◻ ☕
🏧 ◉ ⬛ 🏧 ⊷ ⬜ ◻
**Nearby Facilities**
**Open** March **to** Oct
**Access** Poor **Site** Level
Situated between moors and sea, this makes

a splendid base from which to explore South Devon. Local attractions include Dart Valley Steamer Trips, Dartmoor Wildlife Park and Miniature Pony Centre. Non members welcome. Booking essential.
**Nearest Town/Resort** Ivybridge
**Directions** From Exeter heading SW on the A38, after 30 miles pass the Woodpecker Inn and after ½ a mile take the slip road onto the A3121. At the top of the slip road turn left following Broad Park sign, at crossroads go straight across, after 2½ miles continue right just past California Cross onto the B3207. Site is on the left after 1 mile.
⇌ Ivybridge

## MODBURY

**Camping & Caravanning Club Site,** California Cross, Modbury, Ivybridge, Devon, PL21 0SG
**Tel:** 01548 821297
www.campingandcaravanningclub.co.uk
**Pitches For** ⋏ ⌑ ⊖ **Total** 80
**Facilities** ⓓ ⨍ 🎔 ⓤ ⚓ ⌐ ☉ 🍴 ⬛ ◻ ☕
🏧 ◉ ⬛ 🏧 ⊷ ⬜ ◻ ☼ ∿ ∪ ♪
**Nearby Facilities** ✓ ∪ ♪
**Acreage** 3¾ **Open** April **to** Nov
**Access** Good **Site** Lev/Slope
Rural setting centrally situated in the South Hams. Close to the beaches of Salcombe and Torbay. Take-away food available two nights a week. 5 miles from Sorley Tunnel Childrens Adventure Park. BTB 4 Star Graded and AA 3 Pennants. Non members welcome.
**Nearest Town/Resort** Ivybridge
**Directions** On the A38 travelling south west take the A3121 to the crossroads, straight across on to the B3196 to California Cross Hamlet. Turn left after California Cross Hamlet but just before the petrol station, site is on the right.
⇌ Ivybridge

## MODBURY

**Pennymoor Caravan Park,** Modbury, Nr Ivybridge, Devon, PL21 0SB
**Tel:** 01548 830542/830020 **Fax:** 830542
**Email:** enquiries@pennymoor-camping.co.uk
www.pennymoor-camping.co.uk
**Pitches For** ⋏ ⌑ ⊖ **Total** 89
**Facilities** ⓓ ⨍ 🎔 ⓤ ⚓ ⌐ ☉ 🍴 ⬛ ◻ ☕
🏧 ◉ ⬛ 🏧 ⊷ ⬜ ☼
**Nearby Facilities** ⌐ ♗
**Acreage** 5 **Open** 15 March **to** 15 Nov
**Access** Good **Site** Level
Peaceful rural site. Only 5 miles from Bigbury-on-Sea (Burgh Island).
**Nearest Town/Resort** Modbury/Ivybridge
**Directions** Approx 30 miles West of Exeter, leave A38 at Wrangaton Cross. Turn left, then straight across at next crossroads and continue for approx 4 miles. Pass petrol garage on left, then take second left, site is 1 mile on the right.
⇌ Ivybridge

## MORTEHOE

**Easewell Farm Holiday Parc & Golf Club,,** Mortehoe Station Road, Mortehoe, Devon, EX34 7EH
**Tel:** 01271 870343 **Fax:** 01271 870089
**Email:** goodtimes@woolacombe.com
www.woolacombe.com
**Pitches For** ⋏ ⌑ ⊖ **Total** 302
**Facilities** ⓓ ⨍ 🎔 ⓤ ⚓ ⌐ ☉ 🍴 ⬛ ◻ ☕
🏧 🏧 ◉ ⬛ ✗ ⟲ 🎔 ♠ ⋒ ⊷ ⬜ ◻ ☼ ♪
**Nearby Facilities** ⌐ ✓ ⩍ ⟲ ∪ ♪ ♗ ♙
**Open** 31 March **to** 4 Nov
**Access** Good **Site** Level
Close to the Blue Flag beach of Woolacombe and spectacular coastal walks. Choice of 4 Parcs and their facilities and entertainment. Fishing nearby. All on Parc.
**Nearest Town/Resort** Woolacombe

**Directions** From Barnstaple take the A361 Ilfracombe road to the junction with the B3343 at Mullacott Cross. Turn first left signposted Woolacombe, after 1¾ miles turn right to Mortehoe. Parc is 1¼ miles on the right.
⚏ Barnstaple

# MORTEHOE

**North Morte Farm Caravan & Camping Park,** North Morte Road, Mortehoe, Woolacombe, North Devon, EX34 7EG
**Tel:** 01271 870381 **Fax:** 01271 870115
**Email:** info@northmortefarm.co.uk
www.northmortefarm.co.uk
**Pitches For** ▲ ⬤ 🚐 **Total** 175
**Facilities** ⬧ ✦ 🚻 🆙 ♨ ⌂ ☺ ✦ ⬛ 🖻 🐟
🅂 🛈 ⬤ ⛱ 🗄 🝉 🖭 🄴 ☀
**Nearby Facilities** ⌐ ✔ ⤣ ∪
**Open** Easter **to** End Sept
**Access** Narrow **Site** Lev/Slope
500 yards from Rockham Beach. Adjoining National Trust land. Ideal walking country.
**Nearest Town/Resort** Woolacombe
**Directions** 14 miles from Barnstaple on the A361 take the B3343 and follow signs to Mortehoe. In the village turn right at the Post Office, park is 500 yards on the left.
⚏ Barnstaple

# MORTEHOE

**Warcombe Farm Camping Park,** Mortehoe, Nr Woolacombe, North Devon, EX34 7EJ
**Tel:** 01271. 870690 **Fax:** 01271 871070
**Email:** info@warcombefarm.co.uk
www.warcombefarm.co.uk
**Pitches For** ▲ ⬤ 🚐 **Total** 200
**Facilities** ⬧ 🖻 🆙 ♨ ⌂ ☺ ⤙ ⬛ 🖭 🐟
🅂 🛈 ✕ 🝉 🗄 🝉 🖭 🄴 ☀
**Nearby Facilities** ⌐ ✔ ⤣ ∪
**Acreage** 19 **Open** 15 March **to** 31 Oct
**Access** Good **Site** Mostly Level
Family run, landscaped site with a beautiful lake and panoramic sea views. 1¼ miles to Woolacombe beach. Brand new facilities for 2004.
**Nearest Town/Resort** Barnstaple
**Directions** Turn left off the A361, Barnstaple to Ilfracombe road at Mullacott Cross roundabout signposted Woolacombe. After 2 miles turn right towards Mortehoe. Site is first on the right in less than a mile.
⚏ Barnstaple

# NEWTON ABBOT

**Compass Caravans,** Teigngrace, Newton Abbot, Devon, TQ12 6QZ
**Tel:** 01626 832792 **Fax:** 01626 832792
enquiries@compasscaravansdevon.com
www.compasscaravansdevon.com
**Pitches For** ▲ ⬤ 🚐 **Total** 34

**Facilities** ⬧ 🚻 🆙 ✦ ⌂ ☺ 🐟 ⬛ 🖭 🐟
🅟
**Nearby Facilities** ⌐ ✔ ∪ 🝉 ✗
**Open** All Year
**Access** Good **Site** Level
Close to Dartmoor National Park, Stover Wildlife Park and 15 miles from Torbay.
**Nearest Town/Resort** Newton Abbot
**Directions** Alongside the A38 westbound, ¼ of a mile before the A382 crosses over. Exit left for Teigngrace.
⚏ Newton Abbot

# NEWTON ABBOT

**Dornafield Touring Park,** Two Mile Oak, Newton Abbot, Devon, TQ12 6DD
**Tel:** 01803 812732 **Fax:** 01803 812032
**Email:** enquiries@dornafield.com
www.dornafield.com
**Pitches For** ▲ ⬤ 🚐 **Total** 135
**Facilities** ⬧ ✦ 🖻 🚻 🆙 ✦ ⌂ ☺ ⤙ ⬛ 🖭 🐟
🅂 🛈 ⬤ ⛱ 🝉 🗄 🝉 🖭 🄴 🅟
**Nearby Facilities** ⌐ ✔ ⤣ ∪ 🝉 ✗
**Acreage** 30 **Open** 20 March **to** 30 Oct
**Access** Good **Site** Level
Beautiful 14th Century farmhouse location with superb facilities to suit discerning caravanners and campers. Tennis court on site. Non members welcome. Booking essential.
**Nearest Town/Resort** Newton Abbot
**Directions** Take the A381 (Newton Abbott

# DEVON

to Totnes), in 2 miles at Two Mile Oak Inn turn right. In ½ mile turn first left, site is 200 yards on the right.

⚶ Newton Abbot

## NEWTON ABBOT

**Lemonford Caravan Park**, Bickington, Newton Abbot, Devon, TQ12 6JR
**Tel:** 01626 821242
**Email:** mark@lemonford.co.uk
www.lemonford.co.uk
Pitches For ▲ ⬛ ⬛ Total 85
Facilities ⅙ ∱ ⬛ ⬛ ⬛ ⌐ ⊙ ⌣ ⬛ ⬛ ⬛
⅍ ⬛ ⬛⌿⬛ ⚡
Nearby Facilities ⌐ ✔ ⅃ ⚓ ∪ ⚘ ✗
Acreage 7 Open Mid March to End October

Access Good Site Level
In a beautiful setting and scrupulously clean. Close to Torbay and the Dartmoor National Park.
**Nearest Town/Resort** Ashburton
**Directions** From Exeter along A38 take A382 turnoff, on roundabout take 3rd exit and follow site signs to Bickington. From Plymouth take A383 turnoff, follow road for ¼ mile and turn left into site.

⚶ Newton Abbot

## NEWTON ABBOT

**Ross Park**, Park Hill Farm, Moor Road, Ipplepen, Newton AbbotDevon, TQ12 5TT
**Tel:** 01803 812983 **Fax:** 01803 812983
**Email:**
enquiries@rossparkcaravanpark.co.uk
www.rossparkcaravanpark.co.uk
Pitches For ▲ ⬛ ⬛ Total 110
Facilities ⅙ ✗ ∱ ⬛ ⬛ ⌐ ⊙ ⌣ ⬛ ⬛ ⬛
⅍ ⅞ ⬛ ⬛ ✗ ⬛ ⬛ ⬛ ⬛ ⬛⌿⬛
Nearby Facilities ⌐ ✔ ⅃ ⚓ ∪ ⚘ ⚡
Acreage 26 Open Mid Feb to 4 Jan
Access Good Site Level
Ideal for touring the South Hams area. 6

miles from Torbay and Dartmoor National Park with a 15 minute drive.
**Nearest Town/Resort** Newton Abbot
**Directions** 3 miles from Newton Abbot and 6 miles from Totnes on the A381. At Park Hill crossroads and Jet Filling Station take the road signposted Woodland and brown tourism sign to Ross Park.

⚶ Newton Abbot

## NEWTON ABBOT

**Woodville Caravan Park**, Totnes Road, Ipplepen, Newton Abbot, Devon, TQ12 5TN
**Tel:** 01803 812240 **Fax:** 01803 813984
**Email:** jo@woodvillepark.co.uk
www.woodvillepark.co.uk
Pitches For ⬛ ⬛ Total 32
Facilities ⅙ ∱ ⬛ ⬛ ⬛ ⌐ ⊙ ⌣ ⬛
⅍ ⬛⌿⬛⌿ ⚡
Nearby Facilities ⌐ ✔ ∪
Acreage 3½ Open 1 March to 1 Jan
Access Good Site Level
ADULT ONLY SITE. Opposite a golf course. All hard standing pitches.
**Nearest Town/Resort** Newton Abbot/Torbay
**Directions** From Newton Abbot take the A381 towards Totnes for 2½ miles. After Fermoys Garden Centre, Woodville Park is situated on the right.

⚶ Newton Abbot

## OKEHAMPTON

**Bridestowe Caravan Park**, Bridestowe, Nr Okehampton, Devon, EX20 4ER
**Tel:** 01837 861261
Pitches For ▲ ⬛ ⬛ Total 53
Facilities ∱ ⬛ ⬛ ⬛ ⌐ ⊙ ⌣ ⬛ ⬛ ⬛
⅍ ⅞ ⬛ ⬛ ⬛⌿⬛ ⚡
Nearby Facilities ⌐ ✔ ∪
Open March to December
Access Good Site Level
Dartmoor National Park 2 miles, ideal for

walking, cycling, horse riding, fishing and touring Devon and Cornwall. Within easy reach of coastal resorts.
**Nearest Town/Resort** Bude
**Directions** Leave M5 for A30 to Okehampton 3 miles west of Okehampton turn off A30 to Bridestowe village, follow camping signs to site.

## OKEHAMPTON

**Bundu Camping & Caravan Park**, Sourton Down, Okehampton, Devon, EX20 4HT
**Tel:** 01837 861611 **Fax:** 01837 861611
**Email:**
frances@bundusargent.wanadoo.co.uk
www.bundu.co.uk
Pitches For ▲ ⬛ ⬛ Total 38
Facilities ∱ ⬛ ⬛ ⬛ ⌐ ⊙ ⌣ ⬛ ⬛
⅍ ⬛ ⬛⌿⬛ ⬛ ⚡
Nearby Facilities ⌐ ✔ ⅃ ∪ ⚘
Acreage 4½ Open All Year
Access Good Site Level
Situated with access to Dartmoor and adjacent to National Cycleway Route 27. Ideal for touring Devon and Cornwall.
**Nearest Town/Resort** Okehampton
**Directions** On the A30 west, turn off at first slip road taking the A386 to Tavistock. Take first turn left to Sourton Down, site is at the end of the lane.

⚶ Okehampton

## PAIGNTON

**Beverley Park Holiday Centre**, Goodrington Road, Paignton, Devon, TQ4 7JE
**Tel:** 01803 661973 **Fax:** 01803 845427
**Email:** info@beverley-holidays.co.uk/ca
www.beverley-holidays.co.uk
Pitches For ▲ ⬛ ⬛ Total 180
Facilities ⅙ ∱ ⬛ ⬛ ⬛ ⌐ ⊙ ⌣ ⬛ ⬛ ⬛
⅍ ⅞ ⬛ ⬛ ✗ ⬛ ⬛ ⬛ ⬛⌿ ⬛ ⬛ ⬛

# HIGHER WELL FARM HOLIDAY PARK

We welcome tourers, tents and motor caravans. A quiet secluded park in lovely Devon countryside. Central for touring south Devon, 4 miles from Torbay beaches and 1 mile from River Dart and Stoke Gabriel. Modern toilet/shower building with family and disabled rooms. Electric hook-ups, hard standings, launderette, shop and payphone. Families and couples only. Dogs on leads welcome.

Also HOLIDAY CARAVANS FOR HIRE

**JOHN & LIZ BALL, Higher Well Farm Holiday Park,**
**Stoke Gabriel, Totnes, Devon TQ9 6RN.   Stoke Gabriel (01803) 782289**

★★★★
HOLIDAY PARK

---

**Nearby Facilities** ୮ ✔ ⚓ ❊ ∪ ⅋ ℛ
**Acreage** 9½ **Open** February **to** December
**Access** Good **Site** Level
Views across Torbay. Indoor heated
swimming pool, tennis court. Sauna.
**Nearest Town/Resort** Paignton
**Directions** 2 miles south of Paignton (ring
road) A3022. Turn left into Goodrington
Road.
⇌ Paignton

**PAIGNTON**
**Byslades International Camping &**
**Touring Park,** Totnes Road, Paignton,
Devon, TQ4 7PY
**Tel:** 01803 555072 **Fax:** 01803 555669
**Email:** info@byslades.co.uk
www.byslades.co.uk
**Pitches For** ▲ ⊕ ⊟ **Total** 190
**Facilities** ⚲ ℯ ⨍ ⊡ ⎁ ♨ ℟ ☉ ⊿ ⚍ ◻ � ♥
ℼ ⊙ ◩ ✗ ▽ ⊞ ⚭ ⩟ ⅋ ❋ ⊟ ⊡ ⊞
**Nearby Facilities** ୮ ✔ ⚓ ❊ ∪ ⅋ ℛ
**Acreage** 23 **Open** May **to** October
**Access** Good **Site** Level
The site is overlooking a beautiful valley
and is centrally situated to visit all parts of
Devon. Tennis on site. No Dogs allowed
from mid July to the end of August.
**Nearest Town/Resort** Paignton
**Directions** 2¼ miles west of Paignton on the
A385.
⇌ Paignton

**PAIGNTON**
**Higher Well Farm Holiday Park,** Stoke
Gabriel, Totnes, Devon, TQ9 6RN
**Tel:** 01803 782289
www.higherwellfarmholidaypark.co.uk
**Pitches For** ▲ ⊕ ⊟ **Total** 80
**Facilities** ⚲ ♨ ⨍ ⊡ ⎁ ♨ ℟ ☉ ⊿ ⚍ ◻ ♥
ℼ ⊙ ◩ ♥ ⊡ ⊟
**Nearby Facilities** ୮ ✔ ⚓ ❊
**Acreage** 8 **Open** Easter **to** October
**Access** Good **Site** Lev/Slope
Within 4 miles of Torbays beaches, 1 mile
from the village of Stoke Gabriel and the
River Dart.
**Nearest Town/Resort** Paignton
**Directions** From Paignton take A385
towards Totnes, turn off left at Parkers Arms.
Go 1½ miles then turn left again, site is 200
yards down road.
⇌ Paignton

**PAIGNTON**
**Hoburne Torbay,** Grange Road,
Goodrington, Paignton, Devon, TQ47 7JP
**Tel:** 01803 558010 **Fax:** 01803 696286
**Email:** enquiries@hoburne.com
www.hoburne.com
**Pitches For** ⊕ ⊟ **Total** 139
**Facilities** ⨍ ⊡ ⎁ ♨ ℟ ☉ ⊿ ⚍ ◻
ℼ ⊙ ◩ ✗ ▽ ⊞ ⚭ ⩟ ❋ ⊟ ⊡ ⊞
**Nearby Facilities** ୮ ✔ ⚓ ❊ ∪ ℛ
**Acreage** 65 **Open** February **to** January

**Access** Good **Site** Lev/Slope
Panoramic views over Torbay, close to
Goodrington beach.
**Nearest Town/Resort** Paignton
**Directions** From junc 31 of M5, travel south
for approx 20 miles on A380 to junction with
A385. Continue south on A380 (Paignton
Ring Road) for 1 mile, turn left into
Goodrington Road by Esso Filling Station.
After ¾ mile turn left into Grange Road.
⇌ Paignton

**PAIGNTON**
**Marine Park,** Grange Road, Paignton,
Devon, TQ4 7JR
**Tel:** 01803 661973 **Fax:** 01803 845427
**Email:** info@beverley-holidays.co.uk
www.beverley-holidays.co.uk
**Pitches For** ⊕ ⊟ **Total** 20
**Facilities** ⨍ ⊡ ⎁ ♨ ℟ ☉ ⊿ ⚍
◻ ℛ ◩ ♥ ⊟ ♨
**Nearby Facilities** ୮ ✔ ⚓ ❊ ∪ ⅋ ℛ
**Open** Easter **to** Oct
**Access** Good **Site** Level
Less than 1 mile from Goodrington Sands.
Wonderful, peaceful setting.
**Nearest Town/Resort** Paignton
**Directions** 2 miles south of Paignton. Take
the A3022 ring road, turn left into
Goodrington Road. At the church turn left into
Grange Road and follow round to the left.
⇌ Paignton

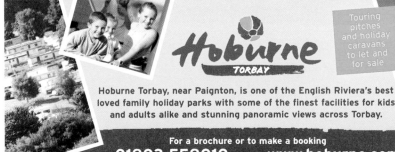

## PAIGNTON

**Whitehill Country Park,** Stoke Road, Paignton, South Devon, TQ4 7PF
**Tel:** 01803 782338 **Fax:** 01803 782722
**Email:** info@whitehill-park.co.uk
www.whitehill-park.co.uk
**Pitches For** ⚠ ⌗ ⛺ **Total** 330
**Facilities** ⌕ 🔣 ♨ ⌂ ⊙ ⌿ ⚊ 🔲 🚐
🔣 ⊙ ⚑ ✕ ⛲ 🛡 ♨ ⚑ 🔾 ⚑ 🔲 🔳 🔲 ⚊ 🔾
**Nearby Facilities** ⌕ ⟋ ⚓ 🔾 ⛵ ⚲ ♇
**Acreage** 30 **Open** 10th May **to** End September
**Access** Good **Site** Lev/Slope
Beautifully situated in rolling Devon countryside yet within easy reach of the sea, Torquay and the Dartmoor National Park.
**Nearest Town/Resort** Paignton
**Directions** Turn off the A385 at Parkers Arms Pub, ½ mile from Paignton Zoo, signposted Stoke Gabriel. Park is 1 mile along this road.
⚡ Paignton

## PAIGNTON

**Widend Touring Park,** Berry Pomeroy Road, Marldon, Paignton, Devon, TQ3 1RT
**Tel:** 01803 550116 **Fax:** 01803 550116
**Pitches For** ⚠ ⌗ ⛺ **Total** 185
**Facilities** ⚻ ⌕ 🔣 ♨ ⌂ ⊙ ⌿ ⚊ 🔲 🚐
🔣 ⊙ ⚑ ✕ ⛲ ⚑ 🔾 ♨ ⚑ 🔲 🔳 ⚊ 🔾 ⚲
**Nearby Facilities** ⌕ ⟋ ⚓ 🔾 ⛵ ♇ ⚲ ♇
**Acreage** 22 **Open** Easter **to** October
**Access** Good **Site** Level
Quiet, family run park for families and mixed couples only. A most central site for most of the sea and country amenities in South Devon. Dogs not allowed from Mid-July to the end of August. Static caravans for holiday letting. Caravan holiday homes for sale.
**Nearest Town/Resort** Paignton/Torquay
**Directions** Turn into Five Lanes Road towards Berry Pomeroy off the main Torquay ring road (A380) new duel carriageway at Marldon.
⚡ Torquay

## PLYMOUTH

**Plymouth Sound Caravan Club Site,** Bovisand Lane, Down Thomas, Plymouth, Devon, PL9 0AE
**Tel:** 01752 862325

www.caravanclub.co.uk
**Pitches For** ⌗ ⛺ **Total** 60
**Facilities** ⌕ ⛱ 🔣 ⊙ ⚑ ♨ ⚊ 🔲 🚐
**Nearby Facilities** ⌕ ⚓ ⚲
**Acreage** 6 **Open** March **to** Oct
**Access** Good **Site** Lev/Slope
¾ miles from a sandy beach. Plenty to see and do in the local area. Near a dry ski slope centre, Tamar Valley Railway, Lydford Gorge, Dartington Crystal and National Marine Aquarium. Own sanitation required. Non members welcome. Booking essential.
**Nearest Town/Resort** Plymouth
**Directions** From east on the A38 turn off at Marsh Mills flyover via slip road, at roundabout turn left onto A374 sp Plymouth City Centre. After 1¾ miles move to offside lane and follow signs for A379 Kingsbridge. At 4th roundabout turn right into Springfield Rd, at lights turn left into Reservoir Rd, by garage turn right into Staddiscombe Rd, after ½ mile turn left sp HMS Cambridge, after 1 mile turn right sp Down Thomas. At village sign turn right into Bovisand Lane (narrow entrance), site is 150 yards on the right.
⚡ Plymouth

## PLYMOUTH

**Riverside Caravan Park,** Longridge Road, Marsh Mills, Plymouth, Devon, PL6 8LD
**Tel:** 01752 344122 **Fax:** 01752 344122
**Email:** info@riversidecaravanpark.com
www.riversidecaravanpark.com
**Pitches For** ⚠ ⌗ ⛺ **Total** 220
**Facilities** ⚻ ⌕ 🔣 ♨ ⌂ ⊙ ⌿ ⚊ 🔲 🚐
🔣 ⊙ ⚑ ✕ ⛲ 🛡 ⚑ 🔾 ♨ ⚑ 🔲 🔳 ⚊ 🔾
**Nearby Facilities** ⌕ ⟋ ⚓ 🔾 ⛵ ♇ ⚲ ♇
**Acreage** 10½ **Open** All Year
**Access** Good **Site** Level
Alongside the River Plym.
**Nearest Town/Resort** Plymouth
**Directions** From the A38 take the slip road to Plymouth, at the roundabout take the third exit onto Plympton road, at trafficlights turn left, then first right.
⚡ Plymouth

## SALCOMBE

**Alston Farm Camping & Caravan Site,** Nr Salcombe, Kingsbridge, Devon, TQ7 3BJ
**Tel:** 01548 561260 **Fax:** 01548 561260

**Email:** alston.campsite@ukgateway.net
www.welcome.to/alstonfarm
**Pitches For** ⚠ ⌗ ⛺ **Total** 200
**Facilities** ⌕ 🔣 ⛱ ♨ ⌂ ⊙ ⌿ ⚊ 🔲 🚐
🔣 ⊙ ⚑ ⛱ 🔲 ♨ 🔲 ⚊
**Nearby Facilities** ⌕ ⟋ ⚓ 🔾 ⛵ ♇ ⚲ ♇
**Acreage** 15 **Open** Easter **to** October
**Access** Good **Site** Level
Secluded, sheltered site. Dish washing facilities. You can also contact us on Mobile: 07808 030921.
**Nearest Town/Resort** Salcombe
**Directions** Signposted on left of A381 between Kingsbridge and Salcombe towards Salcombe.
⚡ Totnes

## SALCOMBE

**Bolberry House Farm Camping & Caravanning Park,** Bolberry, Malborough, Nr Kingsbridge, Devon, TQ7 3DY
**Tel:** 01548 561251
**Email:** bolberry.house@virgin.net
www.bolberryparks.co.uk
**Pitches For** ⚠ ⌗ ⛺ **Total** 70
**Facilities** ⌕ 🔣 ⛱ ♨ ⌂ ⊙ ⌿ ⚊ 🔲 🚐
🔣 🔲 ⊙ ⚑ 🔲 ♨ 🔲
**Nearby Facilities** ⌕ ⟋ ⚓ 🔾 ⛵ ♇ ⚲ ♇
**Acreage** 6 **Open** March **to** October
**Access** Good **Site** Level
A friendly and peaceful, family run park on a coastal farm. Mostly level. Wonderful sea views and stunning cliff top walks. Safe sandy beaches 1 mile at the quaint old fishing village of Hope Cove. Salcombe's scenic and pretty estuary, a boating paradise - 2½ miles. AA 3 Pennants and ETC 3 Rosettes.
**Nearest Town/Resort** Salcombe
**Directions** Take the A381 from Kingsbridge to Malborough. Turn right through the village, follow signs to Bolberry ¾ mile.
⚡ Totnes

## SALCOMBE

**Higher Rew Touring Caravan & Camping Park,** Malborough, Kingsbridge, Devon, TQ7 3DW
**Tel:** 01548 842681 **Fax:** 01548 843681
**Email:** enquiries@higherrew.co.uk
www.higherrew.co.uk
**Pitches For** ⚠ ⌗ ⛺ **Total** 80

## Hope Cove KARRAGEEN Salcombe

**www.karrageen.co.uk**

*NOT AN OPEN FIELD BUT TERRACED, LEVEL AND TREE LINED PITCHES - A SITE WITH CHARACTER AND VIEWS*

*Special Rates for the Over 50's from £50 per week (not High Season)*

Secluded and peaceful family run park situated in beautiful South Devon countryside. Closest park to the beaches at the old fishing village of Hope Cove, one mile away. Surrounded by superb National Trust coastline walks and only four miles from the boating and sailing facilities at Salcombe.

Tiled toilet block offering first class facilities with showers incl. parents and baby room, disabled/family shower room and fully equipped laundry room. Licenced shop at reception with quality hot take-away food. Electric hook-ups for caravans and tents. **Luxury Caravans for hire from £250 per week.**

*For colour brochure please contact:* **PHIL & NIKKI HIGGIN, KARRAGEEN, BOLBERRY, MALBOROUGH, KINGSBRIDGE, DEVON TQ7 3EN**
Tel: **(01548) 561230** Fax: **(01548) 560192** E-mail: **phil@karrageen.co.uk**

---

Facilities ⚡ 🖥 ♿ ☎ ⊙ 🍴 ⚡ 🛒 🚩
📶 🛢 🔥 ♨ 📶 📞 ⚡ ♨ ⚡ ♨
**Nearby Facilities** 🏌 ⛵ 🎣 🚣
**Acreage** 5 **Open** Mid March **to** End Oct
**Access** Good **Site** Terraced
A family run park in an area of outstanding natural beauty on a farm. 1 mile from beaches and beautiful cliff walks. Tennis court on site. ETB 4 Star Graded.
**Nearest Town/Resort** Salcombe
**Directions** When approaching from Kingsbridge on the A381 to Salcombe, turn right at Malborough and follow signs to Soar for approx. 1 mile then turn left at Rew Cross. Higher Rew is then the first turning on the right.
✈ Totnes

### SEATON
**Ashdown Caravan Park,** Colyton Hill, Colyton, Devon, EX24 6HY
**Tel:** 01297 20292
**Email:** ashdowncaravans@tiscali.co.uk
**Pitches For** 🏕 🚐 **Total** 90
**Facilities** ⚡ 🖥 ♿ 🍴 ⊙ 🚩 📶 🛢 🚿 ⚡ ♨ ✂
♨
**Nearby Facilities** 🏌 ⛵ ♿ 🚣 ♨
**Acreage** 9 **Open** April **to** October
**Access** Good **Site** Level
Lovely coastal walks and beaches. Near the picturesque villages of Beer, Colyton and Branscombe.
**Nearest Town** Seaton/Beer/Colyton
**Directions** 3 miles north west of Seaton. Signposted off the A3052 Exeter to Lyme Regis road, at Stafford Cross.
✈ Axminster/Honiton

### SEATON
**Berry Barton Caravan Park,** Berry Barton, Branscombe, Seaton, Devon, EX12 3BD
**Tel:** 01297 680208

---

**Pitches For** 🏕 🚐 🚐
Facilities ⚡ 🖥 ♿ 🍴 ⊙ 🚩 ⚡ 🛒 🚩 🎣 📦
**Nearby Facilities** 🏌 🎣 🚣 ♨
**Acreage** 16 **Open** 15 March **to** 15 Nov
**Access** Good **Site** Level
Situated on a farm in an area of outstanding natural beauty. 1 mile of coastline and the Jurassic Coast for good walks.
**Nearest Town/Resort** Seaton/Sidmouth
**Directions** From the M5 at Exeter take the A3052 to Branscombe turning, go to Fountain Head and turn right just after the pub, Berry Barton is at the top of the hill on the right.
✈ Honiton

### SEATON
**Leacroft Touring Park,** Colyton Hill, Colyton, Devon, EX24 6HY
**Tel:** 01297 552823
**Pitches For** 🏕 🚐 🚐 **Total** 138
Facilities ⚡ 🖥 ♿ 🍴 ⊙ 🚩 ⚡ 🛒 🚩
📶 🛢 🔥 ♨ 📶 📞 ⚡ ✂ ♨
**Nearby Facilities** 🏌 🎣 🚣 ♨
**Acreage** 10 **Open** End March **to** October
**Access** Good **Site** Lev/Slope
Quiet, peaceful site in open countryside. Picturesque villages to explore and woodland walks nearby.
**Nearest Town/Resort** Seaton/Beer
**Directions** A3052 Sidmouth to Lyme Regis road, 2 miles west of Seaton. Turn left at Stafford Cross international caravan sign, site is 1 mile on the right.
✈ Axminster

### SEATON
**Manor Farm Camping & Caravan Site,** Seaton Down Hill, Seaton, Devon, EX12 2JA
**Tel:** 01297 21524
**Email:** tim.salter@talk21.com
**www.manor-farm.net**

---

**Pitches For** 🏕 🚐 🚐 **Total** 180
Facilities ♿ ⚡ 🖥 ♿ 🍴 ⊙ 🚩 ⚡ 🛒 🚩
📶 🛢 🔥 ♨ 📶 📞 ⚡ ♨
**Nearby Facilities** 🏌 ⛵ 🎣 🚣 ♨ 🏇 ♨
**Acreage** 22 **Open** 15 March **to** 31 Oct
**Access** Good **Site** Sloping
Alongside the Jurassic Coast for beaches and walks.
**Nearest Town/Resort** Seaton
**Directions** 1 mile from Seaton on the A3052.
✈ Axminster

### SIDMOUTH
**Kings Down Tail Caravan & Camping Park,** Salcombe Regis, Sidmouth, Devon, EX10 0PD
**Tel:** 01297 680313 **Fax:** 01297 680313
**Email:** info@kingsdowntail.co.uk
**www.uk.parks.co.uk/kingsdowntail**
**Pitches For** 🏕 🚐 🚐 **Total** 100
Facilities ♿ ⚡ 🖥 ♿ 🍴 ⊙ 🚩 ⚡ 🛒 🚩
📶 🛢 🔥 ♨ 📶 📞 ⚡ ♨
**Nearby Facilities** 🏌 🎣 🚣 ♨
**Acreage** 5 **Open** 15 March **to** 15 Nov
**Access** Good **Site** Level
Heated shower block. Local fishermen are happy to take people out on boat trips. Ideal centre for East Devon and West Dorset. Pets are welcome if kept on a lead.
**Nearest Town/Resort** Sidmouth
**Directions** On the A3052 3 miles east of Sidmouth, opposite Branscombe Water Tower. Please note that we are NOT in Salcombe Regis Village.

### SIDMOUTH
**Oakdown Touring & Holiday Home Park,** Weston, Sidmouth, Devon, EX10 0PH
**Tel:** 01297 680387 **Fax:** 01297 680541
**Email:** enquiries@oakdown.co.uk
**www.oakdown.co.uk**
**Pitches For** 🏕 🚐 🚐 **Total** 100

---

KINGS DOWN TAIL Caravan & Camping Park

Salcombe Regis, Sidmouth, Devon EX10 0PD Tel/Fax: 01297 680313

*Quiet, tree sheltered, 5 acre park, personally operated by the proprietors Ian & Sue McKenzie Edwards.*

www.kings-down-tail.co.uk

E-mail: info@kingsdowntail.co.uk

- Ideal centre to explore East Devon
- Close to World Heritage Coastline with its geological wonders.
- Easy access
- Two well equipped toilet blocks
- Heated Shower block
- Games Room & Children's Play Area
- Rallies catered for
- Secure caravan storage available

**Facilities**
**Nearby Facilities**
**Acreage** 13 **Open** April **to** October
**Access** Good **Site** Level
Oakdown the Excellence in England Caravan Holiday Park of the Year 2003. Sidmouths Award Winning park near Jurassic Coast World Heritage Site and beautiful Weston Valley - lovely cliff walks. Oakmead Par 3 Golf Course now open. Field trail to nearby world famous Donkey Sanctuary. Caravan holiday homes to let. Awards for 2005 - ETB 5 Star Grading, AA 4 Pennant De-Luxe Park, David Bellamy Gold Conservation Award, Loo of the Year Award, Calor Gas Best Park in England 1999, Devon & Cornwall Police Gold Award for Security.
**Nearest Town/Resort** Sidmouth
**Directions** 1½ miles east of Sidford on A3052, take the second Weston turning at the Oakdown sign. Site 50 yards on left. Also signposted with international Caravan/ Camping signs.
≠ Honiton

## SIDMOUTH

**Putts Corner Caravan Club Site,** Sidbury, Sidmouth, Devon, EX10 0QQ
**Tel:** 01404 42875
**www.**caravanclub.co.uk
**Pitches For** **Total** 113
**Facilities**
**Nearby Facilities**
**Acreage** 7 **Open** March **to** Oct
**Access** Good **Site** Lev/Slope
Quiet site in pretty surroundings where wildlife and flowers abound. Plenty of walks from the site. Boules pitch, water softening plant and water supply from borehole. 200 yards from a pub. Near the Donkey Sanctuary. Non members welcome. Booking essential.
**Nearest Town/Resort** Sidmouth
**Directions** From east on the A30 Honiton bypass, turn off via slip road at signpost Sidmouth A375, at end of slip road turn left then 100 yards and turn left again, after 350 yards turn right onto the A375. At Hare & Hounds Inn turn right onto the B3174, site is ¼ mile on the right.
≠ Sidmouth

## SIDMOUTH

**Salcombe Regis Camping & Caravan Park,** Salcombe Regis, Sidmouth, Devon, EX10 0JH
**Tel:** 01395 514303 **Fax:** 01395 514314
**Email:** sidmouthcamping@btconnect.com
**www.**salcombe-regis.co.uk
**Pitches For** **Total** 100
**Facilities**
**Nearby Facilities**
**Acreage** 16 **Open** 3 April **to** 28 Oct
**Access** Good **Site** Level
A park with peace and quiet. Just a 5 minute walk from the Jurassic Coastal Path, and a 5-10 minute drive from 'Select Sidmouth'. Ideally based for touring East Devon.
**Nearest Town/Resort** Sidmouth
**Directions** From Exeter M5 take the A3052 through Sidford towards Lyme Regis. Take second turning to Salcombe Regis, on the left after Golf Range.
≠ Honiton or Exeter

## SLAPTON

**Sea View Campsite,** Newlands Farm, Slapton, Nr Dartmouth, Devon, TQ7 2RB
**Tel:** 01548 580366
**Email:** cades@devon-camping.co.uk
**www.**camping-devon.com
**Pitches For** **Total** 45
**Facilities**
**Nearby Facilities**
**Acreage** 10 **Open** 23 May **to** September
**Access** Good **Site** Level
We have a friendly, uncommercialised, quiet site overlooking beautiful countryside and sea. Within 1 mile of glorious beaches, cliff walks and a nature reserve. Woodlands Leisure Centre is close by with fun for all the family.
**Nearest Town/Resort** Dartmouth
**Directions** From Totnes take the A381 towards Kingsbridge, after Halwell Village take the fourth left signposted Slapton. Go 4 miles to Buckland Cross, proceed for ¼ mile, site is on the left hand side.

## SOUTH MOLTON

**Romansleigh Holiday Park,** Odam Hill, South Molton, North Devon, EX36 4NB
**Tel:** 01769 550259
**Email:** romhols@lineone.net
**Pitches For** **Total** 20
**Facilities**
**Nearby Facilities**
**Acreage** 2 **Open** 15 March **to** 31 October
**Access** Good **Site** Level
Secluded, wooded valley with grounds of 14 acres. Easy access to Exmoor and the North Devon coast. Magnificent views.
**Nearest Town/Resort** Barnstaple
**Directions** Take the B3137 South Molton to Witheridge road. Site is signposted right approximately 4 miles from South Molton and 2 miles past Alswear.
≠ Umberleigh

## SOUTH MOLTON

**Yeo Valley Holiday Park,** c/o Blackcock Inn, Molland, South Molton, North Devon, EX36 3NW
**Tel:** 01769 550297 **Fax:** 01769 550101


Salcombe Regis

SIDMOUTH
DEVON EX10 0JH
01395 514303
FREE COLOUR BROCHURE

"The Discerning Campers Choice"

- Spacious Level Site
- Hardstandings with taps & soakaways at no extra cost
- Heated Amenity Block
- Tranquil setting within walking distance of the sea
- Caravan Storage available
- 10 Luxury Holiday Homes available for Hire

E-mail: contact@salcombe-regis.co.uk www.salcombe-regis.co.uk

# Harford Bridge Holiday Park

Beautiful family run park set in Dartmoor National Park, with delightful views of Cox Tor. The River Tavy forms a boundary offering riverside camping and other level, spacious pitches. Luxury self catering caravan holiday homes, open all year. *2 miles from Tavistock, off the A386 Okehampton road, take the Peter Tavy turning.*

**Harford Bridge Holiday Park, Peter Tavy, Tavistock, Devon PL19 9LS**
**Tel: 01822 810349   Fax: 01822 810028**
**www.harfordbridge.co.uk**
**E-mail: enquiry@harfordbridge.co.uk**

ROSE AWARD
CARAVAN HOLIDAY PARK

**Email:** info@yeovalleyholidays.com
**www.**yeovalleyholidays.com
**Pitches For** ▲ ♦ ⇌ **Total** 65
**Facilities** ✹ ⌂ ⌷ ♨ ⌒ ⌐ ⬚ ▣ ☎ ⚥ ⊙ ⬚ ✕ ⓟ ♠ ⋔ ⩣ ⊣⊟⊡ ☀ ⚘
**Nearby Facilities** ┏ ✗ ∪
**Acreage** 7 **Open** All Year
**Access** Good **Site** Gently Sloping
Quiet secluded valley on the edge of Exmoor. Ideal for walking, cycling and outdoor pursuits.
**Nearest Town/Resort** South Molton
**Directions** Signposted clearly from the A361 just east of South Molton.
⇻ Tiverton Parkway/Barnstaple

## STOKENHAM

**Old Cotmore Farm,** Old Cotmore Farm, Stokenham, South Devon, TQ7 2LR
**Tel:** 01548 580240 **Fax:** 01548 580875
**Email:** graham.bowsher@btinternet.com
**www.**oldcotmorefarm.co.uk
**Pitches For** ▲ ♦ ⇌ **Total** 30
**Facilities** ⚥ ⊙ ⬚ ♠ ⋔ ⩣⊟⊡ ☀ ⚘
**Nearby Facilities** ┏ ✗ ⚘ ↯ ∪ ⚘ ♬
**Acreage** 10 **Open** March to November
**Access** Good **Site** Lev/Slope
Small, family run, picturesque, peaceful site with views over farms and fields. Cliff walks, beaches, diving, fishing and bird watching. Excellent pubs.
**Nearest Town/Resort** Kingsbridge/Salcombe
**Directions** Take the A379 Kingsbridge to Dartmouth road, at the Carehouse Cross in Stokenham turn right signposted Beesands. Farm is 1 mile on the right and is signposted.
⇻ Totnes

## TAVISTOCK

**Harford Bridge Holiday Park,** Peter Tavy, Tavistock, Devon, PL19 9LS
**Tel:** 01822 810349 **Fax:** 01822 810028
**Email:** enquiry@harfordbridge.co.uk
**www.**harfordbridge.co.uk
**Pitches For** ▲ ♦ ⇌ **Total** 120
**Facilities** ⚥ ✹ ⌷ ⌂ ⬚ ♨ ⌒ ⊙ ⊣ ⬚ ⊡ ☎ ⬚ ⓟ ♠ ⋔ ⊣⊟⊡ ⬚
**Nearby Facilities** ┏ ✗ ∪ ♬
**Acreage** 16½ **Open** March to November

**Access** Good **Site** Level
Beautiful, family run park with scenic views, riverside pitches, fishing and tennis. Ideal for touring Dartmoor National Park. Rose Award. Self catering available all year.
**Nearest Town/Resort** Tavistock
**Directions** A386 Okehampton road 2 miles north of Tavistock.
⇻ Plymouth

## TAVISTOCK

**Higher Longford,** Moorshop, Tavistock, Devon, PL19 9LQ
**Tel:** 01822 613360
**Email:** stay@higherlongford.co.uk
**www.**higherlongford.co.uk
**Pitches For** ▲ ♦ ⇌ **Total** 52
**Facilities** ⚥ ✹ ⌂ ⌷ ⬚ ♨ ⌒ ⊙ ⊣ ⬚ ⊡ ☎ ⚥ ⊙ ⬚ ✕ ⓟ ♠ ⋔ ⩣⊟⊡ ∪ ☀ ⚘
**Nearby Facilities** ┏ ✗ ∪ ♬
**Acreage** 6 **Open** All Year
**Access** Good **Site** Level
4 Star Deluxe Park in the foothills of Dartmoor. Excellent facilities, free water and showers, take-away including freshly baked bread and pastries, shop and off licence. Ideal for touring Devon and Cornwall.
**Nearest Town/Resort** Tavistock.
**Directions** Tavistock/Princetown road, 2 miles from Tavistock on the B3357.
⇻ Plymouth.

## TAVISTOCK

**Langstone Manor Caravan & Camping Park,** Langstone Manor, Moortown, Tavistock, Devon, PL19 9JZ
**Tel:** 01822 613371 **Fax:** 01822 613371
**Email:** web@langstone-manor.co.uk
**www.**langstone-manor.co.uk
**Pitches For** ▲ ♦ ⇌ **Total** 40
**Facilities** ✹ ⌂ ⌷ ⬚ ♨ ⌒ ⊙ ⊣ ⬚ ⊡ ☎ ⚥ ⊙ ⬚ ✕ ⓟ ♠ ⋔ ⊣⊟⊡ ⬚
**Nearby Facilities** ┏ ✗ ⚘ ∪ ♬ ♬
**Acreage** 5½ **Open** 15 March to 15 Nov
**Access** Good **Site** Level
Direct access onto Dartmoor. Quiet, friendly park with views over moor and farmland. Bar and evening meals. Dogs welcome. ETB 4 Star Graded and AA 3 Pennants.

**Nearest Town/Resort** Tavistock
**Directions** Take the B3357 from Tavistock towards Princetown, after approx. 2 miles turn right at crossroads, pass over the cattle grid, continue up the hill then turn left following signs for Langstone Manor. We are ½ mile on the right.
⇻ Plymouth

## TAVISTOCK

**Woodovis Park,** Tavistock, Devon, PL19 8NY
**Tel:** 01822 832968 **Fax:** 01822 832948
**Email:** info@woodovis.com
**www.**woodovis.com
**Pitches For** ▲ ♦ ⇌ **Total** 50
**Facilities** ⚥ ✹ ⌂ ⌷ ⬚ ♨ ⌒ ⊙ ⊣ ⬚ ⊡ ☎ ⚥ ⊙ ⬚ ♠ ⋔ ⊣⊟⊡ ∪ ☀ ⚘
**Nearby Facilities** ┏ ✗ ∪ ♬
**Acreage** 14 **Open** April to October
**Access** Good **Site** Lev/Slope
5 Star BTB Graded Park. Quiet, rural site with outstanding views. Near to Dartmoor, coasts and Cornwall. Excellent facilities, free showers, laundry/washing-up room. Shop, off-license, farm produce, bread/croissants baked on site. Heated indoor pool, sauna and jacuzzi. Pitch and putt.
**Nearest Town/Resort** Tavistock
**Directions** Take A390 Liskeard road from Tavistock. Site signposted right in 3 miles.
⇻ Plymouth/Gunnislake

## TEIGNMOUTH

**Coast View Holiday Park,** Torquay Road, Shaldon, South Devon, TQ14 0BG
**Tel:** 01626 872392 **Fax:** 01626 872719
**Email:** info@coastview.co.uk
**www.**coastview.co.uk
**Pitches For** ▲ ♦ ⇌ **Total** 250
**Facilities** ✹ ⌷ ♨ ⌒ ⊙ ⊣ ⬚ ⊡ ☎ ⚥ ⊙ ⬚ ✕ ⓟ ⓣ ♠ ⋔ ⩣ ☀ ⬚
**Nearby Facilities** ┏ ∪
**Acreage** 18 **Open** 18 March
**Access** Good **Site** Lev/Slope
Near the beach with fantastic views.
**Nearest Town/Resort** Teignmouth
**Directions** On the A379 between Teignmouth and Torquay.
⇻ Teignmouth

---

## Higher Longford Caravan & Camping Park   01822 613360

*Nestled in the foothills of Dartmoor*  **Moorshop • Tavistock • Devon • PL19 9LQ**

Family run site with 80 level pitches, including multiserviced, hardstanding and grass pitches. Storage also available. Super toilet block with excellent free full en-suite facilities, plus extra toilets and washbasins. Also bathroom and babychanging facilities. Shop. Games Room. Take-Away Meals.   See our website **www.higherlongford.co.uk**

*Open All Year*

**TIVERTON**

**Minnows Caravan Park,** Sampford Peverell, Tiverton, Devon, EX16 7EN
**Tel:** 01884 821770
www.ukparks.co.uk/minnows
**Pitches For** ▲ ⚲ ⛟ **Total** 45
**Facilities** ⚅ ⚘ ⚑ ▯ ☐ ☒ ♨ ⌂ ⊙ ◨ ☏
▯ ⊙ ⚘ ⚙ ✦ ▤ ⊟
**Nearby Facilities** ⌂ ✧ ⚘ ∪ ℘
**Acreage** 5½ **Open** March **to** Nov
**Access** Good **Site** Level
Alongside the Grand Western Canal Country Park, ideal for walking, cycling and fishing. Village with pub and shops ½ mile along the canal. Discount for Caravan Club Members. Non members welcome. Booking essential.
**Nearest Town/Resort** Tiverton
**Directions** Leave the M5 at junction 27 and take the A361 signposted Tiverton and Barnstaple. After 440 yards take the slip road signposted Sampford Peverell, turn right at the mini roundabout, site is immediately ahead on the left.
⇌ Tiverton Parkway

**TIVERTON**

**West Middlewick Farm Caravans & Camping,** West Middlewick Farm, Nomansland, Tiverton, Devon, EX16 8NP
**Tel:** 01884 861235 **Fax:** 01884 861235
**Email:** stay@westmiddlewick.co.uk
www.westmiddlewick.co.uk
**Pitches For** ▲ ⚲ ⛟ **Total** 25
**Facilities** ⚑ ☐ ☒ ♨ ⌂ ⊙ ☏ ▯▲▯
**Nearby Facilities** ✧ ∪ ℘
**Acreage** 3½ **Open** All Year
**Access** Good **Site** Level
Working family farm with lovely walks. Ideal touring.
**Nearest Town/Resort** Tiverton
**Directions** Leave the A361 at junction 27 for Tiverton, then take the B3137 to Witheridge. 9 miles from Tiverton.
⇌ Tiverton Parkway

**TIVERTON**

**Zeacombe House Caravan Park,** East Anstey, Nr Tiverton, Devon, EX16 9JU
**Tel:** 01398 341279
**Email:** enquiries@zeacombeadultretreat.co.uk
www.zeacombeadultretreat.co.uk
**Pitches For** ▲ ⚲ ⛟ **Total** 50
**Facilities** ⚑ ☐ ☒ ♨ ⌂ ⊙ ⚘ ▤ ☐ ▯
☒ ⊙ ⚙ ☐ ☐ A ℘
**Nearby Facilities** ⌂ ✧ ∪
**Acreage** 4½ **Open** 31 Mar **to** 31 Oct
**Access** Good **Site** Level
ADULTS ONLY site near to Exmoor, Tarr Steps, National Trust properties, Tarka Trail and Rosemoor Gardens. Ideal for walking. Evening meal service. AA 4 Pennants and a BH&HPA Member.
**Nearest Town/Resort** Tiverton
**Directions** Leave the M5 at junction 27 and take the A361 to Tiverton. At the roundabout turn right signposted the A396 to Minehead.

IT'S FUN FOR ALL THE FAMILY

# WOOLACOMBE SANDS
## HOLIDAY PARK

## NEAREST HOLIDAY PARK TO THE BEACH

Heated Indoor & Outdoor Swimming Pools, Licensed Club-Nightly Entertainment, Amusement Arcade, Indoor & Outdoor Play Areas, Crazy Golf & Bowling.

### TOURING & CAMPING

Designated areas for Tents and Tourers, Showers, Toilets, Wash basins, Hair dryers, Launderette. Electric Hook Ups available.

### CHALETS / CARAVANS / COTTAGES

Up to 8 people, ALL facilities including Colour TV, Private Bathroom, set in beautiful countryside overlooking the sea & miles of golden sands.

# 01271 870569
## www.woolacombe-sands.co.uk
Woolly Bear Club:- www.woolly-bear.co.uk

## Beach Rd, Woolacombe, N. Devon EX34 7AF

# DEVON

and Dulverton. After 5 miles turn left at the Exeter Inn, after 1¾ miles turn left at the Black Cat onto the B3227, 5 miles to Knowstone and the site is on the left.
🚂 Tiverton

## TORQUAY

**Manor Farm Camp Site,** Manor Farm, Daccombe, Newton Abbot, Devon, TQ12 4ST
**Tel:** 01803 328294 **Fax:** 01803 328294
**Email:** daccombe1@btopenworld.com
**Pitches For** 🛆 ⚌ **Total** 75
**Facilities** 🅿 ⚓ ⌁ ⊙ ⚐ 🖸 🛇 ⊙ ⚐🖸
**Nearby Facilities** ⌐ ✓ ⚓ ⚞ ♞
**Acreage** 3 **Open** Easter **to** Sept
**Site** Sloping
Working farm set in picturesque countryside.
**Nearest Town/Resort** Torquay
**Directions** From Newton Abbot take the A380 for Torquay. Go through roundabout at Kerswell Gardens to next set of traffic lights, turn left into Kingskerswell Road, follow camp signs.
🚂 Torquay

## TORQUAY

**Widdicombe Farm Touring Park,** The Ring Road (A380), Compton, Marldon, TorquayDevon, TQ3 1ST
**Tel:** 01803 558325 **Fax:** 01803 559526
**Email:** enq@widdicombefarm.co.uk
**www.**widdicombefarm.co.uk
**Pitches For** 🛆 ⚌ ⚌ **Total** 160
**Facilities** ⚓ ⌁ 🅿 ⚓ ⚓ ⌁ 🅿 ⊙ ⚐ 🖸 🍴
🛇 ⚑ ⚓ ✕ ⚐ 🖸 ⚐ 🖸
**Nearby Facilities** ⌐ ✓ ⚓ ⚞ ⋃ ♞ ♞
**Acreage** 8 **Open** Mid March **to** Mid Oct
**Access** Good **Site** Level
A very friendly family run park. Lovely countryside setting, yet so near to Torquay. Restaurant serving home cooked food. Club House with good entertainment, mid and high season. Separate Adult Only field. No narrow country lanes. Bargain Breaks from £48.00 per week inc. electric hook-up and awning. Luxury at the right price.
**Nearest Town/Resort** Torquay/Paignton
**Directions** From Exeter take the A380 to Torquay, at the large roundabout controlled by traffic lights follow signs for Torquay. At next roundabout turn right into Hamlyn Way, go to the top of the hill and at the next roundabout go straight on. Look to the right to see our park, proceed to the next roundabout and double back to Widdicombe Farm.
🚂 Torquay/Paignton

## TOTNES

**Steamer Quay Caravan Club Site,** Steamer Quay Road, Totnes, Devon, TQ9 5AL
**Tel:** 01803 862738
**www.**caravanclub.co.uk
**Pitches For** ⚌ ⚌ **Total** 40
**Facilities** ⚓ ⌁ 🅿 ⊙ ⚐ 🖸 🍴 🛇 ⚐🖸 🖸
**Nearby Facilities** ⌐ ✓
**Acreage** 3 **Open** March **to** Oct
**Access** Good **Site** Level
Quiet site with lovely views, just a short walk from Totnes centre. Close to Paignton Zoo, Dart River Cruises and South Devon Railway. Non members welcome. Booking essential.
**Nearest Town/Resort** Totnes
**Directions** From the A38 take either the A384 at Buckfastleigh or the A385 at South Brent, both roads become the A385 at Dartington. In Totnes cross the railway bridge and turn right at the roundabout, after 300 yards turn left over the bridge, turn right into

Seymour Road, turn right into Steamer Quay Road, site entrance is on the left.
🚂 Totnes

## UFFCULME

**Waterloo Cross Caravan Park,** Waterloo Cross, Uffculme, Devon, EX15 3ES
**Tel:** 01884 841342
**Pitches For** 🛆 ⚌ ⚌ **Total** 50
**Facilities** ⌁ 🅿 ⚓ ⚓ ⌁ 🅿 ⊙ ⚐ ⚐ 🍴
🛇 ⚓ ✕ ⚐ ⚐ 🖸
**Nearby Facilities** ⌐ ✓ ⋃ ♞
**Open** All Year
**Access** Good **Site** Level
**Nearest Town/Resort** Cullompton
**Directions** 5 miles from Cullompton.
🚂 Parkway Station

## UMBERLEIGH

**Camping & Caravanning Club Site,** Over Weir, Umberleigh, Devon, EX37 9DU
**Tel:** 01769 560009
**www.**campingandcaravanningclub.co.uk
**Pitches For** 🛆 ⚌ ⚌ **Total** 60
**Facilities** ⚓ ⌁ 🅿 ⚓ ⚓ ⌁ 🅿 ⊙ ⚐ ⚐ 🖸
🛇 ⚑ ⊙ ⚐ ⚓ ✕ ⚐ ⚐ 🖸 ⚞ 🖸
**Nearby Facilities** ⌐ ✓ ⚓
**Acreage** 3 **Open** April **to** Oct
**Access** Good **Site** Lev/Slope
The site enjoys a peaceful and relaxing atmosphere, situated between Exmoor and Dartmoor National Park. Superb golden beaches nearby. BTB 4 Star Graded and AA 3 Pennants. Non members welcome.
**Nearest Town/Resort** Barnstaple
**Directions** From Barnstaple take the A377 and turn right at 'Umberleigh' nameplate.
🚂 Barnstaple

## WESTWARD HO!

**Braddicks Holiday Centre,** Merley Road, Westward Ho!, North Devon, EX39 1JU
**Tel:** 01237 473263 **Fax:** 01237 477709
**Email:** holidays@braddicksholidaycentre.co.uk
**www.**braddicksholidaycentre.co.uk
**Pitches For** 🛆 ⚌ ⚌ **Total** 40
**Facilities** 🅿 ⚓ 🅿 ⚓ ⚓ ⚞
**Nearby Facilities** ⌐ ✓ ⚓ ⚞ ⋃ ♞ ♞
**Open** May **to** October
**Access** Good **Site** Lev/Slope
Beside the Blue Flag beach and on the South West Coastal Path. Nightly entertainment during high season. Just a 5 minute walk from the centre of Westward Ho! Village.
**Nearest Town/Resort** Westward Ho!
🚂 Barnstaple

## WOOLACOMBE

**Damage Barton,** Mortehoe, Woolacombe, North Devon, EX34 7EJ
**Tel:** 01271 870502 **Fax:** 01271 870712
**Email:** info@damagebarton.co.uk
**www.**damagebarton.co.uk
**Pitches For** 🛆 ⚌ ⚌ **Total** 155
**Facilities** ⚓ ⌁ 🅿 ⚓ ⚓ ⌁ 🅿 ⊙ ⚐ ⚐ 🖸
🛇 ⚑ ⚑ ⊙ ⚐🖸 ⚞ 🖸
**Nearby Facilities** ⌐ ✓ ⚓ ⋃ ♞
**Acreage** 16 **Open** 15 March **to** 5 Nov
**Access** Good **Site** Lev/Slope
Peaceful site with good views, wild flowers and birds. Access to a network of footpaths including the coastal path.
**Nearest Town/Resort** Woolacombe
**Directions** Take the A361 from Barnstaple and turn left at the Mullacott Cross roundabout onto the B3343 signposted Woolacombe and Mortehoe. After 1¾ miles turn right signposted Mortehoe, site is on the right after approx. 1 mile.
🚂 Barnstaple

## WOOLACOMBE

**Europa Park,** Beach Road, Woolacombe, North Devon, EX34 7AN
**Tel:** 01271 871425
**Email:** holidays@europapark.co.uk
**www.**europapark.co.uk
**Pitches For** 🛆 ⚌ ⚌
**Facilities** ⚓ ⌁ 🅿 ⚓ ⚓ ⌁ 🅿 ⊙ ⚐ 🖸 ⚞
🛇 ⚑ ⊙ ⚓ ✕ ⚐ ⚓ ⚑ ⚐ 🖸 ⚞ ⚑ 🖸
⚞
**Nearby Facilities** ⌐ ✓ ⚓ ⋃ ♞ ♞
**Acreage** 16 **Open** All Year
**Access** Good **Site** Lev/Slope
Superb views of surrounding countryside and Woolacombe Bay.
**Nearest Town/Resort** Woolacombe/ Ilfracombe
**Directions** Take the A361 Barnstaple to Woolacombe road, at Mullacott Cross roundabout turn onto the B3343 to Woolacombe. Europa Park is on the right.
🚂 Barnstaple

## WOOLACOMBE

**Golden Coast Holiday Village,** Woolacombe, Devon, EX34 7HW
**Tel:** 01271 870343 **Fax:** 01271 870089
**Email:** goodtimes@woolacombe.com
**www.**woolacombe.com
**Pitches For** 🛆 ⚌ ⚌ **Total** 91
**Facilities** ⌁ 🅿 ⚓ ⚓ ⌁ 🅿 ⊙ ⚐ ⚐ 🖸
🛇 ⚑ ⊙ ⚓ ✕ ⚐ ⚓ ⚑ ⚞ ⚐ 🖸 ⚞ 🖸
**Nearby Facilities** ⌐ ✓ ⚓ ⋃ ♞ ♞ ♞
**Open** Feb **to** Jan
**Access** Good **Site** Lev/Slope
Close to the Blue Flag beach of Woolacombe, bus service to the beach. Choice of four parcs and their facilities, entertainment and accommodation.
**Nearest Town/Resort** Woolacombe
**Directions** Take the A361 to Barnstaple and follow Ilfracombe signs, take the Woolacombe junction from Mullacott Cross.
🚂 Barnstaple

## WOOLACOMBE

**Little Roadway Farm,** Woolacombe, North Devon, EX34 7HL
**Tel:** 01271 870313 **Fax:** 01271 871085
**Pitches For** 🛆 ⚌ ⚌ **Total** 200
**Facilities** ⌁ 🅿 ⚓ ⚓ ⌁ 🅿 ⊙ ⚐ ⚞
🛇 ⚑ ⊙ ⚓ ✕ ⚐🖸
**Nearby Facilities** ⌐ ✓ ⚓ ⋃ ♞ ♞ ♞
**Acreage** 20 **Open** March **to** Nov
**Access** Good **Site** Lev/Slope
Within 1 mile of Woolacombe beach. Easy access to Putsborough, Croyde, Saunton and Exmoor.
**Nearest Town/Resort** Woolacombe
**Directions** Take the A361 to Mullacott Cross roundabout and turn left towards Woolacombe, follow tourism signs and turn left on the B3231, Little Roadway Farm is on this road.
🚂 Barnstaple

## WOOLACOMBE

**Twitchen Parc,** Mortehoe, Woolacombe, North Devon, EX34 7ES
**Tel:** 01271 870343 **Fax:** 01271 870089
**Email:** goodtimes@woolacombe.com
**www.**woolacombe.com
**Pitches For** 🛆 ⚌ ⚌ **Total** 339
**Facilities** ⌁ 🅿 ⚓ ⚓ ⌁ 🅿 ⊙ ⚐ ⚐ 🖸
🛇 ⊙ ⚓ ✕ ⚐ ⚓ ⚑ ⚑ ⚐ 🖸 ⚞ ⚑ 🖸
**Nearby Facilities** ⌐ ✓ ⚓ ⋃ ♞ ♞
**Acreage** 20 **Open** March **to** October
**Access** Good **Site** Sloping
Rural, scenic setting, close to Woolacombe's glorious sandy beach and spectacular coastal walks.
**Nearest Town/Resort** Woolacombe
**Directions** From Barnstaple/Ilfracombe road

CAMPING TOURING
FROM ONLY £5 per person a night
FROM ONLY £15 per van a night

the
fun
comes free!!

Four award winning Holiday Parcs set in delightful surroundings, all beside 3 miles of golden Blue Flag sandy beach in Devon & next to the Tarka Trail.

Camping and Touring also Luxury Lodges and Seaview Holiday Homes

- 10 PIN BOWLING
- 17th Century Inn
- Waves Ceramic Studio
- Crèche
- Indoor Bowls Rinks
- Golf Club
- Restaurants/Bars
- Activities Programme

Supersite Pitches • Sauna • Steam Room • Individual Showers
Electric hook-ups • Laundry facilities • On-site shop
CARAVAN STORAGE & SEASONAL PITCHES AVAILABLE

## All this is FREE!!

10 Heated Pools • Nightly Entertainment • Cinema
Waterslides • Health Suite • Crazy Golf • Tennis
Kid's Indoor & Outdoor Play Areas • Kid's Club
Coarse Fishing Lake • Snooker ... Plus much more!

WOOLAC MBE BAY

01271 870 343
www.woolacombe.com

(A361) to junction with B3343 at Mullacott Cross, first left signposted Woolacombe for 1¾ miles, then right signposted Mortehoe. Park is 1¼ miles on left.
✚ Barnstaple

## WOOLACOMBE
**Woolacombe Bay Holiday Village,** Sandy Lane, Woolacombe, Devon, EX34 7AH
**Tel:** 01271 870343 **Fax:** 01271 870089
**Email:** goodtimes@woolacombe.com
www.woolacombe.com
**Pitches For** ⋏ **Total** 150
**Facilities** ⏚ ⸑ ⓤ ⛟ ⌐ ☉ ⌥ ⧉ ▣ ⛟
⛬ ⓘ ⏚ ⊙ ✕ ⛏ ⛢ ⛟ ⋔ ⟲ ⌦ ⊡ ⊟
**Nearby Facilities** ⋔ ✔ ⚓ ⚲ ∪ ♪ ⚘ ↑
**Open** 31 March **to** 4 Nov
Close to the Blue Flag beach of Woolacombe and spectacular coastal walks. Choice of 4 Parcs and their facilities and entertainment. Fishing nearby. Golf on Parc.
**Nearest Town/Resort** Woolacombe
**Directions** From Barnstaple take the A361 Ilfracombe road to the junction of the B3343 at Mullacott Cross. Turn first left signposted Woolacombe, after 1¾ miles turn right to Mortehoe, Parc is 1 mile on the left.
✚ Barnstaple

## WOOLACOMBE
**Woolacombe Sands Holiday Park,** Beach Road, Woolacombe, North Devon, EX34 7AF
**Tel:** 01271 870569 **Fax:** 01271 870606
**Email:** lifesabeach@woolacombe-sands.co.uk
www.woolacombe-sands.co.uk
**Pitches For** ⋏ ⊞ ⛟ **Total** 137
**Facilities** ⏚ ⸑ ⓤ ⛟ ⌐ ☉ ⌥ ⧉ ▣ ⛟
⛬ ⓘ ⊙ ⊗ ✕ ⛢ ⛟ ✢ ⧾ ⊡ ⊟
♪
**Nearby Facilities** ⋔ ✔ ⚓ ⚲ ∪ ♪ ⚘
**Acreage** 20 **Open** April **to** October
**Access** Good **Site** Lev/Slope
Nearest holiday park to Woolacombe's main beach. Outstanding views.
**Nearest Town/Resort** Woolacombe
**Directions** Take the A361 from Barnstaple, at Mullacott Cross roundabout take the B3343. Site is on the left just before Woolacombe on the bend. 4 Flagpoles.
✚ Barnstaple

> ## REMEMBER, IT IS ALWAYS ADVISABLE TO BOOK IN PEAK SEASON.

# DORSET
## BLANDFORD
**The Inside Park,** Blandford, Dorset, DT11 9AD
**Tel:** 01258 453719 **Fax:** 01258 459921
**Email:** inspark@aol.com
www.http://members.aol.com/inspark/inspark
**Pitches For** ⋏ ⊞ ⛟ **Total** 100
**Facilities** ⏚ ⸑ ⓤ ⛟ ⌐ ☉ ⌥ ▣ ⛟
⛬ ⊙ ⊗ ⛏ ⛢ ⋔ ⊡ ♪
**Nearby Facilities** ⋔ ✔ ∪ ⚘
**Acreage** 13 **Open** Easter **to** October
**Access** Good **Site** Lev/Slope
Rural environment with extensive wildlife.
**Nearest Town/Resort** Blandford Forum
**Directions** 1¼ miles south west of Blandford on the road to Winterborne Stickland. Signposted from junction of A350 and A354 on Blandford bypass.

## BOURNEMOUTH
**St. Leonards Farm,** Ringwood Road, West Moors, Ferndown, Dorset, BH22 0AQ
**Tel:** 01202 872637 **Fax:** 01202 855683
**Email:** james@love5.fsnet.co.uk
www.stleonardsfarm.biz
**Pitches For** ⋏ ⊞ ⛟
**Facilities** ⏚ ⸑ ⓤ ⛟ ⌐ ☉ ⌥ ⧉ ▣ ⛟
⛬ ⊙ ⊞ ⟲ ⛟ ⊡ ✂ ♪
**Nearby Facilities** ⋔ ✔ ⚓ ⚲ ∪ ♪ ⚘
**Acreage** 12 **Open** April **to** October
**Access** Good **Site** Level
**Nearest Town/Resort** Bournemouth
**Directions** On the A31 4 miles west of Ringwood, opposite West Moors Garage.
✚ Bournemouth Central

## BRIDPORT
**Binghams Farm Touring Caravan Park,** Binghams Farm, Melplash, Bridport, Dorset, DT6 3TT
**Tel:** 01308 488234
**Email:** enquiries@binghamsfarm.co.uk
www.binghamsfarm.co.uk
**Pitches For** ⋏ ⊞ ⛟ **Total** 111
**Facilities** ⏚ ⸑ Ⓕ ⧉ ⓤ ⛟ ⌐ ☉ ⌥ ⧉ ▣ ⛟
⛬ ⊙ ⊗ ✕ ⛟ ✢ ⧾ ⊟ ⌐ ⌁
**Nearby Facilities** ⋔ ✔ ⚓ ⚲ ∪ ♪ ⚘
**Acreage** 5 **Open** March **to** Oct
**Access** Good **Site** Level
EXCLUSIVELY FOR ADULTS. An Award Winning Park set in an area of outstanding natural beauty yet only 3 miles from the coast. An ideal base to explore Dorset. All modern heated facilities.
**Nearest Town/Resort** West Bay/Bridport.
**Directions** Turn off A35 in Bridport at the roundabout onto A3066, signposted Beaminster. In 1¼ miles turn left into Farm Road.
✚ Dorchester

## BRIDPORT
**Eype House Caravan Park,** Eype, Bridport, Dorset, DT6 6AL
**Tel:** 01308 424903 **Fax:** 01308 424903
**Email:** enquiries@eypehouse.co.uk
www.eypehouse.co.uk
**Pitches For** ⋏ ⛟ **Total** 20
**Facilities** ⓤ ⏚ ⸑ ⌐ ⌥ ⧉ ▣ ⛟
⛬ ⊙ ⊗ ✕ ⧾
**Nearby Facilities** ⋔ ✔ ⚓ ∪
**Acreage** 4 **Open** Easter **to** 30 October
**Site** Sloping
On a coastal path only 200 yards from the beach. Sorry, NO touring caravans.
**Nearest Town/Resort** Bridport
**Directions** Signposted Eype off the A35, follow signs to the sea.
✚ Dorchester/Crewkerne

## BRIDPORT
**Freshwater Beach Holiday Park,** Burton Bradstock, Bridport, Dorset, DT6 4PT
**Tel:** 01308 897317 **Fax:** 01308 897336
**Email:** enquiries@freshwaterbeach.co.uk
www.freshwaterbeach.co.uk
**Pitches For** ⋏ ⊞ ⛟ **Total** 500
**Facilities** ⏚ ⸑ Ⓕ ⛟ ⌐ ☉ ⌥ ⧉ ▣ ⛟
⛬ ⊙ ⊗ ✕ ⛏ ⛢ ⋔ ✢ ⧾ ⊡ ⊟
**Nearby Facilities** ⋔ ✔ ⚓ ⚲ ∪
**Acreage** 40 **Open** Easter **to** October
**Access** Good **Site** Level
Own private beach. Free family entertainment (SBH to Mid Sept). Good cliff walks. Golf course adjoining park.
**Nearest Town/Resort** Bridport
**Directions** From Bridport take B3157 towards Weymouth site 2 miles on right.
✚ Dorchester

## BRIDPORT
**Home Farm Caravan & Campsite,** Rectory Lane, Puncknowle, Nr Dorchester, Dorset, DT2 9BW
**Tel:** 01308 897258
**Pitches For** ⋏ ⊞ ⛟ **Total** 42
**Facilities** ⸑ ⓤ ⏚ ⌐ ☉ ⛟ ⊙ ⊗ ⧾ ⊟ ✂
**Nearby Facilities** ⋔ ✔ ∪
**Acreage** 5 **Open** 1 April **to** 25 Oct
**Access** Good **Site** Lev/Slope
In a beautiful area, 1½ miles from the Heritage Coast. Ideal touring.
**Nearest Town/Resort** Weymouth
**Directions** Take the A35 towards Bridport, before entering the dual carriageway turn left to Litton Cheney and follow the road to Puncknowle. 12 miles from Dorchester.
✚ Weymouth/Dorchester

**family seaside fun!**

- Ideal base for many sites and attractions in Dorset
- Club Complex with licensed restaurant and bars
- Nightly Family Entertainment (*Spring BH – Mid Sept)
- Heated outdoor swimming pools
- Children's activities and amusements
- Beach fishing and wind-surfing
- Pony-trekking and horse & cart rides
- Fine country and cliff walks
- Golf course adjoining park
- Self-catering holiday homes
- Caravan Sales

**Family-owned park with large touring and camping field Own private beach on Dorset's World Heritage Coast**

# FRESHWATER BEACH HOLIDAY PARK
**Burton Bradstock, Nr. Bridport Dorset DT6 4PT**

Tel: 01308 897317 · email: info@freshwaterbeach.co.uk
Look on the internet: www.freshwaterbeach.co.uk

Dorset's **Golden Coast**
A World Heritage Destination

**AA**

**Free entertainment Free club membership**

# DORSET

## BRIDPORT

**Highlands End Farm Holiday Park,** Eype, Bridport, Dorset, DT6 6AR
**Tel:** 01308. 422139 **Fax:** 01308 425672
**Email:** holidays@wdlh.co.uk
www.wdlh.co.uk
**Pitches For** ▲ ⊕ ⊟ **Total** 195
**Facilities** ♿ ⨍ ⊟ ⊞ ⬚ ♨ ⌂ ☉ ⤵ ⬛ ◻ ☂
♒ ⓒ ⓖ ⬛ ✗ ♈ 🎣 ⟰ ⚞ ⛽ ⤝ ⊟ ⬛ ⋇
**Nearby Facilities** ⌐ ⟋ ⥬ ∪ ℛ
**Acreage** 8 **Open** March **to** October
**Access** Good **Site** Level
Exceptional views across Lyme Bay, 500 metres from the beach. Heated swimming pool, steam room and sauna. Tennis and Pitch & Putt on site. All weather awning areas.
**Nearest Town/Resort** Bridport
**Directions** On approach to Bridport from east (Dorchester) on A35 turn left at roundabout, follow Bridport By-pass. Second roundabout take third exit signposted A35 West 1 mile turn left to Eype and follow signposts.
⇾ Axminster

## BRIDPORT

**West Bay Holiday Park,** West Bay, Bridport, Dorset, DT6 4HB
**Tel:** 01308 422424 **Fax:** 01308 421371
**Email:** enquiries@parkdeanholidays.com
www.parkdeanholidays.co.uk
**Pitches For** ▲ ⊕ ⊟ **Total** 128
**Facilities** ⨍ ⊞ ⬚ ⌂ ☉ ⤵ ⬛ ◻ ☂
♒ ⓒ ⬛ ✗ ♈ 🎣 ⟰ ⚞ ⛽ ⤝ ⊟ ⬛ ⋇
**Nearby Facilities** ⌐ ⟋ ℛ
**Acreage** 30 **Open** March **to** Oct
**Access** Good **Site** Level
Situated in the heart of West Bay, beside the beach, harbour and picturesque village.
**Nearest Town/Resort** Bridport
**Directions** Take the M3 towards Winchester, then follow the M27 then the A31. Join the A35 to Dorchester and head west to Bridport, then head into West Bay.
⇾ Dorchester

## CHARMOUTH

**Camping & Caravanning Club Site,** Monkton Wylde Farm, Nr. Charmouth, Dorset, DT6 6DB
**Tel:** 01297 32965
www.campingandcaravanningclub.co.uk
**Pitches For** ▲ ⊕ ⊟ **Total** 80
**Facilities** ⨍ ⊟ ⊞ ♨ ⌂ ☉ ⤵ ⬛ ◻ ☂
⬚ ⓒ ⬛ ⟰ ⚞ ⊟ ⬛ ⋇
**Nearby Facilities** ⌐ ⟋ ⥬ ∪ ℛ ⟰ ⚘
**Acreage** 12 **Open** 25 March **to** 1 Nov
**Access** Good **Site** Level
5 miles from Forde Abbey and Charmouth's fossil beach. 7 miles from Cricket St. Thomas Wildlife Park. BTB 4 Star Graded, AA 4 Pennants and David Bellamy Gold Award. Non members welcome.
**Nearest Town/Resort** Charmouth
**Directions** From Dorchester take the A35, turn right onto the B3165 signposted Hawkchurch, site is on the left within ¼ of a mile.
⇾ Axminster

## CHARMOUTH

**Manor Farm Holiday Centre,** Manor Farm, Charmouth, Bridport, Dorset, DT6 6QL
**Tel:** 01297 560226 **Fax:** 01297 560429
**Email:** enq@manorfarmholidaycentre.co.uk
www.manorfarmholidaycentre.co.uk
**Pitches For** ▲ ⊕ ⊟ **Total** 345
**Facilities** ♿ ⨍ ⊟ ⊞ ⬚ ♨ ⌂ ☉ ⤵ ⬛ ◻ ☂
♒ ⓒ ⬛ ✗ ♈ 🎣 ⟰ ⚞ ⛽ ⤝ ⊟ ⬛ ⋇
**Nearby Facilities** ⌐ ⟋ ⚘ ⥬ ∪ ℛ ⚘
**Acreage** 30 **Open** All Year
**Access** Good **Site** Lev/Slope

Ten minutes level walk to beach, alongside river. In area of outstanding natural beauty. Ideal touring.
**Nearest Town/Resort** Charmouth
**Directions** Come off the Charmouth bypass at east end Manor Farm is ¾ mile on right, in Charmouth.
⇾ Axminster

## CHARMOUTH

**Monkton Wyld Farm,** Charmouth, Dorset, DT6 6DB
**Tel:** 01297 34525
**Email:** holidays@monktonwyld.co.uk
www.monktonwyld.co.uk
**Pitches For** ▲ ⊕ ⊟ **Total** 60
**Facilities** ♿ ⨍ ⊟ ⊞ ♨ ⌂ ☉ ⤵ ⬛ ◻ ☂
♒ ⓒ ⬛ ⬛ ♈ ⤝ ⊟ ⬛ ⌂
**Nearby Facilities** ⌐ ⟋ ⥬ ∪ ℛ
**Acreage** 6 **Open** Easter **to** 30 Oct
**Access** Good **Site** Level
Beautifully landscaped pitches with room to relax, and space for children to play. Friendly, helpful wardens offer every assistance. Spotless shower block. One bedroom self contained flat for rent and B&B in the farmhouse.
**Nearest Town/Resort** Charmouth
**Directions** Take the A35 from Axminster towards Charmouth, cross the county boundary into Dorset and almost immediately turn left down an unmarked lane. Brown tourist sign only.

## CHARMOUTH

**Newlands Holiday Park,** Charmouth, Nr. Bridport, Dorset, DT6 6RB
**Tel:** 01297 560259 **Fax:** 01297 560787
**Email:** enq@newlandsholidays.co.uk
www.newlandsholidays.co.uk
**Pitches For** ▲ ⊕ ⊟ **Total** 200
**Facilities** ♿ ⨍ ⊟ ⊞ ⬚ ♨ ⌂ ☉ ⤵ ⬛ ◻ ☂
♒ ⓒ ⬛ ✗ ♈ 🎣 ⟰ ⚞ ⛽ ⤝ ⊟ ⬛ ⋇

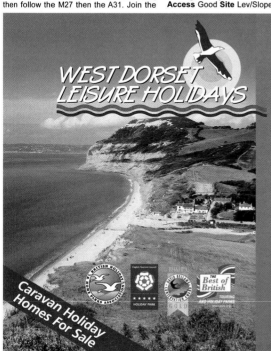

# DORSET

**Nearby Facilities** ⌐ ✔ ⚓ ⤫ ∪ ♫ ♪
**Acreage** 23 **Open** All Year
**Access** Good **Site** Terraced
Situated in the Heritage Coast village of
Charmouth, near Lyme Regis. Wonderful
views and walks through National Trust
land. A short stroll to the village centre and
safe beach.
**Nearest Town/Resort** Lyme Regis
**Directions** Turn off the A35 at the eastern
exit for Charmouth, Newlands is situated a
short distance on the left hand side.
⇞ Axminster

## CHARMOUTH
**Wood Farm Caravan & Camping Park,**
Axminster Road, Charmouth, Bridport,
Dorset, DT6 6BT
**Tel:** 01297 560697 **Fax:** 01297 561243
**Email:** holidays@woodfarm.co.uk
www.woodfarm.co.uk
**Pitches For** ▲ ♥ ⇗ **Total** 216
**Facilities** ♿ ⨏ 🖩 🔲 📺 ♣ ⌐ ⊙ ⊣ ♨ 🔲 ♥
♏ ⅃℞ 🕓 ⊕ ♠ ⚌ 𝄞 ⤳╅🎏 🔲 ╬
**Nearby Facilities** ⌐ ✔ ⚓ ⤫ ∪ ♫ ♪
**Acreage** 12 **Open** March to Oct
**Access** Good **Site** Terraced
Beach ¾ mile. Country setting. Tennis and
coarse fishing ponds on site. Indoor
heated swimming pool. Non members
welcome. Booking essential.
**Nearest Town/Resort** Charmouth
**Directions** On A35, ½ mile west Charmouth.
⇞ Axminster

## CHIDEOCK
**Golden Cap Holiday Park,** Seatown,
Chideock, Nr Bridport, Dorset, DT6 6JX
**Tel:** 01308 422139 **Fax:** 01308 425672
**Email:** holidays@wdlh.co.uk
www.wdlh.co.uk
**Pitches For** ▲ ♥ ⇗ **Total** 120

**Facilities** ⨏ 🔲 📺 ♣ ⌐ ⊙ ⊣ ♨ 🔲 ♥
🕓 ⊕ ♠ ⚌ 🎏 🔲 ╬
**Nearby Facilities** ⌐ ✔ ♪
**Acreage** 10 **Open** March to October
**Access** Good **Site** Level
100 metres from beach, overlooked by the
famous Golden Cap cliff top. Indoor
swimming pool available 5 minutes
travelling time. All weather awning areas.
Unique location on the Heritage Coastline.
**Nearest Town/Resort** Bridport
**Directions** On approach to Bridport from
east (Dorchester) follow A35 signs around
Bridport by-pass. After 2 miles west of
Bridport turn left for Seatown, at Chideock
park is signposted.

## CHRISTCHURCH
**Holmsley Caravan & Camping Site -**
**Forestry Commission,** Forest Road,
Holmsley, Christchurch, Dorset, BH23 7EQ
**Tel:** 0131 314 6505
**Email:** info@forestholidays.co.uk
www.forestholidays.co.uk
**Pitches For** ▲ ♥ ⇗ **Total** 700
**Facilities** ♿ ⨏ 🔲 📺 ♣ ⌐ ⊙ ⊣ ♨ 🔲 ♥
🕓 ⊕ ♠ ⚌ ╅🎏 🔲 ╬
**Nearby Facilities** ∪
**Acreage** 89 **Open** 25 March to 31 Oct
**Access** Good **Site** Level
Coast within 5 miles. Shop and fast food
takeaway on site.
**Nearest Town/Resort** Christchurch
**Directions** Turn west 8 miles southwest of
Lyndhurst off the A35 and follow Holmsley
Camp Site signs.
⇞ New Milton

## CHRISTCHURCH
**Longfield,** Matchams Lane, Hurn,
Christchurch, Dorset, BH23 6AW
**Tel:** 01202 485214

**Pitches For** ♥ ⇗ **Total** 20
**Facilities** ⨏ 📺 ♣ ⌐ ⊙ ⊣ ♨ ♥ ⊕ ♠ ⤫╅
♪
**Nearby Facilities** ⌐ ✔ ⚓ ⤫ ∪
**Acreage** 2½ **Open** All Year
**Access** Good **Site** Level
**Nearest Town/Resort** Christchurch
**Directions** A338 into Bournemouth. Hurr
road, Christchurch, Wessex Way.
⇞ Christchurch

## CHRISTCHURCH
**Meadowbank Holidays,** Stour Way,
Christchurch, Dorset, BH23 2PQ
**Tel:** 01202 483597 **Fax:** 01202 483878
enquiries@meadowbank-holidays.co.uk
www.meadowbank-holidays.co.uk
**Pitches For** ♥ ⇗ **Total** 41
**Facilities** ⨏ 🔲 📺 ♣ ⌐ ⊙ ⊣ ♨ 🔲 ♥
🕓 ⅃℞ ⊕ ♠ ⚌ 🔲 🔲
**Nearby Facilities** ⌐ ✔ ⚓ ⤫ ∪ ♫ ♪
**Acreage** 2 **Open** March to October
**Access** Good **Site** Level
Riverside setting. Close to Bournemouth,
Christchurch and the New Forest.
**Nearest Town/Resort** Bournemouth
**Directions** From Ringwood take the A33ε
towards Bournemouth and turn off fo
Christchurch, follow caravan signs.
⇞ Bournemouth

## CHRISTCHURCH
**Mount Pleasant Touring Park,** Matchams
Lane, Hurn, Christchurch, Dorset, BH23 6AW
**Tel:** 01202 475474
**Email:** enq@mount-pleasant-cc.co.uk
www.mount-pleasant-cc.co.uk
**Pitches For** ▲ ♥ ⇗ **Total** 150
**Facilities** ♿ ⨏ 📺 ♣ ⌐ ⊙ ⊣ ♨ 🔲 ♥
🕓 ⅃℞ ⊕ ♠ ✕ ╅🎏 🔲 ╬
**Nearby Facilities** ⌐ ✔ ⚓ ⤫ ∪ ♫ ♪
**Acreage** 10 **Open** March to October
**Access** Good **Site** Level

Exceptionally clean park. Closest camping
o Bournemouth. Near to lovely forest
walks. ETB 5 Star 'Excellent' Graded and
AA 4 Pennants.
**Nearest Town/Resort** Bournemouth
**Directions** From Ringwood take the A338,
exit at the Christchurch/Airport signs. Follow
signs for the Airport until you reach a mini
roundabout, then follow camping signs.
⇌ Christchurch

## CORFE CASTLE
**Burnbake Campsite,** Rempstone, Corfe
Castle, Dorset, BH20 5JJ
**Tel:** 01929 480570 **Fax:** 01929 480926
**Email:** info@burnbake.com
www.burnbake.com
**Pitches For** ⋏ ⌂ **Total** 130
**Facilities** ⊞ ⚡ ⌐ ⊙ ⊣ ⌑ ⛽ ⛺ ⋒ ❀⚘
**Nearby Facilities** ⌐ ⋏ ⚓ ↘ ∪ ⋔ ♪ ⋏
**Acreage** 12 **Open** April **to** September
**Site** Lev/Slope
A quiet, secluded site in woodlands with a
stream. 4 miles from Studland with its
three miles of sandy beach and excellent
safe bathing. 4 miles from Swanage.
**Nearest Town/Resort** Swanage
**Directions** Between Corfe Castle and
Studland just off the B3351. From Wareham
take the A351 to Corfe Castle, turn left under
the castle onto the Studland road, through
the old railway arches, and take the third
turning left signposted Rempstone.
⇌ Wareham

## CORFE CASTLE
**Knitson Farm Tourers Site,** Knitson
Farm, Corfe Castle, Dorset, BH20 5JB
**Tel:** 01929 425121
www.knitsonfarm.co.uk
**Pitches For** ⋏ ⌂ ⌂ **Total** 60
**Facilities** ⛽ ⋔ ⅊ ⌂ ⊙ ❀⊣⊟ ⚶
**Nearby Facilities** ⌐ ⋏ ⚓ ↘ ∪ ⋔ ♪ ⋏
**Acreage** 5½ **Open** Easter **to** October
**Site** Lev/Slope
Set in very beautiful countryside with many
walks radiating from the field, including
Swanage and Studland beaches.
**Nearest Town/Resort** Swanage
**Directions** Take the A351 to Swanage
outskirts, turn first left into Wash Pond Lane.
Continue until the lane finishes at a T-
Junction turn left. Site is approx. ½ mile
further on, on the left hand side.
⇌ Wareham

## CORFE CASTLE
**Woodland Caravan & Camping Park,**
Parsonage Coppice, Globe Farm,
Bucknowle, WarehamDorset, BH20 5PQ
**Tel:** 01929 480280 **Fax:** 01929 480280
**Email:** hazelparker@btconnect.com
**Pitches For** ⋏ ⌂ **Total** 65

**Facilities** ⅊ ⚡ ⊞ ⚡ ⌐ ⊙ ⊣ ⚡
⛽ ⅊ ⊙ ⛺ ⋒ ⚶ ⌑
**Nearby Facilities** ⌐ ⋏ ⚓ ↘ ∪ ♪ ♪
**Acreage** 5 **Open** Easter **to** End Oct
**Access** Good **Site** Lev/Slope
Family site in a secluded area, ideal for walking,
beaches, etc.. Jurassic Coast within 5 miles.
**Nearest Town/Resort** Swanage
**Directions** From Wareham take the A351
signposted Swanage for 4 miles until you
reach Corfe Castle ruins, turn right and Park
is on the right after ¾ miles.
⇌ Wareham

## DORCHESTER
**Clay Pigeon Touring Park,** Wardon Hill,
Dorchester, Dorset, DT2 9PW
**Tel:** 01935 83492 **Fax:** 01935 83492
**Email:** cheryl@claypigeoncp.wanadoo.co.uk
**Pitches For** ⋏ ⌂ ⌂ **Total** 60
**Facilities** ⚡ ⅊ ⊞ ⊞ ⚡ ⌐ ⊙ ⊣ ⚡ ⌑ ⚡
⌂ ⚡ ⚡ ⋒ ⌂ ⚶ ⚘
**Nearby Facilities** ⌐ ⋏ ⚓ ↘ ∪ ♪ ♪
**Acreage** 10 **Open** All Year
**Access** Good **Site** Level
Views across Dorset countryside. 16 miles
from Weymouth.
**Nearest Town/Resort** Dorchester
**Directions** On the A37 midway between
Dorchester and Yeovil.
⇌ Maiden Newton

## DORCHESTER
**Crossways Caravan Club Site,**
Crossways, Dorchester, Dorset, DT2 8BE
**Tel:** 01305 852032
www.caravanclub.co.uk
**Pitches For** ⌂ ⌂ **Total** 122
**Facilities** ⚡ ⅊ ⊞ ⚡ ⚡ ⌐ ⌑ ⚡
⅊ ⊙ ⚡ ⋒ ⊣⊟
**Nearby Facilities**
**Acreage** 35 **Open** March **to** Oct
**Access** Good **Site** Level
Landscaped site set in 35 acres of
woodland. So much to see and do in the
local area. 8½ miles from Weymouth
beach and attractions. Non members
welcome. Booking essential.
**Nearest Town/Resort** Dorchester
**Directions** From north east on the A31, at
the roundabout on the outskirts of Bere Regis
turn right onto the A35. At Tolpuddle Ball
junction turn left onto slip road signposted
Warmwell, at T-junction turn left, at next T-
junction turn right, site is 4 miles on the left
(entrance through garage forecourt).
⇌ Dorchester

## DORCHESTER
**Giants Head Caravan & Camping Park,**
Old Sherborne Road, Dorchester, Dorset,
DT2 7TR
**Tel:** 01300 341242

**Email:** holiday@giantshead.co.uk
www.giantshead.co.uk
**Pitches For** ⋏ ⌂ ⌂ **Total** 50
**Facilities** ⅊ ⊞ ⚡ ⌐ ⊙ ⊣ ⚡ ⌂ ⚡
⅊ ⊙ ⊣⊟ ⚡
**Nearby Facilities** ⌐ ⋏ ∪ ♪
**Acreage** 3 **Open** March **to** October
**Access** Good **Site** Lev/Slope
Ideal touring, wonderful views, good
walking. Car is essential. Chalets available
for hire.
**Nearest Town/Resort** Dorchester
**Directions** From Dorchester avoiding
bypass, at top of town roundabout take
Sherborne Road approx 500 yards fork right
at Loaders Garage signposted. From Cerne
Abbas take the Buckland Newton road.
⇌ Dorchester

## DORCHESTER
**Lyons Gate Caravan Park,** Lyons Gate,
Nr. Dorchester, Dorset, DT2 7AZ
**Tel:** 01300 345260
**Email:** info@lyons-gate.co.uk
www.lyons-gate.co.uk
**Pitches For** ⋏ ⌂ □ **Total** 90
**Facilities** ⅊ ⊞ ⚡ ⌐ ⊙ ⊣ ⚡ ⌂ ⚡
⛽ ⊙ ⊣⊟ ⚶
**Nearby Facilities** ⌐ ∪
**Acreage** 12 **Open** All Year
**Access** Good **Site** Level
Four coarse fishing lakes on site. Ideal for
visiting Dorchester, Yeovil, Weymouth and
Bridport.
**Nearest Town/Resort** Dorchester
**Directions** On the A352 between Dorchester
and Sherborne.
⇌ Sherborne

## DORCHESTER
**Moreton Camping & Caravanning Club
Site,** Station Road, Moreton, Nr
Dorchester, Dorset, DT2 8BB
**Tel:** 01305 853801
www.campingandcaravanningclub.co.uk
**Pitches For** ⋏ ⌂ ⌂ **Total** 118
**Facilities** ⚡ ⅊ ⊞ ⚡ ⚡ ⌐ ⊙ ⊣ ⚡ ⌂ ⚡
⅊ ⊙ ⋒ ⊣⊟⊟ ⚡
**Nearby Facilities** ⚓
**Acreage** 7 **Open** March **to** Nov
**Access** Good **Site** Sloping
A lovely, leafy site on the outskirts of
Dorchester. One holiday bungalow to let.
BTB 5 Star Graded, AA 3 Pennants and Loo
of the Year Award. Non members welcome.
**Nearest Town/Resort** Dorchester
**Directions** Take the A35 from Poole,
continue past Bere Regis then turn left onto
the B3390 signposted Alfpuddle. After
approx. 2 miles the site is on the left before
Moreton Station, adjacent to the Frampton
Arms public house.
⇌ Moreton

## DORCHESTER

**Warmwell Country Touring Park,** Warmwell Road, Warmwell, Dorchester, Dorset, DT2 8JD
**Tel:** 01305 852313 **Fax:** 01305 851824
**Email:** stay@warmwell-country-touring-park.co.uk
www.warmwell-country-touring-park.co.uk
**Pitches For** ⊕ ⊟ **Total** 170
**Facilities** ⫪ ⬚ ♨ ⌂ ☉ ⎺ ⊿ ▱ ⧠ ☔
⑁ ❍ ⊟ ✖ ♀ ⌦ ⊟ ⚹
**Nearby Facilities** ⌐ ✔ ⊥ ∪ ⇗
**Acreage** 15 **Open** 1 March **to** 1 Jan
**Access** Good **Site** Level
6 miles from Weymouth beach. Many fishing lakes within 10 miles.
**Nearest Town/Resort** Weymouth
**Directions** From the A353 at Weymouth take the B3390 signposted Warmwell.
✈ Moreton

## LULWORTH COVE

**Durdle Door Holiday Park,** Lulworth Cove, Wareham, Dorset, BH20 5PU
**Tel:** 01929 400200 **Fax:** 01929 400260
**Email:** durdle.door@lulworth.com
www.lulworth.com
**Pitches For** ⋏ ⊕ ⊟ **Total** 175
**Facilities** ⫴ ⫪ ♨ ⌂ ☉ ⎺ ⊿ ▱ ⧠ ☔
⑁ ⑀ ❍ ✖ ♀ ⌦ ⊟ ⊟
**Nearby Facilities** ⌐ ✔ ⊥ ⤮ ∪
**Acreage** 45 **Open** March **to** October
**Access** Good **Site** Lev/Slope
Unique cliff top position overlooking the famous landmark of Durdle Door. Sea view hook-ups for motor homes and touring caravans only.
**Nearest Town/Resort** Wareham
**Directions** Take the B3077 Wool to West Lulworth road, fork right in West Lulworth Village, entrance is at the top of the hill.
✈ Wool

## LYME REGIS

**Cummins Farm,** Penn Cross, Charmouth, Bridport, Dorset, DT6 6BX
**Tel:** 01297 560898
**Pitches For** ⋏ ⊕ ⊟ **Total** 30
**Facilities** ⧠ ⌐ ☔ ▨⤮▱
**Nearby Facilities** ⌐ ✔ ⊥ ∪
**Acreage** 5½ **Open** Easter **to** End Sept
**Access** Good **Site** Level
Quiet farm site in a rural setting.
**Nearest Town/Resort** Lyme Regis
**Directions** Midway between Charmouth and Lyme Regis, 200 metres from the A3052.
✈ Axminster

## LYME REGIS

**Hook Farm Camping & Caravan Park,** Gore Lane, Uplyme, Lyme Regis, Dorset, DT7 3UU
**Tel:** 01297 442801 **Fax:** 01297 442801
**Email:** information@hookfarm-uplyme.co.uk
www.hookfarm-uplyme.co.uk
**Pitches For** ⋏ ⊕ ⊟ **Total** 100
**Facilities** ⫴ ⫪ ⫪ ♨ ⌂ ☉ ⎺ ⊿ ▱ ☔
⑁ ⑀ ❍ ⊟ ⧠ ▨⤮▱ ⊟
**Nearby Facilities** ⌐ ✔ ⊥ ⤮ ∪ ⇗ ⇗
**Acreage** 5¾ **Open** 1 March **to** 15 Nov
**Access** Good **Site** Level/Terraced
The closest campsite to Lyme Regis (1 mile). Peaceful, tranquil site in an area of outstanding natural beauty. Many national footpaths are accessible from the park.
**Nearest Town/Resort** Lyme Regis
**Directions** From the centre of Lyme Regis take the B3165 to Uplyme (1 mile). In Uplyme turn left opposite the Talbot Arms Pub into Gore Lane. The Park is 300 yards on the right hand side.
✈ Axminster

## LYME REGIS

**Shrubbery Touring Park,** Rousdon, Lyme Regis, Dorset, DT7 3XW
**Tel:** 01297 442227
www.ukparks.co.uk/shrubbery
**Pitches For** ⋏ ⊕ ⊟ **Total** 120
**Facilities** ⫴ ⫪ ♨ ⌂ ☉ ⎺ ⊿ ▱ ⧠ ☔
⑁ ❍ ⊟ ⧠ ▨⤮▱ ⊟ ☔
**Nearby Facilities** ⌐ ✔ ⊥ ⤮ ∪ ⇗ ⇗
**Acreage** 10 **Open** March **to** November
**Access** Good **Site** Level
Sheltered site. Ideal base for fossil hunters.
**Nearest Town/Resort** Lyme Regis
**Directions** 3 miles west of Lyme Regis on the A3052 coast road.
✈ Axminster

## OWERMOIGNE

**Sandyholme Holiday Park,** Moreton Road, Owermoigne, Nr Dorchester, Dorset DT2 8HZ
**Tel:** 01305 852677
**Email:** smeatons@sandyholme.co.uk
www.sandyholme.co.uk
**Pitches For** ⋏ ⊕ ⊟ **Total** 60
**Facilities** ⫴ ⫪ ⫞ ⫪ ♨ ⌂ ☉ ⎺ ⊿ ▱ ☔
⑁ ❍ ⊟ ✖ ♀ ♠ ⧠ ▨⤮▱ ⊟ ⊟
**Nearby Facilities** ⌐ ✔ ⊥ ∪
**Acreage** 6 **Open** Easter **to** October
**Access** Good **Site** Level
Quiet family park in Hardy countryside, ideal touring spot with all facilities, situated between Lulworth Cove and Weymouth. Restaurant and licenced club at peak times only. Swimming pool nearby. Long waiting list for Seasonal Pitches.
**Nearest Town** Dorchester/Weymouth
**Directions** Situated off the A352 Dorchester Wareham Road - 1 mile through the pretty village of Owermoigne.
✈ Moreton

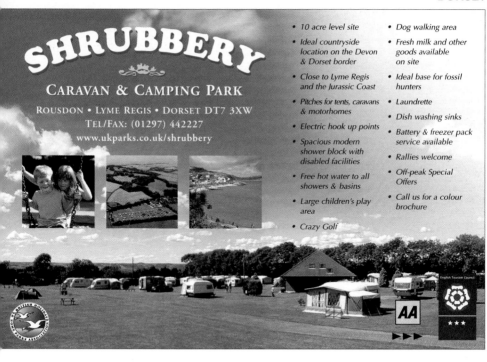

# DORSET

## POOLE

**Beacon Hill Touring Park,** Blandford Road North, Poole, Dorset, BH16 6AB
**Tel:** 01202 631631 **Fax:** 01202 625749
**Email:** bookings@beaconhilltouringpark.co.uk
www.beaconhilltouringpark.co.uk
**Pitches For** ⚠ ⛺ 🚐 **Total** 170
**Facilities** ⚓ ⨍ 🚻 ⒲ ♨ 🅟 ☉ ⤴ 🔌 ◻ 📞
♒ ⊙ ⊞ ✗ ♀ ⊞ ♤ ⩗ ↯ ✲⚓ 🔲 ☀
**Nearby Facilities** ⌐ ✔ ⚓ ↘ ∪ ♘ ♪ ♬
**Acreage** 30 **Open** Easter **to** Sept
**Access** Good **Site** level
Partly wooded, lovely peaceful setting, scenic views. Proximity to main routes. Ideal touring base for Bournemouth, New Forest and Dorset. Coarse fishing, tennis and childrens play areas on site. Take away meals and coffee shop in high season. ETB 3 Star Graded, Bellamy Conservation Gold Award Park, AA 3 Pennants and ANWB Listed.
**Nearest Town/Resort** Poole/Bournemouth
**Directions** Situated on the A350 ¼ mile north of the junction with the A35, between Poole and Blandford.
⇥ Poole

## POOLE

**Huntick Farm Caravans,** Huntick Farm, Lytchett Matravers, Poole, Dorset, BH16 6BB
**Tel:** 01202 622222
**Email:** caravans@huntick622222.fsnet.co.uk
**Pitches For** ⚠ ⛺ 🚐 **Total** 30
**Facilities** ⨍ 🚻 ⒲ ♨ 🅟 ☉ ⤴ 🔌 ⚓ 📞
◻ ♤ ✲⚓ ♪
**Nearby Facilities** ⌐ ✔ ⚓ ↘ ∪ ♪
**Acreage** 3 **Open** April **to** October
**Access** Good **Site** Level
Small, quiet, level grassed site in wooded surroundings. Within 6 miles of a sandy

beach. 10% reduction for O.A.P's.
**Nearest Town/Resort** Poole
**Directions** Off the A350 Blandford to Poole road. Take the turning for Lytchett Matravers and at the Rose & Crown Pub turn down Huntick Road. The site is approx. ¾ miles on the right.
⇥ Poole/Wareham

## POOLE

**Merley Court Touring Park,** Merley, Wimborne, Nr Poole, Dorset, BH21 3AA
**Tel:** 01202 881488 **Fax:** 01202 881484
**Email:** holidays@merley-court.co.uk
www.merley-court.co.uk
**Pitches For** ⚠ ⛺ 🚐 **Total** 160
**Facilities** ⚓ ⨍ 🚻 🚻 ⒲ ♨ 🅟 ☉ ⤴ 🔌 ◻ 📞
♒ ⊙ ⊞ ✗ ♀ ⊞ ♤ ⩗ ✲⚓ 🔲 ♪
**Nearby Facilities** ⌐ ✔ ⚓ ↘ ∪ ♪ ♪
**Acreage** 20 **Open** 1 March **to** 7 Jan
**Access** Good **Site** Level
AA 5 Pennant Premier park. Bournemouth 8 miles, Poole 4 miles, Purbeck and New Forest 7 miles. Caravan Magazine 'Readers' Site of the Year 2001, AA Campsite of the Year 1999, Practical Caravan Magazine 'Best Family Park' 1993 and 1997. Includes a Leisure Garden set in a beautifully landscaped walled garden, with croquet, petanque, beach volleyball, crazy golf and attractive gardens to explore. Pets are welcome but not between 19th July and 29th August.
**Nearest Town/Resort** Poole
**Directions** Direct access from the A31 Wimborne bypass and the A349 Poole junction.
⇥ Poole

## POOLE

**Organford Manor Caravans & Holidays,** Organford, Poole, Dorset, BH16 6ES
**Tel:** 01202 622202
**Email:** organford@lds.co.uk
www.organfordmanor.co.uk

**Pitches For** ⚠ ⛺ 🚐 **Total** 70
**Facilities** ⚓ ⨍ 🚻 ⒲ 🅟 ☉ ⤴ 🔌 ◻ 📞
⊙ ⒲ ⊙ ⊞ ♨⤴ 🔲 ✲⚓ ♪
**Nearby Facilities** ⌐ ✔ ⚓ ↘ ∪ ♪ ♪ ♪
**Acreage** 3 **Open** 15 March **to** 31 Oct
**Access** Good **Site** Level
Quiet, secluded site in wooded grounds of 11 acres. Seasonal site shop. Site within 10 miles of good beaches, Bournemouth to Swanage. Good facilities for the disabled, few motorcycles accepted at Proprietors discretion.
**Nearest Town/Resort** Poole
**Directions** Approaching from the Poole direction on the A35. At the Lytchet roundabout/junction of the A35/A351 continue on the A35 (signposted Dorchester) for ¼ mile. Take the first left, site firs entrance on right.
⇥ Poole/Wareham

## POOLE

**Pear Tree Touring Park,** Organford Road, Holton Heath, Poole, Dorset, BH16 6LA
**Tel:** 01202 622434 **Fax:** 01202 631985
**Email:** info@visitpeartree.co.uk
www.visitpeartree.co.uk
**Pitches For** ⚠ ⛺ 🚐 **Total** 125
**Facilities** ⚓ ⨍ 🚻 🚻 ⒲ ♨ 🅟 ☉ ⤴ 🔌 ◻ 📞
⊙ ⒲ ⊙ ⊞ ♨⤴ 🔲 ✲⚓ ♪
**Nearby Facilities** ⌐ ✔ ⚓ ↘ ∪ ♪ ♪
**Acreage** 7½ **Open** April **to** October
**Access** Good **Site** Level
A quiet, sheltered, family park, set out in level, landscaped terraces, mainly grass with many hard standings and fully serviced pitches. Beautiful countryside views. Ideal for relaxing or exploring. Low season discounts.
**Nearest Town/Resort** Poole
**Directions** Take the A35 from Poole towards Dorchester. Turn left at the A351 towards Wareham. Turn right at the first set of traffic

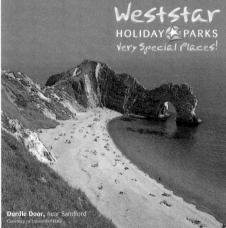

...ghts and the site is on the left hand side
after ½ a mile.
⚬ Wareham/Poole

## POOLE

**Rockley Park,** Napier Road, Hamworthy,
Poole, Dorset, BH15 4LZ
**Tel:** 01202 679393 **Fax:** 01202 683159
**Email:** sharon.greenwood@bourne-leisure.co.uk
**www.touringholidays.co.uk**
**Pitches For** ⚬ ⚬ ⚬ **Total** 75
**Facilities** ...
**Nearby Facilities** ...
**Open** March **to** October
**Access** Good **Site** Sloping
Direct access to the beach. Kids Club and
full family entertainment programme.
Watersports, bowling, multisports court
and rural beach on park. Boat storage
facilities. Rose Award. Pets are welcome
but not during July and August.
**Nearest Town/Resort** Poole
**Directions** From town centre go over lifting
bridge and follow road to traffic lights. Turn
left and follow signs for the park.
⚬ Poole

## POOLE

**Sandford Holiday Park,** Holton Heath,
Poole, Dorset, BH16 6JZ
**Tel:** 0870 066 7793 **Fax:** 01202 625678
**Email:** touring@weststarholidays.co.uk
**www.weststarholidays.co.uk**
**Pitches For** ⚬ ⚬ ⚬ **Total** 500
**Facilities** ...
**Nearby Facilities** ...
**Acreage** 64 **Open** March **to** Oct
**Access** Good **Site** Level
Tucked away in a beautiful woodland
setting. Spacious, level, private, serviced
- super-serviced pitches. Free modern
showers and toilets. Free live
entertainment and kids clubs.
**Nearest Town/Resort** Poole
**Directions** Located on the A351 (signposted
Wareham) which branches off the A35
approx. 5 miles west of Poole. Turn right at
Holton Heath traffic lights by the petrol
station, park is on the left.
⚬ Wareham

## POOLE

**South Lytchett Manor Caravan &
Camping Park,** Dorchester Road, Lytchett
Minster, Poole, Dorset, BH16 6JA
**Tel:** 01202 622577 **Fax:** 01202 622620
**Email:** slmcp@talk21.com
**www.eluk.co.uk/camping/dorset/slytchett**
**Pitches For** ⚬ ⚬ ⚬ **Total** 150

**Facilities** ...
**Nearby Facilities** ...
**Acreage** 11 **Open** Mid March **to** Mid Oct
**Access** Good **Site** Level
Popular, rural site set in lovely parkland
surroundings. Ideal base for exploring Poole,
Bournemouth and the Purbecks. Within easy
reach of beautiful beaches, sailing and wind
surfing. Take-away food in high season. AA
3 Pennants.
**Nearest Town/Resort** Poole
**Directions** From Poole take the A35 dual
carriageway to the roundabout at the end.
Take the third exit into and through Lytchett
Minster, the site is situated on the left 600
yards out of the village.
⚬ Poole

## SHAFTESBURY

**Blackmore Vale Caravan Park,**
Sherborne Causeway, Shaftesbury, Dorset,
SP7 9PX
**Tel:** 01747 852573/851523 **Fax:** 851671
**www.**caravancampingsites.co.uk/dorset/
blackmorevale
**Pitches For** ⚬ ⚬ ⚬ **Total** 50
**Facilities** ...
**Nearby Facilities** ⚬
**Open** All Year
**Access** Good **Site** Level
Scenic views, ideal touring.
**Nearest Town/Resort** Shaftsbury
⚬ Gillingham

## SIXPENNY HANDLEY

**Church Farm Caravan & Camping Park,**
The Bungalow, Church Farm, Sixpenny
Handley, Nr SalisburyWiltshire, SP5 5ND
**Tel:** 01725 552563 **Fax:** 01725 552563
**Email:** churchfarmcandpark@yahoo.co.uk
**www.**churchfarmcandcpark.co.uk
**Pitches For** ⚬ ⚬ ⚬ **Total** 20
**Facilities** ...
**Nearby Facilities** ⚬ ⚬ ⚬
**Acreage** 4 **Open** All Year
**Access** Good **Site** Level
In an area of outstanding natural beauty.
Ideal for walking, cycling and touring.
**Nearest Town/Resort** Salisbury
**Directions** Sixpenny Handley is 1 mile west
on the B3081 road to Shaftesbury and 11
miles from Salisbury on the A354.
⚬ Salisbury

## ST. LEONARDS

**Back-of-Beyond Touring Park,** 234
Ringwood Road, St Leonards, Dorset,
BH24 2SB
**Tel:** 01202 876968 **Fax:** 01202 876968
**Email:** melandsuepike@aol.com
**www.**backofbeyondtouringpark.co.uk

**Pitches For** ⚬ ⚬ ⚬ **Total** 80
**Facilities** ...
**Nearby Facilities** ⚬ ⚬ ⚬ ⚬ ⚬ ⚬ ⚬
**Acreage** 28 **Open** 1 March **to** 31 Oct
**Access** Good **Site** Level
Quiet ADULTS ONLY country and
woodland site with new facilities. Central
for the New Forest, Bournemouth and the
World Heritage coast. Golf on site.
**Nearest Town/Resort** Ringwood
**Directions** Off the A31 at Boundary Lane
roundabout in St. Leonards.
⚬ Bournemouth

## ST. LEONARDS

**Shamba Holidays,** 230 Ringwood Road,
St Leonards, Ringwood, Hampshire, BH24
2SB
**Tel:** 01202 873302
**Email:** enquiries@shambaholidays.co.uk
**www.**shambaholidays.co.uk
**Pitches For** ⚬ ⚬ ⚬ **Total** 150
**Facilities** ...
**Nearby Facilities** ⚬ ⚬ ⚬ ⚬ ⚬
**Acreage** 7 **Open** March **to** October
**Access** Good **Site** Level
Close to the New Forest and
Bournemouth. AA 3 Pennants.
**Nearest Town/Resort** Ringwood
**Directions** Just off the A31 midway between
Ringwood and Wimborne.
⚬ Bournemouth

## SWANAGE

**Cauldron Barn Farm Caravan Park,**
Cauldron Barn Road, Swanage, Dorset,
BH19 1QQ
**Tel:** 01929 422080 **Fax:** 01929 427870
**Email:** cauldronbarn@fsbdial.co.uk
**www.**cauldronbarncaravanpark.com
**Pitches For** ⚬ ⚬ ⚬ **Total** 20
**Facilities** ...
**Nearby Facilities** ⚬ ⚬ ⚬ ⚬ ⚬ ⚬ ⚬
**Acreage** 5 **Open** Mid March **to** Mid Nov
**Access** Good **Site** Level
A rural site only 800 yards from the beach.
**Nearest Town/Resort** Swanage
**Directions** Turn left off Victoria Avenue into
Northbrook Road, take the third left into
Cauldron Barn Road.
⚬ Wareham

## SWANAGE

**Downshay Farm,** Haycrafts Lane,
Swanage, Dorset, BH19 3EB
**Tel:** 01929 480316
**Email:** downshayfarm@tiscali.co.uk
**www.**downshayfarm.co.uk
**Pitches For** ⚬ ⚬ ⚬ **Total** 12

Facilities ∮ 🛍 🚿 ⌐ ⊙🍴🚻🔲
Nearby Facilities ⌐ ✈ ⚓ 🎣 ∪ ♪ ♫ ♀
Acreage 1 Open Easter to End Oct
Access Good Site Level
Nearest Town/Resort Swanage
Directions Take the A351 Corfe to Swanage road, at Harmans Cross turn right, site is ½ a mile up Haycrafts Lane on the right hand side.
🚉 Wareham

**SWANAGE**
Haycraft Caravan Club Site, Haycrafts Lane, Swanage, Dorset, BH19 3EB
Tel: 01929 480572
www.caravanclub.co.uk
Pitches For 🚐 🚍 Total 53
Facilities ⚹ ∮ 🛍 🛍 🚿 ⌐ 🍴 🔲 🍴
🛍 ⊙🚿🚻🔲
Nearby Facilities ⌐ ✈ ⚓ ⚓
Acreage 6 Open March to Oct
Access Good Site Level
Tranquil site set in the heart of Purbeck countryside, 3 miles from the beach. Ideal for walkers. Just a few minutes walk from the Swanage Light Railway. Non members welcome. Booking essential.
Nearest Town/Resort Swanage
Directions From the A352, at the mini roundabout on the outskirts of Wareham turn onto the A351 signposted Swanage. After 6¾ miles at Harmans Cross, just before the petrol station, turn right into Haycrafts Lane, site is ½ mile on the left.
🚉 Swanage

**SWANAGE**
Swanage Coastal Park, Priests Way, Swanage, Dorset, BH19 2RS
Tel: 01590 648331 Fax: 01590 645610
Email: holidays@shorefield.co.uk
www.shorefield.co.uk

Pitches For 👤 🚐 🚍 Total 62
Facilities ∮ 🛍 🛍 🚿 ⌐ ⊙🍴 🔲 🍴
🛍 🛍 🚻🔲
Nearby Facilities ⌐ ✈ ⚓ 🎣 ∪ ♪ ♫ ♀
Acreage 15 Open April to October
Access Good Site Lev/Slope
Views of Swanage Bay and the Purbeck Hills, lovely cliff walks. 1 mile from the beach. Next door to a public indoor swimming pool.
Nearest Town/Resort Swanage
Directions Take the A351 from Wareham, 1 mile past 'Welcome to Swanage' sign take the right hand fork into High Street, then the first right into Bell Street. Continue up the hill then turn first left into Priests Road and first right into the Park. 5 minute drive from the town and beach.
🚉 Wareham

**SWANAGE**
Tom's Field Camping & Shop, Tom's Field Road, Langton Matravers, Swanage, Dorset, BH19 3HN
Tel: 01929 427110 Fax: 01929 427110
Email: tomsfield@hotmail.com
www.tomsfieldcamping.co.uk
Pitches For 👤 🚍 Total 100
Facilities ⚹ ∮ 🛍 🚿 ⌐ ⊙🍴 🍴
🛍 🛍 ⊙🚿🚻🔲
Nearby Facilities ⌐ ✈ ⚓ 🎣 ∪ ♪ ♫ ♀
Acreage 4½ Open Mid March to End Oct
Site Lev/Slope
Set in beautiful countryside, an area of outstanding natural beauty. Coastal walk can be reached in 15 minutes. Only 20 minutes from the Jurassic Coast, Englands only natural world heritage site. Pets are welcome if kept on leads. Walkers' Barn available all year by prior arrangement only.
Nearest Town/Resort Swanage
🚉 Wareham

**SWANAGE**
Ulwell Cottage Caravan Park, Ulwell, Swanage, Dorset, BH19 3DG
Tel: 01929 422823 Fax: 01929 421500
Email: enq@ulwellcottagepark.co.uk
www.ulwellcottagepark.co.uk
Pitches For 👤 🚐 🚍 Total 70
Facilities ⚹ ∮ 🛍 🛍 🚿 ⌐ ⊙🍴 🔲 🍴
🛍 ⊙🛍🚿♀🍴🛍🚿🚻🔲🍴
Nearby Facilities ⌐ ✈ ⚓ 🎣 ∪ ♪ ♫
Open March to 7 January
Access Good Site Lev/Slope
Near sandy beaches, scenic walks and ideal for all water sports. Rose Award.
Nearest Town/Resort Swanage
Directions 1½ miles from Swanage on Studland Road. Turn left by telephone box (left hand side) on side of road.
🚉 Wareham

**THREE LEGGED CROSS**
Woolsbridge Manor Farm Caravan Park, Three Legged Cross, Wimborne, Dorset, BH21 6RA
Tel: 01202 826369
Email: woolsbridge@btconnect.com
www.woolsbridgemanorcaravanpark.co.uk
Pitches For 👤 🚐 🚍 Total 60
Facilities ⚹ ∮ 🛍 🛍 🚿 ⌐ ⊙🍴 🔲 🍴
🛍 ⊙🛍🔲🚻⚡🍴 ♪
Nearby Facilities ⌐ ✈ ⚓ 🎣 ∪ ♪ ♫
Acreage 6¾ Open March to Oct
Access Good Site Level
Nearest Town/Resort Ringwood
Directions Take the A31 west, 1 mile past Ringwood follow the sliproad, at the roundabout turn right signposted Three Legged Cross, site is 2 miles along this road on the right hand side.
🚉 Bournemouth

## WAREHAM
**Birchwood Tourist Park**, Bere Road, Coldharbour, Wareham, Dorset, BH20 7PA
**Tel:** 01929 554763 **Fax:** 01929 556635
www.birchwoodtouristpark.co.uk
**Pitches For** ▲ ⌘ ⊞ **Total** 175
**Facilities** ⸴ 🅿 🄷 🆄 ⚓ ⌐ ⊙ ⌣ 🛆 ⬚ 🍴
🕮 🄾 🄶 🆎 🄼 ⚒ ⫱🅿🄳 🄴 ☼ ♬
**Nearby Facilities** ⌐ 🖊 ⚓ ⤳ Ụ
**Acreage** 27 **Open** March to Oct
**Access** Good **Site** Lev/Slope
Situated in Wareham Forest with direct access to forest walks. Ideal for touring the whole of Dorset.
**Nearest Town/Resort** Wareham
**Directions** Located 3 miles north-west of Wareham on the Bere road (unclassified) in Wareham Forest.
⇸ Wareham

## WAREHAM
**Lookout Holiday Park**, Stoborough, Wareham, Dorset, BH20 5AZ
**Tel:** 01929 552546 **Fax:** 01929 556662
**Email:** enquiries@caravan-sites.co.uk
www.caravan-sites.co.uk
**Pitches For** ▲ ⌘ ⊞ **Total** 150
**Facilities** ⸴ 🄷 🆄 ⚓ ⌐ ⊙ ⌣ 🛆 ⬚ 🍴
🕮 🄾 🄶 🆎 🄼 ⫱🅿🄳 🄴 ☼ ♬
**Nearby Facilities** ⌐ 🖊 ⚓ ⤳ Ụ ⚡ 🎣 ⚐
**Acreage** 15 **Open** All Year
**Access** Good **Site** Level
Ideal for touring the Purbecks and Studland Bay. For Touring Caravans we re open All Year, Static Caravans ebruary to the end of November.
**Nearest Town/Resort** Wareham
**Directions** 1 mile south of Wareham on the swanage road.
⇸ Wareham

## WAREHAM
**Luckford Wood Farm Caravan & Camping Park**, Holme Lane, East Stoke, Wareham, Dorset, BH20 6AW
**Tel:** 01929 463098 **Fax:** 01929 405715
**Email:**
infoandbookings@luckfordleisure.co.uk
www.luckfordleisure.co.uk
**Pitches For** ▲ ⌘ ⊞ **Total** 20
**Facilities** ⸴ 🄷 🆄 ⚓ ⌐ ⊙ ⌣ 🛆 ⬚ 🍴
🕮 🄵 🄾 ⫱🄳 🄴 ☼ ♬
**Nearby Facilities** ⌐ 🖊 ⚓ ⤳ Ụ ⚡ 🎣 ⚐
**Acreage** 6 **Open** March to Oct
**Access** Good **Site** Level
Quiet, family run park, close to beauty spots and places of interest. Well placed for inland and Jurassic Coast walks. Ideally situated for literary lovers of T.S.Elliot, Thomas Hardy and William Barnes. Adults Onlt Area. Caravan rallies held all year. Boat storage. Camp fires and Hogroasts by arrangement. Planning for a new state of the art facility block in progress.
**Nearest Town** Wareham/Lulworth Cove
**Directions** Take the B3070 to Lulworth, take second right at West Holme crossroads into Holme Lane, site is 1 mile on the right after left hand bend.
⇸ Wool/Weymouth

## WAREHAM
**Manor Farm Caravan Park**, 1 Manor Farm Cottage, East Stoke, Wareham, Dorset, BH20 6AW
**Tel:** 01929 462870
**Email:** info@manorfarmcp.co.uk
www.manorfarmcp.co.uk
**Pitches For** ▲ ⌘ ⊞ **Total** 50
**Facilities** ⸴ ⚹ 🄷 🆄 ⚓ ⌐ ⊙ ⌣ 🍴
🕮 🄾 🄶 🄼 ⫱🅿🄳 🄴 ☼ ♬
**Nearby Facilities** ⌐ 🖊 ⤳ Ụ ⚐

**Acreage** 2½ **Open** Easter to October
**Access** Good **Site** Level
Flat, grass touring park in a rural area of outstanding natural beauty, central for most of Dorset. Family run park with clean facilities. Good walking area near beaches. Close to Monkey World and Bovington Tank Museum. Resident Proprietors David & Gillian Topp. RAC Appointed - Alan Roger Good Sites Guide. No rallies.
**Nearest Town/Resort** Wareham/Lulworth Cove
**Directions** From Wareham take the A352 then the B3070. Turn into Holme Lane, at the crossroads turn right signposted Manor Farm CP. Or from Wool signposted down Bindon Lane, at the crossroads turn left signposted Manor Farm CP, site is 300 yards on the left.
⇸ Wool/Wareham

## WAREHAM
**Wareham Forest Tourist Park**, North Trigon, Wareham, Dorset, BH20 7NZ
**Tel:** 01929 551393 **Fax:** 01929 558321
**Email:** holiday@wareham-forest.co.uk
www.wareham-forest.co.uk
**Pitches For** ▲ ⌘ ⊞ **Total** 200
**Facilities** ⸴ 🅿 🄷 🆄 ⚓ ⌐ ⊙ ⌣ 🛆 ⬚ 🍴
🕮 🄾 🄶 🆎 🄼 ⚒ ⫱🅿🄳 🄴 ☼ ♬
**Nearby Facilities** ⌐ 🖊 ⚓ ⤳ Ụ ♬
**Acreage** 40 **Open** All Year
**Access** Good **Site** Level
Tranquil, family owned park set in the forest. Ideal for relaxing and walking. Central location for exploring East Dorset and the Purbeck coastline.
**Nearest Town/Resort** Wareham
**Directions** Located midway between Wareham and Bere Regis in Wareham Forest.
⇸ Wareham

## WAREHAM

**Ridge Farm Camping & Caravan Park,** Barnhill Road, Ridge, Wareham, Dorset, BH20 5BG
Tel: 01929 556444
Email: info@ridgefarm.co.uk
www.ridgefarm.co.uk
Pitches For ▲ ♥ ♥ Total 60
Facilities ⬚ ☐ ⬚ ♥ ⬚ ♨ ⬚ ☐ ☎
⬚ ⊘ ☐ ☐ ※ ♨
Nearby Facilities ⌐ ✔ ⬚ ↻ ☰ ♪ ⚡
Acreage 3½ Open Easter to Sept
Access Good Site Level
Peaceful, family run site adjacent to a working farm and RSPB Reserve. In an area of outstanding natural beauty and ideally situated for the Purbeck Hills, Poole Harbour and the coast. Boat launching nearby.
Nearest Town/Resort Wareham
Directions Approx. 1½ miles south of Wareham turn left in the village of Stoborough towards Ridge. Follow signs down Barnhill Road to Ridge Farm at the end of the lane.
⇌ Wareham

## WEYMOUTH

**Bagwell Farm Touring Park,** Bagwell Farm, Chickerell, Weymouth, Dorset, DT3 4EA
Tel: 01305. 782575
Email: enquiries@bagwellfarm.co.uk
www.bagwellfarm.co.uk
Pitches For ▲ ♥ ♥ Total 320
Facilities ⬚ ⌐ ☐ ☐ ♥ ⬚ ♨ ⬚ ☐ ☎
⬚ ⊘ ☐ ✗ ⬚ ♨ ⬚ ☰ ♨ ♨ ♨
Nearby Facilities ⌐ ✔ ⬚ ↻ ↻ ☰ ♪ ⚡
Acreage 14 Open All Year
Access Good Site Lev/Slope
Views of The Fleet and Chesil Beach. Bar with restaurant on site. Take-away food available.
Nearest Town/Resort Weymouth

**Directions** On the B3157, 4 miles west of Weymouth, 500 yards past the Victoria Inn on the left.
⇌ Weymouth

## WEYMOUTH

**East Fleet Farm Touring Park,** Fleet Lane, Chickerell, Weymouth, Dorset, DT3 4DW
Tel: 01305 785768
Email: enquiries@eastfleet.co.uk
www.eastfleet.co.uk
Pitches For ▲ ♥ ♥ Total 350
Facilities ⬚ ⬚ ♥ ⬚ ♨ ⬚ ☐ ☎
⬚ ⊘ ☐ ✗ ♥ ⬚ ☰ ⬚ ☐ ☐ ※
Nearby Facilities ⌐ ✔ ⬚ ↻ ☰ ♪ ⚡
Acreage 20 Open 16 March to 15 Jan
Access Good Site Lev/Slope
On edge of Fleet Water. Area of outstanding natural beauty.
Nearest Town/Resort Weymouth
Directions 3 miles west of Weymouth on the B3157, left at Chickerell T.A. Camp.
⇌ Weymouth

## WEYMOUTH

**Littlesea Holiday Park,** Lynch Lane, Weymouth, Dorset, DT4 9DT
Tel: 01305 774414 Fax: 01305 783683
www.touringholidays.co.uk
Pitches For ▲ ♥ ♥ Total 150
Facilities ⬚ ⌐ ☐ ☐ ♥ ⬚ ♨ ⬚ ☐ ☎
⬚ ⬚ ⊘ ☐ ✗ ⬚ ⬚ ♨ ♨ ☰ ♨ ☐ ☐
Nearby Facilities ⌐ ✔ ⬚ ↻ ↻ ☰ ♪ ⚡
Open Beg April to End Oct
Access Good Site Lev/Slope
Overlooking Chesil Beach.
Nearest Town/Resort Weymouth
Directions Leave the M5 and follow signs for Weymouth, very well signposted.
⇌ Weymouth

## WEYMOUTH

**Osmington Mills Holidays Ltd.,** Ranch House, Osmington Mills, Weymouth, Dorset, DT3 6HB
Tel: 01305 832311 Fax: 01305 835251
Email: holidays@osmingtonmills.fsnet.co.uk
www.osmington-mills-holidays.co.uk
Pitches For ▲ ♥ ♥ Total 225
Facilities ⬚ ⌐ ⊘ ☐ ⬚ ☐ ♨ ↻ ☐
Nearby Facilities ⌐ ✔ ⬚ ↻ ♪ ⚡
Acreage 13 Open Easter to 31 Oct
Access Good Site Lev/Slope
Situated on coastal footpaths.
Nearest Town/Resort Weymouth
Directions 5 miles east of Weymouth on the A353, after Osmington Village turn right into Mills Road, ½ mile to the camping park, right turn.
⇌ Weymouth

## WEYMOUTH

**Pebble Bank Caravan Park,** 90 Camp Road, Wyke Regis, Weymouth, Dorset, DT4 9HF
Tel: 01305 774844
Email: info@pebblebank.co.uk
www.pebblebank.co.uk
Pitches For ▲ ♥ ♥
Facilities ⬚ ☐ ♥ ⌐ ☐ ♨ ⬚ ☐ ☎
☐ ☐ ♥ ⬚ ☰ ☐ ☐ ♨
Nearby Facilities ⌐ ✔ ⬚ ↻ ↻ ♪ ⚡
Acreage 8 Open Easter to 1st Week Oct
Access Good Site Level
Quiet family park in a picturesque setting with superb sea views. Close to Weymouth Town Centre.
Nearest Town/Resort Weymouth
Directions From harbour roundabout go up the hill to a mini roundabout, turn right onto Wyke Road. Camp Road is 1 mile at the apex of a sharp right hand bend, at the bottom of hill.
⇌ Weymouth

## WEYMOUTH

**Portesham Dairy Farm Camp Site,**
Bramdon Lane, Portesham, Weymouth,
Dorset, DT3 4HG
**Tel:** 01305 871297
**Email:** Malcolm.Doble@talk21.com
**Pitches For** ▲ ⊡ ⊟ **Total** 60
**Facilities** ⨍ ⊡ ⊞ ⊞ ♨ ſ ⊙ � ⊟ ⊡ ⊡
⊠ ⊙ ⋔⊟ ≈ ⌁
**Nearby Facilities** ⋏ ⊥ ∪ ⊰ ♪
**Acreage** 3 **Open** 16 March **to** 31 Oct
**Access** Good **Site** Level
Ideal touring for Chesil area. Public
telephone and café/restaurant nearby.
**Nearest Town/Resort** Weymouth
**Directions** 7 miles from Weymouth on
B3157 Coast road.
⋇ Weymouth

## WEYMOUTH

**Seaview Holiday Park,** Preston,
Weymouth, Dorset, DT3 6DZ
**Tel:** 01305 833037 **Fax:** 01305 835101
www.touringholidays.co.uk
**Pitches For** ▲
**Facilities** ⨍ ⊞ ♨ ſ ⊙ ⊿ ⊟ ⊡ ⊡
⊠ ⊡ ⊙ ⊟ ⊞ ⋇ ⊡ ⊡ ♩ ⊠ ⊡ ⊡ ⊡
**Nearby Facilities** ⋏ ⊥ ∪ ⊰ ⊁
**Open** Easter **to** October
**Site** Terraced & Flat
Nestles on a hillside looking out over the
charming Bowleaze Cove.
**Nearest Town/Resort** Weymouth
**Directions** Take the A353 from the centre
of Weymouth, along the seawall to Preston.
Seaview is ½ mile beyond the village, up the
hill on the right.
⋇ Weymouth

## WEYMOUTH

**Waterside Holiday Park,** Bowleaze Cove,
Weymouth, Dorset, DT3 6PP
**Tel:** 01305 833103 **Fax:** 01305 832830
**Email:** info@watersideholidays.co.uk
www.watersideholidays.co.uk
**Pitches For** ⊡ ⊟ **Total** 70
**Facilities** ⊡ ⨍ ⊞ ♨ ſ ⊙ ⊿ ⊟ ⊡ ⊡
⊠ ⊙ ⊠ ⋇ ⊡ ♩ ⊠ ⊡ ♩ ⊠ ⊡ ⊡
**Nearby Facilities** ⋏ ⊥ ⋇ ∪ ⊰
**Acreage** 4
**Access** Good **Site** Level
Located right on the beach at Bowleaze
Cove, Waterside is Weymouth's only 5 Star
Park as graded by Visit Britain.
**Nearest Town/Resort** Weymouth
**Directions** From Dorchester take the A354
to Weymouth, then take the A353 east to
Wareham. At the end of the sea wall turn
right to Bowleaze Cove.
⋇ Weymouth

## WIMBORNE

**Charris Camping & Caravan Park,**
Candy's lane, Corfe Mullen, Wimborne,
Dorset, BH21 3EF
**Tel:** 01202 885970
**Email:** charris@breathe.com
www.charris.co.uk
**Pitches For** ▲ ⊡ ⊟ **Total** 45
**Facilities** ⨍ ⊞ ⊞ ♨ ſ ⊙ ⊿ ⊟ ⊡ ⊡
⊠ ⊡ ⊙ ⊠ ⋔⊟ ⊡
**Nearby Facilities** ſ ⋏ ⊥ ⋇ ∪ ⊰
**Acreage** 3 **Open** March **to** January
**Access** Good **Site** Lev/Slope
4 Star Graded Park, Caravan Club listed,
Caravan and Camping Club listed. Good
central site convienient for coast and New
Forest. Poole 7½ miles, Bournemouth 8¼
miles. Cafe/restaurant close by.
**Nearest Town/Resort** Wimborne
**Directions** A31 Wimborne bypass 1 mile
west of Wimborne. Signs for entrance.
⋇ Poole.

## WIMBORNE

**Springfield Touring Park,** Candy's Lane,
Corfe Mullen, Wimborne, Dorset, BH21 3EF
**Tel:** 01202 881719
**Pitches For** ▲ ⊡ ⊟ **Total** 45
**Facilities** ⊡ ⨍ ⊞ ⊞ ♨ ſ ⊙ ⊿ ⊟ ⊡ ⊡
⊠ ⊡ ⊙ ⊠ ⋔⊟ ⊡
**Nearby Facilities** ſ ⋏ ⊥ ⋇ ∪ ⊰ ♪
**Acreage** 3½ **Open** April **to** October
**Access** Good **Site** Lev/Slope
Family run park, overlooking the Stour
Valley. Free showers and awnings.
Convenient for the coast, New Forest, also
ferry. Low Season Offers - £50, any 7 days
for 2 adults including electric. Members of
the BH & HPA.
**Nearest Town/Resort** Wimborne
**Directions** 1¼ miles west of Wimborne just
off main A31.
⋇ Poole

## WIMBORNE

**Verwood Camping & Caravanning Club
Site,** Sutton Hill, Woodlands, Wimborne,
Dorset, BH21 8NQ
**Tel:** 01202 822763
www.campingandcaravanningclub.co.uk
**Pitches For** ▲ ⊡ ⊟ **Total** 150
**Facilities** ⊡ ⨍ ⊞ ⊞ ♨ ſ ⊙ ⊿ ⊟ ⊡ ⊡
⊠ ⊙ ⊠ ⊟ ⋔⊟ ⊡ ⊡ ≈ ⌁
**Nearby Facilities** ſ ∪
**Acreage** 12 **Open** March **to** Nov
**Access** Good **Site** Gentle Slope
Beautifully situated next to Ringwood
Forest. Miles of safe, sandy beaches at
Poole and Bournemouth are a reasonable
distance. BTB 4 Star Graded and AA 3
Pennants. Non members welcome.
**Nearest Town/Resort** Ringwood

**Directions** From Salisbury take the A354
after 13 miles turn left onto the B3081, site
is 1½ miles west of Verwood.
⋇ Bournemouth

## WIMBORNE

**Wilksworth Farm Caravan Park,**
Cranborne Road, Wimborne, Dorset, BH21
4HW
**Tel:** 01202 885467
**Pitches For** ▲ ⊡ ⊟ **Total** 85
**Facilities** ⊡ ⨍ ⊡ ⊞ ⊞ ♨ ſ ⊙ ⊿ ⊟ ⊡
⊠ ⊡ ⊙ ⊠ ⋇ ⊡ ♩ ⊰ ⋔⊟ ∪ ⊰ ♪ ⊰
**Nearby Facilities** ſ ⋏ ⊥ ⋇ ∪ ⊰ ♪
**Acreage** 11 **Open** 1 April/Easter **to** 30 Oct
**Access** Good **Site** Level
8 miles from Poole and 10 miles from
Bournemouth.
**Nearest Town/Resort** Wimborne
**Directions** 1 mile north of Wimborne on the
B3078.
⋇ Poole

## WOOL

**Whitemead Caravan Park,** East Burton
Road, Wool, Dorset, BH20 6HG
**Tel:** 01929 462241 **Fax:** 01929 462241
**Email:** whitemeadcp@aol.com
www.whitemeadcaravanpark.co.uk
**Pitches For** ⊡ ⊟ **Total** 95
**Facilities** ⨍ ⊞ ♨ ſ ⊙ ⊿ ⊟ ⊡ ⊡
⊠ ⊡ ⊙ ⊠ ⊡ ♩ ⋔⊟ ⊡ ⋇
**Nearby Facilities** ſ ⋏ ⊥ ⋇ ∪ ⊰ ♪ ⊰
**Acreage** 5 **Open** April **to** End October
**Access** Good **Site** Level
Woodland site with several secluded
pitches. Off licence and take-away food
available on site.
**Nearest Town/Resort** Wareham
**Directions** Off the A352 Wareham to
Weymouth road. 5 miles west of Wareham
and 5 miles north of Lulworth Cove.
⋇ Wool

# DURHAM

## BARNARD CASTLE

**Camping & Caravanning Club Site,**
Dockenflatts Lane, Lartington, Barnard
Castle, Co. Durham, DL12 9DG
**Tel:** 01833 630228
www.campingandcaravanningclub.co.uk
**Pitches For** ▲ ⊡ ⊟ **Total** 90
**Facilities** ⊡ ⨍ ⊡ ⊞ ⊞ ♨ ſ ⊙ ⊿ ⊟ ⊡
⊠ ⊙ ⊠ ⊟ ⋔⊟ ⊡ ≈ ⌁ ⊰
**Nearby Facilities** ſ ⊿ ∪ ⊰
**Acreage** 10 **Open** March **to** Nov
**Site** Level
Well placed for exploring the Pennines and
the city of Durham. BTB 4 Star Graded, AA
4 Pennants and Loo of the Year Award.
Non members welcome.

**Directions** On approach from Scotch Corner take the second turn right for Middleton in Teesdale and Barnard Castle. On approach from Penrith take the B6277 to Middleton in Teesdale. In approx 1 mile take turn off left signposted Raygill Riding Stables. The site is 500 metres on the left.
⇌ Darlington

## BARNARD CASTLE
**Cote House Caravan Park,** Middleton-in-Teesdale, Barnard Castle, Co. Durham, DL12 0PN
**Tel:** 01833 640515
**Pitches For** ⊕ ⊜ **Total** 20
**Facilities** ⬚ ⚓ ſ ⊙⊰ ⵊ ⵰ ↯
**Nearby Facilities** ſ ✔ ⚓ ∪ ₰
**Acreage** 16 **Open** March **to** Oct
**Access** Good **Site** Lev/Slope
By the River Lune.
**Nearest Town/Resort** Barnard Castle
**Directions** 1 mile out of Mickleton, by Grassholme Reservoir.
⇌ Darlington

## BARNARD CASTLE
**Hetherick Caravan Park,** Marwood, Barnard Castle, Co. Durham, DL12 8QX
**Tel:** 01833 631173 **Fax:** 01388 488384
**Email:** info@hetherickcaravanpark.co.uk
www.hetherickcaravanpark.co.uk
**Pitches For** ⚑ ⊕ ⊜ **Total** 41
**Facilities** ⚲ ſ ⬚ ⚓ ſ ⊙⊰ ▢ ☎
**Nearby Facilities** ſ ✔ ∪ ₰
**Acreage** 22 **Open** March **to** October
**Access** Good **Site** Level
Pleasant park situated on a working farm, in the heart of beautiful Teesdale. 3 miles from the pretty market town of Barnard Castle.
**Nearest Town/Resort** Barnard Castle
**Directions** Take the B6278 from Barnard Castle towards Eggleston and Middleton-in-Teesdale, once past the golf course take the second right turn towards Kinninvie and Woodland.
⇌ Darlington

## BARNARD CASTLE
**Pecknell Farm Caravan Site,** Pecknell Farm, Lartington, Barnard Castle, Co. Durham, DL12 9DF
**Tel:** 01833 638357
**Pitches For** ⊕ ⊜ **Total** 15
**Facilities** ſ ⬚ ⬚ ⚓ ſ ⊙⊰ ⊜ ⛺
**Nearby Facilities** ſ ✔ ∪ ₰
**Acreage** 1½ **Open** April **to** October
**Access** Good **Site** Level
Ideal walking area, very attractive walk into historic Barnard Castle. Within easy reach of many attractions.
**Nearest Town/Resort** Barnard Castle
**Directions** 1½ miles from Barnard Castle on the B6277 to Lartington, we are the first farm on the right.
⇌ Darlington

## BARNARD CASTLE
**West Roods Working Farm,** Mrs Margaret Lowson, West Roods Farm, Boldron, Barnard CastleCo. Durham, DL12 9SW
**Tel:** 01833 690116

**Pitches For** ⚑ ⊕ ⊜ **Total** 5
**Facilities** ſ ⬚ ⚓ ſ ⊙⊰ ⛺ ⵰ ▢ ↯
**Nearby Facilities** ſ ✔ ⚓ ∪ ₰ ₰
**Acreage** ½ **Open** May **to** October
**Access** Good **Site** Sloping
Fantastic views of green countryside. Bird watching and walks. Near to Bowes Museum and Highforce Waterfall. Learn water dowsing for £10.00 per hour. 56 miles to the north east coast. Some facilities for the disabled. One hard standing available.
**Nearest Town/Resort** Barnard Castle
**Directions** On the north side of the A66. 2½ miles east of Bowes and 3 miles from Barnard Castle.
⇌ Darlington

## BARNARD CASTLE
**Winston Caravan Park,** The Old Forge, Winston, Darlington, Co. Durham, DL2 3RH
**Tel:** 01325 730228 **Fax:** 01325 730228
**Email:** m.willetts@ic24.net
www.touristnetuk.com/ne/winston
**Pitches For** ⚑ ⊕ ⊜ **Total** 21
**Facilities** ſ ⬚ ⬚ ⚓ ſ ⊙⊰ ⊜ ▢ ☎
⊙⵰▢▢
**Nearby Facilities** ſ ✔ ⚓ ∪ ₰
**Open** March **to** October
**Access** Good **Site** Level
Ideally situated for exploring the many attractions in County Durham.
**Nearest Town/Resort** Darlington
**Directions** From Darlington take the A67 west for 10 miles, turn left onto the B6274 into Winston Village, site is 400 yards on the right hand side.
⇌ Darlington

## BEAMISH
**Bobby Shafto Caravan Park,** Cranberry Plantation, Beamish, Co. Durham, DH9 0RY
**Tel:** 0191 370 1776 **Fax:** 0191 370 1783
**Pitches For** ⚑ ⊕ ⊜ **Total** 75
**Facilities** ⚲ ſ ⬚ ⬚ ⚓ ſ ⊙⊰ ⊜ ▢ ☎
⵰⵰✆▥⚲☐⊟☐⵰
**Nearby Facilities** ſ ✔ ∪ ₰
**Acreage** 10 **Open** March **to** October
**Access** Good
**Nearest Town/Resort** Chester-le-Street
**Directions** Leave the A1(M) at junction 63 (Chester-le-Street) and follow signs along the A68 or A693 to Beamish Museum, then follow brown tourism signs for ¾ miles to the caravan park.
⇌ Durham

## BISHOP AUCKLAND
**Craggwood Caravan Park / Riverside Touring Caravan Park,** Craggwood Caravan Park, Gordon Lane, Ramshaw, Bishop AucklandCo. Durham, DL14 0NS
**Tel:** 01388 835866 **Fax:** 01388 835866
**Email:** billy6482@btopenworld.com
www.craggwoodcaravanpark.co.uk
**Pitches For** ⚑ ⊕ ⊜
**Facilities** ⚲ ⵰ ſ ⬚ ⚓ ſ ⊸ ▢ ☎
⵰⵰✆▥⚲☐⊟☐⵰
**Nearby Facilities** ſ ✔ ∪
**Open** March **to** October
**Access** Good **Site** Level

A river runs down the side of the site, and there is 38 acres of woodland for walks.
**Nearest Town/Resort** Bishop Auckland
**Directions** From Bishop Auckland take the A688 towards Barnard Castle, after approx 3 miles we are s.p. to the right, follow signs.
⇌ Bishop Auckland

## BISHOP AUCKLAND
**Witton Castle Caravan & Camping Site,** Witton Le Wear, Bishop Auckland, Co. Durham, DL14 0DE
**Tel:** 01388 488230 **Fax:** 01388 488008
www.wittoncastle.com
**Pitches For** ⚑ ⊕ ⊜ **Total** 280
**Facilities** ſ ⬚ ⬚ ⚓ ſ ⊙⊰ ⊜ ▢ ☎
⵰⊟☐✆▥⚑⵰☐⊹⊕▥⵰⵰₰
**Nearby Facilities** ſ ✔ ∪ ₰
**Acreage** 30 **Open** March **to** October
**Access** Good **Site** Lev/Slope
Set in central Co Durham in an area of outstanding natural beauty.
**Nearest Town/Resort** Bishop Auckland
**Directions** On A68 signposted between Toft Hill and Witton le Wear.
⇌ Bishop Auckland

## CONSETT
**Manor Park Caravan & Camping Park,** Manor Park Limited, Broadmeadows, Near Castleside, ConsettCo. Durham, DH8 9HD
**Tel:** 01207 501000 **Fax:** 01207 599779
**Pitches For** ⚑ ⊕ ⊜ **Total** 40
**Facilities** ſ ⬚ ⚓ ſ ⊙⊰ ⊜ ▢ ☎
⊟⊟☐⵰✆⚲▥⵰₰
**Nearby Facilities** ſ ✔
**Acreage** 7 **Open** May **to** Sept
**Access** Good **Site** Lev/Slope
Quiet countryside site. Close to Rowley C to C Cycle Route (1½ miles).
**Nearest Town/Resort** Consett
**Directions** Just off the A68, 3 miles south of Castleside and 5 miles north of Tow Law.
⇌ Durham

## DURHAM
**Finchale Abbey Caravan Park,** Finchale Abbey Farm, Co. Durham, DH1 5SH
**Tel:** 0191 386 6528 **Fax:** 0191 386 8593
**Email:** godricawatson@hotmail.com
www.finchaleabbey.co.uk
**Pitches For** ⊕ ⊜ **Total** 40
**Facilities** ſ ⬚ ⬚ ⚓ ſ ⊙⊰ ⊜ ▢ ☎
⵰✕▥⊟☐⊟☐
**Nearby Facilities** ſ ✔
**Acreage** 6 **Open** All Year
**Access** Good **Site** Level
Set in the meander of the River Wear. Ideally situated to visit most of the North East's highlights.
**Nearest Town/Resort** Durham City
**Directions** Leave the A1M at junction 63 and head south on the A167. At Armson roundabout follow signs for Finchale Priory, site is at the same place.
⇌ Durham City

## DURHAM
**Grange Caravan Club Site,** Meadow Lane, Durham, Co. Durham, DH1 1TL
**Tel:** 0191 384 4778
www.caravanclub.co.uk

# DURHAM, ESSEX

## DURHAM, ESSEX

**Pitches For** ▲ ⌂ ⛺ **Total** 75
**Facilities** ⫣ 🅗 🆆 ⚓ 🏧 🔲 🅟 ⬚ 🛢 ⤫🔲 ♿
**Nearby Facilities** ⌂ ✔
**Acreage** 12 **Open** All Year
**Access** Good **Site** Level
Only 3 miles from the city of Durham with its castle and cathedral. Beamish Open Air Museum nearby. Non members welcome. Booking essential.
**Nearest Town/Resort** Durham
**Directions** Leave the A1(M) via slip road onto the A690 signposted Durham. Immediately move to the outside lane to turn right in 50 yards at brown caravan sign into Meadow Lane, site entrance is ahead.
⇌ Durham

## DURHAM

**Strawberry Hill Farm Caravan & Camping Park,** Old Cassop, Durham, Co. Durham, DH6 4QA
**Tel:** 0191 372 3457 **Fax:** 0191 372 2512
**Email:** howarddunkerley@strawberryhillfarm.freeserve.co.uk
**www.**ukparks.com
**Pitches For** ▲ ⌂ ⛺ **Total** 45
**Facilities** ⬚ ⫣ 🅗 🆆 ⚓ 🏧 ⊙ ⤸ 🛢 🔲 ☕
⛽ 🔵 🛢 ⤫🔲 🅟 🔲
**Nearby Facilities** ⌂ ✔
**Acreage** 6 **Open** March **to** Dec
**Access** Good **Site** Level
Approx. 4 miles from Durham City, World Heritage Site, Castle and Cathedral.
**Nearest Town/Resort** Durham City
**Directions** Leave the A1M at junction 61 signposted A177 Peterlee. Turn first right at Jennings Pub and continue to staggered crossroads, turn right onto the A181 and the Park is 1½ miles on the left.
⇌ Durham City

## HARTLEPOOL

**Crimdon Dene Holiday Park,** Blackhall Rocks, Hartlepool, Co. Durham, TS27 4BN
**Tel:** 01429 267801 **Fax:** 01429 261899
**Email:** holidaysales.crimdondene@park-resorts.com
**www.**park-resorts.com
**Pitches For** ⌂ ⛺ **Total** 20
**Facilities** ⬚ ⫣ 🅗 🆆 ⚓ 🏧 ⊙ ⤸ 🔲 ☕
⛽ 🔵 🛢 ⤫ 🍴 🔵 🎣 🛢 🎢 🔲 🔲 ⤫
**Nearby Facilities** ⌂ ✔ ⚲ ∪
**Open** Easter **to** Oct
**Access** Good **Site** Level
Situated on Durham's heritage coast with fine views and access to a sandy beach. Newly refurbished lounge bar with live music most weekends. Sun patio, mini market, childrens entertainment with Dylan the Dinosaur, adventure playground and Pony World.
**Nearest Town/Resort** Hartlepool

**Directions** From the A19 just south of Peterlee, take the B1281 sp Blackhall. Drive through Castle Eden and after approx ½ a mile turn left sp Blackhall. After 3 miles at the T-junction turn right onto the A1086. After 1 mile Park entrance is sp on the left, beside the Seagull Public House.
⇌ Hartlepool

## MIDDLETON-IN-TEESDALE

**Mickleton Mill Caravan Park,** The Mill, Mickleton, Barnard Castle, Co. Durham, DL12 0LS
**Tel:** 01833 640317 **Fax:** 01833 640317
**Email:** mickletonmill@aol.com
**Pitches For** ⌂ ⛺ **Total** 75
**Facilities** ⫣ 🅗 🆆 ⚓ 🏧 🅟 ⊙ ⤸ 🛢 🔲 ☕
⛽ 🔵 🛢 🔲 🔲 ⤫
**Nearby Facilities** ⌂ ✔ ⚲ ∪ ⌖
**Acreage** 7½ **Open** April **to** October
**Access** Fair **Site** Level
Set on the banks of the River Lune. Pitches for 4 tourers.
**Nearest Town/Resort** Barnard Castle
**Directions** From Barnard Castle take the B6277. In Mickleton take the first turn right past Blacksmiths Arms, go down the bank and bear left at the bottom of the hill.
⇌ Darlington

## WOLSINGHAM

**Bradley Mill Caravan Park,** Wolsingham, Bishop Auckland, Co, Durham, DL13 3JJ
**Tel:** 01388 527285 **Fax:** 01388 527285
**Email:** stay@bradleyburn.co.uk
**www.**bradleyburn.co.uk
**Pitches For** ⌂ ⛺ **Total** 12
**Facilities** ⫣ 🅗 ⚓ 🏧 ⊙ 🔲 ☕
🔵 🛢 🔲 ⤫🔲 ⤫
**Nearby Facilities** ⌂ ✔ ∪ ⌖
**Open** March **to** October
**Access** Good **Site** Lev/Slope
**N.B.** This is a STATIC holiday park with a few pitches available for tourers.
**Nearest Town/Resort** Wolsingham
**Directions** 2 miles east of Wolsingham on the A689 and 2 miles west of the A68/A689 junction.
⇌ Bishop Auckland

# ESSEX

## BRENTWOOD

**Kelvedon Hatch Camping & Caravanning Club Site,** Warren Lane, Doddinghurst, Brentwood, Essex, CM15 0JG
**Tel:** 01277 372773
**www.**campingandcaravanningclub.co.uk
**Pitches For** ▲ ⌂ ⛺ **Total** 90
**Facilities** ⬚ ⫣ 🅗 🆆 ⚓ 🏧 ⊙ ⤸ 🛢 🔲 ☕
🔵 🛢 🔵 🛢 🍴 🔵🔲 🔲 ⤫ ♿

**Nearby Facilities** ⌂ ✔ ∪ ♪
**Acreage** 12 **Open** March **to** Nov
**Access** Fair **Site** Level
Peaceful site, good for country walks. 20 miles from the centre of London. Plenty of sporting activities within easy reach. BTB 3 Star Graded and AA 3 Pennants. Non members welcome.
**Directions** Leave the M25 at junction 28 and take the A1023 towards Brentwood. Turn left onto the A128 to Ongar, the site is 3 miles on the right, signposted.
⇌ Brentwood

## CLACTON-ON-SEA

**Highfield Holiday Park,** London Road, Clacton-on-Sea, Essex, CO16 9QY
**Tel:** 0870 442 9287 **Fax:** 01255 689805
holidaysales.highfield@park-resorts.com
**www.**park-resorts.com
**Pitches For** ⌂ ⛺ **Total** 42
**Facilities** ⫣ 🅗 🆆 ⚓ 🏧 🅟 ⊙ 🔲 ☕
⛽ 🔵 🛢 🍴 🔵 🎣 🛢 🎢 🔲 ⤫
**Nearby Facilities** ⌂ ✔ ⚲ 🔵 ∪ ♪ ♪
**Open** March **to** Jan
**Access** Good **Site** Level
Near the beach, great for family activities, sensational fun in the evening. Local attractions including the pier, Colchester Zoo, Seaquarium and more.
**Nearest Town/Resort** Clacton-on-Sea
**Directions** From the M25 take the A12 then the A120 leading to the A133 directly to Clacton. Situated on the B1441 approx. 2 miles before the town centre on the left hand side (well signposted).
⇌ Clacton-on-Sea

## CLACTON-ON-SEA

**Silver Dawn Touring Park,** Jaywick Lane, Clacton-on-Sea, Essex, CO16 8BB
**Tel:** 01255 421856
**Pitches For** ⌂ ⛺ **Total** 38
**Facilities** ⫣ ⚓ 🏧 ⊙ ⤸ 🔲 ☕
🔵 🔵 🔵 🛢 ⤫ ⤫
**Nearby Facilities** ⌂ ✔ ⚲ 🔵 ∪ ♪ ♪
**Acreage** 3 **Open** April **to** October
**Access** Good **Site** Level
David Bellamy Silver Award for Conservation.
**Nearest Town/Resort** Clacton-on-Sea
**Directions** Take the A12 then the A120 to Clacton.
⇌ Clacton-on-Sea

## CLACTON-ON-SEA

**Tower Holiday Park,** Belsize Avenue, Jaywick, Clacton-on-Sea, Essex, CO15 2LF
**Tel:** 0870 442 9290 **Fax:** 01255 820060
**Email:** holidaysales.tower@park-resorts.com

# ESSEX

www.park-resorts.com
Pitches For ⌑ ⊟ Total 100
Facilities ⚲ ∮ Ⓦ ♨ ⌂ ⊙ ⊸ ⊒ ◻ ☕
℉ ⓘ ⊗ ⊠ ✕ 📶 ♠ ⚲ ⚘ ⊬ 🄳 ⊟ ☀
Nearby Facilities ⌕ ✦ ⚓ ⚲ ∪ ♪
Open March to Oct
Access Good Site Level
Next to the beach and only 3 miles from
Clacton town. Ideal base for touring East
Anglia.
Nearest Town/Resort Clacton-on-Sea
Directions From the A12 take the A120 then
the A133 to Clacton seafront. Turn right and
follow signs through Jaywick.
➥ Clacton-on-Sea

## COLCHESTER
Colchester Camping Caravan Club Site,
Cymbeline Way, Colchester, Essex, CO3
4AG
Tel: 01206 545551 Fax: 01206 710443
Email:
enquiries@colchestercamping.co.uk
www.colchestercamping.co.uk
Pitches For ⚠ ⌑ ⊟ Total 168
Facilities ⚷ ∮ 🄳 Ⓗ Ⓦ ♨ ⌂ ⊙ ⊸ ⊒ ◻ ☕
℉ ⓘ ⊗ ⊠ ⚲ 🄳 ⊟ ⊬ ♪
Nearby Facilities ⌕ ✦ ⚓ ⚲ ∪ ♪
Acreage 12 Open All Year
Access Good Site Level
Within easy walking distance of
Colchester, England's oldest city. Ideal
base to explore Constable country. Close
to Braintrees Working Silk Museum and
Colchester Zoo. Convenient for ferry ports.
Non members welcome. Booking essential.
Nearest Town/Resort Colchester
Directions Well signposted by brown tourism
signs. From London on the A12, leave
signposted Colchester Central A133, at large
roundabout turn right signposted Lexden &
Stanway, site is 100 yards on the right.
➥ Colchester

## COLCHESTER
Mill Farm Camping, Mill Farm, Harwich
Road, Great Bromley, ColchesterEssex,
CO7 7JQ
Tel: 01206 250485 Fax: 01206 252040
Pitches For ⚠ Total 10
Facilities Ⓦ ♨ ⌂ ⊙ ⊸ ℉ ⊟
Nearby Facilities ✦ ⚓
Acreage 2 Open May to Sept
Access Fair Site Sloping
Quiet site in a rural setting. No club house.
Nearest Town/Resort Colchester
Directions Take the A120 towards Harwich,
signposted.
➥ Wivenhoe

## HALSTEAD
Gosfield Lake Resort, Church Road,
Gosfield, Nr Halstead, Essex, CO9 1UE
Tel: 01787 475043 Fax: 01787 478528
Email: turps@gosfieldlake.co.uk
www.gosfieldlake.co.uk
Pitches For Total 25
Facilities ∮ Ⓦ ⌂ ⊙ ⊗ ✕ 🄳 ⊟
Nearby Facilities ⌕ ✦ ∪ ♪
Acreage 7 Open All Year
Access Good Site Level
Near a lake for water-skiing.
Nearest Town/Resort Halstead
Directions A120, A131 and A1017 from
Braintree, 5 miles A1024, Sible Hedingham
A1017.
➥ Braintree

## HARWICH
Dovercourt Caravan Park, Low Road,
Harwich, Essex, CO12 3TZ
Tel: 01255 243433 Fax: 01255 241673
Email: enquiries@dovercourtcp.com

www.dovercourtcp.com
Pitches For ⌑ ⊟ Total 60
Facilities ⚷ ∮ Ⓦ ♨ ⌂ ⊙ ⊸ ⊒ ◻ ☕
℉ ⓘ ⊗ ⊠ ✕ 📶 ♠ ⚲ ⊬ 🄳 ⊟ ☀
Nearby Facilities ⌕ ✦ ⚓ ⚲ ∪ ♪
Acreage 80 Open to Oct
Access Good Site Level
Adjacent to the beach. Close to Harwich
Port ferry terminal.
Nearest Town/Resort Dovercourt
Directions From Colchester take the A120
towards Harwich, at Ramsey roundabout turn
right and follow brown tourism signs to
Dovercourt Caravan Park.
➥ Harwich International

## MALDON
Barrow Marsh Caravan Park, Goldhanger
Road, Heybridge, Maldon, Essex, CM9
4RA
Tel: 01621 852859 Fax: 01621 853593
Pitches For ⚠ ⌑ ⊟ Total 15
Facilities ∮ Ⓦ ♨ ⌂ ⊙ ⊸ ◻ ⓘ ⊗ ⊠ 🄳 ⊟
Nearby Facilities ✦ ⚓ ⚲
Acreage 14 Open 1 April to 30 Oct
Access Good Site Level
Situated by Blackwater Estuary. 16 miles
from the historic town of Colchester.
Nearest Town/Resort Maldon
Directions From Maldon travel towards
Heybridge and turn onto the B1026
Goldhanger Road to Mill Beach. Site is 3
miles from Maldon on the left hand side.
➥ Witham

## MERSEA ISLAND
Fen Farm Camping & Caravan Site, Fen
Farm, East Mersea, Colchester, Essex,
CO5 8UA
Tel: 01206 383275 Fax: 01206 386316
Email: fenfarm@talk21.com
www.mersea-island.com/fenfarm
Pitches For ⚠ ⌑ ⊟ Total 95
Facilities ⚷ ∮ 🄳 Ⓗ Ⓦ ♨ ⌂ ⊙ ⊸ ⊒ ◻ ☕
🄰 ⓘ ⊗ ⊠ 🄳 ⊟ ⊬ ♪
Nearby Facilities ✦ ⚓ ⚲ ⊬
Acreage 5 Open March to September
Access Good Site Level
Quiet, rural, family site by the beach and
on an estuary. Close to a country park.
Nearest Town/Resort West Mersea
Directions Take the B1025 from Colchester,
take the left fork to East Mersea, take the
first turn right past the Dog & Pheasant Public
House, signposted.
➥ Colchester

## MERSEA ISLAND
Seaview Holiday Park, Seaview Avenue,
Mersea Island, Colchester, Essex, CO5
8DA
Tel: 01206 382534 Fax: 01206 385936
Email: info@westmersea.com
www.www.westmersea.com
Pitches For ⚠ ⌑ ⊟ Total 120
Facilities ⚷ ∮ 🄳 Ⓗ Ⓦ ♨ ⌂ ⊙ ⊸ ⊒ ◻ ☕
℉ ⓘ ⊗ ⊠ ✕ 🄳 ⊟ ⊬
Nearby Facilities ⌕ ✦ ⚓ ⚲ ∪ ♪ ♪
Acreage 30 Open 15 March to 14 Jan
Access Good Site Level
Private beach. Wooded park with pitches
very near the beach. Boat launching
facilities. Static Homes and Exclusive
Pitches available. Licenced Clubhouse.
Ideal for touring.
Nearest Town/Resort Colchester
Directions From Colchester take the B1025
to Mersea Island. Following signs turn left
off the causeway, then turn right, turn right
then left into Seaview Avenue.
➥ Colchester

## MERSEA ISLAND
Waldegraves Holiday & Leisure Park,
Mersea Island, Colchester, Essex, CO5
8SE
Tel: 01206 382898 Fax: 01206 385359
Email: holidays@waldegraves.co.uk
www.waldegraves.co.uk
Pitches For ⚠ ⌑ ⊟ Total 200
Facilities ⚷ ∮ 🄳 Ⓗ Ⓦ ♨ ⌂ ⊙ ⊸ ⊒ ◻ ☕
℉ ⓘ ⊗ ⊠ ✕ 📶 ♠ ⚲ ⚘ ⊬ 🄳 ⊟ ☀
♪
Nearby Facilities ⌕ ✦ ⚓ ⚲ ∪ ⊬
Acreage 45 Open March to November
Access Good Site Level
Ideal family grass park, surrounded by
trees and lakes. Safe private beach,
fishing. Heated swimming pool and an
undercover golf driving range. Holiday
homes for hire and sale. Weekend breaks
available.
Nearest Town/Resort Mersea
Directions From Colchester take B1025, 10
miles to West Mersea. Take left fork to East
Mersea, second road to right.
➥ Colchester

## ROYDON
Roydon Mill Park, Roydon, Essex, CM19
5EJ
Tel: 01279 792777 Fax: 01279 792695
Email: info@roydonpark.com
www.roydonpark.com
Pitches For ⚠ ⌑ ⊟ Total 110
Facilities ∮ Ⓗ Ⓦ ♨ ⌂ ⊙ ⊸ ⊒ ◻ ☕
🄸 ⓘ ⊗ ⊠ ⚲ 📶 🄳 ⊟ ⊬
Nearby Facilities ⌕ ✦ ∪
Acreage 11 Open All Year
Access Good Site Level
Riverside park with a direct train service to
London from the adjacent railway station.
Nearest Town/Resort Harlow
Directions From the A414 between the A10
and Harlow, follow brown and white tourist
signs to the Park.
➥ Roydon

## SOUTHEND-ON-SEA
Riverside Village Holiday Park, Creeksea
Ferry Road, Wallasea Island, Rochford,
Essex, SS4 2EY
Tel: 01702 258297 Fax: 01702 258555
Pitches For ⚠ ⌑ ⊟ Total 60
Facilities ∮ Ⓦ ♨ ⌂ ⊙ ⊸ ⊒ ◻ ☕
℉ ⓘ ⊗ ⊠ 🄳 ⊟ ⊬ ♪
Nearby Facilities ⌕ ✦ ⚓ ⚲ ∪
Acreage 25 Open March to October
Access Good Site Level
Alongside the River Crouch and
surrounded by SSSI and nature reserves.
Part of the Crouch Valley Way, a ramblers
delight. Marinas, country pubs and
restaurants nearby.
Nearest Town/Resort Southend-on-Sea
Directions From A127 through Rochford,
follow caravan signs for Ashingdon then
Wallasea Island. From Chelmsford left at
Battlesbridge, past Hullbridge for Ashingdon
then Wallasea.
➥ Rochford

## SOUTHMINSTER
Steeple Bay Holiday Village, Steeple,
Southminster, Essex, CM0 7RS
Tel: 01621 773991 Fax: 01621 773967
Email: info@cinqueportsleisure.com
www.cplholidays.com
Pitches For ⚠ ⌑ ⊟ Total 60
Facilities ⚷ ⚲ ∮ 🄳 Ⓗ Ⓦ ♨ ⌂ ⊙ ⊸ ◻ ☕
℉ ⓘ ⊗ ⊠ ✕ 📶 ♠ ⚲ ⚘ ⊬ 🄳 ⊟ ☀
Nearby Facilities ⌕ ✦ ⚓ ⚲ ∪ ♪
Open March to Nov
Access Good Site Level
Alongside the River Blackwater.

**Homestead Lake Park**

Thorpe Rd (B1033)
Weeley
Clacton-on-Sea
Essex
CO16 9JN
Tel: 01255 833492
Fax: 01255 831406
email: lakepark@homesteadcaravans.co.uk

www.homesteadlake.co.uk

★★★ TOURING PARK

**Nearest Town/Resort** Southminster
**Directions** Turn off the A12 onto the A414, then take the B1010/B1012 to Latchington, follow signs through Mayland then Steeple Village. After Steeple Village turn left and the site is 1 mile down the lane.
≠ Southminster

## SOUTHMINSTER

**Waterside Holiday Park,** Main Road, St Lawrence Bay, Southminster, Essex, CM0 7LP
**Tel:** 0870 442 9298 **Fax:** 01621 778106
**Email:** holidaysales.waterside@park-resorts.com
www.park-resorts.com
**Pitches For** ♠ ⊕ ♥ **Total** 170
**Facilities** ♿ ∮ 🔲 ⏴ ♣ 𝄐 ☉ 🍴 🛁 🖵 💧
𝄐 ⊙ 🔲 ✕ 🍴 🔲 🔦 🛒 ⅗ ↴🔲 🖵 ⋇
**Nearby Facilities** ✓ ⏴ ⅗ ⟳
**Acreage** 45 **Open** April **to** October
**Access** Good **Site** Lev/Slope
Situated on the Black Water Estuary with own slipway and beach. Beautiful green park with great views. Bird watching (SSSI). Ideal for water sports, subject to weather.
**Nearest Town/Resort** Southminster
**Directions** Head south from Maldon on the B1018, go through Mundon to Latchingdon then bear left towards St Lawrence Bay, site is signposted.
≠ Southminster

## WALTON-ON-THE-NAZE

**Naze Marine Holiday Park,** Hall Lane, Walton-on-the-Naze, Essex, CO14 8HL
**Tel:** 0870 442 9292 **Fax:** 01255 820060
**Email:** holidaysales.nazemarine@park-resorts.com
www.park-resorts.com
**Pitches For** ♠ ⊕ ♥ **Total** 44
**Facilities** ∮ 🔲 ⏴ ♣ 𝄐 ☉ 🛁 🖵 💧
𝄐 ⊙ 🔲 ✕ 🍴 🔲 🔦 ↴🔦
**Nearby Facilities** ✓
**Access** Good **Site** Level
A delightful park adjacent to a nature reserve. On the edge of Walton town with its traditional seaside delights.
**Nearest Town/Resort** Clacton-on-Sea
**Directions** From the A12 take the A120 Harwich road to the A133. Follow as far as Weeley then take the B1033 to Walton sea front, Naze Marine is on the left.
≠ Clacton-on-Sea

## WEELEY

**Green Lane Touring Caravan Park,** Green Lane, Off Mill Lane, Weeley Heath, Essex, CO15 9BZ
**Tel:** 01255 830232
**Email:** wittsend@hotmail.com
**Pitches For** ♠ ⊕ ♥ **Total** 8

**Facilities** ∮ 🔲 🔲 ⏴ ♣ 𝄐 🛁 🛒 ♥
𝄐 ⌂ ♀ 🔲 ⅗ 🔲 ⋇ 🔦 🔦 𝒫
**Nearby Facilities** ✓ ✓ ⏴ ⅗ ⟳
**Acreage** 1 **Open** Easter **to** October
**Access** Good **Site** Level
Peaceful location. Near to several beaches and a fishing lake. Indoor heated swimming pool and clubhouse on site.
**Nearest Town/Resort** Clacton-on-Sea
**Directions** Leave the M25 at junction 28 and take the A12 to junction 29, then take the A120 then the A133 Clacton/Weeley pass. After Macdonalds on the right take the fourth turning on the right.
≠ Weeley/Clacton

## WEELEY

**Homestead Lake Park,** Thorpe Road (B1033), Weeley, Clacton-on-Sea, Essex, CO16 9JN
**Tel:** 01255 833492 **Fax:** 01255 831406
**Email:**
lakepark@homesteadcaravans.co.uk
www.homesteadlake.co.uk
**Pitches For** ♠ ⊕ ♥ **Total** 50
**Facilities** ♿ ∮ 🔲 🔲 ⏴ ♣ 𝄐 ☉
𝄐 ⌂ ✕ ↴🔦 🔲 🖵
**Nearby Facilities** ✓ ✓ ⏴ ⅗ ⟳ 𝒫 𝒫
**Open** March **to** October
**Access** Good **Site** Sloping
Quiet and relaxing site with a fishing lake. 10 miles from historic Colchester. Beaches and piers of Clacton and Walton within 8 miles. Constable country and Ipswich within 25 miles.
**Nearest Town/Resort** Clacton-on-Sea
**Directions** From the A12 take the A120 towards Harwich then the A133 towards Weeley and Clacton. Then take the B1033 towards Walton, go past the second roundabout and the site entrance is ¼ mile on the left hand side. Entrance through Homestead Caravans.
≠ Weeley

## GLOUCESTERSHIRE
### CHELTENHAM

**Cheltenham Racecourse Caravan Club Site,** Prestbury Park, Cheltenham, Gloucestershire, GL50 4SH
**Tel:** 01242 523102
www.caravanclub.co.uk
**Pitches For** ⊕ ♥ **Total** 69
**Facilities** ∮ 🔲 🔲 ⏴ ♣ 𝄐 ☉ ♥ 𝄐 ⌂ ⊙ 🛒 ↴🔦🔲
**Nearby Facilities** ✓
**Acreage** 7 **Open** April **to** Oct
**Access** Good **Site** Lev/Slope
Set on the edge of elegant Cheltenham with panoramic views of the Cleeve Hills. Free racing, putting course adjacent (small charge). Non members welcome. Booking essential.

**Nearest Town/Resort** Cheltenham
**Directions** From west on the A40, 1½ miles past M5 junction at Benhall roundabout turn left into Princess Elizabeth Way. At the roundabout continue straight into Kingsditch Industrial Estate, after ½ mile turn right, at roundabout turn left into racecourse and follow signs.
≠ Cheltenham

## CIRENCESTER

**Hoburne Cotswold,** Broadway Lane, South Cerney, Cirencester, Gloucestershire, GL7 5UQ
**Tel:** 01285 860216 **Fax:** 01285 868010
**Email:** enquiries@hoburne.com
www.hoburne.com
**Pitches For** ♠ ⊕ ♥ **Total** 189
**Facilities** ∮ 🔲 🔲 ⏴ ♣ 𝄐 ☉ 🍴 🛁 🖵 💧
𝄐 ⌂ ♀ 🔲 ⏴ 🔦 ⅗ 🛒 𝒫
**Nearby Facilities** ✓ ✓ ⏴ ⅗ ⟳
**Acreage** 70 **Open** March **to** October
**Access** Good **Site** Level
In the centre of the Cotswold Water Park - and ideal base for all watersports and nature lovers. Tennis on site.
**Nearest Town/Resort** Cirencester
**Directions** 4 miles south of Cirencester on the A419, follow signs to Cotswold Hoburne, in the Cotswold Water Park.

## CIRENCESTER

**Mayfield Touring Park,** Cheltenham Road, Perrotts Brook, Cirencester, Gloucestershire, GL7 7BH
**Tel:** 01285 831301
**Email:** mayfield-park@cirencester.fsbusiness.co.uk
www.mayfieldpark.co.uk
**Pitches For** ♠ ⊕ ♥ **Total** 76
**Facilities** ∮ 🔲 🔲 ⏴ ♣ 𝄐 ☉ 🛁 🖵 💧
𝄐 ⏴ ⌂ 🛒 🔲 🖵 ⅗ 𝒫
**Nearby Facilities** ✓ ✓ ⏴ ⅗ ⟳ 𝒫 𝒫
**Acreage** 10 **Open** All Year
**Access** Good **Site** Lev/Slope
In a position central to the Cotswolds with pleasant views and a warm welcome. This site benefits from having a variety of pitch types with something to suit every need.
**Nearest Town/Resort** Cirencester
**Directions** On A435, 13miles Cheltenham and 2miles Cirencester. From Cirencester by-pass A419/A417 take the Burford Road exit then follow camping and caravan signs.
≠ Kemble

## CIRENCESTER

**Second Chance Caravan Park,** Nr Marston Meysey, Wiltshire, SN6 6SN
**Tel:** 01285 810675/810939
**Pitches For** ♠ ⊕ ♥ **Total** 26
**Facilities** ∮ 🔲 🔲 ⏴ ♣ 𝄐 ☉ 🛁 🖵 💧
🔲 🔲 ⅗ ⋇

Set in the Cotswold Water Park with its own four tranquil lakes teeming with wildlife this friendly park offers a terrific range of facilities in and around our Lakeside Club. Great for families, ideal for walkers, nature lovers and birdwatchers too!

**For a brochure or to make a booking**
Call: **01285 860216** or visit: **www.hoburne.com**

**Nearby Facilities** ┌ ✦ ⚓ ❋ ⚵
**Acreage** 2 **Open** March **to** November
**Access** Good **Site** Level
Riverside location with private fishing and access for your own canoe. The first camping/caravan park on the Thames Path, great for exploring the upper reaches of the Thames. Ideal base for touring the Cotswolds and visiting Cirencester. AA 3 Pennants.
**Nearest Town/Resort** Castle Eaton/ Fairford
**Directions** Between Swindon and Cirencester on the A419. Turn off at the Fairford/Marston Meysey exit and follow the caravan park signs. Proceed approx. 3 miles then turn right at the Castle Eaton signpost. We are on the right.
⚏ Swindon

## COLEFORD

**Bracelands - Forestry Commission Caravan & Camping Site,** Christchurch, Forest of Dean, Coleford, Gloucestershire, GL16 7NN
**Tel:** 0131 314 6505
**Email:** info@forestholidays.co.uk
www.forestholidays.co.uk
**Pitches For** ▲ ♚ ⚘ **Total** 520
**Facilities** ᵭ ∱ ⒲ ♣ ┌ ⊙ ⌿ ▣ ☎ ▨◀┤▣ ☪ ⚲
**Nearby Facilities** ✦ U ♫ ❋
**Acreage** 14 **Open** 18 March **to** 1 Nov
**Access** Good **Site** Sloping
Panoramic views over the magnificent countryside, Highmeadow Wood and the Wye Valley. Watch Peregrines at Symonds Yat, plus a host of outdoor activities.
**Nearest Town/Resort** Coleford
**Directions** At the crossroads of the A4136 and minor road at the Pike House Inn (1 mile north of Coleford), go north for ½ mile following campsite signs. Reception for Bracelands is at the Christchurch site.
⚏ Gloucester

## COLEFORD

**Christchurch - Forestry Commission Caravan & Camping Site,** Christchurch, Coleford, Gloucestershire, GL16 7NN
**Tel:** 0131 314 6505
**Email:** info@forestholidays.co.uk

www.forestholidays.co.uk
**Pitches For** ▲ ♚ ⚘ **Total** 280
**Facilities** ᵭ ∱ ⒲ ♣ ┌ ⊙ ⌿ ⚐ ▣ ☎ ⚲ ⒧ ⓖ ⚲ ⚎ ▣ ▣ ⚲
**Nearby Facilities** ┌ ✦ ⚵ U ♫ ❋
**Open** 18 March **to** 1 Nov
**Access** Good **Site** Sloping
Situated high above the beautiful Wye Valley, with waymarked walking routes down to the river through the surrounding woodland. Near to Clearwell Caves ancient iron mines. Laundry service. Sorry No dogs.
**Nearest Town/Resort** Coleford
**Directions** At the crossroads of the A4136 1 mile north of Coleford, go north for ½ mile following signs to the campsite. Reception is on the left.
⚏ Gloucester

## COLEFORD

**Woodlands - Forestry Commission Caravan Site,** Christchurch, Forest of Dean, Coleford, Gloucestershire, GL16 7NN
**Tel:** 0131 314 6505
**Email:** info@forestholidays.co.uk
www.forestholidays.co.uk
**Pitches For** ♚ ⚘ **Total** 90
**Facilities** ∱ ☎▨◀┤▣ ☪ ⚲
**Nearby Facilities** ✦ U ♫ ❋
**Acreage** 22 **Open** 18 March **to** Oct
**Access** Good **Site** Level
A superbly wooded site with pitches set amongst trees. Ideal for a peaceful, tranquil break. Note : This site has NO toilets.
**Nearest Town/Resort** Coleford
**Directions** At the crossroads of the A4136 and a minor road at Pike House Inn, 1 mile north of Coleford, go north for ½ mile following campsite signs. Reception for Woodlands is at Christchurch site.
⚏ Gloucester

## COLEFORD

**Woodlands View Caravan Park,** Sling, Coleford, Gloucestershire, GL16 8JA
**Tel:** 01594 835127
**Pitches For** ▲ ♚ ⚘ **Total** 20
**Facilities** ∱ ⒲ ⒧ ♣ ┌ ⊙ ⌿ ☎ ⒮ ⓖ ⚎ ▣ ▣ ⚲

**Nearby Facilities** ┌ ✦ U ♫
**Acreage** 1½ **Open** April **to** October
**Access** Good **Site** Level
Near to Clearwell Caves, Puzzle Wood, Dean Heritage Centre and Dean Forest Railway. You can also telephone us on 01989 750468.
**Nearest Town/Resort** Coleford
**Directions** From Coleford take the B4228 towards Chepstow, after ½ a mile you will pass Puzzle Wood on the right, we are signposted ½ mile on the left.
⚏ Lydney

## DURSLEY

**Hogsdown Caravan & Camping,** Hogsdown Farm, Lower Wick, Dursley, Gloucestershire, GL11 6DD
**Tel:** 01453 810224
**Pitches For** ▲ ♚ ⚘ **Total** 45
**Facilities** ∱ ⒧ ⒲ ♣ ┌ ⊙ ⌿ ▣ ☎ ⒮ ⓖ ⚎ ▣ ▣ ⚲ ⚲
**Nearby Facilities** ┌ ✦
**Open** All Year **Access** Good **Site** Level
Ideal for Gloucester, Bath and Bristol.
**Nearest Town/Resort** Berkley
**Directions** Follow signs from Berkley on the A38.
⚏ Dursley

## GLOUCESTER

**The Red Lion Inn Caravan & Camping Park,** Wainlode Hill, Norton, Gloucestershire, GL2 9LW
**Tel:** 01452 730251
www.redlioninn-caravancampingpark.co.uk
**Pitches For** ▲ ♚ ⚘ **Total** 109
**Facilities** ᵭ ∱ ⒧ ⒲ ♣ ┌ ⊙ ⌿ ▣ ☎ ⒮ ⓖ ⚲ ✗▨◀┤▣ ☪ ⚲ ⚲ ⚲
**Nearby Facilities** ┌ ✦ ⚵ U ♫
**Acreage** 10 **Open** All Year
**Access** Good **Site** Level
On the banks of the River Severn with a riverside pub.
**Nearest Town/Resort** Gloucester/ Tewkesbury
**Directions** From Tewkesbury take the A38 south for 3 miles, turn right onto the B4213. After 3 miles turn left to Wainlode Hill, 350 yards alongside the River Severn, park is on the left.
⚏ Gloucester

## Tudor Caravan & Camping Park

**Shepherds Patch, Slimbridge, Gloucester GL2 7BP**  Tel: (01453) 890483

**www.tudorcaravanpark.com**

Quiet, country site under the personal supervision of resident owners Keith, Joan & Robin Fairall. Shepherds Patch is a small community skirting one side of the Gloucester - Sharpness Ship Canal (for a spot of fishing). On the far side of the canal is the World famous Slimbridge Wild Fowl Trust, a sanctuary to many thousands of migratory birds and the largest collection of resident ducks, geese and swans in the World.

- *OPEN ALL YEAR* • *SEPARATE AREA FOR ADULTS ONLY*
- *SEPARATE RALLY FIELD* • *PETS WELCOME*
- *DAVID BELLAMY GOLD WINNERS SINCE 2000*

---

## LECHLADE

**Bridge House Campsite,** Bridge House, Lechlade, Gloucestershire, GL7 3AG
**Tel:** 01367 252348 **Fax:** 01367 252348
Pitches For ▲ ⬟ ⬤ **Total** 51
Facilities ⬤ ⬤ ⬤ ⬤ ⬤ ⬤ ⬤ ⬤ ⬤ ⬤
**Nearby Facilities** ✦ ⬤
**Acreage** 3½ **Open** March **to** October
**Site** Level
Ideal for touring Cotswolds and Upper Thames.
**Nearest Town/Resort** Lechlade
**Directions** Lechlade A361 to Swindon. Opposite Riverside car park.
⬤ Swindon

## MORETON VALENCE

**Gables Farm Caravan & Camping Site,** Moreton Valence, Gloucestershire, GL2 7ND
**Tel:** 01452 720331
Pitches For ▲ ⬟ ⬤ **Total** 30
Facilities ⬤ ⬤ ⬤ ⬤ ⬤ ⬤ ⬤ ⬤ ⬤ ⬤
**Nearby Facilities** ✦
**Acreage** 3 **Open** March **to** Nov
**Access** Good **Site** Level
**Nearest Town/Resort** Gloucester
**Directions** Leave the M5 at junction 12 or 13 and take the A38 for 1½ miles. 6 miles south of Gloucester.

⬤ Gloucester

## MORETON-IN-MARSH

**Cross Hands Inn,** Salford Hill, Moreton-in-Marsh, Gloucestershire, GL56 0SP
**Tel:** 01608 643106
**Email:** crosshandsinn@hotmail.com
**www.crosshandsinn.co.uk**
Pitches For ▲ ⬟ ⬤ **Total** 18
Facilities ⬤ ⬤ ⬤ ⬤ ⬤ ⬤ ⬤ ⬤ ⬤
**Nearby Facilities** ⬤ ✦ ⬤ ⬤
**Open** All Year
**Access** Good **Site** Level
Ideal for touring the Cotswolds.
**Nearest Town/Resort** Chipping Norton
**Directions** On the A44 between Chipping Norton and Moreton-in-Marsh.
⬤ Kingham

## MORETON-IN-MARSH

**Moreton-In-Marsh Caravan Club Site,** Bourton Road, Moreton-in-Marsh, Gloucestershire, GL56 0BT
**Tel:** 01608 650519
**www.caravanclub.co.uk**
Pitches For ⬟ ⬤ **Total** 182
Facilities ⬤ ⬤ ⬤ ⬤ ⬤ ⬤ ⬤ ⬤ ⬤

---

**Nearby Facilities** ✦
**Acreage** 21 **Open** All Year
**Access** Good **Site** Level
Attractive, wooded site offering crazy golf, 5-a-side football, volleyball and a boules pitch. Near Batsford Arboretum & Falconry Centre and Sleepy Hollow Farm Park. Non members welcome. Booking essential.
**Nearest Town/Resort** Moreton-in-Marsh
**Directions** Leave Evesham on the A44, site entrance is on the left approx. 1¼ miles past Bourton-on-the-Hill and 150 yards before Moreton-in-Marsh sign. NB: No arrivals before 1pm at weekends and in peak periods.

## SLIMBRIDGE

**Tudor Caravanning & Camping Park,** Shepherds Patch, Slimbridge, Gloucestershire, GL2 7BP
**Tel:** 01453 890483
**Email:** cades@tudorcaravanpark.co.uk
**www.tudorcaravanpark.com**
Pitches For ▲ ⬟ ⬤ **Total** 75
Facilities ⬤ ⬤ ⬤ ⬤ ⬤ ⬤ ⬤ ⬤ ⬤ ⬤
**Nearby Facilities** ⬤ ✦ ⬤
**Acreage** 7¼ **Open** All Year
**Access** Good **Site** Level
Sharpness Canal next property to Wetlands Centre. AA 3 Pennants.
**Nearest Town/Resort** Dursley/Gloucester
**Directions** Leave the M5 at junction 13 and follow signs for 'WWT Wetlands Centre, Slimbridge'. 1½ miles off the A38 at the rear of the Tudor Arms Pub.
⬤ Dursley

## TEWKESBURY

**Croft Farm Leisure & Water Park,** Brendons Hardwick, Tewkesbury, Gloucestershire, GL20 7EE
**Tel:** 01684 772321 **Fax:** 01684 773379
**Email:** alan@croftfarmleisure.co.uk
**www.croftfarmleisure.co.uk**
Pitches For ▲ ⬟ ⬤ **Total** 60
Facilities ⬤ ⬤ ⬤ ⬤ ⬤ ⬤ ⬤ ⬤ ⬤ ⬤
**Nearby Facilities** ⬤ ✦ ⬤ ⬤ ⬤ ⬤
**Acreage** 10 **Open** 1 March **to** 30 Nov
**Access** Good **Site** Level
Lakeside location with own watersports lake for sailing, windsurfing and canoeing.
**Nearest Town/Resort** Tewkesbury
**Directions** 1½ miles north-east of Tewkesbury on B4080.
⬤ Ashchurch

---

## TEWKESBURY

**Dawleys Caravan Park,** Owls Lane, Shuthonger, Tewkesbury, Gloucestershire, GL20 6EQ
**Tel:** 01684 292622 **Fax:** 01684 292622
**www.ukparks.co.uk/dawleys**
Pitches For ▲ ⬟ ⬤ **Total** 20
Facilities ⬤ ⬤ ⬤ ⬤ ⬤ ⬤ ⬤ ⬤ ⬤
**Nearby Facilities** ⬤ ✦ ⬤ ⬤ ⬤
**Acreage** 3 **Open** April **to** Sept
**Access** Fair **Site** Sloping
secluded rural site, near a river. Close to the M5 and M50.
**Nearest Town/Resort** Cheltenham/Gloucester
**Directions** A38 north from Tewkesbury, approximately 2 miles on the left hand side. Or 1¼ miles south on A38 from M50 junction 1.
⬤ Cheltenham

## TEWKESBURY

**Mill Avon Holiday Park,** Gloucester Road, Tewkesbury, Gloucestershire, GL20 5SW
**Tel:** 01684 296876
Pitches For ⬟ ⬤ **Total** 24
Facilities ⬤ ⬤ ⬤ ⬤ ⬤ ⬤ ⬤ ⬤ ⬤ ⬤
⬤ ⬤ ⬤ ⬤ ⬤
**Nearby Facilities** ⬤ ✦ ⬤ ⬤ ⬤
**Open** March **to** Oct
**Access** Good **Site** Level
Alongside the River Avon.
**Nearest Town/Resort** Tewkesbury
**Directions** On the A38, ¼ of a mile south of the town centre.
⬤ Tewkesbury

## TEWKESBURY

**Tewkesbury Abbey Caravan Club Site,** Gander Lane, Tewkesbury, Gloucestershire, GL20 5PG
**Tel:** 01684 294035
**www.caravanclub.co.uk**
Pitches For ▲ ⬟ ⬤ **Total** 160
Facilities ⬤ ⬤ ⬤ ⬤ ⬤ ⬤ ⬤
**Nearby Facilities** ⬤ ✦
**Acreage** 9 **Open** April **to** Oct
**Access** Good **Site** Lev/Slope
Situated adjacent to the ancient Abbey. Many interesting walks, historic buildings and museums locally. Near the Battle Trail and Royal Worcester Factory. Non members welcome. Booking essential.
**Nearest Town/Resort** Tewkesbury
**Directions** Leave the M5 at junction 9 and take the A438 signposted Tewkesbury. At the traffic lights by Safeway go straight on, at the town centre crossroads keep left and after 200 yards turn left into Gander Lane, site is on the left.
⬤ Tewkesbury

---

### TEWKESBURY

**Winchcombe Camping & Caravanning Club Site,** Brooklands Farm, Alderton, Nr Tewkesbury, Gloucestershire, GL20 8NX
Tel: 01242 620259
www.campingandcaravanningclub.co.uk
Pitches For ▲ ♦ ♦ Total 80
Facilities ⬥ ♪ 🖿 🖩 ♨ ♪ 🖂 ⊙ ⊿ 🝰 ⊙ ♥
🝰 ⊙ 🝰 ♠ 🝰 ⊕ 🖂 🖳 ⊡ ⚥ ⏃
Nearby Facilities ✓
Acreage 20 Open March to Jan
Access Good Site Level
Set amidst the lovely Cotswold countryside, with its own fishing lake. BTB 4 Star Graded, AA 3 Pennants and David Bellamy Gold Award. Non members welcome.
**Nearest Town/Resort** Tewkesbury
**Directions** From Tewkesbury take the A46, at the roundabout go straight over then take the B4077 to Stow-on-the-Wold, site is on the right in 3 miles.
⚐ Tewkesbury

# HAMPSHIRE

### ASHURST

**Ashurst Caravan & Camping Site - Forestry Commission,** Lyndhurst Road, Ashurst, Hampshire, SO42 7QH
Tel: 0131 314 6505
Email: info@forestholidays.co.uk
www.forestholidays.co.uk
Pitches For ▲ ♦ ♦ Total 280
Facilities ⬥ 🖩 ♨ ♪ 🖂 ⊙ ⊿ 🝰 ⊙ ♥
🝰 ⊡ 🖂 ⚥
Nearby Facilities ⌐ U
Acreage 23 Open 25 March to 27 Sept
Access Good Site Level
10 minutes walk to the shops in Ashurst Village.
**Nearest Town/Resort** Lyndhurst
**Directions** 5 miles southwest of Southampton on the A35, signposted.
⚐ Ashurst

### BEAULIEU

**Decoy Pond Farm,** Beaulieu Road, Beaulieu, Brockenhurst, Hampshire, SO42 7YQ
Tel: 023 8029 2652
Pitches For ♦ ♦ Total 4
Facilities 🖩 ♨ ♪ ♥ ♪
Nearby Facilities ⌐ ⚓ U
Acreage ½ Open March to October
Access Good Site Level
Ideal for the New Forest.
**Nearest Town/Resort** Lyndhurst
**Directions** From Lyndhurst take the B3056, after crossing railway bridge, first on the left.

### BRANSGORE

**Harrow Wood Farm Caravan Park,** Poplar Lane, Bransgore, Nr Christchurch, Dorset, BH23 8JE
Tel: 01425 672487 Fax: 01425 672487
Email: harrowwood@caravan-sites.co.uk
www.caravan-sites.co.uk
Pitches For ♦ ♦ Total 60
Facilities ♪ 🖩 🖩 ♨ ♪ 🖂 ⊙ ⊿ 🝰 ⊙
🝰 ⊙ 🝰 ⊡ ⏃
Nearby Facilities ⌐ ✓ ⚓ ✚ U
Acreage 6 Open 1 March to 6 January
Access Good Site Level

Within easy reach of the New Forest and the sea.
**Nearest Town/Resort** Christchurch/ Bournemouth
**Directions** On the A35, 11 miles south-west of Lyndhurst turn right at the Cat & Fiddle Public House. Go 2 miles to Bransgore and turn first right after the school into Poplar Lane.
⚐ Hinton Admiral

### BROCKENHURST

**Aldridge Hill - Forestry Commission Caravan & Camping Site,** Brockenhurst, Hampshire, SO42 7QD
Tel: 0131 314 6505
Email: info@forestholidays.co.uk
www.forestholidays.co.uk
Pitches For ▲ ♦ ♦ Total 200
Facilities ♥ 🝰 🖂 ⊡ 🖂
Nearby Facilities U
Acreage 22
Access Good Site Level
In a heathland clearing in the heart of the New Forest, on the edge of Blackwater Stream. Note : This site has NO toilets.
SITE OPENS: 26 May to 6 June then 16 June to 5 September.
**Nearest Town/Resort** Brockenhurst
**Directions** At the Ford in Brockenhurst turn right, the site is 1 mile on the right.
⚐ Brockenhurst

### BROCKENHURST

**Hollands Wood Caravan & Camping Site - Forestry Commission,** Lyndhurst Road, Brockenhurst, Hampshire, SO42 7QH
Tel: 0131 314 6505
Email: info@forestholidays.co.uk
www.forestholidays.co.uk
Pitches For ▲ ♦ ♦ Total 600
Facilities ⬥ 🖩 ♨ ♪ 🖂 ⊙ ⊿ 🝰 ⊙ ♥
🝰 ⊕ 🖂 ⚥
Nearby Facilities ⌐ U
Acreage 168 Open 25 March to 27 Sept
Access Good Site Level
Sheltered site in an oak woodland. Special 'dog free' area. Brockenhurst Village nearby.
**Nearest Town/Resort** Brockenhurst
**Directions** ½ mile north of Brockenhurst on the A337, signposted.
⚐ Brockenhurst

### BROCKENHURST

**Roundhill Caravan & Camping Site - Forestry Commission,** Beaulieu Road, Brockenhurst, Hampshire, SO42 7QL
Tel: 0131 314 6505
Email: info@forestholidays.co.uk
www.forestholidays.co.uk
Pitches For ▲ ♦ ♦ Total 500
Facilities ⬥ 🖩 ♨ ⊙ ♥ 🝰 ♠ 🝰 ⊕ 🖂 ⚥
Nearby Facilities ⌐ U
Acreage 156 Open 25 March to 27 Sept
Access Good Site Level
Wide open heathland site in the heart of the New Forest. Junior fishing on site. Speacial dog free area.
**Nearest Town/Resort** Brockenhurst
**Directions** On the B3055, 2 miles south east of Brockenhurst off the A337, signposted.
⚐ Brockenhurst

### CADNAM

**Ocknell/Longbeech Caravan & Camping Sites - Forestry Commission,** Fritham, Nr Lyndhurst, Hampshire, SO43 7HH
Tel: 0131 314 6505
Email: info@forestholidays.co.uk
www.forestholidays.co.uk
Pitches For ▲ ♦ ♦ Total 480
Facilities 🖩 ♨ ♥ 🝰 ♠ 🝰 ⊡ 🖂
Nearby Facilities ⌐ ✓ U
Acreage 48 Open 25 March to 26 Sept
Access Good Site Level
Two contrasting sites. Ocknell has spectacular views over the surrounding countryside and Longbeech is set in an ancient oakwood. Toilets at Ocknell only.
**Nearest Town/Resort** Lyndhurst
**Directions** From the A31 at Cadnam take the B3079, then the B3078 via Brook and Fritham (signposted).

### FAREHAM

**Dibles Park,** Dibles Road, Warsash, Southampton, Hampshire, SO31 9SA
Tel: 01489 575232
Pitches For ▲ ♦ ♦ Total 14
Facilities ♪ 🖩 ♨ ♪ 🖂 ⊙ ⊿ 🝰 ⊙ ♥
🝰 ⊙ 🝰 ⊕ 🖂
Nearby Facilities ⌐ ✓ ⚓ ✚ U ♪
Acreage ¾ Open All Year
Access Good Site Level
Shingle beach 1½ miles.
**Nearest Town/Resort** Fareham
**Directions** Turn left off the A27 (Portsmouth to Southampton) opposite Lloyds Bank into Locks Road (sinposted Warsash). In about 1½ miles at the T-Junction turn right into Warsash Road, in about 300yds turn left into Fleet End Road. Take the second right and we are on the right.
⚐ Swanwick

### FORDINGBRIDGE

**Sandy Balls,** Godshill, Fordingbridge, Hampshire, SP6 2JZ
Tel: 01425 653042 Fax: 01425 653067
Email: post@sandy-balls.co.uk
www.sandy-balls.co.uk
Pitches For ▲ ♦ ♦ Total 233
Facilities ⬥ ♪ 🖯 🖩 🖩 ♨ ♪ 🖂 ⊙ ⊿ 🝰 ⊙ ♥
🝰 ⚥ ⊙ 🝰 ✗ ♪ 🖩 🝰 ♪ 🝰 ⚒ 🝰 ✚ 🖂 ⊕
Nearby Facilities ⌐ ✓ U ↺
Acreage 120 Open All Year
Access Good Site Level
Situated between the Hampshire Avon and the New Forest, ideal for exploring the New Forest and surrounding area.
**Nearest Town/Resort** Fordingbridge
**Directions** Take the B3078 east from Fordingbridge, 1½ miles to Godshill.
⚐ Salisbury

### HAMBLE

**Riverside Holidays,** Satchell Lane, Hamble, Hampshire, SO31 4HR
Tel: 023 8045 3220 Fax: 023 8045 3611
Email: enquiries@riversideholidays.co.uk
www.riversideholidays.co.uk
Pitches For ▲ ♦ ♦ Total 77
Facilities ⬥ ♪ 🖩 🖩 ♨ ♪ 🖂 ⊙ ⊿ 🝰 ⊙ ♥
🝰 ⊙ ✚ 🖂 ⊡ 🖂 ⚥ ♪ ⏃
Nearby Facilities ⌐ ✓ ⚓ ✚ U
Acreage 2 Open March to October

A delightful, tranquil setting adjoining a tidal creek of Chichester harbour. Short walk to beaches, restaurants & bars. Free slipway and fishing. Modern toilet blocks/Free showers. Shop. Children's play area.

**100 Fishery Lane, Hayling Island, Hants PO11 9NR**
Tel: 023 9246 2164  E-mail: camping@fisherycreek.fsnet.co.uk  www.keyparks.co.uk

**Access** Good **Site** Lev/Slight Slope Overlooking the River Hamble with a marina below the park. In the very pretty village of Hamble.
**Nearest Town/Resort** Southampton
**Directions** Leave the M27 at junction 8, follow signs for Hamble Village on the B3397 for approx. 2 miles, then turn left into Satchell Lane. Riverside is on the left hand side of Satchell Lane above Mercury Marina.
🚌 Hamble

**HAYLING ISLAND**
**Fishery Creek Caravan & Camping Park,** 100 Fishery Lane, Hayling Island, Hampshire, PO11 9NR
**Tel:** 023 9246 2164 **Fax:** 023 9246 0741
**Email:** camping@fisherycreek.co.uk
www.keyparks.co.uk
**Pitches For** ▲ ⊕ 🚐 **Total** 165
**Facilities** ⅄ ∤ 🆄 ♨ 🏧 ⊙ ⌿ 🔲 📞 🏧 🎪 🗑 🏠 🅰️ ⌂ ⊞ 🄰 ✄ ♒
**Nearby Facilities** 🏊 ✦ 🛝 🛶 ∪ ⋥ 🅿️
**Acreage** 8 **Open** March to October
**Access** Good **Site** Level
Alongside a beautiful tidal creek, offering peace and tranquility. Own slipway, short path to beach. Luxury tent rental available.
**Nearest Town/Resort** Hayling Island
**Directions** Turn off the A27 at Havant, take the A3023 to Hayling Island. Turn left at the first roundabout and follow brown tourism signs to Fishery Creek, left after Mengham Town, left into Fishery Lane, park is at the end of the lane.
🚌 Havant

**HAYLING ISLAND**
**Fleet Park,** Yew Tree Road, Hayling Island, Hampshire, PO11 0QF
**Tel:** 02392 463684
**Email:** lowertye@aol.com
www.haylingcampsites.co.uk
**Pitches For** ▲ ⊕ 🚐 **Total** 75
**Facilities** ∤ ∤ 🆄 ♨ ⌿ ⊙ ⌿ 🔲 🏧 🅰️ ⊞ 🄰 ✄
**Nearby Facilities** 🏊 ✦ 🛝 🛶 ∪ ⋥ 🅿️
**Acreage** 3 **Open** March to October
**Access** Good **Site** Level
Quiet family site on a creek. Near a Ferry Port. Ideal for Portsmouth, Southsea and the Isle of Wight. Easy touring for New

Forest and Beaulieu.
**Nearest Town/Resort** Havant/Southsea
**Directions** Follow A3023 from Havant. Approx. 2 miles on Island turn left into Copse Lane then first right into Yew Tree Road.
🚌 Havant

**HAYLING ISLAND**
**Lower Tye Camp Site,** Copse Lane, Hayling Island, Hampshire, PO11 0QB
**Tel:** 023 9246 2479 **Fax:** 023 9246 2479
**Email:** lowertye@aol.com
www.haylingcampsites.co.uk
**Pitches For** ▲ ⊕ 🚐 **Total** 150
**Facilities** ∤ 🆄 ♨ 🏧 ⊙ ⌿ 🔲 📞 🏧 🅰️ 🗑 🅰️ ⊞ 🄰 ✄ 🎪
**Nearby Facilities** 🏊 ✦ 🛝 🛶 ∪ ⋥ 🅿️
**Acreage** 5 **Open** March to November
**Access** Good **Site** Level
Heated swimming pool on site. Near to Portsmouth, the Isle of Wight, Singlton Open Air Museum, Chichester, an excellent Blue Flag beach and all water sports.
**Nearest Town/Resort** Havant
**Directions** Exit the M27 or the A3M motorway at Havant. Follow the A3023 from Havant, turn left into Copse Lane. You will see the sign after being on Hayling Island for approx 1¼ miles.
🚌 Havant

**HAYLING ISLAND**
**Oven Camping Site,** Manor Road, Hayling Island, Hampshire, PO11 0QX
**Tel:** 02392 464695 **Fax:** 02392 462479
**Email:** lowertye@aol.com
www.haylingcampsites.co.uk
**Pitches For** ▲ ⊕ 🚐 **Total** 330
**Facilities** ∤ 🆄 ♨ 🏧 ✖ 🔲 🅰️ ♨ ⚡ 🗑 🅰️ ⊞ 🄰 ✄ 🎪
**Nearby Facilities** 🏊 ✦ 🛝 🛶 ∪ ⋥ 🅿️
**Acreage** 10 **Open** March to Dec Incl.
**Access** Good **Site** Level
Heated swimming pool. Excellent touring area for Portsmouth, Chichester, New Forest etc. Safe, clean, Blue Flag beaches, excellent for water sports. Excellent Rally site at discount prices. We accept motorcycles at our discretion.
**Nearest Town/Resort** Havant
**Directions** Exit M27 or the A37 at Havant. Take the A3023 from Havant, approx 3 miles

after crossing bridge onto Hayling Island bear right at the roundabout. Site is on the left in 450yds.
🚌 Havant

**LYNDHURST**
**Denny Wood - Forestry Commission Caravan & Camping Site,** Nr Lyndhurst, Hampshire, SO43 7AA
**Tel:** 0131 314 6505
**Email:** info@forestholidays.co.uk
www.forestholidays.co.uk
**Pitches For** ▲ ⊕ 🚐 **Total** 170
**Facilities** 📞 🏧 🔲 🄰 🎪
**Nearby Facilities** ∪
**Acreage** 27 **Open** 25 March to 26 Sept
**Access** Good **Site** Level
Peaceful, grassland site among scattered oaks. New Forest ponies roam free around the site. Note : This site has NO toilets.
**Nearest Town/Resort** Lyndhurst
**Directions** Take the B3056 from Lyndhurst, the site is 2½ miles on the right.
🚌 Brockenhurst

**LYNDHURST**
**Matley Wood - Forestry Commission,** Nr Lyndhurst, Hampshire, SO32 7FZ
**Tel:** 0131 314 6505
**Email:** info@forestholidays.co.uk
www.forestholidays.co.uk
**Pitches For** ▲ ⊕ 🚐 **Total** 70
**Facilities** 📞 🏧 🔲 🄰 🎪
**Nearby Facilities**
**Acreage** 5 **Open** March to Sept
**Access** Good **Site** Level
A small, secluded site within the natural woodland of the New Forest. Note : This site has NO toilets.
**Nearest Town/Resort** Lyndhurst
**Directions** Take the B3056 from Lyndhurst, the site is 2 miles on the left. Reception for Matley Wood is at Denny Wood.
🚌 Brockenhurst

**MILFORD-ON-SEA**
**Lytton Lawn,** Lymore Lane, Milford-on-Sea, Hampshire, SO41 0TX
**Tel:** 01590 648331 **Fax:** 01590 645610
**Email:** holidays@shorefield.co.uk
www.shorefield.co.uk
**Pitches For** ▲ ⊕ 🚐 **Total** 136

# HAMPSHIRE

**Facilities** ⚗ ☆ ╪ 🖃 🅷 🆄 ⚓ ⌂ ⊙ ⤸ 🚃 ▢ 🛁 ⚸ 🛈 ⚙ 🏧 ⌷ ✿⤝🖃 🖸
**Nearby Facilities** ⌂ ✔ ⚓ 🜨 🜉
**Acreage** 4 **Open** 10 Feb **to** 3 Jan
**Access** Good **Site** Lev/Slope
Views of the Isle of Wight. 1 mile from the beach and 2 miles from the New Forest. FREE membership to the leisure club, restaurant, licensed club, colour TV, games room, indoor/outdoor swimming pools and tennis are available at our sister site Shorefield Country Park (2½ miles).
**Nearest Town/Resort** Lymington
**Directions** From Lymington take the A337 towards Everton. Turn left onto the B3058 towards Milford-on-Sea and take the second left into Lymore Lane.
⚡ New Milton

## NEW MILTON

**Hoburne Bashley,** Sway Road, New Milton, Hampshire, BH25 5QR
**Tel:** 01425 612340 **Fax:** 01425 632732
**Email:** enquiries@hoburne.com
**www.hoburne.com**
**Pitches For** ⌷ 🚃 **Total** 307
**Facilities** ╪ 🖃 🅷 🆄 ⚓ ⌂ ⊙ ⤸ 🚃 ▢ 🛁 ⚙ 🏦 ⚸ ✕ ▽ 🛈 🉐 ⋔ ⌵ ╈⤝🖃 🖸
**Nearby Facilities** ⌂ ⚓ 🜨 🜉 🜉
**Access** Good **Site** Lev/Slope
New Forest - 2 miles from the beach and 10 miles from Bournemouth. Own golf course and tennis. Many facilities.
**Nearest Town/Resort** New Milton
**Directions** From the A35 Lyndhurst/Bournemouth road, take the B3055 signposted Sway. Over crossroads at 2¼ miles. Park is ½ mile on left.
⚡ New Milton

## NEW MILTON

**Setthorns Caravan & Camping Site - Forestry Commission,** Wootton, New Milton, Hampshire, BH25 5WA
**Tel:** 0131 314 6505
**Email:** info@forestholidays.co.uk
**www.forestholidays.co.uk**
**Pitches For** ⚗ ⌷ 🚃 **Total** 320
**Facilities** ╪ 🚃 🛁 ⤝🖃 🖸 ⚹
**Nearby Facilities** ⌂ 🜨
**Acreage** 60 **Open** All Year
**Access** Good **Site** Level
Open woodland site with pitches nestling among pine and oak trees. Select pitches available with electric hook-up, picnic table and more space. This site has NO toilet facilities.
**Nearest Town/Resort** New Milton
**Directions** Take the A35 from Lyndhurst, signposted 7 miles south of Lyndhurst.
⚡ New Milton

## OWER

**Green Pastures Farm,** Ower, Romsey, Hampshire, SO51 6AJ
**Tel:** 023 8081 4444
**Email:** enquiries@greenpasturesfarm.com
**www.greenpasturesfarm.com**
**Pitches For** ⚗ ⌷ 🚃 **Total** 45
**Facilities** ⚗ ╪ 🅷 🆄 ⚓ ⌂ ⊙ ⤸ ▢ 🛁
**Nearby Facilities** ⌂ ✔ 🆄 🜉
**Acreage** 5 **Open** 15 March **to** 31 October
**Access** Good **Site** Level
A grassy site on family run farm, within easy reach of the New Forest. Paultons Park 1 mile. Convenient for ferries. Ample space for children to play in full view of units. Separate toilet/shower room for the disabled. Day-kennelling available.
**Nearest Town/Resort** Romsey
**Directions** Leave the M27 at junction 2 and follow signposts for Salisbury for ½ a mile. Then start to follow our own signs. Also signposted from the A36 and the A3090 at Ower.
⚡ Romsey

## RINGWOOD

**Forest Edge Touring Park,** St Leonards, Ringwood, Hampshire, BH24 2SD
**Tel:** 01590 648331 **Fax:** 01590 645610
**Email:** holidays@shorefield.co.uk
**www.shorefield.co.uk**
**Pitches For** ⚗ ⌷ 🚃 **Total** 195
**Facilities** ╪ 🅷 ⚓ ⌂ ⊙ ⤸ 🚃 ▢ 🛁 🏦 ⚸ ⤝🖃 🖸
**Nearby Facilities** ⌂ ✔ 🆄
**Acreage** 8 **Open** 1 Feb **to** 1 Jan
**Access** Good **Site** Level
Close to Avon Forest and 9 miles from Bournemouth's beaches.
**Nearest Town/Resort** Ringwood
**Directions** 3 miles west of Ringwood off the A31. Turn left at second roundabout on the A31.
⚡ Bournemouth

## RINGWOOD

**Oakdene Forest Park,** St Leonards, Ringwood, Hampshire, BH24 2RZ
**Tel:** 01590 648331 **Fax:** 01590 645610
**Email:** holidays@shorefield.co.uk
**www.shorefield.co.uk**
**Pitches For** ⚗ ⌷ 🚃 **Total** 38
**Facilities** ╪ 🚃 🅷 🆄 ⚓ ⌂ ⊙ ⤸ 🚃 ▢ 🛁 🏦 ⚸ ✕ ▽ 🉐 🏧 ⋔ ✕⤝🖃 🖸
**Nearby Facilities** ⌂ ✔ 🆄
**Acreage** 55 **Open** 4 Feb **to** 4 Jan
**Access** Good **Site** Level
Bordering Avon Forest, surrounded by parkland and Forestry Commission land. 9 miles from Bournemouth beaches. Indoor

and outdoor swimming pools, plus flume, gym, sauna and steam room.
**Nearest Town/Resort** Ringwood/Bournemouth
**Directions** 3 miles west of Ringwood off the A31 just past St Leonards Hospital.
⚡ Bournemouth

## RINGWOOD

**The Red Shoot Camping Park Ltd.,** Linwood, Nr Ringwood, Hampshire, BH24 3QT
**Tel:** 01425 473789 **Fax:** 01425 471558
**Email:** enquiries@redshoot-campingpark.com
**www.redshoot-campingpark.com**
**Pitches For** ⚗ ⌷ 🚃 **Total** 130
**Facilities** ⚗ ╪ 🅷 ⚓ ⌂ ⊙ ⤸ 🚃 ▢ 🛁 ⚸ 🏦 ⋔ ⤝🖃 🖸
**Nearby Facilities** ⌂ ✔ 🜨 🆄 🜉 🜉
**Acreage** 4 **Open** March **to** October
**Access** Good **Site** Lev/Slope
Situated in a beautiful part of the New Forest. Half hour drive to Bournemouth coast, Salisbury and Southampton. Good pub adjacent. Mountain bike hire. Off peak tariff early and late season.
**Nearest Town/Resort** Ringwood.
**Directions** Fron Ringwood take A338, 2 miles north of Ringwood take right turn signed Moyles Court and Linwood. Follow signs to Linwood.
⚡ Brockenhurst.

## RINGWOOD

**Tree Tops Touring Caravan Park,** Hurn Road, Avon Castle, Matchams, RingwoodHampshire, BH24 2BP
**Tel:** 01425 475848
**Pitches For** ⚗ ⌷ 🚃
**Facilities** ☆ ╪ 🅷 🆄 ⚓ ⌂ ⊙ ⤸ 🚃 ▢ 🛁 ⚙ ▢ 🛁 🉐 A
**Nearby Facilities** ⌂ ✔ 🜨 🜉
**Open** Easter **to** Sept
**Access** Good **Site** Level
STRICTLY ADULTS ONLY. Ideal for touring Dorset and Hampshire. Sorry no dogs.
**Nearest Town/Resort** Ringwood
**Directions** Take the A31, at Ringwood filter left and follow signs to Matchams, site is 2 miles on the left.
⚡ Bournemouth

## ROMSEY

**Hill Farm Caravan Park,** Branches Lane, Sherfield English, Romsey, Hampshire, SO51 6FH
**Tel:** 01794 340402 **Fax:** 01794 342358
**Email:** gjb@hillfarmpark.com
**www.hillfarmpark.com**
**Pitches For** ⚗ ⌷ 🚃 **Total** 150
**Facilities** ⚗ ╪ 🖃 🅷 🆄 ⚓ ⌂ ⊙ ⤸ 🚃 ▢ 🛁

# HILL FARM
## Caravan Park

Branches Lane, Sherfield English,
Romsey, Hampshire SO51 6FH
Tel: 01794 340402   Fax: 01794 342358
E-mail: gjb@hillfarmpark.com
Web Site: www.hillfarmpark.com

A peaceful retreat away from the crowds. Set in 11 acres of beautiful countryside on the edge of the New Forest. 4 miles North West of Romsey and within easy reach of Salisbury, Winchester, Southampton and the South Coast. Family run site surrounded by fields and woodland. An ideal base to visit the South of England.

* Children's Play Area & Trampoline
* Two Toilet Blocks
* Food available on the Patio and to take away
* Launderette
* 9 Hole Pitch 'n' Putt Golf Course
* Licensed Convenience Store

**AA** ⊷

---

## You couldn't get closer to the beach...

A fully equipped 12 acre site right by the Solent. Touring and luxury caravans, heated outdoor pool. Only 10 minutes from cross-channel ferries. Restaurant and bar, park shop, all modern facilities. Special off-season rates. Discount for OAPs & CC members.

Southsea Leisure Park
Quote CADES06
Melville Road
Southsea
Hampshire PO4 9TB

**Southsea Leisure Park**

© **023 9273 5070**
Fax  023 9282 1302
email: info@southsealeisurepark.com
www.southsea-caravans-ltd.co.uk

---

## Red Shoot Camping Park

English Tourist Board

★★★★

### LINWOOD, NEAR RINGWOOD, HAMPSHIRE BH24 3QT
### TELEPHONE: (01425) 473789   FAX: (01425) 471558
enquiries@redshoot-campingpark.com   www.redshoot-campingpark.com

### APPROVED SITE FOR TENTS, CARAVANS AND MOTOR HOMES

Beautifully situated in the NEW FOREST, with lovely walks from the camp site gate. Ideal centre for walking, touring and for nature lovers, yet only half hours drive from Bournemouth and the sea.

❑ Excellent Toilet/Shower Facilities ❑ Electric Hook-ups ❑ Well Stocked Shop & Off Licence
❑ Children's Play Area ❑ Laundry Room ❑ Facilities for the Disabled ❑ Mountain Bike Hire
❑ Special Off Peak Tariff ❑ Owner supervised to high standard.

'Red Shoot Inn' lies adjacent to the camp site, and is an attractive old pub serving real ales, good food and welcoming families.

**For Details and Brochure send a S.A.E. to:**
**Nick & Jaqui Oldfield at the above address.**

*This popular little site has been owned and managed by the same family for over 30 years.*

🕭 🛇 🛒 ✕ ⌂ ✿ ⭢ 🏠 🖳 ⭧ ♨ ⌀
**Nearby Facilities** Г ✔ U ♬
**Acreage** 11 **Open** March **to** October
**Access** Good **Site** Lev/Slope
Set in beautiful Hampshire countryside we
offer a quiet, rural location. Just 3 miles
north of the New Forest and only 20
minutes from Salisbury, Winchester and
Southampton.
**Nearest Town/Resort** Romsey
**Directions** From Romsey take the A3090
west, turn right onto the A27 towards
Salisbury. In Sherfield English at the first
crossroads turn right into Branches Lane, site
is approx. 1 mile.
✈ Romsey

## SOUTHSEA
**Southsea Leisure Park,** Melville Road,
Southsea, Hampshire, PO4 9TB
**Tel:** 023 9273 5070 **Fax:** 023 9282 1302
**Email:** info@southsealeisurepark.com
www.southsealeisurepark.com
**Pitches For** ⚠ ⊕ 🚐 **Total** 216
**Facilities** ⏚ ∮ ⯐ 🖳 🛒 Г ⊙ ↲ 🛒 📺 🛒
🕭 � 🛇 🛒 ✕ ⵝ 🖻 🛒 ⯑ ⭢ 🖳 🖳 ⭧ ♨
**Nearby Facilities** Г ✔ ⅃ ㆞ ♬
**Acreage** 12 **Open** All Year
**Access** Good **Site** Level
Located beside the beach at the quieter
end of historic Portsmouth. Only 10
minutes from cross-channel ferries. Fully
equipped, modern touring facilities.
**Nearest Town/Resort** Portsmouth
**Directions** From M27/A27/A3M take
southbound A2030 for 4 miles, turn left onto
the A288 and follow signs.
✈ Portsmouth Harbour

## WINCHESTER
**Morn Hill Caravan Club Site,** Morn Hill,
Winchester, Hampshire, SO21 1HL
**Tel:** 01962 869877
www.caravanclub.co.uk
**Pitches For** ⚠ ⊕ 🚐 **Total** 140
Facilities ⏚ ∮ 🖳 🛒 Г ⎚ 🛒
ⅰ 🛇 🛒 ⌂ ⭢ 🖳 🖻
**Nearby Facilities** Г ✔
**Acreage** 9 **Open** March **to** Oct
**Access** Good **Site** Level
Large site. Near Paultons Leisure Park,
Marwell Zoo, Beaulieu, New Forest,
Broadlands and Watercress Railway Line.
Non members welcome. Booking essential.
**Directions** Leave the M3 at junction 9, at
roundabout keep left onto the A33 signposted
Southampton. At Spitfire roundabout turn left
onto the A31 signposted Alton, at next
roundabout follow signs for Easton, turn
immediately right in front of Percy Hobbs
Public House, site is 100 yards.
✈ Winchester

# HEREFORDSHIRE
## BROMYARD
**Boyce Caravan Park,** Stanford Bishop,
Bringsty, Nr Worcester, Worcestershire,
WR6 5UB
**Tel:** 01886 884248
**Email:** ah.richards@btopenworld.com
**Pitches For** ⊕ 🚐 **Total** 18

**Facilities** ⏚ ∮ 🖳 🛒 Г ⎚ ↲ 🛒 📺 🛒
🛇 🛒 ⌂ ⭢ 🖳 ⭧
**Nearby Facilities** ✔
**Acreage** 1½ **Open** March **to** October
**Access** Good **Site** Level
Ideal for exploring the heart of England
and the Welsh Marches etc.. Dogs are
welcome by arrangement. Booking is
advisable.
**Nearest Town/Resort** Bromyard
**Directions** 3 miles east of Bromyard off the
B4220. Follow official signs from the A44/
B4220 junction.

## BROMYARD
**Bromyard Downs Caravan Club Site,**
Brockhampton, Bringsty, Worcester, WR6
5TE
**Tel:** 01885 482607
www.caravanclub.co.uk
**Pitches For** ⊕ 🚐 **Total** 40
**Facilities** ∮ ⌂ ⅰ ⊙ ⭢
**Nearby Facilities** ✔
**Acreage** 4 **Open** March **to** Oct
**Access** Good **Site** Lev/Slope
Rural, woodland site situated in beautiful
countryside. Ideal for walkers. Many
historic houses, museums and steam
railways nearby. Own sanitation required.
Non members welcome. Booking essential.
**Nearest Town/Resort** Bromyard
**Directions** From Leominster on the A44, on
the outskirts of Bromyard follow signs for
Worcester round Bromyard Bypass, DO NOT
go into Bromyard. Site entrance is on the
approx. 1½ miles past Bromyard (¼ mile past
the B4220 junction and immediately past
road signposted Bromyard Downs).

## CRASWALL
**Old Mill Caravan Park,** Old Mill, Craswall,
Herefordshire, HR2 0PN
**Tel:** 01981 510226
**Email:** gjwatkins@tinyworld.co.uk
**Pitches For** ⚠ ⊕ 🚐
**Facilities** ∮ 🛒 ⊙ ⅰ ⭢ 🖻 ⭧
**Nearby Facilities** Г ✔ U
**Acreage** 2 **Open** Easter **to** October
**Access** Good **Site** Level
Near Offas Dyke path and alongsidea
river. Scenic views of the Black Mountains.
**Nearest Town/Resort** Hereford.
**Directions** 8 miles off the A465 at Pandy.
✈ Hereford.

## HAY-ON-WYE
**Penlan Caravan Park,** Penlan, Brilley,
Hay-on-Wye, Herefordshire, HR3 6JW
**Tel:** 01497 831485 **Fax:** 01497 831485
**Email:** peter@penlan.org.uk
www.penlancaravanpark.co.uk
**Pitches For** Total 12
**Facilities** ✗ ∮ 🖳 🛒 Г ⊙ 🖻 🛒 ⭢ ⭧
**Nearby Facilities** Г ✔ ㆞ ㋡ U
**Acreage** 2½ **Open** Easter **to** October
**Access** Fair **Site** Lev/Slope
Peaceful and relaxing site. Ideal for
exploring Mid Wales and the black and white
villages of Herefordshire. National Trust
small holding. Advance booking essential.
**Nearest Town/Resort** Hay-on-Wye
**Directions** From Kington Church follow the

Brilley to Whitney-on-Wye road for 4 miles.
Look for National Trust signs on the left, turn
sharp left into Apostles Lane, Penlan is first
on the right.
✈ Hereford

## HEREFORD
**Cuckoo's Corner,** Moreton-on-Lugg,
Herefordshire, HR4 8AH
**Tel:** 01432 760234
**Email:** cuckoos.corner@ic24.net
www.caravancampsites.co.uk
**Pitches For** ⚠ ⊕ 🚐 **Total** 20
**Facilities** ⏚ ∮ 🖳 🛒 Г ⊙ ⭧
ⅰ 🛇 🛒 ⌂ ⭢ 🖻
**Nearby Facilities** Г ✔ ㋡ U
**Acreage** 1½ **Open** All Year
**Access** Good **Site** Level
Friendly family site with pleasant views.
Archery and croquet on site. Farm animals
and pet exercise area. Good touring area.
Shop, chip shop and pub nearby.
**Nearest Town/Resort** Hereford
**Directions** 4 miles north of Hereford on the
A49, 100 yards beyond signpost Village
Centre and Marden. Or 10 miles south of
Leominster opposite advance sign Village
Centre and Marden.
✈ Hereford

## HEREFORD
**Lucksall Caravan & Camping Park,**
'Lucksall', Mordiford, Hereford,
Herefordshire, HR1 4LP
**Tel:** 01432 870213 **Fax:** 01432 870213
**Email:** enquiries@lucksallpark.com
www.lucksallpark.co.uk
**Pitches For** ⚠ ⊕ 🚐 **Total** 80
**Facilities** ⏚ ✗ ∮ 🖳 🖳 🛒 Г ⊙ ↲ 🛒
🖻 🛒 🕭 🛇 🛒 ⌂ ⭢ 🖳 🖻 🖻 ⭧ ♨
**Nearby Facilities** Г ㋡
**Acreage** 12 **Open** 1 March **to** 30 Nov
**Access** Good **Site** Level
On the banks of the River Wye, ideal for
canoeing and walking. ETC 5 Star Graded.
**Nearest Town/Resort** Hereford
**Directions** On the B4224 between Hereford
(5 miles) and Ross-on-Wye (9 miles).
✈ Hereford

## HEREFORD
**Ridge Hill Caravan & Camp Site,** c/o 38
Gorsty Lane, Hereford, Herefordshire, HR1
1UN
**Tel:** 01432 351293
**Email:** ridgehill@fsmail.net
www.ridgehillcaravanandcampsite.co.uk
**Pitches For** ⚠ ⊕ 🚐
**Facilities** 🛒
**Nearby Facilities** Г ✔ ㋡ ♬
**Acreage** 1¼ **Open** Mid March **to** Oct
**Access** Good **Site** Lev/Slope
Ideal for walking, cycling or visiting
Hereford City and market towns.
**Nearest Town/Resort** Hereford
**Directions** From Hereford take the A49
south, then take the B4399 signposted
Rotherwas. At the first roundabout follow
signs for Dinedor and Little Dewchurch, 2
miles to Ridge Hill, Twyford, turn right at the
phone box.
✈ Hereford

# HEREFORDSHIRE

## HEREFORD

**The Millpond**, Little Tarrington,
Herefordshire, HR1 4JA
**Tel:** 01432 890243 **Fax:** 01432 890243
**Email:** enquiries@millpond.co.uk
www.millpond.co.uk
**Pitches For** ⚠ ⌂ ⛟ **Total** 55
**Facilities** ⚹ �ℹ ⓤ ⚓ ⌂ ⊙⚿ ⛺ ⬛⛽⊡ ⚸
**Nearby Facilities** ⌐ ⤢
**Acreage** 6 **Open** March **to** Oct
**Access** Good **Site** Level
Alongside a picturesque lake.
**Nearest Town/Resort** Hereford/Ledbury
**Directions** Leave the M50 at junction 2 and take the A417 to Ledbury, go around the by-pass and drive west on the A438/A417 to Trumpet crossroads. Take the A438 toward Hereford and turn second right to Millpond.
⚑ Hereford/Ledbury

## HEREFORD

**Upper Gilvach Farm**, St Margarets,
Vowchurch, Hereford, Herefordshire, HR2 0QY
**Tel:** 01981 510618
**Pitches For** ⚠ ⌂ ⛟ **Total** 20
**Facilities** ⓤ ⌐⚿ ⛺⚿⊡ ⚸ ⤢
**Nearby Facilities** ⌐ ⤢ ⓤ ⚲ ⤧
**Open** Easter **to** October
**Access** Good **Site** Level
Very quiet and basic farm site.
**Nearest Town/Resort** Hereford.
**Directions** 4 miles off the B4348.
⚑ Hereford.

## KINGTON

**Fleece Meadow Caravan & Camping Park**, Mill Street, Kington, Herefordshire, HR5 3AL
**Tel:** 01544 231235
**Pitches For** ⚠ ⌂ ⛟ **Total** 30
**Facilities** ⚹ ⚹ ⓤ ⚓ ⌐ ⊙⚿ ⛺ ⬛⚿⊡
**Nearby Facilities** ⌐
**Acreage** 3 **Open** April **to** Oct
**Access** Good **Site** Level
Within easy walking distance of the town centre and recreation ground. Ideal for walking on Offas Dyke and the Mortimer Trail.
**Nearest Town/Resort** Kington
**Directions** From Kington High Street bear left at town clock ito Mill Street, after 200 yards turn left through the bus depot, site is by the river.
⚑ Leominster/Hereford

## LEOMINSTER

**Arrow Bank Holiday Park**, Nun House Farm, Eardisland, Nr Leominster, Herefordshire, HR6 9BG
**Tel:** 01544 388312 **Fax:** 01544 388312
**Email:** enquiries@arrowbankholidaypark.co.uk

---

**Pitches For** ⚠ ⌂ ⛟ **Total** 34
**Facilities** ⚹ ⓤ ⚓ ⌐ ⊙ ⚿ ⚓ ⛺ ⊡ ⛽
**Nearby Facilities** ⌐ ⤢ ⓤ ⚷
**Acreage** 5 **Open** March **to** October
**Access** Good **Site** Level
Peaceful, landscaped park with very spacious and level pitches, set in a beautiful 'Black and White' village. Ideal holiday base.
**Nearest Town/Resort** Leominster
**Directions** 6 miles west of Leominster, off the A44 Rhayadr/Brecon road.
⚑ Leominster

## LEOMINSTER

**Nicholson Farm**, Docklow, Nr Leominster, Herefordshire, HR6 0SL
**Tel:** 01568 760346
**Pitches For** ⚠ ⌂ ⛟ **Total** 7
**Facilities** ⚹ ⓤ ⚓ ⌐ ⊙⚿
**Nearby Facilities** ⌐ ⤢ ⓤ ⚷
A working dairy farm between the small towns of Leominster and Bromyard. Ideal for countryside walking. 5 miles from Hereford and 20 miles from Worcester.
**Nearest Town/Resort** Leominster
**Directions** Off the A44 between Leominster and Bromyard.
⚑ Leominster

## LEOMINSTER

**Pearl Lake Leisure Park**, Shobdon, Leominster, Herefordshire, HR6 9NQ
**Tel:** 01568 708326 **Fax:** 01568 708408
**Email:** info@pearllake.co.uk
www.bestparks.co.uk
**Pitches For** ⚠ ⌂ ⛟ **Total** 15
**Facilities** ⚹ ⚹ ⌐ ⓤ ⬛ ⚓ ⌐ ⊙⚿ ⚓ ⛽ ⬛ ⛺
⬛ ⓒ ⚓ ⚹ ⚲ ⚓ ⚕ ⚿⊡ ⬛ ⤢
**Nearby Facilities** ⌐ ⤢ ⓤ
**Acreage** 80 **Open** March **to** 30 November
**Access** Good **Site** Level
Outstanding park in a beautiful setting with a 15 acre lake, 9 hole golf course, bowling green, woodland, restaurant and bar. ETB Graded 5 Star Excellent.
**Nearest Town/Resort** Leominster
**Directions** Take the A44 from Leominster for 2 miles, turn right onto the B4529, then take the A4110 to Mortimers Cross and turn left onto the B4362, park is on the right as you are leaving Shobdon Village.
⚑ Leominster

## LEOMINSTER

**Townsend Touring Park**, Townsend Farm, Pembridge, Leominster, Herefordshire, HR6 9HB
**Tel:** 01544 388527
**Email:** info@townsendfarm.co.uk
www.townsendfarm.co.uk
**Pitches For** ⚠ ⌂ ⛟ **Total** 62

---

**Facilities** ⚹ ⚹ ⌐ ⌂ ⬛ ⚓ ⌐ ⊙⚿ ⛺ ⬛ ⛽
⚲ ⓒ ⚓ ⚓ ⛺⚿⊡ ⬛ ⤢
**Nearby Facilities** ⌐ ⤢ ⓤ ⚲
**Acreage** 12 **Open** 1 March **to** 15 Jan
**Access** Good **Site** Level
On the edge of one of Herefordshires most beautiful black and white villages, Pembridge. Luxurious heated facilities block. On site farm shop and full butchery.
**Nearest Town/Resort** Leominster
**Directions** From Leominster take the A44 west for 6½ miles to the village of Pembridge. Townsend is located 40 metres into the 30mph speed limit.
⚑ Leominster

## ORLETON

**Orleton Rise Holiday Park**, Green Lane, Orleton, Ludlow, Shropshire, SY8 4JE
**Tel:** 01584 831617 **Fax:** 01584 831617
www.lucksallpark.co.uk
**Pitches For** ⌂ ⛟ **Total** 16
**Facilities** ⚹ ⚲ ⚹ ⓤ ⬛ ⚓ ⌐ ⊙⚿ ⚓ ⬛ ⛽
⚹ ⓒ ⚓⛽⊡ ⬛ ⚸
**Nearby Facilities** ⌐ ⤢ ⓤ ⚷ ⓤ
**Open** March **to** Jan
**Access** Good **Site** Level
Set in 9 acres of immaculately kept parkland. Adjacent to Mortimers Trail. 5 Star Graded Park.
**Nearest Town/Resort** Ludlow
**Directions** Take the A49 Ludlow to Leominster road and turn off at Woofferton (Salwes Arms and Little Chef) onto the B4362. At the T-junction turn left towards Leominster B4361. At the Maidenhead Inn turn right, site is ½ mile along Green Lane.
⚑ Ludlow

## PETERCHURCH

**Poston Mill Park**, Peterchurch, Golden Valley, Herefordshire, HR2 0SF
**Tel:** 01981 550225 **Fax:** 01981 550885
**Email:** enquiries@poston-mill.co.uk
www.bestparks.co.uk
**Pitches For** ⚠ ⌂ ⛟ **Total** 64
**Facilities** ⚹ ⚹ ⌐ ⌂ ⬛ ⚓ ⌐ ⊙⚿ ⚓ ⬛ ⛽
⚹ ⓒ ⚲ ⓒ ⚓ ⚓ ⚹ ⬛ ⚓ ⚓⛽⊡ ⬛ ⚸
**Nearby Facilities** ⌐ ⤢ ⓤ ⚲ ⤧
**Acreage** 33 **Open** All Year
**Access** Good **Site** Level
Highly recommended, beautiful, well maintained park with electric, water and T.V. (inc. Satellite) connections on all pitches. Set on the banks of the River Dore. Adjacent to an excellent restaurant/bar.
**Nearest Town/Resort** Hereford
**Directions** On B4348. 11 miles from Hereford and 11 miles from Hay on Wye.
⚑ Hereford

---

# Townsend Touring Park   01544 388527
## Townsend Farm, Pembridge, Leominster, Herefordshire HR6 9HB
## www.townsend-farm.co.uk   email: info@townsendfarm.co.uk

Spacious 12 acre, 62 pitch Caravan Park. Luxurious heated facilities block comprising of Showers, Wash Cubicles, Toilets, Disabled Room, Family Room, Laundry and Washing-Up Area. Fully serviced, hard standing pitches including electricity, water, waste water hook-ups. Onsite award winning Farm Shop & Butchery. Minutes walk from the centre of the medieval village of Pembridge.

## ROSS-ON-WYE

**Broadmeadow Caravan Park,** Broadmeadows, Ross-on-Wye, Herefordshire, HR9 7BW
**Tel:** 01989 768076 **Fax:** 01989 566030
**Email:** broadm4811@aol.com
www.broadmeadow.info
**Pitches For** ⅄ ⚲ 🚐 **Total** 150
**Facilities** ⅄ 🍴 🗄 📼 🚿 ♨ ⌴ ⊙ 🍴 ⌂ ▣ 🐕
🏪 ⊙ 🏪 🏧 ✴ ⊞
**Nearby Facilities** ⌵ ⚘ 🏊 ∪ ♬ ⚹
**Acreage** 16 **Open** Easter/1st Apr **to** Sept
**Access** Good **Site** Level
Lake walks. Fishing on site. Only 10 minutes to the centre of Ross-on-Wye. Ideal touring and walking in the Wye Valley. ETB 5 Star Graded.
**Nearest Town/Resort** Ross-on-Wye
**Directions** Adjacent to the A40 Ross relief road. Access from Pancake roundabout off relief road turning into Ross. Take the first turning right into Ashburton Estate Road, then turn right by Safeway Supermarket.
✈ Gloucester

## ROSS-ON-WYE

**Lower Ruxton Farm,** Kings Caple, Herefordshire, HR1 4TX
**Tel:** 01432 840223
**Pitches For** ⅄ 🚐 **Total** 20
**Facilities** ⚲ 🐕 🏧 ⊞
**Nearby Facilities**
**Acreage** 8 **Open** Mid July **to** End Aug only
**Site** Level
Alongside a river.
**Nearest Town/Resort** Ross-on-Wye
**Directions** A49 from Ross-on-Wye, 1 mile turn right follow signs for Hoarwithy (Kings Caple 4 miles) across river bridge ½ mile sign to Ruxton second farm on right.
✈ Hereford

## SYMONDS YAT

**Symonds Yat Caravan & Camping Limited,** Symonds Yat West, Nr Ross-on-Wye, Herefordshire, HR9 6BY
**Tel:** 01600 890883/891069
**Email:** geoff@campingandcaravan.com
www.campingandcaravan.com
**Pitches For** ⅄ ⚲ 🚐 **Total** 35
**Facilities** ⅄ 🗄 📼 🚿 ♨ ⌴ ⊙ 🍴 🐕
🏪 🏧 ⊞ 🏪 ⚹
**Nearby Facilities** ⌵ ✔ ⚹
**Acreage** 1 **Open** March **to** October
**Access** Good **Site** Level
In an area of outstanding natural beauty, adjacent to the River Wye which is ideal for walking, canoeing and fishing. Good for touring the Forest of Dean.
**Nearest Town/Resort** Monmouth
**Directions** A40, 7 miles to Ross-on-Wye and 4 miles to Monmouth. Park is ¼ mile from the A40.
✈ Hereford

## SYMONDS YAT WEST

**Doward Park Camp Site,** Great Doward, Symonds Yat West, Nr Ross-on-Wye, Herefordshire, HR9 6BP
**Tel:** 01600 890438
**Email:** enquiries@doward-park.co.uk
www.doward-park.co.uk
**Pitches For** ⅄ 🚐 **Total** 27
**Facilities** ⅄ 📼 ♨ ⌴ ⊙ 🐕 🏧 ⊞ ⚹
**Nearby Facilities** ⌵ ✔ ⚹ ♬ ⚹
**Acreage** 4 **Open** March **to** Oct
**Access** Good **Site** Level
Very scenic and peaceful site with excellent, clean facilities. Close to the River Wye with woodland and river walks. Ideal base for touring the Wye Valley and the Forest of Dean.

**Nearest Town/Resort** Monmouth
**Directions** On the A40 between Ross-on-Wye and Monmouth. Turn off at Symonds Yat West and follow signs for The Doward.
✈ Hereford

## WHITCHURCH

**Sterrett's Caravan Park,** Symonds Yat (West), Nr Ross-on-Wye, Herefordshire, HR9 6BY
**Tel:** 01594 832888
www.ukparks.co.uk/sterretts
**Pitches For** ⅄ 🚐
**Facilities** ⅄ 🗄 📼 ♨ ⌴ ⊙ 🍴 ⌂ ▣ 🐕
🏪 🏧 ⊞ ⊞
**Nearby Facilities** ⌵ ✔ ∪ ⚹
**Acreage** 6 **Open** Feb **to** November
**Access** Good **Site** Level
Near a river. Ideal for touring the Forest of Dean.
**Nearest Town/Resort** Ross-on-Wye
**Directions** Take the A40 from Ross-on-Wye or Monmouth to Whitchurch, turn off and go over a small roundabout by the school, after 200 yards you will come to a large car park, drive through.
✈ Hereford

# HERTFORDSHIRE

## BALDOCK

**Radwell Mill Lake,** Radwell Mill, Baldock, Hertfordshire, SG7 5ET
**Tel:** 01462 730253 **Fax:** 01462 733421
**Pitches For** ⅄ ⚲ 🚐 **Total** 20
**Facilities** 📼 ⌴ 🐕 ⚹ ⚹
**Nearby Facilities**
**Acreage** 3 **Open** Easter **to** November
**Access** Good **Site** Level
Quiet site with a lake and orchard. Good for bird watching. New Motorway Services (½ mile away) with café/restaurant, shops and take-away food.
**Nearest Town/Resort** Baldock
**Directions** Junction 10 A1(M) then the A507, ½ mile towards Baldock take a lane signed "Radwell OnlyG to the lake and site.
✈ Baldock

## HEMEL HEMPSTEAD

**Breakspear Way Caravan Club Site,** Buncefield Lane, Breakspear Way, Hemel Hempstead, Hertfordshire, HP2 4TZ
**Tel:** 01442 268286
www. caravanclub.co.uk
**Pitches For** ⚲ 🚐 **Total** 60
**Facilities** ⅄ 🗄 ♨ 🗄 ⊙ 🏪 🏧 ▣ ♨ 🏧 ⊞
**Acreage** 4½ **Open** March **to** Oct
**Access** Good **Site** Level
Surrounded by countryside. Nearby town offers a bowling green, crazy golf, paddling pool and playground. Plenty of activities and amenities within 2 miles. Near Whipsnade Zoo. Own sanitation required. Non members welcome. Booking essential.
**Nearest Town/Resort** Hemel Hempstead
**Directions** Leave the M1 at junction 8 and take the A414 signposted Hemel Hempstead. At second roundabout turn and return on the A414 towards the M1, after ½ mile (immediately past petrol station) turn left into Buncefield Lane, site is 100 yards on the left.
✈ Hemel Hempstead

## HERTFORD

**Camping & Caravanning Club Site,** Mangrove Road (Not Ball Park), Hertford, Hertfordshire, SG13 8QF
**Tel:** 01992 586696
www. campingandcaravanning.co.uk
**Pitches For** ⅄ ⚲ 🚐 **Total** 250
**Facilities** ⅄ 🗄 📼 🚿 ♨ ⌴ ⊙ 🍴 ⌂ ▣ 🐕
🏪 ⊙ 🏪 🏧 ⊞ ▣ 🐕 ⚹ ♬

**Nearby Facilities** ⌵ ✔ ∪ ♬
**Open** All Year **Site** Level
Set in acres of meadowland. 5 miles from Hatfield House and 20 miles from London. BTB 4 Star Graded, AA 4 Pennants and David Bellamy Gold Award. Non members welcome.
**Directions** From the A10 follow the A414 Hertford signs to the next roundabout (Foxholes) and go straight across, after 200 yards turn left signposted Balls Park and Hertford University. Turn left at the T-Junction into Mangrove Road, go past Simon Balle School, University and Cricket Ground, site is 400 yards past the cricket club on the left.
✈ North & East Hertford

## WALTHAM CROSS

**Theobalds Park Camping & Caravanning Club Site,** Bulls Cross Ride, Waltham Cross, Hertfordshire, EN7 5HS
**Tel:** 01992 620604
www. campingandcaravanning.co.uk
**Pitches For** ⅄ ⚲ 🚐 **Total** 90
**Facilities** ⅄ 📼 ♨ ⌴ ⊙ 🍴 ⌂ ▣ 🐕
🏪 ⊙ 🏪 🏧 ▣ ▣ 🐕
**Nearby Facilities** ⌵ ✔ ∪
**Acreage** 14 **Open** March **to** Nov
**Access** Good **Site** Level
Leafy site just 13 miles from London. Plenty of wildlife to see on the site including birds, foxes, deer and rabbits. Lee Valley nearby which is ideal for boating, sailing and swimming. BTB 3 Star Graded and AA 2 Pennants. Non members welcome.
**Nearest Town/Resort** Waltham Cross
**Directions** Leave the M25 at junction 25, take the A10 towards London keeping to the right hand lane, turn right at the first set of traffic lights signposted Crews Hill. Turn right at the T-Junction (opposite Pied Bull), turn right behind the dog kennels, site is towards the top of the lane on the right.
✈ Waltham Cross

# ISLE OF MAN

## LAXEY

**Laxey Commissioners Campsite,** Quarry Road, Minorca Hill, Laxey, Isle of Man, IM7 4BG
**Tel:** 01624 861241 **Fax:** 01624 862623
**Email:** laxeycommissioners@manx.net
**Pitches For** ⅄ ⚲ 🚐 **Total** 20
**Facilities** 📼 ♨ ⌴ 🐕
**Nearby Facilities** ✔ ⚘ ⚹ ♬
**Acreage** 2 **Open** May **to** Sept
**Access** Good **Site** Level
Near the beach and harbour. Ideal touring.
**Nearest Town/Resort** Douglas
**Directions** Turn off the main Douglas to Ramsey road at Fairy Cottage Filling Station, go over the bridge and up Minorca Hill, turn left before the tram bridge.

## UNION MILLS

**Glenlough Farm Campsite,** Union Mills, Isle of Man, IM4 4AT
**Tel:** 01624 822372/852057 **Fax:** 01624 822372
**Email:** glenloughcampsite@manx.net
**Pitches For** ⅄ 🚐 **Total** 350
**Facilities** ⅄ 🗄 📼 ♨ ⌴ ⊙ 🏪 🏪 🏧 ⊞
**Nearby Facilities**
**Acreage** 15 **Open** May **to** Sept
**Site** Level
Family run, sheltered site on the T.T. Course. Located in the scenic central valley. Everyone welcome.
**Nearest Town/Resort** Douglas
**Directions** 3 miles from Douglas on the A1 Douglas to Peel road.
✈ Douglas

# ISLE OF WIGHT

## ATHERFIELD

**Chine Farm Camping Site**, Military Road, Atherfield Bay, Nr Chale, VentnorIsle of Wight, PO38 2JH
**Tel:** 01983 740228
www.chinefarmcamping.co.uk
Pitches For ▲ ⊕ ⊞ Total 80
Facilities 🆄 ♨ ſ ☉ ♥ ⊖ 🗛ﬣ🖃
Nearby Facilities ✓
**Acreage** 10 **Open** May to Sept
**Access** Good **Site** Level
Sea views and a footpath to beach.
**Nearest Town/Resort** Newport
**Directions** East of Freshwater 8 miles on the A3055 Coast Road.
⇌ Ryde

## BEMBRIDGE

**Whitecliff Bay Holiday Park**, Hillway, Whitecliff Bay, Bembridge, Isle of Wight, PO35 5PL
**Tel:** 01983 872671 **Fax:** 01983 872941
**Email:** holiday@whitecliff-bay.com
www.whitecliff-bay.com
Pitches For ▲ ⊕ ⊞ Total 400
Facilities ♿ ⅋ 🖃 🞲 🆄 ♨ ſ ☉ ↲ 🛲 🖳 🖵 ☎
🕱 ⊖ ⊛ ✕ 🖵 ♠ ⋔ ⅗ ﬣﬣ🖃 🖃 ⚡ ↗
Nearby Facilities ſ ∪ ♪
**Acreage** 15 **Open** March to Oct
**Access** Good **Site** Lev/Slope/Terraces
Situated in pleasant countryside adjoining Whitecliff Bay with own sandy private beach. Indoor pool and leisure centre, family owned and managed. Pets are welcome off-peak.
**Nearest Town/Resort** Sandown
**Directions** Take the A3055 from Ryde to Sandown, in Brading turn left onto the B3395 and follow signposts.
⇌ Brading

## BRIGHSTONE BAY

**Grange Farm Caravan & Camping Site**, Military Road, Brighstone Bay, Brighstone, Isle of Wight, PO30 4DA
**Tel:** 01983 740296 **Fax:** 01983 741233
**Email:**
grangefarm@brighstonebay.fsnet.co.uk
www.brighstonebay.fsnet.co.uk
Pitches For ▲ ⊕ ⊞ Total 60
Facilities ⅋ 🆄 ♨ ſ ☉ ↲ 🛲 🖳 ☎
🕱 🅑 ⊖ ⊛ 🗛 ﬣﬣ🖃 🖃
Nearby Facilities ſ
**Acreage** 2 **Open** March to End October
**Access** Good **Site** Level
Family run park on a small working farm with unusual farm animals. Situated right by the sea, just a minute walk to the beach. South facing. Self catering accommodation also available. Fishing, sailing, boating, fossil hunting, a walkers paradise. ETB 3 Star Graded and David Bellamy Silver Award for Conservation. No motorcycle groups.
**Nearest Town/Resort** BrighstoneNewport
**Directions** On coastal road A3055 midway from Freshwater to Chale (approx 5mls).

## COWES

**Thorness Bay Holiday Park**, Thorness Lane, Thorness, Nr Cowes, Isle of Wight, PO31 8NJ
**Tel:** 01983 523109 **Fax:** 01983 822213
holidaysales.thornessbay@park-resorts.com
www.park-resorts.com
Pitches For ▲ ⊕ ⊞ Total 85
Facilities ⅋ 🖃 🆄 ♨ ſ ☉ ↲ 🛲 🖳 ☎
🕱 ⊖ ⊛ ✕ 🖵 ♠ ⋔ ⅗ﬣﬣ🖃 🖃 ⚡
**Open** March to Oct
**Access** Good **Site** Lev/Slope
In a rural setting amidst woodland running down to the sea.
**Nearest Town/Resort** Cowes
**Directions** From Newport take the A3054

towards Yarmouth. After 1 mile take the first turning right and follow signs to Thorness.
⇌ Ryde

## COWES

**Waverley Park Holiday Centre**, 51 Old Road, East Cowes, Isle of Wight, PO32 6AW
**Tel:** 01983 293452 **Fax:** 01983 200494
**Email:** sue@waverley-park.co.uk
www.waverley-park.co.uk
Pitches For ▲ ⊕ ⊞ Total 45
Facilities ♿ ⅋ 🆄 ♨ ſ ☉ ↲ 🛲 🖳 ☎
🕱 🅑 ⊛ ✕ 🖵 ♠ 🗛 ⅗ﬣ🖃 🖃
Nearby Facilities ſ ✓ ⚓ ⚲ ∪ ♪ ♪
**Acreage** 10½ **Open** March to October
**Access** Good **Site** Sloping
Panoramic views over the Solent.
**Nearest Town/Resort** Cowes
**Directions** Signposted from Red Funnel Ferries, only 500 yards from the East Cowes Terminal.
⇌ Ryde

## FRESHWATER

**Heathfield Farm Camping**, Heathfield Road, Freshwater, Isle of Wight, PO40 9SH
**Tel:** 01983 756756 **Fax:** 01983 756756
**Email:** web@heathfieldcamping.co.uk
www.heathfieldcamping.co.uk
Pitches For ▲ ⊕ ⊞ Total 60
Facilities ♿ ⅋ 🆄 ♨ ſ ☉ ↲ 🛲 🖳 ☎
🅑 ⊖ ⊛ﬣ🖃
Nearby Facilities ſ ✓ ⚓ ⚲ ∪ ♪ ♪
**Acreage** 10 **Open** May to Sept
**Access** Good **Site** Level
Ideal walking and cycling area.
**Nearest Town/Resort** Freshwater
**Directions** From Yarmouth take the A3054 to Freshwater. After Golden Hill Fort turn left into Heathfield Road, 200 yards to site entrance.

## NEWCHURCH

**Southland Camping Park,** Winford Road, Newchurch, Isle of Wight, PO36 0LZ
**Tel:** 01983 865385 **Fax:** 01983 867663
**Email:** info@southland.co.uk
www.southland.co.uk
**Pitches For** ▲ ⊕ ⊜ **Total** 120
**Facilities** & ƒ ▥ ♨ ⌐ ⊙ ┘ ◢ ▣ ☻
♋ ▮ ◎ ⊜ ▥ ┅ ▣ ⌐
**Nearby Facilities** ┌ ✔ ⚓ ⚘ ∪ ⚲ ♪
**Acreage** 9 **Open** Easter **to** September
**Access** Good **Site** Level
Sheltered, secluded touring park, generous level pitches. Far reaching views over Arreton Valley.
**Nearest Town/Resort** Sandown/Shanklin
**Directions** Newport to Sandown road A3056/A3055 through Arreton, after Fighting Cocks Public House take the second left. Continue along road for 1 mile, site is on the left.
⇌ Lake

## RYDE

**Beaper Farm Camping & Caravan Park,** Nr Ryde, Isle of Wight, PO33 1QJ
**Tel:** 01983 615210/875184
**Email:** beaper@btinternet.com
**Pitches For** ▲ ⊕ ⊜ **Total** 150
**Facilities** & ƒ ▥ ♨ ⌐ ⊙ ┘ ◢ ▣ ☻
◎ ⊼ ▣ ⌐ ♪
**Nearby Facilities** ┌ ✔ ⚓ ⚘ ∪ ⚲
**Acreage** 13 **Open** May **to** September
**Access** Good **Site** Level
Near to beaches, golf, water sports, fishing trips, horse riding, ice skating, ten pin bowling and nightclubs, plus Isle of Wight Steam Railway.
**Nearest Town/Resort** Ryde
**Directions** On the main A3055 Ryde to Sandown road, go past Tesco roundabout for ½ mile, Beaper Farm is second on the left.
⇌ Ryde

## SANDOWN

**Adgestone Camping & Caravanning Club Site,** Lower Adgestone Road, Adgestone, Isle of Wight, PO36 0HL
**Tel:** 01983 403432
www.campingandcaravanningclub.co.uk
**Pitches For** ▲ ⊕ ⊜ **Total** 270
**Facilities** & ƒ ▥ ♨ ⌐ ⊙ ┘ ◢ ▣ ☻
♋ ▮ ◎ ⊜ ✕ ♨ ▥ ┑ ▥ ▣ ⌐ ♪
**Nearby Facilities** ┌ ✔ ⚓ ⚘ ⚲ ♪
**Acreage** 22 **Open** March **to** Oct
**Access** Difficult **Site** Level
One of the best locations on the Isle of Wight, 1 mile from Sandown. Adjacent to the River Yar and nestled in the valley beneath Brading Downs, an area of natural beauty. BTB 4 Star Graded and AA 5 Pennants. Non members welcome.
**Nearest Town/Resort** Sandown
**Directions** Turn off the A3055 Sandown to Shanklin road at Manor House Pub in Lake. Go past the school and golf course on the left and turn right at the T-Junction, park is 200 yards on the right.

## SANDOWN

**Old Barn Touring Park,** Cheverton Farm, Newport Road, Sandown, Isle of Wight, PO36 9PJ
**Tel:** 01983 866414 **Fax:** 01983 865988
**Email:** oldbarn@weltinet.com
www.oldbarntouring.co.uk
**Pitches For** ▲ ⊕ ⊜ **Total** 60
**Facilities** & ƒ ▤ ▥ ▥ ♨ ⌐ ⊙ ┘ ◢ ▣ ☻
▮ ◎ ⊜ ▥ ♨ ⊼ ▣ ▣ ⌐
**Nearby Facilities** ┌ ✔ ⚓ ⚘ ∪ ♪
**Acreage** 5 **Open** 1 May **to** 25 Sept
**Access** Good **Site** Level
1½ miles from the seaside towns of Sandown and Shanklin. Grade II Listed Barn used as a TV and games room.
**Nearest Town/Resort** Sandown

**Directions** From Newport take the A3056, Park is on the right ½ mile after Apse Heath mini roundabout.
⇌ Lake

## SANDOWN

**Queen Bower Dairy Caravan Park,** Alverstone Road, Queen Bower, Sandown, Isle of Wight, PO36 0NZ
**Tel:** 01983. 403840
**Email:** queenbowerdairy@aol.com
www.queenbowerdairy.co.uk
**Pitches For** ▲ ⊕ ⊜ **Total** 20
**Facilities** ⚲ ƒ ▥ ☻ ▥ ⊼ ▣
**Nearby Facilities** ┌ ✔ ⚓ ⚘ ⚲ ♪
**Acreage** 2¼ **Open** May **to** October
**Access** Good **Site** Level
Scenic views, ideal touring. Sell our own produced Dairy products (milk and cream). Public telephone ¼ mile.
**Nearest Town/Resort** Sandown
**Directions** On the A3056 Newport to Sandown road, turn into Alverstone Road at Apse Heath crossroads. Park is 1 mile on the left.
⇌ Sandown

## SANDOWN

**Village Way Caravan & Camping Park,** Newport Road, Apse Heath, Sandown, Isle of Wight, PO36 9PJ
**Tel:** 01983 863279
**Pitches For** ▲ ⊕ ⊜ **Total** 14
**Facilities** ƒ ▥ ♨ ⌐ ⊙ ┘ ◢ ▣ ☻
▮ ◎ ⊜ ⊼ ▣ ☀
**Nearby Facilities** ┌ ⚓ ⚘ ∪ ⚲ ♪ ⚒
**Open** All Year
**Access** Good **Site** Level
Near the beach. Free carp fishing on site. Beautiful country walks to the woods and within walking distance of a garden centre and Safeways. The Heights Leisure Centre is only a mile away.

**Nearest Town/Resort** Sandown
**Directions** From Newport take the A22 to Blackwater then the A3056 to Apse Heath. We are on the main A3056.

## SHANKLIN
**Landguard Camping Park,** Landguard Manor Road, Shanklin, Isle of Wight, PO37 7PH
**Tel:** 01983 867028 **Fax:** 01983 865988
**Email:** landguard@weltinet.com
www.landguard-camping.co.uk
**Pitches For ▲ ⚲ ⊟ Total** 150
**Facilities** ♿ �ℱ ▥ ⚑ ♠ ☊ ⊙ ♨ ◢ 🗐 ▣ ☎
℠ ▣ ⬚ ✕ ⬗ ▣ ▣
**Nearby Facilities** ♄ ✦ ⊥ ⚓ ∪ ♪
**Acreage** 7 **Open** May to Sept
**Access** Good **Site** Level
Only 10 minutes walk into Shanklin town with its 'Old Village' and seaside entertainment.
**Nearest Town/Resort** Shanklin
**Directions** From Newport take the A3056 signposted Sandown. After Safeways at Lake turn right into White Cross Lane and follow signs.
⚓ Shanklin

## SHANKLIN
**Lower Hyde Holiday Park,** Landguard Road, Shanklin, Isle of Wight, PO37 7LL
**Tel:** 01983 866131 **Fax:** 01983 862532
**Email:** holidaysales.lowerhyde@park-resorts.com
www.park-resorts.com
**Pitches For ▲ ⚲ ⊟ Total** 100
**Facilities** ℱ ▥ ▣ ⚑ ♠ ☊ ⊙ ♨ ◢ 🗐 ▣ ☎
℠ ▣ ⬚ ✕ ⬗ ♒ ▣ ✦ ➹ 🕂 ▣ ▣ ☀
**Open** March to Oct
**Site** Lev/Slope
Close to the sandy sunshine beaches of south east Wight and family attractions.

**Nearest Town/Resort** Shanklin
**Directions** From Ryde take the A3055 towards Shanklin. From Lake take the A3056 towards Newport. After ¾ of a mile turn left into Whitecross Lane, park is 1 mile on the right.
⚓ Shanklin

## SHANKLIN
**Ninham Country Holidays,** Shanklin, Isle of Wight, PO37 7PL
**Tel:** 01983 864243/866040 **Fax:** 868881
**Email:** info@ninham.fsnet.co.uk
www.ninham-holidays.co.uk
**Pitches For ▲ ⚲ ⊟ Total** 98
**Facilities** ✦ ▣ ▥ ♠ ☊ ⊙ ♨ ◢ 🗐 ▣ ☎
▣ ▣ ⬚ ♒ ⧑ ➹ ♠ ▣ ▣ ☀ ✎
**Nearby Facilities** ♄ ✦ ⊥ ⚓ ∪ ➹ ♪
**Acreage** 10 **Open** Easter to 30 Sept
**Access** Very Good **Site** Level
Country park setting close to Islands premier seaside resort. Ferry inclusive holidays. Indoor pool and health suite, water sport school and mountain biking nearby.
**Nearest Town/Resort** Shanklin
**Directions** Signposted off Newport/Sandown road (A3056). Site entrance is ¼ mile west of Safeway's on the left.
⚓ Shanklin

## ST. HELENS
**Carpenters Farm Camp Site,** Carpenters Farm, St Helens, Ryde, Isle of Wight, PO33 1YL
**Tel:** 01983 874557
**Pitches For ▲ ⚲ ⊟ Total** 70
**Facilities** ℱ ▥ ♠ ☊ ⊙ ♨ ◢ 🗐 ▣ ☎
▣ ▣ ⬚ 🕂 ▣
**Nearby Facilities** ⊥ ⚓ ∪
**Acreage** 12½ **Open** End May to Oct
**Access** Good **Site** Sloping
**Nearest Town/Resort** Sandown

**Directions** On the B3330, 3 miles from Sandown or Ryde.
⚓ Brading

## ST. HELENS
**Nodes Point Holiday Park,** Nodes Road, St Helens, Ryde, Isle of Wight, PO33 1YA
**Tel:** 01983 872401 **Fax:** 01983 874696
**Email:** nodes.point@park-resorts.com
www.park-resorts.com
**Pitches For ▲ ⚲ ⊟ Total** 177
**Facilities** ℱ ▥ ♠ ☊ ⊙ ♨ ◢ 🗐 ▣ ☎
℠ ▣ ▣ ✕ ♒ ▥ ⧑ ➹ 🕂 ▣ ▣ ☀
**Nearby Facilities** ∪
**Open** March to Oct
**Access** Good **Site** Lev/Slope
Spectacular position overlooking Bembridge Bay and set in 65 acres of parkland. Close to the beach and attractions.
**Nearest Town/Resort** Ryde
**Directions** Approach Ryde on the A3054 to join the A3055 in town. At Bishop Lovett School (on the left) go straight onto the B3330 towards St. Helens. After approx. 2 miles turn left to the park.
⚓ Ryde

## TOTLAND
**Stoats Farm Camping,** Stoats Farm House, Weston Lane, Totland, Isle of Wight, PO39 0HE
**Tel:** 01983 755258
**Email:** david@stoats-farm.co.uk
www.stoats-farm.co.uk
**Pitches For ▲ ⚲ ⊟ Total** 100
**Facilities** ♿ ℱ ▥ ♠ ☊ ⊙ ♨ ◢ 🗐 ▣ ☎
℠ ♠ 🕂 ▣ ▣ ☀
**Nearby Facilities** ♄ ✦ ⊥ ⚓ ∪ ♪
**Acreage** 10 **Open** March to October
**Access** Good **Site** Lev/Slope
Situated under Tennyson Downs, ½ a mile from beaches and The Needles.

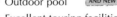

**Nearest Town/Resort** Totland Bay
**Directions** Off the B3014 at the junction of Weston Lane, Moons Hill and Alum Bay Old Road.

## YARMOUTH
**The Orchards Holiday Caravan & Camping Park,** Newbridge, Yarmouth, Isle of Wight, PO41 0TS
**Tel:** 01983 531331 **Fax:** 01983 531666
**Email:** info@orchards-holiday-park.co.uk
www.orchards-holiday-park.co.uk
**Pitches For** ▲ ⇗ ⇋ **Total** 175
**Facilities** ⅄ ✦ 🏠 🎱 📷 ⚓ ♈ ⊙ ⅃ ⚙ 🔲 💂
🏪 🎱 🅿 🚽 🍴 🔥 🚿 ⚡ ⤴ 🚻 🔲 ▣
**Nearby Facilities** ♈ ✦ ⅄ ⋃ ♬
**Acreage** 8 **Open** 20 February **to** 2 January
**Access** Good **Site** Lev/Slope
Good views of the Downs and Solent. Bookings inclusive of car ferries throughout season. Outdoor swimming pool from late May to early September, indoor swimming pool all season. Take-away food, self-service shop and coarse fishing on site. Battery charging, small function/meeting room. Rallies welcome. Ideal for rambling and cycling. Non members welcome. Booking essential.
**Nearest Town/Resort** Yarmouth
**Directions** 4 miles east of Yarmouth and 6 miles west of Newport on B3401. Entrance opposite Newbridge Post Office.
⇥ Lymington

# KENT
## ASHFORD
**Broadhembury Caravan & Camping Park,** Steeds Lane, Kingsnorth, Ashford, Kent, TN26 1NQ
**Tel:** 01233 620859 **Fax:** 01233 620918
**Email:** holidays@broadhembury.co.uk
www.broadhembury.co.uk
**Pitches For** ▲ ⇗ ⇋ **Total** 80
**Facilities** ⅄ ✦ 🏠 🎱 📷 ⚓ ♈ ⊙ ⅃ ⚙ 🔲 💂
🏪 🎱 🅿 🚽 🍴 🔥 🚿 ⚡ ⤴ 🚻 🔲 ▣ 🚿
**Nearby Facilities** ♈ ✦ ⋃ ♬
**Acreage** 8 **Open** All Year
**Access** Good **Site** Level
Quiet, Award Winning park in Kentish countryside with every modern amenity. Central to many places of interest. Convenient for all Channel crossings.
**Nearest Town/Resort** Ashford
**Directions** Leave the M20 at junction 10, take the A2070 following signs for Kingsnorth. Turn left at the second crossroads in the village.
⇥ Ashford

## ASHFORD
**Dunn Street Farm,** Westwell, Ashford, Kent, TN25 4NJ
**Tel:** 01233 712537
**Pitches For** ▲ ⇗ ⇋ **Total** 40
**Facilities** ✦ 🎱 🅿 ⊙ 🚿 💂
**Nearby Facilities** ♈ ⋃ ♬
**Acreage** 5 **Open** April **to** October
**Access** Fair **Site** Level
Ideal for walking and cycling. Central for Canterbury, Sissinghurst, Weald of Kent and general touring of the North Downs.
**Nearest Town/Resort** Ashford
**Directions** Leave the M20 at junction 9 and take the A20 west. After 2 miles turn right into Watery Lane to Westwell. At the crossroads in the village take Gold Hill, turn first left up the hill, at the top of the hill turn left, site is 50 yards on the right.
⇥ Ashford

## BIDDENDEN
**Woodlands Park,** Tenterden Road, Biddenden, Ashford, Kent, TN27 8BT
**Tel:** 01580 291216 **Fax:** 01580 291216
**Email:** woodlandsp@aol.com
www.campingsite.co.uk
**Pitches For** ▲ ⇗ ⇋ **Total** 200
**Facilities** ⅄ ✦ 🎱 📷 ⚓ ♈ ⊙ ⅃ ⚙ 🔲 💂
🏪 🎱 🅿 🚽 🔲 ▣ 🚿
**Nearby Facilities** ♈ ✦ ♬
**Acreage** 10 **Open** March **to** October
**Access** Good **Site** Level
Quiet, country site. Ideal for tourist centre.
**Nearest Town/Resort** Tenterden/Leeds Castle
**Directions** On A262, 3 miles north of Tenterden. 15 miles south of Maidstone.
⇥ Headcorn

## BIRCHINGTON
**Quex Caravan Park,** Park Road, Birchington, Kent, CT7 0BL
**Tel:** 01843 841273 **Fax:** 01227 740585
**Email:** info@keatfarm.co.uk
www.keatfarm.co.uk
**Pitches For** ⇗ ⇋ **Total** 50
**Facilities** ⅄ ✦ 🎱 📷 ⚓ ♈ ⊙ ⅃ ⚙ 🔲 💂
🏪 🎱 🅿 🚽 🔲 ▣ 🚿 ♬
**Nearby Facilities** ♈ ✦ ⅄ ⋃ ♬
**Acreage** 3 **Open** 7 March **to** 7 November
**Access** Good **Site** Level
Ideal base for touring Thanet and Canterbury areas.
**Nearest Town/Resort** Margate/Ramsgate
**Directions** Follow road signs to Margate. When in Birchington turn right at mini roundabout (signposted Margate). Approximately 100yds after roundabout take the first turning on the right and then right again as directed by Tourist Board signs.
⇥ Birchington

## BIRCHINGTON
**Two Chimneys Caravan Park,** Shottendane Road, Birchington, Kent, CT7 0HD
**Tel:** 01843 841068/843157 **Fax:** 01843 848099
**Email:** info@twochimneys.co.uk
www.twochimneys.co.uk
**Pitches For** ▲ ⇗ ⇋ **Total** 200
**Facilities** ⅄ ✦ 🎱 📷 ⚓ ♈ ⊙ ⅃ ⚙ 🔲 💂
🏪 🎱 🅿 🚽 🍴 🔥 🚿 ⚡ ⤴ 🚻 🔲 ▣
**Nearby Facilities** ♈ ✦ ⅄ ⋃ ♬ ♬
**Acreage** 30 **Open** March **to** October
**Access** Good **Site** Level
Country site near lovely beaches. Swimming pool with retractable roof, adventure play area and tennis court on site.
**Nearest Town/Resort** Margate
**Directions** 1½ miles Birchington, turn right into park lane at Birchington Church, left fork "RAF ManstonG. First left onto B2048 site ½ mile on right.
⇥ Birchington

## CANTERBURY
**Ashfield Farm Caravan & Camping Site,** Ashfield Farm, Waddenhall, Petham, CanterburyKent, CT4 5PX
**Tel:** 01227 700624
**Email:** mpatterson@ashfieldfarm.freeserve.co.uk
**Pitches For** ▲ ⇗ ⇋ **Total** 30
**Facilities** ⅄ ✦ 🎱 ⚓ ♈ ⊙ ⅃ 💂
🎱 🅿 🚽 🔲 ▣
**Nearby Facilities** ♈ ✦ ⋃
**Acreage** 4 **Open** April **to** November
**Access** Good **Site** Level
Situated in an area of outstanding natural beauty. Close to Canterbury and the Kent coast.
**Nearest Town/Resort** Canterbury
**Directions** From Canterbury take the B2068, site is approx. 6 miles on the right. Or leave the M20 at junction 11 and take the B2068, site is approx. 8 miles on the left.
⇥ Canterbury

## CANTERBURY
**Camping & Caravanning Club Site,** Bekesbourne Lane, Canterbury, Kent, CT3 4AB
**Tel:** 01227 463216
www.campingandcaravanningclub.co.uk
**Pitches For** ▲ ⇗ ⇋ **Total** 200
**Facilities** ⅄ ✦ 🎱 📷 ⚓ ♈ ⊙ ⅃ ⚙ 🔲 💂
🏪 🎱 🅿 🚽 🔲 ▣ 🚿 ♬
**Nearby Facilities** ♈
**Acreage** 20 **Open** All Year
**Site** Lev/Slope
Close to Canterbury and within easy reach of the Channel ports. 2 miles from Canterbury Cathedral and Howletts Wildlife

Park. BTB 4 Star Graded, AA 3 Pennants and David Bellamy Gold Award. Non members welcome.
**Directions** From Canterbury follow the A257 towards Sandwich, turn right opposite the golf course.
⚏ Canterbury

## DEAL

**Clifford Park Caravans,** Clifford Park, Thompson Close, Walmer, DealKent, CT14 7PB
**Tel:** 01304 373373
**Pitches For** ▲ � ⛺ **Total** 15
**Facilities** ⫶ 🄷 � ⚒ ⌿ ⊙⫶🔥 ⓘ 🄾 🄱 🄿
**Nearby Facilities** 🏌 ⌿ ⚓ ⚒ ∪ ⌐
**Open** March **to** Oct
**Access** Good **Site** Level
Just 2 minutes from the village. Ideal for touring and close to ferry ports for the continent.
**Nearest Town/Resort** Deal
**Directions** On the A258, 1 mile from Deal and 5 miles from Dover.
⚏ Walmer

## DOVER

**Hawthorn Farm,** Martin Mill, Dover, Kent, CT15 5LA
**Tel:** 01304 852658 **Fax:** 01304 853417
**Email:** info@keatfarm.co.uk
www.keatfarm.co.uk
**Pitches For** ▲ ⌷ ⛺ **Total** 250
**Facilities** ⫶ 🄷 ⓘ ⚒ ⌿ ⊙ ⛏ 🔥 🄾 🔔
🅂🄸 🄾 ⓐ⛒🄷🄳🄴 ⚒⌐ ⌿
**Nearby Facilities** 🏌 ⌿ ⚓ ∪
**Acreage** 27 **Open** March **to** December
**Access** Good **Site** Level
Beautiful Award Winning park in a quiet and peaceful location. Superb toilet and shower facilities.
**Nearest Town/Resort** Dover
**Directions** Martin Mill is approx. 3 miles from Dover, signposted along the main A258 towards Deal.
⚏ Martin Mill

## DOVER

**Sutton Vale Caravan Park & Country Club,** Vale Road, Sutton-By-Dover, Kent, CT15 5DH
**Tel:** 01304 366233 **Fax:** 01304 381132
**Email:** office@sutton-vale.co.uk
www.sutton-vale.co.uk
**Pitches For** ⌷ ⛺
**Facilities** ⚓ ⚔ ⫶ 🄵 🄷 🅆 ⚒ ⌿ ⌐ ⊐ 🄾 🅂🄸 🄾
🄰⚒ ⌿ 🄾 🄺 🄽 🔥 ⛏⛒🄷🄳🄴 ⚒⌐ ⌿
**Nearby Facilities** 🏌 ⌿ ⚓ ⚒ ∪ ⌿ ⌐
**Open** March **to** January inc.
**Access** Good **Site** Level
Own local village 17th Century pub, swimming pool and sports field. Next door to horse riding stables.

**Nearest Town/Resort** Deal/Sandwich
**Directions** From the A2 Canterbury to Dover road, 5 miles from Dover at the Whitfield roundabout (McDonalds) take first exit, after 20 yards turn right into Archers Court Road, exactly 4 miles on the left.
⚏ Deal

## DYMCHURCH

**New Beach Holiday Village,** Hythe Road, Dymchurch, Kent, TN29 0JX
**Tel:** 01303 872234 **Fax:** 01303 872939
**Email:** info@cinqueportsleisure.com
www.cplholidays.com
**Pitches For** ▲ ⌷ ⛺
**Facilities** ⚓ ⫶ 🅆 ⚒ ⌿ ⌐ ⊐ ⌐ 🄾 🔔
🅂🄸 🄾 ⚒⚔ ⛏ 🅆 ⛒ ⚒ 🄷⛒🄳🄴 ⚒⌐
**Nearby Facilities** 🏌 ⌿ ⚓
**Open** March **to** Nov
**Access** Good **Site** Level
Near the beach, miniature railway, Port Lymmpe Zoo & Castle, coastal park and market. Winter storage available.
**Nearest Town/Resort** Dymchurch
**Directions** On the A259 coastal road between Hythe and Dymchurch.
⚏ Folkestone

## EASTCHURCH

**Warden Springs Caravan Park,** Thorn Hill Road, Warden Point, Eastchurch, Isle of SheppeyKent, ME12 4HF
**Tel:** 0870 442 9281 **Fax:** 01795 880218
www.park-resorts.com
**Pitches For** ▲ ⌷ ⛺ **Total** 37
**Facilities** ⚓ ⫶ 🄵 🅆 ⚒ ⌿ ⊙ ⌐ 🄾 🔔
🅂🄸 🄾 ⚒⚔ ⛏ 🅆 🔥⛒ ⚒ 🄷⛒🄳🄴 ⚒⌐
**Nearby Facilities** 🏌 ⌿ ⚒ ∪
**Open** March **to** October
**Access** Good **Site** Sloping
Overlooking the sea and surrounded by picturesque countryside.
**Nearest Town/Resort** Eastchurch
**Directions** From Sittingbourne head north on the A249, after 8 miles turn right onto the B2231 to Eastchurch. Turn left at Eastchurch and follow signs to Warden Springs for 2 miles.
⚏ Sheerness

## FOLKESTONE

**Black Horse Farm Caravan Club Site,** 385 Canterbury Road, Densole, Folkestone, Kent, CT18 7BG
**Tel:** 01303 892665
www.caravanclub.co.uk
**Pitches For** ▲ ⌷ ⛺ **Total** 140
**Facilities** ⚓ ⫶ 🅆 ⚒ ⌿ 🄾 🔔
🄸 🄾 ⓐ 🄼⛒🄷🄳
**Nearby Facilities** 🏌 ⌿
**Acreage** 11 **Open** All Year
**Access** Good **Site** Level
Situated in the heart of farming country.

Limited hard standings available March to October only. Close to Canterbury, Dover Castle and the Channel Tunnel. Non members welcome. Booking essential.
**Nearest Town/Resort** Folkestone
**Directions** Leave the M20 at junction 13 (at end) and continue onto the A20. Past the end of the tunnel turn off via slip road and roundabout onto the A260 signposted Canterbury, go through Hawkinge into Densole. Site is on the left 200 yards past the Black Horse Inn.
⚏ Folkestone

## FOLKESTONE

**Camping & Caravanning Club Site,** The Warren, Folkestone, Kent, CT19 6NQ
**Tel:** 01303 255093
www.campingandcaravanningclub.co.uk
**Pitches For** ▲ ⌷ ⛺ **Total** 80
**Facilities** ⚓ ⫶ 🅆 ⚒ ⌿ ⊙ ⌐ ⌐ 🄾 🔔
🅄 🄾 ⓐ⛒🄷🄳🄴 ⚒⌐
**Nearby Facilities** 🏌 ⌿ ⚒ ⌿ ⚔
**Open** March **to** Nov
**Access** Difficult **Site** Lev/Slope
Just a short walk to the beach. On a clear day you can see France. Fishing off the site on the sea front, 50 yards. BTB 4 Star Graded, AA 3 Pennants and Loo of the Year Award. Non members welcome.
**Directions** From the M2 and Canterbury on the A260 take a left turn at the roundabout into Hill Road, Folkestone. Go straight over the crossroads into Wear Bay Road, turn second left past Martello Tower, site is ½ mile on the right.
⚏ Folkestone

## FOLKESTONE

**Folkestone Racecourse Caravan Club Site,** Westenhanger, Hythe, Kent, CT21 4HX
**Tel:** 01303 261761
www.caravanclub.co.uk
**Pitches For** ▲ ⌷ ⛺ **Total** 44
**Facilities** ⫶ 🅆 ⚒ ⌿ 🄾 ⓐ⛒🄷
**Nearby Facilities** 🏌 ⌿ ⚒ ⚔
**Acreage** 4 **Open** March **to** Sept
**Access** Good **Site** Level
Near the beach for safe bathing and wind surfing. Near to Romney Hythe & Dymchurch Miniature Railway, Port Lympne Zoo and children's farms. Non members welcome. Booking essential.
**Nearest Town/Resort** Folkestone
**Directions** Leave the M20 at junction 11 and follow signs for Hythe, at the A20 roundabout follow signs for Sellindge. At start of dual carriageway turn right signposted Racecourse, site is ½ mile on the left.
⚏ Folkestone

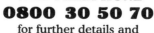

## FOLKESTONE

**Little Satmar Holiday Park,** Winehouse Lane, Capel-le-Ferne, Nr Folkestone, Kent, CT18 7JF
**Tel:** 01303 251188 **Fax:** 01303 251188
**Email:** info@keatfarm.co.uk
www.keatfarm.co.uk
**Pitches For ▲ ⌂ ⊟ Total** 40
**Facilities** ⌁ 🚿 ♨ ┌ ⊙ ┘ ⊿ ▢ ☎
🕮 ⊟ 🎿 ♨ 📶 ⛽ 🎣 ⊟
**Nearby Facilities** ┌ ⊿ ⚲ ∪
**Acreage** 6 **Open** March to October
**Access** Good
Quiet, secluded park. Convenient for Channel ports and Tunnel.
**Nearest Town/Resort** Folkestone
**Directions** Travelling towards Folkestone on the A20 from Dover, exit left signposted Capel-le-Ferne onto the B2011. After 1 mile turn right into Winehouse Lane.
➤ Folkestone

## FOLKESTONE

**Little Switzerland Caravan & Camping Park,** Little Switzerland, Wear Bay Road, Folkestone, Kent, CT19 6PS
**Tel:** 01303 252168
**Email:** littleswitzerland@lineone.net
www.caravancampingsites.co.uk
**Pitches For ▲ ⌂ ⊟**
**Facilities** ⌁ 🚿 ♨ ┌ ⊙ ┘ ⊿ ▢ ☎
🕮 ⊟ ♨ ✗ 📶 ⛽ 🎣 ⊟
**Nearby Facilities** ┌ ⊿ ⚲ ∪ ∕ ♪ ⚑
**Open** March to October
**Access** Good **Site** Level
**Nearest Town/Resort** Folkestone
**Directions** From Dover follow Folkestone signs then Country Park signs.
➤ Folkestone

## HERNE BAY

**Southview Camping,** Southview, Maypole Lane, Hoath, CanterburyKent, CT3 4LL
**Tel:** 01227 860280
**Email:** southviewcamping@aol.com
**Pitches For ▲ ⌂ ⊟ Total** 45
**Facilities** ⌁ ┌ 🕮 🚿 ♨ ┌ ⊙ ┘ ⊿ ▢ ☎
🕮 ⊟ 🎿 ♨ ✆
**Nearby Facilities** ┌ ⊿ ⚲ ⚲ ∪ ♪ ♪
**Acreage** 3 **Open** April to October
**Access** Good **Site** Level
Quiet, rural setting. Public house nearby. Very central location for Canterbury and the beautiful beaches of Thanet. Public telephone 100yds. Sorry no dogs allowed.
**Nearest Town/Resort** Canterbury
**Directions** Well signed from the A299 at Herne Bay or the A28 near Canterbury.
➤ Herne Bay

## LEYSDOWN-ON-SEA

**Priory Hill Holiday Park,** Wing Road, Leysdown-on-Sea, Isle of Sheppey, Kent, ME12 4QT
**Tel:** 01795 510267 **Fax:** 01795 511503
**Email:** philip@prioryhill.co.uk
www.prioryhill.co.uk
**Pitches For ▲ ⌂ ⊟ Total** 50
**Facilities** ⅃ ⌁ 🚿 ♨ ┌ ⊙ ┘ ⊿ ▢ ☎
🕮 ⊟ ♨ ✗ ♈ 📶 ⚑ 🎣 ⊟
**Nearby Facilities** ┌ ⊿ ⚲ ∪ ⚲ ♪ ♪
**Acreage** 15½ **Open** March to October
**Access** Good **Site** Level
Seaside park with a clubhouse, indoor heated swimming pool and entertainment on site. Please see our Web Site for details.
**Nearest Town/Resort** Leysdown-on-Sea
**Directions** From the M2 or M20 onto the A249 then the B2231 to Leysdown, follow tourism signs to Priory Hill.
➤ Sheerness

## MAIDSTONE

**Pine Lodge Touring Park,** Ashford Road A20, Hollingbourne, Kent, ME17 1XH
**Tel:** 01622 730018 **Fax:** 01622 734498
booking@pinelodgetouringpark.co.uk
www.pinelodgetouringpark.co.uk
**Pitches For ▲ ⌂ ⊟ Total** 106
**Facilities** ⅃ ⌁ 🚿 🕮 🚿 ♨ ┌ ⊙ ┘ ⊿ ▢ ☎
🕮 ⊟ 🎿 ♨ 📶 ⚑ ⊟
**Nearby Facilities** ┌ ⊿ ∪ ∪ ♪
**Acreage** 7 **Open** All Year
**Access** Good **Site** Lev/Slope
Good position for exploring 'The Garden of England'. 1 mile from Leeds Castle. Ideal stop to and from the Euro Tunnel and ferry ports.
**Nearest Town/Resort** Maidstone
**Directions** Leave the M20 at junction 8, at the next roundabout turn right towards Bearsted and Maidstone. Park is ½ a mile on the left.
➤ Bearsted

## MARDEN

**Tanner Farm Touring Caravan & Camping Park,** Tanner Farm, Goudhurst Road, Marden, Kent, TN12 9ND
**Tel:** 01622 832399 **Fax:** 01622 832472
**Email:** enquiries@tannerfarmpark.co.uk
www.tannerfarmpark.co.uk
**Pitches For ▲ ⌂ ⊟ Total** 100
**Facilities** ⅃ ⌁ ┌ 🕮 🚿 ⅃ 🚿 ♨ ┌ ⊙ ┘ ⊿ ▢ ☎
🕮 ⊟ 🎿 ♨ 📶 ⊟
**Nearby Facilities** ∕
**Acreage** 15 **Open** All Year
**Access** Good **Site** Level
Peaceful, secluded park in the centre of a 150 acre farm, shire horses kept. ETC 5 Star Graded Park and David Bellamy Gold Award. Non members welcome.

Booking essential.
**Nearest Town/Resort** Maidstone/ Tunbridge Wells
**Directions** From the A262 or A229 onto the B2079. Midway between the village of Marden and Goudhurst.
➤ Marden

## MINSTER-ON-SEA

**Riverbank Park,** The Broadway, Minster-on-Sea, Isle of Sheppey, Kent, ME12 2DB
**Tel:** 01795 870300 **Fax:** 01795 871300
**Email:** bookings.riverbankpark@virgin.net
**Pitches For ▲ ⌂ ⊟ Total** 70
**Facilities** ⅃ ⌁ 🚿 ♨ ┌ ⊙ ┘ ⊿ ▢ ☎
⊟ ⊟ 🎿 ♨ ♪
**Nearby Facilities** ∕ ⚲ ∪
**Acreage** 6 **Open** March to Oct
**Access** Good **Site** Level
Site caters mainly for adults. Near the beach with streams on two sides of the park. Wild life ponds. Holiday bungalows and motel rooms for hire.
**Nearest Town/Resort** Sheerness
**Directions** From Sheerness follow the sea front, to join The Broadway/The Leas in Minster.
➤ Sheerness

## NEW ROMNEY

**Marlie Farm Holiday Village,** Dymchurch Road, New Romney, Kent, TN28 8UE
**Tel:** 01797 363060 **Fax:** 01797 367054
**Email:** info@cinqueportsleisure.com
www.cplholidays.com
**Pitches For ▲ ⌂ ⊟ Total** 325
**Facilities** ⅃ ⌁ 🚿 ♨ ┌ ⊙ ┘ ⊿ ▢ ☎
🕮 ⊟ 🎿 ♨ ✗ 📶 ♈ 🎣 📶 ⚑ ⊟ 🎿
**Nearby Facilities** ┌ ∕ ⚲ ⚲ ∕
**Acreage** 8 **Open** March to Oct
**Access** Good **Site** Level
Set in open countryside near a sandy beach.
**Nearest Town/Resort** New Romney
**Directions** On the A259 coast road.
➤ Folkestone

## RAMSGATE

**Manston Caravan & Camping Park,** Manston Court Road, Manston, Ramsgate, Kent, CT12 5AU
**Tel:** 01843 823442
**Email:** roy@manston-park.co.uk
www.manston-park.co.uk
**Pitches For ▲ ⌂ ⊟ Total** 100
**Facilities** ⌁ 🚿 ♨ ┌ ⊙ ┘ ⊿ ▢ ☎
🕮 ⊟ 🎿 ♨ ⊟ ♪
**Nearby Facilities** ┌ ∕ ⚲ ⚲ ∪ ♪ ♪
**Acreage** 7 **Open** April to October
**Access** Good **Site** Level
Quiet, family park. Motorcycles are sometimes accepted.

# KENT

**Nearest Town/Resort** Ramsgate
**Directions** From the M2 follow the A299 and join the A253 towards Ramsgate. Turn left onto the B2048 then first right onto the B2190 towards KIA. Turn right onto the B2050 across the airfield passing the entrance to KIA. Take the first turning left into Manston Court Road, park is 500 yards on the right.
⚬ Ramsgate

## RAMSGATE

**Nethercourt Touring Park,** Nethercourt Hill, Ramsgate, Kent, CT11 0RX
**Tel:** 01843 595485 **Fax:** 01843 595485
**Email:** petebarrowcliffe@aol.com
**Pitches For** ▲ � ♠ **Total** 52
**Facilities** ♿ ⚑ 🏠 📷 🍴 ⌕ ⊙ ⊿ 🗑 📺 🛒
📶 🚿 🅿
**Nearby Facilities** ⏵ ✓ ⚓ ∪ ♪
**Acreage** 2 **Open** April **to** October
**Access** Good **Site** Level
1¼ miles from the beach and harbour. Sea fishing 1 mile.
**Nearest Town/Resort** Ramsgate
**Directions** Off the main London road on the outskirts of the town.
⚬ Ramsgate

## ROCHESTER

**Woolmans Wood Tourist Caravan Park,** Rochester Road (B2097), Chatham, Kent, ME5 9SB
**Tel:** 01634 867685 **Fax:** 01634 867685
**www.**woolmans-wood.co.uk
**Pitches For** ▲ ♠ **Total** 60
**Facilities** ⚑ 🏠 📷 🍴 ⌕ ⊙ ⊿ 🗑 📺 🛒
📶 🚿 🅿
**Nearby Facilities** ⏵ ✓ ⚓ ∪ ♪
**Acreage** 5 **Open** All Year
**Access** Good **Site** Level
ADULTS ONLY SITE. Rochester Castle and Cathedral, and Chatham Naval Base.
**Nearest Town/Resort** Rochester
**Directions** Take the A229 from the M2 junction 3 or the M20 junction 6. Follow caravan signs to the B2097. Park is ¼ mile on the right hand side.
⚬ Chatham

## SEVENOAKS

**East Hill Farm Caravan Park,** East Hill, Nr Otford, Sevenoaks, Kent, TN15 6YD
**Tel:** 01959 522347
**Pitches For** ▲ **Total** 30
**Facilities** 🏠 ⛱ 🛒 🅿
**Nearby Facilities** ⏵ ∪
**Acreage** 6 **Open** April **to** October
**Access** Good **Site** Level
**Nearest Town/Resort** Sevenoaks
**Directions** Please telephone for directions.
⚬ Otford

## SEVENOAKS

**Gate House Wood Touring Park,** Ford Lane, Wrotham Heath, Sevenoaks, Kent, TN15 7SD
**Tel:** 01732 843062
**Pitches For** ▲ ♠ **Total** 60
**Facilities** ♿ ⚑ 🏠 📷 🍴 ⊙ ⊿ 🗑 🛒
📶 🚿 🅿
**Nearby Facilities** ⏵ ∪
**Acreage** 3½ **Open** April **to** November
**Access** Good **Site** Level
Conveniently situated for Channel ports and sightseeing in South East London (45 minutes by train). Many country pubs, restaurants and take-away nearby.
**Nearest Town/Resort** Maidstone/ Sevenoaks
**Directions** From Maidstone take the M20 and exit at junction 3 onto the M26, within ½ mile take junction 2A. At the roundabout take the A20 signposted Paddock Wood, continue straight through the traffic lights at Wrotham Heath and take the first turn left signposted Trottiscliffe. After 50 yards turn left into Ford Lane and the park is 100 yards on the left.
⚬ Borough Green

## SEVENOAKS

**Oldbury Hill Camping & Caravanning Club Site,** Styants Bottom, Seal, Sevenoaks, Kent, TN15 0ET
**Tel:** 01732 762728
**www.**campingandcaravanningclub.co.uk
**Pitches For** ▲ ♠ **Total** 60
**Facilities** ⚑ 🏠 📷 🍴 ⊙ ⊿ 🗑 🛒
📶 ⊙ 🚿 📺 🅿 🅿
**Nearby Facilities** ∪
**Acreage** 6 **Open** March **to** Oct
**Access** Difficult **Site** Sloping
Set in a quiet countryside location, close to a number of National Trust properties. BTB 4 Star Graded and AA 3 Pennants. Non members welcome.
**Nearest Town/Resort** Sevenoaks
**Directions** From Sevenoaks take the A25 towards Borough Green, turn left just after the Crown Point Inn, go down the lane into Styants Bottom, site is on the left.
⚬ Borough Green

## SEVENOAKS

**Thriftwood Caravan & Camping Park,** Plaxdale Green Road, Stansted, Sevenoaks, Kent, TN15 7PB
**Tel:** 01732 822261 **Fax:** 01732 824636
**Email:** booking@thriftwoodleisure.co.uk
**www.**thriftwoodleisure.co.uk
**Pitches For** ▲ ♠ ♠ **Total** 150
**Facilities** ♿ ⚑ 🏠 🏠 📷 🍴 ⌕ ⊙ ⊿ 🗑 🛒
📶 ⊙ 🚿 🍺 📷 🛒 ⊿ 📺 🅿 ⋈ ♪
**Nearby Facilities** ⏵ ✓ ∪ ♪
**Acreage** 12 **Open** March **to** Jan

**Access** Good **Site** Lev/Slope
Ideal for visiting many Kentish attractions, as well as London and day trips to France.
**Nearest Town/Resort** Borough Green/ Wrotham
**Directions** From the M20 follow the A20 towards West Kingsdown then follow camping signs.
⚬ Borough Green

## SHEERNESS

**Sheerness Holiday Village,** Halfway Road, Minster-on-Sea, Sheerness, Kent, ME12 3AA
**Tel:** 01795 662638 **Fax:** 01795 661483
**Email:** info@cinqueportsleisure.com
**www.**cplholidays.com
**Pitches For** ♠ ♠ **Total** 86
**Facilities** ♿ ⚑ ⚑ 🏠 📷 🍴 ⊿ 🗑 🛒
🅿 ⊙ 🍺 ✗ ⊟ 🍴 ♠ ⋈ 📷 📺 ⋈ ♪
**Nearby Facilities** ⏵ ✓ ⚓ ⋈
**Open** April **to** Oct
**Access** Good **Site** Level
**Nearest Town/Resort** Sheerness
**Directions** From the M2 and A2 follow signs to Sheerness. Site is ½ a mile from the town on the right.
⚬ Sheerness

## TUNBRIDGE WELLS

**Fairdene,** Palmers Farm, Coopers Lane, Fordcombe, Tunbridge WellsKent, TN3 0RN
**Tel:** 01892 740209 **Fax:** 01892 740209
**Pitches For** ▲ ♠ ♠ **Total** 20
**Facilities** 🛒 ⋈ 🅿
**Nearby Facilities** ⋈
**Acreage** 3 **Open** April **to** Sept
**Access** Poor **Site** Sloping
Ideal for visiting stately homes.
**Nearest Town/Resort** Tunbridge Wells
**Directions** From Tunbridge Wells take the A264 then the B2188.
⚬ Ashurst

## WHITSTABLE

**Primrose Cottage Caravan Park,** Golden Hill, Whitstable, Kent, CT5 3AR
**Tel:** 01227 273694
**Pitches For** ▲ ♠ ♠ **Total** 12
**Facilities** ⚑ 🏠 📷 🍴 ⊙ ⊿ 🅿
📶 🚿 🏠 🛒 🅿
**Nearby Facilities** ⏵ ✓ ⚓ ∪ ♪ ♪
**Acreage** ½ **Open** March **to** October
**Access** Good **Site** Level
**Nearest Town/Resort** Whitstable
**Directions** On A2990, 1 mile east of Whitstable roundabout.
⚬ Whitstable

## WHITSTABLE
**Seaview Holiday Village,** St Johns Road, Swalecliffe, Whitstable, Kent, CT5 2RY
**Tel:** 01227 792246 **Fax:** 01227 792247
**Email:** info@cinqueportsleisure.com
www.cplholidays.com
**Pitches For** ⚡ ⛺ **Total** 171
**Facilities** 🚿 ⚡ 🚻 ⛽ 🍴 ⊙ ⬅ 🔲 🛍️
🏪 🅿️ 🔥 ✖ 🛒 🎣 🎮 ⭐ 🚲 🔲 🍴 ☀️
**Nearby Facilities** 🎣 ✗ ⚓ 🏌️ 🏊
**Acreage** 8 **Open** March to Oct
**Access** Good **Site** Level
On the beach.
**Nearest Town/Resort** Whitstable
**Directions** Off the A2990, at the double roundabout turn left and go under the railway bridge, at the mini roundabout turn right, after 600m turn left down lane to the park (signposted).
🚉 Swalecliffe

# LANCASHIRE

## BENTHAM
**Riverside Caravan Park,** High Bentham, Lancaster, Lancashire, LA2 7LW
**Tel:** 015242 61272 **Fax:** 015242 62163
**Email:** info@riversidecaravanpark.co.uk
www.riversidecaravanpark.co.uk
**Pitches For** ⚡ ⛺ **Total** 60
**Facilities** 🚿 ⚡ 🚻 ⛽ 🍴 ⊙ ⬅ 🔲 🛍️
🏪 ⊙ 🔥 🛒 🔲 🍴 ☀️
**Nearby Facilities** 🎣 ✗
**Acreage** 10 **Open** March to October
**Access** Good **Site** Level
Fishing for trout and sea trout on the site. Electric points for tourers. New toilet and shower block now open.
**Nearest Town/Resort** High Bentham
**Directions** Follow caravan signs off the B6480 at the Black Bull Hotel in Bentham.
🚉 Bentham

## BLACKPOOL
**Gillett Farm Caravan Park,** Peel Road, Nr Blackpool, Lancashire, FY4 5JU
**Tel:** 01253 761676
**Pitches For** ⚡ ⛺ **Total** 76
**Facilities** 🚿 ⚡ 🚻 ⛽ 🍴 ⊙ ⬅ 🔲 🛍️
🏪 ⊙ 🔥 🛒 🔲 🍴 ☀️
**Nearby Facilities** 🎣 ✗ ⚓ 🏌️ 🏊
**Acreage** 12 **Open** March to October
**Access** Good **Site** Slightly Sloping
Within easy reach of Blackpool, Lytham St Annes and Fleetwood.
**Nearest Town/Resort** Blackpool
**Directions** Blackpool junction 4 on M55 turn left to Kirkham 400yds, straight on at the roundabout to traffic lights. Turn right and immediate left into Peel Road. 350yds second site on the right.
🚉 Blackpool

## BLACKPOOL
**Mariclough - Hampsfield,** Preston New Road, Peel, Blackpool, Lancashire, FY4 5JR
**Tel:** 01253 761034
**Email:** tony@mariclough.fsnet.co.uk
www.maricloughhampsfieldcamping.co.uk
**Pitches For** ⚡ ⛺ **Total** 50
**Facilities** ⚡ 🚻 ⛽ 🍴 ⊙ ⬅ 🛍️ 🛒
🔲 🍴 🅿️ ☀️
**Nearby Facilities** 🎣 ✗ ⚓ 🏌️ 🏊
**Acreage** 2 **Open** Easter to October
**Access** Good **Site** Level
Exclusively for ADULTS ONLY. Flat, mown grass, sheltered park. Off license. Please telephone before 8pm.
**Nearest Town/Resort** Blackpool
**Directions** M55 junction 4, first left onto the A583. Go through traffic lights, site 200yds on the left.
🚉 Blackpool/Kirkham

## BLACKPOOL
**Marton Mere Holiday Village,** Mythop Road, Blackpool, Lancashire, FY4 4XN
**Tel:** 01253 767544 **Fax:** 01253 791252
www.touringholidays.co.uk
**Pitches For** ⚡ ⛺ **Total** 204
**Facilities** 🚿 ⚡ 🚻 ⛽ 🍴 ⊙ ⬅ 🔲 🛍️
🏪 🅿️ ⊙ ✖ 🛒 🔥 🎮 ⭐ 🚲 🔲 🍴 ☀️
**Nearby Facilities**
**Acreage** 93 **Open** March to October
**Access** Good **Site** Level
A sanctuary for birds and wildlife with spectacular views. Kids Club, family entertainment, bowling, tennis, amusements and crazy golf.
**Nearest Town/Resort** Blackpool
**Directions** Take the A583 towards Blackpool, turn right at Clifton Arms traffic lights onto Mythop Road, park is 150 yards on the left.

## BLACKPOOL
**Newton Hall Holiday Centre,** Staining Road, Staining, Blackpool, Lancashire, FY3 0AX
**Tel:** 01253 882512 **Fax:** 01253 893101
**Email:** reception@newtonhall.net
www.newtonhall.net
**Pitches For** ⛺ ⛽ **Total** 35
**Facilities** 🚿 ⚡ 🚻 ⛽ 🍴 ⊙ ⬅ 🔲 🛍️
🏪 ⊙ ✖ 🛒 🔥 🎮 🔲 ☀️ 🎣
**Nearby Facilities** 🎣 ✗ 🏊
**Open** 1 March to 15 Nov
**Access** Good **Site** Level
Ideal for Blackpools Pleasure Beach and Stanley Park.
**Nearest Town/Resort** Blackpool
**Directions** Leave the M55 at junction 4 and head for Blackpool. At the second set of traffic lights turn right into Mythop Road, at

T-junction turn left into Chain Lane, follow road through Staining Village and Park is on the left.
🚉 Blackpool

## BLACKPOOL
**Pipers Height Caravan & Camping Park,** Peel Road, Peel, Blackpool, Lancashire, FY4 5JT
**Tel:** 01253 763767
**Pitches For** ⚡ ⛺ **Total** 100
**Facilities** 🚿 ✖ ⚡ 🚻 ⛽ 🍴 ⊙ ⬅ 🔲 🛍️
🏪 ⊙ ✖ 🛒 🔥 🔲 ☀️
**Nearby Facilities** 🎣 ✗ ⚓ 🏌️ 🏊
**Acreage** 11 **Open** March to November
**Access** Good **Site** Level
Static caravan sales.
**Nearest Town/Resort** Blackpool
**Directions** Exit M55 junction 4 take the first turning left on the A583. At the first set of lights turn right then sharp left. Site is first on the right. Site is ½ a mile from the M55.
🚉 Blackpool

## BLACKPOOL
**Windy Harbour Holiday Park,** Little Singleton, Nr Blackpool, Lancashire, FY6 8NB
**Tel:** 01253 883064 **Fax:** 01253 892562
**Email:** info@windyharbour.net
www.windyharbour.net
**Pitches For** ⚡ ⛺ **Total**
**Facilities** 🚿 ✖ ⚡ 🚻 ⛽ 🍴 ⊙ ⬅ 🔲 🛍️
🏪 ⊙ 🔥 ✖ 🛒 🔲 🎮 🚲 🔲 🍴 ☀️ 🎣
**Nearby Facilities** 🎣 ✗ ⚓ 🏌️
**Open** 1 March to 15 Nov
**Access** Good **Site** Level
Alongside the River Wyre. Close to Blackpool and Cleveleys. Easy access to the M55.
**Nearest Town/Resort** Blackpool
**Directions** Leave the M55 at junction 3 and take the A585 to Fleetwood. Follow for approx. 3 miles, go straight on at the traffic lights and the park entrance is approx. 300m straight ahead.
🚉 Poulton-le-Fylde

## CARNFORTH
**Bolton Holmes Farm,** Bolton-le-Sands, Carnforth, Lancashire, LA5 8ES
**Tel:** 01524 732854
**Pitches For** ⚡ ⛺ **Total** 30
**Facilities** ✖ ⚡ 🚻 ⛽ 🍴 ⊙ ⬅ 🏪 ⊙ 🔲 ☀️
**Nearby Facilities** ✗ 🏊
**Open** April to September
**Access** Good **Site** Sloping
On the shore side with scenic views.
**Nearest Town/Resort** Lancaster/Morecambe
**Directions** Travel north on A6. Take first left after Royal Hotel, Mill Lane, Bolton-le-Sands.
🚉 Carnforth

# OLD HALL CARAVAN PARK  *www.oldhall.uk.com*

**Luxury Holiday Homes For Sale.** Touring Caravans & Motor Caravans Welcome on this quiet, secluded family run park surrounded by 80 acres of woodland in unspoilt countryside. Extended season - Optional. Conveniently situated close to the Lakes and Yorkshire Dales. Easy access being only 3 miles from M6 J35.

**Capernwray, CARNFORTH, Lancashire LA6 1AD**    Telephone **01524 733276** for details or a brochure

## CARNFORTH
**Capernwray House,** Capernwray, Carnforth, Lancashire, LA6 1AE
**Tel:** 01524 732363
**Email:** mel@capernwrayhouse.com
www.capernwrayhouse.com
**Pitches For** Å ⌖ ➡ **Total** 60
**Facilities** ⌂ 🅱 🆎 ☎ ſ ☺ ⌣ 🔟 ☎
🅂🅁 🎦 🎱 🎰 ♨🔫📼 ⚡ ♨
**Nearby Facilities** ſ ✔ ⚲ ∪ ⚓
**Acreage** 18 **Open** March **to** October
**Access** Good **Site** Lev/Slope
Near a canal, beautiful scenery and good walking. Holiday homes for sale. Bed & Breakfast available.
**Nearest Town** Carnforth/Kirby Lonsdale
**Directions** Leave the M6 junction 35 and follow signs for Over Kellet. At the village green turn left signposted Capernwray. Site is 2 miles on the right.
🚋 Carnforth

## CARNFORTH
**Detron Gate,** Bolton-le-Sands, Carnforth, Lancashire, LA5 9TN
**Tel:** 01524 732842
**Pitches For** Å ⌖ ➡ **Total** 150
**Facilities** ⌂ 🅱 🆎 ſ ☺ ⌣ 🔟 ☎
🅂🅁 🎱 🅰🎰 ♨ ♨
**Nearby Facilities** ſ ✔ ∪ ℛ
**Acreage** 10 **Open** April **to** October
**Access** Good **Site** Lev/Slope
**Nearest Town/Resort** Morecambe
🚋 Carnforth

## CARNFORTH
**Hollins Farm,** Far Arnside, Off Cove Road, Silverdale, CarnforthLancashire, LA5 0SL
**Tel:** 01524 701767
**Pitches For** Å ⌖ ➡
**Facilities** 🅱 🆎 ☺ 🔫📼 🖷
**Nearby Facilities**
**Acreage** 5 **Open** March **to** Oct
**Access** Good **Site** Lev/Slope
Situated in an area of outstanding natural beauty, near the shore and a bird reserve.
**Nearest Town/Resort** Arnside
**Directions** Leave the M6 at junction 35 into Carnforth, follow signs for Silverdale. Go over the level crossing and bear right, after ¾ miles bear left and after ¼ of a mile fork right into Cove Road.
🚋 Arnside/Silverdale

## CARNFORTH
**Old Hall Caravan Park,** Capernwray, Carnforth, Lancashire, LA6 1AD
**Tel:** 01524 733276 **Fax:** 01524 734488
**Email:** oldhall@charis.co.uk
www.oldhall.uk.com
**Pitches For** ⌖ ➡ **Total** 38
**Facilities** & ſ ⌂ 🅱 🆎 ſ ☺ ⌣ 🔟 ☎
🌇 🎱 🎰🔫📼 🖷 ♨
**Nearby Facilities** ſ ✔ ∪ ≵
**Open** 1 March **to** 10 January
**Access** Good **Site** Level
Quiet, peaceful, woodland retreat.
**Nearest Town/Resort** Carnforth
**Directions** Leave the M6 at junction 35, go to Over Kellet. Turn left in the village of Over Kellet and the park is 1½ miles on the right.
🚋 Carnforth

## CARNFORTH
**Red Bank Farm,** The Shore, Bolton-le-Sands, Carnforth, Lancashire, LA5 8JR
**Tel:** 01524 823196 **Fax:** 01524 824981
**Email:** archer_mark@lycos.co.uk
www.redbankfarm.co.uk
**Pitches For** Å ➡ **Total** 50
**Facilities** 🆎 ſ ☺ ⌣ 🔫📼 🖷
**Nearby Facilities** ſ ✔
**Acreage** 3 **Open** Easter **to** October
**Site** Lev/Slope
On the shore side of Morecambe Bay. Camp on our organic field and see our organically fed animals, (ie milking cows and sheep).
**Nearest Town/Resort** Morecambe
**Directions** From the A6 at Bolton-le-Sands, take the A5105 to Morecambe. After 500yds sharp right and right again at the railway bridge, turn left along the shore into the farm.
🚋 Lancaster/Morecambe

## CARNFORTH
**Sandside Caravan & Camping Site,** The Shore, Bolton-le-Sands, Nr Carnforth, Lancashire, LA5 8JS
**Tel:** 01524 822311 **Fax:** 01524 822311
**Pitches For** Å ⌖ ➡ **Total** 70
**Facilities** 🆎 ſ ⌂ 🅱 🆎 ſ ☺ ⌣ 🔟 ☎
🅂🅁 🎦 🎱 ♨🔫📼 ⚡ ♨
**Nearby Facilities** ſ ✔ ⚲ ⚓ ∪ ♫ ℛ
**Acreage** 9 **Open** March **to** Oct
**Access** Good **Site** Level
100 yards from the shore.
**Nearest Town/Resort** Morecambe
**Directions** Leave the M6 at junction 35 and follow the A6 Carnforth road to Bolton-le-Sands, turn right at the the Far Pavillion Indian Restaurant (on the left), go over the railway line and the site is up the hill on the right.
🚋 Carnforth

## CLITHEROE
**Camping & Caravanning Club Site,** Edisford Road, Clitheroe, Lancashire, BB7 3LA
**Tel:** 01200 425294
www.campingandcaravanningclub.co.uk
**Pitches For** Å ⌖ ➡ **Total** 80
**Facilities** & ſ 🅱 🆎 ſ ☺ ⌣ 🔟 ☎
🅸 🎱 🎰🔫📼 🖷 🖷
**Nearby Facilities** ſ ℛ ℛ
**Acreage** 6 **Open** May **to** Nov
**Site** Lev/Slope
In the Ribble Valley, on the banks of a river. Local ghost walks on a weekly basis. Near Clitheroe Castle. BTB 3 Star Graded and AA 3 Pennants. Non members welcome.
**Directions** Nearest main road is the A59. From the west follow the A671 into Clitheroe. Look for the signpost indicating a left turn to Longridge/Sports Centre, turn into Greenacre Road approx 25 metres beyond the pelican crossing. Continue until the T-Junction at Edisford Road, turn left and continue past the church on the right, look for the Sports Centre on the right and car park opposite.
🚋 Clitheroe

## CLITHEROE
**Three Rivers Country Park,** Eaves Hall Lane, West Bradford, Clitheroe, Lancashire, BB7 3JG
**Tel:** 01200 423523 **Fax:** 01200 442383
**Email:** enquiries@threeriverspark.co.uk
www.threeriverspark.co.uk
**Pitches For** Å ⌖ ➡ **Total** 100
**Facilities** ſ ⌂ 🅱 🆎 ſ ☺ ⌣ 🔟 ☎
🅂🅁 🎱 🎦 🎰 ♨ 🎰🔫📼 🖷 🖷 ♨
**Nearby Facilities** ſ ✔ ∪
**Acreage** 45 **Open** March **to** 7 Nov
**Access** Good **Site** Level
Forest and the Trough of Bowland. Explore picturesque villages, Clitheroe Castle and Ingleton Waterfalls. Easy driving distance to the Yorkshire Dales and Skipton.
**Nearest Town/Resort** Clitheroe
**Directions** A59 'Clitheroe North' turning, through the village to a T-Junction and turn left for West Bradford. Go past the Three Millstones Pub on the left, go round the s-bend and take the first turn right. ½ mile along this lane on the right is Three Rivers.
🚋 Clitheroe

## GARSTANG
**Wyreside Farm Park,** Allotment Lane, St Michael's-on-Wyre, Garstang, Lancashire, PR3 0TZ
**Tel:** 01995 679797
**Email:** penny.wyresidefarm@freenet.co.uk
www.ukparks.co.uk/wyresidefarm
**Pitches For** Å ⌖ ➡ **Total** 16
**Facilities** ſ ⌂ 🆎 ſ ☺ ♨ 🎦 ♨🔫📼 🖷
**Nearby Facilities** ſ ✔ ⚲ ⚓ ∪ ℛ ♫
**Acreage** 4½ **Open** March **to** October
**Access** Good **Site** Level
On the banks of the River Wyre. Mowed field to play in. Central for Blackpool, the Lakes and the Trough of Bowland.
**Nearest Town/Resort** Garstang/Blackpool
**Directions** Leave the M6 at junction 32 and take the A6 north for 3½ miles. West at Guys Thatch hamlet into St. Michael's Road, 3½ miles to the mini roundabout on an A586, north over the bridge, past grapes, first right after right hand bend.
🚋 Preston

## LANCASTER
**New Parkside Farm Caravan Park,** Denny Beck, Caton Road, Lancaster, Lancashire, LA2 9HH
**Tel:** 01524 770723/770337
www.ukparks.co.uk/newparkside
**Pitches For** Å ⌖ ➡ **Total** 40
**Facilities** & ſ ⌂ 🆎 ſ ☺ ⌣ ☎ 🔫📼 🖷 ♨
**Nearby Facilities** ſ ✔
**Acreage** 4 **Open** March **to** October
**Access** Good **Site** Lev/Slope
A working farm with beautiful views of Lune Valley. On the edge of Forest of Bowland and close to historic Lancaster and Morecambe Bay. Central for lakes and dales.
**Nearest Town/Resort** Lancaster
**Directions** Leave the M6 at junction 34 and take the A683 towards Kirkby Lonsdale. Park is situated 1 mile on the right.
🚋 Lancaster

## LANCASTER

**Wyreside Lakes Fishery,** Sunnyside Farmhouse, Bay Horse, Lancaster, Lancashire, LA2 9DG
**Tel:** 01524 792093
**Email:** wyreside2003@yahoo.co.uk
www.wyresidelakes.co.uk
**Pitches For** ⚠ ⛟ ☗ **Total** 50
**Facilities** ⚃ ⛏ 🄵 ⓗ ⛢ ⌐ ☉ ⌐ ⛟ ☗
🛉 ⚐ ✕ ⚑ ⍥ ♨ ⚡ ✻
**Nearby Facilities** ↾ ∪
**Acreage** 10 **Open** All Year
**Access** Good **Site** Lev/Slope
Set in the beautiful Wyreside Valley with views of the Bowland Fells. 13 lakes to walk around and the beautiful Foxes Wood.
**Nearest Town/Resort** Garstang
**Directions** Leave the M6 at junction 33, turn left towards Garstang and follow brown tourism signs.
⭜ Lancaster

## MORECAMBE

**Glen Caravan Park,** Westgate, Morecambe, Lancashire, LA3 3EL
**Tel:** 01524 423896
**Pitches For** ⛟ ☗ **Total** 10
**Facilities** ⚃ ⓗ ⛢ ⌐ ☉ ⌐ ☖ ⌐ ☗ ⚒ ✻
**Nearby Facilities** ↾ ∫ ∟ ∪ ♪
**Acreage** ½ **Open** March **to** October
**Access** Good **Site** Level
15 minutes walk Morecambe Promenade.
**Nearest Town/Resort** Morecambe
**Directions** In Morecambe itself close to promenade, Regent Road and Westgate.

## MORECAMBE

**Melbreak Caravan Site,** Carr Lane, Middleton, Nr Morecambe, Lancashire, LA3 3LH
**Tel:** 01524 852430

**Pitches For** ⚠ ⛟ ☗ **Total** 55
**Facilities** ⚃ ⛏ 🄵 ⓗ ⛢ ⌐ ☉ ⌐ ⛟ ☗
🛉 ⚐ ⍲ ✻
**Nearby Facilities** ↾ ∫
**Acreage** 2 **Open** March **to** October
**Access** Good **Site** Level
Site is 1 mile from Middleton beach.
**Nearest Town/Resort** Morecambe
**Directions** Leave the M6 at junction 34 and take the A683 for 3 miles, at the second roundabout turn left, after 4 miles turn left for Middleton. Turn right by the church and site is ½ mile on the left.
⭜ Morecambe

## MORECAMBE

**Ocean Edge Leisure Park,** Moneyclose Lane, Heysham, Lancashire, LA3 2XA
**Tel:** 0870 774 4024 **Fax:** 01524 732034
**Email:** enquiries@southlakeland-caravans.co.uk
www.southlakeland-caravans.co.uk
**Pitches For** ⚠ ⛟ ☗ **Total** 126
**Facilities** ⚃ ⓗ ⛢ ⌐ ☉ ⌐ ⛟ ☗
🛉 ⚐ ⚒ ✕ ⚐ ⍥ ♨ ⚐ ✻ ♪ ☗
**Nearby Facilities** ↾ ∫ ∟ ⚲ ∪ ♪
**Acreage** 20 **Open** March **to** Jan
**Access** Good **Site** Level
Coastal park with bars, entertainment and cabaret, kiddies disco, amusements and day-time activities. Indoor pool and sauna, mini-market, indoor and outdoor play areas. A complete family park. Ideal touring centre. Holiday Home hire and sales.
**Nearest Town/Resort** Morecambe/Lancaster
**Directions** M6 junction 34, follow signs for Port of Heysham, site signed from 2 miles.
⭜ Morecambe

## MORECAMBE

**Venture Caravan Park,** Langridge Way, Westgate, Morecambe, Lancashire, LA4 4TQ
**Tel:** 01524 412986 **Fax:** 01524 422029
**Email:** mark@venturecaravanpark.co.uk
www.venturecaravanpark.co.uk
**Pitches For** ⚠ ⛟ ☗
**Facilities** ⚃ ⛏ 🄵 ⓗ ⛢ ⌐ ☉ ⌐ ⛟ ☗
🛉 ⚐ ✕ ⚐ ⍲ ♨ ⚐ ⚒ ⚐ ☗ ✻
**Nearby Facilities** ↾ ∫ ∟ ⚲ ∫ ♪
**Open** All Year
**Access** Good **Site** Level
**Nearest Town/Resort** Morecambe
⭜ Morecambe

## ORMSKIRK

**Abbey Farm Caravan Park,** Dark Lane, Ormskirk, Lancashire, L40 5TX
**Tel:** 01695 572686 **Fax:** 01695 572686
**Email:** abbeyfarm@yahoo.com
www.abbeyfarmcaravanpark.co.uk
**Pitches For** ⚠ ⛟ ☗ **Total** 104
**Facilities** ⚃ ⛏ 🄵 ⓗ ⛢ ⌐ ☉ ⌐ ⛟ ☗
🛉 ⚐ ⚒ ⍲ ⚐ ☗ ☗ ✻
**Nearby Facilities** ↾ ∫ ∪ ♪
**Acreage** 6 **Open** All Year
**Access** Good **Site** Level
Peace and quiet in a rural setting. Ideal touring centre. Family bathroom available. Off license on site. A Countryside Discovery Park, David Bellamy Environment Award and Merseyside Caravan Park of the Year 1995.
**Nearest Town/Resort** Southport
**Directions** From the M6 junction 27 onto the A5209 to Newburgh and Parbold. After 4½ miles turn left onto the B5240 and turn immediate right into Hobcross Lane. Site is 1½ miles on the right.
⭜ Ormskirk

## Abbey Farm Caravan Park

**Dark Lane, Ormskirk, Lancashire L40 5TX**

Award winning, family run park in peaceful surroundings.

www.abbeyfarmcaravanpark.co.uk

Tel/Fax: 01695 572686   E-mail: abbeyfarm@yahoo.com

Children's Playground & Recreation Room
Heated Facilities
Family Bathroom

**OPEN ALL YEAR**

### PILLING

**Glenfield Caravan Park,** Smallwood Hey Road, Pilling, Nr Blackpool, Lancashire, PR3 6HE
**Tel:** 01253 790782
**Email:** petercottam@tiscali.co.uk
www.ukparks.co.uk/glenfield
**Pitches For** ⌖ ⛺ **Total** 8
**Facilities** ⌗ ▥ ♨ ⌒ ☉ ▨ ⬚ ⍾ ▨ ⌗▣ ⌇
**Nearby Facilities** ⌘ ⟋ ⚓ ∪ ⏋
**Acreage** 8 **Open** March **to** October
**Access** Good **Site** Level
Flat site on the coast. Ideal for walking and cycling.
**Nearest Town/Resort** Blackpool
**Directions** In the village of Pilling just off the A588 Lancaster to Blackpool main road. 10 miles from Lancaster and Blackpool.
⌁ Poulton-le-Fylde

### PREESALL

**Maaruig Caravan Park,** 71 Pilling Lane, Preesall, Poulton-le-Fylde, Lancashire, FY6 0HB
**Tel:** 01253 810404
**Pitches For** ⌖ ⛺ **Total** 31
**Facilities** ⌗ ▥ ♨ ⌒ ☉ ⬚ ▢ ⬚ ▨⌗▣ ⍾
**Nearby Facilities** ⌘ ⟋ ⚓ ∪ ⌇
**Acreage** 1 **Open** 1 March **to** 4 Jan
**Access** Good **Site** Level
Near the beach, ideal walking. Central location for Blackpool, Preston, Lancaster and drive to the Lake District. Less than 1 hours drive to the Lake District.
**Nearest Town/Resort** Blackpool
**Directions** Leave the M55 at junction 3 and take the A585 towards Fleetwood. At the third set of traffic lights turn right onto the A588. Follow Knott End (B5377) up to the T-Junction, turn left then the first right into Pilling Lane.
⌁ Poulton-le-Fylde

### PRESTON

**Beacon Fell View Caravan Park,** Higher Road, Longridge, Nr Preston, Lancashire, PR3 2TF
**Tel:** 01772 783233 **Fax:** 01772 784204
**Email:** beaconfell@hagansleisure.co.uk
www.hagansleisure.co.uk
**Pitches For** ⌖ ⛺ ⛺
**Facilities** ⌗ ▥ ▤ ▥ ♨ ⌒ ⬚ ⬚ ▢ ▢ ▨ ☉ ⬚ ▥ ♨ ⌖ ⬚ ⍾ ⬚⌗▣ ▣
**Nearby Facilities** ⌘ ⟋ ∪ ⌇ ⍺
**Acreage** 30 **Open** March **to** Oct
**Access** Good **Site** Sloping
Overlooking the Ribble Valley. 30 minutes from the bright lights of Blackpool. Ideal touring destination for the Lake District and the Yorkshire Dales.
**Nearest Town/Resort** Longridge
**Directions** In Longridge go straight across the roundabout and keep left at the White Bull Pub, park is 1 mile on the right.
⌁ Preston

### SOUTHPORT

**Riverside Holiday Park,** Harrison Leisure UK Ltd, Southport New Road, Banks, SouthportMerseyside, PR9 8DF
**Tel:** 01704 228886 **Fax:** 01704 505886
**Email:** karen@harrisonleisureuk.com

www.harrisonleisureuk.com
**Pitches For** ⌖ ⛺ ⛺ **Total** 200
**Facilities** ⌗ ▥ ♨ ⌒ ⬚ ☉ ⬚
▧ ☉ ⬚ ▥ ▤ ⍾ ▥ ☐ ⬚ ⍾
**Nearby Facilities** ⌘ ⟋ ⚓ ∪ ⌇
**Open** 1 March **to** 7 Jan
**Access** Good **Site** Level
Night clubs, lounge bar and family room. Bus on site with direct transport to Southport which runs every ½ an hour. Large area for touring.
**Nearest Town/Resort** Southport
**Directions** Leave the M6 at junc 27 and take the A5209 towards Parbold and Burscough. At the junction turn right onto the A59 and continue to the traffic lights in Tarleton, turn left onto the A5105. Continue to the dual carriageway, at the roundabout go straight across and the site is approx. 1 mile on the left.
⌁ Southport

### THORNTON

**Kneps Farm Holiday Park,** River Road, Stanah, Thornton-Cleveleys, BlackpoolLancashire, FY5 5LR
**Tel:** 01253 823632 **Fax:** 01253 863967
**Email:** enquiries@knepsfarm.co.uk
www.knepsfarm.co.uk
**Pitches For** ⌖ ⛺ ⛺ **Total** 60
**Facilities** ⌗ ⌀ ⌗ ▥ ▤ ▥ ♨ ⌒ ☉ ⬚
▢ ⍾ ▧ ☉ ⬚ ▥⌗▣ ⍾
**Nearby Facilities** ⌘ ⟋ ⚓ ⌇
**Acreage** 3½ **Open** March **to** Mid Nov
**Access** Good **Site** Level
Situated adjacent to the Stanah Amenity and Picnic Area, forming part of the River Wyre Estuary Country Park. A rural retreat close to Blackpool.
**Nearest Town/Resort** Blackpool
**Directions** 5 miles north north east of Blackpool. From the M55 junction 3 take the A585 Fleetwood road to the River Wyre Hotel on the left, turn right at the roundabout onto the B5412 signposted Little Thornton. Turn right at the mini-roundabout after the school onto Stanah Road, go straight over the next roundabout leading to River Road.
⌁ Poulton-le-Fylde

### THORNTON

**Stanah House Caravan Park,** River Road, Thornton, Cleveleys, FY5 5LR
**Tel:** 01253 824000
**Email:** stanahhouse@talk21.com
**Pitches For** ⌖ ⛺ ⛺ **Total** 50
**Facilities** ⌗ ▥ ▤ ♨ ⌒ ☉ ⬚ ▥ ▢ ⬚ ▥
⬚ ▥⌗▣ ▣ ⍾
**Nearby Facilities** ⌘ ⟋ ⚓ ∪ ⌇
**Acreage** 7 **Open** March **to** Oct
**Access** Good **Site** Lev/Slope
Alongside the River Wyre and Wyreside Ecology Centre. Only 3½ miles from Blackpool.
**Nearest Town/Resort** Blackpool
**Directions** From South: Leave the M6 at junc 32 joining the M55, exit at junc 3 and take the A585 following signs to Fleetwood. At the traffic lights by Shell bear right, go straight through the next lights, at roundabout by the River Wyre Hotel turn right for Little Thornton and Stanah Picnic Area. After 1 mile turn right

into Stanah Road which continues into River Road. You will reach the Wyre Estuary Country Park and the site entrance is third on the right.
⌁ Poulton-le-Fylde

### WARTON

**Oakland Caravan Park,** Lytham Road, Warton, Preston, Lancashire, PR4 1AH
**Tel:** 01772 634459 **Fax:** 01772 679000
**Pitches For** ⌖ ⛺ ⛺ **Total** 60
**Facilities** ⌗ ⍾ ⌗ ▥ ▤ ▥ ♨ ⌒ ☉ ⬚ ▢ ⬚
▨ ☉ ⬚ ▥⌗▣ ⌇
**Nearby Facilities** ⌘ ⟋ ⚓ ∪ ⌇ ⍺
**Acreage** 9 **Open** 22 Dec **to** 8 Nov
**Access** Good **Site** Lev/Slope
2 miles from the Pleasure Beach, Blackpool Tower, Sandcastle and beach.
**Nearest Town/Resort** Blackpool/Preston
**Directions** Leave the M6 at junction 31 and take the A583 towards Blackpool. Turn left onto the A584, come off at Warton and the site is 1 mile on the right from the roundabout.
⌁ Wesham

## LEICESTERSHIRE

### CASTLE DONINGTON

**Donington Park Farmhouse Hotel,** Melbourne Road, Isley Walton, Castle Donington, Leicestershire, DE74 2RN
**Tel:** 01332 862409 **Fax:** 01332 862364
**Email:** info@parkfarmhouse.co.uk
www.parkfarmhouse.co.uk
**Pitches For** ⌖ ⛺ ⛺ **Total** 60
**Facilities** ⍾ ⌗ ▥ ▤ ▥ ♨ ⌒ ⬚ ⬚ ▢ ⬚
▧ ☉ ⬚ ▥ ✕ ⬚⌗▣ ▣
**Nearby Facilities** ⌘
**Acreage** 7 **Open** All Year
**Access** Good **Site** Sloping
Donington Park Race Circuit and Car Museum.
**Nearest Town/Resort** Castle Donington
**Directions** On the A453 at Isley Walton take the Melbourne turning, site is ½ a mile down this road at the competitors entrance to Donington Park.
⌁ Derby

### LEICESTER

**Hill Top Caravan & Leisure Park,** Hill Top, 67 Old Gate Road, Thrussington, Leicestershire, LE7 4TL
**Tel:** 01664 424357 **Fax:** 01664 424357
www.caravancampingsites.co.uk/ leicestershire
**Pitches For** ⛺ ⛺ **Total** 10
**Facilities** ⍾ ⌗ ▥ ▤ ▥ ⌒ ⬚⌗▣
**Nearby Facilities** ⌘ ⟋ ⚓ ∪ ⌇ ⍺
**Acreage** 1 **Open** All Year
**Access** Good **Site** Level
Within walking distance of two country pubs and a general store. Archery on site. 5 minutes drive to two golf courses. Close to Belvoir Castle, Rutland Water, Ragdale Hall Health Spa, National Space Centre and much more.
**Nearest Town/Resort** Leicester
**Directions** 9 miles north of Leicester on the A46 Newark road. At Thrussington Rearsby sign turn right, on entering Thrussington turn sharp left at 30mph sign into Old Gate Road, site is 500 yards on the right.
⌁ Syston

## LUTTERWORTH

**Ullesthorpe Garden Centre,** Lutterworth Road, Ullesthorpe, Nr Lutterworth, Leicestershire, LE17 5DR
Tel: 01455 202144 Fax: 01455 202585
enquiries@ullesthorpegardencentre.co.uk
www.ullesthorpegardencentre.co.uk
Pitches For ♥ ♠ Total 162
Facilities ♿ ⚡ ⚘ ⛗ ⛱ ⛏ ✕ ♨ ☐ ▣
Nearby Facilities ⛳ ✦ ✈ ∪
Open April to Sept
Access Good Site Level
In the countryside. Only 12 electric hook-ups available.
Nearest Town/Resort Lutterworth
⚑ Rugby

## MARKET BOSWORTH

**Bosworth Water Trust,** Far Cotton Lane, Market Bosworth, Leicestershire, CV13 6PD
Tel: 01455 291876 Fax: 01455 291876
Email: info@bosworthwatertrust.co.uk
www.bosworthwatertrust.co.uk
Pitches For ▲ ♥ ♠ Total 76
Facilities ♿ ⚡ ⛗ ⚘ ⛱ ⛏ ✕ ♨ ❄ ♨ ☐ ▣
Nearby Facilities ⛳ ✦ ⚓ ⛏ ∪ ♨ ⚲
Acreage 50 Open All Year
Access Good Site Level
50 acre park with a 5 acre caravan park.
£3 per car to enter, £4 on Sundays and

Bank Holidays. Battlefields of Market Bosworth, Twycross Zoo and steam railway.
Nearest Town/Resort Market Bosworth
Directions From Hinckley A447, left onto the B585 to Market Bosworth. From Nuneaton A444 and cross the A5, right onto the B585 to Market Bosworth.
⚑ Hinckley/Nuneaton

# LINCOLNSHIRE

## ALFORD

**Woodthorpe Hall Leisure Park,** Woodthorpe Hall, Woodthorpe, Alford, Lincolnshire, LN13 0DD
Tel: 01507 450294 Fax: 01507 450885
enquiries@woodthorpehallleisure.co.uk
www.woodthorpehallleisure.co.uk
Pitches For ▲ ♥ ♠ Total 60
Facilities ♿ ⚡ ⛗ ⚘ ⛗ ⛏ ♨ ⊙ ⊣ ☐ ▣
⛗ ▣ ⓖ ⛱ ✕ ♨ ⛱ ☐ ▣ ♨ ⚘ ✈
Nearby Facilities ⛳ ✦ ✈ ∪
Open 1 March to 3 Jan
Access Good Site Level
Golf course and fishing lakes on site. 6 miles from the beach and 10 miles from the Georgian market town of Louth.
Nearest Town/Resort Alford
Directions Just off the B1373, 1½ miles from Withern Village and 3½ miles from the market town of Alford.
⚑ Skegness

## BARTON-UPON-HUMBER

**Silver Birches Caravan Park,** Waterside Road, Barton-Upon-Humber, North Lincolnshire, DN18 5BA
Tel: 01652 632509 Fax: 01652 632509
www.silverbirchescaravanpark.co.uk
Pitches For ▲ ♥ ♠ Total 25
Facilities ♿ ⚡ ⛗ ⚘ ⛏ ♨ ⊙ ⚘ ♨ ▣ ⛱
Nearby Facilities ⛳ ✦ ⚓ ⛏
Acreage 1½ Open March to Nov
Access Good Site Level
Set on manicured lawns. Ideal location for touring. Local attractions include nature reserves and Watersedge Country Park. Spectacular views of the Humber Bridge, beautiful walks.
Nearest Town/Resort Hull/Cleethorpes
Directions From the A15 or the A1077, once in Barton follow Humber Bridge Viewing Area signs and Watersedge signs, site is just past the Sloop Inn public house.
⚑ Barton-Upon-Humber

## BOSTON

**Midville Caravan Park,** Hobhole Bank, Midville, Boston, Lincolnshire, PE22 8HW
Tel: 01205 270316
Pitches For ▲ ♥ ♠ Total 24
Facilities ♿ ⚡ ⛗ ⚘ ⛏ ♨ ⊙ ⊣ ⚘ ☐ ♨
⛗ ⛱ ⓐ ❄ ♨ ☐ ♨
Nearby Facilities ⛳ ✦ ⚓ ⛏ ∪ ♨ ⚲ ⚑

# LINCOLNSHIRE

**Open** March **to** Nov
**Access** Good **Site** Level
On site public house. Fishing just outside the site.
**Nearest Town/Resort** Skegness
**Directions** 12 miles from Boston on the A16 or the A52.
✈ Skegness

## BOSTON

**Pilgrims Way Camping Park,** Church Green Road, Fishtoft, Boston, Lincolnshire, PE21 0QY
**Tel:** 01205 366646
**Email:** info@pilgrimswaylincs
www.pilgrims-way.co.uk
**Pitches For** ▲ ⬟ ⬟ **Total** 20
**Facilities** ♿ ╏ ▥ ⓤ ♨ ╎ ⊙ ↺ ⬚ ☎
▯▮ ⬟ ⬟★▤▱ ☀ ⌇ ⚘
**Nearby Facilities** ╎ ✔ ∪ ♬
**Acreage** 1 **Open** Easter **to** End September
**Access** Good **Site** Level
Quiet park. 20 minutes from Skegness. Close to Bowling, swimming and historical sites. AA 4 Pennants De Lux.
**Nearest Town/Resort** Boston/Skegness
**Directions** Take the A52 Boston to Skegness road, 1 mile out of town turn right at Ball House Pub, follow signs to camping park.
✈ Boston

## BOSTON

**White Cat Caravan & Camping Park,** Shaw Lane, Old Leake, Boston, Lincolnshire, PE22 9LQ
**Tel:** 01205 870121
**Email:** kevin@klannen.freeserve.co.uk
www.whitecatpark.com
**Pitches For** ▲ ⬟ ⬟ **Total** 40
**Facilities** ╏ ▥ ▯ ⓤ ╎ ⊙ ↺ ☎
▮ ▯▮ ⬟ ⬟ ▥ ⬚★✔▤ ▣ ⬚
**Nearby Facilities** ╎ ✔ ∪ ♬
**Acreage** 2½ **Open** Mid March **to** 31 Oct
Ideal for touring the Fens, wild life marshes and Skegness resort. Permanent tourer sites and caravan hire available.
**Nearest Town/Resort** Boston/Skegness
**Directions** 8 miles from Boston on the A52 Skegness road. At Old Leake follow signs to a right turn into Shaw Lane, site is 300 yards on the left.
✈ Boston

## CLEETHORPES

**Thorpe Park Holiday Centre,** Thorpe Park, Humberston, Cleethorpes, North East Lincolnsh, DN35 0PW
**Tel:** 01472 210083 **Fax:** 01472 211241
**Email:** sharon-lee@bourne-leisure.co.uk
www.touringholidays.co.uk
**Pitches For** ▲ ⬟ ⬟ **Total** 85
**Facilities** ♿ ╏ ▥ ⓤ ♨ ╎ ⊙ ↺ ⬚ ☎
▯▮ ▮ ⬟ ✔ ▥ ⬚ ⬟ ♋ ⬚★✔▣ ▣ ☎
**Nearby Facilities** ↘ ∪ ♩ ♬
**Open** March **to** September
**Access** Good **Site** Level
Next to Pleasure Island. Near the beach. Kids Club and a full family entertainment programme. Fishing lake, pets corner, golf, crazy golf and a mini park train.
**Nearest Town/Resort** Cleethorpes
**Directions** From the M180 take the A180 and follow signs for Grimsby and Cleethorpes. In Cleethorpes town centre follow signs for the park.
✈ Cleethorpes

## GRANTHAM

**Woodland Waters,** Willoughby Road, Ancaster, Grantham, Lincolnshire, NG32 3RT
**Tel:** 01400 230888 **Fax:** 01400 230888
**Email:** info@woodlandwaters.co.uk
www.woodlandwaters.co.uk
**Pitches For** ▲ ⬟ ⬟ **Total** 84
**Facilities** ♿ ╏ ▥ ⓤ ♨ ╎ ⊙ ↺ ⬚ ☎
▮ ▯▮ ⬟ ⬟★✔ ▥ ⬚ ♋ ⬚★✔▣
**Nearby Facilities** ╎ ∪ ♬
**Acreage** 72 **Open** All Year
**Access** Good **Site** Level
Bar and restaurant, five fishing lakes and lovely woodland walks on site.
**Nearest Town/Resort** Grantham/Sleaford
**Directions** On the A153 midway between Grantham and Sleaford.
✈ Grantham/Sleaford

## HORNCASTLE

**Ashby Park,** West Ashby, Nr Horncastle, Lincolnshire, LN9 5PP
**Tel:** 01507 527966
**Email:** ashbyparklakes@aol.com
www.ukparks.co.uk/ashby
**Pitches For** ▲ ⬟ ⬟ **Total** 80
**Facilities** ♿ ╏ ▥ ⓤ ♨ ╎ ⊙ ↺ ⬚ ☎
▮ ▯▮ ⬟ ⬟★✔▣ ▣ ☀ ⌇ ⚘
**Nearby Facilities** ╎ ✔ ∪
**Acreage** 70 **Open** All Year
**Access** Good **Site** Level
Seven fishing lakes, pub and restaurant ½ mile, swimming pool 1¾ miles. 23 miles to the coast. Static caravans for sale. ETB 4 Star Graded and David Bellamy Gold Award for Conservation.
**Nearest Town/Resort** Horncastle
**Directions** 1¾ miles north of Horncastle between the A153 and the A158.
✈ Lincoln

## HORNCASTLE

**The Golfers Arms,** Horncastle Golf & Country Club, Shearmans Wath, West Ashby, HorncastleLincolnshire, LN9 5PP
**Tel:** 01507 526800
www.horncastlegolfclub.com
**Pitches For** ⬟ ⬟ **Total** 10
**Facilities** ╏ ▥ ⓤ ☎ ⬟★✔ ▥ ⬚ ☀
**Nearby Facilities**
**Acreage** 10½ **Open** All Year
**Access** Good **Site** Level
Golf, restaurant and bar on site. Enjoy the wildlife and river walks. Country & Western and Rock 'n' Roll weekends.
**Nearest Town/Resort** Lincoln/Boston
**Directions** On the main A158 Lincoln to Skegness road.
✈ Lincoln/Boston

## HUTTOFT

**Jolly Common Caravan Park,** Jolly Common, Sea Lane, Huttoft, AlfordLincolnshire, LN13 9RW
**Tel:** 01507 490236
www.jollycommoncaravanpark.co.uk
**Pitches For** ⬟ ⬟ **Total** 60
**Facilities** ╏ ▥ ⓤ ♨ ╎ ⊙ ↺ ☎ ▯▮ ⬟★✔▤A
**Nearby Facilities** ╎ ✔ ⬚ ∪ ♬
**Acreage** 9 **Open** 15 March **to** 30 Oct
**Access** Good **Site** Level
ADULTS ONLY SITE, suitable for mature couples. Spacious ptches set in peaceful countryside. One mile from sandy beaches and an 18 hole golf course. Private well-stocked fishing lake.
**Nearest Town/Resort** Sutton-on-Sea
**Directions** 4 miles after Sutton-on-Sea, in Huttoft, take the first left down Sea Lane. After ½ a mile turn right into Jolly Common, site entrance is 200 metres on the left.
✈ Skegness

## INGOLDMELLS

**Bridge End Touring Site,** Boltons Lane, Ingoldmells, Lincolnshire, PE25 1JJ
**Tel:** 01754 872456
**Pitches For** ⬟ ⬟ **Total** 40
**Facilities** ╏ ▥ ♨ ╎ ⊙ ⬟ ☎ ▯▮ ▣
**Nearby Facilities** ╎ ✔ ⬚ ★ ∪ ♮ ♬
**Acreage** 3 **Open** Easter **to** Oct
**Access** Good **Site** Level
FAMILIES ONLY. Quiet family run site on the edge of the busy resort of Ingoldmells. Open country views from the site. Easy walk to the beach. Near Fantasy Island. No children's play area.
**Nearest Town/Resort** Skegness
**Directions** Situated 3 miles north of Skegness at the junction of the A52 and Boltons Lane.
✈ Skegness

## INGOLDMELLS

**Hardy's Touring Site,** Sea Lane, Ingoldmells, Skegness, Lincolnshire, PE25 1PG
**Tel:** 01754 874071
**Pitches For** ⬟ ⬟ **Total** 112
**Facilities** ╏ ▥ ♨ ╎ ⊙ ⬚ ▥ ☎
▮ ▯▮ ⬟ ✕ ▥★✔▣
**Nearby Facilities** ╎ ✔ ∪ ♮ ♬
**Acreage** 5 **Open** Easter **to** October
**Access** Good **Site** Level
5 minutes walk from the beach. Next to Fantasy Island and 10 minutes from an animal farm.
**Nearest Town/Resort** Skegness/Ingoldmells
**Directions** Take the A52 north from Skegness to Ingoldmells. At the Ship Inn in Ingoldmells turn right down Sea Lane, towards the sea. Site is ½ mile on the right.
✈ Skegness

## INGOLDMELLS

**Valetta Farm Caravan Site,** Mill Lane, Addlethorpe, Skegness, Lincolnshire, PE24 4TB
**Tel:** 01754 763758
**Pitches For** ▲ ⬟ ⬟ **Total** 35
**Facilities** ♿ ╏ ▥ ⓤ ♨ ╎ ⊙ ⬚ ▥★✔ ⬚ ☀ ⚘
**Nearby Facilities** ╎ ✔ ⬚ ∪ ♬
**Acreage** 2 **Open** 25 March **to** 20 October
**Access** Good **Site** Level
Quite a pretty site in the country, 1 mile from the beach.
**Nearest Town/Resort** Skegness
**Directions** Turn left off the A158 (Horncastle to Skegness road) in Burgh-le-Marsh at the signpost Ingoldmells and Addlethorpe. Follow signposts for Ingoldmells for 3 miles, turn right by disused mill into Mill Lane. Site is on the left in 150yds.
✈ Skegness

## LINCOLN

**Hartsholme Country Park,** Skellingthorpe Road, Lincoln, Lincolnshire, LN6 0EY
**Tel:** 01522 873578
www.lincoln.gov.uk
**Pitches For** ▲ ⬟ ⬟ **Total** 50
**Facilities** ♿ ╏ ▥ ♨ ╎ ⊙ ☎
▮ ✕ ▥ ⬚★✔▣
**Nearby Facilities**
**Acreage** 2½ **Open** March **to** October
**Access** Good **Site** Level
Set amongst mature woodland with a large picturesque lake, as well as open grassland. Adjacent to Swanholme Lakes local nature reserve. Also open for Lincoln's Christmas Market.
**Nearest Town/Resort** Lincoln
**Directions** 2½ miles south west of Lincoln city centre. Signposted from the A46, on the B1378.
✈ Lincoln

## LINCOLN

**Oakhill Leisure,** Norton Disney, Lincoln, Lincolnshire, LN6 9QG
**Tel:** 01522 868771
**Email:** ron@oakhill-leisure.co.uk
www.oakhill-leisure.co.uk
**Pitches For** ▲ ⚏ ⚏ **Total** 60
**Facilities** ⚙ ⏚ 🚽 🅿 ⚡ ⊙ ↵ ◻ 🍴 ♨ ✈ ♪
**Nearby Facilities** ✓
**Acreage** 10 **Open** All Year
**Access** Good **Site** Level
Peaceful woodland site with a fishing lake.
**Nearest Town/Resort** Lincoln
**Directions** From the A46 turn off at the roundabout signposted Thurlby and Norton Disney. At the T-junction turn right and site is 1 mile on the right.
✈ Lincoln

## LINCOLN

**Shortferry Caravan Park,** Ferry Road, Fiskerton, Lincoln, Lincolnshire, LN3 4HU
**Tel:** 01526 398021 **Fax:** 01526 398102
**Email:** kay@shortferrycp.co.uk
www.shortferry.co.uk
**Pitches For** ⚏ ⚏ **Total** 75
**Facilities** ⚙ ⏚ 🚽 🅿 ⚡ ⚡ ⊙ ↵ ◻ 🍴 ◻ ⚡
🏧 🅱 ⊙ 🏪 ✖ ♀ 🍴 ♨ ✈ 🎣 ◻ ⚡
**Nearby Facilities** ↑ ✓ ∪
**Acreage** 80 **Open** All Year
**Access** Good **Site** Level
Situated by a river with 2 fishing ponds. Fishing tackle and bait shop. Entertainment most weekends. Bar meals and take-away in our public house. 9 hole pitch 'n' putt golf course and a bowling green on site. Seasonal outdoor heated swimming pool.
**Nearest Town/Resort** Lincoln
**Directions** From the A46 Lincoln ring road take the A158 towards Skegness. After approx. 5 miles turn right at Shortferry sign, continue to follow signs for approx. 5 miles.
✈ Lincoln

## MABLETHORPE

**Camping & Caravanning Club Site,** Highfield, 120 Church Lane, Mablethorpe, Lincolnshire, LN12 2NU
**Tel:** 01507 472374
www.campingandcaravanningclub.co.uk
**Pitches For** ▲ ⚏ ⚏ **Total** 105
**Facilities** ⚙ ⏚ 🚽 ⚡ ⊙ ↵ 🍴 ◻ ⚡
🏧 🅸 ⊙ 🅱 ♨ ✈ ◻
**Nearby Facilities** ↑ ✓ ✓ ♪
**Acreage** 6 **Open** March **to** Oct
**Access** Difficult **Site** Level
Just 1 mile from the sea and award winning beaches. Ideal for cyclists. Near the Lincolnshire Wolds. BTB 4 Star Graded and AA 3 Pennants. Non members welcome.
**Nearest Town/Resort** Mablethorpe

**Directions** On the outskirts of Mablethorpe, on the A1104. Turn into Church Lane after the petrol station on the right, site is 800 yards along the lane on the right hand side.
✈ Cleethorpes

## MABLETHORPE

**Denehurst Guest House & Camping Touring Site,** Alford Road, Mablethorpe, Lincolnshire, LN12 1PX
**Tel:** 01507 472951 **Fax:** 01507 472951
www.denehurstguesthouse.co.uk
**Pitches For** ▲ ⚏ ⚏ **Total** 20
**Facilities** ⏚ 🚽 ⚡ ⊙ ↵ ♨ ⚡
🅱 ✖ ♀ 🍴 ◻ ⚡
**Nearby Facilities** ↑ ✓
**Acreage** 1 **Open** March **to** December
**Access** Good **Site** Level
One mile to the beach and shops.
**Nearest Town/Resort** Mablethorpe
**Directions** On the A1104 Alford road, west of Mablethorpe ¾ mile. A157 from Louth.
✈ Skegness

## MABLETHORPE

**Dunes Holivan Estate,** Quebec Road, Mablethorpe, Lincolnshire, LN12 1QH
**Tel:** 01507 473327 **Fax:** 01507 473327
**Email:** holivans@enterprise.net
www.holivans.co.uk
**Pitches For** ⚏ ⚏ **Total** 25
**Facilities** ⏚ 🚽 ⚡ ⊙ ◻ ⚡
⊙ ♀ ◻ ♨ ✈ ◻
**Nearby Facilities** ✓
**Acreage** 10 **Open** Easter **to** October
**Access** Good **Site** Level
Adjacent to dunes and beaches.
**Nearest Town/Resort** Mablethorpe
**Directions** Go into Mablethorpe on the A1104, up to the pullover and turn left into Quebec Road. After ¾ mile turn into the caravan park.
✈ Skegness/Grimsby

## MABLETHORPE

**Golden Sands Holiday Park,** Quebec Road, Mablethorpe, Lincolnshire, LN12 1QJ
**Tel:** 01507 477871 **Fax:** 01507 472066
www.touringholidays.co.uk
**Pitches For** ⚏ ⚏ **Total** 169
**Facilities** ⚙ ⏚ 🚽 🅿 ⚡ ⚡ ⊙ ↵ ◻ ⚡
🏧 🅸 ⊙ 🅱 ✖ ♀ 🍴 ♨ 🔺 ♨ ✈ ✈ ◻ ⚡ ◻
**Nearby Facilities** ✓
**Acreage** 10 **Open** Easter **to** October
**Access** Good **Site** Level
Situated close to a fine sandy beach, with excellent facilities for all the family, providing a fun packed holiday.
**Nearest Town/Resort** Mablethorpe
**Directions** From Mablethorpe town centre, follow the sea front road to the north end for Golden Sands.
✈ Skegness

## MABLETHORPE

**Grange Farm Leisure Ltd.,** Alford Road, Mablethorpe, Lincolnshire, LN12 1NE
**Tel:** 01507 472814
www.ukparks.co.uk/grangefarm
**Pitches For** ⚏ ⚏ **Total** 35
**Facilities** ⚙ ⏚ 🚽 🅿 ⚡ ⊙ ↵ ◻ ⚡
⊙ 🅱 ✖ ♀ ◻
**Nearby Facilities**
**Open** March **to** Nov
**Access** Good **Site** Level
Set in open farmland. 4 coarse fishing lakes, carp lake and fly fishing lake for fishing all year round. Tackle shop. Public Bar on premises with food available. Pets are welcome by arrangement.
**Nearest Town/Resort** Mablethorpe
**Directions** Situated on the A1104 between Mablethorpe and Maltby-le-Marsh. Approx. 1½ miles from the centre of Mablethorpe.
✈ Skegness

## MARKET DEEPING

**The Deepings Caravan Park,** Outgang Road, Market Deeping, Lincolnshire, PE6 8LQ
**Tel:** 01778 344335 **Fax:** 01778 344394
**Email:** info@thedeepings.com
www.thedeepings.com
**Pitches For** ▲ ⚏ ⚏ **Total** 45
**Facilities** ⚙ ⏚ 🚽 ⚡ ⊙ ⚡
🏧 🅸 ⊙ ♨ ✈ ♨ ♪
**Nearby Facilities** ✓ ∪ ♪
**Open** February **to** December
**Access** Good **Site** Level
**Nearest Town/Resort** Market Deeping
**Directions** Park is 2 miles from Market Deeping on the B1525. Take the first left after The Goat Inn.
✈ Peterborough

## MARKET RASEN

**Manor Farm Caravan & Camping Site,** Manor Farm, East Firsby, Market Rasen, Lincolnshire, LN8 2DE
**Tel:** 01673 878258 **Fax:** 01673 878310
**Email:** info@lincolnshire-lanes.com
www.lincolnshire-lanes.com
**Pitches For** ▲ ⚏ ⚏ **Total** 21
**Facilities** ⚙ ⏚ 🚽 ⚡ ⊙ ↵ ◻ ◻ ⚡
🏧 ⊙ ♨ ✈ ◻
**Nearby Facilities** ↑ ✓
**Acreage** 3 **Open** All Year
**Access** Good **Site** Level
Small site shop. ETB 3 Star Graded and Welcome Host.
**Nearest Town/Resort** Market Rasen/Lincoln
**Directions** Take the A15 north from Lincoln, 2½ miles past RAF Scampton turn right and follow brown tourism signs to the site entrance.
✈ Market Rasen/Lincoln

# LINCOLNSHIRE

## MARKET RASEN

**Market Rasen Racecouse Caravan Club Site,** Legsby Road, Market Rasen, Lincolnshire, LN8 3EA
**Tel:** 01673 842307
**Email:** marketrasen@rht.net
www.marketrasenraces.co.uk
**Pitches For** ▲ ⚌ ⚌ **Total** 55
**Facilities** ♿ ⓕ 🔟 ⚓ ⌐ ⊙ ⏚ ⌑ ☎
⓲ ⊘ ⓐ ⊞ 🔲 ⊟
**Nearby Facilities** ⌐ ✓
**Acreage** 3 **Open** March to Oct
**Access** Good **Site** Level
At the edge of the lovely Lincolnshire Wolds. Discounts for racing and the adjacent 9 hole golf course. Ideal walking and cycling. Non members welcome. Booking essential.
**Directions** Travelling from the West on the A361, go into Market Rasen and through the traffic lights. After 400 yards turn right signposted Legsby, site entrance is on the left within ¾ miles.
⚌ Market Rasen

## METHERINGHAM

**White Horse Caravan Park,** Dunston Fen, Metheringham, Lincoln, Lincolnshire, LN4 3AP
**Tel:** 01526 399919 **Fax:** 01526 399919
**Email:** whitehorse@dunstonfen.co.uk
www.dunstonfen.co.uk
**Pitches For** ▲ ⚌ ⚌ **Total** 8
**Facilities** ⓕ 🔟 ⚓ ⌐ ⊙ ⏚ ⚌ ⌑ ☎
⊘ ⓐ ⚓ ⚓ 🔲 ⌐ ⊟ ⊟
**Nearby Facilities** ⌐ ✓ ⚐ ↝ ∪
**Acreage** 1 **Open** Feb to Dec
**Access** Good **Site** Level
Alongside a river. Ideal for fishing, walking and cycling. Licensed pub on site.
**Nearest Town/Resort** Lincoln
**Directions** From Lincoln take the B1188 towards Sleaford, turn right at sign for Dunston and follow brown tourism signs.
⚌ Metheringham

## NORTH SOMERCOTES

**Lakeside Park,** North Somercotes, Nr Louth, Lincolnshire, LN11 7RB
**Tel:** 01507 358428 **Fax:** 01507 358135
**Email:**
lakeside@donamottcaravans.ndirect.co.uk
www.donamott.com
**Pitches For** ⚌ ⚌ **Total** 140
**Facilities** ♿ ⓕ 🔲 🔲 🔟 ⚓ ⌐ ⊙ ⊟ ☎
⓲ ⓲ ⊘ ⓐ ✕ 🔲 🔲 ⚓ ⊹ ⚓ ⌐ ⊟ ⊟ ⊰
**Nearby Facilities** ⌐ ✓ ℛ
**Acreage** 15 **Open** 15 March to 30 Oct
**Access** Good **Site** Level
Near the coast.
**Nearest Town/Resort** Louth
**Directions** From Louth take the B1200 through Saltfleet to join the A1031, turn left and the Park is 2 miles on the right.
⚌ Grimsby

## SALTFLEET

**Sunnydale Holiday Park,** Sea Lane, Saltfleet, Lincolnshire, LN11 7RP
**Tel:** 0870 442 9293 **Fax:** 01507 339100
www.park-resorts.com
**Pitches For** ⚌ ⚌ **Total** 30
**Facilities** ♿ ⚓ ⓕ 🔟 ⚓ ⌐ ⊙ ⌑ ☎
⓲ ⓲ ⊘ ⓐ ⚓ 🔲 ⚓ ⚓ ⌐ ⊟ ⊟ ⊰
**Nearby Facilities** ⌐ ✓
**Open** March to November
**Access** Good **Site** Level
Attractive touring park ideal for exploring the beauty of Lincolnshire. Quality on park facilities. Close to summer seaside attractions and picturesque market towns.
**Nearest Town/Resort** Louth
**Directions** Head towards Louth on the A16, take the B1200 through Manby and Saltfleetby. Drive through Saltfleet and turn off along Sea Lane, the park is 400 yards on the left.
⚌ Cleethorpes

## SCUNTHORPE

**Brookside Caravan & Camping Park,** Stather Road, Burton-Upon-Stather, Scunthorpe, Lincolnshire, DN15 9DH
**Tel:** 01724 721369
**Email:** brooksidecp@aol.com
**Pitches For** ▲ ⚌ ⚌ **Total** 35
**Facilities** ♿ ⓕ 🔲 🔟 ⚓ ⌐ ⊙ ⚌ ⚓ ⌑ ☎
⓲ ⚓ ⊟
**Nearby Facilities** ⌐ ✓ ∪ ℛ
**Acreage** 6 **Open** All Year
**Access** Good **Site** Level
Our family run, superbly equipped park, set in an area of outstanding beauty, is the ideal location for visiting North Lincolnshire. 4½ miles from Scunthorpe town centre. Bank Holidays - Adults only.
ETB 5 Star Graded.
**Nearest Town/Resort** Scunthorpe
**Directions** B1430 from Scunthorpe Town centre to Burton-Upon-Stather (4 miles) turn left in front of the Sheffield Arms public house. Down the hill past the Ferry Boat Inn, entrance to park 100yds further on right.
⚌ Scunthorpe

## SKEGNESS

**Butlins Skyline Limited,** Butlins, Skegness, Lincolnshire, PE25 1NJ
**Tel:** 01754 762311 **Fax:** 01754 767833
**Pitches For** ⚌ ⚌
**Facilities** ♿ ⓕ 🔟 ⚓ ⌐ ⊙ ⚌ ⚓ ⌑ ☎
⓲ ⓲ ⊘ ⓐ ✕ ⚓ ⚓ 🔲 ⊹ ⊹ ⚓ ⌐ ⊟
**Nearby Facilities** ⌐ ✓ ⚐ ∪ ⚐ ℛ
**Access** Good **Site** Level
Full use of Butlins Resort facilities at no additional cost for entrance.
**Nearest Town/Resort** Skegness
**Directions** From Skegness take the A52 north for approx. 3 miles, site is on the left hand side opposite the main entrance.
⚌ Skegness

# Lincolnshire's Jewel in the Crown

Set amidst beautiful manicured gardens and dramatic water features, Lakeside is Lincolnshire's premier location for Touring and Motorcaravans.

## Lakeside Park

- TROPICANA INDOOR POOL COMPLEX
- 7 ACRE FISHING LAKE
- 9 HOLF GOLF COURSE
- 'SUPER' PITCHES
- THE WATERFRONT BAR & GRILL
- OSCAR'S NIGHT CLUB
- TENNIS COURTS
- BOWLING GREEN
- CHILDRENS ADVENTURE AREA

*Phone for a brochure or call and see it for yourself:*
*Lakeside Park, North Somercotes, Near Louth, Lincolnshire LN11 7RB*
*Tel: 0845 456 5268 Email: parks@donamott.com Website: www.donamott.com*

# Manor Farm Caravan Park *Anderby* 01507 490372

Peaceful, rural surroundings with plenty of open space. Modern toilet/shower block.
Within easy reach of Skegness and beaches. *We look forward to seeing you.*

**MANOR FARM CARAVAN PARK, Sea Road, Anderby, SKEGNESS, Lincs PE24 5YB**

## SKEGNESS

**Country Meadows Holiday Park,** Anchor Lane, Ingoldmells, Skegness, Lincolnshire, PE25 1LZ
**Tel:** 01754 874455
**Email:** info@countrymeadows.co.uk
www.countrymeadows.co.uk
**Pitches For** Å ♀ ⚪ **Total** 200
**Facilities** ⅃ ⚪ ⚑ ♨ ⌂ Ⓟ ⊙ ⌿ ⚏ ◻ ♥
Ⅱ ⚪ ⛺ ⋔ ┼ ▣
**Nearby Facilities** Γ ✔ ⚑ ∪ ⋗ ♬
**Acreage** 10 **Open** March to October
**Access** Good **Site** Level
5 minutes walk from the beach and a 10 minute walk to Fantasy Island. Adjacent to an animal farm.
**Nearest Town/Resort** Skegness
**Directions** On the A52 4 miles north of Skegness. ¾ mile out of Ingoldmells Village turn right into Anchor Lane, go 1 mile down toward the sea and the site is on the left hand side.
⚡ Skegness

## SKEGNESS

**Homelands Caravan Park,** Sea Road, Anderby, Skegness, Lincolnshire, PE24 5YB
**Tel:** 01507 490511
www.caravancampingsites.co.uk
**Pitches For** Å ♀ ⚪ **Total** 10
**Facilities** ✔ ⚑ ♨ ⌂ Ⓟ ⊙ ⌿ ⚏ Ⅱ ⚪ ┼ ▣
**Nearby Facilities** Γ ✔

**Acreage** 1 **Open** March to November
**Access** Good **Site** Level
Quiet, friendly site in the countryside. Within walking distance of a sandy beach. 4 Berth Static Van also available for hire.
**Nearest Town/Resort** Skegness/ Mablethorpe
**Directions** From Skegness take the A52 coast road to Mablethorpe, approx. 10-12 miles from Skegness.
⚡ Skegness/Mablethorpe

## SKEGNESS

**North Shore Holiday Centre,** Elmhirst Avenue, Roman Bank, Skegness, Lincolnshire, PE25 1SL
**Tel:** 01754 763815 **Fax:** 01754 761323
reception@northshore-skegness.co.uk
www.northshore-skegness.co.uk
**Pitches For** ♀ ⚪ **Total** 200
**Facilities** ⅃ ✔ ⚑ ♨ ⌂ Ⓟ ⊙ ⌿ ⚏ ♥
SⅩ Ⅱ ⚪ ⛺ ✕ ▽ ⋔ ┼ ▣
**Nearby Facilities** Γ ✔ ⚑ ⋗ ∪ ⋗ ♬
**Open** Mid March to End Oct
**Access** Good **Site** Level
Just a short walk to both the beach and Skegness centre. Set well back from the main road, ideal family holiday base. Pitch & Putt and Miniature Golf on site. All weather touring pitches now available.
SORRY NO TENTS.
**Nearest Town/Resort** Skegness

**Directions** A52 towards Mablethorpe, 500yds from the A158 junction.
⚡ Skegness

## SKEGNESS

**Riverside Caravan Park,** Wainfleet Bank, Wainfleet, Skegness, Lincolnshire, PE24 4ND
**Tel:** 01754 880205
**Pitches For** Å ♀ ⚪ **Total** 30
**Facilities** ✔ ⚑ ⚪ ♨ ⌂ Ⓟ ⊙ ⌿ ⚏ ◻ ⋗ ♬
**Nearby Facilities** Γ ✔ ⚑ ⋗
**Acreage** 1.4 **Open** 15 March to 31 Oct
**Access** Good **Site** Level
1967 to 2006. Alongside a river for fishing and boating. Beach 6 miles.
**Nearest Town/Resort** Skegness
**Directions** A52 Boston to Skegness. Turn left onto the B1195 to Wainfleet All Saints and follow brown signs.
⚡ Wainfleet

## SKEGNESS

**Skegness Sands,** Winthorpe Avenue, Skegness, Lincolnshire, PE25 1QZ
**Tel:** 01754 761484
www.caravanclub.co.uk
**Pitches For** ♀ ⚪ **Total** 80
**Facilities** ⅃ ✔ ⚑ ⚪ ♨ ⌂ Ⓟ ⊙ ⌿ ⚏ ◻ ♥
Ⅱ ⚪ ⛺ ⋔ ┼ ▣
**Nearby Facilities** Γ ✔ ⚑ ⋗
**Acreage** 3½ **Open** All Year

# *Butlins*
## kids love it

Caravan pitches (no tents) from only £6 per person per night based on 4 sharing, inclusive of electric hook up and space for awning. Renowned entertainment and many great facilities including bars and restaurants, Splash Waterworld and a great range of shops.

For full details and to book your pitch contact your chosen Resort.

✉ Butlins Minehead, Somerset, TA24 5SH

 **01643 700 515**
Please call to check opening times and prices

📱 Jane.barron@bourne-leisure.co.uk

✉ Butlins Skegness, Lincolnshire, PE25 1NJ

 **01754 762 311**
Please call to check opening times and prices

📱 cashiers.skegness@bourne-leisure.co.uk

## Tel: 01507 490750 — Ronam Cottage — ★ Open All Year ★
### Pinfold Lane, Anderby, Nr. Skegness, Lincolnshire PE24 5YA

Quiet park with beautiful views of open countryside. Good facilities and a high standard of cleanliness.
This highly regarded Camping & Caravanning Club Site welcomes members and non-members alike.
We look forward to seeing you.

**Access** Good **Site** Level
Easy access to the beach and private access to the promenade. Only 2 miles from the centre of Skegness. Close to Butlins Funcoast World, Natureland Marine Zoo, Hardy's Animal Farm, Fantasy Island and Gibraltar Point Nature Reserve. Non members welcome. Booking essential.
**Nearest Town/Resort** Skegness
**Directions** Fron Skegness take the A52, at the Garden City Pub (on the left) turn right into Winthorpe Avenue, site is 200 yards on the left.
☀ Skegness

### SKEGNESS
**Ronam Cottage,** Pinfold Lane, Anderby, Skegness, Lincolnshire, PE24 5YA
**Tel:** 01507 490750
**Pitches For** Å ⊕ ⊟
**Facilities** ∮ ⓊⒺ ♨ ⌐ ⚑ ⊬
**Nearby Facilities** ⌐ ✔
**Acreage** 1½ **Open** All Year
**Access** Good **Site** Level
Near to Anderby Creek and beach. Countryside walks. 2 hard standings available. Rally Field available. Camping & Caravanning Club site, non members welcome.
**Nearest Town/Resort** Skegness/Mablethorpe
**Directions** From Alford take the A1104 and turn onto the A1111 to Bilsby. Turn right onto the B1449 then left onto the A52, turn first right to Anderby. After 1½ miles turn left on the bend, site entrance is 50 yards on the right.
☀ Skegness

### SKEGNESS
**Skegness Water Leisure Park,** Walls Lane, Skegness, Lincolnshire, PE25 1JF
**Tel:** 01754 899400 **Fax:** 01754 897867
enquiries@skegnesswaterleisurepark.co.uk
www.skegnesswaterleisurepark.co.uk
**Pitches For** Å ⊕ ⊟ **Total** 200
**Facilities** ⚭ ∮ ⓊⒺ ♨ ⌐ ⊙ ⌕ ⊒ ⚑ ⊠ ☎
⛟ ⓏⒺ ❌ ⚑ ⋈ ⊟ ⊡ ⊬ ♫
**Nearby Facilities** ⌐ ✔ ∪
**Acreage** 133 **Open** 6 March to 30 October
**Access** Good **Site** Level
Near the beach and a fishing lake. Water-skiing lake on site. Near Funcoast World (Butlins).
**Nearest Town/Resort** Skegness/Ingoldmells
**Directions** Conveniently situated 3 miles north of Skegness just off the A52, 400 yards from Butlins. Once you reach the outskirts of Skegness follow the brown information signs.
☀ Skegness

### SKEGNESS
**The Elms Touring Caravan Site,** Orby Road, Addlethorpe, Skegness, Lincolnshire, PE24 4TR
**Tel:** 01754 872266
**Email:** sue@elms1010.fsnet.co.uk
**Pitches For** Å ⊕ ⊟ **Total** 200
**Facilities** ⚭ ∮ ⓊⒺ ♨ ⌐ ⊙ ⊠ ☎ ⚑ ⋈ ⊬ ♫
**Acreage** 10 **Open** Mid March to Mid Oct
**Access** Good **Site** Level
1 mile from the beach, Ingoldmells and Fantasy Island.
**Nearest Town/Resort** Skegness
**Directions** Take the A158 heading towards Skegness, turn first left after Gunby roundabout to Orby and Ingoldmells.
☀ Skegness

### SKEGNESS
**Topyard Farm Caravan Site,** Croft Bank, Croft, Skegness, Lincolnshire, PE24 4RL
**Tel:** 01754 880109
**Email:** topyardfarm@croft252.fsnet.co.uk
**Pitches For** Å ⊕ ⊟ **Total** 40
**Facilities** ⚭ ∮ ⓊⒺ ♨ ⌐ ⊒ ⊬ ☎
⛟ ⓏⒺ ⚑ ⋈ ⊟ ⊬ ∪
**Nearby Facilities** ⌐ ✔ ⋈ ∪
**Acreage** 2½ **Open** Mid March to Mid Nov
**Access** Good **Site** Level
Close to the beach, town, fishing, golf and Fantasy Island.
**Nearest Town/Resort** Skegness
**Directions** 2 miles from the centre of Skegness on the main A52.
☀ Skegness

### SLEAFORD
**Low Farm Touring Park,** Spring Lane, Folkingham, Sleaford, Lincolnshire, NG34 0SJ
**Tel:** 01529 497322
**Pitches For** Å ⊕ ⊟ **Total** 36
**Facilities** ∮ ⓊⒺ ♨ ⌐ ⊙ ⊠ ☎ ⛟ ⋈ ⊟ ⊡ ⊬ ♫
**Nearby Facilities** ✔
**Acreage** 2¼ **Open** Easter to End Sept
**Access** Good **Site** Lev/Slope
**Nearest Town/Resort** Sleaford
**Directions** 9 miles south of Sleaford on the A15. Go through village, turn right by the Village Hall.
☀ Sleaford

### SPALDING
**Delph Bank Touring Caravan & Camping Park,** Old Main Road, Fleet Hargate, Holbeach, Nr Spalding Lincolnshire, PE12 8LL
**Tel:** 01406 422910
**Email:** enquiries@delphbank.co.uk
www.delphbank.co.uk
**Pitches For** Å ⊕ ⊟ **Total** 45

**Facilities** ∮ ⓊⒺ ♨ ⌐ ⊙ ⊒ ⊠ ☎
⛟ ⓏⒺ ⚑⊟ ⊟ A ⊬ ♫ ♪
**Nearby Facilities** ⌐ ✔
**Acreage** 3 **Open** March to November
**Access** Good **Site** Level
ADULTS ONLY PARK. An attractive, quiet, tree lined site, convenient for touring the Fens and Lincolnshire/Norfolk coastal resorts. Pubs and eating places within walking distance. BH & HPA Member. ETB 4 Star Graded and AA 3 Pennants.
**Nearest Town/Resort** Holbeach
**Directions** From Kings Lynn take the A17, Turn left in the village of Fleet Hargate on right, site is on the left. From Spalding take the A151 to Holbeach, continue a further 3 miles to Fleet Hargate, turn right into the village and look for our sign on the right.
☀ Spalding

### SPALDING
**Foremans Bridge Caravan Park,** Sutton Road, Sutton St James, Spalding, Lincolnshire, PE12 0HU
**Tel:** 01945 440346
**Email:** ann@anegus.wanadoo.co.uk
www.foremans-bridge.co.uk
**Pitches For** Å ⊕ ⊟ **Total** 40
**Facilities** ∮ ⓊⒺ ♨ ⌐ ⊙ ⊒ ⊠ ☎
⛟ ⓏⒺ ⚑ ⋈ ⊟ ⊬ ♫
**Nearby Facilities** ⌐ ✔ ∪
**Open** March to Nov
**Access** Good **Site** Level
Alongside a river and a cycle route. Near to market towns.
**Nearest Town/Resort** Long Sutton
**Directions** From the A17 Holbeach to Kings Lynn road, take the B1390 at the roundabout to Sutton St James. The site is on the left after approx. 2 miles, immediately after the river bridge.
☀ Spalding

### SPILSBY
**Meadowlands,** Monksthorpe, Great Steeping, Spilsby, Lincolnshire, PE23 5PP
**Tel:** 01754 830794
**Pitches For** Å ⊕ ⊟ **Total** 20
**Facilities** ∮ ⓊⒺ ♨ ⌐ ⊒ ⊟ ⛟ ⚑⊟ ⊟ ⊬
**Nearby Facilities** ✔ ∪
**Acreage** 5 **Open** All Year
**Access** Good **Site** Level
Quiet site in a rural setting. Ideal for walking and cycling. Handy for Skegness and the beautiful Wolds. 3 miles from Spilsby.
**Nearest Town/Resort** Spilsby
**Directions** Take the A16 into Spilsby town then take the Wainfleet road, pass The Bell Inn and after approx. 1 mile turn left at AA sign, site is on the right.
☀ Wainfleet

## STAMFORD

**Road End Farm Caravan Park,** Road End Farm, Great Casterton, Stamford, Lincolnshire, PE9 4BB
**Tel:** 01780 763417 **Fax:** 01780 489212
**Email:** colintlamb@aol.com
**Pitches For** ▲ ⊞ 🚐 **Total** 12
**Facilities** 🕯 🗓 ⚓ 🏪 🛒 ⊙ ➡ 🖃
**Nearby Facilities** ┏ ✓ ⚓ ⅄
**Acreage** 4 **Open** All Year
**Access** Good **Site** Lev/Slope
Close to Rutland Water which is the largest man-made lake in Europe.
**Nearest Town/Resort** Stamford
**Directions** 1 mile north of Stamford on the B1081, turn right at sign for Little Casterton, site is 100 yards on the right.
⚍ Stamford

## SUTTON-ON-SEA

**Cherry Tree Site,** Huttoft Road, Sutton-on-Sea, Lincolnshire, LN12 2RU
**Tel:** 01507 441626
**Email:** murray.cherrytree@virgin.net
www.cherrytreesite.co.uk
**Pitches For** ⊞ 🚐 **Total** 60
**Facilities** ⚓ 🕯 🗓 🗓 ⚓ ┏ ⊙ ➡ 🛒 🖃 🍴
🏪 🛒 ⊙ ➡ 🖃 🄲 ▲ ⅃⅄
**Nearby Facilities** ┏ ✓ ∪ ⅄
**Acreage** 3 **Open** March to October
**Access** Good **Site** Level
ADULTS ONLY SITE. Beach, golf course and Lincolnshire Wolds. ETB 4 Star Graded.
**Nearest Town/Resort** Sutton-on-Sea
**Directions** Take the A52 south from Sutton-on-Sea, 1½ miles on the left hand side. Entrance via a lay-by. Tourist Board signs on road.
⚍ Skegness

## SUTTON-ON-SEA

**Kirkstead Holiday Park,** North Road, Trusthorpe, Sutton-on-Sea, Lincolnshire, LN12 2QD
**Tel:** 01507 441483
**Email:** mark@kirkstead.co.uk
www.kirkstead.co.uk
**Pitches For** ▲ ⊞ 🚐 **Total** 60
**Facilities** ⚓ 🕯 🗓 🗓 ⚓ ┏ ⊙ ➡ 🛒 🖃 🍴
🕮 🄲 🛒 🍴 🎯 🏪 ▲ 🍴 ➡ 🖃 🄲 ⅄ ⅃
**Nearby Facilities** ┏ ✓ ∪ ⅄
**Acreage** 6 **Open** March to 1 December
**Access** Good **Site** Level
10 minute walk to the beach. Clubhouse, new shower block. Familys welcome.
**Nearest Town/Resort** Sutton-on-Sea
**Directions** Take the A52 coast road from Sutton to Mablethorpe, turn off left at Trusthorpe. Signposted from the A52.
⚍ Skegness

## TATTERSHALL

**Willow Holt Caravan & Camping Park,** Lodge Road, Tattershall, Lincolnshire, LN4 4JS
**Tel:** 01526 343111 **Fax:** 01526 345391
**Email:** enquiries@willowholt.co.uk
www.willowholt.co.uk
**Pitches For** ▲ ⊞ 🚐 **Total** 100
**Facilities** 🕯 🗓 🗓 ⚓ ┏ ⊙ ➡ 🛒 🖃 🍴
🄲 🄲 🛒 🎯 🏪 ➡ 🖃 ⅄ ⅃ 🄟
**Nearby Facilities** ┏ ✓ ⚓ ⅄ ∪ ⅃ ⅄
**Acreage** 25 **Open** 1 March to 5 Jan
**Access** Good **Site** Level
Peaceful site, all level pitches, abundant wildlife. Ten acres of fishing lakes on site, free to site occupants for 2005. New lakeside statics for sale.
**Nearest Town/Resort** Lincoln/Boston
**Directions** Take the A153 Sleaford/Skegness road, in Tattershall turn at the market place onto country road signposted Woodhall Spa. In 1½ miles site is on the left. Good wide entrance.

## WAINFLEET ALL SAINTS

**Swan Lake Caravan Park,** Culvert Road, Wainfleet, Skegness, Lincolnshire, PE24 4NJ
**Tel:** 01754 881456
www.swan-lake.co.uk
**Pitches For** ▲ ⊞ 🚐 **Total** 25
**Facilities** 🕯 🗓 ⚓ ┏ ⊙ ➡ 🛒 🍴 ⊞ 🍴 🖃
**Nearby Facilities** ┏ ✓
**Acreage** 7 **Open** March to November
**Access** Good **Site** Level
Near the River Steeping. Caravans for sale and hire. Ideal touring. Sorry, no dogs allowed.
**Nearest Town/Resort** Skegness
**Directions** Follow brown tourism signs from the A52, between Skegness and Boston.
⚍ Thorpe Culvert

## WOODHALL SPA

**Bainland Country Park,** Horncastle Road, Woodhall Spa, Lincolnshire, LN10 6UX
**Tel:** 01526 352903 **Fax:** 01526 353730
**Email:** bookings@bainland.co.uk
www.bainland.co.uk
**Pitches For** ▲ ⊞ 🚐 **Total** 150
**Facilities** ⚓ 🕯 🖃 🗓 🗓 ⚓ ┏ ⊙ ➡ 🛒 🖃 🍴
🕮 🄲 🄲 🛒 ✕ ┏ 🏪 ⚓ 🄟 🎯 ➡ 🖃 🄲 ⅄
🄟
**Nearby Facilities** ┏ ✓ ⚓ ⅄ ∪ ⅃ ⅄
**Acreage** 12 **Open** All Year
**Access** Good **Site** Level
Situated on the edge of the Wolds, surrounded by woodland. Ideally central for touring this delightful county. Golf and tennis on site.
**Directions** Situated on the B1191, 1½ miles

from Woodhall Spa towards Horncastle. Just before petrol station.
⚍ Metheringham

## WOODHALL SPA

**Camping & Caravanning Club Site,** Wellsyke Lane, Kirkby-on-Bain, Woodhall Spa, Lincolnshire, LN10 6YU
**Tel:** 01526 352911
www.campingandcaravanningclub.co.uk
**Pitches For** ▲ ⊞ 🚐 **Total** 90
**Facilities** ⚓ 🕯 🗓 ⚓ ┏ ⊙ ⊙ 🄲 🛒 🏪 ➡ 🖃 🄲
**Nearby Facilities** ┏
**Acreage** 6½ **Open** March to Oct
**Access** Good **Site** Level
A nature lovers dream with many varieties of birds seen on site. BTB 5 Star Graded, David Bellamy Gold Award and AA 3 Pennants. Non members welcome.
**Nearest Town/Resort** Horncastle
**Directions** From Sleaford or Horncastle take the A153 to Haltham. At the garage turn left towards Kirkby-on-Bain. At the Ebrington Arms turn right, site is 1 mile.
⚍ Metheringham

## WOODHALL SPA

**Jubilee Park Camping & Caravanning Park,** Stixwould Road, Woodhall Spa, Lincolnshire, LN10 6QH
**Tel:** 01526 352448
**Pitches For** ▲ ⊞ 🚐 **Total** 88
**Facilities** ⚓ 🕯 🗓 ⚓ ┏ ⊙ ➡ 🛒 ✕ ⅃ ⅄ ⚓ ⅄ ⅃⅄
**Nearby Facilities** ┏ ✓ ⅄
**Open** April to October
**Access** Good **Site** Level
Ideal touring centre.
**Nearest Town/Resort** Horncastle
**Directions** 6 miles from Horncastle on the B1191 Sleaford road.
⚍ Lincoln

# LONDON

## ABBEY WOOD

**Abbey Wood Caravan Club Site,** Federation Road, Abbey Wood, London, SE2 0LS
**Tel:** 020 8311 7708 **Fax:** 020 8311 1465
www.caravanclub.co.uk
**Pitches For** ▲ ⊞ 🚐 **Total** 220
**Facilities** 🕯 🗓 🗓 ⚓ ┏ 🄲 🛒 🍴
🄲 🄲 🛒 🄟 ➡ 🖃 🄲
**Nearby Facilities** ┏ ▲ ⅄
**Acreage** 9 **Open** All Year
**Access** Good **Site** Lev/Slope
Spacious site screened by mature trees. Within walking distance of railway link to central London for its attractions. Near the London Eye, Thames Barrier and Splash World at Woolwich. Non members welcome. Booking essential.

**Directions** From central London on A2 turn off at A221 junc into Danson Rd, follow signs for Bexleyheath to Crook Log (A207 junc). At lights turn right and immediately left into Brampton Rd. After 1½m at lights turn left into Bostal Rd (A206), at lights turn right into Basildon Rd (B213). In 300yds turn right into McLeod Rd, at roundabout turn right into Knee Hill, turn second right into Federation Rd, site is 50yds on the left.

⚌ Abbey Wood

## CRYSTAL PALACE

**Crystal Palace Caravan Club Site,**
Crystal Palace Parade, London, SE19 1UF
**Tel:** 020 8778 7155 **Fax:** 020 8676 0980
www.caravanclub.co.uk
**Pitches For** ▲ ⊞ ☻ **Total** 150
**Facilities** ⅃ ♨ ⌂ ⒁ ♣ ⌐ ⊙ ⅃ ☎ ▣ ☂
⌘ ⓪ ☻ ☒ ⌂ ⌂
**Nearby Facilities** ⌐ ⅃ ⌃ ∪
**Acreage** 6 **Open** All Year
**Access** Good **Site** Level
On the edge of a pleasant park. Ideal for the sights of central London which is easily accessible by public transport (Travelcards sold on site April to November). Non members welcome. Booking essential.
**Nearest Town/Resort** London
**Directions** Site entrance is off the A212 at the junction of Crystal Palace Parade and Westwood Hill.

⚌ Crystal Palace

## LOUGHTON

**The Elms Caravan & Camping Park,**
Lippitts Hill, High Beach, Loughton, Essex, IG10 4AW
**Tel:** 020 8502 5652
**Email:** info@theelmscampsite.co.uk
www.theelmscampsite.co.uk
**Pitches For** ▲ ⊞ ☻ **Total** 50
**Facilities** ⅃ ♨ ⌂ ⒁ ♣ ⌐ ⊙ ⅃ ☎
⌘ ⓪ ☻ ✕ ▣ ☀ ☒ ⌂
**Nearby Facilities** ⌐ ⅃ ⌃ ∿ ∪ ⌐ ♫ ⌘
**Acreage** 3 **Open** March to Oct
**Access** Good **Site** Level
A forest location with wildlife and many varieties of birds, deer, etc.. Motorcycles welcome.
**Nearest Town/Resort** Loughton
**Directions** There is an Elms link from the station. If travelling by road The Elms is in between the A104 Epping New Road and the A112 Seawardstone Road.

⚌ Loughton

## MANCHESTER
### LITTLEBOROUGH

**Hollingworth Lake Caravan Park,** Round House Farm, Rakewood, Littleborough, OL15 0AT
**Tel:** 01706 378661
**Pitches For** ▲ ⊞ ☻ **Total** 45
**Facilities** ⅃ ♨ ⌂ ⒁ ♣ ⌐ ⊙ ⅃ ☒ ☂
⌘ ⓪ ☻ ▣
**Nearby Facilities** ⌐ ⅃ ⌃ ∿ ∪
**Acreage** 3 **Open** All Year
**Access** Good **Site** Level
Near a large lake that covers 120 acres.
**Nearest Town/Resort** Rochdale
**Directions** Leave the M62 at junction 21, Milnrow B6255. Follow Hollingworth Lake Country Park signs to The Fisherman's Inn. Take Rakewood Road, then the second on the right.

⚌ Littleborough

## STOCKPORT

**Elm Beds Caravan Park,** Elm Beds Road, Poynton, Stockport, Cheshire, SK12 1TG
**Tel:** 01625 872370

www. ukparks.co.uk/elmbeds
**Pitches For** ▲ ⊞ ☻ **Total** 20
**Facilities** ♨ ⒁ ♣ ⌐ ⊙ ⅃ ☂
⌘ ⓪ ☻ ☒ ▣ ☀ ⌂
**Nearby Facilities** ⌐ ⅃ ⌃ ∪
**Acreage** 2 **Open** March to October
**Access** Uneven **Site** Lev/Slope
Adjacent to Macclesfield Canal. Near the Peak District National Park.
**Nearest Town/Resort** Stockport
**Directions** Take the A6 from Stockport and join the A523 to Poynton, at traffic lights turn east, straight on for 2 miles.

⚌ Poynton/Middlewood

# MERSEYSIDE
## KIRBY

**Wirral Country Park Caravan Club Site,**
Station Road, Thurstaston, Wirral, Merseyside, CH61 0HN
**Tel:** 01516 485228
www. caravanclub.co.uk
**Pitches For** ⊞ ☻ **Total** 93
**Facilities** ♨ ⒁ ♣ ⌐ ⊙ ⅃ ☎ ▣ ☂
⌘ ⓪ ☻ ⌂ ☒ ⌂
**Nearby Facilities** ⌐ ⅃ ⌃ ∿ ∪
**Acreage** 8 **Open** March to Oct
**Access** Good **Site** Level
Set in an area of great natural beauty with sea views. Easy access to the Dee Estuary. Ideal for sports and water sports enthusiasts. Several swimming pools and sports centres nearby. Non members welcome. Booking essential.
**Nearest Town/Resort** Thurstaston
**Directions** Leave M6 onto M56 Westbound, at the end turn left signposted Queensferry. At the roundabout turn right onto A540 and stay on this road ignoring signs for Wirral Country Park. Just past Heswall at crossroads in Thurstaston turn left into Station Rd, after 150yds turn right and keep left, after ¾m (immediately after bridge) turn right into site road, site is on the left.

⚌ Thurstaston

# NORFOLK
## ACLE

**Broad Farm Trailer Park,** Fleggburgh, Burgh St Margaret, Great Yarmouth, Norfolk, NR29 3AF
**Tel:** 01493 369273
**Pitches For** ▲ ⊞ ☻ **Total** 350
**Facilities** ♨ ⒁ ♣ ⌐ ⊙ ⅃ ☎ ▣ ☂
⌘ ⓪ ☻ ✕ ▣ ☀ ⌐ ☒ ⌂ ☀ ⌂
**Nearby Facilities** ⌐ ⅃ ⌃
**Acreage** 30 **Open** May Day W/E to 30 Sept
**Access** Good **Site** Level
Situated in the countryside. Ideal for visiting Norfolk's many attractions.
**Nearest Town/Resort** Great Yarmouth
**Directions** 7 miles from Great Yarmouth taking the A1064 when you reach Caister-on-Sea.

⚌ Acle

## ATTLEBOROUGH

**Oak Tree Caravan Park,** Norwich Road, Attleborough, Norfolk, NR17 2JX
**Tel:** 01953 455565
**Email:** oaktree.cp@virgin.net
www.oaktree-caravan-park.co.uk
**Pitches For** ▲ ⊞ ☻ **Total** 30
**Facilities** ♨ ⒁ ♣ ⌐ ⊙ ⅃ ▣ ⓪ ☒ ⌂
**Nearby Facilities** ⌐ ⅃ ⌃ ∪
**Acreage** 5 **Open** All Year
**Access** Good **Site** Level
**Nearest Town/Resort** Attleborough
**Directions** Turn right off the A11 (Thetford to Norwich road) signposted Attleborough, in 2 miles continue through Attleborough

passing Sainsburys, fork left immediately past the church at T-junction, site is on the right in ½ mile.

⚌ Attleborough

## AYLSHAM

**Top Farm Camping & Caravan Site,** Top Farm, Kittles Lane, Marsham, NorwichNorfolk, NR10 5QF
**Tel:** 01263 733962 **Fax:** 01263 732282
**Email:** clive@top-farm.info
www.top-farm.info
**Pitches For** ▲ ⊞ ☻ **Total** 25
**Facilities** ♨ ⒁ ♣ ⌐ ⊙ ⅃ ▣ ☒ ☀ ⌂
**Nearby Facilities** ⌐ ⅃ ⌃ ∿ ∪ ⌐ ♫ ⌘
**Acreage** 7 **Open** All Year
**Access** Good **Site** Level
Site adjoins heathland and meadows, walks on private land and common heathland. A short drive away from the Norfolk Broads, beaches, the city of Norwich and market towns.
**Nearest Town/Resort** Aylsham
**Directions** Leave Aylsham on the A140, the next village is Marsham, turn right and follow the road for ¾ miles, turn right into Sandy Lane and Kittles Lane.

⚌ Norwich

## BURGH ST. PETER

**Waveney River Centre,** Staithe Road, Burgh St Peter, Beccles, Suffolk, NR34 0BT
**Tel:** 01502 677343 **Fax:** 01502 677566
**Email:** info@waveneyrivercentre.co.uk
www.waveneyrivercentre.co.uk
**Pitches For** ▲ ⊞ ☻
**Facilities** ♨ ⒁ ♣ ⌐ ⊙ ⅃ ☎ ▣ ☂
⌘ ⓪ ☻ ✕ ▣ ☀ ⌐ ☒ ▣ ⌂ ☀
**Nearby Facilities** ⌐ ⅃ ⌃ ∪
**Open** Easter to 31 Oct
**Access** Poor **Site** Lev/Slope
All touring pitches overlook the River Waveney.
**Nearest Town/Resort** Beccles
**Directions** From the A143 follow brown tourism signs to Haddiscoe Village. Stay on this road (Wiggs Road) for 2 miles, turn left into Burgh Road, site is 2¼ miles.

⚌ Haddiscoe

## CAISTER-ON-SEA

**Grasmere Caravan Park,** Bultitudes Loke, Yarmouth Road, Caister-on-Sea, Great YarmouthNorfolk, NR30 5DH
**Tel:** 01493 720382
**Pitches For** ⊞ ☻ **Total** 46
**Facilities** ♨ ⒁ ♣ ⌐ ⊙ ⅃ ☒ ☀ ⌂
⌘ ⓪ ☻ ⌂ ▣
**Nearby Facilities** ⌐ ⅃ ⌃ ∿ ∪ ⌐
**Acreage** 2 **Open** April to Mid October
**Access** Good **Site** Level
½ mile from beach, 3 miles to centre of Great Yarmouth. Advance bookings taken for touring site pitches. Each pitch with it's own electric, water tap and foul water drain. Some hard standings.
**Nearest Town/Resort** Great Yarmouth
**Directions** Enter Caister from roundabout near Yarmouth Stadium at Yarmouth end of bypass. After ½ mile turn sharp left just before the bus stop.

⚌ Great Yarmouth

## CLIPPESBY

**Clippesby Hall,** Clippesby, Norfolk, NR29 3BL
**Tel:** 01493 367800 **Fax:** 01493 367809
**Email:** holidays@clippesby.com
www.clippesby.com
**Pitches For** ▲ ⊞ ☻ **Total** 100
**Facilities** ⅃ ♨ ⌂ ⒁ ♣ ⌐ ⊙ ⅃ ☒ ☀ ⌂
⌘ ⓪ ☻ ✕ ▣ ☀ ⌐ ♫ ⌘ ☒ ▣ ⌂ ☀

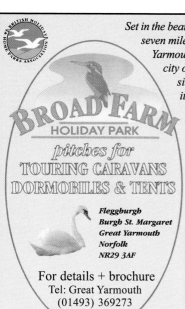

**Nearby Facilities** ⌐ ✦ ⚓ ⚡ ∪ ♫
**Acreage** 30 **Open** Easter **to** Mid Sept
**Access** Good **Site** Level
Set in the heart of the Norfolk Broads National Park. Near to nature reserves and tourist attractions. Bellamy Gold Award for Conservation.
**Nearest Town/Resort** Great Yarmouth
**Directions** From the A47 Norwich bypass follow tourism signs to the 'The Broads'. At Acle take the A1064, after 2½ miles turn left onto the B1152, after ½ a mile turn left at the Clippesby Village sign, after 400 yards turn right.
⇌ Acle

### CROMER
**Deer's Glade Caravan & Camping Park,**
White Post Road, Hanworth, Norwich, Norfolk, NR11 7HN
**Tel:** 01263 768633 **Fax:** 01263 768328
**Email:** info@deersglade.co.uk
www.deersglade.co.uk
**Pitches For** ⋏ ⊡ **Total** 125
**Facilities** ⚹ ∤ Ⓗ Ⓦ ⚓ ⌐ ☺ ⅃ ⚐ ⌷ 🍴
♒ ⊘ ⚓ ⋔ ⊣⊟ ⊡ ☼ ♫
**Nearby Facilities** ⌐ ✦ ⚓ ⚡ ∪ ♫
**Open** All Year
**Access** Good **Site** Level
**Nearest Town/Resort** Cromer
**Directions** 5 miles inland off the A140 Cromer to Norwich road.
⇌ Cromer

### CROMER
**Forest Park Caravan Site Ltd.,**
Northrepps Road, Cromer, Norfolk, NR27 0JR
**Tel:** 01263 513290 **Fax:** 01263 511992
**Email:** forestpark@netcom.co.uk
www.forest-park.co.uk

**Pitches For** ⋏ ⊡ ♿ **Total** 355
**Facilities** ⚹ ∤ Ⓦ ⚓ ⌐ ☺ ⅃ ⚐ ⌷ 🍴
♒ ⊘ ⚓ ✗ ∇ Ⓜ ⚓ ⋔ ⌇⊣⊟ ⊡ ☼
**Nearby Facilities** ⌐ ✦ ⚓ ⚡ ∪ ♫
**Acreage** 90 **Open** 15 March **to** 15 Jan
**Access** Good **Site** Sloping
Overlooking Cromer Golf Course and surrounded by forest with many woodland walks.
**Nearest Town/Resort** Cromer
**Directions** Go through the town centre until you reach traffic lights, turn left into Overstrand Road. Follow until you reach a right hand fork featuring a horse trough, turn right and Forest Park is on the left.
⇌ Cromer

### CROMER
**Ivy Farm Holiday Park,** 1 High Street, Overstrand, Nr Cromer, Norfolk, NR27 0PS
**Tel:** 01263 579239
**Email:** enquiries@ivy-farm.co.uk
www.ivy-farm.co.uk
**Pitches For** ⋏ ⊡ ♿ **Total** 43
**Facilities** ∤ Ⓦ ⚓ ⌐ ☺ ⅃ ⚐ ⌷ 🍴
⊘ ⚓ ⋔ ⚡ ⊣⊟ ⊡ ☼ ♫
**Nearby Facilities** ⌐ ✦ ⚓ ⚡ ∪ ♫
**Acreage** 4 **Open** 20 March **to** 31 October
**Access** Good **Site** Lev/Slope
Just a 2 minute walk to the beach. Country walks.
**Nearest Town/Resort** Cromer
**Directions** Take the coast road from Cromer towards Mundesley and Overstrand is the next village. Pass the church on the left, pass the garden centre on the right, turn next left into Carr Lane. Entrance is half way down on the right.
⇌ Cromer

### CROMER
**Manor Farm Caravan & Camping Site,** Manor Farm, East Runton, Cromer, Norfolk, NR27 9PR
**Tel:** 01263 512858
**Email:** manor-farm@ukf.net
www.manorfarmcaravansite.co.uk
**Pitches For** ⋏ ⊡ ♿ **Total** 130
**Facilities** ⚹ ⚓ ∤ Ⓦ ⚓ ⌐ ☺ ⅃ ⚐ ⌷ ⋔ ⊣⊟
**Nearby Facilities** ⌐ ✦ ∪ ♫
**Acreage** 16 **Open** Easter **to** October
**Access** Good **Site** Lev/Slope
Panoramic sea and woodland views. Spacious, quiet, family run farm site. Ideal for families. Separate field for dog owners.
**Nearest Town/Resort** Cromer
**Directions** 1½ miles west of Cromer, turn off the A148 at signpost 'Manor Farm'.
⇌ Cromer

### CROMER
**West Runton Camping & Caravanning Club Site,** Holgate Lane, West Runton, Cromer, Norfolk, NR27 9NW
**Tel:** 01263 837544
www.campingandcaravanningclub.co.uk
**Pitches For** ⋏ ⊡ ♿ **Total** 200
**Facilities** ⚹ ∤ Ⓦ ⚓ ⌐ ☺ ⅃ ⚐ ⌷ 🍴
⚐ ⊘ ⚓ ⋔ ⊣⊟ ⊡ ♫
**Nearby Facilities** ⌐ ✦ ⚓ ⚡ ∪ ♫
**Acreage** 15 **Open** March **to** Nov
**Access** Difficult **Site** Lev/Slope
Panoramic view of the countryside. Just 1 mile from the sea. BTB 4 Star Graded and AA 3 Pennants. Non members welcome.
**Nearest Town/Resort** Cromer
**Directions** Take the A148 from Kings Lynn, on approaching West Runton turn left at the Roman Camp Inn, ½ a mile along the track, on the crest of the hill, is the site entrance.
⇌ West Runton

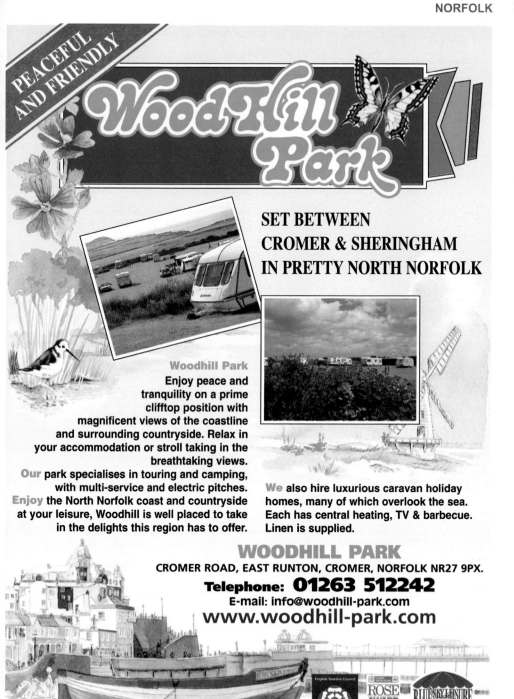

**PEACEFUL AND FRIENDLY**

# WoodHill Park

## SET BETWEEN CROMER & SHERINGHAM IN PRETTY NORTH NORFOLK

**Woodhill Park**

Enjoy peace and tranquility on a prime clifftop position with magnificent views of the coastline and surrounding countryside. Relax in your accommodation or stroll taking in the breathtaking views. Our park specialises in touring and camping, with multi-service and electric pitches. Enjoy the North Norfolk coast and countryside at your leisure, Woodhill is well placed to take in the delights this region has to offer.

We also hire luxurious caravan holiday homes, many of which overlook the sea. Each has central heating, TV & barbecue. Linen is supplied.

## WOODHILL PARK

CROMER ROAD, EAST RUNTON, CROMER, NORFOLK NR27 9PX.

**Telephone: 01263 512242**

E-mail: info@woodhill-park.com

**www.woodhill-park.com**

A Blue Sky Leisure Park

# SEACROFT
## CAMPING PARK

*A touring park ideally placed for a family holiday with sandy beaches well within walking distance.*

Runton Road, Cromer, Norfolk NR27 9NH
**Tel: (01263) 511722   Fax: (01263) 511512**

* Tents, Motorhomes, Caravans all welcome
* Toilet block with Showers
* Two individual washing cubicals in ladies
* Heated Swimming Pool
* Large Recreation Field
* Licenced Bar (Food Served), Take-Away Food and Shop
* Conservatory
* Laundry room with Washing Machine and Drier
* Washing-up Sinks
* Facilities for the Disabled
* Games Room
* Family Entertainment in High Season
* Baby Changing Facility

## CROMER

**Woodhill Park,** Cromer Road, East Runton, Cromer, Norfolk, NR27 9PX
**Tel:** 01263 512242 **Fax:** 01263 515326
**Email:** info@woodhill-park.com
www.woodhill-park.com
**Pitches For** A ⚑ ⛺ **Total** 300
**Facilities** ⛲ ⧗ 🏠 📶 ♨ ⌂ ⊙ 🔌 ▢ ☎
📶 🚾 🖳 🍴 🎣 ⚡ 🛒 ▣ 📧
**Nearby Facilities** ⛵ 🏊 🏔 🎿 ∪ ♪
**Acreage** 32 **Open** March **to** Oct
**Access** Good **Site** Lev/Slope
Peaceful and tranquil, set in countryside overlooking the sea, developed to highest standards. Multi-service and super size hook-up pitches. Rose Award.
**Nearest Town/Resort** Cromer
**Directions** Set between East and West Runton on the seaside of the A149 Cromer to Sheringham road.
⇌ West Runton

## DISS

**Applewood Caravan & Camping Park,** The Grove, Banham, Norwich, Norfolk, NR16 2HE
**Tel:** 01953 887771 **Fax:** 01953 887445
**Email:** info@banhamzoo.co.uk
www.banhamzoo.co.uk
**Pitches For** A ⚑ ⛺ **Total** 145
**Facilities** ⛲ ⧗ 🏠 📶 ♨ ⌂ ⊙ 🔌 ▢ ☎
📶 🚾 🖳 🍴 ✗ 🎣 ⚡ 📧 ♪
**Nearby Facilities** ⛵ 🏊
**Acreage** 13 **Open** Easter **to** Oct
**Access** Good **Site** Level
Adjacent to Banham Zoo.
**Nearest Town/Resort** Diss
**Directions** Banham is situated between Attleborough and Diss on the B1113 Norwich to Bury St Edmunds road. Follow the brown tourist signs.
⇌ Diss

## DISS

**The Willows Camping & Caravan Park,** Diss Road, Scole, Diss, Norfolk, IP21 4DH
**Tel:** 01379 740271 **Fax:** 01379 740271
**Pitches For** A ⚑ ⛺
**Facilities** ⧗ 🏠 🚾 ♨ ⌂ ⊙ 🔌
🖳 ⌂ ♨ 🛒 ▣ 📧 ♪
**Nearby Facilities** ⛵ 🏊 ∪
**Open** Easter **to** Oct

**Access** Good **Site** Level
Alongside the River Waveney.
**Nearest Town/Resort** Diss
**Directions** 1½ miles from Diss.
⇌ Diss

## DISS

**Waveney Valley Holiday Park,** Airstation Farm, Airstation Lane, Rushall, DissNorfolk, IP21 4QF
**Tel:** 01379 741690 **Fax:** 01379 741228
**Email:** waveneyvalleyhp@aol.com
www.caravanparksnorfolk.co.uk
**Pitches For** A ⚑ ⛺ **Total** 45
**Facilities** ⧗ 🏠 🚾 ♨ ⌂ ⊙ 🔌 ▢ ☎
📶 🚾 ⊙ ✗ 🎣 🖳 ♨ 🛒 ▣ 📧 ♪
**Nearby Facilities** ⛵ 🏊
**Acreage** 4 **Open** April **to** October
**Access** Good **Site** Level
Family run site in a rural position. Horse riding for all ages and abilities on site.
**Nearest Town/Resort** Harleston
**Directions** From Diss take the A140, at Dickleburgh in Rushall turn at telephone box towards Pulham, turn into Airstation Lane and site is on the right.
⇌ Diss

## DOCKING

**The Garden Caravan Site,** Barmer Hall, Syderstone, Kings Lynn, Norfolk, PE31 8SR
**Tel:** 01485 578220/178 **Fax:** 578178
**Email:** nigel@mason96.fsnet.co.uk
www.gardencaravansite.co.uk
**Pitches For** A ⚑ ⛺ **Total** 30
**Facilities** ⛲ ⧗ 🏠 🚾 ♨ ⌂ ⊙ 🔌 🖳 🏠 ⊙ 🛒 ▣
**Nearby Facilities** ⛵ 🏊 🏔 🎿 ∪ ♪
**Open** March **to** November
**Access** Good **Site** Lev/Slope
A lovely secluded and sheltered site in a walled garden. Close to the famous North Norfolk coast.
**Nearest Town/Resort** Fakenham
**Directions** From Fakenham or Kings Lynn take the A148, then take the B1454 towards Hunstanton, 4 miles on the right hand side.

## DOWNHAM MARKET

**Grange Farm,** Whittington Camp Site, Whittington Hill, Whittington, Kings LynnNorfolk, PE33 9TF
**Tel:** 01366 500075

**Email:** whittington.campsite@tesco.net
**Pitches For** A ⚑ ⛺
**Facilities** ⛲ ⧗ 🏠 ♨ ⌂ 🔌 🖳 🏠 📧 🎿 ♪
**Nearby Facilities** ⛵ 🏊 🎿
**Open** February **to** Dec
**Access** Good **Site** Level
Alongside a river. Within 1 hours drive of Hunstanton, Sheringham, Cromer and Great Yarmouth.
**Nearest Town/Resort** Downham Market
**Directions** From the A134 take the A1122 left to Downham Market.
⇌ Downham Market

## FAKENHAM

**Crossways Caravan & Camping Park,** Crossways, Holt Road, Little Snoring, Norfolk, NR21 0AX
**Tel:** 01328 878335 **Fax:** 01328 878335
**Email:** hollands@mannasolutions.com
**Pitches For** A ⚑ ⛺ **Total** 26
**Facilities** ⧗ 🏠 🚾 ♨ ⌂ ⊙ 🔌 🖳 ⌂ ☎
📶 🚾 ⊙ 🛒 ▣ 📧 🎿 ♪
**Nearby Facilities** ⛵ 🏊
**Acreage** 2 **Open** All Year
**Access** Good **Site** Level
Quiet, family run site. Central to North Norfolk, ideal for touring.
**Nearest Town/Resort** Fakenham
**Directions** On the A148 Kings Lynn to Cromer road, 2 miles from Fakenham. Situated in Little Snoring behind the village store.
⇌ Kings Lynn

## FAKENHAM

**Fakenham Racecourse Caravan Club Site,** Pudding Norton, Fakenham, Norfolk, NR21 7NY
**Tel:** 01328 862388 **Fax:** 01328 855908
**Email:**
caravan@fakenhamracecourse.co.uk
www.fakenhamracecourse.co.uk
**Pitches For** A ⚑ ⛺ **Total** 116
**Facilities** ⛲ ⧗ 🏠 🚾 ♨ ⌂ ⊙ 🔌 ▢ ☎
📶 ⊙ ✗ 🛒 ▣ 📧 🎿
**Nearby Facilities** ⛵ 🏊
**Acreage** 11½ **Open** All Year
**Access** Good **Site** Level
Ideal site for a relaxing or active holiday, in comfortable and picturesque surroundings.

# WAVENEY VALLEY HOLIDAY PARK
**Tel: (01379) 741228     Fax: (01379) 741228**
**Airstation Lane, Rushall, Diss, Norfolk IP21 4QF**
*Leave the A140 for Dickleburgh, travel 2 miles east to Rushall.*
Large level site with Electric hook-ups available, Flush Toilets, H&C Water Showers,
Shaver Point, Site Shop, Gas, Laundry Room, Licensed Bar, Restaurant,
www.caravanparksnorfolk.co.uk     Outdoor Swimming Pool and Horse Riding.

Local attractions include Norfolk Broads, Sandringham House, Holkham Hall, Thursford Steam Engine Collection and Pensthorpe Waterfowl Park. Non members welcome. Booking essential.
**Nearest Town/Resort** Fakenham
**Directions** On approaching Fakenham from all directions, follow "Campsite" and international caravan/camping signs, they all refer to this site.
⚆ King's Lynn

## FAKENHAM

**Manor Park,** Manor Farm, Tattersett, Kings Lynn, Norfolk, PE31 8RS
**Tel:** 01485 528310
**www.**manorparktouringcaravans.co.uk
**Pitches For** ▲ ⚎ ☗ **Total** 30
Facilities
Nearby Facilities
**Acreage** 4 **Open** March to October
**Access** Good **Site** Lev/Slope
15 minutes from beaches, Wells-Next-the-Sea, etc..
**Nearest Town/Resort** Fakenham
**Directions** From Kings Lynn take the A148 to Coxford, 15 miles. From Fakenham take the A148, 5 miles.
⚆ Kings Lynn

## FAKENHAM

**The Old Brick Kilns,** Little Barney Lane, Barney, Fakenham, Norfolk, NR21 0NL
**Tel:** 01328 878305 **Fax:** 01328 878948
**Email:** enquires@old-brick-kilns.co.uk
**www.**old-brick-kilns.co.uk
**Pitches For** ▲ ⚎ ☗ **Total** 65
Facilities
Nearby Facilities

**Acreage** 13 **Open** 1 March **to** 6 Jan
**Access** Good **Site** Level
Beaches within 20 minutes drive. Near to Sandringham, Blicking Hall, Houghton Hall, Thursford, Walsingham and Norwich.
**Nearest Town/Resort** Fakenham
**Directions** From the A148 Fakenham to Cromer road, take the B1354 to Melton Constable. After 300 yards turn right to Barney, then turn first left down Little Barney Lane, Park is at the end in ¾ miles.
⚆ Kings Lynn

## GREAT HOCKHAM

**Puddledock Farm Camp Site,**
Puddledock Farm, Great Hockham, Thetford, Norfolk, IP24 1PA
**Tel:** 01953 498455
**Pitches For** ▲ ⚎ ☗ **Total** 30
Facilities
Nearby Facilities
**Acreage** 5 **Open** March **to** Nov
**Access** Good **Site** Level
Very quiet site with an abundance of birds and wildlife. Backs onto the forest for walks. Putting green on site. Children by arrangement.
**Nearest Town/Resort** Thetford
**Directions** Midway between Thetford and Watton on the A1075. Turn left at 83 past Forestry Commission picnic site, no roadside sign.
⚆ Thetford

## GREAT YARMOUTH

**Breydon Water Holiday Park,** Butt Lane, Burgh Castle, Great Yarmouth, Norfolk, NR31 9QB
**Tel:** 01493 780357 **Fax:** 01493 782383
**Email:** holidaysales.breydonwater@park-resorts.com

**www.**park-resorts.com
**Pitches For** ▲ ⚎ ☗ **Total** 150
Facilities
Nearby Facilities
**Acreage** 20 **Open** March **to** October
**Access** Good **Site** Level
Set in countryside yet only ten minutes from Great Yarmouth. Two bars with entertainment, amusements, swimming pool with slide, Kids Club and play area.
**Nearest Town/Resort** Great Yarmouth
**Directions** From Great Yarmouth follow signs for Lowestoft, at the third roundabout look for the sign for Burgh Castle. Follow for 2½ miles to the T-junction and follow brown tourism signs.
⚆ Great Yarmouth

## GREAT YARMOUTH

**Burgh Castle Marina,** Butt Lane, Burgh Castle, Norfolk, NR31 9PZ
**Tel:** 01493 780331 **Fax:** 01493 780163
**Email:** info@burghcastlemarina.co.uk
**www.**burghcastlemarina.co.uk
**Pitches For** ▲ ⚎ ☗ **Total** 45
Facilities
Nearby Facilities
**Acreage** 19 **Open** Easter **to** Oct
**Access** Good **Site** Level
Riverside location, easy stroll to the magnificent Roman ruins and spectacular marshland views. RSPB Reserves nearby. Exhibition on the area in the parks reception.
**Nearest Town/Resort** Gorleston-on-Sea
**Directions** Approach on the A143 Beccles to Great Yarmouth road. 2 miles south of the A12 intersection follow brown marina signs to Belton. After ¾ miles turn right for Burgh Castle.
⚆ Great Yarmouth

## GREAT YARMOUTH
**Drewery Caravan Park,** California Road, California, Great Yarmouth, Norfolk, NR29 3QW
**Tel:** 01493 730845 **Fax:** 01493 731968
**Pitches For** ▲ ⇔ **Total** 135
**Facilities** ఉ ≬ 🔟 ♨ ୮ ⊙ ┙ ⊿ ◙ ☎ ♨ ⑥ ☂ ♉
**Nearby Facilities** ୮ ✔ ⚐ ⚲ ∪ ♫
**Acreage** 4 **Open** Easter to October
**Access** Good **Site** Level
Near the beach. Ideal for Norfolk Broads and Great Yarmouth.
**Nearest Town/Resort** Great Yarmouth
**Directions** Take the A149 from Great Yarmouth, at the Greyhound Stadium roundabout turn left, at next roundabout take the second exit onto the B1159. Go to roundabout and take the second exit, after ¼ mile turn right into California Road and follow to the end. Site is opposite California Tavern. 6 miles from Great Yarmouth.
⇻ Great Yarmouth

## GREAT YARMOUTH
**Great Yarmouth Racecourse Caravan Club Site,** Jellicoe Road, Great Yarmouth, Norfolk, NR30 4AU
**Tel:** 01493 855223
www.caravanclub.co.uk
**Pitches For** ⇔ ⇔ **Total** 115
**Facilities** ≬ 🔟 ♨ ୮ ◙ ☎ ♉ ⑥ ⊜ ♨ ┉ ┫ ⊟
**Nearby Facilities** ୮ ✔ ⚐ ⚲
**Acreage** 5¼ **Open** March to Nov
**Access** Good **Site** Level
300yds from the lively seafront. Adjacent to a racecourse and golf course. Near the Norfolk Broads and Pleasurewood Hills. Dogs on leads at all times. Non members welcome. Booking essential.
**Nearest Town/Resort** Great Yarmouth
**Directions** From north on the A149, at the traffic lights on the south skirts of Caister turn left into Jellicoe Road. After ¼ mile turn left into the Racecourse entrance (BEWARE of blind turning), go across the racetrack to the site.
⇻ Great Yarmouth

## GREAT YARMOUTH
**Rose Farm Touring & Camping Park,** Stepshort, Belton, Great Yarmouth, Norfolk, NR31 9JS
**Tel:** 01493 780896 **Fax:** 01493 780896
www.rosefarmtouringpark.co.uk
**Pitches For** ▲ ⇔ ⇔ **Total** 80
**Facilities** ఉ ≬ 🔟 ♨ ୮ ⊙ ┙ ⊿ ◙ ☎ ⑥ ⑪ ♉ ⋒ ┫ ⊟ ⊟ ♨
**Nearby Facilities** ୮ ✔ ⚐ ⚲ ∪ ♪ ♫
**Acreage** 6 **Open** All Year
**Access** Good **Site** Level
A clean site in peaceful surroundings.
**Nearest Town/Resort** Gorleston

**Directions** From Great Yarmouth on the bypass take the A143 to Beccles, through Bradwell up to the small dual carriageway. Turn right into new road signposted Belton and Burgh Castle. Down New Road first right at Stepshort, site is first on right.
⇻ Great Yarmouth

## GREAT YARMOUTH
**The Grange Touring Park,** Yarmouth Road, Ormesby St Margaret, Great Yarmouth, Norfolk, NR29 3QG
**Tel:** 01493 730306 **Fax:** 01493 730188
**Email:** info@grangetouring.co.uk
www.grangeouring.co.uk
**Pitches For** ▲ ⇔ ⇔ **Total** 70
**Facilities** ≬ 🔟 ♨ ୮ ⊙ ┙ ⊿ ◙ ☎ ♉ ⑥ ⊜ ♨ ⋒ ┫ ⊟
**Nearby Facilities** ୮ ✔ ⚐ ⚲ ∪
**Acreage** 3½ **Open** Easter to End Sept
**Access** Good **Site** Level
Rural, sheltered site, very convenient for Great Yarmouth and the Norfolk Broads.
**Nearest Town/Resort** Great Yarmouth
**Directions** 2 miles north of Great Yarmouth, by the roundabout on the B1159 at the north end of Caister bypass.
⇻ Great Yarmouth

## GREAT YARMOUTH
**Vauxhall Holiday Park,** Acle New Road, Great Yarmouth, Norfolk, NR30 1TB
**Tel:** 01493 857231 **Fax:** 01493 331122
**Email:** info@vauxhallholidays.co.uk
www.vauxhall-holiday-park.co.uk
**Pitches For** ▲ ⇔ ⇔ **Total** 210
**Facilities** ఉ ≬ 🔟 ♨ ୮ ⊙ ┙ ⊿ ◙ ☎ ♉ ⑥ ⊜ ♨ ✗ ∇ ⑪ ⋒ ♨ ⊛ ⊟ ◙
**Nearby Facilities** ୮ ✔ ⚐ ⚲ ∪
**Acreage** 48 **Open** Easter then Mid May to Sept
**Access** Good **Site** Level
Ideal centre for attractions of Great Yarmouth and for exploring the famous Norfolk Broads.
**Nearest Town/Resort** Great Yarmouth
**Directions** Situated on the A47.
⇻ Great Yarmouth

## GREAT YARMOUTH
**Wild Duck Holiday Park,** Howards Common, Belton, Great Yarmouth, Norfolk, NR31 9NE
**Tel:** 01493 780268 **Fax:** 01493 782308
www.touringholidays.co.uk
**Pitches For** ▲ ⇔ ⇔ **Total** 100
**Facilities** ఉ ≬ 🔟 ♨ ୮ ⊙ ┙ ⊿ ◙ ☎ ♨ ♉ ⑥ ⊜ ✗ ∇ ⑪ ⋒ ⊛ ┫ ┫ ⊟ ⊟
**Nearby Facilities** ୮ ✔ ⚐ ⚲ ∪ ♫
**Open** March to End Oct
**Access** Good **Site** Level
5/10 minutes drive to the nearest beach.

Close to Great Yarmouth, Norwich, Norfolk Broads, Bygone Village, Lowestoft and Suffolk Wildlife Park.
**Nearest Town/Resort** Great Yarmouth
**Directions** 3 miles outside Great Yarmouth on the A143, turn right off the dual carriageway and follow brown tourism signs through Belton Village.
⇻ Great Yarmouth

## GREAT YARMOUTH
**Willowcroft Camping & Caravan Park,** Staithe Road, Repps with Bastwick, Potter Heigham, Norfolk, NR29 5JU
**Tel:** 01692 670380 **Fax:** 01692 670380
camping@willowcroft4.freeserve.co.uk
www.willowcroft4.freeserve.co.uk
**Pitches For** ▲ ⇔ ⇔ **Total** 44
**Facilities** ≬ 🔟 ♨ ୮ ⊙ ┙ ⊿ ⑥ ⑪ ♨ ┫ ⊟
**Nearby Facilities** ✔ ⚐ ⚲
**Acreage** 2 **Open** All Year
**Access** Good **Site** Level
Quiet park, just a two minute walk to a river for fishing. Excellent for canoeing, bird watching, walking and cycling etc..
**Nearest Town/Resort** Potter Heigham
**Directions** 10 miles from Great Yarmouth on the Potter Heigham road, into Church Road, then Staithe Road.
⇻ Acle

## HARLESTON
**Little Lakeland Caravan Park,** Wortwell, Harleston, Norfolk, IP20 0EL
**Tel:** 01986 788646 **Fax:** 01986 788646
**Email:** information@littlelakeland.co.uk
www.littlelakeland.co.uk
**Pitches For** ⇔ ⇔ **Total** 40
**Facilities** ఉ ≬ 🔟 ♨ ୮ ⊙ ┙ ⊿ ◙ ☎ ♉ ⑥ ⑪ ♨ ┫ ╳
**Nearby Facilities** ୮ ✔ ⚐ ⚲ ∪
**Acreage** 4 **Open** March to October
**Access** Good **Site** Level
Half acre fishing lake, site library.
**Nearest Town/Resort** Harleston
**Directions** Turn off A143 (Diss to Lowestoft) at roundabout signposted Wortwell. In village turn right about 300 yards after Bell P.H. at bottom of lane turn right into site.
⇻ Diss

## HEMSBY
**Long Beach Caravan Park,** Hemsby, Great Yarmouth, Norfolk, NR29 4JD
**Tel:** 01493 730023 **Fax:** 01493 730188
**Email:** info@long-beach.co.uk
www.long-beach.co.uk
**Pitches For** ▲ ⇔ ⇔ **Total** 100
**Facilities** ఉ ≬ 🔟 ♨ ୮ ⊙ ┙ ⊿ ◙ ☎ ♨ ♉ ⑥ ⊜ ∇ ⑪ ⋒ ♨ ┫ ⊟ ⊟ ♨ ♫ ♪
**Nearby Facilities** ୮ ⚐ ⚲ ∪
**Acreage** 5 **Open** Mid March to End Oct

# NORFOLK

**Access** Good **Site** Level
Park adjoins its own private sandy beach and dunes.
**Nearest Town/Resort** Great Yarmouth
**Directions** 5 miles north of Great Yarmouth, turn east from the B1159 at Hemsby.
⚌ Great Yarmouth

## HEMSBY

**Newport Caravan Park (Norfolk) Ltd.,**
Newport Road, Hemsby, Great Yarmouth, Norfolk, NR29 4NW
**Tel:** 01493 730405
**Pitches For** ⚌ ⚌ **Total** 90
**Facilities** ⌿ ⬛ ⚊ ⌐ ⊙ ⬛ ⬛ ⬛ ⬛
⬛ ⬛ ⬛ ⬛ ⬛ ⬛
**Nearby Facilities** ⌐ ⚊ ⚊ ⚊ U
**Open** Easter **to** End October
500yds from the beach, 6 miles from Great Yarmouth. Convenient base for visiting the Broads, North Norfolk and Norwich.
**Nearest Town/Resort** Great Yarmouth
**Directions** Take the A149 from Great Yarmouth, B1159 follow signs for Hemsby/Winterton-on-Sea, turn right to Newport Road.
⚌ Great Yarmouth

## HOLT

**Kelling Heath Holiday Park,** Weybourne, Holt, Norfolk, NR25 7HW
**Tel:** 01263 588181 **Fax:** 01263 588599
**Email:** info@kellingheath.co.uk
www.kellingheath.co.uk
**Pitches For** ⚌ ⚌ **Total** 300
**Facilities** ⬛ ⌿ ⬛ ⚊ ⌐ ⊙ ⬛ ⬛ ⬛
⬛ ⬛ ⬛ ⬛ ⬛ ⬛ ⬛ ⬛ ⬛ ⬛ ⬛ ⬛ ⬛ ⬛
**Nearby Facilities** ⌐ ⚊ ⚊ ⚊ U ⚊ ⚊
**Acreage** 250 **Open** 1 March **to** Dec
**Access** Good **Site** Level
A 250 acre estate of woodland and heather, with magnificent views of the Weybourne coastline. Rose Award.

**Nearest Town/Resort** Sheringham
**Directions** Turn north at site sign at Bodham on the A148 or turn south off the A149 at Weybourne Church.
⚌ Sheringham

## HORSEY

**Waxham Sands Holiday Park,** Warren Farm, Horsey, Norfolk, NR29 4EJ
**Tel:** 01692 598325 **Fax:** 01692 598325
**Pitches For** ⚌ ⚌ **Total** 200
**Facilities** ⬛ ⚊ ⌐ ⊙ ⬛ ⬛ ⬛
⬛ ⬛ ⬛ ⬛ ⬛ ⬛ ⬛
**Nearby Facilities** ⌐ ⚊ ⚊ ⚊ U
**Acreage** 25 **Open** Spring Bank Holiday **to** 30 Sept
**Access** Good **Site** Level
We have our own beach and are adjacent to a nature reserve. Good location for attractions of Norfolk. Close to the Norfolk Broads.
**Nearest Town/Resort** Great Yarmouth
**Directions** Situated on the B1159 main coast road, 12 miles north of Great Yarmouth.
⚌ Great Yarmouth

## HUNSTANTON

**Manor Park Holiday Village,** Manor Road, Hunstanton, Norfolk, PE36 5AZ
**Tel:** 01485 532300 **Fax:** 01485 533881
**Email:** info@manor-park.co.uk
www.manor-park.co.uk
**Pitches For** ⚌ ⚌ **Total** 64
**Facilities** ⬛ ⌿ ⬛ ⚊ ⌐ ⊙ ⬛ ⬛ ⬛
⬛ ⬛ ⬛ ⬛ ⬛ ⬛ ⬛
**Nearby Facilities**
**Open** March **to** October
**Access** Good **Site** Level
**Nearest Town/Resort** Hunstanton
⚌ Kings Lynn

## HUNSTANTON

**Searles Leisure Resort,** 3 South Beach Road, Hunstanton, Norfolk, PE36 5BB
**Tel:** 01485 534211 **Fax:** 01485 533815
**Email:** bookings@searles.co.uk
www.searles.co.uk
**Pitches For** ⚌ ⚌ ⚌
**Facilities** ⬛ ⌿ ⬛ ⬛ ⬛ ⚊ ⌐ ⊙ ⬛ ⬛ ⬛ ⬛
⬛ ⬛ ⬛ ⬛ ⬛ ⬛ ⬛ ⬛ ⬛ ⬛ ⬛ ⬛ ⬛
**Nearby Facilities** ⌐ ⚊ ⚊ U ⚊
**Open** Mid March **to** Early Nov
**Access** Good **Site** Level
Family park 200 metres from the beach, with excellent camping and touring facilities. Pools, Clubhouse, Entertainment, Hair & Beauty Salon and a Golf Course.
**Nearest Town** Hunstanton/King's Lynn
**Directions** From King's Lynn take the A149 to Hunstanton. In Hunstanton at the first roundabout turn signposted South Beach. Go straight over the next roundabout and Searles is on the left.
⚌ King's Lynn

## KINGS LYNN

**Gatton Water Touring Caravan & Camping Site,** Hillington, Nr Sandringham, King's Lynn, Norfolk, PE31 6BJ
**Tel:** 01485 600643
**Email:** gatton.waters@virgin.net
www.gattonwaters.co.uk
**Pitches For** ⚌ ⚌ ⚌ **Total** 90
**Facilities** ⬛ ⌿ ⬛ ⚊ ⌐ ⊙ ⬛ ⬛ ⬛
⬛ ⬛ ⬛ ⬛ ⬛ ⬛ ⬛ ⬛ ⬛
**Acreage** 24 **Open** April **to** October
**Access** Good **Site** Level
ADULTS ONLY SITE. Most pitches overlook a lake.
**Nearest Town/Resort** Kings Lynn
**Directions** 8 miles from Kings Lynn on the A148 (Kings Lynn/Cromer road).
⚌ Kings Lynn

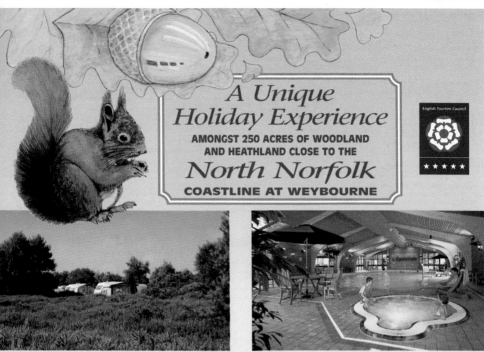

*A Unique Holiday Experience*

**AMONGST 250 ACRES OF WOODLAND AND HEATHLAND CLOSE TO THE**

*North Norfolk*

**COASTLINE AT WEYBOURNE**

### AN AWARD WINNING ENVIRONMENT

- Winner **Holiday Park of the Year** – Safeway Excellence in England Awards for Tourism 2002
- Winner of the **British Airways Tourism for Tomorrow** award for protection of the environment.
- A **David Bellamy "Gold"** conservation award.

### TOURING PITCHES

Set amongst rare open heathland enjoying backdrops of mature pine and native woodland. Electric hook-up points and fully equipped amenity buildings with disabled facilities are available.

### LUXURY HOLIDAY HOMES

Enjoy short breaks or longer stays in luxurious holiday homes set amongst mixed woodland and heathland. Sleeping up to eight each home has full central heating and uPVC double-glazing.

### RELAX AND ENJOY

- Nature trails and woodland walks with magnificent views of the Weybourne coastline
- Tutored rambles, pond dipping and other activities at certain times of the year
- A range of environmental activity using self-guided leaflets available
- Cycle routes on park, or the quiet country lanes surrounding Kelling Heath
- Tennis courts, trim trail, orienteering course and petanque

**KELLING VILLAGE SQUARE** with:-
- Health & Fitness Club with indoor pool, sauna and steam rooms and gym.
- Free outdoor leisure pool
- Village Store
- The Forge Bars, with meals available and entertainment if you choose
- The Folly with traditional entertainment in the open air from jazz bands to folk at selected times of the year

# KELLINGHEATH

**WEYBOURNE, HOLT, NORFOLK NR25 7HW**
**E-mail: info@kellingheath.co.uk**
☎ **01263 588181**
**www.kellingheath.co.uk**

A Blue Sky Leisure Park

## Sandy Gulls Caravan Park    01263 720513
### Cromer Road, Mundesley-on-Sea, North Norfolk NR11 8DF

*The areas only cliff top touring park.* Sandy Gulls caters for customers who value a tranquil location, and seek their own personal space! We do not cater for children or teenagers.
Superb location with spacious pitches, all with uninterrupted sea views and beach access. Electric and TV Hook-ups. Spacious Shower Block.
Blue Flag Beach. Village shops selling local produce. Choice of good local restaurants & pubs serving delicious meals. In the evenings why not realx, watch the End of Pier Show or visit the multi-screen Regal Cinema.
Whilst here why not visit the famous Steam Railway at Sheringham, the Shire Horse Centre, Blickling and Felbrig Halls, The Norfolk Broads, see the seals at Blakeney Point, visit nature reserves and bird sanctuaries, or travel by train to the interesting city of Norwich.

### KINGS LYNN
**Kings Lynn Caravan & Camping Park,** Parkside House, New Road, North Runcton, Kings LynnNorfolk, PE33 0QR
**Tel:** 01553 840004
**Email:** klynn_campsite@hotmail.com
**Pitches For** ▲ ⊞ ⊞ **Total** 35
**Facilities** ┆ ⓌⓌ ▲ ↑ ⊙ ⌐ ☎ ℞↤🗎⊟🔲
**Nearby Facilities** ┌ ✔ ⚓ ↰ ∪ ≱ ♫
**Acreage** 3½ **Open** All Year
**Access** Good **Site** Level
Situated in a beautiful parkland setting with mature trees. Well situated for Kings Lynn, inland market towns, the North Norfolk coast, watersports and good pubs. Tesco's nearby. Rallies welcome.
**Nearest Town/Resort** Kings Lynn
**Directions** 1½ miles from the A17, A47, A10 and A149 main Kings Lynn Hardwick roundabout. Take the A47 towards Swaffham and take the first right at North Runcton.
➔ Kings Lynn

### KINGS LYNN
**Pentney Park,** Main Road, Pentney, King's Lynn, Norfolk, PE32 1HU
**Tel:** 01760 337479 **Fax:** 01760 338118
**Email:** holidays@pentney.demon.co.uk
www.pentney-park.co.uk
**Pitches For** ▲ ⊞ ⊞ **Total** 200
**Facilities** ⚒ ⊙ ⛱ ✕ ♠ ⬙ ⑂ ↑ ↤🗎⊟🔲✄
**Nearby Facilities** ┌ ✔ ∪ ≱
**Acreage** 16 **Open** All Year
**Access** Good **Site** Level
Near the River Nar Valley Walk, linking to Peddars Way Walk. Ideal base for visiting beautiful Norfolk.
**Nearest Town/Resort** King's Lynn
**Directions** Situated on the A47 9 miles east of Kings Lynn and 7 miles west of Swaffham. Turn onto the B1153 to Gayton, entrance is 200 yards.
➔ King's Lynn

### MUNDESLEY
**Sandy Gulls Cliff Top Touring Park,** Cromer Road, Mundesley, Norfolk, NR11 8DF
**Tel:** 01263 720513
**Pitches For** ⊞ ⊞ **Total** 40
**Facilities** ⚓ ┆ ⊞ Ⓦ ▲ ↑ ⊙ ⌐ ⌐ ☎
℞ 🗎 ⛲↤🗎⊟
**Nearby Facilities** ┌ ✔ ⚓ ↰ ∪ ♫
**Acreage** 2½ **Open** Easter **to** October
**Access** Good **Site** Level
Cliff top location, overlooking the beach. Near to the Broads National Park. Children are not catered for. TV Hook-ups. ETB 3 Star Graded Park.
**Nearest Town/Resort** Cromer.
**Directions** South along the coast road for 4 miles.
➔ Cromer

---

# GOLDEN BEACH HOLIDAY PARK
### Sea Palling, Norwich, Norfolk NR12 0AL  Tel: (01692) 598269  Fax: (01692) 598693

A lovely quiet park in a small unspoiled village just behind sand dunes which border miles of golden beaches with excellent sea fishing, therefore making it the ideal location for family holidays and weekends. The Norfolk Broads with its numerous boating, fishing and wildlife attractions are only 4 miles away. We accommodate 112 fully serviced static holiday caravans plus touring caravan and tenting section. Our facilities include a children's play area, resident's lounge bar, shop, launderette and restaurant.
**Luxury self catering holiday homes available for hire or for sale.**
### Write or phone for a free colour brochure.

---

## NORTH WALSHAM
**Two Mills Touring Park,** Yarmouth Road, North Walsham, Norfolk, NR28 9NA
**Tel:** 01692 405829 **Fax:** 01692 405829
**Email:** enquiries@twomills.co.uk
**www.twomills.co.uk**
Pitches For ▲ ✿ ☗ Total 55
Facilities ⚿ ∦ ⊟ ⊞ ⅏ ♨ 𝖗 ☉ ❏ ▰ ◙ ❦
⚑ ⓖ ☕ ❦⅋⊟ ❏ ☖ Ⓐ ⚘ ♪
Nearby Facilities 𝖗 ✓ ⚠ ↘ ∪
Acreage 6 Open 1 March to 3 Jan
ADULTS ONLY. Ideally situated for visiting North Norfolk's many attractions.
Nearest Town/Resort North Walsham
Directions Follow Hospital signs passing the Police Station on route. 1 mile on the left from the town centre.
⚗ North Walsham

## NORWICH
**Camping & Caravanning Club Site,**
Martineau Lane, Norwich, Norfolk, NR1 2HX
**Tel:** 01603 620060
**www.campingandcaravanningclub.co.uk**
Pitches For ▲ ✿ ☗ Total 50
Facilities ∦ ⅏ ♨ 𝖗 ☉ ❧ ❏ ▰
⚑ ⓖ ☕⅋⊟ ❏
Nearby Facilities 𝖗 ✓ ⚠ ♪
Acreage 2½ Open March to Oct
Access Good Site Level
A rural location close to the city of Norwich. Near to the Norfolk Broads. BTB 3 Star Graded and AA 2 Pennants. Non members welcome.
Nearest Town/Resort Norwich
Directions From the A47 join the A146 towards Norwich city centre. At the traffic lights turn left, then left again at the Cock Public House. Site is 150 yards on the right.
⚗ Thorpe

## NORWICH
**Haveringland Hall Park,** Cawston, Norwich, Norfolk, NR10 4PN
**Tel:** 01603 871302 **Fax:** 01603 879223
**Email:** info@haveringlandhall.co.uk
**www.haveringlandhall.co.uk**
Pitches For ▲ ✿ ☗ Total 100
Facilities ∦ ⅏ ♨ 𝖗 ☉ ❧ ▰ ◙ ❦
⚑ ⓖ ☕⅋⊟ ❏ ⚘
Nearby Facilities 𝖗 ✓
Acreage 120 Open Easter to Oct
Access Good Site Level
Set in the grounds of an old country estate. 120 acres of peace and tranquility with lots of woodland and two lakes. David Bellamy Silver Award for Conservation.
Nearest Town/Resort Cawston
Directions From Norwich take the A140 north, then fork left onto the B1149. Turn left signposted Eastgate, at Ratcatchers Public House crossroads turn left, after 800 yards turn left and go through lodge gates.
⚗ Norwich

## NORWICH
**Norfolk Showground Caravan Club Site,**
Royal Norfolk Agricultural, Association Showground, Long Lane, Bawburgh, Norwich Norfolk, NR9 3LX
**Tel:** 01603 742708

**www.caravanclub.co.uk**
Pitches For ✿ ☗ Total 60
Facilities ⚿ ∦ ⊟ ⅏ ♨ 𝖗 ☉ ❦
⚑ ⓖ ☕⅋⊟ ❏
Nearby Facilities 𝖗 ✓ ↘
Acreage 5 Open March to Oct
Access Good Site Lev/Slope
Secluded and charming site set in country parkland. Various events held at the showground. Riverside walks. Close to Norwich with its Norman castle, two cathedrals and many historic buildings. Non members welcome. Booking essential.
Nearest Town/Resort Norwich
Directions From north on the A140 at ring road traffic lights continue right on a A140, at next roundabout turn right onto the A1074 signposted Swaffham. At Longwater Intersection roundabout turn left and cross over the A47, at next roundabout turn left signposted Bawburgh, site is ¼ mile on the right.
⚗ Norwich

## NORWICH
**Swans Harbour Caravan & Camping Park,** Barford Road, Marlingford, Norwich, Norfolk, NR9 4BE
**Tel:** 01603 759658
**Email:** info@swansharbour.co.uk
**www.swansharbour.co.uk**
Pitches For ✿ ☗ Total 30
Facilities ⚿ ∦ ⊟ ⅏ ♨ 𝖗 ☉ ❧ ❦ ☕⚘
Nearby Facilities 𝖗 ✓
Acreage 4 Open All Year
Access Good Site Level
Alongside a river with own fishing rights. Hard standing available.
Nearest Town/Resort Norwich
Directions Turn off the B1108 (Norwich to Watton road). 3 miles past Southern Bypass turn right signposted Marlingford. Follow brown tourist signs to the site.
⚗ Wymondham

## POTTER HEIGHAM
**Causeway Cottage Caravan Park,** Bridge Road, Potter Heigham, Nr Great Yarmouth, Norfolk, NR29 5JB
**Tel:** 01692 670238
Pitches For ✿ ☗
Facilities ∦ ⅏ ♨ 𝖗 ☉ ❧ ❦ ⓖ⚘⊟ ❏
Nearby Facilities 𝖗 ✓ ⚠ ↘
Access Good Site Level
Nearest Town/Resort Great Yarmouth
Directions Potter Heigham is between Great Yarmouth and Norwich. Turn off the A149 at Potter Heigham, we are 250yds from the river and old bridge.
⚗ Acle

## SANDRINGHAM
**Camping & Caravanning Club Site,** The Sandringham Estate, Double Lodges, Sandringham, Norfolk, PE35 6EA
**Tel:** 01485 542555
**www.campingandcaravanningclub.co.uk**
Pitches For ▲ ✿ ☗ Total 275
Facilities ⚿ ∦ ⅏ ♨ 𝖗 ☉ ❧ ▰ ◙ ❦
⚑ ⓖ ☕⊞⅋⊟ ❏ ♪
Nearby Facilities 𝖗 ∪
Acreage 28 Open February to Nov
Access Good Site Lev/Slope

In the grounds of the Royal Estate. BTB 5 Star Graded, David Bellamy Gold Award and AA 4 Pennants. Non members welcome.
Nearest Town/Resort Kings Lynn
Directions From the A148 Kings Lynn to Cromer road, turn left onto the B1440 signposted West Newton. Follow signs indicating tents and caravans to reach the site.
⚗ Kings Lynn

## SANDRINGHAM
**Sandringham Estate Caravan Club Site,** Glucksburg Woods, Sandringham, Norfolk, PE35 6EZ
**Tel:** 01553 631614
**www.caravanclub.co.uk**
Pitches For ✿ ☗ Total 136
Facilities ⚿ ∦ ⊟ ⅏ ♨ 𝖗 ☉ ❦
⚑ ⓖ ☕⊞⅋⊟ ❏
Nearby Facilities
Acreage 13 Open March to Jan
Access Good Site Lev/Slope
Set in the heart of the Royal estate, with Sandringham House, museum and grounds on the doorstep. Then theres the Country Park with nature trails, train ride, Visitor Centre, tea room, gift shop and flower stall. Non members welcome. Booking essential.
Nearest Town/Resort Sandringham
Directions From north on the A149, at the end of Dersingham bypass turn left onto the B1439 at signpost for West Newton, site is within ½ a mile on the left at rustic signpost SECC.

## SCRATBY
**Green Farm Caravan Park,** Scratby, Great Yarmouth, Norfolk, NR29 3NW
**Tel:** 01493 730440
**Email:** geoff@greenfarm-holidays.co.uk
**www.greenfarmcaravanpark.com**
Pitches For ▲ ✿ ☗ Total 200
Facilities ∦ ⊟ ⅏ ♨ 𝖗 ☉ ❧ ▰ ◙ ❦
⚑ ⚑ ⓖ ☕ ❦ ✗ ⅏ ♠ ⚑⅋⊟ ❏
Nearby Facilities 𝖗 ✓ ⚠ ↘ ∪
Acreage 20 Open 26 March to October
Access Good Site Level
Near the beach. ETC 5 Star Graded.
Nearest Town/Resort Great Yarmouth
Directions 4 miles north of Great Yarmouth on the B1159.
⚗ Great Yarmouth

## SCRATBY
**Scratby Hall Caravan Park,** Thoroughfare Lane, Scratby, Great Yarmouth, Norfolk, NR29 3PH
**Tel:** 01493 730283
Pitches For ▲ ✿ ☗ Total 108
Facilities ∦ ⅏ ♨ 𝖗 ☉ ❧ ▰ ◙ ❦
⚑ ⓖ ☕ ♠ ⅏⅋⊟ ❏
Nearby Facilities 𝖗 ✓ ↘ ∪
Acreage 4½ Open Easter to Early Oct
Access Good Site Level
½ a mile from the beach. Convenient for the Norfolk Broads.
Nearest Town/Resort Great Yarmouth
Directions Approx. 5 miles north of Great Yarmouth. From the A1064 take the B1159, signposted.
⚗ Great Yarmouth

## SEA PALLING

**Golden Beach Holiday Centre,** Beach Road, Sea Palling, Norwich, Norfolk, NR12 0AL
**Tel:** 01692 598269 **Fax:** 01692 598693
**Pitches For** ▲ ⚌ ⚌ **Total** 50
**Facilities** ⬧ ⬧ ▯ ▯ ⬧ ⌐ ☉ ⬧ ⬧ ▯ ☎
⬧ ▯ ⬧ ⬧ ✕ ⬧ ▯ ▯ ⬧ ⬧ ⬧
**Nearby Facilities** ⬧ ⬧ ⬧ ⬧ ⬧
**Acreage** 7 **Open** March **to** 1 November
**Access** Good **Site** Level
Family site with a family atmosphere, 200 yards from the beach. New toilets.
**Nearest Town/Resort** Stalham
**Directions** Follow the coast road to Stalham then follow caravan and camping signs to Sea Palling. Turn down Beach Road, site is on the left 200 yards from the beach.
⚏ Wroxham

## STANHOE

**The Rickels Caravan & Camping Site,** Bircham Road, Stanhoe, Kings Lynn, Norfolk, PE31 8PU
**Tel:** 01485 518671
**Pitches For** ▲ ⚌ ⚌ **Total** 30
**Facilities** ⬧ ▯ ⬧ ⌐ ☉ ⬧ ☎ ▯ ⬧ ▯ ⬧ ▯
**Nearby Facilities** ⬧ ⬧ ⬧ ⬧ ⬧ ⬧
**Acreage** 2¼ **Open** March **to** October
**Access** Good **Site** Lev/Slope
Local beaches, stately homes, Sandringham and market towns. Childrens Television. Dogs 50p per night, short dog walk.
**Nearest Town/Resort** Hunstanton
**Directions** From Kings Lynn take the A148 to Hillington, turn left onto the B1153 to Great Bircham. Fork right onto the B1155 to the crossroads, straight over. Site is 100yds on the left.
⚏ Kings Lynn

## SWAFFHAM

**Breckland Meadows Touring Park,** Lynn Road, Swaffham, Norfolk, PE37 7PT
**Tel:** 01760 721246
**Email:** info@brecklandmeadows.co.uk
**www.**brecklandmeadows.co.uk
**Pitches For** ▲ ⚌ ⚌ **Total** 45
**Facilities** ⬧ ⬧ ▯ ▯ ⬧ ⌐ ☉ ⬧ ⬧ ▯ ☎
▯ ⬧ ▯ ⬧ ▯ ⬧ ⬧ ⬧
**Nearby Facilities** ⬧ ⬧ ⬧ ⬧ ⬧
**Acreage** 3 **Open** All Year
**Access** Good **Site** Level
Small, friendly and very clean park. Within walking distance of the town centre for shops, pubs, restaurants, etc.. Dog walk adjacent to the park. Central for touring Norfolk. Ideal for walking and cycling.
**Nearest Town/Resort** Swaffham/ Hunstanton
**Directions** Take the A47 from Kings Lynn to Swaffham, approx 15 miles. Take the first exit off the dual carriageway, site is ¾ miles before Swaffham town centre.
⚏ Kings Lynn

## THETFORD

**Lowe Caravan Park,** Ashdale, 134 Hills Road, Saham Hills (Nr Watton), ThetfordNorfolk, IP25 7EW
**Tel:** 01953 881051

**Pitches For** ▲ ⚌ ⚌ **Total** 20
**Facilities** ⬧ ▯ ▯ ⬧ ⌐ ☉ ⬧ ⬧ ☎ ▯ ⬧
**Nearby Facilities** ⬧
**Acreage** 2 **Open** All Year
**Access** Good **Site** Level
Quiet, relaxing site in the countryside.
**Nearest Town/Resort** Watton
**Directions** Take the A11 from Thetford then take the road to Watton. Go through the high street and take second turn into Saham Road (past the golf club). Take the third turning on the right, site is ½ a mile on the right.
⚏ Thetford/Norwich

## THETFORD

**The Covert Caravan Club Site,** High Ash, Hilborough, Thetford, Norfolk, IP26 5BZ
**Tel:** 01842 878356
**www.**caravanclub.co.uk
**Pitches For** ⚌ ⚌ **Total** 103
**Facilities** ⬧ ▯ ⬧ ▯ ☉ ⬧ ⬧ ▯ ▯ ⬧
**Nearby Facilities** ⬧
**Acreage** 9½ **Open** March **to** Oct
**Access** Good **Site** Level
Quiet, secluded site set in Forestry Commission woodland. Ideal for wildlife lovers. Within easy driving distance of Swaffham, Norwich and Kings Lynn. Close to Banham Zoo. Own sanitation required. Non members welcome. Booking essential.
**Nearest Town/Resort** Thetford
**Directions** From Thetford take the A134, at the roundabout in Mundford turn right onto the A1065 signposted Swaffham. Site entrance is on the left within 2 miles by the WWII tank.
⚏ Thetford

## THETFORD

**The Dower House Touring Park,** Thetford Forest, East Harling, Norwich, Norfolk, NR16 2SE
**Tel:** 01953 717314 **Fax:** 01953 717843
**Email:** info@dowerhouse.co.uk
**www.**dowerhouse.co.uk
**Pitches For** ▲ ⚌ ⚌ **Total** 140
**Facilities** ⬧ ⬧ ▯ ▯ ⬧ ⌐ ☉ ⬧ ⬧ ▯ ☎
▯ ⬧ ▯ ⬧ ⬧ ⬧ ⬧ ⬧ ▯ ⬧ ⬧ ⬧
**Nearby Facilities** ⬧ ⬧
**Acreage** 20 **Open** 18th March **to** 2nd Oct
**Access** Good **Site** Level
Set in Thetford Forest, the site is spacious and peaceful. Although we have a bar, we have no amusement arcade or gaming machines.
**Nearest Town/Resort** Thetford
**Directions** From Thetford take A1066 East for 5 miles, fork left at camping sign onto unclassified road, site on left after 2 miles, signposted.
⚏ Harling Road

## THETFORD

**Thorpe Woodlands - Forestry Commission,** Shadwell, Thetford, Norfolk, IP24 2RX
**Tel:** 01842 751042
**Email:** info@forestholidays.co.uk
**www.**forestholidays.co.uk
**Pitches For** ▲ ⚌ ⚌ **Total** 138
**Facilities** ⬧ ☎ ⬧ ⬧ ⬧ ⬧ ▯ ⬧
**Nearby Facilities**
**Open** 25 March **to** 1 Nov

**Access** Good **Site** Level
In Thetford Forest Park, on the banks of the River Thet. A good base for visiting the Norfolk Broads. Note : This site has NO toilets.
**Nearest Town/Resort** Thetford
**Directions** Take the A1066 from Thetford after 5 miles bear left to East Harling. The site is ¼ mile on the left.
⚏ Thetford

## WELLS-NEXT-THE-SEA

**Pinewoods Holiday Park,** Beach Road, Wells-Next-the-Sea, Norfolk, NR23 1DR
**Tel:** 01328 710439 **Fax:** 01328 711060
**Email:** holiday@pinewoods.co.uk
**www.**pinewoods.co.uk
**Pitches For** ▲ ⚌ ⚌
**Facilities** ⬧ ⬧ ▯ ▯ ▯ ⬧ ⌐ ☉ ⬧ ⬧ ▯ ☎
⬧ ▯ ☉ ⬧ ✕ ▯ ▯ ⬧ ⬧
**Nearby Facilities** ⬧ ⬧ ⬧ ⬧ ⬧
**Open** 15 March **to** Oct
**Access** Good **Site** Level
**Nearest Town/Resort** Wells-Next-the-Sea
**Directions** From Wells Quay site is ¾ miles down Beach Road.
⚏ Sheringham

## WELLS-NEXT-THE-SEA

**Stiffkey Campsite,** The Greenway, Vale Farm, Stiffkey, Wells-Next-the-SeaNorfolk, NR23 1QP
**Tel:** 01328 830235 **Fax:** 01328 830119
**Pitches For** ▲ ⚌ ⚌ **Total** 80
**Facilities** ▯ ⬧ ⌐ ☉ ⬧ ▯ ⬧ ☉ ⬧
**Nearby Facilities** ⬧ ⬧ ⬧ ⬧ ⬧
**Acreage** 6 **Open** April **to** October
**Site** Lev/Slope
Adjoining marsh saltings and the beach. Near to steam and miniature railway. Good shop and pub in the village.
**Nearest Town/Resort** Wells-Next-the-Sea
**Directions** Take the A149 east towards Cromer, Stiffkey is the next village 3½ miles from Wells.
⚏ Kings Lynn/Cromer

# NORTHAMPTONSHIRE

## CORBY

**Top Lodge Caravan Club Site,** Fineshade, Corby, Northamptonshire, NN17 3BB
**Tel:** 01780 444617
**www.** caravanclub.co.uk
**Pitches For** ⚌ ⚌ **Total** 83
**Facilities** ⬧ ▯ ⬧ ☉ ⬧ ⬧ ▯ ⬧ ⬧
**Nearby Facilities** ⬧ ⬧
**Acreage** 5½ **Open** March **to** Oct
**Access** Good **Site** Level
Tranquil, meadowland site surrounded by woodland. Ideal for walking, cycling and bird watching. Within easy reach of the Fens and Rutland Water. Own sanitation required. Non members welcome. Booking essential.
**Nearest Town/Resort** Corby
**Directions** From north on the A43, 2¼ miles past the roundabout at the A47 junction turn left signposted Fineshade. After crossing the railway bridge turn left in front of Forestry Commission Station into site.
⚏ Corby

# NORTHUMBERLAND

## ALNWICK

**River Breamish Caravan Club Site,**
Powburn, Alnwick, Northumberland, NE66
4HY
**Tel:** 01665 578320
www.caravanclub.co.uk
**Pitches For** ▲ ♣ ➡ **Total** 74
**Facilities** ⚙ ✚ 🚿 ♨ ⌂ 🔴 ☎ 🅿 ⬛ Ⓜ✚🔲🔲
**Nearby Facilities**
**Acreage** 10 **Open** March **to** Oct
**Access** Good **Site** Level
Set amid the Cheviot Hills, ideal for
walking and cycling. A footbridge in
Branton (1 mile) spans over the river into
Breamish Valley. Close to Alnwick Castle,
Chillingham Castle and Wallington House.
Non members welcome. Booking essential.
**Nearest Town/Resort** Alnwick
**Directions** From the A1 take the A697 for
Wooler. After going through Powburn,
immediately after Hedgeley Service Station,
turn left signposted Branton, site is ½ mile
on the right.
➥ Alnwick

## AMBLE

**Rose Cottage Camp Site,** Rose Cottage,
Birling, Warkworth, Morpeth,
Northumberland, NE65 0XS
**Tel:** 01665 711459
**Email:** anne.foreman@virgin.net
**Pitches For** ▲ ➡ **Total** 14
**Facilities** 🆘 ♨ ⌂ 🔴➥🔲
**Nearby Facilities**
**Open** April **to** September
**Site** Level
Near the beach. Ideal touring.
**Nearest Town/Resort** Alnwick
**Directions** On the A1068 7 miles south of
Alnwick.
➥ Alnmouth

## ASHINGTON

**Sandy Bay Holiday Park,** North Seaton,
Ashington, Northumberland, NE63 9YD
**Tel:** 0870 442 9310 **Fax:** 01670 812705
**Email:** holidaysales.sandybay@park-
resorts.com
www.park-resorts.com
**Pitches For** ♣ ➡ **Total** 50
**Facilities** ✚ 🆘 ♨ ⌂ 🔴 ➥ 🔲 ☎
🍴 🔴 ☎ ✖ ⬛ 🐾 ♨ 🦌 ♨➥🔲 ☀
**Nearby Facilities** ┏ ✔ U
**Acreage** 2 **Open** March **to** November
**Access** Good **Site** Level
Located next to the beach and on the
mouth of the River Wansbeck. A perfect
holiday haven offering something for the
whole family.
**Nearest Town/Resort** Ashington/
Newbiggin-by-Sea

**Directions** From the A1 take the A19, at the
roundabout turn onto the A189 heading
north. At next roundabout turn right onto the
B1334 towards Newbiggin-by-Sea, Sandy
Bay is on the right.
➥ Morpeth

## BAMBURGH

**Glororum Caravan Park,** Glororum,
Bamburgh, Northumberland, NE69 7AW
**Tel:** 01668 214457 **Fax:** 01668 214622
**Email:** info@glororum-caravanpark.co.uk
www.glororum-caravanpark.co.uk
**Pitches For** ▲ ♣ ➡ **Total** 100
**Facilities** ✚ ✚ 🆘 ♨ ⌂ 🔴 ➥ 🔲 ☎
🍴 Ⓟ 🔴 ☎ Ⓜ✚🔲🔲
**Nearby Facilities** ┏ ✔ ⚓ ♨ ┛ ♪ ♨
**Acreage** 22 **Open** April **to** October
**Access** Good **Site** Level
1 mile from the beach. Water sports, hill
walking, pony trekking and many historic
castles nearby. Fishing and boat trips to
Farne Island.
**Nearest Town/Resort** Bamburgh
**Directions** Situated 1 mile from Bamburgh
on the B1341 Adderstone road. From the A1
take the B1341 at Adderstone Garage and
continue for 4 miles.
➥ Berwick-upon-Tweed

## BAMBURGH

**Waren Caravan & Camping Park,** Waren
Mill, Bamburgh, Northumberland, NE70 7EE
**Tel:** 01668 214366 **Fax:** 01668 214224
**Email:** waren@meadowhead.co.uk
www.meadowhead.co.uk
**Pitches For** ▲ ♣ ➡ **Total** 180
**Facilities** ⚙ ✚ ☐ 🆘 ♨ ⌂ 🔴➥🔲 🔲 ☎
🍴 Ⓟ 🔴 ✖ Ⓟ ⬛ ♨ 🦌 ♨➥🔲🔲
**Nearby Facilities** ┏ ✔ ⚓ U
**Acreage** 4 **Open** March **to** Oct
**Access** Good **Site** Level
Close to the Heritage Centre, Seahouses,
Bamburgh Castle and Lindisfarne Island.
Ideal for fishing, seeing seabirds and seal
sanctuary trips.
**Nearest Town/Resort** Bamburgh
**Directions** Take the A1 heading north, 15
miles before Berwick-upon-Tweed.
➥ Berwick-upon-Tweed

## BEADNELL BAY

**Camping & Caravanning Club Site,**
Beadnell, Chathill, Northumberland, NE67
5BX
**Tel:** 01665 720586
www.campingandcaravanningclub.co.uk
**Pitches For** ▲ 🆘 **Total** 150
**Facilities** 🆘 ♨ ⌂ 🔴 ➥ 🔲 ☎
Ⓟ 🔴 ☎➥🔲🔲
**Nearby Facilities** ┏ ✔ ⚓ ♨ U ♪
**Acreage** 6 **Open** May **to** Sept
**Site** Lev/Slope

2 miles of sandy beach just over the road.
6 miles from Bamburgh Castle. BTB 3 Star
Graded and AA 2 Pennants. Non members
welcome.
**Directions** From south leave the A1 and
follow the B1430 signposted Seahouses. At
Beadnell ignore signs for Beadnell Village,
site is on the left after the village, just beyond
the left hand bend. From north leave the A1
and follow the B1342 via Bamburgh and
Seahouses, site is on the right just before
Beadnell Village.

## BELLINGHAM

**Brown Rigg Caravan & Camping Park,**
Tweed House, Brown Rigg, Bellingham,
HexhamNorthumberland, NE48 2JY
**Tel:** 01434 220175
**Email:**
enquiries@northumberlandcaravanparks.com
www.northumberlandcaravanparks.com
**Pitches For** ▲ ♣ ➡ **Total** 70
**Facilities** ✚ ☐ 🆘 ♨ ⌂ 🔴 ➥ 🔲 ☎
🍴 🔴 ☎ ⬛ Ⓜ✚🔲🔲 ♨ ♨
**Nearby Facilities** ┏ ✔ ⚓ ♨ U
**Acreage** 5 **Open** 31 March **to** 31 Oct
**Access** Good **Site** Level
Ideal for touring Hadrians Wall, Kielder
Water and Forest and the Borders region.
**Nearest Town/Resort** Kielder
**Directions** Take the A69, after Hexham in ½
mile turn right signposted Acomb, Chollerford
and Bellingham. At Chollerford turn left onto
the B6318, go over the river and turn second
left onto the B6320 signposted Wark and
Bellingham.
➥ Hexham

## BELLINGHAM

**Demesne Farm Campsite,** Demesne
Farm, Bellingham, Hexham,
Northumberland, NE48 2BS
**Tel:** 01434 220258/220107
**Email:** telfer@demesne.plus.com
www.demesnefarmcampsite.co.uk
**Pitches For** ▲ ♣ ➡ **Total** 30
**Facilities** ☐ 🆘 ⌂ 🔴 ♨
**Nearby Facilities** ┏ ✔ ⚓ ♨ U ♪ ♨
**Acreage** 2 **Open** April **to** Nov
**Access** Good **Site** Level
Close to Hadrians Wall, Kielder Water,
Scottish Borders, Metro Centre,
Northumberland National Park and
National Trust properties. Also available is
a Bunk House which sleeps 15 people,
please phone for details. You can also
telephone us on Mobile 07967 396345.
**Nearest Town/Resort** Hexham
**Directions** From Hexham take the B6320
north for 17 miles into Bellingham village
centre. Turn right and site is 75 metres on
the right.
➥ Hexham

# NORTHUMBERLAND

## BERWICK-UPON-TWEED

**Beachcomber Campsite**, Goswick, Berwick-upon-Tweed, Northumberland, TD15 2RW
**Tel:** 01289 381217
**Email:** johngregson@micro-plus-web.net
**Pitches For** ▲ ♦ ⚌ **Total** 50
**Facilities** ⌁ ▥ ♨ ⌂ ⊙↲ ⎚ ☎ ⚇ ⊬⊟
**Nearby Facilities** ↾ ⤧
**Acreage** 4 **Open** Easter to End September
**Access** Good **Site** Level
Quiet, family run site situated behind the dunes (50 metre walk) of a very large sandy beach. Horse riding on site. Golf within ½ mile.
**Nearest Town/Resort** Berwick-upon-Tweed
**Directions** From Berwick-upon-Tweed take the A1 south, after approx. 1 mile take a left turn signposted Goswick and Cheswick. Follow this country road for approx. 4 miles to the Campsite.
⚏ Berwick-upon-Tweed

## BERWICK-UPON-TWEED

**Haggerston Castle**, Beal, Nr Berwick-on-Tweed, Northumberland, TD15 2PA
**Tel:** 01289 381333 **Fax:** 01289 381337
**Email:** becky.roberts@british-holidays.co.uk
www.touringholidays.co.uk
**Pitches For** ♦ ⚌ **Total** 159
**Facilities** ♨ ⚘ ⌁ ▥ ▥ ♨ ↾ ⊙↲ ⚑ ⎚ ☎
⚇ ⅋ ⊙ ⚉ ✕ ⎍ ⍾ ♣ ⍟ ❊ ⛄ ⊬⊟ ⊡ ▤
**Nearby Facilities** ↾ ↙ ∪ ♪
**Open** March to October
**Access** Good **Site** Level
Situated in an area of great heritage interest. Lots of on park facilities. Kids Club. A full family entertainment programme. Golf, horse riding, tennis, bowls, boating, bikes and heated swimming pools. ETB 5 Star Park, Rose Award and David Bellamy Conservation Award.
**Nearest Town/Resort** Berwick-upon-Tweed
**Directions** On A1, 7 miles south of Berwick-upon-Tweed.
⚏ Berwick

## BERWICK-UPON-TWEED

**Ord House Country Park**, East Ord, Berwick-upon-Tweed, Northumberland, TD15 2NS
**Tel:** 01289 305288 **Fax:** 01289 330832
**Email:** enquiries@ordhouse.co.uk
www.ordhouse.co.uk
**Pitches For** ▲ ♦ ⚌ **Total** 60
**Facilities** ♨ ⌁ ▥ ▥ ♨ ↾ ⊙↲ ⚑ ⎚ ☎
⚇ ⊙ ⚉ ✕ ⅋ ⍾ ⊛⊬⊟ ⊡ ⛄
**Nearby Facilities** ↾ ↙ ⚠ ↘ ∪
**Acreage** 42 **Open** All Year
**Access** Good **Site** Lev/Slope

Award Winning park with an 18th century mansion house containing a licenced club.
**Nearest Town** Berwick-upon-Tweed
**Directions** Take East Ord road from bypass, follow caravan signpost.
⚏ Berwick-upon-Tweed

## BERWICK-UPON-TWEED

**Seaview Caravan Club Site**, Billendean Road, Spittal, Berwick-upon-Tweed, Northumberland, TD15 1QU
**Tel:** 01289 305198
www.caravanclub.co.uk
**Pitches For** ▲ ♦ ⚌ **Total** 100
**Facilities** ♨ ⌁ ▥ ▥ ♨ ↾ ⎚ ☎
⚇ ⊙ ⚉⊬⊟ ⎚
**Nearby Facilities** ↾ ↙ ⚠ ↘
**Acreage** 6 **Open** March to Oct
**Access** Good **Site** Lev/Slope
Overlooking a river estuary with views of Holy Island. Just a short walk into Berwick. Near a safe sandy beach. Close to Swan Leisure Pool, Lindisfarne Priory and Paxton House. Non members welcome. Booking essential.
**Nearest Town/Resort** Berwick-upon-Tweed
**Directions** From the A1 take the A1167 signposted Spittal, at the roundabout turn right into Billendean Terrace, site is ½ mile on the right.
⚏ Berwick-upon-Tweed

## DUNSTAN HILL

**Camping & Caravanning Club Site**, Dunstan Hill, Dunstan, Alnwick, Northumberland, NE66 3TQ
**Tel:** 01665 576310
www.campingandcaravanningclub.co.uk
**Pitches For** ▲ ♦ ⚌ **Total** 150
**Facilities** ♨ ⌁ ▥ ▥ ♨ ↾ ⊙↲ ⚑ ⎚ ☎
⚇ ⊙ ⚉ ⎍⊬⊟ ⛄ ♪
**Nearby Facilities** ↾ ↙
**Acreage** 14 **Open** March to Oct
**Access** Good **Site** Level
In north east England just 1 mile from the coast. One of the Parks major attractions is Kielder Water, Europe's largest man made lake. Access to Dunstanburgh Castle from the site. BTB 4 Star Graded and AA 3 Pennants. Non members welcome.
**Nearest Town/Resort** Alnwick
**Directions** Travelling north on the A1 take the B1340 signposted Seahouses, follow to the T-Junction at Christon Bank and turn right, take the next right signpost Embleton, turn right at the crossroads then first left signposted Craster. Travelling south on the A1 take the B6347 through Christon Bank, take a right turn to Embleton, turn right at the crossroads, then first left signposted Craster, site is 1 mile on the left.
⚏ Alnmouth

## FALSTONE

**Kielder Water Caravan Club Site**, Leaplish Waterside Park, Falstone, Hexham, Northumberland, NE48 1AX
**Tel:** 01434 250278
www.caravanclub.co.uk
**Pitches For** ▲ ♦ ⚌ **Total** 80
**Facilities** ♨ ⌁ ▥ ▥ ♨ ↾ ⎚ ☎
⚇ ⊙ ⚉⊬⊟ ⚘
**Nearby Facilities** ⚠ ↘ ∪
**Acreage** 12 **Open** March to Oct
**Access** Good **Site** Lev/Slope
Peaceful site overlooking Kielder Water. Just a short walk to a swimming pool, restaurant and crazy golf. Ideal for walking and cycling. Adventure playground right outside the site. Non members welcome. Booking essential.
**Nearest Town/Resort** Hexham
**Directions** Leave M6 at junc 44 (end) and turn right onto A7 signposted Hawick. After 9¼ miles turn right onto B7201 signposted Kielder Water, in Canonbie keep right onto B6357 and follow signs for Kielder Water. Approx. 5 miles past Kielder Village turn left signposted Leaplish Waterside Park, site is ¼ mile on the right.
⚏ Hexham

## HALTWHISTLE

**Camping & Caravanning Club Site**, Burnfoot Park Village, Haltwhistle, Northumberland, NE49 0JP
**Tel:** 01434 320106
www.campingandcaravanningclub.co.uk
**Pitches For** ▲ ♦ ⚌ **Total** 50
**Facilities** ⌁ ▥ ▥ ♨ ↾ ⊙↲ ⚑ ⎚ ☎
⚇ ⊙ ⚉⊬⊟ ⎚ ⛄
**Nearby Facilities** ↙
**Acreage** 3½ **Open** March to October
**Site** Level
On the banks of the River South Tyne for fishing on site. Close to the Pennine Way. BTB 4 Star Graded and AA 3 Pennants. Non members welcome.
**Directions** Follow signs from the A69 by-pass, DO NOT go into Haltwhistle.
⚏ Haltwhistle

## HALTWHISTLE

**Seldom Seen Caravan Park**, Haltwhistle, Northumberland, NE49 0NE
**Tel:** 01434 320571
www.ukparks.com
**Pitches For** ▲ ♦ ⚌ **Total** 20
**Facilities** ⌁ ▥ ▥ ♨ ↾ ⊙ ☎
⚇ ⊙ ⚉ ⎍⊬⊟ ⛄
**Nearby Facilities** ↾ ↙ ∪ ♪
**Open** March to January
**Access** Good **Site** Level
Central touring area, Roman wall. David Bellamy Gold Award for Conservation.

**Nearest Town/Resort** Haltwhistle
**Directions** Off the A69 east of Haltwhistle, signposted.
⇒ Haltwhistle

## HALTWHISTLE

**Yont the Cleugh Caravan Park,** Coanwood, Haltwhistle, Northumberland, NE49 0QN
**Tel:** 01434 320274
**Email:** yontthecleugh@yahoo.co.uk
www.yontthecleugh.co.uk
**Pitches For** ▲ ♥ ⊕ **Total** 30
**Facilities** ⚡ ▥ 🅆 🏧 ↑ ⊙ ⌔ ⬛ 🔲 ⬛
⬛ 🏪 🛒 ▥ 🏧 🅰 🍴 🕀 🔾 ⋇
**Nearby Facilities** ┌ ✓ U
**Acreage** 2 **Open** March **to** Nov
**Access** Good **Site** Lev/Slope
Surrounded by woodland. Near to Hadrians Wall.
**Nearest Town/Resort** Haltwhistle
**Directions** Turn off the A69 just past Haltwhistle signposted Coanwood, Alston and caravan sites. Follow the road for 4 miles keeping left.
⇒ Haltwhistle

## HAYDON BRIDGE

**Poplars Riverside Caravan Park,** Eastland Ends, Haydon Bridge, Hexham, Northumberland, NE47 6BY
**Tel:** 01434 684427
**Pitches For** ▲ ♥ ⊕ **Total** 14
**Facilities** ⚡ 🅆 🏧 ↑ ⊙ ⌔ ⬛ 🔲 ⬛
🛒 ⊙ 🏪 🅰 ↑🔲 ⋇
**Nearby Facilities** ┌ ✓ U ℘
**Acreage** 2½ **Open** March **to** October
**Access** Good **Site** Level
Small, peaceful site close to the village. Near to Hadrians Wall.
**Nearest Town/Resort** Hexham
**Directions** Take the A69 Newcastle to Carlisle road, follow signs from the bridge in the village.
⇒ Haydon Bridge

## HEXHAM

**Ashcroft Farm Caravan Site,** Ashcroft Farm, Bardon Mill, Hexham, Northumberland, NE47 7JA
**Tel:** 01434 344409
**Pitches For** ♥ ⊕ **Total** 5
**Facilities** ⚡ ℞ **Nearby Facilities** ┌ ✓ U
**Acreage** 2 **Open** May **to** September
**Access** Good **Site** Level
Riverside site, close to the village and it's amenities. 2 miles from the Roman Wall.
**Nearest Town/Resort** Hexham
**Directions** Take the A69 to Bardon Mill, turn into the village and turn first left.
⇒ Bardon Mill

## HEXHAM

**Causey Hill Caravan Park,** Causey Hill, Hexham, Northumberland, NE46 2JN
**Tel:** 01434 602834 **Fax:** 01434 602834
**Email:** causeyhillcp@aol.com
www.causeyhill.co.uk
**Pitches For** ▲ ♥ ⊕ **Total** 75
**Facilities** ⚡ ⅃ 🅆 🏧 ↑ ⊙ ⌔ ⬛ 🔲 ⬛
🛒 ⊙ 🏪 🅰 ↑🔲 ⋇
**Nearby Facilities** ┌ ✓ U

**Acreage** 18 **Open** March **to** Oct
**Access** Good **Site** Level
Set in quiet countryside and surrounded by sheltered woodland for walks. Stunning views and pond features. 1½ miles from the town centre. Near Hadrians Wall.
**Nearest Town/Resort** Hexham
**Directions** From Hexham town centre take the B6306, turn first right and after 1½ miles turn right at crossroads, turn right down Causey Hill and after 200 yards turn left. Near Hexham Racecourse.
⇒ Hexham

## HEXHAM

**Hexham Racecourse Caravan Site,** High Yarridge, Hexham, Northumberland, NE46 2JP
**Tel:** 01434 606847 **Fax:** 01434 606847
**Pitches For** ▲ ♥ ⊕ **Total** 48
**Facilities** ⚡ 🏧 ↑ ⊙ ⌔ ⬛ 🔲 ⬛
⬛ 🏪 🅰 🍴 ↑🔲 ⋇
**Nearby Facilities** ┌ ✓ ⚓ ⋇ U ℘
**Acreage** 8 **Open** May **to** Sept
**Access** Good **Site** Sloping
**Nearest Town/Resort** Hexham
**Directions** Travel west on Hexham main street, go to the traffic lights and bear left onto the B6305 for Allendale. After 3 miles turn left at signed T-Junction, site is 1½ miles.
⇒ Hexham

## HEXHAM

**Springhouse Farm Caravan Park,** Slaley, Hexham, Northumberland, NE47 0AW
**Tel:** 01434 673241
**Email:** enquiries@springhousecaravanpark.co.uk
www.springhousecaravanpark.co.uk
**Pitches For** ▲ ♥ ⊕ **Total** 20
**Facilities** ⚡ 🅆 🏧 ↑ ⊙ ⌔ ⬛ 🔲 ⬛
⬛ 🏪 🅰 🍴 🕀 🔲 ⋇
**Nearby Facilities** ┌ ✓ ⋇ U
**Open** March **to** October
**Access** Good **Site** Sloping
Quiet, surrounded by forest. Panoramic views, excellent country walks.
**Nearest Town/Resort** Hexham
⇒ Hexham Station

## MORPETH

**Bockenfield Country Park,** Bockenfield, Felton, Northumberland, NE65 9QJ
**Tel:** 01670 786010
**Email:** bockenfieldpark@aol.com
www.bockenfieldcountrypark.co.uk
**Pitches For** ♥⊕ **Total** 55
**Facilities** ⚡ ⅃ 🅆 🏧 ↑ ⊙ ⌔ ⬛ 🔲 ⬛
⬕ ⅃↑🔲 ⬛ ⋇
**Nearby Facilities** ┌ ✓ ⚓ ⋇ U ℘ ⚘
**Acreage** 10 **Open** March **to** Jan
**Access** Good **Site** Level
A peaceful, rural, family run site. Easy access to the A1, ideal for touring. Close to many places of interest including Alnwick Gardens. Separate areas for Adults/ Families. Dogs must be pre-booked.
**Nearest Town/Resort** Morpeth
**Directions** Off the A1 just south of Felton Village, turn at signpost for Bockenfield and site is on the left.
⇒ Morpeth

**Forget-Me-Not Holiday Park,** Croftside, Longhorsley, Morpeth, Northumberland, NE65 8QY
**Tel:** 01670 788364
**Email:** info@forgetmenotholidaypark.co.uk
www.forgetmenotholidaypark.co.uk
**Pitches For** ▲ ♥ ⊕ **Total** 67
**Facilities** ⚡ ⅃ 🅆 🏧 ↑ ⊙ ⌔ ⬛ 🔲 ⬛
⬛ 🏪 ✗ 🛒 🅰 🏧 ⌂ 🕀 ⋇ ⋇ ℘
**Nearby Facilities** ┌ ✓ U
**Acreage** 26 **Open** March **to** October
**Access** Good **Site** Level
On the edge of a national park, ideal touring. 7 miles from the beach.
**Nearest Town/Resort** Morpeth
**Directions** From the A1 take the A697 to Longhorsley, turn left in Longhorsley towards Netherwitton, park is 1¼ miles on the right.
⇒ Morpeth

## OTTERBURN

**Border Forest Caravan Park,** Cottonshope Burnfoot, Nr Otterburn, Northumberland, NE19 1TF
**Tel:** 01830 520259
**Email:** borderforest@btinternet.com
www.borderforest.com
**Pitches For** ▲ ♥ ⊕ **Total** 36
**Facilities** ⚡ ⅃ 🅆 🏧 ↑ ⊙ ⌔ ⬛ 🔲 ⬛
⬛ 🏪↑🔲 ⬛ ⋇ ℘ ⋇
**Nearby Facilities** ┌ ✓ ⚓ ⋇ U ⚘ ⋇
**Acreage** 3 **Open** 1st March **to** 31st October
**Access** Good **Site** Level
Situated in Kielder Forest Park and surrounded by Cottonshope, Burn and River Rede. Ideal walking and touring base. 6 miles south of the Scottish Border at Carter Bar.
**Nearest Town/Resort** Jedburgh/Hexham
**Directions** Adjacent to A68 - 17 miles to Jedburgh, 28 miles to Hexham, 38 miles to Newcastle.
⇒ Hexham

## OVINGHAM

**The High Hermitage Caravan Park,** The Hermitage, Ovingham, Prudhoe, Northumberland, NE42 6HH
**Tel:** 01661 832250 **Fax:** 01661 834848
**Email:** highhermitage@onetel.com
**Pitches For** ▲ ♥ ⊕ **Total** 43
**Facilities** ⅃ 🅆 🏧 ↑ ⊙ ⌔ ⬛ 🔲
⬕ ⊙ 🏪 🔲 ⋇
**Nearby Facilities** ┌ ✓ ⋇ U ℘
**Acreage** 2½ **Open** April **to** October
**Access** Good **Site** Gently Sloping
Quiet, rural, riverside site with extensive wildlife. Grassy slope sheltered by trees on north, east and west sides. Giant chess and draughts. Ideal for touring the Roman Wall and associated sites plus gorgeous Northumberland countryside and beaches. ETB 3 Star Graded.
**Nearest Town/Resort** Prudhoe
**Directions** Take the A69 from Newcastle or Hexham and take exit to Wylam. Go straight ahead at first crossroads to Wylam, follow road and turn right at the bottom to Ovingham, site entrance is 1½ miles down this river road opposite water intake area.
⇒ Wylam/Prudhoe

### ROTHBURY
**Coquetdale Caravan Park,** Whitton, Rothbury, Morpeth, Northumberland, NE65 7RU
**Tel:** 01669 620549 **Fax:** 01669 620559
**Email:** enquiry@coquetdalecaravanpark.co.uk
**www.**coquetdalecaravanpark.co.uk
**Pitches For** ♥ ♠ **Total** 40
**Facilities** ⌀ ⚏ ♨ ⌂ ☉ ⌣ ▱ ◎ ☎
♨ ⏣ ⊙ ⌤ ⌦ ◱ ◳
**Nearby Facilities** ↾ ✔ ∪ ♪ ⅄
**Acreage** 1½ **Open** May **to** Sept
**Access** Good **Site** Level
Beautiful views. Ideal situation for touring Borders and coast. All units are strictly for families and couples only.
**Nearest Town/Resort** Rothbury
**Directions** ½ mile southwest of Rothbury on road to Newtown.
⇆ Morpeth

### ROTHBURY
**Nunnykirk Caravan Club Site,** Nunnykirk, Morpeth, Northumberland, NE61 4PZ
**Tel:** 01669 620762
**www.**caravanclub.co.uk
**Pitches For** ♥ ♠ **Total** 84
**Facilities** ⌀ ◎ ☖ ◳
**Nearby Facilities** ✔
**Acreage** 14 **Open** March **to** Oct
**Access** Good **Site** Level
Attractive and peaceful site, a wildlife and bird watchers paradise. Simonside Hills nearby, perfect for hill walkers. Close to Hadrians Wall and Wallington Hall & Gardens. Own sanitation required. Non members welcome. Booking essential.
**Nearest Town/Resort** Morpeth
**Directions** From A1 take A696 signposted Jedburgh, after approx. 19¼ miles turn right at Knowesgate Hotel signposted Scots Gap. After 2¼ miles turn left onto B6342, after 6 miles cross the bridge at foot of the hill and turn right into a private road, site is ¼ mile on the right.
⇆ Morpeth

### SEAHOUSES
**Seafield Caravan Park,** Seafield Road, Seahouses, Northumberland, NE68 7SP
**Tel:** 01665 720628 **Fax:** 01665 720088
**Email:** info@seafieldpark.co.uk
**www.**seafieldpark.co.uk
**Pitches For** ♥ ♠ **Total** 18
**Facilities** ⊾ ⚏ ⌀ ⚏ ▱ ⚏ ♨ ↾ ☉ ⌣ ▰
◎ ☎ ⏣ ◎ ⚏ ⌥ ⌦ ◱ ◳
**Nearby Facilities** ↾ ✔ ⅄ ⚓ ∪ ♪
**Acreage** 1 **Open** Feb **to** Jan
**Access** Good **Site** Level
In the centre of the village, near to a beach, scenic views and the harbour.
**Nearest Town/Resort** Seahouses
**Directions** B1340 east off the main A1 to the coast.
⇆ Chathill

### WOOLER
**Highburn House Caravan & Camping Park,** Wooler, Northumberland, NE71 6EE
**Tel:** 01668 281344
**Email:** relax@highburn-house.co.uk
**www.**highburn-house.co.uk
**Pitches For** ▲ ♥ ♠ **Total** 100
**Facilities** ⊾ ⚏ ⌀ ▱ ⚏ ⌂ ♨ ↾ ☉ ⌣ ▰
◎ ☎ ⏣ ◎ ⚏ ⌥ ⌦ ◱ ◳
**Nearby Facilities** ↾ ✔ ∪ ♪ ⅄
**Acreage** 12 **Open** April **to** December
**Access** Good **Site** Level
Stream runs through middle of site, beautiful view over hills and valley.
**Nearest Town/Resort** Wooler

**Directions** Off A1 take A697 to Wooler town centre, at the top of Main Street take left turn, 400 metres on left is our site.
⇆ Berwick

### WOOLER
**Riverside Park,** Brewery Road, Wooler, Northumberland, NE71 6QG
**Tel:** 01668 281447 **Fax:** 01668 282142
**Pitches For** ♥ ♠ **Total** 55
**Facilities** ⊾ ⚏ ▱ ⌀ ⚏ ♨ ↾ ☉ ⌣ ▰ ◎ ☎
♨ ◎ ⚏ ✕ ▾ ⌥ ⏣ ⌦ ◱ ◳
**Nearby Facilities** ↾ ✔ ∪
**Open** 16 March **to** 6 Jan
**Access** Good **Site** Level
In a historic area, near a river with free fishing and the coast.
**Nearest Town/Resort** Berwick-upon-Tweed
**Directions** 29 miles from Morpeth straight up the A697.
⇆ Berwick-upon-Tweed

# NOTTINGHAMSHIRE

### CARLTON-ON-TRENT
**Carlton Manor Touring Park,** Ossington Road (off A1), Carlton-on-Trent, Nr Newark, Nottinghamshire, NG23 6NU
**Tel:** 01530 835662
**Pitches For** ▲ ♥ ♠ **Total** 22
**Facilities** ⚏ ▱ ⌀ ♨ ↾ ☉ ☎
♨ ✕ ⌥ ▾ ⌦ ⚏ ♪
**Nearby Facilities** ↾ ✔
**Acreage** 2 **Open** April **to** Nov
**Access** Good **Site** Level
Clean site with spotless toilets. Warden on site at all times. Train spotting on site. We do allow individual motorcyclists, but no groups. Emergency phone on site at Wardens. Hotel opposite open all day for food and drink etc.. Shops, fishing and doctor in village. Pubs, library, hairdressers etc. all nearby. Shop (Co-Op) open between 8am and 8pm. 10 miles from Robin Hood country, 12 miles from Lincoln and 50 miles from Skegness. You can also contact Mrs Goodman on MOBILE 07870 139256.
**Nearest Town/Resort** Newark
**Directions** From Newark take the A1 north towards Doncaster, site is 6 miles, signposted.
⇆ Newark Village

### NEWARK
**Milestone Caravan Park,** Great North Road, Cromwell, Newark, Nottinghamshire, NG23 6JE
**Tel:** 01636 821244
**Pitches For** ♥ ♠ **Total** 120
**Facilities** ⊾ ⚏ ⌀ ▱ ⚏ ♨ ↾ ☉ ⌣ ☎
♨ ◎ ⚏ ⌥ ⌦ ◱ ♪
**Nearby Facilities** ↾ ✔ ∪ ♪
**Acreage** 8 **Open** All Year
**Access** Good **Site** Level
Small and pretty site with a coarse fishing lake and picnic area. Specialist fishing lakes in the village. Just a short distance to Sherwood Forest, Nottingham Castle, Newark Castle & Museums and Lincoln Cathedral & Castle. Non members welcome. Booking essential.
**Nearest Town/Resort** Newark
**Directions** A1 south take the signpost for Cromwell, site is ½ mile on the left. A1 north take the signpost for Cromwell Doll Museum, over the flyover and the site is on the left in 500 yards.
⇆ Newark

### NEWARK
**New Hall Farm,** New Hall Lane, Edingley, Newark, Nottinghamshire, NG22 8BS
**Tel:** 01623 883041
**Email:** new.hall@care4free.net
**www.** newhallfarm.co.uk
**Pitches For** ▲ ♥ □ **Total** 25
**Facilities** ⚏ ⌀ ▱ ♨ ↾ ☉ ⌣ ▱ ◎ ☎
♨ ⏣ ♨ ⚏ ⌀ ♪
**Nearby Facilities** ↾ ✔ ⅄ ∪ ♪ ♪
**Acreage** 2 **Open** March **to** November
**Access** Good **Site** Sloping
ADULTS ONLY SITE with panoramic views across open countryside. Ideal for walking.
**Nearest Town/Resort** Southwell
**Directions** 3 miles from both Southwell and Farnsfield, along New Hall Lane.
⇆ Newark

### NOTTINGHAM
**Riverdale Park,** Gunthorpe Bridge, Gunthorpe, Nottinghamshire, NG14 7EY
**Tel:** 01332 810818 **Fax:** 01332 810818
**Pitches For** ♥ ♠ **Total** 6
**Facilities** ⚏ ⌀ ♨ ↾
**Nearby Facilities**
**Open** 1 March **to** 6 Jan
**Access** Good **Site** Level
Near the River Trent. You can also telephone us on 0115 966 5173.
**Nearest Town/Resort** Nottingham
**Directions** Take the A612 east from Nottingham, go through Burton Joyce to Lowdham, then take the A6097 to the village of Gunthorpe.
⇆ Radcliffe-on-Trent/Nottingham

### NOTTINGHAM
**Thornton's Holt Camping Park,** Stragglethorpe, Radcliffe-on-Trent, Nottinghamshire, NG12 2JZ
**Tel:** 0115 933 2125 **Fax:** 0115 933 3318
**Email:** camping@thorntons-holt.co.uk
**www.** thorntons-holt.co.uk
**Pitches For** ▲ ♥ ♠ **Total** 155
**Facilities** ⊾ ⚏ ⌀ ▱ ⚏ ♨ ↾ ☉ ⌣ ▱ ◎ ☎
♨ ⏣ ◎ ⚏ ⌀ ♨ ⚏ ✔ ⅄ ⌥ ⌦ ◱ ♪
**Nearby Facilities** ↾ ✔ ⅄ ⚓ ∪ ♪ ♪
**Acreage** 15 **Open** All Year
**Access** Good **Site** Level
Only 3 miles from Nottingham. Ideal base for touring Sherwood Forest and the Vale of Belvoir. Pub and restaurant nearby.
**Nearest Town/Resort** Nottingham
**Directions** 3 miles east of Nottingham turn south off A52 towards Cropwell Bishop. Park is ¼ mile on left.
⇆ Radcliffe-on-Trent

### RATCLIFFE ON SOAR
**Red Hill Marina,** Ratcliffe-on-Soar, Nottinghamshire, NG11 0EB
**Tel:** 01509 672770
**Pitches For** ▲ ♥ ♠ **Total** 5
**Facilities** ⚏ ◎ ✕ ⚏ ◳
**Nearby Facilities** ⅄
**Open** All Year
**Access** Good **Site** Level
By a river.
**Nearest Town/Resort** Nottingham
**Directions** Leave the M1 at junction 24 and take the A453, 1½ miles on the left hand side.
⇆ Loughborough

### SUTTON-IN-ASHFIELD
**Shardaroba Caravan Park,** Silverhill Lane, Teversal, Nr Sutton-in-Ashfield, Nottinghamshire, NG17 3JJ
**Tel:** 01623 551838 **Fax:** 01623 552174
**Email:** stay@shardaroba.co.uk
**www.** shardaroba.co.uk

## THORNTON'S HOLT CAMPING PARK

STRAGGLETHORPE, RADCLIFFE ON TRENT,
NOTTINGHAM NG12 2JZ
Tel: *0115 933 2125*  Fax: *0115 933 3318*
E-mail: *camping@thorntons-holt.co.uk*
Web Site: *www.thorntons-holt.co.uk*

*Situated where the peace of the countryside meets the culture and life of the City of Nottingham, this sheltered park offers the following attractions:-*
∗ 155 PITCHES, 135 ELECTRIC HOOK-UPS, 35 HARDSTANDINGS
∗ GOOD CENTRAL AMENITIES ∗ PLAY AREA ∗ INDOOR HEATED SWIMMING POOL ∗ SHOP & INFORMATION CENTRE
∗ PUB & RESTAURANT WITHIN 150 METRES

Pitches For ▲ ⊞ ⊞ Total 100
Facilities
Nearby Facilities
Acreage 6 Open All Year
Gold Award Caravan Holiday Park of the Year 2005.
Nearest Town/Resort Sutton-in-Ashfield
⇻ Mansfield

### TUXFORD
Greenacres Caravan & Touring Park,
Lincoln Road, Tuxford, Newark,
Nottingham, NG22 0JN
Tel: 01777 870264 Fax: 01777 870264
Email: bailey-security@freezone.co.uk
www. http://members.freezone.co.uk/
bailey-security/
Pitches For ▲ ⊞ ⊞ Total 67
Facilities
Nearby Facilities
Acreage 4½ Open Mid March to End Oct
Access Good Site Level
Ideal for night halt or for touring Robin Hood country. Static caravans for sale and hire. Secure Storage during Winter.
Nearest Town/Resort Retford
Directions From A1 (north or south) follow signs. Park is on the left 250yds after Fountain Public House.
⇻ Retford

### TUXFORD
Orchard Park Touring Caravan & Camping, Orchard Park, Marnham Road, Tuxford, NewarkNottinghamshire, NG22 0PY
Tel: 01777 870228
Email: info@orchardcaravanpark.co.uk
www. orchardcaravanpark.co.uk
Pitches For ▲ ⊞ ⊞ Total 60
Facilities
Nearby Facilities
Acreage 7 Open March to November
Access Good Site Level
A quiet, sheltered park, spaciously set in an old fruit orchard. Central for Sherwood Forest, Clumber Park, Lincoln and Nottingham.
Nearest Town/Resort Newark
Directions Turn off the A1 dual carriageway at Tuxford, when you reach the T-Junction in the village turn right signposted Lincoln (A57). In ¼ mile turn right signposted Marnham, site is ½ a mile on the right.
⇻ Retford

### WORKSOP
Clumber Park Caravan Club Site, Lime Tree Avenue, Clumber Park, Worksop, Nottinghamshire, S80 3AE
Tel: 01909 484758
www. caravanclub.co.uk
Pitches For ⊞ ⊞ Total 183
Facilities
Nearby Facilities
Acreage 20 Open All Year
Access Good Site Level
Situated in 4000 acres of parkland (once part of Sherwood Forest), ideal for walking and cycling. Visitor Centre 10 minutes away. Close to Creswell Crags Cave Tours. Non members welcome. Booking essential.
Nearest Town/Resort Worksop
Directions From the A1, at the roundabout junction of the A57 and the A614 turn onto the A614 signposted Nottingham. After ½ a mile turn right into Clumber Park through a stone arch, after 1 mile turn right, site is 50 yards on the left.
⇻ Worksop

### WORKSOP
Riverside Caravan Park, Central Avenue, Worksop, Nottinghamshire, S80 1ER
Tel: 01909 474118
Pitches For ▲ ⊞ ⊞ Total 60
Facilities
Nearby Facilities
Acreage 5 Open All Year
Access Good Site Level
Alongside a canal for fishing. Golf courses.

# OXFORDSHIRE

## ABINGDON
Bridge House Caravan Site, Clifton Hampden, Abingdon, Oxfordshire, OX14 3EH
Tel: 01865 407725
Pitches For ▲ ⊞ ⊞
Facilities
Nearby Facilities
Open April to October
Access Good Site Level
On the banks of the Thames River.
Nearest Town/Resort Abingdon
Directions On the A415 from Abingdon.
⇻ Culham

## BANBURY
Barnstones Caravan Site, Barnstones, Main Street, Great Bourton, Nr BanburyOxon, OX17 1QU
Tel: 01295 750289
Pitches For ▲ ⊞ ⊞ Total 50
Facilities
Nearby Facilities
Acreage 3 Open All Year
Access Good Site Level
Cotswolds, Oxford, Stratford-upon-Avon and Warwick Castle. 40 pitches are hard standing with a grass area for awnings. 20 pitches are fully serviced. Food now available on site.
Nearest Town/Resort Banbury
Directions Leave Banbury on the A423 to Southam, in 3 miles turn right signposted Great Bourton. Site entrance is 100yds on the right.
⇻ Banbury

## BENSON
Benson Waterfront, Benson, Oxon, OX10 6SJ
Tel: 01491 838304 Fax: 01491 836738
Email: bensonwaterfront@btopenworld.com
www.waterfrontcafe.co.uk
Pitches For ▲ ⊞ ⊞ Total 20
Facilities
Nearby Facilities
Acreage 1 Open April to October
Access Good Site Level
On the banks of the beautiful River Thames.
Nearest Town/Resort Benson/Wallingford
Directions On the A4074 Oxford to Reading road, opposite the B4009.
⇻ Cholsey

## BLETCHINGDON
Greenhill Leisure Park, Greenhill Farm, Station Road, Bletchingdon, Oxfordshire, OX5 3BQ
Tel: 01869 351600 Fax: 01869 350918
Email: info@greenhill-leisure-park.co.uk
www.greenhill-leisure-park.co.uk
Pitches For ▲ ⊞ □ Total 40
Facilities
Nearby Facilities
Acreage 7 Open All Year
Access Good Site Lev/Slope
Quiet and spacious farm site. Pets Corner, farm animals and riverside walks. Rally field available. 3 miles from Blenheim Palace. Ideal for touring the Cotswolds.
Nearest Town/Resort Woodstock
Directions 3 miles east of Woodstock and 8 miles north of Oxford on the B4027. 2½ miles from the A34 and 7 miles south of the M40 junction 9.
⇻ Islip

## BURFORD
Burford Caravan Club Site, Bradwell Grove, Burford, Oxfordshire, OX18 4JJ
Tel: 01993 823080
www.caravanclub.co.uk
Pitches For ⊞ ⊞ Total 120
Facilities
Nearby Facilities
Acreage 10 Open March to Oct
Access Good Site Level
Attractive and spacious site. Area for volleyball, netball and football (goal posts). Opposite Cotswold Wildlife Park. Non members welcome. Booking essential.
Directions Leave Oxford on A40, after approx. 23 miles at large roundabout in Burford turn left onto A361 and follow signs for Cotswold Wildlife Park. After 2 miles at crossroads turn right, DO NOT turn right into New Bradwell Village, site is 70 yards on the right opposite entrance to Wildlife Park.

## CHIPPING NORTON

**Camping & Caravanning Club Site,** Chipping Norton Road, Chadlington, Chipping Norton, Oxon, OX7 3PE
**Tel:** 01608 641993
www.campingandcaravanningclub.co.uk
**Pitches For** ▲ ⊕ ☞ **Total** 105
**Facilities** ⅍ ✦ ⅏ ⅓ ⌐ ☉ ◔ ☜ ◙ ☎
⅊ ☉ ☎ ➤ ⊟ ☐ ☞
**Nearby Facilities** ⌐ ∪
**Open** March **to** October **Site** Lev/Slope
Perfect for exploring the Cotswolds. 11 miles from Blenheim Palace. BTB 4 Star Graded and AA 3 Pennants. Non members welcome.
**Directions** Take the A44 or the A361 to Chipping Norton. Pick up the A361 Burford road, turn left at the crossroads and the site is 150 yards. From Burford stay on the A361 and turn right at the sign for Chadlington.

## HENLEY-ON-THAMES

**Swiss Farm International,** Marlow Road, Henley-on-Thames, Oxfordshire, RG9 2HY
**Tel:** 01491 573419
**Email:** enquiries@swissfarmcamping.co.uk
www.swissfarmcamping.co.uk
**Pitches For** ▲ ⊕ ☞ **Total** 160
**Facilities** ✦ ⅏ ⅓ ⅎ ⌐ ☉ ◔ ☜ ◙ ☎
⅊ ☉ ☎ ▽ ⊞ ♣ ⅍ ⊟ ☐ ☞ ☇
**Nearby Facilities** ⌐ ⅄
**Acreage** 20 **Open** March **to** October
**Access** Good **Site** Sloping
Ideal for visiting London, Oxford, Windsor and South East England.
**Nearest Town/Resort** Henley-on-Thames
**Directions** From Henley take the A4155 towards Marlow, site is 500 yards on the left after the rugby club.
⚆ Henley-on-Thames

## OXFORD

**Camping & Caravanning Club Site,** 426 Abingdon Road, Oxford, Oxfordshire, OX1 4XG
**Tel:** 01865 244088
www.campingandcaravanningclub.co.uk
**Pitches For** ▲ ⊕ ☞ **Total** 85
**Facilities** ✦ ⅏ ⅓ ⌐ ☉ ◔ ☜ ◙ ☎
⅊ ☉ ☎▽ ⊟ ☐ ☞ ℘
**Nearby Facilities** ✦ ℘
**Acreage** 5 **Open** All Year

## WALLINGFORD

**Access** Good **Site** Level
In one of Britain's most popular tourist destinations, this university city has a lot more to offer with more than 650 listed buildings. BTB 4 Star Graded and AA 3 Pennants. Non members welcome.
**Nearest Town/Resort** Oxford
**Directions** From the M40 take the A34 at the A423, turn left immediately after junction into Abingdon Road, site is on the left behind Touchwood Sports.
⚆ Oxford

## WALLINGFORD

**Bridge Villa Camping & Caravan Park,** Crowmarsh Gifford, Wallingford, Oxfordshire, OX10 8HB
**Tel:** 01491 836860 **Fax:** 01491 836793
**Email:** lindsaytownsend@btopenworld.com
**Pitches For** ▲ ⊕ ☞ **Total** 111
**Facilities** ⅍ ✦ ⅏ ⅓ ⌐ ☉ ◔ ☜
⅊ ⅊ ☉▽⊟ ☐ ☐ ☇ ℘
**Nearby Facilities** ⌐ ✦ ⊿ ⅄ ∪ ♪ ℛ
**Acreage** 4 **Open** Feb **to** Dec
**Access** Good **Site** Level
**Directions** On the east side of Wallingford, go over Wallingford Bridge and the site is 100 metres on the right hand side.
⚆ Cholsey

## WITNEY

**Hardwick Parks,** Downs Road, Standlake, Nr Witney, Oxon', OX29 7PZ
**Tel:** 01865 300501 **Fax:** 01865 300037
**Email:** info@hardwickparks.co.uk
www.hardwickparks.co.uk
**Pitches For** ▲ ⊕ ☞ **Total** 214
**Facilities** ⅍ ✦ ⅏ ⅓ ⌐ ☉ ◔ ☜ ◙ ☎
⅊ ⅊ ☉ ☎ ✕ ▽ ⅏ ⅍ ⅎ ⊟ ☐ ☇ ☇
**Nearby Facilities** ⌐ ✦ ⊿ ⅄ ∪ ♪ ℛ
**Acreage** 40 **Open** April **to** October
**Access** Good **Site** Level
On the edge of the Cotswolds. Ideal for all watersports, two lakes on park for fishing, sailing, boating, jet-skiing and water-skiing. Holiday homes for hire.
**Nearest Town/Resort** Witney
**Directions** A415 Witney to Abingdon road, signposted 4 miles out of Witney on the main road.
⚆ Oxford

## WITNEY

**Lincoln Farm Park,** High Street, Standlake, Nr Witney, Oxfordshire, OX29 7RH
**Tel:** 01865 300239 **Fax:** 01865 300127
**Email:** info@lincolnfarm.touristnet.uk.com
www.lincolnfarmpark.co.uk
**Pitches For** ▲ ⊕ ☞ **Total** 90
**Facilities** ⅍ ✦ ⊟ ⅏ ⅓ ⌐ ☉ ◔ ☜ ◙ ☎
⅊ ⅊ ☉ ⅏ ⅓ ✦ ⅎ ⊟ ☐ ☞
**Nearby Facilities** ⌐ ✦ ⊿ ⅄ ∪ ♪ ℛ
**Acreage** 8 **Open** 1 February **to** Mid Nov
**Access** Good **Site** Level
Leisure centre with two indoor swimming pools, saunas, spa and fitness centre.
**Nearest Town/Resort** Witney
**Directions** On the A415 5 miles from Witney and 9 miles from Abingdon.
⚆ Oxford

# SHROPSHIRE

## BISHOPS CASTLE

**Cwnd House Farm,** Wentnor, Bishops Castle, Shropshire,
**Tel:** 01588 Linley 650237
**Pitches For** ▲ ⊕ ☞ **Total** 10
**Facilities** ⅏ ⅓ ✦ ⅎ
**Nearby Facilities** ✦ ∪
**Acreage** 2 **Open** May **to** October
**Access** Good **Site** Level
Farm site with scenic views. Ideal touring centre.
**Nearest Town/Resort** Church Stretton
**Directions** Cwnd House Farm is on Longden Pulverbatch road from Shrewsbury (13 miles) Bishops Castle is southwest. From Crave Arms take the A489 to Lydham Heath, turn right, site is about 1 mile past the Inn on the Green on the right.
⚆ Church Stretton

## BISHOPS CASTLE

**Daisy Bank Touring Caravan Park,** Snead, Montgomery, Powys, SY15 6EB
**Tel:** 01588 620471
**Email:** j.spurgeon@tesco.net
www.daisy-bank.co.uk
**Pitches For** ⊕ ☞ **Total** 55
**Facilities** ⅍ ✦ ⊟ ⅏ ⅓ ⅏ ⅓ ✦ ⌐ ☉ ◔ ☜ ◙ ☎
⅊ ☉ ☎ ➤ ⊟ ☐ ☇ ☇ ℘

## DAISY BANK TOURING CARAVAN PARK

**Exclusively for Adults**

SNEAD • MONTGOMERYSHIRE
POWYS • SY15 6EB

www.daisy-bank.co.uk

*Tel: 01588 620471*

E-mail: enquiries@daisy-bank.co.uk

*Offa's Dyke country, an area rich in history.*

Beautifully landscaped park with panoramic views of the Welsh and Shropshire hills.

- All 55 Pitches are fully serviced with Electric Hook-up, water and grey waste drain
- Large fenced-in Dog Walk • Free Putting Green
- Winner of Loo of the Year Award 2004 - Caravan Parks Category Wales
- Heated disability-friendly wet rooms
- Excellent touring and walking area • **OPEN ALL YEAR**

**Nearby Facilities** ↑ ✔
**Acreage** 5 **Open** All Year
**Access** Good **Site** Lev/Slope
ADULT ONLY park, in an area of natural beauty. Situated in the heart of the Camlad Valley with scenic views.
**Nearest Town/Resort** Bishops Castle
**Directions** Situated off the A489, between Craven Arms and Churchstoke. 2 miles east of Churchstoke.
⚞ Craven Arms

### BISHOPS CASTLE

**Poplar Farm Caravan & Camping**, Poplar Farm, Prolley Moor, Wentnor, Bishops CastleShropshire, SY9 5EJ
**Tel:** 01588 650383 **Fax:** 01588 650381
**Email:** poplarfarm99@aol.com
www.poplarfarm99.com
**Pitches For** ▲ ☲ ⊜ **Total** 28
**Facilities** ƒ �📶 Ⓦ ☎ ↑ ⊙ ⅃ ⚍ ▣ ☕
Ⓢ 🕈 ⌖ ♿ ⌂ ▣ ☕ ⚘
**Nearby Facilities** ↑ ✔ ∪
**Acreage** 1½ **Open** March to Nov
**Access** Good **Site** Sloping
Situated on the western slope of Shropshire's Long Mynd, this is both an area of special scientific interest and one of outstanding natural beauty. Cycle hire on site. Gliding and hang gliding nearby.
**Nearest Town/Resort** Bishops Castle
**Directions** From north on the A49, pass through Church Stretton and turn at Marshbrook (right hand) onto the B4370. At T-junction with the A489 turn right towards Bishops Castle, after approx. 2 miles turn right signposted Asterton, 3¼ miles to the site.
⚞ Church Stretton

### BISHOPS CASTLE

**The Green Caravan Park**, Wentnor, Bishops Castle, Shropshire, SY9 5EF
**Tel:** 01588 650605
**Email:** info@greencaravanpark.co.uk
www.greencaravanpark.co.uk
**Pitches For** ▲ ☲ ⊜ **Total** 140
**Facilities** ƒ 🕈 Ⓦ ☎ ↑ ⊙ ⅃ ▣ ☕
Ⓢ 🕈 ✗ ▽ ♿ ⌂ ▣ ☕ ⚘ ⚘
**Nearby Facilities** ↑ ✔ ∪ ⚘
**Open** Easter to October
**Access** Good **Site** Level
Picturesque, riverside site in an area of outstanding natural beauty. Superb walking in the countryside. Excellent birdlife. Central for touring. David Bellamy Gold Award for Conservation.
**Nearest Town/Resort** Bishops Castle
**Directions** Follow brown tourism signs from the A488 and the A489.
⚞ Craven Arms

### BRIDGNORTH

**Stanmore Hall Touring Park**, Stourbridge Road, Bridgnorth, Shropshire, WV15 6DT
**Tel:** 01746 761761
**Email:** stanmore@morris-leisure.co.uk
www.morris-leisure.co.uk
**Pitches For** ▲ ☲ ⊜ **Total** 131
**Facilities** ♿ ƒ ⅏ Ⓦ ☎ ↑ ▣ ☕
Ⓢ ❍ ⌂ ♿ ⌂ ▣ ☕
**Nearby Facilities** ↑ ✔
**Acreage** 12½ **Open** All Year
**Access** Good **Site** Level
Set in the beautiful grounds of Stanmore Hall which now houses the Midland Motor Museum. Conservatory overlooking the 2 acre lake with its water lilies and resident peacocks. 30 pitch ADULT ONLY area on site. Non members welcome. Booking essential.
**Nearest Town/Resort** Bridgnorth
**Directions** On the A442, at the roundabout in Bridgnorth turn onto the A458 signposted Stourbridge, site is 1½ miles on the right.
⚞ Bridgnorth

### BRIDGNORTH

**The Riverside Caravan Park**, Kidderminster Road, Bridgnorth, Shropshire, WV15 6BY
**Tel:** 01746 762393
**Pitches For** ☲ ⊜ **Total** 8
**Facilities** ƒ ☎ Ⓢ ❍ ⌂ ▽ ⍩
**Nearby Facilities** ↑ ✔ ⚑ ⚘ ∪
**Open** March to January
**Access** Good **Site** Level
On the banks of the River Severn. Just a 10 minute walk to Bridgnorth. Watch the Severn Valley Railway steam by.
**Nearest Town/Resort** Bridgnorth
**Directions** From Bridgnorth on the A442 road to Kidderminster, take the first turning on the right (150 metres).
⚞ Telford

### CHURCH STRETTON

**Small Batch**, Little Stretton, Church Stretton, Shropshire, SY6 6PW
**Tel:** 01694 723358
**Pitches For** ▲ ☲ ⊜ **Total** 40
**Facilities** ƒ Ⓦ ☎ ↑ ⊙ ⅃ ▣ ☕
**Nearby Facilities**
**Acreage** 1½ **Open** Easter to End Sept
**Access** Good **Site** Level
Scenic views and ideal touring.
**Nearest Town/Resort** Church Stretton
**Directions** A49 south, 2 miles south of Church Stretton turn right onto the B5477. Take the second left, at T-Junction turn right up to site through stream.
⚞ Church Stretton

### CRAVEN ARMS

**Kevindale**, Broome, Craven Arms, Shropshire, SY7 0NT
**Tel:** 01588 660199
**Pitches For** ▲ ☲ ⊜ **Total** 12
**Facilities** ♿ ☎ ↑ ⊙ ⅃ ▣ ☕
**Nearby Facilities** ↑ ✔ ∪
**Acreage** 2 **Open** April to October
**Access** Good **Site** Level
Scenic views, near village inn with good food. Close to Mid Wales Border, ideal walking. Two acre rally field.
**Nearest Town/Resort** Craven Arms
**Directions** From Craven Arms which is situated on the A49 Hereford to Shewsbury road, take the B4368 Clun/Bishops Castle road in 2 miles take B4367 Knighton road 1¼ miles turn right into Broome Village.
⚞ Broome

### ELLESMERE

**Fernwood Caravan Park**, Lyneal, Nr Ellesmere, Shropshire, SY12 0QF
**Tel:** 01948 710221 **Fax:** 01948 710324
**Email:** fernwood@caravanpark37.fsnet.co.uk
www.ranch.co.uk
**Pitches For** ☲ ⊜ **Total** 60
**Facilities** ♿ ƒ ⅏ ☎ ↑ ⊙ ⚍ ▣ ☕
Ⓢ ❍ ⌂ ♿ ⌂ ▣ ☕ ⚘
**Nearby Facilities** ↑ ✔ ⚐ ⚘
**Acreage** 7 **Open** March to November
**Access** Good **Site** Lev/Slope
40 acres of woodland open to caravanners. Lake with wildfowl and coarse fishing.
**Nearest Town/Resort** Ellesmere
**Directions** A495 from Ellesmere signposted Whitchurch. In Welshampton, right turn on B5063 signed Wem. Over canal bridge right sign Lyneal.
⚞ Wem

### LUDLOW

**Westbrook Park**, Little Hereford, Ludlow, Shropshire, SY8 4AU
**Tel:** 01584 711280 **Fax:** 01584 711460
**Email:** info@bestparks.co.uk
www.bestparks.co.uk
**Pitches For** ▲ ☲ ⊜ **Total** 52
**Facilities** ♿ ƒ 🕈 Ⓦ ☎ ↑ ⊙ ⅃ ⚍ ▣ ☕
🕈 ⌂ ♿ ⌂ ▣ ☕
**Nearby Facilities** ↑ ✔ ⚘ ∪ ⚘
**Acreage** 6 **Open** 1 March to End Nov
**Access** Good **Site** Level
Very well maintained quality park, in a pretty orchard, on the banks of the River Teme, with excellent fully serviced pitches. Short walk to the local inn for good food. ½ mile of
**Nearest Town/Resort** Ludlow

# SHROPSHIRE

**Directions** 3 miles west of Tenbury Wells on the A456, enter the village of Little Hereford. Turn left after passing over River Teme bridge, travel 300yds and turn left onto the park.
⚒ Ludlow

## MUCH WENLOCK

**Mill Farm Holiday Park,** Hughley, Nr Shrewsbury, Shropshire, SY5 6NT
**Tel:** 01746 785208
**Email:** mail@millfarmcaravanpark.co.uk
www.millfarmcaravanpark.co.uk
**Pitches For** ▲ ⬛ ⬛ **Total** 125
**Facilities** ⚒ ∤ ⬛ ⬛ ⬛ ⬛ ♠ ⌐ ☺ ⬛ ⬛ ⬛
⬛ ⬛ ⤑ ⬛ ⬏ ⬟
**Nearby Facilities** ┏ ✦ ∪ ⬚ ♪
**Acreage** 20 **Open** 1 March **to** 28 Jan
**Access** Good **Site** Lev/Slope
**Nearest Town/Resort** Shrewsbury
**Directions** From Much Wenlock take the A458 to Harley, turn left at Harley and follow signs to Hughley, caravan park is on the left.
⚒ Church Stretton

## MUCH WENLOCK

**Presthope Caravan Club Site,** Stretton Road, Much Wenlock, Shropshire, TF13 6DQ
**Tel:** 01746 785234
www.caravanclub.co.uk
**Pitches For** ⬛ ⬛ **Total** 73
**Facilities** ∤ ⬛ ⬛ ⬛ ⬛ ⬛⤑⬛ ⬛
**Nearby Facilities** ✦
**Acreage** 10 **Open** March **to** Oct
**Access** Good **Site** Level
Interesting site with abundant wildlife, set on the slopes of Wenlock Edge. A walkers paradise. Close to Ironbridge Gorge, museum and bridge. Near Severn Valley Railway and Blists Hill Open Air Museum. Own sanitation required. Non members welcome. Booking essential.
**Nearest Town/Resort** Much Wenlock
**Directions** Leave M54 at junction 6 and take A5223 signposted Ironbridge, watch for change of signs from Ironbridge to Much Wenlock. At Jiggers roundabout turn right onto A4169, after 1¾ miles turn left (still on A4169) signposted Much Wenlock. At T-junction opposite Gaskell Arms turn right onto A458, after ¼ mile turn left onto B4371, site is 3 miles on the left.
⚒ Much Wenlock

## OSWESTRY

**Ebnal Touring Park,** Rhos-Y-Gadfa, Gobowen, Oswestry, Shropshire, SY10 7BL
**Tel:** 01691 661274
**Email:** kathy.cap@btinternet.com
**Pitches For** ▲ ⬛ **Total** 20

**Facilities** ⬛ ∤ ⬛ ⬛ ⬛ ♠ ⌐ ☺ ⬛ ⬛ ⬛
**Nearby Facilities** ┏ ✦ ⬚
**Acreage** 2 **Open** Easter **to** 31 Oct
**Access** Good **Site** Level
Near to the Shropshire Union Canal, Chirk Castle, Erddig Hall, roman Chester and medieval Shrewsbury.
**Nearest Town/Resort** Oswestry
**Directions** 5 miles from Oswestry. Take the A5 for Wrexham into Gobowen Village, at the roundabout take the B5069 to Overton & St. Martins. After 1 mile turn right for Ebnal and Rhos-Y-Gadfa.
⚒ Gobowen

## SHREWSBURY

**Beaconsfield Farm Holiday Park,** Battlefield, Shrewsbury, Shropshire, SY4 4AA
**Tel:** 01939 210370 **Fax:** 01939 210349
**Email:** mail@beaconsfield-farm.co.uk
www.beaconsfield-farm.co.uk
**Pitches For** ▲ ⬛ ⬛ **Total** 60
**Facilities** ⬛ ∤ ⬛ ⬛ ⬛ ♠ ⌐ ☺ ⬛ ⬛ ⬛ ⬛
⬛ ⬛ ⬛ ✕ ✦ ⬛ ⬛ ⬛ ⬛ ⤑
**Nearby Facilities** ┏ ✦ ∪ ⬚ ♪
**Acreage** 15 **Open** All Year
**Access** Good **Site** Level
Exclusively for ADULTS over 21 years. 5 Star, well landscaped, level park with fly and coarse fishing and a bowling green. A La Carte restaurant on the park. 1½ miles to Park & Ride. Ideal base for Shrewsbury and the Welsh border. Holiday homes for sale and hire.
**Nearest Town/Resort** Shrewsbury
**Directions** 1½ miles north of Shrewsbury on the A49.
⚒ Shrewsbury

## SHREWSBURY

**Cartref Caravan & Camping Site,** Cartref, Fords Heath, Nr Shrewsbury, Shropshire.
**Tel:** 01743 821688
www.caravancampingsites.co.uk/cartref
**Pitches For** ▲ ⬛ ⬛ **Total** 35
**Facilities** ⬛ ∤ ⬛ ⬛ ♠ ⌐ ☺ ⬛ ⬛ ⬛
⬛ ⬛ ⬛ ⤑ ⬛ ⬛ ⬛
**Nearby Facilities** ┏ ✦ ⬚
**Acreage** 1½ **Open** Easter **to** October
**Access** Good **Site** Level
Peaceful countryside. Ideal for touring or an overnight stop.
**Directions** From Shrewsbury bypass A5 trunk road take the A458 Welshpool West. 2 miles to Ford Village, turn south at Ford, follow camp signs. Signposted from the A5 bypass on the Montgomery junction B4386.
⚒ Shrewsbury

## SHREWSBURY

**Ebury Hill Camping & Caravanning Club Site,** Ebury Hill, Ring Bank, Haughton, Telford TF6 6BU
**Tel:** 01743 709334
www.campingandcaravanningclub.co.uk
**Pitches For** ▲ ⬛ ⬛ **Total** 100
**Facilities** ∤ ⬛ ⬛ ⬛ ⬛ ⬛ ⬛ ⤑ ⬛ ⬛ ✕ ♪
**Nearby Facilities**
**Acreage** 18 **Open** March **to** Nov
**Access** Good **Site** Lev/Slope
Set on an ancient Iron Age hill fort, with panoramic views. Close to Shrewsbury and Ironbridge Gorge. Fishing on site. BTB 4 Star Graded, David Bellamy Gold Award and AA 1 Pennant. Non members welcome.
**Nearest Town/Resort** Shrewsbury
**Directions** From the A5/A49 take the B5062 signposted Newport, pass Haughmond Abbey and turn left signposted Hadnall. Site is on the left in approx. 1 mile.
⚒ Shrewsbury

## SHREWSBURY

**Hollies Farm,** 16 Valeswood, Little Ness, Shrewsbury, Shropshire, SY4 2LH
**Tel:** 01939 261046
**Pitches For** ⬛ ⬛ **Total** 5
**Facilities** ⬛ ∤ ⬛ ⬛ ✕ ♠
**Nearby Facilities** ┏ ✦ ∪
**Acreage** 1 **Open** Easter **to** Nov
**Access** Good **Site** Level
ADULTS ONLY site with spectacular views. On the edge of a country park. Ideal for touring and walking. You can also contact us on Mobile: 07962 121652.
**Nearest Town/Resort** Shrewsbury
**Directions** Little Ness is 2 miles off the A5 at Nescliffe, midway between Shrewsbury and Oswestry.
⚒ Shrewsbury

## SHREWSBURY

**Middle Darnford Farm,** Ratlinghope, Pontesbury, Shrewsbury, Shropshire, SY5 0SR
**Tel:** 01694 751320
**Pitches For** ▲ ⬛ **Total** 20
**Facilities** ⬛ ⤑ ∤ ⬛ ⤑
**Nearby Facilities** ┏ ∪
**Acreage** 2 **Open** April **to** Nov
**Site** Lev/Slope
Close to the walks at Long Myn.
**Nearest Town/Resort** Church Stretton
**Directions** From Church Stretton follow the road across Long Myn through to Ratlinghope, site is ¼ of a mile after leaving Long Myn.
⚒ Church Stretton

## SHREWSBURY

**Severn House,** Montford Bridge, Shrewsbury, Shropshire, SY4 1ED
Tel: 01743 850229
Email: severnhouse@tiscali.co.uk
www.severnhousecaravans.co.uk
Pitches For A ♥ ₩ Total 25
Facilities ∱ ▯ ▥ ⚓ ſ ⊙ ⬅ ☕
⬛▨☕⊣▣⤫ ⌓
Nearby Facilities ⌘
Acreage 2½ Open April to October
Access Good Site Level
Riverside site with 300 metres of river for fishing. Dog walk, local shop, buses, pub and meals nearby. Regular bus service.
Nearest Town/Resort Shrewsbury
Directions 4 miles north west of Shrewsbury on the A5 towards Oswestry and North Wales. At signposts for the site turn onto the B4380 and Montford Bridge is ½ mile.
⚏ Shrewsbury

## TELFORD

**Pool View Caravan Park,** 3 Pool View Park, Buildwas, Telford, Shropshire, TF8 7BS
Tel: 01952 433946
Pitches For A ♥ ₩ Total 15
Facilities ∱ ▥ ⚓ ſ ⊣▣ ⤫ ⌓
Nearby Facilities ✓
Open End Feb to End Oct
Access Good Site Level
Panoramic views of fields and countryside. Short walk from the Buildwas Nature Trail, museum and Ironbridge Bridge itself. Caravan storage available.
Nearest Town/Resort Telford
Directions From Ironbridge follow the main road through the village (with the main car park on your left), go over the roundabout to the T-junction and turn left. Go over the Buildwas Bridge (approx 150 yards) to the private road on your left. Follow the road straight up to the Park and follow signs to the Wardens Home at No.3.
⚏ Telford/Wellington

## TELFORD

**Severn Gorge Park,** Bridgnorth Road, Tweedale, Telford, Shropshire, TF7 4JB
Tel: 01952 684789
Email: info@severngorgepark.co.uk
www.severngorgepark.co.uk
Pitches For A ♥ ₩ Total 50
Facilities ♿ ∱ ▯ ▥ ⚓ ſ ⊙ ⬅ ▣ ◻ ☕
⬛▨☕✕⊣▣ ⌓
Nearby Facilities ⌘ ✓ ⚲ ⤬ U ♞
Acreage 4 Open All Year
Access Good Site Level
Ironbridge, Gorge and museums.
Nearest Town/Resort Telford
Directions From the M54 junction 4, follow

signs (A442) for Kidderminster for 1 mile. Then take the A442 signposted Kidderminster to the first roundabout Brockton roundabout 2¾ miles. Follow brown Severn Gorge Caravan Park signposts, 1 mile to the site.
⚏ Telford

## WEM

**Lower Lacon Caravan Park,** Wem, Shropshire, SY4 5RP
Tel: 01939 232376 Fax: 01939 233606
Email: info@llcp.co.uk
www.llcp.co.uk
Pitches For A ♥ ₩ Total 270
Facilities ♿ ∱ ▯ ▥ ⚓ ſ ⊙ ⬅ ▣ ◻ ☕
⬛▨☕✕▽ ▥ ⬛⤻⊣▣ ⤫ ⌓
Nearby Facilities ſ ✓
Acreage 48 Open All Year
Access Good Site Level
Nearest Town/Resort Wem
Directions 1 mile from Wem on the B5065. From the A49 then the B5065, 3 miles.
⚏ Wem

## WHITCHURCH

**Green Lane Farm Caravan & Camp Site,** Green Lane Farm, Prees, Whitchurch, Shropshire, SY13 2AH
Tel: 01948 840460
Email: gqgreenlanefarm@aol.com
www.greenlanefarm.northshropshire.biz
Pitches For A ♥ ₩ Total 22
Facilities ♿ ∱ ▥ ⚓ ſ ⊙ ▣ ⬛ ⌓ ⤻▣ ⌓
Nearby Facilities ſ ✓ U
Acreage 2½ Open March to Oct
Access Good Site Level
Central for all local attractions, Hawkstone, Shrewsbury, Chester, Llangollen, Nantwich, etc..
Nearest Town/Resort Whitchurch
Directions 350 yards off the main A41 between Whitchurch and Newport.
⚏ Whitchurch

## WHITCHURCH

**Roden View Caravan & Camping,** Roden View, Dobsons Bridge, Whixall, WhitchurchShropshire, SY13 2QL
Tel: 01948 710320 Fax: 01948 710320
Email: jean@roden-view.co.uk
Pitches For A ♥ ₩ Total 7
Facilities ∱ ▥ ⚓ ſ ⊙ ⬅ ☕ ⬛▨☕⤻▣
Nearby Facilities ſ ✓ ⚲
Acreage 4½ Open All Year
Access Good Site Level
Near to the Shropshire Union Canal and Whixall Moss. 5 miles from Ellesmere, Shropshire's Lake District. There is a washing machine available for use. Bed & Breakfast (4 Diamond) available all with en-suite.

**Nearest Town/Resort** Wem
**Directions** From Shrewsbury Wem Church turn left after second garage, then turn right for Whixall, at the next T-Junction turn left then immediately right, 2½ miles to the next T-Junction turn right. ½ mile the house is on the right before Dobsons Bridge.
⚏ Wem

# SOMERSET
## BATH

**Bath Chew Valley Caravan Park,** Ham Lane, Bishop Sutton, North East Somerset, BS39 5TZ
Tel: 01275 332127 Fax: 01275 332664
Email: enquiries@bathchewvalley.co.uk
www.bathchewvalley.co.uk
Pitches For ♥ ₩ Total 33
Facilities ∱ ▯ ▥ ⚓ ſ ⊙ ⬅ ▣ ◻ ☕
▨ ⊙ ☕⤻▣ ▨ ☕⤫
Nearby Facilities ſ ✓ ⚲ ⤬ U ♞ ♪
Acreage 2¼ Open All Year
Access Good Site Level
ADULTS ONLY PARK. A site for peace and tranquility, set in an area of outstanding natural beauty. Featured on BBC's Gardeners World. ETB 5 Star Graded, the only 5 Star Park in North East Somerset.
Nearest Town/Resort Bath
Directions Approaching Bath on the A37 or the A38 Bristol to Wells or Bristol to Taunton roads, take the A368 which links both to Bishop Sutton, turn opposite the Red Lion Pub.
⚏ Bath

## BATH

**Bury View Farm,** Corston Fields, Nr. Bath, Somerset, BA2 9HD
Tel: 01225 873672 Fax: 01225 874188
Email: salbowd@btinternet.com
Pitches For ♥ ₩ Total 15
Facilities ∱ ▥ ⚓ ſ ⊙ ⬅ ☕ ▨ ⊙ ⤻▣
Nearby Facilities ſ ✓ U
Acreage 2 Open All Year
Access Good Site Level
Quiet farm site, 5 miles from Bath City and close to Cheddar, Wells and Bristol.
Nearest Town/Resort Bath
Directions 5 miles from Bath. From Bristol take the A4, at the Globe (Newton St. Loe roundabout) take the A39, 1½ miles to the site.
⚏ Bath/Keynsham

**BATH**
**Newton Mill Camping & Caravan Park,**
Newton Road, Bath, Somerset, BA2 9JF
Tel: 01225 333909
Email: newtonmill@hotmail.com
www.campinginbath.co.uk
Pitches For ▲ ⊞ ⊟ Total 195
Facilities ⬧ ∤ ⊞ ⓤ ♨ ⌐ ☉⌐ ⬛ ◻ ☎
⛊ ◉ ⬛ ✗ ⛲ ⊞ ⬥ ⌂ ┿ ☐ ⊟
Nearby Facilities ⌐ ∤ ∪ ♟
Acreage 42 Open All Year
Access Good Site Level
A beautiful, idyllic setting in a hidden valley, close to the city centre. Superb heated toilets, Awarded 5 Star loo of the Year 2005, include showers and bathrooms. Very frequent bus service. Near to the traffic free Bath to Bristol cycle path.
Nearest Town/Resort Bath
Directions On the A4 Bath to Bristol road, at the roundabout by the Globe Public House take the exit signposted Newton St. Loe, Park is 1 mile on the left.
⇆ Bath

**THANK YOU FOR CHOOSING CADE'S**

**BREAN SANDS**
**Channel View Caravan Park,** Warren Road, Brean, Burnham-on-Sea, Somerset, TA8 2RR
Tel: 01278 751055 Fax: 01278 751055
Pitches For ▲ ⊞ ⊟ Total 50
Facilities ⬧ ∤ ⊞ ♨ ⌐ ☉⌐ ☎ ⬛ ┿ ◻ ⛌ ♟
Nearby Facilities ⌐ ∤ ∪ ♏ ∪
Acreage 3 Open April to Mid Oct
Access Good Site Gentle Slope
Quiet and friendly site, on the beach side overlooking farmland.
Nearest Town/Resort Brean Sands
Directions Leave the M5 at junction 22 and follow signs to Burnham-on-Sea, Berrow and Brean. Site is ¼ mile past the Brean Down Inn on the left hand side.
⇆ Highbridge

**BREAN SANDS**
**Holiday Resort Unity at Unity Farm,**
Coast Road, Brean Sands, Somerset, TA8 2RB
Tel: 01278 751235 Fax: 01278 751539
Email: admin@hru.co.uk
www.hru.co.uk
Pitches For ▲ ⊞ ⊟ Total 800
Facilities ⬧ ∤ ⊞ ⊞ ⓤ ♨ ⌐ ☉⌐ ⬛ ◻ ☎
⛊ ⛣ ⓛ ◉ ⬛ ✗ ⛲ ⊞ ⬥ ⌂ ┿ ☐ ⬛ ⛌

**Nearby Facilities** ⌐ ∤ ⬥ ⏄ ∪ ♏ ♟ ⅄
Acreage 200 Open February to Nov
Access Good Site Level
200yds from 7 mile beach, own leisure centre with 30 fun fair attractions, pool complex with 3 giant water slides, 18 hole golf course, lake for fishing, horse riding and 10 Pin Bowling. Family entertainment Easter to November. Special offers for young families and OAPs in June and Sept.
Nearest Town/Resort Burnham-on-Sea
Directions Leave M5 at junction 22. Follow signs for Berrow and Brean Leisure Park, sit on right 4½ miles from M5.
⇆ Weston-Super-Mare

**BREAN SANDS**
**Northam Farm Caravan & Touring Park,**
Brean, Nr Burnham-on-Sea, Somerset, TA8 2SE
Tel: 01278 751244 Fax: 01278 751150
Email: enquiries@northamfarm.co.uk
www.northamfarm.co.uk
Pitches For ▲ ⊞ ⊟ Total 350
Facilities ⬧ ⛣ ∤ ⊞ ⓤ ♨ ⌐ ☉⌐ ⬛ ◻ ☎
⛊ ◉ ⬛ ✗ ⊞ ⬥ ┿ ☐ ⊟
Nearby Facilities ⌐ ⏄ ⬥ ∪ ⅄
Acreage 30 Open Easter to October
Access Good Site Level
Ideal base for seeing Somerset. 6 miles of

sandy beach. Our Seagull Inn with family entertainment is within easy walking distance. Excellent facilities, fishing lake and a café with take-away food on park. ETC 4 Star Graded and AA 3 Pennants. Winter Secure Storage.
**Nearest Town/Resort** Burnham-on-Sea
**Directions** M5 Junction 22. Follow signs to Brean, ¼ mile past Leisure Park on righthand side.
⚇ Weston-super-Mare

**BREAN SANDS**
**Warren Farm Holiday Centre,** Brean Sands, Burnham-on-Sea, Somerset, TA8 2RP
**Tel:** 01278 751227 **Fax:** 01278 751033
**Email:** enquiries@warren-farm.co.uk
www.warren-farm.co.uk
**Pitches For** ▲ ⚎ ⚎ **Total** 500
**Facilities** 🚿 🎣 ⚏ 🚽 🔥 ⌂ ⌁ ⚎ ◻ ⚐ 🍴

**Nearby Facilities** ⌐ ✓ ⚓ ⚘ ∪
**Acreage** 50 **Open** April **to** End Oct
**Access** Good **Site** Level
Flat, grassy, family park with excellent facilities including an indoor play area and family entertainment at the Beachcomber Inn. 100 metres from 5 miles of sandy beach. Dogs are welcome free in designated areas. AA Holiday Centre.
**Nearest Town/Resort** Burnham-on-Sea
**Directions** Leave M5 at junction 22, follow signs to Burnham-on-Sea, Berrow and Brean on the B3140. Site is 1¼ miles past the leisure centre.
⚇ Weston-super-Mare

**BRIDGWATER**
**Currypool Mill,** Cannington, Bridgwater, Somerset, TA5 2NH
**Tel:** 01278 671135

**Email:** currypool.mill@btopenworld.com
www.currypoolmill.co.uk
**Pitches For** ▲ ⚎ ⚎ **Total** 35
**Facilities** 🚽 ⚏ 🔥 ⌂ ⌁ ◻ 🍴
🚿 ⚏ ⚏ 🎣 ⚘ ⚎ ⚐
**Nearby Facilities** ⌐ ✓ ⚓ ⚘ ∪ ℛ
**Open** Easter **to** Mid Nov
**Access** Good **Site** Level
Quiet location near the Quantock Hills and Somerset coast. Set amongst streams and waterfalls. Dog walking fields, putting and croquet.
**Nearest Town/Resort** Bridgwater
**Directions** From Bridgwater take the A39 Minehead road, after approx. 5 miles take a left hand turning signposted Spaxton and Aisholt. Currypool is approx. ½ a mile on the left.
⚇ Bridgwater

# Northam Farm
## CARAVAN & TOURING PARK

**Brochure Hotline**
**01278 751244**
www.northamfarm.co.uk

### Brean Sands
*Where the sea meets the countryside*

- 5 miles of sandy beach
- Children's outdoor play areas
- Restaurant/Take-away
- Nightly entertainment in the Seagull Inn (a short walk away)
- Shop with off-licence
- Fishing Lake & Dog walks
- Family owned and operated for over 50 years

Mr, Mrs, M. Scott & Family, Northam Caravan & Touring Park, Brean, Near Burnham-on-sea, Somerset, TA8 2SE, Tel: (01278) 751244 Fax: (01278) 751150, email: enquiries@northamfarm.co.uk

# SOMERSET

## BRIDGWATER
**Fairways International Touring Caravan Park,** Bath Road, Bawdrip, Bridgwater, Somerset, TA7 8PP
**Tel:** 01278 685569 **Fax:** 01278 685569
**Email:** fairwaysint@btinternet.com
www.fairwaysint.btinternet.co.uk
**Pitches For** ▲ ⚌ ⚌ **Total** 200
**Facilities** ⬡ ⬡ ⬡ ⬡ ⬡ ⬡ ⬡ ⬡ ⬡ ⬡
⬡ ⬡ ⬡ ⬡ ⬡ ⬡ ⬡ ⬡ ⬡ ⬡ ⬡
**Nearby Facilities** ⬡ ⬡ ⬡ ⬡ ⬡ ⬡
**Acreage** 5¾ **Open** March **to** Nov
**Access** Good **Site** Level
Ideal touring, within easy reach of Cheddar, Wells, Glastonbury, Mendip Hills and Burnham-on-Sea. Fishing locally.
**Nearest Town/Resort** Bridgwater
**Directions** Leave the M5 at junction 23 and take the A39 towards Glastonbury, at the junction of the B3141.
⚞ Bridgwater

## BRIDGWATER
**Hawkridge Farm,** Lawyers Hill, Spaxton, Bridgwater, Somerset, TA5 1AL
**Tel:** 01278 671341 **Fax:** 01278 671341
**Email:**
carolling@fortress49.freeserve.co.uk
**Pitches For** ⚌ **Total** 5
**Facilities** ⬡ ⬡ ⬡ ⬡ ⬡
**Nearby Facilities** ⬡ ⬡ ⬡
**Acreage** 1½ **Open** Easter **to** End Dec
**Access** Good **Site** Sloping
Tranquil site with panoramic views over Hawkridge Reservoir. Quantock Hills, an area of outstanding natural beauty. Trout fishing at the reservoir.
**Nearest Town/Resort** Bridgwater
**Directions** Leave the M5 at junction 23 and take the A38 towards Bridgwater. Continue straight until you pass Morrisons and B&Q, at the next traffic lights turn left into West Street. Go through the village and continue up the hill and fork right signposted Nether Stowey. Site entrance is on the right just past Hawkridge Reservoir.
⚞ Bridgwater

## BRIDGWATER
**Mill Farm Caravan & Camping Park,** Fiddington, Bridgwater, Somerset, TA5 1JQ
**Tel:** 01278 732286 **Fax:** 01278 732281
www.mill-farm-uk.com
**Pitches For** ▲ ⚌ ⚌ **Total** 200
**Facilities** ⬡ ⬡ ⬡ ⬡ ⬡ ⬡ ⬡ ⬡ ⬡ ⬡
⬡ ⬡ ⬡ ⬡ ⬡ ⬡ ⬡ ⬡ ⬡ ⬡ ⬡
**Nearby Facilities** ⬡ ⬡ ⬡ ⬡ ⬡
**Open** All Year
**Access** Good **Site** Level
Unique, quiet, friendly and sheltered country park. Situated at the foot of the beautiful Quantock Hills and beside a picturesque stream. The ideal family site.
**Nearest Town/Resort** Bridgwater
**Directions** Leave the M5 at junction 23 or 24 and go through Bridgwater. Follow the A39 towards Minehead for 6 miles. At Keenthorne turn right for Fiddington, Mill Farm is 1 mile.
⚞ Bridgwater

## BRUTON
**Batcombe Vale Caravan & Camping Park,** Batcombe, Shepton Mallet, Somerset, BA4 6BW
**Tel:** 01749 830246
**Email:** donaldsage@compuserve.com
www.batcombevale.co.uk
**Pitches For** ▲ ⚌ ⚌ **Total** 32
**Facilities** ⬡ ⬡ ⬡ ⬡ ⬡ ⬡ ⬡ ⬡
⬡ ⬡ ⬡ ⬡ ⬡
**Nearby Facilities** ⬡ ⬡ ⬡
**Acreage** 7 **Open** May **to** September
**Access** Good **Site** Level
Own secluded valley of lakes and wild gardens. Fishing and boating on site. Near Longleat, Stourhead and Glastonbury. All shops are 2 miles away. Jet skiing nearby.
**Nearest Town/Resort** Bruton
**Directions** Access must be via Bruton or Evercreech from where it is well signed.
⚞ Bruton

## BURNHAM-ON-SEA
**Burnham-on-Sea Holiday Village,** Marine Drive, Burnham-on-Sea, Somerset, TA8 1LA
**Tel:** 01278 783391 **Fax:** 01278 793776
**Email:**
burnham@bourneleisuregroup.co.uk
www.touringholidays.co.uk
**Pitches For** ▲ ⚌ ⚌ **Total** 75
**Facilities** ⬡ ⬡ ⬡ ⬡ ⬡ ⬡ ⬡ ⬡ ⬡ ⬡
⬡ ⬡ ⬡ ⬡ ⬡ ⬡ ⬡ ⬡ ⬡ ⬡
**Nearby Facilities** ⬡ ⬡ ⬡ ⬡ ⬡ ⬡
**Acreage** 95 **Open** March **to** November
**Access** Good **Site** Level
Near the beach. Fishing, golf, tennis and an all-weather multi-sports court on park. Cafe bar, mini-market, bakery, gift shop, off licence and two entertainment venues.
**Nearest Town/Resort** Burnham-on-Sea
**Directions** Leave the M5 at junction 22, turn left at the roundabout onto the A38 to Highbridge. Continue over the mini roundabout and railway bridge, turn next left onto the B3139 to Burnham-on-Sea. Turn left at the Total Garage into Marine Drive and the park is 400 yards on the left.
⚞ Highbridge

## BURNHAM-ON-SEA
**Diamond Farm Caravan & Touring Park,** Diamond Farm, Weston Road, Brean, Nr Burnham-on-SeaSomerset, TA8 2RL
**Tel:** 01278 751263
**Email:**
trevor@diamondfarm42.freeserve.co.uk
www.diamondfarm.co.uk
**Pitches For** ▲ ⚌ ⚌ **Total** 100
**Facilities** ⬡ ⬡ ⬡ ⬡ ⬡ ⬡ ⬡ ⬡ ⬡ ⬡
⬡ ⬡ ⬡ ⬡ ⬡ ⬡ ⬡ ⬡ ⬡ ⬡
**Nearby Facilities** ⬡ ⬡ ⬡ ⬡ ⬡ ⬡ ⬡
**Acreage** 6 **Open** April **to** 15 October
**Access** Good **Site** Level
A quiet, family site alongside River Axe and only 800yds from the beach. All modern facilities.
**Nearest Town/Resort** Burnham-on-Sea
**Directions** M5 junction 22, follow signs to Brean, ½ mile past leisure park turn right to Lympsham/Weston-super-Mare. Diamond Farm is 800yds on the left hand side.
⚞ Weston-super-Mare

## BURNHAM-ON-SEA
**Home Farm Holiday Park,** Suremine Limited, Edithmead, Burnham-on-Sea, Somerset, TA9 4HD
**Tel:** 01278 788888 **Fax:** 01278 780113
**Email:** info@homefarmholidaypark.co.uk
www.homefarmholidaypark.co.uk
**Pitches For** ⚌ ⚌ **Total** 650
**Facilities** ⬡ ⬡ ⬡ ⬡ ⬡ ⬡ ⬡ ⬡ ⬡ ⬡
⬡ ⬡ ⬡ ⬡ ⬡ ⬡ ⬡ ⬡ ⬡ ⬡ ⬡
**Nearby Facilities** ⬡ ⬡ ⬡ ⬡ ⬡ ⬡ ⬡
**Acreage** 44 **Open** Feb **to** Dec
**Access** Good **Site** Level
**Nearest Town/Resort** Burnham-on-Sea
**Directions** Just off the M5 Junction 22.
⚞ Burnham-on-Sea

## BURNHAM-ON-SEA
**Southfield Farm Caravan Park,** Weston Road, Brean, Burnham-on-Sea, Somerset, TA8 2RL
**Tel:** 01278 751233
**Email:** office.southfield@btinternet.com
**Pitches For** ▲ ⚌ ⚌ **Total** 200
**Facilities** ⬡ ⬡ ⬡ ⬡ ⬡ ⬡ ⬡ ⬡ ⬡ ⬡
⬡ ⬡ ⬡ ⬡ ⬡ ⬡ ⬡
**Nearby Facilities** ⬡ ⬡
**Acreage** 15 **Open** Whitsun **to** 30 Sept
**Access** Fair **Site** Level
Direct access to the beach from the site.
**Nearest Town/Resort** Brean
**Directions** Leave the M5 at junction 22 and follow signs to Brean. Turn right at the village hall and site is 50 metres on the right.
⚞ Weston-super-Mare

**WELCOME TO SOMERSET'S ULTIMATE FAMILY DESTINATION**

**Home Farm HOLIDAY PARK and COUNTRY CLUB**

FREE COLOUR BROCHURE

**PARK FEATURES...**

☆ AMPLE HOOK UPS
☆ HARD STANDINGS
☆ BATHROOMS & LAUNDERETTE
☆ DISABLED FACILITIES
☆ OPEN AIR SWIMMING POOL
(HEATED IN PEAK TIMES)
☆ CABARET CLUB & RESTAURANT
☆ SUPERMARKET
☆ GUESTS WITH PETS AREA
☆ FISHING LAKES
☆ TAKE-AWAY FOOD

Set in 44 acres of beautiful parkland HOME FARM is one mile from the quaint resort of Burnham-on-Sea which offers miles of golden sand.

**HOME FARM HOLIDAY PARK & COUNTRY CLUB
EDITHMEAD, BURNHAM-on-SEA,
SOMERSET TA9 4HD
Tel: 01278 78 88 88** www.homefarmholidaypark.co.uk

---

**CHARD**

**Alpine Grove Touring Park,** Forton, Chard, Somerset, TA20 4HD
**Tel:** 01460 63479 **Fax:** 01460 63479
**Email:** stay@alpinegrovetouringpark.com
**www.**alpinegrovetouringpark.com
**Pitches For** ▲ ⚌ ⚌ **Total** 40
**Facilities** ⌁ 🏠 🚽 🔥 🏕 ⊙ ⚌ ⚌ ◻ 🐕
🏌 ⊙ 🏊 ⊼ ⊬ ▣ ▤
**Nearby Facilities** ⌁ ✓ ∪ ♫
**Acreage** 8 **Open** 1 April **to** 30 Sept
**Access** Good **Site** Level
Ideal for woodland walks and fossil hunting. 20 minutes from the World Heritage coastline. ETC 4 Star Graded, AA Pennants and Silver David Bellamy award.
**Nearest Town/Resort** Chard
**Directions** From Chard take the A30 signposted Cricket St Thomas, turn right onto the B3167 and follow brown tourism signs.
⇷ Crewkerne

**CHARD**

**Five Acres Caravan Club Site,** Beetham, Chard, Somerset, TA20 3QA
**Tel:** 01460 234519
**www.**caravanclub.co.uk
**Pitches For** ⚌ ⚌ **Total** 74
**Facilities** ⌁ 🏠 🚽 🔥 🏕 ⊙ ⚌ ⚌ ◻ 🐕
🏌 ⊙ 🏊 ▣ ▤
**Nearby Facilities** ⌁
**Acreage** 5 **Open** March **to** Oct
**Access** Good **Site** Level
Peaceful and pleasant park set in South Somerset countryside. Near Chard Reservoir & Nature Reserve which hosts 50 species of bird including Osprey. Close to Montacute House and Cricket St. Thomas Wildlife Park. Non members welcome. Booking essential.

**Nearest Town/Resort** Chard
**Directions** From east on the A303, at the crossroads at the end of Ilminster bypass turn left by the thatched cottage into a narrow lane signposted Crickleaze. Site is second entrance on the left (250 yards). NB: DO NOT use first entrance as its difficult to back out.
⇷ Chard

**CHARD**

**Snowdon Hill Farm,** Snowdon Hill Farm, Chard, Somerset, TA20 3PS
**Tel:** 01460 63213 **Fax:** 01460 61933
**Facilities** ⌁ 🐕 🍴 🏕 ⊼ ▣ ▤ ▤
**Nearby Facilities** ⌁ ✓ ⚊ ⊼ ∪ ♫
**Acreage** 5 **Open** All Year
**Access** Good **Site** Lev/Slope
Quiet location with exceptional views. 30 minutes drive from the coast. Farm shop with local produce on site. Maize Maze from July to September.
**Nearest Town/Resort** Chard
**Directions** ¾ miles west of Chard on the A30 turn right into Barleymow's Farm Shop.
⇷ Crewkerne

**CHARD**

**South Somerset Holiday Park,** A30 Exeter Road, Howley, Nr Chard, Somerset, TA20 3EA
**Tel:** 01460 66036
**Email:** sshpturnpike@aol.com
**Pitches For** ▲ ⚌ ⚌ **Total** 110
**Facilities** ⚫ ⌁ 🏠 🚽 🔥 🏕 ⊙ ⚌ ⚌ ◻ 🐕
🏌 ⊙ 🏊 ⊼ ⊬ ▣ ▤ ⚘
**Nearby Facilities** ⌁ ✓ ⚊ ⊼ ∪ ♫ ⚹
**Acreage** 7½ **Open** All Year
**Access** Good **Site** Gentle Slope
Central location, 20 minutes drive from the south coast.

**Nearest Town/Resort** Chard
**Directions** 3 miles west of Chard on the A30.
⇷ Crewkerne

**CHEDDAR**

**Netherdale Caravan & Camping Site,** Bridgwater Road, Sidcot, Winscombe, Somerset, BS25 1NH
**Tel:** 01934 843007
**Email:** camping@netherdale.net
**www.**netherdale.net
**Pitches For** ▲ ⚌ ⚌ **Total** 25
**Facilities** ⌁ 🏠 🔥 🏕 ⊙ ⚌ 🐕
🏌 ⊙ 🏊 ▣ ▤
**Nearby Facilities** ⌁ ✓ ⚊ ⊼ ∪ ♫ ⚹
**Acreage** 3½ **Open** March **to** October
**Access** Good **Site** Lev/Slope
Excellent walking area, footpath from site to valley and Mendip Hills adjoining. Good views. Ideal touring centre for Somerset. Many historical places and beaches within easy reach of site. Deep sinks and tumble drier for laundry purposes. Pets welcome on a lead. Only individual motorcycles accepted, not groups. 3 miles from a dry ski slope and a well equipped sports centre.
**Nearest Town/Resort** Cheddar
**Directions** Site is midway between Bristol and Bridgwater on the A38. From Weston-super-Mare follow the A371 to join the A38 at Sidcot Corner, site is ¼ of a mile south. From Wells and Cheddar follow the A371 westwards to join the A38, a mile south of site.
⇷ Weston-super-Mare

**SOMERSET ENTRIES CONTINUE ON PAGE 164**

## CHEDDAR
**Bucklegrove Caravan & Camping Park,**
Rodney Stoke, Cheddar, Somerset, BS27
3UZ
**Tel:** 01749 870261 **Fax:** 01749 870101
**Email:** info@bucklegrove.co.uk
www.bucklegrove.co.uk
Pitches For ▲ ♚ ♞ Total 125
Facilities ⓑ ⸙ ⬚ ⬚ ⬚ ⌐ ⊙⌣ ⬚ ⬚ ☎
⬚ ⬚ ⬚ ⬚ ⬚ ⬚ ⬚ ⬚ ⬚ ⬚ ⬚
**Nearby Facilities** ⌐ ✎ ⌁ ⬚ ∪ ℛ ⚡
**Open** March **to** December
**Access** Good **Site** Level/Gently Sloping
Friendly, family run park with a free indoor
heated pool. Ideal touring centre on the
south side of the Mendip Hills with scenic
views and walking.
**Nearest Town/Resort** Wells/Cheddar
**Directions** Midway Between Wells and
Cheddar on the A371.
✳ Weston Super Mare

## CHEDDAR
**Rodney Stoke Inn,** Rodney Stoke, Nr
Cheddar, Somerset, BS27 3XB
**Tel:** 01749 870209 **Fax:** 01749 870406
Pitches For ▲ ♚ ♞ Total 31
Facilities ⸙ ⬚ ⬚ ⌐ ⬚ ✕ ⬚ ⬚ ⬚ ⬚
**Nearby Facilities** ⌐ ✎ ⌁ ∪ ⚡
**Acreage** 2 **Open** All Year
**Access** Good **Site** Level
Central location for Cheddar Gorge and
Caves, the City of Wells and Wookey Hole
Caves.
**Nearest Town/Resort** Cheddar
**Directions** Take the A371 from Cheddar
towards Wells for 3 miles.
✳ Weston-Super-Mare

## CHEDDAR
**Splott Farm,** Blackford, Nr Wedmore,
Somerset, BS28 4PD
**Tel:** 01278 641522
Pitches For ▲ ♚ ♞ Total 32
Facilities ⸙ ⬚ ⬚ ⌐ ⊙⬚ ⬚ ⬚ ⬚ ⬚ ✤⬚ ⚡
⚡
**Nearby Facilities** ⌐ ✎ ⌁ ⬚ ∪ ⚡ ⚡ ⚡
**Acreage** 4¼ **Open** March **to** November
**Access** Good **Site** Gentle Slope
Very peaceful site with views of the Mendip
Hills (and Quantocks), very rural area.
Ideal touring, Weston-super-Mare, Wells,
Cheddar, Burnham-on-Sea, Wookey.

**Nearest Town** Burnham-on-Sea/Cheddar
**Directions** Leave M5 at junction 22, 2 miles
to Highbridge, take B3139 Highbridge/Wells
road, about 5 miles.
✳ Highbridge

## CONGRESBURY
**Oak Farm Touring Park,** Weston Road,
Congresbury, Somerset, BS49 5EB
**Tel:** 01934 833246
Pitches For ▲ ♚ ♞ Total 40
Facilities ⸙ ⬚ ⬚ ⌐ ⊙⬚ ⬚ ⬚ ⬚ ⬚ ⬚⬚ ⚡
**Nearby Facilities** ⌐ ✎ ⌁ ⬚ ∪ ⚡ ⚡
**Open** 31st Mar **to** October
**Access** Good **Site** Level
Pub and restaurant close by. You can also
call us on Mobile 07989 319686.
**Nearest Town/Resort** Weston-super-Mare
**Directions** 4 miles from junc. 21 on M5, on
the A370 midway between Bristol and
Weston-super-Mare.
✳ Yatton

## CROWCOMBE
**Quantock Orchard Caravan Park,**
Flaxpool, Crowcombe, Taunton, Somerset,
TA4 4AW
**Tel:** 01984 618618 **Fax:** 01984 618442
**Email:** qocp@flaxpool.freeserve.co.uk
www.quantockorchard.co.uk
Pitches For ▲ ♚ ♞ Total 77
Facilities ⓑ ⸙ ⬚ ⬚ ⬚ ⌐ ⊙⬚ ⬚ ⬚ ⬚ ☎
⬚ ⬚ ⬚ ⬚ ⬚ ⬚ ⬚ ⬚ ⬚ ⬚ ⚡
**Nearby Facilities** ⌐ ✎ ⌁ ⬚ ∪ ℛ ⚡
**Acreage** 7½ **Open** All Year
**Access** Good **Site** Level
Quantock Hills and steam railway.
Seasonal Pitches from September to July.
**Nearest Town/Resort** Taunton/Minehead
✳ Taunton

## DULVERTON
**Exe Valley Caravan Site,** Bridgetown,
Somerset, TA22 9JR
**Tel:** 01643 851432
**Email:** paul@paulmatt.fsnet.co.uk
www.exevalleycamping.co.uk
Pitches For ▲ ♚ ♞ Total 30
Facilities ⓑ ⸙ ⬚ ⬚ ⬚ ⌐ ⊙⬚ ⬚ ⬚ ⬚ ☎
⬚ ⬚ ⬚ ⬚✚⬚ ⬚ ⚡
**Nearby Facilities** ⌐ ✎ ⌁ ⬚ ∪
**Acreage** 4 **Open** March **to** October
**Access** Good **Site** Level

ADULTS ONLY. Most improved site in
Exmoor. Within Exmoor National Park.
Free fly fishing on site. Just a few minutes
walk from the local pub serving good food.
**Nearest Town/Resort** Dulverton
**Directions** Leave the M5 at junction 27 and
take the A361 towards Tiverton. From the
roundabout on the Tiverton by-pass take the
A396 signposted Minehead. Take care after
7 miles to stay on the A396 at the Black Cat
filling station, and DO NOT go through
Dulverton. Turn left 100 yards beyond
Badgers Holt Pub in the centre of
Bridgetown.

## DULVERTON
**Exmoor House Caravan Club Site,**
Dulverton, Somerset, TA22 9HL
**Tel:** 01398 323268
www.caravanclub.co.uk
Pitches For ♚ ♞ Total 64
Facilities ⓑ ⸙ ⬚ ⬚ ⬚ ⌐ ⬚ ☎
⬚ ⬚ ⬚✚⬚
**Nearby Facilities** ✎
**Acreage** 4 **Open** March **to** Jan
**Access** Good **Site** Level
Quiet and pretty site with valley views. 200
yards from the village. Ideal base to
explore Exmoor National Park. Near the
Lorna Doone Trail, Dunster Castle and
Knightshayes Court. Non members
welcome. Booking essential.
**Nearest Town/Resort** Dulverton
**Directions** Leave M5 at junc 27 and take
A361 sp Barnstaple, after 6 miles at the
roundabout turn right onto A396. At
roundabout by Exeter Inn turn left so
Dulverton, at Black Cat junction on sharp left
hand bend bear right to crossroads and
continue straight on A396. After 2¾ miles by
Exebridge Petrol Station fork left onto B3222
after 3 miles turn left by the Bridge Inn, site
is 200 yards.

## DULVERTON
**Lakeside Caravan Club Site,** Higher
Grants, Exebridge, Dulverton, Somerset,
TA22 9BE
**Tel:** 01398 324068
www.caravanclub.co.uk
Pitches For ♚ ♞ Total 50
Facilities ⓑ ⸙ ⬚ ⬚ ⬚ ⌐ ⬚ ☎
⬚ ⬚ ⬚ ⬚✚⬚ ⬚ ⚡

# SOMERSET

**Nearby Facilities** ✓
**Acreage** 11 **Open** March **to** Oct
**Access** Good **Site** Level
Situated in a quiet village with lovely views towards Exmoor. Ideal for keen anglers. Within easy reach of Exmoor National Park and Lorna Doone country. Near Rosemoor Gardens, Dunkery Beacon and Dunster Castle. Non members welcome. Booking essential.
**Nearest Town/Resort** Dulverton
**Directions** Leave M5 at junc 27 and take A361 towards Barnstaple. After 6 miles at the roundabout turn right onto A396, at the roundabout by Exeter Inn turn left sp Dulverton. At Black Cat junction on sharp left hand bend keep right, at crossroads by Exebridge Petrol Station continue on A396. Site is 2½ miles on the left.

## EMBOROUGH

**Old Down Touring Park,** Old Down House, Emborough, Radstock, Nr BathSomerset, BA3 4SA
**Tel:** 01761 232355 **Fax:** 01761 232355
**Email:** olddown@talk21.com
www.olddowntouringpark.co.uk
**Pitches For** ▲ ⊟ **Total** 30
Facilities ∮ 🖽 🆙 ▲ ୮ ⊙ ⊒ ☎
🏵 🛇 🛎 🍴 ⤋ 🄳 🄴 🌣
**Nearby Facilities** ୮ ✓ ⚡
**Acreage** 4 **Open** March **to** November
**Access** Good **Site** Level
Convenient for Bath, Wells and the Mendip Hills.
**Nearest Town/Resort** Wells
**Directions** From Shepton Mallet head north on the A37 towards Bristol. After 6 miles turn right onto the B3139. Old Down Inn is on the left, site entrance is 50 yards along on your right.
⇌ Bath

## EXFORD

**Westermill Farm,** Exford, Exmoor, Somerset, TA24 7NJ
**Tel:** 01643 831238 **Fax:** 01643 831216
**Email:** cad@westermill.com
www.westermill.com
**Pitches For** ▲ ⊟ **Total** 60
Facilities 🆙 ▲ ୮ ⊙ ⊒ 🛲 🄾 ☎
🏵 🅸 🛇 🛎 🍴 🄳 🌣
**Nearby Facilities** ✓ ∪
**Acreage** 6 **Open** All Year
**Access** Good **Site** Level
Beautiful, secluded site beside a river for fishing, bathing and paddling. Fascinating 500 acre farm with Waymarked walks. Centre Exmoor National Park. Free hot showers. Camp fire areas. Log cottages and farmhouse cottage for hire. Holder of the Gold David Bellamy Award for Conservation.
**Nearest Town/Resort** Exford

**Directions** Leave Exford on the Porlock road. After ½ mile fork left, continue for 2 miles along valley until 'Westermill' is seen on a tree and fork left.
⇌ Taunton

## FROME

**Seven Acres Touring Caravan & Camping Park,** West Woodlands, Frome, Somerset, BA11 5EQ
**Tel:** 01373 464222
**Pitches For** ▲ ⊕ ⊟ **Total** 32
Facilities ઠ ∮ 🄷 🆙 ▲ ୮ ⊙ ⊒ ☎
🅸 🄰 🍴 🄳 🄴
**Nearby Facilities** ୮ ✓ ∪ ⚡
**Acreage** 7 **Open** March **to** October
**Access** Good **Site** Level
As seen on national television. Acres of level, landscaped grounds with a stream meandering through. On the outskirts of the Longleat Estate and within easy reach of Stourhead, Cheddar Caves and Stonehenge.
**Nearest Town/Resort** Frome
**Directions** From the Frome by-pass take the B3092 towards Maiden Bradley and Mere. Seven Acres is situated approx. 1 mile from the by-pass.
⇌ Frome

## GLASTONBURY

**Orchard Camping,** The Inn, Catcott Road, Burtle, Somerset, TA7 8NG
**Tel:** 01278 722269 **Fax:** 01278 722269
**Email:** chris@theburtleinn.co.uk
www.theburtleinn.co.uk
**Pitches For** ▲ **Total** 25
Facilities ઠ 🆙 ▲ ୮ ⊙ ⊒ ☎
🅸 🄰 🍴 🄼 🄳 🄴 🄳
**Nearby Facilities** ୮ ✓ ⚡ ⤋ ∪ ⚡ 🏃
**Acreage** 1 **Open** All Year
**Access** Good **Site** Level
Located in a cider apple orchard.
**Nearest Town/Resort** Burnham-on-Sea
⇌ Highbridge

## GLASTONBURY

**The Old Oaks Touring Park,** Wick Farm, Wick, Glastonbury, Somerset, BA6 8JS
**Tel:** 01458 831437
**Email:** info@theoldoaks.co.uk
www.theoldoaks.co.uk
**Pitches For** ▲ ⊟ **Total** 80
Facilities ઠ ∮ 🄵 🄷 🆙 ▲ ୮ ⊙ ⊒ 🛲 🄾 ☎
🏵 🛇 🛎 🍴 🄶 🄴 🄰 ⚡
**Nearby Facilities** ✓
**Acreage** 10 **Open** 18 March **to** 2 Oct
**Access** Good **Site** Level
An ADULT ONLY park set in tranquil, unspoilt countryside with panoramic views, lovely walks, spacious pitches and excellent amenities.
**Nearest Town/Resort** Glastonbury

**Directions** From Glastonbury take the A36 Shepton Mallet road. In 2 miles turn left signposted Wick 1, site is on the left in 1 mile.
⇌ Castle Cary

## HIGHBRIDGE

**Greenacre Place Touring Caravan Park,** Bristol Road, Edithmead, Highbridge, Somerset, TA9 4HA
**Tel:** 01278 785227
**Email:** sm.alderton@btopenworld.com
www.greenacreplace.com
**Pitches For** ⊕ ⊟ **Total** 10
Facilities ∮ 🆙 ▲ ୮ ⊙ ☎ 🅸 🄶 ⤋ 🄳 🄰
**Nearby Facilities** ୮ ✓ ⚡ ∪ ⚡ 🏃
**Acreage** 1 **Open** March **to** November
**Access** Good **Site** Level
ADULTS ONLY. Small, peaceful caravan park with easy access. Short drive to sandy beaches. Ideally placed for touring Somerset.
**Nearest Town/Resort** Burnham-on-Sea
**Directions** Just off the M5 junction 22.
⇌ Highbridge

## ILMINSTER

**Thornleigh Caravan Park,** Hanning Road, Horton, Ilminster, Somerset, TA19 9QH
**Tel:** 01460 53450 **Fax:** 01460 53450
**Email:** ken-shirl@supanet.com
www.thornleigh-cp.fsnet.co.uk
**Pitches For** ▲ ⊕ ⊟ **Total** 20
Facilities ઠ ∮ 🆙 ▲ ୮ ⊙ ⊒ ☎ 🅸 🆙 🄳 🄴
**Nearby Facilities** ୮
**Acreage** 1¼ **Open** March **to** October
**Access** Good **Site** Level
Flat site in a village location, ideal for touring Somerset and Devon. Sauna on site. Heated shower block. ½ hour drive to the south coast. 6 miles to Cricket St Thomas Wildlife Park. National Trust properties nearby. Restaurant and public telephone nearby. Ideal rally site with village hall close by.
**Nearest Town/Resort** Ilminster
**Directions** A303 West Ilminster, take the A358 signposted Chard. ¼ mile turn right signposted Horton and Broadway. Site on the left opposite the church, ¾ mile.
⇌ Crewkerne

## LANGPORT

**Bowdens Crest Caravan & Camping Park,** Bowdens, Langport, Somerset, TA10 0DD
**Tel:** 01458 250553 **Fax:** 01458 253360
**Email:** bowcrest@btconnect.com
www.bowdenscrest.co.uk
**Pitches For** ▲ ⊕ ⊟ **Total** 30
Facilities ઠ ∮ 🄷 🆙 ▲ ୮ ⊙ ⊒ 🛲 🄾 ☎
🏵 🛇 🛎 🍴 🄼 🄰 🄳 🄴 🄳 🌣
**Nearby Facilities** ୮ ✓ ⚡
**Acreage** 2½ **Open** All Year

**Access** Good **Site** Level
Tranquil countryside site overlooking
Somerset levels.
**Nearest Town/Resort** Langport
**Directions** On the A372 Langport to
Bridgwater road, 1½ miles out of Langport
turn right up the hill as signposted.
≠ Bridgwater

## LANGPORT

**Thorney Lakes Caravan Site,** Thorney
Farm, Muchelney, Langport, Somerset,
TA10 0DW
**Tel:** 01458 250811
**Pitches For** ▲ ⊞ ⊕ **Total** 36
**Facilities** ʃ �W ♣ ſ ⊙⊣ ☻➔⊞
**Nearby Facilities** ſ ✔
**Acreage** 7 **Open** March to November
**Access** Good **Site** Level
Site is an orchard on Somerset Moors.
Ideal for walking and cycling.
**Nearest Town/Resort** Langport
**Directions** Turn off the A303 dual
carriageway signposted Martock, Ash and
Kingsbury Episcopi. Follow signs to
Kingsbury Episcopi, at the T-Junction in the
village turn right, site is 1 mile on the right.
≠ Yeovil/Taunton

## MARTOCK

**Southfork Caravan Park,** Parrett Works,
Martock, Somerset', TA12 6AE
**Tel:** 01935 825661 **Fax:** 01935 825122
**Email:** southforkcaravans@btconnect.com
**www.**ukparks.co.uk/southfork
**Pitches For** ▲ ⊞ **Total** 25
**Facilities** ʃ W ♣ ſ ⊙⊣ ☻ ⊞ ☻
☍ ⊕ ☻ Д ➔⊞ ☻
**Nearby Facilities** ſ ✔ ♣
**Acreage** 2 **Open** All Year
**Access** Good **Site** Level
Set in open countryside near River Parrett.
Numerous places of interest nearby for all

age groups. Ideal base for touring. 3 new
holiday homes and 3 static caravans for
hire. ETC 4 Star Graded.
**Nearest Town/Resort** Martock/Yeovil
**Directions** Situated 2 miles north west of
A303 (between Ilchester and Ilminster). From
A303 east of Ilminster, at roundabout take
first exit signposted South Petherton and
follow camping signs. From A303 west of
Ilchester, after Cartgate roundabout (junction
with A3088 to Yeovil) take exit signposted
Martock and follow camping signs.
≠ Yeovil

## MINEHEAD

**Butlins Minehead,** Warren Road,
Minehead, Somerset, TA24 5SH
**Tel:** 01643 703331
**www.**butlins.com
**Pitches For** ⊕□ **Total** 70
**Facilities** ♿ ʃ ⊟ ☳ W ♣ ſ ⊙⊣ ☻ ☎ ☻
⊠ ☻ ✖ ☐ W ♠ Д ╲ ⚓ ➔☐⊞ ☀
**Nearby Facilities** ſ ✔ ⚓ ↖ ∪ ♪ ♣ ♣
**Open** All Year
**Access** Good **Site** Level
An all Butlins resort.
**Nearest Town/Resort** Minehead
**Directions** Well signposted.
≠ Taunton

## MINEHEAD

**Camping & Caravanning Club Site,** Hill
Road, North Hill, Minehead, Somerset,
TA24 5LB
**Tel:** 01643 704138
**www.**campingandcaravanningclub.co.uk
**Pitches For** ▲ ⊞ **Total** 60
**Facilities** ʃ ⊟ W ♣ ſ ⊙⊣ ☻ ☎ ☻
⊠ ☻ ☻➔⊞ ☀
**Nearby Facilities** ſ ✔ ⚓ ↖ ∪ ♣
**Acreage** 3¾ **Open** April to Oct
**Access** Poor **Site** Sloping
In Exmoor National Park with fine views of

the town of Minehead. Sloping site, chocks
required. BTB 4 Star Graded and AA 3
Pennants. Non members welcome.
**Nearest Town/Resort** Minehead
**Directions** From the A39 head towards the
town centre, in the main street turn opposite
W.H.Smith into Blenheim Road, after 50
yards turn left again. Go up the hill and left
around a hairpin bend, turn right at the
cottages. Go past the church on the right and
continue round two bends, site is on the right.
≠ Minehead

## MINEHEAD

**Hoburne Blue Anchor,** Blue Anchor Bay,
Nr Minehead, Somerset, TA24 6JT
**Tel:** 01643 821360 **Fax:** 01643 821572
**Email:** enquiries@hoburne.com
**www.**hoburne.com
**Pitches For** ⊕ ⊞ **Total** 103
**Facilities** ʃ ⊟ W ♣ ſ ⊙⊣ ☻ ☎ ☻ ☻
⊠ ☻ ☻ Д ⊕ ⊟ ☻
**Nearby Facilities** ſ ✔ ⚓ ↖ ∪ ♪ ♣
**Acreage** 29 **Open** March to October
**Access** Good **Site** Level
On waters edge, an ideal base from which
to explore Exmoor and this beautiful
coastline.
**Nearest Town/Resort** Minehead
**Directions** Leave the M5 at junction 25 and
take the A358 signposted Minehead. After
approx 12 miles, at Carhampton, turn left
onto the B3191 signposted Blue Anchor. Park
is 1½ miles on the right.
≠ Minehead

SOMERSET ENTRIES
CONTINUE ON PAGE 168

## MINEHEAD
**Minehead & Exmoor Caravan Park,**
Porlock Road, Minehead, Somerset, TA24 8SW
**Tel:** 01643 703074
**Pitches For** ▲ ⚑ ⚑ **Total** 50
**Facilities** ⚒ ∮ ⑩ ♨ ⌂ ☉ ⌣ ⚍ ⚑
⚏ ⚉ ⚑ ⚑ ⌂ ⚏ ⚞ ⚲
**Nearby Facilities** ⌂ ✦ ⚓ ⚵ ∪ ⚘
**Acreage** 3 **Open** 1 March **to** 1 Nov
**Access** Good **Site** Level/Terraced
1 mile from the centre of Minehead, near the beach and all local attractions.
**Nearest Town/Resort** Minehead
**Directions** 1 mile west of the centre of Minehead, official signposts on the A39.
⚍ Minehead

## MINEHEAD
**St. Audries Bay Holiday Club,** West Quantoxhead, Minehead, Somerset, TA4 4DY
**Tel:** 01984 632515 **Fax:** 01984 632785
**Email:** mrandle@staudriesbay.co.uk
www.staudriesbay.co.uk
**Pitches For** ▲ ⚑ ⚑ **Total** 20
**Facilities** ⚒ ∮ ⑩ ♨ ⌂ ☉ ⌣ ⚍ ⚑ ⚑
⚏ ⚑ ✗ ⚎ ⑩ ⚑ ⚑ ⚞ ⚏ ⌂ ⚑
**Nearby Facilities** ⌂ ✦ ⚵ ∪ ⚘
**Acreage** 12 **Open** Easter **to** Oct
**Access** Good **Site** Level
Near the beach with lovely views across the sea. Friendly family run site. Family entertainment during school holidays.
**Nearest Town/Resort** Minehead
**Directions** 15 miles from the M5 junction 23, off the A39. 15 miles from Taunton, follow the A358 to Williton then the A39.
⚍ Taunton

## PORLOCK
**Burrowhayes Farm Caravan & Camping Site & Riding Stables,** West Luccombe, Porlock, Nr Minehead, Somerset, TA24 8HT
**Tel:** 01643 862463
**Email:** info@burrowhayes.co.uk
www.burrowhayes.co.uk
**Pitches For** ▲ ⚑ ⚑ **Total** 140
**Facilities** ⚒ ∮ ⑩ ♨ ⌂ ☉ ⌣ ⚍ ⚑ ⚑
⚏ ⚑ ⚉ ⚑ ⚑ ⌂ ⚞ ⚏
**Nearby Facilities** ⌂ ✦ ⚓ ⚵ ⚘
**Acreage** 8 **Open** 15 March **to** 31 October
**Access** Good **Site** Lev/Slope
Real family site set in glorious National Trust scenery on Exmoor. Ideal for walking. Riding stables on site.
**Nearest Town/Resort** Minehead
**Directions** 5 miles west of Minehead on A39, left hand turning to West Luccombe, site ¼ mile on the right.
⚍ Taunton

## PORLOCK
**Porlock Caravan Park,** Highbank, Porlock, Nr Minehead, Somerset, TA24 8ND
**Tel:** 01643 862269 **Fax:** 01643 862269
**Email:** info@porlockcaravanpark.co.uk
www.porlockcaravanpark.co.uk
**Pitches For** ▲ ⚑ ⚑ **Total** 40
**Facilities** ∮ ⚑ ⑩ ♨ ⌂ ☉ ⌣ ⚑ ⚑
⚏ ⚉ ⚑ ⚑ ⚞ ⚲
**Nearby Facilities** ⌂ ✦ ⚵ ∪ ⚘
**Acreage** 3½ **Open** Mid March **to** October
**Access** Good **Site** Level
Scenic views, Ideal touring and walking.
**Nearest Town/Resort** Minehead
**Directions** A39 from Minehead to Lynton, take the B3225 in Porlock to Porlock Weir. Site signposted.
⚍ Taunton

## SHEPTON MALLET
**Greenacres Camping,** Barrow Lane, North Wootton, Nr Shepton Mallet, Somerset, BA4 4HL
**Tel:** 01749 890497
**Pitches For** ▲ ⚑ **Total** 30
**Facilities** ∮ ⑩ ♨ ⌂ ☉ ⌣ ⚍ ⚑ ⚏ ⚑ ⚑ ⚑
**Nearby Facilities** ⌂ ✦ ∪
**Acreage** 4¼ **Open** April **to** October
**Site** Level
An award winning family site. Peacefully set within sight of Glastonbury Tor. Some electric hook-ups available.
**Nearest Town/Resort** Wells
**Directions** From Wells take the A39, tur left at Brownes Garden Centre. Sit signposted in the village.
⚍ Castle Cary

## SHEPTON MALLET
**Manleaze Caravan Park,** 4 Cannards Grave, Shepton Mallet, Somerset, BA4 4LY
**Tel:** 01749 342404
**Pitches For** ▲ ⚑ ⚑
**Facilities** ∮ ⑩ ⌂ ☉ ⚞ ⚑
**Nearby Facilities** ⌂
**Acreage** 1 **Open** All Year
**Access** Good **Site** Level
**Nearest Town/Resort** Shepton Mallet
⚍ Castle Cary

## SHEPTON MALLET
**Phippens Farm,** Stoke St Michael, Radstock, Somerset, BA3 5JH
**Tel:** 01749 840395
**Email:** jennifer@francis1973.freeserve.co.uk
**Pitches For** ▲ ⚑ ⚑ ⚑ **Total** 20
**Facilities** ∮ ⑩ ⌂ ⚞ ⚏

# Burrowhayes Farm
## Caravan & Camping Site & Riding Stables

**West Luccombe, Porlock, Near Minehead, Somerset TA24 8HT    Tel: 01643 862463**

- Popular family site in a delightful National Trust setting on Exmoor, just 2 miles from the coast. • Surrounding moors and woods provide a walkers paradise and children can play and explore safely.
- Riding Stables offer pony trekking for all abilities.
- New heated shower block with disabled and baby changing facilities, launderette and pot wash. • Sites for Touring Caravans, Tents & Motorhomes with 16 amp hook-ups. • Caravan Holiday Homes for Hire.

*In the heart of Exmoor Country*    E-mail: info@burrowhayes.co.uk    www.burrowhayes.co.uk

---

**Nearby Facilities**
**Acreage** 4 **Open** March **to** October
Quiet farm site. 2 hard standings available.
**Nearest Town/Resort** Shepton Mallet
**Directions** From Bath take the A367 towards Shepton Mallet for 14 miles, turn left in Oakhill, 1 mile. Or from Bristol take the A37, turn left onto the A367 then right in Oakhill.
✠ Castle Cary

## SPARKFORD
**Long Hazel International Caravan & Camping Park,** High Street, Sparkford, Nr Yeovil, Somerset, BA22 7JH
**Tel:** 01963 440002 **Fax:** 01963 440002
**Email:** longhazelpark@hotmail.com
www.sparkford.f9.co.uk/lhi.htm
**Pitches For** ▲ ⊕ ⬛ **Total** 75
**Facilities** & ∱ 🅗 🆄 ♣ ⌐ ⊙ ⌐ 🔲 ☎
⊕ 🔳 ⬛ ✖ 🄳 ☀
**Nearby Facilities** ⌐ ✔ ∪
**Acreage** 3½ **Open** 16 Feb **to** 16 Jan
**Access** Good **Site** Level
Full disabled shower unit. Near to an inn and restaurant. Ideal for touring or an overnight halt. Haynes Motor Museum and Fleet Air Arm Museum nearby. 3 static caravans available, one pine lodge for hire and 12 pine lodges for sale as second holiday homes.
**Nearest Town/Resort** Yeovil/Sherborne
**Directions** From Wincanton take the A303 to the end of Sparkford by-pass. At the roundabout turn left into Sparkford Village, site is approx. 400 yards on the left.
✠ Yeovil/Sherborne/Castle Cary

## STREET
**Bramble Hill Camping Site,** Bramble Hill, Walton, Nr Street, Somerset, BA16 9RQ
**Tel:** 01458 442548
www.caravancampingsites.co.uk
**Pitches For** ▲ ⊕ ⬛
**Facilities** ✖ ∱ 🅗 ⬛ ♣ ⌐ ⊙ ⌐ ☎ 🄳 ☀ ₽
**Nearby Facilities** ⌐ ✔ ∪
**Acreage** 3½ **Open** April **to** September
**Access** Good **Site** Level
Quiet site. Dogs are welcome on leads only. Ideal site for visiting Clarks Village - 1 mile. Near to Sainsburys, restaurants and swimming pools (1 mile).
**Nearest Town/Resort** Street
**Directions** A39 1 mile from Street, 2 miles from Glastonbury.
✠ Castle Cary/Taunton

## TAUNTON
**Ashe Farm Caravan & Camp Site,** Ashe Farm, Thornfalcon, Taunton, Somerset, TA3 5NW
**Tel:** 01823 442567 **Fax:** 01823 443372
**Email:** camping@ashe-farm.fsnet.co.uk

**Pitches For** ▲ ⊕ ⬛ **Total** 30
**Facilities** ∱ 🅗 🆄 ♣ ⌐ ⊙ ⌐ ⚄ 🔲 ☎
🄸 ⊕ ♣ 🄳 🄴 ☀
**Nearby Facilities** ⌐ ✔ ∪ ₽
**Acreage** 7 **Open** April **to** October
**Access** Good **Site** Level
Ideal touring centre, easy reach of Quantock and Blackdown Hills.
**Nearest Town/Resort** Taunton
**Directions** 4 miles southeast Taunton on A358, turn right at 'Nags Head' towards West Hatch, ¼ mile on right.
✠ Taunton

## TAUNTON
**Cornish Farm Touring Park,** Cornish Farm, Shoreditch, Taunton, Somerset, TA3 7BS
**Tel:** 01823 327746 **Fax:** 01823 354946
**Email:** info@cornishfarm.co.uk
www.cornishfarm.com
**Pitches For** ▲ ⊕☐ **Total** 50
**Facilities** & ∱ 🅗 🆄 ♣ ⌐ ⊙ ⌐ 🔲 ☎
🄸 ✖ 🄳 🄴
**Nearby Facilities** ⌐ ₽
**Acreage** 3½ **Open** All Year
**Access** Good **Site** Level
Excellent facilities. Ideal touring park. Good for the racecourse and Somerset County Cricket Ground. AA 3 Pennants.
**Nearest Town/Resort** Taunton
**Directions** Leave the M5 at junction 25, at first traffic lights turn left, turn third left into Ilminster Road. At the roundabout turn right, next roundabout turn left, at the T-Junction follow brown tourism signs to the site. Total of 3 miles from the M5.
✠ Taunton

## TAUNTON
**Holly Bush Park,** Culmhead, Taunton, Somerset, TA3 7EA
**Tel:** 01823 421515
**Email:** info@hollybushpark.com
www.hollybushpark.com
**Pitches For** ▲ ⊕ ⬛ **Total** 40
**Facilities** ∱ 🅗 🆄 ♣ ⌐ ⊙ ⌐ 🔲 ☎
🄢 ⊕ ♣ 🄳 🄴 ☀ ₽
**Nearby Facilities** ⌐ ✔ ∪ ₽
**Acreage** 2¼ **Open** All Year
**Access** Good **Site** Level
Area of Outstanding Natural Beauty.
**Nearest Town/Resort** Taunton
**Directions** From Taunton follow signs for the Racecourse and Corfe on the B3170, 3½ miles from Corfe turn right at crossroads towards Wellington. Turn right at the next T-Junction, site is 200yds on the left.
✠ Taunton

## TAUNTON
**Tanpits Farm Caravan & Camp Site,** Dyers Lane, Bathpool, Taunton, Somerset, TA2 8BZ
**Tel:** 01823 270663 **Fax:** 01823 270663
**Pitches For** ▲ ⊕ ⬛ **Total** 20
**Facilities** & ∱ 🅗 🆄 ♣ ⌐ ⊙ ⌐ 🄳 🄴 ✖
**Nearby Facilities** ✔
**Acreage** 1 **Open** March **to** Nov
**Access** Good **Site** Level
Within walking distance of pubs, a cinema, bowling anf supermarkets. Near to the Quantock Hills for walking.
**Nearest Town/Resort** Taunton
✠ Taunton

## TAUNTON
**Waterrow Touring Park,** Waterrow, Wiveliscombe, Taunton, Somerset, TA4 2AZ
**Tel:** 01984 623464 **Fax:** 01984 624280
www.waterrowpark.co.uk
**Pitches For** ▲ ⊕ ⬛ **Total** 45
**Facilities** & ∱ 🄵 🅗 🆄 ♣ ⌐ ⊙ ⌐ ⚄ 🔲 ☎
⊕ ✖ 🄳 ⬛ ☀
**Nearby Facilities** ⌐ ✔ ⚓ ∪ ₽
**Acreage** 8 **Open** All Year
**Access** Good **Site** Sloping
EXCLUSIVELY FOR ADULTS. In a peaceful, attractive location alongside the River Tone with a woodland river walk. New heated facilities. Good pub nearby. Watercolour painting holidays. Day kennels. Ideal touring base.
**Nearest Town/Resort** Taunton
**Directions** Leave the M5 at junction 25 and take the A358 signposted Minehead. Then take the B3227 signposted Wiveliscombe, 3 miles after Wiveliscombe you will pass the Rock Pub, the park is on the left within 300 yards.
✠ Taunton/Tiverton

## WELLINGTON
**Cadeside Caravan Club Site,** Nynehead Road, Wellington, Somerset, TA21 9HN
**Tel:** 01823 663103
www.caravanclub.co.uk
**Pitches For** ⊕ ⬛ **Total** 17
**Facilities** ∱ 🄸 🄲 ⊕ ✖ 🄳 ⬛ ₽
**Nearby Facilities** ⌐
**Acreage** 4¾
**Access** Good **Site** Level
Rural site with countryside views. Surrounded by Quantock Hills, Brendon Hills and Blackdown Hills. Open March and then all year. Non members welcome. Booking essential.
**Nearest Town/Resort** Wellington
**Directions** Leave the M5 at junction 26 and take the A38 signposted Wellington, at roundabout turn onto the B3187 signposted Wellington. After ½ mile turn right signposted Nynehead, site is 80 yards on the right.

# SOMERSET

## WELLINGTON

**Gamlins Farm Caravan Park,** Gamlins
Farmhouse, Greenham, Wellington,
Somerset, TA21 0LZ
**Tel:** 01823 672859 **Fax:** 01823 672859
**Pitches For** ▲ ⊞ ⊟ **Total** 25
**Facilities** ∫ 🅗 🆄 ▲ ୮ ☉ ⊐ ◢ ◨ ☂
🅘⊁⊡ ♪
**Nearby Facilities** ୮ ✔ ∪
**Acreage** 3 **Open** Easter **to** September
**Access** Good **Site** Level
Scenic valley setting with a Free coarse
fishing lake. Half an hour from the coast.
Ideal for touring, Exmoor, Quantocks and
The Blackdowns. You can also telephone
us on mobile: 07986 832516.
**Nearest Town/Resort** Wellington
**Directions** Take the M5 to junction 26
Wellington, then take the A38 towards
Tiverton and Exeter. On the dual carriageway
turn right to Greenham, go over two sets of
crossroads, round a bend and the site is on
the right.
⇌ Taunton/Tiverton

## WELLS

**Cheddar Camping & Caravanning Club
Site,** Mendip Heights, Townsend, Priddy,
WellsSomerset, BA5 3BP
**Tel:** 01749 870241
www.campingandcaravanningclub.co.uk
**Pitches For** ▲ ⊞ ⊟ **Total** 90
**Facilities** ∫ 🅗 🆄 ▲ ୮ ☉ ⊐ ◢ ◨ ☂
🆂🅘 ☉ 🅐 🅜⊁⊡ ⊟ ⅀ ♪
**Nearby Facilities** ✔ ∪
**Acreage** 4½ **Open** March **to** Nov
**Access** Good **Site** Lev/Slope
Situated in a designated area of
outstanding natural beauty, in the heart of
the Mendip Hills. Non members welcome.
**Nearest Town/Resort** Wells
**Directions** From Wells take the A39 north
east for 3½ miles, then take the B3135
towards Cheddar for 4½ miles. Signposted
¼ mile north west of Priddy.

## WELLS

**Haybridge Caravan Park,** Haybridge Farm,
Haybridge, Wells, Somerset, BA5 1AJ
**Pitches For** ▲ ⊞ ⊟ **Total** 35
**Facilities** ⊟ ▲ ୮ ☉ ☂
**Nearby Facilities** ୮ ✔ ∪
**Acreage** 4 **Open** All Year
**Access** Good **Site** Lev/Slope
Close to Wells and Wookey Hole Caves,
ideal touring position.
**Nearest Town/Resort** Wells
**Directions** On the main A371 Wells to
Cheddar road, just outside the Wells
boundary.
⇌ Bristol

## WELLS

**Homestead Park,** Wookey Hole, Wells,
Somerset, BA5 1BW
**Tel:** 01749 673022
**Email:** enquiries@homesteadpark.co.uk
www.homesteadpark.co.uk
**Pitches For** ▲ ⊞ ⊟ **Total** 30
**Facilities** ∫ 🆄 ▲ ୮ ☉ ☂ 🅘 ☉ 🅐⊁⊡ ⊠A
**Nearby Facilities** ୮ ✔ ∪
**Acreage** 2 **Open** Easter **to** October

**Access** Good **Site** Level
ADULTS ONLY - Sorry no children.
Sheltered site on the banks of the River
Axe. Ideal for Wookey Hole Caves,
National Trust sites, Mendip Hills, walking
and climbing. Leisure centre nearby.
**Nearest Town/Resort** Wells
**Directions** Leave Wells by A371 towards
Cheddar, turn right for Wookey Hole. Site 1¼
miles on left in village.
⇌ Bristol/Bath

## WESTON-SUPER-MARE

**Country View Holiday Park,** Sand Road,
Sand Bay, Weston-super-Mare, Somerset,
BS22 9UJ
**Tel:** 01934 627595
**Pitches For** ▲ ⊞ ⊟ **Total** 120
**Facilities** ⚲ ∫ 🅗 🆄 ▲ ୮ ☉ ⊐ ◢ ◨ ☂
⅀ 🅘 ☉ 🅐 🆅 🅜 ⅂⊁⊡ ☼ ♪
**Nearby Facilities** ୮ ✔ ⚓ ∪ ⇗ 🏃 ⚘
**Acreage** 10 **Open** March **to** 31 Jan
**Access** Good **Site** Level
Near the beach.
**Nearest Town/Resort** Weston-super-Mare
**Directions** Leave the M5 at junction 21,
follow signs to Sand Bay along The
Queensway into Lower Norton Lane, turn
right into Sand Road.
⇌ Weston-super-Mare

## WESTON-SUPER-MARE

**Dulhorn Farm Holiday Park,** Weston
Road, Lympsham, Weston-super-Mare,
North Somerset, BS24 0JQ
**Tel:** 01934 750298 **Fax:** 01934 750913
**Pitches For** ▲ ⊞ ⊟
**Facilities** ∫ 🆄 ▲ ୮ ☉ ⊐ ◢ ☂ 🅐⊁⊡ ☼
**Nearby Facilities** ୮ ✔ ⚓ ∪ ⇗ 🏃 ⚘
**Open** March **to** Oct
**Access** Good **Site** Level
Midway between Weston-super-Mare and
Burnham-on-Sea. Ideal for beaches,
touring and fishing.
**Nearest Town/Resort** Weston-super-Mare
**Directions** Leave the M5 at junction 22 and
take the A38 towards Bristol. At the next
roundabout take the A370 to Weston-super-
Mare, site is on the left approx. 1¼ miles after
the traffic lights.
⇌ Weston-super-Mare

## WESTON-SUPER-MARE

**Sand Farm,** Sand Farm Lane, Sand Bay,
Weston-super-Mare, Somerset, BS22 9UF
**Tel:** 01934 620995
**Pitches For** ▲ ⊞◻ **Total** 11
**Facilities** ⚲ ∫ 🆄 ▲ ୮ ☉ ☂ ♣⊁⊡ ☼
**Nearby Facilities** ୮ ✔ ⚓ ∪ ⇗ 🏃 ⚘
**Acreage** 1¼ **Open** Easter **to** Oct
**Access** Good **Site** Level
Quiet, farm site, 100 yards from the beach.
Ideal for touring and walking. Regular
(open top) bus service to W-S-M, 2½ miles
from the town centre. Static caravans
available for hire. Ralleys welcome. 'Bring
Your Horse On Holiday', stables available.
You can also contact us on Mobile: 07949
969722.
**Nearest Town/Resort** Weston-super-Mare
**Directions** Leave the M5 at junction 21 and
head towards W-S-M, then take the slip road

for Sand Bay. Follow all signs to Sand Bay
until the beach is in front of you, turn right
into Beach Road then next right into Sand
Farm Lane.
⇌ Weston-super-Mare

## WESTON-SUPER-MARE

**West End Farm Caravan & Camping
Park,** Locking, Weston-super-Mare,
Somerset, BS24 8RH
**Tel:** 01934 822529
**Pitches For** ▲ ⊞ ⊟
**Facilities** ∫ 🅗 🆄 ▲ ୮ ☉ ⊐ ◢
◨ ☂ 🅘 ☉ 🅐 🅜⊁⊡ ⊟ ☼
**Nearby Facilities** ୮ ✔ ⚓ ∪ ⇗ 🏃 ⚘
**Access** Good **Site** Level
Ideal for touring.
**Directions** Leave the M5 at junction 21 and
follow signs for Weston-super-Mare, follow
the signs for International Helicopter Museum
and turn right immediately after Helicopter
Museum and follow signs for site.
⇌ Weston-super-Mare

## WESTON-SUPER-MARE

**Weston Gateway Tourist Park,** Westwick,
Weston-super-Mare, Somerset, BS24 7TF
**Tel:** 01934 510344 **Fax:** 01934 511978
**Pitches For** ▲ ⊞ ⊟ **Total** 175
**Facilities** ⚲ ∫ 🆄 ▲ ୮ ☉ ⊐ ◢ ◨ ☂
🅘 ☉ 🅐 🆅 🅜 ⅂⊁⊡ ☼
**Nearby Facilities** ୮ ✔ ⚓ ∪ ⇗ 🏃 ⚘
**Acreage** 15 **Open** End March **to** End Oct
**Access** Good **Site** Level
Ideal, sheltered park with many famous
tourist attractions within easy driving
distance. No singles and no commercial
vehicles. Open weekends only during April
and October.
**Nearest Town/Resort** Weston-super-Mare
**Directions** From the M5 junction 21, follow
signs for Westwick approx. ¾ miles. From
Weston-super-Mare take the A370 to the
motorway interchange then follow signs to
Westwick.
⇌ Weston-super-Mare

## WILLITON

**Home Farm Holiday Centre,** St Audries
Bay, Williton, Somerset, TA4 4DP
**Tel:** 01984 632487 **Fax:** 01984 634687
**Email:**
mike@homefarmholidaycentre.co.uk
www.homefarmholidaycentre.co.uk
**Pitches For** ▲ ⊞ ⊟ **Total** 40
**Facilities** ∫ 🅗 🆄 ▲ ୮ ☉ ⊐ ◢ ◨ ☂
⅀ 🅘 ☉ 🅐 🆅 🅜 ⅂⊁⊡ ☼
**Nearby Facilities** ୮ ✔ ⚓
**Open** All Year
**Access** Good **Site** Terraced
Private beach, good base for touring
Exmoor. 2 miles from West Somerset
Railway. Holiday caravans and chalets for
hire.
**Nearest Town/Resort** Williton / Watchet
**Directions** Leave M5 at Junction 23, follow
A39 towards Minehead for 17 miles. At West
Quantoxhead take first right turn after St.
Audries Garages (signposted Blue Anchor,
Doniford and Watchet) B3191 take first right
turning in ½ mile to our drive.
⇌ Taunton

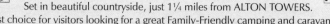

# The Star Caravan & Camping Park
## The Closest Touring Park to Alton Towers!

Set in beautiful countryside, just 1¼ miles from ALTON TOWERS.
First choice for visitors looking for a great Family-Friendly camping and caravanning experience. The Star offers excellent value and good facilities in the best location.

Loo of the Year Award 5 Stars ✦ Free hot showers ✦ Disabled Shower with parking outside ✦ Launderette
Children's Play Area ✦ Milk, Tea, Coffee & Sugar on sale ✦ Electric Hook-ups
Waste Disposal ✦ Calor Gas & Camping Gaz sales ✦ 300 yards from a Pub & Restaurant

LOO OF THE YEAR 2005 ★★★★★

Nr. Alton Towers • Stoke-on-Trent • Staffordshire • ST10 3DW
Bookings: 01538 702219     www.starcaravanpark.co.uk

## WINCANTON

**Wincanton Racecourse Caravan Club Site,** Wincanton, Somerset, BA9 8BJ
**Tel:** 01963 34276
www.caravanclub.co.uk
**Pitches For** ▲ ⊟ ⚬ **Total** 57
**Facilities** ⚭ ╏ ▥ ⚑ ⌐ ▣ ▯ ⊙ ⛟ ▥⤬▣ ▢
**Nearby Facilities** ⌐
**Acreage** 5 **Open** March **to** Oct
**Access** Good **Site** Level
Attractive site with beautiful views of Bruton Forest and the Downs. Close to Stourhead House, Hadspen Garden and Haynes Motor Museum. 9 hole Pay & Play golf adjacent, discounts available. Non members welcome. Booking essential.
**Nearest Town/Resort** Wincanton
**Directions** From east on the A303 take the B3081 signposted Wincanton Racecourse, follow signs for the racecourse through Charlton Musgrove. At junction turn left signposted racecourse, site is 1½ miles on the right.
➹ Wincanton

## WINSFORD

**Halse Farm Caravan & Tent Park,** Halse Farm, Winsford, Exmoor, Somerset, TA24 7JL
**Tel:** 01643 851259 **Fax:** 01643 851592
**Email:** cad@halsefarm.co.uk
www.halsefarm.co.uk
**Pitches For** ▲ ⊟ ⚬ **Total** 44
**Facilities** ⚭ ╏ ▥ ▥ ⚑ ⌐ ⊙ ⛟ ⚑ ▢ ▢
**Nearby Facilities** ✓ ∪ ♪
**Acreage** 3 **Open** 19 March **to** 31 October
**Access** Good **Site** Lev/Slope
In Exmoor National Park, on working farm with beautiful views. For those who enjoy peaceful countryside. Quality heated toilet block and FREE showers. David Bellamy Gold Award for Conservation and ETC 4 Star Graded.
**Nearest Town/Resort** Dulverton
**Directions** Signposted from the A396 Tiverton to Minehead road. In Winsford take small road in front of Royal Oak Inn. 1 mile up hill and over cattle grid, our entrance is immediately on the left.
➹ Taunton

---

**PLEASE REMEMBER, BOOKING IS ALWAYS ADVISABLE IN PEAK SEASON**

---

# STAFFORDSHIRE

## ALTON

**Star Caravan & Camping Park,** Nr Alton Towers, Stoke-on-Trent, Staffordshire, ST10 3DW
**Tel:** 01538 702219
www.starcaravanpark.co.uk
**Pitches For** ▲ ⊟ ⚬ **Total** 188
**Facilities** ⚭ ╏ ▥ ▥ ⚑ ⌐ ⊙ ⛟ ⚑ ▢ ▯
▯ ▣ ▢ ✕ ▥⤬▣ ⚬
**Nearby Facilities** ⌐ ✓ ⚤ ∪ ♪ ⚻
**Acreage** 50 **Open** March **to** Oct
**Access** Good **Site** Lev/Slope
Situated in the centre of beautiful countryside within 9 miles of Leek, Uttoxeter and Ashbourne Town. Within easy reach of the Peak District and Dovedale. Cafe/Restaurant nearby. 6 static caravans for hire. Disabled toilet/shower facilities. Motorcycles are welcome. Pets must be kept on leads at all times. AA 3 Pennants and ETB 4 Star Graded.
**Nearest Town/Resort** Cheadle
**Directions** Situated off the B5417, 1¼ miles from Alton Towers.
➹ Stoke

## BURTON-ON-TRENT

**Willowbrook Farm,** Alrewas, Burton-on-Trent, Staffordshire, DE13 7BA
**Tel:** 01283 790217
**Pitches For** ▲ ⊟ ⚬ **Total** 10
**Facilities** ╏ ▥ ⌐ ⚑ ⛟ ▣ ▥⤬▣
**Nearby Facilities** ⌐ ✓
**Acreage** 4 **Open** All Year
**Access** Good **Site** Level
Alongside the River Trent and lakes. Near the National Memorial Arboretum.
**Nearest Town/Resort** Burton-on-Trent/Lichfield
**Directions** 6 miles from Burton-on-Trent on the A38 southbound, on the A38 side of the River Trent.
➹ Burton-on-Trent/Lichfield

## CANNOCK

**Camping & Caravanning Club Site,** Old Youth Hostel, Wandon, Rugeley, Staffordshire, WS15 1QW
**Tel:** 01889 582166
www.campingandcaravanningclub.co.uk
**Pitches For** ▲ ⊟ ⚬ **Total** 60
**Facilities** ⚭ ╏ ▥ ▥ ⚑ ⌐ ⊙ ⛟ ⚑ ▢ ▯
▯ ▣ ⚑⤬▣ ▢ ✕ ⚬
**Nearby Facilities** ⌐ ✓ ∪ ♪
**Acreage** 5 **Open** March **to** October
**Site** Sloping
On the edge of Cannock Chase. 12 miles from Drayton Manor Park. BTB 4 Star Graded and AA 3 Pennants. Non members welcome.

---

**Directions** Take the A460 to Hednesford, turn right at signpost Rawnsley/Hazelslade, then turn first left, site is ½ mile past the golf club.
➹ Rugeley Town

## LEEK

**Blackshaw Moor Caravan Club Site,** Leek, Staffordshire, ST13 8TW
**Tel:** 01538 300203
www.caravanclub.co.uk
**Pitches For** ⊟ ⚬ **Total** 89
**Facilities** ⚭ ╏ ▥ ▥ ⚑ ⌐ ▣ ⚬
▯ ▣ ▥⤬▣ ⚬
**Nearby Facilities** ⌐ ✓ ⚤ ⚻
**Acreage** 8½ **Open** March **to** Oct
**Access** Good **Site** Level
Situated on the edge of the Peak District with lovely views and walks. Just a short walk from Tittesworth Reservoir & Nature Reserve. Only 9 miles from Alton Towers. Non members welcome. Booking essential.
**Nearest Town/Resort** Leek
**Directions** From Leek take the A53, site is on the right ¼ mile past the Three Horseshoes Inn.
➹ Leek

## LEEK

**Camping & Caravanning Club Site,** Blackshaw Grange, Blackshaw Moor, Leek, Staffordshire, ST13 8TL
**Tel:** 01538 300285
www.campingandcaravanningclub.co.uk
**Pitches For** ▲ ⊟ ⚬ **Total** 70
**Facilities** ⚭ ╏ ▥ ▥ ⚑ ⌐ ⊙ ⛟ ⚑ ▢ ▯
▯ ▣ ▥⤬▣ ▢ ✕
**Nearby Facilities** ⌐ ✓ ⚻
**Acreage** 6 **Open** All Year
**Site** Lev/Slope
On the edge of the Peak District. Ideal for visiting Alton Towers. BTB 4 Star Graded and AA 3 Pennants. Non members welcome.
**Directions** Just 2 miles from Leek on the A53 Leek to Buxton road. The site is located 200 yards past the sign for 'Blackshaw Moor' on the left hand side.
➹ Buxton

## LEEK

**Glencote Caravan Park,** Station Road, Nr Leek, Staffordshire, ST13 7EE
**Tel:** 01538 360745 **Fax:** 01538 361788
**Email:** canistay@glencote.co.uk
www.glencote.co.uk
**Pitches For** ▲ ⊟ ⚬ **Total** 70
**Facilities** ╏ ▥ ▥ ⚑ ⌐ ⊙ ⚑ ▢ ⚬
⊙ ▣ ▥⤬▣ ▢ ✕
**Nearby Facilities**
**Acreage** 6 **Open** March **to** Oct
**Access** Good **Site** Level

**Enjoy the beautiful Churnet Valley**  **01538 360745**

Canalside pubs nearby. Ideal location for walkers. Fishing on site.
Central for The Potteries, Alton Towers, Staffordshire Moorlands
and the Peak District National Park.

**Glencote Caravan Park**  Station Road • Cheddleton • Leek • Staffs • ST13 7EE

www.glencote.co.uk  E-mail: canistay@glencote.co.uk

Situated in the heart of the Churnet Valley.
Close to the Heritage Railway and
canalside pubs. Ideal base for the Peak
District and Potteries.
**Nearest Town/Resort** Leek
**Directions** 3½ miles south of Leek off the
A520 Stone to Leek road.
⇒ Stoke-on-Trent

## LONGNOR

Longnor Wood 'Just For Adults'
**Caravan Park,** Longnor Wood, Longnor,
Near Buxton, Derbyshire, SK17 0NG
**Tel:** 01298 83648
**Email:** enquiries@longnorwood.co.uk
www.longnorwood.co.uk
**Pitches For** ▲ ⊕ ⇔ **Total** 48
**Facilities** ∮ 🖪 �📺 ♨ ↑ ⊙ ⊒ ⊿ 🖸 ☻
𝕊⌷ 🖸 ☻ ✿ ↦🄳⚊Ａ
**Nearby Facilities** ↑ ✔ ∪ ⅄
**Acreage** 10 **Open** April to Oct
**Access** Good **Site** Level
ADULTS ONLY PARK set in the Peak
National Park.
**Nearest Town/Resort** Buxton
**Directions** From Buxton take the A53
towards Leek, at the junction just before the
Winking Man Pub turn left (signposted
Longnor 4½ miles). Turn right at the brown
caravan and camping sign, then turn right
again.
⇒ Buxton

## RUGELEY

**Park View Farm,** Little Haywood, Stafford,
Staffordshire, ST18 0TR
**Tel:** 01889 808194
**Pitches For** ▲ ⊕ ⇔ **Total** 11
**Facilities** �📺 ☻↦🄳
**Nearby Facilities**
**Acreage** 1 **Open** All Year
**Access** Good **Site** Level
Within walking distance of Shugborough
Hall. Convenient for Alton Towers.
**Nearest Town/Resort** Rugeley
**Directions** 3 miles north of Rugeley. Leave
the A51 by-pass to villages of Colwich, Little
and Great Haywood, aite is at the top of the
hill between Little and Great Haywood. Turn
into farm drive adjacent to Jubilee Playing
Field.
⇒ Rugeley/Stafford

## TAMWORTH

**Drayton Manor Park,** Nr Tamworth,
Staffordshire, B78 3TW
**Tel:** 01827 287979 **Fax:** 01827 288916
**Email:** info@draytonmanor.co.uk
www.draytonmanor.co.uk
**Pitches For** ▲ ⊕ ⇔ **Total** 75
**Facilities** & 📺 ♨ ↑ ⊙ ⊒ ☻ 𝕊⌷ ⌿☻ ☻
**Nearby Facilities** ↑ ✔ ⅄ ∪ ⅃ ℛ
**Open** Easter to October
**Access** Good **Site** Lev/Slope
On site Theme Park and Zoo with over 100
rides and attractions.
**Nearest Town/Resort** Tamworth
**Directions** On the A4091 near junctions 9
or 10 of the M42 or exit T2 of the M6 Toll.
⇒ Tamworth

## UTTOXETER

**Uttoxeter Racecourse Caravan Club
Site,** Wood Lane, Uttoxeter, Staffordshire,
ST14 8BD
**Tel:** 01889 564172
www.caravanclub.co.uk
**Pitches For** ▲ ⊕ ⇔ **Total** 76
**Facilities** ∮ 📺 ♨ ↑ ⊙ ⌿☻ ☻ 𝁊↦🄳🄲
**Nearby Facilities** ↑
**Acreage** 3 **Open** March to Nov
**Access** Good **Site** Level
Surrounded by the Weaver Hills. Free
admission to racecourse, bar, betting area,
picnic area and play area. Golf course
adjacent. Close to Alton Towers, Lichfield
Cathedral and Sudbury Hall. Non members
welcome. Booking essential.
**Nearest Town/Resort** Uttoxeter
**Directions** From the A50 take the A518
signposted Racecourse, site is 1½ miles on
the left. Turn into third gate at Caravan Club
sign.
⇒ Uttoxeter

## SUFFOLK

## BECCLES

**Beulah Hall Caravan Park,** Dairy Lane,
Mutford, Beccles, Suffolk, NR34 7QJ
**Tel:** 01502 476609 **Fax:** 01502 476453
**Email:** carol.stuckey@fsmail.net
**Pitches For** ▲ ⊕ ⇔ **Total** 30
**Facilities** ∮ 📺 ♨ ↑ ⊙ ⌿☻ ☻ ↦🄳 ☀
**Nearby Facilities** ↑ ✔ ⚓ ⅄ ∪ ℛ
**Acreage** 2½ **Open** April to October
**Access** Good **Site** Level
Near to Award Winning beaches and the
Broads. Ideal base for touring the area.
**Nearest Town/Resort** Lowestoft
**Directions** Halfway between Lowestoft and
Beccles on the A146. At signpost to Mutford
take 'New Road', 500 yards to the T-junction
and turn right, 300 yards to the site.
⇒ Oulton Broad South

## BECCLES

**Fox Country Caravan Park,** The Fox Inn,
London Road, Shadingfield,
BecclesSuffolk, NR34 8DD
**Tel:** 01502 575610
**Pitches For** ▲ ⊕ ⇔ **Total** 30
**Facilities** ∮ 📺 ♨ ↑ ⊙ ⌿ ☻ ⊙ ☻ ✕ ⅄ 𝁊↦
**Nearby Facilities** ✔ ⚓ ⅄
**Acreage** 2 **Open** All Year
**Access** Good **Site** Level
Quiet country site, 8 miles from the beach
and 4 miles from the Broads.
**Nearest Town/Resort** Beccles
**Directions** 4 miles from Beccles on the
A145.
⇒ Beccles

## BURY ST EDMUNDS

**The Dell Touring Park,** Beyton Road,
Thurston, Bury St Edmunds, Suffolk, IP31
3RB
**Tel:** 01359 270121
**Email:** thedellcaravanpark@btinternet.com
**Pitches For** ▲ ⊕ ⇔ **Total** 100
**Facilities** ∮ 📺 �📺 ♨ ↑ ⊙ ⌿ ☻ ⊒ 🖸 ☻
🅿☻ ☻ ✿↦🄳🄱 ℛ

**Nearby Facilities** ✔ ℛ
**Open** All Year
**Access** Good **Site** Level
Ideal for touring East Anglia. 1 hour from
Cambridge, Norwich and coast. New hard
standing pitches. New toilet block.
**Nearest Town/Resort** Bury St Edmunds
**Directions** Take A14 eastbound 6 miles from
Bury follow Thurston signs.
⇒ Thurston

## DARSHAM

**Haw-Wood Farm Caravan & Camping
Park,** Haw-Wood Farm, Darsham,
Saxmundham, Suffolk, IP17 3QT
**Tel:** 01986 784248
**Pitches For** ▲ ⊕ ⇔ **Total** 100
**Facilities** & ∮ 📺 ♨ ↑ ⊙ ⌿ ☻ 🖸 ☻
𝕊⌷ 🖸 ☻ ✕ 📺↦🄳🄱 ☻ ☀
**Nearby Facilities** ↑ ✔ ⅄ ⅃
**Acreage** 15 **Open** March to Jan
**Access** Good **Site** Level
5 miles from the beach. Near to a golf club,
fishing and clay pigeon shooting.
**Nearest Town/Resort** Southwold
**Directions** Turn off the A12 100 yards north
of the junction with the A144 at the Little
Chef, ¼ mile on the right.
⇒ Darsham

## DUNWICH

**The Cliff House Holiday Park,** Minsmere
Road, Dunwich, Suffolk, IP17 3DQ
**Tel:** 01728 648282 **Fax:** 01728 648996
**Email:** info@cliffhouseholidays.co.uk
www.cliffhouseholidays.co.uk
**Pitches For** ▲ ⊕ ⇔ **Total** 93
**Facilities** & ∮ 📺 �📺 ♨ ↑ ⊙ ⌿ ☻ ⊒ 🖸 ☻
𝕊⌷ 🖸 ☻ ✕ ⅄ 📺 ♜ 📺↦🄳🄱 ☀ ℛ
**Nearby Facilities** ↑ ✔ ⚓ ∪ ℛ
**Acreage** 30 **Open** March to Oct
**Access** Good **Site** Level
Woodland setting close to the beach with
sea views, in an area of outstanding
natural beauty. Bar, restaurant and small
shop on site.
**Nearest Town/Resort** Leiston
**Directions** Follow signs from the A12.
⇒ Darsham

## EYE

**Honeypot Caravan & Camping Park,**
Wortham, Eye, Suffolk, IP22 1PW
**Tel:** 01379 783312 **Fax:** 01379 783312
**Email:** honeypotcamping@talk21.com
www.honeypotcamping.co.uk
**Pitches For** ▲ ⊕ ⇔ **Total** 35
**Facilities** ∮ 📺 ♨ ↑ ⊙ ⌿ ☻ ⊿ 🖸 ☻
🅿🖸 ☻ ✕ 📺↦🄳🄱 ℛ
**Nearby Facilities**
**Acreage** 4 **Open** Mid April to Mid Sept
**Access** Good **Site** Level
Highly recommended site with plenty of
peace and quiet.
**Nearest Town/Resort** Eye
**Directions** Four miles south west of Diss,
on the south side of the A143.
⇒ Diss

## FELIXSTOWE

**Peewit Caravan Park,** Walton Avenue, Felixstowe, Suffolk, IP11 2HB
**Tel:** 01394 284511
**Email:** peewitpark@aol.com
www.peewitcaravanpark.co.uk
**Pitches For** A ⚐ ⛟ **Total** 40
**Facilities** ⚿ � Ⓜ ⚒ ☂ Ⓟ ⊙ ⌁ ☎ Ⓓ ☎
⬚ Ⓣ ☕ ⚑ ⚑Ⓗ
**Nearby Facilities** ⌜ ⚲ ⚓ ⚅ ♪
**Acreage** 3 **Open** Easter/1 April **to** 31 Oct
**Access** Good **Site** Level
Quiet and secluded setting, 900 metres from the seafront. Central for North Essex and coastal Suffolk.
**Nearest Town/Resort** Felixstowe
**Directions** Take the A14 to Felixstowe Docks, at Gate No.1 turn towards the town centre, site is 100 metres on the left.
⚉ Felixstowe

## FELIXSTOWE

**Suffolk Sands Holiday Village,** Carr Road, Felixstowe, Suffolk, IP11 2TS
**Tel:** 01394 273434 **Fax:** 01394 671269
**Email:** info@cinqueportsleisure.com
www.cplholidays.com
**Pitches For** A ⚐ ⛟ **Total** 47
**Facilities** ⚿ � Ⓜ ⚒ ☂ Ⓟ ⊙ ⌁ Ⓓ ☎
⬚Ⓞ☕X⚑⚑⚑Ⓗ☐
**Nearby Facilities** ⌜ ⚲ ⚓
**Open** March **to** Jan
**Access** Good **Site** Level
Near the beach. Two fully serviced pitches available.
**Nearest Town/Resort** Felixstowe
**Directions** Off the A14 just south of Felixstowe.
⚉ Felixstowe

## HADLEIGH

**Polstead Touring Park,** Holt Road, Polstead, Nr Colchester, Suffolk, CO6 5BZ
**Tel:** 01787 211969 **Fax:** 01787 211969
**Email:** alangell2000@yahoo.co.uk
www.polsteadtouring.co.uk
**Pitches For** A ⚐ ⛟ **Total** 30
**Facilities** ⚿ Ⓕ Ⓜ Ⓜ ⚒ ☂ Ⓟ ⊙ ⌁ Ⓓ ☎
⚿⬚ ☕⚑⚑A ⚒ ♪
**Nearby Facilities** ⌜ ∪
**Acreage** 3½ **Open** All Year
**Access** Good **Site** Lev/Slope
ADULTS ONLY SITE. Ideal for touring Constable country.
**Nearest Town/Resort** Hadleigh
**Directions** Between Hadleigh and Boxford on the A1071, opposite 'The Brewers Arms Inn' (signposted).
⚉ Sudbury

## IPSWICH

**Low House Touring Caravan Centre,** Low House, Bucklesham Road, Foxhall, IpswichSuffolk, IP10 0AU
**Tel:** 01473 659437 **Fax:** 01473 659880
**Email:** low.house@btopenworld.com
**Pitches For** A ⚐ ⛟ **Total** 30
**Facilities** ⒻⒻ Ⓜ ⚒ ☂ Ⓟ ⊙ ⌁ ☎
⬚Ⓞ☕⚑Ⓗ☐ ♪
**Nearby Facilities** ⌜ ⚲ ⚓ ⚅ ∪ ♪
**Acreage** 3½ **Open** All Year
**Access** Good **Site** Level
Camp in a beautiful garden packed with ornamental trees and plants, arches and bower doves, rabbits, bantams and guinea fowl. Wildlife all around. Ornamental Tree Walk and Pets Corner. Heated toilet and shower block. Electric hook-ups available on ALL pitches. Calor Gas and Camping Gaz available on site.
**Nearest Town/Resort** Ipswich/Felixstowe

**Directions** Turn off the A14 Ipswich Ring Road (South) via slip road onto the A1156 (signposted East Ipswich). In 1 mile turn right (signposted), in ½ mile turn right signposted Low House, site is on the left in ¼ mile.
⚉ Ipswich

## IPSWICH

**Orwell Meadows Leisure Park,** Priory Lane, Ipswich, Suffolk, IP10 0JS
**Tel:** 01473 726666 **Fax:** 01473 721441
**Email:** david@orwellmeadows.co.uk
**Pitches For** A ⚐ ⛟ **Total** 80
**Facilities** ⚿ Ⓕ Ⓜ ⚒ ☂ Ⓟ ⊙ ⌁ Ⓓ ☎
⬚ Ⓣ Ⓞ ☕ X ☂ Ⓣ ⚑ ⚑ ⚑ ⚑Ⓗ☐ ♪
**Nearby Facilities** ⌜ ⚲
**Acreage** 17
**Access** Good **Site** Level
A quiet, family run park, ideally situated for touring beautiful Suffolk. Adjacent to the Orwell Country Park. Forest and river walks.
**Nearest Town/Resort** Ipswich
**Directions** From A14 towards Felixstowe take first exit after Orwell Bridge, at roundabout turn left and first left again then follow signs.
⚉ Ipswich

## IPSWICH

**Priory Park,** Ipswich, Suffolk, IP10 0JT
**Tel:** 01473 727393 **Fax:** 01473 278372
**Email:** jwl@priory-park.com
www.priory-park.com
**Pitches For** A ⚐ ⛟ **Total** 75
**Facilities** Ⓕ Ⓜ Ⓜ ⚒ ☂ Ⓟ ⊙ ⌁ Ⓓ ☎
⬚Ⓞ☕X⚑⚑♪⚑⚑Ⓗ☐
**Nearby Facilities** ⌜ ⚲ ⚓ ⚅ ∪ ♪
**Acreage** 100 **Open** Easter **to** End October
**Access** Good **Site** Level
Superb historic setting. Frontage onto River Orwell. Magnificent south facing

# SUFFOLK

panoramic views. 9 hole golf course and hard tennis court within the park grounds. Club adventure play area, nature trails, access to foreshore. NEW toilets, showers and laundry facilities for 2001. Holiday Homes for sale.
**Nearest Town/Resort** Ipswich
**Directions** Travelling east along A14 Ipswich southern by-pass take first exit after River Orwell Road bridge, turn left towards Ipswich following caravan/camping signs. 300yards from by-pass on left, follow signs to Priory Park.
⚑ Ipswich

## IPSWICH
**The Oaks Caravan Park,** Chapel Road, Bucklesham, Near Ipswich, Suffolk, IP10 0BT
**Tel:** 01394 448837
**Email:** oakscaravanpark@aol.com
www.oakscaravanpark.com
**Pitches For** ⚑ ▢ Total 100
**Facilities** ⚑ 🅼 ⚡ ⌂ ⊙⌷ 🍴 ⌷⊁⌷ ▣ A ⚡
**Nearby Facilities** ⌇ ⟋ ⚓ U
**Acreage** 5½ **Open** April **to** Oct
**Access** Good **Site** Level
An exclusively ADULTS ONLY touring park with excellent amenities, a park that is focused on peace and tranquillity.
**Nearest Town/Resort** Felixstowe
**Directions** On the A14 towards Felixstowe go over the Orwell Bridge and take the third sliproad signposted Bucklesham. After 1 mile take the third right signposted Kirton, The Oaks is a further ½ a mile on the left.
⚑ Felixstowe

## KESSINGLAND
**Camping & Caravanning Club Site,** Suffolk Wildlife Park, Whites Lane, Kessingland, Nr LowestoftSuffolk, NR33 7SL
**Tel:** 01502 742040
www.campingandcaravanningclub.co.uk
**Pitches For** ⚑ ⚑ Total 90
**Facilities** ⚑ ⚡ 🅼 ⚡ ⌂ ⊙⌷ 🍴 ▣ ⚡ ▢ 🅰⌷▣ ⌷
**Nearby Facilities** ⌇ ⟋ ♿
**Acreage** 5 **Open** March **to** October
**Access** Good **Site** Level
Next to Suffolk Wildlife Park. Set in a quiet seaside resort, close to Great Yarmouth. 5 miles from Pleasurewood Hills. BTB 4 Star Graded, AA 4 Pennants and Loo of the Year Award. Non members welcome.
**Nearest Town/Resort** Lowestoft
**Directions** From Lowestoft on the A12, leave at roundabout in Kessingland following Wildlife Park signs. Turn right through park entrance.
⚑ Lowestoft

## LOWESTOFT
**Beach Farm Residential & Holiday Park Ltd.,** Arbor Lane, Pakefield, Lowestoft, Suffolk, NR33 7BD
**Tel:** 01502 572794 **Fax:** 01502 537460
**Email:** beachfarmpark@aol.com
www.beachfarmpark.co.uk
**Pitches For** ⚑ ⚑ **Total** 10
**Facilities** ⚑ 🅼 ⚡ ⌂ ⊙⌷ 🍴 ⚡ ▣ ⚡
**Nearby Facilities** ⌇ ⟋ ⚓ ⚓ U ♿
**Acreage** 5 **Open** March **to** October
**Access** Good **Site** Level
¼ mile from the beach. Close to all amenities. Club, heated pool and a fast food restaurant on park.
**Nearest Town/Resort** Lowestoft
**Directions** Main roundabout Kessingland Lowestoft A12 fourth exit, from Lowestoft first exit.
⚑ Lowestoft

## LOWESTOFT
**Chestnut Farm,** Gisleham, Lowestoft, Suffolk, NR33 8EE
**Tel:** 01502 740227
**Pitches For** ⚑ ⚑ ⚑ **Total** 40
**Facilities** ⚑ 🅼 ⚡ ⌂ ⊙⚡🍴⌷
**Nearby Facilities** ⌇ ⟋ ⚓ ⚓ U ♿
**Acreage** 3 **Open** March **to** Oct
**Access** Good
Close to the beach, Kessingland, the Broads, Lowestoft and Great Yarmouth.
**Nearest Town/Resort** Lowestoft/ Kessingland
**Directions** South of Lowestoft on the A12 at the Wildlife roundabout off Kessingland bypass turn off signposted Gisleham, Rushmere and Mutford, then turn second left.
⚑ Oulton Broad

## LOWESTOFT
**Kessingland Beach Holiday Park,** Beach Lane, Nr Lowestoft, Suffolk, NR33 7RN
**Tel:** 01502 740636 **Fax:** 01502 740907
**Email:** kessingland.beach@park-resorts.com
www.park-resorts.com
**Pitches For** ⚑ ⚑ ⚑ **Total** 90
**Facilities** ⚑ 🅼 ⚡ ⌂ ⊙⌷ 🍴 ⚡ ▣ ⚡
**Nearby Facilities** ⚑ ⌂ ⚡ 🅼 ⌷ ♿⌷ 🍴⌷⊁⌷▣⌷▣ ⚡
**Nearby Facilities**
**Open** March **to** Oct
**Site** Level
A lively park close to sandy beaches and attractions.
**Nearest Town/Resort** Lowestoft
**Directions** From Ipswich take the A12 north, at Kessingland roundabout take the third exit, follow road through the village, at the beach follow the road to the right and take the left fork.
⚑ Lowestoft

## MILDENHALL
**Round Plantation Caravan Club Site,** Brandon Road, Mildenhall, Bury St Edmunds, Suffolk, IP28 7JE
**Tel:** 01638 713089
www.caravanclub.co.uk
**Pitches For** ⚑ ⚑ **Total** 98
**Facilities** ⚑ ⌂ 🅻 ⌂ ⚡⌷▣ ▣
**Nearby Facilities** ⌇ ⟋
**Acreage** 15 **Open** March **to** Sept
**Access** Good **Site** Level
Pleasant, landscaped, forest site, ideal for bird watching and peaceful walks. US Air Force Base adjacent (periodic aircraft noise). Only a short drive to Duxford Aircraft Museum. Near West Stow Anglo-Saxon Village and Medieval Lavenham. Own sanitation required. Non members welcome. Booking essential.
**Nearest Town/Resort** Mildenhall
**Directions** From Mildenhall take the A1101 towards Bury St. Edmunds. On the outskirts of Mildenhall turn left at the roundabout by the Half Moon Pub into Brandon Road, site is ¾ miles on the right.
⚑ Mildenhall

## NAYLAND
**Rushbanks Farm,** Bures Road, Wiston, Colchester, Essex, CO6 4NA
**Tel:** 01206 262350
**Pitches For** ⚑ ⚑ ⚑ **Total** 15
**Facilities** 🅼 ⚡
**Nearby Facilities** ⌇ ⟋ ⚓
**Access** Good **Site** Level
Attractive site on the north banks of the River Stour. Suitable for canoeing and fishing.
**Nearest Town/Resort** Colchester
**Directions** From Colchester take the A134 towards Sudbury. In Nayland turn left towards Bures.
⚑ Colchester

## SAXMUNDHAM
**Carlton Park Camping & Caravan Site,** Sports Grounds, North Approach, Saxmundham, Suffolk, IP17 1AT
**Tel:** 01728 604413
**Email:** info@carltonpark.info
www.carltonpark.info
**Pitches For** ⚑ ⚑ **Total** 75
**Facilities** ⚑ 🅼 ⚡ ⌂ ⊙⌷ ⚡ ⚡▣ ⚡
**Nearby Facilities** ⌇ ⟋ ⚓ ⚓ U ♿ ⚡ ♿
**Acreage** 6½ **Open** Easter/1 April **to** 31 Oct
**Access** Good **Site** Sloping
Situated in rolling countryside, close to the coast.
**Nearest Town/Resort** Aldeburgh
**Directions** On the B1121 on the north side of Saxmundham.
⚑ Saxmundham

## SAXMUNDHAM

**Homelands,** Main Road, Yoxford, Nr Saxmundham, Suffolk, IP17 3HE
**Tel:** 01728 668348
**Pitches For** ▲ ⬛ ⬛ **Total** 20
**Facilities** � ⬛ ⬛ ⌐ ⬛ ⬛ ⬛ ⬛
**Nearby Facilities** ⌐ ✗ ∪ ♪
**Acreage** 10 **Open** March to October
**Access** Good **Site** Lev/Slope
**Nearest Town/Resort** Aldburgh
**Directions** On the main A12 north of Saxmundham.
⇥ Darsham

## SAXMUNDHAM

**Whitearch Touring Park,** Main Road, Benhall, Saxmundham, Suffolk, IP17 1NA
**Tel:** 01728 604646
www.caravancampingsites.co.uk
**Pitches For** ▲ ⬛ ⬛ **Total** 40
**Facilities** ⬛ ⬛ ⬛ ⬛ ⌐ ⬛ ⬛ ⬛ ⬛ ⬛ ⬛ ⬛ ⬛ ⬛ ⬛ ⬛ ⬛
**Nearby Facilities** ✗ ♪
**Acreage** 14½ **Open** April to October
**Access** Good **Site** Level
Fishing and tennis on site. Suffolk coast, Snape Maltings Concert Hall, Minsmere Bird Reserve, American Theme Park and castles.
**Nearest Town/Resort** Saxmundham
**Directions** Just off the main A12 junction with the B1121 at the Ipswich end of Saxmundham by-pass.
⇥ Saxmundham

## SHOTLEY

**Shotley Caravan Park,** Gate Farm Road, Shotley, Suffolk, IP9 1QH
**Tel:** 01473 787421
www.shotleycaravanpark.com
**Pitches For** ⬛ ⬛
**Facilities** ✗ ⬛ ⬛ ⬛ ⬛ ⬛

**Nearby Facilities** ✗ ⬛ ✗
**Acreage** 7 **Open** March to October
**Access** Good **Site** Lev/Slope
Enjoy peace and tranquillity in this area of outstanding natural beauty, with panoramic views over the River Orwell. Ideal site for the over 50's. Tourers/rallies welcome. Close to a marina, restaurants, pubs, fish & chips, church, doctors and garage. Easy access from the A12/A14.
**Nearest Town/Resort** Ipswich/Felixstowe
**Directions** From Orwell Bridge take exit A137 and follow the B1456 once in Shotley (10 miles from Ipswich). Go past the Rose Pub on the right and after 1 mile turn left into Gate Farm Road and go through white gate.
⇥ Ipswich

## SUDBURY

**Willowmere Caravan Park,** Bures Road, Little Cornard, Sudbury, Suffolk, CO10 0NN
**Tel:** 01787 375559 **Fax:** 01787 375559
**Pitches For** ▲ ⬛ ⬛ **Total** 40
**Facilities** ⬛ ⬛ ⬛ ⌐ ⬛ ⬛ ⬛ ⬛ ⬛ ⬛
**Nearby Facilities** ⌐ ✗ ∪ ♪
**Acreage** 2 **Open** Easter to 1 October
**Access** Good **Site** Level
Quiet, country park near a river.
**Nearest Town/Resort** Sudbury
**Directions** Leave Sudbury on the B1508 to Bures and Colchester, 1 mile from Sudbury.
⇥ Sudbury

## THEBERTON

**Cakes & Ale,** Abbey Lane, Theberton, Suffolk, IP16 4TE
**Tel:** 01728 831655
**Email:** cake.ale@virgin.net
**Pitches For** ▲ ⬛ ⬛ **Total** 50
**Facilities** ⬛ ⬛ ⬛ ⬛ ⬛ ⌐ ⬛ ⬛ ⬛ ⬛
**Nearby Facilities** ⌐ ✗ ⬛ ✗ ∪ ♪

**Acreage** 6 **Open** April to October
**Access** Good **Site** Level
1 mile from Leiston Abbey ruins and 3 miles from Minsmere Bird Sanctuary. Central for the Heritage Coast.
**Nearest Town/Resort** Saxmundham
**Directions** Take the A12 to Saxmundham then the B1119 towards Leiston, follow brown tourism signs.
⇥ Saxmundham

## WOODBRIDGE

**Moat Barn Touring Caravan Park,** Dallinghoo Road, Bredfield, Woodbridge, Suffolk, IP13 6BD
**Tel:** 01473 737520
www.moatbarn.co.uk
**Pitches For** ▲ ⬛ **Total** 25
**Facilities** ⬛ ⬛ ⬛ ⌐ ⬛ ⬛ ⬛ ⬛ ⬛ ⬛
**Nearby Facilities** ⌐ ✗ ⬛ ✗ ∪ ♪ ♪
**Acreage** 2 **Open** March to January
**Access** Good **Site** Level
Quiet, family run park in a rural location. No facilities for children. No large campers vans accepted. Ideal for touring and exploring the Heritage Coast.
**Nearest Town/Resort** Woodbridge
**Directions** On the A12 midway between Wickham Market and Woodbridge turn to Bredfield. Turn right at Village Pump and go through the village past the pub and church, follow road through the S bend and Park is 150 yards on the left.
⇥ Woodbridge

## WOODBRIDGE

**Run Cottage Touring Park,** Alderton Road, Hollesley, Woodbridge, Suffolk, IP12 3RQ
**Tel:** 01394 411309
**Email:** contact@run-cottage.co.uk
www.run-cottage.co.uk
**Pitches For** ⬛ ⬛ **Total** 20

# MOON & SIXPENCE
## NEAR WOODBRIDGE, SUFFOLK

Secluded tourer sites and a good choice of caravan holiday homes for sale, owner occupiers, close friends and family. Superb, tranquil, landscaped parkland of 85 acres. 9 hole practice compact golf course. Lake, fishing during Sept. & Oct. Sandy beach, woods and meadows. Dog walks and cycle trails. Recreation area. Tennis, volleyball and basketball courts. Petanque. Attractive Lounge and Bar. Located in unspoilt Suffolk, close to Woodbridge and the River Deben.

### Colour brochure from:
**Moon & Sixpence, Waldringfield, Woodbridge, Suffolk IP12 4PP.**
**Tel: 01473 736 650   Fax: 01473 736 270**
**Web Site: www.moonsix.dircon.co.uk   E-mail: moonsix@dircon.co.uk**

**Facilities** ⚒ ♿ ⌂ ☒ ♨ ⌐ ⊙ ⌐ ☏ ☖ ⊬
**Nearby Facilities** ⌐ ✗ ⏚ ⤬ ∪
**Acreage** 3½ **Open** All Year
**Access** Good **Site** Level
Quiet, peaceful and secluded site set in
2½ acres of parkland. On Suffolk's
Heritage Coast, ideal for walking, cycling
and bird watching.
**Nearest Town/Resort** Woodbridge
**Directions** Turn off the A12 at Melton onto
the A1152, at next roundabout turn right onto
the B1083. Turn next left to Hollesley then
turn right into The Street at Hollesley, go
through the village and over the small bridge,
site is 100 yards on the left.
⚏ Woodbridge

## WOODBRIDGE

**St. Margaret's Caravan & Camping Site,**
St Margaret's House, Hollesley Road,
Shottisham, WoodbridgeSuffolk, IP12 3HD
**Tel:** 01394 411247
**Email:** ken.norton@virgin.net
**www.st-margarets-house.co.uk**
**Pitches For** ▲ ⚏ ⊟ **Total** 30
**Facilities** ♿ ☒ ⚒ ⌐ ⊙ ⌐ ☏ ⊙ ⊬ ⌐ ☈ ☄
**Nearby Facilities** ⌐ ✗ ⏚ ⤬ ∪ ♪ ♫
**Acreage** 10 **Open** Easter/April **to** End Oct
**Access** Good **Site** Level
Situated on the edge of a small village, in
an area of outstanding natural beauty. Very
quiet site, just birds, rabbits, deer, squirrels
and foxes. 3½ miles from a shingle beach.
Large grassy field adjacent for children to
play in. Excellent walking and cycling area
with forest, river and heathland trails. Milk
and dairy produce are available from the
house (by order). 150 metres from The
Sorrel Horse Public House which serves
very good meals and snacks.
**Nearest Town/Resort** Woodbridge
**Directions** Turn off the A12 onto the A1152,
then take the B1083. In the village of
Shottisham go past the Sorrel Horse Public
House, site is on the left in 150 metres.
⚏ Woodbridge

## WOODBRIDGE

**The Moon and Sixpence,** Newbourne
Road, Waldringfield, Woodbridge, Suffolk,
IP12 4PP
**Tel:** 01473 736650
**Email:** moonsix@dircon.co.uk
**www.moonsix.dircon.co.uk**
**Pitches For** ▲ ⚏ ⊟ **Total** 75
**Facilities** ⌐ ☒ ♿ ⚒ ⌐ ⊙ ⌐ ☏ ☄ ⌐ ☈ ☄
☏ ⊙ ⚒ ⌁ ♪ ⌐ ⌐ ☈ ⌐ ☈ ☈
**Nearby Facilities** ⌐ ✗ ⏚ ⤬ ∪ ♪ ♫
**Acreage** 5 **Open** April **to** October
**Access** Good **Site** Level
Picturesque location. Sheltered, terraced
site. Own private lake and sandy beach.
**Nearest Town/Resort** Woodbridge
**Directions** Turn off A12, Ipswich Eastern By-
Pass, onto unclassified road signposted
Waldringfield, Newbourn. Follow caravan
direction signs.
⚏ Woodbridge

# SURREY

## CHERTSEY

**Camping & Caravanning Club Site,**
Bridge Road, Chertsey, Surrey, KT16 8JX
**Tel:** 01932 562405
**www.campingandcaravanningclub.co.uk**
**Pitches For** ▲ ⚏ ⊟ **Total** 200
**Facilities** ⚒ ♿ ⌂ ☒ ⚒ ⌐ ⊙ ⌐ ☏ ☄ ⌐ ☈ ☏
☏ ⊙ ☈ ⊟ ⌐ ♪ ⌐ ☈ ⌐ ⊟ ♫ ⌐
**Nearby Facilities** ⌐ ✗ ✗ ⏚ ∪

**Acreage** 8 **Open** All Year
**Site** Level
On the banks of the River Thames, fishing
on site. Table tennis on site. 4 miles from
Thorpe Park. Close to London. BTB 3 Star
Graded and AA 3 Pennants. Non members
welcome.
**Directions** Leave the M25 at junction 11 and
follow the A317 to Chertsey. At the
roundabout take the first exit to the traffic
lights and go straight across to the next set
of traffic lights, turn right and after 400 yards
turn left into the site.
⚏ Chertsey

## HAMBLEDON

**The Merry Harriers,** Hambledon, Surrey,
GU8 4DR
**Tel:** 01428 Wormley 682883
**Email:** merry.harriers@virgin.net
**Pitches For** ▲ ⚏ ⊟ **Total** 25
**Facilities** ♿ ⚒ ⌐ ⊙ ⌐ ☏ ☄ ⌐ ✗ ⌐ ☈ ⌐
**Nearby Facilities** ⌐
**Acreage** 1 **Open** All Year
**Access** Good **Site** Level
Unspoilt countryside, opposite country pub.
**Nearest Town/Resort** Godalming
**Directions** Leave Godalming on B2130 and
follow Hambledon signs approx. 4 miles.
⚏ Witley

## HORSLEY

**Camping & Caravanning Club Site,**
Ockham Road North, East Horsley, Surrey,
KT24 6PE
**Tel:** 01483 283273
**www.campingandcaravanningclub.co.uk**
**Pitches For** ▲ ⚏ ⊟ **Total** 130
**Facilities** ⚒ ♿ ⌂ ☒ ⚒ ⌐ ⊙ ⌐ ☏ ☄ ⌐ ☈ ☏
☏ ⊙ ☈ ⌐ ⌐ ♪ ⌐ ☈ ⌐ ⊟ ⌐
**Nearby Facilities** ⌐ ✗ ∪ ♪
**Acreage** 9½ **Open** March **to** October
**Access** Good **Site** Level
Peaceful site, only 40 minutes from
London by train. Fishing lake on site. Non
members welcome.
**Nearest Town/Resort** Guildford
**Directions** Leave the M25 at junction 10 and
travel south on the A3. Turn off and drive
through Ripley Village, turn left onto the
B2039, site is third on the right.
⚏ East Horsley

## LINGFIELD

**Long Acres Caravan & Camping Park,**
Newchapel Road, Lingfield, Surrey, RH7
6LE
**Tel:** 01342 833205 **Fax:** 01622 735038
**Pitches For** ▲ ⚏ ⊟ **Total** 60
**Facilities** ⌐ ♿ ⌂ ☒ ⚒ ⌐ ⊙ ⌐ ☈ ☄ ⌐ ☈ ⊟
☏ ⊙ ☈ ⌐ ⊟ ⌐
**Nearby Facilities** ⌐ ✗
**Acreage** 7 **Open** All Year
**Access** Good **Site** Level
Ideal for visiting Surrey, Kent, Sussex,
Hever Chartwell, Ardingly Showground,
Wakehurst Place and many other
attractions.
**Nearest Town/Resort** East Grinstead
**Directions** From the M25 junction 6 take the
A22 south towards East Grinstead. At
Newchapel roundabout turn left onto the
B2028 to Lingfield, site is 700 yards on the
right.
⚏ Lingfield

## REDHILL

**Alderstead Heath Caravan Club Site,**
Dean Lane, Redhill, Surrey, RH1 3AH
**Tel:** 01737 644629
**www.caravanclub.co.uk**
**Pitches For** ⚏ ⊟ **Total** 85

**Facilities** ⚒ ♿ ⌂ ☒ ⚒ ⌐ ⌐ ☏
☏ ⊙ ☈ ⌐ ⊟ ⌐ ☈
**Nearby Facilities** ⌐ ✗
**Acreage** 30 **Open** All Year
**Access** Good **Site** Level
Quiet, level pitched site which drops into
rolling wooded countryside, and has
wonderful views of the North Downs. Close
to Wisley Gardens, NT Chartwell, Thorpe
Park and Chessington World of Adventure.
Non members welcome. Booking essential.
**Nearest Town/Resort** Redhill
**Directions** Leave M25 at junction 8 and take
A217 signposted Reigate, after 300yds fork
left signposted Merstham. At T-junction turn
left onto A23, after ½ mile turn right into
Shepherds Hill signposted Caterham, after
1 mile turn left into Dean Lane (DO NOT turn
into Dean Lane at Little Chef), site is 175yds
on the right.
⚏ Redhill

# SUSSEX (EAST)

## BATTLE

**Brakes Coppice Park,** Forewood Lane,
Crowhurst, East Sussex, TN33 9AB
**Tel:** 01424 830322
**Email:** brakesco@btinternet.com
**www.brakescoppicepark.co.uk**
**Pitches For** ▲ ⚏ ⊟ **Total** 30
**Facilities** ⚒ ♿ ⌂ ☒ ⚒ ⌐ ⊙ ⌐ ☏ ☄ ⌐ ☈
☏ ⊙ ☈ ⌐ ⊟ ⌐ ☈ ☈
**Nearby Facilities** ⌐ ✗ ⏚ ∪ ♪
**Acreage** 3¼ **Open** March **to** October
**Access** Good **Site** Sloping
Secluded, 11 acre, woodland park with
level pitches. TV aerial point to serviced
pitches.
**Nearest Town/Resort** Battle
**Directions** Turn right off the A2100 (Battle
to Hastings road) 2 miles from Battle. Follow
signs to Crowhurst, 1¼ miles turn left into
site.
⚏ Crowhurst

## BATTLE

**Crazy Lane Tourist Park,** Whydown Farm,
Crazy Lane, Sedlescombe, East Sussex,
TN33 0QT
**Tel:** 01424 870147
**www.crazylane.co.uk**
**Pitches For** ▲ ⚏ ⊟ **Total** 36
**Facilities** ⚒ ♿ ⚒ ♿ ⌂ ☒ ⚒ ⌐ ⊙ ⌐ ☏ ☄
☏ ⊙ ☈ ⌐ ⊟ ⌐ ☈ ☄
**Nearby Facilities** ⌐ ✗ ⏚ ∪ ♪ ♫
**Acreage** 3 **Open** 1 March **to** 31 Oct
**Access** Good **Site** Level
Ideal touring, 15 minutes to the beach.
Countryside and Hastings.
**Nearest Town/Resort** Battle/Hastings
**Directions** Travelling south on A21, turn left
into Crazy Lane, 100 yds past junction A21/
B2244, opposite Black Brooks Garden
Centre.
⚏ Battle

## BATTLE

**Normanhurst Court Caravan Club Site,**
Stevens Crouch, Battle, East Sussex,
TN33 9LR
**Tel:** 01424 773808
**www.caravanclub.co.uk**
**Pitches For** ⚏ ⊟ **Total** 150
**Facilities** ⚒ ♿ ⌂ ☒ ⚒ ⌐ ⌐ ☏ ☄ ⌐ ☈
☏ ⊙ ☈ ⌐ ⊟ ⌐ ☈ ⊟ ⌐
**Nearby Facilities** ⌐ ✗
**Acreage** 18 **Open** March **to** Oct
**Access** Good **Site** Lev/Slope
Set in a former garden with splendid trees
and shrubs, and lovely views of the Downs.
Close to Battle Abbey, Hastings, Rye and

Sussex vineyards. Non members welcome. Booking essential.
**Nearest Town/Resort** Battle
**Directions** From the A269 in Ninfield take the B2204 signposted Battle. Just past Catsfield keep left, after 1¼ miles turn left onto the A271 signposted Eastbourne, site is ½ mile on the left.
✈ Battle

## BEXHILL-ON-SEA

**Cobbs Hill Farm Caravan & Camping Park,** Watermill Lane, Bexhill-on-Sea, East Sussex, TN39 5JA
**Tel:** 01424 213460
**Email:** cobbshillfarmuk@hotmail.com
www.cobbshillfarm.co.uk
**Pitches For** ▲ ⊕ ⊕ **Total** 55
**Facilities** ƒ 🅗 🆖 🛉 ſ ⊙ ⅃ ▣ ☎
🅿 🅖 🚻 🛒 🔥 ⊕ 🗡 🏊 ⌓
**Nearby Facilities** ſ ✔ ⚓ ⚡ ∪ ♪
**Acreage** 7 **Open** April to October
**Access** Good **Site** Level
Situated on a small farm in quiet countryside. Large tent field at peak times.
**Nearest Town/Resort** Bexhill-on-Sea
**Directions** From Bexhill take the A269, turn right into Watermill Lane. Site is 1 mile on the left.
✈ Bexhill-on-Sea

## BRIGHTON

**Sheepcote Valley Caravan Club Site,** East Brighton Park, Brighton, East Sussex, BN2 5TS
**Tel:** 01273 626546
www.caravanclub.co.uk
**Pitches For** ▲ ⊕ ⊕ **Total** 170
**Facilities** & ƒ 🄵 🅗 🆖 🛉 ⊙ ⌓
🅿 🅖 🛒 🕅 ⊣ ▣ ☎
**Nearby Facilities** ſ ⚓ ✔
**Acreage** 17 **Open** All Year
**Access** Good **Site** Level
Situated in the South Downs, adjacent to recreation grounds. Only 2 miles from Brighton with its beach, pier, pavilion, sea life centre, boutiques and seafront attractions. Non members welcome. Booking essential.
**Nearest Town/Resort** Brighton
**Directions** From A27 take B2123 signposted Falmer, at lights by Downs Hotel turn right into Warren Road. At next lights turn left into Wilson Avenue, cross the racecourse and after 1¼ miles turn left at foot of the hill (last turn before the lights) into East Brighton Park, site is ½ mile on the left.
✈ Brighton

## CROWBOROUGH

**Camping & Caravanning Club Site,** Goldsmith Recreation Ground, Crowborough, East Sussex, TN6 2TN
**Tel:** 01892 664827
www.campingandcaravanningclub.co.uk
**Pitches For** ▲ ⊕ ⊕ **Total** 90
**Facilities** & ƒ 🅗 🆖 🛉 ſ ⊙ ⌓ ▣ ☎
🅿 🅖 🕅 🕅 ⊣ ▣ 🗡 ⌓
**Nearby Facilities** ſ ✔ ∪ ✈
**Acreage** 13 **Open** March to December
**Site** Lev/Slope
On the edge of Ashdown Forest. Adjacent

to a sports centre. BTB 4 Star Graded and AA 3 Pennants. Non members welcome.
**Directions** Take the A26 turn off into the entrance to 'Goldsmiths Ground' signposted leisure centre, at the top of the road turn right into site lane.
✈ Jarvis Brook

## EASTBOURNE

**Fairfields Farm Caravan & Camping Park,** Eastbourne Road, Westham, Pevensey, East Sussex, BN24 5NG
**Tel:** 01323 763165
**Email:** enquiries@fairfieldsfarm.com
www.fairfieldsfarm.com
**Pitches For** ▲ ⊕ ⊕ **Total** 60
**Facilities** ƒ 🅗 🆖 🛉 ſ ⊙ ⌓ ▣ ☎
🏊 🅖 🛒 🕅 🅖 ⌓
**Nearby Facilities** ſ ✔ ⚓ ✗ ∪ ♪
**Acreage** 3 **Open** April to October
**Access** Good **Site** Level
A quiet country touring site on a working farm. Near to Eastbourne and a good base for exploring the diverse scenery and attractions of South East England.
**Nearest Town/Resort** Eastbourne
**Directions** On the B2191 in Westham. Signposted on the east side of Eastbourne and from the A27 Pevensey roundabout - Pevensey Castle direction.
✈ Pevensey/Westham

## EWHURST GREEN

**Lordine Court Caravan Park,** Staplecross, Nr Robertsbridge, East Sussex, TN32 5TS
**Tel:** 01580 831792 **Fax:** 01580 831792
**Email:** enquiries@lordine-court.co.uk
www.lordine-court.co.uk
**Pitches For** ▲ ⊕ ⊕ **Total** 120
**Facilities** ✗ ƒ 🄵 🅗 🆖 🛉 ſ ⊣ ▣ ☎
🅘 🅿 🅖 ✗ ⛾ 🛒 🔥 🕅 ⊰ 🅗 ▣ ⌓
**Nearby Facilities** ſ ✔ ∪
**Acreage** 30 **Open** 1 March to 15 Jan
**Access** Good **Site** Sloping
Country station, yet only 10 miles from the sea. Seasonal Pitches (when available) require prior booking. NB: Site open for tourers 1st March to 31st October. Pre-booking is required.
**Nearest Town/Resort** Battle/Rye/Hastings
**Directions** From London take the A21 to Johns Cross, stay on the A21 and turn left to Cripps Corner, at the crossroads turn left onto the B2165 to Northiam. Park is 1 mile out of Staplecross on the B2165.
✈ Robertsbridge

## HAILSHAM

**Peel House Farm Caravan Park,** Sayerlands Lan (B2104), Polegate, East Sussex, BN26 6QX
**Tel:** 01323 845629 **Fax:** 01323 845629
**Email:** peelhocp@tesco.net
**Pitches For** ▲ ⊕ ⊕ **Total** 20
**Facilities** ƒ 🅗 🆖 🛉 ſ ⊙ ⌓ ▣ ☎
🏊 🅖 🛒 🕅 🅖 🅗 ▣ ⌓
**Nearby Facilities** ſ ✔ ⚓ ✗ ∪ ♪
**Acreage** 3 **Open** April/Easter to End Oct
**Access** Good **Site** Level
Quiet, rural site with views over the Downs. Footpath and Cuckoo Trail for walking and

cycling. Many places to visit nearby. Small shop and garden produce. ETB 4 Star Grading.
**Nearest Town/Resort** Hailsham/Eastbourne
**Directions** Off the A22 at South Hailsham roundabout. Turn right at mini roundabout by the BP Station onto the B2104 signposted Pevensey. We are on the right ½ mile after Cuckoo Trail Crossing.
✈ Polegate

## HAILSHAM

**The Old Mill Caravan Park,** Chalvington Road, Golden Cross, Hailsham, East Sussex, BN27 3SS
**Tel:** 01825 872532
**Email:** lucy@jasminewindmill.com
www.jasminewindmill.com
**Pitches For** ▲ ⊕ ⊕ **Total** 8
**Facilities** ƒ 🅗 🆖 🛉 ſ ⊙ ⅃ 🛒 ☎
🅘 🅖 🛒 🕅 🅖 🗡
**Nearby Facilities** ſ ✔ ∪
**Acreage** 2 **Open** April to October
**Access** Good **Site** Level
Ideal for the beach, downland and countryside, as well as Eastbourne, Brighton and Lewes. Static holiday caravans sold and sited.
**Nearest Town/Resort** Eastbourne
**Directions** 4 miles north west of Hailsham. Turn left off the A22 just before Golden Cross Inn car park. Site is 150yds on the right of Chalvington Road.
✈ Polegate

## HENFIELD

**Farmhouse Caravan & Camping Site,** Tottington Drive, Small Dole, Henfield, East Sussex, BN5 9XZ
**Tel:** 01273 493157
**Pitches For** ▲ ⊕ ⊕ **Total** 45
**Facilities** ƒ 🅗 🛉 ſ ☎ 🅘 🅖 🕅 🅗 ▣ ⌓
**Nearby Facilities** ſ ✔ ∪
**Acreage** 4 **Open** March to November
**Access** Good **Site** Level
Small farm site near South Downs. Beach 5 miles, Brighton and Worthing 10 miles.
**Nearest Town/Resort** Brighton
**Directions** Turn first left off A2037 (Henfield/ Upperbeeding). After Small Dole sign into Tottington Drive, farm at end.
✈ Shoreham

## HORAM

**Horam Manor Touring Park,** Horam, Nr Heathfield, East Sussex, TN21 0YD
**Tel:** 01435 813662
**Email:** camp@horam-manor.co.uk
www.horam-manor.co.uk
**Pitches For** ▲ ⊕ ⊕ **Total** 90
**Facilities** & ƒ 🅗 🛉 ſ ⊙ ⅃ 🛒 ▣ ☎
🅘 🅖 🛒 🅗 ▣
**Nearby Facilities** ſ ✔ ♪
**Acreage** 7 **Open** March to October
**Access** Good **Site** Lev/Slope
A tranquil rural setting, but with plenty to do on the estate, and many places to visit.
**Nearest Town/Resort** Heathfield/ Eastbourne
**Directions** On A267, 3 miles south of Heathfield, 10 miles north of Eastbourne.
✈ Eastbourne

## PEVENSEY

**Normans Bay Camping & Caravanning Club Site**, Normans Bay, Pevensey, East Sussex, BN24 6PR
Tel: 01323 761190
www.campingandcaravanningclub.co.uk
Pitches For ▲ ⊕ ➡ Total 200
Facilities ♿ ∱ 🚿 ♨ ↑ � ⊙ ☕ ⚑ 🔲 🕿
♨ 🅿 🖸 🛒 ♨ 🏪 ⤋⌂🔲 ⌕
Nearby Facilities ✔
Acreage 13 Open March to Oct
Access Good Site Level
Site has its own beach and is close to where the Normans landed. BTB 4 Star Graded and AA 3 Pennants. Non members welcome.
Nearest Town/Resort Pevensey
Directions From the A259 in Pevensey Bay Village take the first turn left (coast road) signed Beachlands only. After 1¼ miles site is on the left hand side.
➡ Normans Bay

## PEVENSEY BAY

**Bay View Caravan & Camping Park**, Old Martello Road, Pevensey Bay, Nr Eastbourne, East Sussex, BN24 6DX
Tel: 01323 768688 Fax: 01323 769637
Email: holidays@bay-view.co.uk
www.bay-view.co.uk
Pitches For ∱ ⊕ ➡ Total 79
Facilities ∱ 🛊 🆄🅱 ♨ ↑ ⊙ ☕ ⚑ 🔲 🕿
♨ 🖸 🛒 🏪 ⤋⌂🔲 ⌕
Nearby Facilities ↑ ✔ ⚓ ⤴ ♪
Acreage 3¼ Open Easter to October
Access Good Site Level
5 Star Award Winning park, next to the beach. Near to Eastbourne's Sunshine Coast. Gold David Bellamy Conservation Award.
Nearest Town/Resort Eastbourne

Directions 2 miles from Eastbourne centre off the A259.
➡ Pevensey Bay

## ROBERTSBRIDGE

**Park Farm Caravan & Camping Site**, Park Farm, Bodiam, East Sussex, TN32 5XA
Tel: 01580 830514 Fax: 01580 830519
Pitches For ▲ ⊕ ➡ Total 50
Facilities ∱ 🛊 🆄🅱 ♨ ↑ ⊙ ☕ 🕿
♨ 🏪⤋🔲 ✂ ⌕
Nearby Facilities ✔
Acreage 10 Open April to October
Access Good Site Level
Riverside walk to Bodiam Castle and many walks around the farm. Camp fires allowed. Winter Storage.
Nearest Town/Resort Hastings
Directions On the B2244 3 miles south of Hawkhurst and 3 miles north of Sedlescombe.
➡ Robertsbridge

## RYE

**Camber Sands Leisure Park**, Lydd Road, Camber, Nr Rye, East Sussex, TN31 7RT
Tel: 0870 442 9284 Fax: 01797 225756
Email: holidaysales.cambersands@park-resorts.com
www.park-resorts.com
Pitches For ∱ ⊕ ➡ Total 70
Facilities ∱ 🖸 🆄🅱 ♨ ↑ ⊙ ☕ 🔲 🕿
♨ 🆁 🛒 ♈ 🛡 🏪 ♨ ⤋🔲 ✂
Nearby Facilities ↑ ✔ ⚓ ♿ ⚓ ♪
Open March to November
Access Good Site Level
Popular touring destination opposite a blue flag sandy beach. Fantastic on-site facilities. Shopping and sightseeing opportunities at Hastings and Canterbury.
Nearest Town/Resort Rye

Directions From the M25 take the M20 and exit at junction 10. Take the A2070 signposted Brenzett, follow signs to Hastings and Rye. Stay on the A2070 until you see the signs for Rye, 1 mile before Rye turn left for Camber, the holiday park is 3 miles along the road.
➡ Rye

## RYE

**Rother Valley Caravan Park**, Station Road, Northiam, East Sussex, TN31 6QT
Tel: 01797 252116 Fax: 01797 252116
Email: info@rothervalley.com
www.rothervalleycamping.co.uk
Pitches For ▲ ⊕ ➡ Total 100
Facilities ∱ 🖸 🆄🅱 ♨ ↑ ⊙ ☕ 🕿
🆁 🖸 🛒 ✕⤋🔲 🈂 ✂ ⌕
Nearby Facilities ↑ ✔ ⚓ ⤴ U ♪
Acreage 10
Access Good Site Lev/Slope
Next to Kent & East Sussex Steam Railway. 500 metres from the River Rother.
Nearest Town/Resort Rye
Directions On the A28 between Tenterden and Hastings.
➡ Etchingham

## UCKFIELD

**Heaven Farm**, Furners Green, Uckfield, East Sussex, TN22 3RG
Tel: 01825 790226 Fax: 01825 790881
Email: butlerenterprises@farmline.com
www.heavenfarm.co.uk
Pitches For ▲ ⊕ ➡ Total 30
Facilities ♿ ∱ 🆄🅱 ♨ ↑ ⊙ ☕ 🕿
♨ 🛒⤋🔲 ⌕
Nearby Facilities ↑ ✔ ⚓ ⤴ U
Acreage 2 Open All Year
Access Good Site Lev/Slope
Popular nature trail and tea rooms. Central for many National Trust gardens etc.. 1 mile from Bluebell Railway.

**Nearest Town/Resort** Uckfield/Haywards Heath
**Directions** On the A275 10 miles north of Lewes and 1 mile south of Danehill. 9 miles from Uckfield and East Grinstead.
⇥ Haywards Heath

## UCKFIELD

**Honeys Green Farm Caravan Park,** Easons Green, Framfield, Uckfield, East Sussex, TN22 5GJ
**Tel:** 01732 860205
**Email:** honeysgreenpark@tiscali.co.uk
**Pitches For** ⚑ 🚐 **Total** 22
**Facilities** ∮ 🖽 �📷 ⚹ ┌ ⊙ ⌿ ⤶ 🎇 🛒 🅿
**Nearby Facilities** ┌ ✈ ∪
**Acreage** 2 **Open** Easter to October
**Access** Good **Site** Level
Small, peaceful, rural park with a coarse fishing lake. Lovely walks.
**Nearest Town/Resort** Uckfield/Lewes
**Directions** Turn off A22 (Uckfield – Eastbourne) at Halland roundabout onto B2192 signposted Blackboys/Heathfield, site ¼ mile on left.
⇥ Uckfield/Lewes

## WINCHELSEA

**Rye Bay Caravan Park Ltd.,** Pett Level Road, Winchelsea Beach, East Sussex, TN36 4NE
**Tel:** 01797 226340 **Fax:** 01797 224699
**Pitches For** ⚑ 🚐 **Total** 40
**Facilities** ⚹ 🖽 ⚹ ┌ ⊙ ⌿ ⤶
**Nearby Facilities** ✈
**Open** May to September
**Access** Good
Near the beach.
**Nearest Town/Resort** Rye
**Directions** 3 miles west of Rye and 7 miles east of Hastings.
⇥ Rye

## SUSSEX (WEST)

## ARUNDEL

**Maynards Caravan & Camping Park,** Crossbush, Arundel, West Sussex, BN18 9PQ
**Tel:** 01903 882075 **Fax:** 01903 885547
**Pitches For** ⚑ ⚑ 🚐 **Total** 70
**Facilities** ⚹ ∮ 🖽 ⚹ ┌ ⊙ ⌿ ⤶
🎇 🛒 ╳ 🅿 ⤶
**Nearby Facilities** ┌ ✈ ⚹ ⌖ ∪
**Acreage** 3 **Open** All Year
**Access** Good **Site** Level
3 miles from a sandy beach. Near Arundel Castle and Wild Fowl Reserve.
**Nearest Town/Resort** Arundel
**Directions** Just off the main A27, turn into the Out & Out Restaurant car park.
⇥ Arundel

## ARUNDEL

**Ship & Anchor Marina,** Heywood & Bryett Ltd, Ford, Arundel, West Sussex, BN18 0BJ
**Tel:** 01243 551262
**Email:** ysm36@dial.pipex.com
**Pitches For** ⚑ ⚑ 🚐 **Total** 160
**Facilities** ⚹ ∮ 🖽 ⚹ ┌ ⊙ ⌿ ⤶
🎇 🛒 ╳ 🅿 ⚹ 🛒 ╱ ⤶ 🎇
**Nearby Facilities** ┌ ✈ ⚹ ⌖ ∪
**Acreage** 12 **Open** March to October
**Access** Good **Site** Level
Beside the River Arun with a public house on site. 3 miles to beaches. Advance booking is advisable for hook-ups and groups.
**Nearest Town/Resort** Arundel/Littlehampton
**Directions** From the A27 at Arundel, follow road signposted to Ford for 2 miles. Site is

on the left after level-crossing at Ford.
⇥ Ford

## BILLINGHURST

**Limeburners (Camping) Ltd.,** Limeburners, Newbridge, Billinghurst, West Sussex, RH14 9JA
**Tel:** 01403 782311
**Email:** chippy.sawyer@virgin.net
**Pitches For** ⚑ ⚑ 🚐 **Total** 40
**Facilities** ∮ 🖽 ⚹ ┌ ⊙ ⌿ 🎇 🛒 ⤶ 🅿
**Nearby Facilities** ╱ ∪ ♿
**Open** April to October
**Access** Good **Site** Level
Public house attached, lunch time and evening food. AA 2 Pennants.
**Nearest Town/Resort** Billinghurst
**Directions** 1½ miles west of billinghurst on A272, turn left on B2133 150yds onleft.

## BOGNOR REGIS

**Rowan Park Caravan Club Site,** Rowan Way, Bognor Regis, West Sussex, PO22 9RP
**Tel:** 01243 828515
www.caravanclub.co.uk
**Pitches For** ⚑ ⚑ 🚐 **Total** 100
**Facilities** ∮ 🖽 🖽 ⚹ ┌ ⊙ 🛒 ⤶
🎇 🛒 ⤶ 🅿 ⤶
**Nearby Facilities** ┌ ✈ ⌖ ♿
**Acreage** 8 **Open** March to Oct
**Access** Good **Site** Level
2 miles from the beach, South Coast World and a leisure centre. Close to Weald & Downland Open Air Museum, D-Day Museum & Battle of Britain Aviation and Amberley Chalk Pits Museum. Non members welcome. Booking essential.
**Nearest Town/Resort** Bognor Regis
**Directions** From north on the A29, ½ mile past Shripney Village at the roundabout turn right into Rowan Way, site is 100 yards on the right, opposite Halfords.
⇥ Bognor Regis

## BOGNOR REGIS

**The Lillies Caravan Park,** Yapton Road, Barnham, Bognor Regis, West Sussex, PO22 0AY
**Tel:** 01243 552081 **Fax:** 01243 552081
**Email:** thelillies@hotmail.com
www.lilliescaravanpark.co.uk
**Pitches For** ⚑ ⚑ 🚐 **Total** 50
**Facilities** ⚹ ∮ 🖽 ⚹ ┌ ⊙ ⌿ ⤶ 🅿
⚹ 🎇 🛒 🛒 ⤶ 🅿 ╱
**Nearby Facilities** ┌ ╱ ⚹ ⌖ ∪ ♿ ♿
**Acreage** 3 **Open** All Year
**Access** Good **Site** Level
Quiet, secluded site within walking distance of Barnham Railway Station where there is a direct line to all main local attractions.
**Nearest Town/Resort** Bognor Regis
**Directions** From Bognor Regis take the A29 to Eastergate, turn right at the War Memorial onto the B2233, 5 miles.
⇥ Barnham

## CHICHESTER

**Bell Caravan Park,** Bell Lane, Birdham, Nr Chichester, West Sussex, PO20 7HY
**Tel:** 01243 512264
**Pitches For** ⚑ 🚐 **Total** 15
**Facilities** ∮ 🖽 ⚹ ┌ ⚹ 🎇 🛒 ⤶ 🅿
**Nearby Facilities** ┌ ╱ ⌖ ⚹ ∪ ♿ ♿
**Acreage** ¼ **Open** March to October
**Access** Good **Site** Level
**Nearest Town/Resort** Chichester.
**Directions** From Chichester take the A286 towards Wittering for approx. 4 miles. At Birdham turn left into Bell Lane, site is 500yds on the left.
⇥ Chichester

## CHICHESTER

**Camping & Caravanning Club Site,** 345 Main Road, Southbourne, Hampshire, PO10 8JH
**Tel:** 01243 373202
www.campingandcaravanningclub.co.uk
**Pitches For** ⚑ ⚑ 🚐 **Total** 58
**Facilities** ⚹ ∮ 🖽 🖽 ⚹ ┌ ⊙ ⌿ 🅿 ⤶
🎇 🛒 🛒 ⤶ 🅿 ⤶
**Nearby Facilities**
**Acreage** 3 **Open** February to November
**Access** Good **Site** Level
500 yards through a footpath to the beach. Ideal touring, well placed for visiting the Sussex Downs and south coast resorts. Close to the City of Portsmouth. BTB 4 Star Graded and AA 3 Pennants. Non members welcome.
**Nearest Town/Resort** Chichester
**Directions** On the A259 from Chichester, site is on the right past Inlands Road.
⇥ Southbourne

## CHICHESTER

**Ellscott Park,** Sidlesham Lane, Birdham, Chichester, West Sussex, PO20 7QL
**Tel:** 01243 512003 **Fax:** 01243 512003
**Email:** camping@ellscottpark.co.uk
www.ellscottpark.co.uk
**Pitches For** ⚑ ⚑ 🚐 **Total** 50
**Facilities** ⚹ ∮ 🖽 ⚹ ┌ ⊙ ⌿ ⤶ 🅿
⚹ 🎇 ⤶ 🅿 ⤶ ♿
**Nearby Facilities** ┌ ╱ ⚹ ⌖ ∪ ♿ ♿
**Acreage** 3 **Open** March to October
**Access** Good **Site** Level
The famous West Wittering beach. 1½ miles from Chichester Harbour for yachting and boating. Ideal site for walking, cycling and sight-seeing.
**Nearest Town/Resort** Chichester
**Directions** From the A27 Chichester by-pass turn south onto the A286 towards Witterings. Travel for approx. 4 miles then turn left towards Butterfly Farm, site is 500 metres on the right.
⇥ Chichester

## CHICHESTER

**Lakeside Holiday Village,** Vinnetrow Road, Chichester, West Sussex, PO20 1QH
**Tel:** 01243 787715 **Fax:** 01243 533643
**Email:** info@cinqueportsleisure.com
www.cplholidays.com
**Pitches For** ⚑ 🚐 **Total** 214
**Facilities** ⚹ ∮ 🖽 ⚹ ┌ ⤶ 🅿 ⚹ 🛒
⚹ 🛒 🎇 ╳ 🅿 ⚹ ⤶ 🛒 ⤶ 🎇
**Nearby Facilities** ╱ ∪ ♿
**Acreage** 220 **Open** All Year
**Access** Good **Site** Level
Surrounded by 12 lakes. Close to Chichester.
**Nearest Town/Resort** Chichester
**Directions** Take the A27 to Chichester until you reach the Bognor Road roundabout, take the Pagham exit which leads to Lakeside.
⇥ Chichester

## CHICHESTER

**Red House Farm,** Earnley, Chichester, West Sussex, PO20 7JG
**Tel:** 01243 512959 **Fax:** 01243 514216
**Email:** clayredhouse@hotmail.com
**Pitches For** ⚑ 🚐 **Total** 100
**Facilities** ⚹ ∮ 🖽 ⚹ ┌ ⊙ ⌿ ⤶ 🅿 🛒 ⤶ 🅿
**Nearby Facilities** ╱ ⌖ ⚹ ∪
**Acreage** 4½ **Open** Easter to October
**Access** Good **Site** Level
Flat and smooth site on a working farm in a country area. 1 mile from the village and beach. No all male or female groups permitted.
**Nearest Town/Resort** Bracklesham Bay

# SUSSEX (WEST)

**Directions** From Chichester take the A286 south to Witterings, after 5 miles turn left onto the B2198 opposite the garage to Bracklesham Bay. After 1 mile on sharp right hand bend turn left to Earnley, site is 200 yards on the left.
⇌ Chichester

## EAST WITTERING

**Gees Camp,** Stubcroft Lane, Bracklesham Bay, Chichester, West Sussex, PO20 8NY
**Tel:** 01243 670223
**Pitches For** ▲ ⊕ ⊞
**Facilities** ⫟ ⬚ ☀ ⌐ ☎ ⊟ ⌂
**Nearby Facilities** ⌐ ✐ ⚓ ⊔ Ո ℛ
**Open** March to Oct
**Access** Good **Site** Level
Approx. 600 yards from a sandy beach.
**Nearest Town/Resort** Chichester
**Directions** From Chichester take the A286 to Birdham, then take the B2198 to Bracklesham Bay.
⇌ Chichester

## GRAFFHAM

**Camping & Caravanning Club Site,**
Great Bury, Graffham, Petworth, West Sussex, GU28 0QJ
**Tel:** 01798 867476
www.campingandcaravanningclub.co.uk
**Pitches For** ▲ ⊕ ⊞ **Total** 90
**Facilities** ⊟ ⫟ ⬚ ☀ ⌐ ☉ ⊔ ☎ ⊡ ☕
☋ ⌨ ⊙ ⊟★⊟⊟ ℛ
**Nearby Facilities** Ո
**Open** March to October
**Site** Sloping
Set in 20 acres of woodland with many walks. BTB 4 Star Graded and AA 3 Pennants. Non members welcome.
**Directions** From Petworth take the A285, pass Badgers Pub on the left and the BP Garage on the right, take the next right turn signposted Selham Graffham (with brown camping sign), follow signs to site. From Chichester take the A285 through Duncton and turn left signposted Selham Graffham (with brown camping sign).
⇌ Chichester

## HENFIELD

**Downsview Caravan Park,** Bramlands Lane, Woodmancote, Nr Henfield, West Sussex, BN5 9TG
**Tel:** 01273 492801 **Fax:** 01273 495214
**Email:** phr.peter@lineone.net
**Pitches For** ▲ ⊕ ⊞
**Facilities** ⚲ ⫟ ⬚ ⬚ ☀ ⌐ ☉ ⊡ ☕
☋ ⌨ ⊙ ⊟★⊟⊟ ⫙
**Nearby Facilities** ⌐ ✐ ⚓ ⊔ Ո ℛ
**Acreage** 4 **Open** 1 April/Easter to 31 Oct
**Access** Good **Site** Level
Small, secluded site in peaceful countryside. Close to the South Downs, yet within 9 miles of Brighton. Close to pubs and local shops. Sorry, no facilities for children.
**Nearest Town/Resort** Brighton
**Directions** Signed off the A281 in the village of Woodmancote. 2½ miles east of Henfield and 9 miles northwest of Brighton centre.
⇌ Brighton/Hassocks

## HORSHAM

**Honeybridge Park,** Honeybridge Lane, Dial Post, Nr Horsham, West Sussex, RH13 8NX
**Tel:** 01403 710923 **Fax:** 01403 710923
**Email:** enquiries@honeybridgepark.co.uk
www.honeybridgepark.co.uk
**Pitches For** ▲ ⊕ ⊞ **Total** 200
**Facilities** ⫟ ⊟ ⬚ ⬚ ☀ ⌐ ☉ ⊔ ☎ ⊡ ☕
☋ ⊙ ⊟ ☀ ⚲ ⌨ ⊡ Ո ★⊟⊟ ⫙ ℛ
**Nearby Facilities** ⌐ ✐ ⊔ Ո ℛ
**Acreage** 15 **Open** All Year
**Access** Good **Site** Level
Delightfully situated in an area of Outstanding Natural Beauty. Rural, relaxed atmosphere, highest standards maintained with generous sized hard standing and grass pitches. Heated amenity blocks; excellent facilities (incl. Disabled) licensed shop and take-away food. Ideal touring base, convenient for the coast and only 1 hour from London and theme parks.
**Nearest Town/Resort** Worthing
**Directions** 10 miles south of Horsham on the A24, turn at Old Barn Nurseries.
⇌ Horsham

## LITTLEHAMPTON

**Daisyfields Touring Park,** Cornfield Close, Worthing Road, Littlehampton, West Sussex, BN17 6LD
**Tel:** 01903 714240 **Fax:** 01903 714240
**Email:** daisyfields@f25.com
www.camping-caravaning.co.uk
**Pitches For** ▲ ⊕ ⊞ **Total** 80
**Facilities** ⫟ ⬚ ☀ ⌐ ☉ ☋ ⊙ ⊟ ⊞ ⬚
★⊟ ⊟ ⫙
**Nearby Facilities** ⌐ ✐ ⚓ ⊔ Ո ℛ
**Acreage** 6½ **Open** All Year
**Access** Good **Site** Level
1½ to sandy beach. 1 mile to River Arun. Open all year dependant on the weather. NEW toilet and shower facilities. Pets welcome with camper vans and caravans only. No commercial vehicles.
**Nearest Town/Resort** Littlehampton
**Directions** The site is situated on the A259 Worthing to Bognor Regis, between two Body Shop roundabouts. 3 miles from Arundel.
⇌ Littlehampton

## LITTLEHAMPTON

**White Rose Touring Park,** Mill Lane, Wick, Littlehampton, West Sussex, BN17 7PH
**Tel:** 01903 716176 **Fax:** 01903 732671
**Email:** snowdondavid@hotmail.com
www.whiterosetouringpark.co.uk
**Pitches For** ▲ ⊕ ⊞ **Total** 135
**Facilities** ⚲ ⫟ ⊟ ⬚ ☀ ⌐ ☉ ⊔ ☎ ⊡ ☕
☋ ⌨ ⊙ ⊟ ★⊟ ⊟ Ո ★⊟⊟
**Nearby Facilities** ⌐ ✐ ⚓ ⊔ Ո ℛ
**Acreage** 6 **Open** 15 March to 14 Dec
**Access** Good **Site** Level
1½ miles from the beach. Close to Arundel and South Downs.
**Nearest Town/Resort** Littlehampton
**Directions** From the A27 take the A284 signposted Littlehampton, site is approx. 1½ miles on the left (first left after Six Bells Public House).
⇌ Littlehampton

## SELSEY

**Warner Farm Touring Park,** Warner Lane, Selsey, West Sussex, PO20 9EL
**Tel:** 01243 604499 **Fax:** 01243 604499
**Email:** touring@bunnleisure.co.uk
www.bunnleisure.co.uk
**Pitches For** ▲ ⊕ ⊞ **Total** 200
**Facilities** ⚲ ⫟ ⊟ ⬚ ⬚ ☀ ⌐ ☉ ⊔ ☎ ⊡ ☕
☋ ⌨ ⊙ ⊟ ☀ ⚲ ⊟ ⬚ Ո ★ ☉ ★⊟⊟ ⫙
**Nearby Facilities** ⌐ ✐ ⊔ ℛ
**Acreage** 10 **Open** March to October
**Access** Good **Site** Level
Near the beach.
**Nearest Town/Resort** Chichester
**Directions** From the A27 Chichester take the B2145 to Selsey. On entering Selsey turn right into School Lane. Follow signs for Warner Farm Touring Park.
⇌ Chichester

## SLINDON

**Camping & Caravanning Club Site,**
Slindon Park, Nr Arundel, West Sussex, BN18 0RG
**Tel:** 01243 814387
www.campingandcaravanningclub.co.uk
**Pitches For** ▲ ⊕ ⊞ **Total** 40
**Facilities** ⫟ ⊟ ⌨ ⊙ ⊟★⊟⊟
**Nearby Facilities**
**Acreage** 2 **Open** March to Sept
**Access** Good **Site** Lev/Slope
Within the National Trust property of Slindon Park. 6 miles from Goodwood Racecourse. BTB 3 Star Graded and AA 1 Pennant. Non members welcome.
**Nearest Town/Resort** Chichester
**Directions** From the A27 Chichester to Fontwell road, turn right into Brittons Lane (second turn left after the B2233 on the right), then take the second turn right to Slindon. Site is on this road.
⇌ Barnham

## WEST WITTERING

**Nunnington Farm Camping Site,**
Nunnington Farm, West Wittering, West Sussex, PO20 8LZ
**Tel:** 01243 514013 No Booking
**Email:** nunningtontonfarm@hotmail.com
www.camping-in-sussex.com
**Pitches For** ▲ ⊕ ⊞ **Total** 125
**Facilities** ⚲ ⫟ ⬚ ☀ ⌐ ☉ ⊔ ☎ ⊡ ☕
☋ ⌨ ⊙ ⊟ ★⊟⊟
**Nearby Facilities** ✐ ⚓ ⊔ Ո
**Acreage** 4½ **Open** Easter to Mid October
**Access** Good **Site** Level
Near the beach.
**Nearest Town/Resort** Chichester
**Directions** 7 miles south of Chichester on the A286 - B2179. 200yds before village on left, look for signs.
⇌ Chichester

## WEST WITTERING

**Wicks Farm Camping Park,** Redlands Lane, West Wittering, Chichester, West Sussex, PO20 8QD
**Tel:** 01243 513116 **Fax:** 01243 511296
www.wicksfarm.co.uk
**Pitches For** ▲ ⊕ ⊞ **Total** 40
**Facilities** ⫟ ⬚ ☀ ⌐ ☉ ⊔ ☎ ⊡ ☕
☋ ⌨ ⊙ ⊟ ☀ ⚲ ⊟⊟

**Nearby Facilities** ⌐ ✔ ⚠ ♟
**Acreage** 2¼ **Open** April **to** October
**Access** Good **Site** Level
**Nearest Town/Resort** West Wittering/Chichester
**Directions** From Chichester take the A286 for Birdham, then take the B2179 for West Wittering.
⇌ Chichester

## WISBOROUGH GREEN

**Bat & Ball Public House,** Newpound, Wisborough Green, West Sussex, RH14 0EH
**Tel:** 01403 700313
**Pitches For** Å ⬜ ⬛ **Total** 25
**Facilities** ⬚ ⚓ ⌐ ☉ ⬛ ⬜ ⬛ ✕ ⬤ ⬤ ♦
⬚ ⬛ ⬜ ⬛
**Nearby Facilities** ⌐ ✔
**Acreage** 3-4 **Open** All Year
**Access** Good **Site** Level
Adjacent to Fishers Farm Park. Good walking area. 30 minutes from the coast.
**Nearest Town/Resort** Billinghurst
**Directions** From Billinghurst take the A272 towards Petworth. After 2 miles take the B2133 and follow signs to the Bat & Ball Public House.
⇌ Billinghurst

## WORTHING

**Northbrook Farm Caravan Club Site,** Titnore Way, Worthing, West Sussex, BN13 3RT
**Tel:** 01903 502962
**www.caravanclub.co.uk**
**Pitches For** ⬜ ⬛ **Total** 129
**Facilities** ⚡ ⬚ ⬚ ⚓ ⌐ ⬜ ⬤
⬚ ⬛ ⬛ ⬚ ⬛ ⬛ ⬜ ⬛
**Nearby Facilities** ⌐ ⚠ ✔ ♟
**Acreage** 12½ **Open** March **to** Oct
**Access** Good **Site** Level
Set in open countryside yet only 2 miles from the coast. West Worthing Tennis Club adjacent for tennis, squash, restaurant and bar. Near to Arundel Castle. Non members welcome. Booking essential.
**Nearest Town/Resort** Worthing
**Directions** From north on A24, in Findon at roundabout junction with A280 turn right sp Chichester. After 4 miles at roundabout take second exit to roundabout on far side of bridge over A27 and turn left (first exit sp Ferring). After ¾ miles at brown sign turn left into Titnore Way, site is 120 yards on the left.
⇌ Worthing

**THANK YOU FOR CHOOSING CADE'S**

## TYNE & WEAR

### SOUTH SHIELDS

**Lizard Lane Caravan Park,** Lizard Lane, South Shields, Tyne & Wear, NE34 7AB
**Tel:** 0191 454 4982
**Pitches For** Å ⬜ ⬛ **Total** 40
**Facilities** ⚡ ⬚ ⚓ ⌐ ☉ ⬛ ⬤ ⬜ ⬤
⬚ ⬛ ⬛ ⬜
**Nearby Facilities** ⌐ ✔ ∪ ♟
**Open** March **to** Oct
**Access** Good **Site** Sloping
**Nearest Town/Resort** South Shields
**Directions** Take the Tyne Tunnel, A185, A194 and A183.
⇌ Newcastle

## WARWICKSHIRE

### BIDFORD-ON-AVON

**Cottage of Content,** Barton, Bidford-on-Avon, Warwickshire, B50 4NP
**Tel:** 01789 772279
**Pitches For** Å ⬜ ⬛ **Total** 25
**Facilities** ⬚ ⚓ ☉ ⬛ ⬜ ⬛ ⬤ ⬛ ✕ ⬚ ⬛ ⬜ ⬛
**Nearby Facilities** ⌐ ✔ ⚠ ✖ ∪ ♟ ⚘ ⋏
**Acreage** 2 **Open** March **to** October
**Access** Good **Site** Sloping
**Nearest Town/Resort** Bidford-on-Avon
**Directions** 1 mile from Bidford follow Honeybourne road for ¾ mile. Turn left at crossroads signposted Barton, situated on bend in ¼ mile.
⇌ Stratford-upon-Avon

### LONG COMPTON

**Mill Farm,** Long Compton, Shipston-on-Stour, Warwickshire, CV36 5NZ
**Tel:** 01608 684663
**Pitches For** Å ⬜ ⬛ **Total** 10
**Facilities** ⬚ ⚓ ☉ ⬛ ⬤ ⬛
**Nearby Facilities**
**Acreage** 3 **Open** March **to** October
**Access** Good **Site** Level
Fringe of the Cotswolds.
**Nearest Town/Resort** Moreton-on-Marsh
**Directions** Turn off A3400 west for Barton-on-the-Heath. Site on right in ½ mile.
⇌ Moreton-in-Marsh

### RUGBY

**Lodge Farm,** Bilton Lane, Long Lawford, Rugby, Warwickshire, CV23 9DU
**Tel:** 01788 560193 **Fax:** 01788 550603
**Email:** alec@lodgefarm.com
**www.lodgefarm.com**
**Pitches For** Å ⬜ ⬛ **Total** 35
**Facilities** ⚓ ⚡ ⬚ ⬜ ⚓ ⌐ ⬤
⬜ ⬚ ⬛ ⬜ ⬛
**Nearby Facilities** ⌐ ✔ ⚠ ✖ ∪

**Acreage** 3 **Open** Easter **to** End Oct
**Access** Good **Site** Lev/Slope
**Nearest Town/Resort** Rugby
**Directions** Take the A428 from Rugby towards Coventry. After 1½ miles turn left at Sheaf & Sickle, site is 400 yards on the left.
⇌ Rugby

### STRATFORD-UPON-AVON

**Dodwell Park,** Evesham Road, Stratford-upon-Avon, Warwickshire, CV37 9SR
**Tel:** 01789 204957 **Fax:** 01926 620199
**Email:** enquiries@dodwellpark.co.uk
**www.dodwellpark.co.uk**
**Pitches For** Å ⬜ ⬛ **Total** 50
**Facilities** ⚡ ⬚ ⬚ ⚓ ⌐ ☉ ⬜ ⬛ ⬤
⚡ ⬚ ⬛ ⬛ ⬜ ⬛
**Nearby Facilities** ⌐ ✔ ✖ ∪ ♟
**Acreage** 2 **Open** All Year
**Access** Good **Site** Lev/Slope
Shakespeare Theatre and Cotswolds.
**Nearest Town/Resort** Stratford-upon-Avon
**Directions** 2 miles southwest of Stratford on B439 (formerly the A439)- Not the racecourse site.
⇌ Stratford-upon-Avon

### STRATFORD-UPON-AVON

**Island Meadow Caravan Park,** Aston Cantlow, Warwickshire, B95 6JP
**Tel:** 01789 488273 **Fax:** 01789 488273
**Email:**
holiday@islandmeadowcaravanpark.co.uk
**www.islandmeadowcaravanpark.co.uk**
**Pitches For** Å ⬜ ⬛ **Total** 34
**Facilities** ⚓ ⚡ ⬚ ⬚ ⚓ ⌐ ☉ ⬛ ⬤ ⬜ ⬤
⚡ ⬚ ⬛ ⬛ ⬜ ⬛
**Nearby Facilities** ⌐ ✔ ∪
**Acreage** 3 **Open** March **to** October
**Access** Good **Site** Level
Small, quiet island, adjacent to a picturesque village. Café/Restaurant and childrens play area nearby. Ideal centre for Shakespeare Country.
**Nearest Town/Resort** Stratford-upon-Avon
**Directions** From the A46 or the A3400 follow signs for Aston Cantlow Village. Park is ½ mile west of the village in Mill Lane.
⇌ Wilmcote

### STRATFORD-UPON-AVON

**Riverside Caravan Park,** Tiddington Road, Stratford-upon-Avon, Warwickshire, CV37 7AG
**Tel:** 01789 292312
**Email:** info@stratfordcaravans.co.uk
**www.stratfordcaravans.co.uk**
**Pitches For** ⬜ ⬛ **Total** 90
**Facilities** ⚓ ⚡ ⬚ ⚓ ⌐ ☉ ⬜ ⬛ ⬤
⚡ ⬚ ⬛ ⬛ ⬜ ⬛ ✕ ⬤ ⬛ ⬜ ⬛ ⬛ ⚘ ⋏
**Nearby Facilities** ⌐ ✔ ✖ ∪
**Acreage** 8 **Open** April **to** October

**Access** Good **Site** Lev/Slope
River Taxi to and from the town centre.
Childrens play area nearby.
**Nearest Town/Resort** Stratford-upon-Avon
**Directions** On the B4086 1¼ miles from the town centre, just before entering Tiddington Village.
⇌ Stratford-upon-Avon

### STUDLEY

**Outhill Caravan Park,** Outhill, Studley, Warwickshire, B80 7DY
**Tel:** 01527 852160
**Pitches For** ⊞ ⊞ **Total** 15
**Facilities** ⊞ ⊁ ⋇
**Nearby Facilities**
**Acreage** 11 **Open** April to October
**Access** Good **Site** Level
Peace and quiet. No electricity and no hot water. Advance booking is essential.
**Nearest Town/Resort** Henley-in-Arden
**Directions** From A435 (Birmingham to Evesham road) turn towards Henley-in-Arden on A4189. Take third turning to the right (approx 1¼ miles), check in at Outhill Farm (first on left).

### WARWICK

**Warwick Racecourse Caravan Club Site,** Hampton Street, Warwick, Warwickshire, CV34 6HN
**Tel:** 01926 495448
www.caravanclub.co.uk
**Pitches For** ⊞ ⊞ **Total** 54
**Facilities** ⊞ ⅃ ⊞ ⊞ ⊞ ⏃ ⌂ ⊞
⊞ ⊞ ⊞ ⊞ ⊟
**Nearby Facilities** ⌐ ⋌
**Acreage** 3¼ **Open** March to Jan
**Access** Good **Site** Level
Grass and tarmac site in the racecourse enclosure. Very short walk to the centre of Warwick and its castle. Only 8 miles from Stratford-upon-Avon. Non members welcome. Booking essential.
**Nearest Town/Resort** Warwick
**Directions** Leave the M40 at junction 15 and take the A429 sp Warwick. After 1 mile at brown camping sign turn left into Shakespeares Avenue, at T-junction turn right onto the B4095, site is ½ mile on the left.
⇌ Warwick

### WOLVEY

**Wolvey Caravan & Camping Park,** Villa Farm, Wolvey, Nr Hinckley, Leicestershire, LE10 3HF
**Tel:** 01455 220493/220630
**Pitches For** ⋏ ⊞ ⊞ **Total** 110
**Facilities** ⊞ ⅃ ⊞ ⊞ ⏃ ⌐ ⊙ ⌐ ⊟ ⊞ ⊞
⊞ ⊞ ⊞ ⊞ ⊞ ⊞ ⊞ ⋇ ⌢
**Nearby Facilities** ⌐ ⋌
**Acreage** 10 **Open** All Year
**Access** Good **Site** Level
A quiet site, ideally situated to explore the many places of interest in the Midlands.
**Nearest Town/Resort** Hinckley
**Directions** Leave the M6 at junction 2 and take the B4065, follow signs for Wolvey and camping signs. Or leave the M69 at junction 1 and take the B4065, follow signs for Wolvey and camping signs.
⇌ Hinckley

---

**IT WILL HELP US TO**

**CONTINUE PROVIDING**

**THIS INFORMATION, IF**

**YOU WOULD KINDLY**

**MENTION CADE'S**

**WHEN REPLYING TO**

**OUR ADVERTISERS.**

**THANK YOU.**

---

## WEST MIDLANDS

### HALESOWEN

**Clent Hills Camping & Caravanning Club Site,** Fieldhouse Lane, Romsley, Halesowen, West Midlands, B62 0NH
**Tel:** 01562 710015
www.campingandcaravanningclub.co.uk
**Pitches For** ⋏ ⊞ ⊞ **Total** 95
**Facilities** ⊞ ⅃ ⊞ ⊞ ⏃ ⌐ ⊙ ⌐ ⊟ ⊞ ⊞
⊞ ⊞ ⊞ ⊞ ⊞ ⊞ ⊞ ⋇ ⌢
**Nearby Facilities** ⌐ ∪
**Acreage** 7½ **Open** March to October
**Access** Good **Site** Sloping
In the heart of the West Midlands. Ideal for walkers and cyclists. BTB 5 Star Graded and AA 4 Pennants. Non members welcome.
**Nearest Town/Resort** Halesowen
**Directions** Travelling northwest on the M5, leave at junction 3 onto the A456. Then take the B4551 to Romsley, turn right at Sun Hotel, take the 5th left turn then the next left and the site is 330 yards on the left hand side.
⇌ Old Hill

### MERIDEN

**Somers Wood Caravan & Camping Park,** Somers Road, Meriden, North Warwickshire, CV7 7PL
**Tel:** 01676 522978 **Fax:** 01676 522978
**Email:** enquiries@somerswood.co.uk
www.somerswood.co.uk
**Pitches For** ⊞ ⊞ **Total** 48
**Facilities** ⅃ ⊞ ⊞ ⏃ ⌐ ⊙ ⌐ ⊟ ⊞
⊞ ⊞ ⊞ ⊞ ⊞ ⊞ ⊟ ⊞ ⊞A
**Nearby Facilities** ⌐ ⋌ ∪
**Acreage** 4 **Open** Feb to 15 Dec inc.
**Access** Good **Site** Level
ADULTS ONLY SITE. Adjacent to a golf course with clubhouse. Approx. 3 miles from the N.E.C. Birmingham. Fishing adjacent.
**Nearest Town/Resort** Solihull
**Directions** Leave the M42 at junction 6, take the A45 to Coventry. Immediately on the left pick up signs for the A452 Leamington. Go to roundabout and turn right onto the A452 signed Leamington/Warwick, at the next roundabout turn left into Hampton Lane. Site is ½ mile on the left hand side.
⇌ Hampton-in-Arden

---

## SUTTON COLDFIELD

**Camping & Caravanning Club Site,**
Kingsbury Water Park, Bodymoor Heath
Lane, Sutton Coldfield, West Midlands,
B76 0DY
**Tel:** 01827 874101
www.campingandcaravanningclub.co.uk
**Pitches For** ▲ ⚕ 🚐 **Total** 150
**Facilities** ⚙ ⒡ 🎲 🖵 ⚓ ⌐ ⊙ ⌣ 🔌 ◻ ☎
🏧 🍴 🛁 🗑 🛈 ▭ ✂ 🔎
**Nearby Facilities** ⌐ 🚶 ⚲
**Open** All Year
**Site** Level
Surrounding the site are the 600 acres of
Kingsbury Water Park. BTB 5 Star Graded,
AA 4 Pennants and Loo of the Year Award.
Non members welcome.
**Directions** Leave the M42 at junction 9 and
take the B4097 towards Kingsbury. At the
roundabout turn left and continue past the
main entrance to the water park, go over the
motorway and turn next right, follow lane for
½ mile to the site.
⚄ Tamworth

## SUTTON COLDFIELD

**Marston Caravan & Camping Park,**
Kingsbury Road, Marston, Near Sutton
Coldfield, West Midlands, B76 0DP
**Tel:** 01299 400787
**Pitches For** ▲ ⚕ ▢ **Total** 120
**Facilities** ⚙ ⒡ 🎲 🖵 ⚓ ⌐ ⊙ ⌣ 🔌 ◻ ☎
🏧 ⒓ 🗑 🛁 🗑 ▭ ✂
**Nearby Facilities** ⌐ 🚶 🚣 ⚲ ⊙ 🎣 ⚲ ✠
**Acreage** 10 **Open** All Year
**Access** Good **Site** Level
Next to Kingsbury Water Parks and near to
Drayton Manor Park. Just a 10 minute
drive from the N.E.C..
**Nearest Town/Resort** Birmingham
**Directions** Leave the M42 at junction 9 and
take the A4097 towards Kingsbury, Marston
Caravan Park is ¾ miles on the left.
⚄ Birmingham

> ALWAYS CHECK
> DIRECTLY WITH THE
> PARK THAT
> ANY FACILITIES YOU
> PARTICULARLY
> REQUIRE WILL BE
> AVAILABLE AT THE
> TIME OF YOUR VISIT.

## WILTSHIRE

### BRADFORD-ON-AVON

**Church Farm Touring Caravan &
Camping Site,** Church Farm, Winsley,
Bradford-on-Avon, Wiltshire, BA15 2JH
**Tel:** 01225 722246
**Email:**
enquiries@churchfarmcamping.co.uk
www.churchfarmcamping.co.uk
**Pitches For** ▲ ⚕ 🚐 **Total** 20
**Facilities** ⒡ 🎲 ⚓ ⌐ ⊙ ⌣ ☎ ⒓ 🏧 ▭ ▣
**Nearby Facilities** ⌐ 🚶 🎣 ∪
**Acreage** 1½ **Open** Easter **to** Oct
**Access** Good **Site** Level
Countryside site on a working farm with
sheep and horses, in an area of
outstanding natural beauty. Approx 500
metres from the village shop and pub. 5
miles from Bath. ¾ miles from Kennet &
Avon Canal for boating, fishing, cycling and
walking. Regular buses.
**Nearest Town/Resort** Bradford-on-Avon
**Directions** On the B3108 between Bradford-
on-Avon and Limpley Stoke. At the
roundabout in Winsley follow exit to Bath and
Limpley Stoke. Church Farm is ¾ miles on
the right.
⚄ Bradford-on-Avon

### CALNE

**Blackland Lakes,** Blackland Leisure Ltd,
Stockley Lane, Calne, Wiltshire, SN11 0NQ
**Tel:** 01249 810943 **Fax:** 01249 811346
**Email:**
blacklandlakes.info@btconnect.com
www.blacklandlakes.co.uk
**Pitches For** ▲ ⚕ 🚐 **Total** 180
**Facilities** ⚙ ⒡ 🎲 🖵 ⚓ ⌐ ⊙ ⌣ 🔌 ◻ ☎
🏧 ⒓ 🏧 🗑 🛁 🗑 ▭ ✂ 🔎
**Nearby Facilities** ⌐ 🎣 ∪ ⚲
**Acreage** 15 **Open** All Year
**Access** Good **Site** Level
A natural, interesting, scenic and secure
site. Three lakes, super coarse fishing. 1
mile perimeter trail for dogs, walking and
cycling. Winter bookings must be pre-paid.
Call our Info Line on 01249 810941.
**Nearest Town/Resort** Calne
**Directions** Signposted from the A4 east of
Calne.
⚄ Chippenham

### CHIPPENHAM

**Piccadilly Caravan Site,** Folly Lane West,
Lacock, Chippenham, Wiltshire, SN15 2LP
**Tel:** 01249 730260
**Email:** piccadillylacock@aol.com
**Pitches For** ▲ ⚕ 🚐 **Total** 40
**Facilities** ⒡ 🎲 🖵 ⚓ ⌐ ⊙ ⌣ 🔌 ◻ ☎
🏧 🍴 🛁 🗑 ▭ ▣
**Nearby Facilities** ⌐ 🚶 ∪

**Acreage** 2½ **Open** April **to** October
**Access** Good **Site** Level
Close National Trust village of Lacock.
Ideal touring centre.
**Nearest Town/Resort** Chippenham/
Melksham
**Directions** Turn right off A350 Chippenham/
Melksham Road, 5 miles south of
Chippenham, close to Lacock. Signposted
to Gastard (with caravan symbol), site is after
the Nurseries.
⚄ Chippenham

### CHIPPENHAM

**Plough Lane Caravan Site,** Kington
Langley, Chippenham, Wiltshire, SN15
5PS
**Tel:** 01249 750146 **Fax:** 01249 750795
**Email:** ploughlane@lineone.net
www.ploughlane.co.uk
**Pitches For** ⚕ 🚐 **Total** 50
**Facilities** ⚙ ⒡ 🎲 🖵 ⚓ ⌐ ⊙ ⌣ 🔌 ◻ ☎
⒓ 🏧 🗑 ▭ 🅿 🅰
**Nearby Facilities** ⌐ 🚶 ⚲
**Acreage** 4 **Open** Mid March **to** Mid Oct
**Access** Good **Site** Level
ADULTS ONLY SITE.
**Nearest Town/Resort** Chippenham
**Directions** Well signposted from the A350
north of Chippenham.
⚄ Chippenham

### DEVIZES

**Camping & Caravanning Club Site,**
Spout Lane, Nr Seend, Melksham,
Wiltshire, SN12 6RN
**Tel:** 01380 828839
www.campingandcaravanningclub.co.uk
**Pitches For** ⚕ 🚐 **Total** 90
**Facilities** ⚙ ⒡ 🎲 🖵 ⚓ ⌐ ⊙ ⌣ 🔌 ◻ ☎
🏧 🍴 🛁 🗑 ▭ ✂
**Nearby Facilities** 🚶
**Open** All Year
**Site** Level
Bordering the Kennett & Avon Canal. BTB
5 Star Graded, AA 4 Pennants and David
Bellamy Silver Award. Non members
welcome.
**Directions** Take the A365 from Melksham,
turn right down the lane beside Three
Magpies Public House, site is on the right.
⚄ Melksham

### DEVIZES

**Foxhangers Canalside Park,** Lower
Foxhangers Farm, Devizes, Wiltshire,
SN10 1SS
**Tel:** 01380 828254
**Email:** selfcatering@foxhangers.co.uk
www.foxhangers.com
**Pitches For** ▲ ⚕ 🚐 **Total** 18

# WILTSHIRE

**Facilities** ! 🏠 ⚡ ☎ ⌂ 🍴 🔥 ⚡ 📶 🚽 🅿 🔌
**Nearby Facilities** ✈
**Acreage** 1¾ **Open** Easter **to** Oct
**Access** Good **Site** Sloping
Near a canal for walking, fishing, cycling,
canoeing and boating.
**Nearest Town/Resort** Devizes
**Directions** 2 miles west of Devizes on the
A361. ½ mile east of A361 and A365 junction.
⚡ Chippenham

## MALMESBURY

**Burton Hill Caravan & Camping Park,**
Arches Lane, Burton Hill, Malmesbury,
Wiltshire, SN16 0EH
**Tel:** 01666 826880
**Email:** stay@burtonhill.co.uk
www.burtonhill.co.uk
**Pitches For** ▲ ⚡ 🚐 **Total** 30
**Facilities** ⚽ ! 🏠 ⚡ ⚡ ☎ ⌂ 🍴 🔥 ⚡ 📶 🅿
🔌 ⚡ 🚽 🅿 🔌 ⚡
**Nearby Facilities** ☎ ✈ ⚡ ⚓ ♨ ∪ ♪
**Acreage** 2 **Open** 1 April/Easter **to** October
**Access** Good **Site** Level
Open views. Many local visitor attractions.
Excellent touring base. New shower block.
**Nearest Town/Resort** Malmesbury
**Directions** ½ mile south of Malmesbury on
the A429, entrance is opposite Malmesbury
Hospital.
⚡ Chippenham

## MARLBOROUGH

**Postern Hill - Forestry Commission,**
Postern Hill, Marlborough, Wiltshire, SN8
4ND
**Tel:** 01672 515195
**Email:** info@forestholidays.co.uk
www.forestholidays.co.uk
**Pitches For** ▲ ⚡ 🚐 **Total** 170
**Facilities** ! ⚡ ⚡ 🍴 🔥 ⚡ 📶 🅿 🔌
**Nearby Facilities**
**Acreage** 28½ **Open** 25 March **to** 18 Oct
**Access** Good **Site** Level
In the heart of Savernake Forest, the ideal
site for exploring historic Wiltshire
including Stonehenge and Salisbury
Cathedral. NB: This site has NO toilets.
**Nearest Town/Resort** Marlborough
**Directions** 1 mile south of Marlborough on
the A346. Just 10 miles from the M4 junction
15.
⚡ Marlborough

## NETHERHAMPTON

**Coombe Caravan Park,** Coombe
Nurseries, Race Plain, Netherhampton,
SalisburyWiltshire, SP2 8PN
**Tel:** 01722 328451 **Fax:** 01722 328451
**Pitches For** ▲ ⚡ 🚐 **Total** 48
**Facilities** ! 🏠 ⚡ ☎ ⌂ 🍴 🔥 ⚡ 📶 🅿 ⚡
🔌 ⚡ ⚡ 🚽 🅿

**Nearby Facilities** ☎ ∪ ♪
**Acreage** 3 **Open** March **to** Oct
**Access** Good **Site** Level
Adjacent to racecourse (flat racing), ideal
touring, lovely views.
**Nearest Town/Resort** Salisbury
**Directions** Take A36-A30 Salisbury - Wilton
road, turn off at traffic lights onto A3094
Netherhampton - Stratford Tony road, cross
on bend following Stratford Tony road, 2nd
left behind racecourse, site on right,
signposted.
⚡ Salisbury

## ORCHESTON

**Stonehenge Touring Park,** Orcheston, Nr
Shrewton, Wiltshire, SP3 4SH
**Tel:** 01980 620304
**Email:**
admin@stonehengetouringpark.com
www.stonehengetouringpark.com
**Pitches For** ▲ ⚡ 🚐 **Total** 30
**Facilities** ! 🏠 ⚡ ⚡ ☎ ⌂ 🍴 🔥 ⚡ 📶 🅿 🔌 ⚡
🔌 🔌 🚽 🅿 🔌
**Nearby Facilities** ☎
**Acreage** 2 **Open** All Year
**Access** Good **Site** Level
5 miles from Stonehenge and Salisbury
Plain. Within easy reach Bath and the New
Forest. ETB 3 Star Graded and AA 3
Pennants.
**Nearest Town/Resort** Salisbury
**Directions** On A360 11 miles Salisbury, 11
miles Devizes.
⚡ Salisbury

## SALISBURY

**Alderbury Park,** Southampton Road,
Whaddon, Salisbury, Wiltshire, SP5 3HB
**Tel:** 01722 710125
**Email:** alderbury@aol.com
www.alderburycaravanpark.co.uk
**Pitches For** ▲ ⚡ 🚐 **Total** 39
**Facilities** ⚽ ! 🏠 ⚡ ☎ ⌂ 🍴 ⊙ ⚡ 🅿 🔌
🔌 🔌 🚽 🅿 🔌
**Nearby Facilities** ☎ ✈ ∪ ♪
**Open** All Year
**Access** Good **Site** Level
Ideal touring base for the New Forest,
Salisbury, Stone Henge, Bournemouth,
Poole, Isle of Wight and Southampton ferry
ports. Free use of microwave and freezer
for campers. AA 3 Pennants.
**Nearest Town/Resort** Salisbury
**Directions** On the A36, approx. 3 miles from
Salisbury.
⚡ Salisbury

## SALISBURY

**Camping & Caravanning Club Site,**
Hudson's Field, Castle Road, Salisbury,
Wiltshire, SP1 3RR
**Tel:** 01722 320713
www.campingandcaravanningclub.co.uk
**Pitches For** ▲ ⚡ 🚐 **Total** 150
**Facilities** ⚽ ! 🏠 ⚡ ⚡ ☎ ⌂ 🍴 ⊙ ⚡ 🅿 🔌 ⚡
🔌 🔌 🚽 🅿 🔌 ✳
**Nearby Facilities** ☎ ∪
**Acreage** 4½ **Open** March **to** Oct
**Access** Good **Site** Lev/Slope
1 mile from Salisbury, plenty to do in the
area. BTB 4 Star Graded and AA 3
Pennants. Non members welcome.
**Nearest Town/Resort** Salisbury
**Directions** 1½ miles from Salisbury and
miles from Amesbury on the A345. Hudson'
Field is a large open field next to Old Sarum
⚡ Salisbury

## SALISBURY

**Greenhill Farm Camping & Caravan
Park,** Greenhill Farm, New Road,
Landford, SalisburyWiltshire, SP5 2AZ
**Tel:** 01794 324117 **Fax:** 02380 813209
**Email:** greenhillcamping@aol.com
www.caravancamping.com
**Pitches For** ▲ ⚡ 🚐 **Total** 100
**Facilities** ! 🏠 ⚡ ⚡ ☎ ⌂ 🍴 ⊙ ⚡ 🅿 🔌 ⚡
🔌 🔌 🚽 🅿 🔌 ⚡ 🅰 ✳ ⚡ 🅿
**Nearby Facilities** ☎ ✈ ⚡ ⚓ ∪ ♪ ♪
**Acreage** 30 **Open** All Year
**Access** Good **Site** Level
ADULTS ONLY SITE with two fishing lakes
to pitch beside. Walks directly to the New
Forest from the site. Good for wildlife.
**Nearest Town/Resort** Salisbury
**Directions** Leave the M27 at junction 2 anc
take the A36 Salisbury road. After 4 miles
there is a BP garage on the left, turn nex
left into New Road signposted Nomans Lanc
site is 1 mile on the left.
⚡ Salisbury

## SALISBURY

**Summerlands Caravan Park,** Rockbourne
Road, Coombe Bissett, Salisbury,
Wiltshire, SP5 4LP
**Tel:** 01722 718259
**Pitches For** ▲ ⚡ 🚐 **Total** 25
**Facilities** ! 🏠 ⚡ ⚡ ☎ ⊙ ⚡ 🔌 🔌 ⚡ ✳ ⚡ 🚽 🅿 🔌 🅿
**Open** April **to** Oct **Access** Good **Site** Level
Extensive views from the site. Ideal for
walking and cycling on 'The Green Roads
of Wessex'. Limited facilities for disabled.
**Nearest Town/Resort** Salisbury
**Directions** From Salisbury take the A354 tc
Coombe Bissett. Leaving church on left
continue on main road and go up the hill
look out for Summerlands sign.
⚡ Salisbury

## TILSHEAD

**Brades Acre,** Tilshead, Salisbury, Wiltshire, SP3 4RX
**Tel:** 01980 Shrewton 620402
**Pitches For** ⋏ ⊕ ⊜ **Total** 35
**Facilities** ♂ ⬛ ♨ ⌐ ☉ ↵ ◻ ☂
⛾ ⬡ ⬛ ✕ ⊞ ◻
**Nearby Facilities** ⌐ ✔ ∪ ♬
**Acreage** 1½ **Open** All Year
**Access** Good **Site** Level
Touring for Stonehenge, Salisbury Cathedral, Wilton and Longleat Houses. Avebury, Orcheston riding.
**Nearest Town/Resort** Salisbury/Devizes
**Directions** A360, 10 miles to Devizes, 13 miles to Salisbury.
⮕ Salisbury

## TROWBRIDGE

**Stowford Manor Farm,** Stowford, Wingfield, Trowbridge, Wiltshire, BA14 9LH
**Tel:** 01225 752253
**Email:** stowford1@supanet.com
www.stowfordmanorfarm.co.uk
**Pitches For** ⋏ ⊕ ⊜ **Total** 12
**Facilities** ♨ ⬛ ⌐ ☂ ✕ ⊞ ◻
**Acreage** 1½ **Open** Easter **to** End Oct
**Access** Good **Site** Level
Situated in the beautiful Frome Valley, next to Medieval farm buildings.
**Nearest Town/Resort** Bradford-on-Avon
**Directions** On the A366 3 miles west of Trowbridge.
⮕ Bradford-on-Avon

## WARMINSTER

**Longleat Caravan Club Site,** Warminster, Wiltshire, BA12 7NL
**Tel:** 01985 844663
www.caravanclub.co.uk
**Pitches For** ⊕ ⊜ **Total** 165

**Facilities** ♂ ♨ ⬛ ⬛ ⬛ ♨ ⌐ ◻ ☂
⬡ ⬛ ⬛ ⤚⊞ ◻ ⬛
**Nearby Facilities** ✔ ⚓ ⬗
**Acreage** 14 **Open** March **to** Oct
**Access** Good **Site** Level
The Caravan Club's most beautiful parkland site, set in the heart of the Longleat Estate. Miles of woodland walks. Just a short walk from Longleat House & Safari Park with its maze and childrens adventure castle. Non members welcome. Booking essential.
**Nearest Town/Resort** Warminster
**Directions** From the A36 Warminster bypass take the A362 signposted Frome. At roundabout turn left into Longleat Estate entrance and follow Longleat House route through the toll booths for 2 miles, then Caravan Club pennant signs for 1 mile.

## WESTBURY

**Brokerswood Country Park,**
Brokerswood, Nr Westbury, Wiltshire, BA13 4EH
**Tel:** 01373 822238 **Fax:** 01373 858474
**Email:** woodland.park@virgin.net
www.brokerswood.co.uk
**Pitches For** ⋏ ⊕ ⊜ **Total** 70
**Facilities** ♂ ♨ ⬛ ⬛ ⬛ ♨ ⌐ ☉ ↵ ☂
⛾ ⬡ ⬛ ✕ ⬛ ⤚⊞ ◻
**Nearby Facilities** ✔
**Acreage** 5 **Open** All Year
**Access** Good **Site** Level
Site adjoins an 80 acre area of forest open to the public together with a museum, lake, Narrow Gauge Railway, etc.
**Nearest Town/Resort** Westbury/Trowbridge
**Directions** 4 miles from Westbury, 5 miles from Trowbridge and 5 miles from Frome. Follow brown tourism signs from the A350 and the A36.
⮕ Westbury

# WORCESTERSHIRE

## BROADWAY

**Leedons Park,** Childswickham Road, Broadway, Worcestershire, WR12 7HB
**Tel:** 01386 852423
**Email:** allenscaravans@btconnect.com
www.allenscaravans.com
**Pitches For** ⋏ ⊕ ⊜ **Total** 350
**Facilities** ♂ ♨ ⬛ ⬛ ⬛ ♨ ⌐ ☉ ↵ ◻ ☂
⛾ ⬡ ⬛ ✕ ⬛ ⬛ ⤚⊞ ◻ ⬛
**Nearby Facilities** ⌐ ∪ ♬
**Open** All Year **Access** Good **Site** Level
Ideal for touring the Cotswolds.
**Nearest Town/Resort** Broadway
**Directions** From Evesham take the A44 towards Oxford, after 5 miles at the main roundabout take the third exit to Broadway Village. After 150 yards turn right into Pennylands Bank, turn left at the T-Junction. Park is 250 yards.
⮕ Evesham

## EVESHAM

**Evesham Vale Caravan Park,** Yessell Farm, Boston Lane, Charlton, Nr EveshamWorcestershire, WR11 6RD
**Tel:** 01386 860377
**Pitches For** ⋏ ⊕ ⊜ **Total** 70
**Facilities** ♨ ⬛ ⬛ ♨ ⌐ ☉ ↵ ⬛ ☂
⛾ ⬡ ⬛ ⬛ ⤚⊞ ◻ ⬛
**Nearby Facilities** ⌐ ✔ ⚓ ∪ ♬
**Acreage** 9 **Open** April **to** October
**Access** Good **Site** Level
On the Blossom Trail route, near a river for fishing. Central for the Cotswolds, Stratford, Worcester, etc..
**Nearest Town/Resort** Evesham
**Directions** From Evesham take the A44, after approx. 1½ miles turn right for Charlton. Park is on the left hand side after approx. ¾ mile.
⮕ Evesham

**CARAVAN PARK** **RANCH** **HOLIDAY CENTRE** NATIONAL CARAVAN COUNCIL LIMITED

* ESTABLISHED FAMILY-RUN PARK
* LOCATED IN THE VALE OF EVESHAM
* TOURERS WELCOME
* MULTI SERVICE PITCHES
* ELECTRIC HOOK-UPS AVAILABLE
* LICENCED CLUB SERVING MEALS
* HEATED OUTDOOR SWIMMING POOL
* SHOP
* LAUNDRY

HONEYBOURNE, EVESHAM, WORCS. WR11 7PR
Tel: (01386) 830744
www.ranch.co.uk

## EVESHAM
**Longcarrant Caravan Park,** 6 Longcarrant Park, Ashton-under-Hill, Evesham, Worcestershire, WR11 7QP
**Tel:** 01386 881724
**Email:** malcolmportman@aol.com
**Pitches For** ▲ ⊞□ **Total** 50
**Facilities** ⌀ ⑱ ⚒ ⌂ ☉ ⊒ ⊖ ☏
▯☮ ☯ △⊬▣ ☀
**Nearby Facilities** ↾ ✔ ⚲ ∪ ⚹
**Acreage** 14 **Open** All Year
**Site** Lev/Slope
**Nearest Town/Resort** Evesham
**Directions** From Evesham take the A46, site is 4 miles on the right.
⚐ Evesham

## EVESHAM
**Ranch Caravan Park,** Station Road, Honeybourne, Nr Evesham, Worcestershire, WR11 7PR
**Tel:** 01386 830744 **Fax:** 01386 833503
**Email:** enquiries@ranch.co.uk
www.ranch.co.uk
**Pitches For** ⊞ ⊟ **Total** 120
**Facilities** ⌀ ⌀ ⊟ ⏢ ⑱ ⚒ ⌂ ☉ ⊒ ⊠ ◎ ☏
⚵ ☮ ☯✕ ☖ ▥ ⚖ △ ⚲⊬▣ ▣
**Nearby Facilities** ↾ ✔ ∪
**Acreage** 48 **Open** March **to** November
**Access** Good **Site** Level
Situated in meadow land in Vale of Evesham on north edge of Cotswolds. Meals available in licensed club.
**Nearest Town/Resort** Evesham
**Directions** From Evesham take B4035 to Badsey and Bretforton. Turn left to Honeybourne. At village crossroads take Bidford direction, site on left in 400 yards.
⚐ Evesham

## GREAT MALVERN
**Camping & Caravanning Club Site,** Blackmore Camp Site No.2, Hanley Swan, Worcestershire, WR8 0EE
**Tel:** 01684 310280
www.campingandcaravanningclub.co.uk
**Pitches For** ▲ ⊞ ⊟ **Total** 200
**Facilities** ⌀ ⌀ ⑱ ⚒ ⌂ ☉ ⊒ ⊠ ◎ ☏
▯☮ ☯ ☀ △⊬▣ ☀ ⚲
**Nearby Facilities** ✔ ∪ ⚲
**Acreage** 17 **Open** All Year
**Access** Good **Site** Level
Close to the River Severn. Situated in the Malvern Hills, ideal walking country. Close to the market towns of Ledbury, Tewkesbury and Evesham. BTB 5 Star Graded and AA 4 Pennants. Non members welcome.
**Nearest Town/Resort** Great Malvern
**Directions** Take the A38 to Upton-on-Severn, turn north over the river bridge, turn second left then first left signposted Hanley

Swan. Site is on the right after 1 mile.
⚐ Malvern

## KIDDERMINSTER
**Wolverley Camping & Caravanning Club Site,** Brown Westhead Park, Wolverley, Nr Kidderminster, Worcestershire, DY10 3PX
**Tel:** 01562 850909
www.campingandcaravanningclub.co.uk
**Pitches For** ▲ ⊞ ⊟ **Total** 120
**Facilities** ⌀ ⌀ ⑱ ⚒ ⌂ ☉ ⊒ ⊠ ◎ ☏
▯☮ ☯ ⏢ ⚖ △⊬▣ ▣ ⚲
**Nearby Facilities** ↾ ✔ ⚲ ∪ ⚲
**Acreage** 12 **Open** March **to** Oct
**Access** Good **Site** Lev/Slope
A quiet and secluded site with pretty walks along the canal, and some excellent pubs. BTB 3 Star Graded and AA 3 Pennants. Non members welcome.
**Nearest Town/Resort** Kidderminster
**Directions** From Kidderminster take the A449 to Wolverhampton, turn left at the traffic lights onto the B4189 signposted Wolverley. Look for brown camping sign and turn right, the site entrance is on the left.
⚐ Kidderminster

## MALVERN
**Kingsgreen Caravan Park,** Berrow, Nr Malvern, Worcestershire, WR13 6AQ
**Tel:** 01531 650272
**Pitches For** ▲ ⊞ ⊟ **Total** 45
**Facilities** ⌀ ⌀ ⑱ ⚒ ⌂ ☉ ⊒ ⊠ ◎ ☏
▯☮ ☯⊬▣ ☀ ⚲
**Nearby Facilities** ↾ ✔
**Acreage** 3 **Open** 1 March **to** End October
**Access** Good **Site** Level
Beautiful walks on the Malvern Hills and Malvern with its famous Elgar Route. Historic Black and White timber towns, Tewkesbury and Upton-on-Severn.
**Nearest Town/Resort** Ledbury/Malvern
**Directions** From Ledbury take the A417 towards Gloucester. Go over the M50 then take the first turning left to Malvern, we are 1 mile on the right. OR M50 Southbound junction 2, turn left onto the A417, in 1 mile turn left to the Malverns.
⚐ Ledbury/Malvern

## MALVERN
**Riverside Caravan Park,** Little Clevelode, Malvern, Worcestershire, WR13 6PE
**Tel:** 01684 310475 **Fax:** 01684 310475
**Pitches For** ▲ ⊞ ⊟ **Total** 70
**Facilities** ⌀ ⑱ ⚒ ⌂ ☉ ⊒ ⊠ ◎ ☏
⚵ ☮ ☯ ⚖ △⊬▣ ☀ ⚲
**Nearby Facilities** ↾ ✔ ∪ ⚲
**Open** April **to** October
**Access** Good **Site** Level
On the banks of the River Severn. New licensed bar and tennis court on site.

**Nearest Town/Resort** Malvern
**Directions** Halfway between Upton-upon-Severn and Callow End on the B4424. 3 miles from Upton and 5 miles from Malvern.
⚐ Malvern

## MALVERN
**The Robin Hood,** Castle Morton, Nr Malvern, Worcestershire, WR13 6BS
**Tel:** 01684 833212
**Pitches For** ▲ ⊞ ⊟ **Total** 15
**Facilities** ⑱ ☏ ▯☮ ⑱✕⊬▣
**Nearby Facilities** ↾ ✔ ⚲ ∪ ⚲ ⚹
**Open** All Year
**Access** Good **Site** Level
Situated at the foot of the Malvern Hills, ideal for walking, riding and cycling.
**Nearest Town/Resort** Malvern/Ledbury
**Directions** The B4208 Worcester to Gloucester road.
⚐ Malvern/Ledbury

## MALVERN
**Three Counties Park,** Sledge Green, Berrow, Worcestershire, WR13 6JW
**Tel:** 01684 833439
**Pitches For** ▲ ⊞ ⊟ **Total** 50
**Facilities** ✔ ⌀ ⑱ ⚒ ⌂ ▯♯ ⊟⊬▣ ⚲
**Nearby Facilities** ✔ ⚲ ∪
**Open** Easter **to** Oct
**Access** Good **Site** Level
Close to the Malvern Hills and the Rivers Severn and Avon.
**Nearest Town/Resort** Tewkesbury
**Directions** On the A438 4 miles from Tewkesbury.
⚐ Malvern

## SHRAWLEY
**Brant Farm Caravan Park,** Shrawley, Worcestershire, WR6 6TD
**Tel:** 01905 621008
**Pitches For** ▲ ⊞ ⊟ **Total** 12
**Facilities** ⑱ ⌂ ⊒ ⊖ ☮ ⊟⊬▣ ☀
**Nearby Facilities** ✔
**Acreage** 1 **Open** April **to** End Oct
**Access** Good **Site** Sloping
Lovely walks in the local woods. Fishing nearby. Bus service to Worcester and Stourport. Friendly pubs on either side of the park which serve food.
**Nearest Town/Resort** Shrawley
**Directions** From Stourport-on-Severn take the B4196, Shrawley is approx. 4 miles. Park lies between the Rose & Crown Pub and the New Inn Pub.
⚐ Kidderminster/Worcester

## STOURPORT-ON-SEVERN

**Lickhill Manor Caravan Park,** Lickhill Manor, Stourport-on-Severn, Worcestershire, DY13 8RL
**Tel:** 01299 871041/877820 **Fax:** 01299 824998
**Email:** excellent@lickhillmanor.co.uk
www.lickhillmanor.co.uk
**Pitches For** ▲ ⊕ ⊜ **Total** 120
**Facilities** ॓ ⨍ ▣ ▥ ⅏ ♨ ┌ ⊙ ⊖ ⊜
⅊ ▤ ⊖ ⌸ ⊕ ▢ ⊟ ⊗
**Nearby Facilities** ┌ ⫐ ⅄ ✕ ∪ ♠
**Acreage** 9 **Open** All Year
**Access** Good **Site** Level
Alongside river (fishing rights held). Walks through the unspoilt Wyre Forest. West Midlands Safari Park and Severn Valley Railway nearby.
**Nearest Town/Resort** Stourport-on-Severn
**Directions** From Stourport take the B4195 to Bewdley, at traffic lights on the crossroads follow caravan signs, after ½ mile turn right at the sign.
⧆ Kidderminster

## STOURPORT-ON-SEVERN

**Lincomb Lock Caravan Park,** Lincomb Lock, Titton, Stourport-on-Severn, Worcestershire, DY13 9QR
**Tel:** 01299 823836
**Email:** lincomb@hillandale.co.uk
www.hillandale.co.uk
**Pitches For** ⊕ ⊜ **Total** 14
**Facilities** ⨍ ▥ ⅏ ♨ ┌ ⊙ ⊜
⅊ ▤ ⌸ ⊟ ⊗
**Nearby Facilities** ┌ ⫐ ⅄ ∪ ♠
**Acreage** 1 **Open** 1 March **to** 6 January
**Access** Good **Site** Level
Alongside a river. Many local attractions including West Midlands Safari Park, Severn Valley Railway, Riverside Amusements, the ancient Wyre Forest and local museums. No young families please.
**Nearest Town/Resort** Stourport-on-Severn
**Directions** 1 mile from Stourport on the A4025 turn right at park signs. Or from the A449 join the A4025 at Crossway Green, after 1 mile turn left at park signs.
⧆ Kidderminster

## TENBURY WELLS

**Knighton on Teme Caravan Park,** Tenbury Wells, Worcestershire, WR15 8NA
**Tel:** 01584 781246 **Fax:** 01584 781246
**Email:** kotcaravans@talk21.com
www.kotcaravans.co.uk
**Pitches For** ▲ ⊕ ⊜ **Total** 5
**Facilities** ⨍ ♨ ┌ ⊙ ⊖ ▢ ⊖ ♠ ⅏ ✕
**Nearby Facilities** ┌ ⫐
**Open** Mid March **to** End Dec
**Access** Good **Site** Sloping
Opposite black and white pub with a bowling green. Fishing and walking in the local area.
**Nearest Town/Resort** Tenbury Wells
**Directions** From Kidderminster take the A456 to Leominster, turn off to Knighton on Teme. Follow brown and white tourism signs. Please telephone for a detailed map.
⧆ Ludlow

## WORCESTER

**Ketch Caravan Park,** Bath Road, Worcester, Worcestershire, WR5 3HW
**Tel:** 01905 820430
**Pitches For** ▲ ⊕ ⊜ **Total** 32
**Facilities** ⨍ ▥ ♨ ┌ ⊙ ⊖ ⊜ ⅊ ▢ ♠ ✕ ⊗
**Nearby Facilities** ┌ ⫐
**Acreage** 6½ **Open** April **to** End October
**Access** Good **Site** Level
On the River Severn.
**Nearest Town/Resort** Worcester

**Directions** Leave the M5 at junction 7 and follow signs for Malvern until you come to the A38. Turn for Worcester and park entrance is approx. 100 yards on the left.
⧆ Worcester

## WORCESTER

**Mill House Caravan & Camping Site,** Mill House, Hawford, Worcestershire, WR3 7SE
**Tel:** 01905 451283 **Fax:** 01905 754143
**Email:** millhousecaravansite@yahoo.co.uk
**Pitches For** ▲ ⊕ ⊜
**Facilities** ⨍ ▥ ♨ ┌ ⊙ ⊖ ⊜
⅊ ▢ ⊗ ▤ ⊖ ▢
**Nearby Facilities** ┌ ⫐ ⅄
**Acreage** 8½ **Open** Easter **to** October
**Access** Good **Site** Level
Please note motocycles are not allowed into field. Dogs must be kept on leads.
**Nearest Town/Resort** Worcester
**Directions** A449 Worcester to Kidderminster.
⧆ Shrubhill/Worcester

## WORCESTER

**Seaborne Leisure,** Court Meadow, Kempsey, Worcester, Worcestershire, WR5 3JL
**Tel:** 01905 820295 **Fax:** 01905 821900
**Pitches For** ⊕ ⊜
**Facilities** ⨍ ▣ ▥ ♨ ┌ ⊙ ⊜
⅊ ✕ ⅄ ▤ ⊖ ⊗ ✎
**Nearby Facilities**
**Acreage** 12 **Open** March **to** Dec
**Access** Good **Site** Level
ADULTS ONLY SITE, No Children Under 14 years of Age. Alongside the River Severn and overlooking the Malvern Hills, spectacular views.
**Nearest Town/Resort** Worcester
**Directions** Leave the M5 at junction 7 and take the A38. 3 miles from Worcester.
⧆ Worcester

## WYTHALL

**Chapel Lane Caravan Club Site,** Chapel Lane, Wythall, Birmingham, B47 6JX
**Tel:** 01564 826483
www.caravanclub.co.uk
**Pitches For** ⊕ ⊜ **Total** 99
**Facilities** ⨍ ▥ ♨ ┌ ⊙ ⊜
⅊ ▤ ⊖ ⌸ ⊟
**Nearby Facilities** ┌ ⫐
**Acreage** 14 **Open** All Year
**Access** Good **Site** Level
Rural and open site set in the shadow of an old chapel. The Transport Museum is adjacent, and a short walk leads you to Becketts Farm Shop which has a restaurant. Only 9 miles from the NEC and close to many museums. Non members welcome. Booking essential.
**Nearest Town/Resort** Birmingham
**Directions** From north on M1 leave at junction 23A and take A42/M42, exit at junction 3 and take A435. At roundabout turn left into Middle Lane, after 150 yards turn left into Chapel Lane, after 300 yards turn right by the church then immediately turn right again into the site.
⧆ Birmingham NEC

# YORKSHIRE (EAST)
## BARMBY MOOR

**The Sycamores Camping & Caravan Park,** Feoffe Common Lane, Barmby Moor, East Yorkshire, YO42 4HT
**Tel:** 01759 388838
www. sycamorescaravans.co.uk
**Pitches For** ▲ ⊕ ⊜ **Total** 36
**Facilities** ⨍ ▥ ♨ ┌ ⊙ ▢ ⊗
⅊ ⊖ ▢ ⊟ ✕
**Nearby Facilities** ┌ ⫐ ⅄ ∪ ♠
**Acreage** 3 **Open** March **to** November
**Access** Good **Site** Level
York City Centre and a gliding club nearby.
**Nearest Town/Resort** York/Bridlington
**Directions** From York take the A1079 (York to Hull road) east for approx. 7 miles, turn sharp left before the Esso Filling Station signposted Yapham, we are 200 yards on the right hand side.
⧆ York

## BEVERLEY

**Lakeminster Park,** Hull Road, Beverley, East Yorkshire, HU17 0PN
**Tel:** 01482 882655
**Pitches For** ▲ ⊕ ⊜
**Facilities** ॓ ♣ ⨍ ▥ ♨ ┌ ⊙ ⊖ ⊜ ⊖ ⊗
⅊ ⊖ ▢ ✕ ⅄ ▤ ⊖ ⊟ ✕ ✎
**Nearby Facilities** ┌ ⫐ ∪
**Open** All Year
**Access** Good **Site** Level
15 minutes from Hornsea. Close to minster and racecourse.
**Nearest Town/Resort** Beverley
**Directions** Off the A1074 main Beverley to Hull road.
⧆ Beverley

## BRANDES BURTON

**Dacre Lakeside Park,** Brandes Burton, Driffield, East Yorkshire, YO25 8RT
**Tel:** 01964 543704 **Fax:** 01964 544040
**Email:** dacresurf@aol.com
www. dacrepark.co.uk
**Pitches For** ▲ ⊕ ⊜ **Total** 120
**Facilities** ॓ ⨍ ▥ ▦ ♨ ┌ ⊙ ⊖ ⊜ ⊖ ▢ ⊗
⅊ ⅊ ⊖ ▢ ⅄ ♣ ✕ ⊛ ⊖ ▢ ✕
**Nearby Facilities** ┌ ⫐ ⅄ ✕ ∪ ⅃ ♠
**Acreage** 10 **Open** March **to** October
**Access** Good **Site** Level
8 acre lake for fishing, wind surfing and sailing.
**Nearest Town/Resort** Beverley
**Directions** From the A1 or M1 take the M62 then the A63 to South Cave. Turn off after junction 38 onto the A1079. Go by Beverley onto the A1035, then onto the A165.
⧆ Beverley

## BRIDLINGTON

**Fir Tree Caravan Park,** Jewison Lane, Bridlington, East Yorkshire, YO16 5YG
**Tel:** 01262 676442 **Fax:** 01262 676442
**Email:** info@flowerofmay.com
www. flowerofmay.com
**Pitches For** ⊕ ⊜ **Total** 46
**Facilities** ⨍ ▥ ▦ ♨ ┌ ⊙ ⊖ ⊜ ⊖ ▢ ⊗
⅊ ⊖ ▢ ⅄ ▤ ⊖ ♠ ⅃ ✕ ⊟ ✕
**Nearby Facilities** ┌ ⫐ ⅄ ✕ ∪ ⅃ ♠
**Acreage** 25 **Open** March **to** November
**Access** Good **Site** Level
Pets are welcome by arrangement only.
**Nearest Town/Resort** Bridlington
**Directions** From roundabout on A165 take B1255 to Flamborough for 2 miles. Jewison Lane is on the left and site is on the left after the level crossing.
⧆ Bridlington

## BRIDLINGTON
**South Cliff Caravan Park,** Wilsthorpe, Bridlington, East Yorkshire, YO15 3QN
**Tel:** 01262 671051 **Fax:** 01262 605639
**Email:** southcliff@eastriding.gov.uk
**www.** southcliff.co.uk
**Pitches For** ▲ ⊕ ⊟ **Total** 184
**Facilities** ⛃ ∤ ⊞ ⍟ ▲ ∫ ⊙ ⌿ ▣ ☎
⓼ ⊘ ⊜ ✗ ♀ ⊞ ♠ ⋔ ⊕ ▣ ⊟ ☀
**Nearby Facilities** ⌁ ⚓ ∪ ⊿ ♪
**Open** March **to** Nov
**Access** Good **Site** Level
Direct access to the beach. Golf course adjacent to the park. Special Offers on touring pitches in low and mid season.
**Nearest Town/Resort** Bridlington
**Directions** Take the A165 main route into Bridlington.
⇏ Bridlington

## BRIDLINGTON
**The Poplars,** 45 Jewison Lane, Sewerby, Bridlington, East Yorkshire, YO15 1DX
**Tel:** 01262 677251
**www.** the-poplars.co.uk
**Pitches For** ▲ ⊕ ⊟ **Total** 30
**Facilities** ∤ ⊞ ⍟ ☎ ∫ ⊙ ☎ ⊘ ⊜⋔▣ ▣
**Nearby Facilities** ⌁ ⚓
**Acreage** 1½ **Open** 1 March **to** 15 Nov
**Access** Good **Site** Level
Small quiet site in a good touring location.
**Nearest Town/Resort** Bridlington
**Directions** From Bridlington take the B1255 towards Flamborough for 1½ miles. Jewison Lane is a left turn off the Z bend.
⇏ Bridlington

## GOOLE
**Dobella Lane Farm,** Rawcliffe, Goole, East Yorkshire, DN14 8SQ
**Tel:** 01405 839261
**Pitches For** ▲ ⊕▢ **Total** 5
**Facilities** ⛃ ∤ ⊞ ⍟ ☎ ⊘ ⊜⋔▣ ▣ ℘
**Nearby Facilities** ⌁ ⚓ ⚓ ⊿ ↖∪ ♪
**Acreage** ½ **Open** All Year
**Access** Good **Site** Level
Very private garden site on a working farm.

English country garden. Pub and restaurant in the village.
**Nearest Town/Resort** Goole
**Directions** Leave the M62 at junction 36 and head towards Selby into Rawcliffe. In the village turn left and follow road for ½ a mile, at the brick bus shelter turn left, go over the motorway and we are the first farm on the right.
⇏ Rawcliffe

## HORNSEA
**Four Acres Caravan Park,** Hornsea Road, Atwick, Driffield, East Yorkshire, YO25 8DG
**Tel:** 01964 536940
**Email:** caravanfouracres@aol.com
**Pitches For** ▲ ⊕ ⊟ **Total** 91
**Facilities** ∤ ⊞ ⍟ ▲ ∫ ⊙ ⌿ ☎
⍼⊘⋔▣⊟☀℘
**Nearby Facilities** ⌁ ⚓ ↗∪
**Acreage** 4 **Open** April **to** October
**Access** Good **Site** Level
Near to the beach, local pub, indoor bowls, swimming baths, shop with Post Office and a Sunday market.
**Nearest Town/Resort** Hornsea
**Directions** As you approach Hornsea turn left at the roundabout on the B1242 for approx 2 miles, site is on the right hand side.
⇏ Bridlington

## HULL
**Sand-le-Mere Caravan Park,** Seaside Lane, Tunstall, Roos, Nr Hull East Yorkshire, HU12 0JQ
**Tel:** 01964 670403 **Fax:** 01964 671099
**Email:** info@sand-le-mere.co.uk
**www.** sand-le-mere.co.uk
**Pitches For** ⊕▢ **Total** 18
**Facilities** ∤ ⊞ ▲ ∫ ⊙ ⌿ ☎ ▣ ☎
⓼ ⊘ ⊜ ✗ ♀ ⊞ ♠ ⋔ ⇥▣ ▣ ⊟ ☀
**Nearby Facilities** ⌁ ⚓ ∪ ♪
**Acreage** 1½
**Access** Good **Site** Level
Near the beach and all facilities.
**Nearest Town/Resort** Withernsea
**Directions** From Hull take the A1033 to Hedon, turn left at the roundabout to Preston and follow signs for Burton Pidsea and Roos.
⇏ Hull

## LITTLE WEIGHTON
**Louvain,** Rowley Road, Little Weighton, East Yorkshire, HU20 3XJ
**Tel:** 01482 848249
**Pitches For** ▲ ⊕ ⊟ **Total** 20
**Facilities** ∤ ⊞ ⍟ ⊙ ⌿ ☎ ⊞⇥▣
**Nearby Facilities** ⌁ ⌿ ∪
**Acreage** 1½ **Open** All Year
**Access** Good **Site** Level
Old Town Beverley. Ideal touring.
**Nearest Town/Resort** Beverley
**Directions** From M62 then A63. At South cave crossroads turn right (Beverley Road) keep on this road for approx 3 miles, turn left at signpost Little Weighton & Rowley.
⇏ Hull

## RUDSTON
**Thorpe Hall Caravan & Camping Site,** Rudston, Driffield, East Yorkshire, YO25 4JE
**Tel:** 01262 420393 **Fax:** 01262 420588
**Email:** caravansite@thorpehall.co.uk
**www.** thorpehall.co.uk
**Pitches For** ▲ ⊕ ⊟ **Total** 92
**Facilities** ⛃ ∤ ⊞ ▲ ∫ ⊙ ⌿ ▣ ☎
⓼ ⊘ ⊜ ♠ ⋔ ▣ ▣ ☎
**Nearby Facilities** ⌁ ⚓ ∪ ♪
**Acreage** 4½ **Open** March **to** Oct
**Access** Good **Site** Level
Countryside site within the Kitchen Garden walls. Excellent discounts for 2 person occupancy, up to 25% at specified times (not Bank Holidays).
**Nearest Town/Resort** Bridlington
**Directions** 4½ miles from Bridlington on the B1253.
⇏ Bridlington

## SKIPSEA
**Mill Farm Country Park,** Mill Lane, Skipsea, East Yorkshire, YO25 8SS
**Tel:** 01262 468211
**Pitches For** ▲ ⊕ ⊟ **Total** 56
**Facilities** ⛃ ∤ ⊞ ⍟ ▲ ∫ ⊙ ☎
⍼⊕⇥▣▣ ☀ ℘
**Nearby Facilities** ⌁ ⌿ ⚓ ↖∪ ⊿ ♪
**Acreage** 6 **Open** 10 March **to** 1 Oct
**Access** Good **Site** Level

# Cawood Park

Ryther Road, Cawood,
The Vale of York,
North Yorks YO8 3TT
enquiries@cawoodpark.com

www.cawoodpark.com

Idyllic and tranquil touring park in a quiet setting yet convenient for York Centre.
• Licensed Bar with first class Cabaret every Saturday night.
• Lake Views. • Fishing Lake. • Lakeside holiday cottages.
• Holiday caravans for sale.

*OPEN ALL YEAR* **01757 268450**

Farm walk, beach nearby. RSPB site at Bempton. Good centre for many places of local interest. Many facilities nearby including an indoor swimming pool ½ mile away.
**Nearest Town/Resort** Hornsea
**Directions** The A165 Hull to Bridlington Road, at Beeford take B1249 to Skipsea. At crossroads turn right, then first left up Cross Street which leads on to Mill Lane, site is on the right.
⇌ Bridlington

## SKIPSEA
**Skipsea Sands Holiday Park,** Mill Lane, Skipsea, Driffield, East Yorkshire, YO25 8TZ
**Tel:** 01262 468210 **Fax:** 01262 468454
**Email:** info@skipseasands.co.uk
**Pitches For** Å ⬛ 🚐 **Total** 90
**Facilities** ⬛ ⬛ ⬛ ⬛ ⬛ ⬛ ⬛ ⬛ ⬛ ⬛ ⬛
⬛ ⬛ ⬛ ⬛ ⬛ ⬛ ⬛ ⬛ ⬛ ⬛ ⬛ ⬛ ⬛
**Nearby Facilities** ⬛ ⬛ ∪
**Acreage** 8 **Open** 1 March **to** 1 Nov
**Access** Good **Site** Level
Coastal park with full facilities for a pleasant family holiday.
**Nearest Town/Resort** Bridlington/Hornsea
**Directions** Off the B1242 Hornsea to Bridlington road. In Skipsea Village follow tourism signs onto Cross Street then into Mill Lane, Park is 1 mile from the village.
⇌ Bridlington

## SKIPSEA
**Skirlington Leisure Park,** Low Skirlington, Skipsea, Driffield, East Yorkshire, YO25 8SY
**Tel:** 01262 468213 **Fax:** 01262 468213
**Pitches For** 🚐 🚐 **Total** 215
**Facilities** ⬛ ⬛ ⬛ ⬛ ⬛ ⬛ ⬛ ⬛ ⬛ ⬛
⬛ ⬛ ⬛ ⬛ ⬛ ⬛ ⬛ ⬛ ⬛ ⬛ ⬛ ⬛ ⬛
**Nearby Facilities** ⬛ ⬛ ∪
**Acreage** 20 **Open** March **to** October
**Access** Good **Site** Level
**Nearest Town/Resort** Bridlington
**Directions** On the B1242 between Hornsea and Skipsea.
⇌ Bridlington

## STAMFORD BRIDGE
**Weir Caravan Park,** Stamford Bridge, East Yorkshire, YO41 1AN
**Tel:** 01759 371377 **Fax:** 01759 371377
**Email:**
enquiries@yorkshireholidayparks.co.uk
**www.** yorkshireholidayparks.co.uk
**Pitches For** 🚐 🚐 **Total** 20
**Facilities** ⬛ ⬛ ⬛ ⬛ ⬛ ⬛ ⬛ ⬛ ⬛
⬛ ⬛ ⬛ ⬛ ⬛
**Nearby Facilities** ⬛ ⬛ ∪
**Acreage** 7 **Open** March **to** Oct
**Access** Good **Site** Level
On the edge of a river. 5 minute walk from the village and shops, pubs, etc..
**Nearest Town/Resort** York
**Directions** From the A166 Bridlington road, turn left before the bridge.
⇌ York

## WILBERFOSS
**Fangfoss Park,** Fangfoss, East Yorkshire, YO41 5QB
**Tel:** 01759 380491
**Email:** info@fangfosspark.co.uk
**www.** fangfosspark.co.uk
**Pitches For** Å 🚐 🚐 **Total** 75
**Facilities** ⬛ ⬛ ⬛ ⬛ ⬛ ⬛ ⬛ ⬛ ⬛ ⬛
⬛ ⬛ ⬛ ⬛ ⬛ ⬛ ⬛
**Nearby Facilities** ⬛ ⬛ ∪
**Acreage** 4 **Open** March **to** Nov
**Access** Good **Site** Level
Ideal for York, North Yorkshire Moors and Castle Howard. 40 minutes from the coast.
**Nearest Town/Resort** York
**Directions** From the A64 take the A1079 towards Hull. After 5 miles turn left into Wilberfoss Village, turn next left and the site is 2 miles.
⇌ York

## WITHERNSEA
**Willows Holiday Park,** Hollym Road, Withernsea, East Yorkshire, HU19 2PN
**Tel:** 01964 612233 **Fax:** 01964 612957
**Email:** info@highfield-caravans.co.uk
**www.** highfield-caravans.co.uk
**Pitches For** 🚐 🚐 **Total** 40
**Facilities** ⬛ ⬛ ⬛ ⬛ ⬛ ⬛ ⬛ ⬛ ⬛
⬛ ⬛ ⬛ ⬛ ⬛ ⬛ ⬛ ⬛ ⬛
**Nearby Facilities** ⬛ ⬛ ∪
**Acreage** 9 **Open** 4 March **to** 31 Oct
**Access** Good **Site** Level
Only a ten minute walk to the beach and a 15 minute walk to the town. Near a Tesco store.
**Nearest Town/Resort** Withernsea
**Directions** Take the M62 to Hull then take the A1033 to Withernsea. Willows is the first site on the left on entering Withernsea.
⇌ Hull

## WITHERNSEA
**Withernsea Holiday Park,** North Road, Withernsea, East Yorkshire, HU19 2BS
**Tel:** 0870 442 9313 **Fax:** 01964 614554
**Email:** holidaysales.withernsea@park-resorts.com
**www.** park-resorts.com
**Pitches For** Å 🚐 🚐 **Total** 40
**Facilities** ⬛ ⬛ ⬛ ⬛ ⬛ ⬛ ⬛ ⬛ ⬛ ⬛
⬛ ⬛ ⬛ ⬛ ⬛ ⬛ ⬛ ⬛ ⬛ ⬛
**Nearby Facilities** ⬛ ⬛ ⬛ ⬛ ∪
**Open** March **to** Dec
**Access** Good **Site** Lev/Slope
Within a 5 minute walk to a sandy/shingle beach.
**Nearest Town/Resort** Withernsea
**Directions** From Withernsea town centre head for the lighthouse and turn right into North Road, site is 500 yards.
⇌ Hull

# YORKSHIRE (NORTH)
## AYSGARTH
**Little Cote Site,** West Burton, Aysgarth, North Yorkshire, DL8 4JY
**Tel:** 01969 663450
**Pitches For** Å 🚐 🚐 **Total** 20
**Facilities** ⬛ ⬛
**Acreage** 2 **Open** March **to** October

**Access** Good **Site** Lev/Slope
Small, quiet site alongside a river. Own car is essential. Ideal touring.
**Directions** From the A684 Aysgarth/ Northallerton road, 2 miles east of Aysgarth take the B6160 to West Burton, fork left Walden for ¾ mile.
⇌ Northallerton

## AYSGARTH
**Street Head Caravan Park,** Newbiggin, Bishopdale, Leyburn, North Yorkshire, DL8 3TE
**Tel:** 01969 663472
**Pitches For** Å 🚐 🚐 **Total** 40
**Facilities** ⬛ ⬛ ⬛ ⬛ ⬛ ⬛ ⬛ ⬛ ⬛
⬛ ⬛ ⬛ ⬛ ⬛ ⬛
**Nearby Facilities**
**Open** March **to** Oct
**Access** Good **Site** Lev/Slope
Yorkshire Dales National Park. 1½ miles from Aysgarth Falls.
**Nearest Town/Resort** Leyburn
**Directions** From Leyburn take the A684 for approx. 9 miles, turn onto the B6160 for approx. 2 miles.
⇌ Darlington/Northallerton

## BARDEN
**Howgill Lodge,** Barden, Nr Skipton, North Yorkshire, BD23 6DJ
**Tel:** 01756 720655
**Email:** info@howgill-lodge.co.uk
**www.howgill-lodge.co.uk**
**Pitches For** Å 🚐 🚐 **Total** 30
**Facilities** ⬛ ⬛ ⬛ ⬛ ⬛ ⬛ ⬛ ⬛ ⬛ ⬛
⬛ ⬛ ⬛ ⬛ ⬛
**Nearby Facilities** ⬛ ⬛
**Acreage** 4 **Open** April **to** 31 Oct
**Site** Terraced
Beautiful views, ideal for walking or touring. David Bellamy Gold Award for Conservation.
**Nearest Town/Resort** Bolton Abbey
**Directions** Turn off B6160 at Barden Tower, site 1 mile on right.
⇌ Skipton

## BEDALE
**Lindale Holiday Park,** Newton Le Willows, Bedale, North Yorkshire, DL8 1TA
**Tel:** 01677 450842 **Fax:** 01677 450869
**Email:** info@lindalepark.co.uk
**www.lindalepark.co.uk**
**Pitches For** Å **Total** 15
**Facilities** ⬛ ⬛ ⬛ ⬛ ⬛ ⬛ ⬛ ⬛ ⬛ ⬛ ⬛
**Nearby Facilities** ⬛ ⬛ ⬛ ∪ ⬛ ⬛
**Acreage** 5 **Open** 1 March **to** 15 Jan
**Site** Level
Peaceful site of importance for nature conservation. Convenient for the Dales, Moors, 'Heartbeat' and 'Herriot' Country. Lots of activities locally.
**Nearest Town/Resort** Bedale
**Directions** From Bedale take the A684 towards Leyburn. After Patrick Brompton turn left for Newton Le Willows, keep on this road past the village for ¾ miles, at sharp left hand bend take the road ahead, Park is 200 metres on the right.
⇌ Northallerton

# YORKSHIRE (NORTH)

## BEDALE

**Pembroke Caravan Park,** 19 Low Street, Leeming Bar, Northallerton, North Yorkshire, DL7 9BW
**Tel:** 01677 422652
Pitches For ▲ ⊡ ⌂ **Total** 25
F a c i l i t i e s ⨍ 🅗 🆖 ♨ ┌ ⊙ ⊡ 🛒
🆂🆀 🅟🅲 ⊙ 🅰 🔌 ⊒ ⚲ ♨
**Nearby Facilities** ┌ ✓ U
**Acreage** 1¼ **Open** March to October
**Access** Good **Site** Slight Slope
Between the Yorkshire Dales and North Yorks Moors. Take-away food available. Caravans for hire.
**Nearest Town/Resort** Bedale
**Directions** A1 Leeming Services, right onto A684 to Leeming Bar. Keep left, crossroads into Leases Road. ½ mile on the right.
⇌ Northallerton

## BENTHAM

**Riverside Caravan Park,** High Bentham, Lancaster, Lancashire, LA2 7LW
**Tel:** 015242 61272 **Fax:** 015242 62163
**Email:** info@riversidecaravanpark.co.uk
www.riversidecaravanpark.co.uk
**Pitches For** ▲ ⊡ ⌂ **Total** 60
Facilities & ⨍ 🅗 🆖 ♨ ┌ ⊙ ⊒ ⚲ ⊡ 🛒
🅟🅲 ⊙ 🅰 ♨ 🅰🔌►🅿🅲 ⚲ ♨
**Nearby Facilities** ┌ ✓ ♨
**Acreage** 10 **Open** March to October
**Access** Good **Site** Level
Riverside site, great for families.
**Nearest Town/Resort** High Bentham
**Directions** Follow caravan signs off the B6480 at The Black Bull Hotel in High Bentham.
⇌ High Bentham

## BOLTON ABBEY

**Strid Wood Caravan Club Site,** Bolton Abbey, Skipton, North Yorkshire, BD23 6AN
**Tel:** 01756 710433
www.caravanclub.co.uk
**Pitches For** ⊡ ⌂ **Total** 57
Facilities & ⨍ 🅗 🆖 ♨ ┌ ⊙ 🛒
⊙ 🛒►🅿🅲
**Nearby Facilities** ✓ ⚓ ⚲
**Acreage** 4 **Open** March to Jan
**Access** Good **Site** Level
Situated in the Bolton Abbey estate, this pretty site is surrounded by woodland and the Yorkshire Dales. Many miles of walks around the site. Close to Bolton Priory and Skipton castle. Non members welcome. Booking essential.
**Nearest Town/Resort** Skipton
**Directions** From the A59 Gisburn to Harrogate road, at Bolton Bridge roundabout take the B6160 signposted Bolton Abbey. After 2¾ miles turn right into Strid car park, go through the double gates ahead into the site.
⇌ Skipton

## BOROUGHBRIDGE

**Blue Bell Caravan Site,** Kirby Hill, Boroughbridge, North Yorkshire, YO51 9DN
**Tel:** 01423 322380
**Pitches For** ⊡ ⌂ **Total** 24
Facilities 🆖 🅟 ♨ ┌ ⊙ 🛒 🅟🅲 ⊙ 🅰 ▣ ►🅿🅲 ⚲
**Nearby Facilities** ┌ ✓ ⚓ ⚲ ♨ ⚓
**Acreage** 2 **Open** April to October
**Site** Sloping
**Nearest Town/Resort** Ripon
**Directions** 1 mile from the A1M junction signposted Boroughbridge.
⇌ Harrogate

## BOROUGHBRIDGE

**Camping & Caravanning Club Site,** Bar Lane, Roecliffe, Boroughbridge, North Yorkshire, YO51 9LS
**Tel:** 01423 322683
www.campingandcaravanningclub.co.uk
**Pitches For** ▲ ⊡ ⌂ **Total** 85
Facilities & ⨍ 🅗 🆖 ♨ ┌ ⊙ ⊒ ⚲ ⊡ 🛒
🆂🆀 🅟🅲 ⊙ 🅰 🅣 ♨ 🅰►🅿🅲 ⚲ ♨
**Nearby Facilities** ✓ ⚲ ♨
**Acreage** 5 **Open** All Year
**Site** Level
On the banks of the River Ure for fishing, boat launching facility. Table tennis and pool table on site. Close to the Yorkshire Dales. BTB 5 Star Graded and AA 4 Pennants. Non members welcome.
**Directions** From junction 48 of the A1M north and southbound slip roads, follow signs for Bar Lane Industrial Estate and Roecliffe Village. Site entrance is ¼ mile from the roundabout.
⇌ Harrogate

## BOROUGHBRIDGE

**The Old Hall Holiday Park,** Langthorpe, Boroughbridge, York, North Yorkshire, YO51 9BZ
**Tel:** 01423 322130 **Fax:** 01423 324552
**Email:** phil.brierley@which.net
www.yhcparks.info
**Pitches For** ▲ ⊡ ⌂ **Total** 16
F a c i l i t i e s ⨍ 🆖 ♨ ┌ ⊙ ⊡ 🛒
🅟🅲 ⊙ 🅰 ♨ 🅰🔌►🅿🅲 ⚲
**Nearby Facilities** ┌ ✓ ⚓ ⚲ U ♨
**Acreage** 7½ **Open** Easter/1 April to Oct
**Access** Good **Site** Level
Near a river. Close to York, Harrogate and Lightwater Valley Theme Park.
**Nearest Town/Resort** Boroughbridge
**Directions** From Boroughbridge take the B6265 towards Ripon. Pass the Anchor Pub on the left hand side, 200 yards further on turn left to Langthorpe, Skelton and Newby Hall. Park is second on the right.
⇌ Knaresborough

## CLAPHAM

**Flying Horseshoe Caravan Site,** Clapham, North Yorkshire, LA2 8ES
**Tel:** 01524 251532 **Fax:** 01535 631547
**Email:** alan@laughing.gravy.co.uk
www.laughing-gravy.co.uk
**Pitches For** ▲ ⊡ ⌂
Facilities ⨍ 🅗 🆖 ♨ ┌ ⊙ 🛒 ▣ 🅿🅲 ⚲
**Nearby Facilities**
**Open** Good Friday to 1 Nov
**Access** Good **Site** Level
Close to the coast and lakes. Ideal for countryside walking, near to Three Peaks Walks.
**Nearest Town/Resort** Settle
**Directions** From the A65 follow signs for Clapham Station, site is behind a hotel opposite the station.
⇌ Clapham (Opposite)

## ELVINGTON

**Elvington Lake Caravan Park,** Lake Cottage, Wheldrake Lane, Elvington, YorkNorth Yorkshire, YO41 4AZ
**Tel:** 01904 608255
**Pitches For** ▲ ⊡ ⌂ **Total** 15
Facilities ⨍ 🅗 🆖 ┌ ⊙ ⊒ 🛒 🅟🅲 ♨
**Nearby Facilities** ┌ ✓ U
**Acreage** 3 **Open** All Year
**Access** Good **Site** Level
Award winning park. The only working windmill water pump. On the shore of a quality coarse fishing lake.
**Nearest Town/Resort** York
**Directions** From York take the A1079 Hull

road, immediately straight over first roundabout then turn right onto the B1228, after 4 miles at the garage on the left, turn right.
⇌ York

## FILEY

**Centenary Way Camping & Caravan Park,** Muston Grange, Filey, North Yorkshire, YO14 0HU
**Tel:** 01723 516415
**Pitches For** ▲ ⊡ ⌂ **Total** 100
F a c i l i t i e s ⨍ 🆖 ♨ ┌ ⊙ ⊡ 🛒
🆂🆀 🅟🅲 ⊙ 🅰 🅰🔌►🅿🅲
**Nearby Facilities** ┌ ✓ ⚓ ⚲ U ♨
**Acreage** 3½ **Open** March to October
**Access** Good **Site** Level
Just a ten minute walk to the beach and Filey town. Handy for Scarborough and Bridlington. 45 minutes to the North Yorkshire Moors, York and Whitby.
**Nearest Town/Resort** Filey
**Directions** Take the A165 from Bridlington, at the roundabout turn right onto the A1039, after 200 yards turn right into Centenary Way, follow lane to the very end.
⇌ Filey

## FILEY

**Filey Brigg Touring Caravan & Camping Park,** North Cliff, Filey, North Yorkshire, YO14 9ET
**Tel:** 01723 513852
**Email:** fileybrigg@scarborough.gov.uk
www.discoveryorkshirecoast.com
**Pitches For** ▲ ⊡ ⌂ **Total** 158
Facilities ⨍ 🆖 ♨ ┌ ⊙ ⊒ ⚲ ⊡ 🛒
🆂🆀 🅟🅲 🅰✗🅰►🅿🅲 ⚲
**Nearby Facilities** ┌ ✓ ⚓ U ♨
**Acreage** 9 **Open** Easter to End Oct
**Access** Good **Site** Level
Set in a public country park and situated less than ½ a mile from Filey town and beach. 6 miles from Scarborough.
**Nearest Town/Resort** Filey
⇌ Filey

## FILEY

**Muston Grange Caravan Park,** Muston Road, Filey, North Yorkshire, YO14 0HU
**Tel:** 01723 512167
www.mustongrange.co.uk
**Pitches For** ⊡ ⌂
Facilities & ⨍ 🅗 🆖 ♨ ┌ ⊙ 🛒
🆂🆀 ⊙►🅲🔌 ⚲ ♨
**Nearby Facilities** ┌ ✓ U ♨
**Open** March to Oct
**Access** Good **Site** Level
Just a 10 minute walk to Filey town and it's glorious sandy beach.
**Nearest Town/Resort** Filey
**Directions** Off the A165 Bridlington to Filey road.
⇌ Filey

## FILEY

**Orchard Farm Holiday Village,** Stonegate, Hunmanby, Filey, North Yorkshire, YO14 0PU
**Tel:** 01723 891582 **Fax:** 01723 891582
**Email:** sharon.dugdale@virgin.net
**Pitches For** ▲ ⊡ ⌂ **Total** 85
Facilities & ⨍ 🅗 🆖 ♨ ┌ ⊙ ⊒ ⚲ ⊡ 🛒
🆂🆀 ⊙ 🅰 ♀ 🅰 🅣►🅿🅲 ⚲
**Nearby Facilities** ┌
**Acreage** 14 **Open** March to Oct
**Access** Good **Site** Level
1 mile from the beach. Ideal base for all North Yorkshire attractions.
**Nearest Town/Resort** Filey
**Directions** From Filey take the A165 towards Bridlington, Hunmanby is 2 miles on the right.
⇌ Hunmanby

## FILEY

**Primrose Valley Holiday Park**, Primrose Valley, Filey, North Yorkshire, YO14 9RF
Tel: 01723 513771 Fax: 01723 513777
www.touringholidays.co.uk
Pitches For ♫ ♨ Total 65
Facilities ⅙ ∫ ⅏ ♣ ⌐ ☉ ◎ ☎
Nearby Facilities ⌐ ⚲ ♪
Open April to October
Access Good Site Level
10 minute walk to sandy beaches. Full on park entertainment and sports facilities.
Directions From the A64 at Staxton roundabout take the A165 signposted Bridlington, park is between Scarborough and Bridlington.
⚞ Filey

## FILEY

**Reighton Sands Holiday Park**, Reighto Gap, Filey, North Yorkshire, YO14 9SJ
Tel: 01723 890476 Fax: 01723 891043
www.touringholidays.co.uk
Pitches For ⋏ ♫ ♨ Total 150
Facilities ⅙ ∫ ⅁ ⅄ ⅏ ♣ ⌐ ☉ ◢ ◎ ☎
⅖ ◎ ⬡ ✕ ⌐ ♈ ⅏ ⅌ ⊣ ⋈ ⌐ ▣ ⬛
Nearby Facilities ⌐ ⚲ ⅂ ⋋ ∪ ⋌
Open Easter to End Oct
Access Good Site Lev/Slope
Near to the beach, Reighton Sands offers six miles of glorious sandy beaches. Free sports and leisure facilities, Free Kids Club and Free entertainment.
Nearest Town/Resort Filey/Scarborough
Directions We are signposted opposite the garage at Reighton, on the A165 Filey to Bridlington road, and are located just 1 mile off this road.
⚞ Filey

## GRASSINGTON

**Hawkswick Cote Caravan Park**, Arncliffe, Skipton, North Yorkshire, BD23 5PX
Tel: 01756 770226 Fax: 01756 770327
Pitches For ⋏ ♫ ♨ Total 50
Facilities ⅙ ∫ ⅁ ⅏ ♣ ⌐ ☉ ◢ ◎ ☎
⅖ ◎ ⬡ ⅏ ⬛ ▣ ⋊
Nearby Facilities ⌐ ⚲ ∪ ⋌
Open 7 March to 9 November
Access Good Site Level
Yorkshire Dales walking area and climbing

at Kilnsey Crag.
Nearest Town/Resort Skipton
Directions Take the B6265 Skipton to Threshfield road, at Threshfield take the B6160 to Kilnsey, after Kilnsey bear left to Arncliffe. Park is 1½ miles on the left.
⚞ Skipton

## GRASSINGTON

**Threaplands Camping & Caravan Park**, Threaplands House, Cracoe, Nr Skipton, North Yorkshire, BD23 6LD
Tel: 01756 730248
Pitches For ♫ ♨ Total 30
Facilities ⅙ ∫ ⅏ ♣ ⌐ ☉ ☎ ⅏ ⅁ ⅌ ⬛
Nearby Facilities ⌐ ⚲ ∪ ⋌
Acreage 8 Open March to October
Access Good Site Level
Scenic views. Ideal for touring and walking.
Nearest Town/Resort Skipton
Directions 6 miles from Skipton on the B6265 to Cracoe. ¼ mile past Cracoe keep going straight on, site is ¼ mile on the left.
⚞ Skipton

## GUISBOROUGH

**Margrove Park Holidays**, Margrove Park, Boosbeck, Saltburn-by-the-Sea, North Yorkshire, TS12 3BZ
Tel: 01287 653616
Email: keith@mangrove.fsnet.co.uk
www.mangroveparkholidays.co.uk
Pitches For ⋏ ♫ ♨ Total 10
Facilities ∫ ⅏ ♣ ⌐ ☉ ☎ ⅁ ⅌ ⋊ ⚲ ♪
Nearby Facilities ⌐ ∪
Open April to Oct
Access Good Site Level
5 miles from Saltburn beach. Good walking, ½ mile from Cleveland Way. Wash-up area.
Nearest Town/Resort Guisborough
Directions From Guisborough follow the A171 towards Whitby, after approx. 2½ miles at Charltons turn left signposted Margrove Park. Site is approx. ½ a mile on the right.
⚞ Saltburn

## HARROGATE

**Bilton Park**, Village Farm, Bilton Lane, Harrogate, North Yorlshire, HG1 4DH
Tel: 01423 863121
Email: biltonpark@tcsmail.net
Pitches For ⋏ ♫ ♨ Total 25

Facilities ∫ ⅏ ♣ ⌐ ☉ ◢ ☎
⅖ ⅊ ◎ ⅏ ⅌ ⬛ ▣ ⋊
Nearby Facilities ⌐ ⚲ ∪
Acreage 8 Open April to October
Access Good Site Level
River. Conference and Exhibition town. Ideal touring.
Nearest Town/Resort Harrogate
Directions On the A59 in Harrogate between the A661 and the A61. Turn at Skipton Inn and site is 1 mile down Bilton Lane.
⚞ Harrogate

## HARROGATE

**Great Yorkshire Showground Caravan Club Site**, Wetherby Road, Harrogate, North Yorkshire, HG3 1TZ
Tel: 01423 560470
www.caravanclub.co.uk
Pitches For ♫ ♨ Total 71
Facilities ∫ ⅁ ⅏ ♣ ⌐ ☉ ⊣ ◎ ⅊ ◎ ⅏ ⅌ ⬛
Acreage 6 Open March to Nov
Access Good Site Level
Only 1½ miles from Harrogate. Many splendid examples of municipal gardens nearby. Close to Lightwater Valley Theme Park, Ripley Castle, Harewood House, Newby Hall (Gobelins Tapestries) and the Yorks Dales. Non members welcome. Booking essential.
Nearest Town/Resort Harrogate
Directions From the A658 Otley to Knaresborough road, at roundabout take the A661 signposted Harrogate. After 1 mile at the traffic lights by Sainsburys turn left, site is 400 yards on the right.
⚞ Harrogate

## HARROGATE

**High Moor Farm Caravan Park**, Skipton Road, Harrogate, North Yorkshire, HG3 2LT
Tel: 01423 563637 Fax: 01423 529449
Pitches For ♫ ♨ Total 300
Facilities ⅙ ∫ ⅁ ⅏ ♣ ⌐ ☉ ◢ ◢ ◎ ☎
⅖ ◎ ⬡ ✕ ♈ ⅏ ⅌ ⬛ ▣ ⋊
Nearby Facilities ⌐ ⚲
Open 1 April/Easter to 31 Oct
Access Good Site Level
Nearest Town/Resort Harrogate
Directions On the A59 4 miles from Harrogate on the left hand side.
⚞ Harrogate

## HARROGATE

**Ripley Caravan Park,** Ripley, Harrogate, North Yorkshire, HG3 3AU
**Tel:** 01423 770050 **Fax:** 01423 770050
**Email:** ripleycaravanpark@talk21.com
**Pitches For** Å ⇔ ⇔ **Total** 100
**Facilities** ⅏ ∮ 🄵 🄷 🆄🄱 ♨ ⌂ ⊙ ↵ ⚊ 🄾 🕿
♒ ⅃⅊ ⌂ 🄱 🅃 ♠ ♫ ↴🛏🄳
**Nearby Facilities** ⌐ ✓ ⭢ ∪ ♪
**Acreage** 18 **Open** Easter **to** October
**Access** Good **Site** Level
Ideal site for touring Dales, Harrogate and York. A level and quiet family site. David Bellamy Gold Conservation Award, AA 5 Pennants and ETB 5 Star Graded Park.
**Nearest Town/Resort** Harrogate
**Directions** From Harrogate take A61 towards Ripon, after 3 miles at Ripley roundabout take the B6165 Knaresborough road, site is 300 yards on the left.
⚏ Harrogate

## HARROGATE

**Rudding Holiday Park,** Follifoot, Harrogate, North Yorkshire, HG3 1JH
**Tel:** 01423 870439 **Fax:** 01423 870859
**Email:** holiday-park@ruddingpark.com
**www.ruddingpark.com**
**Pitches For** Å ⇔ ⇔ **Total** 141
**Facilities** ⅏ ∮ 🄵 🄷 🆄🄱 ♨ ⌂ ⊙ ↵ ⚊ 🄾 🕿
♒ ⅃⅊ ⌂ 🄱 ✗ ♈ 🅃 ♠ ♫ ↴🛏🄿 🄱 🄶 ↴
♫
**Nearby Facilities** ⌐ ✓ ⚓ ⭢ ∪ ♪
**Acreage** 30 **Open** March **to** Jan
**Access** Good **Site** Level
Ideal location for exploring the Moors, Dales and cities. Only 3 miles from the Spa town of Harrogate.
**Nearest Town/Resort** Harrogate
**Directions** From the A1 take the A59 to the A658 and turn south signposted Bradford. Continue for 4½ miles then turn right and follow signs.
⚏ Harrogate

## HARROGATE

**Shaws Trailer Park,** Knaresborough Road, Harrogate, North Yorkshire, HG2 7NE
**Tel:** 01423 884432
**www.residentialsite.uk**
**Pitches For** Å ⇔ ⇔ **Total** 77
**Facilities** ∮ 🄷 🆄🄱 ♨ ⌂ ⊙ ↵ 🄾 🕿
⅃⅊ ⌂ ↴🛏 🄱 🄰 ♫
**Nearby Facilities** ⌐ ✓ ⭢ ∪ ♪
**Acreage** 11 **Open** All Year
**Access** Good **Site** Level
A quiet and peaceful ADULTS ONLY park. Ideal for touring Yorkshire Dales, spa town of Harrogate (1 mile) and gardens, Knaresborough (4 miles) and historic York. Health centre next door and a bus stop at

the gateway.
**Nearest Town/Resort** Harrogate
**Directions** On the A59 between Harrogate and Starbeck Railway Station. Entrance is adjacent to Johnsons Cleaners, 100 yards south of the Ford garage.
⚏ Starbeck

## HARROGATE

**The Yorkshire Hussar Inn Holiday Caravan Park,** Markington, Harrogate, North Yorkshire, HG3 3NR
**Tel:** 01765 677327
**Email:** yorkshirehussar@yahoo
**www.ukparks.co.uk/yorkshirehussar**
**Pitches For** Å ⇔ ⇔ **Total** 20
**Facilities** ∮ 🄵 🄷 🆄🄱 ♨ ⌂ ⊙ ↵ ⚊ 🄾 🕿
⅃⅊ ⌂ 🄸 🅈 ∪ ♠ ♫ ⚘
**Nearby Facilities** ⌐ ✓ ∪ ♪ ⚘
**Acreage** 5 **Open** April **to** October
**Access** Good **Site** Level
Ideal touring centre. Site at rear of Inn. Garden setting in village. Ideal touring centre for the Dales. Fountains Abbey 1¼ miles. Holiday vans for hire.
**Nearest Town/Resort** Harrogate/Ripon
**Directions** 1 mile west of A61 (Harrogate/Ripon road). Ripon 5 miles. Harrogate 7 miles.
⚏ Harrogate

## HAWES

**Bainbridge Ings Caravan & Camping Site,** Hawes, North Yorkshire, DL8 3NU
**Tel:** 01969 667354
**Email:** janet@bainbridge-ings.co.uk
**www.bainbridge-ings.co.uk**
**Pitches For** Å ⇔ ⇔ **Total** 80
**Facilities** ∮ 🄷 🆄🄱 ♨ ⌂ ⊙ ↵ 🄾 🄱 🄶 ↴🛏🄿 🄱
**Nearby Facilities** ✓
**Acreage** 5 **Open** April **to** October
**Access** Good **Site** Level
A quiet, clean, family run site with beautiful views and only ½ mile from Hawes. Motorcycles are accepted but not in groups of more than two.
**Nearest Town/Resort** Hawes
**Directions** Approaching Hawes from Bainbridge on the A684 turn left at the signpost marked Gayle and we are 300yds on at the top of the hill.
⚏ Garsdale

## HAWES

**Honeycott Caravan Park,** Ingleton Road, Hawes, North Yorkshire, DL8 3LH
**Tel:** 01969 667310
**Email:** info@honeycott.co.uk
**www.honeycott.co.uk**
**Pitches For** ⇔ ⇔ **Total** 18
**Facilities** ∮ 🄵 🄷 🆄🄱 ♨ ⌂ ⊙ ↵
⅃⅊ ⌂ ↴🛏 🄿 🄱 ⚘

**Nearby Facilities** ✓
**Acreage** 2½ **Open** March **to** October
**Access** Good **Site** Lev/Slope
On the Pennine Way, ideal for walking, fishing, local attractions and touring. Within the Dales National Park area. Short steep hill into park.
**Nearest Town/Resort** Hawes
**Directions** ¼ mile out of Hawes on the B6255 Hawes to Ingleton road.
⚏ Garsdale

## HAWES

**Shaw Ghyll,** Simonstone, Hawes, North Yorkshire, DL8 3LY
**Tel:** 01969 667359 **Fax:** 01969 667894
**Email:** rogerstott@aol.com
**www.yorkshirenet.co.uk/accgde/ydcotts.htm**
**Pitches For** Å ⇔ ⇔ **Total** 30
**Facilities** ∮ 🆄🄱 ♨ ⌂ ⊙ ↵ 🄾 🕿 🄱 ↴🛏🄿 ⚘
**Nearby Facilities** ✓ ⭢ ♪
**Acreage** 2½ **Open** March **to** October
**Access** Good **Site** Level
Quiet sheltered site, ideal for walks and families, pleasant aspect, river and lovely scenic walks.
**Nearest Town/Resort** Hawes
**Directions** 2 miles north of Hawes following the Muker road.

## HELMSLEY

**Foxholme Touring Caravan & Camping Park,** Harome, Helmsley, North Yorkshire, YO62 5JG
**Tel:** 01439 770416/771241 **Fax:** 01439 771744
**Pitches For** Å ⇔ ⇔ **Total** 60
**Facilities** ∮ 🆄🄱 ♨ ⌂ ⊙ ↵ ⚊ 🄾 🕿
⅃⅊ ⌂ ↴🛏🄰 ⚘ ♫
**Nearby Facilities** ⌐ ∪ ♪
**Acreage** 6 **Open** Easter **to** October
**Access** Good **Site** Level
ADULTS ONLY PARK in an ideal touring area. Near National Park, Abbeys and Herriot country. Use of an indoor swimming pool in a hotel in Harome.
**Nearest Town/Resort** Helmsley
**Directions** A170 towards Scarborough ½ mile turn right to Harome, turn left at church, through village, follow caravan signs.
⚏ Malton

## HELMSLEY

**Golden Square Caravan Park,** Oswaldkirk, York, North Yorkshire, YO62 5YQ
**Tel:** 01439 788269 **Fax:** 01439 788236
**Email:** barbara@goldensquarecaravanpark.freeserve.co.uk
**www.goldensquarecaravanpark.com**
**Pitches For** Å ⇔ ⇔ **Total** 110

**Facilities** [icons]
**Nearby Facilities** [icons]
**Acreage** 10 **Open** 1 **March to** 31 October
**Access** Good **Site** Level
Secluded site with magnificent views of North Yorkshire Moors. Indoor/Outdoor play areas. Regional Winner Loo of the Year Award. De-Lux all service pitches. Swimming nearby.
**Nearest Town/Resort** Helmsley
**Directions** 2 miles south of Helmsley. First right off the B1257 to Ampleforth.
⚍ Thirsk/Malton

## HELMSLEY

**Wombleton Caravan Park,** Moorfield Lane, Wombleton, Kirkbymoorside, North Yorkshire, YO62 7RY
**Tel:** 01751 431684
**Email:** info@wombletoncaravanpark.co.uk
**www.**wombletoncaravanpark.co.uk
**Pitches For** ▲ ⬛ ⬛ **Total** 118
**Facilities** [icons]
**Nearby Facilities** [icons]
**Acreage** 5 **Open** March **to** October
**Access** Good **Site** Level
Ideal for North Yorkshire Steam Railway, Duncombe Park, Nunnington Hall, Rievauly Abbey, Helmsley Castle and Flamingo Land.
**Nearest Town/Resort** Helmsley
**Directions** Leave Helmsley by A170 for 4 miles, turn right for Wombleton go through Wombleton ½ mile on left
⚍ Helmsley

## HELMSLEY

**Wren's of Ryedale,** Gale Lane, Nawton, North Yorkshire, YO62 7SD
**Tel:** 01439 771260
**Email:** dave@wrensofryedale.fsnet.co.uk
**www.**wrensofryedale.fsnet.co.uk
**Pitches For** ▲ ⬛ ⬛ **Total** 45
**Facilities** [icons]
**Nearby Facilities** [icons]
**Acreage** 3½ **Open** April **to** October
**Access** Good **Site** Level
Attractive, quiet, family run site. Situated on edge of Yorkshire Moors National Park. Very good centre for touring.
**Nearest Town/Resort** Scarborough/York
**Directions** Leave Helmsley by the A170. 2½ miles to Beadlam, pass the church on left, in 50 yards turn right. Site is 700 yards down the lane.
⚍ Malton

## INGLETON

**The Trees Caravan Park,** Westhouse, Ingleton, North Yorkshire, LA6 3NZ
**Tel:** 015242 41511
**Email:** stocks@greenwoodleghe.co.uk
**Pitches For** ⬛ ⬛ **Total** 29
**Facilities** [icons]
**Nearby Facilities** [icons]
**Acreage** 3 **Open** April **to** October
**Access** Good **Site** Level
Set in beautiful country scenery. Ideal for walking and touring. Mountains, caves and waterfalls nearby. Website: www.caravancampingsites.co.uk/northyorkshire/thetrees.htm
**Nearest Town/Resort** Ingleton
**Directions** From Ingleton, travel 1¼ miles along the A65 towards Kirkby Lonsdale about ¼ mile past the A687 junction - Country Harvest). Turn left at signpost for Lower Westhouse, site is on the left in 50yds.
⚍ Bentham

## KNARESBOROUGH

**Allerton Park Caravan Park,** Allerton Mauleverer, Nr Knaresborough, North Yorkshire, HG5 0SE
**Tel:** 01423 330569 **Fax:** 01759 371377
**Email:** enquiries@yorkshireholidayparks.co.uk
**www.**yorkshireholidayparks.co.uk
**Pitches For** ▲ ⬛ ⬛ **Total** 30
**Facilities** [icons]
**Nearby Facilities** [icons]
**Acreage** 17 **Open** 1 February **to** 3 January
**Access** Good **Site** Level
Woodland park with plenty of wildlife and walks. David Bellamy Gold Award for Conservation.
**Nearest Town/Resort** Knaresborough
**Directions** A59 York to Harrogate road, ½ mile east of Aim.
⚍ Harrogate

## KNARESBOROUGH

**Kingfisher Caravan & Camping Park,** Low Moor Lane, Farnham, Knaresborough, North Yorkshire, HG5 9JB
**Tel:** 01423 869411
**Pitches For** ▲ ⬛ ⬛ **Total** 50
**Facilities** [icons]
**Nearby Facilities** [icons]
**Acreage** 10 **Open** March **to** October
**Access** Good **Site** Level
Ideal touring base for the Dales, convenient for Harrogate and York. Adjacent to a golf range.
**Nearest Town/Resort** Knaresborough
**Directions** From Knaresborough take the A6055. In 1¼ miles turn left to Farnham Village, in Farnham turn left, park is approx. 1 mile on the left.
⚍ Knaresborough

## KNARESBOROUGH

**Knaresborough Caravan Club Site,** New Road, Scotton, Knaresborough, North Yorkshire, HG5 9HH
**Tel:** 01423 860196
**www.**caravanclub.co.uk
**Pitches For** ▲ ⬛ ⬛ **Total** 62
**Facilities** [icons]
**Nearby Facilities** [icons]
**Acreage** 8 **Open** March **to** Beg Jan
**Access** Good **Site** Lev/Slope
Surrounded by mature trees and hedges. Riverside walks, tennis, pitch 'n' putt and boating in the local area. Close to Ripley Castle, Old Court House Museum and Old Mother Shipton's Cave. Non members welcome. Booking essential.
**Nearest Town/Resort** Knaresborough
**Directions** Leave A1 at junc 47 and take A59 sp Knaresborough. At roundabout turn right onto A59 and continue through Knaresborough, at junction with traffic lights turn left and continue on A59. At next lights turn right onto B6165, at petrol station turn right into New Road, site is 50 yards on the right.
⚍ Knaresborough

## LEYBURN

**Constable Burton Hall Caravan Park,** Leyburn, Wensleydale, North Yorkshire, DL8 5LJ
**Tel:** 01677 450428
**Pitches For** ⬛ ⬛ **Total** 120
**Facilities** [icons]
**Nearby Facilities** [icons]
**Acreage** 10 **Open** April **to** October
**Access** Good **Site** Lev/Slope
Ideal for walking and touring. Many castles, gardens and historic houses nearby. No childrens play area and strictly no games.
**Nearest Town/Resort** Leyburn
**Directions** From the A1 take the A684 for 8 miles.

## LEYBURN

**Lower Wensleydale Caravan Club Site,** Harmby, Leyburn, North Yorkshire, DL8 5NU
**Tel:** 01969 623366
**www.**caravanclub.co.uk
**Pitches For** ▲ ⬛ ⬛ **Total** 89
**Facilities** [icons]
**Nearby Facilities** [icons]
**Acreage** 10 **Open** March **to** Nov
**Access** Good **Site** Level
Situated in the hollow of a disused quarry, now overrun with wild flowers and mosses. Ducks and rabbits roam the site freely. Ideal for walking. Close to Constable Burton Gardens, Bolton Castle and Middleham Castle. Non members welcome. Booking essential.
**Nearest Town/Resort** Leyburn
**Directions** From the A684, in Harmby turn off by the Pheasant Inn, cross the railway bridge and immediately turn left at brown caravan sign. Follow signs to the entrance.
⚍ Leyburn

## MALTON

**Ashfield Caravan Park,** Kirby Misperton, Malton, North Yorkshire, YO17 6UU
**Tel:** 01653 668555
**Email:** mail@ashfieldcaravanpark.co.uk
**www.**ashfieldcaravanpark.co.uk
**Pitches For** ▲ ⬛ ⬛ **Total** 40
**Facilities** [icons]
**Nearby Facilities** [icons]
**Acreage** 6 **Open** March **to** October
**Access** Good **Site** Level
Ideal for Flamingo Land, North Yorkshire Moors Railway, Scarborough, York and Eden Camp.
**Nearest Town/Resort** Pickering
**Directions** From the A64 take the A169, turn off to Flamingo Land and Park is opposite the main entrance. 4 miles from Pickering.
⚍ Malton

## MALTON

**Lakeside Holiday Park,** Castle Howard Estate Ltd, York, North Yorkshire, YO60 7DA
**Tel:** 01653 648316 **Fax:** 01653 648316
**Email:** lakeside@castlehoward.co.uk
**www.**castlehoward.co.uk
**Pitches For** ▲ ⬛ ⬛ **Total** 60
**Facilities** [icons]
**Nearby Facilities** [icons]
**Acreage** 4 **Open** March **to** October
**Access** Good **Site** Level
Castle Howard House, grounds, gardens, lakes, stable/courtyard shops and cafes.
**Nearest Town/Resort** Malton
⚍ Malton

## MASHAM

**Black Swan Holiday Park,** Fearby, Masham, Ripon, North Yorkshire, HG4 4NF
**Tel:** 01765 689477
**Email:** welcome@blackswanholiday.co.uk
**www.**blackswanholiday.co.uk
**Pitches For** ▲ ⬛ ⬛ **Total** 50
**Facilities** [icons]
**Nearby Facilities** [icons]

**Acreage** 2½ **Open** March **to** Oct
**Access** Good **Site** Lev/Slope
Close to the Black Sheep and Theakstons Breweries, Lightwater Valley, Forbidden Corner and Ariel Extreme.
**Nearest Town/Resort** Masham
**Directions** Enter Masham on the A6108 and follow brown tourism signs for Black Swan.
➤ Northallerton

## MASHAM
**Old Station Caravan & Camping Park,** Old Station, Low Burton, Masham, North Yorkshire, HG4 4DF
**Tel:** 01765 689569 **Fax:** 01765 689569
**Email:** oldstation@tiscali.co.uk
**www.oldstation-masham.co.uk**
**Pitches For** ▲ ⊡ **Total** 50
**Facilities** & ∮ 🖫 🖩 ▥ ▲ ┌ ⊙ ⌿ ◢ ▢ ☎
🕿 ⑫ ✕ 🆗 ⧖
**Nearby Facilities** ┌ ⌿ ∪ ♪
**Acreage** 3 **Open** March **to** Nov
**Access** Good **Site** Level
Picturesque and peaceful countryside site just outside the town, with Dales scenery. Bus route to the Dales. Convenient for local events and attractions.
**Nearest Town/Resort** Masham
**Directions** From Ripon take the A6108 north west for 8 miles. Or from Bedale take the B6268 south west for 4 miles. Or from Leyburn take the A6108 south for 8 miles.
➤ Northallerton

## MUKER
**Usha Gap Caravan & Camp Site,** Usha Gap, Muker, Richmond, North Yorkshire, DL11 6DW
**Tel:** 01748 886214
**Email:** ushagap@btinternet.com
**www.ushagap.btinternet.co.uk**
**Pitches For** ▲ ⊞ ⊟ **Total** 24
**Facilities** 🖫 🖩 ▲ ┌ ⊙ ⌿ ☎ ⊬
**Nearby Facilities** ✗
**Acreage** 1 **Open** All Year
**Access** Good **Site** Level
Alongside a small river. Shops and a pub ¼ mile. Ideal touring and good walking.
**Nearest Town/Resort** Hawes
➤ Darlington

## NORTHALLERTON
**Cote Ghyll Caravan & Camping Park,** Osmotherley, Northallerton, North Yorkshire, DL6 3AH
**Tel:** 01609 883425 **Fax:** 01609 883425
**Email:** hills@coteghyll.com
**www.coteghyll.com**
**Pitches For** ▲ ⊞ ⊟ **Total** 77
**Facilities** & ∮ 🖫 🖩 ▥ ▲ ┌ ⊙ ⌿ ◢ ▢ ☎
🕿 ⑫ ✕ 🆗 ⧖
**Nearby Facilities** ┌ ⌿ ∪ ♪ ✗

**Acreage** 7 **Open** 1 March **to** 31 Oct
**Access** Good **Site** Level
Beautiful site in a peaceful valley location within the North York Moors National Park. New luxury heated shower block for 2006. Play area and stream. Excellent walking and cycling area. Village pubs and shops just a 10 minute walk. Luxury holiday homes for hire and sale.
**Nearest Town/Resort** Northallerton
**Directions** Exit the A19 dual carriageway at the A684 Northallerton junction. Follow signs into Osmotherley Village. At the T-junction in the centre of the village turn left. On leaving the village the site is ¼ mile on the right.
➤ Northallerton/Thirsk

## PATELEY BRIDGE
**Heathfield Caravan Park,** Ramsgill Road, Pateley Bridge, Harrogate, North Yorkshire, HG3 5PY
**Tel:** 01423 711652 **Fax:** 01423 711652
**Pitches For** ⊞ ⊟
**Facilities** ∮ 🖫 🖩 ▲ ┌ ⊙ ⌿ ◢ ▢ ☎
🕿 ⑫ ⊙ 🖩 ⧗ ▲ 🆗 ⧖
**Nearby Facilities** ⌿ ⊥ ❀ ∪ ♪ ✗
**Open** March **to** October
**Access** Good **Site** Sloping
Set in the beautiful Nidderdale within the Yorkshire Dales. On Nidderdale Way for great walking and breathtaking views.
**Nearest Town/Resort** Pateley Bridge
**Directions** From Nidderdale Motors turn off along Low Wath Road. Follow for approx. 2 miles, pass the Bridge Inn and go over the bridge, follow signs.
➤ Harrogate

## PATELEY BRIDGE
**Manor House Farm Caravan Park,** Manor House Farm, Summerbridge, Harrogate, North Yorkshire, HG3 4JS
**Tel:** 01423 780322
**Pitches For** ▲ ⊞ ⊟
**Facilities** ∮ 🖫 🖩 ▥ ▲ ┌ ⊙ ⌿ ◢ ▢ ☎
⊙ 🖩 ⧖ ℘
**Nearby Facilities** ⌿ ∪ ♪ ✗
**Open** March **to** October
**Access** Good **Site** Level
Near the River Nidd. Good walking country.
**Nearest Town/Resort** Harrogate
**Directions** Situated on the B6165, 5 miles from Ripley and Pateley Bridge.
➤ Harrogate

## PATELEY BRIDGE
**Riverside Caravan Park,** Low Wath Road, Pateley Bridge, Harrogate, North Yorkshire, HG3 5HL
**Tel:** 01423 711383 **Fax:** 01423 712778
**Email:** riverside-cp@lineone.net
**Pitches For** ▲ ⊞ ⊟

**Facilities** ∮ 🖫 🖩 ▲ ┌ ⊙ ⌿ ◢ ▢ ☎
⑫ ⊙ 🖩 ⧖ ⧖
**Nearby Facilities** ⌿ ⊥ ❀ ∪ ♪ ✗
**Open** 1 April/Easter **to** Oct
**Access** Good **Site** Level
Situated amidst beautiful scenery by the River Nidd, yet only a 5 minute walk from Pateley Bridge. Ideal centre for walking and touring. Indoor swimming pool, childrens play area and sports area are all nearby.
**Nearest Town/Resort** Pateley Bridge
**Directions** Take the B6265 or the B61650 into Pateley Bridge. Go down the main street and over the bridge over River Nidd, turn right into Low Wath Road. Park is approx. ¼ mile on the right.
➤ Harrogate

## PATELEY BRIDGE
**Studfold Farm Caravan & Camping Park,** Studfold Farm, Lofthouse, Harrogate, North Yorkshire, HG3 5SG
**Tel:** 01423 755210 **Fax:** 01423 755311
**Email:** ianwalker@studfold.fsnet.co.uk
**www.studfoldfarm.co.uk**
**Pitches For** ▲ ⊞ ⊟
**Facilities** ∮ 🖩 ▲ ┌ ⊙ ☎
🕿 ⑫ ⊙ 🖩 🆗 ⧖
**Nearby Facilities** ⌿ ∪ ✗
**Acreage** 2 **Open** April **to** Oct
**Access** Good **Site** Level
Set on a working farm. Near to Howstean Gorge. Ideal for walking and visiting the Dales. Very small site shop.
**Nearest Town/Resort** Harrogate
**Directions** From Harrogate take the B6265 to Pateley Bridge, then 7 miles to Lofthouse. Take the left fork beyond the village signposted Stean, site is 200 yards on the right.
➤ Harrogate

## PATELEY BRIDGE
**Westfield,** Westfield Farm, Heathfield, Pateley Bridge, HarrogateNorth Yorkshire, HG3 5BX
**Tel:** 01423 711880
**Pitches For** ▲ ⊞ ⊟
**Facilities** & ∮ 🖩 ▲ ┌ ⊙ ⌿ 🖩 ⧖
**Nearby Facilities** ✗
**Acreage** 3 **Open** April **to** October
**Access** Single Track. **Site** Lev/Slope
Small farm site alongside a stream, in a quiet Yorkshire Dales location.
**Nearest Town/Resort** Pateley Bridge
**Directions** From Pateley Bridge 1 mile turn left to Heathfield after 100yds turn left to continue on this road through Heathfield caravan site. We are the third site.
➤ Harrogate

## PICKERING

**Overbrook Caravan Park,** Malton Gate, Thornton-le-Dale, Nr Pickering, North Yorkshire, YO18 7SE
**Tel:** 01751 474417
**Email:**
enquiry@overbrookcaravanpark.co.uk
www.overbrookcaravanpark.co.uk
Pitches For ⌂ ⊞ Total 50
Facilities ⌕ 🄷 🆄🅲 ♨ ⌿ ⊙ ⌁ ⚑ ☎
🄸🄴 ⊙ ➡🄳🄰 ⅍
**Nearby Facilities** ⌕ ✓ ∪ ♪
**Acreage** 3 **Open** March to October
**Access** Good **Site** Level
ADULTS ONLY park in one of North Yorkshires prettiest villages. Peaceful location. Level, well drained site. Ideal for touring and walking.
**Nearest Town/Resort** Pickering
**Directions** From A1 follow A64 to A169, 4 miles turn right to Thornton Dale, follow road for 3½ miles. The site is opposite the village road sign Thornton Dale, turn right into the railway station.
⚏ Malton

## PICKERING

**Rosedale Caravan Park,** Rosedale Abbey, Pickering, North Yorkshire, YO18 8SA
**Tel:** 01751 417272 **Fax:** 01751 417272
**Email:** info@flowerofmay.com
www.flowerofmay.com
Pitches For ▲ ⊞ ⊞ Total
Facilities ⌕ 🄷 🆄🅲 ♨ ⌿ ⊙ ⌁ ⚑ 🄾 ☎
🄸🄴 ⊙ ⚙ ♨ 🄼 ➡🄴 ⅍
**Nearby Facilities** ⌕ ✓ ∪
**Open** Easter to End October
**Access** Good **Site** Level
Idyllic retreat. Ideal for walking and hiking through the beautiful North Yorkshire Moors.
**Nearest Town/Resort** Pickering
**Directions** Turn off the A170 towards Rosedale.
⚏ Malton

## PICKERING

**Spiers House Caravan & Camping Site -** Forestry Commission, Cropton, Pickering, North Yorkshire, YO18 8ES
**Tel:** 01751 417591
**Email:** info@forestholidays.co.uk
www.forestholidays.co.uk
Pitches For ▲ ⊞ ⊞ Total 150
Facilities ⌕ 🄷 🆄🅲 ♨ ⌿ ⊙ ⌁ ⚑ 🄾 ☎
🄸🄴 ⊙ ⚙ 🄼 ➡🄴 ⅍
**Nearby Facilities** ⌕ ∪
**Acreage** 10 **Open** 25 March to 26 Sept
**Access** Good **Site** Lev/Slop
Site located in an extensive open grassland area and there are several way-

marked walks in the adjoining forest. An ideal base to explore the surrounding moors and coast.
**Nearest Town/Resort** Pickering
**Directions** Take A170 westwards from Pickering and at Wrelton turn north to Cropton, continue from there on the Rosedale Road for 1 mile where site is signposted at the edge of Cropton Forest.
⚏ Malton

## PICKERING

**The Black Bull Caravan Park,** Malton Road, Pickering, North Yorkshire, YO18 8EA
**Tel:** 01751 472528
www.blackbullpark.co.uk
Pitches For ▲ ⊞ ⊞ Total 72
Facilities ⌕ 🆄🅲 ⌿ ⊙ ⌁ 🄾 ☎
🄸🄴 ⊙ ⚑ ✕ ♨ 🄼 ♨ ➡🄴 ⅍
**Nearby Facilities** ⌕ ✓ ∪
**Acreage** 4 **Open** March to October
**Access** Good **Site** Level
Ideal base for touring the North Yorkshire Moors.
**Nearest Town/Resort** Pickering
**Directions** 1 mile south of Pickering on the Malton road, behind The Black Bull Public House.
⚏ Malton

## PICKERING

**Upper Carr Chalet & Touring Park,** Upper Carr Lane, Malton Road, Pickering, North Yorkshire, YO18 7JP
**Tel:** 01751 473115 **Fax:** 01751 473115
**Email:** harker@uppercarr.demon.co.uk
www.uppercarr.demon.co.uk
Pitches For ▲ ⊞ ⊞ Total 80
Facilities ⌖ ⌕ 🆄🅲 ♨ ⌿ ⊙ ⌁ ⚑ 🄾 ☎
🆂🄸 ⊙ ⚑ 🄼 ➡🄴 ⅍
**Nearby Facilities** ⌕ ✓ ∪ ♪
**Acreage** 6¼ **Open** March to October
**Access** Good **Site** Level
Ideal for Whitby, Scarborough, historic York and North Yorkshire Moors. Golf and tennis opposite. Steam Railway in Pickering. 3 miles from Flamingo Land.
**Nearest Town/Resort** Pickering
**Directions** 1½ miles south of Pickering on the A169 Malton road, opposite the Black Bull Pub.
⚏ Malton

## PICKERING

**Vale of Pickering Caravan Park,** Carr House Farm, Allerston, Pickering, North Yorkshire, YO18 7PQ
**Tel:** 01723 859280 **Fax:** 01723 850060
**Email:** tony@valeofpickering.co.uk
www.valeofpickering.co.uk
Pitches For ▲ ⊞ ⊞ Total 120

Facilities ⌖ ⌕ 🄷 🆄🅲 ♨ ⌿ ⊙ ⌁ ⚑ 🄾 ☎
🆂🄸 ⊙ ⚑ 🄼 ♨ ➡🄴 ⅍ ♪
**Nearby Facilities** ⌕ ✓ ∪
**Acreage** 8 **Open** 1 March to 8 Jan
**Access** Good **Site** Level
Superb play area and games area. Extensive improvements to shower blocks. ETB 5 Star Graded.
**Nearest Town/Resort** Scarborough
**Directions** From Pickering take the A170 to Allerston, turn right opposite Cayley Arms Hotel, due south 1¼ miles.
⚏ Malton

## PICKERING

**Wayside Caravan & Camping Park,** Wrelton, Pickering, North Yorkshire, YO18 8PG
**Tel:** 01751 472608 **Fax:** 01751 472608
**Email:** waysideparks@freenet.co.uk
www.waysideparks.co.uk
Pitches For ▲ ⊞ ⊞ Total 72
Facilities ⌖ ⌕ 🆄🅲 ♨ ⌿ ⊙ ⌁ ⚑ 🄾 ☎
🆂🄸 ⊙ ⚑ ♨ 🄼 ➡🄴 ⅍
**Nearby Facilities** ⌕ ✓ ∪
**Acreage** 5 **Open** Easter to Early Oct
**Access** Good
Ideal for touring the North York Moors. Walks nearby and historic steam railway.
**Nearest Town/Resort** Pickering
**Directions** 2½ miles west of Pickering off the A170 at Wrelton, turn right off the by-pass.
⚏ Malton

## RICHMOND

**Brompton Caravan Park,** Brompton-on-Swale, Easby, Richmond, North Yorkshire, DL10 7EZ
**Tel:** 01748 824629 **Fax:** 01748 826383
**Email:**
brompton.caravanpark@btinternet.com
www.bromptoncaravanpark.co.uk
Pitches For ▲ ⊞ ⊞ Total 217
Facilities ⌖ ⌕ 🄷 🆄🅲 ♨ ⌿ ⊙ ⌁ ⚑ 🄾 ☎
🆂🄸 ⊙ ⚑ 🄼 ➡🄴 ⅍
**Nearby Facilities**
**Acreage** 10 **Open** Mid March to End Oct
**Access** Good **Site** Level
Perfectly situated for the Dales. No teens, children up to 12 years only. Take-away on site.
**Nearest Town/Resort** Richmond
**Directions** Leave the A1 at Catterick A6136. Follow the B6271 to Richmond and drive through Brompton-on-Swale. Park is 1 mile on the left.
⚏ Darlington

# YORKSHIRE (NORTH)

## RICHMOND
**Fox Hall Caravan Park,** Ravensworth, Richmond, North Yorkshire, DL11 7JZ
Tel: 01325 718344
**Pitches For** ⚠ ⬛ 🚐 **Total** 10
**Facilities** ⚒ ∮ 🚻 🚿 🛁 ☎ ⌂ ☉ 🛒
🚰 ⊡ 🛒
**Nearby Facilities** ⌂ ✦ ∪ ♪
**Acreage** 4 **Open** April **to** Oct
**Access** Good **Site** Level
Quiet, wooded site with separate pitches.
**Nearest Town/Resort** Richmond
**Directions** From Scotch Corner take the A66 west for 5 miles, take the first turning to Ravensworth and the park is 300 yards on the right.
⚏ Darlington

## RICHMOND
**Hargill House Caravan Club Site,** Gilling West, Richmond, North Yorkshire, DL10 5LJ
Tel: 01748 822734
www.caravanclub.co.uk
**Pitches For** ⬛ 🚐 **Total** 66
**Facilities** ⚒ ∮ 🚻 🚿 🛁 ☎ ⌂ 🛒
⽥ 🚰 ⊡
**Nearby Facilities** ⌂ ✦
**Acreage** 4½ **Open** March **to** Nov
**Access** Good **Site** Lev/Slope
Situated in Herriot country with wonderful views of the Yorkshire Dales National Park. Non members welcome. Booking essential.
**Nearest Town/Resort** Richmond
**Directions** Leave the A1 at Scotch Corner and take the A66 signposted Penrith. At the crossroads turn left signposted Gilling West, site is 100 yards on the left.
⚏ Richmond

## RICHMOND
**Orchard Caravan Park,** Reeth, Richmond, North Yorkshire, DL11 6TT
Tel: 01748 884475
**Pitches For** ⚠ ⬛ 🚐 **Total** 56
**Facilities** ∮ 🚻 ⌂ 🛒 ⽥ 🚰 ⊡ 🛒
Nearby Facilities ∮
**Acreage** 3½ **Open** 1 April **to** 31 October
**Access** Good **Site** Level
Near a river and hills for walking. Pets are welcome if kept on leads.
**Nearest Town/Resort** Richmond
**Directions** Approx. 11½ miles from Richmond.
⚏ Darlington

## RICHMOND
**Scotch Corner Caravan Park,** Scotch Corner, Richmond, North Yorkshire, DL10 6NS
Tel: 01748 822530
Email: marshallleisure@aol.com
www.scotchcornercaravanpark.co.uk
**Pitches For** ⚠ ⬛ 🚐 **Total** 75
**Facilities** ⚒ ∮ 🚻 🚿 🛁 ☎ ⌂ ☉ 🛒 🚰 ⊡ 🛒
⽥ ⊡ 🚰 ✕ ⽥ ⊡ 🛒 ≋ 🛒
**Nearby Facilities** ⌂ ✦ ∪ ♪
**Acreage** 7 **Open** Easter **to** End Oct
**Access** Good **Site** Level
Ideal night halt en-route to and from Scotland. Good base for exploring the Yorkshire Dales and Moors.
**Nearest Town/Resort** Richmond
**Directions** Leave the A1 at Scotch Corner and take the A6108 Richmond road. After 250 yards cross to the opposite carriageway and return 200 yards to the site entrance.
⚏ Darlington

## RICHMOND
**Swale View Caravan Park,** Reeth Road, Richmond, North Yorkshire, DL10 4SF
Tel: 01748 823106
**Pitches For** ⬛ 🚐 **Total** 50

## RICHMOND
**Facilities** ⚒ ∮ 🚻 🚿 🛁 ☎ ⌂ ☉ 🛒 🚰 ⊡ 🛒
⽥ ⊡ 🚰 🛒 ⽥ ⊡ 🚰 ≋ ⌀
**Nearby Facilities** ⌂ ✦ ⚓ ∪ ♪ ✈
**Open** March **to** October
On the banks of the River Swale, in the heart of the Yorkshire Dales.
**Nearest Town/Resort** Richmond
**Directions** On the A6108, 2½ miles on the right hand side.
⚏ Darlington

## RICHMOND
**Tavern House Caravan Park,** Newsham, Nr Richmond, North Yorkshire, DL11 7RA
Tel: 01833 621223
**Pitches For** ⚠ ⬛ 🚐 **Total** 6
**Facilities** ∮ 🚻 ⌂ ☉ 🛒 🚰 ⽥ ⚠ ≋
**Nearby Facilities** ⌂ ✦ ∪
**Acreage** 1½ **Open** March **to** October
**Access** Good **Site** Lev/Slope
ADULTS ONLY. Walking, fishing and historic towns. Static caravan for hire.
**Nearest Town/Resort** Barnard Castle/Richmond
**Directions** 7 miles west from Scotch Corner on the A66 turn left, 1 mile into the middle of the village, on the right.
⚏ Darlington

## RIPON
**Church Farm Caravan Park,** Church Farm, Bishop Monkton, Harrogate, North Yorkshire, HG3 3QQ
Tel: 01765 677668 Fax: 01765 677668
**Pitches For** ⚠ ⬛ 🚐 **Total** 40
**Facilities** ⚒ ∮ 🚻 🛁 ☎ ⌂ ☉ 🛒 ⽥ ⊡
**Nearby Facilities** ⌂ ✦ ∪ ♪
**Acreage** 2/3 **Open** March **to** October
**Access** Good **Site** Level
Set in a picturesque village with a stream, two pubs and a shop. Ideal for touring the Yorkshire Dales.
**Nearest Town/Resort** Ripon
**Directions** Left off the Ripon bypass leads straight to Bishop Monkton, camp site is opposite the church.
⚏ Harrogate

## RIPON
**River Laver Holiday Park,** Studley Road, Ripon, North Yorkshire, HG4 2QR
Tel: 01765 690508 Fax: 01765 698708
Email: riverlaver@lineone.net
www.riverlaver.co.uk
**Pitches For** ⬛ 🚐 **Total** 50
**Facilities** ⚒ ∮ 🚻 🛁 ☎ ⌂ ☉ 🛒 🚰 ⊡ 🛒
🛒 ⊡ 🚰 ⽥ ⊡ 🛒 ≋
**Nearby Facilities** ⌂ ✦ ♪
**Acreage** 5 **Open** 1 March **to** 3 January
**Access** Good **Site** Level
Ideal base for the Yorkshire Moors and Dales. Easy access to Fountains Abbey and road network.
**Nearest Town/Resort** Ripon
**Directions** ½ mile from Ripon on the B6265 towards Fountains Abbey.
⚏ Harrogate

## RIPON
**Riverside Meadows Country Caravan Park,** Ure Bank Top (Dept No.1), Ripon, North Yorkshire, HG4 1JD
Tel: 01765 602964 Fax: 01765 604045
Email: info@flowerofmay.com
www.flowerofmay.com
**Pitches For** ⬛ 🚐 **Total** 400
**Facilities** ∮ 🚻 🛁 ☎ ⌂ ☉ 🛒 🚰 ⊡ 🛒
🛒 ⊡ 🚰 ⊡ 🛒 ⽥ 🔔 ⽥ ⊡ ≋
**Nearby Facilities** ⌂ ✦ ∪ ♪
**Acreage** 28 **Open** March **to** October
**Access** Good **Site** Lev/Slope
Countryside park alongside a river. Ideal

for touring the Yorkshire Dales. NEW bar complex for all the family. Pets are welcome by arrangement.
**Nearest Town/Resort** Ripon
**Directions** Leave the A1 onto the A61 north of Ripon town centre, ½ mile.
⚏ Harrogate

## RIPON
**Sleningford Watermill,** North Stainley, Ripon, North Yorkshire, HG4 3HQ
Tel: 01765 635201
www.ukparks.co.uk/sleningford
**Pitches For** ⚠ ⬛ 🚐 **Total** 80
**Facilities** ⚒ ∮ 🚻 🛁 ☎ ⌂ ☉ 🛒 🚰 ⊡ 🛒
🛒 ⽥ ⊡ 🚰 ⊡ 🛒 ≋ ⌀
**Nearby Facilities** ⌂ ✦ ⚓ ∪ ♪
**Acreage** 14 **Open** Easter **to** October
**Access** Good **Site** Level
Picturesque, rural, riverside site. Fly fishing and canoe access. Quiet - birds, wild flowers etc. David Bellamy Gold Award. Central for the Dales.
**Nearest Town/Resort** Ripon
**Directions** 5½ miles N.W. of Ripon (turning at clock tower) onto A6108, between North Stainley and West Tanfield. Or by following Lightwater Valley signs which is 1½ miles along the same road.

## RIPON
**Woodhouse Farm Caravan & Camping Park,** Winksley, Ripon, North Yorkshire, HG4 3PG
Tel: 01765 658309
Email: woodhouse.farm@talk21.com
www.woodhousewinksley.com
**Pitches For** ⚠ ⬛ 🚐 **Total** 150
**Facilities** ∮ 🚻 🛁 ☎ ⌂ ☉ 🛒 🚰 ⊡ 🛒
🛒 ⊡ 🚰 ✕ ⽥ 🔔 ⽥ ⊡ 🛒 ≋ ⌀
**Nearby Facilities** ⌂ ✦ ∪ ♪
**Acreage** 20 **Open** March **to** Oct
**Access** Good **Site** Lev/Slope
Close to Fountains Abbey and Brimham Rocks.
**Nearest Town/Resort** Ripon
**Directions** From Ripon take the B6265 towards Pateley Bridge, after passing Fountains Abbey take the second turning right and follow signs.
⚏ Harrogate

## SCARBOROUGH
**Blue Dolphin Holiday Centre,** Gristhorpe Bay, Filey, North Yorkshire, YO14 9PU
Tel: 01723 515155 Fax: 01723 512059
www.touringholidays.co.uk
**Pitches For** ⚠ ⬛ 🚐 **Total** 311
**Facilities** ⚒ ∮ 🚻 🚿 🛁 ☎ ⌂ ☉ 🛒 🚰 ⊡ 🛒
🛒 ⊡ 🚰 ✕ 🍴 ⽥ ⌀ ⊡ ⚤ 🔔 ⽥ ⊡ 🛒 ≋
**Nearby Facilities** ⌂ ✦ ⚓ ∪ ♪
**Acreage** 5 **Open** 23 March **to** 25 Oct
**Access** Good **Site** Lev/Slope
We are an "All Action" centre. Our tariff does include up to four entertainment passes. BBQ's permitted.
**Nearest Town/Resort** Filey
**Directions** 2½ miles north of Filey off the A165 coast road.
⚏ Filey

## SCARBOROUGH
**Brown's Caravan Park,** Mill Lane, Cayton Bay, Scarborough, North Yorkshire, YO11 3NN
Tel: 01723 582303
www.brownscaravan.co.uk
**Pitches For** ⬛ 🚐 **Total** 35
**Facilities** ∮ 🚻 🛁 ☎ ⌂ ☉ 🛒 🚰 ⊡ 🛒
🛒 ⊡ 🚰 ✕ ⌀ 🔔 ⽥ ⊡ 🛒 ≋
**Nearby Facilities** ⌂ ✦ ∪ ♪ ⚃ ♪
**Acreage** ¼ **Open** April **to** September
**Access** Good **Site** Level

# YORKSHIRE SAND, SEA & SUN

To make the most of your holiday, including indoor heated swimming pool, jacuzzi, 10 pin bowling, superb squash courts, games room with pool and snooker.

- ■ Heated Indoor Pool & Jacuzzi ■ 9 Hole Golf Course
- ■ Supermarket ■ Family Bar and Entertainment
- ■ Excellent Touring Facilities ■ Seasonal Tourers
- ■ Luxury Holiday Homes for Sale or Hire
- ■ Exciting Playground with safety surface

*Special terms early and late season - send for details.*

*Please send for colour brochure from the resident proprietors.*

Mr J.G. Atkinson,
Dept. I. Flower of May,
Lebberston Cliff,
Scarborough  YO11 3NU
Telephone (01723) 584311

*AA* WINNER 1995
BEST CAMPSITE
NORTHERN ENGLAND

RAC

---

## THE FRIENDLY FAMILY PARK

FIR TREE CARAVAN PARK

- ■ Luxury Caravans for Sale or Hire ■ Touring Pitches
- ■ New Indoor Pool ■ "The Harbour"
- New bars for everyone ■ Shop & Launderette
- ■ New Adventure Playground

*AA* ▶▶▶

Nearby Amenities Include:
*Golf • Bird Sanctuary • Sewerby Park*
*• Beaches • Beautiful Views & Walks*

Dept. I.
Jewison Lane
Sewerby
Bridlington
YO16 6YG

Telephone:
(01262) 676442

---

## RELAX IN THE COUNTRY

RIVERSIDE COUNTRY CARAVAN PARK

- ■ Touring Pitches ■ Seasonal Pitches
- ■ Luxury Caravans for Sale

*AA* ▶▶▶

Nearby Amenities Include:
*Walking • Fishing • Historic Towns & Villages*
*Studley Royal & Harlow Carr,*
*Gardens of International Repute*

Dept. I.
Ure Bank Top
Ripon
HG4 1JD

Telephone:
(01765) 602964

---

## UNWIND IN IDYLLIC SETTINGS

ROSEDALE COUNTRY CARAVAN PARK

- ■ Touring Pitches ■ Tent Pitches
- ■ Seasonal Pitches ■ All main facilities

*AA* ▶▶▶

Nearby Amenities Include:
*Walking on the Moors • Fishing • Pickering Attractions,*
*York and Helmsley Country Houses,*
*Museums and History*

Dept. I.
Rosedale Abbey
Pickering
YO18 8SA

Telephone:
(01751) 417272

---

E-Mail: info@flowerofmay.com      www.flowerofmay.com

# CAYTON VILLAGE CARAVAN PARK

**TOURING PARK**

## MILL LANE, CAYTON BAY, SCARBOROUGH YO11 3NN
### THE VERY BEST OF COAST AND COUNTRY...
So near to major attractions. A lovely setting, in the shadow of Cayton Village Church, provides acres of beautifully planned space for touring caravans, tents and motor homes. Super Savers and special OAP rates in low season.

**OPEN 1st March to 4th January**      **Tel: 01723 583171**

E-mail: info@caytontouring.co.uk  Website: www.caytontouring.co.uk

---

Close to beach. Ideal touring centre for North Yorkshire Moors. ETB 5 Star Grading. **Nearest Town/Resort** Scarborough **Directions** 3 miles south of Scarborough just off A165.

≠ Scarborough

## SCARBOROUGH

**Camping & Caravanning Club Site,** Field Lane, Burniston Road, Scarborough, North Yorkshire, YO13 0DA
**Tel:** 01723 366212
www.campingandcaravanningclub.co.uk
Pitches For ▲ ⊕ ⊟ **Total** 300
Facilities ⓗ ⌇ ⓗ ⓤ ♨ ⌠ ⊙ ⌐ ⊿ ☎
⊟ ♠ ♫ ✿ ⊬ ⊞ ⊟ ⊱ ⌇
**Nearby Facilities**
**Acreage** 20 **Open** March to 1 Nov
Near the beach and the North Yorks Moors National Park. Non members welcome.
**Nearest Town/Resort** Scarborough
**Directions** Located 1 mile north of Scarborough on the west side of the A165.
≠ Scarborough

## SCARBOROUGH

**Cayton Village Caravan Park,** Mill Lane, Cayton Bay, Scarborough, North Yorkshire, YO11 3NN
**Tel:** 01723 583171
**Email:** info@caytontouring.co.uk
www.caytontouring.co.uk

Pitches For ▲ ⊕ ⊟ **Total** 200
Facilities ⓗ ⌇ ⓗ ⓤ ♨ ⌠ ⊙ ⌐ ⊿ ⊡ ☎
⏱ ⓘ ⊟ ♠ ⋔ ✿ ♫ ⊞ ⊟ ⊱ ⌇
**Nearby Facilities** ⌐ ✓ ⏶ ⋏ ∪ ⇃ ♣
**Acreage** 11 **Open** 1 March to 4 Jan
**Access** Good **Site** Level
5 Star sheltered park adjoining Cayton Church, village inns, fish shop and bus service. ½ mile to the beach. 4 acre dog walk. Family bathroom, luxurious shower blocks, central heating and dishwashing. Super Saver and O.A.P. Weeks. Open for Christmas and New Year.
**Directions** On the A165, 3 miles south of Scarborough turn inland at Cayton Bay. The park is on the right hand side in ½ mile. From the A64 take the B1261 signposted Filey. At Cayton take the second left at the Blacksmiths Arms onto Mill Lane, the park is on the left hand side.
≠ Seamer

## SCARBOROUGH

**Crows Nest Caravan Park,** Gristhorpe, Filey, North Yorkshire, YO14 9PS
**Tel:** 01723 582206 **Fax:** 01723 582206
**Email:**
enquiries@crowsnestcaravanpark.com
www.crowsnestcaravanpark.com
Pitches For ▲ ⊕ ⊟
Facilities ⋏ ⌇ ⓗ ⓤ ♨ ⌠ ⊙ ⌐ ⊿ ⊡ ☎
⏱ ⓘ ⊟ ♀ ⓘ ♠ ♫ ⊱ ♫ ⊞

Nearby Facilities ⌐ ✓ ⏶ ⋏ ∪ ⇃ ♣
**Acreage** 12 **Open** March to October
**Access** Good **Site** Lev/Slope
AA 4 Pennants and BTA 4 Star Graded.
**Nearest Town/Resort** Filey/Scarborough
**Directions** Off A165 north of Filey, south of Scarborough.
≠ Scarborough

## SCARBOROUGH

**Flower of May Holiday Park,** Lebberston Cliff, Scarborough, North Yorkshire, YO11 3NU
**Tel:** 01723 584311 **Fax:** 01723 581361
**Email:** info@flowerofmay.com
www.flowerofmay.com
Pitches For ▲ ⊕ ⊟ **Total** 300
Facilities ⓗ ⋆ ⌇ ⓗ ⓤ ♨ ⌠ ⊙ ⌐ ⊿
⊡ ⏱ ⏱ ⊟ ♀ ⊟ ♠ ⓘ ⋔ ✿ ♫⊞ ⊱
**Nearby Facilities** ⌐ ✓ ⏶ ⋏ ∪ ⇃ ♣
**Acreage** 13 **Open** Easter to October
**Access** Good **Site** Level
Winner AA Best Holiday Park Northern England 95. Family run park with superb facilities. Exciting playground, luxury leisure centre with indoor pool and golf. Family bars. Supermarket. Pets are welcome by arrangement.
**Nearest Town/Resort** Scarborough
**Directions** 3 miles south of Scarborough off A165 signposted at roundabout.
≠ Scarborough

---

Information correct as of date of print

# Lebberston Touring Park

### Filey Road, Lebberston, Scarborough YO11 3PE
### Tel: 01723 585723   www.lebberstontouring.co.uk
### E-mail: info@lebberstontouring.co.uk

Overlooking the Yorkshire Wolds, our gently sloping park is the perfect place for a quiet, relaxing break. Catering for the more mature visitor and young families, we offer the ideal base for exploring the Heritage Coast, North Yorkshire Moors and seaside towns of Scarborough, Filey and Whitby, along with the many other attractions that wonderful North Yorkshire has to offer.

**AA**

---

## SCARBOROUGH
**Jacobs Mount Caravan Park,** Stepney Rd, Scarborough, North Yorkshire, YO12 5NL
**Tel:** 01723 361178 **Fax:** 01723 361178
**Email:** jacobsmount@yahoo.co.uk
**www.jacobsmount.co.uk**
**Pitches For** ▲ ⬤ ⬤ **Total** 140
**Facilities** ☆ ♂ 🖪 🅗 🆄 ♨ ⌐ ☉ ╝ 🔲 ♒
🖫 🕻 ⬤ 🔾 ✕ 🗍 🕅 🕂 🔲 🖪 🌿 ♒
**Nearby Facilities** ⌐ ✎ ⚓ ∪ ♫
**Acreage** 14 **Open** 5 March **to** 6 Nov
**Access** Good **Site** Level
Only 2 miles from the beach. All pitches are fully serviced hardstandings. Awards include David Bellamy Gold Award, Yorkshire Caravan Park of the Year 2004 and Excellence in England Silver Award 2005. Winner of Yorkshire in Bloom. Personal supervision. Please send SAE for brochure.
**Nearest Town/Resort** Scarborough
**Directions** 2 miles west of Scarborough on the A170 Thirsk to Pickering road, on the left hand side.
⚏ Scarborough

## SCARBOROUGH
**Jasmine Park,** Cross Lane, Snainton, Scarborough, North Yorkshire, YO13 9BE
**Tel:** 01723 859240 **Fax:** 01723 859240
**Email:** info@jasminepark.co.uk
**www.jasminepark.co.uk**
**Pitches For** ▲ ⬤ ⬤ **Total** 70
**Facilities** ☆ ♂ 🅗 🆄 ♨ ⌐ ☉ ╝ 🔲 ♒
🖫 🕻 ⬤ 🔲 🕂 🔲 🖪 🌿 ♒
**Nearby Facilities** ⌐ ✎ ⚓ ∪
**Acreage** 5 **Open** March **to** December
**Access** Good **Site** Level
Picturesque, quiet park with newly refurbished facilities. Awards include David Bellamy Gold Award, Yorkshire Caravan Park of the Year 2004 and Excellence in England Silver Award 2005. Winner of Yorkshire in Bloom. Personal supervision. Please send SAE for brochure.
**Nearest Town** Scarborough/Pickering
**Directions** Turn off the A170 in Snainton Village opposite junior school, ¾ mile signposted.
⚏ Scarborough

## SCARBOROUGH
**Killerby Old Hall Caravan Park,** Killerby Old Hall, Killerby, Cayton, ScarboroughNorth Yorkshire, YO11 3TW
**Tel:** 01723 583799
**www.killerby.com**
**Pitches For** ⬤ **Total** 20
**Facilities** ♂ 🅗 🆄 ♨ ⌐ ☉ ⬤ 🔲 ♒
🖫 🕻 ⬤ 🔲 🔲 🖪 ♒ ♒
**Nearby Facilities** ⌐ ✎ ⚓ ∪ ♫
**Open** March **to** Oct
**Access** Good **Site** Level
1½ miles from the coast. Ideal for walking, fishing, golf and cricket.
**Nearest Town/Resort** Scarborough
**Directions** From York take the A64 through Staxton Village, at roundabout turn right onto the A1039. Go through Flixton and turn left in Folkton, go over the level crossing to Gayton, turn right at Haw Road, site is 500 metres on the left.
⚏ Scarborough

## SCARBOROUGH
**Lebberston Touring Park,** Filey Road, Lebberston, Scarborough, North Yorkshire, YO11 3PE
**Tel:** 01723 585723
**Email:** info@lebberstontouring.co.uk
**www.lebberstontouring.co.uk**
**Pitches For** ⬤ ⬤ **Total** 125
**Facilities** ☆ ♂ 🅗 🆄 ♨ ⌐ ☉ ╝ 🔲 ♒
🖫 🕻 ⬤ 🔲 🔲 🌿 ♒
**Nearby Facilities** ⌐ ✎ ⚓ ∪ ♫
**Acreage** 7½ **Open** March **to** October
**Access** Good **Site** Lev/Slope
Quiet, country park. Well spaced pitches with extensive views over Vale of Pickering and the Yorkshire Wolds. All pets on a lead. Dog area. Trailer tents accepted. AA 4 Pennants.
**Nearest Town/Resort** Scarborough/Filey

## Directions
**Directions** From A64 or A165 take B1261 to Lebberston and follow signs.
⚏ Scarborough

## SCARBOROUGH
**Scalby Close Park,** Burniston Road, Scarborough, North Yorkshire, YO13 0DA
**Tel:** 01723 365908
**Email:** info@scalbyclosepark.co.uk
**www.scalbyclosepark.co.uk**
**Pitches For** ▲ ⬤ ⬤ **Total** 42
**Facilities** ☆ ♂ 🖪 🅗 🆄 ♨ ⌐ ☉ ╝ 🔲 ♒
⬤ 🗍 🕂 🔲 🖪 🌿 ♒
**Nearby Facilities** ⌐ ✎ ⚓ ∪ ♫
**Acreage** 3 **Open** March **to** October
**Access** Good **Site** Level
Sheltered, tree lined, level pitches. Ideal for touring North Yorkshire Moors and the coast. Near to Scarborough.
**Nearest Town/Resort** Scarborough
**Directions** 2 miles north of Scarborough's North Bay, signed 400 yards.
⚏ Scarborough

## SCARBOROUGH
**St. Helens Caravan & Camping,** Wykeham, Scarborough, North Yorkshire, YO13 9QD
**Tel:** 01723 862771 **Fax:** 01723 862771
**Email:** caravans@ynyerham.co.uk
**www.sthelenscaravanpark.co.uk**
**Pitches For** ▲ ⬤ ⬤ **Total** 250
**Facilities** ☆ ♂ 🅗 🆄 ♨ ⌐ ☉ ╝ 🔲 ♒
🖫 🕻 ⬤ 🔲 ✕ 🗍 🕅 ♒ 🕂 🔲 ∪
**Nearby Facilities** ⌐ ✎ ⚓ ∪
**Acreage** 36 **Open** 15 Feb **to** 15 Jan
**Access** Good **Site** Level
Family park near the North Yorkshire Moors and beaches. Ideal base for touring.
**Nearest Town/Resort** Scarborough
**Directions** 5 miles west of Scarborough on the A170, 12 miles east of Pickering.
⚏ Scarborough

---

# YORKSHIRE (NORTH)

### SELBY

**Oakmere Caravan Park & Coarse Fishery,** Hill Farm, Skipwith, Selby, North Yorkshire, YO8 5SN
**Tel:** 01757 288910 **Fax:** 01757 288910
Pitches For ⚏ ⛟
Facilities ⚹ ♿ ▯ ▯ ⚓ ⌂ ⛱ ◨ ▢ ⛟ ▯ ⚓ ◨ ⚑ ✂ ♒
Nearby Facilities ⌐ ✈ ∪
Open March to Oct
Access Good Site Level
Set in the middle of Skipwith Nature Reserve with 9 acres of landscaped fisherys. Near to historic York. ETB 4 Star Graded Site.
**Nearest Town/Resort** York/Selby
**Directions** From York take the A19 down to Escrick, turn left to Skipwith. After approx. 3 miles, Oakmere is just outside Skipwith Village.
⚐ York/Selby

### SETTLE

**Knight Stainforth Hall,** Stainforth, Settle, North Yorkshire, BD24 0DP
**Tel:** 01729 822200 **Fax:** 01729 823387
**Email:** info@knightstainforth.co.uk
**www.knightstainforth.co.uk**
Pitches For ▲ ⚏ ⛟ Total 100
Facilities ⚹ ♿ ▯ ▯ ⚓ ⌂ ⛱ ◨ ⚑ ◨ ⚐ ◨ ▯ ⚓ ▢ ⛟ ▯ ⚓ ◨ ✂ ♒
Nearby Facilities ⌐ ✈
Acreage 6 Open March to October
Access Good Site Sloping
Riverside site, near to potholes. Ideal walking and touring.
**Nearest Town/Resort** Settle
**Directions** Turn off the A65 Settle/Kendal road into Settle, then turn opposite Settle High School. 2½ miles along Stackhouse Lane.
⚐ Settle

### SKIPTON

**Eshton Road Caravan Site,** Eshton Road, Gargrave, Nr Skipton, North Yorkshire, BD23 3PN
**Tel:** 01756 749229 **Fax:** 01756 748060
Pitches For ▲ ⚏ ⛟ Total 20
Facilities ♿ ▯ ▯ ⚓ ⌂ ⛱ ◨ ▢ ⚑ ◨ ⚐ ◨
Nearby Facilities ⌐ ✈ ✗
Acreage 3 Open All Year
Access Good Site Level
Alongside the Leeds Liverpool Canal. Ideal for touring the Yorkshire Dales.
**Nearest Town/Resort** Skipton
**Directions** From Skipton take the A65, 4 miles.
⚐ Gargrave

### SKIPTON

**Tarn Caravan Park,** Stirton, Skipton, North Yorkshire, BD23 3LQ
**Tel:** 01756 795309
Pitches For ▲ ⚏ ⛟
Facilities ✗ ♿ ▯ ▯ ⚓ ⌂ ⛱ ◨ ▢ ⚑ ✗ ◨ ✂ ♒
Nearby Facilities ⌐
Open March to Nov
Access Good Site Level
Ideal for touring. Near to Skipton.
**Nearest Town/Resort** Skipton
**Directions** Situated 1¼ miles north west of the Skipton By-Pass. On the by-pass north roundabout head south west on a minor road signposted 'local traffic only'. After 200 yards turn right and follow signs.
⚐ Skipton

### SLINGSBY

**Camping & Caravanning Club Site,** Railway Street, Slingsby, North Yorkshire, YO62 4AA
**Tel:** 01653 628335
**www.campingandcaravanningclub.co.uk**
Pitches For ▲ ⚏ ⛟ Total 60
Facilities ♿ ▯ ▯ ⚓ ⌂ ⛱ ◨ ▢ ⚑ ◨ ▯ ⚓ ▢ ⛟ ⚑ ✂
Nearby Facilities ⌐
Acreage 3 Open March to Oct
Access Good Site Level
An ideal base to discover the North Yorkshire Moors. York with all its attractions is just a short drive away. BTB 5 Star Graded and AA 3 Pennants. Non members welcome.
**Directions** From the A64 turn left s.p. Castle Howard, drive through Castle Howard Estate until you reach the Malton to Helmsly road. Go straight into Slingsby Village, go round the bend onto Railway Street and continue through the village ¼ mile to the site entrance.
⚐ Malton

### SLINGSBY

**Robin Hood Caravan & Camping Park,** Green Dyke Lane, Slingsby, North Yorkshire, YO62 4AP
**Tel:** 01653 628391
**Email:** info@robinhoodcaravanpark.co.uk
**www.robinhoodcaravanpark.co.uk**
Pitches For ▲ ⚏ ⛟ Total 48
Facilities ♿ ✗ ⚹ ♿ ▯ ▯ ⚓ ⌂ ⛱ ◨ ⚑ ▢ ⛟ ▯ ⚓ ▯ ⚓ ▢ ⚑ ✂
Nearby Facilities ⌐ ✈ ∪ ♒
Acreage 4 Open March to October
Access Good Site Level
In the heart of picturesque Ryedale, this privately owned park offers peace and tranquillity. An ideal centre for York, the Moors, 'Heartbeat' country and the seaside resorts of Scarborough, Whitby and Filey.
**Nearest Town/Resort** Malton
**Directions** From Malton take B1257 westwards 6 miles to Slingsby. Turn right into caravan park.
⚐ Malton

### SNEATON

**Low Moor Caravan Club Site,** Sneaton, Whitby, North Yorkshire, YO22 5JE
**Tel:** 01947 810505
**www.caravanclub.co.uk**
Pitches For ⚏ ⛟ Total 93
Facilities ♿ ▯ ⛟ ▯ ⚓ ▢ ⚑ ◨ ▯ ◨
Nearby Facilities ✈
Acreage 12 Open March to Nov
Access Good Site Level
Tranquil site in the North Yorks Moors National Park (Heartbeat country). 5 miles from a sandy beach. Ideal for walkers. Boules pitch and mini golf on site. Own sanitation required. Non members welcome. Booking essential.
**Nearest Town/Resort** Whitby
**Directions** From the A171 take the B1416 signposted Ruswarp, after 3¾ miles on a sharp left hand bend continue through red gates signposted Maybeck (care required), site is ½ mile on the right.
⚐ Whitby

### TADCASTER

**Whitecote Caravan Park,** Ryther Road, Ulleskelf, Nr Tadcaster, North Yorkshire, LS24 9DY
**Tel:** 01937 835231
Pitches For ▲ ⚏ ⛟
Facilities ♿ ▯ ⚓ ⌂ ⛱ ◨ ▯ ⚓ ▢ ⚑ ▯ ⚓ ◨
Nearby Facilities ⌐ ✈
Open 1 March to 28 Feb
Access Good Site Level
**Nearest Town/Resort** York
⚐ Ulleskelf

### THIRSK

**Sowerby Caravan Park,** Sowerby, Thirsk, North Yorkshire, YO7 3AG
**Tel:** 01845 522753
Pitches For ⚏ ⛟ Total 25
Facilities ⚹ ✗ ⚹ ♿ ▯ ▯ ⚓ ⌂ ⛱ ◨ ▢ ⛟ ▯ ⚓ ▢ ⚑ ▯ ⚓ ▢ ⚑ ◨
Nearby Facilities ⌐ ✈ ∪
Acreage 1½ Open March to October
Access Good Site Level
Alongside a river. Ideal location for touring.
**Nearest Town/Resort** Thirsk
**Directions** From Thirsk go through Sowerby towards Dalton, the park is ½ mile south of Sowerby on the right.
⚐ Thirsk

### THIRSK

**Thirsk Racecourse Caravan Club Site,** Thirsk, North Yorkshire, YO7 1QL
**Tel:** 01845 525266
**www.caravanclub.co.uk**
Pitches For ▲ ⚏ ⛟ Total 60
Facilities ♿ ▯ ▯ ⚓ ⌂ ⛱ ◨ ▯ ◨ ▢ ⚑ ▯ ⚑ ◨
Nearby Facilities ⌐
Acreage 3 Open March to Oct
Access Good Site Level
Situated in the racecourse, surrounded by the Dales and Moors. Just a 5 minute walk to Thirsk town centre. Close to Rievaulx Abbey. Non members welcome. Booking essential.
**Nearest Town/Resort** Thirsk
**Directions** From north on the A1 turn off onto the B6267 signposted Thirsk. After 2¼ miles at the T-junction turn left onto the A61, site is 4¼ miles on the left, just past racecourse buildings.
⚐ Thirsk

### THIRSK

**York House Holiday Park,** Balk, Nr Bagby, Thirsk, North Yorkshire, YO7 2AQ
**Tel:** 01845 597495 **Fax:** 01423 324641
**Email:** phil.brierley@which.net
**www.yhcparks.info**
Pitches For ▲ ⚏ ⛟ Total 20
Facilities ♿ ▯ ⚓ ⌂ ⛱ ◨ ▢ ⚑ ▯ ⚓ ▢ ⚑ ◨ ⚑
Nearby Facilities ⌐ ✈ ∪
Acreage 20 Open 1 April/Easter to Oct
Access Good Site Level
Ideal for North Yorkshire National Park, York and Harrogate.
**Nearest Town/Resort** Thirsk
**Directions** From Thirsk take the A170 towards Sutton Bank, after approx. 2 miles take right turn signposted Bagby, Balk and Kilburn. Continue into Balk (approx. 1 mile).
⚐ Thirsk

### THORNABY-ON-TEES

**White Water Caravan Club Park,** Tees Barrage, Stockton-on-Tees, North Yorkshire, TS18 2QW
**Tel:** 01642 634880
**www.caravanclub.co.uk**
Pitches For ▲ ⚏ ⛟ Total 115
Facilities ♿ ▯ ▯ ⚓ ⌂ ⛱ ◨ ⚑ ▢ ⚑ ▯ ⚓ ▢ ✗ ▯ ⚓ ▢ ⚑ ◨
Nearby Facilities ⌐ ✈ ∪
Acreage 15 Open All Year
Access Good Site Level
Part of the largest white water canoeing and rafting course in Britain. Teeside Park nearby provides shopping, cinema and bowling alley. Just a short drive to the coast. Non members welcome. Booking essential.
**Nearest Town/Resort** Stockton-on-Tees
**Directions** From A19 take A66 sp Darlington. Follow signs for Teeside Retail Park, continue

**Open 1st March to 4th January**

## Middlewood Farm
### HOLIDAY PARK
**Tel: 01947 880414**

*A walkers, artists & wildlife paradise*

Small, peaceful Family Park with magnificent, panoramic views of sea, moors and 'Heart Beat' Country. 5 minute walk to the village PUB and shops, 10 minute walk to the BEACH.

*Robin Hood's Bay, Whitby, North Yorkshire YO22 4UF*
*www.middlewoodfarm.com*

• SUPERB heated facilities
• FREE HOT SHOWERS
• Private bathrooms
• Electric Hook-ups
• Hardstandings available
• Children's Adventure Play Area
• SUPERIOR LUXURY CARAVANS for HIRE

**AA**

*We're waiting to make you Welcome!*

---

in nearside lane and after 200yds take first exit sp Teeside Retail Park. At lights turn right over A66, cross railway bridge, go straight over mini roundabout and cross Tees Barrage Bridge, site is on the right past Talpore Pub.
⚆ Stockton-on-Tees

### WHITBY
**Abbot's House Farm Camping & Caravan Site,** Abbot's House Farm, Goathland, Whitby, North Yorkshire, YO22 5NH
**Tel:** 01947 896270/896026
**Email:** goathland@enterprise.net
www.abbotshouse.org.uk
**Pitches For** ⚊ ⚆ ⚎ **Total** 30
**Facilities** 🚿 ⚒ ⚑ ⚐ ⚑ ⚑ ⚑ ⚑ ⚑ ⚑
**Nearby Facilities** ⚑ ✔ ⚓ ⚓
**Acreage** 2½ **Open** Easter to October
**Access** Good **Site** Level
The North Yorkshire Moors Steam Railway runs through the farm. Yorkshire Televisions 'Heartbeat' country. 9 miles from Whitby, 25 miles from Scarborough and 40 miles from York.
**Nearest Town/Resort** Whitby
**Directions** From Whitby take the A171 west for approx. 3 miles, turn south onto the A169, after approx. 6 miles turn right signposted Goathland. Turn left opposite Goathland Garage.
⚆ Goathland

### WHITBY
**Brow House Farm Campsite,** Brow House Farm, Goathland, Whitby, North Yorkshire, YO22 5NP
**Tel:** 01947 896274
**Pitches For** ⚊ ⚆ ⚎ **Total** 30
**Facilities** ⚓ ⚑ ⚑ ⚐ ⚑ ⚑ ⚑ ⚑ ⚑
**Nearby Facilities** ⚑ ✔ ⚓ ⚓ ⚑
**Acreage** 4½ **Open** March to October
**Access** Good **Site** Level
North Yorkshire Moors and steam railway. Good walking area. Café nearby.
**Nearest Town/Resort** Whitby
**Directions** Leave Whitby on the A171, then take the A169 towards Pickering. Turn left at Goathland turn off and follow the road past the shops and the church to the top of the hill.
⚆ Grosmont

### WHITBY
**Burnt House Holiday Park,** Ugthorpe, Nr Whitby, North yorkshire, YO21 2BG
**Tel:** 01947 840448
**Pitches For** ⚊ ⚆ ⚎ **Total** 70
**Facilities** ⚑ ⚑ ⚑ ⚑ ⚑ ⚑ ⚐ ⚑ ⚑ ⚑
⚑ ⚑ ⚑ ⚑ ⚑ ⚑
**Nearby Facilities** ⚑ ✔ ⚓ ⚓

**Acreage** 7 **Open** March to October
**Access** Good **Site** Level
Ideal base for touring coast or countryside, 4 miles to beach. Fully serviced static caravans for sale. Holiday cottage to let.
**Nearest Town/Resort** Whitby
**Directions** 8½ miles north of Whitby on A171, towards Guisborough, signposted Ugthorpe Village.
⚆ Whitby

### WHITBY
**Grouse Hill Touring Caravan & Camping Park,** Fylingdales, Whitby, North Yorkshire, YO22 4QH
**Tel:** 01947 880543
www.grouse-hill.co.uk
**Pitches For** ⚊ ⚆ ⚎ **Total** 198
**Facilities** ⚓ ⚑ ⚑ ⚑ ⚑ ⚐ ⚑ ⚑
⚑ ⚑ ⚑ ⚑ ⚑
**Nearby Facilities** ⚑ ✔ ⚓ ⚓
**Open** Easter to 1st Tues Oct
**Access** Good **Site** Lev/Slope
Expansive views of woodland and moorland. Ideal for families. 40 extra level pitches with electric and water points. Close to moorland walks. AA 3 Pennants.
**Nearest Town** Scarborough/Whitby
**Directions** 12 miles from Scarborough and 8 miles from Whitby. Signed off the A171 just north of the Flask Inn.

### WHITBY
**Hollins Farm,** Glaisdale, Whitby, North Yorkshire, YO21 2PZ
**Tel:** 01947 897516
**Pitches For** ⚊ **Total** 25
**Facilities** ⚑ ⚑ ⚑ ⚑ ⚐ ⚑ ⚑ ⚑ ⚑ ⚑
**Nearby Facilities** ✔ ⚓ ⚑
**Acreage** ½ **Open** All Year
**Site** Lev/Slope
Set in the heart of Glaisdale Valley. Lovely walks and a pub. 8 miles from the beach. Steam railway. Bed & Breakfast also available.
**Nearest Town/Resort** Whitby
**Directions** From the A171 turn to Egton, then take the road to Glaisdale. In Glaisdale turn opposite the phone box, continue up around the church for 1½ miles, look for camping sign.
⚆ Glaisdale

### WHITBY
**Ladycross Plantation,** Egton, Whitby, North Yorkshire, YO21 1UA
**Tel:** 01947 895502
**Email:** enquiries@ladycrossplantation.co.uk
www.ladycrossplantation.co.uk
**Pitches For** ⚊ ⚆ ⚎ **Total** 120
**Facilities** ⚑ ⚑ ⚑ ⚑ ⚑ ⚐ ⚑ ⚑ ⚑ ⚑ ⚑
⚑ ⚑ ⚑ ⚑ ⚑ ⚑ ⚑
**Nearby Facilities** ✔ ⚑

**Acreage** 12 **Open** March to October
**Access** Good **Site** Level
Ideal for exploring national park and the north east coast. David Bellamy Gold Award for Conservation.
**Nearest Town/Resort** Whitby
**Directions** Take the A171 Whitby to Teeside road, 5 miles from Whitby turn left signposted Egton, Grosmont, North Yorks Moors Railway and Ladycross.
⚆ Egton Bridge

### WHITBY
**Middlewood Farm Holiday Park,** Middlewood Lane, Fylingthorpe, Robin Hood's Bay, WhitbyNorth Yorkshire, YO22 4UF
**Tel:** 01947 880414 **Fax:** 01947 880871
**Email:** info@middlewoodfarm.com
www.middlewoodfarm.com
**Pitches For** ⚊ ⚆ ⚎ **Total** 120
**Facilities** ⚓ ⚑ ⚑ ⚑ ⚑ ⚐ ⚑ ⚑ ⚑ ⚑
⚑ ⚑ ⚑ ⚑ ⚑ ⚑ ⚑ ⚑
**Nearby Facilities** ⚑ ✔ ⚓ ⚓ ⚑
**Acreage** 7 **Open** 1 March to 4 Jan
**Access** Good **Site** Level
Peaceful family park, 10 minutes walk to the beach, pubs, shops and Robin Hood's Bay. Only 5 miles from Whitby. Magnificent views and walks.
**Nearest Town/Resort** Whitby
**Directions** Signposted. Take the A171 Scarborough to Whitby road, 3 miles south of Whitby take the Fylingthorpe and Robin Hood's Bay road. At Fylingthorpe Post Office turn onto Middlewood Lane, park is 500 yards on the left.
⚆ Whitby

### WHITBY
**Northcliffe Holiday Park,** High Hawsker, Whitby, North Yorkshire, YO22 4LL
**Tel:** 01947 880477 **Fax:** 01947 880972
**Email:** enquiries@northcliffe-seaview.com
www.northcliffe-seaview.com
**Pitches For** ⚊ ⚆ ⚎ **Total** 82
**Facilities** ⚓ ⚑ ⚑ ⚑ ⚑ ⚑ ⚐ ⚑ ⚑ ⚑ ⚑
⚑ ⚑ ⚑ ⚑ ⚑ ⚑ ⚑ ⚑
**Nearby Facilities** ⚑ ✔ ⚓ ⚓ ⚑
**Open** Mid March to End Oct
**Access** Good
Exclusive Seasonal Touring Park. Luxury Award Winning park with panoramic sea views. All weather, all mains, individual plots. We're a Double Winner - YTB and ETC. Caravan Holiday Park of the Year 1999. Woodland Shop/cafe/take-away. New childrens play park.
**Nearest Town/Resort** Whitby
**Directions** South from Whitby 3 miles, turn left B1447 to Robin Hood's Bay.
⚆ Whitby

---

## Cawood Park

**www.cawoodpark.com**

Ryther Road, Cawood,
The Vale of York,
North Yorks YO8 3TT
enquiries@cawoodpark.com

Idyllic and tranquil touring park in a quiet
setting yet convenient for York Centre.
• Licensed Bar with first class Cabaret every Saturday night.
• Lake Views. • Fishing Lake. • Lakeside holiday cottages.
• Holiday caravans for sale.

**OPEN ALL YEAR**    **01757 268450**

---

### WHITBY
**Rigg Farm Caravan Park,** Stainsacre,
Whitby, North Yorkshire', YO22 4LP
**Tel:** 01947 880430 **Fax:** 01947 880430
**Pitches For** ▲ ⊞ 🚐 **Total** 35
**Facilities** ⸼ 🛉 ⅏ ⅏ ♿ 📶 ⅃ ⬛ 💻 ☎
⬛ 🅿 ♣ 🅰 ┽⊞ 🔲
**Nearby Facilities** 🟊 🟋 ⅏ ∪
**Acreage** 2/3 **Open** 1 March **to** 31 Oct
**Access** Good **Site** Level
Small select caravan park situated in a
National Park, yet close to unspoilt,
picturesque Whitby Harbour. Ideal for
woodland walking. Steam Railway and
"Heartbeat" Country within a few miles.
Pets are welcome by arrangement.
**Nearest Town/Resort** Whitby
**Directions** Approx. 4 miles from Whitby
town. Signposted on the A171 at the junction
with Low Hawsker. Also signposted on the
B1416 at the junction with Sneatonthorpe.
⇌ Whitby

### WHITBY
**Sandfield House Farm Caravan Park,**
Sandsend Road, Whitby, North Yorkshire,
YO21 3SR
**Tel:** 01947 602660
**Email:** info@sandfieldhousefarm.co.uk
www.sandfieldhousefarm.co.uk
**Pitches For** ⊞ 🚐 **Total** 50
**Facilities** ⸼ ⅏ 🛉 🛉 ♿ 📶 ⅃ ⬛ 💻 ☎
⅏ 🅿 ⬛ ❀┽⊞ ⅏
**Nearby Facilities** 🟊 ⅃ ⅏ 🟋 ∪ ⅏
**Acreage** 12 **Open** March **to** October
**Access** Good **Site** Level
Set in undulating countryside with sea
views, ¼ mile from a 2 mile long sandy
beach.
**Nearest Town/Resort** Whitby
**Directions** 1 mile north of Whitby on the
A174 coast road.
⇌ Whitby

### WHITBY
**Serenity Touring Caravan & Camping
Park,** High Street, Hinderwell, Whitby,
North Yorkshire, TS13 5JH
**Tel:** 01947 841122
**Email:** patandni@aol.com
**Pitches For** ▲ ⊞ 🚐 **Total** 20
**Facilities** ⸼ 🆄 ♿ 📶 ⊙ ┽ ⅏ 🟋 ⅃ ┽⊞ ⅏
**Nearby Facilities** 🟊 ⅃ ⅏ 🟋 ∪ ⅏
**Acreage** 3 **Open** March **to** October
**Access** Good **Site** Level
A very quiet, sheltered and secure,
predominately adult site with lovely country
views. ½ mile from the sea. Spectacular
coastal, country and moorland walks.
Village shops and pubs all nearby. Touring
caravan available for hire.
**Nearest Town/Resort** Whitby
**Directions** Take B1266 off A171 Whitby to
Guisborough Moor road. To T-Junction turn
left onto A174. 1 mile Hinderwell. Site
entrance in village on left signed 'Serenity'.
⇌ Whitby

### WHITBY
**York House Caravan Park,** Hawsker,
Whitby, North Yorkshire, YO22 4LW
**Tel:** 01947 880354

---

**Pitches For** ▲ ⊞ 🚐 **Total** 59
**Facilities** ♿ ⸼ 🛉 🆄 ♿ ⅃ ⊙ ┽ ⅃ 🔲 ☎
🟊 🆄 ⊙ ⬛ ❀┽🔲 ⅏
**Nearby Facilities** 🟊 ⅃ ⅏ 🟋 ∪ ⅏ 🟋
**Acreage** 4¼ **Open** March **to** October
**Access** Good **Site** Lev/Slope
Scenic views of the sea, Whitby and North
Yorkshire Moors.
**Nearest Town/Resort** Whitby
**Directions** 3 miles south of Whitby on the
A171, signposted.
⇌ Whitby

### YORK (Near)
**Alders Caravan Park,** Home Farm, Alne,
York, North Yorkshire, YO61 1RY
**Tel:** 01347 838722 **Fax:** 01347 838722
**Email:** enquiries@homefarmalne.co.uk
www.alderscaravanpark.co.uk
**Pitches For** ⊞ 🚐 **Total** 40
**Facilities** ♿ ⸼ 🛉 🆄 ♿ ⅃ ⊙ ┽
⬛ 🅿 ┽⊞ ⅏ ⅏
**Nearby Facilities** 🟊 ⅃ ∪
**Acreage** 6 **Open** March **to** October
**Access** Good **Site** Level
On a working farm, in historic parkland
where visitors may enjoy peace and
tranquility. York (on bus route), Moors,
Dales and coast nearby.
**Nearest Town/Resort** York
**Directions** 9 miles north of York on the A19,
turn left. Or south of Easingwold on the A19,
turn right. Alders is 2¼ miles in the centre of
the village in Monk Green.
⇌ York

### YORK (Near)
**Cawood Park,** Caravan & Camping
Centre, Ryther Road, Cawood, Vale of
YorkNorth Yorkshire, YO8 3TT
**Tel:** 01757 268450
**Email:** cawood@aol.com
www.cawoodpark.com
**Pitches For** ▲ ⊞ 🚐 **Total** 60
**Facilities** ♿ ⸼ 🛉 🆄 ♿ ⅃ ⊙ ┽ ⅃ 🔲 ☎
🟊 🟋 ⊙ ⬛ ♀ 📶 ♣┽🔲 🔲 ⅏ ⅏
**Nearby Facilities** 🟊 ⅃ ⅏ 🟋 ⅏
**Acreage** 8 **Open** All Year
**Access** Good **Site** Level
Here at Cawood Holiday Park, we have
worked hard to create an environment
which keeps its natural simplicity to provide
a trouble free holiday. Some pitches have
views over our fishing lake. A quiet rural
park.
**Nearest Town/Resort** Selby/York
**Directions** From York or the A1 take the
B1222 to Cawood traffic lights, turn onto the
B1223 signed Tadcaster for 1 mile, park is
on the left.
⇌ Selby

### YORK (Near)
**Home Farm Camping & Caravan Park,**
Moreby, Stillingfleet, York, North Yorkshire,
YO19 6HN
**Tel:** 01904 728263 **Fax:** 01904 720059
**Email:**
homefarm_camping@btopenworld.com
**Pitches For** ▲ ⊞ 🚐 **Total** 25
**Facilities** ⸼ 🆄 ♿ ⅃ ⊙ ┽ ⬛ 🅿 ⬛ ❀┽🔲 🔲
**Nearby Facilities** ⅃ ∪

---

**Acreage** 3 **Open** February **to** December
**Access** Good **Site** Level
Alongside the River Ouse. Ideal base to
tour York and surrounding Dales and North
Yorkshire Moors. 4 miles to the nearest
shop or supermarket.
**Nearest Town/Resort** York
**Directions** On the B1222 between the village
of Naburn and Stillingfleet. 6 miles south of
York City walls.
⇌ York

### YORK (Near)
**Sheriff Hutton Camping & Caravanning
Club Site,** Bracken Hill, Sheriff Hutton,
North Yorkshire, YO60 6QG
**Tel:** 01347 878660
www.campingandcaravanningclub.co.uk
**Pitches For** ▲ ⊞ 🚐 **Total** 90
**Facilities** ⸼ 🛉 🆄 ♿ ⅃ ⊙ ┽ ⅃ ⬛ 💻 ☎
🟋 ⊙ ⬛ 🅰 ┽🔲 🔲 ⅏ ⅏
**Nearby Facilities** ⅃
**Acreage** 10 **Open** March **to** Oct
**Access** Good **Site** Level
Close to the city of York. BTB 4 Star
Graded, AA 3 Pennants and Loo of the
Year Award. Non members welcome.
**Nearest Town/Resort** York
**Directions** From York follow signposts for
Earswick Strensall, keep left at the filling
station and Ship Inn, site is second on the right.
⇌ York

### YORK (Near)
**The Ponderosa Caravan Park,** East Moor,
Sutton-on-the-Forest, Nr York, North
Yorkshire, YO61 1ET
**Tel:** 01347 810744 **Fax:** 01347 810744
**Pitches For** ▲ ⊞ 🚐 **Total** 40
**Facilities** ⸼ 🛉 🆄 ♿ ⅃ ⊙ ┽ ⬛ 💻 ☎
⬛ 🅿 ♣ ✕ ⅃ 🅰┽⅏
**Nearby Facilities** ⅃
**Acreage** 3 **Open** All Year
**Access** Good **Site** Level
Near to the historic city of York, North
Yorkshire Moors and many local
attractions.
**Nearest Town/Resort** York
**Directions** Signposted 800 yards off the
B1363 Wigginton to Helmsley road, 6 miles
from York.
⇌ York

### YORK (Near)
**Willow House Caravan Park,** Wigginton
Road, Wigginton, York, North Yorkshire,
YO32 2RH
**Tel:** 01904 750060 **Fax:** 01904 767030
www.willowhouseyork.co.uk
**Pitches For** ▲ ⊞🔲 **Total** 32
**Facilities** ♿ ⸼ 🆄 ♿ ⅃ ⊙ ┽⅃ 🔲 🅰 ⊙ ┽🔲 ⅏
**Nearby Facilities** ⅃ ⅏
**Acreage** 4 **Open** April **to** Oct
**Access** Good **Site** Level
ADULTS ONLY SITE. 3 miles from the
centre of York and 40 minutes from the
coast.
**Nearest Town/Resort** York
**Directions** From York take the A1237 bypass
to the B1363 Wigginton Road, site is ½ a
mile on the right.
⇌ York

---

# YORK (County of)

## YORK

**Acomb Grange,** Grange Lane, York, YO23 3QZ
**Tel:** 01904 797387
**Email:** pbrown@acomb-grange.freeserve.co.uk
www.go.to/york
**Pitches For** Å ⊕ ⊜ **Total** 5
**Facilities** ∫ ⅏ ♨ ⌓ ⌂ ⊖ ♨ ₤
**Nearby Facilities** ┌ ⌿ ♫
**Acreage** 2 **Open** All Year
**Access** Fair **Site** Level
Near the City of York, North Yorkshire Moors and Dales. Self Catering accommodation also available.
**Nearest Town/Resort** York
**Directions** Take the A59 to Harrogate and follow signs to Acomb. Turn into Askham Lane then turn into Grange Lane.
⇌ York

## YORK

**Beechwood Grange Caravan Club Site,** Malton Road, York, YO3 9TH
**Tel:** 01904 424637
www.caravanclub.co.uk
**Pitches For** ⊕ ⊜ **Total** 111
**Facilities** ⅙ ∫ ⌷ ⅏ ♨ ⌓ ◖ ♨
**Nearby Facilities** ┌ ⌿
**Acreage** 11 **Open** March **to** Nov
**Access** Good **Site** Level
Set in open countryside, yet only 3 miles from York. Boules pitch on site. Plenty to do and see in York from river cruises to the Jorvik Viking Centre and the National Railway Museum. Non members welcome. Booking essential.
**Nearest Town/Resort** York
**Directions** Turn off the A64 onto the A1237 signposted Thirsk. At roundabout turn right into road signposted local traffic only, site is at the end of the drive.
⇌ York

## YORK

**Chestnut Farm Holiday Park,** Acaster Malbis, York, YO23 2UQ
**Tel:** 01904 704676 **Fax:** 01904 704676
enquiries@chestnutfarmholidaypark.co.uk
www.chestnutfarmholidaypark.co.uk
**Pitches For** Å ⊕ ⊜ **Total** 81
**Facilities** ⅙ ∫ ⌷ ⅏ ♨ ⌓ ⊖ ♨ ◖ ☐ ♨
♨ ₤ ⊖ ♨⌂☐ ◖ ✻
**Nearby Facilities** ┌ ⌿ ∪
**Acreage** 5 **Open** March **to** End Nov
**Access** Good **Site** Level
Peaceful family run park in a pretty village by the River Ouse. Only 3 miles from the centre of York. Ideal for touring the Dales, Moors and coast.
**Nearest Town/Resort** York

## YORK

**Directions** Travelling east on the A64 towards York, turn left signposted Copmanthorpe and Acaster Malbis. Follow signs to Acaster Malbis for 2 miles.
⇌ York

## YORK

**Moorside Caravan Park,** Lords Moor Lane, Strensall, York, YO32 5XJ
**Tel:** 01904 491865/491208
www.moorsidecaravanpark.co.uk
**Pitches For** Å ⊕ ⊜ **Total** 50
**Facilities** ⅙ ∫ ⌷ ⅏ ♨ ⌓ ⊖ ♨ ⌂ ☐ ♨
₤ ⊖ ♨⌂☐ ◖ ⌀
**Nearby Facilities** ┌ ⌿
**Open** March **to** October
**Access** Good **Site** Level
NO CHILDREN. Fishing lake on site. Near York Golf Course.
**Nearest Town/Resort** York
**Directions** Take the A1237, then take the Strensall turn and head towards Flaxton.
⇌ York

## YORK

**Naburn Lock Caravan Park,** Naburn, York, YO19 4RU
**Tel:** 01904 728697
**Email:** petercatherine@naburnlock.co.uk
www.naburnlock.co.uk
**Pitches For** ⊕ ⊜ **Total** 100
**Facilities** ⅙ ⌿ ∫ ⅏ ♨ ⌓ ⊖ ♨ ⌂ ☐ ♨
♨ ₤ ⊖ ♨☐ ◖
**Nearby Facilities** ┌ ⌿ ⅃ ✻ ∪ ≈ ♫
**Open** 1 March **to** 6 Nov
**Access** Good **Site** Level
Close to the historic City of York. One hours drive from the Yorkshire Dales and seaside resorts.
**Nearest Town/Resort** York
**Directions** 4 miles south of York. Take the A19 towards Selby then the B1222 to Naburn. Landmarks are McArthur Glen Designer Outlet.
⇌ York

## YORK

**Rawcliffe Caravan Co. Ltd.,** Manor Lane, Shipton Road, York, YO30 5TZ
**Tel:** 01904 640845
www.lysanderarms.co.uk
**Pitches For** Å ⊕ ⊜ **Total** 13
**Facilities** ⅙ ∫ ⌷ ⅏ ♨ ⌓ ⊖ ♨ ⌂ ☐ ♨
◖ ✕ ∪ ⅏☐ Å ♨⌂ ☐ Å
**Nearby Facilities** ┌ ⌿ ✻ ∪ ♫
**Open** All Year
**Access** Good **Site** Level
ADULTS ONLY. Just a 2 minute drive from the Park & Ride into York. Grass and hardstanding pitches, all fully serviced with satellite TV.
**Nearest Town/Resort** York
**Directions** 3 miles north of York on the A19.

2 minutes off the A1237 York ring road and the A19 Thirsk road.
⇌ York

## YORK

**Riverside Caravan & Camping Site,** York Marine Services, Ferry Lane, Bishopthorpe, York, YO23 2SB
**Tel:** 01904 704442
**Pitches For** Å ⊕ ⊜ **Total** 25
**Facilities** ∫ ⅏ ♨ ⌓ ⊖ ♨ ☐ ♨
₤ ⊖ ☐ ⌂ ⅏ ✻ ⌀
**Nearby Facilities** ┌ ⌿ ✻ ⅃
**Acreage** 1 **Open** Easter **to** Oct
**Access** Good **Site** Level
Riverside site, 2 miles from York.
**Nearest Town/Resort** York
**Directions** Take the A64 to Bishopthorpe, from Main Street turn into Acaster Lane then Ferry Lane.
⇌ York

## YORK

**Rowntree Park Caravan Club Site,** Terry Avenue, York, YO23 1JQ
**Tel:** 01904 658997
www.caravanclub.co.uk
**Pitches For** Å ⊕ ⊜ **Total** 102
**Facilities** ⅙ ∫ ⌷ ⅏ ♨ ⌓ ◖ ♨
⊖ ♨⌂☐ ◖
**Nearby Facilities** ┌ ⌿ ⅃ ✻
**Acreage** 4 **Open** All Year
**Access** Good **Site** Level
On the banks of the River Ouse. Within walking distance of York. Close to York Minster, Jorvik Viking Centre, Castle Howard, York Castle Museum and The Shambles. Non members welcome. Booking essential.
**Nearest Town/Resort** York
**Directions** From A64 south of York take A19 sp York Centre, DO NOT turn onto A1237. After 2 miles join the one-way system sp City Centre, at Mecca Bingo keep left and continue over bridge. Turn left immediately before Swan Pub, after 250 yards turn right into Terry Avenue, site is on the right.
⇌ York

## YORK

**Swallow Hall Caravan Park,** Crockey Hill, York, North Yorkshire, YO19 4SG
**Tel:** 01904 448219
**Pitches For** ⊕ ⊜ **Total** 35
**Facilities** ∫ ⅏ ♨ ⌓ ⊖ ✕ ⅄ ⎚ ⌀
**Open** Easter **to** Early Oct
**Access** Good **Site** Level
Golf on site.
**Nearest Town/Resort** York
**Directions** From York take the A19 south off the A64. After 2 miles turn left signposted Wheldrake and Thorganby, after 2 miles turn left signposted Swallow Hall.
⇌ York

# YORKSHIRE (SOUTH)

## BARNSLEY

**Greensprings Touring Park,** Rockley
Lane, Worsbrough, Barnsley, South
Yorkshire, S75 3DS
**Tel:** 01226 288298 **Fax:** 01226 288298
**Pitches For ▲ ⊕ ⊕ Total** 60
**Facilities** ∮ ⌂ ⊞ ♨ ⌐ ⊙ ⊒ ☎
⌷ ⊘ ⅋ ⊡ ⋇
**Nearby Facilities** ⌐ ✔ ∪ ⋎
**Acreage** 4 **Open** April **to** October
**Access** Good **Site** Lev/Slope
Country site, well wooded, pleasant walks.
Convenient from M1. Ideal location for
Sheffield venues. TV Hook-up.
**Nearest Town/Resort** Barnsley
**Directions** Junction 36 on M1. A61 to
Barnsley, take left turn after ¼ mile signed
to Pilley. Site is 1 mile along this road.
⇌ Barnsley

## DONCASTER

**Waterfront Country Park,** The Marina,
West Stockwith, Doncaster, South
Yorkshire, DN10 4ET
**Tel:** 01427 890000 **Fax:** 01427 890000
**Email:** waterfrontpark@aol.com
www.waterfrontpark.co.uk
**Pitches For ⊕ ⊕ Total** 110
**Facilities** ∮ ⌂ ⊞ ⌷ ⊘ ⊦⊡ ⊡ ⋇
**Nearby Facilities** ⌐ ✔ ∪
**Acreage** 5½ **Open** All Year
**Access** Good **Site** Level
Adjacent to the Chesterfield Canal and the
River Trent. Ideal for walking, fishing,
cycling and local pubs.
**Nearest Town/Resort** Doncaster
**Directions** From the A161 Gainsborough to
Goole road, approx. 4 miles north of
Gainsborough in Misterton take turning to
West Stockwith, site is 1 mile (behind the
Waterfront Inn).
⇌ Gainsborough

## ROTHERHAM

**Thrybergh Country Park,** Doncaster
Road, Thrybergh, Rotherham, South
Yorkshire, S65 4NU
**Tel:** 01709 850353 **Fax:** 01709 851532
**Email:**
thrybergh.countrypark@rotherham.gov.uk
www.rotherham.gov.uk
**Pitches For ▲ ⊕ ⊕ Total** 25
**Facilities** ⊘ ∮ ⌂ ⊞ ⌐ ⊙ ⊒ ☎ ✕ ⌳ ⊦⊡
**Nearby Facilities** ⌐ ✔ ⚓ ∪ ♪ ♫
**Acreage** 1 **Open** All Year
**Access** Good **Site** Level
The caravan site forms an integral part of
the country park along with the reservoir
providing fly fishing for trout. A circular
walk of 1¾ miles. 24 Hour access to toilets
and showers.
**Nearest Town/Resort** Rotherham
**Directions** Thrybergh Country Park is
conveniently situated 5 miles from the A1(M)
and M1 and 3 miles from the M18 on the
main Rotherham to Doncaster road the A630.
The entrance is well signposted from both
directions. Grid Ref 111:475 960
⇌ Rotherham

## SHEFFIELD

**Fox Hagg Farm,** Lodge Lane, Rivelin,
Sheffield, South Yorkshire, S6 5SN
**Tel:** 0114 230 5589
**Pitches For ▲ ⊕ ⊕ Total** 60
**Facilities** ∮ ⌂ ⊞ ♨ ⌐ ⊙ ⊒ ☎ ⌷⊦⊡
**Nearby Facilities** ⌐ ✔ ⚓ ∪ ⋎
**Acreage** 2 **Open** April **to** October
**Access** Good **Site** Level
On the outskirts of the Peak District, scenic
views and nature walks. Ideal touring. Post

Office and Wash room.
**Nearest Town/Resort** Sheffield
**Directions** Off the A57
⇌ Sheffield

## THORNE

**Elder House Touring Park,** Elder House,
Sandtoft Road, Thorne, DoncasterSouth
Yorkshire, DN8 5TD
**Tel:** 01405 813173
**Pitches For ⊕ ⊕ Total** 10
**Facilities** ⌖ ∮ ⌂ ⊞ ♨ ⌐ ⊙⊒ ☎⊦⊡
**Nearby Facilities** ⌐ ✔
**Acreage** 2 **Open** All Year
**Access** Good **Site** Level
Peaceful, landscaped, rural and natural
site. Near to Doncaster Racecourse,
Transport Museum and Epworth Home of
The Wesleys. Disabled toilet and shower.
ETB 4 Star Graded Site.
**Nearest Town/Resort** Thorne
**Directions** Leave the M180 at junction 1 and
take the A18 towards Scunthorpe. 2 miles
after the roundabout, at the Black Bull Inn,
turn right. After ½ mile turn left into farm drive
and follow through to the park.
⇌ Thorne South

# YORKSHIRE (WEST)

## ELLAND

**Elland Hall Farm Caravan Site,** Exley
Lane, Elland, West Yorkshire, HX5 0SL
**Tel:** 01422 372325
**Pitches For ⊕ ⊕ Total** 10
**Facilities** ∮ ⊞ ♨ ⌐ ⊙ ⊘ ⊡
**Nearby Facilities**
**Acreage** 1 **Open** April **to** Oct
**Access** Good **Site** Level
**Nearest Town/Resort** Elland
**Directions** From Elland take the Brighouse
road, at the railway bridge turn left into Exley
Lane.
⇌ Halifax

## HEBDEN BRIDGE

**Lower Clough Foot Caravan Club Site,**
Cragg Vale, Hebden Bridge, West
Yorkshire, HX7 5RU
**Tel:** 01422 882531
www.caravanclub.co.uk
**Pitches For ⊕ ⊕ Total** 45
**Facilities** ∮ ⌂ ⊞ ♨ ⌐ ⊙ ⊒⊦⊡
**Nearby Facilities** ⌐ ✔ ⚓ ⋎
**Acreage** 2½ **Open** March **to** Nov
**Access** Good **Site** Level
Screened site bordered by a stream. Three
walks adjacent to the site. Visit Brontes
Haworth Parsonage, walk the Moors and
Pennine Way. Horse drawn canal boat
rides available at Hebden Bridge (2½
miles). Own sanitation required. Non
members welcome. Booking essential.
**Nearest Town/Resort** Hebden Bridge
**Directions** Leave the A646 in Mythomroyd
Village and take the B6138 signposted
Rochdale (care required, narrow bridge). Site
is 1 mile on the right.
⇌ Hebden Bridge

## HEBDEN BRIDGE

**Pennine Camp & Caravan Site,** High
Greenwood House, Heptonstall, Hebden
Bridge, West Yorkshire, HX7 7AZ
**Tel:** 01422 842287
**Pitches For ▲ ⊕ ⊕ Total** 50
**Facilities** ⊞ ♨ ⊙ ⊘ ⊡
**Nearby Facilities** ✔ ∪ ⋎
**Open** April **to** October
**Site** Lev/Slope
Booking for dates is advisable.

**Nearest Town/Resort** Hebden Bridge
**Directions** From Hebden Bridge take
Heptonstall road then follow tent and caravan
signs.
⇌ Hebden Bridge

## HOLMFIRTH

**Holme Valley Camping & Caravan Park,**
Thongsbridge, Holmfirth, West Yorkshire,
HD9 7TD
**Tel:** 01484 665819 **Fax:** 01484 663870
**Email:** enquiries@holmevalleycamping.com
www.holmevalleycamping.com
**Pitches For ▲ ⊕ ⊕ Total** 62
**Facilities** ⊘ ∮ ⌂ ⊞ ♨ ⌐ ⊙ ⊒ ☎ ⌷ ⚹
⊠ ⌷ ⊘ ⊕⌳⊦⊡ ⊡ ⋇
**Nearby Facilities** ⌐ ✔ ⚓
**Acreage** 4½ **Open** All Year
**Access** Good **Site** Lev/Slope
In the heart of 'Last of the Summer Wine'
country. River and picturesque former mill
dam.
**Nearest Town/Resort** Holmfirth
**Directions** Off the A6024, 6 miles south of
Huddersfield and 1 mile north of Holmfirth.
Follow private road down into valley bottom.
(Note bottle banks at double entrance to
lane).
⇌ Brockholes

## KEIGHLEY

**Upwood Holiday Park,** Blackmoor Road,
Haworth, West Yorkshire, BD22 9SS
**Tel:** 01535 644242
**Email:**
caravans@upwoodholidaypark.fsnet.co.uk
www.upwoodholidaypark.fsnet.co.uk
**Pitches For ▲ ⊕ ⊕ Total** 150
**Facilities** ⊘ ∮ ⌂ ⊞ ♨ ⌐ ⊙ ⊒ ⊒ ⊡ ⋇
⊠ ⌷ ⊘ ✕ ♥ ⌳ ⊦⊡ ⋇
**Nearby Facilities** ⌐ ✔ ⚓ ⋎ ∪ ♪
**Acreage** 16 **Open** March **to** 5 Jan
**Access** Good **Site** Lev/Slope
Pleasantly situated close to the Yorkshire
Dales National Park. Beautiful, panoramic
views over the surrounding countryside.
One mile from the Bronte Village of
Haworth and Worth Steam Railway. ETB 4
Star Graded and David Bellamy Gold
Award for Conservation.
**Nearest Town/Resort** Keighley
**Directions** Situated off the A629 Keighley
to Halifax road. It is recommended that
caravans enter via Flappit Pub. On the B6144
Blackmoor Road is the first left after approx.
¾ miles. Upwood is approx. 1 mile on the
left.
⇌ Oxenhope

## LEEDS

**Glenfield Caravan Park,** Blackmoor Lane,
Bardsey, Leeds, West Yorkshire, LS17 9DZ
**Tel:** 01937 574657
**Email:** glenfieldcp@aol.com
www.ukparks.com
**Pitches For ⊕ ⊕ Total** 30
**Facilities** ⊘ ∮ ⌂ ⊞ ♨ ⌐ ⊙ ⊒ ⊡ ⊡
⌷ ⊘ ⊜⊦⊡ ⋇ ⌷
**Nearby Facilities** ⌐ ✔ ∪ ♪
**Acreage** 4 **Open** All Year
**Access** Good **Site** Level
Beautifully kept park. Lovely walks and
places to eat nearby. Easy access and
ideal touring base. New 5 Star heated
shower block with toilets and laundry.
**Nearest Town/Resort** Leeds
**Directions** From Leeds take the A58 towards
Wetherby, after approx 8 miles turn left at
Shadwell Harewood sign. After 1 mile take
right hand fork, continue for 1 mile and site
is on the left at the bottom of the hill.
⇌ Leeds

## LEEDS

**Moor Lodge Caravan Park,** Blackmoor Lane, Bardsey, Leeds, West Yorkshire, LS17 9DZ
**Tel:** 01937 572424
**Email:** moorlodgecp@aol.com
www.ukparks.co.uk/moorlodge
**Pitches For** ▲ ⚐ ⊟ **Total** 12
**Facilities** ⚡ ∮ ▯ ▣ ⑭ ♨ ⌐ ⊙ ⊿ ▣ ☕
▮ ⓪ ☕ ⊁ ⊟ A
**Nearby Facilities** ┏ ✓ ∪ ♪ ⚡
**Acreage** 8 **Open** All Year
**Access** Good **Site** Level
ADULTS ONLY. Immaculate countryside park.
**Nearest Town/Resort** Leeds
**Directions** Turn off the A1 at Wetherby and take the A58 towards Leeds for 4 miles, turn right after the Bracken Fox Pub (Ling Lane). At the crossroads turn right and Moor Lodge is at the bottom of the hill on the right.
⚞ Leeds

## OTLEY

**St. Helena's Caravan Park,** Otley Old Road, Horsforth, Leeds, West Yorkshire, LS18 5HZ
**Tel:** 0113 284 1142
**Pitches For** ▲ ⚐ ⊟ **Total** 60
**Facilities** ⚘ ∮ ▯ ♨ ⌐ ⊙ ⊿ ▣ ☕
☕ ⊁ ⊟ A
**Nearby Facilities** ┏ ✓
**Open** April to October
**Access** Good **Site** Level
ADULTS ONLY. Ideal for touring the Dales, central for Leeds, Bradford and Harrogate.
**Nearest Town/Resort** Horsforth
**Directions** From Leeds take the A660 or the A65, then take the A658.
⚞ Horsforth

## OTLEY

**Stubbings Farm,** Leeds Road, Otley, West Yorkshire, LS21 1DN
**Tel:** 01943 464168
**Pitches For** ▲ ⚐ ⊟ **Total** 20
**Facilities** ▣ ⑭ ♨
**Nearby Facilities** ┏ ✓ ⚑ ⚡ ∪ ♪ ⚡
**Acreage** 3 **Open** All Year
**Access** Good **Site** Lev/Slope
Rural site with beautiful views over the Wharfe Valley.
**Nearest Town/Resort** Otley
**Directions** Off the A660, 1 mile outside Otley.
⚞ Burley-in-Wharfedale

## SHIPLEY

**Dobrudden Caravan Park,** Baildon Moor, Baildon, Shipley, West Yorkshire, BD17 5EE
**Tel:** 01274 581016 **Fax:** 01274 594351
**Email:** liz@dobrudden.co.uk
www.dobrudden.co.uk
**Pitches For** ▲ ⚐ ⊟ **Total** 40
**Facilities** ∮ ▣ ⑭ ♨ ⌐ ⊙ ⊿ ▣ ☕
▮ ⓪ ☕ ⊁ ⊟ ☼ ♪
**Nearby Facilities** ┏ ✓ ⚑ ∪ ♪ ⚡
**Acreage** 9 **Open** March to Dec
**Access** Good **Site** Lev/Slope
In the middle of the Moors. Some facilities for the disabled.
**Nearest Town/Resort** Baildon
⚞ Baildon

## SILSDEN

**Brown Bank Caravan Park,** Brown Bank Lane, Silsden, West Yorkshire, BD20 0NN
**Tel:** 01535 653241
**Email:** timlaycock@btconnect.com
**Pitches For** ▲ ⚐ ⊟ **Total** 15
**Facilities** ∮ ⑭ ♨ ⌐ ⊙ ⊿ ☕
⓪ ☕ ⊟ A ☼ ♪
**Nearby Facilities** ┏ ✓ ∪ ⚡
**Acreage** 12 **Open** April to October

**Access** Good **Site** Level
On the edge of Ilkley Moor with good views and excellent walks. Ideal base for touring. Many attractions within 15 miles.
**Nearest Town/Resort** Silsden
**Directions** From Silsden take the A6034, turn right on the bend into Brown Bank Lane, site is 1½ miles on the right. Also signposted from Addingham on the A6034.
⚞ Steeton

## SILSDEN

**Dales Bank Holiday Park,** Low Lane, Silsden, Keighley, West Yorkshire, BD20 9JH
**Tel:** 01535 653321/656523
**Pitches For** ▲ ⚐ ⊟ **Total** 52
**Facilities** ⚘ ∮ ▣ ⑭ ♨ ⌐ ⊙ ⊿ ☕
▮ ⓪ ☕ ✗ ♈ ▯ ♨ ⊁ ⊟ ☕ ☼ ♪
**Nearby Facilities** ┏ ✓ ⚑ ∪ ♪ ⚡
**Acreage** 5 **Open** April to Oct
**Access** Good **Site** Level
Central for Ilkley, Craven Dales and Bronte Country.
**Nearest Town/Resort** Silsden
**Directions** In Silsden turn up one way street 'Briggate', after 100 yards turn into Bradley Road, after ¾ miles turn right, site entrance is third on the right.
⚞ Steeton

## SILSDEN

**Lower Heights Farm,** Silsden, West Yorkshire, BD20 9HW
**Tel:** 01535 653035
**Pitches For** ▲ ⚐ ⊟ **Total** 5
**Facilities** ∮ ♨ ♨ ⌐ ♨ ▮ ⑭ ♨
**Nearby Facilities** ∪
**Acreage** 2 **Open** Easter to Oct
**Access** Good **Site** Level
Quiet site with good views. Only 5 caravan pitches but any number of tents.
**Nearest Town/Resort** Skipton
**Directions** 1 mile from Silsden off A6034.
⚞ Steeton

## WAKEFIELD

**Nostell Priory Holiday Park,** Doncaster Road, Nostell, Wakefield, West Yorkshire, WF4 1QE
**Tel:** 01924 863938 **Fax:** 01924 864045
**Email:** info@nostellprioryholidaypark.co.uk
www.nostellprioryholidaypark.co.uk
**Pitches For** ▲ ⚐ ⊟ **Total** 50
**Facilities** ⚘ ∮ ▣ ⑭ ♨ ⌐ ⊙ ⊿ ▣ ☕
♈ ⓪ ☕ ♨ ⊁ ⊟ ☼ ♪
**Nearby Facilities** ✓
**Open** March to October
**Access** Good **Site** Level
Set in peaceful countryside with abundant wildlife. Lakeside walks. Nostell Priory House & Gardens nearby.
**Nearest Town/Resort** Wakefield
**Directions** From Wakefield take the A638 towards Doncaster, site is 4 miles.
⚞ Wakefield

## WETHERBY

**Maustin Caravan Park,** Kearby with Netherby, Nr Wetherby, West Yorkshire, LS22 4DA
**Tel:** 0113 288 6234 **Fax:** 0113 288 6133
**Email:** info@maustin.co.uk
www.maustin.co.uk
**Pitches For** ⚐ ⊟ **Total** 25
**Facilities** ∮ ⑭ ♨ ⌐ ⊙ ⊿ ▣ ☕
⓪ ☕ ✗ ♈ ▯ ⊟ ☕ ♪
**Nearby Facilities** ┏ ✓ ∪
**Acreage** 2 **Open** March to Jan
**Access** Good **Site** Level
Quiet site, suits couples. Excellent restaurant/bar open weekends. Flat green bowling. Harewood House nearby. Good touring centre. Holiday homes for sale and

hire. Gold Award for Conservation.
**Nearest Town/Resort** Harrogate/Wetherby
**Directions** A61 three right turns, after crossing River Wharfe at bottom of Harewood Bank. A1 from Wetherby through Sicklinghall to Kearby.

# WALES

## ANGLESEY

### AMLWCH

**Point Lynas Caravan Park,** Llaneilian, Amlwch, Anglesey, LL68 9LT
**Tel:** 01407 831130 **Fax:** 01248 853832
**Email:** peter@pantysaer.freeserve.co.uk
www.pointlynas.com
**Pitches For** ▲ ⚐ ⊟ **Total** 15
**Facilities** ⚡ ∮ ▣ ⑭ ♨ ⌐ ⊙ ⊿ ▣ ☕
☕ ⊁ ⊟ ▣ ☼
**Nearby Facilities** ┏ ✓ ⚡ ♪
**Acreage** 1¼ **Open** Late March to October
**Access** Good **Site** Level
Family park 200 yards from Porth Eilian Cove.
**Nearest Town/Resort** Amlwch
**Directions** Turn off the A5025 at Anglesey Mowers towards the sea. Follow signs for Llaneilian/Porth Eilian. Pass the phone box, entrance is 300yds on the left.
⚞ Bangor

### AMLWCH

**Tyn Rhos,** Penysarn, Amlwch, Anglesey, LL69 9YR
**Tel:** 01407 830574
**Pitches For** ▲ ⚐ ⊟ **Total** 30
**Facilities** ∮ ⑭ ♨ ⌐ ⊙ ♨ ▮ ⑭ ⊟ ☼
**Nearby Facilities** ┏ ✓ ⚑ ⚡ ♪
**Acreage** 2 **Open** Easter to September
**Access** Good **Site** Level
Near the village shops, post office and inn. Sports centre, beaches and swimming all 2 miles. Cafe/restaurant and licensed club within 200yds. 6 berth caravan available for hire, all mod cons.
**Nearest Town/Resort** Amlwch
**Directions** A5025 turn off bypass to village of Penysarn. Take the first right after Y Bedol Public House and cross the cattle grid. 100yds up the drive.
⚞ Bangor

### BEAUMARIS

**Kingsbridge Caravan Park,** Llanfaes, Beaumaris, Anglesey, LL58 8LR
**Tel:** 01248 490636
**Email:** info@kingsbridgecaravanpark.co.uk
www.kingsbridgecaravanpark.co.uk
**Pitches For** ▲ ⚐ ⊟ **Total** 48
**Facilities** ∮ ⑭ ♨ ⌐ ⊙ ⊿ ☕
♈ ▮ ⓪ ☕ ♨ ⊁ ⊟
**Nearby Facilities** ┏ ✓ ⚑ ⚡ ∪ ⚒ ⚡
**Acreage** 14 **Open** March to October
**Access** Good **Site** Level
Fishing, scenic views, historical sites. Ideal for touring and bird watching. Brochure sent on request.
**Nearest Town/Resort** Beaumaris
**Directions** 1¼ miles past Beaumaris Castle. At crossroads turn left, 400yds to the site.
⚞ Bangor

# ANGLESEY

## BENLLECH
**Ad Astra Caravan Park,** Brynteg, Nr Benllech, Anglesey, LL78 7JH
**Tel:** 01248 Tynygongl 853283
**Email:** brian@brynteg53.fsnet.co.uk
www.adastracaravanpark.co.uk
**Pitches For** ▲ ⊆ ⊟
**Facilities** ⌇ 🄵 🄷 🆄🄲 ⚓ 🎢 ⊙ ⊿ 🔲 🚻
🍴 ⊖🠘 ☕ 🆇
**Nearby Facilities** ⌇ 🏊 ⚓ 🠔 ⛵ 🏌 🎣
**Acreage** 3 **Open** March **to** October
**Access** Good **Site** Level
Scenic views, ideal base for touring.
**Nearest Town/Resort** Benllech
**Directions** Turn left up the hill from Benllech Village square onto the B5108. Drive 1½ miles to California Inn, turn left onto the B5110. Park is 500 yards on right hand side.
✈ Bangor

## BENLLECH
**Bodafon Caravan & Camping Park,** Bodafon, Benllech, Anglesey, LL74 8RU
**Tel:** 01248 852417
**Email:** robert@bodafonpark.fsnet.co.uk
www.bodafonpark.co.uk
**Pitches For** ▲ ⊆ ⊟ **Total** 50
**Facilities** ⌇ 🄷 🆄🄲 ⚓ 🎢 ⊙ ⊿ 🚻
⊖ 🆇 🠘🖃
**Nearby Facilities** ⌇ 🏊 ⚓ 🠔 ⛵ 🏌
**Acreage** 5 **Open** March **to** October
**Access** Good **Site** Lev/Slope
Quiet family site with good views, ¾ miles from the beach. Ideal touring.
**Nearest Town/Resort** Benllech Bay
**Directions** A5025 through Benllech, ¼ mile on left going through 30mph signs.
✈ Bangor

## BENLLECH
**Cae Mawr Caravan Club Site,** Llangefni Road, Marianglas, Anglesey, LL73 8NY
**Tel:** 01248 853737
www.caravanclub.co.uk
**Pitches For** ⊆ ⊟ **Total** 76
**Facilities** ⌇ 🄷 🆄🄲 🄸🄲 ⊙ ⊖🠘🖃
**Nearby Facilities** ⌇ 🏊 ⚓ 🠔
**Acreage** 6½ **Open** March **to** Oct
**Access** Good **Site** Level
A sheltered site with cheerful hydrangers. 1 mile from the beach. Close to Beaumaris Castle, Butterfly Palace, Sea Zoo and NT Plas Newydd. Own sanitation required. Non members welcome. Booking essential.
**Nearest Town/Resort** Benllech
**Directions** From A55 on approaching Bangor continue onto A5 sp Holyhead. Cross Britannia Bridge and leave dual carriageway via second slip road and turn right onto A5025. In Benllech continue on A5025 (DO NOT turn left) then turn left onto B5110. Site is on the right by Parciau Arms Pub.
✈ Benllech

## BENLLECH
**Garnedd Touring Park,** Lon Bryn Mair, Brynteg, Anglesey, LL78 8QA
**Tel:** 01248 853240 **Fax:** 01248 853240
**Email:** mmpicomac@aol.com
**Pitches For** ▲ ⊆ ⊟ **Total** 20
**Facilities** ⌇ 🆄🄲 ⚓ 🎢 ⊙ ⊿ 🔲 🚻
🍴🠘 🆇
**Nearby Facilities** ⌇ 🏊 ⚓ 🠔 ⛵ 🏌
**Acreage** 9 **Open** March **to** October
**Access** Good **Site** Level
Five beaches within 5 minutes of the site. Wonderful views. Cottage and static caravan available for hire. You can also call us on Mobile: 07973 156371.
**Nearest Town/Resort** Benllech

## BENLLECH
**Directions** From Menai Bridge take the A5025 signposted Amlwch and Benllech. After entering Benllech turn left at Londis Garage, turn into the fourth lane, site is 600 yards on the right (third site).
✈ Benllech

## BENLLECH
**Golden Sunset Holidays,** Benllech, Anglesey, LL74 8SW
**Tel:** 01248 852345
**Pitches For** ▲ ⊆ ⊟ **Total** 120
**Facilities** 🍴 ⌇ 🆄🄲 ⚓ 🎢 ⊙ ⊿ 🚻 🄸🄲 ⊖🠘🖃
**Nearby Facilities** ⌇ 🏊
**Acreage** 20 **Open** May **to** Sept Inc.
**Access** Good **Site** Lev/Slope
Close to the village and beach.
**Nearest Town/Resort** Benllech
**Directions** Turn right off the A5025 in the centre of Benllech and turn immediately left into site entrance.
✈ Bangor

## BENLLECH
**Home Farm Caravan Park,** Marianglas, Anglesey, LL73 8PH
**Tel:** 01248 410614 **Fax:** 01248 410900
**Email:** enq@homefarm-anglesey.co.uk
www.homefarm-anglesey.co.uk
**Pitches For** ▲ ⊆ ⊟
**Facilities** ⚒ ⌇ 🄵 🄷 🆄🄲 ⚓ 🎢 ⊙ ⊿ 🔲 🚻
🄸🄲 ⊖ 🆇 🠘🖃 🏧
**Nearby Facilities** ⌇ 🏊 ⚓ 🠔 ⛵ 🏌 🎣
**Open** April **to** Oct
**Access** Good **Site** Level
1 to 1½ miles from various beaches.
**Nearest Town/Resort** Benllech
**Directions** Follow the A5025 from bridge for 11 miles, go through Benllech, keep left at the roundabout towards Amlwch. Park is ½ mile on the left, 300 yards after the church.
✈ Bangor

## BENLLECH
**Penrhos Caravan Club Site,** Brynteg, Benllech, Anglesey, LL78 7JH
**Tel:** 01248 852617
www.caravanclub.co.uk
**Pitches For** ⊆ ⊟ **Total** 93
**Facilities** ⚒ ⌇ 🄷 🆄🄲 ⚓ 🎢 🄸🄲 ⊖ 🆇 🠘🖃
**Nearby Facilities** ⌇ 🏊 ⚓
**Acreage** 9 **Open** March **to** Oct
**Access** Good **Site** Lev/Slope
2 miles from a safe sandy beach. Near a farm trail, bird sanctuary, Beaumaris Castle and Sea Zoo. Take a trip on Snowdon's rack and pinion mountain railway for breathtaking views. Non members welcome. Booking essential.
**Nearest Town/Resort** Benllech
**Directions** On A55 approaching Bangor continue on A5 sp Holyhead. Cross Britannia Bridge and leave dual carriageway via second slip road and turn right onto A5025. In Benllech continue on A5025 (DO NOT turn left) and turn left onto B5110. At crossroads with California Pub go straight on and site is ½ mile on the right.
✈ Benllech

## BENLLECH
**Plas Uchaf Caravan & Camping Park,** Benllech Bay, Benllech, Anglesey, LL74 8NU
**Tel:** 01407 763012
**Pitches For** ▲ ⊆ ⊟ **Total** 88
**Facilities** ⚒ ⌇ 🄷 🆄🄲 ⚓ 🎢 ⊙ ⊿ 🚻
🄸🄲 🔲 ⚓ 🌢🠘🖃
**Nearby Facilities** ⌇ 🏊 ⚓ 🠔 ⛵ 🏌
**Acreage** 11 **Open** March **to** October
**Access** Good **Site** Level
Well sheltered, family park, under a mile from the beach. Tarmac roads, close mown grass, picnic tables, street lighting,

freezers etc.. Perimeter parking.
**Nearest Town/Resort** Benllech
**Directions** ¼ mile from Benllech, signposted just after fire station on the B5108.
✈ Bangor

## BENLLECH
**St. David's Park,** Red Wharf Bay, Isle of Anglesey, LL75 8RJ
**Tel:** 01248 852341 **Fax:** 01248 852777
**Email:** paul@stdavidspark.com
www.stdavidspark.com
**Pitches For** ▲ ⊆ **Total** 130
**Facilities** ⌇ 🄷 🆄🄲 ⚓ 🎢 ⊙ ⊿ 🔲 🚻
🆂 ⊙ ⚓ ✗ 🍴 🄸🄲 ⚓ 🄬 🌢🠘🖃 🆇
**Nearby Facilities** ⌇ 🏊 ⚓ 🠔 ⛵
**Acreage** 3 **Open** March **to** Sept
**Site** Sloping
Private beach, fully licenced bars and entertainment. NEW toilet & shower facilities.
**Nearest Town/Resort** Benllech
**Directions** On the A5025 1 mile south of Benllech.
✈ Bangor

## BENLLECH
**Ty Newydd Leisure Park,** Llanbedrgoch, Anglesey, LL76 8TZ
**Tel:** 01248 450677 **Fax:** 01248 450711
**Email:** mike@tynewydd.com
www.tynewydd.com
**Pitches For** ▲ ⊆ ⊟ **Total** 45
**Facilities** ⚒ ⌇ 🄷 🆄🄲 ⚓ 🎢 ⊙ ⊿ 🔲 🚻
🆂 🄸🄲 ⊙ ⚓ ✗ 🍴 🄬 🄭 🌢🠘🖃 🆇 🠘🖃 🆇🌢
🎣
**Nearby Facilities** ⌇ 🏊 ⚓ 🠔 ⛵ 🏌 🎣
**Acreage** 9 **Open** March **to** Oct
**Access** Good **Site** Level
**Nearest Town/Resort** Benllech
**Directions** Take the A5025 and go through Pentreath, turn left at the lay-by and park is through the village on the right.
✈ Bangor

## BRYNSIENCYN
**Fron Caravan & Camping Site,** Brynsiencyn, Anglesey, LL61 6TX
**Tel:** 01248 430310 **Fax:** 01248 430310
**Email:** mail@froncaravanpark.co.uk
www.froncaravanpark.co.uk
**Pitches For** ▲ ⊆ ⊟ **Total** 70
**Facilities** ⚒ ⌇ 🆄🄲 ⚓ 🎢 ⊙ ⊿ 🔲 🚻
🆂 🄸🄲 ⊙ ⚓ 🄬 🌢🠘🖃
**Nearby Facilities** ⌇ 🏊 ⚓ 🠔 ⛵ 🏌 🎣
**Acreage** 5¼ **Open** Easter **to** September
**Access** Good **Site** Level
Ideal for touring Anglesey and North Wales. Wales Tourist Board 4 Star Grading.
**Nearest Town/Resort** Llanfairpwllgwyn
**Directions** At start of Llanfairpwllgwyn turn left onto A4080 to Brynsiencyn follow road through village site is on the right ¼ mile after village.
✈ Bangor

## LLANFAIRPWLL
**Plas Coch Caravan & Leisure Park,** Llanedwen, Llanfairpwll, Anglesey, LL61 6EJ
**Tel:** 01248 714346
**Pitches For** ▲ ⊆ ⊟
**Facilities** ⌇ 🆄🄲 ⚓ 🎢 ⊙ ⊿
🄸🄲 ⊙ 🍴 🄬 🄭 🌢🠘🖃 🆇🌢
**Nearby Facilities** ⌇ 🏊 ⚓ 🠔 ⛵ 🏌 🎣
**Open** April **to** Sept
**Access** Good
½ mile frontage on the Menai Straits for fishing, boating, water skiing, etc..
**Nearest Town/Resort** Menai Bridge
**Directions** Turn left at first sliproad after Menai Bridge, keep left to Llanfairpwll. Turn left at the 30mph sign, turn left at first crossroads, site is approx. 1½ miles.
✈ Llanfairpwll

## LLANFWROG

**Penrhyn Bay Caravan Park,** Llanfwrog, Holyhead, Anglesey, LL65 4YG
**Tel:** 01407 730496
**Email:** penrhyn.bay@btinternet.com
www.penrhynbay.com
**Pitches For** ▲ ⊞ ⬛ **Total** 175
**Facilities** ⬛ ⁄ 🚻 ♨ ▮ ☎ ⊙ ⚊ ▨ 🖵 ◨ ⟁ ❄ 🔌 ⬛ ♨ ⬛ ✕ 🛒 ⬛ ⚊ ❄
**Nearby Facilities** ⟊ ✎ ⚓ ⤳ ⛳
**Acreage** 15 **Open** March **to** End Oct
**Access** Good **Site** Level
Situated between farmland and the sea. Camping and touring van area is on a field next to the beach. Plenty of coastal walks. Tennis on site.
**Nearest Town/Resort** Holyhead
**Directions** Take the A55 to Anglesey, take exit 3 to Valley, turn right at the traffic lights onto the A5025 and go through Llanfachraeth. Take the first turn left and follow signs for Penrhyn Bay Caravan Park.
⇌ Valley/Holyhead

## LLANGEFNI

**Mornest Caravan Park,** Pentre Berw, Gaerwen, Anglesey, LL60 6HU
**Tel:** 01248 421725
**Pitches For** ▲ ⊞ ⬛ **Total** 45
**Facilities** ⁄ 🚻 ♨ ▮ ☎ ⊙ ⚊ 🖵 ◨ ☂ ⚊ 🐾 ❄ ♨
**Nearby Facilities** ⟊ ✎ ⚓ ⤳ ∪ ⛳
**Open** 17 March **to** 31 Oct
**Access** Good **Site** Lev/Slope
**Nearest Town/Resort** Llangefni
**Directions** Go over Menai Bridge and take exit 7 off and follow signs through Gaerwen.
⇌ Bangor

## MOELFRE

**Capel Elen Caravan Park,** Lligwy Bay, Dulas, Anglesey, LL70 9PQ
**Tel:** 01248 410670 **Fax:** 01248 410670
**Email:** john@capelelen.co.uk
www.capelelen.co.uk
**Pitches For** ▲ ⊞ ⬛ **Total** 40
**Facilities** ⁄ 🚻 🚻 ♨ ▮ ☎ ⊙ ⚊ ⚊ ▨ 🖵 ◨ ▮ ⬛ ⚊ ✕ ⚊ 🖵 ⚊ ❄
**Nearby Facilities** ⟊ ✎ ⚓ ⤳ ∪ ⛳ ✗
**Acreage** 2 **Open** Easter/1 April **to** Sept
**Access** Poor **Site** Sloping
½ a mile from a large sandy beach.
**Nearest Town/Resort** Llangefni
**Directions** After the bridge onto Anglesey take the A5025 towards Amlwch. Turn right at Brynrefail and the site is 300 yards down the narrow lane.
⇌ Bangor

## MOELFRE

**Melin Rhos Caravan Park,** Lligwy, Moelfre, Anglesey, LL24 8RU
**Tel:** 01248 852417 **Fax:** 01248 853417
**Email:** robert@bodafonpark.co.uk
www.bodafonpark.co.uk
**Pitches For** ▲ ⊞ ⬛ **Total** 40
**Facilities** ⁄ 🚻 ♨ ▮ ☎ ⊙ ⚊ ⚊ ⬛ 🛒 ⬛ 🖵 ❄ ♨
**Nearby Facilities** ⟊ ✎ ✗ ∪ ⛳ ✗
**Acreage** 4 **Open** March **to** Oct
**Access** Good **Site** Level
Quarter of an hours walk to a lovely beach.
**Nearest Town/Resort** Benllech
**Directions** From Benllech continue along the A5025, at the roundabout turn left, after 2 miles go down a three lane hill and back up, at the top of the hill turn right and the site is approx. ½ a mile on the left.
⇌ Bangor

## MOELFRE

**Tyddyn Isaf Camping & Caravan Park,** Lligwy Bay, Dulas, Anglesey, LL70 9PQ
**Tel:** 01248 410203 **Fax:** 01248 410667
**Email:** enquiries@tyddynisaf.demon.co.uk
www.tyddynisaf.demon.co.uk
**Pitches For** ▲ ⊞ ⬛ **Total** 80
**Facilities** ⁄ 🚻 🚻 ♨ ▮ ☎ ⊙ ⚊ ⚊ ▨ 🖵 ◨ ⬛ ⊙ ❄ 🛒 ▮ ⚊ ⬛ 🐾 ❄ ♨
**Nearby Facilities** ⟊ ✎ ⚓ ⤳ ∪ ⛳ ✗
**Acreage** 16 **Open** March **to** October
**Access** Good **Site** Sloping
Family run park with a private footpath to a fine, sandy beach. "Loo of the Year" Winner, AA 4 Pennant Premier Park, David Bellamy Gold Award, Welcome Host Award, Calor Gas Best Touring Park in Wales Finalist 2003 and WTB 5 Star Graded.
**Nearest Town/Resort** Benllech
**Directions** Take the A5025 from Britannia Bridge, go through Benllech approx. 8 miles, continue to Moelfre Island via left staying on the main road to Brynrefail Village. Turn right opposite the telephone box and International camping sign, we are ½ mile on the right down the lane.
⇌ Bangor

## MOELFRE

**Tyn Rhos Caravan Park,** Moelfre, Anglesey, LL72 8NL
**Tel:** 01248 852417 **Fax:** 01248 852417
**Email:** robert@bodafon.fsnet.co.uk
www.bodafonpark.co.uk
**Pitches For** ▲ ⊞ ⬛ **Total** 50
**Facilities** ⁄ 🚻 ♨ ▮ ☎ ⊙ ⚊ ⚊ ⬛ ⚊ 🛒 ⬛ 🖵 ❄ ♨
**Nearby Facilities** ⟊ ✎ ⚓ ⤳ ∪ ⛳
**Acreage** 10 **Open** March **to** October
**Access** Good **Site** Level
Near Lligwy Beach. Surrounded by numerous footpaths, including coastal path, fishing and ancient monuments.
**Nearest Town/Resort** Benllech
**Directions** From Benllech proceed along the A5025 to the roundabout, turn right to Moelfre and at MDM Design turn left for 2 miles, site is on the right.
⇌ Bangor

## NEWBOROUGH

**Awelfryn Caravan Park,** Newborough, Anglesey, LL61 6SG
**Tel:** 01248 440230
**Email:** awelfryncp@aol.com
**Pitches For** ▲ ⊞ ⬛ **Total** 24
**Facilities** ⁄ 🚻 ♨ ☎ ⬛ 🖵 ❄
**Nearby Facilities** ✎ ⤳ ∪ ⛳
**Acreage** 2 **Open** 1 March **to** 31 Oct
**Access** Good **Site** Lev/Slope
Beauty spot on the edge of Forestry Commission land. 1½ miles from the beach. Llanddwyn Island.
**Nearest Town/Resort** Bangor
**Directions** On the A4080 from Britannia Bridge take a left by a tall column, and follow the A4080 through to Newborough. Turn left at the crossroads for Beach Road, site is on the left after ¼ mile.
⇌ Bangor

## PENTRAETH

**Clai Mawr Caravan Park,** Pentraeth, Anglesey, LL75 8DX
**Tel:** 01248 450467 **Fax:** 01248 450467
**Email:** claimawr@talk21.com
www.walestouristsonline.co.uk/anglesey
**Pitches For** ⊞ ⬛ **Total** 8
**Facilities** ⁄ 🚻 🚻 ♨ ▮ ☎ ⊙ ⚊ ⚊ ⬛ ⚊ 🛒 ⬛ 🖵 ◨ ⬛ 🛒 🖵 ❄
**Nearby Facilities** ⟊ ✎ ⚓ ⤳ ∪ ⛳

**Acreage** 1½ **Open** March **to** October
**Access** Good **Site** Lev/Slope
Quiet, family run site overlooking Red Wharf Bay and the Snowdon Mountains.
**Nearest Town/Resort** Benllech/Llangefni
**Directions** From Bangor take the A55 across Britannia Bridge then take the second exit onto the A5025. Go through Pentraeth to the end of 40mph sign, Clai Mawr entrance is on the right.
⇌ Bangor

## PENTRAETH

**Rhos Caravan Park,** Rhos Farm, Pentraeth, Anglesey, LL75 8DZ
**Tel:** 01248 450214
**Pitches For** ▲ ⊞ ⬛ **Total** 90
**Facilities** ⁄ 🚻 ♨ ▮ ☎ ⊙ ⚊ ⚊ ⬛ ⚊ 🛒 ⬛ 🖵 ◨ ❄
**Nearby Facilities** ⟊ ✎ ⚓ ⤳ ∪ ⛳
**Acreage** 6 **Open** March **to** October
**Access** Good **Site** Level
Near beach and central location for Anglesey, good views of Snowdonia.
**Nearest Town/Resort** Red Wharf Bay
**Directions** Through Pentraeth on A5025 main road. Site entrance on left 1 mile north of Pentraeth.
⇌ Bangor

## RHOSNEIGR

**Bodfan Farm,** Rhosneigr, Anglesey, LL64 5XA
**Tel:** 01407 810706
**Email:** wap@llynfor.freeserve.co.uk
**Pitches For** ▲ ⊞ ⬛ **Total** 100
**Facilities** ⁄ 🚻 ♨ ▮ ☎ ⊙ ⚊ ⚊ ⬛ 🖵 🐾 🖵
**Nearby Facilities** ⟊ ✎ ⚓ ⤳ ∪ ⛳ ✗
**Acreage** 12 **Open** Easter **to** End Sept
**Access** Good **Site** Sloping
Excellent beaches. Ideal for touring Anglesey and Snowdonia. Plenty of open spaces for children to play.
**Nearest Town/Resort** Rhosneigr
**Directions** Leave the A55 at junction 5 and follow the A4080 to Rhosneigr. We are next to the school on Sandy Lane.
⇌ Rhosneigr

## RHOSNEIGR

**Shoreside Camp & Caravan Park,** Station Road, Rhosneigr, Anglesey, LL64 5QX
**Tel:** 01407 810279
**Email:** shoreside@amserve.net
www.shoresidecamping.co.uk
**Pitches For** ▲ ⊞ ⬛ **Total** 100
**Facilities** ⁄ 🚻 ♨ ▮ ☎ ⊙ ⚊ ⬛ ⚊ 🛒 ⬛ 🖵 ❄ ♨
**Nearby Facilities** ⟊ ✎ ⚓ ⤳ ∪ ⛳ ✗
**Acreage** 6 **Open** Easter **to** October
**Access** Good **Site** Lev/Slope
Riding centre on site, bowling and tennis. Near the beach and opposite a golf club. 10 miles from Holyhead, day trips to Dublin.
**Nearest Town/Resort** Rhosneigr
**Directions** Take the A55 to junction 5, then take the A4080 to Rhosneigr, opposite the golf club.
⇌ Rhosneigr

## RHOSNEIGR

**Ty Hen,** Station Road, Rhosneigr, Anglesey, LL64 5QZ
**Tel:** 01407 810331
**Email:** bernardtyhen@hotmail.com
www.tyhen.com
**Pitches For** ▲ ⊞ ⬛ **Total** 38
**Facilities** ⬛ ⁄ 🚻 🚻 ♨ ▮ ☎ ⊙ ⚊ ⚊ ⬛ ⚊ 🛒 ⬛ ♨ ⬛ 🖵 ◨ ⬛ ⚊ 🖵
**Nearby Facilities** ⟊ ⚓ ⤳ ∪ ⛳ ✗
**Acreage** 50 **Open** April **to** October
**Access** Good **Site** Level

On the banks of a 65 acre lake, great for walks, wildlife and fresh air. Five Seaside Award beaches. Golf and sub-aqua. David Bellamy Gold Award for Conservation.
**Nearest Town/Resort** Rhosneigr
**Directions** Take the A55 across Anglesey, turn left onto the A4080 for Rhosneigr. Turn right at Llanfaelog Post Office, Ty Hen is next to the Railway Station, up the drive ½ mile.
➤ Rhosneigr

## RHOSNEIGR

**Tyn Llidiart Camping Site,** Tyn Llidiart, Tywyn Trewan, Bryngwran, Anglesey, LL65 3SW
**Tel:** 01407 810678
**Email:** 106110.521@compuserve.com
**Pitches For** ▲ ⊞ ➡ **Total** 5
**Facilities** ∤ ⅏ ⌐ ⏚ ⅋ ⏚⌂🄿
**Nearby Facilities** ┌ ✔ ⚓ ∪ ⅃ ⅋ ⚞
**Acreage** ¾ **Open** All Year
**Access** Fair **Site** Level
Pleasant, quiet site near the beach.
**Nearest Town/Resort** Rhosneigr
**Directions** Take the A5 to Bryngwran, turn by the Post Office, after approx. 1 mile you will pass garage on the left and three white cottages on the right, at third cottage turn right, fork right over cattle grid and site is on the left.
➤ Holyhead

## TREARDDUR BAY

**Tyn Rhos Camping Site,** Ravenspoint Road, Trearddur Bay, Holyhead, Anglesey, LL65 2BQ
**Tel:** 01407 860369
**Pitches For** ▲ ⊞ ➡ **Total** 200
**Facilities** ∤ ⅏ ⅋ ⌐ ⊙ ⏚ 🄿 ⊡ 🆒
**S⅃** 🅡 ⅋ ⏚⌂🄿 ▨
**Nearby Facilities** ┌ ✔ ⚓ ∪ ⅃ ⚞
**Acreage** 20 **Open** March to October
**Access** Good **Site** Lev/Slope
Well established family run site, rural location with modern facilities. Views of Snowdonia, coastal walks, sandy beaches (Blue Flag Award) 10 minutes. Ideal touring base, Holyhead port town to Ireland - 3 miles. Separate rally field also available. WTB 2 Star Graded.
**Nearest Town/Resort** Holyhead
**Directions** Follow the A55 across Anglesey. Leave the A55 at junction 3 and follow signs (A5) for Valley. Turn left at Valley onto the B4545 for Trearddur Bay. Turn left onto Ravenspoint Road, ¾ miles to the shared entrance, take left hand branch.
➤ Holyhead

## VALLEY

**Bodowyr Caravan Park,** Bodowyr, Bodedern, Anglesey, LL65 3SS
**Tel:** 01407 741171
**Email:** bodowyr@yahoo.com
**www.1stopindex.co.uk/bodowyr**
**Pitches For** ▲ ⊞ ➡ **Total** 30
**Facilities** ∤ ⅏ ⅋ ⌐ ⊙ ⏚ 🄿 ⊡ 🆒
⅃🅡⅊🅇⏚⌂🄿🆗 ▨ 🖉
**Nearby Facilities** ┌ ✔ ⚓ ∪ ⅃ ⅋ ⚞
**Open** March to November
**Access** Good **Site** Level
Very handy for ferries to Ireland. Close to beaches and a wide range of sporting facilities.
**Nearest Town/Resort** Holyhead
**Directions** From Holyhead take the A55, turn off at the Bodedern exit (junction 4) and turn left for Bodedern. Bodowyr is the first turning on the left. Site has international camping signs from the A5 junction.
➤ Valley

# BLAENAU GWENT

## TREDEGAR

**Parc Bryn Bach,** The Countryside Centre, Merthyr Road, Tredegar, Blaenau Gwent, NP22 3AY
**Tel:** 01495 711816 **Fax:** 01495 725093
**Email:** parcbrynbach@blaenau-gwent.gov.uk
**Pitches For** ▲ ⊞ ➡ **Total** 42
**Facilities** ⅊ ∤ ⅏ ⅏ ⏚ ⌐ ⊙ ⏚ 🄿 ⊡
⅊🅇⏚⌂🄿
**Nearby Facilities** ┌ ✔ ⚓ ⅋
**Acreage** 400 **Open** All Year
**Access** Good **Site** Level
Ideally situated on the edge of Brecon Beacons National Park.
**Nearest Town/Resort** Tredegar
**Directions** Just off the A465 Heads of the Valley road at Tredegar.
➤ Rhymney

# BRIDGEND

## PORTHCAWL

**Brodawel Camping Park,** Brodawel House, Moor Lane, Nottage, PorthcawlBridgend, CF36 3EJ
**Tel:** 01656 783231 **Fax:** 01656 783231
**Pitches For** ▲ ⊞ ➡ **Total** 100
**Facilities** ⅊ ∤ ⅏ ⏚ ⌐ ⊙ ⏚ ⅊ ⏚ 🆒
⅊⅃ 🅡 ⅊ ⅊ 🅇 ⏚⌂🄿 🆗 🆒
**Nearby Facilities** ┌ ✔ ⚓ ∪ ⅃ ⅋ ⚞
**Acreage** 5 **Open** April to October
**Access** Good **Site** Level
Convenient to all beaches, very central for touring area. Off Licence. Designer Village Wales 3 miles.
**Nearest Town/Resort** Porthcawl
**Directions** Leave the M4 at junction 37, turn onto the A4229 for Porthcawl for 2 miles, signposted Moor Lane.
➤ Pyle

# CAERPHILLY

## BARGOED

**Parc Cwm Darran,** Deri, Bargoed, Caerphilly, CF81 9NR
**Tel:** 01443 875557 **Fax:** 01443 836944
**Email:** honeym@caerphilly.gov.uk
**www.caerphilly.gov.uk**
**Pitches For** ▲ ⊞ ➡ **Total** 30
**Facilities** ⅊ ∤ ⅏ ⏚ ⌐ ⊙ ⏚ 🆒
⅃🅇⏚⌂🄿
**Nearby Facilities** ┌ ✔ ⅋
**Acreage** 2¾ **Open** Good Friday to 30 Sept
**Access** Good **Site** Sloping
Situated in an 800 acre country park with a fishing lake and nature reserve. Close to Brecon Beacons.
**Nearest Town/Resort** Bargoed
**Directions** Take the A469 from Bargoed and Pontlottyn, site is ¾ miles north of Deri.
➤ Pontlottyn

# CARDIFF

## CARDIFF

**Pontcanna Caravan Site,** Pontcanna Fields, Off Sophia Close, Pontcanna, Cardiff, CF11 9LB
**Tel:** 029 2039 8362 **Fax:** 029 2039 8362
**Pitches For** ▲ ⊞ ➡ **Total** 94
**Facilities** ∤ ⅏ ⅊ ⅏ ⌐ ⊙ ⏚ ⅊ ⏚ 🆒
⅃ 🅡 ⅊⏚⌂🄿
**Nearby Facilities** ∪ 🖉
**Acreage** 6 **Open** All Year
**Access** Good **Site** Level
Fully equipped for the disabled including specially adapted bikes (available for hire).
**Nearest Town/Resort** Cardiff

**Directions** Leave the M4 and follow signs for Cardiff City Centre. On reaching the city centre stay in the right hand lane, go over the bridge and to traffic lights, turn right into Cathedral Road. At next traffic lights turn right into Sophia Close and Sophia Gardens, turn left at the Welsh Institute of Sport, the Park is on this road on the left hand side.
➤ Cardiff Central

# CARDIGANSHIRE (CEREDIGION)

## ABERAERON

**Aeron Coast Caravan Park,** North Road, Aberaeron, Ceredigion, SA46 0JF
**Tel:** 01545 570349
**Email:** aeroncoastcaravanpark@aberaeron.freeserve.co.uk
**Pitches For** ▲ ⊞ ➡ **Total** 100
**Facilities** ⅊ ⅋ ∤ ⅏ ⌐ ⊙ ⏚ ⅊ ⏚ 🆒
⅊⅃ 🅡 ⅊🅇⏚⌂🄿 ▨
**Nearby Facilities** ┌ ✔ ⚓ ∪ ⅃ ⅋
**Acreage** 8 **Open** Easter to End October
**Access** Good **Site** Level
Aberaeron is a recognised beauty spot. Picturesque harbour, coastal and river walks, Tennis court on park. Only 200yds from shops. 4 Star Graded.
**Nearest Town/Resort** Aberaeron
**Directions** Main coastal road A487 on northern edge of Aberaeron. Filling station at entrance.
➤ Aberystwyth

## ABERPORTH

**Caerfelin Caravan Park,** Aberporth, Ceredigion, SA43 2BY
**Tel:** 01239 810540
**Email:** bright@caerfelin.fsbusiness.co.uk
**Pitches For** ⊞ ➡ **Total** 5
**Facilities** ⅊ ∤ ⅏ ⏚ ⌐ ⊙ ⏚ ⅊ 🆒
⅃⅊ 🆒
**Nearby Facilities** ┌ ✔ ⚓ ∪ ⚞
**Acreage** 11½ **Open** Mid March to End Oct
**Access** Good **Site** Lev/Slope
Well sheltered site, five minutes walk to sandy beaches and the village of Aberporth.
**Nearest Town/Resort** Aberporth
**Directions** Turn off A487 at Blaenannerch onto B433, enter village of Aberporth. Turn right at St. Cynwyls Church, park 200 yards on left.
➤ Carmarthen

## ABERPORTH

**Maes Glas Caravan Park,** Penbryn, Sarnau, Llandysul, Ceredigion, SA44 6QE
**Tel:** 01239 654268 **Fax:** 01239 654268
**Email:** enquiries@maesglascaravanpark.co.uk
**www.maesglascaravanpark.co.uk**
**Pitches For** ▲ ⊞ ➡ **Total** 10
**Facilities** ∤ ⅏ ⌐ ⊙ ⏚ ⅊ ⏚ 🆒
⅊⅃ ⅊ ⅊ 🅇 ⏚⌂🄿 ∪
**Nearby Facilities** ┌ ✔ ⚓ ∪
**Acreage** 4 **Open** March to October
**Access** Good **Site** Level
Near Penbryn beach. David Bellamy Gold Award for Conservation.
**Nearest Town/Resort** Llangrannog
**Directions** Turn off the A487 between Cardigan and New Quay in the village of Sarnau by the old church, signposted Penbryn. Follow the road down for ¾ mile to the telephone box, at next junction bear left and the park entrance is on the right.
➤ Aberystwyth

**Glan-y-Mor LEISURE PARK**
Clarach Bay
Nr Aberystwyth SY23 3DT
**Tel: 01970 828900**

★★★★ EXCELLENCE GRADING

Mid-Wales seaside holiday parks - Facilities include: indoor swimming pools, licensed family clubrooms, nightly entertainment, children's play areas, shops, restaurants, launderettes, take-aways, free hot showers & washing-up facilities, flush toilets, electric hook-ups and facilities for the disabled.

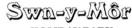

**Swn-y-Môr HOLIDAY PARK**
Borth,
Ceredigion SY24 5JU
DRAGON AWARD
**Tel: 01970 871233**

---

## ABERPORTH

**Pilbach Holiday Park,** Betws Ifan, Rhydlewis, Aberporth, Ceredigion, SA44 5RT
**Tel:** 01239 851434 **Fax:** 01239 851969
**Email:** info@pilbach.com
www.pilbach.com
**Pitches For** ▲ ⚎ ⌂ **Total** 65
**Facilities** ⏚ ⌂ ⊞ ⏤ ⏦ ▯ ⌂ ⊡ ⍽ ⊠ ⏛
♨ ⊗ ✕ ⏁ ⊞ ⋏ ⤧ ♿ ⊡ ⊞ ⋇
**Nearby Facilities** ⏁ ⟋ ⚓ ⌖ ∪ ⟲ ⤢
**Acreage** 15 **Open** March **to** Oct
**Access** Good **Site** Level
Close to Cenarth Water Falls and Aberporth's sandy beaches.
**Nearest Town/Resort** Aberporth/Cardigan
**Directions** From the A487 junction at Aberporth turn left onto the B4333 Newcastle Emlyn road. Turn first left, then after 700 metres turn right, after 300 metres turn left and the park is on the right.
✈ Aberystwyth

## ABERYSTWYTH

**Aeron View Caravan Site,** Blaenpennal, Aberystwyth, Ceredigion, SY23 4TW
**Tel:** 01974 251488
**Email:** aeronview@hotmail.com
www.aeronview.com
**Pitches For** ▲ ⚎ ⌂ **Total** 12
**Facilities** ⏚ ⊞ ⏤ ⌂ ⏦ ▯ ⏤ ⌂ ⊡ ⏛ ⏚
**Nearby Facilities** ⟋
**Acreage** 2 **Open** March **to** Oct
**Access** Good **Site** Level
Quiet site situated in the scenic Aeron Valley, famous for the Red Kite. Ideal for walking, cycling and touring. 8 miles from the beach.
**Nearest Town/Resort** Aberystwyth
**Directions** Leave Aberystwyth on the A487 coast road towards Cardigan, after approx. 2 miles turn left onto the A485 signposted Tregaron. Continue for approx. 8 miles, 2 miles after the village of Bronant turn right at the signpost to Blaenpennal, site is ½ a mile.
✈ Aberystwyth

## ABERYSTWYTH

**Clarach Bay Holiday Village,** Clarach, Aberystwyth, Ceredigion, SY23 3DT
**Tel:** 01970 828277 **Fax:** 01970 820771
**Email:** info@clarach-bay.com
www.clarachbay.com
**Pitches For** ▲ ⚎ ⌂ **Total** 30
**Facilities** ⏚ ⊞ ⌂ ⏦ ▯ ⏤ ⌂ ⊡ ⏛
♨ ⊗ ✕ ⏁ ⊞ ⋏ ⤧ ♿ ⊞
**Nearby Facilities** ⏁ ⟋ ⚓ ⌖ ∪ ⟲ ⤢
**Acreage** 43 **Open** Easter **to** Oct
**Access** Good **Site** Level
In the famous university town of Aberystwyth with it's old ruins and castle. Near to Aberystwyth Cable Car to Construction Hill and the worlds largest Camera Obscura.
**Nearest Town/Resort** Aberystwyth
**Directions** From the A44 follow signs to Bow Street, turn left at the Welsh Black Pub and follow the lane to the crossroads, go straight over and the site is on the left.
✈ Aberystwyth

## ABERYSTWYTH

**Morfa Bychan Holiday Park,** Aberystwyth, Ceredigion, SY23 4QQ
**Tel:** 01970 617254 **Fax:** 01970 624249
**Email:** morfa@hillandale.co.uk
www.hillandale.co.uk
**Pitches For** ▲ ⚎ ⌂ **Total** 50
**Facilities** ⏚ ⟋ ⊞ ▯ ⏤ ⌂ ⊡ ⏛ ⏚
♨ ⊗ ⏁ ⊗ ⏁ ⋏ ⤧ ♿ ⊞ ⊡ ⋇ ⏚
**Nearby Facilities** ⏁ ⟋ ⚓ ⌖ ∪ ⟲
**Acreage** 5 **Open** March **to** October
**Access** Good **Site** Sloping
100 acre park overlooking Cardigan Bay with our own private beach. Heated swimming pool, water hook-ups.
**Nearest Town/Resort** Aberystwyth
**Directions** Take the A487 south from Aberystwyth, after ½ mile signposted to the right, but this is NOT suitable for touring caravans who should continue for 2½ miles and turn right at the second sign. Follow signs for 1½ miles.
✈ Aberystwyth

## ABERYSTWYTH

**Ocean View,** North Beach, Clarach Bay, Aberystwyth, Ceredigion, SY23 3DT
**Tel:** 01970 828425
**Email:** alan@grover10.freeserve.co.uk
www.oceanviewholidays.com
**Pitches For** ▲ ⚎ ⌂ **Total** 24
**Facilities** ⏚ ⊞ ⌂ ⏦ ▯ ⏤ ⌂ ⊡ ⏛ ⏚
♨ ⊗ ⊞ ⋏ ⤧ ♿ ⋇
**Nearby Facilities** ⏁ ⟋ ⚓ ⌖ ∪ ⟲ ⤢
**Open** March **to** October
**Access** Good **Site** Level
Small select park, short walk to popular beach. Glorious views, ideal touring area of magic Mid-Wales.
**Nearest Town/Resort** Aberystwyth
**Directions** Take the A487 Aberystwyth to Machynlleth road. Turn in Bow Street for Clarach Bay. Follow road to the beach. Ocean View is on the right.
✈ Aberystwyth

## BORTH

**Brynowen Holiday Park,** Borth, Aberystwyth, Ceredigion, SY24 5LS
**Tel:** 01970 871366 **Fax:** 01970 871125
**Email:** holidaysales.brynowen@park-resorts.com
www.park-resorts.com
**Pitches For** ⚎ **Total** 16
**Facilities** ⏚ ⊞ ⌂ ⏦ ▯ ⏤ ⌂ ⊡ ⏛
♨ ⏚ ⊗ ✕ ⏁ ⋏ ⊞ ⤧ ♿ ⋇
**Nearby Facilities** ⏁ ⟋
**Open** Easter **to** Oct
**Access** Good **Site** Sloping
Close to the National Library of Wales, Centre for Alternative Technology and King Arthurs Labyrinth.
**Nearest Town/Resort** Aberystwyth
**Directions** Turn off the A487 between Aberystwyth and Machynlleth onto the B4353, park is located here.
✈ Borth

## BORTH

**Glanlerry Caravan Park,** Borth, Ceredigion, SY24 5LU
**Tel:** 01970 871413
**Email:** cath.richards.gcp@talk21.com
www.glanlerrycaravanpark.co.uk
**Pitches For** ▲ ⚎ ⌂
**Facilities** ⏚ ⟋ ⊞ ⌂ ▯ ⏤ ⌂ ⊡
⊞ ⏚ ⊗ ⊞ ⋏ ⊞ ⊞ ⋇ ⏚ ∪ ⟲ ⤢
**Nearby Facilities** ⏁ ⟋ ⚓ ∪ ⟲
**Open** April **to** October
**Access** Good **Site** Level
Family only camping site. Sheltered touring area, alongside a river bank with spectacular scenery. ½ a mile from the beach.
**Nearest Town/Resort** Borth
✈ Borth

## BORTH

**Ty Mawr Holiday Home & Touring Park,** Ynyslas, Borth, Ceredigion, SY24 5LB
**Tel:** 01970 871327
**Pitches For** ▲ ⚎ ⌂ **Total** 20
**Facilities** ⏚ ⊞ ⌂ ⏦ ▯ ⏤ ⌂ ⊡ ⏛ ⏚
⊞ ⏚ ⊗ ⊞ ⋏ ⊞ ⋇ ⏚
**Nearby Facilities** ⏁ ⟋ ⚓ ⌖ ∪ ⟲ ⤢ ⏁
**Acreage** 4 **Open** March **to** September
**Access** Good **Site** Level
Fabulous views. NO club, just peace and quiet. Close to a nature reserve and the beach for safe bathing. David Bellamy Gold Award for Conservation. Booking is essential.
**Nearest Town/Resort** Aberystwyth/Borth
**Directions** Take the A487 from Machynlleth or Aberystwyth, turn onto the B4353 at Tre'r-Ddol signposted Borth and Ynyslas. After 2 miles Ty Mawr is on the left.
✈ Borth

## CARDIGAN

**Allt-y-Coed,** St Dogmaels, Cardigan, Ceredigion, SA43 3LP
**Tel:** 01239 612673
**Pitches For** ▲ ⚎ ⌂
**Facilities** ⊞ ⌂ ⏁ ⏦ ⤧
**Nearby Facilities** ⏁ ⟋ ⚓ ⌖ ∪ ⟲ ⤢ ⟲
**Acreage** 2 **Open** All Year
**Access** Good **Site** Level
Pembrokeshire coast path goes past the site. Dolphins, seals, falcons, rare birds, wild flowers and panoramic views. Long and short term parking for walks along the coastal path. Ample parking. You can also contact us on Mobile Telephone 07970 221548.
**Nearest Town/Resort** Cardigan
**Directions** Cardigan/St. Dogmaels/Poppit Sands coast road from Poppit Sands, past Youth Hostel for 1 mile. Over the cattle grid and follow coastal footpath signs. Ordanance Survey Grid Ref : (Sheet 145) 135 495. Narrow lane from Poppit Sands, NOT suitable for big caravans.
✈ Fishguard

# CARDIGANSHIRE

## CARDIGAN

**Blaenwaun Caravan Park**, Mwnt, Verwig, Cardigan, Ceredigion, SA43 1QF
**Tel:** 01239 612165/613456
**Email:** eleriblaenwaun@btinternet.com
www.blaenwaunfarm.com
**Pitches For** ▲ ⊕ �§ **Total** 20
**Facilities** ⚫ ⛽ ⓦ ♨ ⌐ ☉ ⌙ ▣ 回 ☂
♨ 回 ⊜ ⋔ ⊞ ▣ ⅍
**Nearby Facilities** ⌐ ✔ ⌶ ➘ ∪ ♫ ⚲
**Acreage** 7 **Open** March to October
**Access** Good **Site** Level
¼ mile from a Blue Flag, award winning beach.
**Nearest Town/Resort** Cardigan
**Directions** From Cardigan take the B4548 for 3½ miles.
⇌ Carmarthen

## CARDIGAN

**Brongwyn Mawr Caravan Park,**
Brongwyn Mawr, Penparc, Cardigan, Ceredigion, SA43 1SA
**Tel:** 01239 613644
**Email:** enquiries@cardiganholidays.co.uk
www.cardiganholidays.co.uk
**Pitches For** ▲ ⊕ ➧ **Total** 20
**Facilities** ⛽ ⓦ ♨ ⌐ ☉ ⌙ ▣ 回 ☂
♨ ⚚ ✕ ♠ ⋔ ⅍ ⊞ ▣ 回
**Nearby Facilities** ⌐ ✔ ⌶ ➘ ∪ ♫
**Acreage** 2 **Open** March to October
**Access** Good **Site** Level
Secluded park in the countryside. Ideal location to explore, discover and enjoy. Only 2½ miles from a beautiful beach where you can sometimes see the Dolphins.
**Nearest Town/Resort** Cardigan
**Directions** 2½ miles north of Cardigan on the A487, turn left at the crossroads in Penparc signed Mwnt and Ferwig. Go straight across the next crossroads and the park is the next lane on the right.
⇌ Aberystwyth/Carmarthen

## CARDIGAN

**Penralltllyn Caravan Park**, Cilgerran, Cardigan, Ceredigion, SA43 2PR
**Tel:** 01239 682350
**Pitches For** ▲ ⊕ ➧ **Total** 20
**Facilities** ⛽ ⓦ ♨ ⌐ ☂
**Nearby Facilities** ⌐ ✔ ⌶ ➘ ∪ ♫
**Acreage** 1 **Open** Easter to Sept/Oct
Approx. 15 minutes from lots of beaches. Plenty of woodland walks and lakes in the valley.
**Nearest Town/Resort** Cardigan
**Directions** 3 miles south east of Cardigan on the A484 (Cardigan to Carmarthen road). Turn over the bridge at Llechryd, site is 1 mile from the bridge.
⇌ Carmarthen

## DEVILS BRIDGE

**Erwbarfe Farm Caravan Park**, Devils Bridge, Aberystwyth, Ceredigion, SY23 3JR
**Tel:** 01970 890665
**Email:**
priscilla@erwbarfefarmcaravanpark.freeserve.co.uk
**Pitches For** ▲ ⊕ ➧ **Total** 50
**Facilities** ⛽ 🔥 ⓗ ⓦ ♨ ⌐ ☉ ⌙ 回 ⚚ ⊞ ⅍
**Nearby Facilities** ⌐ ✔ ∪ ♫
**Acreage** 5 **Open** March to Oct
**Access** Good **Site** Level
Ideal for hill walking, bird watching and fishing. Red Kite area. Near Nant-Yr-Arian Mountain Biking Centre.
**Nearest Town/Resort** Aberystwyth
**Directions** From Aberystwyth take the A44, in Ponterwyd turn right onto the A4120. Site is between Ponterwyd and Devils Bridge.
⇌ Aberystwyth

## DEVILS BRIDGE

**Woodlands Caravan Park**, Devils Bridge, Aberystwyth, Ceredigion, SY23 3JW
**Tel:** 01970 890233 **Fax:** 01970 890233
**Email:** woodlandscp@btclick.com
www.woodlandsdevilsbridge.co.uk
**Pitches For** ▲ ⊕ ➧ **Total** 60
**Facilities** ⛽ ⓗ ⓦ ♨ ⌐ ☉ ☂
♨ ⅍ 回 ⊜ ✕ ♠ ⋔ ♨ ⊞ 回 ⅍
**Nearby Facilities** ⌐ ✔ ∪
**Acreage** 8 **Open** Easter to October
**Access** Good **Site** Level
Quiet country site adjoining farm. Excellent mountain bike trail nearby and bike shelter on site. Ideal for walking, bird watching touring, fishing.
**Nearest Town/Resort** Devils Bridge
**Directions** 12 miles East of Aberystwyth on A4120 in Devils Bridge village and 300yds from bridge. Or 3 miles south west of Ponterwyd, turn off A44 at Ponterwyd.
⇌ Devils Bridge

## LAMPETER

**Hafod Brynog Caravan Park**, Ystrad Aeron, Felinfach, Lampeter, Ceredigion, SA48 8AE
**Tel:** 01570 470084
**Email:** amies@hafodbrynog.fsnet.co.uk
**Pitches For** ▲ ⊕ ➧ **Total** 30
**Facilities** ⛽ ⓦ ♨ ⌐ ☉ ⌙ 回 ☂
回 ⚚ ⊜ ♠ ⋔ ⊞ ⅍
**Nearby Facilities** ⌐ ✔ ⌶ ➘ ∪ ♪ ♫
**Acreage** 8 **Open** Easter to End Sept
**Access** Good **Site** Lev/Slope
A quiet site with beautiful views. 6 miles from Cardigan Bay. Ideal for coastal and inland touring, or just relaxing.
**Nearest Town/Resort** Aberearon
**Directions** On the main A482 Lampeter to Aberaeron road, 6 miles from both. Site entrance is opposite the church and next to the pub in the village of Ystrad Aeron.
⇌ Aberystwyth

## LLANARTH

**Shawsmead Caravan Club Site**, Oakford, Llanarth, Ceredigion, SA47 0RN
**Tel:** 01545 580423
www.caravanclub.co.uk
**Pitches For** ⊕ ➧ **Total** 46
**Facilities** ⚫ ⛽ ⓗ ⓦ ♨ ⌐ ☉ ⌙ 回 ☂
回 ☉ ⋔ ⊞ 回
**Nearby Facilities** ⌐ ✔ ⌶ ➘
**Acreage** 4 **Open** March to Oct
**Access** Good **Site** Level
Peaceful meadowland site with pleasant views of the coast and Cardigan Bay. 4 miles from the coast. Ideal for bird watching including Red Kite. Close to two cheese factories and local craft centres. Non members welcome. Booking essential.
**Nearest Town/Resort** Llanarth
**Directions** From the A487, in Llwyncelyn turn onto the B4342 signposted Ystrad Aeron. At the crossroads go straight on, site is 1¼ miles on the right.
⇌ Llanarth

## LLANON

**Woodlands Caravan Park**, Llanon, Nr Aberystwyth, Ceredigion, SY23 5LX
**Tel:** 01974 202342
**Email:**
ianlampert@dolcledan300.fsnet.co.uk
**Pitches For** ▲ ⊕ ➧ **Total** 40
**Facilities** ⛽ ⓗ ⓦ ♨ ⌐ ☉ ⌙ 回 ☂
♨ 回 ⊞ 回
**Nearby Facilities** ⌐ ✔ ➘ ∪ ♫
**Acreage** 4 **Open** April to October
**Access** Good Site Level

Tree screened site with a small river. 250 yards from the beach, 300 yards from the main road.
**Nearest Town/Resort** Aberaeron
**Directions** 5 miles north of Aberaeron on the A487, turn left at the sign.
⇌ Aberystwyth

## LLANRHYSTUD

**Morfa Caravan Park**, Morfa, Llanrhystud, Ceredigion, SY23 5BU
**Tel:** 01974 202253 **Fax:** 01974 202352
**Email:** morfa@morfa.net
www.morfa.net
**Pitches For** ▲ ⊕ ➧ **Total** 30
**Facilities** ⛽ ⓗ ⓦ ♨ ⌐ ☉ ⌙ 回 ☂
♨ 回 ⊜ ♠ ⋔ ⊞ ⅍
**Nearby Facilities** ⌐ ⌶ ∪ ♫
**Open** April to Oct
**Access** Good **Site** Level
Alongside the beach with a tennis court, snooker room and slipway for boats.
**Nearest Town/Resort** Aberystwyth
**Directions** 9 miles south of Aberystwyth on the A470. In Llanrhystud turn right opposite the petrol station, site is ¾ miles.
⇌ Aberystwyth

## LLANRHYSTUD

**Pengarreg Caravan Park**, Llanrhystud, Ceredigion, SY23 5DJ
**Tel:** 01974 202247
**Pitches For** ▲ ⊕ ➧ **Total** 50
**Facilities** ⚫ ⛽ ⓗ ⓜ ⓦ ♨ ⌐ ☉ ⌙ 回 ☂
♨ 回 ⊜ ✕ ♈ ⋔ ♨ ⊞ ⅍
**Nearby Facilities** ⌐ ✔ ⌶ ➘ ∪ ♫
**Acreage** 6 **Open** 1 March to 2 Jan
On the beach and by a river in Llanrhystud Village. Hill walks. Boating ramp.
**Nearest Town/Resort** Aberystwyth
**Directions** 9 miles south of Aberystwyth on the A487.
⇌ Aberystwyth

## NEW QUAY

**Cardigan Bay Camping & Caravanning Club Site**, Llwynhelyg, Cross Inn, Ceredigion, SA44 6LW
**Tel:** 01545 560029
www.campingandcaravanningclub.co.uk
**Pitches For** ▲ ⊕ ➧ **Total** 90
**Facilities** ⚫ ⛽ ⓗ ⓦ ♨ ⌐ ☉ ⌙ 回 ☂
♨ 回 ⊜ ⋔ ⊞ 回
**Nearby Facilities** ✔ ➘ ∪ ♫
**Acreage** 14 **Open** March to Oct
**Access** Difficult **Site** Lev/Slope
Near to golden beaches, forests and lakes. 3 miles from horse racing and close to many attractions. BTB 4 Star Graded and AA 3 Pennants. Non members welcome.
**Directions** From the A487 Cardigan to Aberystwyth road, at Synod Inn turn left onto the A486 signposted New Quay. After 2 miles in the village of Cross Inn turn left after the Penrhiwgated Arms Pub, site is on the right after approx. ¾ miles.
⇌ Aberystwyth

## NEW QUAY

**Cei Bach Country Club**, Parc-Y-Brwcs, Cei Bach, New Quay, Ceredigion, SA45 9SL
**Tel:** 01545 580237 **Fax:** 01545 580237
**Email:** paul@ceibach.freeserve.co.uk
www.cei-bach.co.uk
**Pitches For** ▲ ⊕ ➧ **Total** 60
**Facilities** ⛽ ⓗ ⓦ ♨ ⌐ ☉ ⌙ 回 ☂
♨ 回 ⊜ ✕ ▽ 回 ♠ ⋔ ♨ ⊞ ⅍
**Nearby Facilities** ⌐ ✔ ⌶ ➘ ∪ ♪ ♫ ⚲
**Acreage** 3 **Open** 1 March to 9 Jan
**Access** Poor **Site** Lev/Slope
Great views of the coast line, safe sandy beach. Coastal walk to Aberaeron.

**Nearest Town/Resort** New Quay
**Directions** From the A487 take the B4342 or New Quay. Follow the road to Quay-West and Cambrian Hotel crossroads, take the road signed for Cei Bach.
✈ Aberystwyth

## NEW QUAY
**Frondeg Caravan Park,** Gilfachreda, Nr New Quay, Ceredigion, SA45 9SP
**Tel:** 01545 580444
**Email:** stevehartley.cbmwc@tiscali.co.uk
**Pitches For** ♚ ➡ **Total** 10
**Facilities** ⚹ ✿ ➡ ☏ ⊙ ⤵ 🖭 ☕
🏠 🛈 ⬤➡🖭 ⚶
**Nearby Facilities** ⌐ ✔ ⚓ ⚄ ∪ ♬ ♬
**Acreage** 1 **Open** Easter **to** October
**Access** Good **Site** Level
Quiet, secluded site near a small river leading to safe, sandy bathing beaches, 10 minutes walk. New Quay harbour town, 2 miles by road. You can also telephone us on Mobile 07796 135490.
**Nearest Town/Resort** New Quay
**Directions** Take A487 from Aberystwyth to Llanarth, then take the B4342 to New Quay for approx. 1 mile to Gilfachreda Village.
✈ Aberystwyth

## NEW QUAY
**Tydu Vale Caravan Park,** Pantrhyn, Cwmtodu, Llwyndafydd, Ceredigion, SA44 6LH
**Tel:** 01545 560494
**Pitches For** ♚ ➡ ➡
**Facilities** ⚹ ✿ ☏ ⊙ ☕ 🏠 🛈 ⚹ ☒ Ⓜ ➡🖭 ⚶
**Nearby Facilities** ⌐ ✔ ⚓ ⚄ ∪ ♬ ♬
**Open** March **to** Oct
**Access** Good **Site** Sloping
200 yards from the beach and a shop. Great for small children and walkers.
**Nearest Town/Resort** New Quay
**Directions** 3½ miles from New Quay and the A487.
✈ Aberystwyth

## NEW QUAY
**Wern Mill Camping Site,** Gilfachreda, New Quay, Ceredigion, SA45 9SP
**Tel:** 01545 580699
**Pitches For** ♚ ➡ ➡ **Total** 50
**Facilities** ⚹ ✿ 🖭 ➡ ☏ ⊙ ⤵ ☕
🏠 🛈 ⬤➡🖭 ⚶
**Nearby Facilities** ⌐ ✔ ⚓ ⚄ ∪ ♬ ♬
**Acreage** 2½ **Open** Easter **to** October
**Access** Good **Site** Level
Very sheltered, family site. ½ mile from two sandy beaches. Idyllic walks. Ideal centre for touring Mid Wales.
**Nearest Town/Resort** New Quay
**Directions** From Aberystwyth take the A487 via Aberaeron to Llanarth. Gilfachrheda is located 1½ miles from Llanarth on the B4342

to New Quay road.
✈ Aberystwyth

## NEWCASTLE EMLYN
**Cenarth Falls Holiday Park,** Cenarth, Newcastle Emlyn, Ceredigion, SA38 9JS
**Tel:** 01239 710345 **Fax:** 01239 710344
**Email:** enquiries@cenarth-holipark.co.uk
www.cenarth-holipark.co.uk
**Pitches For** ♚ ➡ ➡ **Total** 30
**Facilities** ⚹ ⚹ ✿ 🖭 ➡ ☏ ⊙ ⤵ 🖭 ☕ 🖭 ☕
🏠 🛈 ⬤ ☒ ⊼ 🏠 ♬ ➡🖭 ⊟ ☕
**Nearby Facilities** ⌐ ✔ ⚓ ⚄ ∪
**Acreage** 2 **Open** March **to** 17 Dec
**Access** Good **Site** Level
Ideal touring location for the coast and countryside. Near Coastal National Park. Indoor swimming pool with sauna, steam rooms, jacuzzi and leisure suite. Holders of numerous awards including Wales in Bloom, Calor Gas Best Park in Britain Award and David Bellamy Gold Award for Conservation.
**Nearest Town/Resort** Newcastle Emlyn
**Directions** 3 miles west of Newcastle Emlyn on the A484. Cross Cenarth Bridge and travel for ¼ mile, turn right at directional signs for the park.
✈ Carmarthen

## SARNAU
**Brynawelon Touring & Camping Park,** Sarnau, Llandysul, Ceredigion, SA44 6RE
**Tel:** 01239 654584
**Email:** info@brynaweloncp.co.uk
www.brynaweloncp.co.uk
**Pitches For** ♚ ➡ ➡ **Total** 40
**Facilities** ⚹ ✿ 🖭 ➡ ☏ ⊙ ⤵ ☕
🏠 🛈 ⬤ 🏠 Ⓜ ➡🖭 ⚶
**Nearby Facilities** ✔ ⚓ ∪
**Acreage** 3 **Open** March **to** October
**Access** Good **Site** Level
Quiet family site with rural surroundings. 2 miles from Penbryn Beach.
**Nearest Town/Resort** Cardigan
**Directions** Travelling north on A487 take a right turn at Sarnau crossroads, site is 550yds on the left.
✈ Carmarthen

## SARNAU
**Dyffryn Bern Caravan Park,** Penbryn, Sarnau, Llandysul, Ceredigion, SA44 6RD
**Tel:** 01239 810900 **Fax:** 01239 811835
**Email:** enquiries@dyffryn.com
**Pitches For** ♚ ➡ ➡
**Facilities** 🖭 ➡ ☏ ⊙ ⤵ 🖭 ☕ 🏠 ♬
**Nearby Facilities** ⌐ ✔ ⚓ ⚄ ∪ ♬
**Acreage** 14 **Open** March **to** October
**Access** Poor **Site** Sloping
**Nearest Town/Resort** Cardigan
**Directions** Off the A487.
✈ Aberystwyth

## SARNAU
**Manorafon Caravan Park,** Sarnau, Llandysul, Ceredigion, SA44 6QH
**Tel:** 01239 810564 **Fax:** 01239 810564
**Email:** info@manorafonholidaypark.co.uk
www.manorafonholidaypark.co.uk
**Pitches For** ♚ ➡ ➡ **Total** 15
**Facilities** ⚹ 🖭 ➡ ☏ ⊙ ⤵ 🖭 ☕
🏠 🛈 ⬤ 🏠 ➡🖭 ⚶
**Nearby Facilities** ⌐ ✔ ⚓ ⚄ ∪ ♬ ♬
**Acreage** 1½ **Open** 1 March **to** 8 Jan
**Access** Average **Site** Sloping
Set in a wooded valley, good for families. ¾ mile from Penbryn beach. Ideal camping and touring for birdwatchers, golfers and walkers. Static caravans and log cabins available to let.
**Nearest Town/Resort** Cardigan
**Directions** Take the A487 north from Cardigan for 7 miles to Tanyagroes, go through the village, second road on the left signed Penbryn/Tresaith. After ½ mile take the first right, after ¾ mile turn second left, we are 200 yards on the right.
✈ Aberystwyth

## SARNAU
**Treddafydd Farm,** Treddafydd, Sarnau, Llandysul, Ceredigion, SA44 6PZ
**Tel:** 01239 654551
**Pitches For** ♚ ➡ ➡ **Total** 10
**Facilities** ⚹ 🖭 ➡ ☏ ⊙ ⤵ 🖭 ☕
**Nearby Facilities** ⌐ ✔ ⚓ ∪
**Acreage** 1 **Open** May **to** Sept
**Access** Good **Site** Sloping
1 mile from sandy Penbryn beach.
**Nearest Town/Resort** Cardigan
**Directions** 1 mile from the A487, in the village of Sarnau turn by the church then first left.
✈ Carmarthen/Aberystwyth

# CARMARTHENSHIRE
## CARMARTHEN
**Coedhirion Farm Parc,** Coedhirion, Llanddarog, Carmarthen, Carmarthenshire, SA32 8BH
**Tel:** 01267 275666
**Pitches For** ♚ ➡ ➡ **Total** 20
**Facilities** ⚹ ✿ 🖭 ➡ ☏ ⊙ ⤵ ☕
🏠 🛈 ⬤➡🖭 ⚶ ♬ ⤵
**Nearby Facilities** ⌐ ✔ ⚓
**Acreage** 5 **Open** Easter **to** Christmas
**Access** Good **Site** Level
Quiet, convenient, woodland site. 5 minutes from the National Botanical Garden of Wales.
**Nearest Town/Resort** Carmarthen
**Directions** 9 miles west of the M4 junction 49, just off the A48 dual carriageway, 6 miles east of Carmarthen.
✈ Carmarthen

# CARMARTHENSHIRE

## CARMARTHEN

**Pant Farm Touring Caravan & Camping Park,** Llangunnor Road, Carmarthen, Carmarthenshire, SA31 2HY
**Tel:** 01267 235665
**Pitches For** ▲ ⊡ ⊟ **Total** 60
**Facilities** ! ⬛ ⚲ ⌐ ⌟ ⚲⊟⊟▲ ⚘
**Nearby Facilities** ⌐ ⚲ ⊿ ⚲ ∪ ♪
**Acreage** 2 **Open** March to Dec
**Access** Good **Site** Level
ADULTS ONLY SITE. Within walking distance of the town. Major shopping centre. Ideal touring base for Southern Wales.
**Nearest Town/Resort** Carmarthen
**Directions** On the B4300 north east of the old Carmarthen Bridge.
⚉ Carmarthen

## CLYNDERWEN

**Derwenlas,** Clynderwen, Carmarthenshire, SA66 7SU
**Tel:** 01437 563504
**Pitches For** ▲ ⊡ ⊟ **Total** 4
**Facilities** ! ⬛ ⚲ ⌐ ⊙ ⚲ ⊡ ⊟
⚋ ⚑ ⊙ ⊟ ⊟ ⊟ ⚘
**Nearby Facilities** ⌐ ⚲ ⊿ ⚲ ∪
**Open** April to September
**Access** Good **Site** Level
**Nearest Town/Resort** Narberth
**Directions** 3 to 3½ miles north of Narberth on the A478.
⚉ Clynderwen

## CROSS HANDS

**Black Lion Caravan & Camping Park,** 78 Black Lion Road, Gorslas, Cross Hands, LlanelliCarmarthenshire, SA14 6RU
**Tel:** 01269 845365
**Email:** blacklionsite@aol.com
**www.** caravansite.com
**Pitches For** ▲ ⊡ ⊟ **Total** 40
**Facilities** ⚋ ! ⊟ ⬛ ⚲ ⌐ ⊙ ⌟ ⚲ ⊡ ⊟
⚋ ⚑ ⊙ ⚊ ⊟ ⚲⊟ ⚘ ♪
**Nearby Facilities** ⌐ ⚲
**Acreage** 7 **Open** April to Oct
**Access** Good **Site** Lev/Slope
Botanic Garden of Wales, Aberglasney a Garden Lost in Time. Four seater spa bath. David Bellamy Silver Award for Conservation.
**Nearest Town/Resort** Cross Hands
**Directions** From Cross Hands follow the brown tourism signs.
⚉ Swansea

## KIDWELLY

**Carmarthen Bay Touring & Camping,** Tanylan Farm, Kidwelly, Carmarthenshire, SA17 5HJ
**Tel:** 01267 267306
**Email:** tanylanfarm@aol.com
**www.** tanylanfarmholidays.co.uk
**Pitches For** ▲ ⊡ ⊟ **Total** 50
**Facilities** ⚋ ! ⬛ ⚲ ⌐ ⊙ ⌟ ⚊ ⊟ ⊟
⚋ ⚑ ⊙ ⚊ ⊟ ⊟ ⊟ ⚘
**Nearby Facilities** ⌐ ⚲ ∪ ♪
**Acreage** 4 **Open** Easter to End Sept
**Access** Good **Site** Level
Level ground on a dairy farm. 200 yards from the beach. Membership to Park Resorts.
**Nearest Town/Resort** Kidwelly
**Directions** In Kidwelly turn left at the Spar Supermarket, take the coastal road to Ferryside for approx. 1 mile and turn left at the duck pond.
⚉ Kidwelly

## LAUGHARNE

**Broadway Caravan Park,** Broadway, Laugharne, Carmarthenshire, SA33 4NU
**Tel:** 01994 427272 **Fax:** 01994 427272
**Pitches For** ▲ ⊡ ⊟ **Total** 6
**Facilities** ⚲ ⌐ ⚑ ⊟ ⊙ ⚊⊟
**Nearby Facilities** ⌐ ⚲ ⊿ ⚲ ∪ ♪ ⚲
**Acreage** 2
**Access** Good **Site** Level
**Nearest Town/Resort** Laugharne
**Directions** Take the A4066 from St. Clears to Laugharne, continue to Pendine and site is ½ mile on the left.
⚉ Carmarthen

## LLANDDEUSANT

**Blaenau Farm,** Llanddeusant, Llangadog, Carmarthenshire, SA19 9UN
**Tel:** 01550 740277
**Pitches For** ▲ ⊡ ⊟ **Total**
**Facilities** ⬛ ⊟
**Nearby Facilities** ⚲ ⚲
**Open** Easter to October
**Access** Poor
Extensive mountain farm site.
**Nearest Town/Resort** Llandovery
**Directions** Approx. 20 miles from the M4.
⚉ Llangadog

## LLANDDEUSANT

**The Black Mountain Caravan & Camping Park,** Llanddeusant, Llangadog, Carmarthenshire, SA19 9YG
**Tel:** 01550 740217 **Fax:** 01550 740621/ 740217
**Email:** davidandsharon@blackmountainholidays.co.uk
**www.** blackmountainholidays.co.uk
**Pitches For** ▲ ⊡ ⊟ **Total** 50
**Facilities** ! ⬛ ⊟ ⚲ ⌐ ⊙ ⌟ ⚊ ⊟ ⊟
⚋ ⚑ ⊟ ⊟
**Nearby Facilities** ⌐ ⚲ ∪
**Acreage** 6½ **Open** All Year
**Access** Good **Site** Lev/Slope
Ideal for walking, fishing and caving.
**Nearest Town/Resort** Llandovery
**Directions** Take the A40 to Llangadog then the A4069 signposted Brynaman. Turn left at a disused pub (Three Horseshoes) and continue for 3½ miles to Cross Inn.
⚉ Llandovery

## LLANDOVERY

**Camping & Caravanning Club Site,** Rhandirmwyn, Llandovery, Carmarthenshire, SA20 0NT
**Tel:** 01550 760257
**www.** campingandcaravanningclub.co.uk
**Pitches For** ▲ ⊡ ⊟ **Total** 90
**Facilities** ⚋ ! ⊟ ⬛ ⚲ ⌐ ⊙ ⌟ ⚊ ⊟ ⊟
⊟ ⊟ ⚑ ⊟ ⊟ ⊟ ⚘ ♪
**Nearby Facilities** ⚲
**Acreage** 11 **Open** March to Oct
**Access** Good **Site** Level
Set in the beautiful Welsh countryside on the banks of the Afon Tywi. Ideal for fishing. BTB 4 Star Graded, AA 3 Pennants, David Bellamy Silver Award and Loo of the Year Award. Non members welcome.
**Nearest Town/Resort** Llandovery
**Directions** From Llandovery take the A483, turn left signposted Rhandirmwyn. Turn left at the Post Office in Rhandirmwyn, site on the left before the river.
⚉ Llandovery

## LLANDOVERY

**Erwlon Caravan & Camping Park,** Brecon Road, Llandovery, Carmarthenshire, SA20 0RD
**Tel:** 01550 720332
**Email:** peter@erwlon.fsnet.co.uk
**www.** ukparks.co.uk/erwlon
**Pitches For** ▲ ⊡ ⊟ **Total** 75
**Facilities** ⚋ ! ⊟ ⬛ ⚲ ⌐ ⊙ ⌟ ⚊ ⊟ ⊟
⚋ ⚑ ⊙ ⚊ ⊟ ⊟ ⚘
**Nearby Facilities** ⌐ ⚲ ∪ ♪
**Acreage** 5 **Open** All Year
**Access** Good **Site** Level
Alongside a river and adjoining the Brecon Beacons National Park. Good public transport. Ideal touring.
**Nearest Town/Resort** Llandovery
**Directions** ½ a mile east of Llandovery on the A40 towards Brecon.
⚉ Llandovery

## LLANGADOG

**Abermarlais Caravan Park,** Nr Llangadog, Carmarthenshire, SA19 9NG
**Tel:** 01550 777868
**www.** ukparks.co.uk/abermarlais
**Pitches For** ▲ ⊡ ⊟ **Total** 88
**Facilities** ! ⊟ ⬛ ⚲ ⌐ ⊙ ⌟ ⚊ ⊟
⚋ ⚑ ⊙ ⚊ ⊟ ⚲⊟ ⊟ ⊟
**Nearby Facilities** ⚲ ∪ ♪
**Acreage** 16 **Open** 15 March to 1 Nov
**Access** Good **Site** Lev/Slope
Alongside a river with scenic views.
**Nearest Town/Resort** Llandovery
**Directions** 6 miles west of Llandovery and 6 miles east of Llandeilo on the A40.
⚉ Llangadog

## NEWCASTLE EMLYN

**Afon Teifi Caravan & Camping Park,** Pentrecagal, Newcastle Emlyn, Carmarthenshire, SA38 9HT
**Tel:** 01559 370532
**Email:** afon.teifi@virgin.net
**www.** afonteifi.co.uk
**Pitches For** ▲ ⊡ ⊟ **Total** 110
**Facilities** ⚋ ! ⊟ ⬛ ⚲ ⌐ ⊙ ⌟ ⚊ ⊟ ⊟
⚋ ⚑ ⊙ ⚊ ⊟ ⚲⊟
**Nearby Facilities** ⌐ ⚲ ♪
**Acreage** 6½ **Open** March to October
**Access** Good **Site** Level
Situated by the River Teifi in the beautiful Teifi Valley. Only 20 minutes from numerous Cardigan Bay beaches. Swimming nearby. Ideal touring centre.
**Nearest Town/Resort** Newcastle Emlyn
**Directions** On the A484 2 miles east of Newcastle Emlyn.
⚉ Carmarthen

## NEWCASTLE EMLYN

**Dolbryn Farm,** Capel Iwan Road, Newcastle Emlyn, Carmarthenshire, SA38 9LP
**Tel:** 01239 710683
**Email:** dolbryn@btinternet.com
**www.** http://uk.geocities.com/dolbryn@btinternet.com
**Pitches For** ▲ ⊡ ⊟ **Total** 40
**Facilities** ⚋ ! ⊟ ⬛ ⚲ ⌐ ⊙ ⌟ ⚊ ⊟ ⊟
⚑ ⚲ ⊟ ⊟ ⊟ ⚘
**Nearby Facilities** ⌐ ⚲ ∪
**Acreage** 4 **Open** Easter to October
**Access** Good **Site** Lev/Slope
Idyllic country site with stream, lakes, hills, etc..
**Nearest Town/Resort** Newcastle Emlyn
**Directions** Turn left off the A484 Carmarthen to Cardigan road at Newcastle Emlyn signposted leisure centre & swimming pool. Follow camping signs for 1½ miles.
⚉ Carmarthen

## NEWCASTLE EMLYN

**Moelfryn Caravan & Camp Park,** Pant-Y-wlch, Newcastle Emlyn, Carmarthenshire, A38 9JE
**Tel:** 01559 371231 **Fax:** 01559 371231
**Email:** moelfryn@tinyonline.co.uk
**Pitches For** ▲ ⚏ ⚏ **Total** 25
**Facilities** ⌁ ⌂ ⌦ ♨ ⌁ ⊙ ⌣ ⬚
**Nearby Facilities** ⌁ ✓ ⚲ ⤢ ⚓ U
**Acreage** 3 **Open** 1 March **to** 10 Jan
**Access** Good **Site** Level
Situated in a tranquil, rural setting with panoramic views for relaxation. Perfect base for exploring the beauty of West Wales.
**Nearest Town/Resort** Newcastle Emlyn
**Directions** From Carmarthen take the A484 to Cynwyl Elfed. Pass the Blue Bell Inn and take the left fork after approx. 200 yards B4333 towards Hermon and stay on this road for 7 miles. There is a brown sign on your left, take that turn and site is ¼ mile on the right.
⚑ Carmarthen

## PEMBREY

**Pembrey Country Park Caravan Club Site,** Pembrey, Llanelli, Carmarthenshire, SA16 0EJ
**Tel:** 01554 834369
**www.** caravanclub.co.uk
**Pitches For** ▲ ⚏ ⚏ **Total** 130
**Facilities** ⅊ ⌁ ⌂ ⌦ ♨ ⌁ ◻ ⬚
⌦ ⊙ ⚏ ⌂ ⌦ ⌦ ⬚
**Nearby Facilities** ⌁ ✓ ⚲ ⤢ U
**Acreage** 12 **Open** March **to** Jan
**Access** Good **Site** Level
Set on the edge of a 520 acre country park. Vast range of outdoor sporting activities available including horse riding, dry slope skiing and toboggan riding, pitch 'n' putt and sea fishing. Ideal for walkers and bird/butterfly watchers. Only 1 mile from a Blue Flag sandy beach. Non members welcome. Booking essential.
**Nearest Town/Resort** Llanelli
**Directions** Leave M4 at junc 48 and take A4138 signposted Llanelli, on the outskirts of Llanelli turn right onto A484. In Pembrey Village turn left at signpost Pembrey Country Park and follow signs to Country Park, site is on the right before park gates.
⚑ Llanelli

## PUMSAINT

**Ogofau Caravan Club Site,** Pumsaint, Llanwrda, Carmarthenshire, SA19 8US
**Tel:** 01558 650365
**Email:** dolaucothi@nationaltrust.org.uk
**Pitches For** ⚏ ⚏ **Total** 34
**Facilities** ⌁ ⌂ ⬚ ⌦ ⌦ ◻ ⬚ ⬚
**Nearby Facilities** ✓ U
**Acreage** 4 **Open** March **to** Oct
**Access** Good **Site** Level
Beautiful setting at the foothills of the Cambrian Mountains, adjacent to the old Roman Gold Mines. Red Kite country by the River Cothi with woodland, flowers and abundant wildlife. Short drive to The National Botanical Garden of Wales. Own sanitation required. Non members welcome. Booking essential.
**Nearest Town/Resort** Pumsaint
**Directions** From the A40, in Llanwrda take the A482 signposted Lampeter. After 7¾ miles turn right at National Trust sign, site is just past the crossroads on the left.

## ST. CLEARS

**Afon Lodge Caravan Park,** Parciau Bach, St Clears, Carmarthenshire, SA33 4LG
**Tel:** 01994 230647
**Email:** yvonne@afonlodge.f9.co.uk
**www.** http://fp.afonlodge.f9.co.uk
**Pitches For** ▲ ⚏ ⚏ **Total** 35
**Facilities** ⌁ ⌂ ⌦ ♨ ⌁ ⊙ ⌣ ◻ ⬚
⌦ ⌦ ⌂ ⌦ ⌦ ◻ ⬚
**Nearby Facilities** ⌁ ✓ ⚲ ⤢ U
**Acreage** 7 **Open** March **to** 9 January
**Access** Good **Site** Lev/Slope
Beautiful tranquil site, ideal touring. T.V. Hook-up.
**Nearest Town/Resort** St. Clears
**Directions** From St. Clears traffic lights take Llanboidy Road. In a 100 yards fork right, then first right, first right.
⚑ Whitland

# CONWY

## ABERGELE

**Gwrych Towers Camp,** Llandulas Road, Abergele, Conwy, LL22 8ET
**Tel:** 01745 832109
**Pitches For** ▲ ⚏ ⚏
**Facilities** ⅊ ⌁ ⌦ ⌁ ⊙ ⚏ ⌦ ⬚
**Nearby Facilities** ⌁ ✓ ⚲
**Acreage** 3 **Open** Spring Bank Hol **to** Beg. Sept
**Access** Good **Site** Level
Near the beach, shops and a golf club. Excellent for touring holiday resorts and enjoying the Welsh scenery. You can also telephone us on: 01829 260210.
**Nearest Town/Resort** Abergele
**Directions** ¼ mile from Abergele on the B5443. Main entrance to Gwrych Castle is also entrance to site.
⚑ Abergele/Pensarn

## ABERGELE

**Owen's Caravan Park,** Gainc Bach, Towyn Road, Towyn, AbergeleConwy, LL22 9ES
**Tel:** 01745 353639
**Pitches For** ⚏ ⚏ **Total** 12
**Facilities** ⌁ ⌦ ⌁ ⊙ ⚏ ◻ ⬚ ⚏ ⌦ ⌂ ⌦
**Nearby Facilities** ⌁ ✓ U
**Open** April **to** October
**Access** Good **Site** Level
**Nearest Town/Resort** Rhyl
**Directions** 2 miles from Rhyl on the coast road to Abergele.
⚑ Rhyl

## ABERGELE

**Roberts Caravan Park,** Waterloo Service Station, Penrefail Cross Roads, Abergele, Conwy, LL22 8PN
**Tel:** 01745 833265
**Email:** gailyroberts@btinternet.com
**Pitches For** ⚏ ⚏ **Total** 40
**Facilities** ⌁ ⌂ ⌦ ♨ ⌁ ⊙ ⌣ ⬚
⌦ ◻ ⌦ ⚏ ⬚
**Nearby Facilities** ⌁ ✓ ⤢ U ♪ ⚲
**Open** Mid March **to** End Oct
**Access** Good **Site** Lev/Slope
A quiet, tidy site with a well stocked shop. Near the beach and within easy reach of the Snowdonia mountain range.
**Nearest Town/Resort** Abergele
**Directions** From Abergele take the A548 Llanrwst road for 2 miles, at the crossroads of the B5381 turn left towards St. Asaph, site is 100 yards on the right of the junction.
⚑ Rhyl

## ABERGELE

**Ty Mawr Holiday Park,** Towyn Road, Towyn, Abergele, Conwy, LL22 9HG
**Tel:** 01745 832079 **Fax:** 01745 827454
**Email:** holidaysales.tymawr@park-resorts.com
**www.** park-resorts.com
**Pitches For** ▲ ⚏ ⚏ **Total** 280
**Facilities** ⌁ ⌂ ⌦ ♨ ⌁ ⊙ ⌣ ⬚ ◻ ⬚
⌦ ◻ ⚏ ✕ ♀ ⌂ ⚑ ⚏ ⬚ ⬚ ⌦ ◻ ⬚
**Nearby Facilities**
**Open** March **to** Oct
**Site** Level
Close to the fun and amusements of seaside Rhyl and scenic Snowdonia.
**Nearest Town/Resort** Rhyl
**Directions** Take the A55 to North Wales past Prestatyn and Rhyl. Leave the dual carriageway at Abergele turning and follow the A548 to Towyn. Park is ¼ of a mile on the right.
⚑ Rhyl

## BETWS-Y-COED

**Riverside Caravan & Camping Park,** Old Church Road, Betws-y-Coed, Conwy, LL24 0AL
**Tel:** 01690 710310
**Email:** riversidecaravanpark@btinternet.com
**Pitches For** ▲ ⚏ ⚏ **Total** 120
**Facilities** ⅊ ⅊ ⌁ ⌂ ⌦ ⌁ ⊙ ⚏ ◻ ⬚
⚏ ⌦ ◻ ⬚
**Nearby Facilities** ⌁ ✓ U ♪
**Acreage** 3 **Open** 14 March **to** 31 Oct
**Access** Good **Site** Level
Adjacent to a golf course and renowned fishing river Conwy.
**Nearest Town/Resort** Betws-y-Coed
**Directions** In the centre of Betws-y-Coed.
⚑ Betws-y-Coed

## BETWS-Y-COED

**Rynys Farm Camping Site,** Rynys Farm, Nr Betws-y-Coed, Llanrwst, Conwy, LL26 0RU
**Tel:** 01690 710218
**Email:** carol@rynys-camping.co.uk
**www.** rynys-camping.co.uk
**Pitches For** ▲ ⚏ ⚏
**Facilities** ⌦ ⌁ ⌁ ⊙ ⚏ ⚏ ◻
**Nearby Facilities**
**Acreage** 6 **Open** All Year
**Access** Good **Site** Level
Very scenic and peaceful site with excellent clean facilities. Central for touring.
**Nearest Town/Resort** Betws-y-Coed
**Directions** 2 miles south of Betws-y-Coed Left by Conway Falls, 200yds from A5.
⚑ Betws-y-Coed

## BETWS-Y-COED

**Tyn Rhos Caravan Park,** Tyn Rhos Farm, Pentrefoelas, Betwys-y-Coed, Conwy, LL24 0LN
**Tel:** 01690 770655 **Fax:** 01690 770655
**Email:** tudur.jones@farming.co.uk
**Pitches For** ⚏ ⚏ **Total** 20
**Facilities** ⌁ ⌦ ⌁ ⚏ ⌦
**Nearby Facilities** ⌁ ✓ ⚲ ⤢ U ⌂
**Open** April **to** October
**Access** Good **Site** Level
Ideal for Snowdonia's mountains and walking. Ideal for touring North Wales. No tents, sorry. Booking by telephone.
**Nearest Town/Resort** Betws-y-Coed
**Directions** 4½ miles from Betws-y-Coed along the A5, in the village of Pentrefoelas.
⚑ Betws-y-Coed

## COLWYN BAY

**Bron-Y-Wendon Touring Caravan Park,** Wern Road, Llanddulas, Colwyn Bay, Conwy, LL22 8HG
**Tel:** 01492 512903 **Fax:** 01492 512903
bron-y-wendon@northwales-holidays.co.uk
www. northwales-holidays.co.uk
**Pitches For** ♥ ♥ **Total** 130
**Facilities** ♿ ⚡ ╏ ⌂ ⛺ ▟ ⌐ ⊙ ◀ ◢ ▣ ☎
♨ ⍢ ⌾ ⓞ ⛿ ⑪ ♠ ╅ ▣ ◻ ▣ ⍬
**Nearby Facilities** ┏ ✔ ⚓ ⅄ ∪ ♪ ♫ ⚡
**Acreage** 8 **Open** All Year
**Access** Good **Site** Lev/Slope
All pitches have coastal views. Just a short walk to the beach. Site is ideal for seaside and touring. 5 Star Graded Park, Welcome Host Gold Award and Top 100 Park.
**Nearest Town/Resort** Colwyn Bay
**Directions** Follow the A55 into North Wales

and take the Llanddulas junction (A547), junction 23. Follow tourist information signs to the park.
⇌ Colwyn Bay

## CONWY

**Conwy Touring Park,** Conwy, LL32 8UX
**Tel:** 01492 592856 **Fax:** 01492 580024
**Email:** sales@conwytouringpark.com
www. conwytouringpark.com
**Pitches For** ⚑ ♥ ♥ **Total** 300
**Facilities** ♿ ⚡ ╏ ▣ ⌂ ⛺ ▟ ⌐ ⊙ ◀ ◢ ▣
▣ ☎ ⍢ ⌾ ⓞ ♠ ⑪ ╅ ▣ ◻ ⌀
**Nearby Facilities** ┏ ✔ ⚓ ⅄ ∪ ♪ ♫ ⚡
**Acreage** 70 **Open** Easter
Scenic views, ideal for touring Snowdonia.
**Nearest Town/Resort** Conwy
⇌ Conwy

## CONWY

**Tyn Terfyn Touring Caravan Park,** Tal Y Bont, Conwy, LL32 8YX
**Tel:** 01492 660525
**Email:** glentynterfyn@tinyworld.co.uk
**Pitches For** ▲ ♥ ♥ **Total** 15
**Facilities** ♿ ⚡ ╏ ▣ ⛺ ⌐ ⊙ ◀ ◢ ▣ ☎
⍢ ⌾ ♠ ╅ ▣
**Nearby Facilities** ┏ ✔ ⚓ ⅄ ∪ ♪ ♫ ⚡
**Acreage** 2 **Open** 14 March **to** October
**Access** Good **Site** Level
Scenic views, good walking, fishing and boating. Ideal touring location.
**Nearest Town/Resort** Conwy
**Directions** From Conwy travel 5 miles (approx) on the B5106 until road sign for Tal y-Bont. First house on the left after sign.

## CONWY

**Wern Farm Caravan Park,** Wern Farm,
Bryn-Y-Groes, Conwy, LL32 8SY
Tel: 01492 650257
Pitches For ⊡ ⊞ Total 24
Facilities ↑ ⌂ Ⓤ ♨ ⌐ ☺♥ ☞⊡
Nearby Facilities ⌐ ✓ ⚓ Ⓤ ⚘
Acreage 2½ Open 14 March to 31 Oct
Access Good Site Sloping
Nearest Town/Resort Conwy
Directions Take the A55 to Conwy then the
B5106 signposted Trefriw. Site is 4 miles (1
mile past the Groes Inn).
⚞ Llandudno Junction

## LLANRWST

**Bodnant Caravan Park,** Nebo Road,
Llanrwst, Conwy Valley, Conwy, LL26 0SD
Tel: 01492 640248
Email: ermin@bodnant-caravan-
park.co.uk
www. bodnant-caravan-park.co.uk
Pitches For ⚑ ⊡ ⊞ Total 54
Facilities ↑ ⚡ ∫ ⊟ ⓊⒷ ♨ ⌐ ☺ ⌐⚐ ☞
☏ ⓪ ☺ ⌂♨⊡
Nearby Facilities ⌐ ✓ ⚓ ⚘ Ⓤ ⚘ ☒ ⚘
Acreage 4 Open March to October
Access Good Site Level
Small, quiet, pretty farm site. Ideal touring
centre. 26 times Winner of Wales in
bloom. 8 multi service pitches. 2 holiday
caravans for hire.
Nearest Town/Resort Llanrwst
Directions Turn off the A470 south in
Llanrwst onto the B5427 signposted Nebo.
Site is 300 yards on the right, opposite the
leisure centre.
⚞ Llanrwst

## LLANRWST

**Glyn Farm Caravans,** Trefriw, Llanrwst,
Conwy, LL27 0RZ
Tel: 01492 640442
Pitches For ⊡ ⊞ Total 28
Facilities ↑ ⊟ ⓊⒷ ♨ ⌐ ☺♨ ☞ ☒⚐⊡
Nearby Facilities ⌐ ✓ Ⓤ ⚘
Open March to October
Access Good Site Level
Beautiful walking country. Centrally
situated for Snowdonia attractions and the
coastal resorts of Llandudno, Colwyn Bay
and the Isle of Anglesey.
Nearest Town/Resort Llanrwst
Directions On the B5106 Betws-y-Coed to
Conwy road, Trefriw Village is 4 miles from
Betws-y-Coed and 8 miles from Conwy. Turn
into the village car park opposite Trefriw
Woollen Mills, site is 200 yards from the main
road.
⚞ Llanrwst

## PENMAENMAWR

**Trwyn Yr Wylfa Farm,** Trwyn Yr Wylfa,
Penmaenmawr, Conwy, LL34 6SF
Tel: 01492 622357
Pitches For ⚑ ⊞ Total 100
Facilities ⚡⚡ ⓊⒷ ⌐ ☺♨
Nearby Facilities ⌐ ✓ ⚓ ⚘ Ⓤ ⚘ ☒
Acreage 10 Open Spring Bank Holiday to
End Aug
Site Level
Secluded site in Snowdonia National Park.

Nearest Town/Resort Penmaenmawr
Directions Leave the A55 at junction 16 for
Penmaenmawr. Turn by Mountain View
Hotel, farm is ¼ mile east.
⚞ Penmaenmawr

## PENMAENMAWR

**Tyddyn Du Touring Park,** Conwy Old
Road, Penmaenmawr, Conwy, LL34 6RE
Tel: 01492 622300 Fax: 01492 622300
www. tyddyndutouringpark.co.uk
Pitches For ⚑ ⊡ ⊞ Total 100
Facilities ⚡ ↑ ∫ ⊟ ⓊⒷ ♨ ⌐ ☺⚐ ☞ ⚐ ⊡
☏ ⓪ ☺⌐ ☒⊡ ⚐ ⚑
Nearby Facilities ⌐ ✓ ⚓ ⚘ Ⓤ ⚘
Acreage 5 Open 22 March to 31 Oct
Access Good Site Lev/Slope
ADULTS ONLY site overlooking Conwy
Bay to Llandudno and Anglesey. NEW
toilet, shower and laundry block added in
2002. Close to the A55 so ideal for touring
Snowdonia.
Nearest Town/Resort Penmaenmawr
Directions 1 mile east of Penmaenmawr.
Take the A55 from Conwy and turn left at the
roundabout after the Little Chef and sharp
left again. Site access is on the right after
Legend Inn.
⚞ Penmaenmawr

## TY-NANT

**Glan Ceirw Caravan Park,** Ty Nant,
Corwen, Conwy, LL21 0RF
Tel: 01490 420346
Email:
glanceirwcaravanpark@tinyworld.co.uk
www. ukparks.com/glanceirw
Pitches For ⚑ ⊡ ⊞ Total 10
Facilities ∫ ⊟ ⓊⒷ ♨ ⌐ ☺⚐ ☞ ⌐⊡ ☞
☏ ☏ ⚑ ☒ ☺ ☒⌐♨☞⊡ ⚒
Nearby Facilities ✓ ⚓ ⚘ ☒
Acreage 1 Open March to October
Access Good Site Level
Picturesque site bordering Snowdonia
National Park. Ideal for touring North and
West Wales.
Nearest Town/Resort Corwen/Betws-y-
Coed
Directions Between Corwen and Betws-y-
Coed just off the A5. Coming from Betws-y-
Coed take the second right after
Cerrigydrudion over a small bridge and
300yds along the lane. From Corwen turn
left after Glan Ceirn signs over a small bridge,
300yds on the left.
⚞ Ruabon

# DENBIGHSHIRE

## CORWEN

**Hendwr Caravan Park,** Llandrillo, Corwen,
Denbighshire, LL21 0SN
Tel: 01490 440210
www. hendwrcaravanpark.freeserve.co.uk
Pitches For ⚑ ⊡ ⊞ Total 40
Facilities ∫ ⓊⒷ ♨ ⌐ ☺⚐ ☞ ⌐⊡ ☞
☒☏ ⌂ ⓪ ☺ ⌂♨⊡ ⚒ ⚒
Nearby Facilities ⌐ ✓ ⚓ ⚘ ⚘
Acreage 2¼ Open April to October
Access Good Site Level
Alongside a river, good walking and fishing.
Wonderful views and an excellent touring
centre for North Wales.

Nearest Town/Resort Corwen/Bala
Directions From Corwen (A5) take the
B4401 for 4 miles, turn right at sign Hendwr.
Site is on the right in ¼ mile. From Bala take
the A494 for 1½ miles, turn right onto the
B4401 via Llandrillo. Site is 1 mile north on
the left.
⚞ Ruabon

## DENBIGH

**Caer Mynydd Park,** Saron, Denbigh,
Denbighshire, LL16 4TL
Tel: 01745 550302 Fax: 01745 550179
Email: kathcaermynydd@aol.com
www.ukparks.com
Pitches For ⚑ ⊡ ⊞ Total 18
Facilities ↑ ∫ ⓊⒷ ♨ ⌐ ☺⊡ ☞
☏ ⚑ ⌂♨⊡
Nearby Facilities ⌐ ✓ ⚓ ⚘ Ⓤ ⚘
Acreage 2 Open March to Oct
Access Good Site Level
Close to Denbigh Moors and Lake Brenig.
Good walking and cycling country. Approx.
15 miles to the nearest coastal resort.
Nearest Town/Resort Denbigh
Directions From the A525 Denbigh to Ruthin
road, at Denbigh Sports Ground turn into
Ystrad Road. Stay on this road for approx. 5
miles.

## DENBIGH

**Station House Caravan Park,** Bodfari,
Denbigh, Denbighshire, LL16 4DA
Tel: 01745 710372
Pitches For ⚑ ⊡ ⊞ Total 26
Facilities ∫ ⓊⒷ ♨ ⌐ ☺⚐ ☞ ☞
☒☏ ⚑ ⌂♨⊡
Nearby Facilities ⌐ ✓ Ⓤ
Acreage 2 Open April to October
Access Good Site Level
Attractive site with scenic views. Ideal touring
centre. Offa's Dyke path 400yds. Close to two
inns (400yds). WTB 3 Star Graded.
Nearest Town/Resort Denbigh
Directions From the A541 Mold to Denbigh
road, turn onto the B5429 in the direction of
Tremeirchion. Site is immediately on the left
by cream house.
⚞ Rhyl

## LLANFERRES

**Bryn-Bowlio Caravan Park,** Tafarn-Y-
Gelyn, Llanferres, Near Mold,
Denbighshire, CH7 5SQ
Tel: 01352 810484 Fax: 01352 810715
Email: brynbowliofarm@tiscali.uk
www.brynbowliocaravanpark.co.uk
Pitches For ⚑⚐ Total 6
Facilities ↑ ∫ ⓊⒷ ♨ ⌐ ☺⊡ ☞ ⚑ ⚘☞⌐⊡
Nearby Facilities ⌐ ✓ Ⓤ
Acreage 3 Open March to Oct
Access Good Site Level
Quiet countryside site in an area of
oustanding natural beauty. . Near
Loggerheads Country Park and Moel
Farm. Great area for hill wlaking.
Nearest Town/Resort Mold
Directions From Mold take the A494 towards
Ruthin. ½ a mile past Loggerheads turn right
signposted Tafarn-Y-Gelyn/Moel Farm. Site
is 500 yards on the left.
⚞ Wrexham

## LLANGOLLEN

**Ddol Hir Caravan Park,** Pandy Road, Glyn Ceiriog, Llangollen, Denbighshire, LL20 7PD
**Tel:** 01691 718681
www.ukparks.co.uk
**Pitches For** ⚠ ⌂ 🚐 **Total** 25
**Facilities** ∮ 🚻 ⚓ ⌂ ☉ 💀 ⛟
🏪 🅾 🚿⇩🖃 ⚡
**Nearby Facilities** ⌂ ✈ ∪ 🅿 ⚘
**Acreage** 6 **Open** March **to** October
**Access** Good **Site** Level
Riverside site in a scenic valley with mountain views. Trout fishing and pony trekking. Within walking distance of shops and pubs.
**Nearest Town/Resort** Llangollen
**Directions** Turn off the A5 at Chirk onto the B4500, park is on the left approx. 6 miles, just through the village of Glyn Ceiriog.
⚡ Chirk

## LLANGOLLEN

**Ty-Ucha Caravan Park,** Maesmawr Road, Llangollen, Denbighshire, LL20 7PP
**Tel:** 01978 860677
**Pitches For** ⌂ 🚐 **Total** 40
**Facilities** ⚡ ∮ 🚻 ⚓ ⌂ ☉ 🚐 🅾 ⚓🖃
**Nearby Facilities** ⌂ ✈ ∪ ⚘
**Acreage** 5 **Open** Easter **to** October
**Access** Good **Site** Level
Quiet site with outstanding panoramic views. Ideal for walking and touring.
**Nearest Town/Resort** Llangollen
**Directions** 1 mile east of Llangollen on the A5, 200 yards signposted.
⚡ Ruabon

## LLANGOLLEN

**Wern Isaf Caravan & Camping Park,**
Wern Isaf Farm, Llangollen, Denbighshire, LL20 8DU
**Tel:** 01978 860632
**Email:** wernisaf@btopenworld.com
www.wernisaf.supanet.com
**Pitches For** ⚠ ⌂ 🚐
**Facilities** ⚓ ∮ 🖻 🚻 🚻 ⚓ ⌂ ☉ 🚐 ⛟
🏪 🅾 🖃🚿 ⚡
**Nearby Facilities** ⌂ ✈ ⚓ ⤬ ∪ 🅿 ⚘
**Acreage** 4 **Open** Easter **to** October
**Access** Good **Site** Lev/Slope
Quiet and very scenic site overlooking Llangollen. Ideal for touring North Wales. Nearby we have horse riding, a steam railway, white water rafting and very scenic walks.
**Nearest Town/Resort** Llangollen
**Directions** In Llangollen turn up behind Bridge End Hotel, go over the canal bridge and turn right into Wern Road, site is ½ a mile on the right.
⚡ Ruabon

## PRESTATYN

**Nant Mill Farm Caravan & Tenting Park,** Nant Mill, Prestatyn, Denbighshire, LL19 9LY
**Tel:** 01745 852360
**Email:** nantmilltouring@aol.com
www.zeropointfive.co.uk/nant_mill/
**Pitches For** ⚠ ⌂ 🚐 **Total** 150
**Facilities** ⚓ ∮ 🚻 ⚓ ⌂ ☉ 💀 ⚓ 🅾 ⛟
🏪 🅾 ⚓ 🖃 ⚓🖃 ⚡
**Nearby Facilities** ⌂ ✈ ⚓ ⤬ ∪ 🅿 ⚘
**Acreage** 5 **Open** Easter **to** October
**Access** Good **Site** Lev/Slope
Near town shops. ½ mile beach, ideal to tour north Wales. Restaurant/bar 200 yards away.
**Nearest Town/Resort** Prestatyn
**Directions** ½ mile east of Prestatyn on A548 coast road.
⚡ Prestatyn

## PRESTATYN

**Presthaven Sands Holiday Park,** Shore Road, Gronant, Prestatyn, Denbighshire, LL19 9TT
**Tel:** 01745 856471 **Fax:** 01745 886646
www.touringholidays.co.uk
**Pitches For** ⌂ 🚐 **Total** 97
**Facilities** ∮ 🖻 🚻 ⚓ ⌂ ☉ 💀 ⛟
🏪 🅾 🅾 ✕ 🛏 📷 ⚓ ⚓🖃 🅾 ⛟
**Nearby Facilities** ⌂ ✈ ⚓ ⤬ ∪ 🅿 ⚘
**Acreage** 12 **Open** Easter **to** Oct
**Access** Good **Site** Level
Alongside 2 miles of beaches and sand dunes.
**Nearest Town/Resort** Prestatyn/Rhyl
**Directions** Take the A548 out of Prestatyn towards Gronant. The park is signposted left, then entrance is ½ mile further on the right.
⚡ Prestatyn/Rhyl

## RHYL

**Clwyd View Touring Park,** Marsh Road, Rhuddlan, Rhyl, Denbighshire, LL18 5UB
**Tel:** 01745 590841
**Email:** viv@clwydview.co.uk
www.clwydview.co.uk
**Pitches For** ⚠ ⌂ 🚐 **Total** 72
**Facilities** ⚓ ∮ 🚻 ⚓ ⌂ ☉ 💀 🅾 ⛟
🏪 🅾 🖃 ⚡
**Nearby Facilities** ⌂ ✈ ∪ 🅿 🅿
**Acreage** 2½ **Open** Easter **to** Oct
**Access** Good **Site** Level
Near the River Clwyd for fishing and 3 miles from the beach. Within walking distance of a castle.
**Nearest Town/Resort** Rhyl
**Directions** 3 miles from Rhyl on the A525.
⚡ Rhyl

## RUTHIN

**Dyffryn Ial Caravan Site,** Troell Yr Alun, Llanarmon-Yn-Ial, Near Mold, Denbighshire, CH7 5TA
**Tel:** 01824 780286 **Fax:** 01824 780286
**Pitches For** ⌂ 🚐
**Facilities** ∮ 🚻 🚻 ⌂ 🏪 ⚡
**Nearby Facilities** ⌂ ✈ ∪
**Open** April to Sept
**Access** Good **Site** Level
Alongside the River Alyn in an area of outstanding natural beauty. Near Offa's Dyke walk and Country Park Loggerheads. Over 100 walks in the area. Ideal for touring North Wales.
**Nearest Town/Resort** Mold/Ruthin
⚡ Wrexham

## ST. ASAPH

**Penisar Mynydd Caravan Park,** Caerwys Road, Rhuallt, St Asaph, Denbighshire, LL17 0TY
**Tel:** 01745 582227 **Fax:** 01745 582227
**Email:** penisarmynydd@btinternet.com
**Pitches For** ⚠ ⌂ 🚐 **Total** 75
**Facilities** ⚓ ∮ 🖻 🚻 🚻 ⚓ ⌂ ☉ 💀 ⚓ 🅾 ⛟
🏪 🅾 ⚓🖃 ⚓ 🅿
**Nearby Facilities** ⌂ ✈ ⚓ ∪
**Acreage** 6 **Open** 1 March **to** 15 Jan
**Access** Good **Site** Sloping
Quiet, rural park. Close to Rhyl and Prestatyn. Ideal for touring the main A55 coastal route to Holyhead.
**Nearest Town/Resort** Prestatyn
**Directions** Leave the A55 Chester to Bangor road at junction 29, park is 500 yards on the right.
⚡ Prestatyn

# FLINTSHIRE

## GRONANT

**Greenacres Caravan Park,** Shore Road, Gronant, Flintshire, LL19 9SS
**Tel:** 01745 854061 **Fax:** 01745 887898
info@greenacrescaravanpark.fsnet.co.uk
**Pitches For** ⌂ 🚐 **Total** 40
**Facilities** ⚓ ∮ 🚻 🚻 ⚓ ⌂ ☉
🏪 🅾 ✕ 🅿 📷 ⚓ ⚓ 🖃
**Nearby Facilities** ⌂ 🅿
**Open** 1 March **to** 31 Oct
**Access** Good **Site** Level
500 yards from the beach. Two licensed premises with live entertainment. Health suite and swimming pool.
**Nearest Town/Resort** Prestatyn
**Directions** 2 miles from Prestatyn off the main A548 coast road.
⚡ Prestatyn

## MOLD

**Fron Farm Caravan & Camping Site,** Fron Farm, Hendre, Mold, Flintshire, CH7 5QW
**Tel:** 01352 741482
**Email:** dylanceriroberts@btinternet.com
**Pitches For** ⚠ ⌂ 🚐 **Total** 40
**Facilities** ⚓ ∮ 🖻 ⌂ 🅾 🏪 🅾 📷 🛏 ⚡
**Nearby Facilities** ✈ ∪
**Acreage** 5 **Open** April **to** Oct
**Access** Good **Site** Lev/Slope
Farm site with animals to see and scenic views. Lovely walks. Ideal touring. No need to book. You can also call us on Mobile: 07710 596463.
**Nearest Town/Resort** Mold/Holywell
**Directions** A541 between Denbigh and Mold, take sign for Rhes-Y-Cae. Fron Farm is the third turning on the right including farm lanes.
⚡ Flint/Chester

# GWYNEDD

## ABERDARON

**Mur Melyn Camping Site,** Mur Melyn, Aberdaron, Pwllheli, Gwynedd, LL53 8LW
**Tel:** 01758 760522
**Pitches For** ⚠ ⌂ 🚐 **Total** 60
**Facilities** 🚻 ⌂ ☉ 🖃🛏
**Nearby Facilities** ✈ ⚓ ⤬ ∪
**Acreage** 2½ **Open** Whitsun **to** September
**Access** Good **Site** Level
Near the beach and a river with scenic views. Ideal for touring Wales.
**Nearest Town/Resort** Pwllheli
**Directions** Take A499 west from Pwllheli then fork onto to B4413 at Llanbedrog about 3 miles before Aberdaron take Whistling Sand road. Turn left at Pen-y-Bont House to site ½ mile.
⚡ Pwllheli

## ABERDARON

**Tir Glyn Caravan Park,** Tir Glyn Farm, Uwchmynydd, Aberdaron, PwllheliGwynedd, LL53 8DA
**Tel:** 01758 760248
jrattirglynaberdaron@btopenworld.com
**Pitches For** ⚠ ⌂ 🚐 **Total** 30
**Facilities** ⚓ ∮ 🚻 ⌂ ☉ 💀 ⛟
🏪 🅾🖃 ⚡
**Nearby Facilities** ⌂ ✈ ⚓ ⤬ ∪
**Acreage** 3 **Open** May **to** October
**Access** Good **Site** Lev/Slope
Surrounded by National Trust land, overlooking the sea for scenic views. Near beaches. Local authority licence.
**Nearest Town** Aberdaron/Abersoch
**Directions** Pwllheli to Abersoch road, take the B4413 at Llanbedrog to Aberdaron. In Aberdaron Village turn right on the bridge

gned Uwchmynydd, keep left then turn first
ft, we are first farm on the left.
⇌ Pwllheli

**BERSOCH**
**each View Caravan Park,** Bwlchtocyn,
bersoch, Gwynedd, LL53 7BT
el: 01758 712956
**itches For ▲ ⌗ ⇌ Total** 47
**a cilities ⚷ ⌇ ⏍ ⚓ ⌐ ⊙ ⊿ ▣ ☂
⌗ ❤ ⛟**
**earby Facilities** ⌐ ⊿ ⚓ ↻ ∪ ⚹
**creage** 5 **Open** Mid March **to** Mid Oct
**ccess** Good **Site** Level
ear the beach. Ideal for touring, fishing,
oating, sailing, wind surfing and golf.
**earest Town/Resort** Abersoch
**irections** Drive through Abersoch and Sarn
ach, go over small crossroads and take next
ft turn signposted Porthtocyn Hotel.
ontinue past the chapel and take next left
urn, continue to Beach View.
⇌ Pwllheli

**BERSOCH**
**Beach View Caravan Park,** Bwlchtocyn,
bersoch, Gwynedd, LL53 7BT
el: 01758 712956
**itches For ▲ ⌗ ⇌ Total** 47
**a cilities ⌇ ⏍ ⚓ ⌐ ⊙ ⊿ ▣ ☂
⌗ ⊙ ❤ ▣ ⛟**
**earby Facilities** ⌐ ⊿ ⚓ ↻ ∪ ⚹ ⚹
**creage** 5 **Open** Mid March **to** Mid Oct
**ccess** Good **Site** Level
ust a very short walk to the beach. Ideal
ouring area.
**earest Town/Resort** Abersoch
**irections** Drive through Abersoch and Sarn
ach, go over the crossroads and turn next
ft signposted Bwlchtocyn and Porthtocyn
otel. Go past the chapel and take left turn
ollowing signs for Porthtocyn Hotel, Beach
iew Park is on the left.
⇌ Pwllheli

**BERSOCH**
**Deucoch Camping & Touring Site,** Sarn
ach, Abersoch, Pwllheli, Gwynedd, LL53
'LD
el: 01758 713293
**Pitches For ▲ ⌗ ⇌ Total** 68
**acilities ⚷ ⌇ ⏍ ⚓ ⌐ ⊙ ⊿ ▣ ☂
⌗ ⚙ ⛟ ▣ ⛟ ⚹**
**Nearby Facilities** ⌐ ⊿ ⚓ ↻ ∪ ⚹ ⚹
**Acreage** 5 **Open** March **to** October
**Access** Good **Site** Level
lear the beach, ideal touring and scenic
iews. Dogs are allowed on leads. Cafe/
estaurant, public telephone and licensed
club nearby.
**Nearest Town/Resort** Abersoch
**Directions** Take Sarn Bach road out of
Abersoch, continue on main road to Sarn

Bach. Turn right in the square.
⇌ Pwllheli

**ABERSOCH**
**Nant-Y-Big,** Cilan, Abersoch, Pwllheli,
Gwynedd, LL53 7DB
**Tel:** 01758 712686 **Fax:** 01758 712193
**Pitches For ▲ ⌗ ⇌ Total** 60
**Facilities ⌇ ⏍ ⚓ ⌐ ⊙ ⊿ ⏍ ▣ ❤ ▣**
**Nearby Facilities** ⌐ ⊿ ⚓ ↻ ∪ ⚹ ⚹ ⚹
**Acreage** 10 **Open** Easter **to** End Oct
200 metres from the beautiful sandy Porth
Ceiriad beach.
**Nearest Town/Resort** Abersoch
**Directions** 2½ miles south of Abersoch. Go
through the next village of Sarn Bach and
follow signposts for Cilan. After approx. 500
metres turn left at No Through Road sign.
⇌ Pwllheli

**ABERSOCH**
**Tan-y-Bryn Farm,** Tan-y-Bryn, Sarn Bach,
Abersoch, Gwynedd, LL53 7DA
**Tel:** 01758 712093
**Pitches For ▲ ⌗ ⇌**
**Facilities ⚷ ⌇ ▣ ⏍ ⚓ ⌐ ⊙ ⊿ ⚙ ▣ ☂
▣ ⛟ ▣ ⚹**
**Nearby Facilities** ⌐ ⊿ ⚓ ↻ ∪ ⚹
**Open** Easter **to** October
**Access** Good **Site** Level
**Nearest Town/Resort** Abersoch
**Directions** 1½ miles south of Abersoch.
⇌ Pwllheli

**ABERSOCH**
**Trem Y Mor,** Sarn Bach, Abersoch,
Pwllheli, Gwynedd, LL53 7ET
**Tel:** 07967 050170 **Fax:** 01758 713243
**Email:** mike.sleigh@tggroup.co.uk
www.tggroup.co.uk
**Pitches For ▲ ⌗ ⇌**
**Facilities ▲ ⌇ ⏍ ▣ ⏍ ⚓ ⌐ ⊙ ⊿ ▣ ☂ ▣
⏍ ▣ ❤ ▣ ▣ ⚹ ℘**
**Nearby Facilities** ⌐ ⊿ ⚓ ↻ ∪ ⚹
**Acreage** 5 **Open** March **to** October
**Access** Good **Site** Sloping
ADULTS ONLY SITE. 15 minutes walk to
the beach.
**Nearest Town/Resort** Abersoch
**Directions** From Abersoch take the road to
Sarn Bach. In Sarn Bach turn left at the
square, Trem Y Mor is the first site on the right.
⇌ Pwllheli

**ABERSOCH**
**Tyn-y-Mur Touring & Camping Park,** Lon
Garmon, Abersoch, Gwynedd, LL53 7UL
**Tel:** 01758 713223
**Email:** info@tyn-y-mur.co.uk
www.tyn-y-mur.co.uk
**Pitches For ▲ ⌗ ⇌**
**Facilities ⚷ ⌇ ▣ ⏍ ⚓ ⌐ ⊙ ⊿ ▣ ☂ ▣
▣ ⏍ ▣ ⚙ ▣ ⚹ ℘**

**Nearby Facilities** ⌐ ⊿ ⚓ ↻ ∪ ⚹
**Open** March **to** October
**Access** Good **Site** Level
Near the beach with superb, uninterrupted,
panoramic coastal views of Abersoch Bay
and Hell's Mouth.
**Nearest Town/Resort** Abersoch
**Directions** On the A499 Pwllheli to Abersoch
road, on approaching Abersoch turn right at
Land & Sea Services Garage, site is then ¾
miles on the left hand side.
⇌ Pwllheli

**ARTHOG**
**Garthyfog Camping Site,** Garthyfog
Farm, Arthog, Gwynedd, LL39 1AX
**Tel:** 01341 Fairbourne 250338
**Email:** abcjohnson@btinternet.com
www.garthyfog.co.uk
**Pitches For ▲ ⌗ ⇌ Total** 20
**Facilities ⏍ ⌐ ⊙ ❤ ▣**
**Nearby Facilities** ⌐ ⊿ ⚓ ↻ ∪ ⚹ ♁ ⚹
**Acreage** 5 **Open** All Year
**Site** Lev/Slope
2 miles from Fairbourne, safe bathing,
sandy beach and shops. Beautiful scenery,
panoramic views. 300 yards from main
road, sheltered from wind. Mains cold
water. Plenty of room for children to play
around the farm, rope-swing, little stream,
etc. One static caravan and two log cabins
available to let.
**Nearest Town/Resort** Barmouth/Dolgellau
**Directions** A493, 6 miles from Dolgellau, left
by Village hall, look for signs on righthand
side.
⇌ Morfa Mawddach

**ARTHOG**
**Graig-Wen,** Arthog, Gwynedd, LL39 1BQ
**Tel:** 01341 250482/250900 **Fax:** 01341
250482
**Email:** graig-wen@supanet.com
www.graig-wen.supanet.com
**Pitches For ▲ ⌗ ⇌**
**Facilities ⏍ ⚓ ⌐ ⊙ ⊿ ▣ ⚙ ❤ ▣ ⚹**
**Nearby Facilities** ⌐ ⊿ ⚓ ↻ ∪ ⚹ ♁ ⚹
**Acreage** 42
**Access** Good **Site** Lev/Slope
Land reaching down to estuary with scenic
views, woodlands and pastures. Ideal for
bird watchers, anglers, nature lovers,
walkers, cyclists and outdoor pursuits.
**Nearest Town/Resort** Fairbourne
**Directions** Between Dolgellau and
Fairbourne on the A493.

**BALA**
**Camping & Caravanning Club Site,**
Crynierth Caravan Park, Cefn-Ddwysarn,
Bala, Gwynedd, LL23 7LN
**Tel:** 01678 530324
www.campingandcaravanningclub.co.uk

# HENDRE MYNACH TOURING CARAVAN & CAMPING PARK

**AA** ⚫⚫ **SITUATED IN SOUTHERN SNOWDONIA**

Award winning site close to the beautiful Mawddach Estuary. 100 metres from a safe sandy beach. Excellent base for walking and cycling, close to Cycle Route 8. All modern amenities. Hard standings available. Pets welcome, dog walk on site. 20 min. pleasant walk along the promenade to Barmouth town centre. Bus service and train station close by. Public house with family rooms just a 20 min. walk. **Disabled facilities are now available.**

*SPECIAL OFFERS AVAILABLE SPRING & AUTUMN*
**PHONE FOR COLOUR BROCHURE**
**Barmouth, Gwynedd LL42 1YR  Tel: 01341 280262**
**www.hendremynach.co.uk  E-mail: mynach@lineone.net**

---

**Pitches For** ⚑ ⚑ ⚑ Total 50
**Facilities** ☐ ⚑ ⚑ ⚑ ⚑ ⚑ ⚑ ⚑ ⚑ ⚑ ⚑
⚑ ⚑ ⚑ ⚑ ⚑ ⚑ ⚑ ⚑
**Nearby Facilities** ⚑ ⚑ ⚑
**Acreage** 4 **Open** March **to** October
**Access** Good **Site** Level
Situated on the edge of Snowdonia National Park. 4 miles from Bala Lake. Good for watersports. Ideal touring site. BTB 5 Star Graded and AA 3 Pennants. Non members welcome.
**Nearest Town/Resort** Bala
**Directions** From the A5 turn onto the A494 to Bala. At signpost Cefn-Ddwysarn turn right before the red phone box, site is 400 yards on the left.
⚑ Ruabon

**BALA**
**Glanllyn-Lakeside Caravan & Camping Park,** Bala, Gwynedd, LL23 7ST
**Tel:** 01678 540227
**Email:** iinfo@glanllyn.com
www.glanllyn.com
**Pitches For** ⚑ ⚑ ⚑ Total 100
**Facilities** ⚑ ⚑ ⚑ ⚑ ⚑ ⚑ ⚑ ⚑ ⚑
⚑ ⚑ ⚑ ⚑ ⚑ ⚑ ⚑ ⚑
**Nearby Facilities** ⚑ ⚑ ⚑ ⚑ ⚑ ⚑ ⚑
**Acreage** 14 **Open** Easter **to** October
**Access** Good **Site** Level
Level parkland with trees. Alongside a lake and river, large launching area for sailing.
**Nearest Town/Resort** Bala
**Directions** 3 miles south west of Bala on the A494, situated on the left alongside Bala Lake.
⚑ Wrexham

**BALA**
**Pen Y Bont Touring & Camping Park,** Llangynog Road, Bala, Gwynedd, LL23 7PH
**Tel:** 01678 520549 **Fax:** 01678 520006
**Email:** penybont@balalake.fsnet.co.uk
www.penybont-bala.co.uk
**Pitches For** ⚑ ⚑ ⚑ Total 95
**Facilities** ☐ ⚑ ⚑ ⚑ ⚑ ⚑ ⚑ ⚑ ⚑ ⚑
⚑ ⚑ ⚑ ⚑ ⚑ ⚑ ⚑ ⚑
**Nearby Facilities** ⚑ ⚑ ⚑ ⚑ ⚑ ⚑ ⚑
**Acreage** 6 **Open** March **to** October
**Access** Good **Site** Level
Nearest park to Bala (10 minute walk) and near to a sailing club. Free showers, separate vanity cubicles and washing areas all under cover. 4 Star Excellent Grading and AA 4 Pennants.
**Nearest Town/Resort** Bala
**Directions** ½ mile from Bala on B4391 to Llangynog.
⚑ Ruabon

**BALA**
**Ty-Isaf Camping Site,** Llangynog Road, Bala, Gwynedd', LL23 7PP
**Tel:** 01678 520574
**Pitches For** ⚑ ⚑ ⚑ Total 30
**Facilities** ⚑ ⚑ ⚑ ⚑ ⚑ ⚑ ⚑ ⚑ ⚑
⚑ ⚑ ⚑ ⚑ ⚑ ⚑
**Nearby Facilities** ⚑ ⚑ ⚑ ⚑ ⚑ ⚑
**Acreage** 2 **Open** April/Easter **to** Oct
**Access** Good **Site** Level
Working farm alongside a stream. Ideal touring.
**Nearest Town/Resort** Bala
**Directions** 2½ miles southeast of Bala on the B4391, near the telephone kiosk and post box.
⚑ Ruabon

**BALA**
**Tyn Cornel Camping & Caravan Park,** Frongoch, Bala, Gwynedd, LL23 7NU
**Tel:** 01678 520759 **Fax:** 01678 520759
**Email:** peter.tooth@talk21.com
www.tyncornel.co.uk
**Pitches For** ⚑ ⚑ ⚑ Total 37
**Facilities** ⚑ ⚑ ⚑ ⚑ ⚑ ⚑ ⚑ ⚑ ⚑ ⚑ ⚑ ⚑
**Nearby Facilities** ⚑ ⚑ ⚑ ⚑ ⚑ ⚑
**Acreage** 10 **Open** March **to** Oct
**Access** Good **Site** Level
Beside the River Tryweryn. Ideally situated for touring North Wales.
**Nearest Town/Resort** Bala
**Directions** 4 miles from Bala on the A4212 Porthmadog road.
⚑ Ruabon

**BANGOR**
**Dinas Farm Camping Site,** Dinas Farm, Halfway Bridge, Bangor, Gwynedd, LL57 4NB
**Tel:** 01248 364227/354614
www.dinasfarmtouringpark.co.uk
**Pitches For** ⚑ ⚑ ⚑ Total 35
**Facilities** ⚑ ⚑ ⚑ ⚑ ⚑ ⚑ ⚑ ⚑ ⚑
⚑ ⚑ ⚑ ⚑ ⚑ ⚑ ⚑ ⚑
**Nearby Facilities** ⚑ ⚑ ⚑ ⚑ ⚑
**Acreage** 4 **Open** Easter **to** October
**Access** Good **Site** Level
Alongside the River Ogwen for salmon and trout fishing (permits sold). Centrally situated for mountains and beaches.
**Nearest Town/Resort** Bangor
**Directions** Take the A5 from the A55 roundabout towards Bethesda, 3 miles south of Bangor turn right at Halfway Bridge towards Tregarth, first farm on the left. 2 miles north of Bethesda.
⚑ Bangor

**BARMOUTH**
**Benar Beach Camping & Touring Site,** Talybont, Barmouth, Gwynedd, LL43 2AR
**Tel:** 01341 247001/247571
**Pitches For** ⚑ ⚑ ⚑
**Facilities** ☐ ⚑ ⚑ ⚑ ⚑ ⚑ ⚑ ⚑ ⚑
⚑ ⚑ ⚑ ⚑ ⚑ ⚑ ⚑
**Nearby Facilities** ⚑ ⚑ ⚑ ⚑ ⚑ ⚑ ⚑
**Acreage** 9 **Open** March **to** October
**Access** Good **Site** Level
Friendly family site 100 yards from miles c golden sand dunes. Ideal base for touring Snowdonia.
**Nearest Town/Resort** Barmouth
**Directions** 5 miles north of Barmouth on th A496 turn left by Llanddwywe Church ½ mil after Talybont Village, site is 100 yards fron the beach on the left.
⚑ Dyffryn Arduudwy

**BARMOUTH**
**Hendre Mynach Touring Caravan & Camping Park,** Barmouth, Gwynedd, LL4 1YR
**Tel:** 01341 280262
**Email:** mynach@lineone.net
www.hendremynach.co.uk
**Pitches For** ⚑ ⚑ ⚑ Total 200
**Facilities** ⚑ ⚑ ⚑ ⚑ ⚑ ⚑ ⚑ ⚑ ⚑ ⚑ ⚑
⚑ ⚑ ⚑ ⚑ ⚑ ⚑ ⚑ ⚑ ⚑ ⚑
**Nearby Facilities** ⚑ ⚑ ⚑ ⚑ ⚑ ⚑ ⚑
**Acreage** 10 **Open** 1 March **to** 9 Jan
**Access** Good **Site** Level
100yds from a safe, sandy beach, 20 minute walk down the promenade to Barmouth tow centre. An excellent base for estuary an mountain walks. Pubs nearby with children room. Near to cycle route 8.
**Nearest Town/Resort** Barmouth
**Directions** ½ a mile north of Barmouth or the A496 Barmouth to Harlech road.
⚑ Barmouth

**BARMOUTH**
**Islwrffordd Caravan Park,** E G Evans & Sons Ltd, Tal-y-Bont, Nr Barmouth, Gwynedd, LL43 2AQ
**Tel:** 01341 247269 **Fax:** 01341 242639
**Email:** info@islawrffordd.co.uk
www.islawrffordd.co.uk
**Pitches For** ⚑ ⚑ ⚑
**Facilities** ⚑ ⚑ ⚑ ⚑ ⚑ ⚑ ⚑ ⚑ ⚑ ⚑ ⚑
⚑ ⚑ ⚑ ⚑ ⚑ ⚑ ⚑ ⚑ ⚑ ⚑ ⚑
**Nearby Facilities** ⚑ ⚑ ⚑ ⚑ ⚑
**Open** March **to** Dec
**Access** Good **Site** Level
Next to the beach with no roads or railway lines to cross.
**Nearest Town/Resort** Barmouth
**Directions** Just off the A496 approx. 4½ miles north of Barmouth in the village of Tal y-Bont.
⚑ Tal-y-Bont

## ARMOUTH

**arc Isaf Farm,** Dyffryn Ardudwy, wynedd, LL44 2RJ
**el:** 01341 247447 **Fax:** 01341 247447
**tches For** ▲ ⚑ ☵ **Total** 30
**acilities** ⌁ ⚏ ☺ ⊙ ♣ ☵
**earby Facilities** ✎ ⚲ ∪ ↑
**creage** 3 **Open** March **to** October
**ccess** Good **Site** Lev/Slope
verlooking Cardigan Bay. Plenty of ountain and woodland walks, Harlech astle and Portmeirion (Italian village).
**earest Town/Resort** Barmouth
**rections** From Barmouth take the A496 north r 5 miles, go through the small village of lybont, ¼ mile on opposite the church on the ft there is a right hand turn through pillar teway. Second farm on the right, signposted.
 Dyffryn Ardudwy/Talybont

## EDDGELERT

**eddgelert - Forestry Commission,** eddgelert, Gwynedd, LL55 4UU
**el:** 0131 314 6505
**mail:** info@forestholidays.co.uk
**ww.**forestholidays.co.uk
**tches For** ▲ ⚑ ☵ **Total** 280
**acilities** ⚒ ⌁ ⚏ ♣ ⌐ ⊙ ⊣ ☵ ▣ ☻
▨ ⊡ ☷ ⋒ ⊣⧠☐ ☵
**earby Facilities** ⚲ ∪ ↑
**creage** 23½ **Open** 1 Jan **to** 1 Nov
**ccess** Good **Site** Level
 the heart of Snowdonia, within walking stance of Snowdon itself. Walking, rcling and canoeing also nearby. New otorhome drive-over waste point.
**earest Town/Resort** Beddgelert
**irections** 1 mile north of Beddgelert Village
 the A4085.

## AERNARFON

**ryn Gloch Caravan & Camping Park,** etws Garmon, Caernarfon, Gwynedd, -54 7YY
**el:** 01286 650216 **Fax:** 01286 650591
**mail:** eurig@bryngloch.co.uk
**ww.**bryngloch.co.uk
**itches For** ▲ ⚑ ☵ **Total** 150
**acilities** ⚒ ⌁ ⚏ ⊞ ⊡ ♣ ⌐ ⊙ ⊣ ⊿ ▣ ☻
▨ ⊡ ⋒ ⋒⧠☐ ☵
**earby Facilities** ✎ ⚲ ⚴ ∗ ∪ ⚹ ↑
**creage** 28 **Open** March **to** Oct
**ccess** Good **Site** Level
ward winning site with scenic views. lenty of flat and mountain walks in the rea. Ideal touring centre. Family owned nd operated. AA 4 Pennants and AA Best ampsite in Wales 2005.
**earest Town/Resort** Caernarfon
**irections** 4½ miles south west of aernarfon on A4085. Site on right opposite etws Garmon church.

## CAERNARFON

**Challoner Caravan Park,** Erw Hywel Farm, Llanrug, Caernarfon, Gwynedd, LL55 2AJ
**Tel:** 01286 672985
**Email:** suechallcouk@supanet.com
**Pitches For** ▲ ⚑ ☵ **Total** 35
**Facilities** ⚒ ⊞ ⚏ ⌐ ⊙ ⌐ ☵⊣☐
**Nearby Facilities** ✎ ⚲ ⚴ ∗ ∪ ♣ ↑
**Open** 1 March **to** 1 Jan
**Access** Good **Site** Level
Ideal for touring Snowdonia. 3 miles from Caernarfon Castle. Bus service runs every 20 minutes from the bottom of the drive.
**Nearest Town/Resort** Caernarfon
**Directions** On the A4086 from Caernarfon towards Llanberis.
⚅ Bangor

## CAERNARFON

**Coed Helen Caravan Club Site,** Coed Helen Road, Caernarfon, Gwynedd, LL54 5RS
**Tel:** 01286 676770
**www.**caravanclub.co.uk
**Pitches For** ⚑ ☵ **Total** 45
**Facilities** ⚒ ⚏ ⊙⊙ ▨ ⊡ ☻ ♈⊣☐
**Nearby Facilities** ✎ ⚲ ⚴ ↑
**Acreage** 2 **Open** March **to** Oct
**Access** Good **Site** Lev/Slope
Just a 10 minute walk to Caernarfon and 5 miles from the beach. Small lounge bar on site. Shop and swimming pool (May to Sept) adjacent. Close to Welsh Highland Railway, Caernarfon Castle and The National Museum of Wales. Non members welcome. Booking essential.
**Nearest Town/Resort** Caernarfon
**Directions** In Caernarfon on the A487, by the River Seiont bridge turn into Fford Pant Road, then turn right into Coed Helen Road. At the T-junction turn left, site is 200 yards on the left.
⚅ Caernarfon

## CAERNARFON

**Cwm Cadnant Valley Camping & Caravan Park,** Llanberis Road, Caernarfon, Gwynedd, LL55 2DF
**Tel:** 01286 673196 **Fax:** 01286 675941
**Email:** cades@cwmcadnant.co.uk
**www.**cwmcadnant.co.uk
**Pitches For** ▲ ⚑ ☵ **Total** 69
**Facilities** ⚒ ⌁ ⊞ ⚏ ♣ ⌐ ⊙ ⊣ ⊿ ▣ ☻
▨ ⊡ ⋒ ⋒⧠☐ ☵
**Nearby Facilities** ✎ ⚲ ⚴
**Open** March **to** Oct
**Access** Good **Site** Sloping
Café/restaurant and indoor swimming pool nearby.
**Nearest Town/Resort** Caernarfon
**Directions** On the A4086, 1km from the town centre.
⚅ Bangor

## CAERNARFON

**Dinlle Caravan Park,** Dinas Dinlle, Near Caernarfon, Gwynedd, LL55 5TW
**Tel:** 01286 830324 **Fax:** 01286 831562
**Email:** enq@thornleyleisure.co.uk
**www.**thornleyleisure.co.uk
**Pitches For** ▲ ⚑ ☵ **Total** 175
**Facilities** ⚒ ⌁ ⚍ ⊞ ⊞ ⚏ ♣ ⌐ ⊙ ⊣ ⊿
▨ ⊡ ⌑ ⊞ ☺ ♈ ⋒ ⊡ ⋒ ⊣ ☐ ☵
**Nearby Facilities** ✎ ⚲ ⚴ ↑
**Acreage** 22 **Open** March **to** Oct
**Access** Good **Site** Level
100 yards from a long, sandy beach.
**Nearest Town/Resort** Caernarfon
**Directions** From Caernarfon take the road towards Pwllheli, after 3 miles turn right for Dinas Dinlle and Caernarfon Airport, along the coast for 300 yards and turn right.
⚅ Bangor

## CAERNARFON

**Llyn-y-Gele Caravan Park,** Pontllyfni, Caernarfon, Gwynedd, LL54 5EL
**Tel:** 01286 660289
**Pitches For** ▲ ⚑ ☵ **Total** 30
**Facilities** ⚒ ⚏ ♣ ⌐ ⊙ ⊣ ▥ ☻
▨ ⊡ ☵⧠☐ ☵
**Nearby Facilities** ✎ ⚲ ⚴ ∗ ∪ ↑
**Acreage** 4 **Open** Easter **to** October
**Access** Good **Site** Level
Panoramic views of Snowdonia range. 7 minute walk to a beach with safe bathing. Fishing ¼ mile. Ideal location for touring Snowdonia. AA and RAC Listed.
**Nearest Town/Resort** Caernarfon
**Directions** Take the A487 out of Caernarfon for 3 miles, onto the A499 for 4 miles. Entrance to the site is the first right by garage and shop in the village of Pontllyfni.
⚅ Bangor

## CAERNARFON

**Llys Derwen Camping & Caravan Site,** Ffordd Bryngwyn, Llanrug, Nr Caernarfon, Gwynedd, LL55 4RD
**Tel:** 01286 673322
**Email:** llysderwen@aol.com
**www.**llysderwen.co.uk
**Pitches For** ▲ ⚑☐ **Total** 20
**Facilities** ⚒ ⚏ ♣ ⌐ ⊙ ⊣ ☵⊣☐
**Nearby Facilities** ✎ ⚲ ⚴ ∗ ∪ ♣ ↑
**Acreage** 4½ **Open** March **to** Oct
**Access** Good **Site** Level
Small family run site. 2 miles from Llanberis and the foot of Mount Snowdon. Static caravans also available for hire.
**Nearest Town/Resort** Caernarfon
**Directions** From Caernarfon take the A4086 towards Llanberis. In the village of Llanrug turn right at the Glyntwrog Public House, site entrance is 100 yards on the right.
⚅ Bangor

# GWYNEDD

## CAERNARFON

**Plas Gwyn Caravan Site,** Plas Gwyn, Llanrug, Caernarfon, Gwynedd, LL55 2AQ
**Tel:** 01286 672619
**Email:** info@plasgwyn.co.uk
www.plasgwyn.co.uk
**Pitches For** Å ⊕ ➡ **Total** 35
**Facilities** ƒ 📺 ♨ ⌂ ⊙ ⌂ ☏ 🏪 ⊙ ➡ ▣ ▣
**Nearby Facilities** ↾ ⌁ ⚓ ◥ ∪ ⚲ 🏇
**Acreage** 4 **Open** March **to** October
**Access** Good **Site** Level
Small, peaceful park. 3 miles from Snowdonia Mountains and 5 miles from the beach. Award winning hire caravans. En-suite bed and breakfast available in the house.
**Nearest Town/Resort** Caernarfon
**Directions** 3 miles from Caernarfon on the A4086, signposted on right.
⇌ Bangor

## CAERNARFON

**Riverside Camping,** Seiont Nurseries, Pontrug, Caernarfon, Gwynedd, LL55 2BB
**Tel:** 01286 678781 **Fax:** 01286 677223
**Email:**
brenda@riversidecamping.freeserve.co.uk
www.riversidecamping.co.uk
**Pitches For** Å ⊕ ➡ **Total** 55
**Facilities** ƒ 📺 ♨ ⌂ ⊙ ⊕ 🖫 ▣
📡 ✕ ⌂ ➡ ▣
**Nearby Facilities** ↾ ⌁ ⚓ ◥ ∪ ⌀ 🏇
**Acreage** 4½ **Open** Easter **to** October
**Access** Good **Site** Level
Secluded, landscaped site, bordered by a salmon river and adjacent to a picturesque garden centre. Mill Café with a spacious balcony serving delicious home made meals. Plenty of space for childrens ball games. Wonderful place to relax after exploring Snowdonia. 2 hard standings available. Permits required for fishing.

**Nearest Town/Resort** Caernarfon
**Directions** 2 miles out of Caernarfon on the righthand side of the A4086 (Llanberis road).
⇌ Bangor

## CAERNARFON

**St Ives Touring Caravan Park,** Lon-Y-Wig, Pontllyfni, Caernarfon, Gwynedd, LL54 5EG
**Tel:** 01286 660347 **Fax:** 01286 660542
**Email:** st.ivestouringpark@btopenworld.com
www.stivestouringcaravanpark.co.uk
**Pitches For** Å ⊕ □ **Total** 19
**Facilities** ƒ 🖾 📺 ♨ ⌂ ⊙ ⊿ ▣ ☏
🏪 🏬 ⊙ ➡ ▣ ✹
**Nearby Facilities** ↾ ⌁ ⚓ ◥ ∪ ⚲ 🏇
**Acreage** 1½ **Open** March **to** Oct
**Access** Good **Site** Gentle Slope
100 yards from the beach. Excellent location for exploring Snowdonia, North Wales and Anglesey. Small shop on site.
**Nearest Town/Resort** Caernarfon
**Directions** From Caernarfon take the A499 towards Pwllheli for 7 miles. On entering Pontllyfni turn right towards the beach.
⇌ Bangor

## CAERNARFON

**Talymignedd Caravan Site,** Nantlle, Caernarfon, Gwynedd, LL54 6BT
**Tel:** 01286 880374
**Pitches For** Å ⊕ ➡
**Facilities** ƒ 🖾 ♨ ⌂ ⊙ ⊕ ☏ ✹
**Nearby Facilities** ↾ ⌁ ⚓ ◥ ∪ ⚲ 🏇
**Open** March **to** Oct
**Access** Good **Site** Level
Mountains and coast very close by. Numerous places of interest nearby to visit. Just a few miles from shopping centres. Very central, ideal for Bangor, Caernarfon, Porthmadog and Pwllheli.
**Nearest Town/Resort** Caernarfon/Porthmadog

**Directions** West of Snowdon on the B44 from Rhyd-ddu to Penygroes. 2 miles fro Rhyd-ddu.
⇌ Porthmadog/Bangor

## CAERNARFON

**Tyn Rhos Farm Caravan Park,** Tyn Rhos Farm, Saron, Llanwnda, CaernarfonGwynedd, LL54 5UH
**Tel:** 01286 830362
**Pitches For** Å ⊕ ➡ **Total** 25
**Facilities** ƒ 🖾 ♨ ⌂ ⊙ ☏
**Nearby Facilities** ↾ ⌁ ⚓ ◥ ∪ ⚲ 🏇
**Acreage** 2 **Open** March **to** Mid Jan
**Access** Good **Site** Level
2½ miles from the beach, 1 mile from steam railway and cycle track.
**Nearest Town/Resort** Caernarfon
**Directions** From Caernarfon take the A48 after passing Tesco go straight on at th roundabout, turn first right to Sarc Llanfaglan, entrance is 3 miles on the left
⇌ Bangor

## CAERNARFON

**Tyn-yr-Onnen Mountain Farm Caravan** & **Camping Park,** Waunfawr, Caernarfon, Gwynedd, LL55 4AX
**Tel:** 01286 650281 **Fax:** 01286 650043
**Email:** tom.griffith1@btopenworld.com
www.tyn-yr-onnen.co.uk
**Pitches For** Å ⊕ ➡ **Total** 60
**Facilities** ♨ ƒ 🖾 ♨ ⌂ ⊙ ⊿ ▣ ▣
🏪 📡 ⊙ ⊕ 🖾 ♨ ⌂ ➡ ▣ ✹ ✹ ∿
**Nearby Facilities** ↾ ⌁ ⚓ ◥ ∪ ⚲ 🏇
**Acreage** 4¼ **Open** 1st May Holiday **to** Sept
**Access** Good **Site** Lev/Slope
A working farm at the foot of a mountain, secluded and peaceful, ideal touring and walking base. Colour brochure only on receiving a S.A.E.. AA 3 Pennants and WTB 3 Star Graded.

**earest Town/Resort** Caernarfon
**rections** A4085 Caernarfon (A487) to eddgelert, left at Waunfawr village church/ ip shop, signposted from that point.
≠ Bangor

## AERNARFON

**hite Tower Caravan Park**, Llandwrog, aernarfon, Gwynedd, LL54 5UH
**el:** 01286 830649
**mail:** whitetower@supanet.com
ww.whitetower.supanet.com
**tches For** A ♥ ♣ **Total** 104
**acilities** ♿ ♣ ⚡ 🔥 🚻 👔 🛒 🎣 ☕ ⚒
🍴 ⚑ ⚏ 🛉 🕭 🏪 ▦ ⚘ 🎯 ⚔ 🔥 🛒 🛒 🕸

**earby Facilities** ⚑ ✔ ♨ 🏊 U ♪ 🎣 ✗
**reate** 6 **Open** March **to** November
**ccess** Good **Site** Level
½ miles beach, 3¼ miles Caernarfon. plendid views of Snowdon. Central for uring Llyn Peninsula, Anglesey and nowdonia.
**earest Town/Resort** Caernarfon
**irections** From Caernarfon follow the A487 orthmadog road for approx ¼ mile, go past e Tesco Supermarket, straight ahead at the undabout and take the first turning on the ght. We are 3 miles on the right.
≠ Bangor

## LYNNOG FAWR

**berafon Camping Site**, Gyrn Goch, aernarfon, Gwynedd, LL54 5PN
**el:** 01286 660295 **Fax:** 01286 660582
**mail:** hugh@maelor.demon.co.uk
ww.maelor.demon.co.uk/aberafon.html
**tches For** A ♥ ♣ **Total** 65
**acilities** ⚡ 🚻 🛒 ⚒ ☕ 🍴 ⚏ ☕
🕭 🕭 ⚏ 🛉 🕭 🔥 🏪 ▦ 🛒 🛒

**earby Facilities** ⚑ ✔ ♨ 🏊 U ♪ 🎣 ✗
**creage** 15 **Open** April **to** October
**ccess** Poor **Site** Level
rivate beach. Boat launching available. hop only open in the main Summer olidays.
**earest Town/Resort** Caernarfon
**irections** From Caernarfon take the A499 wards Pwllheli. 1 mile after Clynnog Fawr n the right hand side.
≠ Pwllheli

## CRICCIETH

**Cae-Canol Caravan & Camping,** Criccieth, Gwynedd, LL52 0NB
**Tel:** 01766 522351
**Pitches For** A ♥ ♣ **Total** 25
**Facilities** ♿ ⚡ 🚻 🛒 🎣 ☕ 🍴 ☕ ⚏ ⚏
**Nearby Facilities** ⚑ ✔ ♨ 🏊 U ♪ ✗
**Acreage** 3 **Open** April to October
**Access** Very Good **Site** Level
Sheltered, grassy site. Private trout fishing available for caravanners and campers. Delightful riverside walk nearby. Ideal for touring.
**Nearest Town/Resort** Criccieth
**Directions** Take the B4411 from Criccieth, 2 miles. Also 2½ miles from the A487 towards Criccieth.
≠ Criccieth

## CRICCIETH

**Eisteddfa Caravan & Camping Site,** Eisteddfa Lodge, Pentrefelin, Criccieth, Gwynedd, LL52 0PT
**Tel:** 01766 522696
**Email:** eisteddfa@criccieth.co.uk
www.eisteddfapark.co.uk
**Pitches For** A ♥ ♣ **Total** 145
**Facilities** ⚡ 🚻 🛒 ⚒ ☕ 🍴 ⚏ ☕
🔭 🛒 🕭 ⚓ 🔥 🏪 ▦ 🛒

**Nearby Facilities** ⚑ ✔ ♨ 🏊 U ♪ 🎣 ✗
**Acreage** 11 **Open** March to October
**Access** Good **Site** Lev/Slope
**Nearest Town/Resort** Criccieth
**Directions** On the A497 Porthmadog to Criccieth road, 1½ miles north east of Criccieth. Entrance is at the west end of Pentrefelin beside the Plas Gwyn Nursing Home.
≠ Criccieth

## CRICCIETH

**Llanystumdwy Camping & Caravanning Club Site**, Tyddyn Sianel, Llanystumdwy, Criccieth, Gwynedd, LL52 0LS
**Tel:** 01766 522855
www.campingandcaravanningclub.co.uk
**Pitches For** A ♥ ♣ **Total** 70
**Facilities** ♿ ⚡ 🚻 👔 🛒 🎣 ☕ 🍴 ⚏ ☕
🕭 ☕ 🛒 🔥 🏪 ▦ 🛒 ⚘ ♪

**Nearby Facilities** ⚑ ✔ U ♪
**Acreage** 4 **Open** March to Oct

**Access** Good **Site** Sloping
Situated just outside Criccieth with scenic coastal views. Nearby attractions include Ffestiniog Railway and Snowdonia National Park. BTB 4 Star Graded and AA 3 Pennants. Non members welcome.
**Nearest Town/Resort** Criccieth
**Directions** From Criccieth take the A497 and turn second right signposted Llanstumdwy, site is on the right.
≠ Criccieth

## CRICCIETH

**Llwyn Bugeilydd**, Criccieth, Gwynedd, LL52 0PN
**Tel:** 01766 522235
**Pitches For** A ♥ ♣
**Facilities** ♿ ⚡ 🚻 🛒 🎣 ☕ 🍴 ☕ 🔥 ▦ 🛒
**Nearby Facilities** ⚑ ✔ ♨ 🏊 U ♪ 🎣 ✗
**Acreage** 5½ **Open** March to October
**Access** Good **Site** Level
Situated away from traffic noise. 1 mile from the beach, shops, pubs and restaurants. You can also contact us on Mobile: 07854 063192.
**Nearest Town/Resort** Criccieth
**Directions** From the A55 take the A487, after Bryncir turn right onto the B4411, site is on the left in 3½ miles. From Porthmadog take the A497 to Criccieth town centre, turn right onto the B4411, site is 1 mile on the right.
≠ Criccieth

## CRICCIETH

**Muriau Bach**, Rhoslan, Criccieth, Gwynedd, LL52 0NP
**Tel:** 01766 530642
**Pitches For** A ♥ ♣ **Total** 30
**Facilities** ⚡ 🚻 🛒 🎣 ☕ 🍴 ⚏ 🕭 🔥 ▦ 🛒
**Nearby Facilities** ⚑ ✔ ♨ 🏊 U ♪ 🎣 ✗
**Acreage** 1¼ **Open** March to October
**Access** Good **Site** Level
Attractive, clean, level site, near to the sea and mountains and central to all places of interest. Commanding the best views in the area, nice walks nearby. Cycle track nearby that leads to Caernarfon. Concessions for pensioners (off peak season). Pets welcome but strictly on a lead. Rock climbing at Tremadog. Bowling green, highland railway and two leisure centres all within easy reach.

# GWYNEDD

**Nearest Town/Resort** Criccieth
**Directions** Coming from Porthmadog on the A487, turn left onto the B4411. Fourth entrance on the left over a cattle grid, with a drive leading up to the site.
⚲ Criccieth

## CRICCIETH

**Mynydd Du Caravan Park,** Porthmadog Road, Criccieth, Gwynedd, LL52 0PS
**Tel:** 07747 033035 **Fax:** 01766 522294
**Email:** w.owen@btconnect.com
**www.mynydd-du-caravansite.co.uk**
**Pitches For** ▲ ⊕ ☻ **Total** 80
**Facilities** ⌇ 🗗 ⅏ ⓌⒺ ♨ ⌐ ☉ ☻ 🏠 ⊁🄿 ⋇ 🖉
**Nearby Facilities** ⌐ ⁄ ⚓ ⌣ ∪ ♉ ⑂
**Acreage** 3½ **Open** March **to** October
**Access** Good **Site** Level
Near the seaside town of Criccieth which has a castle, pubs, restaurants and gift shops.
**Nearest Town/Resort** Criccieth
**Directions** From Criccieth take the A487 towards Porthmadog. Site is 1 mile on the left before the village of Pentre Felin.
⚲ Criccieth

## CRICCIETH

**Tyddyn Cethin Caravan Park,** Criccieth, Gwynedd, LL52 0NF
**Tel:** 01766 522149
**Pitches For** ▲ ⊕ ☻ **Total** 45
**Facilities** ⌇ ⅏ ⌐ ☉ ☻ ☻
**Nearby Facilities** ⌐ ⁄ ⚓ ⌣ ∪ ♉ ⑂
**Acreage** 8 **Open** April **to** Oct
**Access** Good **Site** Level
Situated on the banks of the River Dwyfor.
**Nearest Town/Resort** Criccieth
**Directions** From Criccieth take the B4411, Park is 1½ miles on the right hand side.
⚲ Criccieth

## CRICCIETH

**Tyddyn Morthwyl,** Criccieth, Gwynedd, LL52 0NF
**Tel:** 01766 522115
**Email:**
trumper@henstabl147.freeserve.co.uk
**Pitches For** ▲ ⊕ ☻ **Total** 40
**Facilities** ⌇ ⅏ ⌐ ☉ ☻ ☻ ⊁🄿 🄿
**Nearby Facilities** ⌐ ⁄ ⚓ ⌣ ∪ ♉ ⑂
**Acreage** 6 **Open** March **to** October
Central for mountains of Snowdonia and beaches of Lleyn Peninsula. Level and sheltered with mountain views.
**Nearest Town/Resort** Criccieth
**Directions** 1½ miles north of Criccieth on B4411 main road to Caernarfon.
⚲ Criccieth

## DINAS MAWDDWY

**Celyn Brithion,** Dinas Mawddwy, Nr Machynlleth, Powys, SY20 9LP
**Tel:** 01650 531344
**Email:** celyn.brithion@btopenworld.com
**www.celynbrithion.co.uk**
**Pitches For** ▲ ⊡ **Total** 16
**Facilities** ⌇ ⅏ ♨ ⌐ ☉ ⌐ ☻ ⅏ ⅏ ☉⊁🄿 ⋇
**Nearby Facilities** ⌐ ⁄ ⚓ ⌣ ∪ ⑂
**Open** March **to** Oct
**Access** Good **Site** Level
Situated within Snowdonia National Park. Within easy reach of the coastal resorts of Barmouth and Aberdovey. Ideal walking and climbing area.
**Nearest Town/Resort** Machynlleth
**Directions** Situated on the A470 between Machynlleth and Dolgellau.
⚲ Machynlleth

## DINAS MAWDDWY

**Tynypwll Caravan & Camping Site,** Dinas Mawddwy, Machynlleth, Gwynedd, SY20 9JF
**Tel:** 01650 531326
**Pitches For** ▲ ⊕ ☻
**Facilities** ⚒ ⌇ ⅏ ♨ ⌐ ☻ ⅏⋈
**Nearby Facilities** ⁄ ⑂
**Acreage** 1 **Open** 30 March **to** End Oct
**Access** Good **Site** Level
Riverside site with lovely scenery. Ideal for walking, fishing and touring. Café/ restaurant nearby.
**Nearest Town** Dolgellau/Machynlleth
**Directions** From the A470 turn right by the Dinas Mawddwy sign, turn right by The Red Lion, site is the first left, entrance over the bridge. 10 miles from Dolgellau and 12 miles from Machynlleth.
⚲ Machynlleth

## DOLGELLAU

**Dolgamedd Camping & Caravan Site,** Dolgamedd, Bontnewydd, Dolgellau, Gwynedd, LL40 2DG
**Tel:** 01341 422624/450356 **Fax:** 01341 422624
**Email:** mail@dolgamedd.co.uk
**www.midwalesholidays.co.uk**
**Pitches For** ▲ ⊕ ☻ **Total** 65
**Facilities** ⚒ ⌇ ⅏ ⓌⒺ ♨ ⌐ ☉ ☻ ⅏ ☻ ☻ ⅏⋈⊁🄿 🄿 ⋇
**Nearby Facilities** ⌐ ⁄ ∪ ⑂
**Acreage** 8 **Open** April **to** October
**Access** Good **Site** Level
Situated on an 84 acre sheep farm alongside a river for fishing and swimming. NEW top class facilities building with campers kitchen. Camp fires allowed on the river bank, barbecues and picnic tables. 11 miles from the coast.
**Nearest Town/Resort** Dolgellau
**Directions** 3 miles from Dolgellau on the A494 towards Bala, turn right at Bontnewydd onto the B4416 towards Brithdir. Continue over the bridge and Dolgamedd is on the left.
⚲ Machynlleth

## DOLGELLAU

**Dolserau Uchaf,** Dolgellau, Gwynedd, LL40 2DE
**Tel:** 01341 422639
**Pitches For** ▲ ⊕ ☻ **Total** 20
**Facilities** ⌇ ⅏ ⓌⒺ ♨ ⌐ ☉ ☻ ⅏⋈🄿
**Nearby Facilities** ⌐ ⁄ ∪
**Acreage** 1¼ **Open** Easter **to** October
**Access** Good **Site** Level
Quiet site with open views of the Cader Idris Range. Ideal for walking and cycling.
**Nearest Town/Resort** Dolgellau
**Directions** 3 miles east of Dolgellau on the A494.
⚲ Barmouth

## DOLGELLAU

**Llwyn-Yr-Helm Farm,** Brithdir, Dolgellau, Gwynedd, LL40 2SA
**Tel:** 01341 450254
**Pitches For** ▲ ⊕ ☻ **Total** 25
**Facilities** ⚒ ⌇ ⅏ ⓌⒺ ♨ ⌐ ☉ ☻ ☻
⊕⅏⋈ ⋇
**Nearby Facilities** ⌐ ⁄ ⚓ ⌣ ∪ ♉ ⑂
**Acreage** 2½ **Open** Easter **to** End October **Site** Level
Friendly, quiet small farm site with scenic views, ideal for walking, touring and sandy beaches. Milk and eggs available from the farm. Well behaved pets welcome.
**Nearest Town/Resort** Dolgellau
**Directions** Take minor road at telephone kiosk off the B4416 which is a loop road from A470 to A494, Dolgellau 4 miles.
⚲ Machynlleth

## DOLGELLAU

**Tanyfron Camping & Caravan Park,** Arran Road, Dolgellau, Gwynedd, LL40 2AA
**Tel:** 01341 422638
**Email:** info@tan-y-fron.co.uk
**Pitches For** ▲ ⊕ ☻ **Total** 43
**Facilities** ⌇ 🗗 ⅏ ⓌⒺ ♨ ⌐ ☉ ☻ ⅏ ☻
⊕ 🏠 ⅏ ⋇
**Nearby Facilities** ⌐ ⁄ ⚓ ∪ ♉ ⑂
**Acreage** 3¼ **Open** 1 March **to** 7 Jan
**Access** Good **Site** Level
10 miles beach with scenic views. Ideal for walking, touring and fishing. Within walking distance of the town. TV hook-ups to touring pitches. En-suite B&B available. WTB 5 Star Graded Park and 2000 Wales in Bloom Award Winners.
**Nearest Town/Resort** Dolgellau
**Directions** From Welshpool take A470, turn for Dolgellau by Hanson Depot. ¼ mile left - Dolgellau straight on ½ mile from site.
⚲ Barmouth

## DOLGELLAU

**Tyddyn Farm,** Islawrdref, Dolgellau, Gwynedd, LL40 1TL
**Tel:** 01341 422472
**Pitches For** ▲ ⊕ ☻
**Facilities** ☻ ⋈
**Nearby Facilities** ⌐ ⁄ ∪
**Acreage** 2 **Open** All Year
**Access** Good **Site** Lev/Slope
Alongside a river at the bottom of Cader Idris Mountain. Beautiful views.
**Nearest Town/Resort** Dolgellau
**Directions** 3 miles from Dolgellau town on Cader road, turn left opposite Penbryn Garage.
⚲ Machynlleth

## DYFFRYN ARDUDWY

**Dyffryn Seaside Estate,** Dyffryn Ardudwy, Gwynedd, LL44 2HD
**Tel:** 01341 247220 **Fax:** 01341 247622
**Email:** info@dyffryn-seaside-estate.co.uk
**www.dyffryn-seaside-estate.co.uk**
**Pitches For** ▲ ⊕ ☻ **Total** 130
**Facilities** ⌇ ⌇ ⓌⒺ ♨ ⌐ ☉ ☻ ⅏ ☻ ⊡
⅏ ⅏ ⊕ ☻ ✕ ⅏ ⅏ ⅏ 🅿⋈🄿 ⊡
**Nearby Facilities** ⌐ ⁄ ⚓ ⌣ ∪ ⑂
**Acreage** 11 **Open** March **to** Oct **Site** Level
Near the beach and 1 mile from a river. Mountain walks.
**Nearest Town/Resort** Barmouth
**Directions** From Barmouth take the A496 north, after 5 miles turn left at the church 1 mile north of Talybont.
⚲ Dyffryn Ardudwy

## DYFFRYN ARDUDWY

**Murmur-yr-Afon Touring Caravan & Camping Site,** Dyffryn Ardudwy, Gwynedd, LL44 2BE
**Tel:** 01341 247353 **Fax:** 01341 247353
**Email:**
mills@murmuryrafon25.freeserve.co.uk
**www.murmuryrafon.co.uk**
**Pitches For** ▲ ⊕ ☻ **Total** 67
**Facilities** ⌇ ⌇ 🗗 ⓌⒺ ♨ ⌐ ☉ ☻ ⅏ ☻ ⊡
⅏ ⊕ ☻ 🏠 ⅏🄿
**Nearby Facilities** ⌐ ⁄ ⚓ ⌣ ∪ ♉ ⑂
**Acreage** 4 **Open** March **to** October
**Access** Good **Site** Level
1 mile from beach. Set in sheltered and natural surroundings, 100yds from village and shops, petrol stations and licensed premises.
**Nearest Town/Resort** Barmouth
**Directions** Take the A496 coast road from Barmouth towards Harlech. Site entrance is 100yds from the Power Garage in Dyffryn Village on the right hand side.
⚲ Dyffryn

## FESTINIOG

echrwd, Maentwrog, Blaenau Ffestiniog,
wynedd, LL41 4HF
l: 01766 Maentwrog 590240
mail: llechrwd@hotmail.com
ww.llechrwd.co.uk
tches For ▲ ⊕ ☻
acilities ⚡ 📠 ♨ ♠ 🏠 ⊙ 🍴 ⊒ 🚿 🏪 🖥
earby Facilities ⌐ ✈ ⋃ ♦ 🏌
ccreage 5 Open Easter to October
ccess Good Site Level
verside camp within Snowdonia National
ark, with meadow walk. Near Ffestiniog
ailway.
irections On the A496. Blaenau Ffestiniog
miles, Porthmadog 8 miles.
☀ Blaenau Ffestiniog

## ARLECH

oodlands Caravan Park, Harlech,
wynedd, LL46 2UE
el: 01766 780419 Fax: 01766 780419
mail: grace@woodlandscp.fsnet.co.uk
ww.woodlandscp.fsnet.co.uk
tches For ⊕ 🚐 Total 37
acilities ⚡ 📠 📠 ♨ ♠ 🏠 ⊙ 🍴 ⊒ 🖥
🏪 ⊕ 🚿 🖥 🌿
earby Facilities ⌐ ✈ ⋃ ♦ 🏌
ccreage 2 Open March to October
ccess Good Site Level
ear the beach, shops and a golf course.
djacent to Harlech Castle. Swimming pool
earby. Centrally heated shower and toilet
uilding. Ideal touring.
earest Town/Resort Harlech
irections Leave A496 at Harlech railway
ossing, site signposted at crossing at foot
f castle.
☀ Harlech

## LANBEDROG

Vern Newydd Caravan & Camping Park,
lanbedrog, Pwllheli, Gwynedd, LL53 7PG
el: 01758 740220 Fax: 01758 740810
mail: office@wern-newydd.co.uk
ww.wern-newydd.co.uk
itches For ▲ ⊕ 🚐 Total 30
acilities ⚡ 📠 📠 ♨ ♠ 🏠 ⊙ 🍴 ⊒ 🖥
🏪 🌿 🚿 🖥 🌿
earby Facilities ⌐ ✈ ⋃ ♦ 🏌
ccreage 2½ Open March to October
ccess Good Site Level
eaceful, secluded park on the beautiful
leyn Peninsula. Just a five minute walk to
e village of Llanbedrog with its shops,
opular country inns and several good
laces to eat. It also boasts a popular,
afe, sandy beach for swimming wind-
urfing and boating. 10 minute walk to
each and 2 miles from Abersoch.
earest Town/Resort Abersoch
irections From Pwllheli take the A499
owards Abersoch, in Llanbedrog turn right
nto the B4413 signposted Aberdaron.
Continue through the village, go past the post
ffice (on the right) then take the first turning
ght onto an unclassified road, site is 700
ards on the right.
☀ Pwllheli/Bangor

## MORFA NEFYN

Graeanfryn Farm, Morfa Nefyn, Gwynedd,
LL53 6YQ
Tel: 01758 720455 Fax: 01758 720485
Email: ian.jan.harrison@tinyworld.co.uk
Pitches For ▲ ⊕ 🚐 Total 20
Facilities ⚡ 📠 ♨ ♠ 🏠 ⊙ 🍴 🏪 🖥
Nearby Facilities ⌐ ✈ ⋃ ♦ 🏌
Acreage 1 Open All Year
Rural location, 1 mile from the beach.
Barbecue area. Café/Restaurant nearby.
Camping and Caravan Club 3 Star Site and
WTB 3 Star Graded.
Nearest Town/Resort Pwllheli
Directions From Pwllheli take the A497 for
5 miles, at the roundabout turn left and then
turn next left. Entrance to the site is 50 yards
on the right.
☀ Pwllheli/Bangor

## PORTHMADOG

Black Rock Sands Camping & Touring
Park, Morfa Bychan, Porthmadog,
Gwynedd, LL49 9YD
Tel: 01766 513919
Pitches For ▲ ⊕ 🚐 Total 140
Facilities ⚡ 📠 ♨ ♠ 🏠 ⊙ 🍴 🖥 🚿
🏪 ⊕ 🅿 🏪 🖥 🌿
Nearby Facilities ⌐ ✈ ⋃ ♦ 🏌 🏊 ♦
Acreage 9 Open March to October
Access Good Site Level
Adjacent to a 7 mile sandy beach.
Nearest Town/Resort Porthmadog
Directions From Porthmadog take the road
to Morfa Bychan, turn right just before the
beach.
☀ Porthmadog

## PORTHMADOG

Glan-Y-Mor Camping Park, Morfa
Bychan, Porthmadog, Gwynedd, LL49 9LD
Tel: 01766 514640
Pitches For ▲ Total 60
Facilities 📠 ♠ 🏠 ⊙ 🍴 🖥
Nearby Facilities ⌐ ✈ ⋃ ♦ 🏌
Acreage 5 Open May to September
Site Level
Adjacent to a 7 mile sandy beach.
Nearest Town/Resort Porthmadog
Directions From Porthmadog take the road
to Morfa Bychan, continue to the beach,
entrance is on the left.
☀ Porthmadog

## PORTHMADOG

Greenacres Holiday Park, Black Rock
Sands, Morfa Bychan, Porthmadog,
Gwynedd, LL49 9YB
Tel: 01766 512781 Fax: 01766 512704
www.touringholidays.co.uk
Pitches For ⊕ 🚐 Total 52
Facilities ♿ ⚡ 📠 ♨ ♠ 🏠 ⊒ 🖥 🚿
🏪 🅿 ⊕ ✗ 🎡 ♦ 🍴 🌿 🍴 🖥 🖥
Nearby Facilities ⌐ ✈ ⋃ ♦ 🏌
Open March to Nov
Access Good Site Level
Near the beach with scenic views. New
sport and leisure facilities including bike
hire, bowling and Pitch & Putt. Kids Club
and a full family entertainment programme.
Ideal touring. Dragon Award.

## PORTHMADOG

Nearest Town/Resort Porthmadog
Directions After going over the toll bridge at
Porthmadog, go along the high street and
turn between the Post Office and
Woolworths. ¼ mile on through the village
of Morfa Bychan, take the right fork to Black
Rock Sands, Greenacres is about 2 miles.
☀ Porthmadog

## PORTHMADOG

Gwyndy Caravan Park, Black Rock
Sands, Morfa Bychan, Porthmadog,
Gwynedd, LL49 9YB
Tel: 01766 512047 Fax: 01766 512047
Email: martin@gwyndycp.fsnet.co.uk
Pitches For ▲ ⊕ 🚐 Total 24
Facilities ⚡ 📠 ♨ ♠ 🏠 ⊙ 🍴 ⊒ 🖥 🚿
🏪 🅿 ⊕ 🚿 🖥 🌿
Nearby Facilities ⌐ ✈ ⋃ ♦ 🏌 🏊 ♦
Acreage 5 Open March to October
Access Good Site Level
Select family run park, just a few minutes
from the beach, with backdrop of mountain
views. Ideal for touring the Snowdonia
area. All super pitches.
Nearest Town/Resort Porthmadog
Directions In Porthmadog turn at
Woolworths to Black Rock Sands follow the
road into the village of Morfa Bychan past
the Spar Supermarket, turn first left and then
second right into road leading into caravan
park, exactly 2 miles from Porthmadog.
☀ Porthmadog

## PORTHMADOG

Tyddyn Adi Camping Park, Morfa
Bychan, Porthmadog, Gwynedd, LL49
9YW
Tel: 01766 512933
Email: tyddynadi@btconnect.com
www.tyddynadicamping.co.uk
Pitches For ▲ ⊕ 🚐 Total 200
Facilities ⚡ 📠 ♠ 🏠 ⊙ 🖥 🚿
🏪 🅿 ⊕ 🎡 ♦ 🍴 🌿 🍴 🖥
Nearby Facilities ⌐ ✈ ⋃ ♦ 🏌 🏊 ♦
Acreage 28 Open Easter to October
Access Good Site Level
Close to Porthmadog attractions and ¼
mile from Black Rock Sands. Ideal for
touring.
Nearest Town/Resort Porthmadog
Directions From Porthmadog take the Morfa
Bychan road 2¼ miles. Follow to the end of
village and there is a large green sign on the
right.
☀ Porthmadog

## PORTHMADOG

Tyddyn Llwyn Caravan Park & Campsite,
Black Rock Road, Porthmadog, Gwynedd,
LL49 9UR
Tel: 01766 512205 Fax: 01766 512205
Email: dt@tyddynllwyn.com
www.tyddynllwyn.com
Pitches For ▲ ⊕ 🚐 Total 153
Facilities ⚡ 📠 ♨ ♠ 🏠 ⊙ 🍴 ⊒ 🖥 🚿
🏪 🅿 ⊕ ✗ 🍴 🎡 ♦ 🍴 🖥 🖥
Nearby Facilities ⌐ ✈ ⋃ ♦ 🏌 🏊 ♦
Acreage 52 Open March to October
Access Good Site Lev/Slope
Only 2 miles from Black Rock Sands. In a
sheltered valley beneath Moel Y Gest

# TYDDYN LLWYN HOTEL & CARAVAN PARK
### Morfa Bychan Road, Porthmadog, Gwynedd LL49 9UR

Situated in a delightful, secluded, wooded valley but close to the town. An ideal centre from which to tour Snowdonia and North Wales. Good facilities and local attractions. Restaurant, Bar and other full facilities at our own hotel.

**For Brochure    Tel: (01766) 512205**
**Fax: (01766) 514601**
Web Site: **www.tyddynllwyn.com**

---

Mountain with beautiful wooded scenery. Limited number of super pitches available. WTB 4 Star Graded.
**Nearest Town/Resort** Porthmadog
**Directions** On high street turn by the Post Office signposted golf course and Black Rock Sands. Park is on the right in under ¼ mile. Verge signs on left.
⇌ Porthmadog

## PWLLHELI
**Abererch Sands Holiday Centre,** Pwllheli, Gwynedd, LL53 6PJ
**Tel:** 01758 612327 **Fax:** 01758 701556
**Email:** enquiries@abererch-sands.co.uk
www.abererch-sands.co.uk
**Pitches For** ▲ ⬜ 🚐
**Facilities** 🏊 🔥 🅶 🆖 🚿 🔥 ☉ ⌒ ⊒ 🍔
🕎 🅾 🚿 🛢 🚾 ⤴ 🗉 🎿
**Nearby Facilities** ⌐ ✔ ⚓ ≺ ∪ ⌓ ℛ
**Open** March to October
**Access** Good Site Level
Near the beach.
**Nearest Town/Resort** Pwhelli
**Directions** On the A499 between Pwllheli and Criccieth. 1 mile from Pwllheli.
⇌ Pwllheli

## PWLLHELI
**Bodfel Hall Caravan Park,** Bodfel Hall, Pwllheli, Gwynedd, LL53 6DW
**Tel:** 01758 613386
**Email:** clive@bodfel.com
www.bodfel.com
**Pitches For** ⬜ 🚐 Total 20
**Facilities** 🏊 🔥 🅶 🆖 🚿 🔥 ☉ ⌒ ⊒ 🍔
🛢 ⤴ 🗉 🎿 ℱ
**Nearby Facilities** ⌐ ✔ ⚓ ≺ ∪ ⌓ ℛ ⤚
**Open** March to October
**Access** Good Site Level
Secluded site, away from the main road. Within easy reach of beaches and mountains.
**Nearest Town/Resort** Pwllheli
**Directions** Leave Pwllheli on the A497 going towards Morfa Nefyn. After 2 miles the Park is on the left after a narrow bridge.
⇌ Pwllheli

## PWLLHELI
**Bodwrog Farm,** Bodwrog, Llanbedrog, Pwllheli, Gwynedd, LL53 7RE
**Tel:** 01758 740341
**Email:** enq@bodwrog.co.uk
www.bodwrog.co.uk
**Pitches For** ▲ ⬜ 🚐 Total 20
**Facilities** 🏊 🆖 🚿 ☉ 🍔 ⌴🗉 🎿
**Nearby Facilities** ⌐ ✔ ⚓ ≺ ∪ ⌓
**Acreage** 2 **Open** 1 March to End Oct
**Access** Good Site Lev/Slope
Superb coastal views. 1½ miles from a sandy, sheltered beach. Quiet, scenic

walks. Local restaurants and pubs within 1 mile. New shower and toilet block with disabled toilets. Very good television reception. Six hard standings.
**Nearest Town/Resort** Pwllheli/Abersoch
**Directions** From Pwllheli take the A499 to Llanbedrog, turn right opposite Glyn-Y-Weddw Pub onto the B4413. After 1 mile site is the third opening on the left after the Ship Inn, cattle grid inside entrance.
⇌ Pwllheli

## PWLLHELI
**Hendre Caravan Park,** Efailnewydd, Near Pwllheli, Gwynedd, LL53 8TN
**Tel:** 01758 613416
**Pitches For** ▲ ⬜
**Facilities** 🏊 🆖 🚿 🔥 ⌒ 🍺 🗉 🍔 🛢
**Nearby Facilities** ⌐ ✔ ⚓ ≺ ∪ ⌓ ℛ ⤚
**Open** March to Oct
**Access** Good Site Level
Quiet, secluded site with ¾ of the space for static vans and a ¼ for touring vans, camper vans and tents. Many beaches and lovely walks locally. Close to the old market town of Pwllheli.
**Nearest Town/Resort** Pwllheli
**Directions** From Pwllheli take the A497 Nefyn road, go across the roundabout to Efailnewydd Village, turn first left and go through the village, take the first left at the bottom of the village.
⇌ Pwllheli

## PWLLHELI
**Porthysgaden Site,** Porthysgaden, Tudweiliog, Pwllheli, Gwynedd, LL53 8PD
**Tel:** 01758 770206
**Pitches For** ⬜ 🚐 🚐 Total 40
**Facilities** 🆖 🔥 ⌒ ☉ ⊒ 🗉 🍔 ⌴
**Nearby Facilities** ⌐ ✔ ⚓ ≺ ∪ ⌓ ℛ ⤚
**Acreage** 4 **Open** April to October
**Access** Good Site Level
¼ mile from the beach, sea, rocks and a slipway for boats. Good fishing.
**Nearest Town/Resort** Pwllheli
**Directions** Follow the B4417 and turn right after the village of Tudweiliog then turn first right to the farm.
⇌ Pwllheli

## PWLLHELI
**Rhosfawr Park,** Rhosfawr, Y Ffor, Pwllheli, Gwynedd, LL53 6YA
**Tel:** 01766 810545
**Pitches For** ▲ ⬜ 🚐 Total 40
**Facilities** 🏊 🔥 🆖 🚿 🔥 ⌒ ☉ 🗉 🍔
🕎 🅾 ⤴ 🗉 🎿
**Nearby Facilities** ⌐ ✔ ⚓ ≺ ∪ ⌓ ℛ ⤚
**Acreage** 2 **Open** March to End Oct
**Access** Good Site Level
Situated in the centre of the beautiful Llyn

Peninsula. Ideal for touring. Shop in site selling basic provisions.
**Nearest Town/Resort** Pwllheli
**Directions** 2 miles from Y Ffor on the B4354 Nefyn road, telephone box on the left, we are just a bit further along on the right.
⇌ Pwllheli

## PWLLHELI
**Ty Mawr Caravan Park,** Bryncroes, Pwllheli, Gwynedd, LL53 8EH
**Tel:** 01248 351537
**Pitches For** ▲ ⬜ □ Total 25
**Facilities** 🏊 🔥 🆖 🚿 🔥 ⌒ ☉ ⌴ 🍔
🛢 🅰 ⤴ 🗉
**Nearby Facilities** ⌐ ✔ ⚓ ≺ ∪ ⌓
**Acreage** 2 **Open** April to October
**Access** Good Site Level
2 miles from Penllech Beach and within 4 miles of Aberdaron and Whistling Sands.
**Nearest Town/Resort** Pwllheli
**Directions** From Pwllheli take the A499 to Llanbedrog, then take the B4413 for approx 9 miles. Site is signposted.
⇌ Pwllheli

## TALSARNAU
**Barcdy Touring Caravan & Camping Park,** Talsarnau, Gwynedd, LL47 6YG
**Tel:** 01766 770736
**Email:** anwen@barcdy.co.uk
www.barcdy.co.uk
**Pitches For** ▲ ⬜ 🚐 Total 78
**Facilities** 🏊 🆖 🔥 ⌒ ☉ ⌴ ⊒ 🍔
🕎 🅾 🗉 🗉 🎿
**Nearby Facilities** ⌐ ✔ ⚓ ≺ ∪ ⌓ ⤚
**Acreage** 12 **Open** April to Sept
**Access** Good Site Lev/Slope
Walks from site to nearby mountains and lakes. Ideal touring Snowdonia.
**Nearest Town/Resort** Harlech
**Directions** From Bala A4212 to Trawsfynydd. A487 to Maentwrog. At Maentwrog left onto A496, signposted Harlech. Site 4 miles.
⇌ Talsarnau

## TYWYN
**Caethle Caravan Park,** Caethle, Aberdyfi Road, Tywyn, Gwynedd, LL36 9HS
**Tel:** 01654 710587 **Fax:** 01654 710587
**Pitches For** ▲ ⬜ 🚐 Total 30
**Facilities** 🏊 🔥 🆖 🚿 🔥 ⌒ ☉ ⌴ 🍔
🕎 🆖 🗉 🗉 🎿
**Nearby Facilities** ⌐ ✔ ⚓ ≺ ∪ ⌓ ℛ ⤚
**Acreage** 4 **Open** April/Easter to End Oct
**Access** Good Site Level
Picturesque, uncommercialised site within the Snowdonia National Park. Near the beach, leisure centre and narrow gauge railway.
**Nearest Town/Resort** Tywyn/Aberdyfi

# Pall Mall Farm Caravan Park
### Near the Beach & the Mountains

Stay at our well maintained site with a great family atmosphere. Tents, Touring Caravans and Motor Caravans welcome. Level site with 40 pitches, electric hook-ups. Seasonal Pitches available.

**Pall Mall Farm, Tywyn, Gwynedd LL36 8RU   01654 71034**

**Directions** On the A493 coast road, 1½ miles from Tywyn and 2 miles from Aberdyfi.
Tywyn/Aberdyfi

## TYWYN
**Cwmrhwyddfor Campsite,** T D Nutting, Talyllyn, Tywyn, Gwynedd, LL36 9AJ
**Tel:** 01654 761286/761380
**Pitches For** ▲ � ♠ **Total** 30
**Facilities** ...
**Nearby Facilities** ...
**Acreage** 6 **Open** All Year
**Access** Good **Site** Level
Very central for Tywyn, Aberdovey, Barmouth. The site runs alongside a stream. Ideal for the mountains and sea. All kept very clean, excellent reputation. TV reception on site. Public telephone and Cafe/Restaurant nearby. Prices on application.
**Nearest Town/Resort** Dolgellau
**Directions** Situated on the A487 between Dolgellau and Machynlleth, at foot of Cader Idris mountain, right at the bottom of Talyllyn Pass, a white house under the rocks.
Machynlleth

## TYWYN
**Dôl Einion,** Tal-y-Llyn, Tywyn, Gwynedd, LL36 9AJ
**Tel:** 01654 761312
**Pitches For** ▲ ♠ ♠
**Facilities** ...
**Nearby Facilities** ...
**Acreage** 3 **Open** All Year
**Access** Good **Site** Level
Flat, grassy site with a stream. At the start of the popular Minffordd path to the summit of Cader Idris. Ideal for walking and touring. Fly fishing ½ mile, narrow gauge railway 3 miles and beach 11 miles. B & B on site. Hotel Restaurant and Bar nearby. Public Telephone nearby.
**Nearest Town/Resort** Dolgellau
**Directions** From Dolgellau take the A470 for 3 miles, turn right onto the A487 and continue for 4 miles. Turn right onto the B4405, site is 300 metres.
Machynlleth

## TYWYN
**Llanywern,** Llanegryn, Tywyn, Gwynedd, LL36 9TH
**Tel:** 01654 782247
**Pitches For** ▲ ♠ ♠ **Total** 20
**Facilities** ...
**Nearby Facilities** ...
**Acreage** 4 **Open** April **to** End Oct
**Access** Good **Site** Level
Alongside the River Dysynni for fishing (Prince Albert Members).
**Nearest Town/Resort** Tywyn/Aberdovey
**Directions** 5 miles north of Tywyn.
Tywyn

## TYWYN
**Llanbwst Farm,** Glasgoed, Llabwst Farm, Rhoslefain, TywynGwynedd, LL36 9NE
**Tel:** 01654 711013
**Pitches For** ▲ ♠ ♠ **Total** 25
**Facilities** ...

**Nearby Facilities** ...
**Acreage** 2½ **Open** Spring Bank Hol **to** Oct
**Access** Fair **Site** Lev/Slope
5 miles from Tywyn beach and 3 miles from Fairbourne. Ideal walking and touring area.
**Nearest Town/Resort** Tywyn
**Directions** From Tywyn take the A493 for 5 miles, in Rhoslefain turn right opposite the white cottage, farm is 400 yards.
Tywyn

## TYWYN
**Pall Mall Farm Caravan Park,** Pall Mall Farm, Tywyn, Gwynedd, LL36 9RU
**Tel:** 01654 710384 **Fax:** 01654 710154
**Pitches For** ▲ ♠ ♠ **Total** 90
**Facilities** ...
**Nearby Facilities** ...
**Acreage** 5 **Open** Easter **to** End Oct
**Access** Good **Site** Level
Near the beach, Tal-y-Llyn Railway and mountains. Ideal for touring, camping and walking.
**Nearest Town/Resort** Tywyn
**Directions** Park is first on the left on the way out of Tywyn on the A493 Dolgellau road.
Tywyn

## TYWYN
**Waenfach Caravan Site,** Waenfach, Llanegryn, Tywyn, Gwynedd, LL36 9SB
**Tel:** 01654 Tywyn 710375
**Email:** waenfach@aol.com
**Pitches For** ▲ ♠ ♠ **Total** 10
**Facilities** ...
**Nearby Facilities** ...
**Open** Easter **to** October
**Access** Good
Small site on a working farm. 3 miles from the sea.
**Nearest Town/Resort** Tywyn
**Directions** 3 miles north of Tywyn on the A493.
Tywyn

## TYWYN
**Ynysymaengwyn Caravan Park,** The Lodge, Tywyn, Gwynedd, LL36 9RY
**Tel:** 01654 710684 **Fax:** 01654 710684
**Email:** rita@ynysy.co.uk
**www.**ynysy.co.uk
**Pitches For** ▲ ♠ ♠ **Total** 80
**Facilities** ...
**Nearby Facilities** ...
**Acreage** 4 **Open** April **to** October
**Access** Good **Site** Level
In the grounds of an old manor house with a river at the bottom of the site for fishing. Near to the beach and shops. Woodland walks. NEW for 2005 Superpitches. Walkers and Cyclists Award. Secure storage for cycles. WTB 4 Star Grading and AA 3 Pennants.
**Nearest Town/Resort** Tywyn
**Directions** Take the A493 from Tywyn to Dolgellau, we are the second caravan park on the left.
Tywyn

# MERTHYR TYDFIL
## MERTHYR TYDFIL
**Grawen Caravan & Camping Park,** Cwm-Taf, Cefn Coed, Merthyr Tydfil, CF48 2HS
**Tel:** 01685 723740 **Fax:** 01685 723740
**Email:** grawen.touring@virgin.net
**www.**walescaravanandcamping.com
**Pitches For** ▲ ♠ ♠ **Total** 50
**Facilities** ...
**Nearby Facilities** ...
**Acreage** 3½ **Open** April **to** 30 October
**Access** Good **Site** Level
Picturesque mountain, forest and reservoir walks inside the Brecon Beacons National Park. A wealth of history can be found in the town of Merthyr Tydfil and the Valleys.
**Nearest Town/Resort** Merthyr Tydfil
**Directions** Easy access along the A470 Brecon Beacons road, 2 miles from Cefn Coed and 4 miles from Merthyr Tydfil. 2 miles off the A465 Heads of the Valleys road, ¼ mile from the reservoir.
Merthyr Tydfil

# MONMOUTHSHIRE
## ABERGAVENNY
**Pandy Caravan Club Site,** Pandy, Abergavenny, Monmouthshire, NP7 8DR
**Tel:** 01873 890370
**www.**caravanclub.co.uk
**Pitches For** ♠ ♠ **Total** 53
**Facilities** ...
**Nearby Facilities** ...
**Acreage** 5 **Open** March **to** Oct
**Access** Good **Site** Level
Pleasant site scattered with mature trees and bounded by the River Honddu. Near Offa's Dyke Path. 50 yards from the Old Pandy Hotel and there are eight pubs in the vicinity. Close to the Brecon Beacons and Tintern Abbey. Non members welcome. Booking essential.
**Nearest Town/Resort** Abergavenny
**Directions** From the A465, DO NOT go into Abergavenny but continue on the A465 following signs for Hereford. After 6¼ miles turn left by the Pandy Inn into a minor road, site is on the left immediately after passing under the railway bridge.
Abergavenny

## ABERGAVENNY
**Pyscodlyn Farm Caravan & Camping Site,** Llanwenarth Citra, Abergavenny, Monmouthshire, NP7 7ER
**Tel:** 01873 853271 **Fax:** 01873 853271
**Email:** pyscodlyn.farm@virgin.net
**www.**pyscodlyncaravanpark.com
**Pitches For** ▲ ♠ ♠ **Total** 60
**Facilities** ...
**Nearby Facilities** ...
**Acreage** 4½ **Open** 1 April **to** 31 Oct

# MONMOUTHSHIRE, NEWPORT, PEMBROKESHIRE

**Access** Good **Site** Level
Ideal for walking, cycling and exploring the Black Mountains and Brecon Beacons National Park.
**Nearest Town/Resort** Abergavenny
**Directions** Situated on A40 (Brecon road), 1½ miles from Nevill Hall Hospital, on the left 50 yards past the telephone box.
⇌ Abergavenny

## ABERGAVENNY

**Rising Sun Caravan & Camping Site,** The Rising Sun, Pandy, Abergavenny, Monmouthshire, NP7 8DL
**Tel:** 01873 890254
**Pitches For** ▲ ⊕ ⇋ **Total** 25
**Facilities** ⌇ ⬚ ⬚ ♨ ⌂ ⊙ ⇋ ☻
⬚ ✗ ⬚ ⚏ ⊬ ⬚ ⊡
**Nearby Facilities** ⌐ ✓ ∪
**Acreage** 2 **Open** All Year
**Access** Good **Site** Level
**Nearest Town/Resort** Abergavenny
**Directions** From Abergavenny take the A465 towards Hereford, The Rising Sun lies approx. 7 miles from Abergavenny.
⇌ Abergavenny

## MONMOUTH

**Bridge Caravan Park & Camping Site,** Dingestow, Monmouth, Monmouthshire, NP25 4DY
**Tel:** 01600 740241
**Email:** info@bridgecaravanpark.co.uk
www.bridgecaravanpark.co.uk
**Pitches For** ▲ ⊕ ⇋ **Total** 123
**Facilities** ∆ ⌇ ⬚ ⬚ ♨ ⌂ ⊙ ⇋ ⬚ ⊡ ✲
**Nearby Facilities** ⌐ ✓ ∪ ♬
**Acreage** 4 **Open** Easter **to** October
**Access** Good **Site** Level
Riverside site. Easy access.
**Nearest Town/Resort** Monmouth
**Directions** 4 miles west of Monmouth.
⇌ Abergavenny

## MONMOUTH

**Glen Trothy Caravan Park,** Mitchel Troy, Monmouth, Monmouthshire, NP25 4BD
**Tel:** 01600 712295
**Email:** enquiries@glentrothy.co.uk
www.glentrothy.co.uk
**Pitches For** ▲ ⊕ ⇋ **Total** 130
**Facilities** ∆ ⌇ ⬚ ⬚ ♨ ⌂ ⊙ ⇋ ⬚ ⊡
⊙ ⬚ ⚏ ⬚ ✲
**Nearby Facilities** ⌐ ✓ ⚓ ∪ ♬ ✗
**Acreage** 6½ **Open** 1 March **to** 31 October
**Access** Good **Site** Level
Alongside a river. Ideal touring. No arrivals before 2pm.
**Nearest Town/Resort** Monmouth
**Directions** From north M5, M50 then A40 taking the left turn after the traffic lights and before reaching road tunnel. From East Gloucester, A40 Ross on Wye,A40 Monmouth. From south and southeast M4 Severn Bridge, A466 Chepstow, Tintern and Monmouth turning left at traffic lights onto A40.
⇌ Abergannny

## MONMOUTH

**Monmouth Caravan Park,** Rockfield Rd, Monmouth, Monmouthshire, NP25 5BA
**Tel:** 01600 714745
**Pitches For** ▲ ⊕ ⇋ **Total** 60
**Facilities** ∆ ⌇ ⬚ ⬚ ♨ ⌂ ⊙ ⇋ ☻
⬚ ⊙ ⬚ ✗ ⬚ ⊬ ⬚ ⊡ ✲
**Nearby Facilities** ⌐ ✓ ⚓ ∪ ♬ ✗
**Acreage** 4 **Open** 1 March **to** 5 Jan
**Access** Good **Site** Level
Within walking distance of the town centre. Ideal for touring the Wye Valley and Forest of Dean.

**Nearest Town/Resort** Monmouth
**Directions** From Monmouth take the B4233, we are ¼ of a mile on the right hand side, opposite the fire station.
⇌ Abergavenny

## MONMOUTH

**Monnow Bridge Caravan Site,** Drybridge Street, Monmouth, Monmouthshire, NP5 3AD
**Tel:** 01600 714004
**Pitches For** ▲ ⊕ ⇋
**Facilities** ⌇ ⬚ ⬚ ♨ ⌂ ⊙ ⇋ ☻ ⬚ ⊕ ⊡
**Nearby Facilities** ⌐ ✓ ⚓ ♬ ✗
**Acreage** 1½ **Open** All Year
**Access** Good **Site** Level
On the banks of the River Monnow and on Offas Dyke Path. Ideal for touring Wye Valley and the Forest of Dean.
**Nearest Town/Resort** Monmouth
**Directions** On the edge of town, 5 minutes from the town centre.
⇌ Newport

## USK

**Chainbridge Inn,** Kemeys Commander, Nr Usk, Monmouthshire, NP15 1PP
**Tel:** 01873 880243 **Fax:** 01873 880910
**Pitches For** ▲ ⊕ ⇋ **Total** 25
**Facilities** ⌇ ⬚ ☻ ⬚ ✗ ⬚ ♠ ⊬ ⊡ ✲
**Nearby Facilities** ⌐ ✓
**Acreage** 3 **Open** March **to** January
**Access** Good **Site** Level
On the banks of the River Usk in a rural setting.
**Nearest Town/Resort** Usk
**Directions** In Usk town turn onto the D4598 Abergavenny road, Chainbridge Inn is 2 miles on the left hand side.
⇌ Abergavenny

# NEWPORT
## NEWPORT

**Pentre-Tai Farm,** Rhiwderin, Newport, NP10 8RQ
**Tel:** 01633 893284 **Fax:** 01633 893284
**Email:** george@pentretai.f9.co.uk
**Pitches For** ▲ ⊕ ⇋ **Total** 5
**Facilities** ⌇ ⬚ ♨ ⌂ ⊙ ⇋ ☻ ⬚ ✲ ⚏
**Nearby Facilities** ⌐ ✓ ∪ ♬
**Acreage** 5 **Open** March **to** October
**Access** Good **Site** Lev/Slope
Ideal for visiting Cardiff and the Welsh castles. Useful stopover for Irish ferry. Good pub nearby. B&B also available (WTB 2 Star).
**Nearest Town/Resort** Newport
**Directions** Leave the M4 at junction 28 and take the A467, at the next roundabout take the A468 for approx. 1 mile. Turn right immediately after 'Rhiwderin Inn' and go straight through the village and on down lane. Farm is on the left.
⇌ Newport

## NEWPORT

**Tredegar House Caravan Club Site,** Coedkernew, Newport, NP10 8TW
**Tel:** 01633 815600
www. caravanclub.co.uk
**Pitches For** ▲ ⊕ ⇋ **Total** 80
**Facilities** ∆ ⌇ ⬚ ⬚ ♨ ⌂ ☻
⊙ ⬚ ✗ ⬚ ⊬ ⬚ ⊡ ⬚
**Nearby Facilities** ⌐ ✓
**Acreage** 7 **Open** March **to** Dec
**Access** Good **Site** Level

Bordered by an ornamental lake by Tredegar House. Tea rooms on site. Adventure playground adjacent. 7 miles from Cardiff. Non members welcome. Booking essential.
**Nearest Town/Resort** Newport
**Directions** Leave the M4 at junction 28 and take the A48 signposted Tredegar House. At the roundabout turn left into the site entrance and follow site signs.
⇌ Newport

# PEMBROKESHIRE
## AMROTH

**Little Kings Park,** Ludchurch, Near Amroth, Pembrokeshire, SA67 8PG
**Tel:** 01834 831330
www.littlekings.co.uk
**Pitches For** ▲ ⊕ ⇋ **Total** 120
**Facilities** ∆ ⌇ ⬚ ⬚ ♨ ⌂ ⊙ ⇋ ⬚ ⊡ ⬚
⚏ ⊙ ⬚ ✗ ⬚ ♠ ⬚ ⚚ ⊡ ⬚
**Nearby Facilities** ⌐ ✓ ⚓ ∪ ♬ ✗
**Acreage** 17 **Open** Easter **to** End Sept
**Access** Good **Site** Level
1¼ miles from the beach at Amroth. 10 minutes from Oakwood Park.
**Nearest Town/Resort** Saundersfoot
**Directions** Take the A477 from St. Clears to Tenby. 2 miles from Llanteg petrol station turn left to Amroth, Wisemans Bridge and Ludchurch, turn first right.
⇌ Kilgetty

## AMROTH

**Pantglas Farm,** Tavernspite, Whitland, Pembrokeshire, SA34 0NS
**Tel:** 01834 831618
**Email:** enquiries@pantglasfarm.co.uk
www.pantglasfarm.com
**Pitches For** ▲ ⊕ ⇋ **Total** 75
**Facilities** ∆ ⌇ ⬚ ⬚ ♨ ⌂ ⊙ ⇋ ⬚ ⊡ ⬚
⚏ ⊙ ⬚ ♠ ⬚ ⊬ ⬚ ✲
**Nearby Facilities** ⌐ ✓ ⚓ ∪ ♬
**Acreage** 8 **Open** Easter **to** October
**Access** Good **Site** Level
A quiet, secluded caravan and camping park. Super play area for children. High standard toilet and shower facilities. Caravan storage available from £3.45 weekly. Within easy reach of Tenby, Saundersfoot and Amroth.
**Nearest Town/Resort** Amroth
**Directions** A477 towards Tenby take the B4314 at Red Roses crossroads to Tavernspite 1¼ miles, take the middle road at the village pump. Pantglas is ½ mile down on the left.
⇌ Whitland

## ANGLE

**Castle Farm Camping Site,** Castle Farm, Angle, Nr Pembroke, Pembrokeshire, SA71 5AR
**Tel:** 01646 641220
**Pitches For** ▲ ⊕ ⇋ **Total** 25
**Facilities** ⌇ ⬚ ♨ ⌂ ⊙ ⬚ ⚏ ☻ ⬚ ✲
**Nearby Facilities** ⌐ ✓ ⚓ ∪ ♬ ✗
**Acreage** 2½ **Open** Easter **to** Oct
**Access** Good **Site** Lev/Slope
Overlooking East Angle Bay and directly behind the church in the village. Approx. ½ mile from a safe, sandy beach. Near 2 public houses and Beach Café. Pets are

welcome if kept on leads.
**Nearest Town/Resort** Pembroke
**Directions** Approx. 10 miles from Pembroke.
≠ Pembroke

## BROAD HAVEN

**Creampots Touring Caravan & Camping Park,** Broadway, Broad Haven,
Haverfordwest, Pembrokeshire, SA62 3TU
**Tel:** 01437 781776
www.creampots.co.uk
**Pitches For** ▲ ⚑ ⚑ **Total** 72
**Facilities** ⅃ 🚻 🅿 🔥 ⌐ ⊙ ⌐ ⚐ 🔲 🏧 🌊 👕
**Nearby Facilities** ┠ ✓ ⚓ 🛉 ∪
**Acreage** 7 **Open** Easter **to** October
**Access** Good **Site** Level
Ideal touring base, 1½ miles from safe sandy beach and coastal path at Broad Haven. WTB 5 Star Graded.
**Nearest Town/Resort** Broad Haven
**Directions** Take B4131 Broad Haven road from Haverfordwest to Broadway (5 miles). Turn left and Creampots is the SECOND site on the right (600yds).
≠ Haverfordwest

## FISHGUARD

**Fishguard Bay Caravan Park,** Garn Gelli, Fishguard, Pembrokeshire, SA65 9ET
**Tel:** 01348 811415 **Fax:** 01348 811425
**Email:** enquiries@fishguardbay.com
www.fishguardbay.com
**Pitches For** ▲ ⚑ ⚑ **Total** 50
**Facilities** ⅃ 🚻 🅿 🔥 ⌐ ⊙ ⌐ ⚐ 🔲 👕
**Nearby Facilities** ┠ ✓ ⚓ 🛉 ∪ ⚓ ♪
**Acreage** 5 **Open** March **to** December
**Access** Good **Site** Lev/Slope
Superb cliff top location offering excellent views and walks along this 'Heritage' coast of Pembrokeshire.
**Nearest Town/Resort** Fishguard
**Directions** Take the A487 Cardigan road from Fishguard for 1½ miles, turn left at sign.
≠ Fishguard

## FISHGUARD

**Rosebush Caravan & Camping Park,** Rhoslwyn, Rosebush, Narberth,
Pembrokeshire, SA66 7QT
**Tel:** 01437 532206
**Pitches For** ▲ ⚑ ⚑ **Total** 45
**Facilities** ⅃ 🚻 🅿 🔥 ⌐ ⊙ ⌐ ⚐ 🔲 👕
**Nearby Facilities**
**Acreage** 15 **Open** March **to** October
**Access** Good **Site** Level
ADULTS ONLY PARK in the centre of Pembrokeshire, 800ft above sea level. 3 acre lake for coarse fishing. Mountain walks. David Bellamy Gold Award for conservation.
**Nearest Town/Resort** Fishguard
**Directions** From the A40 take the B4313 near Narberth to Fishguard. 1 mile from the A329 Haverfordwest to Cardigan road.
≠ Clynderwen

## HAVERFORDWEST

**Brandy Brook Caravan & Camping Site,** Rhyndaston, Hayscastle, Haverfordwest,
Pembrokeshire, SA62 5PT
**Tel:** 01348 840272
**Pitches For** ▲ **Total** 40
**Facilities** 🔥 🚻 🔥 ⌐ ⊙ ⌐ 👕
🚿 🍴 🅿 🔥 ⚐ 👕
**Nearby Facilities** ┠ ✓ ⚓ 🛉 ∪ ⚓ ♪
**Acreage** 5 **Open** Easter **to** October
**Access** Poor **Site** Lev/Slope
**Nearest Town/Resort** Haverfordwest
**Directions** From Haverfordwest take the A487 west towards St. Davids, turn right at Roch Motel, signposted.
≠ Haverfordwest

## HAVERFORDWEST

**Nolton Cross Caravan Park,** Nolton, Haverfordwest, Pembrokeshire, SA62 3NP
**Tel:** 01437 710701 **Fax:** 01437 710329
**Email:** noltoncross@nolton.fsnet.co.uk
www.noltoncross-holidays.co.uk
**Pitches For** ▲ ⚑ ⚑ **Total** 15
**Facilities** ⅃ 🚻 🅿 🔥 ⌐ ⊙ ⌐ ⚐ 🔲 👕
🚿 🍴 🅿 🔥 🔥 ⚐ 🔲 👕
**Nearby Facilities** ✓ ∪
**Acreage** 1½ **Open** March **to** December
**Access** Good **Site** Level
Set in open countryside. 1½ miles from the coast.
**Nearest Town/Resort** Haverfordwest
**Directions** Take the A487 from Haverfordwest towards St Davids, after 5 miles at Simpson Cross turn left for Nolton, follow for 1 mile to the next crossroads and turn left, entrance is 100 yards on the right.
≠ Haverfordwest

## HAVERFORDWEST

**Rising Sun Inn Caravan & Camp Site,** Pelcomb Bridge, St Davids Road,
Haverfordwest, Pembrokeshire, SA62 6EA
**Tel:** 01437 765171
**Pitches For** ▲ ⚑ ⚑ **Total** 24
**Facilities** ⅃ 🚻 🔥 ⌐ ⊙ ⌐ 👕
🔥 🔥 ✕ 🔥 ⚐ 🌊
**Nearby Facilities** ┠ ✓ ⚓ 🛉 ∪ ⚓ ♪ ✶
**Acreage** 2 **Open** Easter **to** October
**Access** Good **Site** Lev/Slope
There is a stream on the boundary of the site. 6 miles from the beach and 4 miles from a golf course.
**Nearest Town/Resort** Haverfordwest
**Directions** From Haverfordwest take the A487 road to St Davids. After 2 miles at Pelcomb Bridge site is on the left hand side.
≠ Haverfordwest

## HAVERFORDWEST

**Scamford Caravan Park,** Keeston, Haverfordwest, Pembrokeshire, SA62 6HN
**Tel:** 01437 710304 **Fax:** 01437 710304
**Email:** holidays@scamford.com
www.scamford.com
**Pitches For** ⚑ ⚑ **Total** 5
**Facilities** ⅃ 🚻 🔥 ⌐ ⊙ ⌐ 🔲 👕
🅿 🔥 🔥 ⚐ 🔲 👕
**Nearby Facilities** ┠ ✓ ⚓ 🛉 ∪ ⚓ ♪ ✶
**Open** March **to** Nov
**Access** Good **Site** Level
Ideal location for many beaches, coastal

path, Preseli Hills and Milford Haven Waterway.
**Nearest Town/Resort** Newgale
**Directions** From Haverfordwest take the A487 towards St. Davids. In approx. 4¼ miles turn right at Keeston, then follow signs for Scamford Caravan Park.
≠ Haverfordwest

## KILGETTY

**Ryelands Caravan Park,** Ryelands Lane, Kilgetty, Pembrokeshire, SA68 0UY
**Tel:** 01834 812369
**Pitches For** ▲ ⚑ ⚑ **Total** 45
**Facilities** ⅃ 🚻 🔥 ⌐ ⊙ 👕 🧺 🔥 🔲 👕
**Nearby Facilities** ┠ ✓ ⚓ 🛉 ∪
**Acreage** 5 **Open** March **to** 30 October
**Access** Good **Site** Lev/Slope
Set in open countryside with views to the west, north and east.
**Nearest Town/Resort** Saundersfoot/Tenby
**Directions** Turn left after railway bridge in Kilgetty into Ryelands Lane. Site in ½ mile on the right.
≠ Kilgetty

## KILGETTY

**Stone Pitt Caravan Park,** Begelly, Kilgetty, Pembrokeshire, SA68 0XE
**Tel:** 01834 811086 **Fax:** 01834 810110
**Email:** info@stonepitt.co.uk
www.stonepitt.co.uk
**Pitches For** ▲ ⚑ ⚑ **Total** 55
**Facilities** ⅃ 🚻 🅿 🔥 ⌐ ⊙ ⌐ ⚐ 🔲 👕
🧺 🅿 🔥 🔥 ⚐ 👕 👕
**Nearby Facilities** ┠ ✓ ⚓ 🛉 ∪
**Acreage** 6 **Open** 1 March **to** 9 Jan
**Access** Good **Site** Lev/Slope
Quiet, peaceful, family run park. Within easy reach of Pembrokeshire's wonderful beaches, Folly Farm, Heatherton, Oakwood, Tenby and Saundersfoot. Ideal touring. All pitches are hardstanding with grey water waste.
**Nearest Town/Resort** Saundersfoot/Tenby
**Directions** From St. Clears take the A477, at the next roundabout turn onto the A478 for Narberth. Go over the next roundabout in Begelly Village, site is ½ a mile on the left.
≠ Kilgetty

## LITTLE HAVEN

**Redlands Touring Caravan & Camping Park,** Hasguard Cross, Nr Little Haven,
Haverfordwest, Pembrokeshire, SA62 3SJ
**Tel:** 01437 781300
**Email:** info@redlandscamping.co.uk
www.redlandstouring.co.uk
**Pitches For** ▲ ⚑ ⚑ **Total** 60
**Facilities** ⅃ 🚻 🔥 ⌐ ⊙ ⌐ ⚐ 🔲 👕
🧺 🅿 🔥 🔥 ⚐ 👕
**Nearby Facilities** ┠ ✓ ⚓ 🛉 ∪ ♪
**Acreage** 5 **Open** March **to** December
**Access** Good **Site** Level
Small well run site in Pembrokeshire National Park, within easy reach of coastal path and superb sandy beaches. Hard standing pitches for winter months.
**Nearest Town/Resort** Little Haven
**Directions** 6½ miles southwest of Haverfordwest, on B4327 Dale Road.
≠ Haverfordwest

# PEMBROKESHIRE

## LITTLE HAVEN

**South Cockett Caravan & Camping Park,**
Broadway, Little Haven, Haverfordwest,
Pembrokeshire, SA62 3TU
**Tel:** 01437 781296/781760 **Fax:** 01437
781296
**Email:** esmejames@hotmail.co.uk
www.southcockett.co.uk
**Pitches For** ▲ ⊞ ☰ **Total** 75
Facilities ⅃ ⅏ ☰ ୮ ⊙ ⊣ ▱ ◨ ☗
◐ ☗☗☗
**Nearby Facilities** ⌿ ✦ ⚓ ∪ ⅃
**Acreage** 6 **Open** Easter to October
**Access** Good **Site** Level
Scenic views, near the beach. Ideal
touring, coastal path nearby.
**Nearest Town/Resort** Broad Haven
**Directions** From Haverfordwest take B4341
road for Broad Haven for about 6 miles, turn
left at official camping signs, site 300yds.
⇥ Haverfordwest

## MILFORD HAVEN

**Sandy Haven Caravan Park,**
Herbrandston, Nr Milford Haven,
Pembrokeshire, SA73 3ST
**Tel:** 01646 698844
www.sandyhavencampingpark.co.uk
**Pitches For** ▲ ⊞ **Total** 50
Facilities ⅏ ☰ ୮ ⊙ ☗ ⅊ ◐ ▱☗☗ ⚘
**Nearby Facilities** ⌿ ✦ ⚓ ∪ ⅃ ⅊ ✠
**Acreage** 3½ **Open** Easter to September
**Access** Good **Site** Lev/Slope
Very quiet and uncommercialised site,
alongside a beautiful beach and sea
estuary. Ideal family holidays, boating,
windsurfing, canoeing, etc.. You can also
call our Answerphone on 01646 698844 or
01646 698083.
**Nearest Town/Resort** Milford Haven
**Directions** Take the Dale Road from Milford
Haven, turn left at Herbrandston School and
follow the village road down to the beach.
⇥ Milford Haven

## NARBERTH

**New Park,** Landshipping, Narberth,
Pembrokeshire, SA67 8BG
**Tel:** 01834 891284 **Fax:** 01834 891284
**Pitches For** ▲ ⊞ ☰ **Total** 40
Facilities ⅃ ⅊ ⅏ ⅏ ☰ ୮ ⊙ ⊣ ◐ ⅊ ▱ ☗ ⚘
⅊
**Nearby Facilities** ⌿ ✦ ⚓ ∪ ⅃
**Open** Easter to End Oct
**Access** Good **Site** Level
Situated in a beautiful rural setting, only 1
mile from the River Cleddau. Located in
mid Pembrokeshire it is ideal for exploring
both the coastal and rural settings.
**Nearest Town/Resort** Narberth
**Directions** Take the A40 west, turn left at
Canaston Bridge onto the A4075. After
approx. 3 miles turn right at Cross Hands,
after approx. 2 miles turn right then left. Site
is 1 mile on the left.
⇥ Narberth

## NARBERTH

**Noble Court Holiday Park,** Redstone
Road, Narberth, Pembrokeshire, SA67
7ES
**Tel:** 01834 861908 **Fax:** 01834 861937
**Email:**
enquiries@noblecourtholidaypark.com
www.noblecourtholidaypark.com
**Pitches For** ▲ ⊞ ☰ **Total** 92
Facilities ⅙ ⅃ ⅏ ☰ ୮ ⊙ ⊣ ▱ ◨ ☗
⅊⅊ ◐ ☗ ⚑ ♠ ⋀ ⚘ ▱ ☗ ⚘
**Nearby Facilities** ⌿ ✦ ⚓ ∪ ⅃ ⅊ ⅊
**Acreage** 40 **Open** March to October
**Access** Good **Site** Lev/Slope
Conveniently situated for travel to all
Pembrokeshire beaches and countryside
also Pembrokeshire National Park. Quiet
family caravan park with amenities for all
ages.
**Nearest Town/Resort** Narberth
**Directions** ½ mile north of Narberth on
B4313 road and ½ mile south of A40 on
B4313.
⇥ Narberth

## NARBERTH

**Wood Office Holiday Park,** Cold Blow,
Narberth, Pembrokeshire, SA67 8RR
**Tel:** 01834 860565
**Pitches For** ▲ ⊞ ☰ **Total** 46
Facilities ⅃ ⅏ ☰ ୮ ⊙ ⊣ ▱ ◨ ☗
⅊ ◐ ☗ ⋀☗
**Nearby Facilities** ⌿ ✦ ⚓ ∪ ()
**Acreage** 5½ **Open** April to End Oct
**Access** Good **Site** Level
Close to Oakwood Park, Folly Farm and
Herons Brook. 5 miles from the beach.
**Nearest Town/Resort** Narberth
**Directions** Heading west on the A40 turn
onto the A478 Tenby road, at Templeton turn
left onto the B4315 to Tavernspite.
⇥ Narberth

## NEWPORT

**Llwyngwair Manor,** Newport,
Pembrokeshire, SA42 0LX
**Tel:** 01239 820498 **Fax:** 01239 821280
**Email:** llwyngwairmanor@aol.com
www.llwyngwairmanor.co.uk
**Pitches For** ▲ ⊞ ☰ **Total** 80
Facilities ⅙ ⅆ ⅃ ⅏ ☰ ୮ ⊙ ⊣ ▱ ◨ ☗
⅊ ⅊ ◐ ☗ ⚘ ♅ ⅂ ♠ ⋀ ⚑ ☗ ▱ ☗ ☗
**Nearby Facilities** ⌿ ✦ ⚓ ∪ ⅊
**Open** March to November
**Access** Good **Site** Level
1 mile from sandy beach. 55 acres of wood
and parkland in Pembrokeshire Coast
National Park, alongside the River Nevern.
Tennis on site.
**Nearest Town/Resort** Newport
**Directions** 1 mile from Newport on the A487
to Cardigan.
⇥ Fishguard

## NEWPORT

**Morawelon Caravan & Camping Site,**
Morawelon, The Parrog, Newport,
Pembrokeshire, SA42 0RW
**Tel:** 01239 820565 **Fax:** 01239 820565
**Pitches For** ▲ ⊞ ☰ **Total** 90
Facilities ⅃ ⅏ ☰ ୮ ⊙ ☗ ⅊ ✠ ▱ ☗
**Nearby Facilities** ⌿ ✦ ⚓ ∪ ⅊
**Acreage** 5 **Open** April to Sept
**Access** Good **Site** Sloping
Ideal family site. Near to the beach with a
slipway for boat launching just outside the
entrance. On the Pembrokeshire Coastal
Path.
**Nearest Town/Resort** Newport
**Directions** A487 from Fishguard, 7 miles t
Newport. A487 from Cardigan, 12 miles t
Newport. Turn right after the garage, continu
into Newport, turn left down Parrog Road
Go down to the bottom and Morawelon is
the house by the slipway.
⇥ Fishguard

## NEWPORT

**Tycanol Farm Camp Site,** Newport,
Pembrokeshire, SA42 0ST
**Tel:** 01239 820264
www.caravancampingsites.co.uk
**Pitches For** ▲ ⊞ ☰ **Total** 40
Facilities ⅙ ⅃ ▱ ⅏ ⅏ ☰ ୮ ⊙ ⊣
⅊ ⅊ ◐ ☗ ⋀ ☗♠☗ ▱
**Nearby Facilities** ⌿ ✦ ⚓ ∪ ⅊ ⅊ ✠
**Acreage** 6 **Open** All Year
**Access** Good **Site** Level
Organic farm, situated on a coastal path
with easy access to beaches and the town.
FREE barbecue nightly.
**Nearest Town/Resort** Ne
wport
⇥ Fishguard

## PEMBROKE

**Freshwater East Caravan Club Site,**
Trewent Hill, Freshwater East, Pembroke,
Pembrokeshire, SA71 5LJ
**Tel:** 01646 672341
www.caravanclub.co.uk
**Pitches For** ▲ ⊞ ☰ **Total** 130
Facilities ⅙ ⅃ ▱ ⅏ ☰ ୮ ◨ ☗
⅊ ◐ ☗ ▱ ☗ ☗
**Nearby Facilities** ⌿ ✦ ⚓
**Acreage** 12½ **Open** March to Oct
**Access** Good **Site** Lev/Slope
Situated at the bottom of a hill in
Pembrokeshire Coast National Park. Just
few minutes from the beach with clifftop
views and coastal walks. Close to the
castles of Pembroke, Carew and
Manorbier. Near Folly Farm and Oakwood
Theme Park. Non members welcome.
Booking essential.
**Nearest Town/Resort** Pembroke
**Directions** From A477 take A4075 s
Pembroke. Immediately after passing und
railway bridge turn left onto A4139.
Lamphey at left hand bend continue on
B4584 sp Freshwater East. After 1¾ miles tu
right sp Stackpole, at the foot of the hill tu
right at Club sign. DO NOT tow to beach are
⇥ Pembroke

---

# LLWYNGWAIR MANOR HOLIDAY PARK
## NEWPORT, PEMBS. SA42 0LX

55 acres of beautiful parkland in Pembrokeshire National Park. Alongside the River Nevern. 1 mile from the sea.
Tennis court, fishing and licensed bars. Electric hook-ups for tourers. Self catering apartments and caravans for rent.

### Telephone: (01239) 820498    Fax: (01239) 821280
### www.llwyngwair.co.uk    E-mail: llwyngwairmanor@aol.com

---

CADE'S CAMPING, TOURING & MOTOR CARAVAN SITE GUIDE 200

## PEMBROKE

**Upper Portclew Farm,** Freshwater East, Pembroke, Pembrokeshire, SA71 5LA
Tel: 01646 672112
Pitches For ▲ ⬜ ⬛ Total 35
Facilities ⬜ ⬛ ♠ ┌ ⊙ ┙ ⬛ ▨⌁⬜
Nearby Facilities
Acreage 4 Open 1 May to Mid Sept
Access Good Site Level
Just a short walk through sand dunes to a safe sandy beach and a short walk to a pub with a beer garden and good food, Post Office, fresh bakers and mini-market.
**Nearest Town/Resort** Pembroke
**Directions** 1½ miles east of Pembroke on the A4139. Go through Lamphey onto Freshwater East, 2 miles on the B4584. 10 miles from Tenby and 1½ miles from Lamphey.
⬛ Lamphey

## PEMBROKE

**Windmill Hill Caravan Park,** Windmill Hill Farm, Pembroke, Pembrokeshire, SA71 5BT
Tel: 01646 682392
Email: wjgibby@btopenworld.com
Pitches For ▲ ⬜ ⬛ Total 60
Facilities ⬜ ⬛ ƒ ⬛ ⬜ ♠ ┌ ⊙ ┙ ⬛ ⬛⌁⬜
Nearby Facilities ┌ ✓ ⬛ ❀ ∪ ♪ ⬛ ⬜
Acreage 6 Open March to October
Access Good Site Level
Numerous excellent beaches, famous climbing area. 3 miles from the Irish ferry terminal.
**Nearest Town/Resort** Pembroke
**Directions** Situated approx. 1 mile from Pembroke town on the B4319 towards Castlemartin.
⬛ Pembroke

## REYNALTON

**Croft Holiday Park,** Reynalton, Kilgetty, Pembroke, SA68 0PE
Tel: 01834 860315 Fax: 01834 860510
mail: enquiries@croftholidaypark.com
www.croftholidaypark.com
Pitches For ▲ ⬜ ⬛ Total 55
Facilities ƒ ⬛ ⬜ ♠ ┌ ⊙ ┙ ◄ ⬛ ⬜
⬛ ⊙ ▨ ✗ ⬜ ♠ ▣ ⬛ ⬜ ☼
Nearby Facilities ┌ ✓ ⬛ ❀ ∪ ♪ ⬛ ⬜
Open March to November
Access Good Site Level
Close to the seaside resorts of Tenby and Saundersfoot, and Pembrokeshire National Park.
**Nearest Town/Resort** Saundersfoot
**Directions** From Narberth take the A478 following signs for Tenby. In Templeton turn second right at the Boars Head towards Jerbeston, turn second left to Reynalton and the park is ½ mile on the right hand side.
⬛ Kilgetty

## SAUNDERSFOOT

**Mill House Caravan Park,** Pleasant Valley, Stepaside, Saundersfoot, Pembrokeshire, SA67 8LN
Tel: 01834 812069
mail: holiday@millhousecaravan.co.uk
www.millhousecaravan.co.uk
Pitches For ▲ ⬜ ⬛ Total 12
Facilities ƒ ⬛ ⬜ ♠ ┌ ⊙ ┙ ◄ ⬛ ⬜
Nearby Facilities ┌ ✓ ⬛ ❀ ∪ ♪ ⬛ ⬜
Acreage 2½ Open March to October
Access Good Site Level
Beautiful and sheltered setting in a wooded valley, next to an old water mill. 15 minute walk to the beach and coastal path.

---

Holiday caravans for hire.
**Nearest Town/Resort** Saundersfoot
**Directions** 13 miles west of St. Clears on the A477 turn left signposted Stepaside. After crossing the bridge turn sharp left then immediately left again signed Pleasant Valley. Site is approx. 500 metres on the left hand side.
⬛ Kilgetty

## SAUNDERSFOOT

**Moreton Farm Leisure Park,** Moreton, Saundersfoot, Pembrokeshire, SA69 9EA
**Tel:** 01834 812016
**Email:** moretonfarm@btconnect.com
www.moretonfarm.co.uk
Pitches For ▲ ⬜ ⬛ Total 60
Facilities ⬛ ƒ ⬛ ⬜ ♠ ┌ ⊙ ┙ ◄ ⬛ ⬜ ⬛
▨ ⊙ ⬛ ▣ ⬛ ☼
Nearby Facilities ┌ ✓ ⬛ ❀ ∪ ♪ ⬛ ⬜
Acreage 12 Open March to October
Access Good Site Level
1 mile of safe golden beach. WTB 4 Star Holiday Touring Park.
**Nearest Town/Resort** Tenby/Saundersfoot
**Directions** From St. Clears o the A477, turn left onto A478 for Tenby. Site is on left 1¼ miles, opposite chapel.
⬛ Saundersfoot

## SAUNDERSFOOT

**Moysland Farm Camping Site,** Tenby Road, Saundersfoot, Pembrokeshire, SA69 9DS
Saundersfoot 812455
Pitches For ▲ ⬜ ⬛ Total 20
Facilities ƒ ⬛ ⬜ ♠ ┌ ⊙ ⬛ ▨⌁⬛⬜
Nearby Facilities ┌ ✓ ⬛ ❀ ∪ ♪
Acreage 3 Open June to September
Access Good Site Level
1 mile from the beach. Ideal centre for touring. Please send S.A.E. for details.
**Nearest Town/Resort** Saundersfoot
**Directions** Leave the M4 and take the A48 and A40 to St. Clears, turn onto the A477 to Kilgetty then take the A478 to Tenby. Site is on right hand side of road before New Hedges roundabout.
⬛ Tenby

## SAUNDERSFOOT

**Trevayne Farm,** Saundersfoot, Pembrokeshire, SA69 9DL
**Tel:** 01834 813402
Pitches For ▲ ⬜ ⬛ Total 100
Facilities ƒ ⬛ ⬜ ♠ ┌ ⊙ ⬛ ▣ ⬛ ☼
Nearby Facilities ┌ ✓ ⬛ ❀ ∪ ♪ ⬛
Acreage 7 Open Easter to October
Access Good Site Level
Situated on coast with lovely sandy beach and scenery. 60 electricity hook-ups available for touring and motor caravans and campers. Newly built toilet block with showers and area for disabled.
**Nearest Town/Resort** Saundersfoot/Tenby
**Directions** A40 to St. Clears A477 to Kilgetty. A478 towards Tenby, approx 2½ miles from Tenby turn left for Saundersfoot, right for New Hedges and left again for Trevayne ¾ mile.
⬛ Tenby

## ST. DAVIDS

**Caerfai Bay Caravan & Tent Park,** St Davids, Pembrokeshire, SA62 6QT
**Tel:** 01437 720274 **Fax:** 01437 720577
**Email:** info@caerfaibay.co.uk
www.caerfaibay.co.uk
Pitches For ▲ ⬜ ⬛
Facilities ƒ ⬛ ⬜ ♠ ┌ ⊙ ┙ ◄ ⬛ ⬜
⬛ ⊙ ⬛⌁⬛⬜
Nearby Facilities ┌ ✓ ⬛ ❀ ♪ ⬛
Acreage 9 Open March to Mid Nov
Site Lev/Slope

---

A family run park with panoramic coastal views. Adjacent to the Pembrokeshire Coastal Path and an award winning beach. Within walking distance of St. Davids, Europe's smallest city. Holiday hire caravans available.
**Nearest Town/Resort** St. Davids
**Directions** Turn off the A487 (Haverfordwest to St. Davids road) at St. Davids Visitor Centre signposted Caerfai. At the end of the road, ¾ miles, turn right into park.
⬛ Haverfordwest

## ST. DAVIDS

**Camping & Caravanning Club Site,** Dwr Cwmdig, Berea St Davids, Haverfordwest, Pembrokeshire, SA62 6DW
**Tel:** 01348 831376
www.campingandcaravanningclub.co.uk
Pitches For ▲ ⬜ ⬛ Total 40
Facilities ƒ ⬛ ♠ ┌ ⊙ ┙ ◄ ⬛ ⬜
⬛ ⊙ ⬛⌁⬛⬜
Nearby Facilities ✓
Acreage 4 Open April to Oct
Access Good Site Sloping
Just 1 mile from the beach. Close to Britains smallest cathedral city. BTB 4 Star Graded and AA 2 Pennants. Non members welcome.
**Nearest Town/Resort** Haverfordwest
**Directions** Travelling south on the A487, in Croesgoch turn right at Glyncheryn Farmers Stores. After approx. 1 mile turn right signposted Abereiddy, at the crossroads turn left and the site is 75 yards on the left hand side.
⬛ Fishguard

## ST. DAVIDS

**Hendre Eynon Camp Site,** Hendre Eynon, St Davids, Pembrokeshire, SA62 6DB
**Tel:** 01437 720474 **Fax:** 01437 720474
Pitches For ▲ ⬜ ⬛ Total 72
Facilities ⬛ ƒ ⬛ ⬜ ♠ ┌ ⊙ ┙ ◄ ⬛ ⬜ ⬛
⬛ ⊙ ⬛⌁⬛ ☼
Nearby Facilities ┌ ✓ ⬛ ❀ ♪
Acreage 7 Open Easter to End Sept
Access Good Site Level
Peaceful site on a working farm. Ideal site for country lovers, good for bird watching and walking.
**Nearest Town/Resort** St. Davids
**Directions** At St Davids take the Fishguard road and fork left at the rugby club signposted Llanrhian. Keep going straight and after approx. 2 miles Hendre Eynon is on the right hand side.
⬛ Haverfordwest

## ST. DAVIDS

**Lleithyr Farm Holiday Park,** Lleithyr Farm, St Davids, Pembrokeshire, SA62 6PR
**Tel:** 01437 720245
**Email:** lleithyr@whitesands-stdavids.co.uk
www.whitesands-stdavids.co.uk
Pitches For ▲ ⬜ ⬛ Total 100
Facilities ⬛ ƒ ⬛ ⬜ ♠ ┌ ⊙ ┙ ◄ ⬛ ⬜
⬛ ⊙ ⬛⌁⬛⬜ ☼
Nearby Facilities ┌ ✓ ⬛ ❀ ♪ ⬛
Open 1 March to 6 Jan
Access Good Site Level
Quiet location, 10 minutes walk from the beach. Cliff walks are accessible through the farm. Large shop with in-store bakery, off-licence and butchers counter.
**Nearest Town/Resort** St. Davids
**Directions** From St. Davids follow signs for Whitesands, after 1 mile turn right at the crossroads, then after 400 yards turn first left.
⬛ Haverfordwest

# PEMBROKESHIRE

## ST. DAVIDS

**Lleithyr Meadow Caravan Club Site,** Whitesands, St Davids, Pembrokeshire, SA62 6PR
**Tel:** 01437 720401
www.caravanclub.co.uk
**Pitches For** ⊕ ⚲ ☰ **Total** 120
F a c i l i t i e s ⚲ ƒ ▥ ⚑ ⌐ ▢ ☻
▯❷ ☺ ▤ ⚲ ⤷ ☐ ▣
**Nearby Facilities** ⌐ ✔ ⚓ ↝ ∪
**Acreage** 8 **Open** March **to** Oct
**Access** Good **Site** Level
Just a short walk to Whitesands Bay. Shop adjacent. Non members welcome. Booking essential.
**Nearest Town/Resort** St. Davids
**Directions** From Haverfordwest take A487, before entering St Davids turn right onto B4583 sp Whitesands, turn left still on B4583. At second crossroads (DO NOT follow Lleithyr Meadow signs at first crossroads) turn sharp right opposite St Davids Golf Club, site is 500 yards on the left.
⚒ St. Davids

## ST. DAVIDS

**Nine Wells Caravan & Camping Park,** Nine Wells, Solva, Nr Haverfordwest, Pembrokeshire, SA62 6UH
**Tel:** 01437 721809
**Pitches For** ⚲ ⊕ ☰ **Total** 70
**Facilities** ƒ ▥ ⚑ ⌐ ☺ ⤷ ☐ ▯❷ ⤷ ☐ ▣
**Nearby Facilities** ⌐ ✔ ⚓ ↝ ∪
**Acreage** 4½ **Open** Easter **to** October
**Access** Good **Site** Lev/Slope
Sandy beach ¾ mile. Walk the coastal footpath to Solva. About 5 minute walk to cove and coastal footpath and Iron Age Fort, down National Trust Valley.
**Nearest Town/Resort** Haverfordwest
**Directions** From Haverfordwest take A487 to Solva. ¼ mile past Solva turn left at Nine Wells. Site clearly signposted.
⚒ Haverfordwest

## ST. DAVIDS

**Park Hall Camping Park,** Maerdy Farm, Penycwm, Haverfordwest, Pembrokeshire,
**Tel:** 01437 721606/721282 **Fax:** 721606
**Pitches For** ⚲ ⊕ ☰ **Total** 100
**Facilities** ƒ ▦ ▣ ▥ ⚑ ⌐ ☺ ⤷ ☐ ☻
▯❷ ☺ ▤ ⤷ ☐ ☼ ♆
**Nearby Facilities** ⌐ ✔ ⚓ ↝ ∪ ♪ ♬ ↑
**Acreage** 7 **Open** March **to** October
**Access** Good **Site** Level
Near the beach with scenic views. Ideal touring. Disabled toilet and shower. Dish washing facilities.
**Nearest Town/Resort** Haverfordwest
**Directions** 12 miles from Haverfordwest on the A487 and 6 miles from St. Davids. Turn at the 14th Signal Regiment Brawdy.
⚒ Haverfordwest

## ST. DAVIDS

**Prendergast Caravan & Camping Park,** Trefin, Haverfordwest, Pembrokshire, SA62 5AJ
**Tel:** 01348 831368
**Pitches For** ⚲ ⊕ ☰ **Total** 12
**Facilities** ⚲ ƒ ▥ ⚑ ⌐ ☺ ☻ ☐
**Nearby Facilities** ⌐ ✔ ⚓ ↝ ∪ ♪ ♬ ↑
**Acreage** ½ **Open** April **to** September
**Access** Good **Site** Lev/Slope
Lovely walks along a coastal path.
**Nearest Town/Resort** St. Davids/Fishguard
**Directions** From Haverfordwest take A40 towards Fishguard, until Letterston. Turn left on B4331 until you reach A487. Turn left for St. Davids in about 2½ miles. Turn right by sign for Trefin.
⚒ Haverfordwest

## ST. DAVIDS

**Rhosson Farm Campsite,** Rhosson Farm, St Davids, Haverfordwest, Pembrokeshire, SA62 6RR
**Tel:** 01437 720335/6
**Pitches For** ⚲ ⊕ ☰
**Facilities** ▥ ⚑ ⌐ ☺ ⤷ ↟
**Nearby Facilities** ⌐ ✔ ⚓ ↝ ♪ ↑
**Acreage** 15 **Open** All Year
**Access** Good **Site** Lev/Slope
Wonderful views of Ramsey Island. ½ a mile form the beach. Near the coastal path, lifeboat station and boat trips. Hourly bus service to St Davids. Ice pack service, You can also contact us on Mobile 07870 500890.
**Nearest Town/Resort** St. Davids
**Directions** From St. Davids follow signs towards St Jusinians, Rhosson Farm is 1 mile on the left.
⚒ Haverfordwest

## ST. DAVIDS

**Rhos-y-Cribid,** St Davids, Haverfordwest, Pembrokeshire, SA62 6RR
**Tel:** 01437 720335/6
**Pitches For** ⚲ ⊕ ☰
**Facilities** ▥ ⚑ ⌐ ☺ ⤷ ↟
**Nearby Facilities** ⌐ ✔ ⚓ ↝ ↑
**Acreage** 10 **Open** All Year
**Access** Good **Site** Level
Very quiet site with wonderful views. Near the harbour. Hourly bus service. You can also contact us on Mobile 07870 500890.
**Nearest Town/Resort** St. Davids
**Directions** From St Davids follow signs for Porthclais, then follow signs for campsite. Approx. 1 mile from St. Davids.
⚒ Haverfordwest

## ST. DAVIDS

**Tretio Caravan & Camping Park,** St Davids, Pembrokeshire, SA62 6DE
**Tel:** 01437 720270/781600 **Fax:** 01437 781594
**Email:** info@tretio.com
www.tretio.com
**Pitches For** ⚲ ⊕ ☰ **Total** 40
**Facilities** ⚲ ⚔ ƒ ▥ ⚑ ⌐ ☺ ⤷ ☐ ☐ ☻
▯❷ ☺ ▥ ⤷ ☐ ☼ ♆
**Nearby Facilities** ⌐ ✔ ⚓ ↝ ↑ ↑
**Acreage** 6 **Open** March **to** Oct
**Access** Good **Site** Level
Family run park with a children's play area and a 9 hole pitch 'n' putt course on the 4 acres adjoining the park. Beautiful views over countryside.
**Nearest Town/Resort** St. Davids
**Directions** Leave St Davids on the A487 towards Fishguard, keep left at St. Davids R.F.C. and continue straight on along the coast road for 3 miles.
⚒ Haverfordwest

## TAVERNSPITE

**South Carvan Caravan Park,** Tavernspite, Whitland, Carmarthenshire, SA34 0NL
**Tel:** 01834 831451
**Pitches For** ⚲ ⊕ ☰ **Total** 65
F a c i l i t i e s ƒ ▥ ⚑ ⌐ ☺ ⤷ ☐ ☻
▯❷ ▣ ✖ ♇ ▥ ⯑ ☆ ✿ ⤷ ☐ ☼
**Nearby Facilities** ✔ ∪
**Acreage** 15 **Open** April **to** October
**Access** Good **Site** Level
Wide screen colour TV in the bar.
**Nearest Town/Resort** Whitland
**Directions** From St. Clears take A477 to Tenby at Red Roses turn right 1¾ miles down road into village of Tavernspite.
⚒ Whitland

## TENBY

**Buttyland,** Manorbier, Tenby, Pembrokeshire, SA70 7SN
**Tel:** 01834 871278
**Email:** buttyland@tesco.net
www.buttyland.co.uk
**Pitches For** ⚲ ⊕ ☰ **Total** 53
**Facilities** ƒ ▥ ⚑ ⌐ ☺ ⤷ ☐ ☐ ☻
▯❷ ✖ ✿ ⤷ ☐
**Nearby Facilities** ⌐ ✔ ∪ ↑
**Acreage** 10 **Open** Easter **to** End September
**Access** Good **Site** Level
Manorbier Beach and the Blue Flag beach of Tenby. Ideal touring.
**Nearest Town/Resort** Tenby
**Directions** Take the A4139 west from Tenby for 6 miles. Turn right by Chapel with red cross, 400yds down the road on the right hand side.

**TENBY**

**Crackwell Holiday Park,** Penally, Tenby, Pembrokeshire, SA70 7RX
**Tel:** 01834 842688 **Fax:** 01834 842688
**Email:** crackwelltenby@aol.com
**Pitches For** ▲ ⬤ ☲ **Total** 100
**Facilities** ⬤ ⌇ ⊡ ⊞ ⬛ ▪ ⌐ ⊙ ⊣ ⬛ ⊡ ☎
**Nearby Facilities** ⌐ ✓ ⚓ ⤴ ∪ ⚲ ♞ ⚹
**Acreage** 8 **Open** April **to** October
**Access** Good **Site** Lev/Slope
Near the beach and Pembrokeshire coastal path. Brand new toilet and shower blocks.
**Nearest Town/Resort** Tenby
**Directions** 2 miles west of Tenby on the A4139 coastal road, between Tenby and Lydstep Haven.
⇥ Penally

**TENBY**

**Hazelbrook Caravan Park,** Sageston, Nr Tenby, Pembrokeshire, SA70 8SY
**Tel:** 01646 651351 **Fax:** 01646 651595
**Pitches For** ▲ ⬤ ☲ **Total** 70
**Facilities** ⬤ ⌇ ⊡ ⊞ ▪ ⌐ ⊙ ⊣ ⬛ ⊡ ☎
**Nearby Facilities** ⌐ ✓ ⚓ ⤴ ∪ ⚲
**Acreage** 7½ **Open** 1 March **to** 9 January
**Access** Good **Site** Level
1 mile from Carew Castle and Mill, 2 miles from Dinosaur Park and 7 miles from Oakwood Theme Park.
**Nearest Town/Resort** Tenby
**Directions** Turn off the A477 at the roundabout turning onto the B4318 for Tenby. Caravan park is 20 yards on the right (60 foot entrance).
⇥ Tenby

**TENBY**

**Kiln Park Holiday Centre,** Marsh Road, Tenby, Pembrokeshire, SA70 7RB
**Tel:** 01834 844121
**www.touringholidays.co.uk
**Pitches For** ▲ ⬤ ☲ **Total** 300
**Facilities** ⬤ ⚹ ⌇ ⊞ ▪ ⌐ ⊙ ⊣ ⬛ ⊡ ☎
**Nearby Facilities** ⌐ ✓ ⚓ ⤴ ∪ ⚲ ♞ ⚹
**Acreage** 150 **Open** March **to** September
**Access** Good **Site** Level
5 minutes walk from sandy beach. Tenby has usual resort amusements. Childrens Club and a full family entertainment programme. Burger King and cafe on park.
**Nearest Town/Resort** Tenby
**Directions** Follow the A478 to Tenby, signposted from Tenby.
⇥ Tenby

**TENBY**

**Manorbier Country Park,** Station Road, Tenby, Pembrokeshire, SA70 7SN
**Tel:** 01834 871952 **Fax:** 01834 871203
**Email:** enquiries@countrypark.co.uk
www.countrypark.co.uk
**Pitches For** ▲ ⬤ ☲ **Total** 50
**Facilities** ⬤ ⌇ ⊡ ⊞ ▪ ⌐ ⊙ ⊣ ⬛ ⊡ ☎
⚸ ⬛ ☓ ✓ ⬛ ▪ ⬛ ⊡ ⬛ ⚹
**Nearby Facilities** ⌐ ∪ ⚲
**Open** March **to** Oct
**Access** Good **Site** Level
1½ miles from the beach and a 20 minute drive from Oakwood and Folly Farm.
**Nearest Town/Resort** Tenby
**Directions** From Tenby take the A4139 towards Pembroke. After passing Penally and Lydstep turn right for Manorbier Station, park is 300 yards.
⇥ Manorbier

**TENBY**

**Masterland Farm Touring Caravan & Tent Park,** Broadmoor, Kilgetty, Pembrokeshire, SA68 0RH
**Tel:** 01834 813298 **Fax:** 01834 814408
**Email:** bonsermasterland@aol.com
www.ukparks.co.uk/masterland
**Pitches For** ▲ ⬤ ☲ **Total** 38
**Facilities** ⌇ ⊡ ⊞ ▪ ⌐ ⊙ ⊣ ⬛ ⊡ ☎
⬛ ⬛ ☓ ✓ ⬛ ▪ ⬛ ⊣⊞ ⚹ ⚸
**Nearby Facilities** ⌐ ✓ ⚓ ⤴ ∪ ⚲ ♞
**Acreage** 8 **Open** 1 March **to** 7 January
**Access** Good **Site** Level
Ideal touring, close to leisure parks etc..
**Nearest Town/Resort** Tenby
**Directions** After Carmarthen take main A40 to St. Clears, then take the A477 to Broadmoor. Turn right at Cross Inn Public House, Masterland Farm is 300yds on your right.
⇥ Kilgetty

**TENBY**

**Milton Bridge Caravan Park,** Milton, Nr Tenby, Pembrokeshire, SA70 8PH
**Tel:** 01646 651204 **Fax:** 01646 651204
**Email:** milton-bridge@tiscali.co.uk
**Pitches For** ⬤ ☲ **Total** 15
**Facilities** ⌇ ⊡ ⊞ ▪ ⌐ ⊙ ⊣ ⬛ ⊡ ☎
⬛ ⬛⊞ ⊡ ⬛ ⚹
**Nearby Facilities** ⌐ ✓ ⚓ ⤴ ∪ ⚲ ♞ ⚹
**Acreage** 3 **Open** March **to** October
**Access** Good **Site** Lev/Slope
Small, friendly park situated on a tidal river. Ideal base for exploring the many attractions in the area.
**Nearest Town/Resort** Tenby
**Directions** Half way between Kilgetty and Pembroke Dock on the A477.
⇥ Lamphey

**TENBY**

**Red House Farm,** Twy Cross, Tenby, Pembrokeshire, SA69 9DP
**Tel:** 01834 813918
**Pitches For** ▲ ⬤ ☲ **Total** 10
**Facilities** ⌇ ⊞ ⌐ ▪ ⊞ ⊡ A
**Nearby Facilities** ⌐ ✓ ⚓ ⤴ ∪ ⚲ ♞
**Acreage** 2 **Open** May **to** September
**Access** Good **Site** Lev/Slope
Very quiet, small, ADULTS ONLY site. Most appreciated by those seeking peace rather than entertainment. Not suitable for small children. Sorry No pets.
**Nearest Town/Resort** Tenby
**Directions** Situated just off the A478, 1½ miles from both Tenby and Saundersfoot. Regular bus service.
⇥ Tenby

**TENBY**

**Rowston Holiday Park,** New Hedges, Tenby, Pembrokeshire, SA70 8TL
**Tel:** 01834 842178 **Fax:** 01834 842179
**Email:** enquiries@rowston-holiday-park.co.uk
www.rowston-holiday-park.co.uk
**Pitches For** ▲ ⬤ ☲ **Total** 120
**Facilities** ⚹ ⌇ ⊡ ⊞ ▪ ⌐ ⊙ ⊣ ⬛ ⊡ ☎
⬛ ⬛ ⬛ ☓ ▪ ⬛ ⊣⊞ ⬛ ⚹
**Nearby Facilities** ⌐ ✓ ⚓ ⤴ ∪ ⚲ ♞
**Open** March **to** Oct
**Access** Good **Site** Sloping
Access from Rowston to Waterwynch Beach. 15-20 minute drive from Oakwood and Folly Farm. 5 minute drive to the beaches at Tenby and Saundersfoot.
**Nearest Town/Resort** Tenby
**Directions** From Kilgetty follow signs for Tenby, at New Hedges roundabout turn left, then turn right into New Hedges and follow signs for Rowston.
⇥ Tenby

**TENBY**

**Sunnyvale Holiday Park,** Valley Road, Saundersfoot, Pembrokeshire, SA69 9BT
**Tel:** 01348 872462 **Fax:** 01348 872351
www.howellsleisure.co.uk
**Pitches For** ⬤ ☲ **Total** 50
**Facilities** ⚹ ⌇ ⊡ ⊞ ▪ ⌐ ⊙ ⊣ ⬛ ⊡ ☎
⬛ ⬛ ⬛ ☓ ✓ ⬛ ▪ ⬛ ⊣⊞ ⊡ ⬛ ⚹ ⌐
**Nearby Facilities** ⌐ ✓ ⚓ ⤴ ∪ ⚲
**Acreage** 5 **Open** March **to** October
**Access** Good **Site** Lev/Slope
Near Tenby, Saundersfoot and numerous golden sandy beaches. Clubhouse with Free nightly live entertainment for adults and children. Pitches from just £7 per night.
**Nearest Town/Resort** Tenby

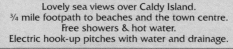

# PEMBROKESHIRE, POWYS

**Directions** Take the A478 to Tenby, proceed through Pentlepoir and take a left turn into Valley Road, Sunnyvale is 300 yards down on the left hand side.
⚡ Kilgetty

### TENBY

**Tudor Glen Caravan Park,** Jameston, Nr Tenby, Pembrokeshire, SA70 7SS
**Tel:** 01834 871417 **Fax:** 01834 871832
**Email:** info@tudorglencaravanpark.co.uk
**www.**tudorglencaravanpark.com
**Pitches For** ▲ ⊕ ➡ **Total** 46
**Facilities** ✦ 🗓 🔟 🎇 ⌂ ☺ ➡ ⬛ 🍴
🕑🏰 🌐🏧🍴 ⟟ 🔥 ⬛
**Nearby Facilities** 🏹 ✈ 🏖 🎿 🛝 🎣 🚣 🏇
**Acreage** 6 **Open** March **to** October
**Access** Good **Site** Lev/Slope
Family run site, ideal touring base.
**Nearest Town/Resort** Tenby
**Directions** From Tenby take the A4139 Coast Road west for 6 miles. Site is on the right before entering village of Jameston.
⚡ Manorbier

### TENBY

**Well Park Caravans,** Tenby, Pembrokeshire, SA70 8TL
**Tel:** 01834 842179
**Email:** enquiries@wellparkcaravans.co.uk
**www.**wellparkcaravans.co.uk
**Pitches For** ▲ ⊕ ➡ **Total** 100
**Facilities** ✦ 🗓 🔟 🎇 ⌂ ☺ ➡ ⬛ 🍴
🕑🏰 🌐🏧🍴 🔥 ⬛ 🎇 ❄
**Nearby Facilities** 🏹 ✈ 🏖 🎿 🛝 🎣 🚣 🏇
**Acreage** 10 **Open** April **to** October
**Access** Good **Site** Lev/Slope
A family run site, situated in pleasant surroundings. Excellent facilities. Very central and convenient for the beautiful beaches and places of interest along the Pembrokeshire coast. AA, Dragon Award and Wales in Bloom Award Winning Park.
**Nearest Town/Resort** Tenby
**Directions** On righthand side of main Tenby (A478) road 1 mile north of Tenby.
⚡ Tenby

### TENBY

**Whitewell Caravan Park,** Lydstep Beach, Penally, Tenby, Pembrokeshire, SA70 7RY
**Tel:** 01834 871569
**Pitches For** ▲ ⊕ ➡ **Total** 120
**Facilities** ✦ 🔟 🎇 ⌂ ☺ ➡ ⬛ 🍴
🕑🏰 🌐🏧🍴 ⬛
**Nearby Facilities** 🏹 ✈ 🏖 🎿 🛝 🎣 🚣 🏇
**Acreage** 13 **Open** April **to** September
**Access** Good **Site** Level
½ mile Lydstep Beach, green countryside on all sides.
**Nearest Town/Resort** Tenby
⚡ Tenby

### TENBY

**Windmills Camping Park,** Tenby, Pembrokeshire, SA70 8TJ
**Tel:** 01834 842200
**Pitches For** ▲ ⊕ ➡
**Facilities** ✦ 🔟 🔟 🎇 ⌂ ☺🍴 🕑🏰 ⬛
**Nearby Facilities** 🏹 ✈
**Acreage** 4 **Open** Easter **to** Oct
**Access** Good **Site** Level
Situated on a hill above Tenby with sea views. Footpath and cycle track down to the town and north beach.
**Nearest Town/Resort** Tenby
**Directions** Approaching Tenby turn left up the lane just past New Hedges Village.
⚡ Tenby

### TENBY

**Wood Park Caravan Park,** New Hedges, Tenby, Pembrokeshire, SA70 8TL
**Tel:** 0845 129 8314 (Lo-call)
**Email:** info@woodpark.co.uk
**www.**woodpark.co.uk
**Pitches For** ▲ ⊕ ➡ **Total** 60
**Facilities** ✦ 🔟 🎇 ⌂ ☺ ➡ ⬛ 🍴
🕑 🏰🌐🏧 ⬛
**Nearby Facilities** 🏹 ✈ 🏖 🎿 🛝 🎣 🚣 🏇
**Acreage** 2 **Open** April **to** October
**Access** Good **Site** Lev/Slope
Quiet, family park ideally situated between Tenby and Saundersfoot. Advanced bookings are not taken for Motor Caravans.
**Nearest Town/Resort** Tenby
**Directions** At the roundabout 2 miles north of Tenby, take the A478 towards Tenby. Take the second turn right and right again.
⚡ Tenby

# POWYS

### BRECON

**Aberbran Caravan Club Site,** Aberbran, Brecon, Powys, LD3 9NH
**Tel:** 01874 622424
**www.**caravanclub.co.uk
**Pitches For** ⊕ ➡ **Total** 24
**Facilities** ✦ 🔟 🕑🏰 🌐🏧➡⬛
**Nearby Facilities** 🏹 ✈
**Acreage** 2 **Open** March **to** Oct
**Access** Good **Site** Level
Small site formerly a railway station, on the edge of Brecon Beacons National Park. Ideal walking and bird watching. Own sanitation required. Non members welcome. Booking essential.
**Nearest Town/Resort** Brecon
**Directions** From the A40 Brecon bypass, at roundabout at end of dual carriageway continue straight on the A40, after 4¼ miles turn right at signpost Aberbran. Site is ½ mile on the left (immediately before demolished railway bridge).
⚡ Brecon

### BRECON

**Brynich Caravan Park,** Brecon, Powys, LD3 7SH
**Tel:** 01874 623325 **Fax:** 01874 623325
**Email:** holidays@brynich.co.uk
**www.**brynich.co.uk
**Pitches For** ▲ ⊕ ➡ **Total** 130
**Facilities** ⚿ ✦ 🔟 🔟 🎇 ⌂ ☺ ➡ ⬛ 🍴
🕑🏰🌐🏧🍴🔥 ⬛
**Nearby Facilities** 🏹 ✈ 🏖 🎿 🛝 🎣 🏇
**Acreage** 20 **Open** 18 March **to** 30 Oct
**Access** Very Easy **Site** Level
Award winning, family run park with spectacular views of the Brecon Beacons. Large pitches, grass and gravel hardstandings, some with waste and water. Adventure playground, recreation field and dog exercise field. Excellent facilities in two heated shower blocks with baby, disabled and family rooms, also laundry and drying room. New indoor soft play barn (extra charge) and restaurant in a converted 17th Century barn.
**Nearest Town/Resort** Brecon
**Directions** 1 mile east of Brecon on A470. 250 yards from A40/A470 roundabout.
⚡ Abergavenny/Merthyr Tydfil

### BRECON

**Lakeside Caravan & Camping Park,** Llangorse Lake, Llangorse, Brecon, Powys, LD3 7TR
**Tel:** 01874 658226 **Fax:** 01874 658430
**Email:** holidays@lakeside.zx3.net

**www.**lakeside-holidays.net
**Pitches For** ▲ ⊕ ➡ **Total** 40
**Facilities** ✦ 🔟 🎇 ⌂ ☺ ➡ ⬛ 🍴
🕑🏰🌐🏧✖🍴🔟🏟🌼🍴⟟⬛ ⬛
**Nearby Facilities** 🏹 ✈ 🏖 🎿 🛝 🎣 🏇
**Acreage** 14 **Open** 31 March **to** 31 Octobe
**Access** Good **Site** Level
The area teems with wildlife, the scenery is outstanding and our welcome is warm. Very near to Llangorse Lake. Rallies welcome.
**Nearest Town/Resort** Brecon
**Directions** From Brecon take the A40 eas for 2 miles, take left hand turn signposte Llangorse, follow signs for 4 miles, turn righ for the lake.
⚡ Abergavenny

### BRECON

**Mill Field Caravan Park,** Mill Service Station, Three Cocks, Brecon, Powys, LD3 0SL
**Tel:** 01497 847381
**Pitches For** ▲ ⊕ ➡ **Total** 40
**Facilities** ✦ 🔟 🎇 🎇 ⌂ 🎇 ❄ 🌼 ⟟
**Nearby Facilities** 🏹 ✈ 🏖 🎿 🛝 🎣 🏇
**Acreage** 2¼ **Open** All Year
**Access** Good **Site** Level
Near to Hay-on-Wye the 'Town of Books'. Easy access to the Black Mountains and Brecon Beacons.
**Nearest Town/Resort** Hay-on-Wye
**Directions** On the A438 between Brecon and Hay-on-Wye, 5 miles from Hay-on-Wye
⚡ Hereford

### BRECON

**Pencelli Castle Caravan & Camp Park,** Pencelli Castle, Pencelli, Brecon, Powys, LD3 7LX
**Tel:** 01874 665451 **Fax:** 01874 665452
**Email:** cades@pencelli-castle.co.uk
**www.**pencelli-castle.co.uk
**Pitches For** ▲ ⊕ ➡ **Total** 80
**Facilities** ⚿ ✦ 🔟 🔟 🎇 ⌂ ☺ ➡ ⬛ 🍴
🕑🏰🌐🏧🌼🍴⬛
**Nearby Facilities** 🏹 ✈ 🏖 🎿 🛝 🎣 🏇
**Acreage** 10 **Open** All Year
**Access** Good **Site** Level
Practical Caravan Top Family Park in Wales 2005/04/03/02, National Tourism Awards for Wales 2003 'Best Place to Stay - Self Catering', AA Best Campsite in Wales 2002 and Calor Gas Best Park in Wales 2001. Peacefully set in the heart of a National Park. Within walking distance of the highest peaks. Adjoining Brecon Canal Village pub 150 yards. Bike hire. On a bus route. Red deer, vintage farm machinery, etc..
**Nearest Town/Resort** Brecon
**Directions** Leave Brecon on the A40 heading east, after 2 miles turn onto the B4558 signposted Pencelli. We are on the outskirts of the village.

### BUILTH WELLS

**Fforest Fields,** Hundred House, Builth Wells, Powys, LD1 5RT
**Tel:** 01982 570406
**Email:** office@fforestfields.co.uk
**www.**fforestfields.co.uk
**Pitches For** ▲ ⊕ ➡
**Facilities** ✦ 🔟 🔟 🎇 ⌂ ☺ ➡ ⬛ 🍴
🕑🏰🌐🏧 ⬛
**Nearby Facilities** 🏹 ✈ 🏖 🎿 🛝 🎣
**Open** Easter/April **to** Nov
**Access** Good **Site** Level
No clubhouse or statics on this very pretty, award winning, family run site. Very rural and peaceful (no traffic noise) with stunning views. Hardstandings for motor caravans. Pristine facilities. Woodland and mountain walks direct from the site. 4 Star

Graded, AA 3 Pennants and Special David Bellamy Gold Award for last five years conservation excellence.
**Nearest Town/Resort** Builth Wells
**Directions** 4 miles east of Builth Wells on the A481, well signposted. Wide entrance.
⇌ Builth Road Station

## BUILTH WELLS
**Irfon Caravan Park,** Upper Chapel Road, Garth, Builth Wells, Powys, LD4 4BH
**Tel:** 01591 620310
**Pitches For** ▲ ⚲ ⌂ **Total** 24
**Facilities** ♪ ⌂ ⬛ ♨ ⌐ ⊙ ⅃ ◪ ▨
🏧 🅾 ☎ ✚ ⛊ 🔄
**Nearby Facilities** ┌ ✓ ∪ ♪
**Acreage** 6½ **Open** Easter **to** October
**Access** Good **Site** Lev/Slope
Quiet site alongside a river with scenic views. Ideal touring in the beauty of the mountains and forest. Convenient for events at the Royal Welsh Showground. Static holiday vans for sale. Fly
**Nearest Town/Resort** Builth Wells
**Directions** 500 yards along the B4519 out of Garth (Garth is 6 miles west of Builth Wells along the A483).
⇌ Garth

## BUILTH WELLS
**White House Caravan & Camp Site,** Builth Wells, Powys, LD2 3BP
**Tel:** 01982 552255
**Email:** info@whitehousecampsite.co.uk
**www.whitehousecampsite.co.uk**
**Pitches For** ▲ ⚲ ⬜ **Total** 30
**Facilities** ♿ ♪ ⌂ ⬛ ♨ ⌐ ⊙ ⅃ ☎ ⊙ ✚ ▨ 🔄
**Nearby Facilities** ┌ ✓ ✇ ♪
**Acreage** 2½ **Open** April **to** Oct
**Access** Good **Site** Level
On the banks of the River Wye. Within walking distance of Royal Welsh Showground. New toilet block. WTB 3 Star Graded.
**Nearest Town/Resort** Builth Wells
**Directions** On the eastern edge of Builth Wells, 300 yards from the A470. Wide entrance.
⇌ Builth Wells

## CRICKHOWELL
**Cwmdu Caravan & Camping Site,** New Road, Cwmdu, Crickhowell, Powys, NP8 1RU
**Tel:** 01874 730441
**Pitches For** ▲ ⚲ ⌂ **Total** 60
**Facilities** ♪ ⬛ ♨ ⌐ ⊙ ⅃ 🕱 🏧 ☎ ✚ ▨
**Nearby Facilities** 
**Acreage** 4 **Open** March **to** Oct
**Access** Good **Site** Lev/Slope
Quiet, peaceful location at the foot of the Black Mountains.
**Nearest Town/Resort** Crickhowell
**Directions** From Crickhowell take the A40 north, turn onto the A479 and the site is in Cwmdu.
⇌ Abergavenny

## CRICKHOWELL
**Riverside Caravan & Camping Park** New Road, Crickhowell, Powys, NP8 1AY
**Tel:** 01873 810397
**Pitches For** ▲ ⚲ ⌂ **Total** 65
**Facilities** ♪ ⌂ ⬛ ♨ ⌐ ⊙ ✚ ▨ ⊡ A
**Nearby Facilities** ┌ ∪ ✗
**Acreage** 3½ **Open** March **to** October
**Access** Good **Site** Level
ADULTS ONLY, No children under 18 years, over 18 years at owners discretion. Near river, mountain and canal walks and pony trekking. Town 5 mins walk, in National Park. New improved toilet, shower block with laundry (with drying facilities).

A.A. 3 Pennants. No hang gliders and paragliders.
**Nearest Town/Resort** Crickhowell
**Directions** Between the A40 and the A4077 at Crickhowell.
⇌ Abergavenny

## LLANBRYNMAIR
**Cringoed Caravan & Camping Park,** Llanbrynmair, Powys, SY19 7DR
**Tel:** 01650 521237
**Email:** cringoedcaravan.park@virgin.net
**Pitches For** ▲ ⚲ ⌂ **Total** 35
**Facilities** ♪ ⌂ ⬛ ♨ ⌐ ⊙ ⅃ ⊙ ▨ ◪ ▨
🏧 🅾 ☎ 🍴 A ↦ ⊡ ☼
**Nearby Facilities** ┌ ✓ ⚓ ∪ ♪
**Acreage** 5 **Open** 7 March **to** 7 January
**Access** Good **Site** Level
Ideal base by the river for touring the many beaches, railways, castles, slate mines, nature reserves and the Alternative Technology Centre.
**Nearest Town/Resort** Newtown
**Directions** Take the A470 from Newtown to Llanbrynmair for 18 miles, turn onto the B4518 for 1 mile, site is on the right.
⇌ Machynlleth

## LLANBRYNMAIR
**Gwern-y-Bwlch Caravan Club Site,** Llanbrynmair, Powys, SY19 7EB
**Tel:** 01650 521351
**www.caravanclub.co.uk**
**Pitches For** ⚲ ⌂ **Total** 38
**Facilities** ⬛ ⌂ ⅃ ⊙ ☎ ✚ ▨
**Nearby Facilities**
**Acreage** 5 **Open** March **to** Oct
**Access** Good **Site** Lev/Slope
Lovely setting with views to the mountains across a valley. Bird hide and feeding station on site, watch for Red Kites. Own sanitation required. Non members welcome. Booking essential.
**Nearest Town/Resort** Llanbrynmair
**Directions** From the A470, 1 mile past Llanbrynmair turn right at Caravan Club sign, site is 50 yards up the hill on the left.
⇌ Llanbrynmair

## LLANDRINDOD WELLS
**Bryncrach Caravan Site,** Bryncrach, Hundred House, Llandrindod Wells, Powys, LD1 5RY
**Tel:** 01982 570291
**Pitches For** ▲ ⚲ ⌂ **Total** 15
**Facilities** ♪ ⌂ ⬛ ♨ ⌐ ⊙ ⅃ ☎
🏧 🅾 ✚ ▨ ☼
**Nearby Facilities** ┌ ✓ ∪ ♪
**Acreage** 1¾ **Open** All Year
**Access** Good **Site** Level
Quiet site with splendid views and walks. Fishing and riding can be arranged. River nearby.
**Nearest Town/Resort** Builth Wells
**Directions** Hundred House is on the A481 between Builth Wells and the A44. Turn left signposted Franks Bridge immediately before the public house, after 250 yards turn left into farm road.
⇌ Llandrindod Wells

## LLANDRINDOD WELLS
**Dalmore Caravan Park,** Howey, Llandrindod Wells, Powys, LD1 5RG
**Tel:** 01597 822483 **Fax:** 01597 822483
**Pitches For** ▲ ⚲ ⌂ **Total** 20
**Facilities** ♪ ⌂ ⬛ ♨ ⌐ ⊙ ⅃ ☎
🏧 🅾 ⊡ A ☼ ✐
**Nearby Facilities** ┌ ✓ ⚓ ∪ ♪
**Acreage** 2 **Open** March **to** October
**Access** Good **Site** Lev/Gentle Slope
ADULTS ONLY ON TOURING PARK. Ideal base for hiking and touring Mid Wales,

scenic views.
**Nearest Town/Resort** Llandrindod Wells
**Directions** 2 miles south of Llandrindod off the main A483, towards Builth Wells.
⇌ Llandrindod

## LLANDRINDOD WELLS
**Disserth Caravan & Camping Park,** Howey, Llandrindod Wells, Powys, LD1 6NL
**Tel:** 01597 860277 **Fax:** 01597 860147
**Email:** m.hobbs@virgin.net
**www.disserth.com**
**Pitches For** ▲ ⚲ ⌂ **Total** 40
**Facilities** ♪ ⌂ ⬛ ♨ ⌐ ⊙ ⅃ ☎ ⊙ ▨ ◪ ▨
🏧 🅾 ☎ ✗ ⛳ ✚ ⊡ ☼
**Nearby Facilities** ┌ ✓ ∪ ♪ ♪
**Acreage** 4 **Open** March **to** Oct
**Access** Good **Site** Level
Small, tranquil, riverside park with wildlife for neighbours.
**Nearest Town/Resort** Llandrindod Wells
**Directions** Heading south on the A483, turn right at Howey signposted Newbridge-on-Wye and Disserth. Park is by the river and church.
⇌ Llandrindod Wells

## LLANFYLLIN
**Henstent Caravan Park,** Llangynog, Nr Oswestry, Powys, SY10 0EP
**Tel:** 01691 860479
**Email:** henstent@mac.com
**www.homepage.mac.com/henstent**
**Pitches For** ▲ ⚲ ⌂ **Total** 35
**Facilities** ♪ ⌂ ⬛ ♨ ⌐ ⊙ ⅃ ☎ ⊙ ▨ ◪ ▨
🏧 🅾 ☎ ✚ ⊡ ☼ ✐
**Nearby Facilities** ┌ ✓ ⚓ ∪ ♪
**Acreage** 1 **Open** March **to** October
**Access** Good **Site** Sloping
Spectacular mountain views with frontage to the River Tanat. Rural location popular with bird watchers and walkers.
**Nearest Town/Resort** Bala
**Directions** Situated on the B4391. Follow signs for Bala from Oswestry. 18 miles from Oswestry, 12 miles from Bala.
⇌ Gobowen

## LLANIDLOES
**Dol-Llys Touring Site,** Dol-Llys Farm, Llanidloes, Powys, SY18 6JA
**Tel:** 01686 412694
**Pitches For** ▲ ⚲ ⌂
**Facilities** ♪ ⌂ ⬛ ♨ ⌐ ⊙ ⅃ ◪ ☎ ✚ ▨
**Nearby Facilities** ┌ ✓ ⚓ ♪
**Acreage** 2 **Open** April **to** October
**Access** Good **Site** Level
Alongside the banks of the River Severn. Campers Kitchen for walkers and cyclists.
**Nearest Town/Resort** Llanidloes
**Directions** From Llanidloes take the B4569, past hospital, fork right onto the Oakley Park Road, Dol-Llys is the first farm on the right.
⇌ Caersws

## LLANSANTFFRAID
**Bryn-Vyrnwy Caravan Park,** Llansantffraid-Ym-Mechain, Powys, SY22 6AY
**Tel:** 01691 828252
**Pitches For** ▲ ⚲ ⌂
**Facilities** ♪ ⌂ ⬛ ♨ ⌐ ☎ ⊙ ♨ 🏧 🅾 ⋒ ↦
**Nearby Facilities** ┌ ✓ ∪
**Acreage** 3 **Open** April **to** October
**Access** Good **Site** Level
On the banks of the River Vyrnwy. Near to excellent golf courses and famous Wales tourist attractions.
**Nearest Town/Resort** Oswestry/Welshpool
**Directions** From Oswestry take the A483 to Welshpool, at Llynclys take the A495 for 3 miles.
⇌ Welshpool

## THE HORSE AND JOCKEY CARAVAN SITE

Tents, Touring Caravans & Motor Caravans welcome. 20 pitches, electric hook-ups available. Pub & Restaurant. Toilets, Showers & Hot Water. Pets Welcome. 12 miles from Newtown on the A490 Churchstoke to Welshpool road. **OPEN ALL YEAR.**

**01588 620060**

Horse & Jockey, Chirbury Road, Churchstoke, Montgomery, Powys SY15 6AE

### LLANWDDYN
**Fronheulog,** Lake Vyrnwy, Via Oswestry, Powys, SY10 0NN
**Tel:** 01691 Llanwyddyn 870662
**Pitches For** ▲ � 🚐 **Total** 22
**Facilities** 🎣🎱👤🚻🛍️🔥🚿🍴🅿️♨️ ♦
**Nearby Facilities** ✓
**Acreage** 2 **Open** March **to** October
**Access** Good **Site** Level
ADULTS ONLY. Pre-booking necessary. RSPB reserve nearby. Ideal centre for touring. Cold water tap. Price Guide £2.50 per person per night.
**Nearest Town/Resort** Lake Vyrnwy
**Directions** 2 miles south of Lake Vyrnwy on B4393. 8 miles from Llanfyllin, Bala 18 miles.

### MACHYNLLETH
**Croeslyn,** Croeslyn, Aberhosan, Machynlleth, Powys, SY20 8SF
**Tel:** 01654 702383
**Pitches For** ▲ ⊑ 🚐
**Facilities** 🅿️
**Nearby Facilities**
**Open** Easter **to** October
**Access** Good **Site** Level
10 miles from the nearest beach. Ideal for walkers and bird watchers.
**Nearest Town/Resort** Machynlleth
**Directions** 4 miles from Machynlleth.
⭐ Machynlleth

### MACHYNLLETH
**Morben Isaf Holiday Home & Touring Park,** Derwenlas, Machynlleth, Powys, SY20 8SR
**Tel:** 01654 781473 **Fax:** 01654 781450
**Email:** manager@morbenisaf.co.uk
**Pitches For** ▲ ⊑ 🚐 **Total** 17
**Facilities** 🅰️ ✆ 🎱 🅿️ 🔥 👤 🚿 🍴 🅿️ 📞
🛁 ♨️ 🚻
**Nearby Facilities** 👤 ✓ ∪
**Open** Mid March **to** 31 Oct
**Access** Good **Site** Level
8 miles from Ynyslas Beach and 3 miles from Ynys-Hir Nature Reserve. Lovely walks starting in Machynlleth.
**Nearest Town/Resort** Machynlleth
**Directions** 2½ miles south of Machynlleth on the A487 Aberystwyth road.
⭐ Machynlleth

### MIDDLETOWN
**Bank Farm Caravan Park,** Middletown, Welshpool, Powys, SY21 8EJ
**Tel:** 01938 570526
**Email:** gill@bankfarmcaravans.fsnet.co.uk
**Pitches For** ▲ ⊑ 🚐 **Total** 20
**Facilities** 🅰️ 🎣 ✆ 🅿️ 🔥 👤 🚿 🍴 🅿️ 📞
🛁 🔥 🐕 🚻 ♨️
**Nearby Facilities** 👤 ✓ ∪
**Acreage** 2 **Open** March **to** October
**Access** Good **Site** Lev/Slope
Scenic views, ideal touring area.
**Nearest Town/Resort** Welshpool
**Directions** On A458 5½ miles east of Welshpool and 13¼ miles west of Shrewsbury.
⭐ Welshpool

### MONTGOMERY
**Bacheldre Watermill Caravan & Campsite,** Churchstoke, Montgomery, Powys, SY15 6TE
**Tel:** 01588 620489 **Fax:** 01588 620105
**Email:** info@bacheldremill.co.uk
www.bacheldremill.co.uk
**Pitches For** ▲ ⊑ 🚐 **Total** 24
**Facilities** ✆ 🅿️ 🔥 👤 🚿 🍴 🅿️ 📞 🚻 ♨️
**Nearby Facilities** 👤 ✓ ∪ ♠
**Acreage** 2 **Open** All Year
**Access** Good **Site** Level
Situated in the Welsh Marches, an area of exceptional beauty. Excellent walking, cycling and exploring. ½ a mile from Offa's Dyke.
**Nearest Town/Resort** Montgomery
**Directions** From Churchstoke take the A489 towards Newtown, after 2 miles turn left at the signpost Bacheldre Mill, site is 50 yards on the right.
⭐ Welshpool

### MONTGOMERY
**Horse & Jockey Caravan Site,** Horse & Jockey, Chirbury Road, Churchstoke, Montgomery, Powys, SY15 6AE
**Tel:** 01588 620060 **Fax:** 01588 620060
**Pitches For** ▲ ⊑ ☐ **Total** 20
**Facilities** 🅰️ ✆ 🅿️ 🔥 🅿️ 👤 🍴 📞
🛁 🍴 🐕 🚻 ♨️
**Nearby Facilities** 👤 ✓ ∪
**Open** All Year
**Access** Good **Site** Level
Near Offa's Dyke Footpath. Ideal for walking and touring.
**Nearest Town/Resort** Newtown
**Directions** 12 miles from Newtown on the A490 Churchstoke to Welshpool road.
⭐ Newtown

### NEW RADNOR
**Old Station Caravan Park,** New Radnor, Powys, LD8
**Tel:** 07891 397719
**Email:** info@oldstationcaravanpark.co.uk
www.oldstationcaravanpark.co.uk
**Pitches For** ▲ ⊑ ☐ **Total** 28
**Facilities** 🅰️ ✆ 🅿️ 🔥 👤 🅿️ 🍴 📞
🛁 🏠 🔥 🐕 🚻 ♨️
**Nearby Facilities** 👤 ✓ ♠ ∪ ♠
**Acreage** 1¾ **Open** March **to** Oct
**Access** Good **Site** Level
Ideal base for walking and cycling. Easy access to Offa's Dyke, Elan Valley Dams and the attractions of Mid Wales.
**Nearest Town/Resort** Kington
**Directions** 6 miles from Kington on the A44 to Rhayader.
⭐ Leominster

### NEWTOWN
**Smithy Caravan Park,** Abermule, Newtown, Powys, SY15 6ND
**Tel:** 01584 711280 **Fax:** 01584 711460
**Email:** info@bestparks.co.uk
www.bestparks.co.uk
**Pitches For** ▲ ⊑ 🚐 **Total** 30
**Facilities** 🅰️ ✆ 🅿️ 🔥 👤 🅿️ 🍴 📞
🛁 🏠 🔥 🐕 🚻 ♨️
**Nearby Facilities** 👤 ✓ ∪ ♠ ♣
**Acreage** 4 **Open** March **to** Nov

**Access** Good **Site** Level
Outstanding quality park, maintained to the highest standards. New toilet and shower block. All pitches are hard standing and fully serviced. 2 miles of River Severn
**Nearest Town/Resort** Newtown
**Directions** Leave the A483 3 miles north Newtown and enter the village of Abermule. Turn down the lane opposite the village shop and Post Office.
⭐ Newtown

### PRESTEIGNE
**Rockbridge Park,** Presteigne, Powys, LD8 2NF
**Tel:** 01547 560300
**Email:** dustinrockbridge@hotmail.com
**Pitches For** ▲ ⊑ 🚐 **Total** 30
**Facilities** 🅰️ 🎣 🅿️ 🔥 🅿️ 👤 🍴 📞
🛁 🔥 🅿️ 🚻 ♨️
**Nearby Facilities** 👤 ✓ ∪ ♠
**Acreage** 6 **Open** April **to** September
**Access** Good **Site** Level
In peaceful surroundings on the upper reaches of the River Lugg.
**Nearest Town/Resort** Presteigne
**Directions** 1 mile west of Presteigne on the B4356 Llanbister road.
⭐ Knighton

### PRESTEIGNE
**Walton Caravan Site,** Court Cottage, Walton, Presteigne, Powys, LD8 2PY
**Tel:** 01544 350259
**Pitches For** ▲ ⊑ 🚐 **Total** 30
**Facilities** 🎣 🅿️ 🔥 🅿️ 👤 🍴 🔥 🅿️ 📞 🚻 ♨️
**Nearby Facilities** 👤
**Acreage** 7 **Open** All Year
**Access** Good **Site** Level
Many walks and rides into the hills. The Crown Hotel (opposite) is excellent for its restaurant.
**Nearest Town/Resort** Kington
**Directions** On the A44 Kington to Aberystwyth road, in the village of Walton opposite the Crown Hotel.
⭐ Knighton

### RHAYADER
**Gigrin Farm,** South Street, Rhayader, Powys, LD6 5BL
**Tel:** 01597 810243 **Fax:** 01597 810357
**Email:** kites@gigrin.co.uk
www.gigrin.co.uk
**Pitches For** ▲ ⊑ 🚐 **Total** 15
**Facilities** 🎣 🅿️ 🔥 🅿️ 🏠 🔥 🚻
**Nearby Facilities** ✓ ∪ ♠
**Acreage** 2 **Open** All Year
**Access** Good **Site** Level
Situated in a beautiful area surrounded by hills. Leisure centre in Rhayader. Red Kite feeding daily. Ideal for walking and cycling in Elan Valley.
**Nearest Town/Resort** Rhayader/Llandrindod Wells
**Directions** Just off the A470 ½ mile south of Rhayader.
⭐ Llandrindod Wells

## RHAYADER

**Wyeside Caravan & Camping Park,** Llangurig Road, Rhayader, Powys, LD6 5LB
**Tel:** 01597 810183 **Fax:** 01597 810183
**Email:** info@wyesidecamping.co.uk
www.wyesidecamping.co.uk
**Pitches For** ⚠ ⚌ ⚌ **Total** 140
**Facilities** ⚒ ⚐ 🚻 🚿 ⌂ 🚽 ⚊ ◻ ☂
🛢 ⊙ 🏪 ⌐ ⊟ 🛒 ⋇
**Nearby Facilities** ⌐ ✔ ∪ ⋏ ⋇
**Acreage** 8 **Open** February **to** Nov
**Access** Good **Site** Level
Set along the banks of the River Wye with excellent facilities. 5 minutes walk to the town centre and 3 miles from Elan Valley.
**Nearest Town/Resort** Rhayader
**Directions** On the A470 north of Rhayader.
⚝ Llandrindod Wells

## WELSHPOOL

**Carmel Caravan Park,** Tynewydd, Cefncoch, Welshpool, Powys, SY21 0AJ
**Tel:** 01938 810542
www.carmelcaravanpark.com
**Pitches For** ⚠ ⚌ ⚌ **Total** 120
**Facilities** ⚒ ⚐ 🚻 ⚿ ⌂ 🚽 ⚊ ◻ ☂
🛢 ⊙ 🏪 ⊟ 🛒 ⋇ ⌐
**Nearby Facilities** ⌐ ✔ ⚓ ∪ ⋏
**Open** 15 March **to** 31 Oct
**Access** Good **Site** Level
Farm site set alongside a river for walks.
**Nearest Town/Resort** Newtown
**Directions** From Welshpool take the A458 to Llanfair Caereinion, turn left over the bridge and follow signs for Cefncoch. Turn left at the pub and follow caravan signs.
⚝ Newtown

## WELSHPOOL

**Dolgead Hall Caravan Park Ltd.,** Llanfair Caereinion, Welshpool, Powys, SY21 0HT
**Tel:** 01938 810335 **Fax:** 01938 810389
**Email:** dolgead@btconnect.com
www.dolgead-hall@demon.co.uk
**Pitches For** ⚌ **Total** 25
**Facilities** ⚒ 🚻 🚿 ⌂ 🚽 ⚊
◻ ⊙ 🏪 🛢 🏪 🏪 ⚐ ❀ 🛒 ⊟ ∪ ⌐
**Nearby Facilities** ⌐ ✔ ∪
**Acreage** 80 **Open** 15 March **to** 15 Sept
**Access** Good **Site** Sloping
Seasonal Pitches Only. 80 acre farm with golf and bowling on site.
**Nearest Town/Resort** Welshpool
**Directions** From Welshpool take the A458 west, go through the village of Llanfair Caereinion. After 1 mile turn right onto the A495, the park is 300 yards on the left.
⚝ Welshpool

## WELSHPOOL

**Henllan Caravan Park,** Llangyniew, Welshpool, Powys, SY21 9EJ
**Tel:** 01938 810554
**Email:** sue@henllancp.fsnet.co.uk
www.henllancaravanpark.co.uk
**Pitches For** ⚠ ⚌ ⚌ **Total** 10
**Facilities** ⚒ ⚐ 🚻 🚿 ⌂ 🚽 ⚊ ◻ ☂
◻ ⊙ 🏪 🏪 🏪 ⚐ ❀ 🛒 ⊟ ⋇
**Nearby Facilities** ⌐ ✔ ∪
**Acreage** ½ **Open** March **to** December
**Access** Good **Site** Level
Alongside the River Banwy. Ideal touring, 9 hole golf course and bowling green. You can also telephone us on Mobile 07907 531331. Contact Sue Evans.
**Nearest Town/Resort** Welshpool
**Directions** 6 miles from Welshpool on the A458.
⚝ Welshpool

## SWANSEA

### GOWERTON

**Gowerton Caravan Club Site,** Pont-y-Cob Road, Gowerton, Swansea, SA4 3QP
**Tel:** 01792 873050
www.caravanclub.co.uk
**Pitches For** ⚌ ⚌ **Total** 130
**Facilities** ⚒ 🚻 🚿 ⌂ 🚽 ⌐ ◻ ☂
◻ ⊙ 🏪 🏪 ⊟ 🛒
**Nearby Facilities**
**Acreage** 17 **Open** March **to** Oct
**Access** Good **Site** Level
Easy drive to many safe sandy beaches. Inland theres the Vale of Neath and Aberdulais Falls. Non members welcome. Booking essential.
**Nearest Town/Resort** Swansea
**Directions** Leave M4 at junc 47 and take A483 sp Swansea. At rndabt turn right onto A484, at next rndabt go straight over, next rndabt turn left onto B4296 sp Gowerton. After passing under railway bridge at lights turn right, next lights turn right into Pont-y-Cob Road, site is ¼ mile on the right.
⚝ Swansea

### HORTON

**Bank Farm,** Horton, Gower, Swansea, SA3 1LL
**Tel:** 01792 390228 **Fax:** 01792 391282
**Email:** bankfarmleisure@aol.com
www.bankfarmleisure.co.uk
**Pitches For** ⚠ ⚌ ⚌ **Total** 230
**Facilities** ⚒ 🚻 🚿 ⌂ 🚽 ⚊ ◻ ☂
◻ ⊙ 🏪 ❌ 🏪 🏪 ⚐ ❀ 🛒 ⊟
**Nearby Facilities** ⌐ ✔ ∪ ⋏
**Acreage** 80 **Open** March **to** 15 November
**Access** Good **Site** Sloping
Overlooking the beach. Heated swimming pool.
**Nearest Town/Resort** Swansea
**Directions** Take the A4118 from Swansea towards Port Eynon, turn left for Horton 1 mile before Port Eynon, turn right at the site entrance after 200 yards.
⚝ Swansea

### LLANGENNITH

**Kennexstone Camping & Touring Park,** Kennexstone Farm, Llangennith, Gower, Swansea, SA3 1HS
**Tel:** 01792 391296
**Email:** david.cgd@tiscali.co.uk
www.gowercamping.co.uk
**Pitches For** ⚠ ⚌ ⚌ **Total** 240
**Facilities** ⚒ 🚻 🚿 ⌂ 🚽 ⚊ ◻ ☂
❀ ⊟ ⋇
**Nearby Facilities** ⌐ ✔ ⚓ ∪ ⋏ ⋇
**Acreage** 12 **Open** Good Friday **to** 1 Oct
**Access** Good **Site** Level
Friendly, family run site thats safe and quiet for children. Ideal for a relaxing holiday. 1½ miles from one of Wales' best surfing beaches. Storage available.
**Nearest Town/Resort** Swansea
**Directions** Leave the M4 at junction 47 and take the A483/A484 to Gowerton, then take the B4295 for 8 miles to Llanrhidian. Follow signs to Llangennith for approx. 2½ miles, at T-junction ½ mile after Burry Green turn right, site is 200 yards.
⚝ Swansea

### OXWICH

**Oxwich Camping Park,** Oxwich, Gower, Swansea, SA3 1LS
**Tel:** 01792 390777
**Pitches For** ⚠ **Total** 180
**Facilities** 🚻 🚿 ⌂ ⊙ ◻ ☂
◻ ⊙ 🏪 ❌ ⍾ 🏪 🏪 ⚐ ❀ ⊟
**Nearby Facilities** ⌐ ✔ ⚓ ∪ ⋏ ⚓ ⋏
**Acreage** 10 **Open** April **to** September

### Site Lev/Slope
Near a sandy beach, water sports and a nature reserve.
**Nearest Town/Resort** Swansea
**Directions** A4118 from Swansea, 10 miles turn left. 1¼ miles turn right at crossroads, ¼ mile on right hand side.
⚝ Swansea

### PORT EYNON

**Newpark Holiday Park,** Port Eynon, Gower, Swansea, SA3 1NP
**Tel:** 01792 390292 **Fax:** 01792 391245
**Email:** newpark@btinternet.com
www.newparkholidaypark.co.uk
**Pitches For** ⚠ ⚌ ⚌
**Facilities** ⚒ 🚻 🚿 ⌂ 🚽 ⚊ ◻ ☂
♿ ⊙ 🏪 🏪 ⊟ ⊟ ⋇
**Nearby Facilities** ⌐ ✔ ⚓ ∪ ⋏ ⋏
**Open** April **to** October
**Access** Good **Site** Lev/Slope
Outstanding views overlooking Port Eynon Bay, which is just a 5 minute walk away.
**Nearest Town/Resort** Swansea
**Directions** Leave the M4 at junction 42 or 47 and head for the A4118.
⚝ Swansea

### RHOSSILI

**Pitton Cross Caravan & Camping Park,** Rhossili, Swansea, SA3 1PH
**Tel:** 01792 390593 **Fax:** 01792 391010
**Email:** enquiries@pittoncross.co.uk
www.pittoncross.co.uk
**Pitches For** ⚠ ⚌ ⚌ **Total** 100
**Facilities** ⚒ ⚐ 🚻 🚿 ⌂ 🚽 ⚊ ◻ ☂
♿ 🎿 ◻ ⊙ 🏪 🏪 ⊟ 🛒
**Nearby Facilities** ⌐ ✔ ⚓ ∪ ⋏ ⋏
**Acreage** 6 **Open** Feb **to** Nov
**Access** Good **Site** Level
Quiet, family friendly park, with a mix of sea views and sheltered areas.
**Nearest Town/Resort** Swansea
**Directions** Just off the B4247.
⚝ Swansea

## VALE OF GLAMORGAN

### BARRY

**Vale Touring Caravan Park,** Port Road (West), Barry, Vale of Glamorgan, CF62 3BT
**Tel:** 01446 719311
**Email:** royphillips@onetel.com
**Pitches For** ⚌ ⚌ **Total** 40
**Facilities** ⚒ ⚐ 🚻 🚿 ⌂ 🚽 ⚊ ☂
◻ ⊙ 🏪 ⊟ 🛒
**Nearby Facilities** ⌐ ✔ ⚓ ∪ ⋏
**Acreage** 2 **Open** March **to** December
**Access** Good **Site** Level
100 yards from a hotel bar open to residents. 2 miles from the beach. Ideal touring.
**Nearest Town/Resort** Barry Island
**Directions** The park is located 2 miles west of Barry on the A4226. When you reach the roundabout with sculpture arrows turn left, park is on your right.
⚝ Barry

### COWBRIDGE

**Llandow Caravan Park,** Llandow, Cowbridge, Vale of Glamorgan, CF71 7PB
**Tel:** 01446 794527
**Email:** enq@llandow.com
www.llandowcaravanpark.com
**Pitches For** ⚠ ⚌ ⚌ **Total** 100
**Facilities** ⚒ ⚐ 🚻 🚿 ⌂ 🚽 ⚊ ◻ ☂
♿ ⊙ 🏪 ⊟ 🛒 ⋇ ⌐
**Nearby Facilities** ⌐ ✔ ∪
**Acreage** 5 **Open** 1 Feb **to** 1 Dec
**Access** Good **Site** Level

## VALE OF GLAMORGAN, WREXHAM

Heritage Coast, 3 miles from beaches and 20 miles from Cardiff.
**Nearest Town/Resort** Cowbridge
**Directions** From the A48 turn onto the B4268/B4270 and follow brown tourism signs to the caravan park.
⚓ Bridgend

### LLANTWIT MAJOR

**Acorn Camping & Caravanning**, Ham Lane South, Llantwit Major, Vale of Glamorgan, CF61 1RP
**Tel:** 01446 794024 **Fax:** 01446 794024
**Email:** info@acorncamping.co.uk
www.acorncamping.co.uk
**Pitches For** ▲ ⛺ ⛟ **Total** 90
**Facilities** ♿ �ℐ 🏪 🏕 🔥 ⌂ ⌐ 🔌 ◻ 🍴
♨ 🛇 🏪 ♨ ⚿ 🄿 🄳 🄲
**Nearby Facilities** ⌐ ✗ ∪ ⚲
**Acreage** 4 **Open** February **to** 8 December
**Access** Good **Site** Level
1 mile from the beach and town. Coastal walks, ideal base for touring. Take-away food available. Holiday hire caravans available, one suitable for wheelchair. David Bellamy Silver Award for Conservation.
**Nearest Town/Resort** Llantwit Major
**Directions** From M4 junction 33 follow signs Cardiff Airport then B4265 for Llantwit Major. Approach via Ham Lane East, through Ham Manor Park. Full directions available from our brochure or web site.
⚓ Barry

### PENARTH

**Marconi Holiday Village**, Lavernock Point, Fort Road, Penarth, Vale of Glamorgan, CF64 5XQ
**Tel:** 029 2070 7310 **Fax:** 029 2070 0509
**Email:** info@lavernockpoint.com
www.lavernockpoint.com
**Pitches For** ▲ ⛟
**Facilities** 🆙 🏕 🄿 ⌐ ⌐ ◻ ♨
♨ 🛇 🏪 ⚿ ♨ 🝙 🕙 🄿 🄲
**Nearby Facilities** ⌐ ✗ ⚓ 🕭 ∪ ⚲ 🄿
**Site** Lev/Slope
Near the beach.
**Nearest Town/Resort** Penarth
**Directions** From Penarth take the B4267 towards Sully, turn left into Fort Road and the site is at the end.
⚓ Penarth

## WREXHAM

### RUABON

**James' Caravan Park**, Llangollen Road, Ruabon, Wrexham, LL14 6DW
**Tel:** 01978 820148 **Fax:** 01978 820148
**Email:** ray@carastay.demon.co.uk
**Pitches For** ⛺ ⛟ **Total** 40
**Facilities** ♿ ℐ 🕙 🆙 🏕 🄿 ⌐ 🍴
🛇 🏪 🝙 🄿 🄲
**Nearby Facilities** ⌐ ✗
**Acreage** 6 **Open** All Year
**Access** Good **Site** Lev/Slope
An attractive park with mature trees. Old farm buildings house the owners collection of old and original farm machinery, carefully restored and maintained, adding charm and interest to the park. 10 minute walk to the village. Near to Ellesmere, Llangollen and Chester.
**Nearest Town/Resort** Wrexham/ Llangollen
**Directions** Situated on the A539 west of the junction with the A483.
⚓ Ruabon

### WREXHAM

**The Plassey Touring Caravan & Leisure Park**, Eyton, Wrexham, LL13 0SP
**Tel:** 01978 780277 **Fax:** 01978 780019
**Email:** enquiries@theplassey.co.uk
www.theplassey.co.uk
**Pitches For** ▲ ⛺ ⛟ **Total** 120
**Facilities** ♿ ⚲ ℐ 🕙 🆙 🏕 🔥 🄿 ⊙ ⌐ ◻ 🍴
♨ 🝙 🛇 🏪 ✗ ⚿ 🕙 ♨ 🝙 🕙 ✈ 🐕 🄿 🄲 ⚓ 🄿
**Nearby Facilities** ∪ 🄿
**Acreage** 10 **Open** 1 March **to** 7 Nov
**Access** Good **Site** Level
On site facilities include a 9 hole golf course, a craft centre with 16 workshops and boutiques, garden centre, hair and beauty studio, restaurant and coffee shop. We even have our own on-site mini real ale brewery!
**Nearest Town/Resort** Wrexham
⚓ Wrexham

# SCOTLAND
## ABERDEENSHIRE

### ABERDEEN

**Lower Deeside Holiday Park,** South Deeside Road, Maryculter, Aberdeen, Aberdeenshire, AB12 5FX
**Tel:** 01224 733860 **Fax:** 01224 732490
**Email:**
enquiries@lowerdeesideholidaypark.com
www.lowerdeesideholidaypark.com
**Pitches For** ▲ ⚑ ⛟
**Facilities** ⨍ ⌂ ⊞ ⒲ ♨ ⌐ ⊙ ⌣ ⊿ ⊡ ☏
⛱ ⊙ ☎ ⛽ ⚑ ⊢⊣⊡ ⊟ ⊱
**Nearby Facilities** ⌐ ✔
**Acreage** 10 **Open** All Year
**Access** Good **Site** Level
Good base to explore the coast and castles.
**Nearest Town/Resort** Aberdeen
**Directions** From Aberdeen take the B9077 at Bridge of Dee roundabout for 6 miles. From Stonehaven take the B979.
⚏ Aberdeen

### ABOYNE

**Aboyne Loch Caravan Park,** Aboyne, Royal Deeside, Aberdeenshire, AB34 5BR
**Tel:** 013398 86244
**Pitches For** ▲ ⚑ ⛟ **Total** 32
**Facilities** ⏣ ⨍ ⌂ ⊞ ⒲ ♨ ⌐ ⊙ ⌣ ⊿ ⊡ ☏
⛱ ⊙ ☎ ⚑ ⛰ ⊢⊣⊱ ⊘
**Nearby Facilities** ⌐ ⏛ ⊥ ∪ ⟋ ⚡
**Open** March **to** Oct
**Access** Good **Site** Level
By Aboyne Loch. Beside two golf courses and two restaurants within walking distance. Boats available to hire. Good area for walking. Dog walk. David Bellamy Gold Award.
**Nearest Town/Resort** Banchory
**Directions** Take the A96 to Ballater.

### ABOYNE

**Camping & Caravanning Club Site,** Tarland By Deeside, Tarland By Aboyne, Aberdeenshire, AB34 4UP
**Tel:** 01339 881388
www.campingandcaravanningclub.co.uk
**Pitches For** ▲ ⚑ ⛟ **Total** 90
**Facilities** ⨍ ⒲ ♨ ⌐ ⊙ ⌣ ⊿ ⊡ ☏
⛱ ⊙ ☎ ⚑ ⛰ ⊢⊣⊱ ⊘
**Nearby Facilities** ⌐
**Acreage** 8 **Open** April **to** Oct
**Access** Good **Site** Level
Close to the village of Tarland and approx. 6 miles from Aboyne. STB 5 Star Graded and AA 3 Pennants. Non members welcome.
**Nearest Town/Resort** Aboyne
**Directions** Take the A93 from Aberdeen, in Aboyne turn right at the Struan Hotel onto the B9094. After 6 miles take the next turn right and then fork left before the bridge, site is on the left in 600 yards.
⚏ Aberdeen

### BRAEMAR

**The Invercauld Caravan Club Site,** Glenshee Road, Braemar, Ballater, Aberdeenshire, AB35 5YQ
**Tel:** 0133 974 1373
www.caravanclub.co.uk
**Pitches For** ▲ ⚑ ⛟ **Total** 97
**Facilities** ⏣ ⨍ ⌂ ⒲ ♨ ⌐ ⊡ ☏
⛱ ⊙ ☎ ⚑ ⊢⊣⊡ ⊟
**Nearby Facilities** ⌐ ✔
**Acreage** 9½ **Open** Dec **to** Oct
**Access** Good **Site** Level

Abundant wildlife can be seen at this gateway to the Cairngorms, ideal for walking and cycling. Near a dry ski slope. Open in December for winter sports. Ski racks, drying room and community room (winter only) on site. Non members welcome. Booking essential.
**Nearest Town/Resort** Braemar
**Directions** Just off the A93 on the outskirts of Braemar Village.

### CRUDEN BAY

**Craig Head Caravan & Camping Park,** Cruden Bay, Peterhead, Aberdeenshire, AB42 0PL
**Tel:** 01779 812251
**Pitches For** ▲ ⚑ ⛟ **Total** 15
**Facilities** ⨍ ⌂ ⒲ ♨ ⌐ ⊙ ⌣ ⊿ ⊡ ☏
⛱ ⊙ ☎ ⚑ ⊢⊣⊡ ⊱
**Nearby Facilities** ⌐ ✔ ⏛ ⊥ ∪ ⟋ ⚡
**Acreage** 5 **Open** All Year
**Access** Good **Site** Level
**Nearest Town/Resort** Peterhead
**Directions** From Peterhead take the A90 south for approx. 9 miles, signposted on the left.
⚏ Aberdeen

### HUNTLY

**Huntly Castle Caravan Park,** The Meadows, Huntly, Aberdeenshire, AB54 4UJ
**Tel:** 01466 794999
**Email:** enquiries@huntlycastle.co.uk
www.huntlycastle.co.uk
**Pitches For** ▲ ⚑ ⛟ **Total** 90
**Facilities** ⨍ ⌂ ⒲ ♨ ⌐ ⊙ ⌣ ⊿ ⊡ ☏
⊙ ☎ ⚑ ⛰ ⊢⊣⊡ ⊟
**Nearby Facilities** ⌐ ✔ ⏛ ⊥ ∪ ⟋ ⚡ ⚡
**Acreage** 15 **Open** March **to** Oct
**Access** Good **Site** Level
Beautifully landscaped site in the Grampian countryside. Base yourself in Huntly where castles, Whisky Trails, Falconry Centre, countryside and the nearby coastline make this the perfect holiday. Rivers Deveron and Bogie nearby for salmon and trout fishing. Non members welcome. Booking essential.
**Nearest Town/Resort** Huntly
**Directions** From Aberdeen on the A96 Huntly bypass, on the outskirts of Huntly at the roundabout, continue on the A96 signposted Inverness. After ¾ miles turn right signposted Huntly, site is ½ mile on the left, just past Huntly Motors.
⚏ Huntly

### JOHNSHAVEN

**Wairds Park,** Beach Road, Johnshaven, Nr Montrose, Aberdeenshire, DD10 0HD
**Tel:** 01561 362395
**Pitches For** ▲ ⚑ ⛟ **Total** 20
**Facilities** ⏣ ⨍ ⒲ ♨ ⌐ ⊙ ⌣ ⊿ ☏
⛱ ⚑ ⊱⊢⊡
**Nearby Facilities** ⌐ ✔
**Acreage** 6 **Open** 1 April **to** 15 October
**Access** Good **Site** Level
Coastal site in a quiet setting. Easy access to tourist routes.
**Nearest Town/Resort** Montrose
**Directions** 10 miles north of Montrose on the A92.
⚏ Montrose

### KINTORE

**Hillhead Caravan Park,** Kintore, Aberdeenshire, AB51 0YX
**Tel:** 01467 632809 **Fax:** 01467 633173
**Email:** enquiries@hillheadcaravan.co.uk
www.hillheadcaravan.co.uk

**Pitches For** ▲ ⚑ ⛟ **Total** 29
**Facilities** ⏣ ⨍ ⌂ ⒲ ♨ ⌐ ⊙ ⌣ ⊿ ⊡ ☏
⛱ ⊙ ☎ ⚑ ⊢⊣⊡ ⊟
**Nearby Facilities** ⌐ ✔ ⚡
**Acreage** 1½ **Open** All Year
**Access** Good **Site** Level
Quiet, sheltered park. Easy access to Castle and Malt Whisky Trails, Aberdeen and Royal Deeside.
**Nearest Town/Resort** Kintore
**Directions** From south leave the A96 at Broomhill roundabouts third exit. From north stay on the A96 past Kintore (DO NOT enter Kintore), leave at Broomhill roundabouts first exit. Follow brown and white caravan signs onto the B994, in ¼ mile turn left onto the B994 signposted Kemnay. After 2 miles turn right signposted Kintore and Hillhead Caravan Park is 1 mile on the right.
⚏ Inverurie

### LAURENCEKIRK

**Brownmuir Caravan Park,** Fordoun, Laurencekirk, Aberdeenshire, AB30 1SJ
**Tel:** 01561 320786 **Fax:** 01561 320786
**Email:**
brownmuircaravanpark@talk21.com
www.brownmuircaravanpark.co.uk
**Pitches For** ▲ ⚑ ⛟ **Total** 10
**Facilities** ⏣ ⨍ ⌂ ⊞ ⒲ ♨ ⌐ ⊙ ⌣ ⊿ ⊡ ☏
⛱ ⊙ ☎ ⚑ ⊢⊣⊡ ⊱ ⊘
**Nearby Facilities** ⌐ ✔ ⚡
**Acreage** 7 **Open** April **to** Oct
**Access** Good **Site** Level
Quiet site. Ideal for cycling and walking. Golf course in the village.
**Nearest Town/Resort** Laurencekirk
**Directions** 4 miles north of Laurencekirk turn left at Fordoun, go past the café and turn left, go over the bridge and the park is 1 mile on the right.
⚏ Stonehaven

### LAURENCEKIRK

**Dovecot Caravan Park,** Northwaterbridge, By Laurencekirk, Aberdeenshire, AB30 1QL
**Tel:** 01674 840630 **Fax:** 01674 840630
**Email:** info@dovecotcaravanpark.com
www.dovecotcaravanpark.com
**Pitches For** ▲ ⚑ ⛟ **Total** 25
**Facilities** ⨍ ⌂ ⒲ ♨ ⌐ ⊙ ⌣ ⊿ ⊡ ☏
⛱ ⊙ ☎ ⚑ ⊢⊣⊡ ⊱
**Nearby Facilities** ⌐
**Acreage** 3 **Open** April **to** Mid Oct
**Access** Good **Site** Level
Alongside the River North Esk. 8 miles from a sandy beach and 10 miles from the Angus Glens. Ideal base for touring.
**Nearest Town/Resort** Laurencekirk
**Directions** From Laurencekirk take the A90 south for 5 miles, at Northwaterbridge turn right to Edzell, site i s 300 metres on the left.
⚏ Montrose

### PETERHEAD

**Lido Caravan Park,** South Road, Peterhead, Aberdeenshire, AB42 2XX
**Tel:** 01779 473358
**Pitches For** ▲ ⚑ ⛟ **Total** 40
**Facilities** ⨍ ⌂ ⊞ ⒲ ♨ ⌐ ⊙ ⌣ ⊿ ⊡ ☏
⛱ ⊡ ⊙ ☎ ⚑ ⊢⊣⊡ ⊱
**Nearby Facilities** ⌐ ✔ ⏛ ⊰
**Open** March **to** Oct
**Access** Good **Site** Level
Alongside the beach and rocks.
**Nearest Town/Resort** Peterhead
**Directions** From Aberdeen take the A90 to Peterhead (well signposted).
⚏ Aberdeen

### PORTSOY

**Sandend Caravan Park,** Sandend, Portsoy, Aberdeenshire, AB45 2UA
**Tel:** 01261 842660
**Pitches For** ▲ ⊕ ⊟ **Total** 52
**Facilities** ⬤ ⁄ 🖪 🄷 🆄🅒 ⚡ ☏ ☺ ⊣ ⬛ ▣ ☎
🛉 ⊕ ⤢▣ ⚹
**Nearby Facilities** ୮ ⁄ ⚓ ⤢
**Acreage** 4½ **Open** April **to** 4 October
**Access** Good **Site** Level
In a conservation village overlooking a sandy beach. Ideal for touring and The Whisky Trail.
**Nearest Town/Resort** Portsoy
**Directions** 3 miles from Portsoy on the A98.
⚞ Keith

### ST. CYRUS

**East Bowstrips Holiday Park,** St Cyrus, Nr Montrose, Aberdeenshire, DD10 0DE
**Tel:** 01674 850328 **Fax:** 01674 850328
**Email:** tully@bowstrips.freeserve.co.uk
www.ukparks.co.uk/eastbowstrips
**Pitches For** ▲ ⊕ ⊟ **Total** 33
**Facilities** ⬤ ⁄ 🄷 🆄🅒 ⚡ ☏ ☺ ⊣ ⬛ ▣ ⚹
🛉 ⁊ ⊕ ⬛ 🄼 ⤢▣ ⚹
**Nearby Facilities** ୮ ⁄
**Acreage** 4 **Open** April **to** October
**Access** Good **Site** Lev/Slope
Quiet park by the coast. Ideal touring base. Excellent facilities. Beautiful sandy beach and nature reserve approx 1 mile. Tourist Board 5 Star Graded and AA 4 Pennants.
**Nearest Town/Resort** Montrose
**Directions** Approx 6 miles north of Montrose. Follow A92, enter village of St. Cyrus, first left after Hotel, second right.
⚞ Montrose

### TURRIFF

**East Balthangie Caravan Park,** East Balthangie, Cuminestown, Turriff, Aberdeenshire, AB53 5XY
**Tel:** 01888 544261 **Fax:** 01888 544921
**Email:** ebc@4horse.co.uk
www.eastbalthangie.co.uk
**Pitches For** ▲ ⊕ ⊟ **Total** 12
**Facilities** ⁄ 🆄🅒 ⚡ ☏ ☺ ☎ 🛉 ⊕ ⤢▣ ⚹ ℘
**Nearby Facilities** ୮ ⁄ ⚓ U
**Acreage** 5 **Open** March **to** October
**Access** Good **Site** Level
Good base for touring.
**Nearest Town/Resort** Turriff
**Directions** Take the A90 from Aberdeen to Ellon, turn onto the B9107 to Cuminestown. After New Deer turn right to New Byth, caravan park is 3 miles on the right.
⚞ Aberdeen

## ANGUS

### ARBROATH

**Elliot Caravan Park,** Dundee Road, Arbroath, Angus, DD11 2PH
**Tel:** 01241 873466
**Pitches For** ⊕ ⊟ **Total** 8
**Facilities** ⁄ 🆄🅒 ⚡ ☏ ☺ ⬛ ▣ ☎
🛉 ⊕ ⬛ 🄼⤢
**Nearby Facilities** ୮ ⁄ ⚓ U ℘ ⤢
**Acreage** 2 **Open** April **to** September
**Access** Good **Site** Level
Near the beach, across from a golf club. Ideal for touring and sea fishing.
**Nearest Town/Resort** Arbroath
**Directions** On the A92, ½ mile from town.
⚞ Arbroath

### ARBROATH

**Red Lion Caravan Park,** Dundee Road, Arbroath, Angus, DD11 2PT
**Tel:** 01241 872038
**Email:** redlion@perthshire-caravans.com
www.perthshire-caravans.com
**Pitches For** ⊕ ⊟ **Total** 40
**Facilities** ⬤ ⁄ 🖪 🆄🅒 ⚡ ☏ ☺ ⊣ ⬛ ▣ ☎
🛉 ⊕ ⬛ ✕ ▽ 🄼⤢▣ ▣ ⚹
**Nearby Facilities** ୮ ⁄ U ℘
**Acreage** 4 **Open** March **to** October
**Access** Good **Site** Level
Adjacent to the seaside and beach.
**Nearest Town/Resort** Arbroath
**Directions** From Dundee take the A92, when entering Arbroath the park is on the left past the first mini roundabout.
⚞ Arbroath

### CARNOUSTIE

**Woodlands Caravan Park,** Newton Road, Carnoustie, Angus, DD7 6HQ
**Tel:** 01241 854430
**Email:** accessconcarnlc@angus.gov.uk
www.angus.gov.uk
**Pitches For** ▲ ⊕ ⊟ **Total** 116
**Facilities** ⬤ ⁄ 🆄🅒 ⚡ ☏ ☺ ⊣ ⬛ ▣ ☎
🛉 ⊕ ⬛ 🄼 ⤢▣ ⚹
**Nearby Facilities** ୮ ⁄ U ℘
**Open** Mid March **to** Mid Oct
**Access** Good **Site** Level
**Nearest Town/Resort** Carnoustie
⚞ Carnoustie

### FORFAR

**Foresterseat Caravan Park,** Arbroath Road, Forfar, Angus, DD8 2RY
**Tel:** 01307 818880
**Email:** emma@foresterseat.co.uk
www.foresterseat.co.uk
**Pitches For** ▲ ⊕ ⊟ **Total** 34
**Facilities** ⬤ ⁄ 🖪 🆄🅒 ⚡ ☏ ☺ ⊣ ⬛ ▣ ☎
🛉 ⊕ ✕ ▽ ⤢▣ ▣ ⚹
**Nearby Facilities** ୮ ⁄ ⚓ ⤢ U ℘
**Acreage** 16 **Open** April **to** October
**Access** Good **Site** Level
Brand new park on the edge of Forfar. Ideal base for touring the Angus Glens and scenic coast. 1 mile from a golf course. Fishing loch and path network nearby. Fully licensed restaurant on site.
**Nearest Town/Resort** Forfar
**Directions** From Forfar take the A932 towards Arbroath, Foresterseat is 1 mile after Cunninghill Golf Course on the right.
⚞ Arbroath

### FORFAR

**Lochlands Caravan Park,** Dundee Road, Forfar, Angus, DD8 1XF
**Tel:** 01307 463621 **Fax:** 01307 469665
**Email:** lochlands@btinternet.com
www.lochlands.co.uk
**Pitches For** ▲ ⊕ ⊟ **Total** 36
**Facilities** ⬤ ⁄ 🆄🅒 ⚡ ☏ ☺ ⊣ ⬛ ▣ ☎
🛉 🄼 ⁊ ⊕ ✕ ⤢▣ ▣ ⚹ ℘
**Nearby Facilities** ୮ ⁄ U
**Acreage** 3 **Open** All Year
**Access** Good **Site** Level
Ideal base for touring, Angus Glens, Glamis Castle and Arbroath. Dundee's many attractions all nearby. Historic St. Andrews, the home of golf, not far away.
**Nearest Town/Resort** Forfar
**Directions** Leave Dundee on the A90 heading towards Aberdeen. After 10 miles take the A932 to Forfar, after 200 yards turn right then right again.
⚞ Dundee

### KIRRIEMUIR

**Drumshademuir Caravan Park,** Roundyhill, By Glamis, Forfar, Angus, DD8 1QT
**Tel:** 01575 573284
**Email:** easson@uku.co.uk
www.drumshademuir.com
**Pitches For** ▲ ⊕ ⊟ **Total** 60
**Facilities** ⬤ ⁄ 🆄🅒 ⚡ ☏ ☺ ⊣ ⬛ ▣ ☎
🛉 ⊕ ⬛ ✕ ▽ 🄼⤢▣ ▣ ⚹ ℘
**Nearby Facilities** ୮ ⁄ ⚓ U ℘ ⤢
**Acreage** 15 **Open** All Year
**Access** Good **Site** Level
Panoramic views. Central location for towns, cities and Angus Glens.
**Nearest Town/Resort** Kirriemuir
**Directions** From the A94 or the A90 take the A928, park is 3 miles north of Glamis Castle.
⚞ Dundee

## ARGYLL & BUTE

### ARROCHAR

**Ardgartan - Forestry Commission,** Ardgartan, Arrochar, Argyll & Bute, G83 7AR
**Tel:** 01301 702293
**Email:** info@forestholidays.co.uk
www.forestholidays.co.uk
**Pitches For** ▲ ⊕ ⊟ **Total** 200
**Facilities** ⁄ 🆄🅒 ⚡ ☏ ☺ ⊣ ⬛ ▣ ☎
🛉 ⊕ ⬛ 🄼⤢▣ ⚹
**Nearby Facilities** ⁄ ⚓ ⤢ ⤢
**Acreage** 17 **Open** 25 March **to** 1 Nov
**Access** Good **Site** Level
On the shores of Loch Long, surrounded by the magnificent mountain scenery of Argyll Forest Park. Ideal for outdoor activities. Slipway for boat launching.
**Nearest Town/Resort** Arrochar
**Directions** 2 miles west of Arrochar on the A83 Glasgow to Inverary road.

### CAMPBELTOWN

**Peninver Sands Holiday Park,** Peninver, By Campbeltown, Argyll & Bute, PA28 6QP
**Tel:** 01586 552262 **Fax:** 01586 552262
**Email:** info@peninver-sands.com
www.peninver-sands.com
**Pitches For** ⊕ **Total** 25
**Facilities** ⁄ 🆄🅒 ⚡ ☏ ☺ ⊣ ⬛ ▣ ☎
⊕ ⬛⤢▣
**Nearby Facilities** ୮ ⁄ ⚓ ⤢ U ℘
**Acreage** 2¾ **Open** 15 March **to** 15 Jan
**Access** Poor **Site** Lev/Slope
Situated right on the beach.
**Nearest Town/Resort** Campbeltown
**Directions** From Campbeltown take the B842 north for 4½ miles. Park is on the right as you enter the village of Peninver.
⚞ Oban

### CARRADALE

**Carradale Bay Caravan Club Site,** Carradale, Campbeltown, Argyll & Bute, PA28 6QG
**Tel:** 01583 431665
**Email:** info@carradalebay.co.uk
www.caravanclub.co.uk
**Pitches For** ▲ ⊕ ⊟ **Total** 60
**Facilities** ⬤ ⁄ 🆄🅒 ⚡ ☏ ☺ ⊣ ⬛ ▣ ☎
⁊ ⊕ ⬛⤢▣ ⚹
**Nearby Facilities** ୮ ⁄ ⚓ ⤢ U ⁊ ℘ ⤢
**Acreage** 8 **Open** March **to** Sept
**Access** Good **Site** Level
Situated facing the Isle of Arran, alongside the River Carra for fishing and theres a safe, sloping, sandy beach. Canoe School on site. Non members welcome. Booking essential.

**Nearest Town/Resort** Campbeltown
**Directions** From Campbeltown B842, turn right onto the B879 (signposted Carradale). In ¼ mile at caravan park sign turn right onto a single track road. Site entrance within ¼ mile.
⇌ Campbeltown

## CONNEL

**Oban Camping & Caravanning Club Site,** Barcaldine By Connel, Argyll, PA37 1SG
**Tel:** 01631 720348
**www.**campingandcaravanningclub.co.uk
Pitches For ⚠ ⚑ ⚌ Total 75
Facilities ⚐ ⸝ ⚍ ⚍ ⚍ ⌂ ⚍ ⚍ ⚍ ⚍ ⚍
⚍ ⚍ ⚍ ✕ ⚍ ⚍ ⚍ ⚍ ⚍ ⚍ ✲ ⚍
**Nearby Facilities** ⚍
**Acreage** 4½ **Open** April **to** Oct
**Access** Good **Site** Level
Set in a delightful walled garden. Superb forest walks are just 5 minutes from the site. A perfect base to explore the Highlands and Islands. STB 4 Star Graded and AA 3 Pennants. Non members welcome.
**Nearest Town/Resort** Loch Linnhe
**Directions** Heading North on the A828, 7 miles from the Connel bridge turn right at the Camping & Caravanning Club sign opposite the Marine Resource Centre, proceed through the large iron gates.
⇌ Oban

## DUNOON

**Cot House Caravan Park,** Kilmun, By Dunoon, Argyll & Bute, PA23 8QS
**Tel:** 01369 840351
Pitches For ⚠ ⚑⚌ Total 20
Facilities ⚐ ⸝ ⚍ ⚍ ⚍ ⌂ ⚍ ⚍ ⚍ ⚍
⚍ ⚍ ⚍ ✕ ⚍ ⚍ ⚍
**Nearby Facilities** ⚍ ⚍ ⚍ ⚍ ⚍
**Acreage** 3½ **Open** 10 Months
**Access** Good **Site** Level
Next to a river and on the edge of the Argyll & Trossachs National Park. Hotel at the entrance to the park which serves excellent meals. Beautiful scenery, salmon fishing, golf and lovely walks. Closed Nov and Feb only.
**Nearest Town/Resort** Dunoon
**Directions** From Dunoon take the A815 to Strachur. The park is situated at the head of Holy Lock.
⇌ Gourock

## GLENBARR

**Killegruer Caravan Site,** Woodend, Glenbarr, Tarbert, Argyll & Bute, PA29 6XB
**Tel:** 01583 421241
**Email:** anne@littleson.fsnet.co.uk
Pitches For ⚠ ⚑ ⚌ Total 25
Facilities ⚐ ⸝ ⚍ ⚍ ⌂ ⚍ ⚍
⚍ ⚍ ⚍ ⚍ ⚍ ⚍ ⚍ ✲
**Nearby Facilities** ⚌
**Acreage** 1¼ **Open** April **to** September
**Access** Good **Site** Level
Overlooking a sandy beach with views of the Inner Hebrides and the Mull of Kintyre. Site facilities have recently been upgraded. Hair dryers available. Close to the ferry link to Arran and Islay Jura & Gigha.
**Nearest Town/Resort** Campbeltown
**Directions** 12 miles north of Campbeltown on the A83.
⇌ Oban

## ISLE OF MULL (CRAIGNURE)

**Shieling Holidays,** Craignure, Isle of Mull, Argyll & Bute, PA65 6AY
**Tel:** 01680 812496
**Email:** Included in Web Site
**www.**shielingholidays.co.uk

Pitches For ⚠ ⚑ ⚌ Total 42
Facilities ⚐ ⸝ ⚍ ⚍ ⚍ ⌂ ⚍ ⚍ ⚍ ⚍ ⚍
⚍ ⚍ ⚍ ⚍ ⚍ ⚍ ⚍ ⚍ ⚍ ⚍
**Nearby Facilities** ⚍ ⚍ ⚍
**Acreage** 7½ **Open** April **to** October
**Access** Good **Site** Level
Enchanting location by the sea. Self Catering Shielings and hostel beds. 5 Star Graded.
**Nearest Town/Resort** Craignure
**Directions** From Craignure Ferry turn left on A849 to Iona for 400 metres, then left again at church.
⇌ Oban

## KILBERRY

**Port Ban Holiday Park,** Kilberry, Tarbert, Argyll & Bute, PA29 6YD
**Tel:** 01880 770224
**Email:** portban@aol.com
**www.**portban.com
Pitches For ⚠ ⚑ ⚌ Total 35
Facilities ⸝ ⚍ ⚍ ⌂ ⚍ ⚍ ⚍ ⚍
⚍ ⚍ ⚍ ✕ ⚍ ⚍ ⚍ ⚍ ⚍ ⚍ ⚍
**Nearby Facilities** ⚍ ⚍ ⚍ ⚍ ⚍ ⚍
**Open** March **to** October
**Access** Fair **Site** Level
Beautiful scenic area by the sea. Remote quiet area of special scientific interest.
**Nearest Town/Resort** Lochgilphead
**Directions** 4 miles outside of Lochgilphead en-route to Campbeltown, turn right onto the B8024 and Park is 1 mile north of Kilberry.
⇌ Oban

## LOCHGILPHEAD

**Lochgilphead Caravan Park,** Bank Park, Lochgilphead, Argyll & Bute, PA31 8NX
**Tel:** 01546 602003 **Fax:** 01546 603699
**Email:** info@lochgilpheadcaravanpark.co.uk
**www.**lochgilpheadcaravanpark.co.uk
Pitches For ⚠ ⚑ ⚌ Total 70
Facilities ⸝ ⚍ ⚍ ⚍ ⌂ ⚍ ⚍ ⚍ ⚍ ⚍ ⚍
⚍ ⚍ ⚍ ⚍ ⚍ ⚍ ⚍ ⚍ ✲
**Nearby Facilities** ⚍ ⚍ ⚍ ⚍ ⚍ ⚍
**Acreage** 7 **Open** April **to** October
**Access** Good **Site** Level
Adjacent to Loch Fyne, Crinan Canal and the town.
**Nearest Town/Resort** Lochgilphead
**Directions** Close to the junction of the A83 and the A816.
⇌ Oban

## LUSS

**Camping & Caravanning Club Site,** Luss, Loch Lomond, Nr Glasgow, Argyll & Bute, G83 8NT
**Tel:** 01436 860658
**www.**campingandcaravanningclub.co.uk
Pitches For ⚠ Total 90
Facilities ⚐ ⸝ ⚍ ⚍ ⌂ ⚍ ⚍ ⚍ ⚍
⚍ ⚍ ⚍ ⚍ ⚍ ⚍ ⚍ ✲
**Nearby Facilities** ⚍ ⚍
**Acreage** 12 **Open** March **to** October
**Access** Good **Site** Level
On the banks of Loch Lomond with good views of Ben Lomond. Fishing (permit required) and watersports. STB 4 Star Graded, AA 4 Pennants, Loo of the Year Award and Babychange Winner 2002. CLUB MEMBER CARAVANNERS & MOTORHOMES ONLY. Non member tents welcome.
**Nearest Town/Resort** Luss
**Directions** Take the A82 from the Erkside Bridge and head north towards Tarbet. Ignore first signpost for Luss. After the bagpipe and kiltmakers workshop take the next turn right signposted Lodge of Loch Lomond and international camping sign, site approx. 200 yards.
⇌ Balloch

## MACHRIHANISH

**Machrihanish Caravan & Camping Park,** East Trodigal, Machrihanish, Campbeltown, Argyll & Bute, PA28 6PT
**Tel:** 01586 810366
**Email:** info@campkintyre.com
**www.**campkintyre.com
Pitches For ⚠ ⚑ ⚌ Total 50
Facilities ⚐ ⸝ ⚍ ⚍ ⌂ ⚍ ⚍ ⚍ ⚍ ⚍
⚍ ⚍ ⚍ ⚍ ⚍ ⚍ ⚍ ✲ ⚍
**Nearby Facilities** ⚍ ⚍ ⚍ ⚍ ⚍
**Acreage** 7 **Open** April **to** Oct
**Access** Good **Site** Level
Overlooking a links golf course with views of the Atlantic and the islands of Islay and Jura. Excellent bar and restaurant within walking distance. ½ a mile from a Blue Cross surfing beach.
**Nearest Town/Resort** Campbeltown
**Directions** Take the A82 Glasgow to Tarbet road, at Tarbet take the A83 and go through Inverary, Lochgilphead and on to Campbeltown. Then take the B843 to Machrihanish for 5 miles.

## MUASDALE

**Muasdale Holiday Park,** Muasdale, Tarbert, Argyll & Bute, PA29 6XD
**Tel:** 01583 421207 **Fax:** 01583 421137
**Email:** enquiries@muasdaleholidays.com
**www.**muasdaleholidays.com
Pitches For ⚠ ⚑ ⚌ Total 15
Facilities ⸝ ⚍ ⌂ ⚍ ⚍ ⚍
⚍ ⚍ ⚍ ⚍ ⚍ ⚍ ⚍
**Nearby Facilities** ⚍ ⚍ ⚍ ⚍
**Acreage** 2 **Open** Easter **to** Sept
**Access** Good **Site** Lev/Slope
Adjoining the beach with views towards Islay, Jura and Gigha. Convenient for ferries to Islay, Jura, Gigha and Arran.
**Nearest Town/Resort** Campbeltown
**Directions** On the A83 at the southern end of the Village, approx. 22 miles from Tarbert.

## OBAN

**North Ledaig Caravan Park,** Connel, By Oban, Argyll & Bute, PA37 1RU
**Tel:** 01631 710291 **Fax:** 01631 710291
Pitches For ⚑ ⚌ Total 260
Facilities ⚐ ⸝ ⚍ ⚍ ⚍ ⌂ ⚍ ⚍ ⚍ ⚍ ⚍
⚍ ⚍ ⚍ ⚍ ⚍ ⚍ ✲
**Nearby Facilities** ⚍ ⚍ ⚍ ⚍ ⚍ ⚍
**Acreage** 30 **Open** 18 March
**Access** Good
Beachside location with superb views. Ideal centre for touring Argyll and the west coast of Scotland.
**Nearest Town/Resort** Oban
**Directions** From Oban take the A85 north, after 4 miles in Connel turn right onto the A828 signposted Fort William. Cross Connel Bridge and the park is 1 mile on the left.
⇌ Connel

## OBAN

**Oban Caravan & Camping Park,** Gallanachmore Farm, Gallanach Road, Oban, Argyll & Bute, PA34 4QH
**Tel:** 01631 562425 **Fax:** 01631 566624
**Email:** info@obancaravanpark.com
**www.**obancaravanpark.com
Pitches For ⚠ ⚑ ⚌ Total 150
Facilities ⸝ ⚍ ⚍ ⚍ ⚍ ⚍ ⌂ ⚍ ⚍ ⚍ ⚍ ⚍
⚍ ⚍ ⚍ ⚍ ⚍ ⚍ ⚍ ✲
**Nearby Facilities** ⚍ ⚍ ⚍ ⚍ ⚍
**Acreage** 15 **Open** Easter/1 April **to** 31 Oct
**Access** Good **Site** Lev/Slope
On the coast with beautiful views. Close to a diving centre and ferry to islands.
**Nearest Town/Resort** Oban
**Directions** Follow signs to the ferry terminal, continue past terminal down Gallanach Road, site is 2½ miles.
⇌ Oban

## OBAN

**Oban Divers Caravan Park,** Glenshellach Road, Oban, Argyll & Bute, PA34 4QJ
**Tel:** 01631 562755 **Fax:** 01631 563583
**Email:** info@obandivers.co.uk
www.obandivers.co.uk
**Pitches For** ▲ ⊕ ➡ **Total** 45
**Facilities** (icons)
**Nearby Facilities** (icons)
**Acreage** 4 **Open** Easter **to** End Oct
**Access** Good **Site** Lev/Slope
Quiet, scenic park on different levels with a stream running through. Just a 30 minute walk to a fresh water loch. Limited facilities only during March and October. STB 4 Star Graded.
**Nearest Town/Resort** Oban
**Directions** From north go through Oban to the traffic island, take ferry and caravan signs into Albany Street then first or second left. take the first right, then first left signposted caravans/tents. Glenshellach Road is 1½ miles.
⇌ Oban

## SOUTHEND

**Machribeg Caravan Site,** Southend, By Campbeltown, Argyll & Bute, PA28 6RW
**Tel:** 01586 830249
**Pitches For** ▲ ⊕ ➡ **Total** 80
**Facilities** (icons)
**Nearby Facilities** (icons)
**Acreage** 4 **Open** Easter **to** September
**Access** Good **Site** Sloping
Near the beach with good views, very quiet location. 18 hole golf course.
**Nearest Town/Resort** Campbeltown
**Directions** Take the B843 from Campbeltown for 10 miles. Site is situated 250yds through Southend Village on the left by the beach.

## TAYINLOAN

**Point Sands Holiday Park,** Tayinloan, Argyll & Bute, PA29 6XG
**Tel:** 01583 441263 **Fax:** 01583 441263
www.pointsands.co.uk
**Pitches For** ▲ ⊕ ➡
**Facilities** (icons)
**Nearby Facilities** (icons)
**Acreage** 14 **Open** April **to** October
**Access** Good **Site** Level
Peaceful site on a safe sandy beach with terrific scenery. Near to island ferries. Ideal for touring and visiting the Isles of Gigha, Arran and Islay. Holiday homes to let.
**Nearest Town/Resort** Tarbert
**Directions** On the A83 Glasgow to Campbeltown road, 17 miles south of Tarbert.

## TAYNUILT

**Crunachy Caravan & Camping Park,** Bridge of Awe, Taynuilt, Argyll & Bute, PA35 1HT
**Tel:** 01866 822612
www.crunachy.co.uk
**Pitches For** ▲ ⊕ ➡ **Total** 80
**Facilities** (icons)
**Nearby Facilities** (icons)
**Acreage** 9 **Open** March **to** November
**Access** Good **Site** Level
Alongside the River Awe at the foot of Ben Cruachan.
**Nearest Town/Resort** Oban
**Directions** Alongside main A85 Tyndrum to Oban 14 miles east of Oban outside the village of Taynuilt.
⇌ Taynuilt

## TAYVALLICH

**Leachive Caravan Site,** Leachive Farm, Tayvallich, By Lochgilphead, Argyll & Bute, PA31 8PL
**Tel:** 01546 870206
**Email:** fiona@leachive.co.uk
**Pitches For** ▲ ⊕ ➡ **Total** 15
**Facilities** (icons)
**Nearby Facilities** (icons)
**Acreage** 4 **Open** April **to** October
**Access** Good **Site** Level
Set beside a sheltered sea loch, ideal for canoeing and sailing. Near a nature reserve with beautiful scenic walks. Numerous forest walks and trails in the near vacinity.
**Nearest Town/Resort** Lochgilphead
**Directions** From Lochgilphead follow signs for Oban for 3 miles, then follow signs for Tayvallich.
⇌ Oban

# AYRSHIRE (NORTH)

## ISLE OF ARRAN

**Lochranza Caravan & Camping,** Lochranza, Isle of Arran, North Ayrshire, KA27 8HL
**Tel:** 01770 830273 **Fax:** 01770 830600
**Email:** office@lochgolf.demon.co.uk
www.lochranzagolf.com
**Pitches For** ▲ ⊕ ➡ **Total** 60
**Facilities** (icons)
**Nearby Facilities** (icons)
**Acreage** 2½ **Open** Easter **to** Late Oct
**Access** Good **Site** Level
Surrounded on three sides by mountains, the sea and a golf course on the fourth. Special location for superb hill walking.
**Directions** Take the ferry from Ardrossan to Brodick, then head north by road for approx. 15 miles.

## ISLE OF ARRAN

**Middleton Caravan & Camping Park,** Lamlash, Isle of Arran, North Ayrshire, KA27 8NQ
**Tel:** 01770 600251/255
**Pitches For** ▲ ⊕ ➡ **Total** 40
**Facilities** (icons)
**Nearby Facilities** (icons)
**Acreage** 3½ **Open** March **to** Sept
**Access** Good **Site** Level
Near the beach and the shops (footpath to the village). Ideal for children. Tennis, putting, bowling and golf course nearby.
**Nearest Town/Resort** Lamlash
**Directions** From ferry terminal in Brodick take the A841 for 4 miles, drive through Lamlash, after the Police Station turn next left, go over the bridge and the site is 2 minutes.

## ISLE OF ARRAN

**Seal Shore Camping & Touring,** Seal Shore, Kildonan, Isle of Arran, North Ayrshire, KA27 8SE
**Tel:** 01770 820320 **Fax:** 01770 820320
**Email:** mdeighton@sealshore.fsnet.co.uk
www.isleofarran.freeserve.co.uk
**Pitches For** ▲ ⊕ ➡ **Total** 43
**Facilities** (icons)
**Nearby Facilities** (icons)
**Acreage** 2¾ **Open** March **to** Oct
**Access** Good **Site** Lev/Slope
Situated on our own private beach. STB 4 Star Graded.

## Nearest Town/Resort Brodick

**Directions** From the ferry turn left, Kildonan is 12 miles.
⇌ Ardrossan

## SALTCOATS

**Sandylands Holiday Park,** Auchenharvie Park, Saltcoats, North Ayrshire, KA21 5JN
**Tel:** 0870 442 9312 **Fax:** 01294 604524
**Email:** holidaysales.sandylands@park-resorts.com
www.park-resorts.com
**Pitches For** ▲ ⊕ ➡ **Total** 25
**Facilities** (icons)
**Nearby Facilities** (icons)
**Open** March **to** October
**Access** Good **Site** Level
Relaxing seaside destination offering great facilities and outstanding views. Great location for visiting beautiful Arran and charming Scottish towns.
**Nearest Town/Resort** Saltcoats
**Directions** Follow signs for Kilmarnock and then Irvine. Follow the A78 signs to Stevenson, go through Stevenson, past the Auchenharvie Leisure Centre and the holiday park is on the left.
⇌ Saltcoats

# AYRSHIRE (SOUTH)

## AYR

**Craig Tara Holiday Park,** Ayr, South Ayrshire, KA7 4LB
**Tel:** 01292 265141 **Fax:** 01292 445206
www.touringholidays.co.uk
**Pitches For** ⊕ ➡
**Facilities** (icons)
**Nearby Facilities** (icons)
**Open** March **to** October
**Nearest Town/Resort** Ayr
**Directions** From the North take the A77 towards Stranraer, after Bankfield roundabout turn second right. From Dooholm Road turn left at the junction and right into Greenfield Avenue, then turn left to Craig Tara.
⇌ Ayr

## AYR

**Craigie Gardens Caravan Club Site,** Craigie Road, Ayr, South Ayrshire, KA8 0SS
**Tel:** 01292 264909
www.caravanclub.co.uk
**Pitches For** ⊕ ➡ **Total** 90
**Facilities** (icons)
**Nearby Facilities** (icons)
**Acreage** 7
**Access** Good **Site** Level
Situated in a beautiful park, just a ten minute walk from Ayr seaside resort. Open March then all year. 40 golf courses in the area. Close to Burns Heritage Trail, Culzean Castle, Vikingar and The Tam O'Shanter Experience. Non members welcome. Booking essential.
**Nearest Town/Resort** Ayr
**Directions** From the A77 Ayr bypass take the A719 signposted Ayr. Just past the racecourse at the traffic lights turn left into Craigie Road, on right bend turn left into Craigie Gardens, keep right and site is 400 yards.
⇌ Ayr

## AYR

**Heads of Ayr Caravan Park,** Dunure Road, Ayr, South Ayrshire, KA7 4LD
**Tel:** 01292 442269 **Fax:** 01292 500298
**Pitches For** ▲ ⊕ ⊕ **Total** 25
**Facilities**
**Nearby Facilities**
**Acreage** 9 **Open** March to October
**Access** Good **Site** Level
Just a 10 minute walk to the beach.
**Nearest Town/Resort** Ayr
**Directions** 5 miles south of Ayr on the A719.
⇌ Ayr

## AYR

**Sundrum Castle Holiday Park,** By Ayr, South Ayrshire, KA6 5JH
**Tel:** 01292 570057 **Fax:** 01292 570065
**Email:** enquiries@parkdeanholidays.com
www.parkdeanholidays.co.uk
**Pitches For** ▲ ⊕ ⊕ **Total** 32
**Facilities**
**Nearby Facilities**
**Acreage** 32 **Open** March to Oct
**Access** Good **Site** Level
Set in attractive Ayrshire countryside, only 4 miles from the beach.
**Nearest Town/Resort** Ayr
**Directions** From Glasgow head south on the A77 to Ayr, then take the A70 to Cumnock. The park is 3 miles along the A70, before Coylton Village.
⇌ Ayr

## BARRHILL

**Queensland Holiday Park,** Barrhill, Girvan, South Ayrshire, KA26 0PZ
**Tel:** 01465 821364 **Fax:** 01465 821364
**Email:** info@queenslandholidaypark.co.uk
www.queenslandholidaypark.co.uk
**Pitches For** ▲ ⊕ ⊕ **Total** 15
**Facilities**
**Nearby Facilities**
**Acreage** 1 **Open** March to October
**Access** Good **Site** Level
Ideal location for walking and cycling in Galloway Forest, or for touring South Scotland. Good local rivers.
**Nearest Town/Resort** Girvan
**Directions** 10 miles south east of Girvan on the A714.
⇌ Barrhill

## GIRVAN

**Windsor Holiday Park,** Barrhill, Nr Girvan, South Ayrshire, KA26 0PZ
**Tel:** 01465 821355 **Fax:** 01465 821355
**Email:**
windsorholidaypark@barrhillgirvan.freeserve.co.uk
www.windsorholidaypark.com
**Pitches For** ▲ ⊕ ⊕ **Total** 30
**Facilities**
**Nearby Facilities**
**Acreage** 6 **Open** March to October
**Access** Good **Site** Level
Ideal area for golf, fishing, walking, cycling and bird watching.
**Nearest Town/Resort** Girvan
**Directions** Situated on the A714 between Newton Stewart and Girvan, 1 mile north of the village of Barrhill.
⇌ Barrhill

## MAYBOLE

**Camping & Caravanning Club Site,** Culzean Castle, Maybole, South Ayrshire, KA19 8JX
**Tel:** 01655 760627
www.campingandcaravanningclub.co.uk

**Pitches For** ▲ ⊕ ⊕ **Total** 90
**Facilities**
**Nearby Facilities** ↾ U
**Acreage** 10 **Open** March to Oct
**Access** Good **Site** Lev/Slope
Set in the grounds of historic Culzean Castle with excellent views and country walks. STB 4 Star Graded and AA 4 Pennants. Non members welcome.
**Nearest Town/Resort** Maybole
**Directions** In Maybole turn right onto the B7023 signposted Culzean and Maidens. After 100 yards turn left, site is 4 miles on the right.
⇌ Maybole

## TROON

**St. Meddans Caravan Site,** Low St Meddans, Troon, South Ayrshire, KA10 6NS
**Tel:** 01292 312957
www.ukparks.co.uk/stmeddans
**Pitches For** ⊕ ⊕ **Total** 25
**Facilities**
**Nearby Facilities**
**Acreage** 1 **Open** 1st Fri March to Last Sun Oct
Just a 5 minute walk from beaches, golf courses and the town centre.
**Nearest Town/Resort** Troon
⇌ Troon

## ·TURNBERRY

**Balkenna Caravan Park,** Girvan Road (A77), Turnberry, South Ayrshire, KA26 9LN
**Tel:** 01655 331692
**Email:** info@balkenna.co.uk
www.balkenna.co.uk
**Pitches For** ▲ ⊕ ⊕ **Total** 15
**Facilities**
**Nearby Facilities** ↾ ⁄
**Acreage** 1½ **Open** All Year
**Access** Good **Site** Level
Magnificent sea views, looking towards the Isle of Arran.
**Nearest Town/Resort** Girvan
**Directions** From Girvan take the A77 north, site is 5 miles on the left just before Turnberry Golf Course.
⇌ Girvan

# CLACKMANNANSHIRE

## ALLOA

**The Woods Caravan Club Site,** Diverswell Farm, Fishcross, Alloa, Clackmannanshire, FK10 3AN
**Tel:** 01259 762802
**Pitches For** ⊕ ⊡ **Total** 105
**Facilities**
**Nearby Facilities** ↾ ⁄
**Acreage** 14 **Open** March to Oct
**Access** Good **Site** Level
Quiet and tranquil site with almost a 180 degree panorama to the Ochil Hills. The view from the caravan window alone is worth the journey. Guided walks and excellent fishing nearby. Ideal touring base where the Lowlands end and the Highlands begin. Non members welcome. Booking essential.
**Nearest Town/Resort** Stirling
**Directions** Leave the M9/M80 at junction 9 and follow signs for Stirling. Pass over a series of roundabouts following signs for the A91 (A914). Pass through Alva then turn right signposted Fishcross, site is ½ a mile on the right.
⇌ Stirling

## DOLLAR

**Riverside Caravan Park,** Dollarfield, Dollar, Clackmannanshire, FK14 7LX
**Tel:** 01259 742896
**Email:** info@riverside-caravanpark.co.uk
www. riverside-caravanpark.co.uk
**Pitches For** ▲ ⊕ ⊕ **Total** 30
**Facilities**
**Nearby Facilities** ↾ ⁄
**Acreage** 7 **Open** April to Sept
**Access** Good **Site** Level
Ideal touring base. Well situated for golfing, hill walking, fishing and bird watching. Dollar Glen and Castle Campbell nearby.
**Nearest Town/Resort** Dollar
**Directions** From Stirling take the A91, in Dollar take the B913 and follow for ½ mile, Park is on the left.
⇌ Stirling

# DUMFRIES & GALLOWAY

## BORGUE

**Brighouse Bay Holiday Park,** Borgue, Kirkcudbright, Dumfries & Galloway, DG6 4TS
**Tel:** 01557 870267 **Fax:** 01557 870319
**Email:** cades@brighouse-bay.co.uk
www.gillespie-leisure.co.uk
**Pitches For** ▲ ⊕ ⊕ **Total** 180
**Facilities**
**Nearby Facilities** ⁄
**Acreage** 25 **Open** All Year
**Access** Good **Site** Lev/Slope
Beautifully situated on a quiet peninsula with its own sandy beach, family park with exceptional on-site recreational facilities including an indoor pool complex, members lounge, spa facilities, fitness room, quad and mountain bikes, pony trekking centre, 18 hole par 73 golf course and driving range, 9 hole par 3 golf course, fishing, nature trails, boating, pond canoes and slipway.
**Nearest Town/Resort** Kirkcudbright
**Directions** Off the B727 Kirkcudbright to Borgue road. Or take the A755 (Kirkcudbright) off the A75 2 miles west of Twynholm, clear signposting for 8 miles.
⇌ Dumfries

## CREETOWN

**Creetown Caravan Park,** Silver Street, Creetown, Dumfries & Galloway, DG8 7HU
**Tel:** 01671 820377 **Fax:** 01671 820377
**Email:** beatrice.mcneill@btinternet.com
www.creetown-caravans.co.uk
**Pitches For** ▲ ⊕ ⊕ **Total** 70
**Facilities**
**Nearby Facilities** ↾ ⁄
**Acreage** 3½ **Open** March to Oct
**Access** Good **Site** Level
Alongside a river. Indoor hot tub on site.
**Nearest Town/Resort** Creetown
**Directions** 5 miles east of Newton Stewart turn into the village of Creetown, turn down at the clock tower and left along Silver Street.
⇌ Dumfries

## CROCKETFORD

**Park of Brandedleys,** Crocketford, Dumfries & Galloway, DG2 8RG
**Tel:** 01387 266700 **Fax:** 01556 690681
**Email:** brandedleys@holgates.com
www.holgates.com
**Pitches For** ▲ ⊕ ⊕ **Total** 80
**Facilities**
**Nearby Facilities** ↾ ⁄ ⚓ U ⁄

## DUMFRIES & GALLOWAY

**Acreage** 10 **Open** All Year
**Access** Good **Site** Lev/Slope
Ideal for touring the south west of
Scotland. Tennis on site.
**Nearest Town/Resort** Dumfries
**Directions** From Dumfries take the A75 west
to the village of Crocketford. In the village
turn left onto minor road, site is 200 metres
on the right.
⚐ Dumfries

### DALBEATTIE

**Glenearly Caravan Park,** Dalbeattie,
Dumfries & Galloway, DG5 4NE
**Tel:** 01556 611393
**Pitches For** ▲ ♙ ➡ **Total** 39
**Facilities** ⅙ ♒ ♿ ⊞ ♨ ⌐ ⊙ ⌐ ⊟ ◻ ☎
▯⌷ ⊖ ♘ ♠ ⚘ ⇥⊞ ⅏
**Nearby Facilities** ⌐ ⚲ ⚘ ⏃ ∪ ⇗ ♪
**Acreage** 10 **Open** All Year
**Access** Good **Site** Level
Peaceful site situated centrally for all local
attractions.
**Nearest Town/Resort** Dalbeattie
**Directions** From Dumfries take the A711
towards Dalbeattie. On approaching
Dalbeattie see signs for Glenearly on the right
hand side.
⚐ Dumfries

### DUMFRIES

**Barnsoul Farm & Wildlife Area,** Barnsoul
Farm, Shawhead, Dumfries, Dumfries &
Galloway, DG2 9SQ
**Tel:** 01387 730249 **Fax:** 01387 730453
**Email:** barnsouldg@aol.com
www.barnsoulfarm.co.uk
**Pitches For** ▲ ♙ ➡ **Total** 50
**Facilities** ⅙ ♒ ⊞ ♿ ♨ ⌐ ⊙ ⌐ ⊟ ◻ ☎
⊜ ▯⇥⊞ ⅏ ⌿
**Nearby Facilities** ⌐ ⚲ ∪ ⇗
**Acreage** 200 **Open** April to Beg Winter
**Access** Good **Site** Lev/Slope

Walking, cycling and fishing nearby.
**Nearest Town/Resort** Dumfries
**Directions** From Dumfries take the A75
towards Stranraer, after 6 miles turn right
towards Shawhead, follow signs for Barnsoul
Farm for 2½ miles.
⚐ Dumfries

### DUMFRIES

**Mouswald Park Caravan Site,** Mouswald
Place, Mouswald, Dumfries, Dumfries &
Galloway, DG1 4JS
**Tel:** 01387 830226 **Fax:** 01387 830666
**Pitches For** ▲ ♙ ➡ **Total** 10
**Facilities** ♒ ⊞ ♿ ♨ ⌐ ◻ ☎
⊖ ⊜ ⇥⊞ ⅏
**Nearby Facilities** ⌐ ⚲ ⏃ ⚘ ∪
**Open** March to October
**Access** Good **Site** Level
Peaceful and quiet site surrounded by
countryside. Log fire in the bar/lounge for
those cool nights.
**Nearest Town/Resort** Dumfries
**Directions** From Dumfries take the A75 for
2½ miles. Take the right fork to Mouswald
and Caravan Park, ¾ mile on the right.
⚐ Dumfries

### ECCLEFECHAN

**Hoddom Castle Caravan Park,** Hoddom,
Lockerbie, Dumfries & Galloway, DG11 1AS
**Tel:** 01576 300251
**Email:** hoddomcastle@aol.com
www.hoddomcastle.co.uk
**Pitches For** ▲ ♙ ➡ **Total** 180
**Facilities** ⅙ ♒ ⊞ ♿ ♨ ⌐ ⊙ ⌐ ⊟ ◻ ☎
⊜ ▯⊖ ⊜ ✗ ⚲ ⊞ ♠ ⊞ ⇥⊞ ⅏ ⌿
**Nearby Facilities** ⌐ ⚲ ♪
**Acreage** 24 **Open** April to October
**Access** Good **Site** Lev/Slope
Quiet site in parkland of a castle. Nature
trails and woodland walks on land
adjoining park. 9 hole golf course on site.
⚐ Dumfries

**Nearest Town/Resort** Lockerbie
**Directions** Exit A74/M74 at Ecclefechan
(junction 19). At church in village turn west
on the B725 (Dalton). 2½ miles to entrance
at Hoddom Bridge.

### GATEHOUSE OF FLEET

**Auchenlarie Holiday Park,** Gatehouse of
Fleet, Castle Douglas, Dumfries &
Galloway, DG7 2EX
**Tel:** 01557 840251
**Email:** enquiries@auchenlarie.co.uk
www.auchenlarie.co.uk
**Pitches For** ▲ ♙ ➡ **Total** 109
**Facilities** ⅙ ♒ ⊞ ♿ ♨ ⌐ ⊙ ⌐ ⊟ ◻ ☎
⊠♁ ⊖ ⊜ ✗ ⊟ ♠ ⊞ ⚲ ⊗ ⇥⊞ ⊡ ⅏
**Nearby Facilities** ⌐ ⚲ ⏃ ⚘ ∪ ⇗ ♪ ⚹
**Acreage** 20 **Open** March to 1 Nov
**Access** Good **Site** Sloping
Our own sandy cove. Good centre for
touring.
**Nearest Town/Resort** Gatehouse of Fleet
**Directions** On the main A75 5 miles west of
Gatehouse of Fleet heading towards
Stranraer.
⚐ Dumfries

### GATEHOUSE OF FLEET

**Mossyard Caravan Park,** Mossyard,
Gatehouse of Fleet, Castle Douglas,
Dumfries & Galloway, DG7 2ET
**Tel:** 01557 840226 **Fax:** 01557 840226
**Email:** enquiry@mossyard.co.uk
www.mossyard.co.uk
**Pitches For** ▲ ♙ ➡ **Total** 30
**Facilities** ⅙ ♒ ♿ ♨ ⌐ ⊙ ⌐ ⊟ ◻ ☎
▯⊖ ⊜ ⇥⊞
**Nearby Facilities** ⌐ ⚲ ⏃ ⚘ ∪ ⇗ ♪ ⚹
**Open** April to End Oct
**Access** Good **Site** Level
Situated on a working farm and set in a
coastal location with a back drop of the
Galloway Hills. Family run business.

## THE BRAIDS CARAVAN PARK ~ GRETNA, SCOTLAND

- Ideal Touring Centre • Caravan Storage • Full Facilities
- Near to the Famous Blacksmith Shop and a Golf Course • Area is popular for birdwatching
- Rallies welcome • **OPEN ALL YEAR**

**AA**

**ANNAN ROAD, GRETNA, DUMFRIES & GALLOWAY DG16 5DQ    TEL/FAX: (01461) 337409**

**Nearest Town/Resort** Gatehouse of Fleet
**Directions** 4 miles west of Gatehouse of Fleet on the A75, turn left at Mossyard sign and follow for 800 yards to reception.
🚉 Dumfries


## GLENLUCE

**Glenluce Caravan Park,** Balkail Avenue, Glenluce, Dumfries & Galloway, DG8 0QR
**Tel:** 01581 300412 **Fax:** 01581 300754
**Email:** enquiries@glenlucecaravans.co.uk
www.glenlucecaravans.co.uk
**Pitches For** ▲ ⊕ ⊟
**Facilities** ⅃ ✦ 🖬 🖾 ⅃ ✦ ⌐ ☉ ↝ ☎ ☏
🏪 ⊙ ≗ ◮ ➡ ⏚
**Nearby Facilities** ⌐ ✦ ∪
**Open** March **to** October
**Site** Level
Secluded suntrap park in the centre of the village. Set in mature grounds. Ideal for walking, fishing and golf.
**Nearest Town/Resort** Stranraer
🚉 Stranraer


## GLENLUCE

**Whitecairn Farm Caravan Park,** Glenluce, Newton Stewart, Dumfries & Galloway, DG8 0NZ
**Tel:** 01581 300267 **Fax:** 01581 300434
**Email:**
enquiries@whitecairncaravans.co.uk
www.whitecairncaravans.co.uk
**Pitches For** ▲ ⊕ ⊟ **Total** 30
**Facilities** ⅃ ✦ 🖬 🖾 ⅃ ✦ ⌐ ☉ ↝ ☎ ☏
🏪 ⊙ ≗ ◮ ➡ ⏚
**Nearby Facilities** ⌐ ✦ ⚓ ∪
**Acreage** 4 **Open** March **to** Oct
**Access** Good **Site** Level
Central location for touring Wigtownshire. Very peaceful park, away from the main road. 2 miles from A75.
**Nearest Town/Resort** Stranraer
**Directions** 1½ miles north of Glenluce village.
🚉 Stranraer


## GRETNA

**Braids Caravan Park,** Annan Road, Gretna, Dumfries & Galloway, DG16 5DQ
**Tel:** 01461 337409 **Fax:** 01461 337409
**Email:**
enquiries@thebraidscaravanpark.co.uk
www.thebraidscaravanpark.co.uk
**Pitches For** ▲ ⊕ ⊟ **Total** 84
**Facilities** ⅃ ✦ 🖬 🖾 ⅃ ✦ ⌐ ☉ ↝ ☎ ☏
🏪 ⊙ ≗ ◮ ⏚
**Nearby Facilities** ⌐ ✦ ∪
**Acreage** 5 **Open** All Year
**Access** Good **Site** Lev/Slope
Ideal touring centre. Good area for bird watching. On board tank waste disposal point. Small rallies welcome, rally building available. STB 4 Star Graded Park.
**Directions** From the M6 run straight onto the A74. Take the A75 signposted Dumfries/ Stranraer. In 1 mile take the second left for Gretna (B721), park is 600yds on the left.
🚉 Gretna Green


## ISLE OF WHITHORN

**Burrowhead Holiday Village,** Tonderghie Road, Isle of Whithorn, Newton Stewart, Dumfries & Galloway, DG8 8JB
**Tel:** 01988 500252 **Fax:** 01988 500855
**Email:** burrowheadhv@aol.com
www.burrowheadholidayvillage.co.uk
**Pitches For** ▲ ⊕ ⊟ **Total** 85
**Facilities** ⅃ 🖾 ⅃ ✦ ⌐ ☉ ↝ ☎ ☏
🏪 ⊙ ≗ ◮ ✕ ♟ 🖬 ♠ ⏏ ↝ ➡ ◨ ⏚
⏚
**Nearby Facilities** ⌐ ✦ ⚓ ↝ ∪ ⚡
**Acreage** 100 **Open** March **to** Oct
**Access** Good **Site** Sloping
Exceptional views overlooking the Solway Firth and across to the Isle of Man.
**Nearest Town/Resort** Isle of Whithorn
**Directions** On entering the Isle of Whithorn take the first turning on the right into Tonderghie Road, Burrowhead is approx. 2 miles.
🚉 Stranraer


## KIPPFORD

**Kippford Holiday Park,** Kippford, Dalbeattie, Dumfries & Galloway, DG5 4LF
**Tel:** 01556 620636 **Fax:** 01556 620607
**Email:** info@kippfordholidaypark.co.uk
www.kippfordholidaypark.co.uk


**Pitches For** ▲ ⊕ ⊟ **Total** 45
**Facilities** ⅃ ✦ 🖬 🖾 ⅃ ✦ ⌐ ☉ ↝ ☎ ☏
🏪 ⅃ ⊙ ≗ ◮ ✦ ➡ ◨ ⏚
**Nearby Facilities** ⌐ ✦ ⚓ ↝ ∪
**Acreage** 18
**Access** Good **Site** Sloping
David Bellamy Gold Award for Conservation, STB 5 Star Graded and Thistle Award. Just a 15 minute stroll to the beautiful seaside village of Kippford. Hilly, part wooded coastal walks. Adventure and Junior playgrounds. Adjacent to a shop, fishing and golf. Free marquee for mini rallies. Level pitches, most with hardstanding and private grassed area to each one, planted around and terraced on sloping ground in small groups.
**Directions** From Dumfries take the A711 to Dalbeattie, then turn left onto the A710 signposted Colvend Coast. The park entrance is on the main road in 3½ miles, 200yds after the branch road to Kippford.
🚉 Dumfries


## KIRKCOWAN

**Three Lochs Holiday Park,** Balminoch, Kirkcowan, Newton Stewart, Dumfries & Galloway, DG8 0EP
**Tel:** 01671 830304 **Fax:** 01671 830335
**Email:** info@3lochs.co.uk
www.3lochs.co.uk
**Pitches For** ▲ ⊕ ⊟ **Total** 80
**Facilities** ⅃ ✦ 🖬 🖾 ⅃ ✦ ⌐ ☉ ↝ ☎ ☏
🏪 ⊙ ≗ ◮ ♠ ♟ ✦ ➡ ◨ ⏚ ⏚
**Nearby Facilities** ⌐ ✦ ⚓ ↝ ∪
**Acreage** 15 **Open** Easter **to** October
**Access** Good **Site** Level
Three Lochs for coarse or trout fishing and sailing. Full size snooker.
**Nearest Town/Resort** Newton Stewart


## KIRKPATRICK FLEMING

**King Robert the Bruce's Cave Caravan & Camping Site,** Cove Farm, Kirkpatrick Fleming, By Lockerbie, Dumfries & Galloway, DG11 3AT
**Tel:** 01461 800285
**Email:** enquiries@brucescave.co.uk
www.brucescave.co.uk
**Pitches For** ▲ ⊕ ⊟ **Total** 40
**Facilities** ⅃ ✦ 🖬 🖾 ⅃ ✦ ⌐ ☉ ↝ ☎ ☏
🏪 ⅃ ⊙ ≗ ✕ ♠ ↝ ➡

# DUMFRIES & GALLOWAY

Nearby Facilities ⌐ ✓ ⌴ ↘ ∪ ♪
Acreage 80 Open All Year
Access Good Site Level
In grounds of 80 acre estate, peacefull and quiet and secluded, famous ancient monument of King Robert the Bruce's cave in grounds of site, free fishing on 3 mile stretch of river for Trout, Sea Trout, Salmon. New disabled toilet block, family shower rooms, laundry room and under 5's park.
Nearest Town/Resort Gretna
Directions Turn off A74 M74 at Kirkpatrick Fleming, then in Kirkpatrick follow all signs to Bruces Cave.
⁑ Annan

## LANGHOLM

Whitshiels Caravan Park, Langholm, Dumfries & Galloway, DG13 0HG
Tel: 01387 380494
Pitches For ▲ ⊕ ⊜ Total 8
Facilities ⨍ ⊟ ⊞ ♨ ⌐ ⊙ ☻
⊙ ⊛ ✕ ⊞ ⊣ ⊟
Nearby Facilities ⌐ ✓ ⌴ ↘ ∪ ♪ ⨯
Acreage ½ Open All Year
Access Good Site Level
Ideal area for fishing, golf, Hadrians Wall, Gretna Green, Borders region and Armstrong Clan Museum. Scenic route to Edinburgh.
Nearest Town/Resort Langholm
Directions 200 yards north of Langholm on the A7.
⁑ Carlisle

## LOCHMABEN

Halleaths Caravan Park, Halleaths, Lochmaben, Lockerbie, Dumfries & Galloway, DG11 1NA
Tel: 01387 810630 Fax: 01387 810005
Email:
halleathscaravanpark@btopenworld.com
www.caravan-sitefinder.co.uk/sites/2436/
Pitches For ▲ ⊕ ⊜ Total 70
Facilities ⨍ ⊞ ♨ ⌐ ⊙ ⊣ ⊠ ⊙ ☻
⊠ ⊠ ⊙ ⊛ ⊞ ⊣ ⊟ ⊟
Nearby Facilities ⌐ ✓ ⌴ ↘ ∪ ⨿ ♪
Acreage 8 Open March to November
Access Good Site Level
Bowling, tennis, yachting, boating, golf and both coarse and game fishing, all within 1 mile of park.
Nearest Town/Resort Lochmaben/Lockerbie
Directions From Lockerbie on M74, take A709 to Lochmaben. ½ mile on the right after crossing the River Annan.
⁑ Lockerbie

## MOFFAT

Camping & Caravanning Club Site, Hammerlands Farm, Moffat, Dumfries & Galloway, DG10 9QL
Tel: 01683 220436
www.campingandcaravanningclub.co.uk
Pitches For ▲ ⊕ ⊜ Total 180
Facilities ⨍ ⊟ ⊞ ♨ ⌐ ⊙ ⊣ ⊠ ⊙ ☻
⊠ ⊟ ⊙ ⊛ ⊞ ⊣ ⊟ ⊟ ⨿ ♪
Nearby Facilities ⌐ ✓ ∪ ♪
Acreage 10 Open March to Oct
Site Level
Set in the Scottish lowlands, the site is perfect for touring Scotland. The local village of Moffat has won awards for 'The Best Kept Village in Scotland'. STB 4 Star Graded and AA 3 Pennants. Non members welcome.
Nearest Town/Resort Moffat
Directions Take the Moffat sign off the A74, in 1 mile turn right by the Bank of Scotland, right again in 200 yards, signposted on the right, follow road round to the site.
⁑ Lockerbie

## MOFFAT

Craigielands Country Park, Beattock, Moffat, Dumfries & Galloway, DG10 9RB
Tel: 01683 300591 Fax: 01683 300591
Email: admin@craigielandsleisure.com
www.craigielands.co.uk
Pitches For ▲ ⊕ ⊜
Facilities ⨍ ⊟ ⊞ ♨ ⌐ ⊙ ⊣ ⊠ ⊙ ☻
⊠ ⊠ ⊙ ⊛ ✕ ✓ ⊞ ♨ ⊣ ⊟ ⊟ ⨿
Nearby Facilities ⌐ ✓ ⌴ ∪ ♪
Acreage 56 Open All Year
Access Good Site Lev/Slope
Own 6½ acre loch. Pub and restaurant on site.
Nearest Town/Resort Dumfries
Directions Leave the M74 at junction 15 Beattock turn off, go to the south end of the village.
⁑ Lockerbie

## MONREITH

Knock School Caravan Park, Monreith, Newton Stewart, Dumfries & Galloway, DG8 8NJ
Tel: 01988 700414/700409
Email: pauline@knockschool.com
www.knockschool.com
Pitches For ▲ ⊕ ⊜ Total 15
Facilities ⨍ⓩ ⨍ ⊞ ♨ ⌐ ⊙ ⊠ ⊣ ⊟ ⊟
Nearby Facilities ⌐ ✓ ⌴
Acreage 1 Open Easter to October
Access Good Site Lev/Slope
Near sandy beaches and golf. Four hard standing pitches available.
Nearest Town/Resort Port William
Directions 3 miles south on A747 at crossroads to golf course.

## NEWTON STEWART

Glentrool Holiday Park, Glentrool, Nr Newton Stewart, Dumfries & Galloway, DG8 6RN
Tel: 01671 840280
Email:
enquiries@glentroolholidaypark.co.uk
www.glentroolholidaypark.co.uk
Pitches For ▲ ⊕ ⊜ Total 14
Facilities ⨍ ⊟ ⊞ ♨ ⌐ ⊙ ⊣ ⊠ ⊙ ☻
⊠ ⊟ ⊙ ⊛ ♖ ⊞ ⊣ ⊟ ⊁ ♪
Nearby Facilities ⌐ ✓ ∪ ♪
Acreage 7½ Open March to October
Access Good Site Level
On the edge of a forest, ideal touring.
Nearest Town/Resort Newton Stewart
Directions Situated off the A714, 9 miles north of Newton Stewart, ½ mile south o Glentrool Village.
⁑ Barhill

## PORT LOGAN

New England Bay Caravan Club Site, Port Logan, Stranraer, Dumfries & Galloway, DG9 9NX
Tel: 01776 860275
www.caravanclub.co.uk
Pitches For ▲ ⊕ ⊜ Total 149
Facilities ⊟ ⨍ ⊞ ♨ ⌐ ⊙ ☻
⊠ ⊟ ⊙ ⊛ ♖ ⊞ ⊣ ⊟ ♪
Nearby Facilities ⌐ ✓ ⌴ ↘ ∪
Acreage 17 Open March to Oct
Access Good Site Level
Set on the edge of Luce Bay with sea views. Direct access to a shingle and sand beach. Boat storage on site. Near a sports centre, bowling green and swimming pool. Close to Mull of Galloway RSPB Sanctuary, Castle Kennedy, Ardwell House and Port Logan Botanic Gardens. Non members welcome. Booking essential.
Nearest Town/Resort Stranraer
Directions Approaching Stranraer on the A77 follow signs for Portpatrick A77, approx 1½ miles past Stranraer continue on the A716 signposted Drummore. Site is 2½ miles past Ardwell on the left.
⁑ Stranraer

## PORTPATRICK

Galloway Point Holiday Park, Portree Farm, Portpatrick, Stranraer, Dumfries & Galloway, DG9 9AA
Tel: 01776 810561 Fax: 01776 810561
www.gallowaypointholidaypark.co.uk
Pitches For ▲ ⊕ ⊜ Total 100
Facilities ⨍ ⊞ ♨ ⌐ ⊙ ⊣ ⊠ ⊙ ☻
♖ ⊠ ⊙ ⊛ ✕ ♐ ⊞ ♨ ⊣ ⊟
Nearby Facilities ⌐ ✓ ⌴ ↘ ∪ ⨿ ♪ ⨯
Acreage 24 Open Easter to Mid October
Access Good Site Lev/Slope
Overlooking Irish Sea. Only ten minutes walk to fishing village of Portpatrick.

Botanical gardens nearby. David Bellamy Silver Award for Conservation, AA 3 Pennants and RAC Appointed.
**Nearest Town/Resort** Portpatrick
**Directions** A75 from Dumfries. A77 from Glasgow and Stranraer. ½ mile south of Portpatrick.
⇌ Stranraer

## PORTPATRICK

**Sunnymeade Caravan Park,** Portpatrick, Nr Stranraer, Dumfries & Galloway, DG9 8LN
**Tel:** 01776 810293
**Email:** info@sunnymeade98.freeserve.co.uk
www.sunny-meade.co.uk
**Pitches For** Å ⊕ □
**Facilities** ∮ ⬛ ⊞ Ⓦ ▲ Γ ⊙ ↲ ◪ ◻ ☎
⬚ ⓖ ⊛ ⊞ ▣
**Nearby Facilities** Γ ✔ ⚓ ✕ U ♪
**Open** May **to** September
**Access** Good **Site** Lev/Slope
Overlooking Irish Sea. Near golf, beach, bowling, fishing etc. Pond
**Nearest Town/Resort** Portpatrick
**Directions** A77 to Portpatrick. First left on entering village, park is ¼ mile on the left.
⇌ Stranraer

## PORTWILLIAM

**West Barr Caravan Park,** West Barr, Portwilliam, Dumfries & Galloway, DG8 9QS
**Tel:** 01988 700367
**Pitches For** Å ⊕ ⊜ **Total** 8
**Facilities** ∮ Ⓦ ▲ Γ ⊙ ↲ ◪ ◻ ☎
**Nearby Facilities** Γ ✔ ⚓ ✕ U ♪
**Open** April **to** October
On the shores of Luce Bay.
**Nearest Town/Resort** Portwilliam
**Directions** From Portwilliam take the A747 towards Glenluce for 1½ miles, first farm on the left.
⇌ Stranraer

## ROCKCLIFFE

**Castle Point Caravan Park,** Rockcliffe by Dalbeattie, Dumfries & Galloway, DG5 4QL
**Tel:** 01556 630248
**Email:** kce22@dial.pipex.com
**Pitches For** Å ⊕ ⊜ **Total** 55
**Facilities** ♿ ∮ Ⓦ ▲ Γ ⊙ ◪ ◻ ☎
⬚ ⓖ ⊛ ⊞ ▣ ▨
**Nearby Facilities** Γ ✔ ⚓ ✕ U
**Acreage** 5 **Open** March **to** October
**Access** Good **Site** Level
Overlooking sea and Rockcliffe Bay, (shore 200yds). Very quiet and well kept park with a lovely view.
**Nearest Town/Resort** Rockcliffe
**Directions** In Dalbeattie take A710. 5 miles turn right to Rockcliffe. Sign for park in 1 mile near entrance to village.
⇌ Dumfries

## SANQUHAR

**Castleview Caravan Site,** Townfoot, Sanquhar, Dumfries & Galloway, DG4 6AX
**Tel:** 01659 50291
**Pitches For** Å ⊕ ⊜ **Total** 15
**Facilities** ⊞ Ⓦ ▲ Γ ⊙ ◻ ☎
⬚ ⬚ ⓖ ⊞ ▣
**Nearby Facilities** Γ ✔ U ♪
**Acreage** 2 **Open** March **to** October
**Access** Good **Site** Level
**Nearest Town/Resort** Sanquhar
**Directions** On the A76 at the south end of Sanquhar, within 30mph.
⇌ Sanquhar

## SOUTHERNESS

**Southerness Holiday Village,** Southerness, By Dumfries, Dumfries & Galloway, DG2 8AZ
**Tel:** 01387 880256 **Fax:** 01387 880249
**Email:** enquiries@parkdeanholidays.co.uk
www.parkdeanholidays.co.uk
**Pitches For** Å ⊕ □ **Total** 100
**Facilities** ♿ ∮ ⬛ ⊞ Ⓦ ▲ Γ ⊙ ↲ ◪ ◻ ☎
⬚ ⓖ ⊛ ✕ Ⓨ ⬛ ▲ ⋔ ▣ ⊞ ▣ ▨
**Nearby Facilities** Γ ✔ ⚓ U
**Acreage** 58 **Open** March **to** Nov
**Access** Good **Site** Level
Beside 2 miles of sandy beach. Superb touring and a choice of nearby golf courses.
**Nearest Town/Resort** Dumfries
**Directions** From Dumfries follow the Solway coast road through New Abbey and follow signs to Southerness Holiday Village for 10 miles.
⇌ Dumfries

## STRANRAER

**Aird Donald Caravan Park,** Stranraer, Dumfries & Galloway, DG9 8RN
**Tel:** 01776 702025
**Email:** enquiries@aird-donald.co.uk
www.aird-donald.co.uk
**Pitches For** Å ⊕ ⊜ **Total** 75
**Facilities** ♿ ∮ Ⓦ ▲ Γ ⊙ ↲ ◪ ◻ ☎
⬚ ⓖ ⊞ ⊞ ▣
**Nearby Facilities** Γ ✔ ⚓ ✕ U ⚲ ♪ ✠
**Acreage** 12 **Open** All Year
**Access** Good **Site** Level
Only 1 mile east of Stranraer town centre. Ideal touring. Also tarmac hard standing for touring caravans in wet weather. Ideal site for ferry to Ireland. Good toilets and facilities. Leisure centre nearby.
**Nearest Town/Resort** Stranraer
**Directions** Off A75 entering Stranraer. Signposted.
⇌ Stranraer

## STRANRAER

**Ryan Bay Holiday Park,** Innermessan, Stranraer, Dumfries & Galloway, DG9 8QP
**Tel:** 01776 889458 **Fax:** 01776 889458
**Email:** ryanbay@hagansleisure.co.uk
www.hagansleisure.co.uk
**Pitches For** Å ⊕ ⊜ **Total** 170
**Facilities** Ⓦ ▲ Γ ↲ ◪ ◻ ☎
⬚ Ⓨ ⬛ ▣ ▣ ▨
**Nearby Facilities** Γ ✔ ✕ U
**Acreage** 11½ **Open** March **to** Oct
**Access** Good **Site** Level
On the beach, overlooking Ryan Bay. Ideal touring centre.
**Nearest Town/Resort** Stranraer
**Directions** From Stranraer take the A77, the park is on the left hand side.
⇌ Stranraer

## THORNHILL

**Penpont Caravan & Camping Park,** Penpont, Thornhill, Dumfries & Galloway, DG3 4BH
**Tel:** 01848 330470
**Email:** penpont.caravan.park@ukgateway.net
www.penpontcaravanandcamping.co.uk
**Pitches For** Å ⊕ ⊜ **Total** 40
**Facilities** ∮ ⊞ Ⓦ ▲ Γ ⊙ ↲ ◻ ☎
⬚ ⓖ ⊞ ▣ ▨
**Nearby Facilities** Γ ✔ U
**Acreage** 1¾ **Open** April **to** October
**Access** Good **Site** Lev/Slope
Quiet and peaceful park in lovely countryside. Ideal touring centre. Cycling, walking, fishing and bird watching. AA Graded.

**Nearest Town/Resort** Thornhill
**Directions** 2 miles west of Thornhill on A702, on the left just before Penpont Village.
⇌ Dumfries

## WHITHORN

**Castlewigg Caravan Park,** Whithorn, Newton Stewart, Dumfries & Galloway, DG8 8DP
**Tel:** 01988 500616 **Fax:** 01988 500616
**Email:** mail@castlewiggcaravanpark.co.uk
www.castlewiggcaravanpark.co.uk
**Pitches For** Å ⊕ ⊜ **Total** 15
**Facilities** ∮ ⊞ Ⓦ ▲ Γ ⊙ ↲ ◪ ◻ ☎
⬚ ⓖ ⬛ ⬛ ⊛ ⊞ ▣ ▨
**Nearby Facilities** Γ ✔ ⚓ ✕ U ♪
**Acreage** 5½ **Open** March **to** October
**Access** Good **Site** Level
Quiet, country site in a central location with scenic views. Beaches nearby.
**Nearest Town/Resort** Newton Stewart
**Directions** From roundabout at Newton Stewart turn onto the A714 to Wigtown. Just before Wigtown take the A746 to Whithorn. 3 miles after Sorbie site on the right.
⇌ Stranraer

# DUNBARTONSHIRE (WEST)

## BALLOCH

**Lagganbeg Caravan Park,** Gartocharn, West Dunbartonshire, G83 8NQ
**Tel:** 01389 830281 **Fax:** 01389 830367
**Email:** info@lagganbeg.co.uk
www.lagganbeg.co.uk
**Pitches For** Å ⊕ □ **Total** 40
**Facilities** ∮ ⊞ Ⓦ ▲ Γ ⊙ ↲ ◪ ◻ ☎
⬚ ⓖ ⊛ ⊞ ▨
**Nearby Facilities** Γ ✔ ⚓ ✕ U ✠
**Acreage** 2 **Open** March **to** Jan
**Access** Good **Site** Level
Near the banks of Loch Lomond.
**Nearest Town/Resort** Balloch
**Directions** Take the A811 to Stirling, site is 4 miles from Balloch.
⇌ Balloch

## BALLOCH

**Lomond Woods Holiday Park,** Tullichewan, Balloch, Alexandria, Loch LomondWest Dunbartonshire, G83 8QP
**Tel:** 01389 755000 **Fax:** 01389 755563
**Email:** lomondwoods@holiday-parks.co.uk
www.holiday-parks.co.uk
**Pitches For** ⊕ ⊜
**Facilities** ∮ ⬛ ⊞ Ⓦ ▲ Γ ⊙ ↲ ◪ ◻ ☎
⬚ ⓖ ⬛ ⬛ ⬛ ⋔ ⊞ ▣ ▨
**Nearby Facilities** Γ ✔ ⚓ ⚲ ✠ ♪
**Acreage** 14 **Open** All Year
**Access** Good **Site** Level
Adjacent to Loch Lomond Shores Visitor Centre. Just a 5 minute walk into the town, railway station and Loch Lomond. Ideal base for touring Scotland.
**Nearest Town/Resort** Balloch
**Directions** 17 miles north of Glasgow turn right off the A82 onto the A811 Balloch and Stirling road. Park is on the left next to Loch Lomond Shores Visitor Centre.
⇌ Balloch

# EDINBURGH (City of)

## EDINBURGH

**Drum Mohr Caravan Park**, Levenhall, Musselburgh, Edinburgh, EH21 8JS
**Tel:** 0131 665 6867 **Fax:** 0131 653 6859
**Email:** bookings@drummohr.org
www.drummohr.org
**Pitches For** ▲ ⬛ ⬛ **Total** 120
**Facilities** ⬛ ⬛ ⬛ ⬛ ⬛ ⬛ ⬛ ⬛ ⬛ ⬛ ⬛ ⬛
⬛ ⬛ ⬛ ⬛ ⬛ ⬛ ⬛ ⬛ ⬛
**Nearby Facilities** ⬛
**Acreage** 10 **Open** March **to** Oct
**Access** Good **Site** Lev/Slope
Close to Edinburgh with an excellent bus service.
**Nearest Town/Resort** Edinburgh
**Directions** From south on the A1, take the A199 to Musselburgh then the B1361 and follow park signs. From west on the A1, exit at the Wallyford slip road and follow park signs.
⇥ Wallyford

## EDINBURGH

**Edinburgh Caravan Club Site**, 35-37 Marine Drive, Edinburgh, City of Edinburgh, EH4 5EN
**Tel:** 0131 312 6874
www.caravanclub.co.uk
**Pitches For** ▲ ⬛ ⬛ **Total** 197
**Facilities** ⬛ ⬛ ⬛ ⬛ ⬛ ⬛ ⬛ ⬛ ⬛
⬛ ⬛ ⬛ ⬛ ⬛
**Nearby Facilities** ⬛ ⬛ ⬛
**Acreage** 12 **Open** All Year
**Access** Good **Site** Level
Situated on the Firth of Forth with easy access to Edinburgh. Visit the castle which houses the Scottish Crown Jewels, Holyroodhouse Palace, Princes Street Gardens, Edinburgh Zoo, Whisky Heritage Centre and Deep Sea World. Non members welcome. Booking essential.
**Nearest Town/Resort** Edinburgh
**Directions** At end of M8 follow onto A720, at Gogar rndbt (end of bypass) turn right sp City Centre A8. After ¼m turn left onto A902, at Barnton junc lights turn left, at Blackhall junc lights fork left into Telford Rd. At Crewe Toll rndbt turn left sp Davidsons Mains, at T-junc lights turn right sp Granton, at next T-junc lights turn left, at rndbt turn right into Marine Drive, site is ½m on the left.
⇥ Edinburgh

## EDINBURGH

**Mortonhall Caravan & Camping Park**, 38 Mortonhall Gate, Frogston Road East, Edinburgh, City of Edinburgh, EH16 6TJ
**Tel:** 0131 664 1533 **Fax:** 0131 664 5387
**Email:** mortonhall@meadowhead.co.uk
www.meadowhead.co.uk

**Pitches For** ▲ ⬛ ⬛ **Total** 250
**Facilities** ⬛ ⬛ ⬛ ⬛ ⬛ ⬛ ⬛ ⬛ ⬛ ⬛ ⬛ ⬛
⬛ ⬛ ⬛ ⬛ ⬛ ⬛ ⬛ ⬛ ⬛ ⬛
**Nearby Facilities** ⬛ ⬛ ⬛ ⬛
**Acreage** 25 **Open** 11 March **to** 5 Jan
**Access** Good **Site** Lev/Slope
**Nearest Town/Resort** Edinburgh
**Directions** From the north or south, Mortonhall is just 5 minutes from the city by-pass. Leave the by-pass at Lothianburn or Straiton Junction and follow signs for Mortonhall. Or from the city take the main roads south from either the east or west end of Princes Street.
⇥ Edinburgh

# FIFE

## GLENROTHES

**Balbirnie Park Caravan Club Site**, Markinch, Glenrothes, Fife, KY7 6NR
**Tel:** 01592 759130
www.caravanclub.co.uk
**Pitches For** ▲ ⬛ ⬛ **Total** 77
**Facilities** ⬛ ⬛ ⬛ ⬛ ⬛ ⬛ ⬛ ⬛
**Nearby Facilities** ⬛ ⬛ ⬛
**Acreage** 8 **Open** March **to** Oct
**Access** Good **Site** Lev/Slope
Set in 400 acres of parkland. Many sporting facilities available in Glenrothes. Near to St. Andrews Golf Course, Royal Palace of Falkland, Deep Sea World Centre, The Secret Bunker, Tarvit House and Anstruther Fisheries Museum. Non members welcome. Booking essential.
**Nearest Town/Resort** Glenrothes
**Directions** From south on A90, after crossing bridge continue onto M90, leave at junction 2A and take A92 sp Glenrothes. Follow signs for Tay Road Bridge staying on A92, at end of dual carriageway turn right onto B9130, after ¾ miles turn left into Balbirnie Park.
⇥ Glenrothes

## LEVEN

**Woodland Gardens Caravan & Camping Park**, Woodland Gardens, Blindwell Road, Lundin Links, LevenFife, KY8 5QG
**Tel:** 01333 360319
**Email:** woodlandgardens@lineone.net
www.woodland-gardens.co.uk
**Pitches For** ▲ ⬛ ⬛ **Total** 20
**Facilities** ⬛ ⬛ ⬛ ⬛ ⬛ ⬛ ⬛ ⬛
⬛ ⬛ ⬛ ⬛ ⬛ ⬛
**Nearby Facilities** ⬛ ⬛ ⬛ ⬛ ⬛ ⬛ ⬛
**Acreage** 1 **Open** April **to** October
**Access** Good **Site** Level
Small, exclusive, quiet site. Adults preferred. Ideal for golfing, walking or relaxing around East Fife. Close to a sandy

beach. Within easy reach of Edinburgh.
**Nearest Town/Resort** Leven
**Directions** On the A915 Kirkcaldy, Leven and St. Andrews road, 3 miles east of Leven at the east end of Lundin Links turn north, signposted.
⇥ Kirkcaldy

## ST. ANDREWS

**Cairnsmill Caravan Park**, Largo Road, St Andrews, Fife, KY16 8NN
**Tel:** 01334 473604 **Fax:** 01334 474410
**Email:** cairnsmill@aol.com
**Pitches For** ▲ ⬛ ⬛ **Total** 80
**Facilities** ⬛ ⬛ ⬛ ⬛ ⬛ ⬛ ⬛ ⬛ ⬛ ⬛ ⬛ ⬛
⬛ ⬛ ⬛ ⬛ ⬛ ⬛ ⬛ ⬛ ⬛ ⬛ ⬛ ⬛ ⬛ ⬛ ⬛
**Nearby Facilities** ⬛ ⬛ ⬛ ⬛
**Acreage** 27 **Open** April **to** Oct
**Access** Good **Site** Level
The home of golf, near a blue flag beach.
**Nearest Town/Resort** St Andrews
**Directions** 1 mile from St. Andrews town centre on the A915.
⇥ Leuchars

## ST. ANDREWS

**Craigtoun Meadows Holiday Park**, Mount Melville, St Andrews, Fife, KY16 8PQ
**Tel:** 01334 475959 **Fax:** 01334 476424
**Email:** craigtoun@aol.com
www.craigtounmeadows.co.uk
**Pitches For** ▲ ⬛ ⬛ **Total** 63
**Facilities** ⬛ ⬛ ⬛ ⬛ ⬛ ⬛ ⬛ ⬛ ⬛ ⬛ ⬛
⬛ ⬛ ⬛ ⬛ ⬛ ⬛
**Nearby Facilities** ⬛ ⬛ ⬛ ⬛
**Acreage** 32 **Open** March **to** Oct
**Access** Good **Site** Lev/Slope
Near the beach and golf in abundance. Ideal touring base.
**Nearest Town/Resort** St. Andrews
**Directions** From St. Andrews (West Port) go via Argyll St and Hepburn Gardens to Craigtoun Meadows.
⇥ Leuchars

## ST. MONANS

**St. Monans Caravan Park**, St Monans, Fife, KY10 2DN
**Tel:** 01333 730778 **Fax:** 01333 730466
**Pitches For** ▲ ⬛ ⬛ **Total** 18
**Facilities** ⬛ ⬛ ⬛ ⬛ ⬛ ⬛ ⬛ ⬛
⬛ ⬛ ⬛ ⬛ ⬛ ⬛ ⬛ ⬛
**Nearby Facilities** ⬛ ⬛ ⬛ ⬛ ⬛ ⬛ ⬛ ⬛
**Acreage** 1 **Open** 21 March **to** October
**Access** Good **Site** Level
Small, quiet park, near the sea and small villages with harbours.
**Nearest Town/Resort** St. Andrews
**Directions** Park is on the A917 at east end of St. Monans.
⇥ Leuchars

# HIGHLAND

## ACHARACLE

**Resipole Farm Caravan & Camping Park,** Loch Sunart, Acharacle, Highland, PH36 4HX
**Tel:** 01967 431235 **Fax:** 01967 431777
**Email:** info@resipole.co.uk
www.resipole.co.uk
**Pitches For** ▲ ⊕ ⊕ **Total** 60
**Facilities** ⬚ ∤ ⬚ ⬚ ⬚ Γ ⊙ ⊒ ⬚ ⬚ ⬚
⬚ ⬚ ⬚ ✕ ⬚ ⬚ ⬚ ⬚ ⬚ ⬚ ⬚ ∪
**Nearby Facilities** Γ ∤ ⬚ ⬚
**Acreage** 6 **Open** April **to** October
Loch side, roomy site with scenic views.
Central for touring the area. Golf on site.
**Nearest Town/Resort** Fort William
**Directions** From Fort William take the A82
south for 8 miles, across Corran Ferry, then
take the A861 to Strontian and Salen. Site is
1¼ miles west of Strontian on the roadside.
⮕ Fort William

## ARISAIG

**Camusdarach Campsite,** Camusdarach,
Arisaig, Inverness-shire, PH39 4NT
**Tel:** 01687 450221
**Email:** camdarach@aol.com
www.camusdarach.com
**Pitches For** ▲ ⊕ ⊕ **Total** 42
**Facilities** ⬚ ∤ ⬚ ⬚ Γ ⊙ ⊒ ⬚ ⬚
⬚ ⬚ ⬚
**Nearby Facilities** Γ ∤ ⬚ ⬚
**Acreage** 2¾ **Open** March **to** October
Near superb white sand beaches, as
featured in the film 'Local Hero'. Perfect
base for exploring the north west
Highlands.
**Nearest Town/Resort** Arisaig
**Directions** 4 miles north of Arisaig on the
B8008, on the seaward side of the road.
⮕ Arisaig

## ARISAIG

**Gorton Sands Caravan Site,** Gorton
Farm, Arisaig, Highland, PH39 4NS
**Tel:** 01687 450283
**Pitches For** ▲ ⊕ ⊕ **Total** 45
**Facilities** ⬚ ∤ ⬚ ⬚ ⬚ Γ ⊙ ⊒ ⬚ ⬚
⬚ ⬚ ⊙ ⬚ ⬚ ⬚
**Nearby Facilities** Γ ∤ ⬚ ⬚ ⬚
**Acreage** 6 **Open** April **to** September
**Access** Good **Site** Level
On sandy beach, views of Isles of Skye,
Eigg and Rhum. Boat trips to Isles, hill
walking, ideal for bathing or boating.
**Nearest Town/Resort** Arisaig
**Directions** A830 Fort William/Mallaig road,
2 miles west of Arisaig, turn left at sign 'Back
of Keppoch', ¾ mile to road end across cattle
grid.
⮕ Arisaig

## AVIEMORE

**Glenmore - Forestry Commission,**
Glenmore, Nr Aviemore, Highland, PH22
1QU
**Tel:** 01479 861271
**Email:** info@forestholidays.co.uk
www.forestholidays.co.uk
**Pitches For** ∤ ⬚ ⬚ **Total** 220
**Facilities** ∤ ⬚ ⬚ ⬚ Γ ⊙ ⊒ ⬚ ⬚ ⬚
⬚ ⬚ ⬚ ⬚ ⬚ ⬚
**Nearby Facilities** ∤ ⬚ ⬚ ∪ ⬚
**Acreage** 20 **Open** 1 Jan **to** 1 Nov
**Access** Good **Site** Level
In the heart of The Cairngorms. Near to
Loch Morlich with its sandy beaches. Ideal
for walking, cycling, mountaineering and
winter sports. Near ski slopes.
**Nearest Town/Resort** Aviemore

---

**Directions** From the A9 turn onto the B9152
south of Aviemore. At Aviemore turn right onto
the B970, site is 5 miles.
⮕ Aviemore

## AVIEMORE

**High Range Touring Caravan Park,**
Grampian Road, Aviemore, Highland,
PH22 1PT
**Tel:** 01479 810636 **Fax:** 01479 811322
**Email:** info@highrange.co.uk
www.highrange.co.uk
**Pitches For** ▲ ⊕ ⊕ **Total** 70
**Facilities** ⬚ ∤ ⬚ ⬚ ⬚ Γ ⊙ ⊒ ⬚ ⬚ ⬚
⬚ ✕ ⬚ ⬚ ⬚ ⬚ ⬚
**Nearby Facilities** Γ ∤ ⬚ ⬚ ∪ ⬚ ⬚
**Acreage** 2 **Open** 1 Dec **to** 31 Oct
**Access** Good **Site** Level
Splendid view of Craigellachie Nature
Reserve, the Lairig Ghru Pass and the
peaks and ski runs of the Cairngorms.
**Nearest Town/Resort** Aviemore
**Directions** Off the B9152 at the south end
of Aviemore, directly opposite the B970.
⮕ Aviemore

## AVIEMORE

**Rothiemurchus Camp & Caravan Park,**
Coylumbridge, Nr Aviemore, Highland,
PH22 1QU
**Tel:** 01479 812800 **Fax:** 01479 812800
**Email:**
lizsangster@rothiemurchus.freeserve.co.uk
www.ukparks.com
**Pitches For** ▲ ⊕ ⊕ **Total** 39
**Facilities** ⬚ ∤ ⬚ ⬚ ⬚ Γ ⊙ ⊒ ⬚ ⬚ ⬚
⬚ ⬚ ⬚ ⬚ ⬚ ⬚
**Nearby Facilities** Γ ∤ ⬚ ⬚ ∪ ⬚ ⬚
**Acreage** 4 **Open** All Year
**Access** Good **Site** Level
Environmentally friendly park alongside a
river, in a pinewood setting. Close to
Aviemore, ideal for ski-ing, bird watching,
walking etc..
**Nearest Town/Resort** Aviemore
**Directions** From Aviemore take the ski road
towards Glenmore. Park on right in 1¼ miles.
⮕ Aviemore

## BALLACHULISH

**Glencoe Camping & Caravanning Club
Site,** Glencoe, Ballachulish, Argyll,
Highlands, PH49 4LA
**Tel:** 01855 811397
www.campingandcaravanningclub.co.uk
**Pitches For** ▲ ⊕ ⬚ **Total** 120
**Facilities** ∤ ⬚ ⬚ ⬚ Γ ⊙ ⊒ ⬚ ⬚ ⬚
⬚ ⬚ ⊙ ⬚ ⬚ ⬚ ⬚
**Nearby Facilities** ∤ ⬚ ⬚
**Acreage** 40 **Open** May **to** Oct
**Access** Good **Site** Lev/Slope
Surrounded by mountains, this quiet site is
situated next to forests. Non members
welcome.
**Nearest Town/Resort** Fort William
**Directions** On the A82, 1 mile south east of
Glencoe Village, follow signs for Glencoe
Visitor Centre.
⮕ Fort William

## BALMACARA

**Reraig Caravan Site,** Balmacara, Kyle of
Lochalsh, Highland, IV40 8DH
**Tel:** 01599 566215
www.reraig.com
**Pitches For** ▲ ⊕ ⊕ **Total** 45
**Facilities** ∤ ⬚ ⬚ Γ ⊙ ⊒ ⬚ ⬚ ⬚ ⬚
**Nearby Facilities**
**Acreage** 2 **Open** Mid April **to** September
**Access** Good **Site** Level
Hotel adjacent to site. Dishwashing sinks,
hairdryers. Forest walks adjacent to site.
No bookings by telephone. No large tents.

---

No awnings during July and August.
**Nearest Town/Resort** Kyle of Lochalsh
**Directions** On the A87, 1¾ miles west of
junction with A890. 4 miles east of the bridge
to the Isle of Skye.
⮕ Kyle of Lochalsh

## BEAULY

**Lovat Bridge Caravan Park,** Lovat Bridge,
Beauly, Inverness-shire, IV4 7AY
**Tel:** 01463 782374
**Email:**
allanlymburn@beauly782.fsnet.co.uk
**Pitches For** ▲ ⊕ ⊕ **Total** 40
**Facilities** ∤ ⬚ ⬚ ⬚ Γ ⊙ ⬚ ⬚ ⬚
⬚ ⬚ ⬚ ✕ ⬚ ⬚ ⬚ ⬚ ⬚ ⬚
**Nearby Facilities** Γ ∤ ⬚ ⬚ ∪ ⬚
**Acreage** 12 **Open** 15 March **to** 15 Oct
**Access** Good **Site** Level
Alongside a river. Ideal touring base.
**Nearest Town/Resort** Beauly
**Directions** 1 mile south of Beauly on the
A862. 11 miles from Inverness.
⮕ Beauly

## BETTYHILL

**Craigdhu Caravan & Camping,** Bettyhill,
Nr Thurso, Highland, KW14 7SP
**Tel:** 01641 521273
**Pitches For** ▲ ⊕ ⊕ **Total** 90
**Facilities** ∤ ⬚ ⬚ ⬚ Γ ⊙ ⊒ ⬚ ⬚ ⬚ ⬚ ⬚ ⬚
⬚
**Nearby Facilities** ∤ ⬚ ∪ ⬚ ⬚
**Acreage** 4½ **Open** April **to** October
**Access** Good **Site** Lev/Slope
Near beautiful beaches and a river for
fishing. Scenic views. Ideal touring. Rare
plants. New swimming pool, telephone,
cafe/restaurant and licensed club nearby.
**Nearest Town/Resort** Thurso
**Directions** Main Thurso/Tongue road.
⮕ Kinbrace

## BOAT OF GARTEN

**Boat of Garten Caravan & Camping
Park,** Boat of Garten, Highland, PH24 3BN
**Tel:** 01479 831652 **Fax:** 01479 831450
**Email:** briangillies@totalise.co.uk
www.campgroundsofscotland.com
**Pitches For** ▲ ⊕ ⊕ ⬚
**Facilities** ⬚ ∤ ⬚ ⬚ ⬚ Γ ⊙ ⊒ ⬚ ⬚ ⬚
⬚ ⬚ ⊙ ⬚ ⬚ ⬚ ⬚ ⬚
**Nearby Facilities** Γ ∤ ⬚ ⬚ ∪ ⬚ ⬚
**Acreage** 7 **Open** All Year
**Access** Good **Site** Level
**Nearest Town/Resort** Aviemore
**Directions** From the A9 take the A95 towards
Grantown-on-Spey and follow signs for Boat
of Garten. Park is situated in the centre of
the village.
⮕ Aviemore

## BRORA

**Dalchalm Caravan Club Site,** Brora,
Highland, KW9 6LP
**Tel:** 01408 621479
www.caravanclub.co.uk
**Pitches For** ▲ ⊕ ⊕ **Total** 52
**Facilities** ⬚ ∤ ⬚ ⬚ ⬚ Γ ⊙ ⊒ ⬚ ⬚ ⬚
⬚ ⬚ ⬚ ⬚ ⬚
**Nearby Facilities** Γ ∤
**Acreage** 5 **Open** March **to** Oct
**Access** Good **Site** Level
300 yards from a safe, sandy beach where
Arctic Tern nest and you can see seals and
dolphins. Play golf directly on the site.
Many picturesque lochs and mountains
nearby. Close to the Clynelish Distillery.
Non members welcome. Booking essential.

# HIGHLAND

**Nearest Town/Resort** Brora
**Directions** From south on the A9, in Brora
1½ miles past the bridge, ignore Dalchalm
sign and turn right at brown caravan sign.
After 350 yards at the T-junction turn left, site
is 150 yards on the right.
⇒ Brora

## CANNICH

**Cannich Caravan Park,** Cannich, By
Beauly, Inverness-shire, IV4 7LN
**Tel:** 01456 415364 **Fax:** 01456 415364
**Email:** enquiries@highlandcamping.co.uk
www.highlandcamping.co.uk
**Pitches For** ⋏ ♨ 🚐 **Total** 43
**Facilities** ✦ 🖪 🄷 🆄 ♨ ⌐ ⊙ ↵ ◢ ▣ ☎
🎗🛁🍴🏪🏧✿⊬🄿🄴
**Nearby Facilities** ⌐ ✔ ∪
**Acreage** 6 **Open** March **to** Oct
**Access** Good **Site** Level
Set in the heart of Strathglass, at the head
of Glen Affric Nature Reserve. Superb
highland and lowland, walking and cycling.
Disabled shower room. Also open winter by
arrangement only.
**Nearest Town/Resort** Drumnadrochit
**Directions** From Inverness take the A82
towards Fort William, at Drumnadrochit take
the A831 signposted Cannich and
Strathglass.
⇒ Beauly

## CULLODEN

**Culloden Moor Caravan Club Site,**
Newlands, Culloden Moor, Inverness,
Highland, IV2 5EF
**Tel:** 01463 790625
www.caravanclub.co.uk
**Pitches For** ⋏ ♨ 🚐 **Total** 97
**Facilities** & ✦ 🄷 🆄 ♨ ⌐ ▣ ☎
🎗⊙⊘🄰↵🄴
**Nearby Facilities** ✓
**Acreage** 7 **Open** March **to** Jan
**Access** Good **Site** Lev/Slope
Breathtaking views over the Nairn Valley. 1
mile from the Culloden battlefield. Only 6
miles from Inverness with its superb
shopping, Whisky trails and Loch Ness.
Basic provisions available on site. Non
members welcome. Booking essential.
**Nearest Town/Resort** Inverness/Culloden
**Directions** From south on the A9 turn off
signposted Hilton (ignoring previous signs for
Culloden Moor), at roundabout turn left onto
the B9006, site is 5¼ miles on the left.
⇒ Inverness

## DINGWALL

**Camping & Caravanning Club Site,**
Jubilee Park Road, Dingwall, Highland,
IV15 9QZ
**Tel:** 01349 862236
www.campingandcaravanningclub.co.uk
**Pitches For** ⋏ ♨ 🚐 **Total** 85
**Facilities** & ✦ 🆄 ♨ ⌐ ⊙ ↵ ◢ ▣ ☎
🎗⊙⊛↵🄿🄴 ℘
**Nearby Facilities** ⌐ ✓
**Acreage** 6½ **Open** April **to** Oct
**Access** Difficult **Site** Level
Central for touring the Highlands. Train and
ferry links to the Isle of Skye. Close to the
city of Inverness. STB 4 Star Graded and
AA 4 Pennants. Non members welcome.
**Nearest Town/Resort** Dingwall
**Directions** From the northwest on the A862
in Dingwall turn right into Hill Street (past the
Shell Filling Station), turn right into High
Street then turn first left after the railway
bridge, site is ahead.
⇒ Dingwall

## DORNIE

**Ardelve,** Dornie, Kyle, Highland, IV40 8DY
**Pitches For** ⋏ ♨ 🚐
**Facilities** ✦ 🖪 🆄 ♨ ⌐ ⊙↵▣
**Nearby Facilities** ∪ ✔
**Acreage** 2 **Open** May **to** September
**Access** Good **Site** Sloping
Ideal for touring Skye. Near Eilan Donan
Castle. Static caravans for hire.
**Nearest Town/Resort** Kyle of Lochalsh
**Directions** Just off A87, Invergarry/Kyle
road.
⇒ Kyle of Lochalsh

## DORNOCH

**Dornoch Caravan & Camping Park,** The
Links, Dornoch, Highland, IV25 3LX
**Tel:** 01862 810423 **Fax:** 01862 810423
**Email:** info@dornochcaravans.co.uk
www.dornochcaravans.co.uk
**Pitches For** ⋏ ♨ 🚐 **Total** 130
**Facilities** ✦ 🖪 🄷 🆄 ♨ ⌐ ⊙ ↵ ◢ ▣ ☎
🎗🛁⊙🄰🏪🏧✿↵🄿🄴⊬
**Nearby Facilities** ⌐ ✓ ℘ ✔
**Acreage** 25 **Open** April **to** 25 Oct
**Access** Good **Site** Level
Beach, championship golf course,
cathedral town. Scenic views, ideal touring.
**Nearest Town/Resort** Dornoch
**Directions** From A9, 6 miles north of Tain,
turn right into Dornoch. Turn right at the
bottom of the square.
⇒ Tain

## DORNOCH

**Grannie's Heilan' Hame Holiday Park,**
Embo, Dornoch, Highland, IV25 3QD
**Tel:** 01862 810383 **Fax:** 01862 810368
**Email:** enquiries@parkdeanholidays.com
www.parkdeanholidays.co.uk
**Pitches For** ⋏ ♨ 🚐 **Total** 220
**Facilities** ✦ 🖪 🆄 ♨ ⌐ ⊙ ↵ ◢ ▣ ☎
🎗🛁⊛✕▽🄰♠🏧✶✿↵🄿🄴⊬℘
**Nearby Facilities** ⌐ ✓ ℘
**Acreage** 60 **Open** March **to** Oct
**Access** Good **Site** Level
Overlooking the beach and close to the
village of Dornoch with its Heritage Centre.
**Nearest Town/Resort** Dornoch
**Directions** Take the A9 north from Inverness.
After approx. 45 minutes turn right onto the
A949 to Dornoch and Embo, after 3 miles
turn right for Embo.
⇒ Tain

## DORNOCH

**Pitgrudy Caravan Park,** Poles Road,
Dornoch, Sutherland, IV25 3HY
**Tel:** 01862 810001 **Fax:** 01862 821382
www.pitgrudycaravanpark.co.uk
**Pitches For** ⋏ ♨ 🚐 **Total** 40
**Facilities** ✦ 🖪 🄷 🆄 ♨ ⌐ ⊙ ↵ ◢ ▣ ☎
🎗⊙🄰🄿🄴⊬
**Nearby Facilities** ⌐ ✓ ⚓ ✶ ∪ ✔
**Acreage** 8 **Open** May **to** September
**Access** Good **Site** Sloping
1 mile from the beach, fishing and golf.
Dornoch town has a cathedral, shops and
many restaurants. Ideal touring centre.
**Nearest Town/Resort** Dornoch
**Directions** From the A9 take road signposted
Dornoch, turn left at the war memorial on the
B9168, park is ½ a mile on the right.
⇒ Ardgay

## DRUMNADROCHIT

**Borlum Farm Camping Park,** Borlum,
Drumnadrochit, Highland, IV63 6XN
**Tel:** 01456 450220 **Fax:** 01456 450358
**Email:** info@borlum.com
www.borlum.com

**Pitches For** ⋏ 🚐 **Total** 25
**Facilities** ✦ 🖪 🄷 🆄 ⌐ ⊙ ↵ ◢ ▣ ☎
🎗↵🄿🄴⊬
**Nearby Facilities** ✓ ∪ ℘
**Acreage** 2 **Open** All Year
**Access** Good **Site** Lev/Slope
Working farm overlooking Loch Ness for
fishing. Ideal base for touring the
Highlands. Riding.
**Nearest Town/Resort** Drumnadrochit
**Directions** Take A82 from Drumnadrochit
towards Fort William site is ¼ mile on the
right hand side after Lewiston Village.
⇒ Inverness

## DUNDONNELL

**Badrallach Bothy & Camp Site,** Croft 9,
Badrallach, Dundonnell, Highland, IV23
2QP
**Tel:** 01854 633281
**Email:** michael.stott2@virgin.net
www.badrallach.com
**Pitches For** ⋏ ♨ 🚐 **Total** 15
**Facilities** & ✦ 🆄 ♨ ⌐ ↵ ◢ ♠ 🏧 🄿🄴 ▣
**Nearby Facilities** ✓ ⚓ ✶ ✔
**Acreage** 1 **Open** All Year
**Access** Poor **Site** Level
Lochshore site on a working croft,
overlooking Anteallach on the Scoraig
Peninsular. Bothy, peat stove. Otters,
porpoises, Golden Eagles and wild flowers
galore. Total peace and quiet - Perfect!
Caravans by prior booking only. STB 4 Star
Graded.
**Nearest Town/Resort** Ullapool/Gairloch
**Directions** Off the A832, 1 mile east of the
Dundonnell Hotel take a left turn onto a single
track road to Badrallach, 7 miles to lochshore
site.
⇒ Garve/Inverness

## DURNESS

**Sango Sands Caravan & Camping Site,**
Durness, Sutherland, Highland, IV27 4PP
**Tel:** 01971 511262/511222 **Fax:** 01971
511205
**Email:** keith.durness@btinternet.com
**Pitches For** ⋏ ♨ 🚐 **Total** 82
**Facilities** ✦ 🖪 🄷 🆄 ♨ ⌐ ⊙ ↵ ◢ ▣ ☎
🎗🛁⊙⊛✕🄰♠↵🄿🄴⊬ ℘
**Nearby Facilities** ⌐ ✓ ⚓ ✶ ✔
**Acreage** 12 **Open** April **to** 15 October
**Access** Good **Site** Level
Overlooking Sango Bay.
**Nearest Town/Resort** Durness
**Directions** On the A838 in the centre of
Durness Village.
⇒ Lairg

## EDINBANE

**Loch Greshornish Caravan & Camp
Site,** Borve, Arnisort, Isle of Skye,
Highland, IV51 9PS
**Tel:** 01470 582230 **Fax:** 01470 582230
**Email:** info@skyecamp.com
www.skyecamp.com
**Pitches For** ⋏ ♨ 🚐 **Total** 130
**Facilities** ✦ 🖪 🄷 🆄 ♨ ⌐ ↵ ◢ ▣ ☎ 🎗 ♠🏧
**Nearby Facilities** ⌐ ✓ ✶ ∪ ✔
**Acreage** 5 **Open** 1 April **to** 15 October
**Access** Good **Site** Level
Alongside a loch with mainly level pitches
and an open outlook. Quiet yet close to the
village of Edinbane (1 mile).
**Nearest Town/Resort** Portree
**Directions** On entry to Portree turn left onto
the A850 to Dunvegan. Follow this road for
approx. 12 miles, campsite is located on the
right hand side.
⇒ Kyle of Lochalsh

## FORT AUGUSTUS

**Fort Augustus Caravan & Camping Park,** Market Hill, Fort Augustus, Highland, PH32 4DS
**Tel:** 01320 366618/366360 **Fax:** 01320 366360
**Email:** info@campinglochness.co.uk
www.campinglochness.co.uk
**Pitches For** ⅄ ⬜ 🚐 **Total** 50
**Facilities** ⅃ 🔥 ⬛ ♨ 𝌎 ⊙ ⛳ ▣ 🚻
**Nearby Facilities** ↑ ✈ ⚓ ↘ U ♪ ♬ ⚐
**Acreage** 3½ **Open** Mid April **to** Sept
**Access** Good **Site** Level
Ideal touring alongside golf course, near Loch Ness, scenic views and hill walking.
**Nearest Town/Resort** Fort Augustus
**Directions** ¼ mile south of Fort Augustus on the A82.
⚶ Spean Bridge

## FORT WILLIAM

**Glen Nevis Holidays,** Glen Nevis, Fort William, Inverness-shire, PH33 6SX
**Tel:** 01397 702191 **Fax:** 01397 703904
**Email:** holidays@glen-nevis.co.uk
www.glen-nevis.co.uk
**Pitches For** ⅄ ⬜ 🚐 **Total** 380
**Facilities** ⅃ ⬛ 🔥 ⬛ ♨ ↑ ⊙ ⛳ ▣ 🚻
𝌎 ▣ 🕭 ✗ 🎾 𝌎 ↘ ▣ 🚻
**Nearby Facilities** ↑ ✈ ⚓ ↘ U ♪
**Acreage** 30 **Open** 15 March **to** 31 Oct
**Access** Good **Site** Level

Spectacularly located at the foot of Britain's highest mountain, Ben Nevis. En-route for the West Highland Way.
**Nearest Town/Resort** Fort William
**Directions** From North or South on the A82, turn at small roundabout signed for Glen Nevis, site is 2 miles into glen.
⚶ Fort William

## FORT WILLIAM

**Linnhe Lochside Holidays,** Corpach, Fort William, Highland, PH33 7NL
**Tel:** 01397 772376 **Fax:** 01397 772007
relax@linnhe-lochside-holidays.co.uk
www.linnhe-lochside-holidays.co.uk
**Pitches For** ⅄ ⬜ 🚐 **Total** 65
**Facilities** ⅃ ▣ 🔥 ⬛ ♨ ↑ ⊙ ⛳ ▣ 🚻
𝌎 ▣ ▣ ⊙ ⬛ 𝌎 ↘ ▣ 🚻
**Nearby Facilities** ↑ ✈ ⚓ ↘ U ♪ ♬
**Acreage** 14 **Open** Easter **to** 31 Oct
**Access** Good **Site** Level
Practical Caravan 'Best in Region 2001' and Calor/STB Best Park in Scotland 1999 Award. Magnificent scenery from this top quality park with a private beach and boat slipway. Mains serviced pitches available. Toddlers play room. Holiday chalets and caravans for hire.
**Nearest Town/Resort** Fort William
**Directions** On the A830, 1 mile west of Corpach village, 5 miles from Fort William.
⚶ Corpach

## FORTROSE

**Fortrose Caravan Park,** Wester Greengates, Fortrose, Highlands, IV10 8TJ
**Tel:** 01381 621927
**Email:** fortrosecaravanpark@hotmail.co.uk
**Pitches For** ⅄ ⬜⬜ **Total** 50
**Facilities** ⬛ ⅃ ⬛ ♨ ↑ ⊙ ⛳ ▣ 🚻
⚐▣ ▣ 🕭
**Nearby Facilities** ↑ ✈ ⚓ ↘ ♪ ⚐
**Acreage** 4 **Open** 1 April **to** 30 Sept
**Access** Good **Site** Level
On the shores of the Black Isle, overlooking Moray Firth. Near to Chanonry Point, one of the best places in Europe to view bottlenose dolphins.
**Nearest Town/Resort** Inverness
**Directions** From the A9 follow signs to Munlochy. Turn right at the Tea Cosy Coffee Shop and the Park is on the right hand side before the golf course and Chanonry Point.
⚶ Inverness

## FORTROSE

**Rosemarkie Camping & Caravanning Club Site,** Ness Road East, Rosemarkie, Fortrose, Highlands, IV10 8SE
**Tel:** 01381 621117
www.campingandcaravanningclub.co.uk
**Pitches For** ⅄ ⬜ 🚐 **Total** 60
**Facilities** ⬛ ⅃ ⬛ ♨ ↑ ⊙ ⛳ ▣ 🚻
𝌎 ⊙ ⬛ 🕭 ▣ 🚻
**Nearby Facilities** ↑ ✈ ↘ ⚐

# HIGHLAND

**Acreage** 4 **Open** April **to** Oct
**Access** Good **Site** Level
On the shores of the Black Isle, overlooking Moray and Cromarty Firths. The spectacular coastline is famous for its bottle nosed dolphins. STB 4 Star Graded, AA 2 Pennants and Loo of the Year Award. Non members welcome.
**Nearest Town/Resort** Rosemarkie
**Directions** From the A9 at Tore roundabout take the A832 Fortrose to Cromarty road. Go through Avoch, in Fortrose turn right at the Police House into Ness Road signposted golf course and leisure centre. Turn first left and the site is 400 yards.
⚏ Inverness

## GAIRLOCH
**Gairloch Holiday Park**, Strath, Gairloch, Highland, IV21 2BX
**Tel:** 01445 712373
**Email:** info@gairlochcaravanpark.com
**www.**gairlochcaravanpark.com
**Pitches For** ▲ ⬛ ⬛ **Total** 75
Facilities ⬛ ⬛ ⬛ ⬛ ⬛
**Nearby Facilities** ⬛ ⬛ ⬛ ⬛ ⬛ ⬛
**Acreage** 6 **Open** April **to** End Oct
**Access** Good **Site** Level
Near the beach. In the village centre for shops, hotels and restaurants. STB 4 Star Graded Park and AA 3 Pennants.
**Nearest Town/Resort** Gairloch
**Directions** Turn off the A832 at Auchtercairn onto the B8021. In approx. ½ mile turn right by Millcroft Hotel then immediately right into the site.
⚏ Achnasheen

## GAIRLOCH
**Sands Holiday Centre**, Gairloch, Highland, IV21 2DL
**Tel:** 01445 712152 **Fax:** 01445 712518
**Email:** litsands@aol.com
**www.**highlandcaravancamping.co.uk
**Pitches For** ▲ ⬛ ⬛ **Total** 250
Facilities ⬛ ⬛ ⬛ ⬛ ⬛
**Nearby Facilities** ⬛ ⬛ ⬛ ⬛ ⬛ ⬛
**Acreage** 55 **Open** April **to** October
**Access** Good **Site** Lev/Slope
Site is near the beach with scenic views, river, loch fishing and launching slip. Underfloor heated toilet and shower room. Tennis and climbing wall in Gairloch Leisure Centre.
**Nearest Town/Resort** Gairloch
**Directions** Turn west off the A832 onto the B8012. Site 3 miles on, beside sandy beach.
⚏ Achnasheen

## GLENCOE
**Invercoe Caravan & Camping Park**, Glencoe, Ballachulish, Highland, PH49 4HP
**Tel:** 01855 811210 **Fax:** 01855 811210
**Email:** invercoe@sol.co.uk
**www.**invercoe.co.uk
**Pitches For** ▲ ⬛ ⬛ **Total** 60
Facilities ⬛ ⬛ ⬛ ⬛ ⬛ ⬛
**Nearby Facilities** ⬛ ⬛ ⬛
**Acreage** 5 **Open** All Year
**Access** Good **Site** Level
Lochside site with beautiful scenery. Ideal centre for touring West Highlands. No advanced bookings.
**Nearest Town/Resort** Fort William
**Directions** Heading north on the A82 turn right at Glencoe crossroads onto the B863.
⚏ Fort William

## GLENCOE
**Red Squirrel Campsite**, Leacantuim Farm, Glencoe, Highland, PH49 4HX
**Tel:** 01855 811256
**Email:** squirrels@amserve.net
**Pitches For** ▲ ⬛
Facilities ⬛ ⬛ ⬛ ⬛ ⬛ ⬛ ⬛
**Nearby Facilities** ⬛ ⬛ ⬛ ⬛ ⬛ ⬛
**Acreage** 20 **Open** All Year
**Site** Lev/Slope
Casual and very different Two Star Site in the centre of the mountains. River for swimming and fishing (salmon permit, must bring your own rods). Meter showers. Emergency telephone on site.
**Nearest Town/Resort** Fort William
**Directions** Turn off the main A82 into Glencoe Village, turn up main street, go over the humpback bridge and park is 1½ miles.
⚏ Fort William

## GRANTOWN-ON-SPEY
**Grantown-on-Spey Caravan Park**, Seafield Avenue, Grantown-on-Spey, Highland, PH26 3JQ
**Tel:** 01479 872474 **Fax:** 01479 873696
**Email:** team@caravanscotland.com
**www.**caravanscotland.com
**Pitches For** ▲ ⬛ ⬛ **Total** 150
Facilities ⬛ ⬛ ⬛ ⬛ ⬛ ⬛
**Nearby Facilities** ⬛ ⬛ ⬛
**Acreage** 23
**Access** Good **Site** Level
Quiet park, central for touring the Highlands. A haven for wildlife, red deer roam freely. Ideal for fishing, walking and golf. Close to the world's only Malt Whisky Trail, the Cairngorms and the skiing village of Aviemore. Open All Year except beg. Nov to mid Dec. Non members welcome. Booking essential.
**Nearest Town/Resort** Grantown-on-Spey
**Directions** From Aviemore take the A9, approx. 1½ miles past Aviemore turn right onto the A95. When in Grantown high street go through the traffic lights and turn left by the Bank of Scotland, site is ½ mile on the right.
⚏ Aviemore

## INVERGARRY
**Faichem Park**, Ardgarry Farm, Faichem, Invergarry, Highland, PH35 4HG
**Tel:** 01809 501226 **Fax:** 01809 501226
**Email:** enquiries@ardgarryfarm.co.uk
**www.**ardgarryfarm.co.uk
**Pitches For** ▲ ⬛ ⬛ **Total** 30
Facilities ⬛ ⬛ ⬛ ⬛ ⬛
**Nearby Facilities** ⬛ ⬛ ⬛ ⬛ ⬛ ⬛
**Acreage** 2 **Open** April **to** October
**Access** Good **Site** Lev/Slope
Panoramic views across Glengarry.
**Nearest Town/Resort** Invergarry
**Directions** From the A82 at Invergarry take the A87, continue for 1 mile. Turn right at Faichem signpost, bear left up hill, first entrance on the right.
⚏ Spean Bridge

## INVERGARRY
**Faichemard Farm Camp Site**, Faichemard Farm, Invergarry, Highland, PH35 4HG
**Tel:** 01809 501314
**Email:** dgrant@fsbdial.co.uk
**www.**host.co.uk
**Pitches For** ▲ ⬛ ⬛ **Total** 35
Facilities ⬛ ⬛ ⬛ ⬛ ⬛ ⬛
**Nearby Facilities** ⬛ ⬛ ⬛ ⬛ ⬛
**Acreage** 10 **Open** April **to** October
**Access** Good **Site** Lev/Slope
ADULTS ONLY SITE. Hill walking, bird watching, space and quiet. Pitch price £5-£8, every pitch has its own picnic table.
**Nearest Town/Resort** Fort William
**Directions** Take A82 to Invergarry (25 miles) travel west on A87 for 1 mile, take side road on right at sign for Faichem, go past Ardgarry Farm and Faichem Park Camp Site to signpost A & D Grant.
⚏ Spean Bridge

## INVERMORISTON
**Loch Ness Caravan & Camping Park**, Invermoriston, Inverness-shire, IV63 7YE
**Tel:** 01320 351207/351399
**Email:** bob@girvan7904.freeserve.co.uk
**www.**lochnesscaravanandcampingpark.co.uk
**Pitches For** ▲ ⬛ ⬛
Facilities ⬛ ⬛ ⬛ ⬛ ⬛ ⬛
**Nearby Facilities** ⬛ ⬛ ⬛ ⬛ ⬛
**Acreage** 8 **Open** 1 March **to** 31 Jan
**Access** Good **Site** Level
The only park on the whole of the loch, with a private beach. Central for touring the Highlands.
**Nearest Town/Resort** Inverness
**Directions** 27 miles from Inverness on the A82.
⚏ Inverness

## INVERNESS
**Auchnahillin Caravan & Camping Park**, Daviot East, Inverness, Highland, IV2 5XQ
**Tel:** 01463 772286 **Fax:** 01463 772282
**Email:** info@auchnahillin.co.uk
**www.**auchnahillin.co.uk
**Pitches For** ▲ ⬛ ⬛ **Total** 100
Facilities ⬛ ⬛ ⬛ ⬛ ⬛ ⬛
**Nearby Facilities**
**Acreage** 10 **Open** March **to** Oct
**Access** Good **Site** Level
Ideal touring area for the Highlands, near lots to see and do. Scenic views.
**Nearest Town/Resort** Inverness
**Directions** Approx. 7 miles south of Inverness take the eastward turning onto the B9154.
⚏ Inverness

## INVERNESS
**Bught Caravan & Tent Park**, Bught Lane, Inverness, Highland, IV3 5SR
**Tel:** 01463 236920 **Fax:** 01463 234093
**Email:**
bookings@invernesscaravanpark.com
**www.**invernesscaravanpark.com
**Pitches For** ▲ ⬛ ⬛ **Total** 140
Facilities ⬛ ⬛ ⬛ ⬛ ⬛ ⬛
**Nearby Facilities** ⬛ ⬛ ⬛ ⬛ ⬛ ⬛
**Acreage** 4½ **Open** Easter **to** Nov
**Access** Good **Site** Level
Bught Park is on the River Ness. Situated in a Tourist Complex with an Aquadome, Cafes, Restaurants, Crazy Golf, Ice Rink, Boating Pond, miniature railway, full size Golf Club, Floral Hall Complex, sports venues and much more.
**Nearest Town/Resort** Inverness
**Directions** Situated inside Inverness city limits, on the A82 Loch Ness road. The park is a 15 minute walk from the railway and bus stations.
⚏ Inverness

**Parkdean Holidays**

# stunning scotland

great locations

great facilities

great fun

Escape with **Parkdean Holidays** to spectacular Scotland, breathtaking views, great facilities and hearty hospitality.

We've five fantastic **4 star** holiday parks: **Sundrum Castle, Southerness, Tummel Valley, Grannie's Heilan' Hame** and **Nairn Lochloy** in lovely beach or woodland locations.

- serviced & standard pitches available
- electricity hook up points
- indoor & outdoor pools
- toilet & shower facilities
- family entertainment
- bars & cafés
- superb sports facilities
- fantastic beach access

# holidays to remember

book now **0870 420 2977** or online www.**parkdean**holidays.co.uk

# HIGHLAND

## INVERNESS

**Torvean Caravan Park,** Glenurquhart Road, Inverness, Highland, IV3 8JL
**Tel:** 01463 220582 **Fax:** 01862 821382
www.torveancaravanpark.co.uk
**Pitches For** ⌖ ♠ **Total 50**
**Facilities** ⌖ ⚲ ⚬ ⌑ ⌾ ♨ ⌦ ⟊ ⬛ ⧠ ♄
⍾ ⌾ ⛺ ⌸ ⌹
**Nearby Facilities** ⌐ ⟋ ⚲ ⚓ ⚬ ⊍ ♞ ⚲
**Acreage** 3 **Open** April **to** October
**Access** Good **Site** Level
Overlooking a canal and golf course. Within walking distance of a theatre, swimming pool, sports centre and Floral Hall. Ideal base for touring the Highlands.
**Nearest Town/Resort** Inverness
**Directions** From the A9 follow signs for the A82 Fortwilliam. 1½ miles from the city centre turn right at Tomnahrich Bridge, opposite Jacobite Cruises and a golf course.
⇥ Inverness

## JOHN O'GROATS

**John O'Groats Caravan & Camping Site,** John O'Groats, Nr Wick, Highland, KW1 4YS
**Tel:** 01955 611329
**Email:** info@johnogroatscampsite.co.uk
www.johnogroatscampsite.co.uk
**Pitches For** ⌖ ♠ **Total 90**
**Facilities** ⚲ ⌑ ⌾ ♨ ⌦ ⟊ ⬛ ⌾ ⧠ ♄
⍾ ⌾ ⛺ ⌸ ⌹ ⌺
**Nearby Facilities** ⟋
**Acreage** 4 **Open** April **to** October
**Access** Good **Site** Level
On sea shore with clear view of Orkney Islands. Day trips to Orkney by passenger terry, jetty nearby. Hotel and snack bar within 150 yards. Cliff scenery and sea birds 1½ miles. STB 3 Star Graded.
**Nearest Town/Resort** John O' Groats
**Directions** End of A99 beside last house.
⇥ Wick

## KINLOCHEWE

**Kinlochewe Caravan Club Site,** Kinlochewe, Achnasheen, Highland, IV22 2PA
**Tel:** 01445 760239
www.caravanclub.co.uk
**Pitches For** ⌖ ♠ **Total 56**
**Facilities** ⚲ ⌑ ⌾ ♨ ⌦ ⟊ ⌾ ♄
⍾ ⌾ ⛺ ⌸ ⌹ ⌺
**Nearby Facilities** ♞
**Acreage** 5 **Open** March **to** Oct
**Access** Good **Site** Level
Peaceful location at the foot of Ben Eighe, surrounded by lochs, woodland and mountains. Close to Victoria Falls and Inverewe Gardens. Butcher calls into site twice a week. Adjacent to a service station and theres a general shop and café in the village. Non members welcome. Booking essential.
**Directions** From Inverness take A9, in Tore at roundabout turn onto A835 sp Maryburgh, in Maryburgh at roundabout continue on A835 sp Ullapool. In Gorstan turn left onto A832, in Achnasheen at roundabout follow signs for Kinlochewe, site is 10 miles on the left.

## LAIDE

**Gruinard Bay Caravan Park,** Laide, Ross-shire, IV22 2ND
**Tel:** 01445 731225
**Email:** gruinard@ecosse.net
www.highlandbreaks.com
**Pitches For** ⌖ ♠ **Total 55**
**Facilities** ⚲ ⌑ ⌾ ♨ ⌦ ⟊ ⬛ ⌾ ♄
⍾ ⍦ ⍾ ⌾ ⛺ ⌸ ⌹

## Nearby Facilities ⌐ ⟋ ⚲ ⊍ ♞
**Acreage** 3 **Open** April **to** October
**Access** Good **Site** Level
By the beach with spectacular views.
**Nearest Town/Resort** Gairloch
**Directions** From Inverness take the A9, then the A835 then the A832. Site is in Laide between the A832 and the beach. 73 miles fro Inverness.
⇥ Inverness

## LAIRG

**Dunroamin Caravan & Camping Park,** Main Street, Lairg, Sutherland, IV27 4AR
**Tel:** 01549 402447 **Fax:** 01549 402784
**Email:** enquiries@lairgcaravanpark.co.uk
www.lairgcaravanpark.co.uk
**Pitches For** ⌖ ♠ **Total 40**
**Facilities** ⚲ ⌑ ⌾ ♨ ⌦ ⟊ ⬛ ⌾ ♄
⍾ ⌾ ⛺ ✕ ⌸ ⌹ ⌺
**Nearby Facilities** ⌐ ⟋ ⚲ ⚲ ⚲ ♞
**Acreage** 4 **Open** April **to** October
**Access** Good **Site** Level
Ideal centre for touring, fishing and sight seeing. Close to Loch Shin and all amenities. Secure Storage during Winter only.
**Nearest Town/Resort** Lairg
**Directions** 300yds east of Loch Shin on the A839 on Main Street Lairg.
⇥ Lairg

## LAIRG

**Woodend Caravan & Camping Park,** Woodend, Achnairn, Lairg, Highland, IV27 4DN
**Tel:** 01549 402248 **Fax:** 01549 402248
**Pitches For** ⌖ ♠ **Total 45**
**Facilities** ⚲ ⌑ ⌾ ♨ ⌦ ⟊ ⬛ ⌾ ♄
⍾ ⛺ ⌸ ⌹
**Nearby Facilities** ⟋ ⚲ ♞
**Acreage** 4 **Open** April **to** September
**Access** Good **Site** Lev/Slope
Overlooking Loch Shin, fishing and scenic views. Campers Kitchen is a small building where campers can take their cooking stores to prepare food, with table, chairs and a dish washing area. Ideal touring centre for north west. AA 3 Pennants. Gold Award for Quality & Service from International Caravan & Camping Guide.
**Nearest Town/Resort** Lairg
**Directions** A836 from Lairg onto A838 and follow site signs.
⇥ Lairg

## MELVICH

**Halladale Inn Caravan Park,** Melvich, Highland, KW14 7YJ
**Tel:** 01641 531282
**Email:** mazfling@tinyworld.co.uk
**Pitches For** ⌖ ♠ **Total 14**
**Facilities** ⌐ ⌑ ⌾ ♨ ⌦ ⟊ ⬛ ⌾ ♄
⍾ ⛺ ✕ ♀ ⌾ ♠ ⌸ ⌹ ⌺
**Nearby Facilities** ⌐ ⟋ ⚲ ⚓ ♞
**Open** April **to** October
**Access** Good **Site** Level
Sandy beaches and sea fishing, wild brown trout and salmon fishing. Bird watching, surfing and diving.
**Nearest Town/Resort** Thurso
**Directions** 17 miles west of Thurso on the A836 north coast road.
⇥ Thurso/Forsinard

## NAIRN

**Camping & Caravanning Club Site,** Delnies Wood, Nairn, Inverness, Highland, IV12 5NX
**Tel:** 01667 455281
www.campingandcaravanningclub.co.uk
**Pitches For** ⌖ ♠ **Total 75**

## Facilities ⌑ ⬛ ⚲ ⌾ ⌾ ♨ ⌦ ⟊ ⬛ ⌾ ♄
⍾ ⌾ ⛺ ♠ ⌸ ⌹ ⌺ ⌺ ♄
**Nearby Facilities** ⌐ ⟋
**Acreage** 14 **Open** April **to** Oct
**Access** Good **Site** Level
Wooded setting just 2 miles from the beach, close to the town of Nairn. STB 4 Star Graded and AA 3 Pennants. Non members welcome.
**Nearest Town/Resort** Nairn
**Directions** Off the A96 Inverness to Aberdeen road 2 miles west of Nairn.
⇥ Nairn

## NAIRN

**Nairn Lochloy Holiday Park,** East Beach, Nairn, Highland, IV12 4PH
**Tel:** 01667 453764 **Fax:** 01667 454721
**Email:** enquiries@parkdeanholidays.com
www.parkdeanholidays.com
**Pitches For** ⌖ ♠ **Total 13**
**Facilities** ⚲ ⌑ ⌾ ♨ ⌦ ⟊ ⬛ ⌾ ♄
⍾ ⍦ ⍾ ⛺ ✕ ♀ ⌾ ♠ ⌾ ⌸ ⌹ ⌺
**Nearby Facilities** ⌐ ⟋ ⚲ ♞
**Acreage** 15 **Open** March **to** Oct
**Access** Good **Site** Level
Situated next to the harbour, beach and the locely village of Nairn.
**Nearest Town/Resort** Nairn
**Directions** Take the A96 from Inverness or Anerdeen. In Nairn follow signs, adjacent to the harbour.
⇥ Nairn

## NEWTONMORE

**Invernahavon Caravan Site,** Glentruim, Newtonmore, Highland, PH20 1BE
**Tel:** 01540 673534/673219 **Fax:** 01540 673219
www.caravanclub.co.uk
**Pitches For** ⌖ ♠ **Total 67**
**Facilities** ⚲ ⌑ ⌾ ♨ ⌦ ⟊ ⬛ ⌾ ♄
⍾ ⌾ ⛺ ♠ ⌸ ⌹
**Nearby Facilities** ⌐ ⟋ ⚲ ⚓ ⊍ ♞ ⚲
**Acreage** 10 **Open** March **to** Oct
**Access** Good **Site** Level
Tranquil and spacious family run site with spectacular views of the 'Monarch of the Glen' country. Heather covered mountains, ideal for walking and wildlife spotting. Adjacent to the Rivers Spey and Truim, fishing permits available. Non members welcome. Booking essential.
**Nearest Town/Resort** Newtonmore
**Directions** 2 miles south of Newtonmore on the A9 turn right onto Glentruim road, site is 400 yards on the right.
⇥ Newtonmore

## ONICH

**Bunree Caravan Club Site,** Onich, Fort William, Highland, PH33 6SE
**Tel:** 01855 821283
www.caravanclub.co.uk
**Pitches For** ⌖ ♠ **Total 99**
**Facilities** ⚲ ⌑ ⌾ ♨ ⌦ ⟊ ⬛ ⌾ ♄
⍾ ⌾ ⛺ ♠ ⌸ ⌹
**Nearby Facilities** ⟋
**Acreage** 7 **Open** March **to** Oct
**Access** Good **Site** Level
Situated at the edge of Loch Linnhe with mountain views. Visit Ben Nevis or take a cable car 2300 feet to Aonach Mor Mountain for fabulous views of the whole mountain range, the Great Glen and islands of Skye and Rhum. Non members welcome. Booking essential.
**Nearest Town/Resort** Onich
**Directions** From south east on the A82, just past Onich turn left at Caravan Club sign into a narrow track with traffic lights and passing places, site is in ¼ mile.

## POOLEWE

**Camping & Caravanning Club Site,**
Inverewe Gardens, Poolewe, Achnasheen,
Highlands, IV22 2LF
Tel: 01445 781249
www.campingandcaravanningclub.co.uk
Pitches For ▲ ⚌ 🚐 Total 55
Facilities ⚪ ∤ 🏠 💷 ♨ 🦺 ⊙ 🕁 🔌 ☎ 🔲 🛢
🖳 ⊙ 🅿 🔲 🕁 ◿
Nearby Facilities ✓ 🏌 ⚓
Acreage 3 Open April to Oct
Site Level
Close to Inverewe Gardens and Loch Ewe.
National Trust Ranger Walks ¼ mile. STB
4 Star Graded and AA 3 Pennants. Non
members welcome.
Directions Site entrance is on the A832,
north of the village of Poolewe.
⚏ Achnasheen

## PORTREE

**Torvaig Caravan & Campsite,** 8 Torvaig,
Portree, Isle of Skye, Highland, IV51 9HU
Tel: 01478 611849
Pitches For ▲ ⚌ 🚐 Total 90
Facilities ∤ 🏠 💷 ♨ 🦺 ⊙ ☎ 🛢 🕁
Nearby Facilities 🏌 ∪ ⚓
Acreage 4½ Open 1 April to 20 Oct
Access Good Site Sloping
Ideal for touring the Isle of Skye.
Nearest Town/Resort Portree
Directions 1 mile north of Portree on the
main A855, on the right.
⚏ Kyle of Lochalsh

## ROY BRIDGE

**Bunroy Park,** Roy Bridge, Inverness-shire,
PH31 4AG
Tel: 01397 712332 Fax: 01397 712045
Email: info@bunroycamping.co.uk
www.bunroycamping.co.uk
Pitches For ▲ ⚌ 🚐 Total 25
Facilities ∤ 🏠 💷 ♨ 🦺 ⊙ 🕁 🔲 🔲
🖳 ⊙ 🅿 🔲 🔲 🔲
Nearby Facilities 🏌 ✓ 🏊 ∪ ⚓
Acreage 4 Open March to October
Access Fair Site Level
Quiet site alongside a river and sheltered
by trees. Ideal for touring, climbing and
walking. STB 4 Star Graded.
Nearest Town/Resort Fort William
Directions 12 miles north east of Fort
William. From Fort William take the A82 to
Spean Bridge, then take the A86 to Roy
Bridge.
⚏ Roy Bridge

## ROY BRIDGE

**Inveroy Caravan Park,** Roy Bridge,
Highland, PH31 4AQ
Tel: 01397 712697 Fax: 01397 712697
Email: renee@rbarberis.freeserve.co.uk
www.rbarberis.freeserve.co.uk
Pitches For ▲ ⚌ 🚐 Total 40
Facilities ∤ 🔲 💷 ♨ 🦺 🕁 🔌 🔲 🛢
🖳 ⊙ 🅿 🔲 ⚪
Nearby Facilities 🏌 ✓ 🏊 ∪ ⚓ 🏌
Open All Year
Access Good Site Level
Centrally situated in the Highlands near
Ben Nevis, abundant wildlife. Ideal for
touring. All facilities nearby, walking,
fishing, canoeing. Static caravans to let.
Nearest Town/Resort Fort William
Directions 14 miles north of Fort William on
the A82.
⚏ Roy Bridge

## SCOURIE

**Scourie Caravan & Camping Park,**
Harbour Road, Scourie, Highland, IV27
4TG
Tel: 01971 502060
Pitches For ▲ ⚌ 🚐 Total 80
Facilities ⚪ ∤ 🏠 💷 ♨ 🦺 ⊙ 🕁 🔌 🔲 🛢
🖳 🛢 ⊙ ✗ 🕁 🔲
Nearby Facilities ✓ 🏊 🏌 🏌 🏌
Acreage 4+ Open Mid April to Sept
Access Good Site Level
Overlooking Scourie Bay. Ideal for hill
walking, bird watching, trout and sea
fishing.
Nearest Town/Resort Scourie
Directions Near Scourie Village, at the
junction of Harbour Road and the A894. 20
miles south of Cape Wrath.
⚏ Lairg

## SHIEL BRIDGE

**Morvich Caravan Club Site,** Inverinate,
Kyle, Highland, IV40 8HQ
Tel: 01599 511354
www.caravanclub.co.uk
Pitches For ▲ ⚌ 🚐 Total 106
Facilities ⚪ ∤ 🏠 💷 ♨ 🦺 🕁 🔌 🔲 🛢
🖳 ⊙ 🛢 🕁 🔲 🔲
Nearby Facilities ✓
Acreage 7 Open March to Oct
Access Good Site Level
Set on a valley floor surrounded by hills
and mountains on National Trust land.
Daily guided walks July and August. Close
to Eilean Castle, Dunvegan Castle, Falls of
Glomach, Talisker Distillery and Isle of
Skye. Non members welcome. Booking
essential.
Nearest Town/Resort Shiel Bridge
Directions From the A87, 1½ miles past
Shiel Bridge at the head of Loch Duich, turn
right by the restaurant into loop road
signposted Morvich, after 1 mile turn right
into road to the site.

## SHIEL BRIDGE

**Shiel Bridge Caravan Park,** Shiel Bridge,
Glenshiel, Kyle of Lochalsh, Ross-shire,
IV40 8HW
Tel: 01599 511221 Fax: 01599 511432
Pitches For ▲ ⚌ 🚐 Total 75
Facilities ⚪ ∤ 🏠 💷 ♨ 🦺 🕁 🔌 🔲 🛢
🖫 🛢 ⊙ ✗ 🕁 🔲
Nearby Facilities ✓ 🏊 ∪
Open 16 March to 16 Oct
Access Good Site Level
Spectacular scenery. Ideal for walking.
Nearest Town/Resort Kyle of Lochalsh
Directions 16 miles east of Kyle of Lochalsh
on the A87.
⚏ Kyle of Lochalsh

## SPEAN BRIDGE

**Gairlochy Holiday Park,** Old Station,
Gairlochy Road, Spean Bridge, Highland,
PH34 4EQ
Tel: 01397 712711 Fax: 01397 712712
Email: theghp@talk21.com
www.theghp.co.uk
Pitches For ▲ ⚌ 🚐 Total 20
Facilities ∤ 🏠 💷 ♨ 🦺 ⊙ 🕁 🔌 🔲 🛢
🛢 🏛 🔲 🔲
Nearby Facilities 🏌 ✓ 🏌
Acreage 1 Open April to October
Access Good Site Level
Nearest Town/Resort Fort William
Directions 1 mile north of Spean Bridge
heading towards Inverness turn onto the
B8004 at the Commando Memorial, site is 1
mile.
⚏ Spean Bridge

## SPEAN BRIDGE

**Stronaba Caravan & Camping Site,**
Stronaba Farm, Spean Bridge, Highland,
PH34 4DX
Tel: 01397 712259
Email: bookings@greatglenholidays.co.uk
Pitches For ▲ ⚌ 🚐 Total 25
Facilities ∤ 🏠 💷 ♨ 🦺 ⊙ 🕁 💷 🕁 🔲
Nearby Facilities 🏌 ✓ 🏊 🏌 ∪ 🏌 🏊 🏌
Acreage 4 Open Easter to October
Access Good Site Lev/Slope
Scenic views, ideal touring. Gas, telephone
and cafe/restaurant all within 2¼ miles.
Site has a flat area.
Nearest Town/Resort Spean Bridge
Directions On the main A82 Fort William to
Inverness road. 2¼ miles north of Spean
Bridge, on the left hand side just beyond AA
phone box.
⚏ Spean Bridge

## STRATHPEFFER

**Riverside Caravan Park,** Contin, By
Strathpeffer, Ross-shire, IV14 9ES
Tel: 01997 421351
Pitches For ▲ ⚌ 🚐 Total 30
Facilities ∤ 🏠 💷 ♨ 🦺 🕁 🔲 ⚪ 🏛 ⊙ 🛢 🐾
Nearby Facilities 🏌 ✓ ∪ 🏌
Open All Year
Access Good Site Level
Riverside site with nice scenery. Ideal for
touring, fishing, shooting, golf and walking.
Nearest Town/Resort Dingwall
Directions From Dingwall take the A835
west towards Ullapool for 7 miles.
⚏ Dingwall

## THURSO

**Dunnet Bay Caravan Club Site,** Dunnet,
Thurso, Highland, KW14 8XD
Tel: 01847 821319
www.caravanclub.co.uk
Pitches For ▲ ⚌ 🚐 Total 45
Facilities ∤ 💷 ♨ 🦺 ⊙ 🕁 🔲 🛢 💷 🏛 🕁 🔲
Nearby Facilities ✓ 🏊 🏌 ∪ 🏌 🏌
Acreage 5 Open March to Oct
Access Good Site Level
Situated on the beach above the sand
dunes. Ideal for bird watching, walking,
guided walks and day trips to the Orkney
Islands. Climb Dunnet Head for
magnificent views over Pentland Firth to
Orkney and the north coast to Ben Loyal
and Ben Hope. Non members welcome.
Booking essential.
Nearest Town/Resort Thurso
Directions From Thurso take the A836, site
is on the left approx. 2½ miles past
Castletown Village.
⚏ Thurso

## UIG

**Uig Bay Camping & Caravan Site,** 10
Idrigill, Uig, Isle of Skye, Highland, IV51
9XU
Tel: 01470 542714 Fax: 01470 542714
Email: lisa.madigan@btopenworld.com
www.uig-camp-skye.com
Pitches For ▲ ⚌ 🚐 Total 50
Facilities ∤ 🔲 🏠 💷 ♨ 🦺 ⊙ 🕁 🔌 🔲 🛢
🖳 🛢 🕁 🔲 ⚪
Nearby Facilities ✓ ∪ 🏌
Acreage 2¼ Open All Year
Access Good Site Level
Close to a pebble beach. Near ferry
terminal to the Western Isles. Ideal for
touring the Highlands. Cycle hire locally.
Nearest Town/Resort Uig
Directions From Portree take the A87 to Uig,
pass the ferry terminal and turn right just
before the pier to the site.
⚏ Fort William

## ULLAPOOL

**Ardmair Point Holiday Centre**, Ardmair Point, Ullapool, Highland, IV26 2TN
**Tel:** 01854 612054 **Fax:** 01854 612757
**Email:** info@ardmair.com
www.ardmair.com
**Pitches For** ▲ ⊕ ⊜ **Total** 45
**Facilities** ⅍ ∮ ◫ ⊞ ⚓ ୮ ⊙ ⌣ ⊠ ◙ ⊟
⊗♨ ◐ ⊛ Δ ❋ ⊞☐ ⋇
**Nearby Facilities** ୮ ✓ ⊿ ⚓ ⅏ ⊁
**Acreage** 7 **Open** May to Sept
**Access** Good **Site** Level
Beautiful location with outstanding views from the site over sea to 'Summer Isles'. Boating centre.
**Nearest Town/Resort** Ullapool
**Directions** 3 miles north of Ullapool on the A835. Enter the park at Ardmair Beach.
⌖ Garve

## ULLAPOOL

**Broomfield Holiday Park**, Shore Street, Ullapool, Highlands, IV26 2SX
**Tel:** 01854 612020 **Fax:** 01854 613151
**Email:** sross@broomfieldhp.com
www.broomfieldhp.com
**Pitches For** ▲ ⊕ ⊜ **Total** 140
**Facilities** ⅍ ∮ ◫ ⚓ ୮ ⊙ ⌣ ⊠ ◙ ⊟
⊗ ◐ ⊛ ✕ Δ ❋ ⊞ ⋇
**Nearby Facilities** ୮ ✓ ∪ ⅏ ⊁
**Acreage** 11 **Open** Easter to September
**Access** Good **Site** Level
On the sea front. Beside a cafe/restaurant and adjacent to a golf course.
**Nearest Town/Resort** Ullapool
**Directions** Turn right past Ullapool Harbour.
⌖ Garve

# LANARKSHIRE (SOUTH)

## ABINGTON

**Mount View Caravan Park**, Abington, By Biggar, South Lanarkshire, ML12 6RW
**Tel:** 01864 502808
**Email:** info@mountviewcaravanpark.co.uk
www.mountviewcaravanpark.co.uk
**Pitches For** ▲ ⊕ ⊜ **Total** 50
**Facilities** ⅍ ∮ ◫ ⊞ ⚓ ୮ ⊙ ⌣ ⊠ ◙ ⊟
⊗ ◐ ⊛ Δ ❋ ⋇
**Nearby Facilities** ୮ ✓ ⅏
**Acreage** 5½ **Open** March to October
**Access** Good **Site** Lev/Slope
Ideal for walking, touring and a quiet family holiday. Well situated for exploring Clyde Valley. One hour from Glasgow, Edinburgh and the Ayrshire coast.
**Nearest Town/Resort** Biggar
**Directions** Leave the M74 at junction 13 and take the A702 south into Abington Village, then follow signs down Station Road.
⌖ Lanark

## LANARK

**Clyde Valley Caravan Park**, 1 Sycamore Grove, Kirkfieldbank, Lanark, South Lanarkshire, ML11 9JW
**Tel:** 01555 663951 **Fax:** 01555 663951
**Pitches For** ▲ ⊕ ⊜ **Total** 100
**Facilities** ⅍ ∮ ◫ ⚓ ୮ ⊙ ⌣ ⊠ ◙ ⊟
⊗ ◐ ⊛ Δ ❋ ⋇ ⋇

**Nearby Facilities** ୮ ✓ ⚓ ∪
**Acreage** 5 **Open** April to October
**Access** Good **Site** Level
Close to Historic Lanark, Fall of Clyde and Lanark Golf Course.
**Nearest Town/Resort** Lanark
**Directions** ½ a mile north of Lanark on the A73, or by the A72 to Kirkfieldbank.
⌖ Lanark

# LOTHIAN (EAST)

## DUNBAR

**Belhaven Bay Caravan Park**, Edinburgh Road, Dunbar, East Lothian, EH42 1TU
**Tel:** 01368 865956 **Fax:** 01368 865022
**Email:** belhaven@meadowhead.co.uk
www. meadowhead.co.uk
**Pitches For** ▲ ⊕ ⊜ **Total** 60
**Facilities** ⅍ ∮ ◫ ⊞ ⚓ ୮ ⊙ ⌣ ⊠ ◙ ⊟
⅏ ◐ ⊛ Δ ❋ ⊞ ⊟
**Nearby Facilities** ୮ ✓ ⚓ ∪ ⅏
**Acreage** 10 **Open** March to Oct
**Access** Good **Site** Level
Near the beach and a park.
**Nearest Town/Resort** Dunbar
**Directions** 2 km west of Dunbar on the Edinburgh road, at West Barns.
⌖ Dunbar

## DUNBAR

**Camping & Caravanning Club Site**, Barns Ness, Dunbar, East Lothian, EH42 1QP
**Tel:** 01368 863536
www.campingandcaravanningclub.co.uk
**Pitches For** ▲ ⊕ ⊜ **Total** 80
**Facilities** ⅍ ∮ ◫ ⊞ ⚓ ୮ ⊙ ⌣ ⊠ ◙ ⊟
⅏ ◐ ⊛ Δ ❋ ⊞ ☐ ⚲
**Nearby Facilities** ✓ ⚓ ∪
**Acreage** 10 **Open** March to October
**Access** Poor **Site** Lev/Slope
Close to the town of Dunbar, on the Scottish coast. STB 3 Star Graded and AA 3 Pennants. Non members welcome.
**Directions** On the A1 approx. 6 miles south of Dunbar (near the Power Station) you will see signs for Barns Ness and Skateraw, turn right at camp site sign towards the lighthouse and take in the views of the sea.
⌖ Dunbar

## DUNBAR

**Thorntonloch Caravan Park**, Innerwick, Dunbar, East Lothian, EH42 1QS
**Tel:** 01368 840236
**Pitches For** ▲ ⊕ ⊜ **Total** 10
**Facilities** ∮ ◫ ⊞ ⚓ ୮ ⊙ ⌣ ⊠ ◙ ⊟
⊗ ◐ ⊛ Δ ❋ ⋇
**Nearby Facilities** ୮ ✓
**Open** 6 March to 27 Oct
**Access** Good **Site** Level
Next to the beach.
**Nearest Town/Resort** Dunbar
**Directions** 7 miles south of Dunbar on the A1.
⌖ Dunbar

## DUNBAR

**Thurston Manor Holiday Home Park**, Innerwick, Dunbar, East Lothian, EH42 1SA
**Tel:** 01368 840643 **Fax:** 01368 840261
**Email:** mail@thurstonmanor.co.uk
www. thurstonmanor.co.uk
**Pitches For** ▲ ⊕ ⊜ **Total** 100
**Facilities** ⅍ ∮ ◫ ⊞ ⚓ ୮ ⊙ ⌣ ⊠ ◙ ⊟
⊗ ◐ ⊛ ✕ ⊽ Ⅲ Δ ❋ ⊞☐ ⋇
**Nearby Facilities** ୮ ✓ ⚓ ∪ ⅏ ⊁
**Acreage** 250 **Open** 1 March to 31 Oct
**Access** Good **Site** Level
5 Star facilities and our own woodland valley of great natural beauty. Ideal touring park.
**Nearest Town/Resort** Dunbar
**Directions** 4 miles south of Dunbar on the A1 take the Innerwick sign. Park is ½ mile on the right. Tourist signs can be seen from the A1.
⌖ Dunbar

## LONGNIDDRY

**Seton Sands Holiday Centre**, Longniddry, East Lothian, EH32 0QF
**Tel:** 01875 813333 **Fax:** 01875 813531
www. touringholidays.co.uk
**Pitches For** ▲ ⊕ ⊜
**Facilities** ⅍ ∮ ◫ ⚓ ୮ ⊙ ⌣ ⊠ ◙ ⊗ ⊛ ⋇
**Nearby Facilities**
**Open** March to Oct
**Access** Good **Site** Level
Picture postcard views over the Firth of Forth. Fabulous beaches nearby.
**Nearest Town/Resort** Edinburgh
**Directions** Take the A1 to the A198, from here turn onto the B6371 for Cockenzie, then turn right onto the B1348. The park is 1 mile on the right hand side. Signposted from the A1 north and south.

## NORTH BERWICK

**Gilsland Caravan Park**, Newhouse Road, North Berwick, East Lothian, EH39 5JA
**Tel:** 01620 892205
**Email:** gilslandcp@ukonline.co.uk
**Pitches For** ▲ ⊕ ⊜ **Total** 33
**Facilities** ∮ ◫ ⊞ ⚓ ୮ ⊙ ⌣ ⊠ ◙ ⊟
◐ ⊛ Δ ❋ ⋇
**Nearby Facilities** ୮ ✓ ⚓ ∪ ⅏ ⊁
**Acreage** 8 **Open** April to Oct
**Access** Good **Site** Level
1 mile from the beach. Town centre, station, indoor pool and sports centre are all within 1 mile.
**Nearest Town/Resort** North Berwick
**Directions** From the centre of North Berwick find the sports centre, we are ½ a mile along Grange Road going west.
⌖ North Berwick

## NORTH BERWICK

**Tantallon Caravan Park**, Dunbar Road, North Berwick, East Lothian, EH39 5NJ
**Tel:** 01620 893348 **Fax:** 01620 895623
**Email:** tantallon@meadowhead.co.uk
www. meadowhead.co.uk
**Pitches For** ▲ ⊕ ⊜ **Total** 150
**Facilities** ⅍ ∮ ◫ ⊞ ⚓ ୮ ⊙ ⌣ ⊠ ◙ ⊟
⊗ ⅏ ◐ ⊛ Ⅲ Δ ❋ ⊞☐ ⊟

**Nearby Facilities** ┌ ✔ ⚓ ኣ ∪ ⚲ ℛ
**Acreage** 20 **Open** March **to** Oct
**Access** Good **Site** Level
Near the beach.
**Directions** 1 km from the town centre.
⌖ North Berwick

## NORTH BERWICK
**Yellowcraig Caravan Club Site,** Dirleton,
East Lothian, EH39 5DS
**Tel:** 01620 850217
**www.** caravanclub.co.uk
**Pitches For** ♥ ⊟ **Total** 78
F a c i l i t i e s ⅙ ∮ ⓗ ⓤ ♨ ┌ ◙ ☗
⅋ ⊙ ⦿ ⋒ ⊬ ⊟ ⊡
**Nearby Facilities** ┌ ⚓ ⚖ ኣ ⚲
**Acreage** 7½ **Open** March **to** Oct
**Access** Good **Site** Level
Attractive site with grass covered sandy
dunes and shrubs. Golden sands and rock
pools nearby. Close to the Scottish Seabird
Centre, Hailes Castle and East Fortune
Museum of Flight. Non members welcome.
Booking essential.
**Nearest Town/Resort** North Berwick
**Directions** From A1 approaching East Linton
turn right onto A198. After approx. 8¾ miles
turn left past railway station, at junction turn
left (still on A198). After 2½ miles turn right
signposted Dirleton, turn right at site sign,
site is 1 mile.
⌖ North Berwick

# LOTHIAN (WEST)
## BLACKBURN
**Mosshall Farm Caravan Park,** Mosshall
Farm, Blackburn, West Lothian, EH47 7DB
**Tel:** 01501 762318
**Pitches For** ♥ ⊟ **Total** 25
**Facilities** ⅙ ∮ ⓗ ⓤ ♨ ┌ ⊙ ☗ ⅋⊬
**Nearby Facilities** ┌ ✔ ⚓ ∪ ℛ
**Acreage** ¾ **Open** All Year
**Access** Good **Site** Level
Situated half way between Edinburgh and
Glasgow.
**Directions** Leave the M8 at junction 4 and
take the road for Whitburn. At T-Junction
A705 take a left turn towards Blackburn, we
are 300 yards on the right.
⌖ Bathgate

## LINLITHGOW
**Beecraigs Caravan & Camping Site,**
Beecraigs Country Park, Nr Linlithgow,
West Lothian, EH49 6PL
**Tel:** 01506 844516 **Fax:** 01506 846256
**Email:** mail@beecraigs.com
**www.** beecraigs.com
**Pitches For** ▲ ♥ ⊟ **Total** 56
**Facilities** ⅙ ∮ ⓗ ⓤ ♨ ┌ ⊙ ☗ ⊿ ◙ ☗
⅋ ⊙ ⦿ ✗ ⋒ ⊬ ⊟ ⊡
**Nearby Facilities** ┌ ✔ ⚓ ኣ ∪ ℛ ⚲
**Acreage** 6½ **Open** All Year
**Access** Good **Site** Level
Within a 913 acre Country Park which
offers a wide range of leisure and
recreational interests - fishing, outdoor
pursuits, play area, Red Deer Farm and
many woodland walks.
**Nearest Town/Resort** Linlithgow
**Directions** From Linlithgow High Street
follow signs for Beecraigs Country Park,
taking you approx. 2 miles up Preston Road.
At the top of the hill turn left and then first
right, take the next right into reception within
the Beecraigs Restaurant.
⌖ Linlithgow

# MIDLOTHIAN
## LOANHEAD
**Slatebarns Caravan Club Site,** Roslin,
Midlothian, EH25 9PU
**Tel:** 0131 440 2192
**www.** caravanclub.co.uk
**Pitches For** ♥ ⊟ **Total** 30
F a c i l i t i e s ⅙ ∮ ⓗ ⓤ ♨ ┌ ◙ ☗
⅋ ⊙ ⦿ ⊟ ⊡
**Nearby Facilities** ┌ ✔
**Acreage** 2½ **Open** March **to** Oct
**Access** Good **Site** Level
Situated beside the delightful Roslin Glen
woods and on the doorstep of Rosslyn
Chapel. Swimming and leisure centre
within easy reach. 4 miles from a dry ski
slope. Non members welcome. Booking
essential.
**Nearest Town/Resort** Edinburgh
**Directions** Leave the A720 Edinburgh
bypass at Straiton Junction and take the
A701 signposted Bilston. In Bilston at
roundabout turn left onto the B7006, at
crossroads in the village go straight on and
site entrance is immediately past the chapel.
⌖ Edinburgh

# MORAYSHIRE
## ABERLOUR
**Camping & Caravanning Club Site,**
Speyside, Archiestown, Aberlour, Moray,
AB38 9SL
**Tel:** 01340 810414
**www.** campingandcaravanningclub.co.uk
**Pitches For** ▲ ♥ ⊟ **Total** 75
**Facilities** ⅙ ∮ ⓗ ⓤ ♨ ┌ ⊙ ☗ ⊿ ◙ ☗
⅋ ⊙ ⦿ ⋒ ⊬ ⊟ ⊡ ⅋ ⚲
**Nearby Facilities** ✔ ℛ
**Acreage** 7 **Open** April **to** Oct
**Access** Good **Site** Level
The surrounding area has historic castles,
National Trust properties and gardens to
visit. Salmon and Whisky are the
specialities of this area of Scotland. STB 4
Star Graded and AA 3 Pennants. Non
members welcome.
**Nearest Town/Resort** Aberlour
**Directions** From the A9 at Carbridge turn
onto the A95 to Grantown-on-Spey then on
to Aberlour. Take the A941 then turn left onto
the B9102 signposted Archiestown, site is on
the left after 3 miles.
⌖ Elgin

## ELGIN
**Riverside Caravan Park,** West Road,
Elgin, Moray, IV30 8UN
**Tel:** 01343 542813
**Pitches For** ▲ ♥ ⊟ **Total** 44
**Facilities** ⅙ ∮ ⓗ ⓤ ♨ ┌ ⊙ ☗ ⊿ ◙ ☗
⅋ ⊙ ⦿ ⋒ ⊬ ⊟ ⊡ ⚲ ⚲
**Nearby Facilities** ┌ ✔ ⚓ ኣ ∪ ℛ ℛ
**Open** April **to** Oct
**Access** Good **Site** Level
Elgin is near to beaches and alongside the
River Lossie. Ideal fun touring base.
Fishing, golfing and plenty of of shops,
restaurants and entertainment for children
nearby.
**Nearest Town/Resort** Elgin
**Directions** Situated off the A96 Aberdeen to
Inverness road. On the western outskirts of
Elgin, 3 minutes drive from the town centre.
⌖ Elgin

# FINDHORN
**Findhorn Bay Holiday Park,** Findhorn,
Forres, Moray, IV36 3TY
**Tel:** 01309 690203 **Fax:** 01309 690933
**Email:** info@findhornbayholidaypark.com
**www.** findhornbayholidaypark.com
**Pitches For** ▲ ♥ ⊟ **Total** 20
F a c i l i t i e s ∮ ⓤ ♨ ┌ ⊿ ◙ ☗
⅋⅌ ⅋ ◙ ⊙ ✗ ⋒ ⊬ ⊟ ⊡ ⚲
**Nearby Facilities** ┌ ✔ ⚓ ኣ ∪ ⚲
**Acreage** 5 **Open** Easter **to** End Oct
**Access** Good **Site** Level
Situated on Findhorn Bay, 1 mile from the
village.
**Nearest Town/Resort** Forres
**Directions** 5 miles from Forres on the B9011.
⌖ Forres

## HOPEMAN
**Station Caravan Park,** Hopeman, Nr
Elgin, Moray, IV30 5RU
**Tel:** 01343 830880 **Fax:** 01343 830880
**Email:** stationcaravanpark@talk21.com
**www.** stationcaravanpark.co.uk
**Pitches For** ▲ ♥ ⊟ **Total** 37
**Facilities** ⅙ ∮ ⓤ ♨ ┌ ⊙ ☗ ⊿ ◙ ☗
⅋ ⊙ ⦿ ⋒ ⊬ ⊟ ⊡ ⚲
**Nearby Facilities** ┌ ✔ ⚓ ኣ ∪ ⚲ ℛ ⚲
**Acreage** 13 **Open** March **to** November
**Access** Good **Site** Level
On a beach on Moray Firth coast.
**Nearest Town/Resort** Elgin
⌖ Elgin

## LOSSIEMOUTH
**Silver Sands Leisure Park,** West Beach,
Covesea, Lossiemouth, Moray, IV31 6SP
**Tel:** 01343 813262 **Fax:** 01343 815205
**Email:** eleanor@silver-sands.fsnet.co.uk
**www.** holidays@silversand.freeserve.co.uk
**Pitches For** ▲ ♥ ⊟ **Total** 140
**Facilities** ⅙ ∮ ⓗ ⓤ ♨ ┌ ⊙ ☗ ⊿ ◙ ☗
⅋⅌ ⅋ ◙ ✗ ⋒ ⊬ ⊟ ⊡ ⚲
**Nearby Facilities** ┌ ✔ ⚓ ኣ
**Acreage** 20 **Open** April **to** Oct
**Access** Good **Site** Level
Near the beach.
**Nearest Town/Resort** Lossiemouth
**Directions** 1 mile from Lossiemouth, well
signposted.
⌖ Elgin

# PERTH & KINROSS
## ABERFELDY
**Glengoulandie Country Park,** By
Pitlochry, Perth & Kinross, PH16 5NL
**Tel:** 01887 830495 **Fax:** 01887 830277
**Email:** info@glengoulandie.co.uk
**www.** glengoulandie.co.uk
**Pitches For** ▲ **Total** 20
F a c i l i t i e s ⅙ ⓤ ♨ ┌ ⊙ ☗ ⊿
◙ ⅋ ◙ ✗ ⋒ ⊬ ⊟ ⊡
**Nearby Facilities** ┌ ✔ ⚓ ኣ ∪ ⚲ ℛ ⚲
**Open** March **to** Oct
**Site** Level
Glengoulandie Country Park has a Deer
Park with Highland cattle, a fishing loch,
coffee shop with a small range of gifts, and
a childrens play area.
**Nearest Town/Resort** Aberfeldy
**Directions** Situated on the B846 Aberfeldy
to Kinloch Rannoch road, approx. 8 miles
from Aberfeldy.
⌖ Pitlochry

# NETHER CRAIG CARAVAN PARK

## Nether Craig, By Alyth, Blairgowrie, Perthshire PH11 8HN

*5 Star Touring Park on the Angus/Perthshire border with panoramic views. Ideal base for touring, hill walking, bird watching, fishing, pony trekking and golf. Tents, Caravans & Motor Caravans welcome March to December.*

**www.nethercraigcaravanpark.co.uk**   *E-mail:* **nethercraig@lineone.net**   Tel: **01575 560204**

### ALYTH

**Five Roads Caravan Park,** Alyth, Blairgowrie, Perth & Kinross, PH11 8NB
**Tel:** 01828 632255
**Email:** steven.ewart@btopenworld.com
www.fiveroadscaravanpark.co.uk
**Pitches For** ▲ ⊞ ☰ **Total** 28
**Facilities** ⚹ ∮ ⌂ ⓘ ⊞ ♣ ⌐ ⊙ ↴ ⬛ ▣ ☎
⌖ ⊟ ⌯ ⊞ ☀
**Nearby Facilities** ⌐ ✔ U ♪ ⚡
**Acreage** 3 **Open** All Year
**Access** Good **Site** Level
Three golf courses within a 1 mile radius.
**Nearest Town/Resort** Alyth
**Directions** From Blairgowrie take the A926, after 4½ miles at the Blackbird Inn turn left.
⚏ Dundee

### BLAIR ATHOLL

**Blair Castle Caravan Park,** Blair Atholl, Pitlochry, Perth & Kinross, PH18 5SR
**Tel:** 01796 481263 **Fax:** 01796 481587
**Email:** mail@blaircastlecaravanpark.co.uk
www.blaircastlecaravanpark.co.uk
**Pitches For** ▲ ⊞ ☰ **Total** 275
**Facilities** ⚹ ∮ ⌂ ⊟ ⓘ ⊞ ♣ ⌐ ⊙ ↴ ⬛ ▣ ☎
⌖ ⌯ ⊙ ⊞ ⓣ ♣ ⋒ ♣ ↵ ▣ ⊟ ☀
**Nearby Facilities** ⌐ ✔ ⚲ U ♪
**Acreage** 35 **Open** March **to** Nov
**Access** Good **Site** Level
Blair Castle, Bruar Falls and the picturesque town of Pitlochry.
**Nearest Town/Resort** Pitlochry
**Directions** Follow A9 north past Pitlochry, after 6 miles turn off following signs to Blair Atholl. After 1¼ miles turn right into caravan park.
⚏ Blair Atholl

### BLAIRGOWRIE

**Ballintuim Caravan Park,** Bridge of Cally, Blairgowrie, Perth & Kinross, PH10 7NH
**Tel:** 01250 886276 **Fax:** 01250 886276
**Pitches For** ▲ ⊞ ☰ **Total** 16
**Facilities** ∮ ⓘ ⊞ ♣ ⌐ ⊙ ↴ ⬛ ▣ ☎
⋒ ↵ ▣ ☀
**Nearby Facilities** ⌐ ✔
**Acreage** 1 **Open** March **to** Oct
**Access** Good **Site** Lev/Slope
Very central location for visiting beauty spots in the renowned area of Perthshire.

### BLAIRGOWRIE

**Nearest Town/Resort** Blairgowrie
**Directions** From Blairgowrie take the A93 towards Braemar, turn left onto the A924 towards Pitlochry for 3 miles.
⚏ Pitlochry

### BLAIRGOWRIE

**Beech Hedge Caravan Park,** Cargill, Perth & Kinross, PH2 6DU
**Tel:** 01250 883249
**Email:** admin@beech-hedge-caravan-park.co.uk
www.beech-hedge-caravan-park.co.uk
**Pitches For** ▲ ⊞ ☰ **Total** 10
**Facilities** ∮ ⓘ ♣ ⌐ ⊙ ↴ ⬛ ▣ ☎ ⊙ ↴ ▣ ☀
**Nearby Facilities** ⌐ ✔ ⚲ U ♪
**Acreage** 3 **Open** Jan **to** Nov
**Access** Good **Site** Level
Near the Rivers Tay and Isla. Woodland walks and cycle hire. Central location.
**Nearest Town/Resort** Blairgowrie
**Directions** On the A93 road to Perth.
⚏ Perth

### BLAIRGOWRIE

**Blairgowrie Holiday Park,** Rattray, Blairgowrie, Perth & Kinross, PH10 7AL
**Tel:** 01250 876666 **Fax:** 01250 874535
**Email:** blairgowrie@holiday-parks.co.uk
www.holiday-parks.co.uk
**Pitches For** ⊞ ☰
**Facilities** ⚹ ∮ ⌂ ⓘ ⊞ ♣ ⌐ ⊙ ↴ ⬛ ▣ ☎
⌖ ⊙ ⊟ ⋒ ↵ ▣ ☀
**Nearby Facilities** ⌐ ✔ U ♪
**Acreage** 15 **Open** All Year
**Access** Good **Site** Lev/Slope
Ideal base for touring the hills, lochs and glens of scenic Perthshire.
**Nearest Town/Resort** Blairgowrie
**Directions** 1 mile north of Blairgowrie town centre off the A93. Turn right (following signs) 100 yards past Keathpark Garage, park is 200 yards on the left.
⚏ Perth

### BLAIRGOWRIE

**Nether Craig Caravan Park,** Alyth, Blairgowrie, Perthshire, PH11 8HN
**Tel:** 01575 560204 **Fax:** 01575 560315
**Email:** nethercraig@lineone.net
www.nethercraigcaravanpark.co.uk
**Pitches For** ▲ ⊞ ☰ **Total** 40
**Facilities** ⚹ ∮ ⌂ ⓘ ⊞ ♣ ⌐ ⊙ ↴ ⬛ ▣ ☎
⌗ ⊙ ⊟ ⋒ ♣ ↵ ▣ ▣ ☀ ⚘
**Nearby Facilities** ⌐ ✔ ⚲ ⚱ U ♪ ⚡
**Acreage** 4 **Open** 15 March **to** Nov
**Access** Good **Site** Level
Quiet, spacious location, away from major roads with picturesque views. Ideal base for touring, hill walking, fishing and golf.
**Nearest Town/Resort** Blairgowrie
**Directions** At the roundabout south of Alyth, join the B954 signposted Glenisla. Follow caravan signs for 4 miles (DO NOT go into Alyth).
⚏ Dundee

### BRIDGE OF CALLY

**Corriefodly Holiday Park,** Bridge of Cally, Perth & Kinross, PH10 7JG
**Tel:** 01250 886236 **Fax:** 01250 874535
**Email:** corriefodly@holiday-parks.co.uk
www.holiday-parks.co.uk
**Pitches For** ⊞ ☰ **Total** 150
**Facilities** ⚹ ∮ ⌂ ⓘ ⊞ ♣ ⌐ ⊙ ↴ ⬛ ▣ ☎
⌖ ⊙ ⊟ ⚑ ⓣ ♣ ⋒ ♣ ↵ ▣ ☀
**Nearby Facilities** ⌐ ✔ U ♪ ⚡
**Acreage** 17½ **Open** All Year
**Access** Good **Site** Level
Riverside setting with scenic views. Level hardstanding pitches. Lounge bar and TV lounge. Ideal touring base.
**Nearest Town/Resort** Blairgowrie
**Directions** From Blairgowrie take A93 north for 6 miles. Turn onto A924 Pitlochry road, site approx 200yds from junction of A93 and A924.
⚏ Perth

### COMRIE

**Twenty Shilling Wood Caravan Park,** St Fillans Road, Comrie, Perth & Kinross, PH6 2JY
**Tel:** 01764 670411
**Email:** alowe20@aol.com
www.ukparks.co.uk/twentyshilling

**Pitches For ♥ ♠ Total** 16
**Facilities** ⚡ ✦ 🅷 🆄 ⚓ ᐓ ⊙ ↰ ⚰ 🅾 ☎
🟍 🅖 ⚘ ᐱ 🅐 🅿 🅲 ⚒ ⚗
**Nearby Facilities** ┏ ✔ ⏚ ⋟ U ♨ ♇ ⚓
**Acreage** 10¼ **Open** Late March **to** 20 Oct
**Access** Good **Site** Level
Family run, spotless all season, peaceful, sheltered, sunny south facing park set in woodlands that are visited by deer and many woodland birds. Individual pitches. Pets permitted. David Bellamy Gold Award for Conservation.
**Nearest Town/Resort** Crieff
**Directions** ¼ mile west of Comrie on A85.
⚓ Perth

## COMRIE
**West Lodge Caravan Park,** Comrie, Perth, Perth & Kinross, PH6 2LS
**Tel:** 01764 670354 **Fax:** 01764 670354
**www.**westlodge.bravehost.com
**Pitches For** ⚊ ♥ ♠ **Total** 20
**Facilities** ⚓ ✦ 🆄 ⚓ ┏ ⊙ ᐓ ⚰ 🅾 ☎
🟍 🅖 ⚘ ᐱ 🅐 🅲 ⚒
**Nearby Facilities** ┏ ✔ ⏚ ⋟ U ♨ ♇ ⚓
**Acreage** 3 **Open** 1 April **to** 31 October
**Access** Good **Site** Level
Sheltered friendly park, set in beautiful country area. Ideal for touring. Caravans for hire nightly or weekly.
**Nearest Town/Resort** Comrie
**Directions** On A85, 5 miles from Crieff. 1 mile east of Comrie.
⚓ Perth

## DUNKELD
**Inver Mill Farm Caravan Park,** Inver, Dunkeld, Perth & Kinross, PH8 0JR
**Tel:** 01350 727477 **Fax:** 01350 727477
**Email:** invermill@talk21.com
**www.**visitdunkeld.com/perthshire-caravan-park.htm
**Pitches For** ⚊ ♥ ♠ **Total** 65
**Facilities** ⚓ ✦ 🆄 ⚓ ┏ ⊙ ᐓ ⚰ 🅾 ☎
🅖 ⚘ ⚒ 🅿 🅲
**Nearby Facilities** ┏ ✔ ⏚ ⋟ U ♨ ♇ ⚓
**Acreage** 5 **Open** End March **to** Mid/End Oct
**Access** Good **Site** Level
Riverside setting. 1 mile from Dunkeld which has many tourist attractions along with walking, fishing, golf and cycling.
**Nearest Town/Resort** Dunkeld
**Directions** From the A9 turn onto the A822 signposted Crieff, turn immediately right following signs to Inver.
⚓ Dunkeld

## INCHTURE
**Inchmartine Caravan Park,** Dundee Road, Inchture, Perth & Kinross, PH14 9QQ
**Tel:** 01821 670212 **Fax:** 01821 670266
**Email:** enquiries@perthshire-caravans.com
**www.**perthshire-caravans.com
**Pitches For** ⚊ ♥ ♠ **Total** 45
**Facilities** ⚓ ✦ 🆄 ⚓ ┏ ⊙ ᐓ 🟍 🅖 ⚒ 🅱
**Nearby Facilities**
**Acreage** 8 **Open** April **to** October
**Access** Good **Site** Level
rural setting.
**Nearest Town/Resort** Dundee
**Directions** Situated just off the A90 northbound, 12 miles north of Perth and 10 miles south of Dundee.
⚓ Perth

## KINLOCH RANNOCH
**Kilvrecht Campsite,** Carie, By Kinloch Rannoch, Perth & Kinross, PH8 0JR
**Tel:** 01350 727284 **Fax:** 01350 727811
**Email:** hamish.murray@forestry.gsi.gov.uk
**Pitches For** ⚊ ♥ ♠ **Total** 90
**Facilities** ⚓ 🆄 ᐓ ☂ ⚒
**Nearby Facilities** ✔ ⏚ ⋟
**Open** Easter **to** 26 Oct
**Access** Good **Site** Level
Quiet and peaceful site in a woodland setting.
**Nearest Town/Resort** Kinloch Rannoch
**Directions** From Pitlochry take the B8019 to Kinloch Rannoch. Go over the bridge and follow road on the south side of the loch for approx. 3 miles. Site is well signposted.
⚓ Pitlochry

## KINROSS
**Gallowhill Caravan & Camping Park,** Gallowhill Farm, Kinross, Perth & Kinross, KY13 0RD
**Tel:** 01577 862364
**Email:** jpaterson21@hotmail.com
**Pitches For** ⚊ ♥ ♠ **Total** 50
**Facilities** ⚓ ✦ 🅷 🆄 ⚓ ┏ ⊙ ᐓ ⚰ 🅾 ☎
🟍 🅖 ᐱ 🅲
**Nearby Facilities** ┏ ✔ U ♇
**Acreage** 4½ **Open** March **to** Oct
**Access** Good **Site** Lev/Slope
Ideal for touring central Scotland.
**Nearest Town/Resort** Kinross
**Directions** Leave the M90 at junction 6 for Kinross and follow signs to the park (1 mile).
⚓ Inverkeithing

## PERTH
**Camping & Caravanning Club Site,** Scone Palace Caravan Park, Scone, Perth & Kinross, PH2 6BB
**Tel:** 01738 552323
**www.**campingandcaravanningclub.co.uk
**Pitches For** ⚊ 🅷 ♥ ♠ **Total** 150
**Facilities** ✦ 🅷 🆄 ⚓ ┏ ⊙ ᐓ ⚰ 🅾 ☎
🟍 🅖 🅖 ⚘ ᐱ 🅐 🅿 🅲 ⚒ ⚗
**Nearby Facilities** ✔
**Acreage** 16 **Open** March **to** Oct
**Site** Lev/Slope
Trout and salmon fishing is available from the nearby River Tay. Just to the north of Perth. Ideal for touring central Scotland. STB 4 Star Graded, David Bellamy Gold Award and AA 3 Pennants. Non members welcome.
**Nearest Town/Resort** Perth
**Directions** From the Motorway follow signs for Scone Palace, after Scone Palace continue for 2 miles then turn left following camp site signs or signs for Stormontfield. After 1 mile turn left into Racecourse Road, site entrance is through the car park.
⚓ Perth

## PITLOCHRY
**Milton of Fonab Caravan Site,** Bridge Road, Pitlochry, Perth & Kinross, PH16 5NA
**Tel:** 01796 472882 **Fax:** 01796 474363
**Email:** info@fonab.co.uk
**www.**fonab.co.uk
**Pitches For** ⚊ ♥ ♠ **Total** 154
**Facilities** ⚓ ⚡ ✦ 🆄 ⚓ ┏ ⊙ ᐓ ⚰ 🅾 ☎
🟍 🅖 ⚘ 🅿 ⚒ ♇
**Nearby Facilities** ┏ ✔ U
**Acreage** 15 **Open** End March **to** Beg Oct
**Access** Good **Site** Level
On the banks of the River Tummel. 5 minute walk to Pitlochry Festival Theatre and a 10 minute walk to Dam and Fish Ladder.

**Nearest Town/Resort** Pitlochry
**Directions** ½ mile south of Pitlochry, opposite Bell's Distillery.
⚓ Pitlochry

## ST. FILLANS
**Loch Earn Caravan Park,** South Shore Road, St Fillans, Perth & Kinross, PH6 2NL
**Tel:** 01764 685270 **Fax:** 01764 679789
**Email:** lochearn@perthshire-caravans.com
**www.**perthshire-caravans.com
**Pitches For** ♥ ♠ **Total** 40
**Facilities** ⚓ ✦ ┏ 🆄 ⚓ ┏ ⊙ ᐓ ⚰ 🅾 ☎
🟍 🅖 ⚘ ✗ ♈ 🅐 🅿 🅲
**Nearby Facilities**
**Acreage** 4 **Open** 31 March **to** 31 October
**Access** Good **Site** Level
Lochside park with boating.
**Directions** From Perth take the A85 and turn off signed South Loch Earn. Before entering St. Fillans turn left over the hump back bridge, Park is 1 mile.
⚓ Perth

## TUMMEL BRIDGE
**Tummel Valley Holiday Park,** Tummel Bridge, Nr Pitlochry, Perth & Kinross, PH16 5SA
**Tel:** 01882 634221 **Fax:** 01882 634302
**Email:** enquiries@parkdeanholidays.com
**www.**parkdeanholidays.co.uk
**Pitches For** ⚊ ♥ ♠ **Total** 33
**Facilities** ✦ 🆄 ⚓ ┏ ⊙ ᐓ ⚰ 🅾 ☎
🟍 ⚘ ✗ ♈ 🅼 🅐 ♒ ⚒ ♋ 🅿 🅲 ⚗
**Nearby Facilities** ✔ ⏚ ⋟
**Acreage** 52 **Open** March **to** Oct
**Access** Good **Site** Lev/Slope
Set on the banks of the River Tummel in the stunning Perthshire countryside.
**Nearest Town/Resort** Pitlochry
**Directions** From Perth take the A9 to Pitlochry, park is 13 miles along this road.
⚓ Pitlochry

---

PLEASE
REMEMBER
IT IS ALWAYS
ADVISABLE TO
BOOK IN PEAK
SEASON

---

# RENFREWSHIRE
## LOCHWINNOCH
**Barnbrock Campsite & Wigwams,** Clyde Muirshiel Regional Park, Barnbrock, Nr Kilbarchan, Renfrewshire, PA10 2PZ
**Tel:** 01505 614791 **Fax:** 01505 613605
**Email:** info@clydemuirshiel.co.uk
**www.**clydemuirshiel.co.uk
**Pitches For** ⚊ **Total** 15
**Facilities** 🆄 ⚓ ┏ ⚰
**Nearby Facilities** ✔ ⏚ ⋟ U
**Acreage** 1 **Open** Easter **to** Oct
**Site** Level
Rural location. Not far from Glasgow. Own transport recommended as the nearest public transport is 4 miles away. NB: This site is only suitable for tents.
**Nearest Town/Resort** Lochwinnoch
**Directions** 4 miles north of Lochwinnoch on the B786. Half way between Lochwinnoch and Kilmacolm. Barnbrock is signposted from the A737 and Lochwinnoch.
⚓ Lochwinnoch

# What you see is what you get at Crossburn.

Come to Crossburn and you won't believe your eyes. That's because our caravan park lies at the heart of the beautiful Scottish Borders.

Soft, rolling hills frame impressive rivers, heritage abounds in our ancient abbeys and historic homes - while the prospect of cycling, walking, fishing and golf is made all the more exciting by the surroundings in which you will be enjoying them all.

*Call us on Peebles (01721) 720501* and discover what a nice place our park can be for making the most of this beautiful area. (You are only 23 miles south of the centre of Edinburgh - Scotland's cosmopolitan capital.)

www.crossburncaravans.co.uk

## SCOTTISH BORDERS

### COCKBURNSPATH

**Chesterfield Caravan Park,** The Neuk, Cockburnspath, Borders, TD13 5YH
**Tel:** 01368 830459 **Fax:** 01368 830394
**Email:** info@chesterfieldcaravanpark.co.uk
www.chesterfieldcaravanpark.co.uk
**Pitches For** ⚠ ⚌ ⚌
**Facilities** ✦ ⬚ ♨ & ♪ ☺ ⌐ ⬚ ⬚ ☻
⬚ ⬚ ☻ ⋒♨⬚⬚ ⋇
**Nearby Facilities**
**Open** April **to** Mid October
**Access** Good **Site** Level
Quiet, tidy, clean, country site with scenic views. Within easy reach of the A1, Scottish Borders, Edinburgh, Berwick-on-Tweed. Nearest beach 3 miles.
**Nearest Town/Resort** Eyemouth
**Directions** From the A1 bypass, follow signs to Abbey St. Bathans. Caravan park is situated ½ mile on the left from this junction.
⚉ Dunbar

### COLDINGHAM

**Scoutscroft Holiday Centre,** St Abbs Road, Coldingham, Eyemouth, Borders, TD14 5NB
**Tel:** 01890 771338 **Fax:** 01890 771746
**Email:** holidays@scoutscroft.co.uk
www.scoutscroft.co.uk
**Pitches For** ⚌ ⚌ **Total** 180
**Facilities** & ✦ ⬚ ♨ ♨ & ♪ ☺ ⌐ ⬚ ⬚ ☻
⬚ ⬚ ☻ ✕ ♈ ⬚ ⋒ ♨ ☀⬚⬚ ⋇ ♪
**Nearby Facilities** ♪ ✦ ⚘ ⚑ ⛰
**Acreage** 16 **Open** March **to** October
**Access** Good **Site** Level
¾ miles from Coldingham Bay.
**Nearest Town/Resort** Eyemouth
⚉ Berwick-on-Tweed

### ETTRICK

**Honey Cottage Caravan Park,** Hope House, Ettrick Valley, Selkirk, Borders, TD7 5HU
**Tel:** 01750 62246
www.honeycottagecaravanpark.co.uk
**Pitches For** ⚠ ⚌ ⚌
**Facilities** ✦ ⬚ ♨ & ♪ ☺ ⌐ ⬚ ⬚ ☻
⬚ ⬚ ☻ ♨⬚⬚ ⋇
**Nearby Facilities** ♪ ✦ ⚘
**Open** All Year
**Access** Good **Site** Level
Alongside a river for fishing. Golf courses within easy reach. Ideal for walking, cycling or just relaxing in open countryside. Restaurant 1 mile.
**Nearest Town/Resort** Hawick/Selkirk

### EYEMOUTH

**Eyemouth Holiday Park,** Fort Road, Eyemouth, Berwickshire, TD14 5BE
**Tel:** 0870 442 9280 **Fax:** 01890 751462
**Email:** holidaysales.eyemouth@park-resorts.com
www.park-resorts.com
**Pitches For** ⚌ ⚌ **Total** 16
**Facilities** & ✦ ⬚ ♨ ♨ & ♪ ☺ ⌐ ⬚ ⬚ ☻
⬚ ⬚ ☻ ✕ ♈ ⬚ ⋒ ♨ ⬚⬚ ⋇
**Nearby Facilities** ♪ ✦ ⚘ ⚑ ⛰
**Acreage** 50 **Open** 6 March **to** 20 Nov
**Access** Good **Site** Level
Cliffside location with superb views of the sea. Private beach, sea angling and a marine reserve.
**Nearest Town/Resort** Eyemouth
**Directions** From the A1 follow signs to Eyemouth on the A1107. On entering the town the park is signposted. Turn right after the petrol station, turn left at the bottom of the hill into Fort Road.
⚉ Berwick-upon-Tweed

### JEDBURGH

**Camping & Caravanning Club Site,** Elliot Park, Jedburgh, Borders, TD8 6EF
**Tel:** 01835 863393
www.campingandcaravanningclub.co.uk
**Pitches For** ⚠ ⚌ ⚌ **Total** 60
**Facilities** ✦ ⬚ ♨ & ♪ ☺ ⌐ ⬚ ⬚ ☻
⬚ ⬚ ☻ ♨⬚⬚ ⋇
**Nearby Facilities** ♪ ✦ ⚘ ⚑
**Acreage** 3 **Open** April **to** Oct
**Access** Good **Site** Level
Quiet, secluded site bounded by the River Jed. Ideal site for picturesque walks. STB 4 Star Graded and AA 3 Pennants. Non members welcome.
**Nearest Town/Resort** Jedburgh
**Directions** On the A68 Newcastle to Edinburgh road, drive to the northern side of Jedburgh and the entrance is opposite the Edinburgh & Jedburgh Woollen Mills.
⚉ Berwick-upon-Tweed

### JEDBURGH

**Lilliardsedge Holiday Park,** Jedburgh, Borders, TD8 6TZ
**Tel:** 01835 830271 **Fax:** 01835 830263
**Pitches For** ⚠ ⚌ ⚌ **Total** 40
**Facilities** & ✦ ⬚ ♨ ♨ & ♪ ☺ ⌐ ⬚ ⬚ ☻
⬚ ⬚ ☻ ✕ ♈ ⬚ ⋒ ♨ ☀⬚⬚ ⋇
**Nearby Facilities** ✦ ⚘
**Open** March **to** Oct
**Access** Good **Site** Level
On St Cuthberts Way with a 9 hole golf course on site. Fishing available locally.
**Nearest Town/Resort** Jedburgh
**Directions** 5 miles north of Jedburgh on the A68.

### KELSO

**Springwood Caravan Park,** Kelso, Borders, TD5 8LS
**Tel:** 01573 224596 **Fax:** 01573 224033
**Email:** admin@springwood.biz
www.springwood.biz
**Pitches For** ⚌ ⚌ **Total** 20
**Facilities** & ✦ ⬚ ♨ & ♪ ☺ ⌐ ⬚ ⬚ ☻
⬚ ⬚ ☻ ⋒ ♨ ☀⬚⬚
**Nearby Facilities** ♪ ✦ ⚘ ⚑
**Acreage** 2 **Open** End March **to** 4th Oct
**Access** Good **Site** Level
Ideal for riverside walks.
**Nearest Town/Resort** Kelso
**Directions** 1 mile south west of Kelso on the A699.
⚉ Berwick-upon-Tweed

### LAUDER

**Camping & Caravanning Club Site,** Carfraemill, Oxton, Lauder, Borders, TD2 6RA
**Tel:** 01578 750697
www.campingandcaravanningclub.co.uk
**Pitches For** ⚠ ⚌ ⚌ **Total** 70
**Facilities** & ✦ ⬚ ♨ & ♪ ☺ ⌐ ⬚ ⬚ ☻
⬚ ⬚ ☻ ♨⬚⬚ ⋇ ♪
**Nearby Facilities** ♪ ✦
**Acreage** 5 **Open** 25 March **to** 1 Nov
**Access** Good **Site** Level
Situated 24 miles south of the vibrant city of Edinburgh. Close to Thirlestane Castle and a good fishing area. Self catering chalets also available to let. STB 4 Star Graded and AA 3 Pennants. Non members welcome.
**Nearest Town/Resort** Edinburgh
**Directions** From Lauder, at the roundabout turn right onto the A697, at the Lodge Hotel turn left and the site is on the right behind Carfraemill Hotel.
⚉ Edinburgh

### MELROSE

**Gibson Park Caravan Club Site,** High Street, Melrose, Borders, TD6 9RY
**Tel:** 01896 822969
www.caravanclub.co.uk
**Pitches For** ⚠ ⚌ ⚌ **Total** 60
**Facilities** & ✦ ⬚ ♨ & ♪ ⌐ ⬚ ☻
⬚ ⬚ ☻ ♨⬚
**Nearby Facilities** ♪ ✦ ⚘
**Acreage** 3 **Open** All Year
**Access** Good **Site** Level
Peaceful site overlooked by the three hills which gave rise to its Roman name of Trimontium. Shops, playing fields and tennis adjacent. Close to Melrose Abbey, Priorwood Gardens and Abbotsford House. Non members welcome. Booking essential.
**Nearest Town/Resort** Melrose

**Directions** From the A68 take the A6091, at roundabout turn right onto the B6374 signposted Melrose. Site is on the right at the petrol station and opposite Melrose Rugby Club.
⇆ Melrose

## PEEBLES

**Crossburn Caravan Park,** Edinburgh Road, Peebles, Borders, EH45 8ED
**Tel:** 01721 720501 **Fax:** 01721 720501
**Email:** enquiries@crossburncaravans.co.uk
www.crossburncaravans.co.uk
**Pitches For** ▲ ⚌ ⚌ **Total** 50
**Facilities** ⚫ ⒡ ⦅ ⦆ ⦆ ⚑ ⌂ ⊙ ⤴ ⚌ ▢ ☏
⦿ ⊘ ⚘ Ⓜ ⟊ ▣
**Nearby Facilities** ⌐ ✓ ∪
**Acreage** 6 **Open** 1 April/Easter **to** Oct
**Access** Good **Site** Level
River nearby. Ideal touring base.
**Nearest Town/Resort** Peebles
**Directions** ½ mile north of Peebles on the A703.
⇆ Edinburgh

## PEEBLES

**Rosetta Caravan & Camping Park,** Rosetta Road, Peebles, Borders, EH45 8PG
**Tel:** 01721 720770 **Fax:** 01721 720203
**Pitches For** ▲ ⚌ ⚌ **Total** 140
**Facilities** ⒡ ⦅ ⦆ ⦆ ⚑ ⌂ ⊙ ⤴ ⚌ ▢ ☏
⦿ ⊘ ⚘ ⟐ ⓣ ⚘ Ⓜ ⟊ ▣ ✕ ∪ ♪
**Nearby Facilities** ⌐ ✓ ⚑ ✕ ∪ ♪
**Acreage** 42 **Open** April **to** October
**Access** Good **Site** Sloping
**Nearest Town/Resort** Peebles
**Directions** Follow Rosetta signs from within the town of Peebles.
⇆ Edinburgh

# STIRLINGSHIRE

## ABERFOYLE

**Cobleland Caravan & Camping Site - Forestry Commission,** Aberfoyle, Stirling, FK8 3UX
**Tel:** 01877 382392
**Email:** info@forestholidays.co.uk
www.forestholidays.co.uk
**Pitches For** ▲ ⚌ ⚌ **Total** 135
**Facilities** ⒡ ⦅ ⦆ ⚑ ⌂ ⊙ ⤴ ⚌ ▢ ☏
⦿ ⊘ ⚘ ⟊ ▣ ✕ ⚘
**Nearby Facilities** ⌐ ✓ ⚑ ∪
**Open** 25 March **to** 26 Sept
**Access** Good **Site** Lev/Slope
Set on the banks of the River Forth amongst majestic oak trees. In the Queen Elizabeth Forest Park with walks direct from the site.
**Nearest Town/Resort** Aberfoyle
**Directions** Just off the A81 on an unclassified road, about 1½ miles south of Aberfoyle.
⇆ Stirling

## ABERFOYLE

**Trossachs Holiday Park,** Aberfoyle, Stirling, FK8 3SA
**Tel:** 01877 382614 **Fax:** 01877 382732
**Email:** info@trossachsholidays.co.uk
www.trossachsholidays.co.uk
**Pitches For** ▲ ⚌ ⚌
**Facilities** ⒡ ⦅ ⦆ ⦆ ⚑ ⌂ ⊙ ⤴ ⚌ ▢ ☏
⦿ ⊘ ⚘ ✕ Ⓜ ⟊ ▣ ✕
**Nearby Facilities** ⌐ ✓ ⚑ ✕ ∪ ♪ ♪ ✕
**Acreage** 40 **Open** March **to** Oct
**Access** Good **Site** Sloping
Environmental park with a David Bellamy Gold Conservation Award. Cycle hire available.
**Nearest Town/Resort** Aberfoyle

**Directions** On the east side of the A81, 3 miles south of Aberfoyle.
⇆ Stirling

## BALMAHA

**Cashel Caravan & Camping Site - Forestry Commission,** Rowardennan, Stirlingshire, G63 0AW
**Tel:** 01360 870234
**Email:** info@forestholidays.co.uk
www.forestholidays.co.uk
**Pitches For** ▲ ⚌ ⚌ **Total** 250
**Facilities** ⚫ ⒡ ⦅ ⚑ ⌂ ⊙ ⤴ ⚌ ▢ ☏
⦿ ⊘ ⚘ Ⓜ ⟊ ▣ ✕ ⚘
**Nearby Facilities** ✓ ⚑ ✕ ✕
**Open** 25 March **to** 1 Nov
**Access** Good **Site** Level
On the shores of Loch Lomond, ideal for watersports (slipway on site), cycling and walking. The West Highland Way passes the entrance and Ben Lomond towers above.
**Nearest Town/Resort** Drymen
**Directions** On the B837 3 miles north of Balmaha.

## CALLANDER

**Gart Caravan Park,** Stirling Road, Callander, Stirling, FK17 8LE
**Tel:** 01877 330002 **Fax:** 01877 330002
**Email:** enquiries@gart-caravan-park.co.uk
www.gart-caravan-park.co.uk
**Pitches For** ⚌ ⚌ **Total** 131
**Facilities** ⚫ ⒡ ⦅ ⚑ ⌂ ⊙ ⤴ ⚌ ▢ ☏
⦿ ⊘ ⚘ Ⓜ ⟊ ▣ ✕
**Nearby Facilities** ⌐ ✓ ⚑ ∪ ✕
**Acreage** 26 **Open** 1 April **to** 15 Oct
**Access** Good **Site** Level
The ideal centre for walking, golf, fishing and exceptional for off-road cycling. Or you can simply relax and enjoy the scenery.
**Nearest Town/Resort** Callander
**Directions** Situated on the main A84, 1 mile east of Callander.
⇆ Stirling

## CALLANDER

**Keltie Bridge Caravan Park,** Callander, Stirling, FK17 8LQ
**Tel:** 01877 330606
**Email:** stay@keltiebridge.co.uk
www.keltiebridge.co.uk
**Pitches For** ⚌ ⚌ **Total** 50
**Facilities** ⚫ ⒡ ⦅ ⚑ ⌂ ⊙ ⤴ ☏ ⦿ ⊘ ⚘ ▣ ✕
**Nearby Facilities** ⌐
**Acreage** 12 **Open** April **to** Oct
**Access** Good **Site** Level
Well situated for exploring Loch Lomond and Trossachs National Park.
**Nearest Town/Resort** Callander
**Directions** Well signposted just off the A84 from Doune towards Callander, 1 mile before Callander.
⇆ Dunblane

## CRIANLARICH

**Glen Dochart Caravan Park,** Luib, Crianlarich, Stirling, FK20 8QT
**Tel:** 01567 820637 **Fax:** 01567 820024
**Email:** info@glendochart.co.uk
www.glendochart.co.uk
**Pitches For** ▲ ⚌ ▢
**Facilities** ⚫ ⒡ ⦅ ⚑ ⌂ ⊙ ⤴ ⚌ ▢ ☏
⦿ ⊘ ⚘ Ⓜ ▣ ✕
**Nearby Facilities** ⌐ ✓ ∪
**Acreage** 7 **Open** March **to** Oct
**Access** Good **Site** Level
Excellent area for touring, walking and fishing.
**Nearest Town/Resort** Stirling
**Directions** From Stirling take the A85 towards Killin. Park is situated midway between Killin and Crianlarich.
⇆ Crianlarich

## DOUNE

**Blair Drummond Caravan Club Site,** Cuthil Brae, Blair Drummond, Stirling, FK9 4UX
**Tel:** 01786 841208
www.caravanclub.co.uk
**Pitches For** ⚌ ⚌ **Total** 88
**Facilities** ⒡ ⦅ ⦆ ⚑ ⌂ ⊙ ⤴ ⚌ ▢ ☏
⚘ ⦿ ⊘ ⚘ Ⓜ ▣ ☏
**Nearby Facilities**
**Acreage** 8½ **Open** March **to** Jan
**Access** Good **Site** Level
Set in and around a walled garden with mature trees and shrubs. Woodland walks. Discounted rates when you visit nearby Blair Drummond Safari Park. Close to Stirling Leisure Complex, Doune Ponds and the castles of Doune and Stirling. Non members welcome. Booking essential.
**Nearest Town/Resort** Doune
**Directions** Leave the M9 at junction 10 and take the A84 signposted Crianlarich. After 4 miles (just past the church) turn right at caravan sign into a private road, site is at the end on the right.
⇆ Stirling

## DRYMEN

**Camping & Caravanning Club Site,** Milarrochy Bay, Balmaha, Near Drymen, Stirling, G63 0AL
**Tel:** 01360 870236
www.campingandcaravanningclub.co.uk
**Pitches For** ▲ ⚌ ⚌ **Total** 150
**Facilities** ⒡ ⦅ ⚑ ⌂ ⊙ ⤴ ⚌ ▢ ☏
⚘ ⦿ ⊘ ⚘ Ⓜ ⟊ ▣ ✕ ♪ ⊙
**Nearby Facilities** ✓ ⚑ ✕ ✕
**Acreage** 12 **Open** March **to** Oct
**Access** Good **Site** Level
On the east bank of Loch Lomond, in the heart of Rob Roy country. Near Queen Elizabeth Forest Park. Boat launching available from site. STB 4 Star Graded and AA 4 Pennants. Non members welcome.
**Nearest Town/Resort** Loch Lomond
**Directions** From the A811 Balloch to Stirling road, take the Drymen turnoff. In Drymen turn onto the B837 (junction is by the War Memorial) to Balmaha. After approx. 5 miles the road turns sharp right up a steep hill, the site is approx. 1½ miles.
⇆ Balloch

## KILLIN

**Cruachan Caravan Park,** Killin, Stirling, FK21 8TY
**Tel:** 01567 820302 **Fax:** 01567 820302
**Email:** info@cruachanfarm.co.uk
www.cruachanfarm.co.uk
**Pitches For** ▲ ⚌ ⚌ **Total** 55
**Facilities** ⚫ ⒡ ⦅ ⦆ ⚑ ⌂ ⊙ ⤴ ⚌ ▢ ☏
⦿ ⊘ ⚘ ✕ Ⓜ ▣ ✕
**Nearby Facilities** ⌐ ✓ ⚑ ✕ ∪ ♪ ♪ ✕
**Acreage** 10 **Open** 15 March **to** End Oct
**Access** Good **Site** Lev/Slope
Working farm set in countryside. Central location for touring, climbing, golf and fishing.
**Nearest Town/Resort** Killin
**Directions** 3 miles east of Killin on the A827.
⇆ Crianlarich

## KILLIN

**High Creagan Caravan Park,** Killin, Stirling, FK21 8TX
**Tel:** 01567 820449
**Pitches For** ▲ ⚌ ⚌ **Total** 30
**Facilities** ⒡ ⦅ ⦆ ⚑ ⌂ ⊙ ⤴ ▢ ☏
⊘ ✕ ▣ ✕
**Nearby Facilities** ⌐ ✓ ⚑ ✕ ∪ ♪ ♪ ✕
**Acreage** 7 **Open** March **to** October
**Access** Good **Site** Level
**Nearest Town/Resort** Killin

**Directions** 2½ miles east of Killin on the left of the A827.
⚓ Crianlarich

### KILLIN
**Maragowan Caravan Club Site,** Aberfeldy Road, Killin, Stirling, FK21 8TN
**Tel:** 01567 820245
www.caravanclub.co.uk
**Pitches For** ⬡ ⬢ **Total** 100
**Facilities** ⬡ ƒ ⬡ ⬡ ⬡ ⬡ ⬡ ⬡ ⬡
⬡ ⬡ ⬡ ⬡ ⬡ ⬡ ⬡
**Nearby Facilities** ⬡ ⬡ ⬡ ⬡ ⬡
**Acreage** 8½ **Open** March **to** Oct
**Access** Good **Site** Level
On the banks of the River Lochay for salmon and trout fishing. Ideal for walkers and wildlife lovers. Close to Archray Forest, Scottish Wool Centre and two Visitor Centres. Non members welcome. Booking essential.
**Nearest Town/Resort** Killin
**Directions** Just off the A827 just outside Killin Village.
⚓ Killin

### STIRLING
**Witches Craig Caravan & Camping Park,** Blairlogie, Stirling, Stirlingshire, FK9 5PX
**Tel:** 01786 474947 **Fax:** 01786 447286
**Email:** info@witchescraig.co.uk
www.witchescraig.co.uk
**Pitches For** ⬡ ⬢ **Total** 60
**Facilities** ⬡ ƒ ⬡ ⬡ ⬡ ⬡ ⬡ ⬡ ⬡ ⬡
⬡ ⬡ ⬡ ⬡ ⬡ ⬡ ⬡
**Nearby Facilities** ⬡ ⬡ ⬡ ⬡ ⬡
**Acreage** 5 **Open** April **to** October
**Access** Good **Site** Level
Situated at the foot of the Ochil Hills with beautiful scenery and many local historical sites. Good hill walking. Ideal touring

centre.
**Nearest Town/Resort** Stirling
**Directions** 3 miles east of Stirling town centre on the A91 Stirling to St. Andrews road.
⚓ Stirling

### STRATHYRE
**Immervoulin Caravan & Camping Park,** Strathyre, Callander, Stirling, FK18 8NJ
**Tel:** 01877 384285 **Fax:** 01877 384390
**Email:** immervoulin@freenetname.co.uk
www.immervoulin-caravan-camping-park.co.uk
**Pitches For** ⬡ ⬡ ⬢ **Total** 56
**Facilities** ⬡ ƒ ⬡ ⬡ ⬡ ⬡ ⬡ ⬡ ⬡ ⬡
⬡ ⬡ ⬡ ⬡ ⬡ ⬡ ⬡
**Nearby Facilities** ⬡ ⬡ ⬡ ⬡ ⬡ ⬡ ⬡
**Acreage** 8 **Open** March **to** Oct
**Access** Good **Site** Level
Alongside the River Balvaig and 300 metres from Strathyre Village. Ideal for walking and cycling.
**Nearest Town/Resort** Stirling
**Directions** On the A84 from Stirling.
⚓ Doune

---

**PLEASE REMEMBER TO MENTION CADE'S WHEN REPLYING TO OUR ADVERTISERS**

---

## WESTERN ISLES
### NORTH SHAWBOST
**Eilean Fraoich Caravan & Camping Park,** North Shawbost, Isle of Lewis, Western Isles, HS2 9BQ
**Tel:** 01851 710504
**Email:** eileanfraoich@btinternet.com
**Pitches For** ⬡ ⬡ ⬢
**Facilities** ⬡ ƒ ⬡ ⬡ ⬡ ⬡ ⬡ ⬡ ⬡ ⬡
⬡ ⬡ ⬡ ⬡ ⬡
**Nearby Facilities** ⬡ ⬡ ⬡ ⬡ ⬡ ⬡
**Open** May **to** October
**Access** Good **Site** Level
Nera to beaches and historical sites. Ideal for hill walking.
**Nearest Town/Resort** Stornoway
**Directions** From Stornoway take the A85 to Barvas, turn left onto the A858 for approx 6 miles, turn left at Shawbost School.

### STORNOWAY
**Laxdale Holiday Park,** 6 Laxdale Lane, Laxdale, Isle of Lewis, Western Isles, HS2 0DR
**Tel:** 01851 706966
**Email:** info@laxdaleholidaypark.com
www.laxdaleholidaypark.com
**Pitches For** ⬡ ⬡ ⬢ **Total** 43
**Facilities** ⬡ ƒ ⬡ ⬡ ⬡ ⬡ ⬡ ⬡ ⬡ ⬡
⬡ ⬡ ⬡ ⬡ ⬡
**Nearby Facilities** ⬡ ⬡ ⬡
**Acreage** 2¼ **Open** March **to** Oct
**Access** Good **Site** Lev/Slope
Peaceful, tree lined site. Centrally located for touring the isles of Lewis and Harris.
**Nearest Town/Resort** Stornoway
**Directions** From Stornoway take the A85 for 1 mile, take the second turning on the left past the hospital.

## INDEX TO PARKS - OPEN ALL YEAR

Simply look for the County you wish to visit below, find the Town and the Park Name, then refer to the relevant County and Town in the main section of the guide for full details.

## ESSEX
COLCHESTER, Colchester C & C Club Site
HALSTEAD, Gosfield Lake Resort
ROYDON, Roydon Mill Pk.

## GLOUCESTERSHIRE
CIRENCESTER, Mayfield Touring Pk.
DURSLEY, Hogsdown C & C
GLOUCESTER, The Red Lion Inn C & C Pk.
MORETON-IN-MARSH, Moreton-In-Marsh C & Club Site
MORETON-IN-MARSH, Cross Hands Inn
SLIMBRIDGE, Tudor C & C Pk.

## HAMPSHIRE
FAREHAM, Dibles Pk.
FORDINGBRIDGE, Sandy Balls
NEW MILTON, Setthorns C & C Site
SOUTHSEA, Southsea Leisure Pk.

## HEREFORDSHIRE
HEREFORD, Cuckoo's Corner
PETERCHURCH, Poston Mill Pk.

## HERTFORDSHIRE
HERTFORD, C & Cning Club Site

## ISLE OF WIGHT
SANDOWN, Village Way C & C Pk.

## KENT
ASHFORD, Broadhembury C & C Pk.
CANTERBURY, C & Cning Club Site
FOLKESTONE, Black Horse Farm Caravan Club Site
MAIDSTONE, Pine Lodge Touring Pk.
MARDEN, Tanner Farm Touring C & C Pk.
ROCHESTER, Woolmans Wood Tourist Caravan Pk.

## LANCASHIRE
LANCASTER, Wyreside Lakes Fishery
MORECAMBE, Venture Caravan Pk.
ORMSKIRK, Abbey Farm Caravan Pk.

## LEICESTERSHIRE
CASTLE DONINGTON, Donington Pk. Farmhouse
LEICESTER, Hill Top Caravan & Leisure Pk.
MARKET BOSWORTH, Bosworth Water Trust

## LINCOLNSHIRE
GRANTHAM, Woodland Waters
HORNCASTLE, Ashby Pk.
HORNCASTLE, The Golfers Arms
LINCOLN, Oakhill Leisure
LINCOLN, Shortferry Caravan Pk.
MARKET RASEN, Manor Farm C & C Site
SCUNTHORPE, Brookside C & C Pk.
SKEGNESS, Ronam Cottage
SKEGNESS, Skegness Sands
SPILSBY, Meadowlands
STAMFORD, Road End Farm Caravan Pk.
WOODHALL SPA, Bainland Country Pk.

## LONDON
ABBEY WOOD, Abbey Wood Caravan Club Site
CRYSTAL PALACE, Crystal Palace Caravan Club Site

## MANCHESTER
LITTLEBOROUGH, Hollingworth Lake Caravan Pk.

## NORFOLK
ATTLEBOROUGH, Oak Tree Caravan Pk.
AYLSHAM, Top Farm C & C Site
CROMER, Deer's Glade C & C Pk.
FAKENHAM, Crossways C & C Pk.
FAKENHAM, Fakenham Racecourse Cara. Club Site
GREAT YARMOUTH, Willowcroft C & C Pk.
GREAT YARMOUTH, Rose Farm T & C Pk.
KINGS LYNN, Pentney Pk.
KINGS LYNN, Kings Lynn C & C Pk.
NORWICH, Swans Harbour C & C Pk.
SWAFFHAM, Breckland Meadows Touring Pk.
THETFORD, Lowe Caravan Pk.,

## NORTHUMBERLAND
BERWICK-UPON-TWEED, Ord House Country Pk.

## NOTTINGHAMSHIRE
NEWARK, Milestone Caravan Pk
NOTTINGHAM, Thornton's Holt Camping Pk.
RATCLIFFE ON SOAR, Red Hill Marina
SUTTON-IN-ASHFIELD, Shardaroba Caravan Pk.
WORKSOP, Clumber Pk. Caravan Club Site
WORKSOP, Riverside Caravan Pk.

## OXFORDSHIRE
BANBURY, Barnstones Caravan Site
BLETCHINGDON, Greenhill Leisure Pk.
OXFORD, C & Cning Club Site

## SHROPSHIRE
BISHOPS CASTLE, Daisy Bank Touring Caravan Pk.
BRIDGNORTH, Stanmore Hall Touring Pk.
SHREWSBURY, Beaconsfield Farm Holiday Pk.
TELFORD, Severn Gorge Pk.
WEM, Lower Lacon Caravan Pk.
WHITCHURCH, Roden View C & C

## SOMERSET
BATH, Bath Chew Valley Caravan Pk.
BATH, Newton Mill C & C Pk.
BATH, Bury View Farm
BRIDGWATER, Mill Farm C & C Pk.
CHARD, Snowdon Hill Farm
CHARD, South Somerset Holiday Pk.
CHEDDAR, Rodney Stoke Inn
CROWCOMBE, Quantock Orchard Caravan Pk.
EXFORD, Westermill Farm
GLASTONBURY, Orchard Camping
LANGPORT, Bowdens Crest C & C Pk.
MARTOCK, Southfork Caravan Pk.
MINEHEAD, Butlins Minehead
SHEPTON MALLET, Manleaze Caravan Pk.
TAUNTON, Waterrow Touring Pk.
TAUNTON, Cornish Farm Touring Pk.

TAUNTON, Holly Bush Pk.
WELLS, Haybridge Caravan Pk.
WILLITON, Home Farm Holiday Centre

## STAFFORDSHIRE
BURTON-ON-TRENT, Willowbrook Farm
LEEK, C & Cning Club Site
RUGELEY, Pk. View Farm

## SUFFOLK
BECCLES, Fox Country Caravan Pk.
BURY ST EDMUNDS, The Dell Touring Pk.
HADLEIGH, Polstead Touring Pk.
IPSWICH, Low House Touring Caravan Centre
WOODBRIDGE, Run Cottage Touring Pk.

## SURREY
CHERTSEY, C & Cning Club Site
HAMBLEDON, The Merry Harriers
LINGFIELD, Long Acres C & C Pk.
REDHILL, Alderstead Heath Caravan Club Site

## SUSSEX, EAST
BRIGHTON, Sheepcote Valley Caravan Club Site
UCKFIELD, Heaven Farm

## SUSSEX, WEST
ARUNDEL, Maynards C & C Pk.
BOGNOR REGIS, The Lillies Caravan Pk.
CHICHESTER, Lakeside Holiday Village
HORSHAM, Honeybridge Pk.
LITTLEHAMPTON, Daisyfields Touring Pk.
WISBOROUGH GREEN, Bat & Ball Public House

## WARWICKSHIRE
STRATFORD-UPON-AVON, Dodwell Pk.
WOLVEY, Wolvey C & C Pk.

## WEST MIDLANDS
SUTTON COLDFIELD, Marston C & C Pk.
SUTTON COLDFIELD, C & Cning Club Site

## WILTSHIRE
CALNE, Blackland Lakes
DEVIZES, C & Cning Club Site
ORCHESTON, Stonehenge Touring Pk.
SALISBURY, Alderbury Pk.
SALISBURY, Greenhill Farm C & C Pk.
TILSHEAD, Brades Acre
WESTBURY, Brokerswood Country Pk.

## WORCESTERSHIRE
BROADWAY, Leedons Pk.
EVESHAM, Longcarrant Caravan Pk.
GREAT MALVERN, C & Cning Club Site
MALVERN, The Robin Hood
STOURPORT-ON-SEVERN, Lickhill Manor Caravan Pk.
WYTHALL, Chapel Lane Caravan Club Site

## YORKSHIRE, EAST
BEVERLEY, Lakeminster Pk.
GOOLE, Dobella Lane Farm
LITTLE WEIGHTON, Louvain

## YORKSHIRE, NORTH
BOROUGHBRIDGE, C & Cning Club Site
ELVINGTON, Elvington Lake Caravan Pk.
HARROGATE, Shaws Trailer Pk.
MUKER, Usha Gap Caravan & Camp Site
SKIPTON, Eshton Road Caravan Site
THORNABY-ON-TEES, White Water Cara. Club Pk.
WHITBY, Hollins Farm
YORK (Near), The Ponderosa Caravan Pk.
YORK (Near), Cawood Pk.

## YORK (COUNTY OF)
YORK, Rowntree Park, Caravan Club Site
YORK, Acomb Grange
YORK, Rawcliffe Caravan Co. Ltd.

## YORKSHIRE, SOUTH
DONCASTER, Waterfront Country Pk.
ROTHERHAM, Thrybergh Country Pk.
THORNE, Elder House Touring Pk.

## YORKSHIRE, WEST
HOLMFIRTH, Holme Valley C & C Pk.
LEEDS, Glenfield Caravan Pk.
LEEDS, Moor Lodge Caravan Pk.
OTLEY, Stubbings Farm,

# WALES

## ANGLESEY
RHOSNEIGR, Tyn Llidiart Camping Site

## BLAENAU GWENT
TREDEGAR, Parc Bryn Bach

## CARDIFF
CARDIFF, Pontcanna Caravan Site

## CARMARTHENSHIRE
LLANDDEUSANT, The Black Mountain C & C Pk.
LLANDOVERY, Erwlon C & C Pk.

## CARDIGANSHIRE (CEREDIGION)
CARDIGAN, Allt-y-Coed

## CONWY
BETWS-Y-COED, Rynys Farm Camping Site
COLWYN BAY, Bron-Y-Wendon Touring Caravan Pk.

## GWYNEDD
ARTHOG, Garthyfog Camping Site
DOLGELLAU, Tyddyn Farm
MORFA NEFYN, Graeanfryn Farm
TYWYN, Cwmrhwyddfor Campsite
TYWYN, Dôl Einion

## INDEX - OPEN ALL YEAR

## INDEX TO ADULTS ONLY PARKS

Simply look for the County you wish to visit below, find the Town and the Park Name, then refer to the relevant County and Town in the main section of the guide for full details.

# ENGLAND

## CAMBRIDGESHIRE
HUNTINGDON, Wyton Lakes Holiday Pk.
HUNTINGDON, Stroud Hill Pk.

## CHESHIRE
CHESTER, Netherwood Touring Site
WINSFORD, Lamb Cottage Caravan Pk.

## CORNWALL
NEWQUAY, Sunnyside Holiday Village
NEWQUAY, Rosecliston Pk.
PENZANCE, Wayfarers Caravan & Camping Pk.
TRURO, Chacewater Camping & Caravan Pk.

## CUMBRIA
KENDAL, Ashes Exclusively Adult Caravan Pk.
MEALSGATE, The Larches Caravan Pk.

## DERBYSHIRE
AMBERGATE, The Firs Farm Caravan & Camping Pk.

## DEVON
CHAGFORD, Woodland Springs Adult Touring Pk.
NEWTON ABBOT, Woodville Caravan Pk.
TIVERTON, Zeacombe House Caravan Pk.

## DORSET
BRIDPORT, Binghams Farm Touring Caravan Pk.
ST. LEONARDS, Back-of-Beyond Touring Pk.
RINGWOOD, Tree Tops Touring Caravan Pk.
ROCHESTER, Woolmans Wood Tourist Caravan Pk.

## LANCASHIRE
BLACKPOOL, Mariclough - Hampsfield

## LINCOLNSHIRE
BOSTON, Pilgrims Way Camping Pk.
HUTTOFT, Jolly Common Caravan Pk.
SPALDING, Delph Bank Touring C & C Pk.
SUTTON-ON-SEA, Cherry Tree Site

## NORFOLK
KINGS LYNN, Gatton Water Touring C & C Site
NORTH WALSHAM, Two Mills Touring Pk.

## NOTTINGHAMSHIRE
NEWARK, New Hall Farm

## OXFORDSHIRE
ABINGDON, Bridge House Caravan Site

## SHROPSHIRE
BISHOPS CASTLE, Daisy Bank Touring Caravan Pk.
SHREWSBURY, Hollies Farm
SHREWSBURY, Beaconsfield Farm Holiday Pk.

## SOMERSET
BATH, Bath Chew Valley Caravan Pk.
DULVERTON, Exe Valley Caravan Site

GLASTONBURY, The Old Oaks Touring Pk.
HIGHBRIDGE, Greenacre Place Touring Caravan Pk.
TAUNTON, Waterrow Touring Pk.
WELLS, Homestead Pk.

## STAFFORDSHIRE
LONGNOR, Longnor Wood 'Just For Adults' Cara. Pk.

## SUFFOLK
HADLEIGH, Polstead Touring Pk.
IPSWICH, The Oaks Caravan Pk.

## WEST MIDLANDS
MERIDEN, Somers Wood Caravan & Camping Pk.,

## WILTSHIRE
CHIPPENHAM, Plough Lane Caravan Site
SALISBURY, Greenhill Farm Camping & Caravan Pk.

## WORCESTERSHIRE
WORCESTER, Seaborne Leisure

## YORKSHIRE, NORTH
HARROGATE, Shaws Trailer Pk.
HELMSLEY, Foxholme Touring C & C Pk.
PICKERING, Overbrook Caravan Pk.
RICHMOND, Tavern House Caravan Pk.
YORK (Near), Willow House Caravan Pk.

## YORK (COUNTY OF)
YORK, Rawcliffe Caravan Co. Ltd.
YORK, Moorside Caravan Pk.

## YORKSHIRE, WEST
LEEDS, Moor Lodge Caravan Pk.
OTLEY, St. Helena's Caravan Pk.
WETHERBY, Maustin Caravan Pk.,

# WALES

## CARMARTHENSHIRE
CARMARTHEN, Pant Farm Touring C & C Pk.

## CONWY
PENMAENMAWR, Tyddyn Du Touring Pk.

## GWYNEDD
ABERSOCH, Trem Y Mor

## PEMBROKESHIRE
FISHGUARD, Rosebush Caravan & Camping Pk.
TENBY, Red House Farm

## POWYS
CRICKHOWELL, Riverside Caravan & Camping Pk.
LLANDRINDOD WELLS, Dalmore Caravan Pk.
LLANWDDYN, Fronheulog

# SCOTLAND
## HIGHLAND
INVERGARRY, Faichemard Farm Camp Site

# INDEX TO PARKS WITH FISHING ON SITE

Use this Index to find Touring Parks with their own fishing facilities.
Simply look for the County you wish to visit below, find the Town and the Park Name, then refer to the relevant County and Town in the main section of the guide for full details.

# INDEX - FISHING ON SITE

## SHROPSHIRE
BISHOPS CASTLE, The Green Caravan Park
BISHOPS CASTLE, Cwnd House Farm
BRIDGNORTH, The Riverside Caravan Park
ELLESMERE, Fernwood Caravan Park
LUDLOW, Westbrook Park
MUCH WENLOCK, Mill Farm Holiday Park
SHREWSBURY, Beaconsfield Farm Holiday Park
SHREWSBURY, Severn House
SHREWSBURY, Ebury Hill C & C Club Site
WHITCHURCH, Roden View C & C

## SOMERSET
BATH, Newton Mill Camping & Caravan Park
BREAN SANDS, Holiday Resort Unity at Unity Farm
BREAN SANDS, Warren Farm Holiday Centre
BREAN SANDS, Northam Farm C & T Park
BRUTON, Batcombe Vale C & C Park
BURNHAM-ON-SEA, Home Farm Holiday Park
BURNHAM-ON-SEA, Diamond Farm C & T Park
DULVERTON, Exe Valley Caravan Site
EXFORD, Westermill Farm
GLASTONBURY, The Old Oaks Touring Park
LANGPORT, Thorney Lakes Caravan Site
TAUNTON, Waterrow Touring Park
WELLINGTON, Gamlins Farm Caravan Park
WILLITON, Home Farm Holiday Centre,

## STAFFORDSHIRE
LEEK, Glencote Caravan Park

## SUFFOLK
EYE, Honeypot C & C Park
FELIXSTOWE, Suffolk Sands Holiday Village
LOWESTOFT, Chestnut Farm
SAXMUNDHAM, Whitearch Touring Park
SUDBURY, Willowmere Caravan Park
WOODBRIDGE, Run Cottage Touring Park

## SURREY
CHERTSEY, C & C Club Site
HORSLEY, C & C Club Site
BATTLE, Brakes Coppice Park
EASTBOURNE, Fairfields Farm C & C Park
ROBERTSBRIDGE, Park Farm C & C Site
UCKFIELD, Heaven Farm
UCKFIELD, Honeys Green Farm Caravan Park

## SUSSEX, WEST
ARUNDEL, Ship & Anchor Marina
CHICHESTER, Lakeside Holiday Village

## WARWICKSHIRE
STRATFORD-UPON-AVON, Island Meadow Cara. Pk
STRATFORD-UPON-AVON, Riverside Caravan Park
WOLVEY, Wolvey C & C Park

## WEST MIDLANDS
SUTTON COLDFIELD, C & C Club Site,

## WILTSHIRE
CALNE, Blackland Lakes
MALMESBURY, Burton Hill C & C Park
SALISBURY, Greenhill Farm Camping & Caravan Park
TROWBRIDGE, Stowford Manor Farm
WESTBURY, Brokerswood Country Park

## WORCESTERSHIRE
MALVERN, Riverside Caravan Park
MALVERN, Kingsgreen Caravan Park
STOURPORT-ON-SEVERN, Lickhill Manor Cara. Park
STOURPORT-ON-SEVERN, Lincomb Lock Cara. Park
WORCESTER, Ketch Caravan Park
WORCESTER, Mill House C & C Site

## YORKSHIRE, EAST
BEVERLEY, Lakeminster Park
BRANDES BURTON, Dacre Lakeside Park
HULL, Sand-le-Mere Caravan Park
RUDSTON, Thorpe Hall C & C Site
SKIPSEA, Skirlington Leisure Park
STAMFORD BRIDGE, Weir Caravan Park
WITHERNSEA, Willows Holiday Park

## YORKSHIRE, NORTH
BENTHAM, Riverside Caravan Park
BOROUGHBRIDGE, C & C Club Site
ELVINGTON, Elvington Lake Caravan Park
FILEY, Orchard Farm Holiday Village
FILEY, Primrose Valley Holiday Park
HARROGATE, High Moor Farm Caravan Park
KNARESBOROUGH, Kingfisher C & C Park
MALTON, Ashfield Caravan Park
PATELEY BRIDGE, Riverside Caravan Park
RICHMOND, Brompton Caravan Park
RICHMOND, Swale View Caravan Park
RIPON, Woodhouse Farm C & C Park
RIPON, Sleningford Watermill
RIPON, River Laver Holiday Park
SCARBOROUGH, St. Helens C & C
SELBY, Oakmere Caravan Park & Coarse Fishery
SETTLE, Knight Stainforth Hall
SKIPTON, Eshton Road Caravan Site
THIRSK, Sowerby Caravan Park
YORK (Near), Home Farm Camping & Caravan Park
YORK (Near), Cawood Park
YORK (Near), The Ponderosa Caravan Park
YORK (Near), Willow House Caravan Park

## YORK (COUNTY OF)
YORK, Moorside Caravan Park
YORK, Riverside C & C Site
YORK, Naburn Lock Caravan Park

## YORKSHIRE, SOUTH
ROTHERHAM, Thrybergh Country Park

## YORKSHIRE, WEST
HOLMFIRTH, Holme Valley Camping & Caravan Park
WAKEFIELD, Nostell Priory Holiday Park,

# WALES

## ANGLESEY
BENLLECH, Golden Sunset Holidays
BENLLECH, St. David's Park
LLANFAIRPWLL, Plas Coch Caravan & Leisure Park
LLANFWROG, Penrhyn Bay Caravan Park
RHOSNEIGR, Ty Hen

## BLAENAU GWENT
TREDEGAR, Parc Bryn Bach

## CAERPHILLY
BARGOED, Parc Cwm Darran

## CARMARTHENSHIRE
LLANDDEUSANT, Blaenau Farm
LLANDOVERY, Erwlon C & C Park
NEWCASTLE EMLYN, Afon Teifi C & C Park
NEWCASTLE EMLYN, Dolbryn Farm

## CARDIGANSHIRE (CEREDIGION)
ABERYSTWYTH, Clarach Bay Holiday Village
ABERYSTWYTH, Morfa Bychan Holiday Park
BORTH, Glanlerry Caravan Park
CARDIGAN, Blaenwaun Caravan Park
CARDIGAN, Penralltllyn Caravan Park
DEVILS BRIDGE, Woodlands Caravan Park
LLANRHYSTUD, Morfa Caravan Park
LLANRHYSTUD, Pengarreg Caravan Park
SARNAU, Dyffryn Bern Caravan Park

## CONWY
TY-NANT, Glan Ceirw Caravan Park

## DENBIGHSHIRE
LLANGOLLEN, Ddol Hir Caravan Park
RUTHIN, Dyffryn Ial Caravan Site

## GWYNEDD
ARTHOG, Graig-Wen
BALA, Glanllyn-Lakeside C & C Park
BALA, Tyn Cornel Camping & Caravan Park
BALA, Ty-Isaf Camping Site
BANGOR, Dinas Farm Camping Site
CAERNARFON, Bryn Gloch C & C Park
CAERNARFON, Riverside Camping
CAERNARFON, Talymignedd Caravan Site
CAERNARFON, Tyn-yr-Onnen Mountain Farm
CLYNNOG FAWR, Aberafon Camping Site
CRICCIETH, Tyddyn Cethin Caravan Park
CRICCIETH, Eisteddfa C & C Site
DINAS MAWDDWY, Celyn Brithion
DINAS MAWDDWY, Tynypwll C & C Site
DOLGELLAU, Dolgamedd Camping & Caravan Site
DOLGELLAU, Tyddyn Farm
PWLLHELI, Abererch Sands Holiday Centre
TYWYN, Dôl Einion
TYWYN, Ynysymaengwyn Caravan Park
TYWYN, Cwmrhwyddfor Campsite
TYWYN, Glanywern

## MONMOUTHSHIRE
MONMOUTH, Monnow Bridge Caravan Site
MONMOUTH, Bridge Caravan Park & Camping Site
MONMOUTH, Glen Trothy Caravan Park
USK, Chainbridge Inn

## NEWPORT
NEWPORT, Pentre-Tai Farm

## PEMBROKESHIRE
FISHGUARD, Rosebush C & C Park
HAVERFORDWEST, Nolton Cross Caravan Park
NARBERTH, Noble Court Holiday Park
NEWPORT, Llwyngwair Manor
NEWPORT, Tycanol Farm Camp Site
TAVERNSPITE, South Carvan Caravan Park

## POWYS
BUILTH WELLS, White House Caravan & Camp Site
BUILTH WELLS, Irfon Caravan Park
LLANDRINDOD WELLS, Disserth C & C Park
LLANFYLLIN, Henstent Caravan Park
LLANIDLOES, Dol-Llys Touring Site
LLANSANTFFRAID, Bryn-Vyrnwy Caravan Park
MACHYNLLETH, Morben Isaf Touring Park
MIDDLETOWN, Bank Farm Caravan Park
NEWTOWN, Smithy Caravan Park
PRESTEIGNE, Rockbridge Park
RHAYADER, Wyeside C & C Park
WELSHPOOL, Dolgead Hall Caravan Park Ltd.
WELSHPOOL, Carmel Caravan Park
WELSHPOOL, Henllan Caravan Park

## WREXHAM
WREXHAM, The Plassey Touring Cara. & Leisure Park

# SCOTLAND

## ABERDEENSHIRE
ABOYNE, Aboyne Loch Caravan Park
PETERHEAD, Lido Caravan Park

## ARGYLL & BUTE
KILBERRY, Port Ban Holiday Park
LOCHGILPHEAD, Lochgilphead Caravan Park
LUSS, C & C Club Site
MUASDALE, Muasdale Holiday Park
OBAN, Oban C & C Park
OBAN, North Ledaig Caravan Park
SOUTHEND, Machribeg Caravan Site,

## AYRSHIRE, NORTH
ISLE OF ARRAN, Seal Shore Camping & Touring

## CLACKMANNANSHIRE
DOLLAR, Riverside Caravan Park

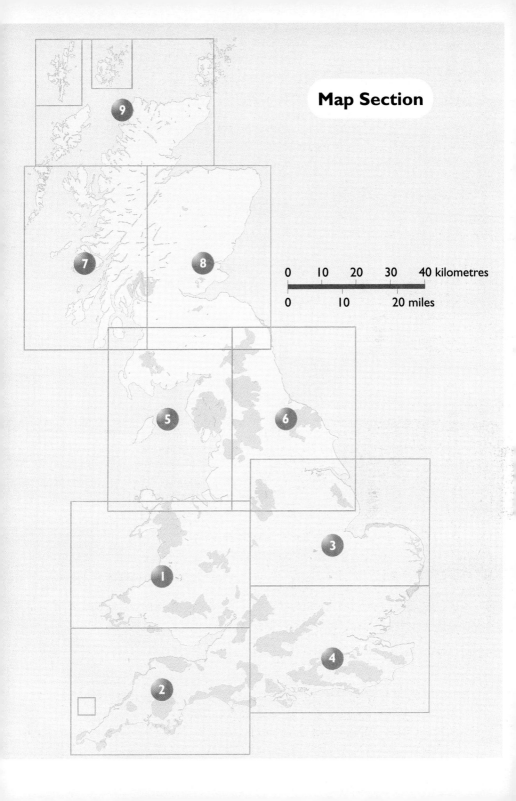

**Map Section**

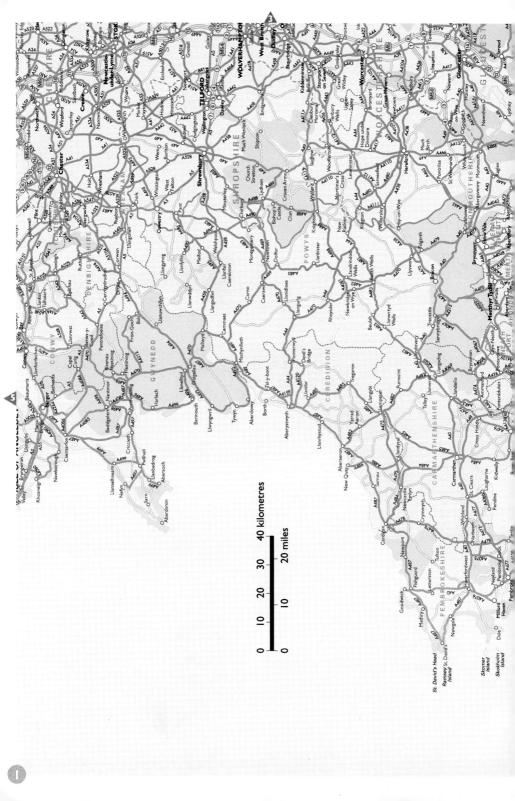

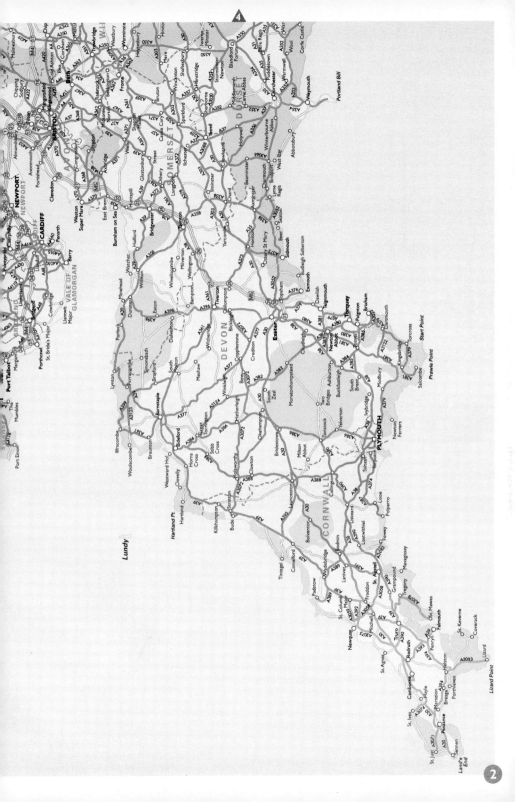

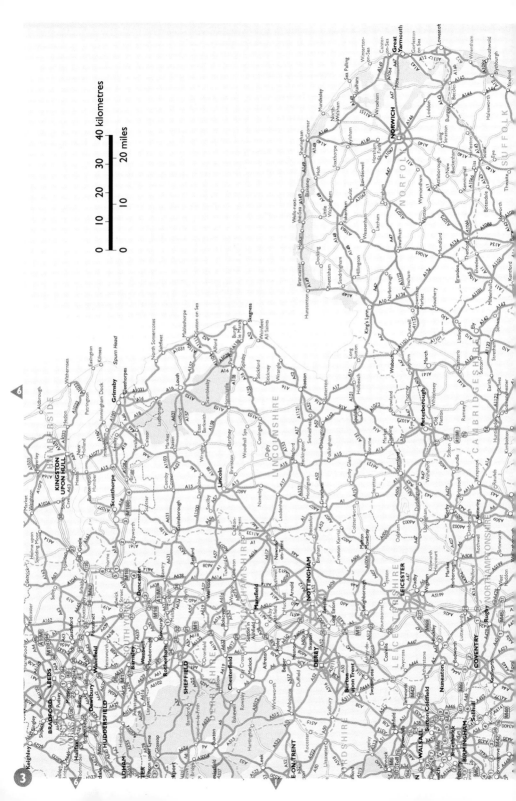

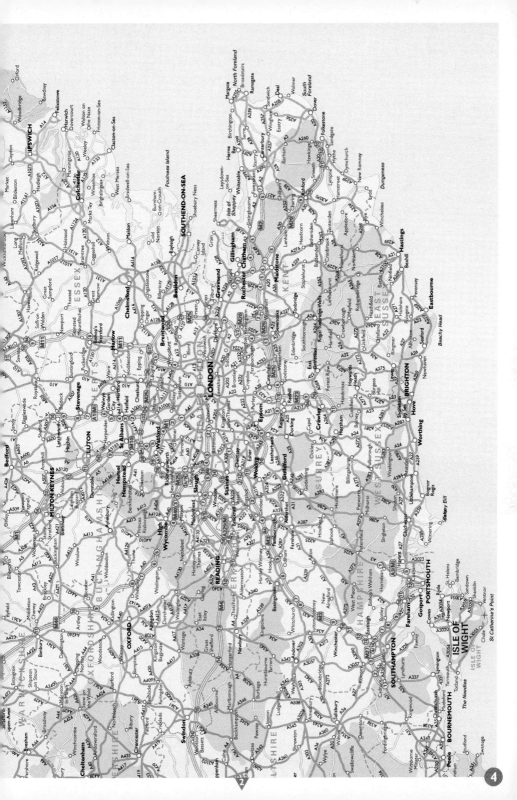

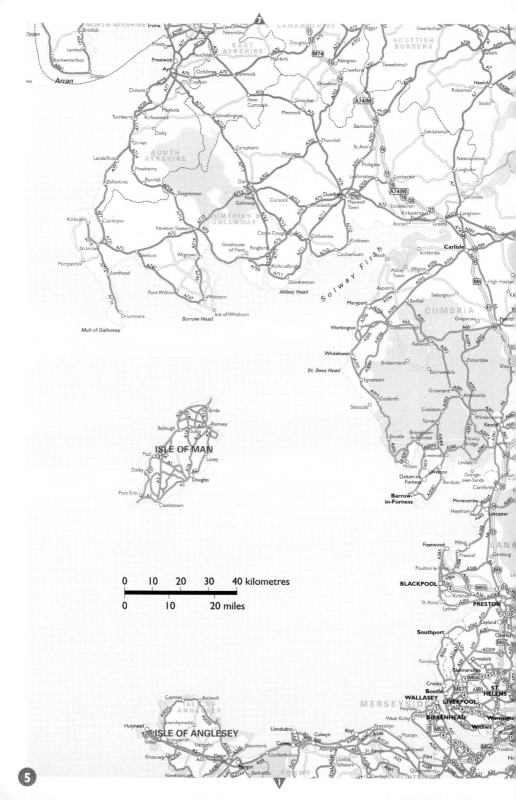

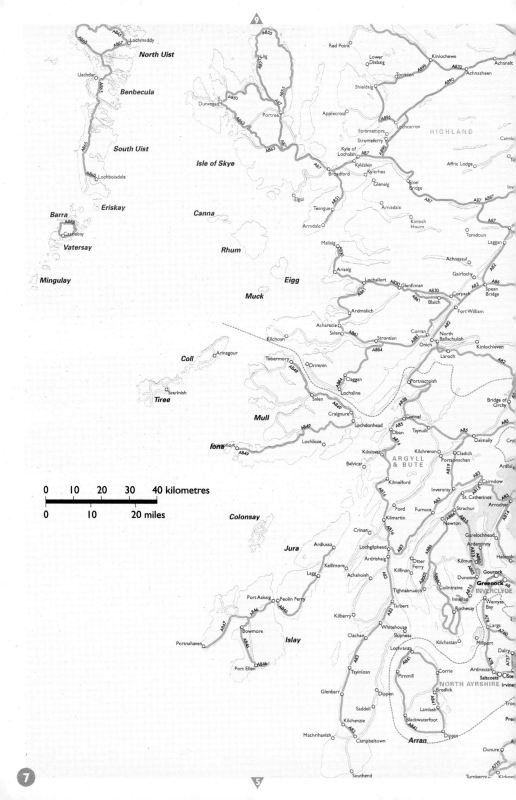

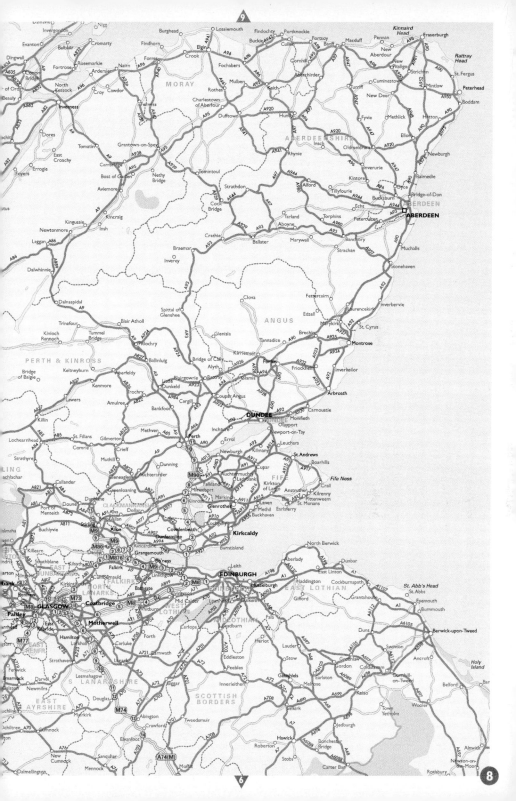

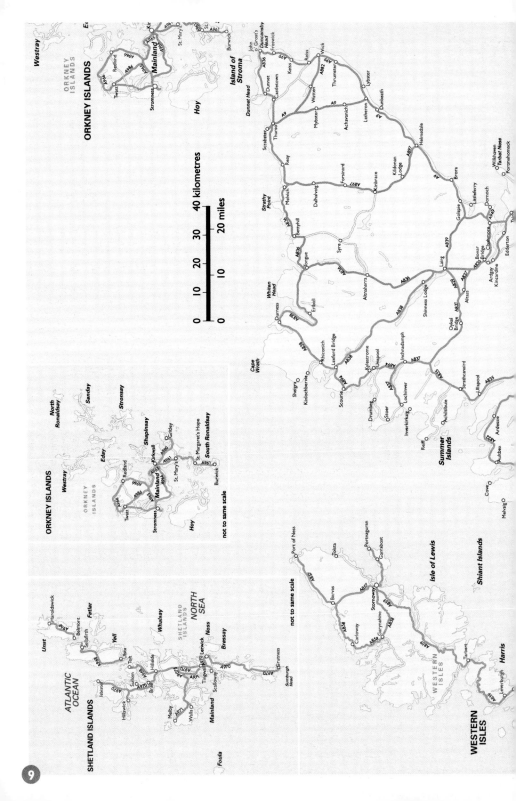

| CADE'S FIFTY PENCE | CADE'S FIFTY PENCE |
|---|---|
| **CAMPING, TOURING & MOTOR CARAVAN SITE GUIDE 2006**<br><br>PRESENT THIS VOUCHER TO THE SITE OPERATOR WHEN PAYING TO RECEIVE FIFTY PENCE DISCOUNT PER VOUCHER, PER NIGHT. SEE CONDITIONS OVERLEAF.<br>VALID UNTIL 31-12-06. | **CAMPING, TOURING & MOTOR CARAVAN SITE GUIDE 2006**<br><br>PRESENT THIS VOUCHER TO THE SITE OPERATOR WHEN PAYING TO RECEIVE FIFTY PENCE DISCOUNT PER VOUCHER, PER NIGHT. SEE CONDITIONS OVERLEAF.<br>VALID UNTIL 31-12-06. |
| CADE'S FIFTY PENCE | CADE'S FIFTY PENCE |
| **CAMPING, TOURING & MOTOR CARAVAN SITE GUIDE 2006**<br><br>PRESENT THIS VOUCHER TO THE SITE OPERATOR WHEN PAYING TO RECEIVE FIFTY PENCE DISCOUNT PER VOUCHER, PER NIGHT. SEE CONDITIONS OVERLEAF.<br>VALID UNTIL 31-12-06. | **CAMPING, TOURING & MOTOR CARAVAN SITE GUIDE 2006**<br><br>PRESENT THIS VOUCHER TO THE SITE OPERATOR WHEN PAYING TO RECEIVE FIFTY PENCE DISCOUNT PER VOUCHER, PER NIGHT. SEE CONDITIONS OVERLEAF.<br>VALID UNTIL 31-12-06. |
| CADE'S FIFTY PENCE | CADE'S FIFTY PENCE |
| **CAMPING, TOURING & MOTOR CARAVAN SITE GUIDE 2006**<br><br>PRESENT THIS VOUCHER TO THE SITE OPERATOR WHEN PAYING TO RECEIVE FIFTY PENCE DISCOUNT PER VOUCHER, PER NIGHT. SEE CONDITIONS OVERLEAF.<br>VALID UNTIL 31-12-06. | **CAMPING, TOURING & MOTOR CARAVAN SITE GUIDE 2006**<br><br>PRESENT THIS VOUCHER TO THE SITE OPERATOR WHEN PAYING TO RECEIVE FIFTY PENCE DISCOUNT PER VOUCHER, PER NIGHT. SEE CONDITIONS OVERLEAF.<br>VALID UNTIL 31-12-06. |
| CADE'S FIFTY PENCE | CADE'S FIFTY PENCE |
| **CAMPING, TOURING & MOTOR CARAVAN SITE GUIDE 2006**<br><br>PRESENT THIS VOUCHER TO THE SITE OPERATOR WHEN PAYING TO RECEIVE FIFTY PENCE DISCOUNT PER VOUCHER, PER NIGHT. SEE CONDITIONS OVERLEAF.<br>VALID UNTIL 31-12-06. | **CAMPING, TOURING & MOTOR CARAVAN SITE GUIDE 2006**<br><br>PRESENT THIS VOUCHER TO THE SITE OPERATOR WHEN PAYING TO RECEIVE FIFTY PENCE DISCOUNT PER VOUCHER, PER NIGHT. SEE CONDITIONS OVERLEAF.<br>VALID UNTIL 31-12-06. |
| CADE'S FIFTY PENCE | CADE'S FIFTY PENCE |
| **CAMPING, TOURING & MOTOR CARAVAN SITE GUIDE 2006**<br><br>PRESENT THIS VOUCHER TO THE SITE OPERATOR WHEN PAYING TO RECEIVE FIFTY PENCE DISCOUNT PER VOUCHER, PER NIGHT. SEE CONDITIONS OVERLEAF.<br>VALID UNTIL 31-12-06. | **CAMPING, TOURING & MOTOR CARAVAN SITE GUIDE 2006**<br><br>PRESENT THIS VOUCHER TO THE SITE OPERATOR WHEN PAYING TO RECEIVE FIFTY PENCE DISCOUNT PER VOUCHER, PER NIGHT. SEE CONDITIONS OVERLEAF.<br>VALID UNTIL 31-12-06. |

## CONDITIONS OF USE

Vouchers will only be redeemed by those sites featuring a ▣ symbol in the *facilities* line of their County entry. Presentation of this voucher to the Site Operator at the time of paying your balance will entitle you to a fifty pence discount per voucher, per night. (Only one voucher per night). Vouchers may be used in multiples i.e. five vouchers presented for a five night stay will entitle you to a discount of £2.50.

A CADE'S CAMPING, TOURING & MOTOR CARAVAN SITE GUIDE 2006 EDITION must be presented at the time of payment. Vouchers are valid for accommodation only. Vouchers may not be exchanged for cash. May not be used with any other offer. Valid until 31-12-06.

## CONDITIONS OF USE

Vouchers will only be redeemed by those sites featuring a ▣ symbol in the *facilities* line of their County entry. Presentation of this voucher to the Site Operator at the time of paying your balance will entitle you to a fifty pence discount per voucher, per night. (Only one voucher per night). Vouchers may be used in multiples i.e. five vouchers presented for a five night stay will entitle you to a discount of £2.50.

A CADE'S CAMPING, TOURING & MOTOR CARAVAN SITE GUIDE 2006 EDITION must be presented at the time of payment. Vouchers are valid for accommodation only. Vouchers may not be exchanged for cash. May not be used with any other offer. Valid until 31-12-06.

## CONDITIONS OF USE

Vouchers will only be redeemed by those sites featuring a ▣ symbol in the *facilities* line of their County entry. Presentation of this voucher to the Site Operator at the time of paying your balance will entitle you to a fifty pence discount per voucher, per night. (Only one voucher per night). Vouchers may be used in multiples i.e. five vouchers presented for a five night stay will entitle you to a discount of £2.50.

A CADE'S CAMPING, TOURING & MOTOR CARAVAN SITE GUIDE 2006 EDITION must be presented at the time of payment. Vouchers are valid for accommodation only. Vouchers may not be exchanged for cash. May not be used with any other offer. Valid until 31-12-06.

## CONDITIONS OF USE

Vouchers will only be redeemed by those sites featuring a ▣ symbol in the *facilities* line of their County entry. Presentation of this voucher to the Site Operator at the time of paying your balance will entitle you to a fifty pence discount per voucher, per night. (Only one voucher per night). Vouchers may be used in multiples i.e. five vouchers presented for a five night stay will entitle you to a discount of £2.50.

A CADE'S CAMPING, TOURING & MOTOR CARAVAN SITE GUIDE 2006 EDITION must be presented at the time of payment. Vouchers are valid for accommodation only. Vouchers may not be exchanged for cash. May not be used with any other offer. Valid until 31-12-06.

## CONDITIONS OF USE

Vouchers will only be redeemed by those sites featuring a ▣ symbol in the *facilities* line of their County entry. Presentation of this voucher to the Site Operator at the time of paying your balance will entitle you to a fifty pence discount per voucher, per night. (Only one voucher per night). Vouchers may be used in multiples i.e. five vouchers presented for a five night stay will entitle you to a discount of £2.50.

A CADE'S CAMPING, TOURING & MOTOR CARAVAN SITE GUIDE 2006 EDITION must be presented at the time of payment. Vouchers are valid for accommodation only. Vouchers may not be exchanged for cash. May not be used with any other offer. Valid until 31-12-06.

## CONDITIONS OF USE

Vouchers will only be redeemed by those sites featuring a ▣ symbol in the *facilities* line of their County entry. Presentation of this voucher to the Site Operator at the time of paying your balance will entitle you to a fifty pence discount per voucher, per night. (Only one voucher per night). Vouchers may be used in multiples i.e. five vouchers presented for a five night stay will entitle you to a discount of £2.50.

A CADE'S CAMPING, TOURING & MOTOR CARAVAN SITE GUIDE 2006 EDITION must be presented at the time of payment. Vouchers are valid for accommodation only. Vouchers may not be exchanged for cash. May not be used with any other offer. Valid until 31-12-06.

## CONDITIONS OF USE

Vouchers will only be redeemed by those sites featuring a ▣ symbol in the *facilities* line of their County entry. Presentation of this voucher to the Site Operator at the time of paying your balance will entitle you to a fifty pence discount per voucher, per night. (Only one voucher per night). Vouchers may be used in multiples i.e. five vouchers presented for a five night stay will entitle you to a discount of £2.50.

A CADE'S CAMPING, TOURING & MOTOR CARAVAN SITE GUIDE 2006 EDITION must be presented at the time of payment. Vouchers are valid for accommodation only. Vouchers may not be exchanged for cash. May not be used with any other offer. Valid until 31-12-06.

## CONDITIONS OF USE

Vouchers will only be redeemed by those sites featuring a ▣ symbol in the *facilities* line of their County entry. Presentation of this voucher to the Site Operator at the time of paying your balance will entitle you to a fifty pence discount per voucher, per night. (Only one voucher per night). Vouchers may be used in multiples i.e. five vouchers presented for a five night stay will entitle you to a discount of £2.50.

A CADE'S CAMPING, TOURING & MOTOR CARAVAN SITE GUIDE 2006 EDITION must be presented at the time of payment. Vouchers are valid for accommodation only. Vouchers may not be exchanged for cash. May not be used with any other offer. Valid until 31-12-06.

## CONDITIONS OF USE

Vouchers will only be redeemed by those sites featuring a ▣ symbol in the *facilities* line of their County entry. Presentation of this voucher to the Site Operator at the time of paying your balance will entitle you to a fifty pence discount per voucher, per night. (Only one voucher per night). Vouchers may be used in multiples i.e. five vouchers presented for a five night stay will entitle you to a discount of £2.50.

A CADE'S CAMPING, TOURING & MOTOR CARAVAN SITE GUIDE 2006 EDITION must be presented at the time of payment. Vouchers are valid for accommodation only. Vouchers may not be exchanged for cash. May not be used with any other offer. Valid until 31-12-06.

## CONDITIONS OF USE

Vouchers will only be redeemed by those sites featuring a ▣ symbol in the *facilities* line of their County entry. Presentation of this voucher to the Site Operator at the time of paying your balance will entitle you to a fifty pence discount per voucher, per night. (Only one voucher per night). Vouchers may be used in multiples i.e. five vouchers presented for a five night stay will entitle you to a discount of £2.50.

A CADE'S CAMPING, TOURING & MOTOR CARAVAN SITE GUIDE 2006 EDITION must be presented at the time of payment. Vouchers are valid for accommodation only. Vouchers may not be exchanged for cash. May not be used with any other offer. Valid until 31-12-06.

| CADE'S  FIFTY PENCE | CADE'S  FIFTY PENCE |
|---|---|
| **CAMPING, TOURING & MOTOR CARAVAN SITE GUIDE 2006** | **CAMPING, TOURING & MOTOR CARAVAN SITE GUIDE 2006** |
| PRESENT THIS VOUCHER TO THE SITE OPERATOR WHEN PAYING TO RECEIVE FIFTY PENCE DISCOUNT PER VOUCHER, PER NIGHT. SEE CONDITIONS OVERLEAF. VALID UNTIL 31-12-06. | PRESENT THIS VOUCHER TO THE SITE OPERATOR WHEN PAYING TO RECEIVE FIFTY PENCE DISCOUNT PER VOUCHER, PER NIGHT. SEE CONDITIONS OVERLEAF. VALID UNTIL 31-12-06. |
| CADE'S  FIFTY PENCE | CADE'S  FIFTY PENCE |
| **CAMPING, TOURING & MOTOR CARAVAN SITE GUIDE 2006** | **CAMPING, TOURING & MOTOR CARAVAN SITE GUIDE 2006** |
| PRESENT THIS VOUCHER TO THE SITE OPERATOR WHEN PAYING TO RECEIVE FIFTY PENCE DISCOUNT PER VOUCHER, PER NIGHT. SEE CONDITIONS OVERLEAF. VALID UNTIL 31-12-06. | PRESENT THIS VOUCHER TO THE SITE OPERATOR WHEN PAYING TO RECEIVE FIFTY PENCE DISCOUNT PER VOUCHER, PER NIGHT. SEE CONDITIONS OVERLEAF. VALID UNTIL 31-12-06. |
| CADE'S  FIFTY PENCE | CADE'S  FIFTY PENCE |
| **CAMPING, TOURING & MOTOR CARAVAN SITE GUIDE 2006** | **CAMPING, TOURING & MOTOR CARAVAN SITE GUIDE 2006** |
| PRESENT THIS VOUCHER TO THE SITE OPERATOR WHEN PAYING TO RECEIVE FIFTY PENCE DISCOUNT PER VOUCHER, PER NIGHT. SEE CONDITIONS OVERLEAF. VALID UNTIL 31-12-06. | PRESENT THIS VOUCHER TO THE SITE OPERATOR WHEN PAYING TO RECEIVE FIFTY PENCE DISCOUNT PER VOUCHER, PER NIGHT. SEE CONDITIONS OVERLEAF. VALID UNTIL 31-12-06. |
| CADE'S  FIFTY PENCE | CADE'S  FIFTY PENCE |
| **CAMPING, TOURING & MOTOR CARAVAN SITE GUIDE 2006** | **CAMPING, TOURING & MOTOR CARAVAN SITE GUIDE 2006** |
| PRESENT THIS VOUCHER TO THE SITE OPERATOR WHEN PAYING TO RECEIVE FIFTY PENCE DISCOUNT PER VOUCHER, PER NIGHT. SEE CONDITIONS OVERLEAF. VALID UNTIL 31-12-06. | PRESENT THIS VOUCHER TO THE SITE OPERATOR WHEN PAYING TO RECEIVE FIFTY PENCE DISCOUNT PER VOUCHER, PER NIGHT. SEE CONDITIONS OVERLEAF. VALID UNTIL 31-12-06. |
| CADE'S  FIFTY PENCE | CADE'S  FIFTY PENCE |
| **CAMPING, TOURING & MOTOR CARAVAN SITE GUIDE 2006** | **CAMPING, TOURING & MOTOR CARAVAN SITE GUIDE 2006** |
| PRESENT THIS VOUCHER TO THE SITE OPERATOR WHEN PAYING TO RECEIVE FIFTY PENCE DISCOUNT PER VOUCHER, PER NIGHT. SEE CONDITIONS OVERLEAF. VALID UNTIL 31-12-06. | PRESENT THIS VOUCHER TO THE SITE OPERATOR WHEN PAYING TO RECEIVE FIFTY PENCE DISCOUNT PER VOUCHER, PER NIGHT. SEE CONDITIONS OVERLEAF. VALID UNTIL 31-12-06. |

## CONDITIONS OF USE

Vouchers will only be redeemed by those sites featuring a 🄱 symbol in the *facilities* line of their County entry. Presentation of this voucher to the Site Operator at the time of paying your balance will entitle you to a fifty pence discount per voucher, per night. (Only one voucher per night). Vouchers may be used in multiples i.e. five vouchers presented for a five night stay will entitle you to a discount of £2.50.

A CADE'S CAMPING, TOURING & MOTOR CARAVAN SITE GUIDE 2006 EDITION must be presented at the time of payment. Vouchers are valid for accommodation only. Vouchers may not be exchanged for cash. May not be used with any other offer. Valid until 31-12-06.

## CONDITIONS OF USE

Vouchers will only be redeemed by those sites featuring a 🄱 symbol in the *facilities* line of their County entry. Presentation of this voucher to the Site Operator at the time of paying your balance will entitle you to a fifty pence discount per voucher, per night. (Only one voucher per night). Vouchers may be used in multiples i.e. five vouchers presented for a five night stay will entitle you to a discount of £2.50.

A CADE'S CAMPING, TOURING & MOTOR CARAVAN SITE GUIDE 2006 EDITION must be presented at the time of payment. Vouchers are valid for accommodation only. Vouchers may not be exchanged for cash. May not be used with any other offer. Valid until 31-12-06.

## CONDITIONS OF USE

Vouchers will only be redeemed by those sites featuring a 🄱 symbol in the *facilities* line of their County entry. Presentation of this voucher to the Site Operator at the time of paying your balance will entitle you to a fifty pence discount per voucher, per night. (Only one voucher per night). Vouchers may be used in multiples i.e. five vouchers presented for a five night stay will entitle you to a discount of £2.50.

A CADE'S CAMPING, TOURING & MOTOR CARAVAN SITE GUIDE 2006 EDITION must be presented at the time of payment. Vouchers are valid for accommodation only. Vouchers may not be exchanged for cash. May not be used with any other offer. Valid until 31-12-06.

## CONDITIONS OF USE

Vouchers will only be redeemed by those sites featuring a 🄱 symbol in the *facilities* line of their County entry. Presentation of this voucher to the Site Operator at the time of paying your balance will entitle you to a fifty pence discount per voucher, per night. (Only one voucher per night). Vouchers may be used in multiples i.e. five vouchers presented for a five night stay will entitle you to a discount of £2.50.

A CADE'S CAMPING, TOURING & MOTOR CARAVAN SITE GUIDE 2006 EDITION must be presented at the time of payment. Vouchers are valid for accommodation only. Vouchers may not be exchanged for cash. May not be used with any other offer. Valid until 31-12-06.

## CONDITIONS OF USE

Vouchers will only be redeemed by those sites featuring a 🄱 symbol in the *facilities* line of their County entry. Presentation of this voucher to the Site Operator at the time of paying your balance will entitle you to a fifty pence discount per voucher, per night. (Only one voucher per night). Vouchers may be used in multiples i.e. five vouchers presented for a five night stay will entitle you to a discount of £2.50.

A CADE'S CAMPING, TOURING & MOTOR CARAVAN SITE GUIDE 2006 EDITION must be presented at the time of payment. Vouchers are valid for accommodation only. Vouchers may not be exchanged for cash. May not be used with any other offer. Valid until 31-12-06.

## CONDITIONS OF USE

Vouchers will only be redeemed by those sites featuring a 🄱 symbol in the *facilities* line of their County entry. Presentation of this voucher to the Site Operator at the time of paying your balance will entitle you to a fifty pence discount per voucher, per night. (Only one voucher per night). Vouchers may be used in multiples i.e. five vouchers presented for a five night stay will entitle you to a discount of £2.50.

A CADE'S CAMPING, TOURING & MOTOR CARAVAN SITE GUIDE 2006 EDITION must be presented at the time of payment. Vouchers are valid for accommodation only. Vouchers may not be exchanged for cash. May not be used with any other offer. Valid until 31-12-06.

## CONDITIONS OF USE

Vouchers will only be redeemed by those sites featuring a 🄱 symbol in the *facilities* line of their County entry. Presentation of this voucher to the Site Operator at the time of paying your balance will entitle you to a fifty pence discount per voucher, per night. (Only one voucher per night). Vouchers may be used in multiples i.e. five vouchers presented for a five night stay will entitle you to a discount of £2.50.

A CADE'S CAMPING, TOURING & MOTOR CARAVAN SITE GUIDE 2006 EDITION must be presented at the time of payment. Vouchers are valid for accommodation only. Vouchers may not be exchanged for cash. May not be used with any other offer. Valid until 31-12-06.

## CONDITIONS OF USE

Vouchers will only be redeemed by those sites featuring a 🄱 symbol in the *facilities* line of their County entry. Presentation of this voucher to the Site Operator at the time of paying your balance will entitle you to a fifty pence discount per voucher, per night. (Only one voucher per night). Vouchers may be used in multiples i.e. five vouchers presented for a five night stay will entitle you to a discount of £2.50.

A CADE'S CAMPING, TOURING & MOTOR CARAVAN SITE GUIDE 2006 EDITION must be presented at the time of payment. Vouchers are valid for accommodation only. Vouchers may not be exchanged for cash. May not be used with any other offer. Valid until 31-12-06.

**CADE'S**  **FIFTY PENCE**

## CAMPING, TOURING & MOTOR CARAVAN SITE GUIDE 2006

PRESENT THIS VOUCHER TO THE SITE OPERATOR WHEN PAYING TO RECEIVE FIFTY PENCE DISCOUNT PER VOUCHER, PER NIGHT. SEE CONDITIONS OVERLEAF. VALID UNTIL 31-12-06.

**CADE'S**  **FIFTY PENCE**

## CAMPING, TOURING & MOTOR CARAVAN SITE GUIDE 2006

PRESENT THIS VOUCHER TO THE SITE OPERATOR WHEN PAYING TO RECEIVE FIFTY PENCE DISCOUNT PER VOUCHER, PER NIGHT. SEE CONDITIONS OVERLEAF. VALID UNTIL 31-12-06.

**CADE'S**  **FIFTY PENCE**

## CAMPING, TOURING & MOTOR CARAVAN SITE GUIDE 2006

PRESENT THIS VOUCHER TO THE SITE OPERATOR WHEN PAYING TO RECEIVE FIFTY PENCE DISCOUNT PER VOUCHER, PER NIGHT. SEE CONDITIONS OVERLEAF. VALID UNTIL 31-12-06.

**CADE'S**  **FIFTY PENCE**

## CAMPING, TOURING & MOTOR CARAVAN SITE GUIDE 2006

PRESENT THIS VOUCHER TO THE SITE OPERATOR WHEN PAYING TO RECEIVE FIFTY PENCE DISCOUNT PER VOUCHER, PER NIGHT. SEE CONDITIONS OVERLEAF. VALID UNTIL 31-12-06.

**CADE'S**  **FIFTY PENCE**

## CAMPING, TOURING & MOTOR CARAVAN SITE GUIDE 2006

PRESENT THIS VOUCHER TO THE SITE OPERATOR WHEN PAYING TO RECEIVE FIFTY PENCE DISCOUNT PER VOUCHER, PER NIGHT. SEE CONDITIONS OVERLEAF. VALID UNTIL 31-12-06.

**CADE'S**  **FIFTY PENCE**

## CAMPING, TOURING & MOTOR CARAVAN SITE GUIDE 2006

PRESENT THIS VOUCHER TO THE SITE OPERATOR WHEN PAYING TO RECEIVE FIFTY PENCE DISCOUNT PER VOUCHER, PER NIGHT. SEE CONDITIONS OVERLEAF. VALID UNTIL 31-12-06.

**CADE'S**  **FIFTY PENCE**

## CAMPING, TOURING & MOTOR CARAVAN SITE GUIDE 2006

PRESENT THIS VOUCHER TO THE SITE OPERATOR WHEN PAYING TO RECEIVE FIFTY PENCE DISCOUNT PER VOUCHER, PER NIGHT. SEE CONDITIONS OVERLEAF. VALID UNTIL 31-12-06.

**CADE'S**  **FIFTY PENCE**

## CAMPING, TOURING & MOTOR CARAVAN SITE GUIDE 2006

PRESENT THIS VOUCHER TO THE SITE OPERATOR WHEN PAYING TO RECEIVE FIFTY PENCE DISCOUNT PER VOUCHER, PER NIGHT. SEE CONDITIONS OVERLEAF. VALID UNTIL 31-12-06.

**CADE'S**  **FIFTY PENCE**

## CAMPING, TOURING & MOTOR CARAVAN SITE GUIDE 2006

PRESENT THIS VOUCHER TO THE SITE OPERATOR WHEN PAYING TO RECEIVE FIFTY PENCE DISCOUNT PER VOUCHER, PER NIGHT. SEE CONDITIONS OVERLEAF. VALID UNTIL 31-12-06.

**CADE'S**  **FIFTY PENCE**

## CAMPING, TOURING & MOTOR CARAVAN SITE GUIDE 2006

PRESENT THIS VOUCHER TO THE SITE OPERATOR WHEN PAYING TO RECEIVE FIFTY PENCE DISCOUNT PER VOUCHER, PER NIGHT. SEE CONDITIONS OVERLEAF. VALID UNTIL 31-12-06.

## CONDITIONS OF USE

Vouchers will only be redeemed by those sites featuring a 🆎 symbol in the *facilities* line of their County entry. Presentation of this voucher to the Site Operator at the time of paying your balance will entitle you to a fifty pence discount per voucher, per night. (Only one voucher per night). Vouchers may be used in multiples i.e. five vouchers presented for a five night stay will entitle you to a discount of £2.50.

A CADE'S CAMPING, TOURING & MOTOR CARAVAN SITE GUIDE 2006 EDITION must be presented at the time of payment. Vouchers are valid for accommodation only. Vouchers may not be exchanged for cash. May not be used with any other offer. Valid until 31-12-06.

## CONDITIONS OF USE

Vouchers will only be redeemed by those sites featuring a 🆎 symbol in the *facilities* line of their County entry. Presentation of this voucher to the Site Operator at the time of paying your balance will entitle you to a fifty pence discount per voucher, per night. (Only one voucher per night). Vouchers may be used in multiples i.e. five vouchers presented for a five night stay will entitle you to a discount of £2.50.

A CADE'S CAMPING, TOURING & MOTOR CARAVAN SITE GUIDE 2006 EDITION must be presented at the time of payment. Vouchers are valid for accommodation only. Vouchers may not be exchanged for cash. May not be used with any other offer. Valid until 31-12-06.

## CONDITIONS OF USE

Vouchers will only be redeemed by those sites featuring a 🆎 symbol in the *facilities* line of their County entry. Presentation of this voucher to the Site Operator at the time of paying your balance will entitle you to a fifty pence discount per voucher, per night. (Only one voucher per night). Vouchers may be used in multiples i.e. five vouchers presented for a five night stay will entitle you to a discount of £2.50.

A CADE'S CAMPING, TOURING & MOTOR CARAVAN SITE GUIDE 2006 EDITION must be presented at the time of payment. Vouchers are valid for accommodation only. Vouchers may not be exchanged for cash. May not be used with any other offer. Valid until 31-12-06.

## CONDITIONS OF USE

Vouchers will only be redeemed by those sites featuring a 🆎 symbol in the *facilities* line of their County entry. Presentation of this voucher to the Site Operator at the time of paying your balance will entitle you to a fifty pence discount per voucher, per night. (Only one voucher per night). Vouchers may be used in multiples i.e. five vouchers presented for a five night stay will entitle you to a discount of £2.50.

A CADE'S CAMPING, TOURING & MOTOR CARAVAN SITE GUIDE 2006 EDITION must be presented at the time of payment. Vouchers are valid for accommodation only. Vouchers may not be exchanged for cash. May not be used with any other offer. Valid until 31-12-06.

## CONDITIONS OF USE

Vouchers will only be redeemed by those sites featuring a 🆎 symbol in the *facilities* line of their County entry. Presentation of this voucher to the Site Operator at the time of paying your balance will entitle you to a fifty pence discount per voucher, per night. (Only one voucher per night). Vouchers may be used in multiples i.e. five vouchers presented for a five night stay will entitle you to a discount of £2.50.

A CADE'S CAMPING, TOURING & MOTOR CARAVAN SITE GUIDE 2006 EDITION must be presented at the time of payment. Vouchers are valid for accommodation only. Vouchers may not be exchanged for cash. May not be used with any other offer. Valid until 31-12-06.

## CONDITIONS OF USE

Vouchers will only be redeemed by those sites featuring a 🆎 symbol in the *facilities* line of their County entry. Presentation of this voucher to the Site Operator at the time of paying your balance will entitle you to a fifty pence discount per voucher, per night. (Only one voucher per night). Vouchers may be used in multiples i.e. five vouchers presented for a five night stay will entitle you to a discount of £2.50.

A CADE'S CAMPING, TOURING & MOTOR CARAVAN SITE GUIDE 2006 EDITION must be presented at the time of payment. Vouchers are valid for accommodation only. Vouchers may not be exchanged for cash. May not be used with any other offer. Valid until 31-12-06.

## CONDITIONS OF USE

Vouchers will only be redeemed by those sites featuring a 🆎 symbol in the *facilities* line of their County entry. Presentation of this voucher to the Site Operator at the time of paying your balance will entitle you to a fifty pence discount per voucher, per night. (Only one voucher per night). Vouchers may be used in multiples i.e. five vouchers presented for a five night stay will entitle you to a discount of £2.50.

A CADE'S CAMPING, TOURING & MOTOR CARAVAN SITE GUIDE 2006 EDITION must be presented at the time of payment. Vouchers are valid for accommodation only. Vouchers may not be exchanged for cash. May not be used with any other offer. Valid until 31-12-06.

## CONDITIONS OF USE

Vouchers will only be redeemed by those sites featuring a 🆎 symbol in the *facilities* line of their County entry. Presentation of this voucher to the Site Operator at the time of paying your balance will entitle you to a fifty pence discount per voucher, per night. (Only one voucher per night). Vouchers may be used in multiples i.e. five vouchers presented for a five night stay will entitle you to a discount of £2.50.

A CADE'S CAMPING, TOURING & MOTOR CARAVAN SITE GUIDE 2006 EDITION must be presented at the time of payment. Vouchers are valid for accommodation only. Vouchers may not be exchanged for cash. May not be used with any other offer. Valid until 31-12-06.

## CONDITIONS OF USE

Vouchers will only be redeemed by those sites featuring a 🆎 symbol in the *facilities* line of their County entry. Presentation of this voucher to the Site Operator at the time of paying your balance will entitle you to a fifty pence discount per voucher, per night. (Only one voucher per night). Vouchers may be used in multiples i.e. five vouchers presented for a five night stay will entitle you to a discount of £2.50.

A CADE'S CAMPING, TOURING & MOTOR CARAVAN SITE GUIDE 2006 EDITION must be presented at the time of payment. Vouchers are valid for accommodation only. Vouchers may not be exchanged for cash. May not be used with any other offer. Valid until 31-12-06.

| | |
|---|---|
| **CADE'S**       **FIFTY PENCE**<br><br>## CAMPING, TOURING<br>## & MOTOR CARAVAN<br>## SITE GUIDE 2006<br><br>PRESENT THIS VOUCHER TO THE SITE OPERATOR WHEN<br>PAYING TO RECEIVE FIFTY PENCE DISCOUNT PER<br>VOUCHER, PER NIGHT. SEE CONDITIONS OVERLEAF.<br>VALID UNTIL 31-12-06. | **CADE'S**       **FIFTY PENCE**<br><br>## CAMPING, TOURING<br>## & MOTOR CARAVAN<br>## SITE GUIDE 2006<br><br>PRESENT THIS VOUCHER TO THE SITE OPERATOR WHEN<br>PAYING TO RECEIVE FIFTY PENCE DISCOUNT PER<br>VOUCHER, PER NIGHT. SEE CONDITIONS OVERLEAF.<br>VALID UNTIL 31-12-06. |
| **CADE'S**       **FIFTY PENCE**<br><br>## CAMPING, TOURING<br>## & MOTOR CARAVAN<br>## SITE GUIDE 2006<br><br>PRESENT THIS VOUCHER TO THE SITE OPERATOR WHEN<br>PAYING TO RECEIVE FIFTY PENCE DISCOUNT PER<br>VOUCHER, PER NIGHT. SEE CONDITIONS OVERLEAF.<br>VALID UNTIL 31-12-06. | **CADE'S**       **FIFTY PENCE**<br><br>## CAMPING, TOURING<br>## & MOTOR CARAVAN<br>## SITE GUIDE 2006<br><br>PRESENT THIS VOUCHER TO THE SITE OPERATOR WHEN<br>PAYING TO RECEIVE FIFTY PENCE DISCOUNT PER<br>VOUCHER, PER NIGHT. SEE CONDITIONS OVERLEAF.<br>VALID UNTIL 31-12-06. |
| **CADE'S**       **FIFTY PENCE**<br><br>## CAMPING, TOURING<br>## & MOTOR CARAVAN<br>## SITE GUIDE 2006<br><br>PRESENT THIS VOUCHER TO THE SITE OPERATOR WHEN<br>PAYING TO RECEIVE FIFTY PENCE DISCOUNT PER<br>VOUCHER, PER NIGHT. SEE CONDITIONS OVERLEAF.<br>VALID UNTIL 31-12-06. | **CADE'S**       **FIFTY PENCE**<br><br>## CAMPING, TOURING<br>## & MOTOR CARAVAN<br>## SITE GUIDE 2006<br><br>PRESENT THIS VOUCHER TO THE SITE OPERATOR WHEN<br>PAYING TO RECEIVE FIFTY PENCE DISCOUNT PER<br>VOUCHER, PER NIGHT. SEE CONDITIONS OVERLEAF.<br>VALID UNTIL 31-12-06. |
| **CADE'S**       **FIFTY PENCE**<br><br>## CAMPING, TOURING<br>## & MOTOR CARAVAN<br>## SITE GUIDE 2006<br><br>PRESENT THIS VOUCHER TO THE SITE OPERATOR WHEN<br>PAYING TO RECEIVE FIFTY PENCE DISCOUNT PER<br>VOUCHER, PER NIGHT. SEE CONDITIONS OVERLEAF.<br>VALID UNTIL 31-12-06. | **CADE'S**       **FIFTY PENCE**<br><br>## CAMPING, TOURING<br>## & MOTOR CARAVAN<br>## SITE GUIDE 2006<br><br>PRESENT THIS VOUCHER TO THE SITE OPERATOR WHEN<br>PAYING TO RECEIVE FIFTY PENCE DISCOUNT PER<br>VOUCHER, PER NIGHT. SEE CONDITIONS OVERLEAF.<br>VALID UNTIL 31-12-06. |
| **CADE'S**       **FIFTY PENCE**<br><br>## CAMPING, TOURING<br>## & MOTOR CARAVAN<br>## SITE GUIDE 2006<br><br>PRESENT THIS VOUCHER TO THE SITE OPERATOR WHEN<br>PAYING TO RECEIVE FIFTY PENCE DISCOUNT PER<br>VOUCHER, PER NIGHT. SEE CONDITIONS OVERLEAF.<br>VALID UNTIL 31-12-06. | **CADE'S**       **FIFTY PENCE**<br><br>## CAMPING, TOURING<br>## & MOTOR CARAVAN<br>## SITE GUIDE 2006<br><br>PRESENT THIS VOUCHER TO THE SITE OPERATOR WHEN<br>PAYING TO RECEIVE FIFTY PENCE DISCOUNT PER<br>VOUCHER, PER NIGHT. SEE CONDITIONS OVERLEAF.<br>VALID UNTIL 31-12-06. |

## CONDITIONS OF USE

Vouchers will only be redeemed by those sites featuring a ▣ symbol in the *facilities* line of their County entry. Presentation of this voucher to the Site Operator at the time of paying your balance will entitle you to a fifty pence discount per voucher, per night. (Only one voucher per night). Vouchers may be used in multiples i.e. five vouchers presented for a five night stay will entitle you to a discount of £2.50.

A CADE'S CAMPING, TOURING & MOTOR CARAVAN SITE GUIDE 2006 EDITION must be presented at the time of payment. Vouchers are valid for accommodation only. Vouchers may not be exchanged for cash. May not be used with any other offer. Valid until 31-12-06.

## CONDITIONS OF USE

Vouchers will only be redeemed by those sites featuring a ▣ symbol in the *facilities* line of their County entry. Presentation of this voucher to the Site Operator at the time of paying your balance will entitle you to a fifty pence discount per voucher, per night. (Only one voucher per night). Vouchers may be used in multiples i.e. five vouchers presented for a five night stay will entitle you to a discount of £2.50.

A CADE'S CAMPING, TOURING & MOTOR CARAVAN SITE GUIDE 2006 EDITION must be presented at the time of payment. Vouchers are valid for accommodation only. Vouchers may not be exchanged for cash. May not be used with any other offer. Valid until 31-12-06.

## CONDITIONS OF USE

Vouchers will only be redeemed by those sites featuring a ▣ symbol in the *facilities* line of their County entry. Presentation of this voucher to the Site Operator at the time of paying your balance will entitle you to a fifty pence discount per voucher, per night. (Only one voucher per night). Vouchers may be used in multiples i.e. five vouchers presented for a five night stay will entitle you to a discount of £2.50.

A CADE'S CAMPING, TOURING & MOTOR CARAVAN SITE GUIDE 2006 EDITION must be presented at the time of payment. Vouchers are valid for accommodation only. Vouchers may not be exchanged for cash. May not be used with any other offer. Valid until 31-12-06.

## CONDITIONS OF USE

Vouchers will only be redeemed by those sites featuring a ▣ symbol in the *facilities* line of their County entry. Presentation of this voucher to the Site Operator at the time of paying your balance will entitle you to a fifty pence discount per voucher, per night. (Only one voucher per night). Vouchers may be used in multiples i.e. five vouchers presented for a five night stay will entitle you to a discount of £2.50.

A CADE'S CAMPING, TOURING & MOTOR CARAVAN SITE GUIDE 2006 EDITION must be presented at the time of payment. Vouchers are valid for accommodation only. Vouchers may not be exchanged for cash. May not be used with any other offer. Valid until 31-12-06.

## CONDITIONS OF USE

Vouchers will only be redeemed by those sites featuring a ▣ symbol in the *facilities* line of their County entry. Presentation of this voucher to the Site Operator at the time of paying your balance will entitle you to a fifty pence discount per voucher, per night. (Only one voucher per night). Vouchers may be used in multiples i.e. five vouchers presented for a five night stay will entitle you to a discount of £2.50.

A CADE'S CAMPING, TOURING & MOTOR CARAVAN SITE GUIDE 2006 EDITION must be presented at the time of payment. Vouchers are valid for accommodation only. Vouchers may not be exchanged for cash. May not be used with any other offer. Valid until 31-12-06.

## CONDITIONS OF USE

Vouchers will only be redeemed by those sites featuring a ▣ symbol in the *facilities* line of their County entry. Presentation of this voucher to the Site Operator at the time of paying your balance will entitle you to a fifty pence discount per voucher, per night. (Only one voucher per night). Vouchers may be used in multiples i.e. five vouchers presented for a five night stay will entitle you to a discount of £2.50.

A CADE'S CAMPING, TOURING & MOTOR CARAVAN SITE GUIDE 2006 EDITION must be presented at the time of payment. Vouchers are valid for accommodation only. Vouchers may not be exchanged for cash. May not be used with any other offer. Valid until 31-12-06.

## CONDITIONS OF USE

Vouchers will only be redeemed by those sites featuring a ▣ symbol in the *facilities* line of their County entry. Presentation of this voucher to the Site Operator at the time of paying your balance will entitle you to a fifty pence discount per voucher, per night. (Only one voucher per night). Vouchers may be used in multiples i.e. five vouchers presented for a five night stay will entitle you to a discount of £2.50.

A CADE'S CAMPING, TOURING & MOTOR CARAVAN SITE GUIDE 2006 EDITION must be presented at the time of payment. Vouchers are valid for accommodation only. Vouchers may not be exchanged for cash. May not be used with any other offer. Valid until 31-12-06.

## CONDITIONS OF USE

Vouchers will only be redeemed by those sites featuring a ▣ symbol in the *facilities* line of their County entry. Presentation of this voucher to the Site Operator at the time of paying your balance will entitle you to a fifty pence discount per voucher, per night. (Only one voucher per night). Vouchers may be used in multiples i.e. five vouchers presented for a five night stay will entitle you to a discount of £2.50.

A CADE'S CAMPING, TOURING & MOTOR CARAVAN SITE GUIDE 2006 EDITION must be presented at the time of payment. Vouchers are valid for accommodation only. Vouchers may not be exchanged for cash. May not be used with any other offer. Valid until 31-12-06.